Social Psychology

Second Edition

Social Psychology

Second Edition

Lawrence S. Wrightsman

University of Kansas

In collaboration with Stuart Oskamp,
Mark Snyder, John O'Connor, Carol Sigelman,
Kay Deaux, and Eric Sundstrom

Brooks/Cole Publishing Company
Monterey, California
A Division of Wadsworth Publishing Company, Inc.

ISBN: 0-8185-0190-1
L.C. Catalog Card No.: 76-12086
Printed in the United States of America

10   9   8   7   6   5   4   3

Manuscript Editor: *Barbara Mountrey*
Production Editor: *Micky Lawler*
Interior & Cover Design: *John Edeen*
Photo Research: *Jamie Brooks*
Cover Photo: *Jim Pinckney*
Part-Opening Photos for Parts 1, 2, 3, 5, and 6:
Jim Pinckney
Part-Opening Photo for Part 4: *Hap
Stewart/Jeroboam Inc.*
Technical Illustrations: *John Foster*

To Stanley Schachter, Stuart W. Cook, and the memory of Fillmore H. Sanford—three quite different social psychologists, each of whom has influenced this book immeasurably.

Preface

Of all the behavioral sciences, social psychology is perhaps most responsive to the *Zeitgeist*, or "spirit of the times." Part of what concerns social psychology is determined by what concerns society in general. If our newspapers and TV reports accentuate terms like *violence* or *pornography* or *quality of life*, so too does social psychology increase its efforts to understand those particular phenomena. But being a behavioral science, social psychology has a second goal: to develop and test theories that aid us in understanding all types of social behavior. Social psychologists constantly develop and revise theories in light of the accumulation of research findings.

A textbook for an introductory course in social psychology must deal with both these concerns. *Social Psychology, Second Edition,* is a comprehensive text that integrates the development of constructs and methodology with our needs as social beings to understand the phenomena around us. Those topics that are traditional in social-psychological research—social perception, attitudes and attitude change, aggression, prejudice, prosocial behaviors, conformity, leadership, group dynamics, and group differences—are fully covered. In surveying these issues, we relate them to the basic theoretical orientations of the field. As a beginning, Chapter 1 introduces five theoretical orientations and, through the use of a fascinating real-world social interaction, shows how each orientation generates different concepts to explain this one interaction. Throughout the book we put these five theories and others to work in explaining various social behaviors and empirical findings. This approach stems from our belief that theories serve as ways of organizing information and of helping us see whether facts and findings do or do not hang together. In the many places where we indicate how different theories would explain a particular process or finding, our goal is to make the reader aware that theoretical explanations are essential but that no one theory is adequate for explaining every type of interpersonal behavior. Such a lack of closure may leave some student readers dissatisfied, but it is an accurate representation of the present state of theory development in social psychology.

Yet social psychology does not thrive by theory and research alone. One of the attractions of the field is that it has something to contribute to the understanding of virtually every social issue that intrudes into our everyday lives. In preparing this text, we have been alert to the changes in the temper and content of the *Zeitgeist*. What people wanted and worried about five years ago is not exactly what they want and worry about now. For example, the predecessor to this text, *Social Psychology in the Seventies*, was prepared and published at a time in which our society was riven by cleavages between groups; many important social issues were those that reflected an uncertain relationship between youth and our tradition-oriented society. The selection of issues covered in that book reflected the *Zeitgeist* realization that conceptions of a traditional male-dominated, White-dominated, middle-age-dominated society were being challenged aggressively and were becoming "inoperative." Topics given extensive exploration included student activism, radical protest, the social-psychological determinants of drug usage, and conflicts among minorities.

Although such issues (and others of similar nature) are still with us, it appears that the *Zeitgeist* has taken an inward turn; people are more concerned with understanding themselves, with their own development and growth and betterment. Of course, these new concerns still fall under the domain of social psychology: people want to understand how they come across to others, how they may influence others to like them. Thus a social-psychology text for these times must reflect this increasing concern with self-examination and self-oriented social relationships. Chapter 4 of this text, on "Impression Management," is an entirely new chapter, and this is the first social-psychology text to deal at length with the means we use to develop favorable images of ourselves in the eyes of others.

Moreover, the nature of each of us as sexual beings continues to demand study. This book includes a new chapter on "The Social Psychology of Sex Roles" plus a chapter on "The Social Psychology of Sexual Behavior," which has been reorganized, revised, and updated from its counterpart in the earlier edition. Living with other people in nontraditional relationships, another theme of the present *Zeitgeist*, is reflected in the latter chapter and in Chapter 17, on "The Behavior of Groups," which discusses communal life. Chapter 17 adds a perspective on the study of social behavior that was lacking in *Social Psychology in the Seventies*. Other new chapters deal with prosocial behavior and with the physical environment.

Four of the five new chapters were drafted by experts on the respective topics and were revised by the senior author so that a continuity of writing style would be present throughout the book. Of the chapter-length topics retained from the previous edition, each one has been thoroughly updated and revised. In two cases, two chapters from *Social Psychology in the Seventies*

were combined into one, leading to Chapter 3 of the present book, on "Social Perception: Forming Impressions of People," and Chapter 13, "Changing Society and Its Institutions." Chapter 12, on "Attitude Change: Outcomes," has been extended in coverage so that it deals with the effects of a number of communication factors on acceptance of a persuasive message. An indication of the extent of revision is the fact that there are approximately 1400 references cited in this text that were not mentioned in *Social Psychology in the Seventies*.

But whereas behaviors change and certain phenomena may wane in interest, basic ways of looking at social behavior remain. Insights about social behavior come from a number of disciplines. The authors of this text are psychologists, and to a great degree that discipline contributes to the orientation of this book. But anthropology, political science, and literature also make contributions. A major theoretical addition in this text is the increased attention devoted to sociological concepts as means of understanding social phenomena. For example, Chapter 1 now covers the concepts of Homans, Mead, and Cooley; Chapter 4 reviews Goffman's provocative ideas on self-presentation as a dramaturgical event. Throughout the book sociological conceptions and explanations are given greater emphasis than before.

Textbooks that attempt to relate theories to real-world phenomena, as this one does, suffer the danger of being provincial, and even ethnocentric, in outlook. The authors are United States citizens, but they aspire to present findings that have application for citizens of other countries as well. Throughout this book we have tried to "decenter" the orientation, in the sense of recognizing our biases and hence not relying completely on happenings and instances from the United States. Careful readers will note that mentions of "our country" (meaning the United States) have been avoided and replaced by the name of the country referred to. Also, a number of appropriate Canadian examples have been added, for which we wish to acknowledge the contributions of T. Edward Hannah of Memorial University of Newfoundland and Daniel Perlman of the University of Manitoba. Sections of this text also deal with certain conditions in the Republic of South Africa and in Northern Ireland, and research by investigators in Great Britain, the Netherlands, West Germany, France, and Australia is cited.

Chapters are organized into six major parts, but each chapter serves as an independent unit. Instructors who used *Social Psychology in the Seventies* reported a number of meaningful orderings of chapters other than the one listed in the table of contents. Cross-referencing of topics and a detailed index will aid those who choose to cover the chapters in an unnumbered order.

We are convinced that the most important benefit of a textbook is that it facilitates the learning process. This book is written in a clear, understandable style. Topics within each chapter are outlined in detail. At the end of each chapter a number of brief statements summarize the central points within it. Important terms are bold-faced in the text and are defined in a Glossary at the end of the book. Suggested readings are indicated with an asterisk in the References. A separate Instructor's Manual provides multiple-choice and discussion questions for each chapter, as well as an extensive set of suggestions for further reading, classroom discussion, demonstration, and individual-involvement exercises.

In addition, a publication entitled *Study Guide for Social Psychology, Second Edition*, includes the following for each chapter: a chapter preview; a list of basic terms, concepts, and theories; a review of key theorists and studies; a set of completion items; a crossword puzzle using terms from the chapter; sample multiple-choice and short-answer questions; and some suggested involvement projects. Prepared by Daniel Perlman, T. Edward Hannah, Carl M. Rogers, and Lawrence S. Wrightsman, this workbook provides an efficient means for students to identify and evaluate their understanding of basic concepts and findings.

These materials have been provided because of our firm belief that a textbook author's responsibility to instructors and students does not end with the preparation of a book. Rather, a book is only the instigator or facilitator of a never-ending search for understanding. We continue our search, and we hope that all these aids will help you in yours.

Lawrence S. Wrightsman

Acknowledgments

For this edition

As we prepared this text, we asked a number of social psychologists in departments of psychology, sociology, and the behavioral sciences in colleges and universities in the United States and Canada to provide criticism and advice. Prior to beginning our task, we obtained suggestions for revising *Social Psychology in the Seventies* from the following: Donald Matlock, Southwest Texas State University; Richard M. Rozelle, University of Houston; Sam G. McFarland, Western Kentucky University; David M. Walton, Marshall University; Candice Ranelli and Leonard Saxe, University of Pittsburgh; Mark Snyder, University of Minnesota; Arthur G. Miller, Miami University; T. Edward Hannah, Memorial University of Newfoundland; Richard C. Noel, California State University at Bakersfield; P. A. Street and John K. Chadwick-Jones, St. Mary's University, Halifax, Nova Scotia; Paul Chris Cozby, California State University at Fullerton; and Robert W. Suchner, Northern Illinois University.

Drafts of individual chapters were read and criticized by the following persons. Chapters 1 and 2: G. R. Ginsburg, University of Nevada at Reno. Chapter 4: David J. Schneider, University of Texas at San Antonio, and Robert W. Suchner, Northern Illinois University. Chapter 6: Mark Freedman, San Francisco, California; Carole Schmidt Kirkpatrick, University of Oregon; Joseph R. Heller, California State University, Sacramento; and Barbara Strudler Wallston, George Peabody College for Teachers. Chapter 7: Ronald W. Rogers, University of South Carolina. Chapter 8: David R. Shaffer, University of Georgia. Chapter 9: Russell D. Clark III, Florida State University; Alan E. Gross, University of Missouri at St. Louis; and Barbara Strudler Wallston, George Peabody College for Teachers. Chapters 10, 11, and 12: Richard D. Ashmore, Livingston College, and Joseph R. Heller, California State University, Sacramento. Chapter 13: Cal R. Regula, Nanticoke, Pennsylvania, and Joseph R. Heller, California State University, Sacramento. Chapter 14: David Walton, Marshall University; Carole Schmidt Kirkpatrick, University of Oregon; Elizabeth Farris, Purdue University; Mary Harris, University of New Mexico; Howard Fromkin, Purdue University; Virginia Abernathy, Vanderbilt University; Norma Fagin, George Peabody College for Teachers; Norma Shosid, Vanderbilt University; Marcie Turner, Murfreesboro, Tennessee; and Barbara Strudler Wallston, George Peabody College for Teachers. Chapter 15: David L. Cole, Occidental College; Glenn Davis, State University of New York at Stony Brook; and Carl Jorgensen, University of California at Davis. Chapter 16: Irwin Altman, University of Utah; Andrew Baum, Trinity College; Joachim F. Wohlwill, Pennsylvania State University; and Daniel S. Stokols, University of California at Irvine. Chapter 17: Marvin E. Shaw, University of Florida. Additionally, George Levinger of the University of Massachusetts critiqued portions of Chapter 5 and made general suggestions for the revision.

The complete manuscript for this edition was read by a number of instructors of social-psychology courses who made suggestions that were incorporated into the final draft. These persons were the following: Paul Chris Cozby, California State University at Fullerton; T. Edward Hannah, Memorial University, Newfoundland; Albert A. Harrison, University of California at Davis; Karen Howe, Trenton State College; Carole S. Kirkpatrick, University of Oregon; Daniel Perlman, University of Manitoba; Lyle Warner, University of Nevada; John Wilson, Cleveland State University; and Bruce C. Wittmaier, Kirkland College.

This being the tenth book the senior author has published with Brooks/Cole, it would seem that some special accolade should be devoted at this point to the staff of that publishing company. Words fail, but let us try to indicate some of the contributions. Bill Hicks has maintained continued supervision of the revision. Claire Verduin has handled the day-to-day activities involved in obtaining reviews and providing feedback to the authors, supervising the selection of artwork, coordinating the task of obtaining permissions, and shepherding the manuscript into production. We are indebted to her for her unfailing willingness to help out and her incredible enthusiasm even during the most despondent of times. Micky Lawler supervised the copy editing, done by Barbara Mountrey, and the production of the book; John Edeen designed the interior and the cover; Jamie Brooks even traveled across the country in the cause of obtaining illustrations. Finally, mention of the Brooks/Cole staff would not be complete without an acknowledgment of the role of Brooks/Cole's Executive Editor, Charles T. Hendrix, who got the Wrightsman book-writing machine started a decade ago. Terry Hendrix has changed the life of at least one author for the better, and we believe the ripple effect of his endeavors has also bettered the lives of innumerable students.

As in the case of nine previous books over the last decade, all translation of yellow-pad scribble into a polished, typed manuscript for this edition has been done by Doreen Lovelace. If she could be paid a dime for every time she has typed "Journal of Personality and Social Psychology" over that decade, she could retire for life. Shirley Wrightsman has once more done a superb index, a feature of the earlier text that caused at least one social psychologist to actually notice the book and hence to read it.

For the first edition (Social Psychology in the Seventies)

It is fitting that the preparation of this social-psychology textbook has been a group enterprise from beginning to end. Although we cannot possibly acknowledge all the participants in our endeavor, we nevertheless want to try.

Barbara Jacobs read drafts of many of the chapters and later corrected galley proofs; her professional experience as an editor and her good grace in modifying inelegancies have helped. The following doctoral students or graduates of Peabody College or Vanderbilt University read and critiqued one or more chapters: Jack Nottingham, Lois Stack, Bill Wright, Jim Cobb, Lee Stewart, Tom Cash, Thomas Caulkins, Susan Falsey, Warren Fitzgerald, Joseph Gaida, Larry Gates, Virginia George, Mary Hannah, Maureen Holovaty, Sandra Hendrix, Rick Jensen, Ann Neeley, Algene Pearson, Barbara Ramsey, Larry Seeman, Harry Spencer, April Westfall, Les Wuescher, Ron Rogers, Bob Claxton, Bert Hodges, and Sam McFarland. Among colleagues at Peabody College we are especially indebted to Frank C. Noble, J. R. Newbrough, Phil Schoggen, Richard Gorsuch, William Bricker, Paul Dokecki, and Hardy Wilcoxon. Chapter 18 on drug usage benefited from comments by Selden Bacon, Richard Blum, Mary L. Brehm, Don Cahalan, Richard Jessor, George Maddox, Lee Robins, and Stan Sadava. Russell D. Clark III of Florida State University, Kenneth Ring of the University of Connecticut, and Bibb Latané of Ohio State University read and commented on one or more chapters.

The entire manuscript in draft form was read and reviewed by Daryl J. Bem of Stanford University, John C. Brigham of Florida State University, Chester A. Insko of the University of

North Carolina at Chapel Hill, Daniel Perlman of the University of Manitoba, and Harry Triandis of the University of Illinois. Their suggestions were followed in preparing a revised manuscript, and Daryl Bem graciously prepared a Foreword.

A special debt of gratitude goes to the eight other authors who not only prepared their own chapters but read and critiqued the other chapters. One of the many pleasures of this enterprise has been the opportunity to work with each chapter author on a mutually rewarding task. The staff members of Brooks/Cole Publishing Company have been a part of this book from the beginning. Charles T. Hendrix, Jack Thornton, Bonnie Fitzwater, and Micky Lawler have offered a gentle nudge or a pellet of reinforcement at the most appropriate times. Doreen Lovelace, the senior author's secretary, has typed magnificently, edited judiciously, and laughed uproariously over parts of the manuscript. Helen King and Carol Bryant assisted in typing and bibliographic work. And, as always, Shirley Wrightsman has made herself available to check references, type drafts, make indexes, prepare test items, and read proofs. All these people share in the causation of whatever desirable qualities this book may possess.

Finally, a word of gratitude for the presence of students and for the opportunity to be with them. Hortense Callisher has written: "The habit of the lectern instills the habit of knowing. The habit of writing instills the habit of finding out." It gives me joy to have become habituated to both.

Contents

PART 1. THEORIES, METHODS, AND ORIENTATION   1

1. Theories as Explanations of Social Behavior   3

    I. Theories in social psychology   6
    II. How did Rasputin gain control over the Tsarina of Russia?   7
    III. Psychoanalytic theory   11
    IV. Role theory   16
    V. Stimulus-response and social-learning theories   19
    VI. Gestalt theory and cognitive theory   21
    VII. Field theory   25
    VIII. A comparison of theories   27
    IX. The future of theories in social psychology   29
    X. What do social psychologists do?   32
    XI. Summary   32

2. Methods of Studying Social Behavior (By Stuart Oskamp)   35

    I. The scientific method   36
    II. Experimental research versus correlational research   42
    III. Major methods of social-psychological research   45
    IV. Research problems in analyzing human products   57
    V. Research problems in asking questions   58
    VI. Research problems in watching people   65
    VII. Research problems in manipulating conditions   67
    VIII. Expectations for the future   73
    IX. Summary   74

PART 2. FORMING AND SUSTAINING RELATIONSHIPS   75

3. Social Perception: Forming Impressions of People   77

    I. The need to predict and understand others   79
    II. The future of our assumptions about human nature   92
    III. Forming an impression of a specific person—like peeling an onion?   95
    IV. The power of first impressions   98
    V. The attribution of cause   100
    VI. The accuracy of our judgments of others   104
    VII. Future trends in the study of social perception   112
    VIII. Summary   113

4. Impression Management (By Mark
   Snyder)   115

   I. The nature of impression
      management 116
   II. Self-presentation: The same person,
      just a different face?   118
   III. In search of a "consistent" public
      image 121
   IV. The quest for social approval   125
   V. Ingratiation   128
   VI. Impression management and social
      influence   134
   VII. Self-disclosure: The private "I" goes
      public   138
   VIII. Detecting impression management in
      others   140
   IX. A time to reflect: Impression
      management and human
      nature   143
   X. Summary   143

5. From Affiliation to Attraction to
   Love   147

   I. Why do we want to be with
      others?   147

   II. Affiliation as a response to
      anxiety   150
   III. Waiting with others—Does it reduce
      anxiety?   154
   IV. The determinants of emotional and
      motivational states   156
   V. Attraction   161
   VI. Love—The ultimate in
      affiliation?   169
   VII. Summary   175

6. The Social Psychology of Sexual
   Behavior   177

   I. The multitude of problems in studying
      sexual behavior   179
   II. Sexual development and
      identity   181
   III. Mistaken beliefs about sexual
      physiology and response   192
   IV. Heterosexual behavior   196
   V. Social influences on sexual
      behavior   204
   VI. Summary   208

PART 3.   BEHAVIOR TOWARD OTHERS   209

7. Aggression and Violence   211

   I. Definitions of aggression   212
   II. Pro-instinct positions and biological
      explanations of aggression   215
   III. Aggression as a possibly innate
      response activated by
      frustration   218
   IV. Prolearning positions   226
   V. A recapitulation and attempt at
      resolution   229
   VI. Violence and the mass media   230
   VII. Collective violence in
      society—Yesterday, today, and
      tomorrow   234

   VIII. Experimental attempts to control
      aggression   239
   IX. Summary   240

8. Moral Judgments and Behavior (By
   John O'Connor)   243

   I. Conceptions of the development of
      morality in Western culture   244
   II. Psychoanalytic explanations of moral
      development   245
   III. Research in psychoanalysis   251
   IV. A critique of the psychoanalytic
      approach to morality   254

V. Cognitive theories of moral
development   254
VI. Research on cognitive
approaches   264
VII. A critique of the cognitive
approach   269
VIII. Social-learning theory   270
IX. Morality research in social
learning   271
X. A critique of social-learning
approaches   273
XI. An attempt at integration   273
XII. Summary   275

9. Prosocial Behavior: Cooperation and
Helping (By Carol Sigelman)   277

I. The importance of prosocial
behavior   279
II. Cooperation: Working for mutual
benefit   283
III. Helping behavior: From handouts to
heroism   287
IV. Toward a prosocial society   308
V. Summary   311

PART 4.   ATTITUDES AND ATTITUDE CHANGE   313

10. Attitudes and Behavior: Prejudice
and Discrimination   315

I. The nature of attitudes   316
II. Distinctions among Terms: Prejudice,
Discrimination, and Racism   322
III. The costs and extent of prejudice,
discrimination, and racism   325
IV. The causes of prejudice and
discrimination   332
V. Social distance: A result of perceived
dissimilarity in beliefs?   337
VI. Attitudes as predictors of
behavior   342
VII. Summary   348

11. Theories of Attitude Change   351

I. Attitude change and
nonchange   352
II. Stimulus-response and reinforcement
theories of attitude change   353
III. The social-judgment theory of attitude
change   357
IV. Consistency theories of attitude
change   364
V. Self-perception theory   379
VI. Functional theories of attitude
change   382
VII. The future of theories of attitude
change   385
VIII. Summary   386

12. Attitude Change: Outcomes   389

I. What causes attitudes to
change?   389
II. Effects of components of the
persuasive communication   392
III. Reducing prejudice: The contact
hypothesis   394
IV. Factors facilitating change in
face-to-face contact   395
V. Bringing the beneficial factors together:
Stuart Cook's study   397
VI. Why do some people change their
attitudes when others do not?   405
VII. Summary   408

13. Changing Society and Its
Institutions   411

I. Pure science or applied science—Or
both?   412
II. Kurt Lewin and action research   416
III. Social psychologists as change
agents   418
IV. "Unplanned" social change   427
V. Examples of social change   432
VI. Youth and social change   435
VII. "Future shock" and the usefulness of
utopias   439
VIII. Summary   443

PART 5.   GROUP DIFFERENCES   445

14. The Social Psychology of Sex Roles (By Kay Deaux)   447

    I. The question of heredity versus environment   448
    II. Sex differences in aptitude and personality   457
    III. Perceptions of sex differences: The eye of the beholder   463
    IV. Equality and the future   467
    V. Summary   472

15. Similarities and Differences among Races and Social Classes   475

    I. The concept of race   475
    II. Racial differences in intelligence-test scores   479
    III. Interpretations of the findings   481
    IV. Comparisons between Whites and races other than Black   495
    V. Social-class similarities and differences   496
    VI. The interpretation of social-class differences in intelligence   499
    VII. A study of race and social class varied concurrently   504
    VIII. Expectations for the future and a final caution   506
    IX. Summary   507

PART 6.   ENVIRONMENTAL AND GROUP INFLUENCES   509

16. Interpersonal Behavior and the Physical Environment (By Eric Sundstrom)   511

    I. Personal space and interpersonal distance   513
    II. Territorial behavior   521
    III. Environmental determination—Effects of physical arrangements on interactions   530
    IV. Crowding: Too many people, not enough space   536
    V. Summary   548

17. The Behavior of Groups   551

    I. What is a group?   551
    II. Do groups have effects beyond those of the individuals in them?   553
    III. Qualities affecting the influence of groups   564
    IV. T-groups and encounter groups   569
    V. Communal groups   572
    VI. Summary   579

18. Authoritarianism, Obedience, and Repression in Our Society   581

    I. Authoritarianism within the person   583
    II. Destructive obedience—A behavioral analogue of authoritarianism?   594
    III. Authoritarianism in our society   600
    IV. Authoritarianism in the future   603
    V. Summary   604

19. Conformity and Social Influence   607

    I. Definitions of conformity and related phenomena   608
    II. Early procedures and findings in the study of conformity (compliance)   611
    III. The extent of conformity   616
    IV. Is there a conforming personality?   620

Contents

V. Is conformity increasing in our society?   624
VI. Unresolved issues in the study of conformity and nonconformity   627
VII. Other effects of social influence: Group risk taking and polarization   628
VIII. Hypnosis: Something more than simply social influence?   633
IX. Summary   634

20. **The Social Psychology of Leadership and Organizational Effectiveness   637**
I. Early approaches to leadership—The search for distinguishing traits   637
II. Leadership as an influence on group functioning   643

III. Fiedler's contingency theory of leadership   648
IV. Leadership, organizational effectiveness, and assumptions about human nature   654
V. Summary   660

Glossary   663

References   673

Author Index   737

Subject Index   751

PART 1
THEORIES, METHODS, AND ORIENTATION

I. Theories in social psychology

II. How did Rasputin gain control over the Tsarina of Russia?

III. Psychoanalytic theory
   A. Basic assumptions and theoretical constructs
   B. Contributions to social psychology
   C. Applications to Rasputin and the Tsarina

IV. Role theory
   A. Basic assumptions and concepts
   B. Contributions to social psychology
   C. Applications to Rasputin and the Tsarina

V. Stimulus-response and social-learning theories
   A. Basic assumptions and concepts
   B. Contributions to social psychology
   C. Applications to Rasputin and the Tsarina

VI. Gestalt theory and cognitive theory
   A. Basic assumptions and concepts
   B. Contributions to social psychology
   C. Applications to Rasputin and the Tsarina

VII. Field theory
   A. Basic assumptions and theoretical position
   B. Influence on social psychology
   C. Applications to Rasputin and the Tsarina

VIII. A comparison of theories
   A. Historical versus contemporary causes of interpersonal behavior
   B. Internal versus situational factors
   C. The units of analysis
   D. Assumptions about human nature

IX. The future of theories in social psychology

X. What do social psychologists do?

XI. Summary

2

Theories as explanations of social behavior

1

I do not say it is good; I do not say it is bad; I say it is the way it is.

Talleyrand

There is nothing so practical as a good theory.

Kurt Lewin

Imagine a trial lawyer sitting alone in her office and planning the strategy she will use in next week's murder trial, in which she will serve as defense attorney. If her client pleads guilty, will the jury show any mercy? At that moment the lawyer's husband is standing before an oil painting he has just finished; he is wondering whether it will earn him a prize and what its sale price should be. Meanwhile, their daughter, a college student, is driving her sports car to the university across town. As she passes through a school zone, she glimpses the "15 MPH" signs, notes that there are no schoolchildren, police, or school patrol present, and speeds ahead, because she is late for class. Are these people's activities appropriate for social-psychological study?

Despite the fact that each member of this family is presently alone, each is engaged in *social behavior*, for their actions reflect the anticipated reactions of others. Their actions are thus the concern of social psychology, because social psychology investigates the effects of other people on an individual's behavior. Gordon Allport (1968) defined the science of social psychology by stating that "social psychologists regard their discipline as an attempt to understand how the *thought, feeling,* and *behavior* of individuals are influenced by the *actual, imagined,* or *implied* presence of others" (p. 3; italics in original). In this useful definition, the term *implied presence* refers to the fact that an individual's actions often reflect an awareness that he or she is a member of a specific cultural, occupational, or social group. Beyond that, our behavior, even when it occurs in isolation, may reflect our awareness of performing a particular role in a complex social structure, thus reflecting the implied presence of others. If we fail at our job, if our physical appearance changes, if we get arrested, our reactions are affected by an awareness of others and our relationships to them.

For us, the ramifications of Allport's definitions are thought provoking. Just how far does the concern of social psychology extend? Clearly within the domain of social psychology is a young man's behavior when he sits on a crowded crosstown bus as a frail old woman stands in the aisle beside him. Does he offer her his seat? Or does he pretend to be engrossed in a book or in the passing street signs? Does he feel any concern about what she thinks of him? When the same young man enters a doctor's office to take an eye examination, his actions may again be affected by the presence of others. The ophthalmologist asks him to look at an eye chart with one eye, trying first one lens and then another. The young man's task seems to be a straightforward one of determining and reporting which lens gives a clearer image, but he may be thinking: "Am I giving the right answer? What if I really can't tell any difference? Does the doctor know if I am making a mistake?" Such questions may reflect a concern over the impression he is making; certainly they demonstrate that responses in a medical examination are social behavior. Even when the patient's responses are accurate, his behavior is influenced to some degree by the presence of this other person.

Certainly not all the activities carried out by humans are social behaviors. If you pick an apple off a tree, eat it, immediately get sick, and thereafter avoid eating apples (at least those straight off the tree), the reactions occur whether others are present or not. Reflex actions, such as removing your hand from a hot stove, are nonsocial; the *immediate* physical response is the same regardless of the awareness of others. But your verbal response to touching a hot stove may well be colored by the presence of others. The very expletives deleted or expressed by some of us may be influenced by who is present. Social psychologists acknowledge that certain internal responses—glandular, digestive, excretory—are often beyond the realm of social psychology. On the other hand, nausea, constipation, or other physical responses may result from tensions associated with the actions or presence of other people. As Figure 1-2 indicates, even the time of dying may be a response to social considerations.

So, perhaps more than you first realized, a great deal of any person's behavior is social. Consider how much other people contribute to

Figure 1-1
What comprises social behavior? Is the behavior of the driver of the empty bus influenced by the implied presence of others? If the driver takes greater risks or drives faster when alone in the bus, his or her behavior is still influenced by the implied presence of others. (Photos by Jim Pinckney.)

Figure 1-2

Is dying a form of social behavior? More specifically, do certain social events
influence the occurrence of death? Historical evidence indicates that some
people "wait to die" until certain major events have occurred. It is perhaps more
than an amazing coincidence that two Presidents of the United States who signed
the Declaration of Independence (John Adams and Thomas Jefferson) *both died
on July 4, 1826, the 50th anniversary of the signing* (Daniels, 1970). More recently,
the research of David Phillips (1970, 1972) has suggested that Jews "postpone"
the date of dying until after significant events, such as Yom Kippur, the Day
of Atonement. In Jewish populations in both New York City and Budapest, he
found a "death dip"—a significant decrease in death rates—during the months
prior to Yom Kippur. Marriott and Harshbarger (1973) and Marriott (1974)
extended this conclusion by finding, among residents of central West Virginia,
that there was a significant peak in deaths approximately two weeks *after*
Christmas. This increase was especially true of women living alone. (Photo by
Jim Pinckney.)

our environment. As opposed to their great-grandparents 100 years ago, contemporary men and women generally do not have to battle an untamed physical environment; their stresses and frustrations are likely to have resulted from dealing with other people rather than with physical objects. Indeed, the degree to which life is successful for most of us is related to how well we are able to understand and predict other people's behavior.

Given that many solitary actions fall within the domain of social psychology, what is the relationship of social psychology to general psychology and to sociology? Gordon Allport, the psychologist who provided us with the comprehensive definition of the field, suggested that social psychology may be best considered a branch of general psychology. He argued (1968, p. 4) that many characteristics of human nature—such as sensory processes, emotional functions, and memory span—need to be studied apart from social considerations. In the present volume, however, we prefer a different orientation. Even though, as abstract phenomena, these processes may not be social, *certainly their observation and measurement are.* That means that it is almost impossible to separate the effects of physical stimuli from the social settings in which they operate. The traditional study of sensation and memory should of course be continued in the experimental psychology laboratory, but a social-psychological approach to the study of these processes should also be pursued. The latter approach might attempt to answer the following questions:

1. How much difference, if any, does the experimenter's manner (friendly versus cold, for example) make in the responses of the subject?
2. Does the setting (doctor's office versus psychology laboratory, for example) influence the subject's perceptions or responses?
3. If the subject has volunteered, are his or her responses different from those that would be given if he or she were a required participant?

We shall see in Chapter 2 how the imagined or implied presence of others can influence the outcome of a seemingly nonsocial experiment. As Krech, Crutchfield, and Ballachey (1962) aver, a social-psychological analysis can give an added degree of understanding to the results of virtually every phenomenon studied in general psychology.

I. Theories in social psychology

Anyone who offers an explanation of why a social relationship exists is reflecting a theory of social behavior. In any science, a theory is a set of conventions, created by the theorist, as a way of representing reality (Hall & Lindzey, 1970). In a sense we are all theorists, as we all have to make explanations for our reality every day (see Chapter 3). Beyond that, there can be no science without theory (Kaufmann, 1973).

Each theory makes a set of assumptions about the nature of the behavior it seeks to describe and explain. It also contains a set of empirical definitions and **constructs**.[1] While the theories developed by different social psychologists may vary in regard to assumptions, constructs, and emphases, all such theories serve common purposes. One of these purposes is to organize and explicate the relationship between diverse bits of knowledge about social phenomena (Hendrick & Jones, 1972). Each of us has a tremendous accumulation of knowledge about the human species as a social organism. Some of this knowledge is based on our personal experience; some is based on contemporary or recent public events; and some is based on what we glean from books, movies, and other mass media. A theory offers us a unified set of constructs and relationships that enables us to handle all these disjointed bits of knowledge. In short, a theory permits us to incorporate known empirical findings within a logically consistent and reasonably

[1]Terms printed in **boldface** are defined in the Glossary.

① aver = to confirm as authentic, valid, true.

simple framework (Hall & Lindzey, 1970, p. 13.).

Another vital function of any theory in social psychology is to indicate gaps in knowledge, so that further scientific research can develop a more comprehensive understanding of social phenomena. The new research generated by a theory may mean that the theory itself ultimately has to be revised or even rejected. A theory is simply a *model* of behavior, and theory construction in social psychology is in such a state of flux that it is not an exaggeration to say that last year's model often gets recalled. Without the use of some theory, however, the task of understanding the innumerable varieties of social phenomena would be tremendously difficult.

The question is: which theory should be used? No one theory adequately accounts for all social phenomena. (This problem is not limited to social psychology; Kaufmann, 1973, notes that there is no all-encompassing theory that can be used throughout the science of physics.) At present the science of social psychology possesses several basic theoretical approaches, each of which contributes in some degree to the understanding of the same phenomena. Even though two theories may rely on different constructs and may offer conflicting explanations of a social interaction, each theory may be *partially correct*, since the actual social behavior may be consistent in some ways with the outcomes predicted by each theory. Furthermore, if one theory is generally successful in explaining phenomena and predicting future outcomes, the success of another approach is not necessarily precluded; even if two theories use different constructs, both could be generally accurate.

We have indicated that theories need to be understood because they offer basic orientations. They also serve as explanations of behavior: they identify mechanisms that generate observable behavior under specified conditions. We are also able to derive from them **hypotheses** that generate further exploration. In addition, the constructs generated by theories serve as tools for the study of social behavior. For these reasons, then, in this chapter we shall describe five broad

theories of social psychology, each of which has a different orientation, set of assumptions, and set of constructs. Our goal is to understand how each of these theories explains the same social behavior. A social relationship that actually existed—the provocative case of Rasputin, the notorious "holy man" who came to control the Tsarina Alexandra of Russia—will serve as our focal point. We shall describe five social-psychological approaches: psychoanalytic theory, role theory, stimulus-response theory, Gestalt theory, and field theory. How does each explain how the despicable Rasputin attained such a powerful position?

II. How did Rasputin gain control over the Tsarina of Russia?

By the year 1905, the future of Tsar Nicholas II's rule of Russia had become uncertain. Unbeknown to the Tsar, the demise of the Russian monarchy was at hand. Even as he and his court enjoyed an opulent world of sparkling palaces, sleek yachts, and enormous estates, many peasants were starving, shivering, and sinking into greater depths of despondency. Although a minor revolution among the masses had forced Nicholas to establish a parliament through which the citizens could voice their grievances, great inequities continued to exist in Russia.

Beyond the political turmoils, Tsar Nicholas and Tsarina Alexandra were anxious about their only male heir. Their first four children were girls, but in August 1904 a male was born. However, when the young Tsarevich Alexis was only six weeks old, he began hemorrhaging from the navel. It was discovered that the crown prince had hemophilia, a condition in which the blood fails to clot, resulting in frequent and profuse bleeding. A normal life for Alexis was impossible; he had to be carefully sheltered and protected. Accidents still occurred, however, and Alexis often suffered agonizing symptoms including high fever, swollen joints, delirium, and excruciating pain. On many occasions the attacks were so crippling that the young prince remained bedridden for several days. Even though Alexis received the best medical attention available, the physicians could do nothing more than wring their hands in sympathy.

As the public began to realize the full implications of Alexis's illness, Rasputin appeared on the scene. In 1905 Rasputin was in his early thirties; he was known throughout Russia for his drunken brawls and his frequent affairs with both willing and unwilling young women. Apparently the essence of vulgarity, he was filthy, rising and sleeping and rising again without bothering to wash or change his crudely made clothes. His hands were grimy; his beard was tangled and encrusted with debris; his hair was straggly and greasy. We are not surprised to learn that he gave off a powerful, acrid smell (Massie, 1967, p. 190). Despite his odious

Figure 1-3
Rasputin and the Tsarina Alexandra. Why was the "mad monk" able to influence the Tsarina of Russia? Various theories of social psychology employ different assumptions and constructs in explaining the relationship. (Photo of Rasputin courtesy of Culver Pictures; photo of Tsarina Alexandra courtesy of the Mrs. Merriweather Post Collection, Hillwood Collections, Smithsonian Institution, Washington, D.C.)

aspects, Rasputin's eyes were his most powerful feature. It was said that anyone who looked at Rasputin eye to eye became extremely responsive to Rasputin's desires.

A brief survey of the background of this charismatic figure tells us that Gregory Efimovitch Rasputin was born in Siberia in 1871, three years after the birth of Tsar Nicholas. As the son of a poor peasant, Rasputin received absolutely no education and never learned to write properly. He fought, drank, stole horses, and debauched and defamed local girls. His usual manner was direct—if talking to a girl did not facilitate achieving his sexual goals, attacking her usually did. He soon had the reputation of being an intemperate satyr; his notoriety was well deserved. In fact, Rasputin was not his true name, but a nickname meaning "dissolute" or "debauched."

By 1904 Rasputin began maintaining vociferously that he had repented; he took up the vows of the church, became a monk, and began a life whose goals were supposed to be poverty, solitude, and austerity.[2] By the time Rasputin arrived in the Russian capital of St. Petersburg in 1905, his reputation as a monk with mystical powers had preceded him. A relative of the royal family, herself caught up in the cultivation of the occult, soon brought Rasputin to the royal family's residence in Tsarskoe Selo, a short distance from the capital city.

Rasputin ingratiated himself with the Tsar and Tsarina by playing with the children and by telling them folktales and anecdotes about village life. More important, he appeared to be able to relieve the suffering of young Alexis. Time and again, after the doctors could do nothing for Alexis's condition, Rasputin seemingly

brought about an improvement. He would visit Alexis in the evening, foretelling that the bleeding and pain would subside by the next morning; often his predictions were correct. Rasputin assured the Tsar and Tsarina that as long as he remained in the palace, no harm would befall Alexis. Was this a case of cause and effect, or was Rasputin simply blessed by coincidence? The Tsarina became convinced that Rasputin was a personal emissary from God. There is no direct evidence that any action of Rasputin's was actually beneficial, but it has been conjectured that Rasputin either hypnotized the child, telling him the bleeding would stop, or simply influenced the prince with personal magnetism and self-confidence. As a matter of fact, we now know that emotional stress can aggravate or even spontaneously induce bleeding in hemophiliac persons; if tension and emotionality can be reduced, the blood flow may also be reduced (Mattson & Gross, 1965a, 1965b; Lucas, Finkelman, & Tocantino, 1962). While hemophilia cannot be completely regulated by voluntary means, Rasputin's charismatic personality could possibly have lessened the child's emotionality.

Whatever his actual effects were, Rasputin established a tremendous influence over the Tsarina—not only in regard to the child, but in the political sphere as well. To a large degree, Rasputin ruled Russia. In 1916, when Russia was involved in World War I, Rasputin instructed the Tsarina as to the timing and direction of military attacks on the German front. The Tsarina in turn transmitted Rasputin's instructions to the Tsar, who had assumed charge of military operations on the front line. In a word, Rasputin's recommendations were calamitous.[3]

The influential monk also became a favorite in the inner circle of the royal court. For many women in the sensation-seeking St. Petersburg

[marginal handwritten note: explanation (attempted) for Rasputin's success w/ Alexis.]

[marginal handwritten note: he was in no position to rule Russia politically just because he gave a child confidence.]

---

[2]Such holy men (or *starets*) were rather numerous in Russia around the turn of the century. A few of them, like Rasputin, subscribed to the beliefs of the Khlysty sect, a group of mystics who believed that God could be permanently incarnated in the individual (Vernadsky, 1944). The Khlysty repudiated marriage, but their secret meetings, in which they tried to call forth the presence of God, often ended in sexual orgies.

[3]Rasputin had advised the Tsar not to plan war, having prophesied that it would mean the end of Russia and the monarchy. The advice was not followed, though, and Rasputin's prophecy proved correct (Lawrence, 1960). Once the war started, Rasputin's advice on tactical matters was not helpful.

society, Rasputin was an exotic diversion. For his part, Rasputin appeared to have an insatiable need to seduce women. To every attractive woman, he proposed that salvation was impossible unless one could be redeemed from sin—and that true redemption was unattainable unless a sin had been committed. Rasputin reputedly offered his women all three: sin, redemption, and salvation (Massie, 1967).

Not all of Rasputin's ventures were successful; some women were absolutely scandalized by his vulgarity and blatant advances. At court banquets, he was unspeakably crude, plunging his filthy hands into bowls of soup or food and scooping up the contents. In fact, by 1911 all of St. Petersburg was in an uproar over Rasputin's excesses. The public reacted to him with both contempt and fear. Common people were indignant that such a grotesque person had influence over the royal family. Having been denounced in a Moscow paper as a conspirator against the Holy Church, Rasputin was then investigated by church authorities. The fact that he was a fraudulent monk—that in reality he was married and had three children in Siberia—was revealed and publicized, and Rasputin's ecclesiastical patrons renounced him.

But these reactions did not change the attitudes of the rulers of Russia. The Tsar and the Tsarina rejected some of this barrage of criticism and suppressed the rest. One high church official was dismissed, and Nicholas announced a fine for any newspaper that continued to mention Rasputin. The royal couple contented themselves by dismissing the charges as false claims brought by worldly men against a holy one. Meanwhile, Rasputin continued in his capacity as court advisor, even while rumors about him increased. Eventually a plot to end Rasputin's life was formulated. Yet even the events associated with Rasputin's assassination convey something about his indefatigable style, his strength, and his zest for life.

A young aristocrat, Prince Felix Yussoupov (or Youssoupoff), felt that Rasputin was demolishing the monarchy and was determined that the monk had to be killed (Massie, 1967, p. 373).

Yussoupov and his fellow conspirators planned the murder for the evening of December 29, 1916. Rasputin was induced to make a midnight visit to Yussoupov's home, lured by the expectation that the prince's attractive young wife would be there to entertain him.[4] Prior to Rasputin's arrival, cyanide of potassium crystals were ground into powder and sprinkled into tasty little cakes that Rasputin enjoyed very much. According to the physician who poisoned the cakes, the dose was so powerful that it would kill several strong men instantly.

Rasputin was escorted to the cellar and offered some of the cakes. He devoured two immediately; but, as Yussoupov watched in amazement, nothing happened. Rasputin then asked for and tossed down two glasses of wine. These, too, had been poisoned. Still nothing happened. (According to Bergamini, 1969, the stomach of about one person out of 20 does not secrete the hydrochloric acid that is necessary to combine with the ingested cyanide in order to create the prussic acid; it is the latter substance that stops the oxidation process, producing almost instant death. This is the best explanation of the present case.)

Still in apparent good health, Rasputin then asked Prince Yussoupov to play his guitar and sing. Completely unnerved, the prince proceeded to entertain Rasputin, while the other conspirators anxiously waited nearby, hearing voices but not knowing what to do. After two hours, Yussoupov could bear the tension no longer; he dashed upstairs, seized a revolver, and returned to the cellar, where he found Rasputin drinking more poisoned wine and planning to seek out companionship among gypsies. Yussoupov led Rasputin to a crucifix, told him to pray, and shot him in the region of the heart (Yussoupov, 1927, p. 169).

Rasputin fell to the floor, after which the other conspirators dashed down to the cellar. The

[4]Prince Yussoupov presented his own account of the assassination in his book *Rasputin: His Malignant Influence and His Assassination* (New York: Cape, 1927). The prince died in 1970 at the age of 80.

doctor felt for Rasputin's pulse and pronounced him dead. The other conspirators took the gun and returned upstairs to prepare to dispose of the body, while Prince Yussoupov remained in the cellar. But the powerful Rasputin was not dead; he opened one eye then the other, leapt to his feet, and began to choke Yussoupov. The prince hastily retreated with Rasputin following. Incredibly, Rasputin made his way to the front entrance of the house and attempted to escape through the courtyard. A conspirator fired four shots as the monk was escaping. One bullet hit him in the shoulder, another apparently in the head; Rasputin fell in the snow, tried to rise, but could not. The assassins dashed over to him, beat him with a club, wrapped his bloody body in a curtain, and tied it with a rope. The body was transported to the frozen Neva River and was clumsily shoved through a hole cut in the ice. When Rasputin's body was discovered three days later, an autopsy revealed that his lungs were full of water. Despite the poison, the bullets, and the beating, Rasputin had died by drowning!

Tsarina Alexandra had Rasputin's body brought to the park at Tsarskoe Selo, where a special chapel was erected and where she went every night to pray over the monk's grave. Within four months of Rasputin's death, revolution broke out, and soon afterward the monarchy was overthrown. The Tsar, the Tsarina, and their children were captured and removed to a remote Ural Mountain village, where in the summer of 1918 they were killed.

Some historians (for example, Vernadsky, 1944) claim that Rasputin's death led to conflict and disorganization within the royal family and that the Tsar ceased to rule after the assassination. It is, of course, a vast oversimplification to assume that it was only Rasputin's domination of the royal family that led to the overthrow of the Romanov dynasty and to the eventual establishment of the Bolshevik government in Russia. Certainly many other factors contributed to the sequence of revolutions in 1917. Famine was rampant in the land, and the major part of the Russian resources and 2 million of its finest

young men had been consumed by a war that was lost. Nevertheless, Rasputin's powerful and unwholesome influence was clearly a part of the downfall of the monarchy. In the presence of Rasputin, Nicholas was incapable of heeding sensible advice until it was too late. In reaction to the powerful monk, the masses abandoned their support of the Tsar and even the Russian parliament.

We have described this incredible account of Rasputin because it contains a social-psychological question that begs for explanation.[5] Despite everything she knew about Rasputin's behavior in the court, Tsarina Alexandra relied on Rasputin not only in the treatment of her son but in her decisions of national importance. The question is: why? In the following sections of this chapter we shall see how each major theoretical approach to social psychology handles this question. Although many concepts will be introduced, they need not be fully understood at this point. Our major objective right now is to show that each theory offers a general explanation (even though each selects a different emphasis) for the same phenomenon. Comparisons of the different approaches will be made at the end of the chapter.

III. Psychoanalytic theory

A. Basic assumptions and theoretical constructs

Psychoanalytic theory, as developed by Sigmund Freud and his followers, is essentially a theory of personality that developed as a part of an approach to psychotherapy. But, as we shall

[5]The "Rasputin phenomenon" may not be only a historical one. While acting as president of Argentina, Mrs. Isabel Peron relied heavily upon José López Rega, who claimed to have co-authored a book with the Archangel Gabriel (Newsweek, September 9, 1974). It was reported that this adviser had an "almost hypnotic" power over the president. Under great pressure from the rest of her cabinet, who threatened to resign, Mrs. Peron officially dismissed López Rega in mid-1975, although he apparently continued to influence her decisions until she was forced to resign in 1976.

see in subsequent paragraphs, it has great applicability to social behavior. One reason for this is that Freud dealt with a basic conflict between the desire to satisfy each impulse and the task of providing a society that meets the needs of all.

According to psychoanalytic theory, the personalities of adults are the results of what happens to them as they pass through childhood, adolescence, and the various stages of development. During the early formative years (ages 1 through 6), each stage of psychological development is related to the child's preoccupation with a different part of the body. Infants, for example, are oriented toward their mouths; in this **oral stage,** the child has oral needs (sucking and biting) that are either sufficiently satisfied or left unsatisfied. According to psychoanalytic theory, all children move through the same series of stages as they grow older—the oral, the **anal,** the **phallic,** and the **genital** stages. (See Chapter 8 for a discussion of these stages.) In each stage, if the relevant needs are not satisfied, some degree of fixation may result, causing some amount of **libido,** or psychic energy, to be committed to that need rather than to a need at the next stage of development. Many adults never reach fully mature psychological development (the genital stage) because much of their psychic energy remains invested in earlier stages.

In conceptualizing the structure of personality, Freud posited three sets of forces—called the **ego,** the **id,** and the **superego**—that are constantly in conflict over the control of behavior. We will examine these forces in detail in Chapters 8 and 18. According to Freud, when the ego has control over the other two sets of forces in the personality, the person has made a rational adjustment to his or her environment. Even though unconscious forces such as aggressive and sexual urges seek discharge, these will be released in healthful, socially acceptable ways if the ego is in control. (Dreams and slips of the tongue, for example, are seen as means by which unconscious urges express themselves.) In essence, the goal of the ego is to steer the individual into activities that permit opportunities for

growth. The ego also utilizes a number of devices, called *defense mechanisms,* that, if used wisely, permit persons to regroup their forces in the face of incipient psychological disturbance.

B. Contributions to social psychology

The contributions of psychoanalytic theory to social psychology have been pervasive. Hall and Lindzey's (1968) review suggests five major contributions of psychoanalytic theory: socialization of the individual, group psychology, a conception of the origin of society, ideas on the nature and functions of culture and society, and family structure and dynamics. Each is described below.

1. *The socialization of the individual* is one basic concern of psychoanalytic theory. **Socialization** is the process of learning what behaviors are appropriate and in other ways becoming assimilated into society. For example, how does a child learn to be a responsible, moral person? According to Freud, the **superego** develops as a result of early socialization processes. The contents of the superego are distilled from the instructions and admonitions of parents, teachers, other authorities, and peers. Eventually these materials become internalized as a conscience. Freud's analysis of the stages of personality development provides a map of the pathways toward being an unselfish, loving, responsible adult, and his conceptualizations have been elaborated on by others (such as Peck & Havighurst, 1960) who are specifically concerned with moral development. Chapter 8 presents these elaborations in detail.

2. A second contribution of psychoanalytic theory is *group psychology.* According to Freud, a group is held together by its system of libidinal ties (Hall & Lindzey, 1968). Freud claimed that when each group member has accepted the group leader as his or her ideal, an identity is formed among all group members. Such an approach might explain the relationships within certain groups, but it has had little influence on social psychologists' conceptualizations of leadership

(see Chapter 20). But the writings of the popular social critic Eric Hoffer (1951, 1964) may have been influenced by Freud's speculations; Hoffer has described the existence of "true believers," who need to affiliate with *some* movement, and do so *regardless* of the particular movement's goals or ideology.

3. Notions about *the origin of society* are a third contribution of psychoanalytic theory. Why do people live together in organized communities? In *Totem and Taboo* (1913) and *Moses and Monotheism* (1939), Freud offered his explanation of how societies evolved. In the beginnings of human society, people lived in small groups under the control of a strong, autocratic, male ruler. When the ruler chose one of his sons to be his successor, the other sons were driven from the tribe; then they banded together to seek the overthrow and destruction of their father. Hence a *social contract* between individuals developed—first, to combine forces to defeat a common enemy who could otherwise not be defeated and, second, to prevent the self-destruction that could result from aggression between brothers.

Something had to be done about controlling those needs—sex and aggression—that, in Freud's view, were innate or *instinctual*. For example, the brothers who banded together renounced the unwarranted expression of aggression toward their companions, in order to prevent self-destruction. The notion of a *social contract* as a means of forming society was, of course, not original with Freud. But what he added was an emphasis on controlling aggressive and other instinctual impulses. Wars with alien tribes served as an acceptable means of draining off instinctual aggression. To Freud, aggression was a basic part of human nature; he believed that wars will always be with us.

4. *The nature and functions of culture and society* is another topic of which psychoanalytic theory has offered its own explanation. As implied in the preceding paragraphs, Freud believed that one function of society is to restrain people from expressing instinctual impulses that are unacceptable in civilized society. Certainly Freud did not think modern men and women are free; rather, he believed that as society becomes more complex, it establishes more prohibitions and more severe punishments for expression of our natural impulses. Hence, to Freud, civilization was inevitably repressive and authoritarian.

5. *The nature of the family* is a final area to which psychoanalytic theory has made contributions. Hall and Lindzey (1968) call Freud's analysis of the structure and dynamics of the family "one of his greatest achievements and his most notable contribution to social psychology" (p. 273). At each stage of personality development, a central concern is the orientation of the child toward each parent. For the male infant, the mother is the child's first libidinal object (that is, recipient of **libido,** or psychic energy), and the father is seen as a rival and interloper. Around age 4 or 5 the boy will begin to identify with his father and vicariously satisfy his libidinal needs. The female child, at this stage, shows an identification with the mother. According to Freud, then, the foundation for future social behavior is firmly laid by the age of 6 or 7.

The impact on subsequent behavior as an adult of the child's orientations toward her or his parents is reflected in the writings of Karen Horney (1937, 1939). Horney is classified as a **neo-Freudian;** that is, she accepts Freud's basic psychoanalytic approach but includes some qualifications and variations in emphasis. According to Horney, a child learns early in life to develop a particular type of response to other people—either moving toward others (affiliation, dependence), moving against others (hostility, rigidity), or moving away from others (isolation, autonomy). Children's characteristic responses to their parents, according to such an analysis, also serve later in life as their characteristic styles of response to others. (Figure 1-4 makes this point in a different way.)

C. Applications to Rasputin and the Tsarina

Let us now consider how the psychoanalytic approach can be employed to explain the relationship between Rasputin and the Tsarina

Alexandra. The psychoanalytic theorist would first seek clues from the Tsarina's childhood. We know that the Tsarina was born in 1872 to German nobility in the city of Darmstadt, Germany.

"Don't you see, Lester? Your lack of control is simply a way of rebelling against both your innate tendency to be neat and orderly and your need to perform up to the expectations of your peer group."

Figure 1-4
Psychoanalytic theory emphasizes internal determinants of behavior in front of an audience. (Drawing by Sidney Harris.)

Both Alexandra's mother and her governess were English, but she adopted the German language, church (Lutheran), and customs. As a child, Alexandra (originally named Alix) was described as a sweet, merry little person who was always laughing. She had the privileges of nobility, but apparently was not overly spoiled. Her governess advocated the maintenance of a strict schedule with fixed hours for every activity—a habit that Alexandra later carried to Russia. As the Tsarina, Alexandra made sure that the Russian royal family ate at the stroke of the hour and that the children's mornings and afternoons were divided into rigid little blocks of time (Massie, 1967).

When Alix (or Alexandra) was 6, an epidemic of diphtheria swept through the German palace. Her 4-year-old sister was the first fatality, followed a week later by Alix's mother. According to Massie (1967), the double tragedy led the young girl "to seal herself off from other people. A hard shell of aloofness formed over her emotions, and her radiant smile appeared less frequently. Although craving intimacy and affection, she held herself back. She grew to dislike unfamiliar places and to avoid unfamiliar people. Only on cozy family gatherings where she could count on warmth and understanding did Alix unwind" (p. 30). After this, the child's grandmother, Queen Victoria of England, took special responsibility for her upbringing and education, although Alix remained in Germany with her father.

Alix met her future husband for the first time while on a visit to Russia when she was 12. Five years later, they not only met again, but began to see each other frequently during Alix's extended visit with her older sister, who had married a member of the Russian royal family. Clearly, Alix and Nicholas were falling in love. Within a year, in fact, they became engaged. They were married on November 26, 1894, in a ceremony that was severely constrained because of the death of Nicholas's father, Tsar Alexander III, three weeks before. Thus within the span of one month the 26-year-old Nicholas and the 22-year-old Alexandra became not only husband and wife but rulers of Imperial Russia as well.

If the reports of witnesses (Mouchanow, 1918; Buxhoeveden, 1930) are correct, the marriage was a happy one throughout its existence. Nicholas and Alexandra were affectionate and devoted to each other; yet there were extensive and difficult adjustments for Alexandra—a new country, a new language, a new religion, a new husband, a new name, and new responsibilities as the empress of Russia! In the spring of the following year, it was learned that Alexandra was carrying a child. Both parents hoped for a male heir, but it was not to be—not then and not for the next three offspring. Not until 1904, when

Alexandra was 32, was the long-awaited but ill-fated male heir born.

In explaining the Tsarina's later actions, the psychoanalytic theorist would also wish to probe Alexandra's relationship with her husband and her children. (Such a retrospective analysis would depend on letters and diaries, if available, in addition to reminiscences by friends and associates.) Several aspects of Alexandra's past and present would be given special emphasis in seeking an understanding of her relationship with Rasputin. For example, the death of her mother might have instilled in Alexandra a feeling of guilt; as a 6-year-old girl at the time of her mother's death, she was working through what Freud termed the **Electra complex;** that is, the child had envied her mother earlier, but at that point was beginning to identify with her. But a residue of hostility may have remained, including earlier unexpressed wishes that her mother were dead. The sudden death of her mother might have caused secret pleasure and hence guilt. *(not pleasure but sorrow that she*

Additionally, the loss of her mother inten-*feel guilt that way.)* sified Alexandra's relationship with her father. The major obstacle to the satisfaction of her libidinal wishes for an intimate relationship with him had been removed. As a father, the Grand Duke was patriarchal, dominant, and strong willed. According to psychoanalytic theory, if the premature death of her mother had caused Alexandra to fixate at the phallic stage of development, she would desire a man who resembled her father. Nicholas apparently did not fit this mold; he is usually described as a well-meaning but rather weak individual who did not possess the strength of will or conviction of purpose necessary for his regal role. Possibly Alexandra's needs for a father figure were met in Rasputin, who clearly possessed the self-confidence and charisma that Nicholas lacked.

Alexandra's personality is another important determinant in the psychoanalytic explanation of her relationship to Rasputin. It is known that the empress was devoted to her family (Almedingen, 1961); she was religious—even pious

—and was attracted to the occult and the spiritual (Wolfe, 1964). She did not get along with her mother-in-law or with her elder sister, who was married to a Russian Grand Duke. With strangers she was shy and aloof; toward her servants she was kind but distant. She was moralistic and prudish—quick to adopt prejudices and slow to shake them. Alexandra saw things in all-or-none terms. People were either entirely good or entirely bad; beyond this, she responded to them emotionally and impulsively, rather than rationally (Buxhoeveden, 1930). Her maid-in-waiting described her as pessimistic, "prone to melancholy," and "never well balanced" (Mouchanow, 1918, pp. 30–31).

The psychoanalytic approach would describe Alexandra as having a weak ego and a strong, primitive superego that caused her to see things in moralistic terms. Although she tried to become acquainted with all the court gossip, she expressed her disgust at what she called the loose morals of St. Petersburg society; but such behavior might have been a reflection of a defense mechanism called **projection.** Discussing the immorality of others may have released some of her own sexual impulses that were castigated by the superego and repressed by the ego.

To the psychoanalyst, the female manifests *penis envy.* But producing a male offspring is a means of fulfilling this desire for a penis. The fact that her one male offspring was so unsatisfactory—and that she was responsible[6]—may have intensified the development of Alexandra's neurotic personality.

The Tsarina's moralistic and mystical orientation implies the presence within her of an *authoritarian personality syndrome.* The theory of the authoritarian personality (Adorno, Frenkel-Brunswik, Levinson, & Sanford, 1950) is based

[6]Alexis's hemophilia was inherited from his mother's side of the family, hemophilia being a sex-linked characteristic that is passed by females to their male offspring. Tsarina Alexandra was the granddaughter of Queen Victoria of Great Britain. Of Queen Victoria's nine children, two daughters (and possibly a third) were carriers, and one son was a victim of hemophilia (McKusick, 1965).

on psychoanalytic theory; it proposes that the authoritarian person identifies with and submits to power, believes in mystical explanations for phenomena, and denies his or her own socially unacceptable feelings.[7] We previously mentioned the Tsarina's way of disparaging the immoral behavior in the Russian court while demonstrating an intense interest in those activities. Alexandra's superstitious nature would confirm her authoritarian acceptance of mysticism and supernatural solutions to problems. She never began a task on Friday; she was always careful to look at the new moon from the right side; she never put on a green dress for fear of bad luck; and the sight of three candles on a table made her absolutely frantic (Mouchanow, 1918).

In summary, we note that the psychoanalytic approach relies almost entirely upon personality factors rather than on situational factors in explaining why the Tsarina was so influenced by Rasputin. The locus of explanation is *within* Alexandra, and Alexandra is seen as a product of her past experiences and development. Thus we say that psychoanalytic theory relies on *historical causation;* of all the approaches it is the most extreme in this regard.

IV. Role theory

A. Basic assumptions and concepts

Role theory, as an explanation of social behavior, possesses two distinctions. First, it is less developed than any other approach considered in this chapter and thus is best considered only to be a loosely linked network of hypotheses and a set of rather broad constructs (Neiman & Hughes, 1951; Shaw & Costanzo, 1970). Second, in contrast to psychoanalytic theory, role theory does not consider any individualized, within-the-person determinants of social behavior. Concepts such as personality, attitudes, and motiva-

tion are not employed; instead, an attempt is made to explain behavior solely in light of the positions held and in terms of the roles, role expectations and demands, role skills, and reference groups operating on the participants in a social interaction. Hence the approach of role theory is the most sociological of the five approaches considered here.

The term **role** is usually defined as the set of behaviors or functions appropriate for a person who holds a particular position within a particular social context (Biddle & Thomas, 1966; Shaw & Costanzo, 1970). Gloria McWilliams, as a student, performs certain behaviors—she attends classes, prepares assignments, makes an application for graduation, and so on. When interacting with Gloria McWilliams in her role as a student, other people assume that she will act in certain ways; these are called *role expectations.* For example, professors expect their students to attend class with some regularity and show some concern over grades; some faculty may expect some degree of deference from their students, while others may not. **Norms** are more general expectations about behaviors that are deemed appropriate for all persons in a social context, regardless of the position they hold. For example, both students and professors are expected to be on time for class (a norm), but the professor is expected to call the class to order (a role expectation).

Role conflict results when a person holds several positions that are incompatible with one another (*interrole conflict*) or when a person in a single position has expectations that are mutually incompatible (*intrarole conflict*). We enact a number of different roles every day, of course. For example, while studying for an important final exam, Gloria McWilliams may receive a call from her mother requiring prolonged discussion about a family problem. Expectations about her role as a student and her role as a member of the family cannot both be satisfied at the same time, and interrole conflict is produced. In contrast, an example of *intrarole* conflict would occur if Gloria McWilliams had to choose between

---

[7]An extensive description of the authoritarian personality is to be found in Chapter 18.

Here's how I really am,
but I look like this . . .

To the Good Rev. Smith   To my son Jimmie   To my boss

To my mother-in-law   To my wife   To my dentist

To Susie — bless her   To Fido   To my banker

Figure 1-5
A person holding one role
can be seen from many
perspectives. Block (1952)
interviewed 23 persons
who interacted with the
same individual. An
analysis of these
interactions revealed five
different roles for this
person in these
interactions; for each there
was a different set of role
expectations.

studying for a history exam or typing a term paper, when both had to be completed by the next morning.

To say that people "perform a series of roles" does not mean that people are pretending; nor does it mean that they necessarily are acting deceitfully or deceptively (Sarbin & Allen, 1968). To a significant extent, we behave in ways that are in accord with the settings we are in and the positions we hold (Barker, 1960). It is true that there is some latitude for what behaviors are considered as acceptable in a particular setting; even an occasional sleeper may be tolerated in some large classes if he or she does not snore too loudly! But the role defines the limits of what is appropriate in the setting.

B. Contributions to social psychology

Role theorists, such as Erving Goffman (1967), point out that our enactment of roles facilitates and "smoothes" social interaction. We have not given this point the importance it deserves here, but in Chapter 4 Goffman's provocative ideas are discussed in detail.

From role enactments, we learn about ourselves, too. In fact, we may develop attitudes about ourselves on the basis of the attitudes of others toward us in given settings. Charles H. Cooley (1922) and George Herbert Mead (1934), two of the founders of the *symbolic-interactionist* approach, noted that a person's self-concept is a social phenomenon; it develops as a result of the variety of roles taken on by the person in social interaction. That is, the self reflects the responses of others toward the person, as colored by the person's own skills in understanding how others see him (Cameron, 1950; Sarbin & Allen, 1968). Charles H. Cooley called the self-concept a "looking-glass self," because it contains our beliefs about how we appear to other persons and our expectations of how those other persons would judge our behavior and appearance.

C. Applications to Rasputin and the Tsarina

The role theorists would conceptualize the relationship of Rasputin and Alexandra in terms of the *roles, role obligations,* and *role expectations* of each. Alexandra's role as a mother demanded that she explore any means of improving her child's health. Beyond that powerful role expectation, Rasputin was introduced to her as a man of the church, and with the royal family he always played the role of a respectful peasant before his sovereign (Buxhoeveden, 1930). Research indicates that clear-cut role expectations for others facilitate the outcome of relationships with them (Smith, 1957; Steiner & Dodge, 1956).

On the basis of Rasputin's sober, solicitous behavior in her presence, Alexandra saw no reason to doubt that the monk possessed the supernatural powers that he was reputed to have. In the opinion of the empress, Rasputin was clearly God's answer to the problems of Imperial Russia. With such expectations, it is no surprise that the Tsarina was so pervasively influenced by Rasputin.

Role theory also notes that when the behavior of one who occupies a certain position is out of line with the behavior that is *expected* of that position, observers believe they know more about the individual (Jones, Davis, & Gergen, 1961). It would be an understatement to describe Rasputin as *unconventional* for his place and time! But the ways in which the monk's actual behaviors deviated from his expected role behaviors may have been part of his attractiveness. In support of this explanation, Alan Moorehead (1958) writes:

> His [Rasputin's] real crime, of course, in the eyes of society was that he broke the conventions, he outraged their way of life. He had a sadistic glee in showing up the pretentiousness, the pomposity and the silliness of his wealthy patrons. Petrograd (St. Petersburg) society was very corrupt and Rasputin knew it. He could degrade and humiliate the sycophants around

the Tsar precisely because they were syco-phants, and therefore venal as well as fright-ened.... He was, moreover, very shrewd. His casual observations about people . . . were ex-tremely revealing, and he could handle back-stairs politics rather more ably than most of the bureaucrats in Petrograd. Finally, he was a su-perb actor; he played his role as though he be-lieved in it absolutely, and perhaps he really did [p. 71 of 1965 edition].

G. H. Mead (1934) considered that role-taking ability was a skill developed as a result of practice in shifting perspectives and having behaved in the past in a variety of ways (Sarbin & Allen, 1968). Rasputin's skill in role-taking seems to have been highly developed.

V. Stimulus-response and social-learning theories

A. Basic assumptions and concepts

A third approach to social behavior, stimu-lus-response theory (abbreviated S-R theory), proposes that social behavior can be understood by studying the associations between stimuli and responses. The approach concentrates on the analysis of these specific units. A **stimulus** is an external or internal event that brings about an alteration in the behavior of the person (Kimble, 1961). This alteration in the person's behavior is called a **response.** If a response leads to a favor-able outcome for the person, a state of **rein-forcement** then exists; that is, the person has been rewarded for his or her response. The de-gree of reinforcement associated with the re-sponse is important in determining whether that same response will be made again. For example, sociologist George Homans has written "If a man takes an action that is followed by a reward, the probability that he will repeat the action in-creases" (1970, p. 321). In contrast, those actions

that are not rewarded tend to be discarded. In more technical words, an S-R association gains strength if its consequences are reinforcing (Shaw & Costanzo, 1970).

To S-R theorists, complex behaviors are seen as chains of simpler S-R associations. Com-plex behaviors may get more complicated but are not seen as being any different "in kind" (Jen-kins, 1974, p. 786). For example, the verbal be-havior employed in giving a complicated answer to a traffic officer's question "Why were you speeding?" may be analyzed on the basis of a chain of specific responses, or verbal associa-tions. But within the stimulus-response frame-work, several viewpoints emphasize different constructs. Varying principles, all assuming the importance of reinforcement, are reflected in Miller and Dollard's emphasis on imitation, in the social-learning theories developed by Ban-dura and by Rotter, and in the various social-exchange theories.

1. Miller and Dollard on imitation. Stimulus-response theory originated with the field of learning, but its applications to social behavior have been rich and varied. More than 30 years ago Neal Miller and John Dollard (1941) pro-posed that *imitation* could be understood by extending the concepts of stimulus-response relationships and reinforcement. Their basic as-sumptions were that imitation, like most human behavior, is learned and that social behavior and social learning could be understood through the use of general learning principles. Miller and Dollard gave imitation a central place in explain-ing how the child learns to behave socially and specifically in how the child learns to talk, which —if you think about it—is a social act. Further-more, they proposed that imitation was impor-tant in maintaining discipline and conformity to the norms of our society. Suppose, for example, that both a young boy and his older brother wait for their father to arrive home from work, since it is the father's custom to bring each son a piece of candy. The older brother starts running toward the garage because he hears a car pull up in the driveway. The younger child imitates his brother's response and discovers that he is rewarded for it. In other situations the younger son continues to emulate his brother's behavior: he reacts to frustration by screaming; he combs his hair the same way; he begins to express the same four-letter words. Imitation has become rewarding, and the imitative response is generalized to many situations.

2. *Social-learning theory.* An extension of the basic stimulus-response approach called social-learning theory (Bandura, 1965b; Bandura & Walters, 1963) is concerned with any learned behavior that occurs as a result of social aspects of the environment—specifically, other people, groups, cultural norms, or institutions (McDavid & Harari, 1974). Bandura and his colleagues (Bandura, 1965a, 1969; Bandura, Ross, & Ross, 1961, 1963) have emphasized the role of *observation* in the learning of responses to social stimuli. They have shown that if a child witnesses an adult being rewarded for making a certain response to frustration, the child is more likely to imitate the adult's response when placed in a similarly frustrating situation. The reinforcement in such instances can be *vicarious* (Berger, 1962). That is the case when the child as an observer makes no response, and so cannot be reinforced, yet learns to make the response, even without a practice trial. Such learning can have embarrassing outcomes; as Kaufmann (1973) notes, a 5-year-old boy may hear certain obscenities expressed at home but give no evidence of having retained them until he explodes with them in front of his Sunday-school teacher and class.

3. *Social-exchange theories.* A third subtype of S-R theories, those that emphasize social exchange, also reflect strong reliance on a principle of reinforcement. For instance, Homans (1958) views social behavior as an exchange of both material and nonmaterial goods (such as approval and prestige). He believes that those who give

to others pressure them for acts of reciprocity, to create an equitable relationship and perhaps a profit (Sahakian, 1974).

Although John Thibaut and Harold Kelley (1959) would not classify themselves as S-R theorists, they, like Homans, have developed a *social-exchange theory* of social interaction that may be translated into S-R principles. To Thibaut and Kelley, each participant in an interpersonal interaction is dependent on each other participant. If for each participant the rewards are greater than the costs, interaction continues; if the costs become greater, interaction is terminated. (Actually, according to Thibaut and Kelley's social-exchange theory, the decision to continue in the social interaction is also a function of the comparison level for alternatives, or the attractiveness of other possible social interactions.) Such an analysis may be applied to a variety of social situations, from the selection of a bridge partner to the maintenance of a marriage.

B. Contributions to social psychology

As Berger and Lambert (1968), Kaufmann (1973), and others indicate, stimulus-response theory deals effectively with many more complex activities than just the maze learning of rats or human muscle twitches. The contributions of S-R theory to the understanding of social behavior are vast; in this section we have not even described the viewpoint of B. F. Skinner (1971), who, while rejecting the label of S-R theorist, has been most influential in applying the principle of reinforcement to a number of tasks, including even the establishment of a hypothetical utopian community (Skinner, 1948). In succeeding chapters examples will be offered showing how stimulus-response theory helps us understand various social phenomena such as our impressions of other people (Chapter 3), our attraction to them (Chapter 5), aggression (Chapter 7), attitude formation (Chapter 10), and attitude change (Chapter 11).

C. Applications to Rasputin and the Tsarina

Let us now turn to a discussion of how the stimulus-response approach can be used to explain the relationship of Rasputin and Tsarina Alexandra, a worried mother who also happened to be an empress. S-R theorists would first note that every one of Alexis's hemophiliac attacks was a stimulus to his mother. Certain responses made by the Tsarina to this stimulus were not successful—included among them were the responses of calling in the physicians, praying, and comforting the child herself. One response—allowing Rasputin to be in the company of the child—was apparently successful. Since the desired outcome was attained, Rasputin was called upon again and again whenever Alexis had another attack. That is, the consequences of calling upon Rasputin were reinforcing, so this particular response emerged as the most likely response to be made whenever a new attack appeared.

The S-R concept of **stimulus generalization** can be used to explain why, in other matters also, Rasputin's advice was followed. After the Tsarina learned that Rasputin could reduce the weight of one problem stimulus (the hemophiliac attacks), it followed that when other problem stimuli occurred, Rasputin would be consulted again. Unfortunately, Alexandra could not determine the desirability of these recommendations (although she followed them anyway) until it was too late; hence the S-R theorists would say that the reinforcement value of these later responses was, for a long time, ambiguous. By this we mean that Rasputin's advice regarding the child could clearly be seen as successful: the child's bleeding and pain decreased. But the wisdom of rejecting a prime minister (as Alexandra did on one occasion because Rasputin felt the candidate was immoral) could not be so easily determined.

The continued interaction between Rasputin and the Tsarina can, according to the social-exchange theory of Thibaut and Kelley, be viewed as a situation in which the rewards for each of the participants were greater than the costs. For Rasputin, the rewards of power and accessibility to women were clearly greater than the costs. For Alexandra, the costs may have been great; but, when placed against the alternatives (the continued suffering of her child), the costs were not sufficient to terminate the relationship.

VI. Gestalt theory and cognitive theory

A. Basic assumptions and concepts

The fourth approach, Gestalt theory, is diametrically opposed to the stimulus-response theories we have just reviewed. **Gestalt** is a German word that is not easily translated into English; generally speaking, it refers to *pattern* or *total whole nature* (Koffka, 1935). A basic assumption of the Gestalt approach is that *the whole is greater than the sum of the parts*—in other words, if we choose to break behavior down into specific stimulus-response associations, we lose its essence and ignore the totality of human experience. Mozart's Piano Concerto No. 23 is more than a sequence of keyboard sounds, just as *Gone with the Wind* is more than a sequence of light frames on a movie screen.

To the Gestaltists, human behavior is integrated, purposeful, and goal oriented; hence Gestalt psychology contrasts with the stimulus-response approach in regard to what is emphasized in the study of social behavior. To Gestaltists, focusing on habits and chains of stimulus-response bonds demeans the human condition, reducing human behavior to a series of passive reactions. Gestalt theorists feel that the S-R approach fails to recognize that at all times human responses are interrelated with one another, moving the person toward goals he or she is striving to achieve.

Gestalt theory also assumes that the brain

actively gives a cognitive structure to sensations and perceptions; for example, when we hear a strange sound in the middle of the night, we not only hear it but interpret it and put it into a context. The nervous system and brain are considered *organizers* and *interpreters*. In contrast, stimulus-response theory focuses on peripheral processes—that is, the actions of receptors and muscle responses. In traditional S-R theory the brain is believed to serve passively as a communication center only. *(& are the ability to interpret organize and understand)*

Some Gestalt theorists use the **phenomenological** approach, which is oriented toward "as naïve and full a description of direct experience as possible" (Koffka, 1935, p. 73). Thus, the phenomenological approach states that knowing how a person *perceives* the world is useful in understanding that person's behavior. In the words of sociologist W. I. Thomas, "situations defined as real are real in their consequences" (quoted in Hollander, 1971). Suppose, for example, that a man comes home from work every day to find that his dinner has been poorly cooked and tastes bad. The man soon begins to believe that the food has been poisoned and that his wife is trying to kill him. In actuality, the wife is concerned about his health and is trying to help him avoid too-rich food. In attempting to understand the man's subsequent behavior—if he were to attack his wife one night—the phenomenological approach would concentrate on his **perceptions** of his wife's intent and of the taste of the food to him, rather than on the actual intent and the nature of the food (Köhler, 1961). (See also Figure 1-6.)

The research of Solomon Asch exemplifies the Gestalt approach. One topic studied by Asch (1946) was how we form our impressions of others. Two groups of students were used as subjects in the study. To one group, Asch read a list of characteristics of a fictitious person that included the words *intelligent, skillful, industrious, warm, determined, practical,* and *cautious.* The same list was read to a second group, with the exception that the word *cold* was substituted for the

word *warm.* This single variation had strong effects; the two groups formed quite different impressions about the imaginary person. Comparable results were obtained in a clever study done by Harold H. Kelley (1950). A guest lecturer in a college class was described to half the class by a list of adjectives that included the word *cold.* The rest of the class was supplied with the same description, with the exception of the substitution of the word *warm.* Not only were there differences between the ratings that the two groups gave the same instructor, but there was also a difference between groups in regard to how many students were willing to ask the lecturer questions after class. To those students who were supplied with the description that included the word *warm,* the instructor actually appeared to be warmer and friendlier; yet all the differences in impressions were solely the result of a single variation in the descriptions given to the students.

These findings give some credence to the Gestalt assumption that a list of descriptive characteristics is not simply an array of words that is added or averaged (Zajonc, 1968b, p. 323). To the contrary, certain characteristics, such as "warm" and "cold," are *central* and have great impact on both the overall impressions and the judgments of specific qualities of another person. Also reflecting the Gestalt assumption is the pervasive **halo effect,** or the tendency to use one's general impression of another person to shape an opinion about a specific characteristic of that person. For example, if someone asks us if our friend Ted is "sensible," we may respond "yes"—not because we have ever observed him in situations requiring good sense, but because our overall impression of him is that "he's a good guy." The phenomenological quality in Gestalt psychology reminds us that our behavior is influenced if we *assume* that things are related, even if in reality they are not.

A more recent development that derives from the Gestalt approach is **attribution theory** (Jones & Davis, 1965; Kelley, 1971); in essence, this theory is concerned with how we impute

Figure 1-6

Even if homosexuals are maladjusted, who's at fault? The phenomenological approach to social behavior proposes that a person's perceptions of reality are important in understanding that person's behavior. Does it affect a man's behavior for him to know that other people know he is a homosexual? The phenomenological approach states that the homosexual would interpret others' actions differently if he knew they were aware of his homosexuality. Some sociologists who have studied "deviance" (for example, Sagarin, 1975; Schur, 1971, 1974) propose that maladjustment or "deviance" is more affected by the public's hostile reaction to the person than it is by the person's nonnormative behavior. This concept, called **secondary deviance** by Lemert (1951), suggests that there is little in many kinds of "deviant behavior" (such as homosexuality or **transsexualism**) that is intrinsically maladjusted, but that the hostile social reaction to this behavior creates in the person a state of self-hate, anger, and suspicion, leading to maladjustment. (Photo by Ellen Shumsky/Jeroboam Inc.)

which means that it is probably a smaller problem and if we accepted them as they were and tried to help them, then they wouldn't have such a hard time getting readjusted.

causes to the actions of other people (Kelley, 1967). For example, if Lisa apparently sees me coming through the cafeteria line but fails to wave me over to her table, how do I interpret her behavior? Do I attribute it to poor vision ("Maybe she really didn't see me"), or to wanting to be alone so she could study for a test? Or do I take it as reflecting something about me personally? Attribution theory reflects the Gestalt assumption that we cannot process stimuli from the outside world apart from other information we have acquired from being perceivers. To say, as the communications theorist Marshall McLuhan (1964) does, that "the medium is the message" is an exaggeration of this viewpoint. But attribution theory does note that the *medium* (that is, the speaker, the source, or the communication mode) clearly influences the perception, interpretation, and acceptance of the message. (See Figure 1-7.)

"I hold that a little rebellion, now and then, is a good thing, and as necessary in the political world as storms are in the physical."

Figure 1-7

Who said it, and what difference does it make? When students read this quotation and were told that Lenin, the leader of the Russian Bolshevik Revolution, had made the statement, they interpreted "rebellion" to mean "revolution" and talked about "purging the old order" or "letting loose of pent-up forces." When told that U.S. President Thomas Jefferson had made the statement, students emphasized "a *little* rebellion" and spoke of a need for "new ideas in government and politics." The effect of substituting one purported author for another was "to alter the cognitive content of the statement" (Asch, 1952, p. 422). Perceivers interpreted the content of the statement according to their assumptions about the author and the author's intent, demonstrating the Gestalt assumption that the whole is greater than the sum of its parts. (The actual author of the statement was Jefferson.)

B. Contributions to social psychology

The interests and assumptions of many social psychologists in the United States, Canada, and Western Europe reflect a basic Gestalt orientation to social behavior, and examples of this orientation will be frequent in forthcoming chapters. Theories of attitude change (Chapter 11) reflect strains toward a "good fit" (Heider, 1958) or attempts to reduce inconsistency (Festinger, 1957). Asch's work has been influential in the study of conformity (Chapter 19). With its strong emphasis on the role of perception in behavior, Gestalt theory has contributed significantly to our understanding of assumptions about other people (Chapter 3), impression management (Chapter 4), attraction (Chapter 5), and prejudice (Chapter 10).

C. Applications to Rasputin and the Tsarina

Returning now to our example of the enigmatic Rasputin, we should note that one of the perplexing aspects of the Rasputin-Tsarina relationship was Alexandra's continued acceptance of the monk in the face of all the negative information that came from others. The Gestalt theorist would point out that Alexandra's general impression of Rasputin was so favorable that she would readily accept his denial of any wrongdoing. The Tsarina was even able to incorporate rumors about Rasputin's drunkenness and sexuality into her conception of the monk as a religious mystic sent by God to help her child. Gestalt principles of *good fit* and *closure* emphasize the human need to make sense out of the world, to fill in the gaps or reinterpret or reject information that cannot be easily integrated with a predominant impression.

As an outgrowth of the Gestalt framework, Festinger's (1957) theory of **cognitive dissonance** proposes that when we hold two cognitions or beliefs that are in opposition to each other, we are motivated to relieve the dissonance that is caused by the conflict between the beliefs. In our example, the Tsarina's knowledge about Rasputin's licentious activities might have been dissonant with her belief that the monk was an agent of God; one means of relieving the dissonance was to reconstrue one of the cognitions. In a message to Nicholas, Alexandra wrote: "They accuse our Friend [Rasputin] of kissing women. Read the apostles; they kissed everybody as a form of greeting" (Moorehead, 1965, p. 73).

The Tsarina also discredited some of the rumors about Rasputin because the criticisms came from persons who, she believed, envied Rasputin (Lawrence, 1960). According to *balance theory* (Heider, 1958), or attribution theory, negative information about someone else that comes from negative sources will be rejected by the recipient. In fact, such information probably intensified the Tsarina's faith in Rasputin: if undesirable people were trying to get rid of the monk, then surely he must be good. *not always true. (also — they were not undesirable people.)*

VII. Field theory

A. Basic assumptions and theoretical position

The last orientation we will consider is that of **field theory.** The Gestalt approach and field theory are similar, but the differences are great enough to warrant separate treatment. The fundamental contribution of field theory, as developed by Kurt Lewin (1946, 1951), is the proposition that human behavior is a function of the person and the environment; expressed in symbolic terms, $B = f(P,E)$. The first implication of this proposition is that a person's behavior is related both to characteristics *within* that person (his or her heredity, abilities, personality, state of health, and so on) *and* to the social situation in which the person presently exists (for example, the presence or absence of others, the extent to which the person's goals may be blocked, the attitudes present in the community, and the like). Such a two-factor explanation of behavior is worthy of special notice because other theories in social psychology sometimes fail to give

definition

$B = f(P, E)$
Behavior = function (People, environment)

weight to *both* aspects. On the one hand, personality theorists—particularly those concentrating on personality traits or personality types—claim that behavior is a result of internal determinants; they give little or no recognition to the social situation as an influence on behavior. On the other hand, role theorists—intent on showing that a person's behavior is a response to the role he or she occupies—fail to recognize individual differences in response to the demands of a role.

A second implication of a field theory of social behavior derives from the earlier use of field theory in physics. As used in physics and as used by Lewin in psychology, field theory assumes that "the properties of any event are determined by its relations to the system of events of which it is a component" (Deutsch, 1968, p. 414). In other words, every action is influenced by the field in which it takes place; this field includes other behaviors by the person as well as other aspects of the environment.

The most basic construct in field theory is the **life space,** the total subjective environment experienced by each of us (Lewin, 1935). All psychological events—including thinking, acting, and dreaming—are theorized to be a function of the life space, "which consists of the person and the environment viewed as one constellation of interdependent factors" (Deutsch, 1968, p. 417). For purposes of research and analysis, the person and the environment are separated, but we must remember that they are clearly interrelated. While the S-R theorists see behavior as a function of the "external stimulus," Lewin claimed that it was meaningless to consider the determinants of behavior without reference to both the individual *and* the environment (Lewin, 1938). Explanations that fail to recognize this interdependence are inadequate. The statement "He became leader of the group because of his aggressiveness" is an unacceptable explanation to field theorists (Deutsch, 1968). Equally simplified and unacceptable is a statement that a "highly cohesive group will be more productive than a less cohesive group."

Another major emphasis of field theory is *the here and now.* To Lewin, psychological events must be explained by properties of the life space that exist in the present. Hence historic causation, a frequent device of psychoanalytic theory, is rejected. According to field theorists, if a 29-year-old male is unmarried, shy, and self-deprecatory in his relationships with others, the fact than an auto accident scarred and permanently disfigured his face at age 12 is not relevant as an explanation. The young man's present reluctance to date women is only a function of contemporary properties of the field, which may include his *present* feelings toward his appearance or his *present memories* of humiliating comments about his face. The past can influence present behavior only indirectly—only as representations or alterations of past events are carried into the present. This operating principle may seem obvious, but it is often violated in other theoretical explanations. An adult's sexual inhibitions, for example, may often be explained in such theories by reference to a past event, such as a man's witnessing his parents in the act of intercourse when he was a 7-year-old child, or a woman's being raped at the age of 15. In contrast to such explanations, Lewinian field theory would emphasize that the present sexual inhibition is a result of *contemporary* expectations, self-evaluations, and memories (and the latter are not 100% accurate representations of what actually happened).

The concept of *tension system* is also basic to field theory. Psychological needs that have been aroused but not yet satisfied create unresolved tension systems; these serve to engage a person in actions that will move her or him toward the goal. According to Lewin, unfinished tasks perpetuate unresolved tension systems; when the task is completed, the associated tension is then dissipated and the task is less well remembered.

B. Influence on social psychology

The present-day influence of field theory on social psychology is very broad. Rychlak (1973) observes that Lewin "probably did more for the establishment and development of social psychology than any other theorist in the history of psychology" (p. 409). He originated the term *group dynamics* and founded the influential Research Center for Group Dynamics (now at the University of Michigan). Lewin and his associates also initiated the T-group movement (see Chapter 17). Lewinian theory has stimulated such diverse approaches to the study of social behavior as Roger Barker's **ecological psychology** (1960, 1963, 1968) and Morton Deutsch's approach to cooperative and competitive goals (1949a, 1949b) (see Figure 1–8). Lewin's theoretical constructs are not central to much current research in social psychology, but his impact is reflected in his general orientation to psychology, which has greatly influenced his colleagues and students (Deutsch, 1968, p. 478).

C. Applications to Rasputin and the Tsarina

Returning once again to an explanation of the influence Rasputin had over the Tsarina, we would first note, in accordance with the precepts of field theory, that the Tsarina's behavior was a result of both her own personality and the situation in which she existed. Part of the Tsarina's motivation came from within herself, including her guilt about being a carrier of hemophilia. In addition, pressures from the external situation—for example, the social importance of providing a living male heir to the monarchy—contributed to Alexandra's acceptance of Rasputin. (We do not know whether Alexandra could have or desired to have any more children, but we know that she did not.) Field theory would note that had the empress given birth to other male offspring or had her son been other than an heir to the Russian Empire, the Tsarina's reaction to Rasputin might have been quite different. A Lewinian representation of the life space of the Tsarina would include an indication of (1) an unresolved tension system oriented toward her goal of a healthy male heir, (2) the blockage of that goal resulting from Alexis's attacks, and (3) the external forces urging Alexandra to move toward her goal. Rasputin would be represented

as a factor that facilitated overcoming the blockage of the goal and further movement toward the goal.

In addition to representing all behavior as responses to tension systems that occur within a field of forces, Lewin contributed a number of other useful constructs to the field of social psychology. He conceptualized conflicts as falling into one of three categories: approach-approach, avoidance-avoidance, or approach-avoidance. In the last type of conflict the person is exposed to opposing forces that possess both positive and negative features (Lewin, 1935, Chapter 4; Deutsch, 1968). For example, the person may seek a desirable region (having a healthy son) that is accessible only by passing through an undesirable region (tolerating Rasputin's crudities). When the goal is a highly desired or important one, as in the case of Alexis's health, the forces that make a region undesirable (Rasputin's vulgarity) tend to diminish or weaken rapidly. In other words, the Tsarina was able to tolerate Rasputin because of the importance of reaching the positive goal of saving Alexis.

VIII. A comparison of theories

While each of the preceding theories aims for comprehensiveness and generality, you have probably concluded that none of them can provide a full explanation for the significant and prolonged interaction between Rasputin and Alexandra. Nor can any one theory deal with all the diverse phenomena that are included within the domain of social psychology. Thus it is unlikely that any broad or grand theory—in its present form—will be considered acceptable by all social psychologists in the near future. In fact, the movement is now toward the development of "theories of the middle level" (Merton, 1968)—that is, theories that seek to explain a narrower band of behavior or a more specific phenomenon. The theory of cognitive dissonance is an example of this approach, concerning itself only with those situations in which a person holds two inconsistent beliefs. As we shall see

Figure 1-8
How much does setting influence behavior? Ecological psychology is the label
given to the approach of social psychologists who use naturalistic observations
to explore the relationship of behavior to the environment in which it takes
place. Developed by Roger Barker and his associates (Barker, 1963, 1965, 1968;
Barker & Schoggen, 1973; Gump, Schoggen, & Redl, 1957; Wicker, 1968, 1969b),
the ecological approach analyzes real-life environments through the use of the
construct **behavior settings**—for example, the grocery store, the high school
English class, the family dinner table, and the dating situation. The principal
assumption of ecological psychology, that much important behavior is related
to the setting in which it occurs, is an extension of Lewinian field theory. (Photos
by Jim Pinckney.)

in Chapter 11, even this level of situation is of sufficient complexity to have caused researchers to revise and revise again Festinger's (1957) initial statement of cognitive-dissonance theory. Conceivably, in the distant future a number of theories of the middle range may be joined together into a grand theory that accounts for the observations we now have (Triandis, 1975), but such a theory will not closely resemble the theories that are available now.

The broad theories presented in this chapter, however, still serve as general orientations toward research problems. As explanations of social behavior, each theory has some successes and some failures. In the case of each theory, there are aspects of the Tsarina-Rasputin relationship that conflict with theoretical explanations. But instead of making a premature decision about the relative adequacy of theories, we should focus on the differences and the unique structure of each. The following paragraphs discuss the basic differences among the theories; these are also summarized in Table 1–1.

(Comparisons)

A. Historical versus contemporary
   causes of interpersonal behavior

Of the five approaches, field theory places the strongest emphasis on the assumption that only present events can explain other present events. In contrast, psychoanalytic theory makes an implicit assumption that present interpersonal behavior is strongly influenced by past events. Stimulus-response theory, while assuming that behavior can be changed through the modification of reinforcements, recognizes that antecedents (or the person's reinforcement history) may be important.

B. Internal versus
   situational factors

It is true that all social-psychological theories lean toward holding individuals (rather than the society in which they live) responsible for their behavior (Caplan & Nelson, 1974). But

psychoanalytic theory gives strongest emphasis to the personality and motives of the participants as determinants of interpersonal behavior. Role theory ignores internal individual differences and sees social behavior as a function of roles, role expectations, and role conflicts. Most comprehensive here is field theory, because of its conviction that every interpersonal action is a result of both the person *and* the environment.

C. The units of analysis

How specific should the units of study be when we consider social behavior? Stimulus-response theory and Gestalt theory represent the range on this issue. S-R theory assumes that social behavior can be adequately described and explained by looking at specific responses. Gestalt theory rejects this assumption, claiming that subdividing behavior into discrete elements destroys its essence.

D. Assumptions
   about human nature

Both reinforcement theory and role theory assume that human nature lacks an essence; rather, people act in response to stimuli (S-R theory) or in response to the expectations of the role they are fulfilling (role theory). Gestalt theory and field theory, however, emphasize that human nature is purposive and goal oriented and that people develop long-term aspirations and act in accordance with these goals. Psychoanalytic theory, as explicated by Sigmund Freud, sees our instinctual nature as selfish and aggressive, but held in abeyance by the restrictions of society.

IX. The future of theories
    in social psychology

We have indicated that there is little likelihood that any one broad theory will come to dominate social psychology in the future. But

Table 1-1
A comparison of theories in social psychology

Theory	Causes of Behavior (Historical or Contemporary)	Internal versus Situational Factors	Units of Analysis	Assumptions about Human Nature
Psychoanalytic theory	Some emphasis on historical but recognition of contemporary	Emphasis on internal factors (personality, motives)	Personality traits and general characteristics	The initially asocial infant learns to control his or her impulses and perhaps becomes an altruistic, loving adult.
Role theory	Contemporary ("You *are* what role you now hold.")	Emphasis on roles and situational influences; internal factors ignored.	Responses to various situations	People act in response to the expectations for roles they hold.
S-R theory	Contemporary, although concerned with antecedents of behavior also	Largely situational (emphasis on reward structure) but recognizes that internal factors may determine what is rewarding	Specific responses, habits— each treated as a unit	People can be molded into almost any behavior pattern through reinforcement.
Gestalt theory	Contemporary; emphasis on phenomenological approach	Both internal and situational factors recognized	More molar behaviors, although often unspecified	Human nature is active and purposive, seeking goals and self-improvement.
Field theory	Strongly contemporary	Emphasis on the place of both types of factors	Great variation in units used, although "life space" is central	There is little in the way of substantive assumptions.

beyond such pessimism, we need to reflect on two current criticisms of social psychology: (1) that the field is in a state of stagnation because it has not provided a level of understanding hoped for by its advocates (Elms, 1975) and (2) that the field of social psychology cannot even be considered as scientific.

Why is it concluded that social psychology is in such a state of stagnation? Triandis (1975) points out deficiencies in both its theories and its methodology. For instance, he notes that the variables emphasized by present theories account for too little of the variance in behavior; as an example, we shall see in Chapter 11 that in the 1960s consistency theories were proposed as an explanation for *all* attitude change. We now realize that they account for a more limited range of phenomena. Beyond that, Triandis proposes that the variables selected for study are often not the important ones in social behavior. Social psychologists sometimes do methodologically impeccable research on variables that are trivial, and as Donald Hebb (1974) has said, "What is not worth doing is not worth doing well."

Critics observe that theories in social psychology often lead to experiments of limited generalization. Both Triandis (1975) and Moscovici (1972) have claimed that much American social psychology is too narrow and culture bound; its concepts and findings may apply only for social behaviors among the middle class in the United States and Canada. For example, a comparative study of interpersonal negotiations that was conducted in eight laboratories in the United States and Europe produced different results in different locations (Kelley, Shure, Deutsch, Faucheux, Lanzetta, Moscovici, Nuttin, Rabbie, & Thibaut, 1970).

Many of these criticisms seem justified. Thorngate's (1973) "Postulate of Commensurate Complexity"—that it is impossible for an explanation of human behavior to be simultaneously general, simple, and accurate—may be sadly correct. Social psychology seeks a new **paradigm**, or set of ground rules as to how to proceed in its search for knowledge (Gergen, 1975; Kuhn, 1970; Secord, 1975); meanwhile, theory-based re-

search continues to use the same paradigm (Levenson, Gray, & Ingram, 1975) and hence to generate knowledge that has severe limits to its generalizability. *maybe it can never really be generalised but is true for the group studied.*

Even more severe is the challenge that social psychology cannot be justified as a scientific field of inquiry. A bold article by social psychologist Kenneth Gergen (1973a) provides the most salient example of this criticism. Gergen proposes that social psychology is primarily a historical inquiry and that it will never be as successful as the natural sciences in building a cumulative structure of knowledge. In Gergen's view, social psychology deals mostly with "facts that are essentially nonrepeatable and which fluctuate markedly over time" (Gergen, 1973a, p. 310). If this is the case, we would have to conclude that principles of social behavior cannot readily be developed, because the facts on which they are based do not remain constant or universal. One reason they are not stable, according to Gergen, is that these facts eventually become public knowledge, and the public changes its social behavior as a result of this knowledge. For example, several decades ago a study (Janis & Field, 1959) concluded that women are more "persuasible" than men. Given this "fact," says Gergen, many women might rebel and overreact, to avoid acting as "persuasible" or suggestible. If that were to happen to any major degree, the sex difference would be reversed, and a completely different "fact" would be established. Thus, according to Gergen, such findings cannot establish principles; instead they are only statements of relationships occurring at a particular time in history.

While many social psychologists have expressed disenchantment during the last decade over the seeming lack of progress in the field (Harré & Secord, 1972; Israel & Tajfel, 1972; McGuire, 1973; Shaver, 1974; Smith, 1972), few were prepared to accept the attack by Gergen on the fundamental scientific orientation of the field. In a detailed critique with which we agree, Schlenker (1974) expresses faith in the traditional scientific approach and judges it to be the best approach to the orderly accumulation of knowledge about social behavior. In response to Gergen's claim that "facts" can be reversed over time, Schlenker notes that one of the necessary conditions for the formulation of generalizable theories is that they be phrased in sufficiently abstract form to allow for the effects of specific contingencies. In effect, he is saying that an acceptable theory can take into account the effects of public knowledge that "women are more persuasible" and predict the future of sex differences in this variable. Other responses note that while "facts" may change over time, the *processes* determining them remain constant. For example, Paige (1970) has shown that while attitudes of Blacks toward Whites changed from the mid-1940s to the mid-1960s, their changes could be understood by considering the political context in which they operated. That is, whatever attitudes were expressed reflected a more general political orientation that specified how to deal with members of the White majority.

Similarly, Perlman (1974) was able to resolve some apparently inconsistent findings on the relationship between self-esteem and sexual permissiveness by relying on a theory of social deviance. This theory predicts that the direction of the relationship between level of self-esteem and sexual permissiveness will depend on what specific cultural norms are operating.

Such a discussion only reaffirms the vast complexity of human behavior; for example, *each* woman who is told that "science says women are more persuasible than men" will probably react in a *somewhat different way*. In a sense all such responses are unique, and the question remains as to whether there is enough communality in such responses to a social stimulus that they can be grouped together and a general scientific law be established (Hendrick, 1974b).

X. What do social psychologists do?

Our extended analysis of the Rasputin-Tsarina relationship may have implied to you that social psychologists spend most of their time attempting to explain—many years after the fact—great and not-so-great happenings from history. This is not the case. The social psychologist's primary activities are the acquisition of knowledge and the application of it to the problems of our world. The knowledge that is accumulated may be theory oriented or atheoretical. Examples of atheoretical research include public-opinion polls, which might ask about a person's preferences among candidates for a political office or reactions to the feminist movement. Comparisons of the attributes of different racial groups (such as IQ differences between Blacks and Whites) or evaluations of the effectiveness of a storefront mental-health clinic may also be atheoretical. Theory-based research seeks to test the utility of a theoretical viewpoint. The typical researcher tends to think in the language of one theory and to rely on it for explanations of findings, rather than mixing concepts from different approaches. While social psychologists may differ in their preferences for a theory explaining social behavior, the preferences of any one social psychologist "do not fluctuate wildly from day to day" (Thorngate, 1973, p. 6).

In attempting to understand social behavior and in testing their theories, social psychologists use a variety of research methods. Observations of people on subways, experiments in psychology laboratories, comparisons of the reactions of persons in different parts of the world, and the ubiquitous questionnaires filled out by college sophomores all reflect social-psychological methodology. These research methods are described in detail in Chapter 2.

XI. Summary

Social psychology is the field of study concerned with interpersonal behavior. It includes in its domain not only actual interpersonal behavior but also any behavior in which the presence of others is imagined or anticipated. Thus very little human behavior escapes the concern of social psychology.

Psychoanalysis, basically a theory of personality structure and development, explains social behavior in terms of the level of personality development and the forces at work within the personality of each participant. Experiences during childhood are considered to be strong determinants of adult social behavior.

Role theory seeks to explain social behavior through an analysis of roles, role obligations, role expectations, and role conflicts. Roles are behaviors a person performs when holding a particular position within a social context.

Stimulus-response theories, in explaining social behavior, study the associations between specific stimuli and responses. These approaches assume that complex social behavior can be understood as a chaining together of simple responses and that the consequences① of a social behavior are highly influential in determining whether similar responses will be made in the future.

Gestalt theory holds that social behavior cannot be properly understood if it is separated, analyzed, and reduced to specific responses. To the Gestalt psychologist, the essence of social behavior is complex, interrelated, and purposive. "The whole is greater than the sum of its parts" is the credo of Gestalt psychology.

A *phenomenological approach* to the study of behavior assumes that understanding a person's perceptions of the environment is more important in explaining that person's social behavior than is objectively describing the environment.

According to *field theory*, social behavior is (real-life situation) always a function of both the person and the environment at a specific point in time. While this is perhaps an obvious assumption, other theories have not studied the effects of both the intraindividual and the situational factors, as field theory does.

No one theory is successful in predicting or explaining all kinds of social behavior. For instance, in the relationship between Rasputin and the Tsarina, each theory highlights different elements, and each fails to explain some aspects. Theories in social psychology differ in regard to historical versus contemporary causation, internal versus situational factors, the unit of analysis, and assumptions about human nature.

At present, the field of social psychology is at a crisis point, for two reasons: (1) Its efforts have failed to produce the level of understanding of social behavior hoped for by its advocates. (2) It has been attacked as failing to meet the criteria for being scientific in approach; rather, it is judged by some to be only a historical inquiry.

① or reinforcements

they all play a part in people's lives.

I. The scientific method

   A. From induction to deduction to verification
   B. Characteristics of the scientific method
   C. Goals of scientific research

II. Experimental research versus correlational research

   A. The experimental method
   B. The correlational (nonmanipulative) method

III. Major methods of social-psychological research

   A. Archival research
   B. The survey
   C. The field study
   D. The natural experiment
   E. Quasi-experimental research
   F. The field experiment
   G. Simulation research
   H. The laboratory experiment

IV. Research problems in analyzing human products
V. Research problems in asking questions

   A. Sampling: Choosing the respondents
   B. Question wording
   C. Memory errors
   D. Social-desirability needs of respondents
   E. Bias from other response sets
   F. Interviewer effects
   G. Other reasons for polling failures

VI. Research problems in watching people
VII. Research problems in manipulating conditions

   A. Use of volunteer subjects
   B. Demand characteristics
   C. Experimenter effects
   D. Internal validity and external validity
   E. A mechanistic view of human nature
   F. Ethical questions
   G. Applicability to major social problems

VIII. Expectations for the future
IX. Summary

Methods of studying social behavior

2

by Stuart Oskamp

The origin of science is in the desire to know causes; and the
origin of all false science and imposture is . . . in the
unwillingness to acknowledge our own ignorance.

William Hazlitt

Social psychologists study human behavior for many reasons. Their motives may be personal interest, scientific curiosity, a desire to help solve society's problems, or a mixture of these reasons. Like most other behavioral scientists, social psychologists believe in Alexander Pope's famous maxim "The proper study of mankind is man." But just *what* phenomena are studied and *how* they are studied differ from one investigation to another.

Four quite different examples will illustrate the range of research questions studied by social psychologists. Each uses a different type of research method, also. In the first, Donley and Winter (1970) used what we call *archival data* to discover how the personal motives of 20th-century U. S. Presidents were related to the actual accomplishments of their respective administrations (see Figure 2-1).

A second research topic of contemporary interest involves aggressive and violent behavior. An *interview study* using a national sample of about 1400 U. S. men (Blumenthal, Kahn, Andrews, & Head, 1972) investigated two separate dimensions of attitudes toward violence. Men who held attitudes that favored the use of violence for social control (as in some police actions) did not necessarily favor the use of violence for

social change (as in riots and violent protests). Interestingly, most men in the study viewed looting and draft-card burning as just as violent as burglary or police beatings of students. Even protests and sit-ins by students were considered violent by many respondents.

As Chapters 10 and 12 reflect, racial prejudice and discrimination are other topics that have been very extensively studied by social psychologists. An *observational* method for studying racial attitudes among college students was developed by Campbell, Kruskal, and Wallace (1966). This method used voluntary seating patterns in college classes to show that in the 1960s there was still a substantial degree of segregation, both by race and by sex, among college students in a Northern U.S. city. However, the voluntary segregation was markedly less at a downtown university that had a decidedly liberal reputation than at a nearby teachers college with a traditional orientation.

Our final example of the research topics studied by social psychologists grew out of the highly publicized incident in which Kitty Genovese was brutally stabbed to death as she returned to her New York City apartment late one night. At least 38 of her neighbors saw the murder from their windows and heard her screams during her half-hour-long struggle with the attacker. Yet not once during that period did any of her neighbors assist her or even call the police. Their failure to intervene stimulated two social psychologists (Latané & Darley, 1970) to begin a program of *experimental research* on the conditions under which people will or will not help others in an emergency.

Social psychologists are not alone in studying human behavior; all of us in our daily lives try to understand other people (see Figure 2-2). The main difference between the social psychologist and the average person, however, is in the methods each uses to seek understanding of other people's behavior. Some of us rely on "authorities" to give us understanding; others

claim to use "common sense." In this chapter, we will describe and evaluate the advantages and limitations of the social psychologist's principal methods. But first, we need to look carefully at the scientific method in general, in order to dispel some of the common misconceptions about the nature of science (Kemeny, 1959; Kuhn, 1970).

I. The scientific method

First of all we should note that the scientific method is *cyclical* in nature: it starts with facts, progresses through theories and predictions, and establishes new facts that form the end of one

Figure 2-1
Are a President's motives revealed here? Donley and Winter (1970) determined the degree to which achievement and power themes were present in the inaugural addresses of U.S. Presidents in this century. Presidents' motives, as shown in their first official statements, were found to correspond closely to the subsequent accomplishments of their administrations. Perhaps this method may also be used to give us predictions of future presidential accomplishments. (Photos by James Brown (left) and Dennis Brack (right), Black Star.)

cycle and the beginning of the next. We may define a **fact** as an observation that has been made (or could be made) repeatedly and consistently by different observers. For example, it is a fact that research subjects who have failed on an experimental task often express anger and hostility toward the experimenter. On the other hand, a **theory** is a creative production defined, very simplistically, as a system of ideas containing some abstract concepts, some rules about the interconnection of these concepts, and some ways of linking these concepts to observed facts

Figure 2-2
Muhammad Ali's theories about people. Theories generate research, and everybody has a theory about people. Invited by the graduating seniors to speak at Harvard University's commencement ceremonies, heavyweight boxing champion Muhammad Ali expressed his theory about people, which is built around four personality types. These are the walnut, "hard on the outside, but soft on the inside"; the prune, "soft on the outside but hard on the inside"; the pomegranate, "hard on the inside and the outside"; and the grape, "soft on the inside and the outside." He also stated that of all the fruits in the bowl the grape is the most attractive. He said that he usually lets the public see only his "walnut" personality, but confessed to being more of a "grape." (Photo courtesy of Wide World Photos.)

(Deutsch & Krauss, 1965). The above fact might be explained by a theory that frustration always leads to some form of aggression.

Two other terms also need a brief definition here. A **hypothesis** is a prediction or guess, often derived from a theory, about what will happen under a given set of circumstances. It is tested by an experiment or by data collection under those specified circumstances. A **law**, as used in science, is a thoroughly demonstrated and accepted conclusion about the relationship between certain events. To become a law, a finding has to be repeated so often that it is no longer open to doubt, except after the discovery of much new and contrary evidence. As a young science, social psychology has very few, if any, laws.

A. From induction to deduction to verification

The scientific method involves three major steps, as illustrated in Figure 2-3. The first step is **induction,** the process of starting with observed patterns and constructing a theory that is consistent with those patterns. Induction is a leap from a set of particular instances to a general rule—a highly creative step of developing a principle or set of principles that could account for the known facts. The second step is **deduction,** the process of logical derivation of some additional consequences of the theory that was in-

duced in step one. These consequences are stated as hypotheses, or predictions of what would happen under certain conditions, still at the abstract or theoretical level. The third step in the scientific method is **verification.** At this point, the method returns to the level of facts and collects new observations to support or refute the predictions made during the deductive step. If, as often happens, there are some discrepancies between the predictions and the verifying observations, these discrepancies become new facts that may demand some insight by the scientist as to how to modify the theory to keep its predictive ability. Thus begins a new cycle of induction, deduction, and verification. Of course, the actual process of scientific work is not usually this neat and orderly. There may be many false starts, intuitive leaps ahead, gaps to be filled in later, and after-the-fact rationalizations. But the three basic steps can usually be identified in any scientific research project.

Let us consider a concrete example of social-psychological research that clearly illustrates the three steps of the scientific method. Our example will be Darley and Latané's study concerning the conditions under which people are willing to help one another. We mentioned the initial facts that stimulated the study earlier: Kitty Genovese was murdered during one-half hour of screams and cries for help; 38 persons witnessed the event; no move was made to help her or to

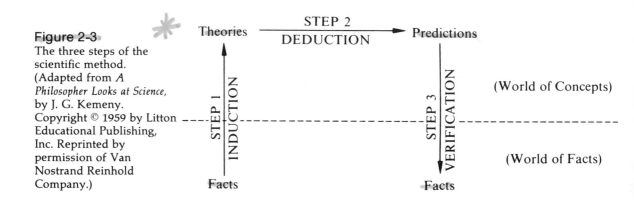

Figure 2-3
The three steps of the scientific method. (Adapted from *A Philosopher Looks at Science,* by J. G. Kemeny. Copyright © 1959 by Litton Educational Publishing, Inc. Reprinted by permission of Van Nostrand Reinhold Company.)

call the police. After considering this situation, Darley and Latané (1968a, 1968b) began to *theorize;* they induced several theoretical propositions—the main one dealing with *diffusion of responsibility* in a social situation. Having induced this principle as a theoretical explanation of the original facts, the researchers deduced other logical consequences from their minitheory and made predictions about what would happen in a laboratory experiment designed to test the theory. Specifically, Darley and Latané deduced that, in an emergency situation, the more witnesses there are who are aware of one another's presence, the less likely it is that any *one* of these witnesses will take helpful action. The experiment controlled conditions by placing the subjects (all males) in separate rooms so that any actions of one subject would not prevent rescue efforts by another. By means of an intercom system, the subjects participated in a group discussion, each speaking in turn about his own problems in adjusting to life at a high-pressure urban university. Some subjects were told that there was only one other discussion participant; some were told that two others were participating; and some were told that five others were participating. In each instance, the number of voices heard matched the instructions.

On the first round of discussion, one participant mentioned, with obvious embarrassment, that he was susceptible to nervous seizures somewhat like epilepsy. On the second round of discussion, the same participant gradually became disorganized in his speech; he stated that his problem was affecting him right now, and he asked for help. He then said something about a seizure, made choking sounds, and finally lapsed into complete silence. During this cry for help, the experimenter waited outside the room of the real subject to see whether he would emerge to offer help and, if so, how soon. As mentioned, the experimenters had predicted that the more people apparently hearing the call for help, the less the likelihood that any one individual would offer help. The results showed that when only one person was present in addition

to the victim, 85% of the subjects tested came out to help within a specified brief period of time. When two people were present (in separate rooms) in addition to the victim, 62% of the subjects offered help; but when five others were separately present, only 31% of the subjects came out to help. Thus the prediction was very strongly verified, and the experimenters' minitheory about the diffusion of responsibility received its initial experimental support. (Darley and Latané's program of research is described further in Chapter 9.)

B. Characteristics of the scientific method

Having defined and illustrated the scientific method, we can now briefly list its unique features.

1. The scientific method must make an assumption of **determinism.** That is, science must assume that nature is orderly and lawful and that, accordingly, events are determined by some cause rather than by chance. Otherwise, we could never develop an understanding of the relationships between phenomena.

2. The scientific method uses the **empirical approach;** that is, it uses an active planned collection of data to verify or disconfirm its hypotheses. This approach is often contrasted with the "armchair" or **rational approach** of the philosopher or literary critic.

3. The scientific method requires the **operational definition** of concepts, in which the concept to be studied is defined by specifying the operations by which it is measured or manipulated. For instance, in the study just described, *helping* was operationally defined as the experimenter's observation that the subject had left the experimental room and had mentioned the emergency within a period of 55 seconds.

4. The scientific method demands **objectivity** in its data and its procedures; that is, different observers must agree on them. Though people using other approaches to knowledge may often make deductions or seek verification

of their ideas, it is the objectivity of the scientist's deductions and—even more—of his or her verifications that sets the scientist apart from the philosopher, the historian, or other nonscientists.

These features of the scientific method give it both advantages and disadvantages as an intellectual tool. On the one hand, the scientific method may limit the focus of study to concepts that can be measured objectively. (Science cannot study the soul, and has great difficulties in studying the content of dreams.) On the other hand, when carefully used, the scientific method provides consistently agreed-upon conclusions, as opposed to the speculative conclusions common in nonscientific fields.

It should be emphasized that the scientific method, defined as the sequence of proceeding from initial facts to new facts by the three steps of induction, deduction, and verification, can occur in any field of study and is not limited to the sciences alone. (The fictional detective Sherlock Holmes was a master of the technique.) Historically, the scientific method was first used in the physical sciences, such as astronomy and physics. It can also be used in the social sciences, such as sociology, psychology, economics, and political science; occasionally it is used even in the humanities.[1]

One final point about the scientific method should be mentioned in order to counteract the possible impression that it is completely objective. Science is, after all, a warm-blooded activity carried on intensively by human beings with their own personal values and preferences and their very human pride, competitiveness, and blind spots (Watson, 1968). As such, its verification phase can never be a completely impartial, value-free activity, no matter how much it strives to be objective and unbiased. Additionally, phi-

losophers of science have pointed out the importance of intuition and hunches, subjective hypotheses, and personal values and beliefs in the creative process of scientific discovery (Polanyi, 1969; Popper, 1972). Also, there are dominant trends and fashions in scientific investigation that may influence both the current methods and the topics chosen for study (Kuhn, 1970). In recent years the availability of government money for research support on certain topics has undoubtedly helped to shape the course of scientific developments.

C. Goals of scientific research

There are at least five possible goals of scientific research. They can be arranged in the following order, moving from a lower to a higher level of scientific development:

1. Description. Collection and classification of factual information constitute the first stage of science, on which the subsequent stages are based.

2. Discovery of relationships. For the social psychologist, the relationships of interest are those between social situations and human behavior and characteristics. Such relationships are often studied using the *correlational method* (see next section), without any implication that the relationships discovered are causal ones. For instance, the study on attitudes toward violence cited at the beginning of this chapter found that Black males in the United States were much more likely than Whites to approve of the use of violence for social change. However, this finding does not mean that they hold such attitudes *because* they are Black.

3. Explanation or understanding. These terms generally are used to refer to the demonstration of a *causal* connection between events. At this stage, the scientist constructs theories about relationships. When the consequences predicted by the theory have been verified, we can claim to have some understanding of the causes of those consequences. For instance, we might conclude

---

[1]Studies investigating the disputed authorship of 12 of *The Federalist Papers* are an example of how the scientific method can be employed in the humanities (Mosteller & Wallace, 1964; Rokeach, Homant, & Penner, 1970). By counting certain key words and value statements, the investigators were able to provide overwhelming support for the view that the papers in dispute were written by James Madison rather than by Alexander Hamilton.

that U. S. Blacks or Canadian separatists who favor the use of violence for social change do so because they have been the victims of discrimination and see little likelihood of improving their lot without some use of violence.

4. *Prediction of events.* Scientific prediction can be of two kinds. *Empirical* prediction merely uses established relationships as its basis (for instance, U. S. Blacks voted heavily Democratic in the last several elections, so they will do so again in the next election). *Rational* prediction is a more advanced stage, which uses a causal theory as the basis for prediction (for example, U. S. Blacks will vote Republican if they are convinced that the Republican Party will do much more than other parties to improve their lot). Although rational predictions are not necessarily any more accurate than empirical predictions, they may have a great advantage whenever new variables enter the picture or relationships between old variables begin to change.

5. *Control or influence over events.* Control is often the ultimate goal of science. Examples of control are successful heart transplants and the landing of astronauts on the moon. In the social sciences, there are so many interacting causes of most human behavior that the degree of control that can be achieved is usually sharply limited. Nevertheless, even the remote prospect of scientific influence on human behavior raises fears in many people's minds of a world like that portrayed in George Orwell's *1984*. On the other hand, B. F. Skinner's *Walden Two* points out that almost all our behavior is already influenced by other people and that scientifically based programs could be used for such beneficial purposes as improving health or reducing prejudice and crime. (See also Figure 2-4.)

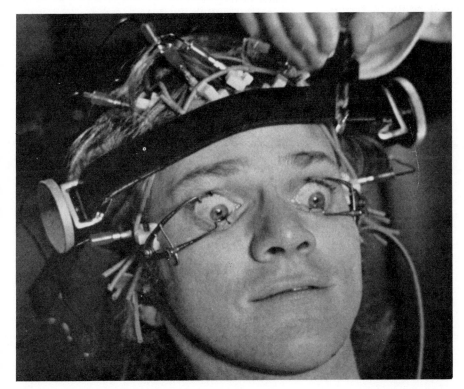

Figure 2-4
Control of behavior in the future? In the futuristic film *A Clockwork Orange*, Alex, who has led a life of violence, is conditioned to respond with nausea anytime he develops a violent thought or a sexual desire. The power of such techniques as a way of controlling behavior is a matter of concern to many people. (Photo courtesy of Warner Bros. Inc.)

II. Experimental research versus correlational research

Following this description of the scientific method in general, let us look briefly at the two major categories of scientific research: experimental research and correlational (or nonexperimental) research.

A. The experimental method

Experimental research on human behavior involves designing situations for observation of behavior in which some aspects of the situation are held constant (controlled) and other aspects are intentionally varied (manipulated). The **experimental method** may be defined as consisting of three components—manipulation of one or more **independent variables,** control of related variables, and observation of one or more **dependent variables.** In Darley and Latané's study there was only one independent variable: the number of other discussion participants in addition to the seizure victim. This variable was given three different values in the experimental design: one, two, and five. Approximately one-third of the subjects took part in each of these three conditions.

Control of related variables—the second component of the experimental method—can include (1) holding some aspects of the situation constant for all subjects, (2) eliminating any aspects that might distort the results, and/or (3) systematically arranging the situation or choosing subjects so that an extraneous variable will have an equal (or a measurable) effect on *every* experimental condition. One of the main variables controlled in the Darley-Latané study was face-to-face interaction of the subjects. It was controlled by eliminating face-to-face interaction and substituting an intercom system. Another factor needing control was the occupation and status of subjects, since such characteristics might affect the subjects' willingness to help a seizure victim. This possibility was controlled by holding the factor constant: all the subjects were students.

Many other factors, such as the subjects' level of anxiety, also might have affected their willingness to help. Although this factor was not mentioned by the researchers, it was nevertheless controlled by means of **randomization**—random assignment of subjects to the three experimental conditions. Random assignment ensures, with a small and specifiable margin of error, that each group has approximately the same percentage of subjects who are quite anxious. The same result could be attained by systematically assigning equal numbers of high- and low-anxiety subjects to each condition, but this procedure would require the prior measurement of the subjects' anxiety levels by some sort of questionnaire or interview. The same goal can be accomplished more simply by randomization, which can also control other extraneous or contaminating variables, including those that the experimenter hasn't even thought of! Random assignment of subjects is a safeguard that is unique to the experimental method, and its importance is very great. It is one of the main reasons why experimentation is the most preferred method of scientific research.

Observation of one or more dependent variables—the third component of the experimental method—requires that there must be at least two clearly distinguishable values or categories into which the dependent variable may fall. Usually the experimenter tries to **measure** the dependent variable—that is, to quantify it on a continuous numerical scale. In the Darley-Latané study there was just one dependent variable, which had only two categories: the subject either did or did not come out of his room to report the emergency during the specified short period of time. This dichotomous (two-point, either-or) dependent variable was converted to a quantitative scale by computing the percentage of subjects in each experimental condition who did come out to help.

As we have seen, in this experiment a very large difference was obtained between the dependent-variable responses for the three independent-variable conditions: 85%, 62%, and 31%.

A final refinement provided by the authors was the subjecting of this difference in percentages to a **statistical test.** The function of such a test (be it a chi-square, an analysis of variance, a t test, or whatever) is to provide a statement of **reliability**—that is, of how likely it is that a difference of this size would occur regularly if the identical experiment were repeated many times. By custom the .05 level of **significance** is accepted in most social-psychological research, which means that a difference as large as the one found could occur by chance only five times out of every 100 occasions. Since the p value (probability that the difference found would occur by chance) for the Darley-Latané experiment was .02—less than .05—we may be confident that the percentages given above represent real, dependable differences in the dependent variable—that the fact that the response rates were different was not just a coincidence. Furthermore, to the extent that other possible contaminating factors have been adequately controlled, we may conclude that these nonchance differences in the dependent variable resulted from the manipulation of the independent variable.

The experiment just described used only one independent variable, but experiments are often constructed to study the effects of two, three, four, or more independent variables. One important advantage of such experiments is that they can show the *interaction* effects of the independent variables in combination with one another, as well as the main effects of each independent variable separately. An **interaction** is a joint effect of two or more variables such that the effect of one variable is different for various levels of the other variable. An example will help to clarify this important statistical concept. Suppose that in the Darley-Latané study we added anxiety of the subjects as a second independent variable. Half of the subjects might be treated as before (the low-anxiety condition), and half might be given an anxiety-arousing experience before the group discussion (the high-anxiety condition). Let us *imagine* that the results for the high-anxiety condition were approximately op-

posite to those for the low-anxiety condition, as shown in Figure 2-5. In this hypothetical example there is no main effect of number of participants (about half of the subjects in each size of group offer help), but there is a pronounced *interaction* of anxiety and number of participants. The low-anxiety subjects are more likely to help when in very small groups than when in larger groups, whereas the high-anxiety subjects are less likely to help when in small groups than when in larger groups.

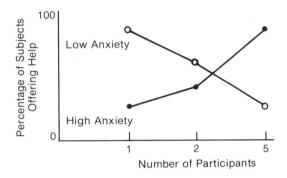

Figure 2-5
An example of an interaction effect

This hypothetical experiment is an example of a **factorial design**—that is, one in which each level of one independent variable is combined with each level of another independent variable (or several others). In this case there were six conditions, combining the two levels of anxiety with the three levels of group size. It is only in factorial experiments that interaction effects of two or more variables can be thoroughly studied.

B. The correlational
(nonmanipulative) method

The experimental method in social psychology is often contrasted with another approach, usually called the **correlational method.** (See, for instance, the detailed comparison by Cronbach, 1957.) The name is somewhat misleading, for it seems to imply the use of correlation coefficients. Since this is not a necessary feature of the method, it might better be named the **nonmanipulative method,** or the nonexperimental method. Whatever it is called, the correlational method studies the *naturally occurring* characteristics of individuals (for example, anxiety, authoritarianism, social class, or race). To use the correlational method, at least two such variables must be measured for each person in the research group, and then the *relationship* between the size of scores on one variable and the size of scores on the other variable is determined.

An imaginary example of correlational research may be given, based on the Darley-Latané study of helping behavior. Suppose the researchers had wanted to study helpfulness in relation to the subjects' social class. They could not manipulate social class, so they would have to use the correlational method. They might maintain the same operational definition of helping as before, using it as an index of the personality trait of helpfulness, and they would probably measure each subject's social class on one of the objective scales that have been developed by past researchers (see Chapter 15). The two sets of scores would then be statistically analyzed to see if they were related, either positively or inversely. Let us suppose that a positive relationship was found (higher-social-class individuals being more helpful) and that the relationship was strong enough to be statistically significant (that is, a dependable nonchance finding).

This example illustrates the most serious problem with the correlational method: *the fact that it often provides few clues as to the direction of causality.* In the hypothetical obtained relationship between these two personal characteristics, helpfulness and social class, which is the independent (or antecedent) variable and which is the dependent (or consequent) variable? In other words, which is cause and which is effect? Perhaps higher social class is the basic causal factor, and helpfulness is the effect. Or perhaps personal helpfulness leads to getting ahead in life and hence to a higher social-class position. Or possibly both variables are effects, resulting from

some other ultimate causal variable, such as the person's level of education. Without more information, we cannot choose among these three hypotheses about the causes.

Despite this drawback of the correlational method, we should not conclude that the experimental method is essential for precise science. A classic example to the contrary is the field of astronomy, which was the first of the physical sciences to emerge into a truly scientific state. Until the post-Sputnik era of artificial satellites, astronomy had to rely almost entirely on the correlational method. After all, scientists cannot manipulate planets or the occurrence of comets to test their theories! But even though astronomy was able to advance by way of the correlational method, scientists prefer the experimental method for one crucial reason: its superiority in allowing us to infer cause and effect.

How is causation determined? Let us hasten to dispel one widespread misconception: contrary to common opinion, experiments do not *prove* cause and effect. Indeed, scientists generally believe that causation can never be proved, since ultimately causation is an *inference* we make from all the data at our disposal. A causal explanation of a phenomenon has to state the necessary and sufficient conditions under which the phenomenon will occur. In addition, some philosophers of science have recently emphasized another requirement of causal explanations: they should specify the **generative mechanism** or process by which the phenomenon is produced (Harré & Secord, 1972).

What are the factors that help us make causal inferences accurately, and why do experiments make it easier than other methods to infer cause and effect? In answering these questions, Selltiz, Wrightsman, and Cook (1976) have listed three factors involved in making causal inferences: concomitant variation, sequence of occurrence of variables, and elimination of other possible causal factors.

Concomitant variation means that two variables vary together in a regular and systematic way—either positively (when variable x is large, variable y is also large) or inversely (when variable x is large, variable y is small), or in any other regular way (for instance, in a curvilinear relationship). Both the correlational method and the experimental method can show concomitant variation.

The sequence of variables is important because, by definition, a cause must occur before or simultaneously with an effect, never after the effect. In correlational research the sequence of variables is sometimes clear (as in Donley and Winter's study of U. S. presidential inaugural addresses and later accomplishments), but in experiments the order of variables is *always* clear, because the experimenter has established the sequence by his or her initial manipulation of the independent variable.

Elimination of other possible causal factors is accomplished through the use of controls in an experiment. Competing causal hypotheses are disproved by holding constant or eliminating the variables that are suggested as causal factors. Nonexperimental studies, by their very nature, cannot be so carefully controlled, but some control can still be exercised. Typical methods include careful selection of subjects and detailed specification of observational methods and conditions, in order to avoid subjects and conditions that might introduce other possible causal factors into the data.

The correlational method will always have a place in social psychology, just as in astronomy, because there are many variables (such as the subject's personality traits or marital status or race) that cannot or should not be manipulated or altered by the experimenter. In such cases we have to use nonexperimental evidence, and consequently we have to be particularly cautious in making causal inferences from our findings.

III. Major methods of social-psychological research

Let us now move from the scientific method in general to the more specific methods of social-psychological research. Basically, there are

only four ways to study human behavior: collecting and analyzing existing products, asking people questions, watching people, and manipulating conditions (experimenting). The four brief research vignettes at the beginning of this chapter were chosen to illustrate these ways of studying people. Two or more of these differing approaches are often combined in a single research project so as to compound their strengths and compensate for their limitations.

The first approach, *collecting and analyzing existing documents and/or artifacts*, is frequently used by historians, archeologists, and biographers but seldom by social psychologists (who should use it more often). The second approach to studying human behavior, *asking people questions*, is a method that includes the familiar gamut of psychological tests, questionnaires, and interviews. The third approach, *watching people*, is an observational method, concentrating on overt behavior rather than on what people say about themselves. Many people can accurately assess their own behavior, so that the asking method is sufficient; but watching is necessary when subjects are unable to describe their behavior or when circumstances (embarrassing situations or fear of social disapproval) might make them unwilling to do so accurately. These three approaches—collecting, asking, and watching—are instances of the correlational method of research, since they do not per se entail any manipulation of conditions by the investigator. However, collected products, questions, and observations can all be used as techniques in the fourth approach to studying human behavior, *experimenting*, which we have already discussed at length.

Within the above ways of studying human behavior, we will distinguish eight specific methods of social-psychological research. These eight methods are archival research, the survey, the field study, the natural experiment, quasi-experimental research, the field experiment, simulation, and the laboratory experiment. Brief examples of research studies will be given to illustrate each method. The order in which the eight methods are presented indicates the different degrees of control of the research conditions they typically possess, with archival research having the least control and the laboratory experiment having the most.

A. Archival research

The way in which preschool picture books teach differential sex-role behavior for boys and girls was the subject of an intriguing report (Weitzman, Eifler, Hokada, & Ross, 1972). These investigators chose to study the supposedly "very best" such books, ones that had won the most coveted prize for preschool books awarded by the American Library Association. Taking the 18 award winners between 1967 and 1971, Weitzman and associates did a content analysis of the titles, illustrations, central characters, and activities described.

Results of this research showed dramatic differences in the portrayals of boys and girls—differences that reflected and reinforced traditional sex-role stereotypes (see Figure 2-6). For instance, many more books were primarily about males than about females (a ratio of 7 to 2). In the books' illustrations females were even less prominent (261 pictures of males to 23 of females, a ratio of 11 to 1). When women or girls did appear, they were much more often in service activities, such as helping, pleasing, or bringing food (a 10-to-1 ratio), whereas boys or men were shown in leadership roles (a 4-to-1 ratio) and in rescue activities (a 9-to-2 ratio). In general boys were active, boisterous, and clever, while girls were passive, pretty, and eager to please. Perhaps the most dramatic finding was that not a single one of the women characters in the books had a job or profession other than being a housewife! (Incidentally, 41% of the books' authors were women.) The researchers concluded that these books show an unrealistically stereotyped picture of the world and teach little girls to have low aspirations and a limited self-image. (We consider such findings in greater detail in Chapter 14.)

This study illustrates many of the characteristics of archival research, which by definition uses the technique of collecting existing ma-

Figure 2-6
Differential sex-role training in preschool picture books. In this typical scene Obadiah has returned from some adventures and is served some hot chocolate by his mother and sister, who are working in the kitchen. (Picture from Brinton Turkle, *Thy Friend, Obadiah.* © 1969 by Viking Press. Used by permission.)

terials. Here, the term **archival research** is used broadly to include analysis of any existing data and not only the records contained in public archives. There is a wide variety in the kinds of data that can be used. Data may be obtained from one individual, or they may be aggregates of information about many individuals. Materials for analysis could include letters written by eminent persons, folk stories of a preliterate society, newspaper editorials, wartime propaganda broadcasts, or public statistics such as suicide rates or stock-market averages.

One of the greatest advantages of archival research is that it uses **unobtrusive measures,** which are **nonreactive** in nature; this means that the act of measuring something for research purposes does not change the phenomenon being measured. (By contrast, asking people's opinions about an issue may often be a **reactive** method, because the people may be induced to think about the issue more than usual and therefore develop or change their opinions.) Another great advantage of archival research is that it makes possible the examination of trends over a period of time. Archival research also allows retrospective studies of past events, which could not be investigated in any other way, and it makes possible cross-cultural comparisons, which would not otherwise be feasible. As this sex-role study shows, archival research permits the testing of hypotheses as well as exploratory and descriptive studies. And, finally, the method can sometimes provide evidence about the direction of causality in relationships—though this kind of evidence is likely to be equivocal. ①

There are also disadvantages to archival research. Often the necessary materials for analysis are difficult to obtain; even if they exist, they may be unknown or unavailable. Also, the researcher can study only those materials that do exist, even though they may not be adequate to test the research hypothesis. Some available materials may contain distortions resulting from their authors' biases (as in some anthropologists' accounts of the customs of a primitive tribe). Content-analysis projects are apt to be lengthy

and expensive, but this problem has been somewhat alleviated by the recent development of computer programs for the analysis of verbal materials. Finally, careful attention must be given to sampling procedures, so that the materials studied are representative of the whole; otherwise researchers cannot generalize from their findings.

B. The survey

The values, attitudes, and beliefs of young people living in the United States in the 1970s were the topic of a large-scale survey by Daniel Yankelovich (1974). The purposes of the study were to compare college students with noncollege youth and to compare responses in 1973 with those from similar surveys of U. S. youth in the 1960s. Interviews were conducted with a representative sample of about 1000 college students and a national cross-section sample of another 2500 young people between the ages of 16 and 25. The questions in the interview had been pretested before the data collection began, and each interview took from one to two hours. Several hundred interviewers conducted the data collection over a period of several weeks. They recorded the respondents' answers on interview forms that were then sent to the study headquarters, where a group of "coders" converted the verbal statements into numerical categories in preparation for computer analysis. *general info of procedure*

A few scattered results from this massive survey will illustrate its findings. A marked change was noted in college students' attitudes since the late 1960s—sharply decreased rebelliousness, lessened criticism of the United States as a "sick society," reduced concern about minorities, but increased acceptance of women's-liberation viewpoints and a dominant interest in finding self-fulfillment *within* a conventional career rather than in place of one. There were some clear differences between college students and noncollege youth; for instance, the noncollege sample was more conservative concerning sex roles and political issues and less satisfied with

① equivocal = having two or more significations; dubious, questionable, of doubtful meaning.

job opportunities. However, perhaps most striking was the finding that the gap between the values of college and noncollege youth has closed markedly in the last few years. The research report stated that "noncollege youth today [1974] is just about where the college population was in 1969. Virtually every aspect of the New Values has deeply penetrated noncollege youth" (Yankelovich, 1974, pp. 23–24).

From this example, we can see many of the characteristics of the **survey method.** By definition, the survey uses the technique of asking, rather than collecting, watching, or experimenting. The questions may be asked orally, as in an interview or test that is administered individually, or the questions may be asked in writing, as in a questionnaire or written test. The subject matter of the questions may vary widely. Surveys most commonly ask about attitudes and opinions, but they can also include questions on knowledge, behavior, personal experiences, environmental situations, and demographic information such as the age and occupation of the respondent. The technique of depth interviewing can also be used to get at important personal motivations, as in the studies of returned Korean War prisoners (E. H. Schein, 1956) and Vietnam veterans (Lifton, 1973). Survey findings may be entirely descriptive in nature, or they may test prior hypotheses; in either case they may be useful for generating theories and hypotheses for further research. Although there are techniques for using repeated survey data from the same group of subjects to indicate causal relationships, surveys usually are much less useful in demonstrating causation than are experiments.

All surveys attempt to make statements about some **population** of respondents; for example, the goal may be to describe the political attitudes of a specific class of people. But the sizes of the populations vary. In public-opinion polls, the population is apt to be very large, such as all the adults in the United States or Canada. In questionnaire studies, the population is apt to be rather small, such as the freshman class of a college. If the population is large, a **sample**

is almost always chosen—that is, a subset of the members of the total population is given the survey interview or questionnaire. (Two of the very few exceptions are the decennial censuses of the United States and Canada, which try to survey the entire populations of each country.) If the population is small, the investigators may choose to contact every member (a 100% sample), or they may decide to contact a smaller group (say, a 10% sample of the members of a freshman class). Such decisions are made primarily on the basis of the cost of data collection as weighed against the degree of precision desired in the final data as an estimate of the true population value. The degree of precision is positively related to the size of the sample and therefore can be estimated in advance by the use of statistical formulas. Wherever sampling is used in a survey, there will be some inaccuracy in applying the results because of **sampling error.** But even in an estimation of the characteristics of very large populations (such as all adults in the United States or Canada), a properly drawn sample of about 1500 cases is enough to give a precise estimate of the total population's views, with a margin for error of less than 3% in either direction.

C. The field study

Fourteen years of field research were reported in the book *Qualities of Community Life* (Barker & Schoggen, 1973). This volume compares aspects of life in a Kansas county seat ("Midwest," population 830) and an English market town ("Yoredale," in North Yorkshire, population 1310). Midwest has been the site of a research field station for many years, while Yoredale was studied intensively during two years a decade apart and for parts of several other years. The research staff members and their families, about 20 people in all, lived in each town and tried to participate normally in community activities according to their interests, avoiding the extremes of either nonparticipating or initiating new activities or procedures. The research purposes and methods were frankly and fully explained to the residents through public meetings, exhibits, and newspaper stories. This procedure was successful in gaining the understanding and cooperation of residents, which was essential in carrying out the research.

A major goal in the investigation was to make a complete inventory and classification of each town's **behavior settings,** defined as public places or occasions that evoke their own typical patterns of behavior. Midwest was found to have nearly 900 public behavior settings and Yoredale about 750, examples being Weylens Grocery, the Odd Fellows Lodge Dinner, Little League baseball practice, King's Arm Pub, and the Church of England Jumble (rummage) Sale. Within these behavior settings the researchers observed and classified people's recurring behavior, recorded the number and characteristics of participants, and classified several levels of participation and leadership.

Though the two towns were found to be similar in many ways, their differences are most interesting. Religious activities were much more prominent in Midwest than in Yoredale, as were educational and governmental activities. However, Yoredale citizens spent more time in activities related to physical health, nutrition (shopping and public eating and drinking), and artistic pursuits. On the average, Midwesterners spent more time than Yoredalers in the public settings of town, their groups were somewhat smaller, and they took more than twice as many leadership roles. The average Yoredaler spent many more hours in settings run by nonlocal authorities (for example, British Railways) and considerably less time in locally run settings. Midwest had more than twice as much public activity involving expression of emotions (for example, athletic contests and plays), and Midwest children got about 14 times as much public attention as Yoredale children.

As shown by this example, a **field study** involves greater depth than a survey but usually less breadth in the sample being studied. Basically, the field study is a watching technique,

though it may often use multiple measurement methods, including collecting and asking techniques. Whereas survey researchers take great pains to ensure the representativeness of their sample, field-study investigators are much less concerned about this aspect of their group. Instead, the aim of the researcher is to understand fully the structural characteristics of a single community or group and/or the dynamic processes that occur there. Since investigators are often involved with the group for long periods of time, they take great care to avoid disrupting or modifying the group processes, and they hope that their presence as observers will eventually be largely ignored by the group members. In addition to the unstructured **participant-observation** method, field studies can incorporate a variety of structured observations, interviews with knowledgeable informants, and questionnaires. Sometimes unobtrusive measures can be taken without the group or individuals concerned having any awareness of the measurement (Heussenstamm, 1971; Wrightsman, 1969). The combination of these methods can give great breadth of coverage and depth of insight into the structure and dynamics of the group under study. Above all, field studies have the advantage that their findings apply directly to the real-life setting in which they were conducted, because their data were directly derived from ongoing everyday activities. The generalizability of the findings to other real groups is a different question, however, and depends mainly on the degree to which the group chosen for study is typical.

The field study isn't as good a method for testing hypotheses as the experiment. The investigator should do pilot work until he or she has some clear-cut hypotheses to test in the field study, but there is still a great temptation to do post hoc (after-the-fact) theorizing on the basis of the data obtained rather than to stick closely to the a priori hypotheses with which the study began. Whether in an experiment or in a field study, such post hoc theorizing is usually very speculative and should not be considered as an

Tally's Corner

adequately tested theory. Another problem with the field study is that it is usually difficult to determine the direction of causality, because the obtained relationships are correlational in nature rather than the result of manipulating variables, as in an experiment. A final problem is that the observer's presence may alter the behavior he or she is observing, since it is rarely possible to make observations without the subjects' knowledge.

D. The natural experiment

A change in the British highway traffic law provided the occasion for a natural experiment by H. L. Ross, Campbell, and Glass (1970). Aiming to lower the highway death rate by getting drunk drivers off the road, the new law authorized police to give an on-the-scene breath test

to drivers who were suspected of being drunk, committing moving-vehicle traffic offenses, or causing an accident. This Breathalyser test measured the percentage of alcohol in the driver's blood. A very stiff and mandatory punishment was established for driving while under the influence of alcohol, and the starting date of the legal crackdown was publicized widely in advance.

The British Ministry of Transport reported a reduction of 1152 highway deaths in the first year of the Breathalyser crackdown. The dramatic drop in injuries and deaths is displayed graphically in the bottom curve of Figure 2-7, which shows the results for weekend nights—the period when drinking drivers are most numerous. By contrast, the upper curve shows the continuing steady level of injuries and deaths during the busy commuting hours (7:00 to 10:00 A.M. and 4:00 to 7:00 P.M.), when British pubs and bars are closed by law. The authors concluded that

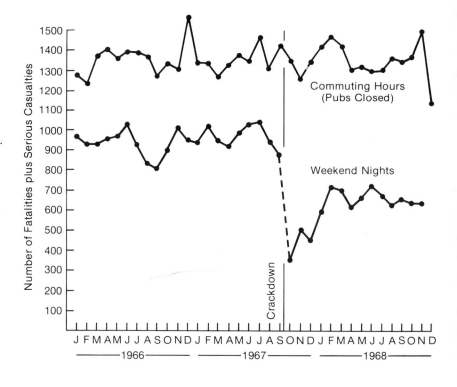

Figure 2-7
Results of the British Breathalyser crackdown. (Adapted from "Determining the Social Effects of a Legal Reform: The British 'Breathalyser' Crackdown of 1967," by H. L. Ross, D. T. Campbell, and G. V. Glass, *American Behavioral Scientist*, 1970, *13*(4), 493–509. Copyright 1970 by Sage Publications, Inc. Used by permission.)

the crackdown had its greatest effect in the first three months and then leveled off, but even at the end of the following year there was a reduction of about 30% in the casualty rate on weekend nights.

As noted previously, the hallmark of any experiment is manipulation of one or more variables. What distinguishes the **natural experiment** from other kinds of experiments is that the manipulation occurs without the intervention of the investigator. It may be a natural event, such as a hurricane or earthquake; it may be an action of governmental policy makers, such as the decision to racially integrate the U. S. armed forces in World War II; or it may be a joint action of many people, such as a national election or a large protest march. In any case the event must be dramatic and clear-cut enough to have an impact on the subjects being studied. The researcher has to obtain measures of the subjects' attitudes or other variables of interest both before and after the experimental event occurs, so that the amount of change caused by the event can be determined. However, to be completely sure that this change is a result of the event in question, the investigator also needs to have a control group of comparable subjects who were not exposed to the event. In the study cited here, all British drivers were exposed to the crackdown, so the control condition chosen was a time period when drinking drivers would be rare.

There are several advantages to using the natural experiment as a research method. Like all experiments, it yields valuable information about the direction of causality; like the field study, it involves little or no disruption of the group by the investigator. Perhaps most important, the natural experiment often involves very strong variables that have powerful effects on people's attitudes and behavior and that could not practically or ethically be manipulated by an experimenter. To counterbalance these advantages, there is the unfortunate fact that natural experiments usually arrive with little or no warning. This means that the investigator must grab the opportunity when it comes, often without

sufficient planning and with inadequate premeasures. It also means that the researcher can study only events that do occur and not other events that might be more illuminating. Many studies, for instance, were carried out to assess the effect of President Kennedy's assassination on the people of the United States (Greenberg & Parker, 1965), but the equally interesting question of how the public would have reacted had the assassination attempt failed could not be answered. A final problem with the natural experiment may occur if the researcher takes any active role in the group of subjects (as in a participant-observation study), thereby risking the introduction of bias.

Another example of a natural experiment on the effects of a legal reform concerned changes in pornography laws in Denmark. Kutchinsky (1973) showed very convincingly that the liberalization of pornography laws and the resulting increase in availability of pornographic books and picture magazines were accompanied by a marked *decrease* in the occurrence of sex crimes, particularly child-molestation offenses. This finding would undoubtedly surprise many moralistic and punitively oriented citizens and legislators, and it emphasizes once again the importance of collecting empirical scientific evidence on the success or failure of political and legal reforms, a procedure that has been advocated by Donald Campbell (1969).

E. Quasi-experimental research

A study of the conformity behavior of automobile drivers (Barch, Trumbo, & Nangle, 1957) provides one example of quasi-experimental research. Its goal was to see if conformity to the state law requiring signaling for a left or right turn would be increased by seeing the driver in the car just ahead give a turn signal. The method used was observation of naturally occurring behavior by drivers at several intersections in Lansing, Michigan. Whenever two successive cars traveling less than 100 feet apart both turned in the same direction, the signaling behavior of the two drivers was recorded. More than 5000 such pairs of cars were counted during a four-week period of daylight, good-weather observations. It was found that the signaling behavior of the first (model) car significantly influenced the behavior of the following driver. However, the amount of influence was relatively small—it accounted for less than a 10% increase in signaling.

The defining characteristics of **quasi-experimental research** are that the investigator does not have full experimental control over the independent variable but does have extensive control over how, when, and for whom the dependent variable is measured (Campbell & Stanley, 1966, p. 34). Under such circumstances, research designs with many of the advantages of true experiments can be used. In the above example, the independent variable was whether the first driver signaled or not, and the dependent variable was whether the second driver did so. The first driver's behavior was not under the investigators' control, but elaborate rules were established specifying the time, place, and conditions for selecting the drivers for whom to record the dependent variable. These data-collection conditions undoubtedly eliminated the operation of many extraneous variables on the data (for example, bad weather conditions, or long distances between cars, which would reduce the modeling influence of the first car). However, it is still conceivable that other uncontrolled extraneous variables could have produced the obtained relationships. Suppose, for example, that many of the observations were made at spots where traffic-control police officers or parked highway-patrol cars were clearly visible to the drivers. Under such conditions most drivers would be likely to give the legally required signal, whereas at observation points where there were no police officers, both drivers of a pair might often neglect to signal. If so, the presence or absence of police might be the real causal variable, producing an apparent (but spurious) influence of the first driver's signaling on the second driver's behavior.

The ideal way to eliminate the effect of possible extraneous variables is to control and randomize the presentation of the independent variable—thus making the study a true experiment rather than a quasi-experiment. In the above research, this could have been done by hiring an assistant to serve as the first driver, returning repeatedly to the same intersection and randomly choosing the trials on which to signal or not signal.

There are many different specific research designs that are quasi-experimental in nature. If you thought carefully about the natural experiment, you may have realized that it is one example of a quasi-experimental method, since the independent variable is not under the control of the investigator. All quasi-experimental methods have some vulnerable points, such as lack of control over certain types of extraneous variables; thus by definition they are less adequate designs than are true experiments. However, they are very useful in situations when better-controlled designs are not feasible. In real-life situations there are often limits on the power of the investigator to manipulate variables or to control the circumstances. In such situations quasi-experimental designs are much better than no research, and their results may be quite conclusive. Usually such studies have the practical purpose of learning something about the particular real-life setting in which the research is conducted, so the problem of generalizing to other settings may be absent or minimal.

Quasi-experimental designs are particularly useful in studying independent variables that are complex and involve long-continued social situations, such as educational methods or institutional environments. For instance, the results of a required high school course in United States or Canadian history could not be tested experimentally, since there would be no comparable untreated control group to compare with the course graduates. A pre/post comparison on a standardized test of U. S. or Canadian history knowledge would not be convincing, since taking the test before the course might sensitize students to facts they should learn in the course. In this situation, the best procedure would be to randomly assign half the class to a precourse history test and the other half to the same test given after the course—a useful quasi-experimental design. However, this design would still be vulnerable to effects of other concurrent experiences, such as many students' seeing a series of television specials on their nation's history. This limitation could be overcome by repeating the design for a second year when the TV specials weren't broadcast, thus ruling out their effect on the postcourse test scores. This example shows how a quasi-experimental design can be "patched up" and strengthened by adding extra measurements or comparison groups that will allow rejection of plausible alternative explanations of the findings.

F. The field experiment

How does the behavior of small crowds of people affect passersby on a busy city street? That was the question asked in a field experiment by Milgram, Bickman, and Berkowitz (1969), which was conducted in downtown New York City during two winter afternoons. At a prearranged signal, a small group of people walked to the middle of a 50-foot section of sidewalk, stopped, and stood looking up at the building across the street. Little was to be seen there except some dim figures at a sixth-floor window (the experimenters) looking back at the sidewalk. After standing in this position for 60 seconds, the group was signaled to disperse. A few minutes later the whole routine was repeated with a different-sized group. Meanwhile motion pictures were taken of the observation area from the window so that raters could later count the number of passersby who stopped and looked up with the crowd or who looked up without stopping.

The independent variable in this experiment was the size of the group looking up. On randomly selected trials the size of the "crowd" was either 1, 2, 3, 5, 10, or 15 people. There were

five trials for each size condition. The results are shown graphically in Figure 2-8. Even one person looking up was enough to produce a similar glance from more than 40% of passersby, while a group of five people could induce almost everyone to follow the direction of their gaze. However, it took much larger crowds to cause many people to stop; even with the largest crowd, 15 people, only 40% of the passersby actually stopped.[2]

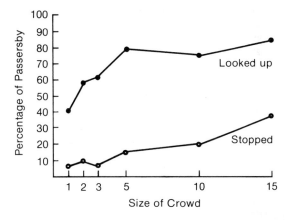

Figure 2-8
Response to crowds. Mean percentages of passersby who looked up and who stopped as a function of the size of the stimulus crowd. (Adapted from "Note on the Drawing Power of Crowds of Different Size," by S. Milgram, L. Bickman, and L. Berkowitz, *Journal of Personality and Social Psychology*, 1969, *13*, 79–82. Copyright 1969 by the American Psychological Association. Used by permission.)

[2]This experiment illustrates a kind of research called a **parametric study**—one in which at least three or more values of the independent variable are used, instead of having a control group that receives no treatment. In a sense, each value of the independent variable provides a control (or comparison) for each of the other conditions. In such research it is possible to study the shape of the curve (or the mathematical function) relating the dependent variable to the independent variable. For instance, in the above study, Figure 2-8 illustrates that the curve for stopping was a rising linear function of the size of crowd, while the graph for looking up was a convex curvilinear function.

As the above example indicates, in the **field experiment** the experimental conditions are planned and introduced by the experimenter, but the setting is a real-life one for the subjects, who may not even be aware that a study is being conducted. This particular experiment was quite a simple one to conduct, but field experiments can be very complex and difficult to conduct, particularly when working within an ongoing organization. The importance of prior planning can hardly be stressed enough. To make such an experiment successful, the investigators must have a great deal of knowledge about the situation and the experimental and control variables, and they need to have done much pilot work and pretesting of their measuring instruments and manipulations. Furthermore, the investigators must have carefully thought through their experimental hypothesis and must have planned their operations at every step of the experiment so as to provide a stringent test of the hypothesis. All this is not an easy task, and there are often other obstacles. Frequently the experimenters must get permission (for instance, from a company president or a commanding general) to do the study, and even then they may not be able to control other crucial variables (such as layoffs in the middle of an assembly-line study or new duty assignments for military subjects).

Other problems can also occur in the field experiment. Often very strong variations in the independent variable may be needed because of relatively insensitive measuring instruments for the dependent variable (for example, worker morale is hard to measure precisely). A dependent variable such as industrial productivity can be influenced by many factors in addition to whatever independent variable is being manipulated. Yet it is frequently impossible to vary the independent variable enough to have a measurable impact on the dependent variable (for instance, if the manipulation were an attempt to change the leadership style of forepersons from authoritarian to democratic, the investigator might find it impossible, in a short time, to create changes great enough to have a significant effect

on morale or productivity). It is particularly difficult to study conflict in organizations because of the sensitive nature of such conflict, and even in relatively conflict-free areas there may often be misunderstandings and suspicion about the investigators' purposes and procedures.

If all these potential obstacles are successfully surmounted, the investigator will have a very powerful research technique that is of practical as well as scientific value. As with the field study, the findings of the field experiment apply to real-life situations, and the problem of generalizability to other settings is small because the study is usually done in the setting that gave rise to the research question in the first place. Thus the field experiment is particularly good for studying complex processes of social change or other problems that are too broad to be studied in a laboratory experiment or that would be changed dynamically if transferred to a laboratory context. Because the field experiment is carried out in a real-life setting, it can study patterns of variables that covary naturally and that might be artificially separated in a laboratory experiment. Like all experiments, the field experiment gives us a relatively clear idea of the direction of causal relationships. In addition, it can sometimes control conditions so as to eliminate the effects of contaminating variables. But it lacks analytical precision, the one great asset of the laboratory experiment.

G. Simulation research

One of the most famous recent studies in social psychology was the prison simulation conducted at Stanford University by Philip Zimbardo and his colleagues (Haney, Banks, & Zimbardo, 1973). The simulation began with wailing police sirens as nine young men were picked up at their homes, spread-eagled and frisked, handcuffed, taken to the police station, fingerprinted and booked, and finally driven blindfolded to a "prison" in the basement of the Stanford psychology building. There three other young men dressed as guards supervised their activities in a small area of the building that had been outfitted with typical prison cells, cots, a small "yard," and even a solitary-confinement "hole."

The subjects in this research project were college students who had answered a newspaper ad for volunteers to take part in a psychological study of "prison life." The many applicants for this $15-per-day summer employment were carefully screened by questionnaires and interviews to select the most mature and stable and least antisocial individuals. The 24 normal, healthy college students who were chosen were randomly divided into "prisoners" and "guards," and they agreed to serve in either role for a two-week period. All were instructed that there would be no use of physical punishment or physical aggression, but in other respects elaborate provisions were made to simulate many of the dehumanizing conditions of prison life. Each prisoner was sprayed with a "delousing" liquid, fitted with a chain and lock around one ankle, dressed only in a loosely fitting smock with no underclothes, and always addressed by his ID number. Guards were issued uniforms, whistles, and nightsticks and told simply to maintain order in the prison during their eight-hour shifts and to be ready to deal effectively with any emergencies that might arise. Videotapes and audio recordings were made of the daily, public behavior of prisoners and guards, and much additional information was gathered from extensive interviews, tests, and observations of all participants.

The realistic prison conditions quickly called forth from the subjects a degree of involvement far beyond mere role-playing. The changes were dramatic: guards increasingly enjoyed asserting their power by issuing commands to do pushups, by refusing requests to go to the toilet, and by other means; prisoners initially resisted but soon lapsed into helplessness and depression. To quote the authors:

> [Within] a surprisingly short period of time, we witnessed a sample of normal, healthy American college students fractionate into a group of prison guards who seemed to derive pleasure from insulting, threatening, humiliating and dehumanising their peers—those who by chance selection had been assigned to the "prisoner" role. The typical prisoner syndrome was one of passivity, dependency, depression, helplessness and self-deprecation. . . . Most dramatic and distressing to us was the observation of the ease with which sadistic behavior could be elicited in individuals who were not "sadistic types" and the frequency with which acute emotional breakdowns could occur in men selected precisely for their emotional stability [p. 89].

By the end of only six days, half the prisoners had become so depressed, angry, or anxious that they had to be "released," and the investigators felt obliged to terminate the whole study at this point because of the increasing emergence of pathological reactions in both prisoners and guards. The researchers held several encounter sessions for the participants to reduce emotional reactions and encourage positive responses to the experience, and they maintained contact with each subject for a year to ensure that the temporary negative effects of the simulation were no longer persisting.

The essential feature of any **simulation** is that it attempts to imitate some crucial aspects of a real-world situation in order to gain more understanding of the underlying mechanisms that operate in that situation. For example, in the prison study, the researchers created conditions of powerlessness, arbitrary control, loss of personal identity symbols, and dependency; and they observed how quickly these social conditions transformed the behavior of both the dominant and the subservient groups of subjects. This was a particularly realistic set of conditions; in many simulations the conditions are not so graphic or compelling. Nevertheless, there is usually a high degree of emotional involvement among the subjects. (Laboratory experiments also attempt to imitate some aspects of a real-world situation and to study the mechanisms that operate there. However, simulation research requires the knowledgeable participation of the subjects in creating the simulation, whereas in most laboratory experiments subjects are unaware of what the experimental setting is intended to represent and to investigate.)

There are several basic types of simulations, ranging from computer models of social processes (for example, friendship-clique formation), through simulation of complex human-machine systems (for example, an air-traffic-control network), to all-human simulations such as the prison study. Another interesting example of the latter type is the Inter-Nation Simulation (Guetzkow, Alger, Brody, Noel, & Snyder, 1963), in which several small groups of subjects make decisions about diplomatic, economic, and military plans for several imaginary nations, and the development of this artificial "world" is observed for trends similar to real-world occurrences. Generally such simulations are run only once; but with sufficient time, energy, and money they can be repeated many times to determine whether their results are stable and reliable, or too variable to yield clear conclusions (for example, Brody, 1963). When a simulation is repeated many times and some of the imposed conditions are systematically manipulated, it becomes a true experiment rather than a one-shot simulation.

Like the field experiment, simulations require much advance planning, and they often permit even greater control of many conditions. As the prison study illustrates, they can sometimes generate very powerful emotions and behavioral influences. They primarily utilize careful control of situational variables, but sometimes personal characteristics of participants may also be controlled or varied by systematic assignment of certain types of individuals to certain conditions. The results of simulations are necessarily suggestive rather than conclusive: they may provide new insights into real-world situations or even dramatic confirmation of expectations, but they cannot demonstrate the correctness of the researcher's theory or hypothesis. The validity and generality of their results are always open to question: Would the same events occur in a real-world setting? Even if they did, would it be because of the factors controlled in the simulation or because of other factors?

H. The laboratory experiment

Darley and Latané's (1968a, 1968b) research on diffusion of responsibility in a potential helping situation will provide our example of a laboratory experiment. Since this study was described in Sections I and II, the description need not be repeated here.

We begin by noting a paradox: laboratory experiments do not have to be done in a laboratory. As a matter of fact, occasionally they can even be conducted in a real-life setting. This is the case because the essential conditions for what we refer to as laboratory experiments are *control* and *precision*. The experimenter designs the situation specifically for his or her purposes, manipulates some variables, and controls other variables as carefully as possible. *Usually* this can be done only in a laboratory. It should also be emphasized that a laboratory experiment is not an attempt to duplicate real-life situations; if that were the purpose, a field study would be conducted. Instead, the laboratory experiment is an attempt to *isolate* factors that may often occur together in real life, to vary some, and to control others, so that the operation of each factor will be seen clearly under pure conditions. The analogy of physics experiments done in a vacuum in order to eliminate air resistance may help illustrate this point. With this degree of control and precision, definitive results are often possible, and conflicting theories can be tested by pitting their predictions against each other. By the choice of research subjects and events the researcher can even control the past history of the experimental group, a technique that would not be possible in any other research method except a simulation.

Despite the many advantages of laboratory experiments, this method poses a number of problems. Its most obvious limitation is the artificiality of the setting—in most laboratory experiments (though definitely not in all) no identical situation and task are apt to be met any-where in the subjects' everyday life, and subjects are very much aware that they are involved in an experiment. To an even greater degree than in the field experiment, researchers using the laboratory experiment must have a great deal of knowledge about the variables involved in the study, and they must have done a great deal of pilot research before the laboratory experiment can be designed effectively. Another persistent problem for laboratory experiments is the effect of the mental set that is brought to the experiment by the subject. The subject's mental set is largely determined by the demand characteristics of the situation, a topic that will be discussed in more detail later in this chapter. Because of the artificiality of the typical experimental situation, it is often difficult to create strong effects by means of experimental manipulations. For instance, it may be possible to create a mild degree of liking between subjects, but we could not possibly manipulate love experimentally. This problem means that nonsignificant results are inconclusive: while they may show that our theory is wrong, *they also may merely indicate that the manipulation is too weak to produce effects on the dependent variable.* To help the investigator decide between these two alternatives, there should be a separate check on whether the manipulation of the independent variable was successful.

An inevitable problem of laboratory experiments is the difficulty in generalizing their results to real-life social situations. If we have artificially isolated the effects of naturally covarying factors, a single experiment will tell us nothing about how these variables interact in real life (Dorris, 1972). The researcher must take the results back to more realistic situations and investigate the interactions of each experimental variable with other related variables. For instance, since experimenters often use groups of subjects that were formed solely for the purposes of the experiment, the researchers need to ask the additional question of whether the results with such groups would hold true for ongoing groups with

a unique history, such as church bowling teams, fraternity groups, or Young Democrats clubs.

On the topic of helping behavior, field experiments have illustrated the importance of checking laboratory results in real-life situations. Piliavin, Rodin, and Piliavin (1969) used New York subway trains as settings for staged emergencies in which a rider suddenly collapsed. In this face-to-face situation, Darley and Latané's diffusion-of-responsibility hypothesis was not supported. (Chapter 9 considers bystanders' reactions to such emergencies in more detail.)

IV. Research problems in analyzing human products

The following four sections of this chapter will look in greater detail at the problems with research methods associated with the four basic ways of studying human behavior mentioned in Section III: analyzing products, asking questions, watching people, and manipulating conditions. This section takes up the problems involved in collecting and analyzing existing human products, particularly the most commonly studied type, written documents.

Content analysis, the method used in the scientific study of documents, may be defined as the objective, systematic, and (usually) quantitative description of verbal communication or other symbolic behavior (for example, drawings or paintings). Its characteristics and uses have been described at length in valuable articles by Berelson (1954) and Holsti (1968). Its major problems, briefly stated, are the following.

1. Obtaining materials. Locations of the needed documents may be unknown, materials out of print, sources of supply uncooperative, and so on. Also, the available materials may not allow an adequate test of the investigator's hypotheses.

2. Sampling. The topic of sampling methods will be discussed at length in Section V. Often sampling decisions must be made at several levels: sources (for example, which newspapers should be chosen in a study of the U. S. press?), specific documents (for example, how many and which issues should be analyzed?), and sections of documents (for example, would just the front page of each issue provide sufficient and appropriate material?).

3. *Choosing coding categories.* The relevant categories into which the material will be coded (di-vided) must be chosen in light of the hypotheses and the material involved. Some typical categories are: subject matter, evaluation (favorable or unfavorable), kinds of people described, values or needs expressed (for example, friendship, power, achievement, wealth), the type of endings (happy, sad, or ambiguous), and so on.

4. *Choosing units* (things) *to be analyzed.* For some purposes the unit of analysis may be large; for example, a whole newspaper article may be classified as political, economic, or social news. For other purposes the unit may be small—for example, individual words whose frequency of occurrence is counted to determine the readability of written material. Often a theme, or assertion about some subject, is the most desirable unit of analysis—for example, "my friend John" (equivalent to "John is my friend") or "Russian policy is pro-Arab."

5. *Choosing what to count.* The choice to be made here is usually among scoring just the appearance or nonappearance of a given theme or coding category, counting the number of times it appears, and rating the intensity with which it is expressed (for example, "slight dislike" or "bitter disapproval").

6. *Demonstrating reliability.* Whenever the coding process involves any subjectivity or use of judgment, it is necessary to show its interrater reliability—that is, the degree of consistency with which two coders will make the same ratings or classifications. Achieving adequate reliability

may often require careful pretraining of coders using material similar to that which they will analyze in the study itself.

7. *Considering the validity of results.* **Validity** refers to the correctness of measurement—that is, the extent to which the method measures what it is intended to measure. Validity should be quantified by whatever means are available. For instance, are the results plausible? To what extent are they related as expected to other relevant data? To what extent are they successful in predicting further events or findings? To what extent are they consistent with established theory?

V. Research problems in asking questions

In the 1970 British elections, the Labour Party, under Harold Wilson, was heavily favored to win. Almost all the major British public-opinion-polling organizations predicted a Labour victory of anywhere from 2% to 9% of the vote. Yet the Conservative Party, under Edward Heath, scored a smashing upset, winning by nearly 5%. How can this failure of scientific polling methods be explained?

Public-opinion polling is one example of the second basic way of studying human behavior, asking questions. This approach is also called the *survey method*, and it includes three of the most popular research techniques of social psychology: polls, interviews, and questionnaires. Since the spectacular failure of polls in the 1970 British election is not the only example that shows that survey findings can be wrong, we must question the basic *validity* of survey methods. The validity of a survey is affected by sampling, question wording, memory errors, respondents' needs for social desirability, bias from other response sets, interviewer effects, and other factors. Failure to use proper safeguards in any one of these aspects may be enough to invalidate the results of an opinion survey, no matter how carefully the other aspects are handled.

A. Sampling: Choosing the respondents

Four different types of sampling will be discussed here: haphazard sampling, systematically biased sampling, quota sampling, and probability sampling. The first, **haphazard sampling,** should always be avoided. As the name implies, haphazard sampling involves an unsystematic approach to the choice of respondents; it is the usual method of inquiring reporters or of television programs such as *Candid Camera,* which choose respondents according to a momentary whim. The key to all sampling procedures is **representativeness:** the sample must be representative of some specifiable population in order to have any usefulness. Since the haphazard sample is not representative of any population, it has no scientific value.

The second type of sampling, **systematically biased sampling,** is also to be avoided. It usually results from an unanticipated error in an attempt to achieve representativeness. A monumental example of biased sampling was displayed in a prediction made by the popular magazine *Literary Digest* in 1936. To predict the results of that year's U. S. presidential elections, the magazine sent out tens of millions of postcard ballots to citizens all around the country. More than 2 million postcards were returned, so the monumental mistake was not due to a small sample! However, there was a serious sampling bias, for the magazine had chosen its respondents from automobile registration listings and telephone books. In 1924, 1928, and 1932, a similar technique had predicted the election successfully, but by 1936 the well-to-do and the poor had divided into quite different political orientations as a result of the Great Depression of the early 1930s. The responses to its poll favored the Republican candidate, Alfred Landon, so the magazine confidently predicted his victory. Instead,

Franklin Roosevelt won by a landslide, carrying all but two states; and confidence in the *Literary Digest* was so badly shaken that the magazine expired two years later.

While the *Literary Digest* was failing so spectacularly, three young pollsters—George Gallup, Archibald Crossley, and Elmo Roper—won wide attention by correctly predicting President Roosevelt's reelection in 1936. These men used the quota method of sampling, which is still used today—with many refinements and improvements—by the major commercial polling organizations. **Quota sampling** seeks to attain representativeness by basing the selection of a sample on major characteristics of the population. First, the population of all registered voters in Canada or the United States is analyzed along several basic dimensions (for example, geographic area of the country, size of city or town, sex, age, and so on). Then a quota is established for the number of respondents in each category so that the sample has the same proportion of people in each category as does the population. This procedure avoids the most frequent sources of systematic bias and thus is more likely to yield accurate predictions than haphazard sampling or systematically biased sampling. However, quota sampling does not avoid some more subtle forms of systematic bias, because it still allows the interviewer a free choice of respondents within the limitations of the quota he or she is assigned. (See Figure 2-9.)

The fourth major type of sampling, **probability sampling,** requires that every member of the population must have a known probability (usually an equal probability) of being contacted. The complex procedures that are necessary to meet this requirement make probability sampling too expensive and too slow for the major commercial pollsters. The greatest advantage to using probability sampling is that the *expected amount of sampling error can be stated exactly,* based on the size of the sample. No other sampling method has this advantage; commercial polling organizations using quota sampling can only es-

Figure 2-9
A source of bias in quota sampling. In quota sampling, the interviewers, within the limits of the quotas prescribed, select their respondents. They may choose to avoid a particular house because of its looks; they may work only at certain times of day; or they may avoid certain kinds of people. Thus, their results can be biased by their selection procedures. (Photo courtesy of Carl Young.)

timate the amount of error in their predictions. In general, however, we must conclude that commercial pollsters have done very well; during the 1950–1970 period, the Gallup Poll erred, on the average, only 1.6% in predicting 11 congressional and presidential elections (Gallup, 1972, p. 234). In the 1972 U. S. presidential election, when Richard Nixon received 61% of the vote, the three major polls predicted he would receive between 59% and 62%. There have also been fiascoes, though, such as the pollsters' prediction that Dewey would defeat Truman in 1948. In a really close election, such as the 1960 contest between Kennedy and Nixon, the pollsters are forced to admit that their data are not precise enough to predict a winner.

A probability sample may be obtained in several ways. The simplest ways are **random sampling** (drawing from a container that has been shaken thoroughly or from a table of random numbers) and **systematic sampling** (picking every nth name from a list). Both of these methods require a complete listing of all the members of the population. When that is impossible—and it usually is!—probability sampling becomes much more difficult and expensive. In that case **stratified random sampling** may be used, in which respondents are randomly chosen from each of several *strata* (categories), which together make up the whole population. The method usually used is **area sampling,** in which the total population is broken down into geographic units such as counties and then broken down again into smaller units such as precincts, census tracts, or portions of these. An enumerator is sent to each of the randomly chosen areas to list every dwelling unit; the sampling directors then make a random choice of a few dwelling units, and interviewers are sent to those specific units with instructions to interview a specific person in each unit. Though area sampling is expensive and slow, it is better than any other method in ensuring the representativeness of the sample.

B. Question wording

Planning and constructing a survey interview is a very large and complicated task, which deserves a more thorough treatment than can be given here. Some of the major problems and considerations in wording interview schedules are the following:

1. *Establishing rapport.* An interview usually begins with an explanation of its purpose and sponsorship, followed by some simple questions to put the respondent at ease.

2. *Format of questions.* Questions may be either **open-ended** (allowing the respondent to answer in his own words) or **closed-ended** (presenting two or more response alternatives for the respondent to choose between). Many interviews use both types, for different purposes.

3. *Order of questions.* A common approach is the **funnel sequence:** broad, open-ended questions first, then somewhat narrower ones, and finally questions focusing on various specific aspects of the topic.

4. *Vocabulary.* Many respondents will have little education, a limited vocabulary, and poor understanding of unusual colloquial or technical terms. *Pretesting* of questions is essential to determine problems in respondents' understanding.

5. *Clarity.* Questions must be kept simple and direct. They should avoid ambiguity, such as double negatives or **double-barreled items**—ones that ask two questions, such as "Do you favor increased U.S. trade with China and Cuba?"

6. *Objective wording.* Avoid bias due to emotionally charged terms (for example, "communist agitators," "police brutality") or the use of prestigious names or concepts (for example, "the President's program," "the American Way of Life").

C. Memory errors

Is the information that people give about themselves in interviews always accurate? Human memory is fallible, and hence many studies have been done to investigate the degree of interviewing errors resulting from faulty memory. Findings show that a number of procedures can be used to improve the respondent's memory accuracy. Two such procedures are asking the respondent to consult available records (diaries, income-tax forms, birth certificates, and the like) and using questions that require recognition of a response (from a list of possible responses) instead of unaided recall (Cannell & Kahn, 1968, p. 562).

D. Social-desirability
   needs of respondents

As we shall see in Chapter 4, most of us are concerned about the impression we make on others—even on pollsters. Many respondents want to be obliging but don't want to show their ignorance or other unfavorable characteristics. In interviews they may be inclined to fake more knowledge than they really have. For instance, "How do you feel about the government's new farm policy?" may evoke the response "I think it's pretty good" from someone who knows nothing about it.

Social-desirability bias is extremely pervasive. On most topics where society's norms dictate or even suggest that most people prefer one kind of behavior over another, we can expect an overreporting of the desirable behaviors and an underreporting of the undesirable ones. Some interesting examples of social-desirability bias are given in Table 2-1.

Several techniques can be used to combat the pervasive social-desirability bias from emerging in interviews. The interviewer should establish good rapport with the respondent and reassure the respondent by the wording of the questions and the manner of asking that a socially undesirable response is perfectly acceptable in the interview situation. Before any detailed questions about a topic, the interview schedule should include questions to determine the respondent's degree of knowledge about and interest in the topic.

Table 2-1

Examples of false interview responses due to social-desirability bias

1. Of 920 Denver adults interviewed in 1949, at least 34% who claimed to have made contributions to the Community Chest (or United Fund drive) had not actually done so according to official records (Parry & Crossley, 1950).
2. Of the same group, 10% falsely claimed to have a driver's license, and 2% reported that they did not when they actually did have one.
3. In a World War II study, 17% of respondents falsely denied having cashed in any war bonds. Among upper-income groups, 43% refused to admit it (Hyman, 1944).
4. With the passage of time, an increasing percentage of respondents report that they voted for the winning candidate in past elections. By 1964, 66% of respondents reported having voted for Kennedy in 1960, although only 50% actually did so.

Source: Personal communication from Angus Campbell (1967).

In questionnaires, other methods can be used to control for social-desirability effects. Allen L. Edwards (1953) suggested use of a *forced-choice* technique in which two items of equal social desirability, but relating to different social needs, are paired together, and the respondent has to pick the item which is more true of himself or herself. Though this was a creative proposal, unfortunately its applications have been disappointing (Barron, 1959, p. 116; W. A. Scott, 1968, p. 241). On both the Minnesota Multiphasic Personality Inventory (MMPI) and the California Psychological Inventory (CPI), a scale was developed to measure *defensiveness*, and scores on this special scale could be used to help interpret results for several other scales on which respondents might be reluctant to admit their own undesirable characteristics (Gough, 1957; McKinley, Hathaway, & Meehl, 1948).

E. Bias from other response sets

Response sets are systematic ways of giving answers that are not directly related to the *content* of the question but are related to the form or characteristics of the alternative answers. We have just discussed the response set of social desirability, or what is sometimes called "faking good." Questionnaire studies particularly, but interviews as well, are also hampered by other kinds of response sets such as carelessness and inconsistency of responses, faking bad, extremity of responses, yea-saying (acquiescence), or nay-saying (opposition). Let us look at each of these problems briefly.

1. Carelessness and inconsistency. When respondents are careless or unmotivated, their answers will be inconsistent from moment to moment or from one testing occasion to another. If this happens often, the questionnaire will be low in reliability (consistency of measurement), and as a result it will also be low in validity (accuracy of measurement). An unreliable measuring device is like a tape measure made of elastic, which stretches a different amount each time it is used; that is, it is very nearly worthless.

2. Faking bad. The response set to give socially unacceptable answers (faking bad) is the opposite of the social-desirability response set. In the general population, this tendency is probably very rare, but in mental health clinics and psychiatric hospitals it is not uncommon to find malingerers (or "goldbrickers," to use the army term) who have something to gain by claiming to be ill or upset. Since the MMPI was developed for use in such settings, it includes a scale to aid in identifying respondents who are faking bad (Hathaway & McKinley, 1951).

3. Extremity of response. This response set can only occur on questionnaire items where there are more than two alternative answers. For instance, what is called a Likert-type attitude scale might have alternatives ranging from $+3$

(strongly agree) to –3 (strongly disagree). Here an *extremity response set* would be displayed if a respondent chose unusually many +3 *or* –3 answers. The effects of the extremity response set on questionnaire validity have been studied very little. These effects can be diminished if equal numbers of items on any given scale are keyed in the positive and negative directions, since the +3 scores will then tend to counterbalance the –3 scores. Another remedy for extreme responding is to eliminate the set altogether by using *dichotomous* items (Yes/No or Agree/Disagree), as is done in many personality inventories.

4. *Acquiescence, or yea-saying.* The acquiescence response set is defined as the tendency to agree with questionnaire items regardless of their content. This response set can be a problem in many attitude and personality scales, and Chapter 18 examines its effects on the California F scale, which was designed to measure authoritarianism. Among others, Bass (1955); Christie, Havel, and Seidenberg (1958); and Gage, Leavitt, and Stone (1957) have evaluated the issue of yea-saying on the F scale, while Block (1965), Jackson and Messick (1965), and Rorer and Goldberg (1965) have reviewed the effects of acquiescence in the MMPI.

5. *Opposition, or nay-saying.* A tendency to disagree with items regardless of their content is opposition, or nay-saying, the opposite of acquiescence. This response set can be measured by low scores on the Couch and Keniston (1960) agreeing-response-set scale. Nay-saying is relatively rare and has been little studied, but it seems somewhat more common among highly educated individuals, as suggested in the old saying that a professor is "someone who thinks otherwise."

Clearly, response sets do affect the answers of some respondents—particularly when the questions are ambiguous or unimportant to the respondent. However, as we have seen, there are ways in which each kind of response set can be detected, controlled, or overcome.

Unobtrusive measures (behavioral measures made without attracting the attention of the people being studied) provide one other way of surmounting the problems and limitations of questionnaires and interviews. A captivating paperback book on this topic (Webb, Campbell, Schwartz, & Sechrest, 1966) offers the following examples of unobtrusive measures: (1) the amount of wear on floor tiles as an indication of the popularity of museum exhibits, (2) the number of whiskey bottles in trashcans as a measure of liquor consumption in an officially dry town, and (3) the index of racial attitudes mentioned at the beginning of this chapter, based on the amount of clustering of Blacks and Whites in college-classroom seating. Further use of such nonreactive observational research methods to supplement verbal methods would give us richer and more valid data.

F. Interviewer effects

A vast body of scientific research shows that the *interviewer's behavior and personal characteristics* can influence the respondent's answers. Some of the most pervasive causes of interviewer effects are the following:

1. *Lack of sensitivity and rapport.* Such interviewer deficits lead to invalid responses (or to no responses at all).

2. *Inadequate training.* Interviewer performance can be greatly improved by careful training (Richardson, 1954).

3. *Variations in stating questions.* Even well-trained interviewers have been found to vary in minor—but influential—ways in their reading of questions and in their use of **probes** (follow-up questions designed to obtain complete answers).

4. *Variations in reinforcing answers.* An interviewer's use of the word "good," for instance, can systematically influence the respondent's subsequent answers (Hildum & Brown, 1956).

5. Interviewer's expectations. Interviewers expect consistency in responses to related questions and consequently often miss inconsistencies that are present (H. L. Smith & Hyman, 1950). Other expectations also undoubtedly decrease validity.

6. Interviewer's attitudes. Interviewers tend to get (or hear) an excess of responses that are similar to their own attitudes. Thus, data obtained by interviewers with opposing opinions are often in strong disagreement (Cannell & Kahn, 1968, p. 549).

7. Interviewer's age. Age may have an effect on information obtained, particularly across the "generation gap" (Erlich & Riesman, 1961).

8. Interviewer's race. Many studies agree that White interviewers get somewhat different responses than Black interviewers. For instance, Schuman and Hatchett (1974) reported that Black interviewers got many more indications of distrust of Whites from Black respondents than did White interviewers. Similar effects have been found for Jewish interviewers asking questions about attitudes toward Jews (Robinson & Rohde, 1946).

The solutions to these problems of interviewer effects are not easy. Sensitive and well-trained interviewers are a first requirement that many polling organizations fail to meet. Training can reduce the usual variations in reading questions, in use of probes, and in use of verbal reinforcement; and to some extent training can alert interviewers to **halo effects** in their expectations about respondents (see Chapter 3). The interviewer's attitudes, social class, sex, and age can be dealt with by the principle of "balanced bias"—that is, by employing equal numbers of interviewers from each class, age group, sex, and so on. However, this is rarely done, and the great majority of interviewers are middle-aged, middle-class women. The problem of the respondent's race (and sometimes also age and social class) can best be met by using interviewers of the same race, age, and social class as the respondent. Encouragingly, this is being done increasingly in recent years, especially with race; and the result is much more valid survey data than in the past. There is, however, still room for improvement.

G. Other reasons for polling failures

Some additional reasons why polling methods sometimes fail are last-minute changes in the respondent's voting intentions, the undecided vote, people who cannot be found at home, the effects of publishing poll results, and differential rates of voter turnouts.

Last-minute changes in voting intentions apparently contributed to the pollsters' wrong predictions in Truman's 1948 defeat of Dewey (Mosteller, Hyman, McCarthy, Marks & Truman, 1949). Since that fiasco, the major commercial polls have continued their polling as close to the election as possible, and some have adopted a "last-minute" telephone poll taken the weekend before the election. The undecided vote was also a major factor in the 1948 election, for an unusually high 19% of voters were still undecided one month before the election (A. Campbell, Gurin, & Miller, 1954). Usually the assumption is made that undecided respondents will split their votes in the same proportion as those who have already decided, but in 1948 most of the undecided votes went to Truman.

Finding no one at home is as frustrating to the pollster as it is the door-to-door salesman. Hilgard and Payne (1944) showed that people who could not be found at home until the second, third, or fourth visit had a number of characteristics that were different from their stay-at-home neighbors. The moral is clear: always call back.

The effects of publishing poll results have not been much studied (J. V. Harrell & Caldwell, 1975), but it is widely believed that polls affect voter turnout and the undecided vote. In the 1970 British election, a dejected Labour Party worker grumbled "They should ban the polls. They lost it for us. Our people just stayed at home, resting on the polls' prediction that it was in the bag" (*Newsweek*, July 6, 1970). Another possible poll effect has occurred in the United States in the last few presidential elections, when national television networks predicted the winning presidential candidate on the basis of East Coast returns well before the close of voting on the West Coast. Although initial studies of the 1964 presidential election showed no significant effect on West Coast voting from such telecasts (W. Weiss, 1969), a number of U. S. legislators have proposed that they be banned, as they are in Canada, until the voting booths are closed.

Differential turnout rates were apparently a major reason for the polling errors in the 1970 British election (*Newsweek*, July 6, 1970). The only polling firm that correctly picked the Conservative Party to win did so because it noted even lower enthusiasm among Labour Party supporters than usual. As the head of the polling firm put it, "We took the calculated risk—we adjusted more than usual for the turnout factor." Apparently taking risks sometimes helps in the polling business. But, in addition, it should be clear by now that there are many ways of substantially reducing every possible source of invalidity. As in other fields, eternal vigilance is the price of polling validity.

VI. Research problems in watching people

The third basic way of studying human behavior is watching people. The **observational method** in science means planned, systematic watching, guided by certain rules and conditions designed to improve accuracy. Since all human beings have lots of experience in observing others, they rarely realize how hard it is to observe completely and accurately. The difficulties in observation will become much more obvious to you if you try to record everything that happens during a grade-school recess period—even

keeping up with a single child may be far more than you can handle! (See Figure 2-10.) **Naturalistic observation** (unselective recording of typical behavior in natural settings) is the favorite method of anthropologists and is also used by psychologists, sociologists, and other social scientists. In social psychology, structured observation may be one of the measurement techniques used in any of the major research methods from the survey to the laboratory experiment. An intensive discussion of the advantages and problems of observational methods is contained in a chapter by Weick (1968). Among the common problems encountered are the following:

1. Awareness of subjects. When subjects are aware of being observed, their behavior may be **reactive**—that is, influenced by the process of observation. Consequently, observers often try to be unobtrusive, and they may maintain secrecy about their activities—though sometimes that can also create problems of suspicion or resistance.

2. Rare occurrence of events. Many kinds of events, such as conflict in interaction or failure in performing tasks, happen rather infrequently in everyday life. Consequently, to observe them, the investigator may need to select their most likely time and setting (such as the dinner-preparation period in a family with young children). An alternative approach is to intervene subtly in the situation in such a way as to increase the frequency of the behavior under study (for instance, by giving subjects a difficult task to perform, or having parents work together with their child on a task). Though the latter approach is no longer completely naturalistic observation, it may be much more fruitful than waiting many hours for the desired behavior to occur.

3. Choosing the time and the medium. Observation may be continuous for an extended period, or it may use **time samples** of many short periods spread over many days or weeks. It may also be done "live," while the action is in progress, or later from some permanent record (film, au-

Figure 2-10
Problems in observation. Trying to record all the behavior of an active child
may be more than one observer can handle. (Photo by Jim Pinckney.)

diotape, or videotape). Each approach has both advantages and disadvantages.

4. *Choosing what to watch.* There are a host of different types of behaviors that can be observed in human interaction. For example, one can focus on nonverbal behavior (facial expressions, glances, or body movements), spatial activity, paralinguistic behavior (the way people speak—pitch, loudness, continuity, and so on), or linguistic communication. Since no observer can watch all these things at once, *systematic* emphasis on what to observe (and what to ignore) will pay off in more reliable and valid data.

5. *Choosing what to record.* At one extreme, the observer can make a **specimen record,** which is a relatively complete, nonselective, sequential,

narrative description of an individual's behavior. Then there are numerous classification systems for recording portions of behavior. Finally, there are judgmental observation systems for rating personality characteristics (such as dominance, aggression, or affiliation). Since the latter systems rely heavily on the observer's subjective feelings, they are usually far less reliable than behavioral-classification systems. Furthermore, behavioral measures can summarize personal traits equally well or better (for instance, children's aggression can be studied by counting the number and intensity of verbal threats, hurtful physical acts, or interference with others' activities).

6. *Choosing coding categories.* There are many well-developed systems of categories for coding

various types of interaction. Researchers can also develop their own set of categories. The purpose of the research and the investigator's prior decisions about what, when, and how to observe will largely determine the choice of recording categories.

7. *Achieving reliability.* Careful and extensive training of observers in what to watch and what to ignore is absolutely essential in observational research. Humans are subject to many sources of perceptual bias, and we are rarely aware of our own biases. Even after careful training, there is still a need for *calibration* of different observers against each other's judgments or against some objective standard (for instance, a manual of scoring examples, or frame-by-frame film analysis).

VII. Research problems in manipulating conditions

The fourth basic way of studying human behavior involves active manipulation of conditions. As stated in Section II, when planned manipulation of conditions is combined with relevant controls and careful observation, we call the process *experimenting.* Though the experiment is the most desirable scientific method for determining cause-and-effect relationships, that does not mean that it has no drawbacks or problems. Indeed, its associated problems are quite proportional to its advantages. Some of the major difficulties with experiments are described below.

A. Use of volunteer subjects

Although volunteers are convenient to use as subjects in experiments because they take part willingly (without need for payment, social rewards, or coercion), their use unfortunately presents a serious problem in the development of general scientific principles. Studies on the characteristics of subjects who have volunteered to participate show that they differ substantially from those who choose not to volunteer (R. Rosenthal & Rosnow, 1969, 1975). For instance, vol-

unteers tend to have more education and a higher occupational status; they usually are more intelligent, have a greater need for approval, and are lower in authoritarianism than nonvolunteers. Since these differences might lead to different reactions in experimental situations, it is safest to avoid using volunteer subjects if one wishes to generalize the results to the entire population.

B. Demand characteristics

Any situation, not only an experiment, has demand characteristics for the people who enter it. For instance, the behavior called forth by entering a classroom is usually to sit in a chair, to watch and listen to the teacher, and perhaps to ask questions, discuss, or take notes. **Demand characteristics** are influences on our behavior in a situation; they are defined as the perceptual cues, both explicit and implicit, that communicate what is expected in the situation (Orne, 1969).

One of the main demand characteristics in an experimental situation, according to Martin Orne, is to be a good subject, to do what the experimenter wants, and perhaps ultimately to provide the experimenter with data that fit the study's hypothesis. Certainly a modicum①of cooperativeness is fine, but cooperativeness can become a problem when it extends to "psyching out" experimenters and giving them the "right" data (or, for that matter, the "wrong" data, as either extreme is just as damaging to scientific validity). Demand characteristics cannot be eliminated from an experimental situation; however, Orne has suggested several ways in which the researcher can attempt to understand how demand characteristics might affect the data and thus take steps to minimize or counterbalance that effect. Other research has led to the encouraging conclusions that subjects are generally conscientious in following the experimental instructions even when they suspect the possibility of deception and that there is little evidence of either overcooperativeness or negativism occurring frequently among experimental subjects (S. J. Weber & Cook, 1972).

① modicum = moderate a small quantity.

C. Experimenter effects

Experimenter effects are changes or distortions in the results of an experiment produced by the characteristics or behavior of the experimenter. Robert Rosenthal (1964, 1966, 1969) and his colleagues have studied these effects very extensively and have classified many different types. Some experimenter effects operate on the data without influencing the subject's behavior. These effects include the researcher's making observation errors, recording errors, computation errors, errors in interpreting the results, and even occasional data faking. However, a greater effect apparently is the experimenter affecting the data by influencing the subject's behavior, in much the same way that interviewers may affect the answers of respondents in polls or interviews. For instance, the experimenter's sex, race, class, warmth or hostility, anxiety, approval needs, authoritarianism, status, and research experience have all been shown to affect the behavior of experimental subjects. However, the degree of influence and the consistency of effects due to these factors vary from one experiment to another. The most stable results have been found for the factors of the experimenter's status and warmth. Rosenthal (1966) concluded that higher-status experimenters tend to obtain more conforming but less pleasant responses from their subjects, while warmer experimenters tend to obtain more competent and more pleasant responses from their subjects.

The experimenter's characteristic that has received the most attention is the experimenter's *expectations* about the subject's responses. (In the scientific literature this is referred to as the "experimenter-expectancy effect.") In investigating this factor, Rosenthal and his colleagues typically use a large number of experimenters, usually undergraduate psychology students, some of whom are given instructions establishing one set of expectations about their subjects' behavior, while the others are given opposite expectations. A typical task used in experiments with human subjects was judging photographs of people's faces on a dimension of success or failure, using a scale from –10 to +10. One group of experimenters was led to expect ratings averaging around –5; the other group expected an average around +5. Results of such experiments have consistently shown significant, but small, differences in the behavior of subjects run by the two groups of experimenters—differences averaging about 1 point on the 20-point scale (Rosenthal, 1966). *Since the experimenters followed a standard script, they could not simply tell their subjects what they expected.* Instead, the expectancies of the experimenters must have been transmitted by subtle cues such as tone of voice, facial expression, and gestures. It has been shown that auditory cues alone are sufficient to affect a subject's behavior, though a much more pronounced effect is obtained when visual cues are added. Amazingly enough, experimenters' expectancies have even been found to affect data obtained in experiments on rats (R. Rosenthal & Fode, 1963). A number of suggestions for controlling experimenter expectancy effects are presented in Table 2-2.

Table 2-2
Suggestions for controlling
experimenter expectancy effects

1. Increase number of experimenters.
2. Observe behavior of experimenters.
3. Analyze experiment for order effects (changes in results between early and late data).
4. Analyze experiment for computational errors.
5. Develop experimenter-selection procedures.
6. Develop experimenter-training procedures.
7. Maintain blind conditions (in which experimenter does not know which group subjects are in).
8. Minimize experimenter-subject contact.
9. Use expectancy control groups (in which expectancies are created or not created to determine their effect separately from the effects of other variables).

Adapted from R. Rosenthal (1966, p. 402).

Another very important part of Rosenthal's research has been the investigation of expectancies on the part of teachers in the public schools. His provocative research report, entitled *Pygmalion in the Classroom* (R. Rosenthal & Jacobson, 1968), suggests that teachers' expectations about their pupils are like self-fulfilling prophecies, making some students successful and other students failures. This dramatic conclusion, like most of Rosenthal's work, has become quite controversial. Snow (1969) has criticized *Pygmalion* for improper statistical procedures, and T. X. Barber and Silver (1968a, 1968b), in an exhaustive analysis of published studies, have concluded that there is still not enough evidence to consider expectancy effects proven phenomena. These critics do not claim, however, that expectancy effects do not or cannot occur.

Overall, Rosenthal's research has made an important contribution to scientific knowledge by demonstrating the possibility of a specific kind of error in research methods. Without question, some of the experimenter errors and influences that he has pointed out do occur, and we must establish safeguards to avoid them wherever possible. Though Rosenthal's conclusions may exaggerate the generality and practical importance of the effects of experimenter bias, in the expectancy area there is little doubt about the possibility of self-fulfilling prophecies (Beez, 1968; LaVoie & Adams, 1973; Rosenthal, 1969; Seaver, 1973).

D. Internal validity
   and external validity

When manipulating conditions experimentally, how correct are we in interpreting our findings? The terms *internal validity* and *external validity*, popularized by Donald Campbell and Stanley (1966), represent two crucial aspects of any research design. **Internal validity** refers to the certainty of the study's conclusions about cause and effect, as opposed to the possibility that some confounding variable may have caused the observed results. Poor internal validity re-sults from lack of adequate control conditions or from careless procedures. For instance, some of the studies that evaluated effects of the Head Start preschool program used control groups that were not really equivalent to the experimental group, and hence they were doomed from the beginning to find small learning effects, or no effects at all—findings that were invalid because of the improper procedures used (D.T. Campbell & Erlebacher, 1970). Internal validity is the most essential characteristic of an experiment, for without it the purported findings cannot be trusted.

External validity is the *generalizability* of the research findings: "To what populations, settings, treatment variables, and measurement variables can this effect be generalized?" (D.T. Campbell & Stanley, 1966, p. 5). Poor external validity can occur even if the experimental procedures are impeccable (Oakes, 1972). A common example is experiments in which bright college students learn lists of nonsense syllables under various conditions. Are their findings applicable to different subjects in other situations, such as slow learners studying reading in a slum-area elementary school? Clearly, external validity is vital if we want to extend our findings beyond the immediate situation and the specific type of subjects on which they were obtained.

Both the internal validity and external validity of experimental findings can be demonstrated by replicating them in further experiments. There are three major types of replications, and their results help to establish the two types of validity. Internal validity can be shown through an *exact replication* of the methods of the original experiment, or through a *modified replication* that uses slightly different procedures or additional conditions to control for possible contaminating variables. In such modified replications the use of different subjects, settings, and experimental procedures can also give evidence of the external validity of the original experimental findings. Finally, *conceptual replications* can help to verify the theory behind the findings by using other treatment manipulations and other measurement techniques that, though clearly different from the original experiment, are related to the same theoretical concepts. For instance, tests of the frustration-aggression theory could operationalize the concept *frustration* by taking toys away from children or by creating disturbances that interfered with the problem-solving activities of college students. Similarly, the concept *aggression* might be measured by the number of times the children hit a bobo doll or by the strength of electric shocks that undergraduates were willing to administer to their frustrator.

E. A mechanistic view of human nature

Because experiments require manipulation of stimulus variables and observation of subject responses, they fit very neatly into the stimulus-response (S-R) theoretical framework described in Chapter 1. In doing so, they may also limit our view of human nature to a mechanistic one; we may see people as creatures completely controlled by their environment. Other theories, which attribute to human nature a more active, stimulus-seeking, goal-directed, or purposive quality, may not be as compatible with the experimental approach, and so may appear to receive less confirmation. That is, fewer investigators may choose to study them, fewer research studies may be done, and weaker research designs may have to be used in some studies. For instance, Gestalt or phenomenological theories may be more difficult to test by means of experiments than S-R theories are. Thus, our choice of research methods can, at least to some extent, influence the degree of confirmation of our theories and the beliefs about human nature that we come to espouse.

F. Ethical questions

When one becomes an experimenter with human subjects and begins to manipulate and control experimental conditions, ethical questions inevitably arise. Historically, social scientists have long recognized the importance of these ethical issues. During the 1960s the professional organizations of anthropologists and of sociologists developed codes of ethics in research. In 1953 and again in 1967, the American Psychological Association (APA) published detailed ethical standards for psychologists. More recently, increased public concern about research practices with human subjects led U.S. psychologists to conduct an intensive, four-year-long campaign to study practices and set standards in this area (APA, 1973). Only a few of the most important issues in conducting social-psychological research can be considered here.

1. Invasion of privacy. The principles of confidentiality and anonymity of clinical and research findings have long been realized as essential safeguards of the privacy of clients and of research subjects. In 1965, both houses of the U.S. Congress held hearings on issues related to invasion of privacy. These hearings raised the threat of future government control over the use of psychological tests and research procedures, and the testimony makes fascinating reading (much of it is reprinted in a special issue of the *American Psychologist*, APA, 1965). Many psychologists testified about safeguards necessary for the proper use of tests in government agencies and in individual clinical work and research, and some reforms were instituted.

2. Informed consent. U. S. government regulations have made the principle of **informed consent** a central ethical consideration in research with human subjects. This means that subjects must be given a choice as to whether they wish to participate in research and that they must be told beforehand about any dangers, unpleasant conditions, or other factors that might make them wish to withdraw. In the case of children, mentally retarded individuals, or others who are not competent to understand the situation, their parent or guardian must be asked for consent. Legislation passed by the U. S. Congress in 1974 further amplified the procedures required to ensure informed consent by research subjects.

3. *Harmful consequences.* In 1966 a major scandal developed over the way some medical research on cancer had been conducted (Lear, 1966). Some very aged and infirm hospital patients had been injected with live cancer cells, after being given only a very cursory description of the research, and without any knowledge that cancer was involved. Partly as a result of the national publicity over this incident, President Johnson appointed a Panel on Privacy and Behavioral Research. The panel's report, dealing at length with questions of informed consent and harmful consequences, was published in *Science* in 1967 and implemented by a ruling of the U. S. Surgeon General.

We can state several ethical rules regarding harmful consequences. First, an experimenter should never subject people or animals to any harmful procedure if it can be avoided. Second, risking harmful effects can only be justified if the experimental goal is of great importance in relation to the degree of risk. Third, if risks are necessary, all possible means should be adopted to minimize them. Fourth, continuing treatment or assistance should be made available to any subjects who have suffered emotionally or physically as the result of an experimental treatment. These rules apply mainly to medical experiments with potentially dangerous drugs or unproven treatments; but occasionally social-psychological experiments involve potential dangers, such as the use of stimulants, the use of electric shock, or unpleasant emotional experiences. An important example is Milgram's (1963) research on the topic of obedience, which is described in Chapter 18. (See also Figure 2-11.)

4. *Deception.* Deception has often been used in social-psychological experiments for two important reasons. First, and most crucial, it is often essential that research subjects be unaware of the hypotheses of experiments if the results of such studies are to be valid. (In fact, the literature on experimenter bias indicates that even the experimenters should *not* know the hypotheses

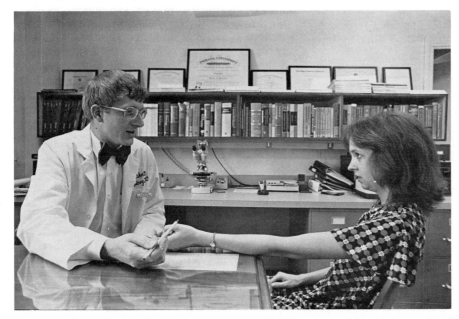

Figure 2-11
Ethics in human research. Getting the research subject's informed consent and preventing any harmful consequences from the research procedures are two important ethical requirements for all researchers. (Photo by Jim Pinckney.)

of the studies!) Second, there is need for **experimental realism** (Aronson & Carlsmith, 1968)—that is, arranging the events of the experiment so that they will seem convincing and have the maximum possible impact on the subjects. Deception may be necessary in many experiments in order to accomplish these goals. A frequent procedure is to present a false "cover story" that will mislead subjects about the main purpose of the experiment and prevent them from guessing the hypotheses being tested. Sometimes deception takes more extensive forms, such as presenting false feedback about the subject's success or failure on a task, or having **confederates** of the experimenter masquerade as other subjects and act or speak in preplanned ways.

Such deception presents important ethical questions (Warwick, 1975). It is generally agreed that deception should not be used if there are other ways of satisfactorily achieving the same end. Also, deception should be used only when the importance of the experimental goal warrants the degree of deception involved, and it should be terminated as soon as possible. However, these principles involve subjective judgments, and there is still controversy not only over the acceptability of deception, but also over its effectiveness (Bickman & Henchy, 1972, p. 3; K. J. Gergen, 1973b; Kelman, 1967). There is general agreement that subjects should be very carefully "debriefed" at the end of an experiment. This means telling the subject the truth about all deceptions, the reasons that made deceptions necessary, and the purpose and goals of the experiment, and then reassuring the subject about any doubts or worries that may have been aroused. If debriefing is done sensitively and thoroughly, most experimenters feel that subjects will accept the necessity of deception and not feel unfairly treated (Aronson & Carlsmith, 1968; Holmes & Bennett, 1974).

5. *Use of research findings.* Just as the atomic scientists became concerned over the use of their research findings, so too have social psycholo-

gists. If research is done for a governmental agency or an industrial corporation, what are investigators' obligations to the sponsor, as contrasted with their obligations to the research subjects who provided them with the data? If the investigators think that their research findings may be used to manipulate people—as in government propaganda, or in selling products that people don't need—do the investigators have a responsibility *not* to do the research? Particularly where research has been done with relatively powerless groups or captive audiences (prisoners, mental patients, minority groups, the poor, and children), it has recently been suggested that researchers have an important responsibility to use the obtained knowledge for the benefit of the particular subject group. This may require investigators to leave their accustomed role of "neutral observers" and become advocates for social change or improvement of the conditions under which powerless or disadvantaged groups have lived. It may even require them to oppose governmental or commercial attempts to use their research findings for repressive or manipulative purposes—an uncomfortable position indeed for an "ivory tower" researcher, but one which may become increasingly imperative in our technological society.

G. Applicability to major social problems

A final problem with experiments is that, by their very nature, most are artificial situations that are not intended to duplicate any situation in the real world. As a technique for basic and theoretical research, the laboratory experiment is not designed to allow direct application of its results to real social situations. Even less is it intended to solve major social problems. Consequently, one should not become irate at experiments that seem far removed from "where it's at" in the real world. It is important to remember that the aim of such experiments is to add a small bit to our basic store of knowledge rather than to solve social problems directly. However, as

Festinger (1953, pp. 169-170) has stated, "Experiments in the laboratory must derive their direction from studies of real-life situations, and results must continually be checked by studies of real-life situations."

One contribution that field experiments and quasi-experimental research can make to solving social problems has been stressed by Donald Campbell (1969). When social reform programs are launched, they can be planned as experiments and their results studied with the most rigorous research designs that are feasible. The study of the British Breathalyser crackdown described in Section III provides one such example. This approach would be a great improvement over the current typical lack of any evaluation, or seat-of-the-pants guesswork, or use of selective testimonials to evaluate a program's effectiveness.

VIII. Expectations for the future

One might expect to see increasing attempts to make experimental studies and other types of research on human behavior relevant to the problems of our society. However, there are opposing arguments indicating that this would be a wasteful way to use our scientific skills. Thomas Kuhn, for instance, writes:

> [T]he insulation of the scientific community from society permits the individual scientist to concentrate his attention upon problems that he has good reason to believe he will be able to solve. Unlike the engineer, and many doctors, and most theologians, the scientist need not choose problems because they urgently need solution and without regard for the tools available to solve them [1970, p. 162].

Despite such arguments, the trend toward greater social relevance of research seems unmistakable. In 1969, for example, a presidential task force was appointed in the United States to develop social indicators to measure the state of citizens' morale, health, and well-being in the same way that the gross national product and the stock market have traditionally measured our economic condition (U. S. Department of Health, Education and Welfare, 1969).

Another trend is the search for more unobtrusive measures to replace or to supplement our traditional reliance on interviews and questionnaires. This tendency will undoubtedly continue, particularly if the concern about testing and invasion of privacy increases in coming years.

A third trend that is developing in social psychology is that toward more research in natural settings and greater integration of field studies with laboratory studies (McGuire, 1967a, 1967b; Bickman & Henchy, 1972). In the past, there has often been little interchange between proponents of the two methods (S. Fried, Gumpper, & Allen, 1973), but now quite a few researchers are trying to use both methods and to check their results back and forth continually between the two settings.

A more radical reorientation has been advocated by the distinguished social psychologist William McGuire (1973), a shift that will undoubtedly take many years to spread throughout the discipline. It involves a systems approach to understanding human behavior, with provisions for complex feedback loops and for two-directional causality between events, so that the "effect" may have an influence back upon the "cause." Within this paradigm, the distinction between independent and dependent variables would be largely discarded, and most research would be done with multiple-variable correlational methods, using large numbers of naturally fluctuating variables.

A final movement, which is growing rapidly, is the concern, both within social psychology and in government circles, for protecting the rights of human subjects and ensuring careful adherence to ethical principles in research. Though this is a healthy corrective to occasional past abuses, the move toward restrictive legislation regarding conditions and methods of research has a great inherent risk of stifling much scientific research, particularly the most innovative and creative approaches. If this should occur, it would be a great loss to our society at a time when we need all the scientific knowledge and skills that are available to help us keep up with the pace of social change.

IX. Summary

The scientific method is a cyclical process of establishing facts about the world. Its main steps are (1) induction of one or more theoretical propositions from observed facts, (2) deduction of some logical consequences of these theoretical propositions, and (3) verification of the predicted consequences by collecting new observations. Distinguishing features of the scientific method are that it is based on the assumption of determinism, uses the empirical approach, requires operational definitions of concepts, and is objective in its deductions and verifications. To the extent that these requirements are met, any field of study can be scientific.

The experimental method consists of (1) manipulation of one or more independent variables, (2) control of related variables, and (3) observation of one or more dependent variables. In contrast, the correlational method is nonmanipulative in nature, for it studies naturally occurring relationships between variables. The correlational method is essential for studying variables, such as personality traits, that cannot be manipulated; it is less satisfactory than the experimental method in providing information on which to base inferences about cause and effect.

This chapter has been organized around the four basic ways of studying human behavior: collecting and analyzing existing products, asking questions, watching people, and manipulating conditions experimentally. Within these basic approaches, eight major research methods of the social psychologist have been described and illustrated: (1) archival research, (2) surveys, (3) field studies, (4) natural experiments, (5) quasi-experimental research, (6) field experiments, (7) simulations, and (8) laboratory experiments.

Problems inherent in each of the basic research approaches have been discussed at length in this chapter. Problems in analyzing documents center around obtaining and sampling the desired materials; choosing categories, units, and scoring systems for the content analysis; and demonstrating the reliability and validity of the results. The survey approach—asking questions—includes three of the most popular social-psychological research techniques: polls, interviews, and questionnaires. The validity of the survey approach depends on many factors, including sampling methods and question wording, memory errors and social-desirability needs of respondents, bias from other response sets, interviewer effects, and other situational factors. Research problems in watching people include subjects' awareness of being observed; the possible rarity of the events of interest; choosing the time and medium for observation; choosing what behaviors to watch and what recording system and coding categories to use; and training and calibrating observers to achieve reliability. Major research problems in manipulating conditions experimentally include the use of volunteer subjects, demand characteristics of the experimental situation, effects caused by the experimenters themselves, and conditions reducing the internal validity of the experiment or the external validity (generalizability) of its findings. Additional problems common in experiments are ethical issues related to the manipulations involved, the question of applicability to any important real-life situations, and the mechanistic view of human nature which they may foster.

Trends that seem to be growing in social-psychological research include the use of unobtrusive behavioral measures, greater integration of laboratory and field studies, and efforts to apply research findings to the problems of society. The increasing concern for ethical safeguards in research may have the unfortunate side effect of culminating in restrictive legislation and the stifling of much valuable research.

PART 2
FORMING AND SUSTAINING RELATIONSHIPS

I. The need to predict and understand others
  A. Philosophies of human nature
  B. Role-construct theory—George Kelly's approach
  C. O. J. Harvey's theory of the development of conceptual systems
  D. Do our assumptions about human nature make any difference?

II. The future of our assumptions about human nature
  A. Our introspective society
  B. Can we blueprint a theory of human nature?
  C. Social psychology's role in determining assumptions about human nature

III. Forming an impression of a specific person—Like peeling an onion?
  A. The use of group stereotypes in forming impressions of individuals
  B. The use of implicit personality theories
  C. Central traits
  D. Adding versus averaging in impression formation

IV. The power of first impressions
V. The attribution of cause
VI. The accuracy of our judgments of others
  A. Procedures for determining accuracy
  B. Characteristics of the task of judging others
  C. Artifacts and components in the measurement of accuracy
  D. Characteristics of a good judge
  E. Generality of our accuracy levels
  F. The accuracy of eyewitnesses

VII. Future trends in the study of social perception
VIII. Summary

Social perception: Forming impressions of people 3

Yond Cassius has a lean and hungry look; . . . such men are
dangerous.
William Shakespeare

You can't treat a kid who grew up knife-fighting in Harlem the
way you treat a blond, four-letter man from Christ Lake,
Wisconsin. I don't want to fit all my players into one mold.
Marquette University basketball coach Al McGuire

It is about 5 P.M. and you have just arrived home by yourself. A man comes to the door and asks to use your phone; he claims his car has broken down and he wants to call for help. What impressions do you form of him? How do you respond? Your reaction probably will be determined to a large degree by your initial judgment of the man's nature. In this chapter we consider how such impressions are formed and just how accurate our perceptions of other people are. Such concerns fall within the area of social perception, a general term for the process of forming judgments about the qualities of other people.

Let us consider the example of the stranger at your door. Your reaction to his request may be influenced by three general considerations: situational factors, your assumptions about

A chapter on Social Perception for the first edition of this book was prepared by Stuart Oskamp. Some material from that chapter has been included in the present chapter, which is an updated and reorganized combination of two chapters from the first edition.

human nature, and your impressions of the stimulus person. By *situational factors* we mean qualities of the environment and the surroundings. For example, if you just heard on the radio that there was a robbery in your neighborhood an hour ago, you probably would be less likely to allow the man to enter. You might even perceive him to be sinister or threatening. Also, if you had just cashed your week's paycheck and had the money lying on the dining-room table, you probably would be less likely to admit a stranger. These and other environmental circumstances can affect our perceptions of others as well as our reactions to others.

However, you probably have general beliefs about the nature of people; most of us do. Can people in general be trusted? Are they sincere? Do they do what they say they will do? These general assumptions can influence our reaction to any specific individual.

But a third factor, your impressions of the person, also will directly affect your response. You probably will gaze at the man's face, observe

77

whether he is nicely dressed or not, and listen for intonations in his voice. From these data—and others—you will form an impression of him that will influence your reaction to him. Before examining the accuracy of our impressions, this chapter will discuss some of the sources of our impressions of others. As we have indicated, all of us possess—to some degree—some basic assumptions about the nature of people in general. Some of us tend to trust other people; some of us do not. (See Figure 3-1 for an example from contemporary literature.) But each person we meet is a *separate stimulus,* and our reactions to

that individual are determined by specific qualities in addition to our general beliefs about human nature. For example, if we know the person is of a certain occupational group, or a certain religion, we probably form impressions of the person on the basis of our **stereotypes** about that group. Similarly, we may assume that all men with beards possess certain qualities, that old people possess other qualities, and so on. Thus we use **group memberships** to aid us in forming impressions of specific people. Beyond these, we make *attributions* about the causes of a person's behavior from the person's specific actions: if we

Figure 3-1
Charlie Brown's assumptions about human nature. (© 1968 by United Feature Syndicate, Inc. Reprinted by permission.)

notice the man constantly looking over his shoulder at the street corner, we may conclude that he is concerned about onlookers, hence not to be trusted. **Attribution theory,** a recently developed viewpoint in social psychology, gives us a framework for studying such judgments. Later in this chapter we will consider all these influences. First, however, we explore the reasons we often form rapid impressions of others and the sources of this impression formation.

I. The need to predict and understand others

Other people significantly influence our successes and failures in life. Teachers' and professors' grading of a student's course work may affect whether or not the student can obtain further schooling, and thus the student's eventual occupation. When we approach others seeking companionship, if they reject us, we are not only left alone but also saddened. Even in something as commonplace as driving down the highway, the behavior of other people can influence what happens to us. A sudden stop by another car or cutting from lane to lane can cause us to be suddenly involved in a serious accident, which may leave us hospitalized and penniless.

Other people play such an influential part in our environment that we need to be able to anticipate their actions. Therefore, we develop broad attitudes about people in general. These attitudes—called **philosophies of human nature** —are expectancies that people possess certain qualities and will behave in certain ways (Wrightsman, 1974). They do not tell us what people *are*, but rather what *we think they are*. Just as we question the performance of our car in preparation for a cross-country trip, we speculate about the performance of people with whom we deal and about the likelihood of their behaving in particular ways. We could not tolerate life if people were constantly surprising us. As we seek to predict their behavior, we may also seek to integrate our impressions into a solidified whole.

Thus we may hence simplify our impressions of the mass of complex human behavior.

A. Philosophies of human nature

If we grant that persons carry around their own beliefs about human nature, how do we conceptualize, define, and measure these beliefs? The framework of philosophies of human nature proposes that even though one person's assumptions may be quite different from another's, what is common to them is that they employ *some* philosophy or set of beliefs about human nature.

An analysis of writings by philosophers, theologians, and social scientists has generated the proposition that our beliefs about human nature have six basic dimensions (Wrightsman, 1964a). Each dimension will be described here, along with some examples of different viewpoints on each dimension and examples of social-psychological findings relevant to each dimension.

The first dimension of a personal philosophy of human nature is *trustworthiness versus untrustworthiness,* or the extent to which one believes that people are basically trustworthy, honest, and responsible, as opposed to untrustworthy, immoral, and irresponsible.

We do not have to look any further than at the influential viewpoints in psychotherapy to see strong differences in assumptions about whether human nature is trustworthy or not. Carl Rogers, the originator of client-centered therapy, has written: "In my experience I have discovered man to have characteristics which seem inherent in his species ... terms such as positive, forward-moving, constructive, realistic, trustworthy" (1957, p. 200). On the other hand, Sigmund Freud, the father of psychoanalysis, wrote in a letter to Fliess that he believed that "with a few exceptions, human nature is basically worthless" (E. L. Freud, 1960). A third major approach, *behavior therapy*, which grew out of the work of B. F. Skinner, assumes that there is no such thing as human nature. Behavior therapy proposes that either trustworthiness *or* deceit can be estab-

Figure 3-2
What assumptions do you make about each of these people? People account
for so much of our everyday existence that it is almost impossible to avoid
forming some impressions of them, based partly on their appearance, sex, race,
or occupation. (Photos by Jim Pinckney.)

lished in any person by rewarding different actions.

As a component of one's philosophy of human nature, belief in trustworthiness is an expectation that other people are honest, moral, and reliable. Julian Rotter (1967, 1971), a contemporary psychologist, has developed a concept somewhat similar to trustworthiness, which he calls *interpersonal trust*. This quality is described as "a person's generalized expectancy that the promises of other individuals or of groups with regard to future behavior can be relied upon" (Hochreich & Rotter, 1970, p. 211). Thus it is a narrower concept than trustworthiness, as it attempts to exclude subjective elements such as positive or negative attitudes toward human nature and focus on the more objective aspects of a situation that may involve trust (Stack, in press). It is objective because it considers only credibility, not morality or honesty. Will the person do what he says he will do? A landlord promises to install a new refrigerator if you rent his apartment. A friend promises to keep a secret. A politician promises to cut taxes if elected. *Interpersonal trust* refers to beliefs about whether such promises can be taken at face value.

The concepts of *interpersonal trust* and *trustworthiness* actually overlap to some degree, and the attitude-scale instruments measuring them correlate at +.76 (Chun & Campbell, 1974). Further evidence for their conceptual similarity is the fact that Hochreich and Rotter (1970) have found that college classes in the late 1960s possessed lower degrees of interpersonal trust than previous classes—a finding that corroborates evidence from another study that freshman classes between the years 1962 and 1968 became progressively more negative in their philosophies of human nature (Baker & Wrightsman, 1974; Wrightsman & Baker, 1969).

The second dimension of philosophies of human nature is *altruism versus selfishness*, or the extent to which one believes that people are basically unselfish and sincerely interested in others as opposed to basically selfish and unconcerned about others.

Well-publicized incidents in which persons seeking help were ignored by many passersby have caused many people to reevaluate their beliefs about the extent of altruism in human nature (see Figure 3-3). The murder of Kitty Genovese, discussed in Chapter 2 and in Chapter 9, is a case in point. This incident deservedly received much publicity, and it has frequently been interpreted as an indication of the growing apathy and indifference to human distress that results from the impersonal complexities of modern life (Wainwright, 1964). The incident also led to a research program by Latané and Darley (1970), who found that one reason that a person fails to act in such a situation may be an awareness that a large number of other people are also watching. (diffusion of responsibility.)

The third dimension of philosophies of human nature is *independence versus conformity to group pressures*, or the extent to which one believes that people can maintain their convictions in the face of pressures to conform from a group, society, or some authority figure. Ours has sometimes been called the age of conformity. William H. Whyte, Jr., in his book *The Organization Man* (1956), deplored the emergence of the person whose advancement through the business organization progresses because he or she can roll with the tides of authority, rather than because of any creativity or effort he or she might possess.

Stanley Milgram's work on obedience (discussed in Chapter 18) likewise elicits a pessimistic view of human nature. In Milgram's project, men from the local community were hired to participate in what appeared to be a learning experiment. Each man had to give a series of shocks (which increased in intensity) to another person in an adjoining room. At a certain point, the person receiving these shocks began screaming and pounding the wall. Milgram's basic research question was what percentage of the sample would continue to obey the experimenter, administering shocks of ever-increasing intensity, even after hearing screams and pounding on the wall. Milgram had asked psychologists

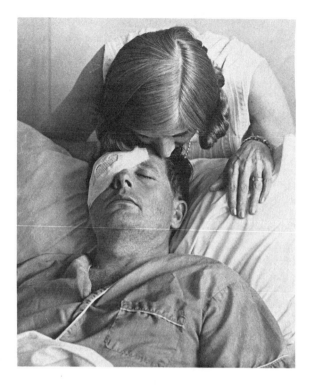

Figure 3-3
No kindness on Human Kindness Day. In the photo,
Steven Laine, public affairs director for the U.S.
Secretary of Agriculture, is comforted by his wife in
a Washington, D.C., hospital. Laine was on his way
home from work on a Saturday in May 1975 when
he was stabbed in the eye in the midst of a crowd
of 125,000 people celebrating "Human Kindness
Day." Laine said he was attacked from behind while
walking through the crowd near the Washington
Monument. When he turned, something sharp and
thin was thrust into his eye. "I said, 'Help me,' and
there was no response," he reported. "I said it
several times and no one did anything." He had to
walk unaided to a first-aid station on the edge of the
crowd. Doctors have told Laine he will lose the
injured eye. Police reported that about 100 persons
were robbed or assaulted during the day of rock
music sponsored by the National Park Service.
(Photo by Margaret Thomas from the *Washington
Post.*)

and Yale undergraduates to estimate what percentage of the subjects would continue administering shocks to the end of the shock series (450
volts); in effect, Milgram asked for a measure
of their beliefs about human nature in a specific
situation. All respondents predicted that only an
insignificant minority of subjects would go to the
end of the shock series. The estimates ranged
from 0% to 3%; in other words, the most pessimistic member of the Yale class predicted that
only 3 out of 100 persons would proceed to give
the most potent shock possible on the shock generator. Yet *26 of Milgram's 40 subjects,* or 65%,
administered shocks all the way through the
450-volt maximum. These people obeyed the experimenter, although they manifested great tension and anguish in many ways—stuttering,
groaning, biting their lips, laughing nervously,
and even having one convulsive seizure. Despite
the qualms we may have about the ethics or
propriety of such experimental manipulations
(the subjects were told afterward that the accomplice did not really get shocked), the outcome
of Milgram's study is provocative and disturbing
evidence of the dominant need to obey and conform to the demands of an authority figure. Not
all the world's Adolf Eichmanns and Lieutenant
Calleys are thousands of miles away from our
own neighborhoods.

The fourth dimension of philosophies of
human nature, *strength of will and rationality versus
an external locus of control and irrationality,* is the
extent to which one believes that people have
control over their own outcomes and understand
the motives behind their behavior. United States
culture, and perhaps to a lesser extent the Canadian culture, has traditionally been characterized
by a belief in the effectiveness of willpower and
motivation. The self-help movement, from Mary
Baker Eddy to Dale Carnegie to Norman Vincent
Peale, has long been a strong force in amateur
North American philosophy. Yet the opposite
view has had its adherents. St. Paul believed that
willpower was not enough: "I can will what is
right, but I cannot do it." The contemporary Ca-

nadian and United States societies with their heavy emphasis on technology also evoke pessimism; with a growing number of skilled jobs and increasing emphasis on aptitude-test results for personnel selection and academic admission, there appears to be less and less room for sheer motivation or willpower as a determinant of success. (See also Table 3-1.)

This fourth dimension of philosophies of human nature also includes beliefs about human rationality and/or irrationality. Rationality here means that one's ego is in control and that cognitions dominate emotions. There seems to be a growing belief among social scientists that people are not basically rational. Leonard Krasner (1965), for instance, views the human species as "being at the robot end of the continuum"; and

Sigmund Freud's similar views have emerged in a posthumously published book about former U. S. President Woodrow Wilson (S. Freud & Bullitt, 1967). In the book, President Wilson's virtues are portrayed as weaknesses and his visions as the fruits of compulsion; his idealization of the League of Nations is interpreted by Freud as evidence of a passive, dependent relationship between Wilson and his father. According to Freud, subconscious factors are the major influence on decisions even at the highest levels of international affairs. Indeed, freedom may be a vanishing orientation, and the rationalist wonders whether there is no place for the rational decisions of free men and women. In a fascinating study, Charlotte Doyle (1965, 1966; see also Walker, 1970) has shown that experimental

---

Table 3-1
Internal versus external locus of control, (reinforcement)

The concept of *internal versus external locus of control* (also called "internal versus external control of reinforcement") developed from Julian Rotter's social learning theory (Rotter, 1954, 1975; Rotter, Chance, & Phares, 1972).

Although the *concept* deals with an intrapersonal orientation, Rotter's (1966) Internal-External (I-E) scale contains statements about both oneself and people in general. For example, the following two pairs of items reflect beliefs about people in general:

1. People's misfortunes result from the mistakes they make.
   versus
   Many of the unhappy things in people's lives are partly due to bad luck.
18. With enough effort we can wipe out political corruption.
   versus
   It is difficult for people to have much control over the things politicians do in office.

The above items contrast with the *personal* orientation of the following internal-external pairs:

19. There is a direct connection between how hard I study and the grades I get.
   versus
   Sometimes I can't understand how teachers arrive at the grades they give.
22. What happens to me is my own doing.
   versus
   Sometimes I feel that I don't have enough control over the direction my life is taking.

The I-E-scale items have been criticized not only for mixing the above types of statements but also for failing to distinguish between two aspects of an external locus: the unpredictability of outcomes versus the situational determinants (Gurin, Gurin, Lao, & Beattie, 1969; Kleiber, Veldman, & Menaker, 1973; Collins, 1974). Nevertheless, the scale has been used extensively, particularly in the last five years (Prociuk & Lussier, in press; Phares, 1976).

psychologists believe more strongly in determinism than do any other academic group. Physical and biological scientists, for example, tend toward the opposite end of the continuum. Experimental psychologists have also been found to believe that freedom is illusory, whereas physical scientists accept freedom as a reality of life.

The "average" person, however, is likely to believe that people are rational and that one's outcomes in life are orderly and even *justified*. In the words of social psychologist Melvin Lerner, "There is an appropriate fit between what [people] do and what happens to them" (1966, p. 3). People cannot believe that they—and their friends and family—live in a world governed mainly by a schedule of random reinforcements. Yet this belief in justice—in other words, the belief that people get what they deserve—leads to some perverse findings.

One commonplace reaction is *blaming the victim* (Ryan, 1971). A psychiatrist named Martin Symonds has interviewed hundreds of victims of rapes, assaults, and kidnappings and finds that many of them receive, instead of sympathy, inquisitions and censure from their friends and family. When a person has been mugged, for example, frequently the response of friends, family, and the police is to interrogate the person relentlessly about *why* he or she got into such an unfortunate situation. "Why were you walking in that neighborhood alone?" "Why didn't you scream?" "Why were you carrying so much money?" Such reactions reflect the pervasive need to find rational causes for apparently senseless outcomes *(Newsweek*, June 17, 1974, p. 66).

There is empirical support for such seemingly bizarre reactions. Lichtman, as cited by Lerner (1966), exposed ninth-grade students to a tape recording of a number of people talking about a particular boy named Bill Johnson. The students learned that Bill had had an automobile accident resulting from a blowout in a front tire of a used car he had recently bought. Bill was hospitalized and suffered two weeks of intense pain, facing the possibility that he would have a permanent limp. All the subjects were led to

believe that Bill had been warned about the tires when he bought the car. One group of subjects was told that Bill bought new tires and that it was one of these that blew out. The other group was told that he had definitely neglected to buy new tires. Couched within this ruse were questions concerning how responsible Bill was for the accident and how attractive he was to the subjects. Surprisingly, Bill was judged to be *less attractive* when it was established that he had bought new tires prior to the blowout. To be sure, he was described as less responsible for his suffering, but also—and most important—he was described as a less attractive, desirable person (Lerner, 1966, p. 6). Can you see why an assumption of a "just world" would lead people to find Bill less likable when he suffered the accident *despite* his good efforts?

One might tend to explain such irrationality about the rendering of justice as simply the product of ninth-grade minds; but Lerner has found similar results with college undergraduates (Lerner, 1970, 1974; Lerner & Simmons, 1966). Figure 3-4 indicates that a significant portion of the United States adult citizenry uses the argument of a "just world" to explain the assassination of a public figure. After a series of intriguing experiments, Lerner concluded that "anyone [who is] suffering is most likely to arouse people's dislike if he conveys the impression that he was a noble victim. He gets off with somewhat less rejection if he appears to be an innocent victim. And finally the victim who allows people to believe that he brought his suffering upon himself will be the best liked" (Lerner, 1966, p. 9). People generally believe that you deserve what you get; if you have a bad experience, you must also be bad.

Lerner and his colleagues have repeatedly shown that a person who suffers a misfortune through no fault of his or her own tends to be devalued and derogated by uninvolved observers (Lerner, 1965; Lerner & Becker, 1962; Lerner & Matthews, 1967; Lerner & Simmons, 1966; Novak & Lerner, 1968). As is noted by Sorrentino and Boutilier (1974), Lerner has explained this reaction by concluding that suffering by an innocent victim threatens the observer's beliefs in a just world. Are there ways that such derogation might be reduced? Two studies used different procedures with some success.

Figure 3-4
Martin Luther King, victim of assassination. In April 1968, right after Dr. King's murder, a representative sample of 1337 American adults were asked: "When you heard the news [of the assassination], which of these things was your strongest reaction: (1) anger, (2) sadness, (3) shame, (4) fear, (5) he brought it on himself?" About one-third (426) of the respondents chose the response "brought it on himself" (Rokeach, 1970). For these respondents, Lerner's "just world" hypothesis applies: since Dr. King was killed, he must have deserved to be killed. (Photo by Charles Moore, Black Star.)

If observers were told to expect a similar fate to that of the victim, they should be less likely to derogate the victim, hypothesized Sorrentino and Boutilier (1974). Subjects in their experiment observed another female undergraduate receive a series of electric shocks as a "learner" in a teaching-effectiveness project. Some of the subjects had been told that they would serve as "learners" later; others had been told that they would not. Anticipation of a similar fate led to significant reductions in the response of devaluing the "learner."

A procedure used by Aderman, Brehm, and Katz (1974) also had female subjects watch another female receive electric shocks in a "learning task," but Aderman and associates used the set given the subjects as a means to develop compassion rather than derogation for the shock victim. Instead of being told "to observe closely the emotional state of the worker and to watch for cues which indicate her state of arousal" (Lerner & Simmons, 1966, p. 206), some of the subjects were told to observe and "imagine how you yourself would feel if you were subjected to that experience" (1974, p. 344). This procedure aimed at developing a state of empathy in the observers. Additionally, some observers in each condition watched by themselves, whereas others watched in groups of three to six people. As the mean scores in Table 3-2 indicate, observers given a set to concentrate on their own feelings in such a situation rated the victim as more attractive than themselves. In contrast, the other subjects, especially those who watched in the presence of others, tended to derogate the victim.

The conceptualization of philosophies of human nature includes the four substantive dimensions mentioned thus far plus two further dimensions that cut across the four substantive dimensions and deal with beliefs about individual differences in human nature. In a sense, these beliefs about individual differences constitute a separate part of one's philosophy of human nature and its effects on behavior. Two college students, for example, may each possess an extremely positive belief about the amount of trust-

(readiness to respond in a certain way to some stimulus situation)

worthiness in human nature; yet they may have divergent beliefs about the extent of individual differences. The student who believes that people are trustworthy and that all people are alike may be less likely to seek information about another person before interacting with that person. The student who believes that each person is different, even though all people are basically trustworthy, may behave differently in various interpersonal situations. Therefore, in arriving at a conceptualization of the philosophies of human nature, we must include beliefs about individual differences as well as the substantive dimensions.

Table 3-2
Mean relative derogation scores for subjects in the study by Aderman, Brehm, and Katz.

| Audience Size | Observational Set | | |
	Empathy ("Imagine Yourself")	Observation ("Watch Her")	Lerner & Simmon's 1966 Data
Alone	5.67	− 2.33	− 2.33
Group	− 0.56	− 7.44	− 8.50

Note: Minus scores indicate that the subjects rated themselves more favorably than they rated the innocent victim. (Adapted from Table 1, p. 345, of Aderman, Brehm, & Katz, 1974.)

The fifth dimension, then, is *similarity versus variability*, or the extent to which one believes that people differ in their basic nature. Most clinical psychologists, at least, would agree that it is desirable to believe that people are different and that each is unique. Yet, with the exception of Gordon Allport's (1961, 1962) consistent advocacy of recognition of uniqueness and the work by social psychologist Howard Fromkin (1973) on the avoidance of similarity and the seeking of "differentness," most personality theorists have taken the easy way out by implying that most people are basically alike.

The sixth and last dimension is *complexity versus simplicity*, or the extent to which one believes that people are complicated and hard to understand as opposed to simple and easy to understand. Most psychologists appear to agree that one goal of psychological training is the development of a strong belief in human complexity. Seward Hiltner (1962) writes that there now seems to be "a greater consensus among psychologists about their view of man than in any previous time in our century, and this view includes more factors of greater complexity" (p. 246). Still, there is little theorizing on the subject of complexity, with the exception of George Kelly's role-construct theory (Bannister, 1970; G. A. Kelly, 1955, 1963) and O. J. Harvey's work (O. J. Harvey, Hunt, & Schroder, 1961) on four levels of conceptual systems. Each of these theories reflects a realization that people differ in regard to how complex they perceive human nature to be.

B. Role-construct theory— George Kelly's approach

George Kelly is one of the few psychologists who has written extensively about our efforts to interpret and understand our world. His is a cognitive theory of human behavior, and it stresses the connections between an individual's perception of stimuli, interpretation of them, and behavior. Kelly asserts:

> Man looks at his world through transparent patterns or templets which he creates and then attempts to fit over the realities of which the world is composed. . . . Let us give the name constructs to these patterns that are tried on for size. They are ways of construing the world [1955, pp. 8–9].

Construct is a key term for Kelly. It is a way of interpreting the world, a concept that a person uses to categorize events and to guide his or her behavior. Kelly's fundamental assumption is that each of us is a scientist. That is, just as a scientist tries to understand, predict, and control events, each human being tries in the very same way to choose constructs that will make the world understandable and predictable. According to Kelly's theory, people do not "strive for reinforcement" or seek to "avoid anxiety"; instead, they try to *validate their own construct systems*. Furthermore, Kelly has discarded the notion of an objective, absolute truth in favor of the principle of phenomenology—that is, that conditions have meaning only as they are construed by the individual.

The fundamental postulate in Kelly's theory is "A person's processes are psychologically channelized by the ways in which he anticipates events" (1955, p. 46). In other words, our expectations direct our behavior. This basic postulate is presented as an underlying assumption, and Kelly makes no attempt to prove it. From this postulate, Kelly evolves 11 corollaries, which form the framework of his system.

According to Kelly, every construct we use (such as "cheap" or "likable") gives us a basis for classifying the similarities and differences between people, objects, or events. Each person has developed only a finite number of constructs. Though some of a person's constructs may be inconsistent with others, there is a tendency toward an overall consistency within the person's construct system. One person's constructs are never completely identical with another's. If one person's constructs are similar to another's, their behavior will also be similar. Finally, if one person understands another person's constructs, he or she will be able to behave appropriately toward the other person.

The relevance of Kelly's theory to conceptions of the complexity of human nature lies in Kelly's recognition that people differ in the *number* of constructs they use in seeking to understand others. At one extreme, a person may label everyone as either "good" or "evil"; for that person, this broad evaluative construct reflects a very simplified conception of the nature of others. Another person may need 20, 50, or hundreds of constructs to deal with the task of describing and understanding others.

A few rudimentary studies have demonstrated the extent of these individual differences in beliefs about the complexity of human behavior. Gordon Allport (1958, 1966) conducted a small investigation showing that when asked to list the essential characteristics of some friend, 90% of the subjects employed between 3 and 10 trait names, the average being 7.2. The difference between 3 and 10, we may agree, is a large difference in complexity.

The method George Kelly developed to measure personal constructs is called the Role Construct Repertory Test, or "Rep Test." On its test form a number of roles are listed (self, spouse, boss, friend, person you dislike, and so on). The subject is asked to name ways in which two of the individuals in these roles are alike and different from a third individual. This process is repeated many times for different combinations of roles, and the traits named most frequently by the subject are his or her major personal constructs. A form appropriate for use by children has also been developed (Vacc & Vacc, 1973).

The Rep Test has been used in empirical studies by many different researchers (see, for example, the compilation by Bannister, 1970). One important variable that the Rep Test illuminated for us is **cognitive complexity,** or "the capacity to construe social behavior in a multidimensional way" (Bieri, Atkins, Briar, Leaman, Miller, & Tripodi, 1966). A cognitively simple person is likely to make only very gross discriminations among dimensions of behavior. A certain politician may be seen as simply "good" or "bad." A good example of the way that cognitive complexity has been linked to other variables in social perception is provided in an experiment on impression formation by Mayo and Crockett (1964). They predicted that subjects who did *not* see social behavior in a very cognitively complex way would show a **recency effect** when presented with two inconsistent sets of information about a hypothetical person. (A recency effect is the tendency to use the most recently received information in forming one's impressions.) The reason for the effect is these subjects' relative inability to assimilate inconsistent information and, thus, their need to reject the first set of information when presented with a second, inconsistent set of data. In contrast, subjects who possessed high degrees of cognitive complexity were expected to incorporate both sets of information into a more balanced impression, since cognitively complex persons believe that both positive and negative traits are present in other people. Results of the study supported both hypotheses. However, a study by Petronko and Perin (1970) found that cognitively simple people give greatest credence to perceptually emphasized information, not necessarily to the most recent information.

C. O. J. Harvey's theory of the development of conceptual systems

Another approach to complexity in assumptions about human nature focuses on the process of moving from early, simplified conceptions to a later, more refined and complex view. The work of O. J. Harvey and his associates (Greaves, 1972; O. J. Harvey, 1966; O. J. Harvey, Hunt, & Schroder, 1961; O. J. Harvey & Ware, 1967; Kaats, 1969) gives attention to this process of forming judgments and changing them as we grow older. In his work on **conceptual systems,** or belief systems, Harvey proposes four different kinds of systems that differ in both structure and content. He states that as one grows older, the systems one uses progress from a more concrete to a more abstract nature, as can be seen in the following descriptions.

System 1. Harvey's first system is a highly concrete and rigid belief system. Emphasis is placed on conforming to rules and on extrinsic rather than intrinsic rewards for good performance. The result is a relatively undifferentiated and poorly integrated conceptual system, with behavioral manifestations that include extrinsic religiosity, authoritarianism, conventionality, and extremes of evaluation in judging others.

System 2. This conceptual system is somewhat more abstract than System 1, but the essential difference is that System 2 possesses a "negative and rebellious orientation toward authority and training agents" (Kaats, 1969, p. 22). The rejection of traditional authority is accompanied by a high degree of anxiety, resulting from the absence of any authoritative guidelines (Felknor & Harvey, 1968). Beyond this, the structural emphasis of the conceptual-systems approach would note that System-2 persons maintain an inflexibility and a lack of differentiation and integration, much as do System-1 persons.

System 3. The third conceptual system is more abstract and has more differentiation and integration and more cognitive planning than the first two systems. The *content* of beliefs about people in System-3 persons is positive. They see other people as likable and attractive. System-3 persons are "thought to manifest both a need to be dependent upon others as well as a need for others to depend upon them" (Kaats, 1969, p. 24). But the respect for other people in System 3 is purposeful—the System-3 person, in the quest for control and interpersonal manipulation, is attracted to others because they can do things for him or her. Helpfulness on the part of System-3 persons is a way to achieve their own goals (Felknor & Harvey, 1968).

System 4. This is the most abstract and highly developed system, characterized by the establishment of interdependent relationships with others, self-confidence, a positive self-concept, an openness to change, and an absence of authoritarianism (Kaats, 1969). System-4 persons are highly differentiated and integrated; they can view another person or an issue from a multitude of varying perspectives. Their rewards stem from internal considerations, rather than from the opinions of others. System 4 is considered by Harvey to be the healthiest of the four systems. While such a position reflects a value judgment on Harvey's part, it agrees with the mass of thinking in social psychology that people with cognitive complexity are better able to adapt to today's world than are those who see other people in highly simplified terms.

In fact, a variety of studies (reviewed by O. J. Harvey, 1969, and by Kaats, 1969) indicate that the level of a person's conceptual system is related to important behaviors. For example, persons with *more concrete* conceptual systems tended to

1. make more extreme, either-or judgments (D. K. Adams, Harvey, & Heslin, 1966; Ware & Harvey, 1967);
2. show more prejudiced racial attitudes (Severy & Brigham, 1971);
3. be more likely to vote for Nixon or Wallace than for Humphrey in the 1968 United States presidential election (Severy & Brigham, 1971);
4. be more likely to vote for Nixon than for McGovern in the 1972 election (Brigham & Severy, 1973);
5. rely more on status and power than on expertise and information as guidelines for their own judgments (O. J. Harvey & Ware, 1967);
6. show less ability to change sets in attacking complex problems that have changing rules (O. J. Harvey, 1966);
7. show more conventional behavior and less creativity (O. J. Harvey, 1966).

Greater abstractness (in other words, Systems 3 and 4) results in the opposite behavior patterns in these and other behavioral tests. Harvey's theory of conceptual systems offers a promising approach to the study of assumptions about people, but further work is necessary to clarify the differentiation between the systems and to specify how a person moves from one system to another.

D. Do our assumptions about human nature make any difference?

Philosophies of human nature have been conceptualized as possessing six dimensions, four of a substantive nature and two reflecting the complexity of human nature. In order to measure these six dimensions, a **Likert-type scale,** referred to hereafter as the PHN scale, was constructed, with six subscales of 14 items each (Wrightsman, 1964a). (See Table 3-3 for a summary of subscales and dimensions.) Relying upon scale scores as operational definitions of philosophies of human nature, we may now indicate some conclusions regarding beliefs about human nature. Pooling together subjects of different ages, sexes, races, and occupations, we find that the average person believes human nature to be (1) neither extremely trustworthy nor extremely untrustworthy; (2) neither extremely altruistic nor extremely selfish; (3) somewhat rational and possessing a moderate degree of strength of will; (4) somewhat more likely to conform to group pressures than to remain independent of group pressures; (5) moderately individualized—that is, that to a moderate degree, people are variable and unique; and (6) moderately complex and hard to understand (Wrightsman, 1974; Wrightsman & Satterfield, 1967).

There are significant—in fact, huge—differences between typical responses at different colleges, particularly in regard to the four substantive dimensions. The student bodies of some institutions have generally positive beliefs about human nature; students in schools in the southern part of the United States, for example, more characteristically have trusting beliefs than do students from eastern U. S. colleges (Wrightsman, 1974). A few college samples have extremely negative beliefs about human nature. The mean scores from these colleges on measures of trustworthiness and altruism are one or more standard deviations below the mean scores of other colleges. One institution with an extremely negative average is a private college in the U. S. Midwest that attracts bright, religiously sophisticated students who have been brought up in a strict Calvinist tradition. In fact, in a doctrinal statement of faith, the catalog of the college states "We believe . . . that human beings are born with a sinful nature, and in the case of all those who reach moral responsibility, become sinners in thought, word, and deed." Thus, it is not surpris-

Table 3-3
The dimensions and subscales of the Philosophies of Human Nature scale

The Philosophies of Human Nature (PHN) scale measures one's beliefs about human nature. It is a Likert-type scale, with each subscale being composed of 14 statements (items). Subjects indicate their agreement or disagreement with each item by circling a number from +3 to −3. The range for each subscale is +42 to −42. The six subscales are:

Substantive characteristics of human nature

1. Trustworthiness versus untrustworthiness
   + =belief that people are trustworthy, moral, and responsible
   − =belief that people are untrustworthy, immoral, and irresponsible
2. Strength of will and rationality versus lack of will power and irrationality
   + =belief that people can control their outcomes and that they understand themselves
   − =belief that people lack self-determination and are irrational
3. Altruism versus selfishness
   + =belief that people are altruistic, unselfish, and sincerely interested in others
   − =belief that people are selfish and self-centered
4. Independence versus conformity to group pressures
   + =belief that people are able to maintain their beliefs in the face of group pressures to the contrary
   − =belief that people give in to pressures of group and society

Individual differences in human nature

5. Variability versus similarity
   + =belief that people are different from each other in personality and interests and that a person can change over time
   − =belief that people are similar in interests and are not changeable over time
6. Complexity versus simplicity
   + =belief that people are complex and hard to understand
   − =belief that people are simple and easy to understand

The first four subscales (T, S, A, and I) can be summed to give a *positive-negative* score (range +168 to −168), indicating general positive or negative beliefs about substantive characteristics of human nature. The last two subscales (V and C) can be summed to give a multiplexity score (range +84 to −84), indicating beliefs about the extent of individual differences in human nature.

ing that these students see human nature (although not necessarily themselves) as selfish, conformist, and untrustworthy.

A person's philosophy of human nature may be changed temporarily by a dramatic piece of information or personal experience. For example, within five days after U. S. President John F. Kennedy's assassination, the PHN scale was readministered to 30 undergraduates who had taken the scale 14 months previously. The students were also asked how upset they were about Kennedy's death. Those (approximately half) who were most disturbed had become more negative than other students in their substantive beliefs about human nature, while the scores of those who were less concerned did not change

significantly. All the subjects were retested again five months later; by that time, those who had become more negative had returned to the beliefs they had held prior to the assassination (Wrightsman & Noble, 1965).

New experiences can also effect a positive change in beliefs about human nature. James Young (1970) administered the PHN scale to 90 undergraduates who participated in a weekend sensitivity-training program. Compared with their pretraining scores, the scores obtained immediately after the sensitivity training indicated that they had developed significantly more favorable beliefs about the trustworthiness of human nature. However, when retested a third time two months later, the participants' scores were, on the average, about halfway between their pre-training scores and the scores obtained immediately after sensitivity training.

More prolonged exposure to a new way of looking at human relationships also can change one's beliefs. Kleeman (1972) completed a comprehensive study in which students at eight colleges took a one-semester sensitivity-training course built around concepts of human growth and potential. Classes in psychology, literature, biology, and history at the same colleges were used as control groups. Both types of students took the PHN scale twice, at the beginning and at the end of the semester. Upon retest, the students in the traditional classes changed on only one subscale: they became slightly more altruistic. In contrast, the students who participated in the human-potential seminar developed significantly more favorable attitudes on each of the four substantive dimensions of the PHN scale.

Kleeman's study indicates that after voluntarily participating in a course directed at self-growth, students changed their beliefs about human nature. Whether the activities of the class were themselves the causes of the changes, we cannot say. It may be that participants expected that their attitudes would be changed by such an experience; hence they responded so as to show changes. But another way of expressing that is to say that they demonstrated a philosophy of human nature that emphasizes an assumption of the possibility of change!

Such studies demonstrate that dramatic or pervasive occurrences can affect one's beliefs about human nature, but we must remember that these effects may be only temporary. Apparently, one's beliefs about human nature become established rather early in life and are quite resistant to permanent change. Evidence for this claim comes from G. W. Baxter's (1968) study of changes in philosophies of human nature in the first one or two years of college. Baxter used students who had taken the PHN scale during freshman orientation week and readministered the scale after these students had completed their first or second year of college. Some students' substantive scores became more favorable, and

others' scores became more unfavorable. There was very little in the way of a consistent direction of change—except that stronger beliefs in the complexity of human nature emerged in all groups. Test-retest correlations over one or two years ranged from $+.45$ to $+.65$, indicating that the typical student showed a moderate degree of consistency from testing to testing. Numerous personality measures were studied to see whether they related to degree or direction of change, but nothing of significance emerged. Contrary to the belief that the first year of college is often a period of dramatic change in one's values, there is little evidence here that predictable changes occur in beliefs about the goodness of human nature. If we wish to induce favorable beliefs about others, we must intervene at an earlier age than late adolescence.

But even when philosophies of human nature are changed by some kind of planned intervention, there is no guarantee that these new attitudes will be reflected in different kinds of behavior. Claxton (1971) gave unskilled male workers in a manpower-retraining program a special attitude-change intervention. He did so because the U.S. Department of Labor has stressed the need to modify workers' attitudes, aspirations, achievement motivation and those other personal qualities that might be social-psychological barriers to finding employment. To the regular training and counseling sessions Claxton added discussions and role-playing activities built around the concepts of trust, altruism, and the complexity of human nature. In retesting on the PHN six months after the beginning of training, those men who had the special sessions had significantly more favorable attitudes about the trustworthiness, altruism, and complexity of human nature. However, there was no relationship between a trainee's PHN scores and whether he was employed three months later.

Yet there remains evidence that philosophies of human nature are related to other orientations. When students are given the opportunity to evaluate their instructor at the end of a course, the favorableness of their evaluation is related to their philosophies of human nature.

In a study by Wrightsman (1964a), groups with favorable and unfavorable beliefs on the PHN scale differed significantly in their evaluations of the instructor; those subjects possessing unfavorable beliefs about human nature gave more negative evaluations of the teacher than students possessing favorable beliefs. Thus, the favorableness of one's beliefs about human nature in general is related to the evaluation one gives a specific individual.

An unusual scheduling of courses provided an opportunity to test the effects of beliefs about the complexity and variability of human nature upon student evaluations of teachers (Wrightsman, 1964b). At the time of the study, education majors at Peabody College were required to take, during the same term, two psychology courses taught by two different instructors. Each course had two sections, one for elementary education majors and one for secondary education majors. At the end of the courses, after each student had been exposed to the two instructors for an entire term, the students completed teacher-evaluation forms for each instructor and the PHN scale. Female elementary education majors saw human nature as significantly more trustworthy, altruistic, and independent than did female secondary education majors. Consistent with previously found sex differences, both female groups had more favorable views of human nature than did males in education classes, who also saw people as less complex than did females.

In this study it was predicted that those students who had more multiplex views of human nature (that is, high complexity and high variability scores) would give evaluations that *differentiated more between the two instructors* than would the evaluations by those students who were low in multiplexity. This expectation was partially confirmed. The correlations between the extent to which individual students differentiated their ratings and their beliefs about the degree of complexity of human nature were +.36, +.35, and –.08 for the three groups of students (males, females in secondary education, and females in elementary education). Thus, two of the three

groups showed the expected relationship to a statistically significant degree. Correlations of the extent of differentiation in ratings between instructors and variability scores were +.12, +.20, and +.39, only one group producing a significant relationship. There is evidence, then, that both the substantive quality of a person's beliefs about human nature and a person's beliefs about the extent of differences in human nature play some role in a person's evaluations of particular individuals.

In summary, people do possess a rather organized, consistent set of beliefs about human nature. The beliefs held by a person are related to his or her reactions to specific individuals. The nature of one's own beliefs is partially accounted for by one's sex, race, and occupational role in society (Wrightsman, 1974). Since a person's beliefs are apparently formed at an early age, interventions during adolescence or adulthood for the purpose of changing these beliefs are only partly successful.

II. The future of our assumptions about human nature

A. Our introspective society

Despite the fact that there are people in the United States, Canada, and every other country who are poorly fed, poorly clothed, and poorly housed, humankind's physical needs are better provided for now than at any time in the past. It might seem to be a period of contentment. Yet even many of those people whose material needs are satisfied have come to realize that a civilization directed toward material improvement is not enough (Heilbroner, 1974). While still concerned with providing physiological and material needs, Canadian and United States societies are beginning to direct more concern to needs of a higher order. That is, even though the needs for food, shelter, and clean air and water are not completely satisfied, these nations have begun to study whether a spirit of community and harmony and morality can be attained. This introspection about the quality of human life is painful but healthy in the long run.

Because of this orientation, we can expect continued concern about incidents that seemingly reflect negatively on human nature—whether these incidents be massacres of unarmed civilians in Southeast Asia or failures to aid a victim attacked on a city street or attempts by government officials to deceive the public.

B. Can we blueprint a theory of human nature?

Even though concerns about our essential nature will increase, a blueprint of humanity's basic social traits is impossible. Although there are consistencies across cultures in some social-psychological characteristics—for example, some type of family structure exists in every society—it appears impossible to extract a basic nature from these human characteristics. Attempts to measure human nature in a way that will enable us to make statements such as "60% of North American adults are trustworthy and 40% are not" are futile. Even if we could agree on what represents trustworthy and untrustworthy behavior, we would find the behavior under study influenced by the nature of the person involved, the nature of the situation, and the recent reinforcement history of the person being studied.

A comprehensive cross-cultural study by Roy E. Feldman (1968) clearly illustrates some of the complexities in seeking an answer to a seemingly simple question: who is more helpful to a stranger—a resident of France, one of Greece, or one of the United States? Feldman employed five behavior settings in Paris, Athens, and Boston, and trained locals and foreigners in the five settings of each city to ask for help. Feldman was interested not only in nationality differences in helping behavior but also in whether a foreign stranger was treated differently from a compatriot. But the results are so inconsistent that only a few general conclusions may be drawn.

In the first behavior setting, for example, the purpose was to determine whether people helped individuals who asked them for directions. Main shopping areas were used in Paris, Athens, and Boston, and only males over age 18 were stopped. Each person who was stopped was asked for directions to a familiar location.

In this setting, both the Parisians and the Athenians gave help to a fellow citizen more frequently than to a foreigner. For example, 24% of the Parisians did not give directions to a compatriot, while 45% did not help a foreigner (or gave the foreigner wrong instructions). (Even if the foreigner asked the question in French, he was less likely to receive helpful information than was a compatriot.) In the Athenian sample, 36% either did not give directions to the foreigner or misdirected him, while 32% did not help fellow Greeks. Of the Bostonians, 20% either did not respond or responded incorrectly to foreigners, while 21% responded not at all or incorrectly to compatriots.

In another behavior setting, Feldman tested whether cashiers in Paris, Athens, and Boston would keep or return an overpayment of money after a small purchase. Again, both compatriots and foreigners did the purchasing; but, in this case, only the language of the host country was used. Pastry shops were used for the setting, since they are numerous in all parts of all three cities, and frequent purchases for small amounts of money could be made. In Paris, 39% of all the pastry shops in a certain neighborhood were used; 31% of the shops in an equivalent area were used in Athens, and 18% in Boston. In making a purchase costing about 20 cents, the purchaser paid a few pennies, centimes, or drachmas above the actual cost and then slowly walked out of the store. The amount of overpayment was always one-fourth to one-third of the purchase price.

No important differences occurred between the ways cashiers treated foreigners and compatriots in any city. In Paris pastry shops, 54% of the cashiers kept the money from both types of purchasers. In Athens, the overpayment was not returned to the foreigner 51% of the time and not returned to the compatriot 50% of the time. In Boston, the money was kept from the compatriot 38% of the time and from the foreigner 27% of the time.

A third behavior setting involved the foreigner or compatriot in a taxi ride: 60 in Paris, 42 in Athens, and 44 in Boston. In each city, half the riders were compatriots and half were foreigners. The foreigner did not simply announce his destination, but read the location of the destination from a slip of paper and then handed the paper to the driver. In neither Boston nor Athens was the foreigner overcharged more often than the compatriot; but in Paris, the foreigner from the United States was overcharged significantly more often than the French compatriot. Of the 30 pairs of equivalent rides in Paris, the foreign rider was charged more than the French rider 18 times, the same amount 7 times, and less 5 times. The French taxi drivers illustrated a wide variety of techniques for increasing the distance traveled and/or fare charged to the foreigner.

Testings of more than 3000 subjects in these and two other behavior settings produced differences that were not consistent from one country or behavior setting to another. When a difference was observed, though, "the Athenians treated the foreigner better than the compatriot, but Parisians and Bostonians treated compatriots better than foreigners" (Feldman, 1968, p. 212). Even within the limited number of settings in Feldman's study, it is impossible to extract consistent human natures across cities or across settings within cities. However, when differences in the five settings are considered, some degree of consistency does emerge. Triandis (1976) suggests that in traditional societies, such as Greece, people cooperate with members of their ingroups but not with members of out-groups; Greeks treat visitors to Greece like members of their own family. Also, the nature of the social setting is crucial. In settings in which the relationship is role related (customer and client), there is more consistency in treatment of locals and foreigners than in situations in which the relationship is unstable (such as passersby on the street).

C. Social psychology's role in determining assumptions about human nature

Despite the cautionary tone of the foregoing section, social psychology as a scientific discipline can still play a role in influencing the popular conception of human nature. George Miller, in his 1969 presidential address to the American Psychological Association, identified two possible sets of beliefs about human nature that could result from the impact of scientific advances in psychology. One set of beliefs emphasizes the control of behavior, the viewpoint that living organisms are nothing but machines, and the impact of external reinforcements in "shaping" our behavior. Miller does not question the validity of this conception, but rather its effect on those who accept it. This image of human nature, Miller states, "has great appeal to an authoritarian mind, and fits well with our traditional competitive ideology based on coercion, punishment, and retribution" (1969, p. 1069). In a similar vein, social psychologist Chris Argyris (1975) has noted the implicit assumptions of *manipulation* and *control* that run through the writings of many social psychologists.

Miller's second set of beliefs about human nature reflects a more humanistic flavor. According to this image, people may be inspired to do well by both the stick and the carrot; they possess degrees of imagination, ingenuity, and creativity that are not well utilized under most working conditions; and they "exercise self-direction and self-control in the service of objectives to which they are committed" (Miller, 1969, p. 1070). For Miller, the challenge to social science is the fostering of a social climate in which this second conception of human nature will take root and flourish. Such a conception is slowly gaining ground, but the traditional view of human nature (that people must be threatened in order to achieve and that they can be successfully controlled) remains pervasive. Perhaps, when recognizing the differences among people, we must conclude that both views of human nature have some validity.

III. Forming an impression of a specific person—Like peeling an onion?

As the above discussion implies, beliefs about human nature are necessary and hence ever present in our society. But as an aid in forming impressions of specific people, they can get us only so far. Our reactions to an individual are not simply a result of our philosophy of human nature or what constructs we use. How do we form an impression of another? We seem to scan the person's surface qualities and then look for less apparent indicators, somewhat as though we were peeling an onion.

A. The use of group stereotypes in forming impressions of individuals

Let us return to our example of the stranger at your front door. Your basic trust in human nature may contribute a little to your decision, but you may also rely on general physical characteristics of the person, such as his or her age, sex, race, and physical appearance. For example, you will of course immediately note that the stranger is a man. Each of us probably possesses some **stereotypes,** or simplified sets of images, of groups of people. To maintain the analogy of judging a specific person as peeling off a series of layers, our assumptions of human nature may be considered the outer layer and our stereotypes about people of that person's sex as a second layer. For example, you may believe that men are aggressive, ambitious, and deceptive. You may thus discount what the stranger is telling you simply because he is a man.

However, there are more specific layers that are deeper and hence more important. Generally, the more specific the information, the more influential it is in forming an impression of a person. For example, the man may mention that he is on his way to an important meeting at the Second Baptist Church, where he is a member of the board of deacons. This informa-

tion may trigger further impressions on your part; you may think, for example, that Baptists are law-abiding, earnest people who are not threats to you. Because not all people are Baptists, the fact that a particular person *is* one will communicate more influential information to you about that person.

Let us further assume that the man mentions that he is the uncle of Carole Kingman, a friend of yours who lives two doors down the street. He has tried to use the phone at Carole's house, but nobody is home. Here is the most specific category yet—a relative of a friend. You like Carole and her parents, and you assume that her uncle is similar to them. You figure you'd like him, too. You welcome him in, show him to the telephone, and offer him coffee and cake while he waits for the tow truck to come. Our initial impression, which leaned toward mistrust —an impression based on the outer layers—has shifted to one of trust.

Thus, in judging others, we extend our analysis beyond group-related layers to more individualized ones. With some people we proceed to the innermost layer right away, because we know them as individuals. If a violent murderer had escaped from the local prison and we had just seen his photo on television, and if he were to show up at our front door, we would not mess around by peeling through layers of his sex, educational level, occupation, or whatever. We would say to ourselves that this particular man is dangerous.

B. The use of implicit personality theories

Stereotyping is not the only process we use in forming impressions of others. We saw that George Kelly proposed that we act as scientists and that we assume relationships among the characteristics or traits possessed by other people. Such a viewpoint claims that each of us has a "layman's theory of personality" (Cronbach, 1955). These assumed relationships are called **implicit personality theories**; they are naïve assumptions that certain characteristics are associated with each other (Bruner & Tagiuri, 1954; Carroll, 1974; D. J. Schneider, 1973). For example, we have observed Helen enough to know that she is quite *timid;* we conclude that she is also *unhappy.* We have no evidence that these two traits are associated in people, but we *assume* that they are. The use of implicit personality theories once more reflects our need to simplify and to integrate information and thus be able to deal with the complexities of human behavior that we encounter daily. If the stranger at your door seeking help happens to use some vulgar language, your "theory of personality" may cause you to see him as a potential thief ("anyone who uses crude language is likely to steal, too").

C. Central traits

Another example of the simplifying and integrating processes involved in impression formation is our reliance on **central traits.** The study of implicit personality theories and centrality of traits reflects a Gestalt orientation to the study of forming impressions. For example, as we indicated in Chapter 1, Solomon Asch (1946) expected that as you form your impression of another person, some pieces of information would carry greater weight and thus modify the whole picture. Asch called such influential characteristics *central traits.* Furthermore, he showed that the *warm-cold* dimension was a central one that markedly affected the organization of people's impressions. For instance, when the adjective *cold* was included in a list of seven words purportedly describing another person, only about 10% of the subjects gave responses stating that the target person would also be *generous* or *humorous.* However, when the adjective *warm* was used instead of *cold,* about 90% of the subjects described the person as *generous,* and more than 75% described the person as *humorous.* Responses to many other traits were also markedly affected by the presence of the word *warm* or *cold* in the brief stimulus list.

By contrast, when the words *polite* and *blunt* were substituted for *warm* and *cold,* respectively, the resulting impressions were not much dif-

associated with low.

ferent from each other. Because of their lack of effect, then, Asch did not consider the terms *polite* and *blunt* to be central traits. The results of Asch's study and those of several other researchers seemed to support the Gestalt theory that Asch advocated.

However, further studies by Wishner (1960), by Warr and Knapper (1968, Experiments 10–13), and by Rosenberg, Nelson, and Vivekananthan (1968) provided a more refined analysis that cast a different theoretical light on the topic. Wishner began by having more than 200 undergraduate psychology students rate their course instructors on 53 pairs of traits used by Asch. From these ratings Wishner then computed the correlation coefficients between each trait and every other trait. That is, he found out to what degree ratings of generosity went hand-in-hand with the ratings of, say, punctuality.

Wishner extracted the following three characteristics from this huge correlation matrix, which helped to explain Asch's findings of the centrality of the *warm-cold* trait in the formation of impressions about personality:

1. The correlations between *warm-cold* and the other six traits on Asch's stimulus list were all relatively low. This means that *warm-cold* was adding new information about the person rather than uselessly repeating information already communicated by the six other stimulus traits.
2. The correlations of the other six stimulus traits with many of the traits on the response checklist used by Asch's subjects were relatively low. This means that these response traits—that is, the impressions of the subjects—were not strongly determined by knowledge of the other six stimulus traits.
3. The correlations between *warm-cold* and most of the traits on the response checklist were rather high.

These three facts explain the centrality of *warm-cold* traits in determining personality impressions in Asch's study. These facts also explain why some traits on the response checklist were not much affected by the *warm-cold* variable. These were cases where the second and/or third characteristic of the correlation matrix did not hold.

As a final demonstration of the power of his analysis, Wishner showed that he could create a situation that would produce exactly the sort of personality impression that he predicted. On the basis of his trait correlation matrix, Wishner picked a new stimulus list and a new response checklist, so that the two lists were relatively uncorrelated. Then he chose *humane-ruthless* as a central trait, which was not correlated with the traits on the stimulus list. Finally, Wishner correctly predicted that this central trait would have great weight in determining responses to the traits with which it was highly correlated, and little weight in determining responses to the traits with which it was not correlated.

Wishner's study has made an important theoretical contribution to our understanding of impression formation. Asch considered the stimulus traits as a Gestalt, which led him to conclude that whether a given trait was central or peripheral in its impact would depend on its relationship to its context—that is, to the other *stimulus* traits. However, Wishner's analysis has shown that stimulus traits are less important in determining centrality than the central trait's relationship with the *response* traits. In this situation, stimulus-response theory seems more successful than a Gestalt analysis.

D. Adding versus averaging in impression formation

Often when we ask what someone is like, we are given a list of traits that supposedly describe the person. For example, we may be told by a mutual friend that our blind date for Friday night is "interesting, creative, and modest, but kind of moody." How do we integrate these pieces of information? We have already seen that the use of central traits and implicit personality theories aid us in this challenging task. More recently, social psychologists have directed their interest toward a process of integrating the information. Two models have been proposed: the *additive model* and the *averaging model* (Brewer, 1968; Hendrick, 1968; Rosnow & Arms, 1968).

To illustrate how these work, let us say that you have been told that your sister's new fiancé is *good humored* and *clever*. How would your impression differ if you had been told he was *good humored, clever, casual,* and *shy*?

The *averaging model* claims that we, in a sense, assign a favorability value to each trait and then use the mean of these values to form our impression of a person (Anderson, 1965, 1974; Anderson & Alexander, 1971). We have been provided a list of favorability or likability of 555 personality traits by Anderson (1968b), a portion of which is included in Table 3-4. In the above example, the averaging model would probably conclude that we would have a more favorable impression of our sister's fiancé when we were told only that he was *good humored* and *clever*, because both of these are very desirable traits. The inclusion of *casual* and *shy* reduces the average, as they are less attractive traits.

The *additive* or *summation* model, in contrast, bases one's overall judgment on the *sum* of the traits' values, not their average (Anderson, 1962). According to this model of information integration, adding the traits *casual* and *shy* should increase the favorability of your overall evaluation. (See also Table 3-5.)

Which model is correct? There is some evidence in support of each. The additive model received support from a study by Fishbein and Hunter (1964), who showed that people who knew five strongly positive characteristics about a target person had a somewhat more positive feeling toward him than did people who possessed only two strongly positive characteristics about him.

On the other hand there is stronger recent evidence for the averaging model (Anderson, 1965; Anderson, Lindner, & Lopes, 1973). It seems correct to say that *part* of our response to others is some kind of averaging of all the information we have about them, in order to form an overall impression. Doubtless the process is not a simple averaging, however. Some information must carry more weight than others.

Probably constructs that are salient or important in our own individualized construct theory (to use George Kelly's approach) are more heavily weighted if an averaging process does occur. Norman Anderson (1968a) has proposed such a weighted-averaging model.

IV. The power of first impressions

Most of us probably exert extra effort to look nice and be charming on the occasion of applying for a job or meeting a blind date. We assume that another person's first impression of us may be an influential one. If we look and act our best, we hope this first impression will be a lasting one. What evidence is there for the power of first impressions? Put another way, is the *first* information **(primacy effect)** or the *latest* information (recency effect) most influential in another person's perception of us?

To study the effects of first impressions, Luchins (1957a, 1957b) wrote two short paragraphs chronologically describing some of the day's activities of a boy named Jim. In one paragraph, Jim walked to school with friends, basked

Table 3-4
The likableness of personality-trait words

What is the "best" thing you can say about someone's personality? What is the "worst"? Norman H. Anderson and his associates have obtained likableness ratings for 555 different words that are used as personality trait descriptions; that is, subjects rated each word on a seven-point scale ranging from "least favorable or desirable" to "most favorable or desirable." The average ratings given each word by the 100 college students form the value for that word. Such a listing is tremendously useful in research on impression formation, for it gives us an empirical indication of the value of different traits. Of course, these likableness ratings are colored by the particular group of raters; some other group might rate "polite" as more or less favorable than this group (which made it 53rd in a list of 555 terms). Also, the likableness of traits can change over time; "logical" may not be as highly valued as it once was (in this group it is 94th).

Such a listing is interesting in what it reveals about our preferences. "Sincere" is rated most favorably of all 555 terms, while "liar" and "phony" are the very least desirable. These say something about our values. Interestingly, the very middle term in the list (278th in ranking) is "ordinary." The entire list cannot be reprinted here, but some extremes and highlights are included.

Rank	Term	Rank	Term	Rank	Term
1.	sincere	80.	ethical	531.	loud-mouthed
2.	honest	100.	tolerant	540.	greedy
3.	understanding	150.	modest	546.	deceitful
4.	loyal	200.	soft-spoken	547.	dishonorable
5.	truthful	251.	quiet	548.	malicious
6.	trustworthy	278.	ordinary	549.	obnoxious
7.	intelligent	305.	critical	550.	untruthful
8.	dependable	355.	unhappy	551.	dishonest
9.	open-minded	405.	unintelligent	552.	cruel
10.	thoughtful	465.	disobedient	553.	mean
20.	kind-hearted	500.	prejudiced	554.	phony
30.	trustful	520.	ill-mannered	555.	liar
40.	clever				

Adapted from "Ratings of Likableness, Meaningfulness, and Likableness Variances for 555 Common Personality Traits Arranged in Order of Decreasing Likableness," by N. H. Anderson, *Journal of Personality and Social Psychology*, 1968, 9, 272–279. Copyright 1968 by the American Psychological Association. Used by permission.

in the sun on the way, talked with acquaintances in a store, and greeted a girl whom he had recently met. In the other paragraph Jim's activities were very similar, but his style was different; he walked home from school alone, stayed on the shady side of the street, waited quietly for service in a store, and did not greet a pretty girl whom he had recently met. The first paragraph (E) made subjects think of Jim as an extrovert; the second paragraph (I) made him seem an introvert.

Luchins then combined the two paragraphs either in the E-I order or in the I-E order. In either case the paragraphs formed a connected, chronological narrative, but they presented sharply conflicting information about Jim. After reading the two paragraphs, subjects were asked to rate Jim on a personality-trait checklist. Luchins reasoned that if the information initially given was most important in determining personality impressions, then the E-I order should produce impressions more like the E paragraph alone, and the I-E order should produce impressions more like those of the I paragraph alone. This result would be called a *primacy effect*. A

recency effect, however, would mean that the second paragraph was more dominant. The results of several experiments were consistent in showing a strong primacy effect. Thus, first impressions are apparently very important in determining our final impressions of other people.

Luchins continued his research and demonstrated that, under the right conditions, the primacy effect could be easily overcome, and a large recency effect could be produced. In this part of the study, subjects were warned about the dangers of being misled by first impressions, and they were asked to perform an unrelated mathematical task for five minutes between their readings of the first and second paragraphs about Jim. Under these conditions, the information most recently read was much more influential in determining impressions about Jim. Also, if some other activity by the subjects is introduced between their exposure to the two parts of the description of Jim, a recency effect is obtained (Luchins, 1957b, 1958; Mayo & Crockett, 1964; Rosenkrantz & Crockett, 1965). But such an experimental procedure has been criticized because it does not ask the subjects to incorporate their

---

Table 3-5
Adding versus averaging in the integration of impressions

When given a list of traits that describe another person, how do we integrate the information given by these traits? The adding model and averaging model agree that we, in effect, assign a value to each trait. But the models differ in regard to how these values are integrated.

Consider the data below, bearing in mind that we have assigned relative likableness values to each trait.

Let us say that we are given the following traits for two men:

Gary		Steve	
Understanding	(+3)	Understanding	(+3)
Poised	(+2)	Sharp-witted	(+2)
Confident	(+1)	Congenial	(+2)
		Resourceful	(+2)
		Loud-mouthed	(−3)

The additive model would sum the values for each stimulus person, giving each a score of +6. Thus the additive model would predict that our overall impressions of both men would be equally favorable. On the other hand, the averaging model would get a mean value for the traits for each, giving Gary a +2 and Steve 1 1/5. The averaging model would predict that our overall evaluation of Gary would be better.

initial impressions into their final impressions. When the instructions stress that the two parts of the description refer to the same person, the recency effect disappears, and most persons attempt to form an integrated impression of Jim (Leach, 1974).

V. The attribution of cause

In most cases we are not content simply to *observe* and *describe* others' personalities and actions. We seek to *understand*. We feel constrained to assign causes to behavior. Why did Joe not call me tonight, as he promised to do? Why is my sister getting a better grade than I am in the physics class? Why did that child drown at the beach when a lifeguard was on duty? A rapidly developing approach to the study of such questions is called *attribution theory*. While the term is new and research using it has emerged within the last 10 or 12 years, the springboard for this approach is found in the seminal writing of Fritz Heider (1944, 1958) more than three decades ago.

Heider stressed the notions that people perceive the behavior of others as being caused and that they attribute the cause either to the person, to the environment, or to a combination of the two. For example, Joe failed to call me last night. I conclude that either he forgot (called a personal or *dispositional* attribution) *or* his car stalled and he couldn't get to a phone (environmental or *situational* attribution) *or* he was mad at me but when he got over being mad the phone at his house was tied up (combination of dispositional and situational attributions).

A central focus of attribution theory is upon our choice of the specific types of dispositional or situational attributions. (See Figure 3-5 for a flow chart of the stages in making a dispositional attribution.) When our sister gets an "A" on the physics midterm, do we attribute it to her ability, energy level, and dedication, or do we speculate that the instructor is being easy on her because she's a sexy female? Heider postulates that a person's effect on events involves both the person's level of ability and the person's amount of effort, and it is only when both factors are present that we hold a person responsible for events and attribute to the person certain dispositional properties or traits (Saxe, Greenberg, & Bar-Tal, 1974). This would say that if we recognize that our sister is both bright and motivated to do well, we make a dispositional attribution as to the source of her "A" grade. Otherwise, we fall back on a situational attribution ("the kindly [or lecherous] instructor").

But we evaluate a person's ability in relation to environmental forces. For instance, even a very competent lifeguard is not blamed when he or she is unable to save a drowning child if, for example, the undertow was so strong that the lifeguard could not combat it. Similarly, we evaluate a person's efforts in regard to two components: his or her intentions and level of exertion. We say that the lifeguard certainly tried hard enough; we make attributions about his or her intentions based on our observations of the lifeguard's behavior.

One of the basic principles generated by attribution theory is that people are more likely to attribute the causes of their own behavior to situational dispositions, whereas observers are more likely to attribute the responsibility for the same behavior to internal dispositions of the actors. First offered by Jones and Nisbett (1971), this actor-observer difference in causal attributions has received some empirical support (McArthur, 1972; Nisbett, Caputo, Legant, & Marecek, 1973; Harvey, Arkin, Gleason, & Johnston, 1974). However, the difference needs to be qualified, as the success or failure of the action interacts with the attribution of causes. When an action is expected to have a positive outcome, actors attribute more responsibility to themselves for a positive outcome than for a negative one. But in the same situation, observers attributed more responsibility to the actor for a negative outcome than for a positive one (Harvey et al., 1974).

Nevertheless, the explanations offered by people for their own behavior and the reasons generated by outside observers are often quite conflicting. West, Gunn, and Chernicky (1975) noted this in regard to the burglary of the Democratic party headquarters in the Watergate Hotel. The mass media attributed the break-in to such causes as the paranoid orientation of the Nixon administration and the recruitment of an amoral staff of campaign workers by the Committee to Re-Elect the President. In contrast, several members of the Nixon administration offered different reasons. For instance, some stated that "these activities were a natural result of the potentially violent plans of the radical left and that given the available alternative courses of action, such activities were demanded by the circumstances" (quoted by West et al., 1975, p. 55). Note that these differences reflect Jones and Nisbett's proposition that those actively involved will be more likely to "blame the environment."

West et al. (1975) felt that it might have been the case that the Watergate crimes were due to severe situational pressures on those involved. These pressures included the normative expectations within the Nixon administration and the payoffs for engaging in such illegal activities or for not doing so. The social psychologists decided to create a miniature Watergate break-in in the laboratory, in order to study the interpretations of situational pressures made by participants and by observers.

College students participated as subjects in the study. They were approached by a local private investigator who told them that he had "a project you might be interested in." The private investigator suggested that they meet at his home or at a local restaurant. If the subject asked about the reason for the meeting, he or she was assured that it would be fully explained at a later time. Every person approached (56 males and 24 females) made an appointment to meet with the private investigator.

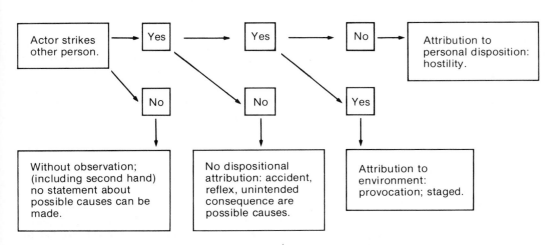

STAGE 1 — Was action observed? STAGE 2 — Was action intended? STAGE 3 — Was action coerced?

Figure 3-5
Flow chart for attribution to a personal disposition of the "actor." (From *An Introduction to Attribution Processes*, by K. G. Shaver. Copyright © 1975 by Winthrop Publishers, Inc. Reprinted by permission of the publisher.)

At the second meeting, the private investigator was accompanied by a confederate. They brought along a briefcase containing elaborate plans for the commission of a burglary at a local advertising agency.

Subjects in different experimental conditions were given different explanations for the reasons for the break-in, as follows:

Condition 1. The burglary was to be committed for a government agency (the Internal Revenue Service) and it was being done for the purpose of microfilming an illegal set of records maintained by the advertising agency. The agency—in actuality a front for a Miami investment corporation—was defrauding the government of 7 million dollars in taxes yearly. Subjects were told that the records had to be microfilmed in order to get a search warrant and subpoena to seize the records. In this condition subjects were told that the government had guaranteed them immunity from prosecution if they were caught.

Condition 2. The same explanation as above was given, except that subjects were warned that there would be no immunity from prosecution if they were captured.

Condition 3. Subjects were told that another advertising firm had offered $8000 for a copy of a set of designs prepared by the first agency. Each subject was told he or she would be paid $2000 for participation in the crime.

Condition 4. In a control condition, subjects were told that the break-in was being committed merely to determine whether the burglary plans designed by the private investigator would work. The subjects were told that although an illegal act, the break-in, would be committed, absolutely nothing would be stolen from the office.

Each subject was introduced to the confederate who was to play the role of the outside lookout on the four-person burglary team. Extensive details about the break-in were presented, including aerial photographs of the building and its surrounding area, routes of city and state patrol cars, and blueprints of the advertising office. The subject's job was to serve as an inside lookout and also to microfilm the advertising agency's records.

After hearing the elaborate description, subjects were encouraged to ask questions. West, Gunn, and Chernicky note that "virtually all of the questions in fact concerned technical details of the plan" (1975, p. 58). Each subject was then asked to come to a final planning meeting of the group. If the subject refused, the private investigator re-emphasized that the plan was foolproof and asked the subject to reconsider his or her decision. If the subject maintained his or her refusal, the experiment was terminated, and the subject was told of the deception and the true purposes of the study.

The major dependent variables of this part of the study were the subject's agreement or refusal to participate and the reasons he or she gave. These 80 subjects served as "actors."

Meanwhile, in a second part of the study, 238 students (92 males and 146 females) served as "observers." Each was given a booklet describing the above procedures and one of the four conditions. Subjects were asked:

1. If 100 students were presented with this proposal, how many (number) would you guess would agree to participate?
2. Would you do it?

These observers were also asked to write comments about a particular student who either did or did not participate. Table 3-6 presents the percentages of actors and observers who agreed or refused.

Analyses of the free responses indicated that actors attributed their behavior to situational causes, and observers attributed the actors' behavior to internal characteristics. Even when observers are forced to put themselves in the role of the actor, they may still give too much weight to dispositions as causes, and not enough to the environment.

The principles of attribution theory have been extended and made more precise in important papers by E. E. Jones and Davis (1965) and by Harold Kelley (1967, 1971, 1972, 1973), and in books by Daryl Bem (1970) and Kelly Shaver (1975). Jones and Davis hold that perceivers first observe a person's actions, then infer the per-

Table 3-6
Responses to break-in proposal

	Condition			
	1 Government Sponsorship with Immunity	2 Government Sponsorship without Immunity	3 Reward	4 Control
Actors (N = 20 in each condition)				
Agreed	45%	5%	20%	10%
Refused	55%	95%	80%	90%
Observers (N = 55 to 57 in each condition)*				
Agreed	28.1%	14.0%	12.2%	18.2%
Refused	71.9%	86.0%	87.8%	82.8%

*Response to question "Would you do it?"

From "Ubiquitous Watergate: An Attributional Analysis," by S. G. West, S. P. Gunn, and P. Chernicky, *Journal of Personality and Social Psychology*, 1975, *32*, 55–65. Copyright 1975 by the American Psychological Association. Reprinted by permission.

son's intentions from his or her actions, and finally infer the person's traits or dispositions from his or her intentions. They suggest four variables that determine the strength and confidence with which such dispositional attributions will be made: social desirability, common effects, hedonic relevance, and personalism.

If the person's actions reflect *social desirability*, we are less confident in making a dispositional attribution about the person's actions. If we tip our hairdresser $5 at Christmas and are effusively thanked and complimented, we still know little about how the hairdresser feels about us and our dandruff. Such a response reflects social desirability and is to be expected from the situation. But if the hairdresser had failed to say thank you or had made a gruff acknowledgment

of the tip, we would be more likely to make a dispositional attribution, to say that something is upsetting him or that he does not think much of us (E. E. Jones & Harris, 1967).

In general, unfavorable information about a person carries more weight in attributing causes to the person's behavior than does favorable information (Hamilton & Huffman, 1971). This apparently occurs because negative information is assumed to have a lower base rate; that is, we assume people to possess desirable qualities rather than undesirable ones (Lay, Burron, & Jackson, 1973).

The *common effects* of two actions provide a basis for attributions about the actor's traits. For instance, the young woman who acts warm and responsive toward her companion on an expensive dinner-and-concert evening *and* on a simple Coke date is seen as genuinely friendly rather than as a gold digger. The other side of this coin is that *noncommon effects* between a chosen action and a nonchosen one provide a basis for attributions. The man who asks a woman only for a drink after work, when he has two tickets to the latest hit play and could have asked her to it, will probably be seen as not seriously interested in her.

The *hedonic relevance* of the person's actions (that is, the extent to which they are rewarding or costly to the perceiver) increases the strength of attributions. If your actions hurt me or help me materially, I am more likely to conclude that you are a harmful or helpful person than I would be if your actions had no effects.

The *personalism* of the other's actions (that is, the extent to which they are seen as being directed specifically at the perceiver) increases the strength of attributions (Potter, 1973). This principle represents an extension of the hedonic-relevance principle. If your actions hurt me and I perceive that they were directed *specifically at me*, I am even more likely to conclude that you are a hurtful person. Or as K. G. Shaver (1975) suggests, if I refuse to play tennis with you by saying that I have to go to the library and then show up on the tennis courts with someone else, you are more likely to make a dispositional attribution, specifically that I don't want to play *with you*.

Extensions of attribution theory by Daryl Bem (1970, 1972b) and Harold Kelley (1967, 1971, 1972) include the conditions for making attributions to external entities, rather than to persons. Kelley suggests that the criteria we use for making an external attribution can be used to organize much of the social-psychological literature on the processes of **social influence** (see Chapters 12 and 19).

An important point made by Bem is that the processes of self-perception and of other-perception are substantially similar. Thus attribution theory can also be applied to research on the self-concept and to therapeutic methods that stress self-awareness. (For more information on this theoretical approach the interested reader is referred to the papers cited above and to clearly organized summaries of research on attribution theory in K. G. Shaver, 1975, and in Hastorf, Schneider, and Polefka, 1970, pp. 70–89).

VI. The accuracy of our judgments of others

In the foregoing discussion we have analyzed the processes of social perception without mentioning the accuracy of our judgments of others' traits. In fact, you may have already expressed the feeling that all the foregoing is irrelevant if people really can't do a very good job of judging other's feelings, attitudes, and abilities. What can we say about people's skills in this regard? Twenty years ago the study of social perception concentrated on the question of accuracy. While some general principles were extracted (which we will review in this section), the general reaction was a great deal of frustration because of the methodological problems involved. Interest in the accuracy of social perception waned for a second reason, too: social psychologists came to recognize that the processes involved in *how* we perceived others were more important than the elusive question of *how well* we did it. As Chandler (1974) puts it, "people are so frequently right for the wrong reasons that being right about another's feelings really tells us very little" (p. 2). Even though there is little advancement presently in the scientific study of accuracy, its investigation reflects the methodological morasses we can get into, and deserves to be discussed.

A. Procedures for determining accuracy

In order to determine the accuracy of impressions, three conditions are needed: a *stimulus person and situation,* a perceptual *response* or judgment by the subject, and a *criterion* with

attribution: opinions of characteristics

which to compare the subject's response. Table 3-7 illustrates the very wide variety of materials that have been used in accuracy studies. In some instances (such as the opinions of informants), the criterion itself may not be very accurate. This limitation must be considered in evaluating research studies in this area. But once a criterion is chosen, the typical research paradigm is simple. The subject's judgments are compared with what the criterion says, and discrepancies on any items are treated as errors. The more errors, and the larger the errors, the poorer is the subject's accuracy score.

Stuart Oskamp[1] has developed a simple exercise that will illustrate some of the procedures and problems encountered in the study of social perception. Choose a person whom you know well, and we will try to determine how accurate your knowledge of that person really is. First, rate this person on the brief set of items listed in Figure 3-6. For each item, put a number in the first column, using the scale that is provided. Next, describe yourself, using the same scale and putting the appropriate numbers in the sec-

[1]Personal communication, July 1, 1972.

Table 3-7
Materials used in studying accuracy of person perception

1. Stimulus information (about the person to be judged)
   photographs of person's face
   motion pictures (either sound or silent)
   observations of live behavior (for instance, through a one-way mirror)
   face-to-face interactions (from brief interviews to long-term friendships)
   tape recordings of conversation
   psychological test protocols
   written materials (from autobiographies to brief descriptive paragraphs)
   personal productions (for example, handwriting, drawings)
   general experience with people in a given culture
2. Perceptual response or judgment (by the subject or judge) (subjective)
   rating of personality traits (such as "talkative")
   postdicting real-life behaviors (of the stimulus person)
   postdicting responses to specific test items
   postdicting psychological test scores (such as intelligence, achievement, or personality tests)
   postdicting the judgments of experts (for instance, psychiatric diagnoses)
   writing descriptive paragraphs (about the stimulus person)
   matching two sets of materials (such as test scores and personality descriptions)
   ranking stimulus persons on a given trait
   forced-choice responses (for example, which of two behaviors is more typical of the person)
3. Criterion information (the "real truth" about the stimulus person) (objective)
   public, factual information (such as age, job title, and the like)
   scores on psychological tests
   self-report data (for example, questionnaire items or interview responses)
   factual information from knowledgeable informants (for instance, information about stimulus person's real-life behavior)
   opinions or judgments from knowledgeable informants (such as job supervisor, wife, family, friends, or psychotherapist)

Adapted from Cline (1964).

① postdicting =

ond column in Figure 3-6. In order to complete this exercise, you will have to ask the target person to describe himself or herself on the same items using the same scale. Be sure that he cannot see your ratings while he is doing this. Then transfer his self-ratings into the third column, which is marked "Friend's Self-Rating."

Now you have all the elements necessary for determining the degree of accuracy of your perception of another person in the manner used in many social-psychological studies. For each characteristic, compare the number in column (a) with that in column (c) and obtain the absolute value of the difference. That is, for each item, subtract the smaller of the two numbers from the larger and record the difference in the margin. Then add up these differences for the 8 items; the result is your *error score*. A perfect score would be 0, and the worst possible score would be 40. A completely chance level of accuracy would be around 24.

Two other types of scores could be obtained using different combinations of the three columns; these scores measure *real similarity* and

assumed similarity. The difference between columns (b) and (c), the two self-ratings, is called **real similarity** because it indicates the degree of similarity between the two individuals' views of themselves. A score of 0 means complete similarity, and a high score means low similarity. The difference between columns (a) and (b) is called **assumed similarity,** or sometimes **projection,** because it shows how much you believe your friend is like yourself. With minor variations, this methodology has been used in many research studies on person perception.

B. Characteristics of the task of judging others

Some items in Figure 3-6 required only simple observation or knowledge on your part, whereas other items demanded a fairly remote inference about your friend and could not be answered directly from any behavior that you could have observed. For instance, "talkative in social groups" is basically an observational item, but "worries very frequently" is an inferential item

Figure 3-6
Social perception form

	(a) Friend	(b) Self	(c) Friend's Self-Rating
1. Is usually well dressed			
2. Enjoys gardening			
3. Would like to be an astronaut or explorer			
4. Is an avid reader			
5. Is quite athletic			
6. Likes little children			
7. Is talkative in social groups			
8. Worries very frequently			

Number Scale

1—strongly untrue of person
2—moderately untrue of person
3—mildly untrue of person
4—mildly true of person
5—moderately true of person
6—strongly true of person

(unless, by chance, your friend has told you about his or her worries in detail). Items 1, 4, 5, and 7 were intended to be primarily observational items, whereas items 2, 3, 6, and 8 were intended to be inferential. You might wish to go back and score these two types of items separately. Was there any substantial difference in the degree of your accuracy on the two types of items? If so, were you more accurate on the observational items or on the inferential ones? (Remember, this is an error score, so a low score means high accuracy.)

Gage and Cronbach (1955) have distinguished three important dimensions of the judgment task: (1) the degree of acquaintance between the judge and the other person, (2) the amount of extrapolation required by the task, and (3) the nature of the other people who are to be described. As regards the first dimension, it makes sense that you would probably make more errors if you try to make judgments about another student whom you barely know.

The second dimension, the amount of extrapolation required by the task, refers to the fact that some tasks may require only *knowledge* based on past experience, while other tasks may require the ability to *observe* and report one's observations, the ability to *infer* personal traits that have not been directly observed, or the combined ability to *observe and infer*. We have no reason to assume that a person who excels in one of these abilities will also excel in the others. Therefore, the nature of the judgment task must be considered in evaluating research results on this topic.

The nature of the other people who are to be described is the third important dimension of the judgment task. Some studies have asked judges to describe the characteristics of people in general (for instance, all citizens of a given country), of a category of persons (for example, college students), or of a particular group of people (for example, your social-psychology class). Such studies tap an ability that has been called **stereotype accuracy,** or the ability to correctly describe the population average or group norm, based on one's stereotype about the particular population or group in question. Other stu-

dies have asked judges to describe how an individual *differs* from his or her group or how an individual's behavior on one item (or trait) differs from his or her behavior on other items (or traits). These studies tap **differential accuracy,** or the ability to make a distinction between a particular individual's score and the norm or average behavior. This separation between stereotype accuracy and differential accuracy is an important one, which will recur often in our subsequent discussions.

A final characteristic of the person-perception task is that it is subject to the influence of response sets. The particular response sets that occur most commonly here are somewhat different from those discussed in Chapter 2. Most troublesome is the assumed similarity effect, or the tendency to rate another person as similar to oneself. This is a major source of fallacious conclusions in interpreting person-perception accuracy scores. Its effects can best be visualized by imagining a person who assumes that everyone whom he rates is completely similar to himself. Such a person would turn out to be highly accurate in judging people *who really are similar to him* (his friends, for instance, or people from similar backgrounds). However, he would be *very inaccurate* in judging people who are really different from him. In both cases, his accuracy score would be the result of his assumed similarity response set; thus, the score would be an *artifact* rather than a true indication of the person's skills.

C. Artifacts and components in the measurement of accuracy

An **artifact** is a research finding that does not reveal the true state of affairs but, instead, reflects the results of an arbitrary methodological approach. As we have seen, a judge's accuracy can be an artifact of a particular response set that he or she uses in making ratings. This fact went unrecognized in the early years of social-perception research, resulting in many spurious and fallacious research findings. It was most clearly spelled out, however, in a brilliant article by Cronbach (1955), who, in a single stroke, made most of the earlier research in this field obsolete.

We can illustrate Cronbach's methodological critique by referring again to the exercise in Figure 3-6 in which you recorded (a) your descriptions of your friend, (b) your descriptions of yourself, and (c) your friend's self-descriptions (the criterion). This criterion, incidentally, is somewhat suspect as an adequate indication of the "real truth" about your friend, since your friend may not completely know himself or herself. *(from page 106.)*

The three sets of scores in columns (a), (b), and (c) were independent sets of data. They were combined by subtracting one column from another, to obtain three *difference scores:* |a–b|, |b–c|, and |a–c| (where the vertical lines mean "the absolute value of"). The crucial point is that these three difference scores are not independent sets of data. When two difference scores have been computed, all three independent scores (a, b, and c) have been used, so the third difference score is already completely determined. This fact has been illustrated in our discussion of the assumed-similarity effect. Our example showed that if *assumed similarity* (a–b) was very high, and *real similarity* (b–c) was also high, then *accuracy* (a–c) was already determined—in other words, it had to be high. Any combination of any two of the factors will completely determine the third. Low assumed similarity in combination with high accuracy means that real similarity must be low; high real similarity combined with low accuracy means that assumed similarity must be low, and so on.

Cronbach's (1955) article showed that the accuracy score could be broken down into four major components. In addition, he demonstrated the mathematical reason for the artifactual connection between accuracy and assumed similarity, proving that some of the components of the accuracy score were also components of the assumed-similarity score. The four major components of the accuracy score are described as follows.

1. *Elevation* reflects the judge's way of using the response scale. It shows whether the judge's average rating (across all items, or traits, and across all persons being rated) is close to the average of all the criterion ratings.
2. *Differential elevation* shows the judge's ability to predict how far a given person's average trait score is above or below the average of the group being noted. That is, can the judge predict differences in the elevation (mean trait score) for individuals?
3. *Stereotype accuracy*, also mentioned in the preceding section on the characteristics of the judgment task, shows a judge's ability to predict the group norm on each trait; it has also been called "accuracy in predicting the generalized other."
4. *Differential accuracy* shows a judge's ability to predict differences between individuals on each trait.

One of the most important conclusions made by Cronbach was that these four components of the accuracy score were all *independent* aspects of interpersonal perceptiveness. Thus, a judge could be good on some items but poor or mediocre on others. Consequently Cronbach recommended (1) that each component be computed and treated separately, (2) that overall accuracy scores be abandoned, because their artifactual nature prevented any meaningful interpretations, and (3) that particular attention be paid to stereotype accuracy and differential accuracy. These recommendations drastically transformed research in the field of social perception.

In a later article Cronbach (1958) made still another dramatic impact on person-perception research by raising cogent objections to the whole idea of computing accuracy scores. Instead, he recommended that we study the perceptual world of each judge separately and intensively before we complicate the research problem by adding another set of scores as a criterion and by studying the judge's accuracy. This recommended approach focuses our attention on the implicit personality theory of each judge—his or her conception of which personality traits typically go together.

D. Characteristics of a good judge

Many studies have asked what kind of person is able to make accurate personal judgments. Unfortunately, most of these studies were done prior to Cronbach's critiques and thus are subject to the criticism of artifactual spurious findings. For this reason, we must be cautious in reaching conclusions. We may, however, tentatively accept Taft's (1955) report that several studies yield rather consistent evidence for each of the following characteristics of good interpersonal judges: (1) high intelligence and academic ability, (2) good emotional adjustment and integration, (3) esthetic and dramatic interests, (4) specialization in the physical sciences rather than in psychology.

How can we explain these paradoxical findings about psychologists being relatively poor judges of people? Taft suggests that psychologists may be too concerned about social relations and not detached or objective enough to be good judges; psychologists may have had too little experience with a wide variety of people. Though there may be a kernel of truth in these suggestions, a more basic reason for psychologists being poor judges of people may be their tendency toward overdifferentiation, a technical problem that will be described next.

Overdifferentiation of the persons being judged has been pointed to by Cronbach (1955) and other researchers as a major source of judgmental errors. The explanation of this is a technical, statistical one, but the basic principle involved is simple. Observers will usually be more accurate if they make most of their judgments close to the average level, for that is where most individuals actually score. If they make many extreme judgments (ones far from the group norm), they may possibly be reacting correctly to the direction of individual differences in the trait, but they are probably over estimating the extent of these differences. As a result, such a judge will have larger errors in his predictions than a person who makes less wide-ranging judgments. Thus, it is quite easy for a person acting as a rater or judge of others to be *oversensitive to individual differences.*

Dramatic evidence of oversensitivity comes from two studies. Gage (1952) had judges (students) make predictions of the questionnaire responses of other students. The judges knew only that the other students were typical undergraduate education majors. Later Gage gave the judges a period of direct contact with these students and had the judges make another set of predictions on this basis. Surprisingly, the later predictions were somewhat *less accurate* than the predictions made from the group-based impressions. Similarly, Crow (1957) gave a group of medical students a special training course on noticing and handling personal relationships with their patients; he then compared their subsequent accuracy of person perception with that of another group of medical students who had not received this training. Again, contrary to the intentions and expectations of the faculty, the trained subjects were somewhat less accurate in their personal judgments than the untrained group. Crow showed that this was due to the trained group's increase in variability of judgment, and he explicitly warned of the dangers of oversensitivity to individual differences as a factor leading to poor judgments about other people.

E. Generality of our accuracy levels

Let us suppose that, despite the many methodological problems involved, we have persevered in a person-perception study and found several judges who were quite accurate in their perceptions. Another important question that we might want to ask is: how general is their accuracy? That is, would these judges remain accurate ones if they were judging other persons or making judgments about different traits? This question has been studied with increasingly sophisticated techniques since Cronbach's (1955) critique. We will briefly describe two such studies with conflicting results and attempt to resolve their differing conclusions.

In the first, Crow and Hammond (1957) concluded that they had found no evidence for generality of accuracy. Their study was done with 72 senior medical students who viewed six-minute sound films of a physician interviewing a medical patient. Altogether, the subjects saw films of 30 different patients, viewing 10 patients on three different occasions six months apart. After each film the subjects had to estimate the self-ratings of the patient on seven personality scales and also the patient's real position on the same seven scales, as indicated by the Minnesota Multiphasic Personality Inventory (MMPI), a well-known personality inventory.

Crow and Hammond computed a measure of *differential accuracy* and three response-set measures that showed the judges' stereotypes about the scores of the patients. Correlations of these measures for the three different testing occasions showed that the response sets were quite stable over time, but the differential-accuracy scores were less stable. Since previous studies had not usually separated response-set components from accuracy scores, Crow and Hammond concluded that past findings of generality of accuracy might have resulted from *the consistency of response sets* rather than from consistency in judging ability.

The second important study, by Cline and Richards (1960), used a somewhat similar methodology, but with some crucial differences. Cline and Richards reached conclusions largely opposed to those of Crow and Hammond's study. These researchers also used short sound movies of interviews as their stimuli, but they went to great pains to improve both the stimulus materials and the response measures. They used color movies of a diverse sample of adults, who ranged from a 65-year-old widow with two married children to a 22-year-old single male Mexican-American working in a meat-packing plant. The interviews concentrated on personality characteristics, values, and interests, which probably gave a more rounded picture of the individual than Crow and Hammond's inter-

views. In addition, the final ten films that were used had been selected on the basis of their power to discriminate between good and poor judges—a procedure akin to improving a test by retaining only the best items. The final ten films were shown to a group of 50 students who were more diverse than the subjects in the Crow and Hammond study. Moreover, the films were all shown at one sitting instead of being spread over 12 months; thus, changes in judging ability over time were not a source of unreliability.

Cline and Richards' judging tasks were very carefully constructed, with a strong emphasis on good criterion information, obtained through very thorough case studies of each interviewee. Five different tasks were developed, and the predictions required of judges were considerably more detailed and varied than in Crow and Hammond's study. Furthermore, the judges in this study were given a chance to tune their perception by briefly inspecting the measuring instruments before seeing the films.

Cline and Richards followed Cronbach's (1955) recommendations by breaking down their judges' trait-rating scores into four basic components. As a result of the correlations obtained between these components and the other four judging tasks, the authors concluded that there is a general ability to perceive others accurately and that this ability is made up of two independent components—stereotype accuracy and differential accuracy. Thus, Cline and Richards found that the accuracy of the judge's social stereotype (which Crow and Hammond had dismissed as a response set) is the most important component of judgmental accuracy and that it helps to produce generality of accuracy. Our conclusion is that the results of the two studies are not at all incompatible but, rather, are quite supportive of one another.

Since the time of these studies, Cline (1964) has continued to find evidence that judging ability is a general trait; he has also found that it is composed of several independent skills rather than a single skill. This seems to be the best conclusion at present.

F. The accuracy of eyewitnesses

United States Senator Robert F. Kennedy was assassinated in the presence of a number of witnesses as he walked through a kitchen of the Ambassador Hotel in Los Angeles (Figure 3-7). Nearly 100 people were in the kitchen when the fatal shots were fired. Many eyewitnesses reported seeing Sirhan Sirhan spring forward, raise his gun, and fire. Yet the eyewitnesses, many of them standing next to each other, apparently saw different specific actions.

Langman and Cockburn (1975), who spent three years investigating the assassination, report:

> The eyewitnesses, many of them standing next to each other, saw—or remembered they

saw—very different things. Against the recollections of the assistant maître d'hôtel, who says that he was holding Kennedy's hand and leading him along—toward Sirhan—one can place the recollections of at least four other people who testified that Kennedy was turning to his left at the time Sirhan fired in order to shake hands with one of the waiters. Frank J. Burns, a friend of Kennedy's, was standing off Kennedy's right shoulder when the shots were fired, and he testified at Sirhan's trial that Kennedy had turned "almost ninety degrees" at the time and therefore was not facing Sirhan's gun muzzle but indeed presenting his right and hinder side to it. It is difficult to find witnesses—apart from the assistant maître d'hôtel—who directly contradict his recollections and those of many others, such as Edward Minasian, Martin Petrusky, Jesus Perez, and Vincent Di Pierro, all employed in the Ambassador's kitchen.

It is, however, impossible to find witnesses who directly corroborate the autopsy evidence that the gun was practically touching Kennedy's head. Their estimates vary wildly. Pete Hamill, the columnist, put Sirhan seven feet from Kennedy. Juan Romero, a busboy who had just shaken hands with Kennedy, estimated "approximately one yard." Valerie Schulte, a college student, said at the trial that "Sirhan's arm and gun" were "approximately five yards from me, approximately three yards, something like that, from the Senator." Edward Minasian, who was walking about a yard in front of Kennedy, thought the barrel of Sirhan's gun was "approximately three feet" from Kennedy. The closest to Kennedy that one can place the gun muzzle, going on these recollections, is about two feet—a distance calculated from one recollection that Sirhan was "three or four" feet away from Kennedy [1975, pp. 18-20].*

Such inconsistencies are not surprising to social psychologists who have conducted careful research on the accuracy of eyewitnesses to sudden events. For example, Buckhout, Alper, Chern, Silverberg, and Slomovits (1974) staged

Figure 3-7
The accuracy of eyewitnesses. (Photo courtesy of United Press International.)

*From "Sirhan's Gun," by B. Langman and A. Cockburn. Copyright 1974 by *Harper's Magazine.* Reprinted from the January 1975 issue by special permission.

crimes to test witnesses' immediate recall and their ability to recognize the lawbreaker in a police lineup. Many witnesses were incorrect in describing what happened immediately afterward, and only 14% of the witnesses were able to pick the culprit out of a police lineup.

In another study Buckhout and his colleagues (Buckhout, Figueroa, & Hoff, 1974) staged an assault on a professor in a classroom in front of 141 students. Seven weeks later the students had to select the assailant from a set of six photographs. More than 60% of the witnesses—including the professor—picked an innocent man. Yet despite numerous demonstrations of the extent of errors (Loftus & Palmer, 1974; Loftus, 1974; Wall, 1971) eyewitness testimony continues to be used as a source of convictions of many innocent people (Levine & Tapp, 1973).

VII. Future trends in the study of social perception

Four main trends may be cited as possible future developments in the area of social perception. First, as a better understanding of the factors in social perception develops, the typical research methodology will continue to become increasingly complex. For example, social psychologists (such as Krupat, 1974) are beginning to study the effects of the context in which social perception occurs. The movement toward more intricate methodologies has been particularly true in the study of person-perception accuracy, where the earlier, simpler methodologies were rendered uninterpretable by the presence of statistical artifacts. Tagiuri (1969) summarizes this trend as follows:

> The technology is by now very complex and tends, at times, to obscure the main issues. Simpler approaches and formulations have not stood up, however, and the current cumbersome methodologies and fragmentation of the problem may be unavoidable until some fresh formulation is reached. . . . The methodological intricacies may, however, be inappro-

priate to the complexity of the process. . . . The subtlety and delicacy of the process of coming to know other persons has never been underestimated, but empirical, naturalistic, and theoretical evidence now available suggests that it is even more complex than one ever dreamt of [p. 432].

Second, there has been a decided lack of theoretical underpinnings for most of the research in social perception. Tagiuri pungently describes the state of affairs as "an excess of empirical enthusiasm and . . . a deficit of theoretical surmise" (1969, p. 433). The recent research stemming from Bem's self-perception theory, from attribution theory, and from George Kelly's personal-construct theory is beginning to fill this void, but there is still a great need for more adequate theoretical bases for many aspects of research in the field.

Third, so far we have only begun to integrate the field of social perception with the more traditional areas of psychology and sociology. Tagiuri indicates that social perception overlaps the following other general areas of study: cognition, perception, learning, concept formation, personality, clinical diagnosis, and quantitative methods. The overlapping that occurs in these areas is worthy of future close attention.

Finally, the relation of social perception to actual interpersonal behavior needs much more thorough study. Dunnette (1968) has suggested broadening our focus to study *interpersonal accommodation*, or the process of back-and-forth interaction that uses perceptual feedback to modify behavior and approach a desired equilibrium state in social interaction. Tagiuri suggests future "studies of the judgments made about persons in the course of ordinary transactions with their environment . . . where people are truly interacting, and where observer and observed are simultaneously judge and object" (1969, p. 435). As has been discovered in the area of attitudes and behavior (Wicker, 1969a), it is possible that we may find major discontinuities between perception and behavior, despite our traditional assumptions and accumulated evidence of their general correspondence.

VIII. Summary

Everyone makes assumptions about the nature of people in general, in order to predict and understand their behavior. One way of conceptualizing these assumptions is to use philosophies of human nature, which are expectancies that people in general possess certain qualities and will behave in certain ways. Six dimensions of philosophies of human nature have been identified; four of these are substantive dimensions, and the other two deal with beliefs about individual differences in human nature. These assumptions about human nature influence our everyday behavior toward others.

Other theories that deal with our general ways of looking at human behavior are George Kelly's role-construct theory and O. J. Harvey's theory of conceptual systems. Kelly proposed that each of us generates his or her own constructs, which we use to describe people and to distinguish between them. Conceptual systems are ways of viewing the world. Harvey has proposed that people move through four stages of conceptual systems.

It is expected that in the future our society will intensify its quest for the satisfaction of human social needs. Social psychology can play a role by creating a climate in which more representative conceptions of human nature can flourish.

Forming an impression of a specific person can be thought of as involving a process of peeling layers. Our initial impressions may be influenced by our general beliefs about all people, mixed with our stereotypes about the groups to which the specific person belongs. In forming impressions of others, most of us use implicit personality theories, or assumptions that certain traits go together.

Central traits such as *warm-cold* are important in forming impressions of people only when the central traits are highly correlated with other traits that we wish to predict, and *not* because of their relationship to other stimulus traits that we have observed.

When we form impressions of a person based on a set of discrete pieces of information about that person, we apparently evaluate the favorability of each piece and average the ratings, rather than summing them, to emerge with an overall impression of the person.

Attribution theory deals with the causes we believe responsible for the behavior of others. Actions may be given either a dispositional attribution (the person is seen as the cause of his or her actions) or a situational attribution (the environment is seen as causing the person's behavior). People tend to make situational attributions for their own behavior, particularly when it is unsuccessful, while observers tend to rely on dispositional attributions.

Research results in the study of the accuracy of social perception have been confused and contradictory because of the marked effects of the different procedures used, the response sets that may influence scores, and the statistical artifacts that are inherent in the method of measurement.

One of the most important characteristics of good (in other words, accurate) judges of other people is that they avoid the mistake of overdifferentiation, or oversensitivity to the individual differences of the people being judged.

Research evidence indicates that the ability to judge other people accurately is, at least partially, a general trait that is relatively stable across various judging tasks and across various people to be judged. This ability has at least two major independent components: *stereotype accuracy*, or the ability to predict the group mean or knowledge of the generalized other, and *differential accuracy*, or the ability to predict differences between individuals on any given trait.

Future trends in the field of social perception are likely to include the continuation of complex methodology to match the subtleties of the processes involved, an increase in theoretical foundations for empirical research, a growing integration with the more traditional areas of sociology and psychology, and more extensive study of the correspondence between social perception and interpersonal behavior.

I. The nature of impression management
   A. Not for hypocrites only
   B. The necessity of impression management

II. Self-presentation: The same person, just a different face?
   A. The other person as an influence
   B. The interaction context: Goals and motives
   C. When saying is believing

III. In search of a "consistent" public image
   A. The "foot-in-the-door" effect
   B. "Bending over backward" to be consistent

IV. The quest for social approval
   A. Success, failure, and approval seeking
   B. Choosing an appropriate sex-role image
   C. Forcing the stigmatized to play their role
   D. Need for approval: Do some people have more than others?

V. Ingratiation
   A. Edward E. Jones's approach to ingratiation
   B. Research on ingratiation: Means and ends
   C. Nonverbal ingratiation
   D. Does ingratiation work if it is obvious?

VI. Impression management and social influence
   A. Machiavelli and company
   B. The successful help seeker

VII. Self-disclosure: The private "I" goes public
   A. Reciprocity and self-disclosure
   B. Liking and self-disclosure
   C. Social approval and self-disclosure
   D. Nonverbal behavior and self-disclosure

VIII. Detecting impression management in others
   A. Deceptive faces and truthful bodies
   B. Nonverbal detection of prejudice
   C. The skilled impression manager

IX. A time to reflect: Impression management and human nature
X. Summary

Impression management
by Mark Snyder

4

The image of myself which I try to create in my own mind in order that I may love myself is very different from the image which I try to create in the minds of others in order that they may love me.

W. H. Auden

The world is governed more by appearances than by realities, so that it is fully as necessary to seem to know something as to know it.

Daniel Webster

We live in a society which has made deception and pretense into art forms, a world in which appearances and outward images are often more important than reality itself. We wear coats which are "not *fur* real," relax in dens panelled in synthetic materials with the look and feel of dark oak, and brush with whitening toothpastes which promise to add sex appeal to our personal images. Advertising seduces us to identify with our society's heroes and heroines by using the products that they endorse. Millions of people buy books and take courses designed to help them create images that will win friends and influence people.

And as the events in recent United States political history associated with "Watergate" suggest, some of the U.S. leaders themselves seemed ready to blur the distinction between truth and lie. A U.S. President whose popularity in the public polls had skidded to record lows talked not about changing himself, but about changing his *image.* His ceremonial visits to foreign lands, somber-faced televised speeches, and heavily edited tape transcripts attempted to create the image of a chief executive too concerned with lofty affairs of state and international diplomacy to have been involved in or even aware of corruption. Yet as the almost daily disclosures made perfectly clear, the same administration that publicly preached law and order privately practiced illegal surveillance, spying, and obstruction of justice. (Nixon)

The gaps and contradictions that often exist between public appearances and private reality have long been favorite themes of fiction. Holden Caulfield, the 16-year-old hero of J. D. Salinger's *Catcher in the Rye,* was repulsed by the apparent phoniness, pretense, and hypocrisy of the adult world he encountered in his wanderings. Adults, from Holden's perspective, talked as if they loved others. But their unloving actions spoke loudly enough to drown out their words. Holden Caulfield decided that he could find sincere love only in children who had not yet learned the rituals

115

of pretense and hypocrisy put on by their elders. *Catcher in the Rye* first appeared in 1951; it is still a favorite today. Apparently this aspect of the world has not changed, and many of us still share Holden Caulfield's concerns.

The world of fiction is populated with masters of the arts of deception, hypocrisy, and pretense. The successful con artist, the artful seducer and charmer, the person of many faces are forever popular. The award-winning film *The Sting,* in which a team of confidence men played by Robert Redford and Paul Newman beat the racketeers at their own confidence game, seems destined to become a movie classic. Similarly, Molière's 17th-century stage comedy *Tartuffe* never fails to charm theatergoers. The title character is a pious-faced hypocrite who, behind a mask of religious propriety, proceeds to dupe the gullible Orgon, taking his property and his wife. Tartuffe shifts among his various faces with the ease of a chameleon switching colors to match its surroundings.

I. The nature of impression management

Why are we so fascinated with hypocrisy and pretense, so intrigued by the wiles and guiles of imposters and con artists? In each case, an individual (whom social psychologists label an *actor*) attempts through careful choice of words and deeds to create a particular image of himself or herself in the mind of another person (called a *perceiver*). The actor may hope also to influence the perceiver's behavior. Thus Tartuffe, who in reality is a small-time criminal, puts on a show of deep religious piety. He hopes that others will accept this image of him and let him live off their wealth. The process of attempting to control the images that others form of us is called **impression management.** Notice that for Tartuffe to be successful, he must be experienced with his targets and know exactly what behaviors on his part will foster the desired image in the eyes of his beholders. He must be skilled at "taking the role of the other" and seeing himself from the other's perspective. He can then proceed to present a convincing performance that will have the desired effect on others.

A. Not for hypocrites only

But is impression management the exclusive province of imposters, snake-oil hucksters, and politicians? Not so. Consider the case of a woman on trial for a crime that she did not commit. Her task on the witness stand is to present herself carefully, so that everything she does and says clearly and unambiguously communicates her true innocence to the jurors, so that they will vote for her acquittal. Chances are good, however, that members of the jury are somewhat skeptical of this defendant's claims of innocence. After all, they might reason to themselves, the district attorney would not have brought this case to trial were the state's case against her not a convincing one. The defendant must carefully manage her verbal and nonverbal behaviors so as to ensure that even a skeptical jury forms a true impression of her innocence. In particular, she must avoid the pitfalls of an image that suggests that she "doth protest [her innocence] too much" and therefore must be guilty. It should be clear, though, that the goal of impression management in this situation is to effectively present a true and honest image to others, one that will not be misinterpreted.

Or, consider a more everyday example of impression management in social interaction. Imagine, if you will, that you are being interviewed for a job. Would you not "put your best foot forward," "show your best profile," and be careful to make the most favorable impression and get the job you want? Would you not also try to size up what type of candidate the interviewer prefers and tailor your image to meet those preferences? Even if you personally would not practice the arts of impression management in this situation, you no doubt can readily appreciate that many others would do so.

B. The necessity of impression management

Many observers of social behavior have suggested that impression management is actually necessary for effective functioning in interpersonal relationships. Theorists of the tradition known as *symbolic interactionism*, notably C. H. Cooley (1922) and G. H. Mead (1934), have stressed that participants in social interaction attempt to "take the role of the other" and see themselves as others see them. This not only allows them to know how they are coming across to others but also permits them to guide their social behavior so that it has its desired effects on others. For example, by taking the role of the other, a politician can choose the right clothes and speech patterns to please rural constituents and then effectively change each of these to court the favor of party bosses. Similarly, by considering the perspective and background of each audience, a physics professor can meaningfully communicate the latest developments in relativity theory to college sophomores in the classroom or to distinguished researchers at a scientific convention. (See also Figure 4-1 for a more fanciful example.)

Impression management is also at the core of Erving Goffman's (1955, 1959, 1963a, 1963b, 1967) theory of the *presentation of self in everyday life*. Goffman has described social interaction as a kind of theatrical performance in which each person acts out a "line." A line is a set of carefully chosen verbal and nonverbal acts that express one's self. Of course, the line can shift from situation to situation as, for example, the role of obedient employee or sensitive friend or aggressive handball player becomes most important. When individuals appear before others, they have many motives for trying to control the impressions that others receive of them and of the nature of their interaction. In particular, the desire for social approval and the wish to control the outcomes of social interaction will result in impression management. Each person in the interaction will attempt to maintain an image appropriate to the current social situation and secure an evaluation from the others that is both pleasant and self-assuring. A participant whose image successfully receives social approval is said to be "in face"; one whose image fails is "out of face." For Goffman, one of the fundamental rules of social interaction is mutual commitment. By this he means that each participant will work to keep each participant in face through impression management. To do so, each participant has a repertoire of face-saving devices, an awareness of the interpretations that others place on his or her acts, a desire to sustain each person's face, and the willingness to use this repertoire of impression-management tactics.

Figure 4-1
One-upsmanship. The late Stephen Potter, the author of *Gamesmanship, One-upsmanship,* and other such books, devoted his life to the development and analysis of successful impression management. Potter's books are full of tricks, rejoinders, and actions that always give one an advantage over others. In this illustration, J. Fitz James has spent weeks studying for final exams under a sunlamp in order both to get all As and to give the impression of having vacationed in the sun while others studied.

Maintaining face is not the goal of social interaction. Rather, it is a necessary background for it to continue. Incidents that threaten the face of a participant also threaten the survival of the relationship. Thus, when events challenge the face of a participant, corrective processes called face-work are initiated to avoid embarrassment that might interfere with the conduct of the relationship. Thus we conspicuously overlook or help others apologize for the social blunders and potentially embarrassing *faux pas* that they commit. (For examples of research on face-saving behavior, see B. R. Brown, 1968, 1970; B. R. Brown & Garland, 1971; Modigliani, 1968.) In short, for Goffman, social interaction requires its participants to be able to regulate their self-presentation so that it will be perceived and evaluated appropriately by others.

In a third approach, Alexander has also suggested impression management as a fundamental facet of social interaction (C. N. Alexander & Knight, 1971; C. N. Alexander & Sagatun, 1973). According to the theory of *situated identities*, there is for each social setting or interpersonal context a pattern of social behavior that conveys an identity that is particularly appropriate to that setting. This behavioral pattern is called a situated identity. Alexander claims that people strive to create the most favorable situated identities for themselves in their social encounters. Thus a college instructor might aim for a somewhat professorial and academic situated identity in lecture, but shift to a more casual and loose situated identity at a social gathering of friends and acquaintances.[1]

These three viewpoints—symbolic interactionism, presentation of self, and situated identities—all have something in common despite their

[1]The reader may note that the concept of situated identity is similar to that of *role*, presented in Chapter 1. But a situated identity is much more tied to a specific situational context than is a role. A more relevant difference is that roles seem to focus on behaviors that are expected or appropriate, while situated identities deal more with the *image* one projects in a particular interaction.

differences in language and emphasis. And that is this: other people are always forming impressions of us and using these impressions to guide their interaction with us (Chapter 3 explores this point in detail). Accordingly, it is to our benefit to understand their perceptions of us and to create images acceptable to us. This makes us better able to predict, understand, and influence the flow of social interaction.

From this perspective, attempts to influence the images others form of us are a direct consequence of the fact that others do form impressions of us and act on those perceptions. Impression management is, quite simply, the inevitable consequence of social perception. What, then, determines the particular image that an individual will present in a particular social situation? How will impression management be used to gain social approval, win friends, and influence others? What causes honest and revealing self-disclosure? Do some people engage in impression management more than others? How are we as perceivers to detect impression management in others so that we can react accordingly? What does impression management imply about human nature? This chapter suggests answers to these and other questions.

II. Self-presentation: The same person, just a different face?

A. The other person as an influence

Would you act the same if confronted with a boastful, conceited person as you would with a modest, self-effacing individual? An experiment by Gergen and Wishnov (1965) simulated precisely this situation and found that subjects presented themselves very differently in the two contexts. Subjects paired with the boastful egotist described their personalities much more positively than they had a month before the experiment. However, those who met a humble and modest partner tended to play down their own virtues and emphasize their shortcomings. Clearly, these subjects chose to project self-images more similar to those of their partners. Perhaps in a situation as novel and unfamiliar as a psychological experiment, subjects were somewhat unsure of how to behave. Thus, they turned to their partners as guides to choosing a self-presentation appropriate to the new situation. Accordingly, they played up either their virtues or their shortcomings, whichever their partners had implied was best to do.

Beliefs about others also influence the way we express and communicate our attitudes about social issues. Imagine that you are a college student during the years of intense United States involvement in the Vietnam War. You have agreed to communicate your opinions on the war to an audience of extreme "hawks" and then to an audience of extreme "doves." You are a moderate on the Vietnam War issue. Might you present your position differently to each audience? The University of Virginia undergraduates studied by Newtson and Czerlinsky (1974) certainly did. These students expressed more "hawkish" views when communicating to a prowar audience and more "dovish" attitudes when addressing a pacifistic audience. In a similar experiment, political "middle-of-the-roaders" became more liberal for an audience of liberals and more conservative for a conservative audience. Even though the students in both studies had been instructed to present their opinions as accurately as possible, they still presented themselves as more similar to each audience than they actually were. Why? Perhaps they were trying to win the liking and social approval of their audiences by exaggerating their similarities. Opinion conformity is certainly one powerful tactic of ingratiation (see Section V of this chapter) that can be used by those out to win the liking and positive regard of others.

Will people always choose those self-presentations that maximize similarity with their interaction partners? What if you were interacting with an obnoxious and unlikable person who nevertheless persisted in expressing attitudes and opinions strikingly similar to yours? Might you not take pains to express your attitudes in such a way as to maximize any differences between you and that obnoxious person? This was precisely the outcome of an experimental investigation by Cooper and Jones (1969). Subjects altered their stated attitudes whenever an obnoxious interaction partner expressed viewpoints similar to their original attitudes. Thus the goals of self-presentation are not always to maximize similarity between ourselves and others. When similarity is not particularly desirable, people may use impression management to establish social distance.

B. The interaction context: Goals and motives

The nature of the interaction environment also helps determine what image a person creates. Gergen and Taylor (1969) arranged for naval cadets to work together on a problem-solving task. For half the groups, social compatibility and solidarity were stressed. For the remaining groups, productivity and output were the primary goals. After the problem had been described to each person and the compatibility or productivity goal orientation explained, each subject was asked to describe himself to his partner. The descriptions were the measure of self-presentation. Those cadets with the productivity orientation became considerably more positive in their self-descriptions; those anticipating a compatibility-oriented setting were quite modest and even self-critical in their self-presentations. Apparently the naval cadets in this study believed that the best guarantee of productivity was letting their partners know their competence and qualifications. However, those who strived for compatibility felt that modesty would be less offensive to their partners than a show of bragging and self-congratulation.

One of the most powerful motivational influences on self-presentation is reference-group identification. One study shows the amount of physical suffering that people will endure in order to present an image that is a credit to their religious group. Lambert, Libman, and Poser (1960) studied the effects of the increased salience of a religious reference group on pain tolerance of Jewish and Protestant college women at McGill University in Montreal. To test pain tolerance, the experimenter wrapped a blood pressure cuff especially equipped with hard rubber projections around each woman's arm and gradually increased the pressure until she reported that the pain was intolerable. This procedure is a standard laboratory method for inducing superficial pain without risk of physical harm. During a five-minute relaxation period the experimenter casually made some remarks designed to make salient each woman's religious affiliation. For example, some Jewish women were told that Jews withstand more pain than Christians; others learned that Christians tolerate more pain than Jews. Similarly, some Protestant women were led to believe that Christians had higher pain tolerance than Jews; other Protestants learned that Jews could withstand more intense pain.

The experimenter then measured pain tolerance again, supposedly for "reliability." Those Jewish women who had been told that Jews typically take more pain than Christians tended to hold the line: they took neither more nor less pain on the second test. However, Jews who had learned of evidence alluding to their possible inferiority actually took considerably more pain before finding it unbearable. The results were somewhat different for the Protestant women. Whether told that Christians typically take less pain or take more pain, the Protestant women substantially increased their pain tolerance in reaction to this information.

Clearly religious-group membership affected self-presentation (here pain tolerance) when this affiliation was made salient. However, the specific influence of reference-group membership differed for Protestant and Jewish subjects. The Jewish women appeared to be interested both in reducing any apparent differences between their religious group and the Protestants and in maintaining any superiority they might have. The Protestant subjects appeared ready to erase any inferiority that their religious group might possess and also to extend any differences when they felt that their group already held the edge. One final note on the subtlety of reference-group identification: Protestants did not withstand more pain when their reference group was identified as Protestant, rather than Christian. Perhaps Protestantism does not function as a reference-group label in the same sense that Judaism and Christianity do.

C. When saying is believing

Some people are quite flexible in their self-presentation. With skill and grace, they can put on a happy face for one person and a sad face for another. What effects do these shifts in public appearances have on the more private reality of the self-concept? In some circumstances we are persuaded by our own appearances: we become the persons we appear to be. This is particularly likely to occur when the image we present wins the approval and favor of those around us. In an experiment by E. E. Jones, Gergen, and Davis (1962), subjects who had been instructed to win approval of an interviewer presented very flattering images of themselves. Half of these subjects (chosen at random) then received favorable reactions from their interviewers; the rest did not. All subjects later estimated how accurately and honestly their self-descriptions had mirrored their true personalities. Those who had won the favor of their interviewers considered their self-presentations to have been the most honest of all. These persons were apparently operating with a rather pragmatic definition of their self-concepts: that which produced the most positive results was considered to be an accurate reflection of their true inner selves (Gergen, 1968).

This suggests that impression management can blur the distinction between public appearance and private reality: *we come to believe our own performance*. Furthermore, the reactions of others can make it all the more likely that we are what we claim to be. If others accept our self-presentations at face value, they may then treat us as if we really were what we pretend to be. For example, if I act as if I like Chris, chances are that Chris will like me. Chris will probably treat me in a variety of friendly ways. As a result of Chris's friendliness I come to like Chris, even though I did not in the first place. Once again appearance has created reality.

III. In search of a "consistent" public image

We generally assume that people are fairly consistent and stable beings. Such assumptions aid us in our quest to make others seem predictable. We expect that the sociable individual is sociable in all—or at least most—social contexts. Yet research on self-presentation suggests that some people are strikingly inconsistent. Like chameleons, they adopt whatever appearance suits the here and now. But one of our most cherished assumptions about human nature is that regularities and consistencies called "personality traits" do exist—that a person who is generous in one situation is likely to be generous in another context, that one who is honest is honest most of the time, that a person who takes a liberal stance today will favor the liberal viewpoint on tomorrow's issues. At times people do appear remarkably consistent, not necessarily because of the influence of these basic traits of character, but because through impression management they strive to present consistent public images and appearances.

A. The "foot-in-the-door" effect

A dramatic demonstration of the lengths to which people will go to present a consistent image is the "foot-in-the-door" effect: a person who can be coaxed into complying with one request for a favor is then much more likely to later comply with a larger and more substantial demand. In one study, J. L. Freedman and Fraser (1966) arranged for two undergraduate experimenters to contact suburban housewives in their homes; first with a small request and later with a larger request. The housewives were first asked either to place a small sign in their window or to sign a petition on the issue of either keeping California beautiful or safe driving. Clearly these were all small and harmless requests. Two weeks later, a different experimenter returned to each home and asked each housewife to place a large and unattractive billboard promoting auto safety on her lawn for the next couple of weeks—a rather substantial request. A control group of different housewives was only contacted about the second, large-billboard request. The results showed a very strong "foot-in-the-door" effect. Subjects who had complied with the earlier trivial request were much more likely to comply with the larger one several weeks later. More intriguing yet was the apparent generality of the effect; even signing an innocuous petition to "keep California beautiful" made a housewife much more likely to agree to place a large ugly billboard reading "Drive Safely" on her lawn when asked to do so weeks later by a different experimenter.

Why does this "foot-in-the-door" effect occur? One explanation offered by social psychologists stresses the desire to be consistent. Having once projected an image of helpfulness and cooperativeness, the typical housewife in this study continued to act helpfully and cooperatively in order to measure up to her image—even if it meant agreeing to a rather burdensome request. Other research evidence supports this interpretation. Individuals who have been induced to project an unhelping, uncooperative image by refusing a rather large request will then refuse a second request, even if it is of perfectly reasonable magnitude (Snyder & Cunningham, 1975). What may be happening here is that subjects try to keep their later actions consistent with the image conveyed by their earlier ones, even if that image is the rather undesirable one of selfishness and uncooperativeness.

It is clear from research of this kind that people try to act consistently with the way they have behaved in the past. What is not so clear is whether they also alter their private self-images or self-concepts. Thus, does the house-wife who *acts* generously because she has done so in the past also come to *believe* that she is a generous and helping person, the kind of altruistic good citizen who gets involved in worthwhile causes? Most "foot-in-the-door" researchers have assumed that such changes in self-perception occur along with the changes in behavior (for example, Freedman & Fraser, 1966; Snyder & Cunningham, 1975). Persons strive not only for consistent public images, but for consistent private images as well. (See also Figure 4-2.)

B. "Bending over backward" to be consistent

What would happen if someone with a favorable self-image did something that cast doubt on that image? For example, Mr. Boss feels that he supports equal-opportunity hiring programs. He turns down a female applicant because there are no openings. As she leaves Mr. Boss's office, the look on her face clearly suggests that she feels she is a victim of sex discrimination. Mr. Boss feels that his nonsexist, equal-opportunity image is threatened. Will he bend over backward to fill the next vacancy in his factory with a female worker? Several studies demonstrate just such a "bending-over-backward" effect in impression management.

1. The "door-in-the-face" effect. Cialdini and his coworkers (1975) first approached college students with a highly socially desirable but personally demanding request: Would they serve as voluntary counselors at a County Juvenile Detention Center for two years? Virtually everyone politely refused. However, most college students wish to appear socially concerned and helpful to those less fortunate than themselves. No doubt when they turned down the request both their self-concepts and their public images were challenged. To restore their own feelings that they were altruistic, socially concerned do-gooders and to ensure that the requester maintained that image of them, most subjects readily agreed to a smaller, more reasonable request that would demonstrate the same form of socially appropriate altruistic concerns. They jumped at the opportunity to chaperone juveniles on a trip to the zoo. Cialdini (1975) has also shown how powerful his technique can be in recruiting volunteer blood donors. Figure 4-3 illustrates how the "door-in-the-face" effect is used to explain the permission to "bug" the Democratic party headquarters in the Watergate Hotel.

2. Reverse discrimination and tokenism. Dutton and Lake (1973) have shown how "bending over backward" to present an unprejudiced image can produce reverse discrimination. The subjects in their study were White undergraduates at the University of British Columbia who valued equality and considered themselves relatively unprejudiced. By means of an ingenious "lie detector" procedure, some subjects were led to believe that they had shown physiological signs of racial prejudice. Other subjects learned that their responses were typical of the unprejudiced person. Afterward, the experimenters arranged for each subject to be approached by either a White panhandler or a Black one. The results were an impressive example of reverse discrimination in action: the Black panhandler received considerably more money from subjects who feared that they might be prejudiced (average donation 47.25¢) than from those who had not had their self-images threatened by the physiological feedback (average donation 16.75¢). The White confederate received about equal amounts of money from subjects in either condition (average donation approximately 28¢).

Clearly the subjects who had been threatened with the possibility of prejudice overreacted and bent over backward to prove to themselves and others that they were unprejudiced—toward

Figure 4-2

Consistency in public image. Under some circumstances people are particularly likely to seek consistent images. Imagine some minor changes in the classic "foot-in-the-door" script. An experimenter asks a suburban homemaker to display a "Keep Our Community Beautiful" sticker. She, not surprisingly, agrees. He then says "You are a generous person. I wish more of the people I met were as charitable as you." Essentially, he publicly labels her as generous, cooperative, and civic minded. What happens the next day when another solicitor asks her to volunteer for work on a community-action project? Will the public labeling motivate this homemaker to comply all the more eagerly with requests that allow her to display a consistently cooperative, community-conscious image? As it happens, this hypothetical script is strikingly similar to a study by Kraut (1973). In his experiment, subjects who gave to charity were either labeled as charitable or not labeled. Similarly, subjects who refused to give to charity were either labeled uncharitable or not labeled. All subjects were later asked by another canvasser to contribute to a second charity. Subjects labeled as charitable gave more and subjects labeled as uncharitable gave less than their respective unlabeled counterparts. It seems that being labeled heightened the motivation to maintain a consistent public image and pattern of social behavior. (Photo by Jim Pinckney.)

Figure 4-3
The "door-in-the-face" effect and Watergate. Why was Gordon Liddy able to
persuade the leaders of the Committee to Re-Elect the President to finance his
attempt to "bug" the offices of the Democratic Party in the Watergate Hotel?
John Mitchell and Jeb Magruder knew such actions were illegal; they also had
little assurance that the bugging would produce anything of value. The way
Magruder explains it in his book, the decision reflected the classic
"door-in-the-face" effect. Magruder writes: "I think the decision was a result
of a combination of pressures that played upon us at the time. For one thing,
I think Liddy put his plan to us in a highly effective way. If he had come to
us at the outset and said, 'I have a plan to burglarize and wiretap Larry
O'Brien's office,' we might have rejected the idea out of hand. Instead, he came
to us with his elaborate call girl/kidnapping/mugging/sabotage/wiretapping
scheme, and we began to tone it down, always with a feeling that we should
leave Liddy a little something—we felt we needed him, and we were reluctant
to send him away with nothing. Whether by accident or design, Liddy had used
an old and effective bureaucratic ploy: he had asked for the whole loaf when
he was quite content to settle for half or even a quarter." (From *An American
Life: One Man's Road to Watergate*, by J. S. Magruder. Copyright © 1974 by Jeb
Stuart Magruder. Reprinted by permission of the publisher, Atheneum
Publishers. Photos courtesy of Wide World Photos.)

Blacks. Reverse discrimination may thus be seen as an attempt by those who consider prejudice to be undesirable—yet are uncertain about their own level of prejudice—to prove that they are free of prejudice. But in their efforts not to discriminate against one group, they discriminated against another.

However, such attempts to appear unprejudiced may produce only token acts, which may later serve as rationalizations for avoiding more significant commitments to eradicating prejudice. See Figure 4-4 for an example of such a rationalization.

IV. The quest for social approval

Why do people engage in impression management? What personal benefits do they receive as a consequence of controlling the way they come across to others with whom they interact? One likely consequence is social approval: by choosing one self-presentation rather than another they hope to win the approval and acceptance of others. In fact, there is clear evidence that people use tactics of impression management when they seek a socially appropriate image and the social approval it brings. E. E. Jones, Gergen, and Davis (1962) studied college women who were about to be interviewed by a trainee in clinical psychology. Half these women were told to say whatever they felt necessary to secure the favorable approval of the interviewer. The other prospective interviewees were told to be candid, honest, and accurate in their self-presentations. Not surprisingly, the women who were seeking approval described themselves much more favorably than those oriented toward candor. Either those searching for approval exaggerated their good qualities, or those striving for accuracy in presenting themselves played down their assets. But despite these differences, the two groups did not differ in how honest they felt they had been with the interviewer.

Figure 4-4
"But I gave at the office." In a follow-up to the experiment described at the end of Section III, Dutton and Lennox (1974) once again used the "lie-detector" technique to convince students that they were prejudiced. Once again, some individuals were approached by a White panhandler, others by a Black. The next day a person apparently not connected with the original study asked each subject to donate time to an interracial-brotherhood effort. Those who previously had been panhandled by the Black were much more stingy with their time than either those who had been approached by the White panhandler or members of a comparison group who had not been panhandled. (Photo by Jim Pinckney.)

Depends on whether you're trying to get the person to like your or not.

A. Success, failure, and approval seeking

When people experience failure, they need reassuring social approval more than when they have been successful. One social psychologist (D. J. Schneider, 1969) built upon this principle to study the effects of the experience of failure on impression management. He arranged for some subjects to fail at a task and for others to succeed at the same task. He then had them describe themselves to another person in a standard self-presentation task. Those who had just failed —and presumably were in need of social approval—described themselves more positively than those who had succeeded. However, this occurred only when the other person was actually capable of providing the social approval they so eagerly sought. When the target could not offer social approval, the failed subjects described themselves more negatively than the successful subjects.

Nonverbal behaviors play an important role in the search for social approval. However, males and females rely on different channels of nonverbal self-presentation. When seeking approval, males use more positive head nods and females use more gestures (Rosenfeld, 1966). Moreover, in evaluative self-presentation settings, males look more at an approving than at a disapproving other, if he is of higher status (Fugita, 1974; no female subjects were observed in Fugita's study).

B. Choosing an appropriate sex-role image

The approval motive can powerfully influence impression management in the domain of sex-role behaviors. (See Figure 4-5.) In one study by Zanna and Pack (1976), female Princeton undergraduates described themselves to a male partner. He was either desirable (a 20-year-old Princeton senior, 6 feet 1 inch tall, with no woman friend and a strong interest in meeting

female college students) or rather undesirable (an 18-year-old non-Princeton freshman, 5 feet 5 inches tall, with a girl friend and no interest in meeting other women). Furthermore, the male's stereotype of the ideal woman either conformed to the traditional female stereotype (that is, the ideal woman should be very emotional, deferent to her husband, home oriented, passive, and so on), or its opposite (that is, the ideal woman should be very independent, very competitive, very ambitious, very dominant, and so on).

What effect did this information about the partner and his beliefs have on the women's self-presentation? When the partner was desirable, the women presented themselves as extremely conventional when his ideology was conventional. However, when the desirable male partner expressed a nontraditional ideology, the

"Have you got something a little more . . . . feminist?"

Figure 4-5
Choosing an appropriate sex-role image. (Drawing by William Hamilton.)

women then presented themselves in much more liberated terms. When the partner was generally undesirable, neither his personal characteristics nor his viewpoints had much impact on the images conveyed by the female subjects.

Clearly, expectations shaped the women's self-presentations. The implications of this research cannot be overestimated. According to this view, many sex differences may be not so much the product of inherent biological or temperamental differences between men and women as the result of differences in the images that people project in their attempts to act out accepted sex-roles. As these stereotypes shift, so too may sex-role behaviors. (See also Chapter 14, which discusses sex roles in depth.)

Sex-role stereotypes are so powerful and far-reaching that they even touch intellectual abilities. For example, when applying for college, men score about 60 points higher than women on the mathematical-aptitude tests of the College Board Exams (R. Brown, 1965). Lest anyone leap to the conclusion that this reflects innate differences in mathematical ability between the sexes, we hasten to point out the following: Women dramatically improve their mathematical performance if the problems are reworded to deal with cooking, gardening, and other domestic activities normally thought to be the province of women (G. A. Milton, 1958, 1959). The abstract mathematical reasoning is the same; only the implications for one's sex role have been changed. We have here a clear example of how attempts to convey an image appropriate to one's gender can affect basic intellectual performance.

C. Forcing the stigmatized to play their role

Stigma are characteristics that are considered to be undesirable by most people. In the United States, Canada, and other nations, being physically or mentally handicapped, non-White, poor, old, or homosexual can sometimes be stigmatizing experiences. The eminent social observer Goffman (1963b) has written insightfully of such experiences. He argues, essentially, that others intentionally or unintentionally "force" the stigmatized to play the role laid down for them. For example, he claims that people want to feel sorry for and charitable to the handicapped. Therefore, such individuals can anticipate sizable gains from behaving in ways that evoke pity. Thus the original stereotype that the handicapped are pitiful is confirmed because they have purposely conformed to those expectations. For the handicapped to behave in an independent manner would only provoke perceptions of ingratitude. The net result is that the handicapped often accept their fate and act out the role society has defined for them. M. S. Weinberg and Williams (1974) have suggested a similar effect. Based on results of extensive cross-cultural survey research on homosexual (gay) males, they have speculated on the ways in which widely held but essentially untrue social stereotypes may shape the behavior of some gay men to fulfill these stereotypes. The impression-management process underlying the influence of each of these stereotypes is the same: "I am X. Everyone believes that all Xs act in some fashion. Therefore I will act that way too." The stereotype is made to come true.

The evidence supports this viewpoint: people made to feel "stigmatized" come to behave as if they were in fact branded with shame and disgrace. For example, Farina, Gliha, Boudreau, Allen, and Sherman (1971) measured the impact on mental patients of believing that others were aware of their psychiatric history. Mental patients interacted with another individual (actually a confederate) in a cooperative task. Half the patients were told that the other person knew that they were patients. The remainder believed that their partners thought that they were nonpatients. Actually the confederate never knew whether or not the person had a psychiatric history. The effects were impressive. Believing that others were aware of their status caused the identified patients to feel less appreciated, to find the task more difficult, and to perform poorly. Moreover, objective observers perceived them to be more tense, more anxious, and more poorly adjusted than the patients who believed that their partners did not know their status. Apparently the belief that others might perceive them as stigmatized individuals caused them to act in ways consistent with such a deviant status.

In another study, Farina, Allen, and Saul (1968) led college students to believe that they had revealed to another that they were stigmatized (a history of either mental illness or homosexual behavior). In fact, the other subject always received the same neutral information. However, merely believing that another person viewed them as stigmatized influenced the subjects' behaviors and caused them to be rejected by the other person. Possibly, stigmatized individuals expect to be viewed negatively by others and rejected by them. Therefore they accept and play the role that leads to this rejection. Ironically, they are probably conforming to these expectations in the vain hope that they will be accepted if they do what others expect of them. In their quest for approval, they actually cause the rejection they seek to forestall. *

the self you project to others.

D. Need for approval:
   Do some people
   have more than others?

It appears that some people have a greater need for approval than others. Such individuals are identified by their high scores on the Marlowe-Crowne Social Desirability Scale, a measure of the tendency to describe oneself in favorable, socially desirable terms (Crowne & Marlowe, 1964). These are people who claim: "I never hesitate to go out of my way to help someone in trouble," "I have never intensely disliked anyone," "I always try to practice what I preach," "I am always courteous to people who are disagreeable," and other characteristics thought by some to be socially desirable. Presumably people who make such claims do so because they crave the social approval they feel is accorded such

That says you are the object of me at this moment

individuals. There is, in fact, considerable evidence that in a wide variety of situations, those with a high need for approval do give socially desirable responses. They conform more than do individuals with a low need for approval, they do not show overt hostility toward one who has insulted and double-crossed them, and they are less likely to speak "dirty" words. Strangely enough, these people who desire social approval so intensely are also social isolates. Their peers describe them as individuals who spend most of their time alone rather than with other people, don't go out of their way to make friends, are not very conversational, and don't act friendly toward others (Crowne & Marlowe, 1964, pp. 162–163). Perhaps it is only the approval of adult experimenters in psychology studies that is reinforcing to those with high scores on the Social Desirability Scale.

V. Ingratiation

The front cover of the 1973 printing of Dale Carnegie's *How to Win Friends and Influence People* (originally published in 1936) claims that more than 7.5 million copies have been sold. This number grows at the rate of more than 250,000 copies each year. Dale Carnegie human relations courses are offered in over a thousand cities in the United States and Canada. (An advertisement is reproduced in Figure 4-6.) The heart of the Dale Carnegie approach is sets of basic rules, each with a specific purpose. For example, Carnegie offers six ways to make others like you:

Rule 1. Become genuinely interested in other people.
Rule 2. Smile.
Rule 3. Remember that a person's name is to that person the sweetest and most important sound in any language.
Rule 4. Be a good listener. Encourage others to talk about themselves.
Rule 5. Talk about things that interest the other person.
Rule 6. Make the other person feel important —and do it sincerely.

"The Dale Carnegie Course gets you to recognize and use your capabilities."

Terri Sopp Rae, Downey, California

Roland Schultz, Professor of Chemistry,
Oklahoma Christian College, Oklahoma City, Oklahoma

■ "I know now that I had a tendency to under-rate my own abilities," recalls Roland Schultz, "but after taking the Dale Carnegie Course, I have the self-assurance to be comfortable and at the same time more effective in putting across ideas to my students.

"This also shows up in my life-style. I have become active in organizations I wouldn't have considered before I took the Course. It's one of the best investments I ever made."

■ Terri Sopp Rae believed she needed to improve her self-image. "In college classes, I was afraid to volunteer even when I knew the answers. I thought I'd make a mistake and everyone would laugh at me.

"After my brother Randy enrolled in the Dale Carnegie Course and I saw what it did for him, I was convinced I could improve with Carnegie training.

In the Course, I developed a much stronger feeling of assurance. Now I can express myself and feel good about it. I find people listen to me, too, even when I'm talking to a group.

"My parents have noticed I'm a lot easier to get along with. I even found that my Dad and I have a lot in common. It's great discussing things with him. I'm really glad I took the Course while I'm young."

The Dale Carnegie Course leads men and women to new confidence, better relationships and greater recognition of their abilities—these and many other benefits can be yours. Dale Carnegie training is offered in more than 1,000 U.S. communities, including all major cities and in 51 other countries. For more information write us today.

DALE CARNEGIE COURSE
SUITE 115T · 1475 FRANKLIN AVENUE · GARDEN CITY, NEW YORK 11530

Figure 4-6
An advertisement for the Dale Carnegie Course in Effective Speaking and Public Relations. (Courtesy of Dale Carnegie & Associates, Inc., Garden City, New York.)

It is all too easy to make light of the Carnegie method because he makes it seem so simple. Yet the advice is eminently reasonable and practical. It also fits well with social-psychological theory and research on communication.

The term **ingratiation** refers to those methods of self-presentation that a person consciously uses to increase a specific target person's liking for him or her.

A. Edward E. Jones's approach to ingratiation

Edward E. Jones (1964) has made an in-depth social-psychological analysis of strategic approaches to interpersonal relationships. He suggests that there are four sets of *tactics* that the budding ingratiator can use to gain the liking of a target person.

Compliments, or other-enhancement. This is outright flattery. This technique assumes that people find it hard to resist liking others who think highly of them. However, the ingratiator must be careful to present these compliments sufficiently credibly that they will be believed and accepted as sincere. Jones believes that flattery will be most effective when the target needs the reassurance that a compliment can provide: "It is a person's doubts about an attribute in which he wishes to excel which render him open to flattery" (1964, p. 29). The ingratiator also should strive to appear discriminating and spontaneous in the use of praise and flattery.

Conformity in opinion, judgment, and behavior. This tactic assumes that we like those with beliefs, attitudes, and behaviors similar to our own. Once again the ingratiator must maintain credibility. One strategy is discriminating conformity: the successful ingratiator will mix disagreements on unimportant points with agreements on crucial issues for which the target will reward social support with liking. (See Figure 4-7.) Another approach is to limit the use of obvious conformity when the target suspects ingratiation (see also Kauffman & Steiner, 1968).

Self-presentation. An ingratiator can court favor by presenting a favorable self-image. That is exactly what subjects did in the Jones, Gergen, and Davis (1962) study: they described themselves in very flattering, self-congratulatory terms when instructed to win the approval of interviewers. However, as Stires and Jones (1969) have pointed out, there are times when modesty is the best policy. Although self-enhancement was the preferred mode of ingratiation in their research, dependent subjects inhibited this tendency in favor of more modest self-presentations when they knew that the target was aware of his power over the ingratiators. Modesty may also be particularly potent in the service of ingratiation when an overly positive self-presentation might threaten the target. Modesty can here play to the target's vanity. Samuel Taylor Coleridge, British poet and philosopher, urged this rule for deciding between modesty and self-enhancement: "If you would stand well with a great mind, leave him with a favorable impression of yourself; if with a little mind, leave him with a favorable impression of himself" (quoted in T. Edwards, 1972, p. 297).

Rendering favors. This is a straightforward application of the everyday principle that people are attracted to those who give them gifts and do other pleasant and rewarding things for them. It is important to distinguish between feelings of social indebtedness and feelings of liking provoked by gifts. Only the latter is correctly called ingratiation. In fact, we tend to react more favorably to those whose gifts we regard as appropriate than to those who make inappropriate offerings to us (S. B. Kiesler, 1966).

What psychological and social goals are met by ingratiation? In other words, why do people ingratiate themselves with others? Jones claims three *motives* for ingratiation: acquisition, protection, and signification.

Acquisition. The ultimate aim here is gain. The ingratiator hopes that liking will lead to favorable treatment from the target person. The employee who ingratiates himself or herself with the boss to get a raise practices acquisitive ingratiation.

Protection. The goal is to keep the target from inflicting either psychological or physical harm on the ingratiator. Jones suggests that those in dependent positions use protective ingratiation to acknowledge the power held by those in control of their fate. The prisoner who curries favor with a sadistic guard engages in protective ingratiation.

Signification. We try to make others like us because of what their liking says about our personal worth. To be genuinely liked by others means that we are worthy of their liking. Perhaps, too, we wish others to like us so that we may like ourselves. There is potential irony here: the harder we work to win another's liking, the less we may value it because we know the high price we have paid for it. However, if the ingratiation attempt succeeds in taking in the target, chances are that the ingratiator will not even be aware of how deceitfully that liking was gained (Jones, Gergen, & Davis, 1962). Self-deception

[handwritten margin note:] But not because they like us, but of our real worth.

"That fine line between gracious attendance and fawning obsequiousness—tell me, sir, how close did I come?"

Figure 4-7
One tactic of ingratiation is to disagree with the other person on unimportant matters but agree on important ones. (Drawing by William Hamilton.)

and ingratiation work hand-in-glove to guarantee that both the ingratiator and the target will have favorable regard for the ingratiator.

Underlying Jones's analysis of ingratiation is a social-exchange model of human interaction: the ingratiator uses tactics designed to increase his or her reward value to the target and the target in turn increases his or her liking for the ingratiator. This "give and get" perspective on social interaction reflects the social-exchange theory (Homans, 1961) briefly described in Chapter 1 as a type of stimulus-response analysis of social behavior.

B. Research on ingratiation: Means and ends

Not only has Jones insightfully analyzed the ingratiation process, but he has also extensively researched the phenomenon in both laboratory and field settings. In one study, E. E. Jones, Gergen, and Jones (1963) studied the effects of position in a status hierarchy on choice of ingratiation tactics. To do this, they paired undergraduate Naval Reserve Officers Training Corps (NROTC) cadets for discussions of opinion issues under controlled conditions designed to maximize or minimize ingratiation motives. One member of each pair was of high status (an upperclassman); the other was of low status (a freshman cadet). In the ingratiation interaction, they were told to be as compatible as possible so that the researchers could study the effects of compatibility on leadership effectiveness. In the noningratiation interaction, honesty and sincerity of self-presentation were stressed. In each interaction, the partners exchanged opinions and self-presentation by passing written messages.

The researchers then coded these messages for signs of opinion conformity, self-presentation, and other-enhancement—three of the major tactics of ingratiation emphasized in Jones's theory. Status clearly made a difference in the forms of ingratiation preferred by the partners.

Opinion conformity. Cadets of low status conformed more than those of high status, particularly on opinions relevant to the Navy and to NROTC (such as whether graduates of the U. S. Naval Academy at Annapolis should be favored over NROTC graduates for positions of authority in the U. S. Navy). There was some tendency for subjects with high status to conform more than persons with low status on items that were peripheral to NROTC concerns (such as opinions about college courses and extracurricular activities).

Self-presentation. Partners of high status in the ingratiation interaction described themselves more positively on important items and somewhat more modestly on unimportant items than they did in the noningratiation situation. Subjects with low status did the opposite: when these cadets were courting the favor of their superiors, they were modest on important items and assertive on unimportant ones.

Other-enhancement. The freshmen were more than willing to flatter their upperclass counterparts and to risk the obviousness of such a blatant ploy.

What this first experiment shows is that people of all levels of status are quite willing to play the ingratiation game—they just play their cards differently. Other research suggests the ends to which ingratiation can be the means. Jones, Gergen, Gumpert, and Thibaut (1965) examined the use of ingratiation by a worker to tease and coax from a supervisor the judgment that the worker had performed his task well. To do this the researchers created the following situation. A worker-subject is involved in an ambiguous problem-solving task. He quickly becomes aware that he is not doing well. He then engages in an interaction with a supervisor. They exchange opinions and self-presentations in the usual message-passing format.

However, a few new twists are added to the ingratiation situation. The worker learns either that the supervisor is free to decide subjectively after each trial whether or not a solution is correct or that the supervisor is bound and committed to a set of solutions worked out in advance. Presumably the worker would be more likely to make ingratiating moves when a supervisor has the freedom to define standards for good performance than when there is little to be gained by ingratiation. Moreover, the supervisor was characterized either as one who valued togetherness and solidarity or as one who cared only for good performance. Presumably, ingratiators would tailor their strategies to the personal orientations of their targets.

The results supported each expectation. The workers were most ingratiating when they felt they could influence the supervisors' judgments. Otherwise they avoided ingratiation. This is a reasonable strategy: few students would waste time ingratiating themselves with a supervisor at the College Board Exams to gain admission to college, but many would put on a good show for an admissions interviewer with the power to pick and choose among prospective applicants.

Moreover, the workers tailored their strategies to their beliefs about the supervisors. When he was togetherness oriented, they sought his approval through conformity with his opinions and attitudes. When he was productivity oriented, many workers chose a self-presentational strategy: they claimed to be efficient, diligent, reliable—in short, they stressed those qualities that define a good worker. This, too, is quite reasonable. A candidate for public office would hardly court favor with the financial backers and the voters in the same fashion—at least not if that politician wanted both substantial donations and a decisive vote.

C. Nonverbal ingratiation

Can nonverbal behaviors such as eye contact, body movements, and facial expressions be used to increase liking? At least one experiment

suggests an affirmative answer (Ellsworth & Carlsmith, 1968). Female interviewers held brief discussions with female undergraduates. These interviews communicated information either favorable or unfavorable to the student. For half the subjects, the interviewer was trained to make frequent eye contact. For the rest of the subjects, she carefully avoided eye contact. Afterward, each subject rated her liking for her interviewer.

Eye contact affected liking, but the effect depended on the nature of the interaction. When the interviewer communicated pleasant information, she made herself most likable by offering frequent eye contact. But when she imparted unpleasant information, she was best liked when she initiated a minimal amount of eye contact. Why? Perhaps there was something unpleasant about a stranger mixing insults and intense eye contact; it may thwart our desire to suffer in private, alone and unwatched. Similarly, there is probably something unnatural about an interviewer who does not personalize her complimentary communications with eye contact. The implication is clear—ingratiators in pleasant situations should seek and sustain eye contact; those in unpleasant contexts should scrupulously avoid eye contact.

D. Does ingratiation work if it is obvious?

Essentially, an ingratiator is out to gain the liking of a target person. To be maximally effective, the ingratiator must hide this manipulative intent and any deceit or pretense involved. Yet even if the target does notice the devious intent of the ingratiator, there may be strong motivation not to challenge the ingratiator. In Emerson's words, "We love flattery even though we are not deceived by it, because it shows we are of importance to be courted" (Emerson, *Essays, Second Series: Gifts,* quoted in E. E. Jones, 1964, p. 164). Thus, even unabashed ingratiation attempts may often bear fruit. Such is the nature of human vanity.

VI. Impression management and social influence

Impression management often plays a tactical role in social interaction. The approval seeker uses it to win social acceptance. The ingratiator uses it to be liked, and on occasion to influence those in positions of power. Impression management is put to even more devious use when the actor's goals include manipulating and controlling others for personal gain. Manipulativeness is often called Machiavellianism, after Niccolò Machiavelli (see Figure 4-8), the 16th-century advocate of the use of manipulation and deceit for personal and political benefit (Christie & Geis, 1970; D. L. Jensen, 1960).

A. Machiavelli and company

The silver-tongued confidence artist is a specialist in the not-always-honest manipulation of others. Yellow Kid Weil is sometimes considered to be the leading con man of the 20th century. He was an equal-opportunity swindler: he dealt indiscriminately in all manner of fraud, including nonexistent properties, paper securities, false letters of credit, and get-rich-quick schemes hatched in the twilight zones of legality. When asked by novelist Saul Bellow to describe his personal philosophy, the Yellow Kid had this to say: "I have never cheated any honest man, only rascals. They may have been respectable, but they were never any good. They wanted something for nothing. I gave them nothing for something" (Bellow, 1956, p. 42). For the Yellow Kid, victims get only what they deserve.

The con artist's world view is not all that different from that of Machiavelli. In *The Prince* (1940), Machiavelli described people as objects to be manipulated with cool calculation and emotional detachment. He had little regard for conventional morality: for Machiavelli, the ends of increased personal and political power almost always justified such means as lying, cheating, and deceit. The inborn baseness and manipulativeness of others were, for Machiavelli, further justifications for a manipulative interpersonal orientation. Whether or not Machiavelli was right about human nature, there are those among us who accept and act on his personal philosophy.

1. Who are the Machiavellians among us? Christie and Geis (1970) have constructed a simple paper-and-pencil scale to measure each person's degree of Machiavellianism. Those with high scores on this Mach scale agree with statements such as "The best way to handle people

Figure 4-8
Niccolò Machiavelli. In his advice to the Prince of Florence, Machiavelli wrote, among other things, "It is safer to be feared than to be loved," "Most men mourn the loss of their patrimony more than the death of their fathers," and "Humility not only is of no service but is actually harmful."

is to tell them what they want," "Anyone who completely trusts anyone else is asking for trouble," and "It is safest to assume that all people have a vicious streak and it will come out when they are given a chance."

By contrast, those with low scores on the Mach scale express very different views about human nature and morality. They prefer a different approach to social interaction: "When you ask someone to do something for you, it is best to give the real reasons rather than giving reasons that might carry more weight," "One should take action only when sure it is morally right," and "There is no excuse for lying to someone."

To some extent, scores on the Mach scale reflect socialization backgrounds. High scorers are more frequently males, often come from urban backgrounds, are relatively young, and tend to be in people-oriented professions such as psychiatry, clinical psychology, and business administration.

2. What do Machiavellians do? Those who endorse Machiavelli's world view are both willing and able to use Machiavellian tactics to outmaneuver, manipulate, and exploit the non-Machiavellians of this world. A fascinating way to witness the Machiavellian in operation is the "ten-dollar bargaining game" (Christie & Geis, 1970). Three people, one with a high score on the Mach scale, one with a medium score, and one with a low score, together face the task of dividing ten dollars among themselves. Easy you say? Not so, for there is a catch. The money must be divided between only *two* of the players. One unfortunate person gets squeezed out.

Not surprisingly, highly Machiavellian persons rush in to exploit this situation and arrange coalitions that profit themselves at the expense of those who are less Machiavellian. The latter refrain from using manipulative tactics that violate their ethical concerns about fighting over money. On the average, High Machs engineered deals that netted them $5.57, Middle Machs walked away with $3.14, and Low Machs con-

tented themselves with $1.29 and the knowledge that they had practiced the morality they preach. (Were Machiavellianism unrelated to success in this game, the average winnings for each player would, of course, have been $3.33). The bargaining game clearly demonstrates the manipulative skill of the Machiavellian.

No doubt some of the Machiavellian's success in "con games" derives from a keen ability to accurately perceive and size up the manipulativeness of others. In fact, non-Machiavellians are noticeably inaccurate in their perceptions of others and tend to consistently (and trustingly) underestimate the Machiavellianism of others (Geis & Levy, 1970).

Machiavellians are not only skilled in the control of others, but also able to successfully resist the attempts of others to influence their attitudes and change their behavior (Christie & Geis, 1970). These steely-eyed people can also cheat on tests and when accused of dishonesty stare their accusers straight in the eye as they coolly deny any complicity (Christie & Geis, 1970). As you might expect, Machiavellians also derive considerable personal satisfaction from their manipulative escapades. (See Figure 4-9 for another example of the Machiavellian in action.)

3. The young Machiavellian. Machiavellian orientations appear even in junior citizens. In one study, Braginsky (1970) offered 10-year-olds five cents for each bitter-tasting cracker they induced another child to eat. Children with high scores on a version of the Mach scale modified for use with youngsters (called the "Kiddie Mach") accepted their mission with zeal. They readily lied about the taste of the crackers, offered bribes, and with straight faces falsely claimed that the experimenter wanted the child to eat the crackers. Their tactics paid off: the budding Machiavellians coaxed, bribed, or coerced their targets to eat an average of 6.46 bitter-tasting crackers. Low Mach children, by comparison, persuaded their targets to eat only 2.79 crackers.

Figure 4-9
Beware the Machiavellian!

Given license to distract a subject taking a test, one highly Machiavellian tester went through the following gestures.

[The tester] rubs hands together in the stereotyped gesture of anticipation, bends over double, unties shoe, shakes foot, reties shoe; jingles contents of pocket noisily, pulls out Chapstick and applies it while staring absentmindedly at ceiling; whistles, slaps leg and straightens up noisily and abruptly in chair; taps pencil rhythmically on table; hums, reaches around divider and carefully knocks it over (this produces a loud crash and sends paper on table flying in all directions); after 10-second dead silence apologizes profusely to [test-taker] for distracting him; erases vigorously on blank margin of [test-taker's] score sheet (divider board prevents [test-taker] from seeing that "examiner" is not erasing actual marks); comments with serious frown at one-way vision mirror, "I feel like I'm on TV, don't you?" (followed by grin at mirror as soon as [test-taker] returns his attention to test booklet); holds matchbook in both hands above divider board in full view of [test-taker] (pretending to ignore stopwatch), tears out matches one by one, dropping each into ashtray; dismantles a ballpoint pen behind divider board, uses spring to shoot it, parts flying, across the room; jumps from chair, dashes across room to retrieve pen parts saying, "Sorry, I'm a little nervous."

All this occurred in the 15 minutes or so necessary to administer ten embedded-figures problems! The innocent subject should indeed beware of the Machiavellian! (From "In Search of the Machiavel," by F. Geis, R. Christie, and C. Nelson. In R. Christie and F. L. Geis (Eds.), *Studies in Machiavellianism.* Copyright 1970 by Academic Press, Inc. Reprinted by permission.)

4. Machiavellianism and modern society. Fortunately for the trusting members of our society, Machiavellians are not always able to put their abilities to work. Their dispositions serve them best in those social situations that provide face-to-face interaction with their targets, some latitude for improvisation and tailoring their tactics to their targets and goals, and opportunities to use emotional arousal to distract their targets and make them more susceptible to control. One implication of this is that Machiavellians should not be able to con their way to success in standardized, objective tests of ability and achievement (J. E. Singer, 1964). In fact, there is no relationship between Machiavellianism and intelligence-test scores. Moreover, Machiavellians would probably not rise to power in tightly structured bureaucratic organizations. They would, however, probably succeed in loosely structured organizations.

In reflecting on years of research on Machiavellianism, Christie and Geis (1970) have suggested that modern society is becoming increasingly Machiavellian. One possible reason is "defensive Machiavellianism." It is easy to understand why non-Machiavellians, faced with frequent manipulative attempts, might adopt manipulative countermeasures to preserve their own independence and autonomy. It is simply a case of the best defense being an offense.

B. The successful help seeker

If the wiles and guiles of the disciples of Machiavelli seem harsh and abrasive, there are more gentle approaches to influencing others. Human relations theorist Dale Carnegie offered twelve ways to win people to your way of thinking and nine ways to change people without giving offense or arousing resentment. Carnegie's approach reflects a view of human nature that contrasts distinctly with that of Machiavelli. According to Carnegie, we should focus on the nobler aspects of others and genuinely try to see things from the other person's point of view. There has, however, been much less research on this personal orientation than on that of Machiavelli.

Are you really out to love others or selfishly gain things for yourself

Furthermore, not all attempts at social influence involve the manipulation and exploitation of others. Very often the goal is to receive help or legitimate favors from those in a position to be generous. What can a help seeker do to increase the chances that the target will help or comply with a request? Research on altruism and compliance suggests at least two strategies of impression management.

1. *The staring hitchhiker.* What can a hitchhiker do to get a ride? One experiment demonstrates the benefit of staring at oncoming drivers. Snyder, Grether, and Keller (1974) studied the behavior of a male and a female hitchhiker as they tried to hitch rides at several different traffic locations. Half of the time, they conspicuously stared directly at oncoming drivers. The rest of the time, they did not. The hitchhikers then counted the number of rides offered as a measure of compliance with their requests.

Staring had a clear and reliable effect. Hitchhikers who stared at oncoming drivers received more than twice as many rides as those who did not stare at approaching drivers. In addition, a female hitchhiker was offered more rides than a male hitchhiker. Contrary to popular belief and hitchhiking folklore, it was no easier for a male-female couple to hitch a ride than for a single male. This surprising result may reflect space limitations in cars: many drivers might have room for one additional passenger but not enough space for two riders.

Why does staring increase compliance in the hitchhiking situation? The researchers assumed that staring had two effects. First, it made drivers uncomfortable, anxious, or tense. Second, it made salient the culturally specified helping norms or altruistic motives that support offering rides to neatly dressed college students near the campus. The driver, in other words, felt singled out by the stare and had a hard time ignoring the helping norm. The driver ended the discomfort produced by the stare and conformed with the helping norm by stopping and offering the staring hitchhiker a ride. Alternately, a driver could have looked the other way and driven on. To do so would have ended the tension produced by the stare, but would probably have produced some unpleasant guilt and regret at having violated the cultural helping norm.

2. *The gift-giving stranger.* It is hard not to like those who give us gifts, presents, and other tokens of affection. It is also hard to refuse the requests they later make of us. Regan (1971) arranged for pairs of college students to participate in an experiment that seemingly concerned aesthetic judgments. Actually, one student was a confederate of the experimenter, and the experiment had little to do with such judgments. However, it set the stage to study the effects of receiving a gift on compliance and helpfulness. During a break in the experiment, the confederate left the room and returned with two Cokes and gave one to the subject. He explained "I asked [the experimenter] if I could get myself a Coke and he said it was okay, so I brought one for you, too." In a comparison condition, it was the experimenter who went away and came back bearing Cokes. He gave one to each student and explained "I brought you guys a Coke." In the third condition, no Cokes were had by anyone.

During another break in the experiment, the confederate passed a note to the subject asking if he would buy raffle tickets to help his hometown high school build a new gym. The note explained that tickets were 25¢ each and the subject should simply write on the note the number he would buy. This number was, of course, the measure of compliance with the request for help.

The results showed the power of a Coke in the hands of the right person. Subjects who had been given a Coke *by the confederate himself* were, relatively speaking, soft touches. They signaled their intention to buy almost twice as many tickets as those given a Coke by the experimenter or those given no Coke at all. In fact, those given a Coke by the experimenter were no more receptive to the confederate's request for help than were those given no Coke at all. The results mean that it is not just the good feeling associated with receiving a gift that increases compliance with the requests of others. The gift apparently must come from the same person who later makes the request. In other words, the gift must set up a bond of obligation between the giver and the receiver. The receiver then pays back or fulfills this debt of obligation by meeting the requests of the giver. Door-to-door brush peddlers who give away free samples have made use of this principle for decades.

VII. Self-disclosure: The private "I" goes public

Not all social communication is impression management. People certainly do make themselves transparent to others and present unvarnished images of themselves. Such self-presentation is called *self-revelation* or *self-disclosure.*

Many psychologists believe that the ability to allow one's true self to be known to at least one significant other is necessary for a "healthy," self-actualized personality. Jourard (1959, 1964) claimed that either too little or too much self-disclosure could cause problems in adjustment. The person who never discloses might be unable to establish any close and meaningful relationships with others. But those who habitually pour out their souls to anyone who will listen may be seen as maladjusted and morbidly preoccupied with themselves. Jourard felt that it would be ideal to disclose a lot to a few close friends and a moderate amount to others. Although Jourard's viewpoint is intuitively appealing, research has yet to fully chart the relationship between self-disclosure and psychological adjustment. However, much is known about the causes and consequences of self-disclosure in interpersonal relationships.

Research suggests both personal and social determinants of self-disclosure. Race (Jourard & Lasakow, 1958; Dimond & Hellkamp, 1969), sex (Jourard, 1964; Dimond & Munz, 1967; Pederson

& Higbee, 1969), and cultural factors (K. Lewin, 1948b; Plog, 1965) are all important. So are social factors that define the social context in which self-disclosure does or does not take place.

A. Reciprocity and self-disclosure

People are most self-revealing in interaction with those who initiate a high level of self-disclosure: we tend to reciprocate or imitate the level of self-disclosure defined as socially appropriate by others (H. J. Ehrlich & Graeven, 1971; Tognoli, 1969; F. M. Levin & Gergen, 1969; Cozby, 1973b). Reciprocity occurs in a wide variety of life settings, including marital relationships, which typically show good correspondence between the levels of self-disclosure of wife and husband (Levinger & Senn, 1967), and therapeutic encounters, in which the clients' amounts of self-disclosure come to match those of their therapists (Truax & Carkhuff, 1965). (See Figure 4-10.)

One theory suggests that reciprocity reflects a trust-building mechanism. According to the theory of social penetration (Altman & Taylor, 1973; D. A. Taylor & Altman, 1975; D. A. Taylor, Altman, & Sorrentino, 1969) relationships begin with low levels of self-disclosure and low levels of trust. When one individual initiates self-disclosure, this signals the beginning of bonds of trust. The other person then responds in kind with equally intimate self-disclosure to signal acceptance of the trust. This back-and-forth trading of self-disclosure continues until a level of mutual intimacy appropriate to the relationship is reached. Any further increases in self-disclosure would be uncomfortable, and the partners would back off to their optimal or equilibrium point of intimacy (Argyle & Dean, 1965).

B. Liking and self-disclosure

Liking and self-disclosure often go hand in hand: when asked whom they like, females usually indicate those individuals to whom they self-disclose (Jourard, 1959; Jourard & Lasakow, 1958). In addition, self-disclosure and satisfaction seem to go together in marriage (Levinger & Senn, 1967). [Closeness, real love and concern

Do we like those who are self-revealing to for us? Not always. Cozby (1972) found that overly the intimate disclosures aroused anxiety in female per- listeners. Moderate disclosers were most popular son.) in his research.

For whatever reasons, liking and self-disclosure seem to be related only for female subjects. Jourard and Landsman (1960) found no relationship at all for males between those whom they liked and those to whom they disclosed. Similarly, Ehrlich and Graeven (1971) could find no influence whatsoever of self-disclosure on liking in research involving male subjects. These sex differences may reflect more general differences in sex-role socialization of the expression of liking and intimacy.

C. Social approval and self-disclosure

Self-disclosure is quite sensitive to the social approval received for being intimate and self-revealing. Taylor, Altman, and Sorrentino

(1969) trained confederates to provide either continuous positive reward, continuous negative feedback, or mixed reactions to subjects with whom they conversed. As expected, those who received either continuous positive approval or increases in social approval over the course of the conversation became increasingly willing to talk about themselves in intimate and revealing fashion.

D. Nonverbal behavior and self-disclosure

The nonverbal behaviors of others also serve as important guides to choosing an appropriate level of self-disclosure and interpersonal intimacy. One such behavior is eye contact. In a study by Ellsworth and Ross (1972), three people were involved in each experimental session: a *talker* talked in intimate terms to a same-sex *listener* while an *observer* recorded the intimacy level of the talker from behind a one-way observation mirror. Half the listeners were instructed to provide a high level of eye contact during the conversation. The remaining listeners were told to keep eye contact to a minimum during the discussion. After the interaction, all three per-

Figure 4-10
Reciprocity in self-disclosure. (Drawing copyright 1971 by G.B. Trudeau. Distributed by Universal Press Syndicate.)

sons rated the intimacy level of the talker's self-disclosure.

The results were quite different for male and female partners. For females, all three participants agreed that the talker was more intimate under conditions of high eye contact. For males, the listener and the observer agreed that the male talker was actually less intimate when he was given frequent eye contact. But the male talker disagreed; he thought he had been more intimate in the high-eye-contact condition. Why this disagreement? Consider the high-eye-contact condition. To the male talker the most obvious feature of the situation was certainly the high level of eye contact maintained by the male listener. Most likely the talker felt uncomfortable because such a high level of eye contact from a previously unknown male listener was inappropriately intimate for such an interaction. Accordingly, the talker tried to reduce the intimacy level of the conversation by reducing the revealingness of his self-presentation. But the listener continued to maintain eye contact throughout the conversation (as he had been instructed to do by the experimenter). In the end, the talker could only infer that he must have been really intimate. Why else, he might have reasoned, would the listener have kept up such a high level of personalizing eye contact? Thus the talker judged his level of self-disclosure by its apparent effects on the listener. The listener and the observer based their judgments on the talker's actual behavior. Because they used different sources of information, they reached different conclusions about the talker's level of intimacy.

Why were the effects of eye contact on self-disclosure different for males and females? Why did females increase their intimacy level in the face of frequent eye contact from another female and males decrease their intimacy in response to eye contact from another male? The answer probably lies in cultural differences in the norms of what is acceptable and appropriate in face-to-face interactions between previously unacquainted male-male and female-female

pairs. Intimacy and eye contact may be quite threatening to those socialized to play a traditionally "masculine" sex role.

VIII. Detecting impression management in others

An insurance salesman compliments me on my taste in furnishing my home. Is this a sincere compliment, or is he softening me up for the big sell? An admirer tells me what beautiful eyes I have. Admiration or seduction? A job applicant recites a litany of impressive credentials. Accurate self-presentation or self-serving impression management? Such is our dilemma when we are perceivers in social interaction. We want to know which of a person's behaviors truly reflect underlying attitudes and feelings and which are impression management designed to create an image. If we know this, we can react appropriately. We can tell truth from deception, treat compliments as admiration rather than ingratiation, and accept gifts that are signs of affection and reject those that have strings attached.

But how are we to read through the masks of impression management? What are the cues that allow us to peel away the cosmetic layers and see the true complexion? Both scientific and everyday observers of social behavior have suggested that nonverbal behaviors such as facial expressions, tone of voice, and body movement reveal meaningful information about a person's feelings, attitudes, and motives (for reviews, see R. P. Harrison, 1974; Knapp, 1972). Much of this interest stems from an assumption that nonverbal behaviors may not be under voluntary control to the same extent that other behaviors are. Nonverbal behaviors might serve as a pipeline, radarscope, or lie-detector route to a person's true inner self. A person might lie to you in words and deeds, but never with body language.

Freud observed "He that has eyes to see and ears to hear may convince himself that no mortal can keep a secret. If his lips are silent, he chatters with his fingertips, betrayal oozes out of him at every pore" (Freud, 1959, p. 94). George Borrow, a 19th-century British author, assured us that "if people would but look each other more in the face, we should have less cause to complain of the deception of the world: nothing [is] so easy as physiognomy nor so useful" (Borrow, 1914, p. 156). Journalist Julius Fast rode the best-seller lists with his *Body Language* (1970). The dust jacket of this "how-to-do-it" book promises answers to questions such as: "Does her body say that she's a loose woman?" "Does his body say he's an easy man to beat?" and "Does your body say that you're lonely?"

Sound promising? It is—but the plot thickens. It is true that nonverbal behaviors may escape attempts at deception and censorship. But some channels of nonverbal expression are more revealing than others, and some people are better than others at consciously controlling the messages that their nonverbal behaviors convey. So, in order to detect deception and impression management in others, a perceiver must focus on the right nonverbal behaviors, and the target must be a person who is not highly skilled in using nonverbal behaviors for purposes of impression management. What are these nonverbal behaviors, and who are these people?

A. Deceptive faces and truthful bodies

Research suggests that individuals engaged in deception are much more successful at controlling their facial expressions than they are at controlling their expressive body movements. In other words, the body provides more clues to deception than does the face. This point is well demonstrated in the research of Ekman and Friesen.

In one of their studies (1974), student nurses participated in two interviews. In one of these they frankly and honestly described their reactions to a pleasant film. In the other, they did their best to express positive feelings toward a distinctly unpleasant film. Observers then watched videotapes of these interviews. One set of tapes showed only the faces of the nurses. The other set of tapes showed only their bodies from the neck down. The observers' task was to decide whether each tape segment reflected honesty or deception. The observers, of course, knew nothing about which film the nurse had actually been watching when the tape was made. Thus they could rely only on nonverbal information in either the face or the body to make their judgments. The results revealed striking differences in the information conveyed by face and body. Observers were considerably more accurate in detecting deceptive impression management when they viewed the body than when they viewed the face. In another study, Ekman and Friesen (1969) showed that it is much easier to tell when psychiatric patients are faking improvement by attending to bodily clues than by attending to facial cues.

There are at least two possible reasons why it is easier to detect impression management from the body than from the face. Subjects may simply be unaware that their body movements can give them away; hence they make little attempt to lie with this channel of communication. Essentially, they remember to put on a happy face but forget to put on a happy body. Alternately, they may actually be *less able* to consciously control body movements for purposes of impression management. In other words, they may be *able to put on a happy face* but *unable to put on a happy body*.

B. Nonverbal detection of prejudice

Another experiment points to the usefulness of nonverbal behaviors as cues to the true attitudes held by those attempting impression management. Weitz (1972) reasoned that on college campuses with strong normative pressures supporting a tolerant and liberal value system, all students would try to avoid saying anything that would indicate racial prejudice—whether or not their private attitudes supported such behavior. In fact, she found that among "liberal" White males at Harvard University, the most prejudiced students (as determined by behavioral measures of actual attempts to avoid interaction with Blacks) bent over backward to *verbally* express liking and friendship for a Black in a simulated interracial encounter. However, their nonverbal behaviors betrayed them. Their true racial attitudes showed through in their tone of voice. Thus, although the prejudiced made every effort to say kind and favorable things, they continued to do so in cool and distant tones of voice. It is as if they knew the words, but not the music—they knew *what* to say but not *how* to say it.

C. The skilled impression manager

A perceiver can learn much about another person's efforts at impression management by closely scrutinizing nonverbal behaviors. This strategy is useful only for those channels of nonverbal expression that are not being used to create an impression.

The perceiver's ability to detect impression management is further limited by the fact that there are striking and important individual differences in the extent to which people can and do control and manage their self-presentation and expressive behaviors. Clearly professional stage actors can do what many of us cannot. Successful politicians have long practiced the art of wearing the right face for the right constituency. Onetime mayor of New York Fiorello La-Guardia was particularly skilled at adopting the expressive mannerisms characteristic of a variety of ethnic groups. In fact, he was so good at this that it is easy to guess whose vote he was soliciting by watching silent films of his campaign speeches. In the late 1960s, a United States presidential candidate successfully used advertising and media experts to help him trade a loser's image for that of a winner and statesman (Witcover, 1970; McGinniss, 1970). For such highly

skilled performers, nonverbal behaviors would tell us little about whether their self-presentations were genuine or contrived to create particular images.

Of course, entertainers and politicians are the exception rather than the rule. Nonetheless, people do differ in the extent to which they can and do exercise control over their verbal and nonverbal self-presentation. These differences are measured by the Self-Monitoring Scale (Snyder, 1974). Self-monitoring individuals (identified by high scores on the Self-Monitoring Scale) are particularly sensitive to the expression and self-presentation of others in social situations and use these cues as guidelines for monitoring or controlling their own verbal and nonverbal self-presentation for purposes of impression management.

According to their peers, self-monitoring individuals are good at learning what is socially appropriate in new situations, have good self-control of their emotional expression, and can effectively use this ability to create the impressions they want. They are also particularly skilled at intentionally expressing and accurately communicating a wide variety of emotions in both the vocal and facial channels of nonverbal expressive behavior. In a self-presentation task, self-monitoring individuals are quite likely to seek out and consult social-comparison information about appropriate patterns of self-presentation. Scores on the Self-Monitoring Scale are unrelated to scores on measures of seemingly related concepts including need for approval, Machiavellianism, locus of control, inner- versus other-directedness, self-esteem, field dependence, hypnotic susceptibility, and many others. Self-monitoring therefore appears to exist as a unique psychological construct.

It appears that self-monitoring individuals are well-suited to practice the arts of impression management. And they do. In one experiment (Snyder & Monson, 1975) group-discussion conditions made salient different peer reference groups that could provide cues to the social appropriateness of self-presentation. Self-monitoring individuals were keenly attentive to these differences: they were conforming when conformity was the most appropriate interpersonal orientation and nonconforming when reference-group norms favored autonomy in the face of social pressure. Non-self-monitoring individuals were virtually unaffected by these differences in social setting; presumably, their self-presentations were more accurate reflections of their true personal attitudes and dispositions. What this means is that those persons who are most skilled at impression management (self-monitoring individuals) are also those most likely to practice impression management. This, of course, only compounds the dilemma of perceivers. In their efforts to detect impression management, they are most likely to encounter performers well skilled in it.

IX. A time to reflect: Impression management and human nature

Impression management is a basic fact of social interaction. There are a variety of ways by which people can and do influence their public images. These strategies and tactics are often used to "win friends and influence people." But is impression management a good thing, something to be valued and prized? Or is it part of the seamier side of human nature?

A skilled wordsmith could give impression management either a bad or a good image. First the bad image: impression management makes humans into social chameleons, forever putting on new faces to tailor themselves to their current settings, forever being molded and shaped like silly-putty creations to be the "right" person in the "right" place at the "right" time. Clearly this is an unflattering view of human nature. Now the good image: impression management gives us the flexibility and adaptiveness to quickly and

consistently cope with the diversity of roles required of the individual in modern society. Impression management allows us to choose with skill and grace the self-presentation and social behaviors appropriate to a wide variety of situations. This is certainly a more comfortable image of human nature.

Is one perspective more "correct" than the other? Of course not, for they both describe impression management. By carefully choosing shades of meaning, the skilled wordsmith can portray impression management either as a virtue or as a vice. It's the same concept; only the words have been changed to make it seem good or bad. Impression management in and of itself is neither good nor bad. The same practices may be applied to creating an honest or a deceptive image, to influence others for altruistic or exploitative purposes. We may or may not approve of any specific goal that impression management serves, but it is certainly an integral part of everyday social relationships and interpersonal behavior.

X. Summary

Impression management refers to all those strategies and techniques used by individuals to control the images and impressions that others form of them during social interaction. In order to successfully practice impression management, individuals must know what behaviors on their part will create what impressions in the eyes and minds of their beholders. They must be skilled at taking the role of the other, and able to convincingly and naturally perform precisely those verbal and nonverbal acts that will create the desired image. The images created by impression management may or may not be accurate reflections of the person's true nature.

Three viewpoints on social interaction—symbolic interactionism, presentation of self, and situated identities—stress the fact that others are always forming impressions of us in their social encounters with us, and using these perceptions as guides to their behavior toward us. Accordingly, it is to our benefit to understand their perceptions of us and act to create impressions acceptable to us. This makes us better able to predict, understand, and influence the flow of social interaction. From this perspective, impression management is a direct consequence of the fact that others do form impressions of us and act on those impressions.

Several factors determine the particular image or self-presentation that a person will choose to offer to another in social interaction. Two of the most powerful influences are *characteristics of the other person* and the *motivational context of the interaction*. In general, people tailor their self-presentations to stress their similarities with what is expected of them, except where it would be personally uncomfortable to feel similar to an undesirable other. Two important motivational determinants of self-presentation are *desire for compatibility and solidarity* and *identification with a reference group*. Although people are quite flexible in their self-presentation, they tend to feel that their various different images are each true reflections of their true selves. They are particularly likely to identify with those self-presentations that secure the social approval of others.

In a variety of contexts, people strive to maintain a consistent public image. One example is the "foot-in-the-door" effect, in which a person who has acted helpfully in one situation will then act helpfully in another situation that calls for substantially greater involvement. People are particularly likely to seek consistent images when they have been publicly labeled with their images. At times, people will also "bend over backward" to maintain a public image that is personally and socially desirable. At times, this can lead to reverse discrimination and tokenism.

One of the most important motivational determinants of impression management is *social approval*. When in need of social approval, people will present particularly favorable images to those they believe are in positions to offer such

approval. The effects of this presentation can be seen in the domain of sex-role images; people strive to act out socially appropriate sex roles. The quest for social approval is also apparent in the self-presentation of the stigmatized (those with characteristics considered to be undesirable by most people). People who are made to feel stigmatized come to behave as if they were in fact stigmatized. Some people are more dependent on approval than others. These individual differences are tapped by the Social Desirability Scale, a measure of the tendency to describe oneself in favorable, socially desirable terms.

Ingratiation refers to those tactics of self-presentation consciously designed to increase the attractiveness of an individual to a specific other person. A social-psychological analysis of ingratiation suggests that there are four major tactics of ingratiation: *compliments* or *other enhancement; conformity in opinion, judgment, and behavior; self-presentation;* and *rendering favors*. This same analysis suggests that the goals of ingratiation are acquisition or self-gain, protection from harm, and signification or sense of self-worth. Research on ingratiation suggests that one's choice of ingratiation tactics depends on one's place within a status hierarchy and on the personal characteristics of the target of the ingratiation attempt.

Impression management can be used for purposes of social influence, including the manipulation and exploitation of others. Manipulativeness or Machiavellianism as a personal orientation is measured by the Mach Scale. Machiavellians outmaneuver non-Machiavellians in bargaining situations, are keen perceivers of manipulative personality in others, and are able to resist the attempts of others to influence their own attitudes and change their behavior. Machiavellianism can be observed in children as well as adults. Other approaches to the role of impression management in social influence suggest the importance of the nonverbal behavior of staring and the giving of gifts as strategies of successfully seeking help or favors from another.

In some social contexts, people will reveal or disclose personal and intimate aspects of their behavior and feelings. Among the factors known to promote such self-disclosure are reciprocity, liking, social approval, and in some cases the nonverbal behavior of others. Some social psychologists believe that self-disclosure is important for psychological adjustment.

One goal of the perceiver in social interaction is to recognize and to detect impression management in others. Nonverbal behaviors may be very helpful in this task. However, some channels of nonverbal expressions (for example, the body) are more informative than others. Moreover, some people are better able than others to consciously control their nonverbal expressive behaviors for purposes of impression management. These individuals are identified by their high scores on the Self-Monitoring Scale and are particularly likely to use their well-developed communication skills for purposes of impression management.

I. Why do we want to be with others?
   A. Reactions to isolation
   B. Our strong need to affiliate—Sometimes, at least
   C. Two kinds of reasons for joining a group
   D. Self-evaluation through social comparison

II. Affiliation as a response to anxiety
   A. Does misery love company?
   B. What kind of company does misery love?
   C. Birth-order differences in the link between anxiety and affiliation

III. Waiting with others—Does it reduce anxiety?

IV. The determinants of emotional and motivational states
   A. Schachter's theory: Physiological arousal plus cognitive state
   B. Cognitive effects of false heart-rate feedback
   C. An alternative explanation: Bem's self-perception theory

V. Attraction
   A. The antecedents of interpersonal attraction
   B. Theory-based explanations for factors in interpersonal attraction

VI. Love—The ultimate in affiliation?
   A. Social-psychological approaches
   B. The measurement of romantic love
   C. Stimulants to romantic love: The Romeo-and-Juliet effect
   D. A theoretical explanation of passionate love
   E. Conclusions

VII. Summary

From affiliation to attraction to love 5

In Chapter 3 we saw how people went about the task of forming impressions of others. In Chapter 4 it was proposed that each of us, to some degree at least, seeks to "manage" the impressions we make on other people. In this chapter we study some of the reasons for both these processes; one reason that we seek to understand people and wish to impress them is that we want to be with them. Many of them we like; some we even love.

Barbra Streisand sings a song that tells us that "people need people." But why? Why do most people seek out other people? Before we discuss why we like or love specific persons, we need to consider why we *affiliate*. Why is prolonged absence from others so intolerable to many people? Such questions are central to social psychology. One of the purposes of this chapter is to suggest answers to such questions and, in doing so, to describe an important program of research initiated by Stanley Schachter.

If affiliation is a basic need that brings us in contact with others, attraction is the next step in forming lasting social relationships. The chapter concludes with a consideration of why we like and love some people and not others.

I. Why do we want to be with others?

A. Reactions to isolation

Suppose you are offered $20 a day to remain in a room by yourself for as long as you wish. The room is without windows but has a lamp, a bed, a chair, a table, and bathroom facilities. Free meals are brought at mealtimes and left outside your door, but you see no one. You are permitted no companions, no telephone, no books, magazines, or newspapers, and no radio or television. Your watch and wallet or pocketbook have been removed and your pockets emptied before you entered. If you were to volunteer for such a project, how long could you remain?

In seeking an understanding of the affiliation need, Schachter (1959) placed five separate students in settings like the one described. All participants were volunteers. One of them was able to remain in the room for only 20 minutes before he had an uncontrollable desire to leave. Three volunteers remained in the room for two days. Afterward, one of these stated that he had become quite uneasy and would not want to do it again, but the other two seemed rather unaffected by their isolation. The fifth subject remained in isolation for eight days. Upon his release this college student admitted that he was growing uneasy and nervous, but the extended isolation did not affect his adjustment.

No one—including Schachter himself—would regard this study as a definitive one. It was simply an exploratory investigation of the reactions of normal people to voluntary social isolation. Yet the enormous differences in the reactions of five volunteers to identical situations constitute a fascinating finding. Some subjects apparently have vastly greater needs than do others for the presence of other people, or for

social surrogates such as radio, television, and telephone. Why?

Social-psychological studies that single out the effects of isolation are quite limited (Suedfeld, 1974). Many of the studies on "isolation" also restrict the environmental stimulation, as Schachter's exploratory study did, and also confound isolation and involuntary confinement (Figure 5-1). If people know they have no choice but to be isolated, they may adapt to this condition fairly well. Suedfeld (1974) notes that Admiral Byrd survived an Antarctic winter completely alone, with his physical and mental faculties intact (Byrd, 1938). Several solitary sailors, including Sir Francis Chichester, have sailed around the world without experiencing or suffering any psychological harm. Prolonged isolation results in an initial stage of a great deal of anxiety, but this dissipates. Periods of calm adaptation and then boredom develop in individuals isolated for

Figure 5-1
The effects of isolation. (Photo by David Powers/Jeroboam Inc.)
(long isolation is definitely not rehabilitative.)

long periods of time. For example, Burney (1961), who spent 526 days in solitary confinement in a Nazi German prison, at first was extremely upset but came to adapt to isolation to such a degree that when he was finally able to have contact with other prisoners, he "found conversation an embarrassment" (1961, p. 146, quoted in Suedfeld, 1974). Perhaps the best summary of the effects of isolation comes from Suedfeld:

> . . . there appears to be trustworthy evidence that isolation disrupts the ordinary everyday coping procedures, and leads to special kinds of psychological events. These frequently include hallucinations and vivid dreams, unusual states of excitement and arousal, and a great openness to experience. These unusual states last for varying, but sometimes quite prolonged, periods. If the individual does not return to the normal social environment, he begins to adapt and to develop habitual methods of behaving in isolation. These may appear bizarre by "normal" standards, but in fact represent a best fit response to a bizarre environment [Suedfeld, 1974, p. 10].

B. Our strong need to affiliate—Sometimes, at least

The data on isolation are an assortment of facts in search of a connecting theory. It may be helpful, then, to use Hebb's (1955) postulate of an optimal level of **arousal** in the organism. Perhaps this postulate can be used to explain momentary differences, within an individual, in the strength of the need to be with others. At times, each of us may experience a state of affiliative surfeit; our social needs are not only met but oversupplied. Perhaps we have gone from a crowded bus to a football game and then to a rock concert. We have to be alone for a while. At other times, a state of inactivity or isolation may have produced a deficit and thus caused us to seek others out. We may even brave the rain or cold to walk to the library or student center in hopes that a friend will be there. But Schachter's study and the work of others shows that individuals differ in just *how much stimulation*

is optimal. For some, the absence of others instigates a need that is as insistent as the pain of a toothache; for others, the affiliative need is less urgent.

Although a notion of optimal levels is a step toward explaining the affiliative motive, the above exposition is grossly inadequate. It fails to provide independent definitions of surfeit and deficit; it posits the presence of individual differences but fails to explain why they occur; and it ignores the fact that there are other needs for which affiliation is instrumental (for example, we may want to be with other people so that they will tell us how brilliant we are or so that they will cook us a meal). Therefore at this point, instead of focusing on affiliation as a broad response, we shall try to narrow matters down by considering the more specific question: why do people join groups?

C. Two kinds of reasons for joining a group

We can distinguish between two general reasons for wanting to become a part of a group (Schachter, 1959). First, social-exchange theory would note that a person may join because the group is a means to an end. In this case, the individual has personal goals that can be met *only* by affiliating with others or by joining a group. Our friend Steve, a tennis buff, needs to have at least one other companion who plays tennis; he may even join a tennis club to achieve his goals. Likewise, in order to get to work economically, Steve may join a car pool in response to the rising costs of gasoline, even though his fellow car poolers might be people Steve would not care to associate with socially. The economic rewards are greater than any "costs" in lowered prestige.

But reinforcement theory would observe that groups may also represent rewards *in and of themselves.* Schachter and others (for example, Burk, Zdep, & Kushner, 1973) suggest that needs such as those for approval and for development of an identity can be met only by other people.

It sometimes is difficult to separate the concepts of *the group as a means* and *the group as an end in itself*, but cases in which the company of others is itself the object reflect the latter goal. The two goals may be fulfilled by the same behavior. Steve may join the car pool partly in response to the energy crisis and partly because his need for prestige is met by associating with others whom he considers prominent people.

D. Self-evaluation through social comparison

Another implicit value of joining a group is that such a process offers a vehicle for self-evaluation. Not only do we want information about how we appear to other people, as Chapter 4 noted, but we want to evaluate our own skills and our beliefs. We want to know how good we are, and how good we should be. It is true that some characteristics can be evaluated with little or no reference to other people. The new bridegroom who has just cooked his first cheese souffle can evaluate his cooking ability by looking at the souffle and tasting it. A 15-year-old boy who cannot do a single chin-up considers himself weak without comparing himself with his friends. Though observing the physical skills of others might confirm his judgment, his initial evaluation is based on nonsocial sources. However, and more importantly for our purposes, the evaluation of many skills, aptitudes, attitudes, and values can be done *only* by *comparing oneself with other people*. Festinger (1954) generated **social-comparison theory** to explain this process. Whether it be one's attitude toward Vietnamese immigrants or one's new hairstyle or one's golf swing, if one has doubts about its appropriateness or correctness, one will be motivated to evaluate one's own beliefs and abilities by comparing them with social reality (Radloff, 1961; Latané, 1966; Singer & Shockley, 1965; J. F. Evans, 1974, 1975).

Self-evaluation through social comparison is more fruitful when we choose to make our comparisons with people who are generally similar to ourselves (Bleda & Castore, 1973; Castore & DeNinno, 1972). A dentist is trying to decide whether he is supporting the "right" candidate for governor; he compares his choice with that of the rest of his golf foursome, or his fellow church members, or other dentists. He does not seek out the opinions of college professors, labor organizers, or country-music stars. Likewise, in evaluating their own athletic abilities, most people prefer to compare themselves with someone of similar age, training, and general skill level. If the average once-a-week duffer seeks self-evaluation through social comparison, playing golf with his 8-year-old daughter would be just as unrewarding as playing with Jack Nicklaus. (See Figure 5-2 for another manifestation of social comparison.)

II. Affiliation as a response to anxiety

We have seen that affiliating with others can aid us in the attainment of many of our goals and that membership in the group in and of itself may serve as a goal. There is justification for an assumption that isolation heightens a state of uneasiness in some persons, especially when such persons are *prevented* from being with others. Schachter's observations caused him to conclude that "one of the consequences of isolation appears to be a psychological state which in its extreme form resembles a full-blown anxiety attack" (1959, p. 12). Where does that lead us? Schachter's response was to explore a transformation of the relationship. If isolation does lead to increased anxiety, would a heightened level of anxiety lead to a greater desire for affiliation? We answer that basic question in this section.

A. Does misery love company?

Anxiety is usually considered to be a generalized, diffuse apprehension about the future. It is usually distinguished from fear, which is more object oriented, more specific, and more reality oriented. A man may fear a visit to the dentist because he knows he will be in pain, but an

anticipated visit to a doctor for a routine physical examination may trigger anxiety or generalized dread that something will turn out badly.
Clearly, the reactions of fear and anxiety are so
overlapping that they often cannot be distinguished. While Schachter's program of research
concerned itself with anxiety as a stimulus to an
increased need to be with others, the experimental
manipulations inevitably triggered fear also. In
fact, Schachter observed "Though we have been

Figure 5-2
Playing "hard to get" and social comparison. According to folklore, men
consider women who are "hard to get" desirable companions. But such a
conclusion needs to be qualified, on the basis of research by social psychologist
Elaine Walster and her colleagues (Walster, Piliavin, & Walster, 1973; Walster,
Walster, Piliavin, & Schmidt, 1973). That is, uniformly "hard to get" women
were often rated by men as being undesirable, because they were "too picky"
or "snotty." The most desired woman was the one who liked the man doing
the rating *but did not like other men.* Walster and her colleagues conclude that
"a woman will be most successful in attracting any given man if she appears
to be highly selective in her expressions of affection" (Walster, Piliavin, &
Walster, 1973, p. 83). Such a finding implies that men employ social comparison
with others in order to evaluate their own attractiveness to women. If a woman
who characteristically rejects other men selects them, it is solid evidence of their
appeal. (Photo by Jim Pinckney.)

free in our use of the term 'anxiety,' it should be clear that the experimental manipulations have involved nothing more than the manipulation of physical fear" (1959, p. 65).

In his initial study, Schachter led introductory-psychology students at the University of Minnesota to believe that they were to receive a series of electric shocks. Those subjects in Schachter's "high-anxiety" condition were told that the shocks would be painful but that there would be no permanent damage (Schachter, 1959, p. 13). By contrast, subjects in the "low-anxiety" condition were led to expect virtually painless electric shocks that would feel like a tickle if they were felt at all. After this initial manipulation of anxiety states, all subjects were treated identically. They were each given a sheet on which to indicate, by checking a place on a five-point scale, just how they felt about being shocked. The reason for this procedure was to check the effectiveness of the experimental manipulation; subjects given the "painful" description reported significantly more negative feelings about the experiment, thus indicating that the manipulation was successful. Another demonstration of the effectiveness of the manipulation was the fact that almost 20% of the high-anxiety subjects chose to withdraw from the experiment halfway through, even though they were told they would be given no experimental credit for participating. (They were given credit anyway.)

The basic purpose of the study was to determine whether anxious subjects would seek the presence of others more than would less anxious subjects. Subjects were told there would be a ten-minute delay while the equipment was set up. Each subject had to choose whether she wanted to wait by herself or wait with some of the other subjects in the same experiment. (Note that this choice pertained to *waiting during a pre-shock period*; the subjects were not given the choice of being shocked alone or in small groups.) After each subject indicated her choice, and after some ancillary responses were gathered, the data collection was over. The participants were told that they would not be shocked, and the true purposes of the study were explained to them.

As expected, the level of situationally induced anxiety influenced the waiting preferences. Of the 32 high-anxiety subjects, 20 wanted to wait with other subjects; only 10 of the 30 low-anxiety subjects chose to wait with others—a difference that was statistically significant. The adage that "misery loves company" was confirmed. Though being in a state of emotional upheaval is not the only reason that people want to be with others, it does have an effect.

B. What kind of company does misery love?

Just what is it about being with others that makes that choice so desirable to highly anxious subjects? Perhaps other people serve as a distraction, or perhaps subjects are unsure of their reactions and hence seek out others in the same plight for social comparison. These are not the only conceivable reasons for the link between anxiety and affiliation, but as two possibilities they can be contrasted and evaluated. Such a study was the next step taken by Schachter in his program of research.

In this second experiment all subjects were told that they would receive painful shocks; all subjects were hence in a high-anxiety condition. Each subject was given the choice of waiting alone or with others, but the characteristics of the others were varied from one condition to another. Subjects in the *same-state condition* were given the choice of waiting alone or with other female students who would be taking part in the same electric-shock experiment. Subjects in the *different-state condition* had a different choice; they could wait alone or wait with female students who were not participating in the experiment but were waiting to see their faculty advisors.

Although this experiment used only a small number of subjects (a total of 20), the difference between conditions was clear-cut and statistically significant. Six of the ten subjects in the same-state condition chose to wait with other potential shock subjects; four chose to wait alone. In the different-state condition all ten subjects chose to wait alone; being with others who were not experiencing the same event as themselves was not an attractive option. The findings imply that *distraction* apparently is not a component in the link between anxiety and affiliation. Thus the old saying that "misery loves company" should be amended to "misery loves equally miserable company." But perhaps the company should not be *too* miserable. Rabbie (1963) found that subjects did not want to wait with others who were extremely fearful, because that might cause their own fears to soar.

Both Schachter's and Rabbie's findings support *social comparison* as an explanation for the link between anxiety and affiliating. Perhaps the distressed person seeks out the presence of others in order to compare his or her reactions with theirs. Perhaps they will provide cues as to the appropriate response, cues that enable the person to evaluate his or her own feelings. Much research (Gerard & Rabbie, 1961; Wrightsman, 1960a; Zimbardo & Formica, 1963; G. Becker, 1967; Firestone, Kaplan, & Russell, 1973) has given support to such an interpretation. At the same time there is evidence that the affiliation may serve other purposes, including meeting needs for approval, dependency, support, and acceptance from others (Helmreich & Collins, 1967; Dittes & Capra, 1962). The latter explanation would imply that the state—the actual experience—was less important than the personalities of the other people. For example, Miller and Zimbardo (1966) discovered that subjects preferred to wait with others who had the same personality but were going to be in another experiment rather than to wait with others who were to undergo the same experiment but had dissimilar personalities. The desire to be with others who are like oneself in personality is a strong one.

It may even be that not all types of anxiety lead to heightened affiliation. Sarnoff and Zimbardo (1961) conducted an experiment that aroused what they called "oral anxiety"; male college students were told that they would have to suck on such objects as baby bottles, pacifiers, lollipops, and breast shields. Subjects in this condition preferred waiting in isolation, while sub-

jects given the usual threat of shock preferred to wait with others. When anxiety generates embarrassment, misery does not love similar company (Teichman, 1973). Or, as Firestone, Kaplan, and Russell (1973) note, the anxious person, afraid of embarrassment, may seek nonmiserable companionship. Such persons may wish to compare themselves with others who have *not* undergone their experience, "a comparison which may allow [them] to see how [they have been affected] and changed by the experience" (Firestone, Kaplan, & Russell, 1973, p. 413).

C. Birth-order differences in the link between anxiety and affiliation

Further analysis of the findings of his two experiments led Schachter to "rediscover" the importance of birth order as a correlate of affiliation. Although assumptions abound in our society about the nature of the "only child," the "youngest child," and so on, early social-psychological research (in the 1920s, 1930s, and 1940s) revealed no personality differences that could be related consistently to birth order. Apparently these early studies did not go far enough. Factors associated with birth order do affect social behavior. Table 5-1 presents the findings from Schachter's initial study. Note that in the high-anxiety condition, 32 of the firstborn subjects preferred to wait together, while only 16 wished to wait alone or did not care. But the later-born subjects, when highly anxious, showed no such proclivities; only 21 of 60 wished to wait together.

At this point, it may be said with some confidence that, compared with later-born individuals, more firstborns seek the company of others when anticipating an anxiety-producing event. Firstborns are also more dependent on others, more easily influenced by others, and more concerned with pleasing others than are later borns. In short, firstborns are more other-oriented people. (See, for example, Table 5-2.) Our best guess is that the causes for these birth-order differences emerge during the first few years of life. For example, research such as that by Hilton (1967) and Rothbart (1971)—observing mother-child interactions in order to understand the concomitants of birth order—shows that mothers treat their firstborns and later borns differently. Mothers interact more with the firstborn and more often challenge the firstborn toward achievement.

III. Waiting with others— Does it reduce anxiety?

We know that some persons—particularly firstborns—*want* to be with others when fearful. But what if they are then placed with others?

Does the presence of others reduce their anxiety? Several studies are relevant to this question; their results are summarized below.

A study by Wrightsman (1960b) had subjects wait either alone or in groups of four while they anticipated an experiment that supposedly would "drastically alter the glucose levels in their blood." It was found that if the subject was firstborn, waiting with others facilitated anxiety reduction more than waiting alone. But if the subject was later born, waiting with others made no particular contribution to anxiety reduction. These findings, which applied to both male and female subjects, corroborated Schachter's conclusions about birth order. Firstborns, when anx-

Table 5-1
Birth-order differences in Schachter's first experiment

Birth Order	High-Anxiety Condition Waiting Preference		Low-Anxiety Condition Waiting Preference	
	Together	Alone or Don't Care	Together	Alone or Don't Care
First and only child	32	16	14	31
Later born	21	39	23	33
	$\chi^2 = 10.70$ $p < .01$		$\chi^2 = 1.19$ $p = $ N.S.	

Adapted from *The Psychology of Affiliation*, by Stanley Schachter, with the permission of the publishers, Stanford University Press. © 1959 by the Board of Trustees of the Leland Stanford Junior University.

The data in this table indicate that the heightened desire to affiliate under conditions of high anxiety occurs predominantly among the firstborns. Moreover, the manipulation of anxiety states has no effect on the group of later borns. Apparently, such a relationship also occurs outside the laboratory. Schachter (1959) has reported an unpublished study by Wiener and Stieper investigating which military veterans applied for free outpatient psychotherapy at a Veterans Administration Center. Between 75% and 89% of the veterans who were firstborn or only children sought out the psychotherapy, while only 59% of the later-born veterans did so. Apparently the anxious firstborn individual depends on other persons as vehicles for anxiety reduction. The student who cannot remain in his solitary dormitory room before an important final exam, choosing to study with others or roam the halls looking for a willing companion, is likely to have been a firstborn child.

Since Schachter's findings were published, a multitude of studies (Sampson, 1965; Warren, 1966; Altus, 1966; Vockell, Felker, & Miley, 1973) have looked at birth-order differences in a variety of qualities (intelligence, college grades, dependence, extroversion, schizophrenia, suicide, and so on). While some reviewers (particularly Panos, 1968, and Schooler, 1972, 1973) interpret the results of these studies as occurring because of statistical **artifacts,** our reading of the studies suggests that firstborns have higher levels of verbal ability and get better grades in college than their IQs would predict, but also are more dependent on others (Breland, 1973).

ious, want to be with other people; and when they are placed with others to wait, they benefit from the presence of others, which later borns do not. One of the conclusions of Wrightsman's study was that firstborns want to affiliate (and benefit from affiliating) for two reasons: (1) they receive direct anxiety reduction (sympathy and reassurance), and (2) they achieve self-evaluation by means of social comparison. Ring, Lipinski, and Braginsky (1965) tested these conclusions by placing subjects in groups of four, in which the other three "subjects" were actually confederates assigned a certain role. Before being placed in the group, each subject was told that she was to participate in an auditory stimulation experiment. In addition to the birth order of the subject, two variables were manipulated in the experiment: (1) how anxious the three confederates in the group were and (2) how hard or easy it was for the subject to evaluate her anxiety level by comparing it with those of others.

Ring and associates confirmed some of the findings of Wrightsman's study—namely, that (1) firstborns are more easily influenced than later borns in an anxiety-producing situation, (2) firstborns do have a need to use other persons as sounding boards (make social comparisons) for self-evaluation, and (3) firstborns are less confident about their self-ratings of emotionality. But Ring and his associates also found that later-born subjects have a *greater need for anxiety reduction* than do firstborns. This conclusion is based on their finding that later-born individuals prefer other people who are seemingly calm, while their firstborns tended in the opposite direction and expressed more liking for those who were less calm.

Although the statement that firstborns, as a group, prefer to be with others and actually benefit by being with others is true for groups of subjects, until rather recently no study had looked at the preferences and the waiting behaviors of the same subjects. MacDonald (1970) did so, using procedures similar to ones used in earli-

---

Table 5-2
Birth order and a Los Angeles earthquake

How would you react if the building you were in began to shake, bookshelves began to tumble, walls began to crack? What would you do if you were alone when these things happened?

The Los Angeles area was jarred by a massive earthquake at 6:01 A.M. local time on Tuesday, February 9, 1971. Two social psychologists at UCLA used this naturally occurring event as an aid in assessing birth-order differences in reactions to this anxiety-producing event. According to previous findings, among those who experienced the earthquake while alone, those who were firstborns should have sought out others more often. Among the questions Hoyt and Raven asked respondents was the number of persons they spoke to within 15 minutes after the quake. The mean numbers and standard deviations were as follows:

	Birth Order			
	Firstborn		Later Born	
Sex	Mean	S.D.	Mean	S.D.
Males	3.58	3.63	2.80	1.90
Females	3.97	3.48	1.67	2.40

Thus for both males and females, those who were firstborn reported speaking to more people—that is, more affiliating. (The birth-order difference was statistically significant only for females, however.)

From "Birth Order and the 1971 Los Angeles Earthquake," by M. F. Hoyt and B. H. Raven, *Journal of Personality and Social Psychology*, 1973, *28*, 126. Copyright 1973 by the American Psychological Association. Reprinted by permission.

er studies (Schachter, 1959; Wrightsman, 1960a). After creating a high-anxiety state in his subjects by describing a threatening electric-shock experiment, MacDonald determined whether each person would prefer to wait alone or with others. Then he had each subject wait five minutes, either alone or with three other naïve subjects, *regardless of the subject's preferences.*

The results provide both consistencies and inconsistencies with previous research. Findings that were generally in line with the results of earlier studies were: (1) later borns who wait alone become less anxious than later borns who wait together, and (2) firstborns who wait together become less anxious than later borns who wait together. However, no birth-order differences were found in *preferences* for waiting together. And, more perplexing, those firstborns who wanted to wait alone but were forced to wait together were the ones who experienced the greatest decrease in anxiety level. MacDonald explained this result by emphasizing the more highly socialized nature of firstborns. In other words, firstborns are more likely to conform to the expectations of adults or of society in general. This analysis may be extended as follows: when waiting in the company of others, firstborns—to a stronger degree than later borns—may respond to demand characteristics of the situation and report greater anxiety reduction. Such an explanation sees the anxiety reduction as an artifact, however; it tells us nothing about actual anxiety reduction.

An even more confusing picture about the effects of birth order emerges from a study by Buck and Parke (1972), who used a confederate to wait with the subject in some conditions. (In another condition the subject waited alone.) Subjects who waited with the confederate were told that he was serving in a control condition and that he would not receive electric shocks, but that they would. In the case of half of the subjects, this confederate expressed a sympathetic comment, thus reflecting Schachter's "direct anxiety reduction," while for the other subjects the confederate remained quiet. Later-born subjects were calmed by the presence of the companion,

but only when he offered a sympathetic comment. The anxiety level of firstborns was not influenced by the presence or absence of the companion. The findings of this study clearly contradict MacDonald's explanation that firstborns would be more responsive to the demands of the social situation.

The general conclusion that being with others is an effective anxiety reducer receives even more serious challenge in a thorough review by Epley (1974), who is quite critical of the methodological flaws he sees in many of the studies reviewed in this section. Even though some of his criticisms are misinformed (see Wrightsman, 1975, and Epley, 1975), his review challenges our assumption that the presence of others *in and of itself* provides comfort and reassurance in times of stress. One of Epley's criticisms is that a number of processes are involved when an anxious person waits with others, and that so far there has been little attempt to separate out the effects of sheer physical presence of others from, for example, a person's tendency to imitate the calm response of companions.

There is no denying that some persons *can* be helped by the presence of others. But it is also possible that the comments and actions of the others can heighten the stress. For example, during the bombing of London during World War II, Schmideberg (1942) noted that those citizens who were severely frightened by the air raids were calmed by the presence of those others who were less frightened, while the presence of fearful others had an opposite effect. We need further study of stressful situations and the persons who are part of them before we can specify the directional effects of the presence of other people.

IV. The determinants of emotional and motivational states

We have seen some of the reasons why we want to be with others. We will soon consider a next step in the general process—that of attraction. But before we do so, we need to understand current thinking about the determinants of our emotions. How do we know what to label the emotional state that we feel? Here, too, the work of Stanley Schachter has been most influential.

A. Schachter's theory: Physiological arousal plus cognitive state

Suppose you are alone, late at night, walking along a dark street in a tumbledown section of a strange city. A man quickly steps from a doorway and tells you to stop. This is clearly an emotion-producing situation, but what emotion is aroused? Is it fear? Anxiety? Anger? Excitement? How do you know what emotion you are experiencing?

For decades, physiologists and psychologists have theorized about the nature of emotion. We know that under conditions of strong emotion, physiological changes occur. The sympathetic nervous system takes over, leading to a slowing down of digestion, a diversion of more blood to the head and the extremities, dilation of the pupils of the eyes, deeper breathing, a higher pulse rate, and an increased galvanic skin response. Attempts to detect different physiological response patterns associated with different emotions have largely been unsuccessful (Ax, 1953), and it now appears that the whole gamut of strong emotions—from joy and elation to excitement, fear, and anger—have very similar consequences in our viscera. This has led several psychologists, including Hunt, Cole, and Reis (1958) and Schachter (1964), to posit cognitive factors as the interpreters of emotional states. Although physiological arousal is necessary for emotional labeling, Schachter suggests that we interpret and identify emotional states on the basis of our present situation and our prior experiences. The label assigned to the felt emotion is determined by the cognitive processing of this information. Thus, Schachter's is a two-factor theory, including both physiological arousal and appropriate cognitive factors.

Schachter and Singer (1962) designed a procedure to test the basic hypothesis that a person's emotional state results from the interaction of a physiological state of arousal and a cognitive state. By injecting some subjects with adrenaline and others with a **placebo,** the researchers varied the physiological states of arousal in different groups of participants. Adrenaline has some transitory effects, including flushing of the face, tremors in the hands, and an accelerated heart rate. Some of the subjects given the drug were told to expect effects that were normal for that drug (the adrenaline-informed condition); other subjects were misinformed about what effects to anticipate. The latter were told to expect side effects such as itching sensations, numbness in the feet, and mild headache (the adrenaline-misinformed condition). A third set of subjects receiving the adrenaline injection were told that the drug was mild and harmless and had no side effects (adrenaline-ignorant condition). The fourth group received a placebo and was told there were no side effects (placebo condition). Thus, Schachter and Singer varied both the degree of physiological arousal (adrenaline injection versus placebo injection) and the cognitive state (expectations of differing drug effects).

After receiving the injection, each subject was directed to join another student in a waiting room while the drug took effect. (The subjects were told that they would be given some vision tests—the supposed purpose of the experiment.) The other student in the waiting room was a confederate of the experimenter who had been trained to act in a certain way. For example, in a seemingly euphoric state of being, the confederate began hula-hooping, fashioning paper airplanes and sailing them about, and playing basketball with pieces of scrap paper. The confederate then invited the subject to join in his pranks.

Other subjects were placed with a confederate who had been instructed to act out the emotion of anger. In this anger condition, both the confederate and the subject were instructed to answer a very long and tedious questionnaire containing several personal and rather insulting items. While filling out the questionnaire, the confederate became more and more angry and finally ripped it up, slammed it to the floor, and stamped out of the room.

The purpose of all these behaviors—in both the euphoric and the anger condition—was to give the subject some input from the situation that might influence his reaction to his physiological effects. Two measures of the subject's reactions were taken; in one measure, the subject's behavior was observed through a one-way mirror, and he was rated on the extent to which he joined in with the confederate in demonstrating either euphoric or angry behavior. Additionally, subjects filled out a questionnaire indicating their mood at the moment. These mood questions along with some of the results are reprinted in Table 5-3. The results for the euphoria condition in Table 5-3 indicate that those subjects who received an injection of the drug and were accurately informed about its side effects were less likely to perceive themselves as feeling happy and good; conversely, subjects in the *misinformed* and *ignorant* conditions were more influenced by the confederate's behavior. Observations of subjects in the anger condition led to the same findings. No adrenaline-misinformed condition was used in this part of the study, but

subjects in the adrenaline-ignorant condition agreed with the confederates' comments more frequently and were angrier more often than placebo subjects or informed subjects.

To determine if the adrenaline actually did produce physiological changes, all subjects' pulse rates were taken both before and after the period of waiting with the confederate. These measures confirmed the expectation that in cases where adrenaline was used, pulse rates would increase, whereas in cases where the placebo was used, pulse rates would not increase.

Schachter and Singer explain the thought-provoking findings of their study by considering (1) the state of physiological arousal induced by the adrenaline and (2) the inadequacy of the explanations provided by the various experimental conditions. Thus, when the individual has no appropriate explanation for his state of arousal (for example, the *misinformed* and *ignorant* conditions), his evaluative needs are manifested. This means that his state of arousal is labeled in accordance with the immediate situation—namely, the behavior of the confederate. Emotional states as different as anger and euphoria can be produced from the same physiological conditions. But when the subject has an appropriate

Table 5-3
Measures and results of Schachter-Singer experiment

How good or happy would you say you feel at present?

I don't feel at all happy or good (0)	I feel a little happy and good (1)	I feel quite happy and good (2)	I feel very happy and good (3)	I feel extremely happy and good (4)

Mean Self-Report Scores for Euphoria Condition

Condition	N	Mean
Adrenaline-Informed	25	0.98
Adrenaline-Ignorant	25	1.78
Adrenaline-Misinformed	25	1.90
Placebo	25	1.61

Adapted from "The Interaction of Cognitive and Physiological Determinants of Emotional State," by S. Schachter. In L. Berkowitz (Ed.), *Advances in Experimental Social Psychology*, Vol. 1. Copyright 1964 by Academic Press. Reprinted by permission.

explanation for his bodily state (as in the *informed* condition), evaluative needs are not elicited. In such a condition, the behavior of the confederate is not imitated.

Let us ask what would happen if the social situation were held constant and only levels of physiological arousal were varied. Schachter and Wheeler (1962) examined this question, by injecting different groups of subjects with different drugs—one that mimics the action of the sympathetic nervous system (adrenaline), one that tranquilizes (chlorpromazine), and one that does nothing (a saline solution). All subjects were told that there would be no side effects; they then watched a slapstick comedy film. As predicted, the greatest amount of observable amusement (as measured by observations of grins, smiles, laughs, and big laughs) was in the adrenaline groups, followed by the placebo group. The tranquilized group showed the least emotional reaction. Thus it was shown that one's degree of emotional behavior is related to the extent of activation of the sympathetic nervous system, or emotional arousal. (See Figure 5-3 for other applications of this principle.)

In more recent years, Schachter and his associates have extended their efforts beyond making demonstrations of the cognitive determinants of emotional states (see also Ross, Rodin, & Zimbardo, 1969). Schachter's theory has been applied to the study of (1) the cognitive effects of false heart-rate feedback, (2) cheating and psychopathy (Dienstbier & Munter, 1971), (3) pain perception (Nisbett & Schachter, 1966; Craig & Neidermayer, 1974), and (4) obesity (Schachter & Rodin, 1974). Only the first of these topics will be reviewed in the next section.

B. Cognitive effects of false heart-rate feedback

In one study, male college students found themselves participating in an apparently pleasant activity of viewing pictures of seminude females (Valins, 1966). Some of the subjects were told that they would hear the sounds of their heartbeats, which were to be amplified electronically. The true purpose of the experiment, however, was to determine what effects a falsified heart rate would have on the subject's evaluations of the pictures. Some subjects heard their heartbeat speed up markedly while viewing certain pictures. In another condition, the subjects heard a sudden decrease in the bogus heart rates for certain pictures, but no change for the other pictures. Stuart Valins, the researcher, hypothesized that a cognition—such as "that girl's picture has affected my heart rate"—would prompt the subject to consider that young woman to be more attractive than some other young woman who apparently caused no effects. Subjects in a control condition were told that the heart rate sounds were extraneous noise; they did not come to perceive the "false-feedback" pictures as being the more attractive ones. But subjects who were told that their heart rates actually increased or decreased did prefer those pictures to a significant degree. Valins accounts for his findings in the light of Schachter's proposition that cognitive representations of internal states are evaluated and labeled in accordance with the predominant characteristics of the environmental situation. Subjects, given the task of explaining to themselves why their heart rates changed, found "it was most appropriate for them to explain their reactions by referring to the [photographs], and to interpret them as indicating varying degrees of attraction" (Valins, 1966, p. 407). A rather perplexing factor, however, is that either an increase or a decrease in heart rate produced the same results; perhaps the change served as a general signal of differential reaction.

More recent work by Valins (1967a, 1967b, 1970) and Schachter (1967, 1971b) has concentrated on the individual differences in utilizing internal sensations as cues for labeling one's own behavior. Valins (1967b) found that unemotional people (measured by paper-and-pencil instruments) tend to ignore their internal states and feel no pressure to evaluate and label their feelings. In laboratory experiments, they were less likely to mimic the behavior of a confederate and did not rate certain photographs of nudes as more attractive merely because their heartbeat supposedly responded differentially. Conversely, people who rely extensively on their internal states to label their emotions and behavior were more influenced by bogus heart rates, emotional confederates, and similar variations.

C. An alternative explanation: Bem's self-perception theory

The same facts can have several differing theoretical explanations, as we saw in Chapter 1. The self-perception theory of Daryl Bem

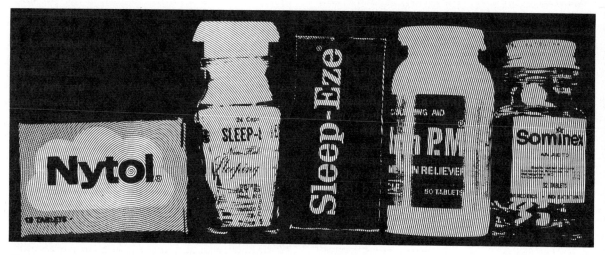

Figure 5-3
Blaming a sleeping pill for lack of sleep. When does taking a sleeping pill lead to greater degrees of insomnia? When the person is told the pill will have beneficial effects that, in fact, it does not have. Storms and Nisbett (1970) recruited chronic insomniacs as volunteer subjects and gave each two pills, with instructions to take one pill a few minutes before going to bed on two consecutive nights. The pills were actually placebos, with no effects, but the subjects were all told that they were sleeping pills. Additionally, some of the subjects were told that the pills would produce an arousal reaction; that is, they would feel an increased heart rate and body temperature. Other subjects were told that the pills would cause a state of relaxation, with a decreased heart rate and body temperature. Those insomniacs who were told the pills would arouse them reported that they got to sleep 25% quicker than normally on the nights that they took the pill. Thus for them, the usual restlessness they suffered when they went to bed and couldn't get to sleep was now "explained" by a "foreign substance"—the pill—so that they did get to sleep more quickly (or at least reported that they did so). But what of those insomniacs who were told that the pill would relax them, when it actually did not have the power to do so? These subjects reported that, on the average, it took them 40% longer than usual to get to sleep on the nights that they took the pill. They apparently experienced their normal restlessness upon going to bed, realized it was *contrary* to the pill's promised effects, and thus became even more aroused. Thus Storms and Nisbett demonstrated that the attributed cause of arousal can either reduce or increase the level of arousal.

(1972b) does not rely on social-comparison theory, as Schachter's does, to explain the findings discussed in this chapter. Instead, Bem proposes that we infer our internal states by observing our own behavior, without necessarily comparing it with anybody else's. He believes that "individuals come to 'know' their own attitudes, emotions, and other internal states partially by inferring them from observations of their own overt behavior and/or the circumstances in which this behavior occurs" (1972b, p. 5). Thus, Bem's theory is a type of attribution theory, discussed in Chapter 3, but the attributions are now made about the causes of our own behavior, rather than about those of someone else's. We will return to self-perception theory as it relates to attitudes and attitude change in Chapters 10 and 11.

V. Attraction

Under certain conditions, many people experience a powerful desire to be with other people. Apparently, others serve as a way of evaluating our own opinions and abilities. It is interesting to ask, however, *which* persons are most attractive to us. Why are we friendly or attracted to some people, while we reject or dislike others? In this section we move from the general nature of affiliation to the specific reaction of attraction. We shall review some of the characteristics of other people that make them attractive. Then several theoretical explanations for the findings will be contrasted.

A. The antecedents of interpersonal attraction

We may say with confidence that a person will usually be attracted to another person who:

- has similar values, beliefs, and personality characteristics;
- satisfies the first person's needs;
- is competent;
- is beautiful or handsome;
- is pleasant or agreeable;
- reciprocates the first person's liking.

Also, by the nature of things, we are more likely to come to like those who are nearby; there is a validity in the song from *Finian's Rainbow* that says "When I'm not near the one I love, I love the one I'm near." We now consider each of these conditions in turn.

Similarity of personality, values, and beliefs. We are attracted to and like people whose attitudes and values appear to agree with ours. We dislike those who seem to disagree with us (Byrne, 1971; Kaplan, 1972; Griffitt, 1974). If their personalities are like ours, the attraction is much stronger. For example, early research in the laboratory, using verbal descriptions of others' attitudes and personalities, found that Whites preferred associating with Blacks who had attitudes like their own, rather than with Whites who had opposing attitudes (Stein, Hardyck, & Smith, 1965; Rokeach, 1968; Byrne & Wong, 1962; see also Moss & Andrasik, 1973). But the value of these procedures has been challenged because of their artificial nature; that is, the "other person" is only described on paper, and the subject is explicitly made aware of the degree of similarity or dissimilarity in attitudes (Levinger, 1972; Wright & Crawford, 1971).

Field studies should help clarify the relationship. In an early one, Newcomb (1961) gave college students free housing in a rooming house in exchange for their willingness to fill out a seemingly endless list of questionnaires and ratings about their attitudes and their liking for their housemates. The results of this massive study are usually interpreted to indicate that those students whose attitudes were similar at the beginning of the semester came to like each other more. However, the results are confusing for, as Griffitt and Veitch (1974) observe, Newcomb's statements about the relationship appear positive at one point (p. 85) and negative at another (p. 261).

To clarify the relationship in the field, Griffitt and Veitch (1974) created a setting in which contact was more than superficial and the attitude similarity would not be salient in the eyes of the participants. They arranged for 13 males who were unacquainted at the beginning of the project to live together for ten days under conditions that simulated living in a fallout shelter. The participants' liking for one another was measured at the end of the first, fifth, and ninth days of confinement. Griffitt and Veitch found that on each of these days, people were somewhat more attracted toward those others whose attitudes were similar to their own.

Complementarity of need systems. In contrast to the preceding condition, there may be cases in which opposites attract. If another person differs from you and if this opposing quality *meets your needs*, that person will be more attractive to you than other people. According to the theory of need complementarity, similarity in certain personality traits and needs does not facilitate two persons' liking each other. A very dominant person may be more likely to be attracted to a submissive partner. Or females with traditional views of their own role may prefer males with traditionally masculine attributes (Seyfried & Hendrick, 1973). The complementarity of need systems could work in both directions—the highly submissive person would be attracted to a marriage partner who would speak out, take responsibility, and make decisions. In regard to marriage selection, Robert Winch (1952; Winch, Ktsanes, & Ktsanes, 1954) has proposed that each person chooses a mate who is most likely to provide the greatest degree of gratification of his or her needs. Winch further suggested that need complementarity was strongest in regard to nurturance/receptivity, as well as the aforementioned dominance/submissiveness.

One careful study has shown, however, that possibly two factors may occur; the personalities and needs of two marriage partners may be similar as well as complementary. In that study, Kerckhoff and Davis (1962) interviewed, tested, and later retested college couples who were seriously considering marriage. These couples were classified either as long term (had gone together 18 months or more) or short term (had gone together less than 18 months). The investigators were interested in whether a similarity of values or a complementarity of needs led to greater progress toward a permanent relationship. To measure degrees of progress, both members of each couple were asked whether their relationship had changed over the seven months since they had first filled out questionnaires measuring needs and values. Three possible answers to the question were: "Yes, we are farther from being a permanent couple"; "No, it is the same"; and "Yes, we are nearer to being a permanent couple."

The length of time that the relationship had existed was a significant **moderator variable** in regard to similarity of values and needs. Those couples who had been going together less than 18 months and who were more similar in values reported greater movement toward a permanent relationship. In the case of these short-term relationships, the presence of complementary needs did not lead to feelings of a more permanent relationship. But among long-term couples, those who experienced a greater complementarity of needs reported greater movement toward permanence. In the longer relationships, possession of similar values did not, at this point, facilitate a move toward marriage. Such findings encourage the development of a minitheory of the *filtering factors of mate selection.* Kerckhoff and Davis propose that the quality of a relationship is assayed by sequentially passing through several filters. The first includes sociological and demographic variables such as socioeconomic status and religion, the second (coming after the couple has dated a little longer) is consensus on values, and the third (coming only after a longer period) is the complementarity of needs.

But only marginal support was found for the "filtering-factors" explanation in a study by Levinger, Senn, and Jorgensen (1970). These researchers suggest that first there is a process of discovering each other's important values, which is followed by a process of developing communality within the pair. This second process reflects greater self-disclosure and also refers to acts of behavior coordination and emotional investment by the two people. Levinger writes "As two persons get to know each other, they learn how to accommodate to each other's responses and preferences. And, as a relationship unfolds, each partner takes increasing pleasure from the other's satisfaction" (1974, p. 106). *(hopefully)*!

Competence. We like people who are intelligent, able, and competent more than we do those who are not. Stotland and Hillmer (1962) report that in the absence of any other information, a subject's liking for another person increases if the person has a high degree of ability. Apparently this is so even when the subject does not expect to benefit from the other person's competence (Iverson, 1964; Stotland & Dunn, 1962). There is also some tendency for men to prefer competent women to incompetent ones (Spence & Helmreich, 1972).

However, as Bramel (1969) points out, there may be limits to this relationship. People who are extremely competent may make us uncomfortable if an atmosphere of social comparison exists. Thus, it must be said that other attributes interact with high ability to influence our liking of a person. When a person of established high ability demonstrates human failings, his attractiveness may actually be enhanced. A real-life example of this phenomenon was the apparent increase in Muhammad Ali's popularity after he lost the world championship boxing match to Joe Frazier. Aronson (1970) notes that a Gallup Poll taken right after the abortive Bay of Pigs invasion of Cuba showed that President John F. Kennedy's personal popularity had increased rather than decreased. Perhaps this was a sympathetic response to his defeat, but Aronson sees it as a reflection of how human fallibility in a person with high ability makes that person even more attractive. Aronson states: "Perhaps President Kennedy was too perfect. He was young, handsome, bright, witty, a war hero, super-wealthy, charming, athletic, a voracious reader, a master political strategist" (1970, p. 148).

Aronson tested his hypothesis under well-controlled laboratory conditions (Aronson, Willerman, & Floyd, 1966). In the study, college students listened to a tape recording purportedly of another student who was seeking a position on the university College Quiz Bowl team. Half of the subjects heard the candidate answer very hard questions in an extraordinarily skillful way; the candidate ended by getting 92 percent of the questions right. The other half of the subjects heard the same voice fail to answer many of the questions; this candidate was correct only 30 percent of the time. For half of the subjects hearing each of these voices, the tapes at this point ended and the subjects were asked, among other things, how much they liked the candidate. Not surprisingly, the person with superior ability was liked somewhat more. (Average attraction ratings were 20.8 for the superior-ability candidate and 17.8 for the average-ability candidate.) The other half of the subjects heard a continuation of the tape and learned that just as the candidate was handed a cup of coffee, he spilled the cup and, amid a great commotion, exclaimed, "Oh, my goodness, I've spilled coffee all over my new suit." These subjects were then asked to rate the candidate. It is interesting to note the effect of this blunder on how much the subjects liked the candidate. The superior-ability candidate now received a mean attraction rating of 30.2 (compared to 20.8 in the absence of the blunder), whereas the average-ability candidate received a mean rating of –2.5 (much below his initial 17.8 rating). Thus, a blunder by a person of high ability enhances his or her appeal, but the same act detracts from the already-less-attractive image of the average person.

we don't want people to be too fabulous us.

We may question whether such a blunder would increase the attractiveness of the competent person for everybody. Helmreich, Aronson, and LeFan (1970) proposed that the observer's level of self-esteem might influence whether a blunder on the part of a competent person increases his attractiveness. The investigators granted that, for persons of average self-esteem (that is, people who see themselves as moderately competent), the blunder of a superior person is endearing because it "not only 'humanizes' the superior, but brings him closer to the 'average' observer" (Helmreich et al., 1970, p. 260). However, the observer who sees himself as highly competent (or rates his own self-esteem as high) may identify with the superior person and be more attracted to him if he maintains a flawless image. It was predicted that observers who are relatively low in self-esteem would also be more attracted to the flawless, competent person than to the fallible one, because of the observer's own need "for someone to take care of him [and] to provide an ideal, a hero" (Helmreich et al., 1970, p. 260).

Another procedure was used to test this extended hypothesis. Subjects watched a videotape of an interview instead of listening to a recording. The person being interviewed had applied for the position of student ombudsman, "the most responsible job a student can hold." The level of competence or superiority of the applicant was varied by information that the applicant reported about himself—grade-point average, class honors, offices held, and high school activities. The blunder was again the act of spilling coffee. Thus, Helmreich and associates varied three conditions: the applicant's level of competence (superior or inferior), the blunder committed by the applicant (present or absent), and the self-esteem of the observer (high, average, or low).

The results are reproduced in Figure 5-4. As indicated in the graph on the left, the competent applicant who commits a blunder becomes more likable for subjects with average levels of self-esteem—a result similar to the findings of subjects in Aronson, Willerman, and Floyd's (1966) study. But subjects who are either high or low in self-esteem respond differently—for them, the presence of the blunder decreases the attractiveness of the competent applicant.

Reactions to the incompetent applicant, as shown in the right-hand side of Figure 5-4, were quite different. As expected, this stimulus person was less attractive for all observers, and the presence or the absence of the blunder had little effect on his attractiveness.

Mettee and Wilkins (1972) have extended this conclusion. They too found that very competent subjects downgrade a person of superior ability who commits a blunder, but such an act does not affect their rating of people of average ability. In contrast, subjects of average ability derogate the person of average competence who blunders, but not the superior person.

Physical attractiveness. Aristotle once wrote that "Beauty is a greater recommendation than any letter of introduction," and things have not changed in the last 2300 years. A beautiful or handsome physical appearance remains a critical determinant of success in our society. The vast amounts of money spent on cosmetics, plastic surgery, diet foods, and contemporary fashions are all very apparent indications of the amounts of money and concern we invest in our appearance (Barocas & Karoly, 1972; Barocas & Vance, 1972).

Such investments seem to pay off, because there is an implicit assumption in our society that "what is beautiful is good" (Dion, Berscheid, & Walster, 1972). As one example, Dion (1972) showed college females photographs of children who, she claimed, had misbehaved. Some of the children were physically attractive; some were not. Particularly when the misbehavior was a severe one, the beautiful children were given the benefit of the doubt. Respondents tended to "explain away" the misbehavior of the attractive children, while ugly children *who committed the same acts* were called maladjusted and deviant.

In fact, it is hard to overestimate the effects of the other's physical appearance on our initial attraction to him or her. (See Figure 5-5.) In a study that randomly assigned blind dates for a dance (Walster, Aronson, Abrahams, & Rottman, 1966), the participants were asked after the dance whether they liked their date and would like to go out together again. The personality and the intelligence of the date did not affect the preference for subsequent interactions; *the person's physical appearance was the only quality that made a difference.* A similar computer-dating study found that the perceived physical attractiveness of a

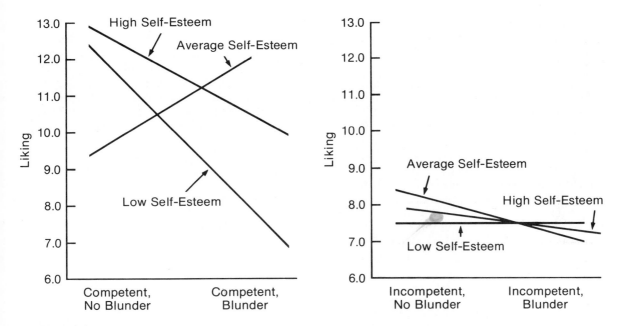

Figure 5-4
Attraction toward the competent stimulus person. Higher scores indicate greater attraction. (From "To Err Is Humanizing—Sometimes: Effects of Self-Esteem, Competence, and a Pratfall on Interpersonal Attraction," by R. Helmreich, E. Aronson, and J. LeFan, *Journal of Personality and Social Psychology*, 1970, *16*, 259–264. Copyright 1970 by the American Psychological Association. Reprinted by permission.)

date correlated .89 with how much the person desired to go out with the date again (Brislin & Lewis, 1968).

One reason we are beckoned by the physically attractive lies in our hope that their attractiveness will "rub off on" us. Many years ago the sociologist W. W. Waller (1937) observed that we gain a great deal of prestige by being seen with an attractive person of the other sex. This "rating and dating complex" has been verified. In one instance, the data show that "students follow prestige lines at all stages in the mate selection process" (Rogers & Havens, 1960, p. 59). Sigall and Landy (1973) found that a male gets the most favorable impression from outside observers when he is accompanied by a good-looking female companion. He is viewed most negatively when his female companion is physically unattractive.

Pleasant or agreeable characteristics. This is a condition that needs little or no elaboration. We like people who are nice or who do nice things.

Reciprocal liking. We are attracted to people who like us. Heider's (1958) balance theory, to be considered in Chapter 11, predicts that if person P likes himself and if person O likes person P, a cognitively balanced state will be introduced in which person P likes person O. Backman and Secord (1959) showed that if members of discussion groups are told that certain other group members liked them very much, these others were more likely to be chosen later when two-

Figure 5-5
How much does physical attractiveness influence choice of a marriage partner?
Bernard I. Murstein (1972) has proposed what he calls a stimulus-value-role (or
SVR) theory of marital choice. According to this theory, the first stage of
attraction involves the other person as a *stimulus*. Murstein proposes that we
choose, as marital partners, other persons of comparable physical attractiveness
to ourselves. That is, beautiful people marry beautiful people, and homely
people marry homely people. Murstein carried out two studies to test his claim.
In the first, 99 couples who were "going steady" rated their partner and
themselves on a five-point scale of physical attractiveness. Also their
photographs were rated by a separate group of people on physical attractiveness.
Since Murstein needed to determine the average amount of similarity in
attractiveness within a pair, he formed a "control group" of pairs by randomly
pairing together males and females from the 99 couples. The photograph-based
attractiveness of the actual couples was significantly less discrepant than that
of artificially paired couples. The self-ratings of actual couples were also less
discrepant from each other than were the artificially formed "couples," but not
to a statistically significant degree. Thus there was empirical support for
Murstein's hypothesis that "likes attract" when it comes to physical
attractiveness. Murstein's second study also had couples rate themselves and
their partners. However, in this case 98 new couples were the subjects. Again,
there was a general similarity of degree of physical attractiveness between the
two people in the same couple. (Photos by Jim Pinckney.)

person teams were formed. The opposite also is the case; Aronson and Cope (1968) have found that "my enemy's enemy is my friend." The latter relationship is also consistent with predictions from Heider's balance theory. In fact, if a person likes someone else, the person may distort the amount of similarity between them (Stephan, 1973) so that the other person appears to be more similar than he or she really is.

Propinquity. Other things being equal, we like people who live close to us better than those who are at a distance from us. For instance, families in a student apartment complex, all of rather homogeneous backgrounds, are more likely to interact with and like those persons living on the same floor in the same building than those families living on other floors or in other buildings (Festinger, Schachter, & Back, 1950). Members of Air Force bomber crews develop closer relationships with coworkers who are stationed near them than with coworkers stationed a few yards away (Kipnis, 1957). A number of other studies also indicate that people tend to become friends with their nearest neighbors (Merton, 1947; Rosow, 1961; Whyte, 1956). Just living close is not sufficient for establishing friendship, however; doubtless propinquity serves as a filter (Athanasiou & Yoshioka, 1973). Even though such findings certainly do not seem surprising, it should be remembered that greater friendships and attractions remain despite the greater frictions that occur from two people living or working closely together.

B. Theory-based explanations for factors in interpersonal attraction

We have seen how a variety of antecedent conditions contribute to interpersonal attraction. (See also Figure 5-6 for the effects of prolonged exposure on attraction.) Let us now explore some possible explanations for these relationships. Like Aronson (1970), one could be tempted to

subsume all these factors under reinforcement theory; that is, we are attracted to people whose behavior is rewarding to us. One type of reinforcement theory—social-exchange theory—provides an example. According to Thibaut and Kelley's (1959) social-exchange theory, a relationship between two persons continues if the rewards from the relationship are greater for each person than the costs. This principle was extended by using a concept of comparison level of alternatives, which postulates that the individual compares the cost/reward ratio of one interaction with the cost/reward ratio of available alternative behaviors. Curry and Emerson (1970) found that social-exchange theory does a good job of explaining why certain persons in a group of strangers come to like certain other persons. Aronson has carefully summarized the application of this theory to factors in interpersonal attraction as follows:

(1) Propinquity is more rewarding, all other things being equal, because it costs less in terms of time and effort to receive a given amount of benefit from a person who is physically close to us than [from] one who is at a distance (Thibaut & Kelley, 1959); (2) people with similar values reward each other through consensual validation (Byrne, 1969); (3) the same would be true for similarity of some personality traits, whereas (4) for some needs, complementarity would be most rewarding—for example, sadism-masochism or nurturance dependency; (5) people perhaps expect to gain more through association with highly competent people than with people of low or moderate competence. That is, in general, our past histories are such that we have usually been more rewarded by people who knew what they were about than by people who tended to blunder frequently; (6) obviously, pleasant, agreeable behavior is more rewarding than unpleasant, disagreeable behavior; and (7) being liked can probably be considered a reward in and of itself—in addition, for most people it also entails a similarity of beliefs because most of us think rather highly of ourselves (Byrne & Rhamey, 1965). [From Aronson, 1970, pp. 144–145.]

Figure 5-6
The effects of repeated exposure. There is a mass of evidence for the "mere
exposure" hypothesis—that is, that repeated exposure to the same stimulus
object leads to a greater attraction to that object (Harrison, 1969; Matlin, 1970;
Wandersman, Schaffner, & Stang, 1974; Zajonc, 1968). The usual experimental
procedure in such studies includes two phases. First, there is an exposure phase
in which several stimulus objects (names, or human faces, for example) are
shown different numbers of times, in a random order. Then, during the test
phase, subjects give their evaluations of the stimuli they previously have seen
(Saegert, Swap, & Zajonc, 1973). Generally there is an increase in the favorable
evaluations given to the stimuli seen most often. Such a conclusion has been
questioned both because of methodological problems (Stang, 1974) and because
of limitations due to the context (Burgess & Sales, 1971; Perlman & Oskamp,
1971). Its effect may well be limited to those objects for which our *initial*
impression is at least slightly favorable. (Photo by Jim Pinckney.)

However, not all findings about attraction
fit this simplified social-exchange explanation;
just as we do not always feel attracted to those
similar to ourselves (S. E. Taylor & Mettee, 1971).
(See also Figure 5-7.) Also, if one has exerted
much effort to achieve a goal or a relationship,
that goal or relationship becomes more attractive
(Aronson, 1961). Likewise, the more severe the
initiation rites necessary to become a member
of a group, the more attractive that group then

becomes (Aronson & Mills, 1959; Gerard & Mathewson, 1966). We find that **cognitive-dissonance** theory, an offspring of the Gestalt approach, more acceptably explains such outcomes, as well as many similar findings dealing with the relationship of effort to evaluation of a goal. Cognitive-dissonance theory is concerned with inconsistencies between two beliefs or behaviors of the same person. The theory predicts that such inconsistencies are so unpleasant that the person is motivated to resolve the resulting dissonance. (See Chapter 11 for details.) Applied to the present case, cognitive-dissonance theory would predict that when we make great efforts to meet another person, we will find the other person more attractive than we would have had our efforts been less concentrated. That is, any realization that the other person is unlikable would be dissonant with the great amount of effort expended in meeting him; hence, we convince ourselves that the other person is attractive.

From the field of sociology, the theory of *symbolic interaction* takes a different perspective in explaining interpersonal attraction. You may recall from Chapter 1 that the symbolic interactionists generally believe that one's self-identity arises through his or her role taking and internalization of the reactions of others (Gecas, 1971; Lewis, 1973). The symbolic-interaction viewpoint is critical of the previous approaches for their obsession with characteristics of the other person and their neglect in studying attraction as a *relationship* between two people (Kerckhoff, 1974). For the symbolic-interaction theorist, the question of why I am attracted to someone else cannot be answered simply by examining the features of that other person. Rather, we must also examine what it is about me that leads me to find those features of the other person attractive (McCall, 1974).

Thus, we discover, as with other phenomena, that it is necessary to utilize several theoretical approaches to understand more thoroughly the nature and determinants of attraction. We may expect that the future will bring about a more precise understanding of the use of each theory in predicting the phenomenon of attraction.

Figure 5-7
When *dis*similars attract—or do they? During a youth rally as a part of the 1972 Republican National Convention at Miami Beach, entertainer Sammy Davis, Jr., embraced then-President Nixon and endorsed him for reelection. It was clearly not a case in which similarity attracts; two people who are more different in life-style and attitudes would be hard to imagine. But Davis did not indicate he liked Nixon, only that he liked him for President. Davis later came to be very disappointed that President Nixon did not provide aid programs for the minorities and the poor. (Photo courtesy of Wide World Photos.)

VI. Love—The ultimate in affiliation?

Perhaps the ultimate in affiliation is love. Many thinkers have asked what love really is; yet, until recently, social psychologists have shied away from the study of love, for a variety of reasons. Berscheid and Walster (1969) report that in the early decades of this century, the scientific study of romantic love was almost a taboo; for example, in the 1920s two professors in the United States were fired from a state university because of their participation in a questionnaire study of attitudes toward sex. But the intervening 50 years have produced ever-increasing freedoms in the study of such attitudes. (See Chapter 6 of this text for examples.)

One reason for avoiding the topic is that, of all the social-psychological constructs, love is perhaps the most difficult to define and measure. Goode (1959), a sociologist, defined love as follows: "A strong emotional attachment, a cathexis, between adolescents or adults of opposite sexes, with at least the components of sex desire and tenderness." Some limitations to this definition are immediately apparent. One drawback is that the use of the phrase *opposite sexes* precludes the consideration that any homosexual relationship —even a long-term one involving both sexual desire and tenderness—could be considered love. Another difficulty with Goode's definition is in the words "at least the components of sex desire and tenderness"; if there are other components we would like to know what they are. A more recent definition by Greenfield, an anthropologist, is in some ways better: "Love [is] a relationship which may be observed and which includes patterned, repetitive and normative behavior and specifiable attitudes and emotional states between persons of the opposite sex or on occasions of the same sex. This actually or potentially includes sexual activity" (Greenfield, 1970, p. 3). Here again, however, qualities other than sexual activity are not described.

By defining love as a "relationship" Greenfield implies that love may not reside in a person but rather is a developing process between people, a state of becoming present in a dyad as a totality. Love, according to this view, is not the attribute of either person separated from the other.

A. Social-psychological approaches

Social psychologists have often either ignored a definition of love or have treated it as merely an intense form of liking. For example, in one experiment specifically concerned with romantic attraction, the measure of the dependent variable was simply a paper-and-pencil measure of liking (Walster, 1965). Heider's (1958) influential theory treats loving as intense liking. Surely, there is more to love than this; the social psychologist's obsession with measurement may be a cause for the predominant orientation. If love is considered as merely an extreme and selective type of liking, its measurement can be achieved by using captive audiences of college sophomores and procedures within the usual social-psychological bag of tricks—questionnaires, rating forms, and the like. But that approach, we believe, is not enough.

B. The measurement of romantic love

Social psychologist Zick Rubin (1970, 1973) has sought an approach that is something of a compromise. Rubin conceptualizes romantic love as something more than intense liking, but he still attempts to assess it through rather traditional techniques. Thus, he has attempted to bring the study of romantic love within the mainstream of social-psychological approaches to interpersonal attraction. Rubin defines love as "an *attitude* held by a person toward a particular other person, involving predispositions to think, feel, and behave in certain ways toward that other person" (1970, p. 265, italics in original.) Notice that this definition is quite different from Greenfield's and from Goode's in particular; it is a nonsubstantive definition, which does not mention any attributes of love such as tenderness or sexual desire. In fact, the same definition that Rubin uses for *love* could be used for *hate*, as well. In Rubin's definition, the nature of love is limited to an attitude, and considerations of love as a part of a person's personality or experience are excluded.

Rubin's first purpose was to devise a love scale that would measure degrees of romantic love (defined by Rubin as "love between unmarried opposite-sex peers, of the sort which could possibly lead to marriage"). A parallel scale for the measurement of liking was developed. Items from these are listed in Figure 5-8; take a moment to read over the statements. Despite his nonsubstantive definition of love, Rubin has included three components in his romantic love scale: (1) affiliative and dependent needs, (2) predisposition to help, and (3) exclusiveness and absorption. The concept of liking, as reflected in the liking-scale items, includes two components: (1) a perception that the target person is similar to oneself and (2) a favorable evaluation of and respect for the target person.

Figure 5-8
Examples of Rubin's measures

Love-Scale Items

1. If I could never be with _____, I would feel miserable.
2. I would forgive _____ for practically anything.
3. I feel that I can confide in _____ about virtually everything.

Liking-Scale Items

1. I think that _____ is unusually well adjusted.
2. Most people would react very favorably to _____ after a brief acquaintance.
3. _____ is the sort of person who I myself would like to be.

Note: Scores on individual items can range from 1 to 9, with 9 always indicating the positive end of the continuum. There are nine items on each scale. From "Measurement of Romantic Love," by Z. Rubin, *Journal of Personality and Social Psychology*, 1970, *16*, 267. Copyright 1967 by the American Psychological Association. Reprinted by permission.

These scales were administered, at the University of Michigan, to 158 couples who were dating but not engaged. They were instructed to answer the love scale and the liking scale with respect to their dating partner and a close friend of the same sex. The means and standard deviations for the men and women respondents are reported in Table 5-4, which indicates that the love scores of men for their dating partners and those of women for their dating partners were almost identical. However, women like their dating partners significantly more than they were liked in return. This difference results from women's rating their male friends higher on task-oriented dimensions such as intelligence and leadership potential.

Means for liking same-sex friends were virtually identical, but women reported greater love toward same-sex friends than did males. As Rubin indicates, this difference is consistent with a cultural stereotype that women express more love toward each other than men do. Thus, we have the beginnings of a conceptual distinction between romantic love and liking. Further evidence that these are separate entities comes from the following findings:

1. The correlation across couples between the extent of the man's and woman's love for each other was $+.42$. The corresponding liking correlation was lower: $+.28$. Thus, there was more similarity in regard to how much the members of a dating couple *love* each other than in how much they *liked* each other.

2. Love scores were highly correlated with estimates of the probability that the current dating partners would marry ($r = +.59$ for each sex). However, liking scores were less correlated with the likelihood of marriage ($+.35$ for men and $+.32$ for women).

The outcomes of Rubin's research project may not extend one's knowledge beyond what can be gained from common observation; that is, the approach to romantic love through the attitude-measurement framework may not be enough by itself. Love may develop as a result of the interaction of many factors. Let us now consider an example of a situational factor that may play a role in the development of love.

C. Stimulants to romantic love: The Romeo-and-Juliet effect

An unintentional implication of the attitudinal approach may be that romantic love is a static, unchanging phenomenon. We realize, of course, that it is not. Romantic love grows and wanes, intensifies and diminishes for a variety

Table 5-4
Love and liking for dating partners and same-sex friends

Index	Women		Men	
	$\overline{X}$	SD	$\overline{X}$	SD
Love for partner	89.46	15.54	89.37	15.16
Liking for partner	88.48	13.40	84.65	13.81
Love for same-sex friend	65.27	17.84	55.07	16.08
Liking for same-sex friend	80.47	16.47	79.10	18.07

Note: Based on responses of 158 couples. (From "Measurement of Romantic Love," by Z. Rubin, *Journal of Personality and Social Psychology*, 1970, *16*, 267–268. Copyright 1970 by the American Psychological Association. Reprinted by permission.)

of reasons. Although loving and liking are qualitatively different, many of the factors associated with the development of attraction or liking probably contribute to the development of love as well. Although all these factors should be considered, for the moment we shall examine one specific determinant. What effect does parental interference have on the feelings of romantic love between a young woman and a young man?

In Chapter 11, we will review Brehm's (1966) theory of **reactance.** This minitheory would predict, among other things, that a threat to one's freedom of choice—as represented by parental interference—would lead to intensified feelings of romantic love between two partners. (We could call this phenomenon the Romeo-and-Juliet effect.) Driscoll, Davis, and Lipetz (1972) set out to test this hypothesis. Ninety-one pairs of married couples and 49 pairs of dating couples participated in the study. The average length of time that the latter couples had been together on a serious basis was eight months, and 18 of the 49 couples were living together at the time of the study. Scales to measure parental interference, various types of love, interpersonal trust, and other factors were administered to each couple. Not surprisingly, a low correlation of +.24 was obtained between degree of parental interference and degree of romantic love in mar-

ried couples. But this correlation was +.50 for the unmarried sample, indicating that unmarried couples who reported greater parental interference were also more in love. From these data, it cannot be said with certainty that heightened parental interference intensified the relationship; but Driscoll and his colleagues repeated the measures six to ten months later to determine changes in responses. Changes in degree of parental interference correlated +.34 with changes in the extent of romantic love experienced by the 29 initially unmarried couples who were retested. Thus, the hypothesis that parental interference intensifies feelings of romantic love is apparently supported. However, we could probably safely assume that had the Montagues and Capulets known of this phenomenon, their reactions to the love affair of Romeo and Juliet would not have changed.

D. A theoretical explanation of passionate love

Walster and Berscheid (Walster, 1971; Walster & Berscheid, 1971) have attempted to relate the determinants of emotional states to the feeling of passionate love—apparently a more transitory phenomenon than romantic love. These researchers first asked if reinforcement theory could explain passionate love and concluded that it cannot. They recognize that we may fall in love with persons who offer us affection or other rewards, but they also point out that we may intensely love those who have rejected us. When a lover has been spurned, his or her feelings may dissipate—or they may grow all the stronger. In one paper, Walster (1971, p. 87) cites an actual incident involving an Italian man who had kidnapped his former sweetheart; the kidnapper tearfully explained "The fact that she rejected me only made me want and love her more."

Evidence from anecdotes may not convince die-hard empiricists, but such stories, along with other data, led Walster and Berscheid to postulate that something besides a straightforward theory of reinforcement is necessary to explain passionate love. Thus, they proposed that Schachter's two-factor theory of emotion might be of use. You will recall from earlier in this chapter that Schachter emphasized that in order to experience emotion, one must not only be physiologically aroused but also possess the appropriate cognitions in order to label the arousal as a particular emotional state. These cognitions are often derived from the situation. Walster and Berscheid noted that two components are also necessary for a passionate experience; the arousal and the appropriate cognitions. Walster wrote:

... perhaps it does not really matter how one produces an agitated state in a lover. Stimuli that usually produce sexual arousal, gratitude, anxiety, guilt, loneliness, hatred, jealousy, or confusion may all increase one's physiological arousal, and thus intensify his emotion experience. As long as one attributes his agitated state to passion, he should experience true passionate love. As soon as one ceases to attribute his tumultuous feelings to passion, love should die [1971, pp. 90–91] (wrong)

Even negative experiences can induce love, because they intensify the component of arousal. For example, the presence of fear or misery can facilitate one's experiencing of love or, at least,

can increase sexual attraction. There is both anecdotal evidence and research support for this effect (Brehm, Gatz, Goethals, McCrimmon, & Ward, 1970). As an example of the first type of evidence, Bertrand Russell, in his autobiography, indicated how an irrelevant, but frightening, event from World War I intensified his passion for his then-current mistress, Colette.

We scarcely knew each other, and yet in that moment there began for both of us a relation profoundly serious and profoundly important, sometimes happy, sometimes painful, but never trivial and never unworthy to be placed alongside of the great public emotions connected with the War. Indeed, the War was bound into the texture of this love from first to last. The first time that I was ever in bed with her (we did not go to bed the first time we were lovers, as there was too much to say), we heard suddenly a shout of bestial triumph in the street. I leapt out of bed and saw a Zeppelin falling in flames. The thought of brave men dying in agony was what caused the triumph in the street. Colette's love was in that moment a refuge to me, not from cruelty itself, which was inescapable, but from the agonizing pain of realizing that is what men are ... [quoted in Walster & Berscheid, 1971, p. 50].

Additionally, Zick Rubin, in his delightful *Liking and Loving* (1973), reminds us that the first-century Roman poet Ovid made a similar observation. In his *Ars Amatoria (The Art of Love)*, Ovid noted that an excellent time for a man to arouse passion in a woman was while she was watching the gladiators disembowel each other in the arena.

Ovid never sought any further empirical evidence for this conclusion, but a much more recent study by Dutton and Aron (1974) has. In what is probably the first study conducted on a wobbly suspension bridge over a canyon, Dutton and Aron had a female interviewer request that males crossing the bridge fill out a brief questionnaire and compose a story based on one of the pictures from the Thematic Apperception Test (TAT). Subjects did this as they stood on the narrow wooden bridge that tilted and wobbled over the rocks 230 feet below. The researchers assumed that such a condition would create fear; they were curious about whether such a reaction would heighten sexual attraction. Such a possibility was confirmed in two ways, using comparisons with another group of male subjects interviewed by the same woman as they crossed a solid, sturdy bridge upstream, which crossed a small stream only 10 feet below it. The fear-arousal subjects showed more sexual imagery in their TAT stories; they were also more likely to contact the female interviewer later. (She had given each subject her name and phone number in case he wanted more information.) Nine of the 18 subjects in the high-fear condition called, while only 2 of 16 in the low-bridge condition did. Thus an unrelated frightening event, which maintains heightened arousal, does seem to be related to increased sexual attraction.

Arousal can be stimulated by an irrelevant emotion that has either a positive or a negative nature. The earlier study by Valins (1966) of reactions to *Playboy* nudes is appropriate here. Men whose heartbeat apparently increased when looking at certain photos of unclad females later rated those photographs as more attractive than did men who did not experience perceptions of an increased heart rate. The false feedback gave meaning to the feelings experienced by the subjects.

All this led Walster and Berscheid to emphasize the role of *labeling* in determining the presence of romantic love. Love does not exist unless the lover defines it as such. If the appropriate cognitions are present, almost any form of heightened arousal can lead the person to label his or her emotion as love. Let us spell out some implications.

First, people are more likely to label their emotions as love if the cognitions are appropriate. For example, consider two male college freshmen who have participated in a computer-dating project. Each male is assigned to one of two identical twins, each of whom is strikingly beautiful but acts in a rather neutral way toward her date. Each young woman talks very little,

expresses very little emotion, yet does not discourage her date in any way. Let us also say that the two males have been told different things about their dates. One is told: "Even though your computer-matched date appears to be rather shy and inexpressive, we are absolutely convinced that she is quite attracted to you." The other is told: "If your date appears shy and inexpressive it means that she is not attracted to you at all." Each couple then goes to a double-feature movie, which includes an X-rated film. As he watches the love-making in the film, each male feels emotion—he gets warm; his face flushes; there may even be sexual arousal. How does he label his emotion? Our guess is that the two freshmen will label the same reaction differently. For one, it may be sexual desire or passionate love; for the other, the reaction will more likely be labeled as embarrassment. The basic difference underlying these different labels is the set of cognitions held by each male in regard to how much his date likes him.

Let us look at other implications of Walster and Berscheid's emphasis on labeling. Some of the exercises involved in **sensitivity training** may lead to arousal. For example, a male and female may be paired off and asked to stare into each other's eyes or may have to touch one another while blindfolded. Again, an excited heartbeat or a feeling of blood rushing to the head may occur. Sexual arousal may even result. Does the person attribute his or her feelings to passionate love? Most probably, he or she would say: "I don't know this person. I don't even know the person's name. How could I be in love?" In short, the cognitions drawn from the situation are inappropriate for labeling the feeling as romantic or passionate love, even though emotional arousal may be present to a high degree. Thus, some other label is sought.

E. Conclusions

In 1958, Harry Harlow, a psychologist, wrote "So far as love or affection is concerned, psychologists have failed in their mission. The little we know about love does not transcend simple observation, and the little we write about *of course.* it has been written better by poets and novelists" (1958, p. 673). After reading this section on love, some readers may conclude that Harlow's statement is still essentially accurate. But there are reasons for optimism. More social psychologists have come to recognize the inadequacies of past research efforts, and the topic is no longer an area restricted by taboo. Interdisciplinary research efforts are being encouraged. Even though it is recognized that no variable is more difficult to define and measure than love, there is increased commitment to studying its important aspects. Social psychologists are beginning to follow Abraham Maslow's mandate: "We must understand love; we must be able to teach it, to create it, to predict it, or else the world is lost to hostility and to suspicion." *only one real way to "create" love.*

VII. Summary

The need to affiliate, or to be with others, is an exceedingly strong one in some individuals. Two reasons for joining a group are (1) that the group is a means to an end and (2) that the group is an end in itself. For example, group membership provides a means for self-evaluation through social comparison.

Under conditions of increased situational anxiety, there is a greater desire to be with others. This is particularly true of persons who are firstborn or only children.

When waiting with others in anticipation of an anxiety-producing event, the typical firstborn person will become less anxious than had he or she been left alone. The presence of others has no such general effect on anxiety reduction in later-born subjects.

Schachter's theory emphasizes the cognitive determinants of emotional states. Emotions are labeled on the basis of physiological arousal plus cognitive factors—the latter being influenced by the situation. Individuals differ in their utilization of internal sensations as cues for developing labels for behavior.

The following factors make another person more attractive to us: similarity of personality, values, or beliefs; complementarity of needs; competence; pleasant or agreeable characteristics or behavior; physical attractiveness; reciprocal liking; and propinquity. Reinforcement theory proposes that we are attracted to people who reward us. There are many cases in which this theory is accurate, but there are also cases in which it does not apply.

Love is conceptualized as being qualitatively different from liking. It is long lasting and includes components of both sexual desire and tenderness.

Romantic love is not a static phenomenon; it grows and wanes for a variety of reasons. One situational determinant of the intensity of romantic love experienced by a couple is the degree of parental influence. Heightened parental interference intensifies the feelings of love.

Explanations of the determinants of romantic or passionate love capitalize on Schachter's two-factor theory of emotion. For instance, Walster and Berscheid have proposed that a person labels his or her feelings as passionate or romantic love if (1) there exists a state of physiological arousal and (2) his or her cognitions are appropriate.

I. The multitude of problems in studying sexual behavior

II. Sexual development and identity
  A. Gender attribution versus choice of sexual partner
  B. Transsexualism
  C. Choice of a homosexual partner
  D. Bisexuality
  E. Sexual aspects of our conceptions of masculinity and femininity

III. Mistaken beliefs about sexual physiology and response

IV. Heterosexual behavior
  A. Kinsey's studies of male and female sexual behavior
  B. Hunt's more recent survey
  C. Changes in sexual attitudes and behavior among college students

V. Social influences on sexual behavior
  A. Erotic stimuli
  B. Environmental effects

VI. Summary

The social psychology of sexual behavior

6

Our sexual behavior is essentially the result of our attitudes toward sex; and these attitudes, in turn, are a product of how we have been brought up.

Allen Fromme

Sexual relationship is an interpersonal relationship, and as such is subject to the same principles of interaction as are other relationships.

Lester A. Kirkendall
R. W. Libby

Human sexuality deserves a place in a social-psychology textbook because sexual identity and behavior are social phenomena. Our sexual attitudes and behavior are controlled by social practices and social expectations; norms and standards apply to sexual behaviors just as they do to any other essential social behaviors. This remains true even today, at a time when it is claimed that there is a revolution in sexual standards.

A second reason that sexuality is an appropriate topic for a social-psychological text is that our assumptions about human nature include beliefs about people as sexual beings. Freud deserves credit (or discredit, some would say) for

A chapter on this topic for the first edition of this book was authored by Gilbert R. Kaats and Keith E. Davis. Portions of that material, in revised form, are included here. The chapter in the first edition was, to the best of our knowledge, the first of its kind in any textbook on social psychology. Drs. Kaats and Davis are acknowledged for their groundbreaking contribution.

stating that sexuality is at the center of human concerns (Gagnon & Simon, 1973). For good or ill, our society reminds us daily of the salience of our sexual nature. Figure 6-1 illustrates just some of the ways that sexual needs, sensuality, and sexual relationships are promoted in our society. Beyond that immense fact, we use our perceptions about the sexual nature of others to form overall impressions of them. Such descriptions as "he's on the make," "she's a flirt," or other evaluations too extreme to mention here reflect the centrality of sexual orientation in determining our reactions to others. Also, rightly or wrongly, we label people as "deviant" or "healthy" on the basis of what we know of their sexual proclivities.

Our assumptions reflect our recognition that the expression of sexual attitudes and behavior has dramatic effects on individuals and the society at large. For this reason, society has long regulated our sexual behavior through its laws, mores, and expressions of morality. Consequent-

Figure 6-1
The salience of sexuality in contemporary society. (Photo by Jim Pinckney.)

ly, sexual practices can lead to crippling feelings of guilt and shame, to scandal, to blackmail, to forced marriages, or to arrest and commitment in mental institutions. But on the positive side, sexual activities can lead to increased self-confidence, feelings of fulfillment, and some of the deepest of human emotions. Sexual behavior can enhance marriage and other relationships, and, of course, it is essential for the survival of the species. The gratification of few other needs has such important consequences for the individual or the society. (Sex is not just for gratification)

Sexual behavior is also fundamentally social in that it has a *symbolic value*, making it capable of fulfilling many other desires and needs. The fact that a man is eating a hearty meal is no guarantee that he is hungry; engaging in sexu-

al intercourse does not indicate what needs the participants are satisfying. Kaats and Davis (1972) noted some of the possibilities. One is *assaultive* sexual behavior, which can result in heinous crimes against another person. *Pathological* sexual behavior, of which the assaultive type may be a subvariety, is a manifestation of some deeprooted neurotic or psychotic disturbance. *Utilitarian* sexual behavior is the use of sex for materialistic or social gains; it includes not only prostitution but also the subtle manipulation of another person for personal gain.

But these are not the only needs met by sexual activity. *Ego sexual behavior* serves one's own psychological needs and is often a way of proving one's masculinity or femininity. There is also *recreational* sex, in which a meaningful relationship exists and sexual behavior is enjoyed as an extension of the participants' liking or caring for each other. This type is not an expression of love in the deepest sense, nor does it include the formal commitments of engagement or marriage. Recreational sexual behavior goes beyond physical gratification in that the nature of the relationship is important, but it falls short of *love* sex. The latter type of sexual behavior represents the expression of some of the deepest of human emotions and is, for many persons, the prerequisite for engaging in sexual intercourse. In contrast, *reproductive* sexual behavior need not necessarily be an aspect of *love* sex, although it most frequently is. For example, Kaats and Davis note that some people may engage in reproductive sex almost exclusively because they hope that creating children will "save our marriage" or "bring us closer together." Unmarried participants may use it as a way of getting a husband or wife.

I. The multitude of problems in studying sexual behavior

Despite our irrepressible sexual habits and their pervasive effects, science has been quite timid in the past in investigating sexual attitudes, behavior, and physiology. For many years, sexual behavior was a taboo topic for the social scientist. Even the teaching of college-level courses on human sexuality is a development of the last decade and a half. Other than a course on sex taught at Indiana University many years ago by the famous sex researcher Alfred Kinsey, apparently the first college course with a title like "human sexuality" was initiated in 1964 by James L. McCary at the University of Houston. The community hostility toward the public discussion of such topics at that time—a little more than a decade ago—is reflected pungently in one of the many letters Dr. McCary received. It reads:

Dear Sir:

I want you to know that as a Christian I resent what you are teaching them boys and girls at that university. Furthermore, I am going to write

the school trustees and let them know what you are doing. I hope you burn and suffer on doomsday, you son-of-a-bitch.
Sincerely yours,
Mr. _____

[Reprinted in McCary, 1975, p. 17.]

One of the reasons that the topic of human sexuality suffered "benign neglect" is that very few investigators were willing to cope with the problems and accusations generated by doing that type of research (Zuckerman, 1971a). It is sadly true that the researcher's decision to study sexual behavior is often interpreted by others as an indication that his or her own sexual behavior is deviant.

Even if a researcher is courageous enough to study sexual behavior while accepting the stigma of doing so, he or she then faces the very likely outcome that the project's findings may overturn people's assumptions about sex and challenge deeply held values and beliefs. Such new findings are not always popular, and society has a tendency to punish the bearer of tidings that conflict with cherished assumptions. Yet the basic principles of science are a commitment to objectivity and a responsibility to disseminate discoveries and findings. What if such actions conflict with the values of society?

For example, we are all aware of the substantial body of research suggesting that one of the most important sources of influence is our peer group. Our clothes, hair styles, modes of speech, and much of our behavior is in step with what is done by our peers (or some subgroup of peers). Recent research has found that women in college tend to underestimate how many of their friends have had sexual intercourse; they also tend to *over*estimate the extent to which their friends would disapprove of them for engaging in such behavior. When such findings are publicized and young women discover the more tolerant attitudes and permissive behavior of their peers, it could remove one source of restraint and lead to more widespread premarital intercourse. Some elements in our society would find such a development disturbing and might seek to punish the scientist "responsible" for it.

The problem of the policy implications in respect to research on sexual behavior also points out the necessity for researchers and disseminators to be scrupulously careful in conducting their projects and reporting their findings. Erroneous data may mislead other researchers as well as the average citizen. One must also be careful to avoid the strong temptation to outrun the data and assume the role of an expert.

An example of succumbing to this temptation is David Reuben's famous book *Everything You Always Wanted to Know about Sex but Were Afraid to Ask*. The book became an immediate best seller when it was published in 1969, and it continues to be referred to quite frequently. Although there is some correct information in the book, the author often generalizes from his personal experience as a psychiatric practitioner. His discussions of homosexuality, prostitution, and impotence reflect his personal values more than the latest research. Table 6-1 lists some of his statements and compares them with what the evidence actually indicates. You might note that Reuben tends to put down any type of sexual

Table 6-1
David Reuben versus the research findings

As a popular guide, the book *Everything You Always Wanted to Know about Sex but Were Afraid to Ask* has been highly successful. Unfortunately, it makes many statements that contradict the empirical evidence (Rollin, 1972). Some of these are listed below:

Dr. Reuben says:

1. About 70% to 80% of Americans engage in simultaneous cunnilingus and fellatio.

2. The best douche available for women is Coca-Cola.

3. After the penis is within the vagina, the woman can, by muscle movements, stroke the penis from tip to base.

4. Gentle stroking of the pubic area of a female initiates erection of the clitoris.

5. There is always bleeding when the hymen breaks.

6. Since the precise moment of orgasm usually brings on the lapse of consciousness, neither partner is able to enjoy the orgasm of the other.

The evidence indicates:

1. Actual rates of *simultaneous* actions are not available. Recent reports of either separately indicate rates of 45% to 65%.

2. Such a procedure could lead to peritonitis, or even to gas embolism, causing death.

3. Masters and Johnson's research indicates that this action is impossible for most women.

4. Masters and Johnson state: "The clitoris does not erect under direct or indirect forms of stimulation." This is a well-established fable usually used in pornography.

5. Innumerable women have lost their hymens without overt evidence of bleeding.

6. Most men and women do *not* lose consciousness during orgasm.

behavior that differs from what—in his personal view—is healthy; he also suggests that psychiatry is the cure-all for sexual problems. Reuben often uses extreme or infrequent cases or problems as examples, without giving the reader any indication of the range, frequency, or variance of such problems. By mixing facts with his own personal opinions that appear to be facts, his book probably has caused some readers anxieties and made them feel less adequate as sexual partners.

For these and other reasons, our society has been in the curious position of knowing very little about something on which it has traditionally placed a great deal of emphasis. Even physicians are often uninformed; as recently as 1967, only 3 of 103 medical schools in the United States offered courses in sexuality (McCary, 1975). Certainly this lack of information did not result from a lack of need for it. Indeed, we have a number of staggering social problems related to sexual behavior.

But slowly the picture has begun to alter, and some impressive changes have occurred in the past two decades. The distinctions between homosexuality, transsexualism, and transvestism are being studied and better understood. Sex-reassignment operations are being performed within legal bounds. Freud's misguided conception of the sexuality of women, long accepted because it was the only theory we had, has been refuted by research on the physiology of sexual behavior. Traditional conceptions of the deleterious effects of pornography are finally being tested in the real world. So are the effects of drugs on sexual arousal and satisfaction. In this chapter we consider each of these developments as it relates to the social-psychological nature of sexual activities.

II. Sexual development and identity

Two of the most emotion-laden tasks in the socialization process are conceiving of oneself as male or female and making the appropriate

choice of a sexual partner. The emotional significance of these processes is revealed in many ways, including the everyday language of insults. To speak of a boy or man as a "sissy," a "fag," or a "queer" or to call a girl or woman a "butch" or a "dyke" is to denigrate that person and, often, to express one's personal disgust.

A. Gender attribution versus choice of sexual partner

In dealing with the topic of sexual development, it is important to distinguish between one's **gender identity** and one's *choice of a sexual partner*. Gender identity refers to one's self-awareness of being male or female (Money & Ehrhardt, 1972), whereas one's choice of a sexual object (or partner) indicates the sex of persons to whom one is sexually attracted. One reason that this distinction is so important is the homosexual object choices, contrary to some popular beliefs, do not imply that the chooser's gender identity is necessarily male or female. A given male may feel adequate in his own manliness, for example, and still prefer men as lovers. *Something is really wrong or sick somewhere though.*

B. Transsexualism

The case in which one's gender identity is in opposition to one's bodily appearance and sexual organs is called **transsexualism** (Benjamin, 1966; Green & Money, 1969). Transsexual persons are convinced that they belong to the other[1] sex than the one as which they are labeled, and they are driven by a compulsion to have the body, appearance, and status of the other sex (Money & Ehrhardt, 1972).

It is important not to confuse transsexual persons with those who possess ambiguous sexual anatomy. For example, **hermaphrodites** have,

[1]We realize that the other sex is usually referred to as "the opposite sex." Such an expression makes a subtle—perhaps insidious—assumption that women and men are basically different. We prefer the term "other" because it leaves open the degree of *similarity* between the sexes.

in varying degrees, a mixture of male and female bodily organs and hormonal patterns, so that their sex cannot be clearly defined as entirely female or entirely male. In contrast, the bodily development of transsexuals is apparently normal and they do not deny this anatomical reality; their complaint is instead a plea that "I am a female soul trapped in a male body" (Person & Ovesey, 1974, p. 5).

Despite the fact that many transsexuals dress up as if they were members of the other sex and engage in sexual intercourse with members of the same sex, they differ from both transvestites and homosexuals. While *transvestites* are sexually aroused by wearing clothing appropriate for the other sex, they never believe themselves to be members of the other sex (Prince & Butler, 1972). In contrast to *homosexuals*, who prefer those of their own sex as sexual partners, the transsexual man, feeling like a woman and calling himself by a woman's name, wants to have a man admire "her" and make love to "her" (Money & Brennan, 1969). The use of the male example is defensible in light of the fact that transsexualism is more frequent in men than in women (Brown & Lynn, 1970).

The proposed causes of transsexualism are many, but proofs are few (Hoenig & Kenna, 1974). Organic causes cannot be ruled out (Blumer, 1969), but psychogenic reasons are more frequently offered (Stoller, 1964). For example, noting that infants of both sexes are attached to their mother or mother-substitute early in life, Brown and Lynn (1970) speculate that transsexualism predominates in males because some males fail to shift from this initial identification to one with the father or father-substitute. In some cases the parents may convey to the child their disappointment that they did not have a child of the other sex (Stoller, 1964). They may even deliberately treat the child in a manner appropriate for the other sex.

The limited research indicates to us that in most cases the biologically determined sexual classification of the infant is a correct one. But for some reason the child learns the personality and role of the other sex. A male transsexual can learn gestures, a voice quality, and a gait that are quite feminine. His adaptation reflects his assumptions about the feminine role. For example, Money and Primrose observe: "His [the male transsexual's] female personality is, in part, his conception of those traits and behavior patterns which typically contribute femininity" (1969, p. 131). But the feelings can be mimicked only so far; Money and Primrose also note that the male transsexual's imitation "excludes traits such as an urge to fondle the newborn or erotic arousal by touch (in contrast to the typical male pattern of arousal by visual or narrative stimuli) because they are normally outside male experience and comprehension" (1969, p. 131). Transsexualism thus seems to reflect the case of a male acting as he thinks a female acts.

Much the same patterns hold for transsexual females. Just as male transsexuals reject the penis and prefer not to use it in intercourse, so female transsexuals loathe their breasts and prefer to take the role of initiator in intercourse. Money and Brennan obtained the following findings in a study of six female transsexuals who wanted to undergo a sex-reassignment operation.

> They scored very low on femininity and fairly high on masculinity on the Guilford-Zimmerman M-F scale. In childhood they had no girlish interests. They were tomboys and prone to fight, usually with boys. Sensory and perceptual erotic arousal thresholds in adulthood conformed more to those of the female than the male, but the imagery of arousal and erotic performance was masculine. . . . Five were living as males. A universal presenting symptom was hatred of the breasts. . . . None of the patients wanted anything to do with pregnancy and motherhood; parental feeling toward infants and children, insofar as it could be estimated, was fatherly rather than motherly [1969, pp. 151–152].

In J. P. Driscoll's (1971) research, a sample of 17 transsexual men were first met when they were dressing as women and engaging in prostitution with men as their clients. Fifteen of the

17 had been raised as girls; all came from broken homes; all had been effeminate in childhood and adolescence; and all learned first to think of themselves as homosexuals, next as transvestites, and finally as transsexuals. A key step in the change in self-attribution was the knowledge that it was possible to have an operation for sex reassignment (often incorrectly called "sex-change operation" in the mass media). Of Driscoll's 17 male interviewees, 12 eventually gave up prostitution and, with hormone treatments and a self-help club, began relatively normal lives as women. Only one, however, had the very expensive operation (costing between $3500 and $12,000) for sexual reassignment and thus became a fully functioning woman.

Most psychiatric specialists (Green & Money, 1969) have come to the conclusion that a change of physical sex structure is preferable to psychotherapy for transsexual persons. One reason is that psychotherapy has proved extremely ineffective in the past, while advances in medical and surgical technology and hormonal treatments have made the successful operation a possibility. It is estimated that more than 3000 such operations have been completed in the United States (Drake, 1974). An artificial vagina can be constructed for men who want to become women. The skin of the amputated penis is used as the lining of the artificial organ, and the new woman may participate fully in sexual intercourse, and, if all goes well, even have orgasms. In reassignment from female to male, the task of achieving a structure that permits some degree of sexual intercourse is a more difficult one. It can be achieved, although erection and ejaculation are not possible. An artificial penis, made from skin taken from the midsection, is fashioned over the clitoris, which has been made larger by hormonal treatment (Drake, 1974).

Perhaps the most famous transsexual was George Jorgensen, who became Christine Jorgensen (1967). Now about 50 years of age, she lives near Los Angeles and lectures on transsexuality at colleges. A more recent case is that of the Britisher James Morris, who became Jan Morris

(see Figure 6-2). He/she had the sexual structure of a boy, was raised as a boy, went to Oxford, joined the British cavalry, married, fathered four children, and later became a very successful globe-trotting newspaper correspondent. For instance, in 1953 Morris climbed 20,000 feet up Mount Everest with Sir Edmund Hillary's expedition. In fact, James Morris would have seemed about as likely as Burt Reynolds to want to start life anew as a woman. Yet Morris claims he/she can recall the moment, as a child, when he/she first felt a desire to be a girl. From then on, life was an agonizing need to unite sex and gender, which was not achieved until the age of 46, when a sex-reassignment operation was completed.

What is the social-psychological relevance of transsexualism? Freud said that "anatomy is destiny," but the evidence of transsexuals indicates that desires, expectations, and other social-psychological considerations can, at times, overrule anatomy. Genetically determined sex, formed at conception, does not inexorably guide sexual development; learning can also play an influential role (Money & Ehrhardt, 1972).

C. Choice of a homosexual partner

Transsexualism is a relatively rare response; perhaps one person in every 50,000 is transsexual. We know that homosexuality is not a rare phenomenon, although accurate estimates of incidence rates are impossible to obtain. In this section we consider homosexuality as one outcome of sexual identity and development.

1. Incidence rates. Given the severe taboos on homosexuality in most U. S. and Canadian communities, we might expect that the available figures would underestimate the actual incidence. Nevertheless, the original Kinsey study found that "four percent of the white males are exclusively homosexual throughout their lives, after the onset of adolescence" (Kinsey, Pomeroy, & Martin, 1948, p. 651). Another 6% of Kinsey's sample reported having been primarily homosexual for at least three years between the ages of 16 and 55. And a considerably larger number of men in Kinsey's sample (37%) had had at least one homosexual experience at some time during their lives.

The number of women in Kinsey's sample who reported having had homosexual experi-ences was considerably lower. For example, only 3% of unmarried women were exclusively homo-sexual (Kinsey, Pomeroy, Martin, & Gebhard, 1953). About 13% stated that they had had at least one homosexual encounter that led to or-gasm. (It should be noted that the latter figure may be an underestimate; there may be many

Figure 6-2
James Morris becomes Jan Morris. As a boy, James Morris prayed daily "Please, God, make me a girl." Unlike most of the transsexuals interviewed by Driscoll and described in the text, Morris was raised as a boy and engaged in active and athletic pursuits (joining the cavalry, climbing mountains, being a war correspondent). Yet at the age of 46 after having spent several years in the attire and life-style of a woman, James Morris became Jan Morris through an operation in Casablanca. (Photo by Bill Brandt.)

orgasm is not the true and complete end of intercourse.

other women who have had homosexual encounters not resulting in orgasm.)

More recently, a comprehensive sample of U. S. adults completed in the mid-1970s (Hunt, 1974) reports somewhat similar incidence rates for homosexuality. Hunt's sample, which we will be discussing at several points in this chapter, included 2026 people in 24 urban areas, generally matching the U. S. adult population in regard to most demographic characteristics. Interestingly, this study was financed by the Playboy Foundation, in an effort to develop a recent and accurate estimate of U.S. sexual attitudes and practices.

According to Hunt's results, homosexuality—although it has increased in visibility—has not become more common in the 25 years since Kinsey's survey. Hunt concludes that some 20% to 25% of males in the United States have had at least one homosexual experience. He also estimates that about one out of every five single women and one in ten married women sooner or later have some homosexual experience. (The fact that Hunt makes a distinction between rates of married and single *women* only reflects our society's emphasis on the marital status of women in our society.) *so unsatisfactory and a gross*

Relatively few people in either Kinsey's or *exp.* Hunt's samples reported being involved in serious, long-term adult homosexual activities; the general estimate for women is from 0.5% to 1% and for men about 2% (Katchadourian & Lunde, 1975). Much of the reported experience is part of adolescent experimentation. Only 1% of the married men and less than 1% of the married women in Hunt's sample reported having had a homosexual experience within the last year. (Of course, even 1% of U. S. married men would mean more than 300,000 people.) For single people, the percentages were 6% for men and 3% for women.

But as important as incidence rates are two conclusions: (1) the number of people who have some homosexual experience is far larger than the number of people who become exclusively homosexual; and (2) people may maintain active heterosexual and homosexual relationships at the same time or in alternation (see the section of this chapter on *bisexuality*.) Choice of a sex object of the same sex is not necessarily incompatible with choice of a sex object of the other sex. M. Hoffman's (1968) research makes it abundantly clear that some happily married fathers who enjoy their heterosexual relations also periodically engage in homosexual behavior. Beyond that, Humphreys's (1975) controversial study of homosexual liaisons in public restrooms shows that there exists a subtype that is represented by married men who do not think of themselves as homosexuals but who allow others to perform fellatio on them in public restrooms. Also, it is a fact that in many prisons, homosexual rape is performed by some older, stronger inmates on younger, weaker men, and yet the initiators do not think of themselves as gay. By raping the other man, they feel they are demonstrating their superiority and masculinity (A. J. Davis, 1968). These are examples of the *assaultive sex* we mentioned at the beginning of the chapter. Finally, male hustlers of the type made famous in John Rechy's novel *City of Night* (1963) typically do not think of themselves as homosexuals, even though they make their living by allowing homosexuals to perform fellatio on them. Indeed, Humphreys (1971) argues that the homosexual world is changing toward a more virile self-image and a more bisexual pattern of object choices.

The variety of actions that fall within the category of *homosexual behavior*, along with the number of people who can comfortably shift their attraction from persons of one sex to those of the other, reaffirm a belief in the malleability of human nature. Assumptions that one sexual orientation is "natural" and another is not are refuted when we examine the diversity of responses across societies or even in the next-door apartment house.

Yet, despite this, our society defines homosexual object choice as "unnatural." Some of those who find themselves engaging in such activities often have great difficulty establishing an unfragmented self-concept. Others become increasingly inner-directed (M. Freedman, 1975).

We consider these reactions in the next section. In doing so, we may seem male chauvinistic, because much more space will be devoted to males than to females. The extent of homosexuality in males is about three times that in females (Cory, 1973); in addition, the research and public focus on male homosexuality is probably *more than* three times as great as that on female homosexuality. Our relative neglect of females is a reflection of our lack of knowledge.

2. Self-identification of male homosexuality. "What am I?" "Am I gay or am I straight?" At first, you might think such questions would be easy for the homosexual person to answer. But because of the stigma attached to this label in our society, there is often great reluctance to call oneself homosexual, even though one recognizes that his or her sexual preference is clearly for people of the same sex. For example, Dank (1971), who interviewed 55 men who are members of a homophile organization, reported that on the average there was a six-year interval between their first sexual feelings toward persons of the same sex and the decision that they were homosexual. Data on lesbian women (Hedblom, 1973) suggests that the same phenomenon exists for them.

There are apparently stages in such self-labeling (Morin & Miller, 1975). First comes a diffuse realization that one is in some way different from the traditional pattern. Yet development of a homosexual identity is frustrated by lack of information about such a role plus the presence of guilt coming from the prejudice associated with the term. At this point many homosexuals seek therapy for their "problem"; but the problem is really one of self-acceptance more than of sexual-object choice (Morin & Miller, 1975). New approaches in psychotherapy seek to help such individuals in "coming out," in accepting homosexuality as a viable life-style and in disclosing their object choice to others. Several people have reserved the term "gay" for those who can accept their homosexual object choice. G. Weinberg (1972) defines a *homosexual* as one with a preference for a person of the same sex,

while a *gay person*, in addition, has managed to reject the negative stereotype associated by our society with being homosexual. Morin and Miller state that males who identify themselves as "gay" possess self-images of being proud, angry, open, visible, political, and healthy and having all the positive qualities not usually a part of the effeminate, limp-wristed, secretive stereotype of the homosexual male.

These authors state that once the stage of self-acceptance is achieved, overidentification as a "gay" should be avoided (Morin & Miller, 1975). The experience of Blacks indicates that there is an optimum level of identification with one's group (Proshansky & Newton, 1968). Militant overidentification as a gay prevents self-actualization and development of a career and a multidimensional life.

Table 6-2
Humphreys's typology of homosexual males

1. *Trade.* These are mostly married men who have little socioeconomic autonomy in their jobs. These men think of themselves as heterosexual but take the inserter role in homosexual acts. (Humphreys's largest category.)
2. *Ambisexuals.* These are often upper-middle-class men who have sufficient security and economic freedom in their jobs to form homosexual groups and to be able to afford to patronize male prostitutes. They have vigorous homosexual and heterosexual lives.
3. *Gays.* These men openly participate in the public world of gay bars and organizations such as the Mattachine Society. They are usually unmarried, think of themselves as homosexuals, and have positive self-concepts.
4. *Closet queens.* These are unmarried, middle-income men who live in fear that their deviance will be discovered. They tend toward patterns of self-hatred and social isolation. Their sexual activities take the form of solitary sexual forays.
5. *Male hustlers.* These men think of themselves as heterosexual but engage in many homosexual activities for pay.

Adapted from Humphreys (1971).

3. *Types of male homosexuality.* In seeking to understand the causes of choosing homosexual sex objects, we need to recognize that no one variable can explain such choices adequately. Most social scientists who have studied homosexuals soon become aware of the very important differences among types of homosexuals—differences that are so marked that it is hardly plausible for all types of homosexuals to have similar life histories or personalities. Even if we restrict our attention to only those men who have "come out"—that is, have acknowledged that they are primarily gay in their object choice and who rarely desire sexual relations with women—we still find considerable diversity (Morin, 1974). Very little of the explanatory work has dealt with these more refined typologies; one such classification, however, is presented in Table 6-2. (See also Figure 6-3.)

Humphreys's classification makes explicit three general variables: (1) *self-label* (as homosexual, heterosexual, or bisexual); (2) *evaluative attitude toward self* (accepting or rejecting); and (3) what we might call *socioeconomic autonomy* (which consists of the relative freedom from detection, along with the monetary power to satisfy one's desires). Since typologies such as Humphreys's have only recently been formulated, their effect has not yet been seen in research findings, which unfortunately lump together all types of persons who are self-designated homosexuals. In the research studies, the trade and hustler types are probably underrepresented, while closet queens probably contribute disproportionately as research subjects because they are most likely to seek professional help.

4. *The personality and background of male homosexuals.* Do homosexual males tend to possess distinctive personality characteristics that are different from those of heterosexuals? Early research, in seeking an answer to this question,

Figure 6-3
The diversity of homosexuals. (Left photo by Peter Gerba; right photo by John Picatti. Both courtesy of Jeroboam Inc.)

made the mistake of using as subjects only those homosexuals who had sought out psychological counseling (Cattell & Marony, 1962; A. Ellis, 1968). It would not surprise us to find that they differed in personality from heterosexuals who were not in need of therapy (Siegelman, 1972). But in a better-designed study, Evelyn Hooker (1957) took 30 men who were homosexual and not seeking psychiatric help and matched them with 30 heterosexuals on the basis of their ages, IQs, and educational attainments. Each man was administered a set of personality diagnostic procedures including the Rorschach Ink Blot Test, the Thematic Apperception Test, and the Make-a-Picture Test. The responses to these personality tests were then evaluated by experienced clinical psychologists who did not know whether the respondent's preference was homosexual or heterosexual. (Such a procedure is called *blind scoring*.) These experts were unable to agree on which subjects were the homosexuals; also, the clinical psychologists did not rate the homosexuals as any less adjusted than the heterosexuals. In both sexual-object groups a wide range of personality types, character structures, and interests were present. Hooker's study leads to a very important conclusion: that homosexuals who are not seeking psychiatric help are no different in personality, as a group, from heterosexuals who are not seeking help. Such a conclusion was perhaps one of the reasons why the American Psychiatric Association in 1973 voted to drop its classification of homosexuality as "a mental disorder" and to reclassify it in some cases as "a sexual-orientation disturbance" and in other cases not even that (see also M. Freedman, 1975). (See also Figure 6-4.)

While the personality-test responses of homosexuals may be indistinguishable from those of heterosexuals, their self-images and remembrances of their parents may be different. For example, R. B. Evans (1969) collected retrospective self-reports of childhood from 43 homosexual males and 142 nonhomosexual males who were not seeking psychiatric help. There was a clear pattern of differences in retrospective reports, supporting a hypothesis that a son is more

likely to become a homosexual when exposed to a situation in which the mother is overprotective and unusually sexually intimate with her son. Such descriptions often picture the father as either uninvolved or actively hostile (the hypothesis is from an interview study by Bieber, Dain, Dince, Drellich, Girand, Gundlach, Kremer, Rifkin, Wilbur, & Bieber, 1962). Supposedly such persons inhibit the expression of masculine behavior in their sons. On the basis of the self-reports he collected, Evans states:

> Specifically, in retrospect, the homosexuals more often described themselves as frail or clumsy as children and less often as athletic. More of them were fearful of physical injury, avoided physical fights, played with girls, and were loners who seldom played baseball and other competitive games. Their mothers more often were considered puritanical, cold toward men, insisted on being the center of the son's attention, made him her confidant, were "seductive" toward him, allied with him against the father, openly preferred him to the father, interfered with his heterosexual activities during adolescence, discouraged masculine attitudes, and encouraged feminine ones. The fathers of the homosexuals were retrospectively considered as less likely to encourage masculine attitudes and activities, and the homosexual subjects spent little time with their fathers, were more often aware of hating him and afraid he might physically harm them, less often were the father's favorite, felt less accepted by him, and in turn less frequently accepted or respected the father [R. B. Evans, 1969, p. 133].

Figure 6-4
A doctor writes to a mother about her homosexual son. Can you guess the name of the doctor writing the letter?

April 9, 19___

Dear Mrs. _____,

I gather from your letter that your son is a homosexual. I am most impressed by the fact that you do not mention this term yourself in your information about him. May I question you, why do you avoid it? Homosexuality is assuredly no advantage, but it is nothing to be ashamed of, no vice, no degradation, it cannot be classified as an illness; we consider it to be a variation of the sexual function produced by a certain arrest of sexual development. Many highly respectable individuals of ancient and modern times have been homosexuals, several of the greatest men among them (Plato, Michelangelo, Leonardo da Vinci, etc.). It is a great injustice to persecute homosexuality as a crime, and cruelty too. If you do not believe me, read the books of Havelock Ellis.

By asking me if I can help, you mean, I suppose, if I can abolish homosexuality and make normal heterosexuality take its place. The answer is, in a general way, we cannot promise to achieve it. In a certain number of cases we succeed in developing the blighted germs of heterosexual tendencies which are present in every homosexual; in the majority of cases it is no more possible. It is a question of the quality and the age of the individual. The result of the treatment cannot be predicted.

What analysis can do for your son runs in a different line. If he is unhappy, neurotic, torn by conflicts, inhibited in his social life, analysis may bring him harmony, peace of mind, full efficiency, whether he remains a homosexual or gets changed. If you make up your mind he should have analysis with me (I don't expect you will!!) he has to come over to [the doctor's city]. I have no intention of leaving here. However, don't neglect to give me your answers.

Sincerely yours with kind wishes,

Dr. _____

As Katchadourian and Lunde (1975) observe, the compassion felt by this doctor is quite apparent. So too is his uncertainty about whether homosexuality is an illness. He first remarks that it "cannot be classified as an illness" but then later contrasts it with "normal heterosexuality." The name of the doctor was Sigmund Freud, as you may have guessed. It was written when he was 79 years of age.

A number of the self-report items from the Evans and the Bieber et al. studies are reproduced in Table 6-3. (Bieber's subjects were patients in psychotherapy, but their responses are quite similar to those of Evans's subjects.) These may tell us more about homosexuals' attempts to justify to themselves the causes for their object choice than anything else. That is, homosexuals know that society considers them deviant, and—as we saw earlier—they have certainly sought explanations of why they are as they are. They know that society "explains" male homosexuality often on the basis of being smothered and overprotected by the mother and ignored by the father. At present there are no data comparing the *actual* childhood environments and experiences of homosexuals and heterosexuals.

Even if there are differences—and we must note that most studies do find that homosexuals *report* more disturbed relationships with parents during childhood (Hooker, 1969)—parental problems do not adequately explain homosexuality. For one thing, as Table 6-3 shows, many heterosexuals report the same kinds of family backgrounds reported for boys who later became homosexual. Second, in too few cases is it clear exactly how the parental practices of those who rear homosexuals differ from those practices that supposedly contribute to other kinds of atypical reactions.

All these facts underline the social-psychological nature of variables that play a role in homosexual object choice. Three very likely components are (1) the source and rewardingness of early sex behavior, (2) peer relations in adolescence and early adulthood, and (3) the social structure of the gay world. M. Hoffman's (1968, pp. 128–153) case studies illustrate the range of contributing factors. In one case, a male adolescent who had been socially isolated and ineffectual at masculine pursuits became friends with another male and eventually engaged in some homosexual acts (mutual masturbation). When such persons discover that these pleasurable acts are classified by society as homosexual, they gradually become confirmed homosexuals. Here, factors (1) and (2) are clearly at work.

Another case is the male prostitute or hustler who starts out merely to make money but who then finds himself the center of attention, favor, and affection. What was initially a

Table 6-3

Differences in self-reports of backgrounds of homosexuals and heterosexual males

Questionnaire Item	Bieber et al. Study				Evans Study			
	Response	Homosexual	Heterosexual	p	Response	Homosexual	Heterosexual	p
Father and mother spent time together	Great deal	1	13		Great deal	16	28	
	Average	42	50		Considerable	53	39	
	Little	36	24		Little	26	23	
	Very little	21	13	.002	Very little	5	9	.23
Mother insisted on being center of son's attention	Yes	64	36		Never	30	18	
	No	36	64	.001	Seldom	37	63	
					Often	16	17	
					Always	16	1	.001
Mother discouraged masculine attitudes/activities	Yes	39	17		Often	5	2	
	No	61	83	.002	Sometimes	21	7	
					Seldom	30	14	
					Never	44	77	.001
Mother's relationships with father/other men	Frigid	72	56		Frigid	12	0	
	Not frigid	28	44	.04	Cold	26	23	
					Warm	63	77	.10
Physical makeup as a child	Frail	50	17		Frail	37	11	
	Clumsy	24	8		Clumsy	14	6	
	Athletic	13	33		Athletic	5	45	
	Well coordinated	13	42	.001	Coordinated	44	38	.001
Played with girls before adolescence	Yes	34	10		Never	9	3	
	No	66	90	.001	Sometimes	49	83	
					Often	40	14	
					Always	2	0	.001

Note: Significance levels based on chi square, with two-fold classifications corrected for continuity. Decimals omitted. Adapted from "Childhood Parental Relationships of Homosexual Men," by R. B. Evans, *Journal of Consulting and Clinical Psychology*, 1969, 33, 129–135. Copyright 1969 by the American Psychological Association. Used by permission.

pragmatic choice may later become a pattern of behavior that leads to higher social status and to more intense and rewarding relationships than could be obtained in the heterosexual world. A handsome stud has a status in the gay world similar to that of a beautiful woman in the heterosexual world. It can be a very appealing status. In such cases, factor (3) seems important. Humphreys's research (1975) indicates that many of the trade homosexuals apparently seek out homosexual release because they have unsatisfactory marital situations and do not have the opportunity or means to get satisfaction from prostitutes. In such cases, their family background as children may be entirely normal. Clearly, no one pattern is dominant.

5. *Female homosexuality.* The majority of lesbians, or female homosexuals, are, like their male counterparts, indistinguishable from the general population in regard to appearance, dress, and mannerisms (Katchadourian & Lunde, 1975). However, there is a greater tendency for pairs of lesbians to form lasting ties and stable relationships. This difference may be to some extent a result of sex differences in role expectations. The lessened harassment of female homosexuals in our society—compared with what men face—may also contribute.

Are the causes of homosexuality in women any different from those of homosexuality in men? Most of the theoretical work focuses on male examples—for example, McCary (1973) says "A boy's parents, wanting a daughter, may have rejected his birth" (p. 372). Certainly the opposite could just as well occur.

Psychoanalytic theory's explanation of female homosexuality utilizes the family's interpersonal dynamics and the quality of life during childhood. Gagnon and Simon (1973), who interviewed lesbians, found two consistent themes emerging: about half of these women reported that their parental homes were broken by death, divorce, or separation, and, second, in almost every case there was a strongly expressed preference for one of the parents. In these cases, atti-

tudes toward the other parent or substitute parent ranged from condescending neutrality to outright hostility. However, the preference for the female parent or the male parent was almost equally divided.

Gagnon and Simon recognize that many of these same conditions are present in the backgrounds of women who opt for a heterosexual orientation. They state:

> Clearly, the term to be underscored is *predisposing.* The question simply stated then becomes: such predisposing factors, plus what, lead to lesbian commitments? And this is a question that is not likely to be answered in any comprehensive way in the near future [1973, p. 191; italics in original].

The fact, mentioned earlier, that female homosexuals do not differ from other females in appearance or mannerism tends to refute the claim that they are "heterosexual rejects"—that is, that they are not sufficiently attractive to "make it" as women (Gagnon & Simon, 1973). Likewise, young girls' being "tomboys" and preferring sports are not correlated with later choice of other women as sexual partners (Katchadourian & Lunde, 1975).

D. Bisexuality

By *bisexuality,* we refer to the object choice of persons whose sexual behavior reflects no clear-cut generalized homosexual or heterosexual preference (G. F. Kelly, 1974). One shorthand label for them is "AC-DC" (for alternating and direct current). Although bisexuality as a lifestyle has received more publicity of late, it has been present for years. Although his figures may be somewhat exaggerated because he sought out some deviant groups, Kinsey reported some degree of bisexual behavior in 33% of the males and 26% of the females he interviewed.

Bisexuality has traditionally been viewed as an indication of an identity crisis or arrested psychosexual development. For example, at one stage in his theory development, Freud interpreted bisexual behavior as a step in the reidentification process that homosexuals completed as they moved toward heterosexual expression. Yet there are indications of a new attitude toward bisexuality emerging in the youth culture. Gary F. Kelly (1974), a counselor, views this new orientation as essentially a hedonistic one in which the sex of one's partner is of little consequence. Others see a bisexual orientation as an advanced state, moving *beyond* heterosexuality, in which the person can respond to and appreciate another as an individual rather than as a representative of one sex. Bisexuality may also be a response to the movement toward "unisex" that seemingly crested in U. S. and Canadian society in the early 1970s. Many traditional differences between men and women are still being changed—in style of dress, in occupation, in language, and in emotional temperament. Men are being encouraged to express gentle, loving emotions. Many women seek to free themselves from the dependent, incompetent image. Bisexuality may be a sexual response that some people make to such changes in expectations.

The presence of bisexuality in our society should remind us of the error in making a dichotomy between homosexual and heterosexual people. We should view sexual preference as a continuum, with some people exclusively heterosexual, a few exclusively homosexual, and many amenable to expressing both orientations. Some of the latter type may be heterosexual most of the time and others homosexual most of the time.

E. Sexual aspects of our conceptions of masculinity and femininity

In our society, a vague sense that one is not the woman or man one ought to be is apparently a more pervasive response than overt homosexuality. Research and thinking within social psychology, in seeking an understanding, have focused on the parental and early childhood antecedents of femininity and masculinity. (It is worthy to note that novels and autobiographical accounts, instead, tend to be concerned with adolescence and early adulthood in both sexes. In them, the issues of being able to win favor and of being popular and respected as a woman or man are central themes.) Unfortunately, very little is known about how the various types of masculinity and femininity measures used in social-psychological research are related to the sexual behavior of the adolescent and young adult. (Chapter 14 will deal with the nonsexual aspects of conceptions of masculinity and femininity.)

Yet, speculating, Kaats and Davis (1972) proposed that adolescents who are worried about their adequacy as men or their attractiveness as women would either avoid the competition of rating and dating or be excessively determined to prove themselves. It is not at all implausible that men who are insecure in their masculinity would either (1) strive to "score" by seducing as many women as possible; (2) avoid the threatening problem by intense dedication to athletic, artistic, or intellectual pursuits; or (3) be more susceptible to the appeals of homosexual love. Rather similar patterns could occur in women. But research has given us little information about how males and females handle their feelings of inadequacy, and we must wait for the future to provide well-grounded answers.

III. Mistaken beliefs about sexual physiology and response

As today's Ann Landers column or tonight's TV situation comedy reminds us, the task of developing an adequate sexual identity can become an obsession for adolescents and adults alike. Yet even those persons who overcome this challenge face another—the misleading information generated by myths about sexual physiology and response. In this context we are reminded of the 19th-century humorist Artemus Ward's statement "It ain't the things you don't know that make you a fool; it's the things you know that ain't so."

Hence we will consider many of these sexual myths in this section; scrutiny of them is appropriate activity for a social-psychological text, because they can be thought of as expectations that influence social behavior. Many of these myths were discredited by the publishing of the results of a seven-year research program on the anatomy and physiology of human sexual response, directed by gynecologist William Masters and psychologist Virginia Johnson. (This team, who later became husband and wife, is pictured in Figure 6-5.)

Figure 6-5
Sex researchers William Masters and Virginia Johnson. (Photo by Bob Levin, Black Star, courtesy of Reproductive Biology Research Foundation.)

Masters and Johnson studied the physiological and psychological responses of men and women prior to, during, and immediately after sexual intercourse and other forms of sexual activity. The recent development of intricate technology permitted them to make observations of even the size of the clitoris and the color of the lining of the vagina during different stages of sexual intercourse. Their study was the first to deal with so many aspects of sexual response simultaneously; that is one reason the findings have provided us so much authenticated information for the first time.

The myth of the male's sexual wisdom. For many readers, this chapter may be the first formal exposure to sex education. Perhaps it will encourage some to look further into the subject, for what you are expected to know or what you expect your partner to know is itself the subject of a widely held cultural myth. As Masters and Johnson (1970) put it:

> The most unfortunate misconception our culture has assigned to sexual functioning is the assumption, by both men and women, that men by divine guidance and infallible instinct are able to discern exactly what a woman wants sexually and when she wants it. *Probably this fallacy has interfered with natural sexual interaction as much as any other single factor.* The second most frequently encountered fallacy, and therefore a constant deterrent to effective sexual expression, is the assumption, again by both men and women, that sexual expertise is the man's responsibility [p. 87; italics added].

Thus both men and women make assumptions about the sexual nature and knowledge of both sexes. It follows that one of the major goals in the understanding of sexual activities is the establishment of lines of communication between men and women so that each may gain a better understanding of the ways in which the other is different and the ways in which both are similar.

On this point, James McCary (1973) writes:

> For a man to become a good sex partner, or a better one, he must first be willing to admit that he does not know all there is to know about human sexuality. Many men, unfortunately, are unwilling to make this admission because it threatens their ego and masculine self-image. Thus entrenched in their sexual ignorance, they stumble along ineptly in their sexual relationships, lending much credence to the French maxim that "there are no frigid women, just clumsy men."
>
> A woman, for her part, often has the romantic yet dangerously mistaken notion that her lover

should anticipate her sexual needs and the unfolding of them with unerring accuracy. She therefore feels that she has no need to verbalize to him what pleases her sexually. Almost every man wants to please his partner. But in his attempt to outguess her, he frequently makes the wrong move and is mutely condemned as an inept lover. And when he does succeed in pleasing her, he is, unfortunately, frequently rewarded only by her silence [p. 149].

The search for aphrodisiacs. Although humans have long searched for an effective aphrodisiac to initiate and prolong the sexual act, their efforts so far have been a failure—at least physiologically. As MacDougald (1973) puts it, "There has been an extraordinary amount of nonsense [written about aphrodisiacs, and] it is evident that there are no traditional 'aphrodisiacs' that can bring about erotic biochemical and/or physiological results" (p. 152). This conclusion appears equally true for such substances as cantharides (Spanish fly) and such "sexual foods" as raw oysters, raw eggs, or truffles. But, even though direct physiological enhancement may not occur, the psychological impact may be significant. Alcohol is an example; it acts physiologically as a depressant that narcotizes the brain, retards reflexes, and dilates the blood vessels, thus interfering with the capacity for erection. In fact, heavy drinking was a frequent trigger of impotence for the males seeking sex therapy in Masters and Johnson's (1970) research. However, although alcohol physically depresses sexual abilities, it also removes feelings of guilt and anxieties about the sexual act—and that often more than compensates for the physiological decrement.

Penis size. Commonplace stereotypes to the contrary, the size of a man's penis has little to do with his sexual effectiveness. For one thing, though there is a great deal of variation in size in the flaccid state, these differences are minimized during erection because the smaller penis grows proportionately larger. Also, the vagina accommodates to any size of penis; and, while

a larger penis does put more pressure on and extend farther into the vaginal barrel, the barrel itself is relatively insensitive and probably adds very little to the experiencing of the sexual act (McCary, 1973). Even the smallest of erect penises can effectively stimulate the clitoris—the structure that is largely responsible for pleasure and orgasm (Masters & Johnson, 1966; R. Wood, 1963). The only qualification is again psychological. A woman who is convinced that she needs a large penis for satisfaction will need one despite the fact that this need is physiologically and anatomically unwarranted.

Masturbation. Hysteria and prohibitions against self-stimulation have been with us for a long time. J. Duffy (1963, 1964; cited in McCary, 1973) tells of the time a century ago when French physicians expressed their concern about a masturbatory occupational hazard peculiar to French seamstresses. The up-and-down rubbing movements of their legs as they treadled their sewing machines often came to elicit orgasms. In at least one factory, a matron was hired to circulate among the seamstresses so as to detect runaway machines as the women became caught up in this "horrible" spinoff of their working task.

Despite centuries of fears, there is not a shred of evidence to suggest that masturbation will cause blindness, acne, insanity, feeblemindedness, the growth of hair in the palms of the hands, or any of a variety of other physical ailments that have been attributed to it. Lest one think that we are exaggerating the myths about the dangers of masturbation, as recently as 1959 Lief found that "a study of medical students from five Philadelphia medical schools revealed that half of them thought—after three or four years of medical school—that masturbation itself is a frequent cause of mental illness. Worse yet, a fifth of the medical school faculty members shared the same misconception" (1966, p. 276).

However, Masters and Johnson (1970) did conclude that youthful sexual experiences that were accompanied by an emphasis on *speed* of ejaculation often led to problems of premature ejaculation in adulthood.

Frequency of sexual activity. There is no evidence to suggest that frequent sexual activity during one's younger years causes one to lose capacity for sexual response. The male is capable of an infinite number of ejaculations, and semen replaces itself as easily as saliva (I. Rubin, 1966). Few people have complained that getting hungry and salivating too often will consume their supply of saliva. In fact, the person who is more active in his or her earlier years will remain more active later in life as well (Kinsey et al., 1948, 1953; I. Rubin, 1966). This is not to suggest that one can *prolong* his or her sexual life by engaging in sex more frequently and at an earlier age. No doubt both tendencies reflect a higher sex drive to begin with. In any case, the evidence casts further doubt on the myth about "burning out."

Two types of orgasm in women. Primarily as a result of Freud's speculations, a widespread conception developed that there existed in women two types of orgasm: clitoral and vaginal. Vaginal orgasm was assumed to be the only psychologically mature type of orgasm, whereas clitoral orgasm was felt to be the result of an inhibition of full sexual expression, brought about by some neurotic problem. Although a number of psychiatrists and psychoanalysts still maintain Freud's point of view, Masters and Johnson's (1966) research suggests that there is no difference between the two. Both are involved in orgasm, and, if anything, the clitoris plays the major role.

Beyond that, the use of different types of stimulation in Masters and Johnson's research showed that the physiological experience of orgasm for the woman was the same whether it was generated by an inserted penis, by a vibrator used by herself or by someone else, or by stimulation of the clitoris. To put it physiologically, "an orgasm is an orgasm is an orgasm." Of course, the source of the stimulation may make

an immense difference in the *psychological* satisfaction experienced. (and thus the vocal physical satisfaction)

Single versus multiple orgasms. Conventional beliefs have always held that a person cannot experience more than one orgasm during one act of sexual intercourse. However, the physiological recordings of Masters and Johnson (1966) indicate that many women, at least, are capable of many orgasms during a single act of intercourse. McCary (1973) has also made the following observation.

> Although men supposedly possess a stronger sex drive, they are not nearly so capable as women of multiple orgasms. Only about 6% to 8% of men are able to have more than one orgasm during each sexual experience, and when the capacity for multiple orgasm exists, it is usually found only in very young men.... Those men who have a second orgasm shortly after the first relate the pleasure of the first is superior to that of the second, in direct contrast to women's subjective reports [p. 195].

Some contemporary writers have criticized the stress placed on orgasm—particularly simultaneous orgasm—that was found in earlier sexual and marriage manuals (A. Ellis, 1960; McCary, 1973). Such earlier viewpoints encouraged many people to use orgasm as a yardstick of personal sexual adequacy or as a measure of the depth of a relationship. Often this objectification tends to pervert the sexual act and gives birth to some rather self-defeating, vicious circles.

Sex as a barometer. We hope and assume that only a very small percentage of marriages begin with sexual problems. Consequently, many couples have used their sexual performance as a barometer of the relationship, or an indication of how they really feel about each other. Such a conclusion is not always justified. As Golden (1971) concludes: "There are couples for whom the only good thing in marriage is sex. And there are sexless marriages which are satisfactory to husband and wife. But both these situations are rare. Usually in a discordant marriage the sex life is unsatisfactory, too" (p. 185). But Golden, as well as some other observers, believes that sexual maladjustments are more likely to be a *result* of interpersonal difficulties. This, however, does not make the converse true; "poor sexual adjustment does not mean that a marriage is going to be shattered or even that the marriage is unhappy" (Golden, 1971, p. 167). And we must remember, as indicated in Chapter 2, that correlation does not imply causality. For that matter, both sexual and interpersonal difficulties may be caused by some third factor such as a temporary stressful situation resulting from loss of job, presence of in-laws in the home, or health worries.

Kaats and Davis (1972) remind us that using sex as a barometer can be a hazardous process and can cause a great deal more difficulty than is warranted. Again, a self-fulfilling prophecy may be instituted here. The most realistic approach is to consider carefully whether sexual maladjustments reflect any other difficulties or whether they represent a problem of their own.

On the basis of a variety of sources (Benjamin & Masters, 1964; Masters & Johnson, 1966, 1970; McCary, 1971, 1973; I. Rubin, 1966; and R. Wood, 1963), we have listed in Figure 6-6 a number of other popular beliefs that are really more myth than reality. Social-psychological work has collaborated with medical research in shattering these long-standing beliefs.

IV. Heterosexual behavior

Who engages in what types of sexual behavior under what circumstances? By phrasing the question that way, we are again reminded of the social-psychological determinants of sexual activity. In seeking its answer, we are aided by the completion in the mid-1970s of a survey of sexual behavior of a representative sample of United States adults (Hunt, 1974). This study is the first systematic investigation to have appeared since the pioneering Kinsey studies (Kin-

sey et al., 1948, 1953). We also have detailed information about the sexual attitudes and behavior of college students—a state that reflects the greater ease of obtaining these subjects, as well as society's general concern regarding premarital sexual behavior.

A. Kinsey's studies of male and female sexual behavior

Because Kinsey's original investigations are benchmark studies in our society and because they were pioneering efforts in the study of sex in any modern society, their major findings are worth reviewing. A few preliminary comments, however, are important. We must always remember that the Kinsey samples were composed of volunteers, selected from diverse sections of the society; they were *not* selected in a fashion designed to ensure the representativeness of the sample. The data were collected in face-to-face interviews. Although there are many possible methodological artifacts in the original Kinsey procedures (sampling bias, interviewer bias, self-report distortion by subjects, and the like) comparisons between the Kinsey findings and those of earlier and subsequent works have produced generally consistent outcomes.

Men. Some of the more general findings of Kinsey and his associates were that 85% of the males studied had had premarital intercourse, and about 50% of all married males had had intercourse with other women since they married. Also, 59% had engaged in heterosexual oral-genital sex; 37% had had at least one homosexual experience; and 70% of the total population had had intercourse with prostitutes. A total of 92% of all males (96% of college graduates) had masturbated to orgasm.

Women. For women in the United States, the data showed that 64% had "responded to orgasm" by one means or another prior to marriage and almost half (48%) had had premarital intercourse. (This figure is biased upward by the small number of older, unmarried women in Kin-

Figure 6-6

The truth about some sexual myths

1. An intact hymen is not proof of virginity, since it can grow back once ruptured. Since it can be ruptured by means other than intercourse, its absence is also not proof of nonvirginity.

2. There is no physiological or medical reason why a woman should avoid any form of sexual activity during menstruation. Some writers suggest it may even have the advantages of (a) relieving discomfort of menstrual cramps, and (b) satisfying sexual desires, which may be at their peak for some women. However, some authorities claim that it is possible—though not likely—for a woman to become pregnant as a result of intercourse during her menstrual period.

3. There is no physiological reason to suggest that sterilization, by such means as the vasectomy, should either enhance or inhibit an individual's sex drive or behavior. Psychologically, it appears to have an enhancing effect for some by eliminating the fear of pregnancy and by removing the discomfort resulting from the use of other forms of birth control. However, some voluntarily sterilized men report negative effects based on the finality of the act.

4. There is no need to avoid sexual intercourse during pregnancy. Unless contraindicated by vaginal bleeding, painful intercourse, or broken membranes, intercourse can take place right up to the moment of labor.

5. From an anatomical and physiological point of view, there is no best or most satisfying sexual position, such as the male-above position that is customary in Western society. However, different positions, by varying stimulation to different parts of the sex organs, may achieve different degrees of satisfaction.

6. Although an effective diuretic, saltpeter (potassium nitrate) is an almost completely neutral chemical; as a sex deterrent, it is a complete failure.

7. Heterosexual oral-genital sexual activity does not indicate latent or overt homosexuality.

8. Although the data and professional opinions are quite mixed, there is some reason to doubt the assertion that all prostitutes are either sick or frigid. Women become prostitutes for a large number of reasons—many of which are quite rational, such as the need for money or enjoyment of sex.

sey's sample.) More than one-fourth of all women (26%) admitted having had extramarital intercourse. Moreover, 43% of the women had had heterosexual oral-genital sex (62% among the higher educated), and 28% had had at least some homosexual experiences. Over two-thirds (69%) of the still unmarried females in the study who had had intercourse insisted that they did not regret the experience. Another 13% expressed some "minor regrets."

For both sexes, socioeconomic status was one of the most significant variables in predicting incidence of most sexual behaviors. Even though as children they had begun most sexual practices later than noncollege persons, college-educated men and women proved less inhibited in most sexual behaviors and were more likely to engage in masturbation, oral-genital sex, homosexuality, and a variety of coital positions. While differences among religious denominations were not striking, those persons who were nonreligious were more likely to masturbate, to pet to orgasm, and to have premarital coitus and extramarital affairs. Here we have persuasive evidence for the social-psychological contributions to sexual activity.

B. Hunt's more recent survey

The survey carried out by Morton Hunt (1974) more than 25 years after Kinsey's shows some changes in rates of heterosexual behavior. For example:

1. The percentage of persons who reported premarital intercourse increased. Kinsey reported that about one-half of the unmarried women in his survey had had sexual intercourse prior to age 25; the figure in Hunt's survey is 75%. (It should be noted, though, that the sexual partner was usually someone the woman expected to marry.) While the percentage of males reporting sexual intercourse prior to marriage increased only slightly—it was 85% in Kinsey's sample—it was beginning earlier and it was more frequent for the average individual. In Hunt's sample, nearly three-fourths of the noncollege-educated males had engaged in intercourse by the age of 17, and more than half of the college-educated males had. (The comparable figure in Kinsey's sample was 25%.)

2. Use of prostitutes by single men has radically decreased. Kinsey stated that 70% of his male subjects reported it; Hunt's figure is less than half of Kinsey's.

3. Among married people, rates of extramarital intercourse in Hunt's sample reflect much more marital fidelity than we might have assumed in an era of "sexual liberation." Kinsey reported that 50% of husbands and 26% of wives had committed adultery; Hunt finds the rates for males to have decreased slightly (41%), while females' rates have remained about the same. However, those who do engage in extramarital sex do so earlier in their marriages than did those in Kinsey's samples. Extramarital sexual activity continues to be a predominantly guilt-ridden and secret activity; only one out of every five spouses knows about it.

4. The higher divorce rates—twice as high as in 1938—reflect one area in which social liberation has taken place. In addition, while Hunt concludes that secret extramarital sex has not changed much, the rates of sexual activity for divorced persons are far higher than those of divorced persons in 1938. Divorced males in Hunt's sample reported a median of 8 sexual partners a year; divorced women mentioned an average of 3.5. Both sexes reported a median of two acts of sexual intercourse per week.

5. Frequency of sexual intercourse between married partners has increased; comparable averages for those married couples ages 26–35 were 2.0 times per week for Kinsey's sample and 2.5 times per week for Hunt's. Today's couples report much greater willingness to experiment with different positions and with other types of heterosexual behavior besides intercourse. The most dramatic changes are in respect to oral-genital contact; among the college educated, the reported rates for males were 45% by Kinsey and 66% by Hunt; for females, 58% and 72%, respectively. Hunt states that nine-tenths of husbands and wives under age 25 report at least occasional fellatio and cunnilingus.

6. With the increase in sexual activity and the receptiveness to new experiences, it is not surprising that more of Hunt's women report experiencing an orgasm almost always or always during sexual intercourse (Kinsey, 45%; Hunt, 53%). On the other hand, such innovations as group marriage and mate swapping are quite infrequent; only 2% of males and an even smaller percentage of women had reported having participated in them, and many of these had done so only once.

C. Changes in sexual attitudes and behavior among college students

We have reviewed findings for incidence of heterosexual behavior in the general population, with a focus on changes in the last three decades. What can we now say about college students and sexual behavior? Is there a revolution taking place?

Kaats and Davis (1972) point out that there are two problems in answering such a question. First, seldom has any attempt been made to clarify the notion of revolution; and, second, concern has been almost exclusively focused on the percentage of virgins and nonvirgins in the college population. A genuine sexual revolution would have to involve a dramatic change in the principles that guide sexual behavior as well as a change in behavior itself. These principles or standards would involve a specification of what kinds of sexual activities are acceptable with specific kinds of persons (other sex, same sex, self) under specific circumstances (being engaged, being in love, having adequate privacy).

From Reiss's pioneering work (1960, 1967) on premarital standards, it is apparent that the dominant standards in the United States and, by extension, in Canada have been abstinence until marriage or a personal acceptance of premarital intercourse when the partners were in love or engaged. The standard for men—held by both men and women—tended to be more permissive in regard to sexual intercourse, either prior to marriage or in the absence of a love relationship. A sexual revolution would imply, among other things, a dramatic change in judgments about what is acceptable premarital behavior. If current college students have come to view love between partners as irrelevant to the decision to engage in intercourse, then a dramatic change in principles would have occurred. But we conclude that, although attitudes about socially acceptable premarital sexual activity have undergone a significant liberalization, the change is not so dramatic as to justify labeling it a revolution (Athanasiou, 1973). Not as yet, at least, though, as McCary (1973) notes, "there are signs that a revolt looms on the horizon" (p. 273).

Standards of conduct. Reiss's volumes (1960; 1967) are the landmark works on sexual standards. The data for the 1967 book were collected in the United States in 1959 and 1963. Smigel

and Seiden (1968) reviewed work done prior to the studies of Reiss and concluded that 40% to 50% of college men and 9% to 14% of college women had endorsed for themselves a standard other than premarital abstinence. Reiss's studies show a noticeable liberalization. The 1959 sample, which included Blacks and Whites, northern and southern parts of the U. S., and high school and college students, showed that 69% of the males endorsed a standard other than abstinence for themselves and 27% of the women accepted premarital intercourse as appropriate for themselves. The increased permissiveness for both men and women apparently came from an increased acceptability of premarital intercourse when the partners were in love, engaged, or strongly affectionate toward each other.

In Reiss's 1963 national probability sample, one can see a dramatic discrepancy between adult and student judgments. At that time 44% of the student women considered premarital intercourse acceptable if the participants were engaged, but only 17% of the adult women did so. About one-fourth of the student women found intercourse acceptable if the participants were strongly affectionate, but only 12% of the adult women did.

An examination of several other studies conducted in the late 1960s and early 1970s reveals that 50% to 80% of the college men felt that premarital intercourse was acceptable —although only about 65% had had intercourse (McCary, 1973; Athanasiou, 1973). Among the men, acceptance of greater intimacy was related to race, age, semester in college, strength of religious feelings, and region of country: older men who were indifferent or hostile to religion and who went to eastern, western, or southern schools were more permissive than younger, religious Midwesterners. Among college women the crucial factor is apparently being "in love" versus "strongly affectionate." In a series of studies at the University of Colorado (Kaats & Davis, 1970) and in surveys by Freeman and Freeman (1966) and by Nutt and Sedlacek (1974), up to 70% of the women endorsed sexual intercourse for themselves if in love, but 40%

or less found it acceptable only if strong affection existed or only if there was no exploitation. Among college women, acceptance of greater intimacy was very strongly related to having been in love two or more times or to being in a significant dating relationship (going steady, pinned, or engaged).

Despite the very noticeable increases in acceptance of premarital sexual behavior, a newly devised assessment of the double standard revealed that approximately half the men held a personal standard that implied greater sexual freedom for men than for women, particularly when the woman in question was a sister or potential spouse. The data in Table 6-4 show that the double standard is upheld by women as well as by men. Both men and women agree that it is important to them that women be virgins at marriage; both would be less willing to encourage their sister than their brother to have intercourse with someone the sibling loved; both would lose more respect for a woman who engaged in sex without love than for a man who did so; and both have higher standards of sexual

Table 6-4

Mean scores for college male and female respondents on items measuring male-female sexual equalitarianism

Item[a]	Males (N = 110)	Females[b] (N = 162)
1. It is important to me to be a virgin at the time of my marriage.	1.80	3.15
2. Virginity in a prospective mate is important to me.	2.92[c]	1.98[c]
3. If he asked my advice about having sexual intercourse, I would encourage a brother of mine *not* to engage in it before marriage.	2.48	2.63
4. If she asked my advice about having sexual intercourse, I would encourage a sister of mine *not* to engage in it before marriage.	3.47[c]	3.65[c]
5. I would lose respect for a male who engaged in premarital intercourse with a girl he did not love.	2.19	2.87
6. I would lose respect for a girl who engaged in premarital intercourse with a boy she did not love.	3.11[c]	3.80[c]
7. I think having sexual intercourse is more injurious to a girl's reputation than to a boy's reputation.	4.26	4.47
8. I have higher standards of sexual morality for females than for males.	3.52	3.79

[a]Subjects indicated their degree of agreement or disagreement to each statement. The choices were keyed as follows: 1 = strongly disagree, 2 = moderately disagree, 3 = neutral, 4 = moderately agree, 5 = strongly agree. Thus, a mean of 1.80 means an average score close to moderate disagreement (2.00) but a little stronger disagreement than that.

[b]Probability levels based on comparisons between Items 1 and 2, Items 3 and 4, and Items 5 and 6 within each group. Differences between groups on Items 7 and 8 are not significant.

[c]$p < .001$

Adapted from "The Dynamics of Sexual Behavior of College Students," by G. R. Kaats and K. Davis, *Journal of Marriage and the Family*, 1970, 32(3), 390–399. Copyright 1970 by the National Council on Family Relations. Reprinted by permission.

morality for females than for males (Kaats & Davis, 1970).

But people's attitudes may not always be reflected in their own behavior. Athanasiou and Sarkin (1974) report that a substantial number of the respondents in their U. S. national sample felt that premarital sex was wrong but still did not wait until marriage to engage in it. At the same time, as Table 6-5 indicates, there is some correspondence between standards regarding premarital intercourse and the locus of the person's first act of sexual intercourse.

A current viewpoint in regard to standards does not evaluate premarital virginity as either "good" or "bad." Instead, it considers desirability to lie in *congruence* between one's attitudes (or values) and one's behavior (Christensen, 1970). If one "believes" in premarital virginity but engages in premarital sexual intercourse, one's beliefs are discrepant with one's behavior. Thus "it is not the sexual act alone that determines the consequences but, more importantly, how this act lines up with the standards held. Norms and values are intervening variables, not only influencing the behavior, but determining in significant ways, the effects that this behavior will have" (Christensen, 1970, p. 149).

Petting behavior. Heavy petting, defined as stimulation of one or both partners' genitals without clothing barriers, has apparently undergone a significant increase in recent years. The Kinsey report on females indicated that 52% of those women who went to college experienced heavy petting. This figure is from 8% to 40% lower than any figures from studies done in the 1960s or later. In the Packard (1968) and the Luckey and Nass (1969) studies, 61% of the junior and senior college women had had such experience. And the U. S. college women were the most conservative of any from the five countries sampled. (The others were Norway, Canada, England, and Germany.) In the work at Kansas State, an identical percentage was found for freshman and sophomore women; a higher rate, 64% to 89%, was found at the University of Colorado. In the 1969 sample (Kaats & Davis, 1970), 57% of the women had experienced heavy petting in high school.

For college women, engaging in heavy petting is strongly correlated with permissive standards for sexual intercourse, dating status, and perceptions of girl friends as having had coital experience. Among those women who considered sexual intercourse acceptable when in love,

---

Table 6-5
Premarital standards and relationship with other person when intercourse first took place

What Is Your Opinion about Premarital Sexual Intercourse?	Locus of First Intercourse				Total	
	Spouse after Marriage (%)	Fiancé(e) (%)	Steady Date (%)	Occasional Date Partner (%)	Percent	No.
1. It is all right for both young people and adults.	12.5	16.8	39.1	31.5	100	(184)
2. It is all right for consenting adults.	24.4	17.5	30.4	26.6	100	(217)
3. It is all right for couples who share affection.	16.3	19.3	40.0	24.5	100	(135)
4. It is all right for couples who are in love.	19.8	29.1	33.7	17.5	100	(86)
5. It is all right for couples who are engaged.	33.3	51.9	14.8	0.0	100	(27)
6. It is wrong . . . should wait until married.	63.9	9.6	16.9	9.6	100	(83)
(N)	(177)	(142)	(239)	(174)		(732)

From "Premarital Sexual Behavior and Postmarital Adjustment," by R. Athanasiou and R. Sarkin, *Archives of Sexual Behavior*, 1974, 3(3), 207–225. Copyright 1974 by Plenum Publishing Corp. Reprinted by permission.

who were highly involved in a dating relationship, and who thought that several of their female friends had experienced sexual intercourse, all but 6% had engaged in heavy petting, and all but 21% had engaged in coitus. Among college women at the opposite extreme (those who did not approve of premarital coitus when in love, who were not dating anyone special, and who thought that almost all their girl friends were still virgins), only 21% had engaged in heavy petting, and all were still virgins.

Further findings (Kaats & Davis, 1970) on the incidence of heavy petting indicate that 28% of the young women had had experience with three or more partners, 55% had engaged in heavy petting with someone they did not love, and almost 25% had petted heavily with two or more partners they did not love. Thus, very intimate petting is not restricted exclusively to loved ones or those to whom one is seriously committed. Apparently, the experience of heavy petting has become acceptable to a substantial majority of college women (60% to 90%).

Coitus: Women. Three classic studies have dealt with the incidence of intercourse among college women. The first of these was the Kinsey study, which reported that 20% of the 20-year-old college women and 27% of the 21-year-old college women had experienced intercourse. The second classic study was the work done by Ehrmann (1959), who reported that 13% of the women sampled were nonvirgins. And, third, Bromley and Britten (1938) found that 25% of the women in their samples were nonvirgins, with variations among colleges ranging from 18 to 36%. In some quarters, it is regarded as an established fact that no significant change in coital rates occurred in the 1960s, despite the increased ease in getting and using birth-control pills. Yet, such a conclusion will hardly stand up under careful scrutiny. The basis for the conclusion that no more than 25% of college women have engaged in intercourse has come from studies of small samples of students—sometimes composed primarily of freshmen—or studies based on data actually collected in the 1950s.

In their examination of the data, Kaats and Davis (1970) found only two substantial, carefully executed studies (J. Katz, 1968; Robinson, King, Dudley, & Cline, 1968) indicating that rates of intercourse for college women were below 30%. Most of the studies showed that between 35% and 50% of college women have experienced sexual intercourse. In Canada the rate is about the same, around 40% (Perlman, 1973). Perhaps, in respect to sampling college students, the most adequate work is the Groves, Rossi, and Grafstein (1970) study. Their data were collected from 8000 first-semester freshmen and juniors. The relevant findings are presented in Table 6-6. The findings for juniors are most comparable to the previously cited data. The rate of coital experience for junior women (36%) is almost twice Kinsey's 20% figure for 20-year-old college women. The Groves et al. figures are very similar to those of Simon and Gagnon in their as yet unpublished study of approximately 1200 college students. Many other studies conducted at colleges in the 1960s (Bell & Chaskes, 1970; Christensen & Gregg, 1970; Kaats & Davis, 1970) also show that between 30% and 50% of undergraduate females have participated in intercourse.

Not having found the right man, or not having developed an acceptable relationship, is the restraining factor for a significant minority of college women. In Kaats and Davis's studies at the University of Colorado and Kansas State, 10% to 20% of the college women who found

Table 6-6
Percentage of unmarried students who report having had sexual intercourse

	Freshman Class	*Junior Class*	*Combined*
Males	42%	59%	50%
Females	29%	36%	32%
Both sexes	36%	50%	42%

Adapted from Groves, Rossi, and Grafstein (1970, p. 4). Used by permission of the author.

premarital coitus acceptable when one is in love or engaged had not yet experienced intercourse. Christensen and Gregg (1970) likewise found that about 10% of the women who approve of premarital intercourse had not yet engaged in it. If one could safely predict future behavior from current judgments of acceptability, then up to 80% of this generation of college women are likely to have premarital sexual intercourse by the age of 25. This would constitute a significant increase over the Kinsey generation, which had a 47% rate of premarital intercourse for those college women married by age 25.

Coitus: Men. As implied in our earlier discussion, on the surface it looks as if the sexual behavior of college men has remained unchanged since the beginning of the 1900s. Almost all studies of male college students yield rates of intercourse hovering around the 60% figure, with significant regional and religious variations. Somewhat lower rates were typical for college men in the Midwest and for men coming from strict religious backgrounds in all areas of the country. In Canada, the rate is about 55% (Perlman, 1973).

There are, however, two important ways in which men's sexual behavior has changed. We have mentioned Hunt's findings that show that for males the age of first experience has decreased. Thus, though no more men are becoming sexually experienced prior to marriage, those who become experienced do so at an earlier age. Research done at the University of Colorado produced findings consistent with Hunt's survey; it was found that more than half the college men who had experienced intercourse had done so prior to attending college (Kaats & Davis, 1970).

Another way in which patterns have changed is in the psychological and emotional setting of sexual experience. One example is the considerable reduction in the use of prostitutes by college men. Kinsey reported that 22% of college-aged men had used prostitutes. In contrast, Packard (1968) found a rate of only 4.2%, and Schofield (1965) found that only 3% of college-aged males used prostitutes. Nonetheless, men

are still much more likely than women to have their first act of sexual intercourse with someone they do not love.

From these and related findings Kaats and Davis (1972) identified situational and intrapersonal factors that would predict the extent of a person's sexual experience. These factors include the person's own judgment about the acceptability of premarital sex, his or her current dating status (not going steady, going steady, pinned, or engaged), and the perception of whether friends have experienced sexual intercourse. In general, the most powerful predictor of the extent of sexual experience among these three factors is the person's own judgment of its acceptability; this, however, is more true for women than for men. Of the women who reject the acceptability of premarital intercourse even when in love, 92% are virgins, whereas only 61% of the men with this attitude are virgins. For men more than for women, beliefs about friends' behavior is an important determinant. For women, the actual degree of sexual experience is best predicted by their attitude and their dating status.

This approach helps us to specify the conditions that make a woman receptive to sexual intercourse when an opportunity materializes. Specifying these conditions for men is a different matter, since almost half of them accept sexual intercourse even when the two participants have no particular affection for each other.

In light of these findings and others, we may summarize the state of sexual attitudes and behavior in contemporary U. S. (and probably Canadian) college students as follows:

1. Judgments of what is acceptable sexual behavior by both men and women have become much more tolerant, but vestiges of a double standard remain. In other words, both men and women are more permissive in their judgments for men than for women.

2. Even though contemporary college women have earlier and more extensive sexual experience with more partners than did college women a generation ago, the vast majority of intimate behavior remains within the context of relationships involving strong affection or love.

3. The major factors in the decision to engage in intercourse can be classified as (a) a practical opportunity, (b) desire, and (c) lack of inhibitions. Moral considerations apparently continue to constitute the major restraints on premarital sexual behavior, but relationship reasons ("not loving the person") and practical fears (of ruined reputation or pregnancy) also continue to be important.

4. Kaats and Davis (1970) found that women judged as physically attractive were less likely to remain virgins and more likely to have had frequent petting experiences. This finding supports a *meaningful opportunity* interpretation. That is to say, the attractive young woman is the target of more frequent and more sincere romantic interactions; hence, she is more likely to be in situations of mutual love and, thus, is more likely to have more practical opportunity for intimacy than the less attractive young woman.

V. Social influences on sexual behavior

Throughout this chapter runs the theme that sexual behavior is social behavior, subject to the scientific laws that control all forms of social behavior. If we recall the definition of social psychology offered in Chapter 1, we note that social behavior is any action affected by the actual or imagined presence of other people. What effects do other people and the environment have on sexual behavior and the interpretations we give to our feelings? What is arousing? Is the state of arousal influenced by the setting in which it occurs? In this section we consider the specific influences of erotic stimuli, and then other environmental influences on sexual response.

A. Erotic stimuli

Contemporary North American society appears to be obsessed with obscenity and pornography. The use of illustrations and other material designed to arouse sexual desires seems to be increasing exponentially in all the media (Goldstein & Wilson, 1973). Do pornographic materials have the effects feared by those who wish to restrict their availability? What happens when a society decides to withdraw all restrictions on sales of such materials?

First we need to distinguish between the terms **obscenity** and **pornography.** The original meaning of the term *obscenity* seems to have referred to that which was considered publicly offensive and proscribed—primarily derogatory statements about the church and government (W. C. Wilson, 1973). The incorporation of sexual terms and activities within the realm of obscenity developed around the middle of the 19th century; more recent developments in the United States have completed the process by limiting legal obscenity to the sexual realm (Bender, 1971).

On the other hand, *pornography* refers to written, oral, or visual materials that are considered to be sexually arousing. Concern with such materials seems to have increased with the widespread use of printing in the 18th century, with the expansion of literacy in the 19th century, and with the advent of inexpensive, high-quality photographic reproduction in the middle of the 20th century (Wilson, 1973). Technical quality aside, much of contemporary pornography continues to picture humans as possessing only one motivation, and much of current written pornography is, in the words of one critic (Marcus, 1966), mere "organ-grinding." *(oversimplification?)*

If, then, the obscene is what is offensive, whereas the pornographic is what is arousing, we will limit our review to the effects of pornography on sexual response. The study of such reactions is still in its infancy (Mosher, 1973). Much of the research—all of which has been done in the last decade—uses the presentation of erotic or pornographic stimuli under controlled conditions in order to determine their effects on sexual arousal. We can divide the potential effects into the following categories: physiological responses, sexual activity, and sex crimes.

1. Physiological responses. There are several methods used in determining physiological reactions to erotic or pornographic stimuli. After Schmidt, Sigusch, and Meyberg (1969) had male college students in Germany view sexually explicit photos, they asked the students to describe their bodily reactions. About four-fifths of the subjects reported that they had had an erection during the viewing, and almost one-fifth reported the emission of some preejaculatory fluid. In a later study in which both males and females viewed erotic movies and slides (Schmidt & Sigusch, 1970) most of the females reported some bodily reactions in the genital area, including feelings of warmth. (Incidentally, this study, published as recently as 1970, appears to be the first to have used *films* as erotic stimuli—and it was done in Germany!)

Mosher (1973) repeated Schmidt and Sigusch's procedure with U.S. college undergraduates and even used the same films (there was no language problem!). Results were similar; they included reports of moderate levels of sexual arousal and genital changes in most subjects as they watched the films. Of the males, three-fourths reported at least a partial erection, about one-fourth reported a full erection, and 5 of 194 males reported preejaculatory secretion. Four-fifths of the women reported "mild genital sensations," and 35 of 183 reported vaginal lubrication. Both these studies indicated that both men and women can be responsive to some erotic stimuli when they are presented in a laboratory setting. Women, however, reported less response to those films portraying oral-genital activity than did men. (visual response)

Direct measurement of physiological responses leads to similar conclusions. In such studies, the content of urine may be analyzed to determine changes in its chemical composition as a result of sexual stimulation (Barclay, 1970). Measurements of sexual organs may also be done; a device—called the penile plethysmograph—can be attached to the penis to measure its volume and size (Freund, Sedlacek, & Knob, 1965; Zuckerman, 1971a, 1971b), and the female's responses can be measured by vaginal contractions and the temperature of the clitoris (Jovanovic, 1971) or by blood volume and pulse pressure in the genital area (Heiman, 1974, 1975).

The general conclusion of a variety of studies using such methodologies and exposing people to prolonged stimulation through visual media (Hain & Linton, 1969; Heiman, 1974, 1975; Howard, Liptzin, & Reifler, 1973; Loiselle & Mollenauer, 1965; Wegner, Averill, & Smith, 1968) indicates that, as one might expect, the usual initial reaction is physiological arousal, but this response decreases over time, even if the viewing of the erotic material is continued. That is, repeated exposure to such materials reduces their effect (Mann, Berkowitz, Sidman, Starr, & West, 1974). For example, in a study done for the U.S. Commission on Obscenity and Pornography, Howard, Liptzin, & Reifler (1971) and Howard, Reifler, & Liptzin (1973) showed how the exposure to erotic material can be satiating. Each subject (who was a male between the ages of 21 and 23) spent 90 minutes a day for three weeks alone in a room that contained a large and diverse collection of erotic materials, including books, photographs, and movies, as well as some noneretic material. All measures—including the amount of urinary acid phosphates secreted by the prostate gland, penile erections, and self-ratings of arousal—decreased over time. Subjects spent less and less time with the erotic material and even resorted to reading *Reader's Digest.* However, the introduction of novel erotic stimulus materials heightened the response once more.

Sexual arousal can, of course, occur without the presence of such erotic materials in the environment. Self-generated fantasies and other cognitive processes can lead to arousal, and their effects on physiological responses can even be demonstrated in a laboratory setting (Geer, 1974). In such a procedure, subjects are asked to sit in a comfortable chair, to imagine a sexual scene, and to "turn themselves on" by doing so. Following such instructions, after about two or three minutes there are changes in the physiological recording devices monitored in another room—changes such as increases in vaginal pressure pulse and in the size of the penis, indicating that the individual is experiencing sexual arousal.

2. Sexual activity. Exposure to explicit sexual materials leads to a state of physiological arousal, but does it lead to increased sexual activity? Certainly the assumption that it does is behind much effort to ban or otherwise censor pornographic materials.

The usual empirical procedure to evaluate the effects of such material first assesses the sexual activity of volunteer subjects (who may be either married or single); these subjects report the frequency and type of sexual activities they have carried out over the last week or month or six months. Then the subjects are shown erotic materials (usually films) and at a later time—perhaps a day later, perhaps a week—are again asked to report on their sexual activities. Sometimes a control group is also included. The procedural and ethical problems in this methodology should be apparent (Amoroso & Brown, 1971). The use of volunteers may mean that the sample contains too high a proportion of sensation-seeking persons. There may be demand characteristics that influence the subjects to engage in or to report more—or less—sexual activity (or more or less variety) after watching the films. In fact, at least one such study (Mann, Sidman, & Starr, 1971, 1973) did find that the stimulation provided by participating in a study led the subjects (couples married more than ten years) to perform more varied and frequent sexual activities than they had before volunteering for the study. Nevertheless, such findings are more reliable than mere speculation.

The results would surprise those who fear the power of pornographic materials. The rather consistent results are the following: (1) heightened sexual activity for only a brief period of time, such as the night the subjects saw the film (Cattell, Kawash, & DeYoung, 1972); (2) no prolonged report of increased sexual activity over a period of 12 weeks, even in response to four

viewings of sexually explicit films (Mann, Sidman, & Starr, 1971, 1973); and (3) no change in *types* of activity (Amoroso, Brown, Pruesse, Ware, & Pilkey, 1971). Mosher (1973), in reviewing studies by others and himself, offers a generalization that "erotic films lead to increased sexual activity immediately following the films only if there is a well-established sexual pattern" (p. 109). And even those mild increases are not found in younger and less experienced viewers.

3. Sex crimes. The greatest fear claimed by the crusaders against pornography is, of course, that its availability would unleash a variety of sex crimes upon the innocent populace. Fortunately we may rely upon the results of a natural experiment to evaluate this assumption. From 1965 through 1969, Denmark withdrew all laws against the distribution and sale of pornographic materials. As can be seen in Figure 6-7, there has been no increase in sex crimes; in fact, they have declined dramatically (Kutchinsky, 1973). From a rather steady average of 85 cases of sexual offenses per 100,000 inhabitants, the number dropped within three years to an average of fewer than 50 cases. Incidence of new cases of specific types of crime also was reduced; for example, between 1965 (the first year of the legal availability of hard-core pornographic photographs) and 1969 (the year of the end of all criminal penalties; also the year of peak production of materials), the number of reported cases of child molestation in Denmark dropped from 220 to 87.

The Danish experience certainly gives no support to traditional fears that the availability of pornographic material may trigger bizarre sexual reactions in certain maladjusted individuals, leading to their committing sex crimes against others. In fact, as Kutchinsky (1973) observes, the data are so impressive as to offer support to an opposing theory, often called the "safety-valve" theory (Kronhausen & Kronhausen, 1964). That is, potential sex offenders may have obtained sufficient sexual satisfaction through the reading or viewing of pornographic materials, most probably combined with masturbation (Kutchinsky, 1973).

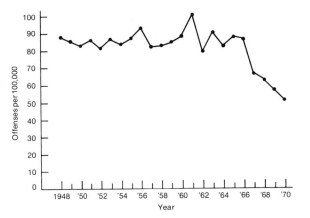

Figure 6-7
Availability of pornography and rate of sex offenses. From 1965 through 1969, Denmark gradually abolished all laws restricting the sale of pornographic books, films, and other materials. The incidence of reported sex crimes dropped after this change. (From "The Effect of Easy Availability of Pornography on the Incidence of Sex Crimes," by B. Kutchinsky, *Journal of Social Issues*, 1973, 29, 163–181. Copyright 1973 by the Society for the Psychological Study of Social Issues. Reprinted by permission.)

(may cause deeper problems, though.)

Probably such empirical data have little effect on those who wish to limit the availability of pornography. They may respond "Still, exposure to pornography can affect *children;* it can lead them to become criminals." What evidence do we have for this claim?

Actually, very little. There have been two studies that relate exposure to pornography during the formative years with subsequent antisocial and criminal behavior (K. E. Davis & Braucht, 1973; Goldstein, 1973). Both studies are retrospective; they rely on adults' remembering and reporting childhood experiences. While the con-

clusions of these two studies are not entirely consistent with each other, neither gives much sup-*but still support.* port for a hypothesis that early exposure to pornography is related to subsequent criminal behavior.

B. Environmental effects

Our subjective reactions to sexual activity can be strongly colored by the setting in which sex occurs. Likewise, components of the setting have great effects. For example, Baron, Byrne, and Griffitt (1974) remind us that music has historically been associated with sexual activity, and in contemporary life the stripteaser, the go-go girls (and boys), and the lyrics of many popular songs verify the association. Yet research supporting this observation is quite limited. Beardslee and Fogelson (1958) report that female and male college students wrote stories containing more sexual symbolism after listening to records of instrumental music that supposedly generated arousing feelings. *(emotions)*

Drugs also have effects. As we noted earlier in the chapter, physiologically alcohol is a depressant that retards sexual arousal. But psychologically it serves as an anxiety reducer, so it releases constraints against exposing oneself to sexual encounters. Marijuana is reported to enhance sexual pleasure and decrease inhibitions (Katchadourian & Lunde, 1975). In their interviewing of heavy drug users, Kaats and Davis (1970) encountered a number of stories suggesting that marijuana seems to drag out time, thus prolonging the subjective experiencing of orgasm and ejaculation and possibly resulting in deeper emotional feelings during sexual activity (see also Athanasiou, Shaver, & Tavris, 1970). In fact, we may not have any empirical data for a while. A study on the effects of smoking marijuana on sexual arousal—funded by the U. S. National Institute on Drug Abuse and to be conducted at Southern Illinois University—was abruptly terminated by an action of the U.S. Congress.

VI. Summary

Sexual identity and sexual behavior are social phenomena, controlled by norms and social practices. Sexual behavior also has symbolic value in the sense that it is capable of fulfilling many other desires and needs.

Sexual attitudes and behavior were not studied much until recently, because of the taboo nature of the topic. This led to a great deal of ignorance about sex, not only on the part of uneducated people but also on the part of physicians, who were expected to be authorities.

In sexual development, we must distinguish between *gender identity* (one's awareness of being male or female) and *choice of a sexual partner.* Transsexualism is the condition in which a person's gender identity is in opposition to his or her physical appearance and sexual structure. Transsexuals are convinced that they belong to the other sex. Some experience sex-reassignment operations, after hormone therapy.

Homosexuality, despite recent publicity, does not appear to be increasing in our society. Homosexuals do not differ in appearance or mannerisms from the general population. The causes of homosexuality are still controversial, but apparently predominant, at least for males, is the mother's relationship to the homosexual during childhood. Homosexuality is no longer classified as a mental illness by the American Psychiatric Association, and some recent therapeutic efforts focus on the encouragement of "coming out," the public declaration of one's homosexuality and acceptance of oneself. For if there is any maladjustment associated with homosexuality, it may have occurred because of the stigma society assigns to that state and the difficulties in resolving one's self-image with that information. *(but it is still wrong, an illness yes.)*

There is a tendency for pairs of lesbians to form more lasting relationships than do male homosexuals. This difference may be a function of sex-role expectations.

Bisexuals are persons whose sexual object choice is not exclusively homosexual or heterosexual. Recent publicity on bisexuality should remind us that distinctions between heterosexuality and homosexuality are false; there is a continuum of sexual preference from one extreme to another.

Some highly popular treatments of sexual behavior contain mixtures of scientific findings and unsupported personal opinions. Masters and Johnson's work on the physiology of sexual behavior has discredited some long-cherished myths, among them the importance of penis size, the impossibility of multiple orgasms, and the supposed distinction between clitoral and vaginal orgasms.

Studies of college students indicate that even though attitudes toward premarital sexual activity have undergone a significant liberalization, the change is not dramatic enough to warrant calling it a sexual revolution.

For women much more than for men, the acceptability of premarital sexual intercourse is still dependent on the experience of love or affection with the sexual partner. Men are much more likely than women to have their first sexual experience with someone they do not love.

Obscene materials are those that are considered offensive, whereas pornographic materials are those whose purpose is to excite or to elicit sexual arousal. Although such materials *are* arousing, their effects are temporary. Satiation continues unless novel types of erotic materials are introduced. The experience of Denmark indicates that the legal availability of pornographic and other erotic materials does not increase the rate of sex crimes; if anything, there is an opposite effect.

The setting in which sexual activity takes place can have great effect on the extent to which it is perceived as satisfying.

PART 3
BEHAVIOR TOWARD OTHERS

I. Definitions of aggression
   A. Aggression: The psychoanalytic definition
   B. Aggression: The ethological definition
   C. Aggression: The social-learning theorists' and experimental social
      psychologists' definition
   D. Differences among the definitions

II. Pro-instinct positions and biological
    explanations of aggression
   A. Orthodox psychoanalysis and neo-Freudian theories
   B. Lorenz and ethology
   C. Territoriality as an instinct and its influence on expression of aggression
   D. Hereditary determinants of aggression

III. Aggression as a possibly innate
     response activated by frustration
   A. The frustration-aggression hypothesis
   B. The instigation of aggression by others
   C. Berkowitz's revised frustration-aggression hypothesis

IV. Prolearning positions
   A. J. P. Scott and animal psychology: Absence of physiological factors
   B. Social-learning theory: Aggressiveness may be modeled
   C. Cross-cultural comparisons: The search for the nonaggressive society

V. A recapitulation and attempt at resolution
VI. Violence and the mass media
VII. Collective violence in society—Yesterday, today, and
     tomorrow
   A. Violence in the past
   B. Changes in violence rates: The problem of assessing crime statistics
   C. The future—How can aggression be controlled?

VIII. Experimental attempts to control aggression
IX. Summary

Aggression and violence 7

Violence is as American as cherry pie.
Rap Brown

Sure we make mistakes. You do in any war.
Police Commissioner of New York City, 1964, after riot in Harlem

In the last 15 years some form of violent mass conflict has occurred between or within 114 of the world's 121 largest countries (Gurr, 1970). Since the turn of the century more than 900,000 civilians in the United States have died as a result of criminal acts. In fact, the United States is apparently the leader among stable industrialized societies in rates of homicide, assault, rape, and robbery.

One could easily conclude from these and other isolated facts that violence and aggression are inevitable facets of human society. Indeed, some behavioral scientists make the assumption that aggression is an inevitable result of some "killer instinct" in human nature. Some of these behavioral scientists assume that aggression is as characteristic in our species as it is in those species from which we have evolved. Other scientists, however, assume that aggression can be completely explained as a result of the frustrations of everyday life or that it is entirely capable of being controlled.

The latter approach—emphasizing a learned reaction—rests upon quite different facts from those presented in the first paragraph. For one, societies do exist in which the commonplace in-

stances of violence—fighting, rape, muggings, and so on—present in our society are unheard of. If one searches far enough, a continuum can be established composed of societies that range all the way from totally warlike to completely pacifistic.

No solitary fact about violence and aggression can be interpreted fully until it is placed in the context of a theory; and when we consider the nature of aggression, we find more than enough theories to go around. These numerous theoretical perspectives differ in the degree to which they assume that instinct plays a role in human aggression. (**Instincts** are unlearned behavior patterns that appear fully in all members of the species when there is an adequate stimulus.) They also differ in the degree to which they see the causes of aggression as coming from within the person as opposed to coming from the situation in which the person lives. This chapter will describe and evaluate three dominant, yet conflicting, assumptions about the nature of aggression—that it is essentially innate, that it is a response activated by frustration, and that it is simply a learned behavior. In addition, the following questions will be answered.

211

1. Is aggression always undesirable or bad, or can it serve adaptive functions? In species other than humans, does aggression serve a survival function?
2. Can examples of entirely peaceful societies be found? If so, why do riots and mass violence occur in some societies and not in others?
3. Is the rate of violence increasing, or has violence always been a prominent part of Western civilization?
4. Does exposure to violence on television and in other mass media encourage the expression of violence in the observer, or does the viewing satisfy aggressive needs so that the viewer is less likely to aggress against others?

Figure 7-1
The costs of violence. Not all the costs of violence, aggression, and war are reported by tabulations of deaths and injuries. Is this man the same person he was before the war? (Photo by Dave Bellak/ Jeroboam Inc.)

Before we look at the multitude of explanations for aggression and violence, some of the semantic problems in this area need to be attacked. A definition of aggression is of the first order of importance.

I. Definitions of aggression

Three theories offer different definitions of aggression and different assumptions about its causes. The psychoanalytic approach sees aggression as an inevitable expression of our energy. The approach of ethology, or the study of different species in their natural settings, sees aggression as serving protective and life-saving functions. The third viewpoint, that of the social-learning theorists and experimental social psychologists, treats aggression as a response to **frustration**. (See also Table 7-1 for another perspective on what is violent and aggressive.)

A. Aggression: The psychoanalytic definition

The orthodox Freudian or psychoanalytic framework assumes that aggressive energy is constantly generated by our bodily processes. For example, any intake of food will eventually lead to the generation of more energy. Aggressive urges, like sexual urges, must be "released"—that is, be expressed directly or indirectly. These urges can be discharged either through socially acceptable actions (such as a debate or some muscular activity) or in less socially desirable ways (insults, fighting, and the like). The destructive release of aggressive urges does not necessarily have to be directed against others; it can be aimed toward the self, as in suicide. (See Figure 7-2.)

Some orthodox Freudians regard aggression as playing a part in ego enhancement, but the typical psychoanalytic view defines aggression as an underlying urge that seeks expression. Hence, aggression can become a problem because it will become destructive to the self or to others whenever it cannot be expressed in socially acceptable ways. Freud believed that one function of society was to keep our natural aggressiveness in its place, restraining its outward expression.

B. Aggression: The ethological definition

The noted ethologist Konrad Lorenz (1966) describes aggression as "the fighting instinct in beast and man which is directed *against* members of the same species" (p. ix; italics in original). According to Lorenz's hypothesis, aggression is not a bad thing in itself; rather, it functions to preserve the species as well as the individual. Fights serve to spread out the species, by reducing the number within a species or by dispersing members over an area so that *the species as an entity* may survive. Through his investigations, Lorenz states, he has found the following:

The danger of too dense a population of an animal species settling in one part of the avail-

Table 7-1
What acts are violent?

A survey of different groups carried out by the Institute for Social Research at the University of Michigan reflects how groups can differ in their judgment of what is a violent act. The percentage of different groups defining certain acts as violence is presented below. ("Reverse discrimination Whites" are persons who, at some point in the interview, expressed fears of being discriminated against by Blacks.)

	College Students (N = 63)	College Degree and over (N = 172)	White Union Members (N = 279)	Reverse-Discrimination Whites (N = 187)	Blacks (N = 303)
Police beating students is violence.	79%	66%	45%	47%	82%
Police shooting looters is violence.	43%	50%	23%	26%	59%
Police frisking is violence	16%	16%	10%	13%	34%
Looting is violence.	76%	79%	91%	89%	74%
Burglary is violence.	47%	54%	67%	73%	70%
Sit-ins are violence.	4%	13%	24%	40%	15%
Draft-card burning is violence.	26%	35%	63%	74%	51%
Denial of civil rights is violence.	54%	45%	40%	42%	70%

From *Justifying Violence: Attitudes of American Men,* by M. D. Blumenthal, R. L. Kahn, F. M. Andrews, and K. B. Head. Copyright 1972. Reprinted by permission of the Institute for Social Research of The University of Michigan.

able biotope and exhausting all its sources of nutrition and so starving can be obviated by a mutual repulsion acting on the animals of the same species, effecting their regular spacing out, in much the same manner as electrical charges are regularly distributed all over the surface of a spherical conductor. This, in plain terms, is the most important survival value of intraspecific aggression [1966, p. 31].

Figure 7-2
Suicide as an aggressive act. The deaths of more than 20,000 United States and 2000 Canadian citizens each year are recorded as suicides; doubtless the number of actual suicides is higher, but many of these deaths are recorded as caused by "accidents" because of the stigma of suicide. Freud interpreted suicide as an aggressive act toward oneself that often was really directed toward others. Many "suicide notes" may seek to induce guilt in those still living. (Photo by Jim Pinckney.)

The dangers of the human population explosion have always been apparent to Lorenz, who supports the notion that increased crowding will lead to increased aggression.

Lorenz concludes that an organism is far more aggressive toward other members of its own species than toward any other species. The basic purpose of such aggression is to keep members of the species separated—to give each member enough area to survive. This intraspecies aggression also affects sexual selection and mating and hence assures the selection of the best and strongest animals for reproduction. In Lorenz's view, aggression becomes undesirable only when the species—the human species, for example—fails to develop the usual instinctual inhibitions against it. Intraspecies fights do not usually end in death, but in acts of appeasement by the loser.[1] If humans had no weapons at their disposal, they would not normally be equipped to kill others of their species. Lacking such innate abilities, the human species has established *no inhibitions.* To Lorenz, all man's "trouble arises from his being a basically harmless, omnivorous creature, lacking in natural weapons with which to kill his big prey, and, therefore, also devoid of the built-in safety devices which prevent 'professional' carnivores from abusing their killing power to destroy fellow members of their own species" (1966, p. 241). What if all killing of other

[1]This is true even for animals as ferocious as wolves. If one wolf triumphs over the other to the point that the loser yields and docilely bares its neck, the winner usually refrains from killing the opponent. A raven could peck out the eye of another raven with one thrust but will not do so. Likewise, animals with idiosyncratic retaliatory powers, such as the skunk, do not usually aggress against other members of their own species in such ways. But sometimes they do. For example, for three years George Schaller (1972) followed prides of lions over the grasslands of Tanzania, in East Africa. Schaller observed several fights between male lions that ended fatally. E. O. Wilson (1973) claims that "murder has been now observed frequently enough in gulls, hyenas, hippopotamuses, macaques, and some other vertebrates to suggest that it is both widespread and, Konrad Lorenz and some other popular writers to the contrary notwithstanding, far more common and hence 'normal' in those species than in man" (p. 466).

people had to be done with our hands and teeth? Would that not only reduce the murder rate but also our desire to kill?

C. Aggression: The social-learning theorists' and experimental social psychologists' definition

In contrast to psychoanalysts, contemporary behavioristic psychologists conceptualize aggression as a *type of behavior*. For example, Leonard Berkowitz, an influential social psychologist, defines aggression as "behavior whose goal response is the inflicting of injury on some object or person" (1969a, p. 3).[2] Aggression, then, may be overt (that is, expressed verbally or through physical action) or covert (that is, not visible, as in the case of hostile thoughts). In Berkowitz's formulation, there is an important distinction between aggression—a behavioral reaction—and the emotional state "which may facilitate and perhaps even 'energize' the aggressive response" (Berkowitz, 1969a, p. 3). This intervening emotional state represents arousal or anger.

D. Differences among the definitions

Each of the three definitions of aggression described above implies a different phenomenon. The psychoanalyst focuses on an unconscious

---

[2]Like any definition, this one elicits borderline examples. Is a nurse acting aggressively when giving a patient a routine injection? No, because the goal of the nurse is not to hurt the patient. But what if the patient has just insulted the nurse, and so the nurse jams the needle in with unnecessary force? Certainly there is a component of aggression in this behavior. What if a woman fights back when an intruder attempts to harm her baby; while this response is adaptive, it is also aggressive. Many examples exist where deliberate acts of harm toward another person occur in the absence of anger (a soldier firing at an enemy on the battlefield, for example). Because of these problems, several writers (Buss, 1961; Schellenberg, 1970) make a distinction between *angry aggression* and *strategic aggression*. The latter refers to cases where others are deliberately hurt, but as a consequence of an attempt to achieve one's own goals.

urge; the ethologist stresses a purposeful belligerence and fighting, particularly among members of the same species; and the experimental social psychologist and social-learning theorist emphasize behaviors that have the goal of inflicting injury on others. These varying emphases must be borne in mind as we proceed to explore the issue of whether aggression is innate or learned. However, the operational definition of aggression used in most of the experiments described subsequently is that of the experimental social psychologist: aggression is an act done primarily to hurt some person or object.

II. Pro-instinct positions and biological explanations of aggression

The psychoanalytic position and the ethological position both assume that the instigation of aggression is instinctual in origin. In this section, these two theories will be described; in addition, an evaluation will be made of viewpoints that emphasize heredity and the biological determinants of aggression.

A. Orthodox psychoanalysis and neo-Freudian theories

Sigmund Freud once wrote "The tendency to aggression is an innate, independent, instinctual disposition in man" (1930, p. 102). Freud was a physician, and his theories of motives and personality were closely tied to knowledge about bodily functions and human physiology. Accordingly, Freud believed that an instinct is a mental entity in the id representing an inner somatic source of stimulation (Hall & Lindzey, 1968); in other words, instincts result from tensions created by biological needs. Expression of aggression is instigated by a "constant, internal, driving force" (Berkowitz, 1965b, p. 304). Aggressive energy thus generated within the body is energy that must be dissipated; it can be either neutralized or discharged (Freud, 1963).

Freud constantly revised his theory, and his more recent followers have introduced further revisions. The **neo-Freudians** have conceptualized aggressive behavior as a part of the ego (or the reality-oriented part of the personality) rather than placing aggression among the irrational processes of the id (Hartmann, Kris, & Loewenstein, 1949). Thus, to the neo-Freudians, aggressive drives are healthy; they are adaptations to the realities of the environment of every human being. This revision of Freud's thought seems to approach the position of those experimental social psychologists, such as Leonard Berkowitz, who see aggression as the result of frustrations derived from the blockage of a goal.

B. Lorenz and ethology

As we indicated earlier, **ethology** is the subfield of biology concerned with the instincts and action patterns common to all members of a species operating in their natural habitat (Eibl-Eibesfeldt, 1970). Much of the work done by the ethologist consists of observing the normal behavior of fish, birds, or animals in the field and attempting to determine similarities and causes in the observed action patterns (see Figure 7-3). As Crook (1973) has stated, in many cases one may justifiably regard these patterns as being under innate or instinctual control. Lorenz (1952, 1966, 1970) has painstakingly observed needlefish, greylag geese, hedgehogs, and Alsatian dogs, noting the characteristic behavior patterns of each species. Without reluctance, Lorenz has applied his conclusions to the human species. However, other ethologists, such as Tinbergen (1968), have emphasized that differences between species may reduce generality and the ability to apply one's conclusions to the more advanced species.

In some ways, Lorenz's approach resembles that of the psychoanalyst. As an ethologist, he uses a hydraulic model of instinctive behavior, in which the expression of any fixed action pattern depends on the accumulation of energy. (In a hydraulic system, the accumulation of energy builds up pressure that forces action or change.) But to the ethologists, release of energy—or the instigation of aggression—occurs *when triggered by some external stimulus* (E. H. Hess, 1962). The con-

Figure 7-3
The noted ethologist Konrad Lorenz at work observing animals in the field. (Photo by Harry Redl/Black Star.)

cept of *releasers* is used by ethologists to explain the relationship between internal factors and external, triggering stimuli. Berkowitz, though not an ethologist, has summarized the theory thus: "A releaser, or sign stimulus, is a cue in the external environment which produces a given reaction from an organism ready to make this response. There is an interaction between the organism's internal condition and the external stimulation" (1965b, p. 304). Essentially, this is a *two-factor theory* of the expression of aggression; it has the advantage over orthodox psychoanalytic theory and the neo-Freudian approach of recognizing the role of environmental changes in contributing to the aggressive response.

Psychologists who have studied aggression in animals often support this proposition that aggression is the result of an interaction between internal factors (such as neurological and endocrine reactions) and external stimuli (Flynn, Edwards, & Bandler, 1971; Moyer, 1971, 1972). To call it just "a need for fighting" overlooks the complexities (Geen, 1972).

Given that aggression is a response to cues from outside, how do releasers, or external sign stimuli, work? Ethologists such as Lorenz (1966) and Tinbergen (1951) have documented many cases in which lower animals respond with aggressive behavior only to specific, delimited stimuli. If the male stickleback fish sees a red spot on the belly of another fish, he perceives it as a rival male and will attack. If the red spot is on the other fish's back, the stickleback does not attack. But the sign stimulus also has no effect if internal conditions in the potential aggressor are not appropriate. The male stickleback will not attack unless it has an accumulation of reproductive hormones at the time.

C. Territoriality as an instinct and its influence on expression of aggression

We may still ask *why* aggression occurs. According to the ethologist, aggression results from the organism's propensity to defend its ter-

ritory. Largely through the efforts of the talented professional writer Robert Ardrey (1961, 1966, 1970), the ethological conception of territoriality as a basic instinct has been popularized. Territoriality is an innate drive to gain and defend property. In some animal species, the owner will mark off its property by urination or other means at its disposal (F. D. Becker, 1973); other members of the species recognize the rights of ownership and withdraw when they approach the owner's territory (Ardrey, 1966; Crook, 1973). In Lorenz's (1966) description, scents act like railway signals that prevent collisions between two trains. This territorial marking not only defends an animal's living area but also serves to signal when the marking animal is likely to attack another member of the same species (Ralls, 1971).

To both the novice and the expert, the territoriality drive manifested by some species is quite impressive in its strength; in the African kob, for example, territoriality overrides even the sexual drive. Ardrey (1966) recounts the observations Helmut Buechner (1961, 1963) made of the Uganda kob, an elegant, rather snobbish antelope:

> Males compete for real estate, never for females. The kob's territorial and sexual appetites are so profoundly intermeshed that fights generate sexual stimulation. The champion whom we watched in a twenty-minute defense of his property had an erection through most of the combat. Nevertheless, when the female arrives on a territory, she becomes the sole if momentary property of the male whose grass she crops. A flourishing arena is a Breughel-like scene of scattered kob couples in various stages of intimate disposal amid a scattering of solitary males paying no regard whatever [Ardrey, 1966, p. 51].

Attachment to a piece of ground is stronger than attraction to a female. If a male kob has mounted a female on his personal land, or "putting green," and she crosses into a neighbor's putting green while still in the act of copulating, the sexually aroused male will not pursue. He takes it with good grace and does not even watch the male on the adjoining putting green take his place and his pleasure.

Ardrey also applies concepts of territoriality to the human species, positing that we are innately aggressive because of territorial needs.[3] Many species of animals do not appear to be territorial (Crook, 1973); however, Ardrey dismisses these cases. (Lorenz, at least, recognizes that territoriality is not basic to many animal species.) Perhaps because of ample living areas, sufficient food supplies, or other reasons, animals including the California ground squirrel, the fieldmouse, the red fox, and—closer to the human species—primates such as the orangutan, the chimpanzee, and the gorilla do not display territorial behavior (Montagu, 1973b, p. 8). Bourlière (1954) observed that "territorial behavior is far from being as important in mammals as in birds" (pp. 99–100). Of the animals closest to the human, only the baboon expresses territoriality.[4] So, despite Ardrey's eloquent case for the importance of territoriality, it is doubtful that its existence in the human species can be demonstrated (Barnett, 1973).

D. Hereditary determinants of aggression

Attempts to breed animals so that they are extremely aggressive or nonaggressive have been partially successful in uncovering hereditary determinants of aggression. Lagarspertz (1961), in

a study reviewed by McClearn and Meredith (1966), used mice in a selective-breeding experiment to develop one highly aggressive strain and one highly unaggressive strain. Aggressiveness was measured, and excessively aggressive mice were bred together, as were unaggressive ones. This procedure was continued through three generations, producing in the last generation significant differences in the aggressiveness of the two groups of mice. There was still some overlap, however, in the aggressiveness ratings of the two third-generation groups. We cannot say whether such results could be applied to human beings. Selective breeding, with control of the infant's environment, is not feasible with human beings, and other sources of information must be used when looking for the possible role of heredity in human aggressiveness.

III. Aggression as a possibly innate response activated by frustration

A. The frustration-aggression hypothesis

In 1939 a group of psychologists at Yale University (Dollard, Doob, Miller, Mowrer, & Sears, 1939) introduced a hypothesis that has continued to influence the direction of psychology, generating more empirical research than any other theory of aggression. Basically, these psychologists hypothesized that frustration instigated aggression. More specifically, this frustration-aggression hypothesis postulated that "the occurrence of aggression always presupposes frustration" (N. E. Miller, 1941, pp. 337–338). A second part of the hypothesis was usually interpreted to mean that any frustrating event inevitably leads to aggression. This part of the hypothesis was later clarified by one of the authors, Neal Miller (1941), who made it clear that there were no implications that frustration had no consequences other than aggression or that aggression would inevitably occur as a response to frustra-

---

[3]Other reasons contribute to Ardrey's conclusion that the human species is innately aggressive. In *African Genesis* (1961), Ardrey describes recent fossil excavations in Africa and concludes that *australopithecus*—an intermediate form between lower animals and man—made use of tools or weapons to kill other animals. Relying on the conclusions of Professor Raymond Dart, Ardrey judged that man's animal ancestors were carnivorous, predatory, and cannibalistic in origin. However, few psychologists believe the evidence is clear enough to warrant any conclusion, particularly Ardrey's (see, for example, Elms, 1972a, 1972b).

[4]J. P. Scott has commented that most observers agree that "baboons resemble human beings in social organization more closely than do the anthropoid apes, which are ecologically adapted for forest living and tend to develop less closely organized groups" (J. P. Scott, 1969, p. 631, quoting K. R. L. Hall, 1964).

tion. The original formulation conceived of frustration as leading to an instigation of aggression but recognized that punishment or inhibitions could suppress any possible expression of aggression. To clarify the frustration-aggression hypothesis, Miller (1941, p. 338) rephrased the formulation, stating that "frustration produces instigations to a number of different types of responses, one of which is an instigation to some form of aggression." Unfortunately, the revised hypothesis is much less testable. Nonetheless, both formulations raise several questions, which we will consider now.

1. *What is frustration?* To say the least, *frustration* is a vague term, which is given various meanings (see Berkowitz, 1969a, for an elucidation of these ambiguities). In common usage, *frustration* may refer either to an external instigating condition or to the organism's reaction to this condition. Suppose a young man is ready to drive his car to the airport to meet a female friend, and he discovers that his car battery is dead. What is the frustration? Is it the dead battery or the fact that the car will not start (the external instigating conditions)? Or is frustration the young man's feeling of increased tension and the pounding of his heart—or does it refer to his pounding on the car? (The last three phenomena are various examples of the organism's reaction to the condition.) Wrightsman and Sanford (1975) tried to separate these two factors by using *frustration* to refer to the *state of being blocked* and *frustration-induced behavior* to refer to the emotional reaction resulting from being blocked or thwarted. Other observers, such as J. S. Brown and Farber (1951) and Amsel (1958, 1962), have viewed frustration as an internal action in response to being blocked. In the original frustration-aggression formulation, the Yale theorists defined frustration as the state that emerges when a goal-response is interfered with—"an interference with the occurrence of an instigated goal-response at its proper time in the behavior sequence" (Dollard et al., 1939, p. 7). Such an emphasis on observables suited the Watsonian

behavioristic orientation of the Yale group at that time, but psychologists who have tested the frustration-aggression hypothesis have not always clearly defined the term *frustration*. This lack of a definition of the term has led Berkowitz (1969a, p. 7) to conclude that many of the failures to verify the frustration-aggression hypothesis reflect the ambiguity and inconsistency in definitions rather than any essential lack of validity in the formulation.

2. *Is the relationship between frustration and aggression innate?* There is a tendency to regard the frustration-aggression relationship as inevitable or instinctual. Perhaps this notion was inadvertently conveyed when Dollard and his colleagues wrote that "the frustration-aggression hypothesis assumes a universal causal relation between frustration and aggression" (Dollard et al., 1939, p. 10). Yet, most probably, no innate link was postulated, since Miller, one of the formulators of the hypothesis, wrote two years later that "no assumptions are made as to whether the frustration-aggression relationship is of innate or of learned origin" (N. E. Miller, 1941, p. 340). At the same time, Miller recognized the possibility of innate causes.

Despite this apologia, more recent critics —at least those of a social-learning orientation—regard the frustration-aggression hypothesis as inadequate, since persons can learn to modify or *inhibit* their reactions to frustration (Bandura, 1973; Bandura & Walters, 1963). For example, a budding short-story writer may learn to swallow her impulses to strike back when her teacher insults her carefully written story. Berkowitz, interpreting the position of Bandura and Walters, has stated that if human beings can learn new reactions (either aggressive or nonaggressive) to frustration, then the possibility of innate behavioral determinants is excluded (Berkowitz, 1969a, p. 4). Yet Berkowitz states that "learning and innate determination can coexist in man" (1969a, p. 4). This is an extremely important point. Learning may alter or modify built-in patterns of behavior, so that each plays a role. While frustration may instinctively heighten the likelihood that a certain type of response (such as aggression) will be instigated, learning may strongly alter or disguise the manifestation of this response. The formulators of the frustration-aggression hypothesis clearly recognized that expression of aggression could be inhibited by anticipation of punishment, but they still insisted on the innate link between frustration and the instigation to react. In 1964, Neal Miller wrote "It seems highly probable that . . . innate patterns exist, that they play an important role in the development of human social behavior, and that these instinctual patterns are modifiable enough so that they tend to be disguised by learning although they may play crucial roles in motivating, facilitating, and shaping socially learned behavior" (p. 160).

3. *Does research verify or disprove the frustration-aggression hypothesis?* A variety of evidence from studies using both human and nonhuman subjects seems to support the notion that aggression may be caused by frustration (see Azrin, Hutchinson, & Hake, 1966; Rule & Percival, 1971). For example, Buss (1963) studied the effect of three kinds of frustration on the expression of aggression in college students; the three frustrations were failing a task, losing an opportunity to win some money, and missing an opportunity to attain a better course grade. Each type of frustration led to the expression of about the same degree of aggression, and each frustration produced more aggression than the control condition. Although the evidence pointed to a link between frustration and physical aggression, the amount of aggression expressed was rather minimal. Possibly only minimal aggression emerged because in this experiment aggression was not useful in overcoming the frustration. In situations where aggression can successfully overcome the interference (called *instrumental aggression*), the stronger the need being blocked, the more intense should be the aggression. Thus, while accepting the value of the frustration-aggression hypothesis, Buss (1961, 1966) concludes that it

is applicable only in cases in which aggression has an instrumental value—in other words, only when aggression can be used to override the frustration. The results of Buss's 1966 study and other more recent ones (Thompson & Kolstoe, 1974) reinforce his conclusion that other determinants of aggression (a physical attack, for example) may be more important than frustration (see for example, Gaebelein & Taylor, 1971; Rule & Hewitt, 1971).

More recently, several studies (Gentry, 1970; S. P. Taylor & Pisano, 1971) have found no increase in aggression as a result of the degrees of frustration produced in human subjects in the laboratory. Real-life frustrations do seem to generate aggressive acts, however, and social psychologists need further study of similarities in processes generated by laboratory frustrations and real-life ones.

Children can also demonstrate the aggressive consequences of frustration (Hanratty, O'Neal, & Sulzer, 1972). In one experiment, Mallick and McCandless (1966) arranged for older children to frustrate (interfere with) or not to frustrate 8- and 9-year-old children who were trying to complete five simple block-construction tasks. (Each subject had been promised a nickel for each task completed within a certain time limit.) Interference caused every subject in the frustration condition to fail to complete any task. In the nonfrustration condition, the older child helped the subject complete the tasks, with no reward promised or given to the helper.

In a later phase of the experiment, each subject was shown the confederate (the older child who had frustrated or facilitated the subject's block building) sitting with his hands touching electrodes attached to an electric shock apparatus. Each subject was told that he could administer as many shocks as he wanted and that the other child would not know who was shocking him. In other experiments within the same study, Mallick and McCandless utilized other procedures to generate frustration and measure aggression. The results across procedures were consistent; frustration led to heightened aggressive feelings, which remained intensified even after subjects were given opportunities to direct aggressive actions toward the source of frustration.

In fact, most homicides can be thought of as aggressive acts that are responses to frustration (Berkowitz, 1974). It appears that only a small proportion of homicides are the result of a well-thought-out determination to kill (Mulvihill & Tumin, 1969; Wolfgang, 1968). It is for this reason that the threat of capital punishment is a relatively ineffectual deterrent to killing (N. Walker, 1965).

B. The instigation of
   aggression by others

Not all cases of frustration-induced aggression involve simply one person setting out to harm another. In some cases a frustrated third party is *the instigator of aggression,* even though

he or she does not commit any aggressive act. (See Figure 7-4.) Husbands or wives arrange for someone to murder their spouses; underworld criminals let out "contracts" on their enemies; in one specific case, a leader of the United Mine Worker's of America local and his family were murdered at the apparent instigation of another mine worker's official (Mander & Gaebelein, 1975).

Given that aggression often involves such a triad, what are some of the variables that influence the instigator's behavior? Gaebelein (1973a, 1973b) has found that two powerful influences are *the degree of the cooperation expressed by the actual aggressor* (or "hit man") and *the provocativeness of the victim.* For example, Gaebelein and Hay (1974) had subjects act as instigators of aggression in a laboratory setting. Their job was to establish levels of shocks to be given to a victim while another "subject" (actually a confederate of the experimenters) was to administer the shocks. In

Figure 7-4
Instigation of aggression by others in the real world. (Drawing by Sidney Harris.)

"I'M AFRAID WE'LL HAVE TO TURN IT OVER TO OUR COLLEAGUES, THE HOSTILE COLLECTION AGENCY."

some cases, the "hit man" refused to administer anything higher than relatively mild shocks. In such cases, the instigators suggested lower shock settings than did instigators who had "cooperative" hit men, even though the victim's behavior encouraged higher degrees of punishment.

If a noncooperative hit man is a deterrent to the advocacy of extreme violence, the provocative behavior of a victim can compensate for such an effect. Victims who continue to attack cause instigators to advocate greater degrees of punishment. In contrast, victims who are compliant and passive deter the instigation of extreme punishments.

C. Berkowitz's revised frustration-aggression hypothesis

Although the essence of the frustration-aggression hypothesis is apparently verifiable, many qualifications remain. The original conception is too simple and at the same time too sweeping (Berkowitz, 1969a). It leads to an unwise assumption that aggression has to be an outgrowth of any frustration. Because of the limitations of the hypothesis, Berkowitz (1965a, 1969a) suggested a revised frustration-aggression formulation that emphasizes *the interaction between environmental cues and the internal emotional state.* The original hypothesis has been modified in the following ways.

First, the reaction to frustration creates "only a *readiness* for aggressive acts. Previously acquired aggressiveness habits can also establish this readiness" (Berkowitz, 1965b, p. 308; italics in original). In other words, Berkowitz says that the occurrence of aggressive behavior is not dependent solely on frustration (a point Neal Miller is willing to grant) and that an intervening variable—a readiness—must be added to the link. We may think of this readiness as *anger arousal* (O'Neal, 1973).

Second, stimulus cues, or external triggers, must be recognized as playing a role in the determination of expressed aggression, even when frustration is present. Frustration creates the readi-

ness of anger; cuing stimuli may actually elicit the aggression. Aggressive behavior is not solely a matter of the individual's being "primed" to respond aggressively; the cuing values of various stimuli also influence the strength of the aggressive response and particularly that of an impulsively aggressive response (Zillman, Katcher, & Milavsky, 1972). Previously, Berkowitz (1965b) has advocated a view that aggressive cues or releasers were *necessary* for aggressive impulses to occur. More recently his position has become somewhat tempered:

> The emotional state arising from the encounter with the aversive stimulus may in itself contain distinctive stimuli which can instigate the aggressive reaction, particularly if the emotion is strong enough; but the presence of appropriate aggressive cues (in the external environment or represented internally in thoughts) increases the probability that an overt aggressive response will actually take place [Berkowitz, 1969a, p. 18].

Note that cues increase the probability of the occurrence of aggression but are not considered to be essential for the expression of aggression. The emotional state itself (anger) may be sufficient for aggression to appear. An important research program at the University of Wisconsin has contributed to the reformulation of the hypothesis. Several of these Wisconsin studies have used the same basic procedures to study the aggressive cue value of a stimulus. In these studies, the subject, a male college student, was introduced to the other subject, who in actuality was an accomplice of the experimenter. The accomplice either made the subject angry or treated him in a neutral manner. Immediately after this act, a seven-minute film clip was shown—the film being either a vicious prizefight scene from the film *Champion* or a neutral film dealing with English canal boats. After viewing one of these films, the subject was given an opportunity to shock the confederate, who had moved to another room. The experimenter presented this opportunity in a way that made the subsequent shocking appear socially acceptable to the subject (Berkowitz, 1965a).

In the first study of this series, the confederate was introduced either as a nonbelligerent speech major or as a physical-education major interested in boxing; the purpose of this manipulation was to vary the aggressive cue value of the confederate in the eyes of the subject. (A real-life analogy might be the difference between being frustrated by a musician or by a policeman.) When the confederate was introduced as a boxer, the subject gave more shocks of a longer duration than when the confederate was introduced as a speech major.[5] These differences support the hypothesis that the degree of aggressive behavior expressed by a person is influenced by the aggressive cue value of a stimulus in his or her environment. It would suggest that frustrations in the real world engendered by stimuli that have aggressive cue values (such as policemen) are more likely to elicit aggression. However, the value of this conclusion is somewhat moderated by the finding that even when the subject is treated neutrally by the accomplice, the boxer is given more shocks than the speech major. Perhaps, as Berkowitz (1965a) postulates, boxers elicit more aggression because of their connection with fighting or because they are disliked by other students. As in any experiment, subjects entered this experiment with certain assumptions. Here, the assumptions about the nature of physical-education majors were uncontrolled possible influences.

A second experiment (Berkowitz & Geen, 1966) used another approach to study the aggressive cue value of the stimulus (the accomplice). In the film clip from Champion, Kirk Douglas,

a well-known actor, played a boxer who was badly mauled in the fight. At the beginning of the experiment, the accomplice was introduced to half of the subjects as Kirk Anderson, while to the other half of the subjects the accomplice's name was Bob Anderson. It was hypothesized that if the accomplice's name was Kirk, he would be associated with the fight scene and hence would elicit more shocks than if his name were unassociated with the fight. (Another, less important change in the procedure of this study was using an exciting but nonaggressive film of a track meet instead of the film on canal boats.) After being angered and having watched an aggressive film, subjects gave the accomplice named Kirk more shocks than the accomplice named Bob. Although alternative explanations may always be advanced to explain such phenomena,[6] the results are clearly in line with an expectation that certain stimuli elicit more aggression than others, when other factors are constant and delimited.

A third experiment (Geen & Berkowitz, 1966) further verified the triggering properties of the aggressor's name. In the Champion movie, Kirk Douglas played a boxer named Midge Kelly, who was given a bloody beating by another boxer named Dunne. One-third of the subjects in both movie conditions were told that the accomplice's name was Bob Kelly, and another third of the subjects were told the accomplice's name was Bob Dunne. The remaining third of the subjects in both film groups were introduced

[5]Questions have been raised by D. P. Hartmann (1970) regarding the adequacy of the measures of aggression used in these and similar studies. Hartmann notes that among the measures used in different studies are the frequency of shocks given, the duration of shocks, the intensity, the pressure exerted on the shock switch, the duration times the intensity, the intensity times frequency, and so on ad infinitum. The correlations between these measures are often low (Geen & O'Neal, 1969: Geen, Rakosky, & O'Neal, 1968).

[6]In this study, subjects in the aggressive-film/Kirk condition were reminded "casually but pointedly" by the experimenter that the first name of the movie actor was the same name as that of the other subject (the accomplice) in the experiment. While this was probably necessary to develop an association between the two, it encouraged different demand characteristics for the subjects in this condition. However, if different demand characteristics were operating here, we would expect angered subjects in the aggressive-film/Kirk condition to express significantly more anger toward the accomplice than would angered subjects in the aggressive-film/Bob condition. This did not happen to a statistically significant degree, although the difference was in this direction.

to an accomplice named Bob Riley, a name that does not appear in either film clip. All subjects in this experiment were angered by the accomplice. It was expected that after witnessing the boxing film, subjects would administer more shocks to Bob Kelly than to any other accomplice. This was the case. When the accomplice's name was the same as the name of the victim in the film, an average of 5.4 shocks was given after the subject had watched the boxing film. When the accomplice's name was irrelevant (Riley) an average of only 4.4 shocks was administered after the boxing film. The neutral name Riley did not produce any significant differences when the subject had watched the track film.

Of interest was the finding that Dunne, the aggressor's name in the film, received fewer shocks than Kelly, the victim in the film. As Berkowitz concludes (1965b), "the confederate's aggressive cue value apparently varied directly with his association with the victim rather than the giver of the observed aggression" (p. 318). Why this unexpected result occurred is unclear. The finding is reminiscent of those in Lerner's "just world" studies. Possibly the subjects associated Kelly with the victim and felt that, as a victim, he must have deserved the beating he was so obviously getting. Therefore, subjects shocked him all the more, merely because he "deserved it."

A related finding (Berkowitz & Alioto, 1973; J. L. Hoyt, 1970; Meyer, 1972) is that after subjects have been attacked, just how aggressive they became toward their attacker depended on the interpretation given to a certain film they had watched. In one study (Geen & Stonner, 1973) all attacked subjects watched the same film clip from *Champion,* but one-third were told that the fight was motivated by a quest for vengeance, one-third were told the boxers were professionals fighting for money, and one-third were shown the film clip without being given an interpretation. Subjects were more aggressive if they had been told that the fight reflected a revenge motive.

More recent research in this productive series of experiments has shown that after a subject is conditioned to have a negative attitude toward a certain name, more aggression is directed toward the frustrator who has the same unfortunate name (Berkowitz & Knurek, 1969). In the study that demonstrated this finding, college males were trained to dislike a given name (either George or Ed) by learning to associate the name with words having unfavorable connotations. Later, half of the subjects were deliberately frustrated by the trainer; then all subjects participated in a supposedly separate study in which they discussed an issue with two other males, one of whom was named either George or Ed. Subjects acted more unfriendly toward the negatively named person than toward the other discussion member. One could apply this finding to the possible causes of unfriendly reactions to members of minority groups.

The weapons effect. Other experiments in this series have shown that the presence of a weapon may instigate the expression of aggression, even if the weapon is not actually used to express aggression (Berkowitz & LePage, 1967). Male university students received either one or seven electric shocks from a fellow student and then were given the opportunity to administer shocks in return. While some subjects participated in the study, a rifle and a revolver were on the table near the shock key; for other subjects, two badminton racquets were on the table; and for a group of control subjects, no object was on the table. As one might expect, more shocks were administered by the strongly aroused subjects (those who had been stung by seven shocks rather than only one); but, more importantly, the presence of the guns increased the average number of shocks given from 4.67 to 6.07 (see Table 7-2).

This "weapons effect" illustrates that if a person's inhibitions toward aggression are rather weak at a particular moment, aggressive cues in the environment can make the expression of aggressive acts more likely. To attribute this re-

Table 7-2
Mean number of shocks given in each condition

Condition	Shocks Received by the Subject	
	One Shock Only	*Seven Shocks*
Associated weapons were present	2.60$_a$	6.07$_d$
Unassociated weapons were present	2.20$_a$	5.67$_{cd}$
No objects present	3.07$_a$	4.67$_{bc}$
Badminton racket present	—	4.60$_b$

Note: Cells having a common subscript are not significantly different at the .05 level by Duncan Multiple Range test. There were 10 subjects in the seven-shocks-received/badminton-racket condition and 15 subjects in each of the other conditions. (From "Weapons as Aggression-Eliciting Stimuli," by L. Berkowitz and A. LePage, *Journal of Personality and Social Psychology*, 1967, 7, 202–207. Copyright 1967 by the American Psychological Association. Reprinted by permission.)

sponse to the presence of weapons has not gone unchallenged, however; several studies have failed to replicate the results of Berkowitz and LePage (Buss, Booker, & Buss, 1972; Page & Scheidt, 1971) and it is also possible that when the effect occurs, subjects are reacting to the demand characteristics of the situation. Berkowitz and LePage recognized this possibility and advanced several reasons why they believe demand characteristics were not a strong influence (1967, pp. 296–207).

Berkowitz (1974) proposes that it is not the presence of weapons that increases aggression, but rather the person's *interpretation of the weapons;* that is, the mere sight of a weapon stimulates the person to greater aggression. Studies testing this interpretation reflect the presence of a "weapons effect" (Fraczek & Macaulay, 1971; Frodi, 1973, cited in Berkowitz, 1974; Turner & Simons, 1974). As Berkowitz has said, "The finger pulls the trigger, but the trigger may also be pulling the finger."

The potential effect of weapons is consistent with the claim by the late J. Edgar Hoover, former director of the U. S. Federal Bureau of Investigation (reported in *Time*, August 12, 1966)

that the availability of firearms has a significant influence on the murder rate in the United States. But beyond this, the presence of firearms appears to lead to more violence even when these weapons are not used in the expression of violence. In Canada, where firearms such as revolvers and submachine guns must be registered and may not be owned for the purposes of "protection," the homicide rate is considerably lower than in the U. S. The fact that the world contains more than 750 million operable military rifles and pistols (Thayer, 1969) should cause us concern for the possibilities of world peace. (See also Figure 7-5 for an example of advertising for international sale of armaments.)

The general findings from the Wisconsin studies support two conclusions: (1) witnessing an aggressively oriented movie lowers one's inhibitions against the expression of aggression resulting from frustration, and (2) certain stimuli have greater cuing properties in the triggering of frustration-engendered aggression than do others. In other words, whether the subject will act aggressively is partially a function of the presence of aggression-cuing stimuli in his or her environment.

the peacekeeper: Bell's air mobility team

Enemy tank attack! You can stop it fast. With the world's most effective anti-tank system. Bell's armed helicopter – the Cobra.

Bell's Cobra offers multiple combinations of the most modern firepower systems. And it can come a long way in a hurry to establish battlefield superiority by furnishing flexible, light fire support for maneuvering troops and heavy fire against hard targets.

The Cobra strikes at long range from concealed defensive positions. Target in view, it leaps up from ground cover. Unleashes its ordnance with precision accuracy. Then leaves. Fast!

It can be rearmed, refueled and maintained in the field. And it comes to you with proven com-

bat reliability, maintainability and survivability.

The Cobra is the firepower member of the Bell team. Bell's OH-58 provides reconnaissance capability, plus command and control from the air. Bell's powerful new 214 provides troop mobility for fast response, battlefield support by moving artillery and supplies, and quick evacuation of the wounded.

Together, they form the world's most effective air mobility team.

peacekeepers the world over depend on Bell HELICOPTER

Figure 7-5

An example of international armament sales—another "defensive" sale from the United States. This is a reproduction of a Bell Helicopter Co. advertisement that appeared recently in several internationally circulated magazines promoting the company's line of combat helicopters for sale. The ad reproduced here was taken from *Modern Asia*, a bimonthly magazine for businesspeople that is published in Hong Kong and circulated in Asian countries. (Used by permission of Bell Helicopter Company.)

IV. Prolearning positions

A. J. P. Scott and animal psychology: Absence of physiological factors

Thus far, we have moved from a single-factor instinctual view to one in which learned responses of aggression are superimposed on a possibly innate reaction to frustration. Let us now explore a position that denies the importance of instincts. In his text *Aggression* (1958, p. 98), psychologist J. P. Scott concluded that "all research findings point to the fact that there is no physiological evidence of any internal need or spontaneous driving force for fighting; that all stimulation for aggression comes eventually from forces present in the external environment." In rejecting the psychoanalytic view, Scott observes that presently no known physiological mechanism serves as an internal drive, without external stimulation.

Although Scott doubts that experience and training can greatly modify the social behavior patterns of lower animals, he observes that domestic animals appear to have much less fixed and ceremonious behavior than do wild ones (1969, p. 622), and that the behavior of mammals is much less instinctual than that of birds or fish. Likewise, when considering territoriality—the cornerstone of the ethologist's views on innate human aggression—Scott finds little indication that territoriality is a basic trait of primates. According to Scott, one cannot conclude at this point whether territoriality is "a cultural or a biological invention. Its existence in precultural man is entirely conjectural" (1969, p. 635).

B. Social-learning theory: Aggressiveness may be modeled

Consider the following situation (from Bandura, Ross, & Ross, 1961): A child in nursery school is brought to an experimental room and asked by the experimenter to join in a game. The experimenter then directs the child to one corner of the room, where there is a small table and chair. The child is instructed in the task of designing pictures, by using potato prints and colorful stickers. After beginning the child in his or her task, the experimenter escorts an adult to an opposite corner of the room that also contains a table and chair, a mallet, Tinker Toys, and a five-foot, inflated Bobo doll. The experimenter tells the child that these materials are there for the adult to play with, and then the experimenter leaves the room.

Half the children in the study were boys and half were girls. Half the children of each sex watched an adult (the model) of the same sex, and half watched an adult of the other sex. During the ten minutes they were together, the model for half the children assembled the Tinker Toys quietly and did not touch or even approach the Bobo doll (nonaggressive condition). The adult model for the other half spent most of the time (nine minutes) attacking the Bobo doll, hitting it, throwing it, laying it on its side, pounding its nose, and otherwise aggressing against it. These actions were interspersed with verbal responses such as "Sock him in the nose," "Pow!" "Kick him," and the like.

The children were then moved to a different experimental room set off from the main nursery; many of the children believed that they were no longer on the nursery school grounds. Each child was subjected to a mild arousal of aggression to instill some reason for acting aggressively. The child was interrupted shortly after he or she had started playing with some favorite toys and was told by the experimenter that those particular toys were reserved for other children. The child could then play with any other toy in the room for 20 minutes; these toys had been previously classified into types that do or do not elicit aggressive play. The aggressive toys were a three-foot Bobo doll, a mallet and pegboard, two dart guns, and a tether ball with a face painted on it, hanging from the ceiling. The nonaggressive toys included crayons and coloring paper, a tea set, a ball, two dolls, three toy bears, plastic farm animals, and a set of cars and trucks. The behavior of each child was rated by observers on a variety of measures including imitation of physical aggression, imitative verbal aggression, imitative nonaggressive verbal responses, and aggressive gun play.[7]

[7]In contrast to Berkowitz's Wisconsin studies, subjects in this study were frustrated *after* witnessing aggression. In Berkowitz's studies subjects were angered and then allowed to witness aggressive or nonaggressive stimuli.

Clearly, watching an aggressive model encourages the expression of aggression in children. Girls who watched an aggressive model averaged 18 aggressive acts with the mallet, while girls with a nonaggressive model made, on the average, less than one response with the mallet. All measures consistently showed that viewing aggressive models encourages more expression of aggression after experiencing frustration. Children who had a nonaggressive model generally displayed the same or a smaller degree of aggression than a control group of children who did not watch a model. Watching another person act violently apparently weakens inhibitions toward the expression of aggression—at least in the case of children. The next question is whether the same results would occur in adults, where the inhibitions are perhaps more entrenched than in children. Observations of mass violence indicate that these *disinhibitory processes* occur in adults too; an initial violent act by one person (such as throwing a brick at a police car) will eradicate the inhibitions of others against such antisocial actions.

Further studies (Bandura, 1965a; D. Z. Kuhn, Madsen, & Becker, 1967; R. Walters & Willows, 1968) indicate that if a child watches a film in which an adult is rewarded for displaying novel, aggressive responses, the child will imitate the adult. Imitation occurs more often when the adult is rewarded than when he or she is punished for expressing aggressive impulses. Posttests indicated that children in all conditions (which varied reward and punishment for adult aggressiveness) equally learned to imitate the aggressiveness. However, if the child witnessed the adult model being punished for aggressiveness, this observation acted as an inhibitor to the child's expression of aggression (Bandura, Ross, & Ross, 1963).

These studies elucidate two processes that contribute to the expression or nonexpression of aggression: *imitation* and *inhibition*. If the child watches the aggressive actions of another person, the "observer may acquire new responses that did not previously exist in his repertoire" (Bandura & Walters, 1963, p. 60). This phenomenon by which the child learns to imitate a response is called **modeling.** Observing another person may reduce inhibitions and lead the child to violence, if the model indicates that violence is permissible. But if the child witnesses another person being punished for aggression, inhibitions against aggression are increased. According to this viewpoint, individual differences in the degree of aggressiveness as a personality trait result from previous learning. Child-rearing practices and imitation of others are important determinants.[8]

C. Cross-cultural comparisons: The search for the nonaggressive society

Those who explain aggression as a learned response claim that if societies exist where no aggressive behavior is manifested, one can conclude that learning, rather than instinct, plays a dominant role in the manifestation of aggressive responses. These observers believe that the existence of nonaggressive societies would, at least, imply that learning can inhibit any aggressive instinct. Although this analysis emphasizes an undesirable "either-or" approach of instinct versus learning, it is, nonetheless, useful to find societies in which aggression is nonexistent. Gorer (1968) has reviewed anthropological investigations of societies whose goal is one of peaceful isolation.[9] These societies include the Arapesh of New Guinea, the Lepchas of Sikkim, in the Himalayas, and the Pygmies in central Africa. A classic study by Margaret Mead (1935)

gives a detailed account of the Arapesh, who live in a mountainous area on the Island of New Guinea. In Arapesh society, helping one's neighbor is considered essential for the survival of both parties. Arapesh men and women both possess gentle personalities, are responsive to others, and are rather maternal in their concern for others.

Mead also compared two other tribes living in New Guinea. The Mundugumor were described as aggressive, overly "masculine" individualists. The Tchambuli were notable because the roles of the two sexes were the reverse of those in Western cultures. Mead capitalized upon these differences to emphasize that "human nature is almost unbelievably malleable," a conclusion with which we agree. Yet Mead's subsequent writings have been somewhat tempered, perhaps in response to criticisms of her earlier work. Fortune (1939), for example, reported that the Arapesh males, despite all their concern for fellow tribal members, were among the most feared headhunters in New Guinea.

The Great Whale River Eskimos, according to Honigmann (1954), insist on total inhibition of the expression of aggression in their children. These parents reprimand fighting and teach their children that physical aggression is the worst thing a child can do.

The societies described by Gorer have several characteristics in common, which facilitate the development and maintenance of their nonaggressive behavior. First, they tend to live in rather inaccessible places, which other groups do not covet as living area. Whenever other groups have invaded their territory, their response as a tribe has been to retreat into even more inaccessible areas. Second, they are oriented toward the concrete pleasures of life—such as eating, drinking, and sex—and, apparently, the supply of these pleasures sufficiently satisfies their needs. It is unlikely that important needs are often frustrated for very long. Achievement or power needs are not encouraged in children; "the model for the growing child is of concrete performance and frank enjoyment, not of metaphysical symbolic achievements or of ordeals to be surmounted" (Gorer, 1968, p. 34). Third, these societies make

---

[8]It should be noted that the thorough study of Sears, Maccoby, and Levin (1957), which dealt with aggressiveness of 5-year-olds in the home, turned up few significant relationships. There was a slight tendency for severely punitive parents to have more aggressive children, but cause and effect cannot be attributed to this relationship. Results of a similar nature, with lower-class children, are reported by McCord, McCord, and Howard (1961).

[9]Isolated communities in the United States and Canada, such as the Amish, the Mennonites, and the Hutterites, also possess these aims. The Hutterites advocate a life of pacifism, and aggressive acts in their society go unrewarded (Eaton & Weil, 1955; cited in Bandura & Walters, 1963).

few distinctions between males and females. Although some distinctions between male and female roles exist in each of these societies, no attempt is made to project, for instance, an image of brave, aggressive masculinity. (In contrast, the Mundugumor cannibals of the New Guinea Highlands idealize a highly competitive, aggressive conception of masculinity.) Among nonaggressive societies, sexual identity is apparently no problem; Gorer claims that no cases of sexual inversion have been reported in these societies.

All these societies are small, weak, and technologically undeveloped. Yet there are isolated groups in North America, especially the Mennonites and Hutterites, that are technologically developed and still live a life free of aggression. Such groups are able to survive when left in relative isolation.

Despite their apparent lack of traits with survival value, the Lepchas and other nonaggressive societies remind one of the malleability of human nature and the great diversity in "normal" behaviors from one society to another (Eisenberg, 1972).

V. A recapitulation and attempt at resolution

At this point, a few conclusions will be offered to summarize our thinking on the diverse causes of aggression.

1. Humans are, of course, one species of animal, and our behavior may partially be accounted for by viewing the human species as a step in an evolutionary sequence. Books such as Desmond Morris's *The Naked Ape* (1967) and *The Human Zoo* (1969) may enlighten the uneducated about our similarities to other primates; but books like these, and even Lorenz's *On Aggression*, do a disservice when they stretch the generalizations from other species to humans. The more advanced the species, the less its behavior relies on innate determinants, and the greater the role of learning. Very few human actions are unaffected by learning (Barnett, 1973).

2. At the same time, there may be in the human species some carry-over from earlier species in regard to innate tendencies toward the instigation of aggression. These innate physiological processes may best be interpreted as the readiness to respond (Megargee & Hokanson, 1970). These processes interact with the situation and the environment to produce behavior. Thus, innate structures are postulated to be more responsive when certain environmental stimuli are present. Both the studies done by Bandura and his associates and those conducted by Berkowitz's group show that the expression of aggression (as opposed to its instigation) is facilitated when aggressive cues are in the immediate environment.

3. The frustration-aggression hypothesis, while sometimes correct, must be restated to be accurate. Miller's (1941) reformulation—that frustration produces instigations to a number of different types of responses, only one of which is aggression—makes more accurate the theorized relationship. For instance, frustration may lead to regression and more infantile behavior, especially in children (Himmelweit, 1950). As Berkowitz (1969a) indicates, aggression is a much more complicated phenomenon than the original frustration-aggression hypothesis would lead us to believe. "The existence of frustration *does not* always lead to some form of aggression, and the occurrence of aggressive behavior *does not necessarily* presuppose the existence of frustration" (Berkowitz, 1969a, p. 2; italics in original). Acts of aggression can be stimulated by rousing speeches or martial music even in the absence of frustration (Geen, 1972). It should be noted that, although the revised hypothesis is more clearly representative of the empirical data, it is also less testable than the original formulation since it is exceedingly difficult to disprove.

4. Laboratory studies consistently indicate that witnessing aggression, particularly when one is frustrated, leads to an increased expression of aggression (Bryan & Schwartz, 1971). Several different intervening processes may be at work here (Geen, 1973). First, *modeling* plays a role; the observer learns to react violently by watching an-

other person do so (Baron, 1974; Baron & Kepner, 1970; Leyens, 1972; L. Wheeler & Smith, 1967). Second, both Berkowitz's and Bandura's studies isolate the process of *disinhibition of aggression:* witnessing aggression reduces one's previously acquired inhibitions against expressing violence (Geen & Stonner, 1973). Third, certain cues in the environment play an *eliciting* role, determining how much aggression the subject expresses after witnessing a violent event under frustrating conditions. Fourth, observing violence may raise the observer's level of autonomic arousal, thus intensifying any response, including aggression (Geen, 1973; Zillman, 1971).

VI. Violence and the mass media

We may question what implications the findings described in the previous section have for watching violent movies or violent programs on television. Movies in the United States and Canada are now rated in regard to their acceptability for children. The degree of sexual content, rather than the degree of violence, in the film appears to be the most influential determinant in the rating. Even though social critics decry the prevalence of violence in television dramas, the industry is slow to reduce a staple on which the viewing audience apparently thrives. Does the portrayal of violence in the mass media encourage the viewer to respond violently? Or is such viewing a healthy channeling of aggressive impulses? (See Figure 7-6.) Those who defend violence on television believe that vicarious participation in the mass output of aggressive acts has a *cathartic* function; that is, the display of violence on television provides a harmless outlet for impulses that would otherwise lead to socially undesirable actions.[10] These observers also note that

throughout history every society has provided children with fictional materials that have a heavy component of violence; fairy tales, for example, involve horrible spiders, powerful giants, and fire-breathing dragons. But the violence of fairy tales differs from the violence on television; fairy tales form a faraway fantasy world, whereas the typical television program depicts human beings with whom the child can identify much more easily (Gentry, 1974).

Figure 7-6
The effects of watching a sports event. Does the chance to yell "Kill the umpire!" or to boo the visiting team at the basketball game serve to release pent-up feelings of aggression, or does it make the spectator more hostile? What are the effects of watching a hard-hitting football game or a fight during a hockey match? Little research is available, but Goldstein and Arms (1971) conclude that hostility is increased as a result of watching an exciting football game, regardless of whether the spectator's team wins or loses. Apparently the act of watching the violence on the field loosens the spectator's own inhibitions against expressing aggression, giving the person a sense of being "free to aggress" (Worchel, 1972).

[10]Schellenberg (1974) has reprinted Alfred Hitchcock's defense of his chilling television programs: "One of television's great contributions is that it brought murder back into the home where it belongs. Seeing a murder on television can be good therapy. It can help work off one's antagonisms. If you haven't any antagonisms, the commercials will give you some" (from *Consumer Reports,* January 1967, p. 6).

Children learn how people behave by watching them; whether the role models are seen live or on television seems to make little difference on the total aggression expressed (Bandura & Mischel, 1965; Bandura, Ross, & Ross, 1963). But probably more input comes to the average child via television than from live observations. In contemporary North American life, it can be said that the television set is indeed a member of the family (D. G. Singer & Singer, 1974). Surveys indicate that children begin watching television at age 2 or 3, and, by the age of 5, are watching two to three hours a day (Siegel, 1969). By the age of 10 or 11, at least in lower-income families, the average viewing time per day is five to six hours (National Commission on the Causes and Prevention of Violence, 1969, p. 193). It is claimed that by the age of 16, the average child has spent more time watching television than in the school classroom and will have witnessed more than 13,000 killings on TV (Waters & Malamud, 1975). Aggressive episodes outweigh protective and affectionate ones by a ratio of 4 to 1. One significant aspect of these programs is the emphasis on violent means to solve problems or conflicts. If witnessing violence is, indeed, therapeutic, children who watch television get plenty of input to satisfy their aggressive needs.

Although evidence on the effects of television watching is only now beginning to accumulate, one pattern that has emerged reveals that witnessing violence leads to the assumption of more violence in ambiguous situations. In an early study (Siegel, 1958), 7-year-old children first listened to radio serials about taxi drivers. In one series the taxi drivers were usually violent; in the other series, they were not. Later, each child was asked to predict the ending of a local newspaper story about a taxi driver. (Only those children who understood that newspaper stories report reality, not make-believe, were used as subjects.) The children who had heard the radio serials about the violent taxi drivers attributed much more violence to the driver in the newspaper story than did the other children. Although demand characteristics or evaluation apprehension may be possible explanations of the differences here, another possible conclusion is that children form their impressions of violence in real life from the fictional representations they have heard or seen. Children's assumptions about the aggressive nature of people are affected by whatever is gleaned from the mass media. (See also Figure 7-7.)

Other evidence (Eron, 1963) shows that those boys who report watching a considerable amount of violence on television are also the ones who are rated by their peers as most aggressive. In fact, there are modest correlations ($+.30$'s) between the amount of TV watched at age 8 and the amount of aggressiveness (as rated by peers) shown *ten* years later (Eron, Huesman, Lefkowitz, & Walder, 1972). Additional research studies (Berkowitz & Geen, 1966, 1967) indicate that, in the case of college students, witnessing an aggression-oriented movie lowers the restraints against expressing frustration-induced tendencies. R. H. Walters, Llewellyn-Thomas, and Acker (1962) found hospital attendants responding in the same manner. Indeed, these restraints are unleashed more quickly when the aggression occurs in a justified context.

Further investigation is needed before we can properly understand this weakening of restraints; yet we are already aware of its tragic real-life examples. One of these occurred in Boston in October 1973. A young woman named Evelyn Wagler was driving through the Roxbury section when her car ran out of gas. Returning to the car with a two-gallon can of gasoline, she was forced into a debris-filled backyard by six young men, who beat her and ordered her to douse herself with the fuel. Then one of them struck a match and tossed it on her. She became a writhing, screaming human torch, and four hours later she was dead.

Just two nights before, a film named *Fuzz* had been shown on a national television network. In this film, which purportedly took place in Boston, a scene pictures youths dousing sleeping tramps with gasoline and setting them afire.

The U. S. National Commission on the Causes and Prevention of Violence (NCCPV,

Figure 7-7

Television violence and identification. Particularly important in the study of television violence is the degree to which the observer can identify with the character (Bryan & Schwartz, 1971); in many cases, perpetrators of violence in television dramas are seen by children as both real (or contemporary and true to life) and ideal (they possess envied attributes). Characters and actions are seen as reflections of the real world, which the viewers, as children, will soon inherit. Such acceptance of this real-world property of television-land is more prevalent in lower-class than in middle-class children. A sample of U. S. teenagers were asked whether they agreed or disagreed with the statements "The programs I see on television tell about life the way it really is" and "The people I see on television programs are just like people I meet in real life." The responses showed that 40% of lower-class Blacks, 30% of lower-class Whites, and 15% of middle-class Whites agreed (NCCPV, 1969). Another deleterious effect of frequently viewing violence is a dulling of the viewers' "emotional reactions to fictional violence [and] to violence in real life, [thus making] them more willing actually to engage in aggressive actions when provoking circumstances arise" (NCCPV, 1969, p. 202). (Photo by Jim Pinckney.)

1969; see also R. K. Baker & Ball, 1969; Berkowitz, 1964; Briand, 1969) collected the testimonies of various persons whose professional work was relevant to the issue of the effects of violence on the mass media. The commission reported that "it is reasonable to conclude that a constant diet of violent behavior on television has an adverse effect on human character and attitudes. Violence on television encourages violent forms of behavior, and fosters moral and social values about violence in daily life which are unacceptable in a civilized society" (NCCPV, 1969, p. 202). However, all of the evidence collected by the commission was indirect or from laboratory studies (see, for example, Cline, Croft, & Courrier, 1973).

Several field experiments have compared the amounts of aggression expressed by children who watch either violent or nonviolent TV programs or films. One of these, by Feshbach and Singer (1970; Feshbach, 1969), found that viewing violent programs resulted in a slight *decrease* in expressed aggression. But more recent field experiments have produced an opposite conclusion.

Feshbach and Singer attempted to control the types of programs watched by boys during a six-week period. These boys were enrolled in one of three private boarding schools or were in one of four state residential schools. Children from ages 10 to 17 and from both the upper and lower socioeconomic levels were participants. Boys were paid ten dollars each for participating in the study. Some boys were allowed to view only those programs high in aggressive content; others, in the control group, were told they could watch only programs without much aggressive content. (However, after protests from the control-group members, they too were permitted to watch a few of their favorite programs, including *Batman*, which was high in aggression.)

Both before and after the six-week viewing period, all the boys completed questionnaires measuring overt and covert hostility, aggression-anxiety, impulsiveness, and aggressive values. The Thematic Apperception Test, a projective measure of aggression, was administered to

each boy, and peer ratings of aggression were collected. The boys rated each television program they watched. Each boy's immediate supervisor recorded daily the boy's number and type of aggressive incidents.

Feshbach and Singer's results were somewhat consistent in indicating that less aggression was expressed by boys who watched aggressive content on television. These boys, for example, engaged in only half as many fist fights as did control group members. "The frequency of both verbal aggression and physical aggression, whether directed toward peers or authority figures, was reliably higher in the control group exposed to the nonaggressive programs as compared to the experimental group who had been placed on the aggressive 'diet' " (Feshbach, 1969, p. 4). The differences were statistically significant in the state residential schools but not in the private schools. However, differences were consistent for boys of junior high school and senior high school age. Only in the expression of aggressive fantasy on the Thematic Apperception Test did the aggressive-TV group score higher than in the controls.

The study was a useful beginning effort in trying to determine the effects of watching violence in a real-life setting that still permitted experimental control. It is not surprising that in such real-life testing methodological limitations occur that limit the confidence we have in the authors' conclusions (Wells, 1973). For example, boys in the two experimental conditions doubtless communicated with each other; those originally prevented from watching violent programs protested. Perhaps the limitation led to expression of more aggression by these nonviolent viewers.

A more recent field experiment (Leyens, Camino, Parke, & Berkowitz, 1975) was able to exert more control over what programs were viewed, perhaps because the study was done in Belgium instead of the United States. The manipulation of violent content was done through the use of a special "Movie Week" in which the boys (aged 14–16) were surveyed about their reactions to films shown nightly. During this week the TV sets in the cottages in which the boys lived were disconnected. The subjects lived in four small dormitories, with from 18 to 32 boys living in each dormitory. Observations of the boys the week before the film showing indicated that in two of the dormitories aggressive behavior was relatively high; in the other two it was not. Therefore, during the week of film watching, one aggressive dormitory and one nonaggressive one saw only films that were saturated with violent content (examples included *Bonnie and Clyde, The Dirty Dozen,* and *Iwo Jima*). The other two dormitories were shown nonviolent films, including *Lili* and *La Belle Américaine*. As had Feshbach and Singer, Leyens and associates had trained observers rate the amount of aggressive behavior shown by each boy during the week of film viewing and the week afterward.

The violent films increased the expression of physical aggression in both the cottages; the authors conclude that "the films evoked among the spectators the kind of aggression they had been exposed to" (Leyens et al., 1975, p. 353). This implies that modeling was occurring; or perhaps the films were providing ideas for activities that the boys had to try out.

Verbal aggression was increased only in the initially aggressive dormitory that had the violent films. The nonaggressive dormitory with the violent films actually decreased the expression of verbal aggression. The effects of the film content were much more extreme immediately after viewing than they were during later observation periods.

Two studies done recently in the United States (Parke, Berkowitz, Leyens, & Sebastian, in press) have also shown that delinquent boys were much more aggressive after watching violent commercial movies than after watching neutral ones. There remain some problems in the methodology of these recent studies (for example, in forming groups of subjects who are equal prior to viewing, and in selecting nonviolent films or TV programs that are as exciting as the violent ones). However, they provide the most solid evidence we have that exposure to the mass

media can encourage the expression of aggression.

Of course, a great deal more research must be done before comprehensive conclusions can be safely drawn (A. H. Stein, 1974). For example, does violence on news programs have the same effect as violence in television dramas? Feshbach (1969) hypothesizes that "violence presented in the form of fiction is much less likely to reinforce, stimulate, or elicit aggressive responses than violence in the form of a news event" (p. 5). Most children can discriminate between fantasy and reality. Yet even fictional shows differ in the extent of fantasy and reality. Watching the real-life, believable violence depicted in *Lassie*, for example, may be more detrimental to children than watching a fantasy film. Likewise, the aesthetic nature of the dramatic event may contribute to its impact in ways that social psychologists are so far unable to measure.

VII. Collective violence in society—Yesterday, today, and tomorrow

The remaining sections of this chapter deal with extreme cases of violent behavior. An attempt will be made to construct a long-range historical view of the incidence of collective violence, from the past to the present. Projections about the future are also proposed.

A. Violence in the past

Collective violence—violence between nations or between identifiable groups within a nation—has always been a part of Western civilization. The United States, in particular, has always been a relatively violent nation (R. M. Brown, 1969; NCCPV, 1969, p. 1). Tilly, in surveying the field, concludes that "historically, collective violence has flowed regularly out of the central political processes of Western countries. Men seeking to seize, hold, or realign the levers of power have continually engaged in collective violence as part of their struggles. The oppressed have struck in the name of justice, the privileged in the name of order, those in between in the name of fear" (1969, pp. 4–5). The freedom of the United States as a nation resulted from a series of violent acts.

An analysis of comparative levels of political violence in the United States (S. G. Levy, 1969) has indicated no general chronological trend in the direction of either greater or less violence. The most violent incidents occurred in the decade between 1879 and 1889, but the subsequent decade, from 1889 to 1899, had a moderate rate of such incidents. The 1940s and 1950s had low rates, but the 1960s had one of the highest rates of violent incidents. Although not "born

out of revolution" and perhaps not as violent on the whole as the U. S., Canada too has had its share of collective violence. Since confederation in 1867, Canadians have fought in four major wars and have rioted over unemployment in the 1930s, over conscription in the 1940s, and over confederation itself in the 1960s.

Certain conditions can precipitate an increased incidence of violence (see Figure 7-8). Revolutions that are massive and powerful enough to overthrow the established government often occur when similar sets of conditions are present. One might predict that a prolonged, severe hardship is all that is necessary to trigger the collective violence of a revolution. Davies

---

Figure 7-8
Ghetto riots—What are the causes?

During the 1960s, riots in Black ghettos struck from one side of the United States to another—from Los Angeles to Detroit, Newark, and even Miami and Orangeburg, South Carolina. In the introduction to a special issue of the *Journal of Social Issues*, Allen (1970b) lists several suggested causes and evaluates each on the basis of what we now know about the riots and the rioters.

1. "The riots were senseless outbursts of violence." The behavioral scientist would reply that every social event has a cause. For example, in the past riots have been used as the way to achieve goals when more legitimate means had failed (Rudé, 1964).

2. "The riots were a part of a large-scale organized conspiracy to overthrow our country." The evidence refutes this explanation also. Most of the riots were spontaneous in origin; many started with a confrontation between a Black person and a policeman (Marx, 1970) and spread from there. The investigations and research of the Kerner Commission (1968) concluded that no conspiracy was present, that the riots were not Communist inspired.

3. "The riots are a reflection of the world-wide revolutionary movement to overthrow the capitalistic system." This claim has similarities to the preceding one and appears equally without substantiation. Allen notes that much of the rioters' behavior signified a desire to share more fully in the benefits of the system, rather than to overthrow it (1970b, p. 3).

4. "The people who participated in the riots were the 'riffraff' of ghetto life"—the deviants, the criminals, the unassimilated migrants (Caplan, 1970). Numerous interview studies and comparisons of rioters and nonrioters deny this; if anything, the opposite is the case (Tomlinson, 1968; McCord & Howard, 1968; Caplan, 1970). In McCord and Howard's samples of Blacks in Houston and Oakland, college-educated respondents were *least* opposed to the use of violence. The poorest of the poor participated less often in the riots (Caplan & Paige, 1968; Murphy & Watson, 1970). The militants in Watts, according to Tomlinson, were "the cream of urban Negro youth in particular and urban Negro citizens in general" (p. 28).

5. "The riots were a protest against conditions of ghetto life." This explanation is the one that is most strongly supported by available evidence. Although it should not be inferred that the rioters did so consciously to obtain specifiable goals, "it is clear that Black ghetto residents have called attention to their plight . . . by violently striking out against the symbols of their discontent" (Allen, 1970b, p. 4). The selectivity in the stores vandalized is only one example of the ways that the protest was shown.

All riots, and the actions of every individual, are responses to a variety of forces. Apparently, frustration and protest against the denial of opportunities are frequent causes.

(1962, 1969), however, concludes that the precipitating factor is a sudden sharp decline in the status of the underprivileged, coming immediately after a steady increase in their status. The earlier increase in their socioeconomic or political satisfaction leads the people to expect the continuation of such improvements (the curve of rising expectations). As we have seen before, *predictability* is important in making our assumptions about human nature. When such expectations are substantially frustrated for many people by an abrupt shift in the opposite direction, a discrepancy termed a *revolutionary gap* results (Tanter & Midlarsky, 1967), and collective violence is more likely to occur. Such people perceive a state of **relative deprivation,** compared to their earlier conditions, or compared to the conditions of others who serve as a reference group. General support for this analysis is found in a variety of cases, including the economic and political conditions of French workers and peasants before the French Revolution of 1789, the changing status of Southerners (as compared with Northerners) before the American Civil War, and the conditions of Black Americans during and after World War II (Davies, 1962; Geschwender, 1964). Similar conditions occurred before the Russian Revolution (Davies, 1969): in the late 1800s, the serfs had been freed and their material conditions improved; but during World War I, the Russian people were called upon to make great physical and material sacrifices. The refusal of the Tsarist government to terminate a disastrous war, along with other factors reviewed in Chapter 1, led to the first Russian Revolution and then to the overthrow of the Kerensky regime.

The hypothesis of relative deprivation as a trigger for collective violence may be verified if large numbers of citizens conclude that conditions in the 1970s are a sudden reversal of the conditions of the 1960s, which saw a steady improvement in job opportunities, income levels, number of material possessions, and other satisfactions. If we are wise, we will pay attention to increased rates of violence, for as the NCCPV report (1969, p. 2) reminds us, the rate of violence is a social bellwether; "dramatic rises in its level or modifications in its form tell us something important is happening in our political and social systems."

B. Changes in violence rates: The problem of assessing crime statistics

According to the Federal Bureau of Investigation and the Royal Canadian Mounted Police, crime rates in the United States and Canada are increasing yearly. Many behavioral scientists, however, are unconvinced of the accuracy of crime-rate comparisons across years. Part of the increase in reported rates may be due to more extensive disclosure of crimes. There may be incentives, such as increased public impatience with law enforcement, for police departments to report more (or fewer) crimes. Different police departments report crimes in different ways, and some do not report their figures to the FBI or RCMP at all. The "FBI crime rate" report usually lumps together major crimes and less serious ones; the latter account for 85% of the total arrests. Altogether, any conclusions about rises in crime rate must be drawn from data other than the FBI crime rates in the United States. It is possible that the homicide rate in the 1960s and early 1970s actually increased, but the best available evidence (Graham & Gurr, 1969) is that the crime rate in the United States is lower than it was 50 years ago. In 1916, the city of Memphis reported a rate for homicides that was seven times the present rate. Similarly, reported rates in Boston, New York, and Chicago during the years 1915 to 1925 showed higher violent-crime rates than those in the first published national crime statistics in 1933 (NCCPV, 1969, p. 20).

C. The future—How can aggression be controlled?

Although some form of violence has always existed in our society, scientists still wonder whether violence in individuals, groups, and nations can be controlled in the future. Can drives to harm others be channeled into socially acceptable behaviors? Each theoretical position has its own answer.

1. The psychoanalytic view. As he grew older, Sigmund Freud became increasingly pessimistic about the possibilities of world peace. World War I had a devastating effect on him. As Grossack and Gardner tell it, "he had spent his formative years in a peaceful world and was tortured by the phenomenon of millions of men confronting one another in combat, and being reduced to subhuman behavior" (1970, p. 12). The termination of World War I brought no optimism, for Freud and other astute observers noted that great conflicts and misunderstandings between the major powers continued to exist. At this point, Freud developed his theory of the **death instinct** —or a compulsion in all human beings "to return to the inorganic state out of which all living matter is formed" (C. S. Hall & Lindzey, 1968, p. 263). He saw aggression as a natural derivation of the death instinct.

Psychoanalysts who adopt this position see little chance of restraining our violent behaviors. Freud himself wrote that there is "no likelihood of our being able to suppress humanity's aggressive tendencies" (quoted in Bramson & Goethals, 1968, p. 76). However, two procedures may offer hope. One, at an international level, is a combining of forces to restrain aggressive actions by powerful nations. At an individual level, Freud, of course, saw the development of the superego as a way of restraining innate aggressive impulses: the child could be so reared that she or he would come to adopt standards and values that would inhibit aggression. Identification with the parent of the same sex, through resolution of the Oedipus conflict, was seen as a step in inhibiting instinctual aggression. Additionally, neo-Freudians advocate participation in socially acceptable aggressive activities (sports, debate, and the like) as ways of releasing aggressive energy.

2. The ethologist's view. If one assumes that aggression is innate (as the ethologists do), then one must conclude that aggression will always be a part of our lives. Our task, then, is to channel aggression into socially acceptable behaviors —a proposal that Lorenz (1966) advocates. Lorenz believes that Olympic games, space races to Mars, and similar international competitions provide opportunities for catharsis admirably, by redirecting fighting behavior into relatively harmless pursuits. The ethologists also encourage us to try to identify, and thus help control, those cues that trigger the expression of aggression.

3. Will overcrowding be our downfall? In analyzing aggression, ethologists use the concept of territoriality. In attempting to predict the rate of collective violence in the future, they give considerable attention to the increase in population. In 1900, the population of the United States was 76 million; in 1960, it was 180 million; in 1970, 205 million. In the year 2000, the projected population is 308 million (Bureau of the Census, U. S. Department of Commerce, 1970). By the year 2000, the population of the world is expected to be 7 billion, double what it is now. By the year 2050, perhaps 30 billion people will be competing for life resources. As the number of people associated with a given living area increases, does the rate of aggression and violence increase? Or is the human species infinitely adaptable? Carstairs (1969) has reviewed evidence from animal behavior indicating that the biological effects of overcrowding increase disruptive behavior. If Norway rats are given ample supplies of food, water, and nesting materials but are crowded together beyond their normal circumstances, infant mortality, cannibalism, and aggression increase (Calhoun, 1962).

But any extrapolation to the human condition at this point is tenuous. The available evidence about the effects of human overcrowding does not come from well-controlled experiments; beyond that, it is quite contradictory. For example, reported crime rates in the United States are clearly much higher, per capita, in urban areas than in rural areas (see Table 7-3). However, in the larger urban centers of Canada (such as Montreal, Toronto, and Vancouver) the rates for every type of violent crime are fractions of those for U. S. cities of equivalent sizes. Also, people in other societies can live in extremely crowded conditions without any increases in rate of crime or in mental disturbances (Draper, 1973); Mitchell (1971) found that in Hong Kong, where almost everyone lives in an overcrowded environment, the conditions did not lead to severe emotional strain.

Table 7-3
Rates for violent crimes in the United States in 1968

Population of Cities	Violent Crimes per 100,000 Persons
Over 250,000	773.2
100,000–250,000	325.3
50,000–100,000	220.5
25,000–50,000	150.8
10,000–25,000	126.6
Under 10,000	111.4
Suburban areas	145.5
Rural areas	96.5

Source: U. S. National Commission on the Causes and Prevention of Violence (1969, p. xvii).

We review the effects of crowding on human behavior in more detail in Chapter 16. At this point we simply note that overcrowding per se—as long as adequate supplies of materials for human needs are maintained—may not have the negative effects assumed by some (Stokols, Rall, Pinner, & Schopler, 1973).

4. *Frustration-aggression theory.* According to an early interpretation of the frustration-aggression hypothesis, the presence of aggression always presupposed frustration. But revisions of the frustration-aggression formulation accentuate the complexities of the relationship. Frustration is only one of the causes of aggression, and aggression is only one of the outcomes of frustration. Still, eliminating frustrations would be one way of reducing violence. Ransford (1968) interviewed Blacks living in the Watts area of Los Angeles and found that those with more intense feelings of dissatisfaction and frustration were more prone to violent action. The attendant violence of Quebec's separatism movement has generally been attributed to social and economic frustrations.

There are numerous actions community leaders do or could take to reduce frustrations. While mayor of New York, John Lindsay "rapped" with the residents of Harlem when frustrations had intensified. In many cities, the availability of playgrounds and swimming pools for people crowded into steamy tenements in the summertime might prevent rioting. Human-relations training for police may likewise reduce public frustrations and hence reduce aggression. In controlling aggression, the experimental social psychologist would also attempt to limit the presence of aggression-eliciting stimuli, including toy guns for children, guns for adults, and aggressive adult models, whether in the mass media or in real life.

5. *Social-learning theory.* Insofar as controlling aggression is concerned, social-learning theorists differ from ethologists on the advisability of advocating competition. The social-learning theorists believe that such activities "merely strengthen aggressive habits and decrease inhibitions against aggression" (Megargee & Hokanson, 1970, p. 34). Through response generalization, the rewarding of such mild aggressive behavior could lead to the development of more extreme, antisocial forms of aggression. Some social psychologists believe this is already happening in the United States and Canada. For instance, rewarding young boys who participate in hard-hitting sports such as hockey, boxing, rugby, and football and encouraging the expression of hostile feelings could lead to more extreme aggression in the future. As you might expect, social-learning theorists reject any notions of the cathartic value of watching violence

on television (Bandura, 1965a). In fact, research indicates that actual expression of aggressive acts does not drain off pent-up aggressive drives but instead encourages further expression of these drives (Bandura & Walters, 1963; Mallick & Mc-Candless, 1966). A detailed statement of social-learning theorists' position on regulating aggression may be found in R. H. Walters (1965), in R. H. Walters and Parke (1964), or in Bandura (1973).

A second means of regulating violence would be to limit the exposure of children to real-life models who act aggressively. Particularly undesirable is the witnessing of violent acts that are rewarded. Even viewing violent acts that are done for good purposes provides the observer with new ways of expressing hostility and violence (R. H. Walters, 1965). Parents who beat their child serve as potent role models for a child who seeks ways to respond to his or her own frustrations (Sears, Maccoby, & Levin, 1957).

Control of violence in the mass media would also be a part of this means. Beginning with the fall 1975 season, television networks in the United States instituted a new policy by which they set aside the first hour of prime-time viewing—between 8 and 9 P.M. in most time zones —for programs "suitable for family viewing." The nature of these programs is a question, however, and even if they remain free of disturbing material, Nielsen surveys indicate millions of children are up watching TV *beyond* this hour (Waters & Malamud, 1975).

As a third means of controlling violence, social-learning theorists would advocate *nonreinforcement* of aggressive responses (P. Brown & Elliott, 1965), along with *retraining*, which would establish new, constructive ways of responding to frustration-inducing events (Davitz, 1952). In fact, Bryan and Schwartz (1971) speculate that in the near future films may be used systematically to reeducate emotionally disturbed persons away from violent reactions to the world, as is prophesied in *A Clockwork Orange*. Social-learning theorists note with interest the research using both children (Deur & Parke, 1970) and adults (Baron, 1973; Donnerstein, Donnerstein, Simon,

& Ditrichs, 1972) indicating that strong and mild forms of punishment (including threats of retaliation) can serve to inhibit future expressions of aggression, temporarily at least.

VIII. Experimental attempts to control aggression

A century ago, a proper English lady, on being introduced to the theory of our evolutionary descent from the apes, responded: "Let us hope it is not true—but if it is, let us pray it will not become generally known!" If the human species possesses an innate component to aggress, we should seek to know about it and recognize its implications. But even if such innate tendencies exist, much harmful aggression is the result of learned reactions and frustrations. Anything that is learned can be manipulated and controlled. The important Robber's Cave field experiment by Sherif and his associates (M. Sherif, 1966; M. Sherif, Harvey, White, Hood, & Sherif, 1961) demonstrates how two groups can be manipulated so that hostilities between the two groups are first escalated and then reduced to the point that the two groups merge into one.[11]

The boys at Robber's Cave were 11- and 12-year-olds, psychologically well adjusted and from stable, middle-class families. Although the boys did not know it, their summer camp was staffed by researchers who manipulated and observed their aggressive behavior.

Two groups of boys were escorted to separate cabins on the first day, each unaware that the other group existed. In order to develop cohesiveness within each group, activities were planned that required the boys to cooperate for mutual benefit—for example, in camping out or cleaning up a beach area. Boys soon came to recognize each other's strengths and weaknesses; leaders and lieutenants emerged on the basis of their contribution to the group. Each group de-

---

[11]The section on Sherif's Robber's Cave experiment was drafted by Carol Sigelman.

veloped a name for itself, group jokes, standards for behavior, and even sanctions for those who "got out of line."

The time then came to introduce intergroup conflict and aggression. All that was necessary was to place the two groups in competition for rewards that only one group could attain. When the groups were brought together for a series of contests, good sportsmanship was quickly replaced by an ethic more akin to that of the former Green Bay Packer coach Vince Lombardi: "Winning isn't everything; it's the only thing." The groups began to call each other derogatory names, pick fights, and raid each other's camps. "Rattlers" downgraded all "Eagles," and vice versa, to the extent that neither group desired further contact with the opposing group. M. Sherif (1966) remarked that if a neutral observer with no knowledge of what had transpired had happened by, these previously wholesome boys would have appeared to be "wicked, disturbed and vicious bunches of youngsters" (p. 58). Yet the escalating hostility between groups appeared to produce a peak of solidarity within each group.

Reducing intergroup aggression was not as simple as producing it. Several strategies were tried and found wanting. The boys attended religious services emphasizing brotherly love and cooperation, but this appeal to moral values did not stop them from going right back to their war strategies after the services. In one phase of the research, the experimenters temporarily reduced conflict by introducing a third group that served as a "common enemy," but this strategy only widened the scope of conflict. Other possible strategies were rejected out of hand. Providing groups with accurate information about each other was not tried because, in an atmosphere of hostility, such information can readily be ignored or twisted. Similarly, conferences between leaders of the two groups were rejected, because concessions by the leaders could only be interpreted by their followers as traitorous sellouts of the group's interest.

Sherif and his colleagues also predicted that intergroup contact under pleasant circumstances

would not work, and they were right. Going to the movies, eating together, and shooting off fireworks on the Fourth of July only provided more opportunities to express hostility. The missing element was a **superordinate goal,** a goal important to all parties that could not be achieved by either group alone. Realizing this, the researchers arranged for a breakdown in the water supply line. Although the boys joined forces to find the leak, they still resumed their conflict when the crisis had passed. The researchers then instigated a whole series of such joint efforts to achieve a superordinate goal, as the groups pooled money to rent a movie and used a rope to pull and start the food supply truck. As a cumulative effect of these joint projects, the boys became friendlier, began to see strengths in their rivals, and even developed friendships across group lines. In fact, the majority chose to return home on the same bus, and the group that had earlier won a five-dollar prize used its money to treat the other group. The introduction of superordinate goals apparently permitted conflict-reduction strategies such as contact, increased knowledge of the other group, and communication to become effective. Although superordinate goals cannot be fabricated, such goals as halting the arms race or solving the energy crisis may help to bring hostile nations into contact and open lines of fruitful communication.

One of the unfortunate side effects of a belief in innate aggression is the tendency to throw one's hands up and say "There's nothing to be done; war is inevitable, and people are just naturally violent." This chapter has indicated that environmental circumstances can inhibit or encourage the expression of detrimental types of hostility and violence. These circumstances should not be overlooked as we seek a more peaceful human existence.

IX. Summary

To Freud and orthodox psychoanalysts, aggression is an urge generated by the body that must eventually find release. The ethologist believes intraspecies aggression has survival value, for it facilitates selective mating and spreading out of the species. On the other hand, most social-learning theorists and experimental social psychologists define aggression as behavior whose goal is to inflict harm or injury on some object or person.

Several viewpoints agree that aggressive behavior is more likely to occur if two types of factors—internal factors and triggering stimuli (or releasers) from the environment—are both present.

In many species of animals and birds, an instinct to defend one's living space, or territoriality, is a dominant force. However, the presence of such an instinctual territorial need in humans is difficult to document.

To some extent, aggressiveness can be produced in lower animals through a procedure of selective breeding over several generations. Thus, in lower animals, the extent of aggressiveness may partially derive from hereditary factors.

The frustration-aggression hypothesis, in its original form, proposed that the occurrence of aggression is a result of frustration and that any frustrating event inevitably leads to aggression. The hypothesis was later altered by its authors, who clarified it by stating that frustration could lead to other outcomes as well as aggression. Berkowitz has further amended the hypothesis, emphasizing that frustration produces a readiness for aggressive acts.

It is fruitless to argue over whether any link between frustration and aggression is innate or learned. While frustration may, in an innate way, heighten the likelihood of an aggressive act, learning may inhibit or alter this aggressive response.

Laboratory studies indicate that (1) witnessing an aggressive event lowers restraints against the witness's expression of aggression, after he or she has been frustrated, and (2) if aggression-cuing stimuli (such as guns) are present but not used, the subject will act more aggressively than if such stimuli were absent.

There are societies of people who live together peacefully. These are primitive tribes whose needs are usually met without frustration. They respond passively to aggression from other groups or retreat further into inaccessible living areas. Although their survival ability is theoretically low, these societies reflect the malleability and diversity of human nature.

If a child is exposed to an aggressive adult model and then frustrated, the child is more likely to act aggressively than if the adult model had acted in a nonaggressive manner. Apparently, inhibitions against aggression in the child are reduced by viewing an aggressive adult model.

The effect of watching violence on television is unclear. Laboratory studies indicate that witnessing violence facilitates expression of aggression by children. But a field study found that watching television programs that were considered highly aggressive reduced the amount of aggression expressed by the viewers (boys aged 10 to 17). The best conclusion at present is a cautionary one that recognizes that viewing aggression may lead to socially undesirable reactions.

Collective violence—or violence between nations or between identifiable groups within a nation—has always been a part of Western civilization. Particularly in the United States, violent means of solving problems have been characteristic.

One explanation for the origin of revolutions and other collective violence uses the concept of relative deprivation. When a group suffers an abrupt shift away from past increases in socioeconomic and political satisfaction, its members are more likely to revolt or express collective violence.

Every theory of aggression makes its own recommendations about the control or rechanneling of violence and aggression. Often these recommendations are in conflict with each other.

I. Conceptions of the development of morality in Western culture

II. Psychoanalytic explanations of moral development
- A. Freudian psychosexual development
- B. Erikson's psychosocial development: A revision and extension of Freud's stages
- C. Superego as values—Wilder's interpretation

III. Research in psychoanalysis
- A. The search for a general trait
- B. Tests of psychoanalytic theory

IV. A critique of the psychoanalytic approach to morality

V. Cognitive theories of moral development
- A. Piaget—Two stages of moral development
- B. Kohlberg—An extension of the cognitive stage approach

VI. Research on cognitive approaches
- A. Attempts to verify Piaget's stage approach
- B. Tests of Kohlberg's theory

VII. A critique of the cognitive approach

VIII. Social-learning theory
- A. The ethical-risk hypothesis
- B. Resistance to temptation
- C. Reactions to transgression

IX. Morality research in social learning
- A. Punishment
- B. Modeling

X. A critique of social-learning approaches

XI. An attempt at integration

XII. Summary

Moral judgments and behavior

by John O'Connor

8

> My impression, in the army, in college, and elsewhere, was that most institutions are political in nature and that you make your way in them only by adroit maneuvering. It seemed to me that . . . most people get along in the world by being flexible in their attitudes, not by moral confrontation. My impression was that it didn't pay to challenge the system, because the system was stronger than any individual.
>
> *Jeb Magruder*

> I said I didn't believe in the war, yet I continued to be an instrument of war without even seeking alternatives. Not to choose *is* to choose. I am responsible for the armor-piercing incendiary fragments and the mesh metal madness. . . . The attitude that one's society is responsible is an inarticulate passing of the buck, a convenient displacement of the blame, an escape mechanism which facilitates the act of war.
>
> *A conscientious objector and former U. S. Air Force flyer*

The two positions quoted above reflect two kinds of moral stances that have reverberated throughout history. Each responds differently to a dilemma central to society's values. How do we develop our own moral stances? Must each of us gain moral maturity on our own, or do conventional values provide acceptable guidelines?

The fact that there exist diverse beliefs about what is "moral" is not new to any of us, but in this chapter we shall seek to understand why these individual differences exist. We shall ask how we learn to participate in society and incorporate its values. How do we attain the state of **socialization,** the acquisition of the behaviors, norms, and values of our society? For we do recognize that each person's moral and ethical stance reflects in some way his or her participation as a member of a given society. But how much of this stance is emotional, how much is learned, and how much is part of a more generalized **cognitive** orientation of the individual? These are the questions that will serve as the focus of the present chapter.

243

I. Conceptions of the development of morality in Western culture

Throughout the recorded history of Western civilization, human beings have been preoccupied with the nature of their own morality in their search for justice and liberty. The ancient Greek philosophers considered reason the highest attribute of the virtuous person. Training and education were seen as the pathways to goodness, even though the skeptical Socrates admitted that he did not know what virtue really was or how it could be taught (Sizer & Sizer, 1970). With the rise of an organized Christian dogma we were given a new definition of moral judgment and conduct. According to doctrines advanced by St. Augustine, every human is born in sin, is basically evil, and can never hope to achieve virtue by power of reason alone. Therefore, people must be educated to faith. During early Christian times, the good person was seen as the one who glorified God; later, the Catholic church taught that moral thought and conduct were the means to ensure a person's eternal salvation. In the era of the Reformation, many people turned to reason and science in their search for an answer to the perplexing question of morality. In short, they came to believe that rationality would ensure morality.

With the writings of Sigmund Freud in the early 1900s, our ability to reach moral decisions through reason alone came into serious question. Civilization was ripe for a more complex, sophisticated analysis of the nature of morality (albeit a more pessimistic one). Had Freud not advanced his theories, someone else doubtless would have. While his concern was with the transformation of the child into a socialized adult, Freud was one of the first to point systematically at irrational psychosexual urges as the primary determinants of behavior and to the apparent necessity for all of us to place constraints on our feelings and behavior.

The early part of the 20th century saw the beginning of a scientific study of morality that derived its impetus not just from the clinical insights of Freud, but from academic social psychology as well. William McDougall (1908) conceptualized the problem in the following way in one of the first textbooks on social psychology:

> The fundamental problem of social psychology is the moralization of the individual into the society into which he is born as an amoral and egoistic infant. There are successive stages, each of which must be traversed by every individual before he can attain the next higher: (1) the stage in which the operation of the instinctive impulses is modified by the influence of rewards and punishments, (2) the stage in which conduct is controlled in the main by anticipation of social praise or blame, (3) the highest stage in which conduct is regulated by an ideal that enables a man to act in the way that seems to him right regardless of the praise or blame of his immediate social environment [p. 6].

While Freud and McDougall share some common assumptions (for example, the amorality of infants and the necessity of the child's developing through a lockstep set of stages), the great differences in their approaches anticipated the conflicting theories of moral development that we consider in this chapter. In more recent times, the differences have been illuminated by researchers who ask whether *emotional-motivational* or *cognitive* or *learning* factors are most important in the development of morality.

The **psychoanalytic theory** of Freud has utilized *emotional* and *motivational constructs* to explain the development of personality and character, while the contrasting *cognitive approach* has concerned itself with different phenomena—*the development of rules, the violation of moral norms, and the acquisition of universal principles.* Cognitive theories hold that these developments serve as coding processes in the child, intervening between stimulus and response (Baldwin, 1969). For example, both Jean Piaget and Lawrence Kohlberg have offered theories about how the individual structures the external moral order and how these structurings change during the process of the individual's development.

A third approach to the study of moral development, exemplified by **reinforcement theories** and **social-learning theories,** has been most interested in other phenomena—how the individual behaves in specific situations, how much of this behavior generalizes to other situations, and how this behavior is *learned*. Reinforcement theorists and social-learning theorists at first rejected the necessity of postulating *any* intervening variables; they chose to study specific aspects of moral behavior directly. Such investigators as Bandura and Walters (1963) and Aronfreed (1968) sought to determine what types of environmental variations change behavior. However, more recent research on learning through observation (Bandura, 1971) and modeling (Crane & Ballif, 1973; McManis, 1974) indicates that consequences do not alter behavior automatically and unconsciously, but are *cognitively* mediated, that is, mediated through some higher-order process in the brain (Bandura, 1974). In its concern with morality, social-learning theory has focused on two major topics: *resistance to temptation* and *reaction to transgression*. **Resistance to temptation** implies suppression of a behavior that would have a high incidence except for the influence of a prohibition or norm. **Reaction to transgression** is normally described as an emotional reaction such as fear, guilt, shame, or self-criticism.

It is necessary to begin our review with these three predominant approaches to moral development and then use these theories to coordinate the scraps of empirical cloth that come to us in different textures, colors, and shapes. After seeing how each theory approaches moral development, we will be prepared to evaluate its contributions to our understanding.

II. Psychoanalytic explanations of moral development

Despite the fact that it has been severely criticized for a number of reasons, Sigmund Freud's psychoanalytic approach cannot be ignored. Its influence on research, in the choice of problems (the concept of conscience, for example), is pervasive, even if not always acknowledged.

A. Freudian psychosexual development

In developing his **emotional-motivational approach to personality and morality,** Freud (1917/1963) postulated that three systems of energies operate within every individual. The interaction of these energy systems accounts for the character and morality shown by a person in his or her dealings with others. Each system—the **id,** the **ego,** and the **superego**—has its own province of the mind, and each functions as a relatively independent system, although continually interacting with the other two systems.

1. The id. In psychoanalytic theory, the id can roughly be equated with the quantity of biologically determined energy in the organism. The id is below the level of awareness (in other words, is part of the **unconscious**) and is the source of irrational impulses that persistently strive for selfish gratification. Not only does the id contain all the various sexual drives manifested by the child during his or her psychosexual development, but it also contains aggressive urges that seek expression. The id remains unconscious, even when the ego is so weakened that it can offer little resistance to the selfish demands of the id. One cannot simply equate the id with the unconscious, however, for the latter also contains portions of the ego and the superego as well as defense mechanisms used in protecting the ego from attack.

2. The ego. While the id is said to be inborn, according to Freudian theory the ego is developed through learning and through encounters with one's environment. The basic purpose of the ego is to maintain the organism on its path toward realistic goals; in doing so, the ego mediates among the "three harsh masters"—the id, the superego, and external reality. As one of its tasks is the minimizing of conflicts among these three entities, the ego serves a synthesizing function as well as an executive one.

The ego is also the principal system by which a person learns about and deals with the reality of the environment. The ego begins to develop at birth, and its development continues throughout life. According to psychoanalytic theory, the ego emerges as a result of the child's failures to gratify his or her needs. Fenichel (1945) has written, for example, that if the needs of the infant (mostly coming from the id) were always satisfied immediately, there would be no ego. This is the case because initially the infant does not differentiate between self and not self; it knows only its own states of tension and relaxation. It is only when the child begins to perceive external objects and other people as sources of gratification that the ego emerges.

In some of his formulations, Freud seemed to conclude that the ego possesses no energies of its own—at least none traceable to biological sources. Supposedly, all the executive powers of the ego were borrowed from the id and the superego, and the ego maintained itself by organizing the dynamic energies of these other two systems. Many social psychologists regard this as a rather curious conclusion, since it suggests that the major integrative and organizing aspect of personality—the ego—is only a derivative of more basic impulses. The **neo-Freudians,** who operate within a basically psychoanalytic framework but disagree with certain of Freud's views, have elevated the status of the ego. Unlike Freud, most neo-Freudians propose that the ego is innate and has a source of energy all its own. In effect, they reject Freud's assumption that humans are passive slaves to primitive instinctual urges (Shaffer, in press). Many current researchers have focused on the concept of the ego and ego development (Haan, Stroud, & Holstein, 1973; Orlofsky, Marcia, & Lesser, 1973); these findings will be discussed in Section III when we examine attempts at verification of the concept of the ego.

3. The superego. The third aspect of Freud's mental triad, the superego, contains the *conscience,* the censorship function of personality. The superego also encompasses the **ego ideal,** the child's perception of the kind of person he or she would like to be. In observing his patients (and perhaps himself), Freud was struck by the impression that censoring or inhibiting forces generated by the superego were often as compelling and irrational as the id impulses themselves —and just as likely to lead to maladjustment. The phenomenon of melancholia or depression, in which the person cruelly punished himself or herself for often trivial shortcomings, especially reflected the dominance of what Freud labeled as the superego.

Parents, teachers, siblings, and others in the environment contribute to the formation of the superego. What the child introjects from these agents is principally *prohibitions.* Since Freud saw the young child as *amoral,* preoccupied with the satisfaction of his or her own impulses, and lacking in any internalized inhibitions, he considered these prohibitions necessary. According to Freud, only parents or others who threaten punishment can effectively control the expression of the child's impulses. At the onset, the child conforms to parental dictates only because he or she fears their punishments. Later, around the age of 6 or 7, if development has been optimal, the child comes to identify with his or her parents (the powerful aggressors), and their image and standards become introjected—or become the child's own.

The reason this change takes place is related to the interest in sexual organs that occurs during the ages of 3 to 6 and the resolution of what Freud called the **Oedipus conflict.** The precise causes of the introjection of parental standards for boys are different from those for girls. The boy has craved his mother and has come to resent his father. According to Freud, he fears that his father will harm him. *Castration anxiety* is the term Freud used to refer to this fear, which leads to a repression of the sexual desire for the mother. In fact, the boy comes to identify with the powerful father and gains vicarious satisfaction for his sexual impulses. The repression of the original sexual desires leads to the final development of the superego.

For girls, the counterpart of castration anxiety is *penis envy.* According to Freud, the girl expresses disappointment upon discovering that a boy has a protruding sex organ, which she apparently lacks or has lost. She blames her mother for this, and shifts her affection to the father, who possesses this valued organ. The development of the superego is facilitated by the identification with the father.

In one sense the child becomes the parent; he or she follows an internalized conscience as though its commands were coming directly from the parent. The most important aspect of this notion of identification and introjection is that the standards embraced by the child continue to operate with all the force they possessed at the time of introjection. The period of introjection is usually a time of great anxiety for the child, and hence the conscience can be excessively severe and unyielding. The child can become excessively self-critical and equally critical of others.

As the preceding paragraphs imply, in the absence of adequate parental figures to emulate, the superego may fail to develop. According to psychoanalytic theory, children raised without adequate identification figures are likely to be deficient in the control of impulses and in concern for others; in extreme cases their adult behavior becomes what we call psychopathic—that is, without any apparent concern about their wrongdoing.

4. *Freudian stages of development.* Freud hypothesized that as a child grows older, his or her psychic energy, or **libido,** is directed toward the satisfaction of needs associated with different parts of the body. The amount of energy available to the child is a finite amount; increased amounts cannot be generated on demand. If a child's needs are not satisfied at a particular stage, a portion of the child's psychic energy re-

mains oriented toward that need (that is, a part of the child's energy fixates), even though biological development also requires the child to pass on to the next stage of development. Coincident with their biological development is the discovery by children that they must adapt their behaviors in order to become members of a community. All children must learn to control their bladders; they must not play with their genitals; and so on. Each stage has new requirements. Freud conceived the following stages, which center on parts of the body and related needs.

The **oral stage** occurs at 1 year of age and is concerned with sucking and biting needs. The **anal stage** occurs between ages 2 and 3 and is centered on toilet training and the regulation of elimination. The **phallic stage,** which takes place between the ages of 4 and 6, centers on an attraction to the other sex and envy of the parent of the same sex (called the Oedipus complex). Between the ages of 6 and 14, the child enters into a **latency period,** or period of quiescence. At around the age of 14 and beyond, the individual enters the **genital stage,** which centers on the development of love for others. According to Freud, fixation at a particular stage means two things: (1) in adulthood, the person will not be able to fully achieve the genital stage (love others and act unselfishly), because a portion of his or her psychic energy will still be devoted to unsatisfied selfish needs; and (2) the adult personality will reflect the presence of these early unsatisfied needs. For example, a man who fixated at the oral stage of development would show his oral needs as an adult by engaging in excessive talking, chewing, or smoking, and by choosing an orally oriented occupation—such as selling, preaching, or teaching.

With this formulation in mind, we can see why psychoanalytic theory proposes that by the age of 6 the nature of an individual's major drives and interpersonal relationships has been established, and that this organization remains fundamental throughout his or her life. However, one of the inadequacies of classical psychoanalytic theory as an explanation of moral development is that, during the so-called latency period, the child's moral development may be accelerating, yet the theory—with its accentuation of psychosexual development—overlooks this. Neo-Freudians, notably Erik Erikson (1963a, 1963b, 1964) and Harry Stack Sullivan (1953), have given more attention to this period of early adolescence as they moved away from a sexually saturated view of development.

B. Erikson's psychosocial development: A revision and extension of Freud's stages

Erikson, who had been a high-school dropout and a wandering artist in his youth (a hippie?), was never a conventional psychoanalyst. For example, his work with the Oglala Sioux Indians (the tribe that killed Custer and were in turn all but destroyed at the Battle of Wounded Knee) and the Yurok Indians of Northern California convinced him that traditional psychoanalytic theory was not adequate for explaining the emotional problems of native North Americans. The Indians' dilemma was that they could neither live as their ancestors had nor identify with White people's values. Their difficulty appeared to have more to do with ego and cultural values than with sexual drives.

1. The study of the ego. Erikson emphasizes three major conceptions in the study of the ego that differ dramatically from Freud's. He suggests that:

a. Along with Freudian psychosexual developmental stages, there are also psychosocial developmental stages. Beyond the early ages, development concentrates on the creative, adaptive, and reality-oriented aspects of personality rather than on sexual drives. The source of the energy for development is not merely displaced sexual energy, as Freud had postulated.

b. Personality development continues *throughout life* and centers on nuclear conflicts particular to each period of development.

c. Each psychosocial stage has a positive as well as a negative component.

2. Psychosocial stages. Erikson's eight stages of development, together with the construct that is achieved through the successful resolution of each stage, are described in Table 8-1. We discuss each in detail below.

a. Trust versus mistrust. Erikson's first stage merits special attention, since it is concerned with trust and mistrust. The infant takes in the world through its senses at the same time it takes in food through its mouth. To Erikson, the basic attitude that should be learned by the infant is that "you can trust the world in the form of your mother, that she will come back and feed you the right thing in the right quantity at the right time" (Erikson, as quoted in R. I. Evans, 1969, p. 15). Basic trust is defined as a correspondence between the infant's needs and its world. Erikson believes that this quality is instinctive in animals, but that it must be learned by humans, and that the mother is the person who must teach it. Mothers of different races, social classes, and cultures will teach it in different ways—but always in the manner that fits the group's perception of the nature of the world.

Basic mistrust is also important, for Erikson does not see each stage as mastered by the complete domination of some positive quality. In the first stage, Erikson proposes that "a certain ratio of trust and mistrust in our basic social attitude is the critical factor" (Erikson, as quoted in R. I. Evans, 1969, p. 15). When we enter a new situation, we must be able to determine how much we can trust and how much we must mistrust. Erikson defines mistrust as a sense of readiness for danger and an anticipation of discomfort. Here again, we learn this readiness from our environment, while in animals this ability is instinctively given. Thus, we may say that Erikson is evolving an orientation toward human nature that says "Trust others when it is appropriate, and distrust them when that is justified."

Erikson is not explicit about what this "certain ratio of trust to mistrust" should be, but clearly the ratio should be favorable—in other words, there should be more trust than mistrust. Only with such a ratio can the construct or goal of hope be realized. Erikson does not see hope as merely some hypothetical construct invented by philosophers and theologians; rather, it is a "very basic human strength without which we couldn't stay alive" (Erikson, as quoted in R. I. Evans, 1969, p. 17).

b. Autonomy versus doubt. According to Erikson, each stage in one's development is structured in the same way. But each builds on the previous ones. For example, a goal of "will" or self-control is achieved during the second stage, which occurs as children learn to master their anal sphincter muscles. Here again, Erikson's ideal is the development of both a positive trait (autonomy) and a negative one (shame or

---

Table 8-1
Erikson's stages and conflicts

Stage of Life (or Nuclear Conflict)	Construct Ideally Realized or Achieved	Age or Equivalent Freudian Stage
1. Acquiring a basic sense of trust versus a sense of mistrust	Hope	Oral-sensory stage
2. Acquiring a sense of autonomy versus a sense of doubt and shame	Will	Anal-muscular
3. Acquiring a sense of initiative versus a sense of guilt	Purpose	Phallic
4. Acquiring a sense of industry versus a sense of inferiority	Competence	Latency period
5. Acquiring a sense of identity versus a sense of identity diffusion	Fidelity	Puberty and adolescence
6. Acquiring a sense of intimacy and solidarity versus a sense of isolation	Love	Young adulthood
7. Acquiring a sense of generativity versus a sense of self-absorption or stagnation	Care	Adulthood
8. Acquiring a sense of integrity versus a sense of despair and disgust	Wisdom	Maturity

doubt), but apparently more autonomy than shame. For autonomy to develop, a firmly developed sense of trust is necessary (Erikson, 1968). Children must be able to have faith in the world to have faith in themselves.

Too much autonomy, however, can be harmful. For example, a girl who uses temper tantrums to control her parents or who cries hysterically to keep her parents home acquires an inflated sense of autonomy. A little doubt and shame is a healthy balance to such an inflated ego. Erikson says that shame assumes that one is completely exposed and capable of being self-conscious. The achievement of willpower is an outgrowth of the development of autonomy.

c. Initiative versus guilt. Erikson suggests that the nuclear conflict appearing at the third stage has initiative at one end and guilt at the other. The parents' responses to the child's self-initiated activities (such as motor development, language, and fantasy) have great importance here. If the child's questions are not rebuffed, and if his or her physical exploits such as rope jumping and bicycle riding are not discouraged, the child will develop a lifelong sense of initiative and purpose. If efforts are discouraged or ridiculed, the child will develop guilt. Erikson says that guilt is a likely development at this stage, because as the child thinks "grand thoughts" of accomplishment, he or she also reflects a fear of having committed deeds that were unacceptable.

d. Industry versus inferiority. The fourth stage is the one in which the child becomes able to use deductive reasoning, and in which he or she learns obedience to rules. This stage has a sense of industry at one extreme and a sense of inferiority at the other. At this stage children are fascinated with what makes things work, with the intricate details in model-airplane building and cooking. Parents who deride all this as messy or clumsy cause the child to develop a sense of inferiority.

e. Identity versus role confusion. According to Freud, identity comes to the young child during the phallic stage, when the child of 4 to 6 years gains vicarious pleasure and power by imag-

ining an association between himself or herself and the parent of the same sex. Erikson (1968) has extended this concept and proposed that the adolescent must also develop an identity. This identity represents more than a rebirth of the phallic-stage adaptation. The problem of the adolescent is not only to control and direct sexual drives but also to establish a selfhood in light of the variety of roles available. Erikson views adolescent love as an attempt at defining one's identity rather than as a purely sexual matter; the adolescent girl, for example, projects her image onto others and in seeing her image reflected is able to clarify her self-concept. This concept is very close to that suggested by George Herbert Mead (1934), who proposed that a child gradually defines the viewpoint of the "generalized other." Mead sees the critical aspect of moral development as empathy, or role-taking ability.

f. Intimacy versus isolation. The nuclear conflict of the sixth stage has intimacy at one extreme and isolation at the other. Classical Freudian theory has little to say about this period of development during early adulthood. Erikson describes intimacy as the ability to care about someone else and share in a companionable way with that person. This is the period of intense marital relations and strong bonds of friendship. Isolation comes from not being able to share with anyone.

g. Generativity versus self-absorption. After marriage, establishment of a family, and beginning of a career, the next conflict centers around growth versus stagnation. Erikson uses the terms generativity—an extension of oneself beyond one's family to a concern for society and the welfare of others—versus self-absorption in one's personal needs.

h. Integrity versus despair. The psychosocial dimension that predominates in maturity has integrity at one extreme and despair at the other. People who can look upon their lives as useful and worthwhile are contrasted with those individuals who see their lives as a waste and despair at what might have been.

The failure to handle any one nuclear conflict adequately can result in a permanent impairment in respect to the problem involved. That is, the failure limits what each person can assimilate from interactions with others. Each level of conflict demands progressively more ego strength for its mastery. Thus, mature integrity depends on the basic development of trust, autonomy, initiative, and other adaptive skills. But mature development is not just a stringing together of all these qualities. Rather, the stages have a snowballing effect; each stage adds something specific to all later stages and creates a new ensemble from earlier ones. This constant transformation of morality is called *epigenesis*. The development at each stage must be supported by strong cultural institutions—first by the parents, and later by all the various aspects of society.

As Elkind (1974) suggests, Erikson's stage approach has virtues that go beyond the Freudian conception of development. Erikson's theory (1) focuses on real emotional problems, not the residuals of psychosexual frustrations; (2) allows for the role of society and the individual's interaction with it, not just parental impositions; and (3) demonstrates that each phase of growth has its positive qualities as well as its dangers. Beyond these specific qualities, Erikson's theory has a liberating orientation that helps the individual to widen his or her options.

Erikson's theory has been with us for more than 20 years, and his thinking has had a slowly increasing influence on social psychology; but at present we still lack well-developed procedures designed to assess the child's resolution of each nuclear conflict. How do we know, for example, whether a 3-year-old boy trusts or mistrusts others, or whether a 15-year-old girl has developed a clear-cut identity for herself? Existing concepts and measures could be used for studying some conflicts and stages. Trust versus mistrust, for example, seems similar to concepts of **interpersonal trust** (Rotter, 1971) and the trustworthiness of human nature (Wrightsman, 1964a, 1974). Constructs at other stages of life might be tapped with a concept of achievement motivation; for example, concerns with *industry*

versus inferiority (latency stage) and *generativity versus stagnation* (adulthood stage) seem particularly fruitful for this approach.

C. Superego as values— Wilder's interpretation

Another neo-Freudian explanation has focused on the superego, suggesting that the superego is synonymous with values (J. Wilder, 1973). According to Wilder, the central problem —at least at the present time—in moral development is not the denial of basic drives, as Freud suggested, but the denial of *values*. Within this orientation, the superego is a system that allows the ego to make decisions with the help of "yardsticks" supplied by the superego. Values serve as yardsticks that change with developmental and environmental circumstances. Wilder suggests that the superego serves to predict what the painful or pleasurable consequences of an action will be. This frame of reference allows the superego not to be fixed at age 6 or so, but to be extended with experience through all life stages. This fascinating interpretation implies that the stable superego of Freud's time reflected the commonly shared values of that religious era. We can anticipate that children's images of the future and their ability to predict consequences will vary considerably, depending on their environments as well as on their "parental" predictions. Children raised in the ghetto may predict the probability of future events differently than upper-class children. The rapidly changing values of the present era probably threaten the predictive capacity of the superego.

III. Research in psychoanalysis

A. The search for a general trait

The psychoanalytic approaches described in Section II assume that there is an overriding consistency to personality, that the forces of id, superego, and ego play predominant roles in determining behavior in a variety of situations. The early empirical studies of morality (then called "character development") caused social psychologists to question this assumption. The most extensive of the empirical studies was the Character Education Inquiry, begun by Hartshorne, May, and Maller in the mid-1920s, which attempted to examine the degree of consistency of moral behavior across situations. Hartshorne and his associates wanted to answer such questions as: How general or how situation-specific is moral behavior? Are children who behave morally or ethically in one situation also moral or ethical in another situation? The Hartshorne et al. project covered five years and examined the conduct of high school students in the classroom, on the playing fields, at parties, at church, and in scouting activities. Almost all the experimental tasks placed the students in different situations that tempted them to act in an immoral way. For example, the students were asked to score their own true-false tests without supervision by the teacher. (The subjects did not know that the researchers had copies of their papers and would know how many changes were made in the process of scoring).[1]

Hartshorne, May, and Maller were unable to find many correlations of great magnitude in the reactions to the different tasks that tempted students to lie, cheat, and steal in a variety of situations. The researchers concluded that expressions of morality exhibit no general consistency at all and that the morality or immorality of a person's behavior is specific to his or her particular situation at the time. The girl who cheated in scoring her test was not the one who stole money from the teacher's desk. When these results were published in the late 1920s and early 1930s, the predominant reaction among social psychologists was that research on moral development was rather futile and the search for any organized system of development, such as Freud's, was fruitless.

But not all social psychologists were content to accept the conclusion that moral behavior is entirely situation-specific. Burton (1963) reanalyzed the Hartshorne-May data and found evidence for a small degree of consistency along a dimension of morality in a subject's response from one situation to another. Later, the team of Nelson, Grinder, and Mutterer, using several methodological approaches, reexamined the issue of generality versus specificity of honesty using sixth-grade children in six different temptation situations. In general, their conclusion was "that temptation behavior is only moderately consistent across a variety of tasks" (1969, p. 265).

Taking another approach, Gordon Allport (1961) pointed out that a consistency of orientation might even exist when the same student cheats on a test but does not steal money from the teacher's desk; in both of these situations the student's behavior may be guided by a motive to please the teacher. In other words, cheating may be a response to the student's desire to achieve the teacher's goals. The example may be far-fetched, but the point is correct enough. Cases of apparently inconsistent behavior may actually reflect consistency at a deeper level.

B. Tests of psychoanalytic theory

Empirical studies specifically directed at testing psychoanalytic theory have also been completed. A massive longitudinal study was carried out by Peck and Havighurst (1960), who tested all the children in a small town, first at age 10 and again six years later. Using a conception of five stages of moral development based on psychoanalytic theory, the researchers found that—as opposed to Freud's postulation—the child's moral growth continues beyond the age of 6. (Peck and Havighurst's stages of development are presented, along with others, in Table 8-2.) Although different 16-year-olds manifested different stages of development, most individuals

---

[1]It is sadly ironic that many scientists who study moral behavior either induce their subjects to cheat and lie or otherwise deceive their subjects during experiments, even while trying to determine the specificity or generality of morality. Scientists lie in the specific situation of the study, and the reader must assume that the scientists lie only when gathering data and not while analyzing or reporting. Indeed, the generality-specificity argument is rather complex.

Table 8-2
A comparison of stages of moral judgment

Theorist	Amoral Type	Fearful-Dependent	Opportunistic	Conforming to Persons	Conforming to Rules	Operating from Principles; Autonomous
McDougall (1908)	1. Instinctive		2. Reward and punishment	3. Anticipating praise and blame		4 Regulation by an ideal
Piaget (1965)	1. Premoral	2. Heteronomous—obedient to adult authority	3. Autonomous—reciprocity and equality oriented			4. Autonomous—ideal reciprocity and equality
Peck & Havighurst (1960)	1. Amoral		2. Expedient	3. Conforming	4. Irrational-conscientious	5. Rational-altruistic
Kohlberg (1963)		1. Punishment	2. Instrumental-relativist orientation; selfish exchange	3. Interpersonal concordance or "good-boy/nice-girl" orientation	4. "Law-and-order" and rule orientation	5A. Social-contract, legalistic orientation 5B. Individual-conscience orientation 6. Orientation to universal ethical principles
Fromm (1955)	1. Receptive	2. Exploitative	3. Marketing	4. Hoarding		5. Productive, autonomous
Riesman (1950)	1. Tradition-directed man		2. Other-directed man			3. Inner-directed man
Harvey, Hunt, & Schroder (1961)	1. System 1: Absolutistic, evaluative	2. System 2: Negativistic		3. System 3: Conforming, people oriented		4. System 4: Integrated, independent

Note: This table compares the terms used by different theorists concerned with the development of moral judgment or character. By reading across from left to right, the different stages for each theory are presented. By reading down one column, the equivalent stages of different theorists are presented. The similarity is impressive. (Figures 8-1 and 8-2 and Tables 8-1, 8-2, and 8-3 are adapted from "Stage and Sequence: The Cognitive-Developmental Approach to Socialization," by L. Kohlberg. In D. A. Goslin (Ed.), *Handbook of Socialization Theory and Research*. Copyright 1969 by Rand McNally & Company, Chicago. Reprinted by permission.)

tended to maintain the motives and attitudes they had held at age 10.

Many other researchers have examined Freud's hypothesis about the development of a conscience—that conscience emerges in the phallic stage as a result of the Oedipus conflict. Sears, Maccoby, and Levin (1957) defined conscience as an internalized control whereby children reward or punish themselves as though their parents' standards had become their own. Conscience was assessed through asking the mother questions about the child's behavior in a task that tempted the child to violate a rule or command. Sears et al. concluded that warm, loving parents and stable relations were most predictive of an advanced stage of moral development, a finding not consistent with Freud's theory. One problem with this study, however, was that the mother was the source of measures both of the child's behavior—through her reports—and of parental attitudes; such a procedure may encourage spuriously high relationships between factors. Some of the more recent studies also indicate that the frequent use of power assertion —in other words, instances in which parents use their physical power to control the child—leads the child to develop a weak conscience (Allinsmith, 1960; Aronfreed, 1961; Hoffman & Saltzstein, 1967; and Holstein, 1969, reviewed by Shoffeitt, 1971). Again, such findings are not consistent with Freud's hypothesis.

Some writers with a psychoanalytic bias interpret the results of studies as indicating support for Freud's ideas about how the superego develops. For example, Kline's (1972) review of the Sears results concludes "that psychoanalytic propositions yielded a rather positive verdict" (cited in R. Carlson, 1975, p. 397). Yet it seems to us that the most conservative evaluation of superego research is that the empirical findings give little support to the predominant place of the superego in morality development.

"Ego" research fared somewhat better. Orlofsky, Marcia, and Lesser (1973) studied Erikson's psychosocial conflict of identity and found some support for the position that genuine intimacy occurred only when a reasonable sense

of identity was established. Toder and Marcia (1973) found more conformity in persons with an "unstable" identity status than in those with a "stable" identity status.

IV. A critique of the psychoanalytic approach to morality

When we look for empirical support for the Freudian proposal that an overriding superego controls morality in every situation, we find very little or no evidence for such a notion. Even recent psychoanalytic theorizing emphasizes ego strength more than the superego. Among the characteristics of the ego that contribute to moral conduct are general intelligence, ability to delay gratification, capacity for focused attention, ability to control socially unacceptable fantasies, and degree of self-esteem (Kohlberg, 1963). Rather than emphasizing an early, fully developed superego evolved from the Oedipal conflict, researchers are currently emphasizing the decision-making capacity of the ego, which develops gradually with age. Yet widespread dissatisfaction with the Freudian theory of moral development still exists, for reasons cited above and because of inconsistent findings from one study to the next. Let us turn, then, to the second major approach, the cognitive approach, to see whether it offers more promise.

V. Cognitive theories of moral development

Jean Piaget, in Switzerland, and Lawrence Kohlberg, in the United States, have done much to elucidate how moral development can be understood through a *cognitive* approach. Such an approach emphasizes thoughts rather than emotions and concentrates on the learning of rules, laws, and higher principles. In this section the contributions of each of these theorists will be reviewed.

They don't think on their own.

A. Piaget—Two stages of moral development

Piaget and Freud, the two leading theoreticians of moral development, were similar in their methodology. Each observed, asked questions, and talked to people who had been ignored by others. Freud spent hours seated by his patients' couch listening to the dream descriptions and free associations of neurotic Viennese women, while Piaget (1926, 1965) squatted on the sidewalks of Geneva playing marbles with children. Both thinkers employed a concept of stages of development, but for Piaget these stages were mental, or cognitive, in nature.

In his more general theory of mental development, Piaget proposed that the child moves through four stages of increasingly abstract reasoning. He believed that all children develop through the same sequence, regardless of the contents of their particular experiences, their family, or their culture. Progressing to a higher stage in respect to this *mental* development is a necessary, but not a sufficient, condition for shifting to a higher stage of *moral* development. Piaget proposed the presence of only two stages of moral development. In the earlier **heteronomous stage,** or the stage of moral realism, the child accepts rules as given from authority. In the second stage, the stage of **autonomous morality,** or moral independence, the individual believes in modifying rules to fit the needs of the situation.

As Piaget (1971) uses the term, "cognitive stages" possess the following characteristics:

1. They imply that children of different ages possess *qualitatively* different ways of thinking and of solving the same problems.

2. These different ways of thinking may be ordered in an **invariant** sequence; that is, there is a consistent series of steps in the sequence, along which each child must progress as he or she gets older (Piaget, 1960).

3. Each way of thinking forms a *structured whole.* That means that, at each stage, the individual beliefs are all organized around that particular way of thinking. Piaget believes that these ways of thinking, or structures, are "really there"

controlling thought, much as the moon is "really there," controlling tides (Brainerd, 1974).

4. Each successive cognitive stage is a hierarchical integration of what has gone before. Higher stages do not replace lower stages but, rather, reintegrate them. Previous ways of doing things are maintained for the functions they serve, but increasingly a solution at the highest level available to the person is preferred.

1. The development of rules. Piaget studied behavior in games, because he wanted to examine how children thought spontaneously and to observe how children conformed to their own conceptions of the rules (Piaget, 1965). Piaget's method was to play marbles and other street games with the children and, in response to his probing questions, let them explain the rules as they played. You might try asking young children "Who makes the rules?" or "Can you change the rules in this game?" and see if you get different explanations from children of different ages.

Piaget observed that when young children (aged 3 years) play marbles together, they have no rules and no cooperative play. Children that young really do not play "together," even if they share the same space at the same time. From ages 3 to 5, some trend toward a group of players emerges, but each child is **egocentric** in the sense that he or she considers his or her own point of view the only possible one. At this age, children lack **empathy** (Shantz, 1974); they are unable to put themselves in someone else's place because they are unaware that the other person has a point of view. Around the age of 7 or 8, *incipient cooperation* emerges—the first incidence of concern about mutual benefits and the unification of rules. However, at this stage the ideas about rules in general are still rather vague. It is not until a later time, the period of *codification of rules*, around age 11 or 12, that every detail of the game is fixed and agreed upon.

While children progress in the practice of rules, their attitudes toward rules are also changing. (Piaget, 1965, called this "the consciousness of rules.") To the 3-year-old, rules are received almost without thought. During the next few years, rules are held to be sacred and untouchable; 4- and 5-year-olds see rules as coming from adults and lasting forever, even though children at this age often break rules indiscriminately. During later ages (10 to 11 years old), a rule is looked upon as a law resulting from mutual consent. At this age, rules are seen as modifiable, but the ones actually agreed upon are adhered to scrupulously. For example, in response to the question "Are you allowed to change the rules at all?" a 13-year-old responds with "Oh, yes, some want to, and some don't. If the boys play that way (changing something), you have to play like that" (Piaget, 1965, p. 68).

2. *Intentions versus consequences.* The child's conception of rules is not the only thing that changes between the stage of moral realism and the stage of moral independence. Conceptions of the seriousness of crimes also change. In seeking to understand these changes in conceptions, Piaget chose to deal with occurrences common to many children—clumsiness and lying. The young of any species are incredibly clumsy; puppies are forever stumbling and crashing into things, much as young children are. A child is constantly dropping, breaking, or soiling things or otherwise disturbing the tranquility of the adult world, and a parent's reaction to a child's spilling milk or knocking the saltshaker off the table is usually an angry one. Thus, clumsiness plays an important part in the lives of children, and the child inevitably attaches some meaning to adults' reactions to his or her transgressions. Piaget asked children to compare and evaluate the seriousness of two kinds of clumsiness—one a well-intentioned act that did considerable damage, the other a disobedient act that had negligible consequences. These were compared by using pairs of stories like those presented in Figure 8-1.

Piaget found that younger children judged actions according to their *material consequences*; to them, the boy who broke the most cups was the naughtiest. Older children took *intentions* into account and judged the second boy in Figure 8-1 (Henry) as committing the more serious offense.

This finding may provoke the question of whether society values intentions or consequences when determining punishment for a crime. What if I want to kill you and I deliberately shoot you, but my aim is so bad that I miss you completely? How does the punishment for that act compare with the punishment for an action where my intention is the same, but my aim is so good that I kill you? What punishment would result if I were showing friends my new gun and it went off, accidentally killing a bystander?

The nature and consequences of lying also showed changes occurring between the stage of moral realism and the stage of moral independence. To find out how children evaluate lying, Piaget asked each child "Do you know what a lie is?" The younger children defined a lie simply as "naughty words" or something bad "like words no one is supposed to say." Intent to deceive did not enter into the younger child's definition of a lie. In somewhat older children, lies were described as "things you can't believe; the more unlikely the lie—the farther from reality—the worse it is." Piaget (1965) compared reactions to a story innocently told about a dog as big as a horse with reactions to a story containing a more believable falsehood told with the deliberate intent to deceive. Younger children judged the farfetched lie to be worse, while older children emphasized the intent and motives involved. The issue of intent versus consequences in determining the morality of an action is very much with us today (Gutkin, 1973). Does helping the energy crisis (a good intention) mean that we should allow unlimited strip mining? Is government secrecy to be permitted if the intention is to protect the democratic way of government?

3. *Two types of punishment: Expiatory and reciprocal.* Piaget and his associates also studied the types of punishment advocated by younger children (up to age 8) and older children (age 8 and older) when rules were broken. Simple stories of natural transgressions centering on parent-child interactions were used to identify the child's conception of *justice.* Piaget classified pun-

ishments into two types: **expiatory punishment** and punishment through **reciprocity.** Expiatory punishments demand—in a rather authoritarian manner—that the transgressor must suffer (Sherwood, 1966); the punishment need not be related to the *content* of the guilty act, but a due proportion should be maintained between the *degree* of suffering inflicted on the transgressor and the gravity of the transgressor's misdeed. Examples of expiatory punishment abound in our society:

A. A little boy who is called John is in his room. He is called to dinner. He goes into the dining room. But behind the door there was a chair, and on the chair there was a tray with fifteen cups on it. John couldn't have known that there was all this behind the door. He goes in; the door knocks against the tray; bang go the fifteen cups, and they all get broken!

B. Once there was a little boy whose name was Henry. One day when his mother was out he tried to get some jam out of the cupboard. He climbed onto a chair and stretched out his arm. But the jam was too high up, and he couldn't reach it and have any. While he was trying to get it, he knocked over a cup. The cup fell down and broke.

Figure 8-1
Piaget's moral-decision stories. (From J. Piaget, *The Moral Judgment of the Child.* Copyright 1935 by Routledge & Kegan Paul, Ltd. Copyright 1965 by The Macmillan Company. Reprinted by permission of the publishers; photo by Jim Pinckney.)

spanking, revoking or decreasing a child's allowance, or placing a child's toys (or the family car)
off limits for a time.

In contrast, reciprocity attempts to relate
the punishment to the crime, so that the rule-
breaker will be able to understand the implications of his or her misconduct. One type of reciprocity involves *restitutive* punishment, such as
having a boy pay for and replace the window
that he broke. *Exclusion* is another type of reciprocity, exemplified by statements such as "I'm
not going to play with you anymore because you
play too rough with me."

Punishment by reciprocity corresponds
with the more advanced stage of moral development—the stage of moral independence. For example, Piaget reports the results of interviewing
about 100 children between the ages of 6 and
12. The reciprocity type of punishment was preferred by only 30% of the 6- and 7-year-olds,
compared to 50% of the 8- and 10-year-olds and
80% of the 11- and 12-year olds.

Along with moral realism and the advocacy
of expiatory punishment, the younger child believes in **immanent justice**—the concept that justice dwells within the things involved and that
misdeeds will be punished by natural acts or
occurrences. If a girl is running across a bridge
when she should be walking, and the bridge happens to collapse at that moment and toss her
into the icy water, younger children will conclude
that the girl was punished for "being bad." Piaget
finds in older children a very clear decrease in
the belief in immanent justice. Almost all young
children believe in immanent justice, while less
than one-fourth of the 11- and 12-year-olds studied believe in it.

*4. Two kinds of distributive justice: Equality and
equity.* In his analysis of justice, Piaget made a
further distinction in respect to beliefs about *distributive justice*, or how punishments and rewards
should be distributed to members of a group.
Two types of distributive justice were distinguished: equality and equity. Equality has the
same meaning in Piaget's system that it does for
most of us: everyone should be treated the same.

There is here a subtle distinction from *equity*,
which allows for consideration of individual circumstances. Piaget measured the children's responses to stories resembling the following:

> On Thursday afternoon, a mother asked her
> little girl and boy to help her about the house
> because she was tired. The girl was to dry the
> plates, and the boy was to fetch in some wood.
> But the little boy (or girl) went and played in
> the street. So the mother asked the other one
> to do all the work. What did this other one say?

In response to stories of this kind, younger
children felt that the child should obey the
mother, while older children (ages 8 to 10) opted
for equality. They said the boy and girl should
still do the same amounts of work. Still older
children (11 and older) gave responses that reflected equity: "It wasn't fair, but she did it to
help her mother." From these responses, Piaget
distinguished three levels in the development of
concepts of distributive justice. At the first level,
just is whatever is commanded by an adult; it's
the law. At the second level, *equality orientation*—or equalitarianism—reigns supreme, even at
the expense of disobedience and punishment. At
the third level, equity dominates—in other words,
equality is never defined without taking into account the way that each individual is situated.
Thus, in Piaget's observations, there emerges a
consistent pattern of movement from one stage
to another that is correlated with age.[2]

Many of the social issues of today center
around the concept of distributive justice. For

[2]Piaget and Freud both describe an ongoing process
whereby rules and commands are "internalized" or "interiorized." There are differences, however, between Freud's
and Piaget's meanings of "interiorized." Roger Brown (1965)
interprets their concepts as being different in the same way
that ingestion is different from digestion. To Brown, Freud's
idea of internalization is like ingestion—a swallowing whole
of adult laws and ideas, which then become a part of the
child without any further process of assimilation. For Piaget,
the process resembles digestion—adult ideas are only food
for the developing moral system, which assimilates and trans-
forms the food before it becomes a part of the child's own
organization. Kohlberg's approach resembles Piaget's in this
regard.

example, should minority students be treated with equality or equity when considered for admittance to college? Should all people pay the same tax rate, or should those with large incomes be taxed at a higher rate than the poor? Apparently reflecting the current shift toward the study of pro-social behavior (see Chapter 9), social psychologists such as Brickman and Bryan suggest that "the fundamental question of nature, and of evolution, is how the resources of the environment are distributed across species and among members of a given species" (Brickman & Bryan, 1975, p. 160). Perhaps this critical question has come forward now because of the widespread realization that our resources, such as land, water, and oil, are finite. People in many countries must decide how the decreasing resources are to be shared and what is a "fair" price.

B. Kohlberg—An extension of the cognitive stage approach

Just as Erikson was a revisionist of Freud, so Kohlberg has extended Piaget's basic theory. While Kohlberg uses Piaget's basic approach of confronting a child with stories that pose a moral dilemma, Kohlberg's stories and situations are more complex than Piaget's. (An example is given in Figure 8-2). The dilemmas posed are challenging to adults as well as children, because they often set up opposition between a law (or norm) and a human need, and they encourage respondents to answer on the basis of their general theory of morality (R. Brown, 1965). Hence it is not surprising that Kohlberg has found greater complexity and more extended moral development than did Piaget. Kohlberg (1958, 1963, 1968) proposes that there are six possible stages of moral development experienced by children as they pass into adolescence and adulthood. In conjunction with the six stages of development, the child passes from one level of moral maturity to a second and then to a third level. These three levels and the two stages within each level are as follows:

1. Preconventional level. At the initial level the child is responsive to cultural rules and labels such as "good" and "bad," or "right" and "wrong"; however, the child interprets these labels in light of the *consequences* of his or her actions (punishment, reward, exchange of favors) or in light of the physical power of those who enunciate the rules and labels. Here, "might means right." This preconventional level is divided into the following two stages.

The first stage is the *punishment and obedience orientation.* To the child at this stage, the consequences of an action determine the goodness or badness of the action, regardless of the human meaning of these consequences. Those actions that can be performed without getting caught are not considered to be bad by the child. Avoidance of punishment and unquestioning deference to power are valued *in their own right;* they are not seen as reflections of an underlying moral order that sometimes employs punishment and authority.

The second stage is the *instrumental-relativist orientation,* or *hedonistic orientation.* At this stage, right action consists of that which satisfies one's own needs and occasionally the needs of others. That is, "unselfish" acts are right only if they will also benefit the actor in the long run. Human relations are viewed in the terms of the marketplace: elements of fairness, reciprocity, and equal sharing are present, but they are always interpreted in a very pragmatic way. "You scratch my back and I'll scratch yours" reflects the orientation of the person at Stage 2 (Kohlberg, 1968).

2. Conventional level. At the conventional level of moral development, maintaining the expectations of one's family, group, or nation is perceived as valuable in its own right, regardless of immediate and obvious consequences. The attitude is not only one of conformity to personal expectations and social order, but also of loyalty. Emphasis is on actively maintaining, supporting, and justifying the social order and identifying with the persons or groups in it. This conventional level encompasses two further stages of moral development.

Figure 8-2
Kohlberg's decision story

Kohlberg's moral-judgment stories tend to set up an opposition between a legal rule or social norm and a human need (R. Brown, 1965). Here is a typical example (from Kohlberg, 1963, 1969):

In Europe, a woman was near death from a special kind of cancer. There was one drug that the doctors thought might save her. It was a form of radium that a druggist in the same town had recently discovered. The drug was expensive to make, but the druggist was charging ten times what the drug cost him to make. He paid $200 for the radium and charged $2,000 for a small dose of the drug. The sick woman's husband, Heinz, went to everyone he knew to borrow money, but he could only get together about $1,000, which is half of what it cost. He told the druggist that his wife was dying, and asked him to sell it cheaper or let him pay later. But the druggist said, "No, I discovered the drug and I'm going to make money from it." So Heinz got desperate and broke into the man's store to steal the drug for his wife.

Should Heinz have done that? Was it actually wrong or right? Why?

Is it a husband's duty to steal the drug for his wife, if he can get it no other way? Would a good husband do it?

Did the druggist have the right to charge that much when there was no law actually setting a limit to the price? Why?

If the husband does not feel very close or affectionate to his wife, should he still steal the drug?

Suppose it wasn't Heinz's wife who was dying of cancer, but it was Heinz's best friend. His friend didn't have any money, and there was no one in his family willing to steal the drug. Should Heinz steal the drug for his friend in that case? Why?

Suppose it was a person whom he knew that was dying but who was not a good friend. There was no one else who could get him the drug. Would it be right to steal it for him? Why?

What is there to be said on the side of the law in this case?

Would you steal the drug to save your wife's life? Why?

If you were dying of cancer but were strong enough, would you steal the drug to save your own life?

Heinz broke in the store and stole the drug and gave it to his wife. He was caught and brought before the judge. Should the judge send Heinz to jail for stealing, or should he let him go free? Why?

The *interpersonal concordance* or *good-boy/nice-girl orientation* is the third stage in Kohlberg's scheme. Moral behavior, in the eyes of the person at Stage 3, is that which pleases, helps, or is approved by others. The individual conforms to his or her assumption of what is normal or natural behavior. The morality of a behavior is frequently judged by the intention behind it. The notion that someone "means well" becomes important for the first time, and one earns approval by being "nice."

The *law-and-order orientation* is Kohlberg's fourth stage. Here the orientation is toward authority, established rules, and the maintenance of the social order. Moral behavior consists of doing one's duty, showing that one respects authority, and maintaining the given social order *because it is* the given social order (Kohlberg, 1968).

3. *Postconventional or principled level.* At the third level, there is a clear effort by the person to define moral values and principles that have validity and application apart from the authority of the groups or persons advocating these principles and apart from the individual's own identification with these groups. This level also has two stages.

The *social-contract, legalistic orientation* falls into this highest level of maturity and is the fifth stage in moral development. This stage generally has utilitarian overtones. Moral action tends to be defined by how well it reflects general individual rights and the standards that have been critically examined and agreed upon by the whole society. The person at Stage 5 has a clear awareness of the individual differences in personal values and opinions; hence this fifth stage emphasizes procedural rules for reaching consensus. Aside from what is constitutionally and democratically agreed upon, this social-contract orientation sees right and wrong as matters of personal values and opinion. Although the legal point of view is accepted at Stage 5, the possibility of changing the law in light of what seems best for society is emphasized (Kohlberg, 1968). (This approach contrasts with the view of morality at the fourth stage, which accepts law as right and does not seek to change it.) The fifth stage represents the "official" morality of democratic governments and the United States Constitution.

The *orientation of universal ethical principles* is the sixth stage in Kohlberg's scheme of moral development. At this highest stage, what is morally right is defined not by laws and rules of the social order but by one's own conscience, in accordance with self-determined ethical principles. Rather than being concrete moral rules, these principles are broad and abstract and might include universal principles of justice, principles of reciprocity and equality of human rights, and respect for the dignity of human beings as individuals.[3] For example, one's position regarding the acceptability of abortion on demand may reflect one's principles about the sanctity of human

life or, conversely, about the rights of individuals to control their own bodies. Kohlberg has found that postconventional morality (both Stage 5 and Stage 6) "is probably attainable only in adulthood and requires some experience in moral responsibility and independent choice" (Kohlberg, 1973, p. 500).

Examples of how persons at each stage would respond to the dilemma posed in Figure 8-2 are shown in Table 8-3. Some statements by participants in the "Watergate cover-up" are scored for stage level in Table 8-4.

Kohlberg also speculates on the presence of a new adult stage, unique to the mature person, which involves adoption of a religious and cosmic perspective. This "guru stage," as it has been called, reflects Kohlberg's belief that ultimately even the person at Stage 6 cannot answer the question "Why be moral?" unless he or she WRONG! has been "principled" for a number of years. These new developments emphasize the changing nature of a theory as new and dynamic as Kohlberg's.

Like Piaget, Kohlberg proposes that if a person is to achieve the highest stage of moral development, he or she must pass through the other five stages in an invariant manner. In doing so, such individuals constantly restructure their experience, and perhaps move toward a more mature level of moral judgment. At the same time, temporary regression is possible, as when a college student at Stage 6 finds society unprepared for his or her principles. Some such students may reject society's values and return to the hedonism of Stage 2. Fixation may occur at any stage and is more likely to occur when no confrontation with higher stages is available.

The notion that an individual must pass through a series of stages in order to achieve moral maturity is quite an assumption, but a comparison of different theorists (presented in Table 8-2) reveals that a variety of viewpoints arrive at the same position—a stage in which principles rather than rules are relied upon and actions are autonomous. But the assumption that a principle-oriented morality is higher than a law-oriented morality is laden with value judg-

---

[3]Several years later Kohlberg (1971) revised his conception to include a subdivision of the fifth stage called an "individual conscience" orientation. This transition period between Stage 5 and Stage 6 is reflected in persons who act on the basis of their own consciences but not out of adherence to a universal moral principle. An example might be a college-age draft resister who says "My conscience makes me do this, but yours may not." Other mixtures and intervening stages are reported in Fishkin, Keniston, and MacKinnon (1973).

Table 8-3
Examples of answers reflecting each stage of Kohlberg's moral-judgment theory

Stage 1: No differentiation is seen between the moral value of life and its physical or social status value.

Tommy, age 10 (Story III. Why should the druggist give the drug to the dying woman when her husband couldn't pay for it?): "If someone important is in a plane and is allergic to heights and the stewardess won't give him medicine because she's only got enough for one and she's got a sick one, a friend, in back, they'd probably put the stewardess in a lady's jail because she didn't help the important one." (Is it better to save the life of one important person or a lot of unimportant people?): "All the people aren't that important because one man has just one house, maybe a lot of furniture, but a whole bunch of people have an awful lot of furniture and some of these poor people might have a lot of money and it doesn't look it."

Stage 2: The value of a human life is seen as instrumental to the satisfaction of the needs of its possessor or of other persons. The decision to save life is relative to, or to be made by, its possessor. (Differentiation of physical and intrinsic value of life, differentiation of its value to self and to others.)

Tommy, age 13 (Story IV. Should the doctor "mercy kill" a fatally ill woman requesting death because of her pain?): "Maybe it would be good to put her out of her pain, she'd be better off that way. But the husband wouldn't want it, it's not like an animal. If a pet dies you can get along without it—it isn't something you really need. Well, you can get a new wife, but it's not really the same."

Jim, age 13 (same question): "If she requests it, it's really up to her. She is in such terrible pain, just the same as people are always putting animals out of their pain."

Stage 3: The value of a human life is based on the empathy and affection of family members and others toward its possessor. (The value of human life, as based on social sharing, community, and love, is differentiated from the instrumental and hedonistic value of life applicable also to animals.)

Tommy, age 16 (same question): "It might be best for her, but not for her husband—and it's a human life—not like an animal. It just doesn't have the same relationship that a human being does to a family. You can become attached to a dog, but nothing like a human you know."

Stage 4: Life is conceived as sacred in terms of its place in a categorical moral or religious order of rights and duties. (The value of human life, as a categorical member of a moral order, is differentiated from its value to specific other people in the family, and so on. The value of life is still partly dependent on serving the group, the state, and God, however.)

Jim, age 16 (same question): "I don't know. In one way, it's murder, it's not a right or privilege of man to decide who shall live and who should die. God put life into everybody on earth and you're taking away something from that person that came directly from God and it's almost destroying a part of God when you kill a person. There's something of God in everyone."

Stage 5: Life is valued both in terms of its relation to community welfare and in terms of being a universal human right. (Obligation to respect the basic right to life is differentiated from generalized respect for the sociomoral order. The general value of the independent human life is a primary autonomous value not dependent on other values.)

Jim, age 20 (same question): "Given the ethics of the doctor who has taken on responsibility to save human life—from that point of view he probably shouldn't but there is another side, there are more and more people in the medical profession who are thinking it is a hardship on everyone, the person, the family, when you know they are going to die. When a person is kept alive by an artificial lung or kidney it's more like being a vegetable than being a human who is alive. If it's her own choice I think there are certain rights and privileges that go along with being a human being. I am a human being and have certain desires for life and I think everyone else does, too, and in that sense we're all equal."

Stage 6: Belief in the sacredness of human life as representing a universal human value of respect for the individual. (The moral value of a human being, as an object of moral principle, is differentiated from a formal recognition of his rights.)

Jim, age 24 (Story III. Should the husband steal the drug to save his wife? How about for someone he just knows?) "Yes. A human life takes precedence over any other moral or legal value, whoever it is. A human life has inherent value whether or not it is valued by a particular individual." (Why is that?): "The inherent worth of the individual human being is the central value in a set of values where the principles of justice and love are normative for all human relationships."

Table 8-4
Morality stages and Watergate

Candee and Kohlberg (1974) analyzed some of the responses of staff members of the Nixon administration to indicate the levels of their moral reasoning. Typical comments and their levels are the following:

Source	Comments (Not Exact Quotes)	Stage
Bart Porter	I felt a deep sense of loyalty to this man (Nixon).	3–4
Bart Porter	Even though I did not think this was quite right, I did nothing because of the fear of group pressures that ensue from not being a team player.	3
E. Howard Hunt	I became engaged in these activities because I believed that the activities that were proposed to me had the sanction of the highest authorities in our country. Secondly, my 26-year record of service to this country predisposed me to accept orders and instructions without question and without debate.	4
John Mitchell	In my mind, the reelection of Richard Nixon, compared with what was available on the other side, was so much more important that I put it in just that context.	2 or 4
Egil Krogh	I now see that the sincerity of my motivation was not a justification but indeed a contributing cause of the incident. I hope that young men and women who are fortunate enough to have an opportunity to serve in government can benefit from this experience and learn that sincerity can often be as blinding as it is worthy. I hope they will recognize that the banner of national security can turn perceived patriotism into actual disservice. When contemplating a course of action, I hope they will never fail to ask "Is this right?"	5

Candee and Kohlberg (1974) view Watergate as an opportunity for national moral growth (as in Krogh's case) and greater faith in our own Stage 5 constitutional system. Other researchers (West, Gunn, & Chernicky, 1975) have used the Watergate incident to explore situational factors that might explain why people violate the law, and the reasons they give. (See Chapter 3.)

ments, and for this reason Kohlberg has received his share of criticisms. Nonetheless, Kohlberg's approach offers an extremely provocative way of looking at morality, and the correctness of his assumptions may, to a large degree, be evaluated by research and empirical work.

VI. Research on cognitive approaches

A. Attempts to verify Piaget's stage approach

During the period between 1946 and 1956, Gesell, Ilg, and Ames (1956) traced the development of children from ages 5 to 16. The researchers found a spiral pattern of development in the morality of an individual from early childhood to age 16, the foundation of moral development being laid during the first five years of life. Two periods or stages were discovered—one covering ages 5 to 10, the other covering ages 10 to 16. Gesell and his coworkers saw this development as sequential and supporting the Piagetian view; they concluded that there is "an unmistakable trend from the specific to the general and from the concrete to the abstract" (1956, p. 73). Also supportive of Piaget's conception is Gesell's conclusion that this development comes about as the result of a tension between stability and conflict in human experience. All in all, Gesell's observations lend positive support to the hypothesis that the development of morality follows a pattern and exhibits clear-cut stages of growth.

Piaget's conclusions have not always been supported in research, however, and many investigators have criticized the two-stage theory as too simplistic (Isaacs, 1966; Kohlberg, 1969; E. Lerner, 1937). Other researchers (MacRae, 1954, for example) have questioned the presence of distinct stages. Apparently the time periods Piaget assigned for the emergence of each stage become less applicable the further one is removed from the locale of Piaget's children in Geneva (Bronfenbrenner, 1970). This implies a strong

cultural influence at work. However, the change to a different type of moral development with increasing age is consistent in every society studied. For example, seeing intention as more important than physical consequences in judging the wrongness of an action is found more often in older children than in younger ones "in every culture, in every social class, in every sex group, and in every subculture studied (Switzerland, United States, Belgium, Chinese, Malaysian-aboriginal, Mexican, Israel, Hopi, Zuni, Sioux, Papago)" (Kohlberg, 1969, p. 374). More recently Hetherington and McIntyre (1975), who summarized the research on role-taking abilities, find that role-taking often comes much earlier than Piaget suggested. They report research results that find role-taking in 3- and 4-year-olds (Flavell, 1973; Shotz & Gelman, 1973), as well as finding support for a sequential model of development (Masangkay, McCluskey, McIntyre, Sims-Knight, Vaughn, & Flavell, 1973; McIntyre, Vaughn, & Flavell, 1973).

There is empirical support for Piaget's assumption that older children place more emphasis on *intentions* in evaluating the seriousness of a mistake. For example, Baer and Wright (1974) discuss a number of studies (including Gutkin, 1972) that found a developmental sequence in judgments about intentions and damage. Intention was found to be more important in the higher stage. Other studies have less dramatic results, but in general lend some support to Piaget's theory.

B. Tests of Kohlberg's theory

The dilemmas posed in the stories used by Piaget and by Kohlberg seek to measure **moral judgment,** or the moral attitudes that determine how a person feels one should respond to a certain situation. But do moral attitudes lead to moral behaviors? Do subjects at different stages of moral judgment respond to the same stimulus with different behaviors? If not, the conception of stages in moral judgment cannot be applied to the prediction of everyday behaviors. A number of researchers have examined behavior in relation to moral-judgment stages. For example, R. Krebs (1967) observed the extent of cheating among sixth-grade children on four tests. The results, reprinted in Table 8-5, indicate that of the five sixth graders who had achieved a principled moral-judgment level, only one (20%) cheated, whereas between 67 and 83% of the children at other moral-judgment levels cheated. A study of cheating by college students (Schwartz, Feldman, Brown, & Heingartner, 1969) also found that principled morality inversely related to cheating.

Table 8-5
Percentage of students cheating

N	Level	Percent Cheating
55	Premoral (Stages 1 and 2)	83
63	Conventional (Stages 3 and 4)	67
5	Principled (Stages 5 and 6)	20

From "Some Relations between Moral Judgment, Attention, and Resistance to Temptation," by R. Krebs. Unpublished doctoral dissertation, University of Chicago, 1967.

The Kohlberg moral-judgment stories were given to college students who had previously participated in Milgram's (1963) obedience study (summarized in Chapter 18). Kohlberg expected that subjects who were more advanced in moral judgment (Stages 5 and 6) would be more likely to refuse to continue giving shocks to another participant after the latter had indicated he was in pain. Although the number of subjects was small—only 34—the results were most revealing. Eight of the subjects were at Stage 5 or Stage 6 in moral judgment; six, or 75%, of these refused to continue giving shocks. Twenty-four subjects were at the conventional level of moral judgment (Stage 3 or Stage 4); only three, or 12.5%, of these refused to continue. Principled morality was strongly related to the refusal to collaborate in an act that inflicted pain on another human

being, while persons at a level of conventional morality were likely to collaborate with the experimenter. Similarly, in a laboratory experiment, Anchor and Cross (1974) found a greater choice of aggressive responses to others by those at a preconventional level.

A comprehensive test of Kohlberg's moral-judgment theory was presented by Haan, Smith, and Block (1968), who related university students' moral-judgment stages to their political behavior, their participation in student protests, their backgrounds, their perceptions of their parents, and their self-descriptions and ideal-self-descriptions. Students from the University of California at Berkeley and from San Francisco State College and Peace Corps volunteers served as subjects. There were 957 respondents. However, only 54% of the subjects gave responses which could reliably be classified in one of the six moral-judgment stages. (Such occurrences indicate either that the measuring instrument is not precise enough to classify every subject or that some subjects are not clearly in a single stage at a given point in time. Probably both possibilities apply.) As shown in Table 8-6, few respondents were at the preconventional stages; about

Table 8-6
Percentages of subjects at each of Kohlberg's stages in the study of university students and Peace Corps volunteers

Stages	Males (N = 253)	Females (N = 257)
1 and 2	7%	3%
3	22%	41%
4	43%	38%
5	21%	14%
6	7%	4%

From "Moral Reasoning of Young Adults: Political-Social Behavior, Family Background, and Personality Correlates," by N. Haan, M. B. Smith, and J. Block, *Journal of Personality and Social Psychology*, 1968, 10, 183–201. Copyright 1968 by the American Psychological Association. Reprinted by permission.

two-thirds of the men and 80% of the women possessed conventional moral judgment (Stages 3 and 4): and 28% of the males and 18% of the females possessed postconventional, or principled, morality. (Kohlberg believes that fewer women achieve higher stages of moral development because allegiance to their children precludes the development of abstract moral principles, although research by Poppen, 1974, suggests that the sex difference is probably caused by Kohlberg's use of male-typed stories.) For respondents at each moral-judgment level, Haan et al. found somewhat different personality and behavior patterns.

1. Preconventional morality (Stages 1 and 2). At this level, males were found to be politically radical, active, and protesting, while the women were found to be moderates and inactive, even though joiners. Persons at the preconventional stages do not endorse the obligation to take the role of others and, instead, are more concerned with their personal fulfillment—"the women by a stubborn practicality and the men for personal flair and expressiveness" (Haan et al., 1968, p. 195).

2. Conventional morality (Stages 3 and 4). Respondents at the conventional level of morality were found to have modeled themselves after their parents and accepted the traditional values of United States society. They reported that their parents provided clear rules, punishments, and rewards (a strategy very similar to the one recommended by social-learning theorists for the development of morality). These respondents were found to have harmonious, nonskeptical relationships with institutions and authority figures.

3. Postconventional morality (Stages 5 and 6). The young people at this principled level of morality were characterized by a firm sense of autonomy in their life patterns and ideological positions. They were found to be candid about themselves and their families and espoused both new values and new politics. Although they rejected the traditional values implicit in the Protestant ethic, they maintained a concern about their responsibilities to others. Their parents

seem to have permitted and perhaps encouraged them to learn from and be challenged by their own life experiences. While males reported that their fathers encouraged them to take chances and try new things, the females reported that their fathers did not give them responsibilities. Respondents at the sixth stage, particularly, showed the self-honesty and self-condemnation consistent with Kohlberg's theory.

Haan, Smith, and Block also reported the extent of participation in the 1965 Berkeley Free Speech Movement sit-in according to moral-judgment levels. The percentages of the moral types arrested at the sit-in are represented in Table 8-7. Among the men who were at preconventional Stages 1 and 2, 60% participated and 40% did not. The percentages of Stage-5 and Stage-6 men who attended the sit-in were also high—41% and 75%, respectively. Participation levels by Stage-3 and Stage-4 men were much lower—18% and 6%, respectively. Percentages of participating women were similar to those of the men in that more preconventional and postconventional women were present at the sit-in than were conventional types.

It appears that preconventional and postconventional types participate in protests for dif-

---

Table 8-7
Percentages of pure moral types arrested in the Berkeley Free Speech Movement sit-in

Stages	Men (N = 117)	Women (N = 97)
1 and 2	60%	33%
3	18%	9%
4	6%	12%
5	41%	57%
6	75%	86%

From "Moral Reasoning of Young Adults: Political-Social Behavior, Family Background, and Personality Correlates," by N. Haan, M. B. Smith, and J. Block, *Journal of Personality and Social Psychology*, 1968, *10*, 183–201. Copyright 1968 by the American Psychological Association. Reprinted by permission.

ferent reasons. The preconventional, Stage-2 types see the protest in terms of a power conflict in which they are out to better their own status. The principled protesters (Stages 5 and 6) are concerned about basic issues of civil liberties and the role of students as citizens within a university community. These findings are consistent with the subjects' reported activities and substantiate the general relationship between moral judgment and behavior. Interestingly enough, the few Stage-3 arrestees stated that they had participated in the sit-in because the University of California administrators had failed as good authorities. Similarly, the few Stage-4 arrestees justified their position by claiming that the administration had violated proper legal procedures. Also interestingly, the stage-6 types sat-in more in sorrow than with the anger of the Stage-2 protestors.

Probably the most important contribution of the study by Haan and associates is the clear differentiation of various stages in regard to empathy. Both conventional and principled morality are made possible by the capacity to assume the role of another—which means that one must be able to extend one's self and not become rigid. Persons at Stage 5, with a strong sense of being contractually obligated, are not able to separate themselves from the social order, even when they recognize its injustices. They may try to change the social order but recognize that an injustice exists because of the will of the majority. In contrast, the Stage-6 orientation in a moral confrontation will draw upon the expression of universal, logically consistent, ideal principles of justice. The Stage-6 person will reject a social contract or law if it violates his or her individual principles but will also understand the essential contractual nature of the social order and human affairs. The question is: how can a Stage-6 person exist in a society that operates on the Stage-4 level? The Stage-6 response is to protest but also to accept the penalties for breaking the law. Martin Luther King's letter from a Birmingham jail (Figure 8-3) is cited by Kohlberg (1970) as an example of the kind of civil disobedience that exemplifies Stage-6 morality.

Figure 8-3
Letter from a Birmingham Jail, by Martin Luther King, Jr.

... there is a type of constructive, non-violent tension which is necessary for growth. Just as Socrates felt it was necessary to create a tension in the mind so that individuals could rise from the bondage of myths and half-truths . . . , so must we see the need for non-violent gadflies to create the kind of tension in society that will help men rise from the dark depths of prejudice and racism. . . .

One may well ask: "How can you advocate breaking some laws and obeying others?" The answer lies in the fact that there are two types of laws: just and unjust. . . . One has not only a legal but a moral responsibility to obey just laws. Conversely, one has a moral responsibility to disobey unjust laws. . . . An unjust law is a human law that is not rooted in eternal law and natural law. Any law that uplifts human personality is just. Any law that degrades human personality is unjust. . . . An unjust law is a code that a numerical or power majority group compels a minority group to obey but does not make binding on itself. This is *difference* made legal. . . .

In no sense do I advocate evading or defying the law, as would the rabid segregationist. That would lead to anarchy. One who breaks an unjust law must do so openly, lovingly, and with a willingness to accept the penalty. I submit that an individual who breaks a law that conscience tells him is unjust, and who willingly accepts the penalty of imprisonment in order to arouse the conscience of the community over its injustice, is in reality expressing the highest respect for law.

From pp. 81–86, "Letter from a Birmingham Jail," in *Why We Can't Wait*, by Martin Luther King, Jr. Copyright 1963 by Martin Luther King, Jr. By permission of Harper & Row, Publishers, Inc. Photo by Vance Allen/Freelance Photographers Guild.

Fishkin, Keniston, and MacKinnon (1973) report two excellent studies of the moral reasoning and political ideology of undergraduates. They found that preconventional and postconventional students espoused a more radical ideology and took more radical action than the conventional students. The Stage-4 students were the least radical. The preconventional and postconventional subjects were most critical of conventional wisdom. They differed however, in acceptance of radical slogans, with preconventional students accepting and postconventional rejecting radical ideology. As in other studies, the female students were predominantly at Stage 3 and the males at Stage 4 (V. Erickson, 1974).

Fontana and Noel (1973) report another study in a college setting that included as subjects students, faculty, and administrators. They found that political leftists were more often at Stage 2 than were rightists. There was no correlation between age of faculty and moral reasoning. The Stage 2 faculty members were less activist than those at Stage 5 or Stage 6 (they postulate that the lower visibility of the Stage 2 faculty was self-serving). Natural-science faculty were predominantly at Stage 4 and social-science and humanities faculty were at Stages 5 and 6.

Kohlberg's proposition that movement through the stages occurs in an invariant sequence has less solid support than his other proposals (Holstein, 1969). **Cross-sectional studies** (Kohlberg, 1969) using children of different ages as subjects found that, on the average, older children are at higher stages of moral development than young children. While the average age at which change takes place is not the same in each society, children in the United States, Taiwan, Great Britain, Mexico, and Turkey show the following patterns of development: from age 10 to age 16, the extent of conventional moral thought (Stages 3 and 4) increases steadily; however, Stage 4 is the dominant stage of most adults. This apparently occurs because of no exposure to reasoning that is representative of higher levels.

Longitudinal studies (Kramer, 1968) indicate some degree of movement consistent with Kohlberg's proposed sequence. Fifty young males were interviewed every 3 years over a 12-year period. At the beginning of the study, the subjects were from ages 10 to 16, and all were in their 20s upon completion of the study. Half the subjects were from middle-class backgrounds, while the others were from lower-class families. Most of the young men remained at the same stage or increased in stage development with age; however, there was a regression or drop in stage level (usually back to the hedonism of Stage 2) in about 50% of the middle-class males between the end of high school and the middle of their college years. This regression was temporary, and these young men increased in moral development after college.

Kohlberg makes a value judgment in stating that Stage 6 comes last and hence is "highest" and "best." Kohlberg himself recognized the possibility that Stage 6 may not be the end point in moral development. Possibly, he says, Stages 4, 5, and 6 are "alternative types of mature response rather than . . . a sequence" (Kohlberg, 1969, p. 385). There is some research that supports such a possibility.

If there is a progression through the stages, as Kohlberg proposed, then those individuals at the higher stages will understand the reasoning at their own stage level and those lower, but not *above* their own level. Yet training sessions that use role playing or discussions along with explanations one stage above the individual's present level may provide development "upward."

In a project designed to test this assumption, Rest (1969, 1973; Rest, Turiel, & Kohlberg,

① p. 665.   ② p. 668.

1969) studied the nature of stage sequence of 12th grade, middle-class students. These subjects were given various ways of thinking about a moral dilemma, including such things as attitudes toward law and the value of life and predispositions to act in certain ways. Rest and his colleagues found the order of difficulty the same as the order of acquiring the structural features of moral thinking, but a detailed examination of the data (Rest, 1969, Table 10) indicates that only two of Rest's Stage-3 subjects did not comprehend Stage-4 reasoning. One Stage-3 subject comprehended Stage-4, but not Stage-3, reasoning. The Stage-4 representatives all comprehended Stage-3 reasoning, but one did not comprehend Stage-4 reasoning. These findings do not seem to lead to a conclusive argument that Stage 4 is above Stage 3.

Blatt and Kohlberg (1969) studied the effects of classroom moral discussion on children's level of moral judgment and in general found clear movement from one stage to the next for the lower stages. But 2 of Blatt's 11 subjects at Stage 4 moved to Stage 3, 1 moved to Stage 5, and 8 remained the same. Arbuthnot (1975) and Small (1974) found that training in role playing or the Kohlberg theory could advance the stage level of college students' responses. In a consistent finding, Maitland and Goldman (1974) indicate that discussions to consensus on issues of moral judgment produced greater increases in moral-judgment scores than did open-ended discussion or sessions in which each subject worked alone.

In a longitudinal study with college-age males (O'Connor, 1971), a greater percentage of Stage-4 respondents moved to Stage 3 than stayed the same or moved to Stage 5. (Of the Stage-4 students, 58% were at Stage 3 two years later.) The Stage-5 representatives in O'Connor's sample fared only slightly better than those at Stage 4, with fully one-third regressing to Stage 3 two years later. Kramer (1968) found continued growth in a similar age group, but it was the result of relatively fewer subjects in lower stages rather than an increase in the number of higher stages.

VII. A critique of the cognitive approach

What is the critical factor that leads some of us to become principled persons while others of us act in selfish, amoral ways? Both Piaget and Kohlberg have proposed that the critical variable in moral development is the exposure of the child to a *variety* of socializing agents (Bronfenbrenner & Devereux, 1965). Behind this assumption are others: that a clear-cut series of stages occurs; that these stages are reflected in our behavior; and that—according to Kohlberg—we all begin at an amoral level.

As we have seen above, it appears that Kohlberg's theory holds up for Stages 1-3, but beyond these there is much less consistency in the progression of the stages.

R. Brown and Herrnstein (1975) question the possibility that content and structure can really be separated. As we have seen from the research on students, individuals at one moral level may take the same action for different reasons, making it very difficult to generalize about what "moral" behavior is at that level. Persons at the same stage may interpret a situation quite differently. Even if they agree, their actions may be different, depending on whether responsibility is clearly defined or left ambiguous. Finally, an actual situation (as in the Milgram obedience study) may involve critical referents not brought out in a story, or the situation may affect the moral-judgment response in other ways (Arbuthnot & Andrasik, 1973). Perhaps if Milgram's subjects had been asked, before the experiment, what they would do in such a situation, they would have agreed with the experimenter that they would not have gone all the way. But they did. Why?

Piaget and Kohlberg differ markedly in their assumptions about where we begin. Kohlberg appears to believe the amoral level is a given. Piaget, however, seems to believe that acquiescence to authority is almost innate. This aspect of moral development has seen little empirical investigation.

Chapter Eight

Other aspects of the Kohlberg approach have also been subject to criticism (Kurtines & Greif, 1974; Simpson, 1974). Kurtines and Greif attack the intuitive method Kohlberg used to derive the six stages and his subjective scoring system. They further argue that reliability estimates fluctuate so greatly that they limit the utility of his instrument. Finally, they point out that predictive and construct validity is severely lacking.

Perhaps the most scathing criticism of the cognitive approach is presented by Elizabeth Simpson (1974), who objects quite vehemently to the theories of both Piaget and Kohlberg. She emphasizes the importance of a person's sex and culture in determining how he or she views moral dilemmas. For example, she claims that in the United States the concept of equality has different specific meanings to persons of different social classes. The working class sees equality as primarily economic, while the upper middle class defines equality socially, not economically. She also sees conceptual differences in how life is valued. For example, the expressed notion that human life is sacred has many socially sanctioned exceptions such as war, self-defense, and responses to rape. The whole notion of a "universal" orientation of "right to property" is hard to define for a group or tribe that has no notion of individual property rights. She also attacks the strong emphasis that Kohlberg places on language ability. Can you be a Stage 5 or Stage 6 only if you have the verbal facility and are a member of the educated elite? The emphasis on problem-solving abilities is particular only to educated Western societies and is not universal. She also argues that "to paraphrase an old line, a good woman is hard to find (Stage 5 or 6) because she has been taught that she is expected *not* to think that way" (p. 98). Simpson would prefer to see scientists search for "alternative and creative modes of coping with the truly universal and external problems of justice and liberty" (1974, p. 103). Such criticisms, rather than destroying the cognitive approaches, will probably generate more study, which will lead to further qualifications of the theories' claims.

VIII. Social-learning theory

The conception of morality offered us by social-learning theory has had very dramatic changes in the past few years. You may recall that the original position of S-R theorists gave total emphasis to environmental determinants of moral behavior. Reflecting such a conception was John B. Watson's statement "Give me a dozen healthy infants, well formed, and my own specified world to bring them up in, and I'll guarantee to take any one at random and train him to become any type of specialist I might select—doctor, lawyer, merchant, chief, and yes, even beggar man and thief, regardless of his talents, peculiarities, tendencies, abilities, vocations, and race of his ancestors" (Watson, 1930, p. 82). It is still the case that some social-learning theorists, in the Skinnerian tradition, reject the need to consider any internal determinants of moral behavior. But others now see moral behavior as cognitively mediated and self-motivated (Bandura, 1974). The latter type recognize the capacity of children to be active agents, interacting with and changing their environments and capable of self-regulation and self-reinforcement. But before we get too involved with the future of social learning, let's examine its approach.

A. The ethical-risk hypothesis

While the Freudian generally interprets morality as a heavy-handed superego dispensing guilt, the social-learning theorist operationally defines morality as resistance to temptation which is accounted for by an *ethical-risk hypothesis* (Rettig & Rawson, 1963). That is, the greater the likelihood of getting caught, the less likely the child is to engage in immoral behaviors. Early social-learning theorists held that the child responds to each situation in these terms, and that hence it was fruitless to expect much generalization of "morality" across tasks or generalized traits of personality over many situations.

Thus, the social-learning theorists initially assumed that "the value of a man's character lies in what he would do if he would not get caught."

The consequences (getting caught) were assumed to alter behavior automatically and unconsciously. Moral behavior would thus follow the same rules as other behavior in that reinforcers applied as soon as possible after a behavior could gradually shape the desired behavior.

B. Resistance to temptation

Resistance to temptation generally refers to a suppression (inhibition) of a behavior that has a high probability of occurring and that can be influenced by a prohibition or norm (Dmitruk, 1973). Two variables that have been widely studied and that influence resistance to temptation are (1) variations in punishment and (2) inhibiting and disinhibiting effects of models. We shall cover each of these as we examine research in social-learning approaches to morality.

C. Reactions to transgression

Aronfreed (1968) defines transgression as "any form of behavior . . . when it has become discriminantly associated with punishment that is sufficiently aversive to produce some degree of behavioral suppression" (p. 169). In classical conditioning terms, the person comes to associate a feeling of "anxiety" with an intention toward the transgression, as well as with the overt behavior itself. In instrumental conditioning terms, the effect is to provide behavioral alternatives to transgression. These alternatives acquire positive value because they reduce anxiety.

Reactions to transgression are the emotional feelings caused after the individual realizes that he or she has "done something wrong." Hence the anxiety. Aronfreed has divided reactions to transgression into two major categories: *internal* and *external.*

Internally, these reactions take on the form of fear, guilt, and shame. Fear is the anticipation of unpleasant consequences associated with the transgression. Guilt is an undifferentiated anxiety, more general in nature, while shame is an affective reaction oriented toward what others

may find out. One of the problems associated with internal reactions is the sequence: stimulus, behavior, and then anxiety reaction. The child must be trained to predict the consequences of his or her behavior. The psychopath, for example, shows little evidence of internalization of anxiety or anticipation of the consequences. Crucial measures of the effectiveness of socialization depend on the discriminative control that the individual has over aversive experiences. If anxiety is indiscriminant, few behavioral options are experienced and there is low resistance to temptation.

Externally, the observable reactions to transgression are confession, restitution, self-criticism, and reactions oriented toward external punishment. Confession allows the individual some control over the outcome and terminates the negative emotion. The parent (and our judicial system) usually treats the confessor more leniently. Restitution has a generally corrective orientation; it also interacts with the negative emotion, but not as clearly as confession. Self-criticism, usually verbal, also has anxiety-reducing value. Punishment seeking or reactions oriented toward external punishment are also internalized and anxiety reducing. The child who transgresses and then ensures that he is "caught" is not uncommon.

From a social-learning perspective, both internal and external reactions to transgression are learned ways of relieving anxiety associated with transgression.

IX. Morality research in social learning

Research within a social-learning framework began by testing Freudian concepts of conscience and internalization but has widened considerably to include empirical examination of cognitive orientations and pursuit of information developed from that research. Most frequently studied have been the suppression effects of punishment and of modeling.

discriminate =

restitution =

A. Punishment

The effects of punishment on resistance to temptation have been widely studied (Cheyne & Walters, 1970; LaVoie, 1973; Parke, 1969). Experiments using both animals and children as subjects have indicated that both the timing and the intensity of the punishment contribute to its effectiveness as a suppressor of behavior (Cheyne & Walters, 1969). Studies have also been conducted to determine whether the timing of the punishment of children influences the degree to which the child internalizes a prohibition. These studies typically use a simple experimental paradigm pairing toys, one more attractive than the other.

Aronfreed (1968) confronted boys with a discrimination-learning task in which each child had to choose between two toys and tell a story about one of the toys. If the child chose the attractive toy, he was sharply told "No! That's for the older boys!" In one condition (pretouching condition), the "No" was uttered just as the child reached for the toy and before he touched it. In a second condition the experimenter said "No" two or three seconds after the child picked up the toy. In a control condition, each boy simply pointed to the toy of his choice, and the experimenter made no comment. Internalization of the proscription against touching the toy was assessed by using a covert marker that could show whether the child had picked up an attractive toy while the experimenter was out of the room. The boys who were punished at the *initiation* of the transgression suppressed their choice of the attractive toy after fewer punishments than did the children who were punished *after* they picked up the toy. The boys in the pretouching condition also transgressed less than the boys who touched the toy in the second condition. In generalizing to natural settings, Aronfreed (1968) suggests that restricting the opportunity to transgress is insufficient, by itself, to bring about an internalized suppression of the child's temptation. Explicit punishment is also necessary.

Although social-learning theorists rely primarily on such factors as the timing and intensity of reinforcements, they also consider cognitive determinants of resistance to temptation in their approach to morality. Aronfreed (1968), for example, finds that children will be more resistant to temptation if they are given a reason for their punishment than if they are given no clue as to why they are being punished. The effects of increased cognitive structure on resistance to temptation suggest that children acquire complex rules as they increase their ability to consider the multiple consequences of their behavior (LaVoie, 1974a, 1974b).

B. Modeling

Experiments on the topic of modeling generally find what is known from everyday observation: by watching others we can learn too. Berger (1962), for example, found that if subjects watch a model being punished by an electric shock, they will also show anxiety to the sound of the buzzer that they heard prior to each shock.

Kimbrell and Blake (1958) studied the effects of a model's behavior and physiological motivation on violating a prohibition. They had subjects serve in a "taste preference" experiment and either do a puzzle or eat various numbers of crackers. Then the subjects were asked to wait in the hall before taking part in "another part of the experiment." A drinking fountain with a sign reading "Do not use this fountain" was nearby. The hall was deserted in one condition; in the other condition, it contained an accomplice who either drank or did not. Most of the very thirsty subjects (those who ate the most crackers) drank, while none of those who worked on the puzzle did. The effect of the model's drinking or not drinking was greatest for those subjects who were somewhat thirsty; none of them drank when the model didn't, but half drank when the model did.

Bandura and McDonald (1963) studied the effects of modeling by using pairs of stories similar to those of Piaget in Figure 8-1. They found they were able to influence children's responses in either direction, contrary to the developmental theory of Piaget. Cowan, Langer, Heavenrick, and

Nathanson (1969) repeated much the same experiment and replicated the basic results of the Bandura-McDonald experiment. But Cowan et al. also examined the stability of the learning involved by a two-week-delayed test. They found that the downward learning was less stable than the upward learning and that the children appeared to be doubtful about the process.

Rosenkoetter (1973) compared the effects of models on disinhibition and inhibition and found that the models had more pronounced effects as disinhibiting agents than as inhibiting agents. Rosenkoetter's findings are fairly typical of experimental results on modeling effects. Models are not particularly effective in suppressing behavior (inhibition) but are effective as deviant models for violating prohibitions (disinhibition).

X. A critique of social-learning approaches

A general statement evaluating the usefulness of a social-learning approach to morality research is difficult to make. Many of the experimental studies directed toward psychoanalytic and cognitive theories appeared to be more concerned with "proving" how wrong those theoretical approaches were than with explaining the phenomenon under investigation. The *ethical-risk hypothesis*, while fairly well supported in the laboratory, has not fared too well in naturalistic settings. Children, and adults for that matter, appear to come into an experimental setting quite willing to attribute good things to the scientist and comply with his or her authority. In some experiments the subject's preconceived notions, or history of reinforcement, appear to be generally ignored. In other experimental settings cheating is almost encouraged. The child usually responds with the apparently expected behavior if others (such as the model) are cheating and the authority doesn't seem to mind.

Social-learning theory that is used to examine conscience structure seems to have been misapplied or is simply not explained in cognitive

terms. For example, Lehrer (1967, cited in Kohlberg, 1969, p. 368) modified a ray-gun test used to measure resistance to temptation and got dramatic changes in cheating (from 80% to 25%). Kohlberg speculated that the imposing appearance of the gun led the children to believe it had score-keeping powers. "Obviously the behavior of the 55% of children who cheat on one machine but not the other is not determined by features of conscience strength" (Kohlberg, 1969, p. 368).

In experimental settings social learning has found moral judgments to be reversible (Bandura & McDonald, 1963; Schleifer & Douglas, 1973), at least during the experiment (Cowan et al., 1969). Cognitive theorists argue that the reversibility, or regression if found, was not "true" regression, and that explanations developed by social-learning theorists for other purposes should not be used to explain cognitive-structural changes, since social learning doesn't admit the existence of structure. However, social learning appears to be moving toward acceptance of cognitive factors in behavior. The imitation studies (modeling), or, as Hetherington and McIntyre (1975) call them, "Whoopee!" studies ("Whoopee! We can condition _____ !"), make it clear that the child can imitate almost anything, including moral judgments (Keasey, 1973; Prentice, 1972; Turiel & Rothman, 1972). But what the developmental or age-related determinants of imitation are and what the specific relationship of moral judgment to behavior may be are not clear at this time.

XI. An attempt at integration

We have now covered the three major orientations of moral development. Which one is most accurate, or most representative of the truth? Each approach is in the dynamic state of modifying and redefining its basic tenets. The original superego postulated by Freud as the basic source of morality is quite different from the superego as interpreted by Wilder, or from the ego functioning of Erikson. Piaget's two rela-

child sees it not as real life but a non-realistic game.

① dynamic = changing, in flux, not static.

tively simple cognitive stages of morality have been expanded to six (or seven) more elaborate stages by Kohlberg. Social learning was originally seen as acquired through successive approximations by means of differential reinforcement (Skinner, 1953). But social-learning theory is now able to demonstrate that a whole class of behaviors can be learned more readily with modeling than with reinforcement (Bandura & McDonald, 1963; L. C. Jensen & Hughston, 1973).

There appears to be some convergence now between these originally divergent approaches. In psychoanalysis, the core of ego functioning is a striving to master, to differentiate and integrate experience. Within the social-learning framework, Bandura (1974) views environmental and personal sources of control as aiding a growth process that seeks to expand individual freedom. Both of these sound quite similar to Kohlberg's (1969) definition of moral growth: "a trend toward an increasing internal orientation to norms" (p. 411).

Both psychoanalytic and cognitive approaches view moral development as occurring in stages. Growth occurs in one set of qualities and is then built upon in the development of another. The exact nature of these qualities has not been identified clearly by research. Each approach views the development as hierarchical in nature, with a proposed invariant sequence. The support for that sequence is far from impressive. Social learning, which now postulates some form of structure as viable, will have to define the nature of that structure. Is it developmental and more complex in older persons?

Kohlberg's hypothetical seventh stage, suggested in his most recent writing (1973), is viewed by Carlson (1975) as a rapprochement with Erikson's theory. But the basic difference of the logical versus the psychological formulation remains. Interestingly, Kohlberg (1973) speculates that responsibility and a commitment to principled living for a period of time appear to be necessary components of Stages 5 and 6. That's very much like Erikson's "self-chosen identification with goals, resulting in relatively permanent choices or commitments; later stages

are more adequate, not in cognitive inclusiveness, but in their ability to order personal experience in more stable, positive, and purposive form" (Erikson, cited in Carlson, 1975, p. 400).

A new theoretical framework that may provide integration of the three major approaches is that of Hogan (1973), who describes moral conduct and character in terms of five concepts: moral knowledge, socialization, empathy, autonomy, and a dimension of moral judgment. Hogan, like Kohlberg and Piaget, considers humans as a rule-formulating species. He sees all purposive social behavior as functioning within human subsystems, with each rule system containing its own ethic. The ethical system is a product of cognitive development and role-taking experience. A unique and fascinating aspect of Hogan's theory is his suggestion of several biological bases for morality, which include "authority-acceptor" and altruism, or should-value, an internal template for comparing and evaluating conduct. Unlike Kohlberg, Hogan sees no clear distinction between social and moral rules, but defines the function of morality as an integral part of social conduct. Hogan's approach contains elements of each of the major orientations presented in this chapter—affective, cognitive, and behavioral—and may provide the integration so needed in this complex area.

Perhaps the rigorous experimental approach of social learning will help us unravel the complex relations between moral judgment and behavior. In the search, however, the following admonition by Simpson seems particularly appropriate to researchers in moral judgment and behavior:

> Because the saber-toothed tiger survived for forty million years, the teeth which finally grew inward and destroyed him could hardly be called maladaptive. But the moral reasoning which we see actively applied today by the Western world, quite apart from highminded professional philosophy, bids fair to destroy man far short of a life span of forty million years. Is there a society with as many concepts for the good as the Eskimos have for snow or the Arabs for horse? Are there functional meth-

ods of conflict resolution and resource allocation in use which would serve people whose present methods are failing? We would do better to explore and analyze differences wherever found, to borrow and adapt, and to nurture invention and cultural mutation as it occurs than to perpetuate the ideology of a suicidal world trying to reconcile its differences through the use of a theoretical framework ill-suited for containing and ordering real human diversity [1974, p. 103].

XII. Summary

In seeking to understand the development of morality, some theorists, such as Freud and Erikson, have emphasized motivational and emotional determinants, while others, including Piaget and Kohlberg, have stressed cognitive factors. Reinforcement theorists and social-learning theorists have tried to avoid introducing any intervening variables, either motivational or cognitive, and have focused on behavior and the changes it undergoes. Resistance to temptation, or the suppression of responses that are prohibited by society, has been studied extensively by these theorists.

Freud proposed that three systems of energy operate within the person and that each system—the *id*, the *ego*, and the *superego*—has its own goals. In addition, Freud posited that a child passes through five stages of personality development—the *oral* stage, the *anal* stage, the *phallic* stage, the *latency* period, and the *genital* stage. Preoccupation with a specific part of the body is central to each stage. If the related needs are not satisfied, part of the person's psychic energy remains oriented toward these needs.

In psychoanalytic theory, morality is seen as a result of the child's identification with the parents and as an outcome of the child's introjection of their standards.

As a neo-Freudian, Erik Erikson has extended the period of psychological development beyond childhood into adolescence, young adulthood, and maturity. Erikson has proposed that each age period has its own *nuclear conflict*

to resolve. In contrast to Freud, Erikson and other neo-Freudians recognize the ego as a stable factor in early development.

Empirical tests of Freud's theory of moral development have been inconsistent in the degree to which their results support the theory. Erikson's theory is just beginning to be tested. The limited results so far are generally positive.

Piaget's theory is an example of a cognitive approach to moral development, emphasizing the acquisition of rules, laws, and principles. Children pass from an earlier stage of *moral realism* (accepting rules as given by authority) to *moral independence* (rules may be altered by consensus to fit the needs of the situation). According to Piaget, as the child moves from one stage to the other, he or she comes to emphasize the intentions rather than the consequences of an act; he or she gradually favors *reciprocity* rather than *expiatory* types of punishment, and finally discards a belief in immanent justice.

Kohlberg has extended Piaget's conception and proposed three levels of moral development: *preconventional*, *conventional*, and *postconventional* (also called the autonomous or principled level). Within these levels, there are six stages of moral development, which (according to Kohlberg) the child must pass through in *invariant* order.

Kohlberg's measurement of moral-judgment levels has been related to moral behavior. Persons at advanced stages of moral judgment have been found to be less likely to cheat on tests or to obey an experimenter who tells them to hurt a fellow subject.

Social-learning theorists are gradually including cognitively mediated behavior as a valid area of research. These theorists have studied two major aspects of morality, *resistance to temptation* and *reactions to transgression*. Studies in experimental settings have generally been more supportive of this approach than has research in naturalistic settings.

There appears to be some convergence of the three approaches toward viewing the human being as striving for competence, but much more research is needed before a definitive statement can be made.

Freud → Erikson   Piaget → Kohlberg

I. The importance of prosocial behavior
  A. Prosocial behavior and social psychology
  B. Prosocial behavior and life
  C. Studying prosocial behavior

II. Cooperation: Working for mutual benefit
  A. Group cohesiveness and productivity
  B. Learning to cooperate and compete

III. Helping behavior: From handouts to heroism
  A. Sizing up the situation
  B. The influence of other people
  C. Psychological states and helping
  D. Finding the Good Samaritan: Background and personality
  E. People who need people: The recipients of help
  F. Explanations of helping behavior

IV. Toward a prosocial society
  A. Teaching cooperation and helping to children
  B. Alms for the poor: Enlisting support for charities
  C. Helping in the helping professions
  D. Urban life and prosocial behavior
  E. Legislating a prosocial society

V. Summary

Prosocial behavior: Cooperation and helping

by Carol Sigelman

9

It is more blessed to give than to receive.
The New Testament, Acts 20:35

If it is more blessed to give than to receive, then most of us
are content to let the other fellow have the greater blessing.
Shailer Mathews

After wallowing in the aggression and violence of Chapter 7 and watching people struggle to resist temptation in Chapter 8, we now have the pleasure of examining positive forms of social behavior. Consider the following vignettes:

As a member of the student government, Susan is assigned to acquaint new students with the various clubs on campus. When she learns that Ron is supposed to acquaint students with committees, she suggests that each of them take half the list of new students and recruit for both clubs and committees. They finish the job much faster this way and recruit record numbers of students to the various organizations.

Faye's flight to Chicago has been delayed, and she sits in the terminal fantasizing about the upcoming weekend. A man approaches and asks if she would mind watching his suitcase for a minute. Faye agrees. When he returns, he mutters thanks and hurries toward the departure gate.

George hears a knock at the door. A stranger explains that she is collecting money for a new program to treat autistic children. George, who has never heard of autism before, becomes interested as she describes the innovative pro-

gram. Although his bank balance is very low, he donates $25.00.

Marcy and Alan are relaxing after a day of wine, cheese, and sun in a wilderness park. Suddenly they hear a scream from the direction of the river. They run to the river and spot a man flailing against the current, his capsized boat downstream. Alan hunts for a rope or pole. When Marcy realizes that the man can no longer stay afloat, she jumps in to rescue him, although she is only a mediocre swimmer. Somehow she drags him close enough to shore so that Alan can reach them both with a pole. They leave as soon as they have delivered the man to the park patrol. They read in the paper the next morning that a Roger Harris was saved from drowning by an unidentified couple in Elmore Park.

We offer these vignettes as examples of "prosocial" forms of behavior. Their common element is that a person's behavior contributed to improving the physical or psychological well-being of another person or persons. Following the lead of Wispé (1972, 1977), we define **prosocial behavior** as behavior that has positive social consequences. A host of behaviors fall into this

277

broad category, among them altruism, aiding, attraction, bystander intervention, charity, cooperation, friendship, helping, rescue, sacrifice, sharing, sympathy, and trust. Although all these behaviors certainly contrast with antisocial forms of behavior, the present chapter will focus on only a few of them.

In the first vignette, Susan and Ron acted in conjunction so that each could recruit students to campus programs. **Cooperation**—that is, working together for mutual benefit—is a prosocial behavior that has received a great deal of attention, particularly as it contrasts with **competi-**

tion—striving to excel in order to obtain an exclusive goal. When two people cooperate, the action of each brings *both* closer to a goal; when two people compete, the behavior of one actually makes it less likely that the other will attain the goal.

Helping behavior, defined generally, is behavior that benefits another person rather than oneself. It may take several forms. In the second vignette, Faye performed a *favor* for a stranger. A *favor* is a helping act that requires little self-sacrifice in time and effort but that benefits another person.

Figure 9-1
Helping behavior, courtesy of United Airlines. In a series of TV commercials, United Airlines has pictured a chain of helping actions, the recipient of the first becoming the help giver in the second, and so on. Social-psychological research indicates that there is something to this idea; people are more likely to help others if they have just been aided themselves. (Photos courtesy of United Airlines.)

The third vignette represents still another form of helping behavior that has attracted considerable research interest. *Donation* is the provision of goods or services to a person or organization in need. It requires material sacrifice, though the degree of sacrifice may be large (as in George's case) or small.

The fourth vignette seems particularly praiseworthy, largely because Marcy risked her life and she and Alan did not ask for a reward. *Intervention in an emergency* is a potentially costly form of helping behavior, performed under stressful conditions, with little possibility of reward. It may cause you to think of the term "altruism." Although some researchers have used altruism to refer to helping behavior in general, most of us use it more narrowly. *Webster's New World Dictionary* defines altruism as "unselfish concern for the welfare of others," suggesting that the term is not applicable if the actor is motivated to achieve personal gain. According to Severy (1974), the essence of altruism is a motivation to help simply because you recognize that another person needs help.

We have no hesitancy about applying the term *altruism* to the action of the Good Samaritan (Luke 10:30–35), who aided a man wounded by thieves. Why is the Samaritan so praiseworthy? Unlike the priest and the Levite who "passed by on the other side," the Samaritan went to the wounded man, carried him to an inn, cared for him, paid the innkeeper, and offered money for any further expenses. Walster and Piliavin (1972) pinpointed why this parable serves as a model of altruism. First, the Samaritan was not responding to pressures or obligations. His act was voluntary and, in fact, nonconforming, since other community leaders failed to help. He was not of the same ethnic group as the victim and had no special responsibility for him. Moreover, his behavior was costly, involving sacrifices on his part of time, effort, and money. Finally, he sought no reward, nor did he receive one. Like the Lone Ranger, he rode away unnamed and unthanked. Taking both the behavior and the motives behind the behavior into account, then, *altruism* is a very special form of helping behavior which is voluntary, costly, and motivated by something other than the anticipation of reward.

I. The importance of prosocial behavior

Violence, war, and corruption make headlines, but our humanity to others is often hidden on the back pages. Social psychologists have also neglected the study of prosocial behavior until the last decade or so, although recently the topic has become one of the liveliest areas of social psychology (Wispé, 1972, 1977). One reason for this new-found interest concerns the profound implications of prosocial behavior for theories of human behavior and our assumptions about human nature. A second reason is more practical than theoretical: antisocial behavior and the lack of prosocial responses to it threaten society enough so that we must find keys to a more prosocial world.

A. Prosocial behavior and social psychology

Prosocial behaviors pose a challenge to social psychologists. Recall two of the major theories presented in Chapter 1. Stimulus-response theory states that we tend to repeat or strengthen those behaviors that are followed by rewarding consequences. How, then, would altruism increase in strength, or even exist, if it is associated with negative consequences—loss of resources, injury, or even death? Or take psychoanalytic theory, which rests on the assumption that human nature is instinctively selfish and aggressive. How can it explain behavior that is apparently unselfish and beneficial to others? The theorist's challenge is to explain why people do something that is apparently not reinforcing or that goes against their hypothetical basic nature.

Various stimulus-response and social-learning theorists have responded to this challenge, some by rejecting the concept of altruism, others by arguing that there are rewards to seemingly altruistic acts but that the rewards are subtle—for example, an increased feeling of self-esteem or even an expectation of reward in an afterlife. But we believe that such arguments are often circular—they seem to assume that since the helping behavior occurred, its consequences *must* have been reinforcing.

Other researchers acting within an S-R framework have tried to demonstrate that helping, like any other learned behavior, is in fact reinforcing. For instance, Weiss, Buchanan, Altstatt, and Lombardo (1971) showed that people will learn a response whose only reinforcement is saving another person from a painful shock. The reinforcement could involve avoiding the upsetting realization of another person's distress, or it might consist of the pleasant anticipation of the other's sigh of relief when the shock is terminated.

But what if people must sacrifice something in order to be helpful? In a study by Aronfreed and Paskal (1965), children were trained in empathy—the vicarious experience of another person's emotions (Aronfreed, 1968). During training, the experimenter expressed joy and hugged the child after pulling a lever which produced a red light. As a result of this training, most children activated the light to make the experimenter happy more often than they pulled the other lever to earn candy for themselves. Aronfreed argued that empathy underlies altruism and is acquired by learning principles. People reduce their own vicarious discomfort by delivering another person from pain, and increase their vicarious happiness by making someone else happy.

However, Tipton and Jenkins (1974) demonstrated that a person who stands to lose by being altruistic is less likely to help. Like Weiss and his associates, they found that subjects would push a button solely to terminate a painful

shock to another person. However, if subjects believed that their performance on a task would suffer if they acted quickly to end the shock, and if they faced an extra hour of work on a dull task as a punishment for poor performance, their rate of altruism dropped off sharply. As we shall see, the more rewarding a helpful act is, the more often it will occur. On the other hand, the greater the costs of helping, the less likely it is that help will be forthcoming. While these generalizations are in line with principles of positive reinforcement and punishment, they do not explain heroic altruism where the costs are immense.

Still another challenge to social psychologists is to determine whether the highest form of prosocial behavior—altruism—is rooted in nature or nurture. Donald Campbell (1965) once argued that altruism in humans is, in part, transmitted genetically from generation to generation, as it is in some animal species, because of the contribution of "altruistic genes" or predispositions to group functioning and survival. However, Campbell (1972, 1977) later declared his theory inoperative. He decided it was impossible for "altruistic" genes to become more prevalent than "cowardly" genes; while altruists might indeed help the group to survive, they would die out faster than the cowards who thought first of themselves and declined to take risks on behalf of others. Campbell concluded that prosocial behavior is taught by society but runs counter to genetically determined dispositions.

Taken together, stimulus-response theory, psychoanalytic theory, and evolutionary theory do not paint a bright picture. Heroic altruism seems to defy many conceptions of human nature. For this very reason, it will continue to be of interest to social psychologists.

B. Prosocial behavior and life

For those who do not relish theoretical debate, there are practical reasons for studying prosocial behavior. First, our very survival may hinge on our ability to restrict antisocial behaviors such as violence and war and increase positive forms of behavior such as cooperation and helping.[1] This is critical in a violent society (see Chapter 7). It becomes increasingly important as we become more urbanized, more crowded, and less self-sufficient. Some argue that changes in our society are actually undermining traditional values of neighborliness and goodwill, making violence a more common occurrence. Perhaps because of this vision of the future, some members of society are rejecting "dog-eat-dog" competitive values and are searching for alternatives in communes, sensitivity-training groups, and neighborhood-action projects (see Chapters 13 and 17 for descriptions of these movements).

Not only do we deplore violence, but we are alarmed when people fail to help when help is needed. An incident that symbolizes this failure occurred in New York City in 1964. The stabbing of Kitty Genovese might have passed for "just another murder" except for some peculiar circumstances:

> For more than half an hour thirty-eight respectable, lawabiding citizens in Queens watched a killer stalk and stab a woman in three separate attacks in Kew Gardens.
>
> Twice the sound of their voices and the sudden glow of their bedroom lights interrupted him and frightened him off. Each time he returned, sought her out and stabbed her again. Not one person telephoned the police during the assault; one witness called after the woman was dead [*New York Times*, March 27, 1964].

[1]As you may have noticed, this chapter reflects our belief that prosocial behavior is morally good. Some social philosophers see it differently. For example, Ayn Rand (1943), in her novels, placed high value on individualism and argued that our responsibility is to look out for ourselves, not for others. We will admit that not all prosocial acts are as moral as they may appear. It sometimes depends on who is defining "positive social consequences." The Spanish Inquisition must have seemed prosocial to some of its perpetrators. And even if we could all agree that the consequences of an act were positive, many of us would hesitate to label an act "prosocial" if we could determine that its motive was greed or hatred.

Police and community experts, including sociologists and psychologists, could offer no real explanation—particularly since witnesses needed only make a call from the safety of their apartments. Most experts pointed to public apathy as the cause, but many of the witnesses appeared to have been genuinely upset, as if they had been locked in a tremendous internal struggle to decide what to do.

New York City was jolted by the episode. As a writer for the *New York Times* concluded, the event was "a symptom of a terrible reality in the human condition—that only under certain situations and only in response to certain reflexes or certain beliefs will a man step out of his shell toward his brother" (A. M. Rosenthal, 1964, p. 81). The task of identifying those conditions was taken on by social psychologists in quite direct response to the Kitty Genovese incident.

We also have a stake in determining why many people do not support charitable causes, why individuals and groups, including nations, do not cooperate with one another, and why even the simple courtesies or favors of life are not always forthcoming.

C. Studying prosocial behavior

Though it is important to study prosocial behavior, it is difficult to do so. For example, researchers cannot simply explain the nature of their research to subjects. Sensitive to the *demand characteristics* of the situation, a subject would be unlikely to say "I wouldn't help" or to deny aid when helping is clearly the subject under investigation. But even those subjects who are unaware of the true nature of the study may be on their best behavior or unsure about the role of "research subject," so that they are eager to please. Of course, natural experiments are an option, and, indeed, sociologists have studied citizens' reactions to major disasters such as tornadoes; but untenured researchers can hardly afford to lurk on street corners waiting for emergencies to occur.

Figure 9-2
Would Kitty Genovese be safe today? The memory of Kitty Genovese lingers. On July 8, 1974, United Press carried a story about an off-duty policeman who trailed three men in Queens (a borough of New York City) as they carried a woman into a building and prepared to rape her. He pulled his gun and held the assailants at bay as he yelled and knocked on apartment doors. For 40 minutes no one even telephoned for police support. As the policeman finally attempted to move the suspects outside by himself, one escaped.

But perhaps there is hope. On December 31, 1974, United Press carried another story, this one about neighbors' responses when a woman's purse was snatched in Detroit. About a hundred people, hearing her shout and blow a special whistle she wore around her neck, joined in chasing the thief. One man even crashed his car into a fence and apartment building when the thief dashed between two houses. Finally, a group cornered the man and held him at bay with a shovel until a police officer arrived on the scene in response to telephone calls.

How can we explain why people ignored a clear call for help in the first situation and responded so effectively in the second? More importantly, what can we do to ensure that future Kitty Genoveses receive help when they need it? (Photo by Jim Pinckney.)

As a result, much research on prosocial behavior has taken the form of field experimentation, in which the experimenter makes a request or stages an incident in a public place. As Chapter 2 indicated, field experimentation has many advantages, but it also poses serious ethical problems. People are transformed into research subjects without their knowledge, much less their informed consent; and very often they are not debriefed afterward, even when they have witnessed such frightening and apparently injurious events as the collapse of an apparently sick person on the street or in the subway.

The justification for such methodology is that it is the best—and sometimes the only—way to determine what people will do and under what circumstances they will do it. Nonetheless, researchers must take every precaution to maintain their responsibilities to their subjects.

What can we learn from research on prosocial behavior? The first topic of this chapter is cooperation, a form of prosocial behavior that has "something in it" for the actor. We will explore the conditions that make people more or less likely to cooperate or to compete, and we will see how these behaviors are learned. Then we will turn to a variety of helping behaviors, including doing small favors, donating to charity, and intervening in emergencies. In explaining these behaviors, we will focus on situational factors, the effects of other people, momentary psychological states, personality characteristics and other background variables, and the characteristics of the recipient of help. Two explanatory models—one pointing to the operation of norms or standards of behavior, the other focusing on the costs and rewards of helping or failing to help—will tie together the loose ends of research findings. Finally, we will apply what we have learned to the task of building a more prosocial society. Although research may not answer all our questions about the deep-seated motives for prosocial behavior, it does suggest ways to change individuals and situations to foster more prosocial behavior in the future.

II. Cooperation: Working for mutual benefit

As noted above, cooperation is a prosocial behavior in which persons act for mutual benefit, as Susan and Ron did when they divided the labor of recruiting students to campus organizations. When people cooperate, they coordinate their efforts so that each individual's actions bring everyone closer to achieving a goal. In fact, people who cooperate can often achieve a goal that none could obtain alone, as when it takes four people pushing together to roll a car out of a muddy rut.

We cannot fully understand cooperation without comparing and contrasting it with competition. When people compete, they strive individually to obtain the same goal, one that not all of them can attain (Deutsch, 1949a). One person's progress toward the goal decreases the probability that other competitors will attain it. We are not suggesting that competition is necessarily antisocial rather than prosocial, for people often have rewarding and positive interactions in the context of competition; but there is often the risk of hostility among competitors, particularly when rewards are highly valued.

Analysis of cooperation and competition is often clouded because the two terms not only describe behavior but also refer to (1) reward structures inherent in a situation and (2) the individual's motives as he or she enters a situation. Consider one very familiar situation—the classroom. A professor may grade on a curve such that only 15% of the students will receive A's in the course. Students then find themselves in a *competitive reward structure* in which the successes of their peers actually decrease their own chances of success (assuming that "success" is

defined as receiving an A grade). College students often have to operate in such situations, competing with others for honors, athletic awards, and job openings that not all of them can attain.

A more inventive professor might introduce a *cooperative reward structure* into the classroom by saying "Each team that I have formed in this classroom must work as a team to complete a series of projects. If the team does good work, everyone on the team will receive an A in the course. If the team produces poor projects, all members will receive F's." As in the competitive reward structure, students' outcomes are interdependent; the actions of one have implications for the outcomes of others. The critical difference is that in a competitive reward structure, one person's gain is another person's loss, while in a cooperative reward structure, one person's contribution increases not only his or her own rewards but also those of other group members (Deutsch, 1949a).

But consider still another commonly employed grading system. The professor says "I reward competent work. If you complete your assignments successfully, you will receive an A. The grade you receive has no bearing on the grades others receive; in fact, I would be happy to see each of you produce high-quality work and receive an A." Here students' outcomes are not interdependent, since goal attainment by one has no effect on the probability of goal attainment by another. In this *individualistic reward structure,* individuals are freer to cooperate or compete with others as they choose, or simply to go about their own business.

In analyzing cooperation and competition, we also need to consider the cognitions and motives of individuals (K. J. Edwards, 1974). Some people always seem to want to share resources and cooperate, while others seem to become cutthroat in even the friendliest of games. In a class with an individualistic reward structure, for example, Fred and Tim might share notes and study together to ensure that they both do better in the course. Tina and Joyce, on the other hand, might compete with each other, compare standings, or even go out of their way to see that the other person does worse. If an individual primarily seeks the outcome most beneficial to all participants, he or she is governed by a *cooperative motive*. A person with a *competitive motive* seeks not only to achieve personal success but also to cause others in the situation to fail. Finally, the person with an *individualistic motive* seeks to optimize personal rewards, without regard to how others fare.

Naturally, a competitive reward structure tends to draw out the competitive motives in students. For example, premed students competing for scarce openings in medical schools sometimes find themselves in a "sort of academic guerilla war" (*Time*, May 20, 1974, p. 62). To further their career chances, students reportedly give up their social lives, emphasize grades over learning, refuse to help other students, deliberately give misleading information to others, tear pages from important library readings, and ruin other students' laboratory experiments. A few students who might have become excellent physicians have dropped out, perhaps because their personal motives clashed with such an intensely competitive reward structure.

However, cooperatively motivated individuals can sometimes alter a competitive reward structure. For example, poker is typically a competitive game, but a sociologist participated in a long-standing poker group in which members cooperated in setting standards of poker play so that all could enjoy the thrill of close competition (Zurcher, 1970). In fact, rather than exploiting "suckers" who did not play well or were too honest to bluff, the group declined to invite such players back.

Of course, in real life we rarely encounter pure cooperative or competitive reward structures. Rather, we enter many mixed-motive situations in which we must choose between cooperating and competing. Consider the predicament called the "Prisoner's Dilemma":

> Two subjects are taken into custody and separated. The district attorney is certain they are guilty of a specific crime, but he does not have adequate evidence to convict them at a trial. He points out to each prisoner that each has two alternatives: to confess to the crime the police are sure they have done or not to confess. If they both do not confess then the district attorney will book them on some very minor trumped-up charge . . . ; if they both confess, they will be prosecuted, (and) he will recommend (a rather severe) sentence; but if one confesses and the other does not, then the confessor will receive rather lenient treatment for turning state's evidence whereas the latter will get the "book" slapped at him [Luce & Raiffa, 1957, p. 95].

Put yourself in the place of one of the prisoners. It seems easy enough to stay quiet, or "stonewall" in Watergate parlance, and receive a light sentence for a minor crime; but if your partner confesses, you will pay dearly. On the other hand, you can confess to gain a lenient sentence and worsen your partner's position relative to yours, but again you run the risk that he will confess also, ensuring that you will both suffer. The Prisoner's Dilemma is a mixed-motive situation precisely because what is the best choice for each individual separately—if chosen by both individuals—results in a losing outcome (Dawes, 1974).

In the Prisoner's Dilemma, concealing the crime is a cooperative choice, while confessing is a competitive choice. Hundreds of college students have played laboratory games involving these two choices, though they play for money or points rather than for prison sentences. Prisoner's Dilemma research tells us a great deal about the determinants of cooperation and competition (the interested reader is referred to Rapoport & Chammah, 1965; Swingle, 1970; and Wrightsman, O'Connor, & Baker, 1972). For example, the strategy of the other player influences one's own tendency to cooperate. Generally people do not act more cooperatively if the other player is cooperative on every trial, but they quickly learn to make more cooperative choices if the other player matches their own choices *rather than all cooperation.*

"tit-for-tat," cooperating in response to a cooperative choice, and competing in response to a competitive choice. Cooperation is also facilitated if players can communicate with one another—provided they do not use the opportunity to communicate to make threats. Personal characteristics also affect rates of cooperation. Whereas some people are cooperatively motivated, others are more competitively motivated, even when the task is not specifically introduced as calling for either cooperative or competitive behavior. A variety of attitudes, personality characteristics, and motives have been shown to influence behavior in Prisoner's Dilemma games. These include Machiavellianism, trusting attitudes, risk taking, and self-concept. Such personal variables interact with characteristics of the situation such as strategy of the other player and opportunity to communicate.

According to some critics, however, Prisoner's Dilemma studies place subjects in an unrealistic situation, do not clearly separate cooperative and competitive motives from a host of other motives, and typically do not permit the kind of communication that facilitates cooperation in real life (Gergen, 1969; Nemeth, 1972; Pruitt, 1967). In this chapter, we will highlight more realistic studies in order to compare cooperation with helping behavior, which is typically studied under the most naturalistic conditions possible. Having introduced the terms we will need, we will now consider the effects of reward structures on group cohesiveness and productivity and the development of cooperative and competitive motives in children.

A. Group cohesiveness and productivity

If a competitive reward structure can produce antisocial behavior among premed students, does a cooperative reward structure lead people to behave more prosocially? The answer is yes, at least for well-developed groups in field situations; cooperative reward structures are associated with increased communication among partici-

pants, greater group cohesiveness, and higher satisfaction (Bramel, 1969; Raven & Eachus, 1963; Rosenblatt, 1964). Even before beginning to work together, group members expecting a cooperative orientation report more attraction to the group (Rabbie, 1974; Rabbie & Wilkens, 1971). For example, Haines and McKeachie (1967) compared methods of running discussion sections in an introductory psychology course by grading individual performance in some groups and group projects in others. Not only was tension higher in the group with the competitive reward structure, but students in the cooperative sections enjoyed their classes more.

Similar differences in atmosphere were found in an employment agency (Blau, 1954). In one section of the agency, an employment interviewer's job security depended on his filling more job openings and serving more clients than did other interviewers in the section. In a second section, the supervisor encouraged interviewers to develop a common purpose and make as many placements as possible without regard to relative standings among interviewers. As expected, interviewers in the first section became competitively motivated. They rarely communicated with one another, and they actually concealed information about job openings. Interviewers in the second section enjoyed each other's company and actually helped one another place clients.

This is all well and good, but an efficiency expert looks for more than group satisfaction and cohesiveness. What about productivity? In Blau's study, the cooperative section actually placed more job applicants than did the competitive section. This relationship between a cooperative reward structure and productivity has provocative implications for classroom instruction. One group of researchers varied the reward structures for four groups of 15 fifth-grade children studying arithmetic (Wodarski, Hamblin, Buckholdt, & Ferritor, 1973). In one reward structure, the student received a dollar in play money (exchangeable for goods) for each problem he or she worked correctly. In another reward structure, a group-shared consequence condition, each student in the group was paid according to the average of the four lowest scorers in the group. In two other conditions, the individual's reward was based on both individual performance and the performance of the four lowest scorers in the group. In two other conditions, the individual's reward was based on both individual performance and the performance of the four lowest scorers. All reward structures produced high rates of studying and low rates of disruptive behavior, but as rewards came to depend more heavily on the performance of low scorers in the group, problem-solving accuracy increased. Although such a cooperative structure may seem unfair to more capable students, their performance actually rose slightly as more of their reward came to depend on the performance of slower students. Most interestingly, they became more likely to help slower students with their work. The slower students, of course, profited most, perhaps because they received more help and worked harder knowing that the whole group depended on them. The unorthodox cooperative reward structure used in this study thus had positive effects on both prosocial behavior and achievement.

What happens if a group with a cooperative reward structure competes with an outside group, as athletic teams do? Dunn and Goldman (1966) divided students taking an introductory psychology course into groups that met once a week to discuss human-relations problems. In addition to establishing individualistic, competitive, and cooperative reward structures, the researchers used an intergroup-competition/intragroup-cooperation reward structure. Students instructed to cooperate with each other in order to best other groups had the highest percentage of mature, goal-oriented comments (65%). The cooperative groups also performed well, with 50% of their comments rated productive; productivity dropped sharply in competitive groups (10%) and individualistic groups (0%). The only disadvantage of the intergroup-competition/intragroup-cooperation structure was that students in these groups were less accepting of fellow group members than were students in the straight cooperative reward structure.

On the whole, competitive reward structures within groups tend to breed distrust, disrupt cohesiveness, and even lower productivity. Cooperative reward structures have positive effects on group cohesiveness, and that may increase productivity (assuming group members do not conspire to produce as little as possible). These effects are most noticeable when the tasks are such that two heads (or pairs of hands) are better than one (Blau, 1954; Crombag, 1966; Raven & Eachus, 1963). When sheer quantity of work is required and individuals can work best without assistance, a competitive reward structure may enhance productivity (L. K. Miller & Hamblin, 1963).

B. Learning to cooperate and compete

How do we learn to cooperate, compete, and decide which to do in a given situation? Children 2 or 3 years old are not capable of cooperation or competition, because both behaviors require coordinating one's actions with the actions of others. Young children, egocentric in their thinking, tend to play alone or to play beside others without really playing *with* them. Jean Piaget (1965), in his observation and questioning of boys playing marbles, found that even 3- to 5-year-olds were too egocentric to play games properly. They had idiosyncratic understandings of the rules and, although they did care about winning, they saw nothing wrong with having several winners—as long as they themselves won. As indicated in Chapter 8, by the age of 5 or 6, the child learns the necessity of cooperation and begins to enjoy demonstrating mastery of skills through competition. Thus we can say that both cooperative and competitive behaviors increase with age.

The more challenging task is learning *when* to cooperate and when to compete. Children's choices have been studied through the use of the game pictured in Figure 9-3.

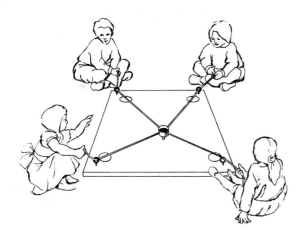

Figure 9-3

Deciding whether to cooperate or compete. Imagine that a child is seated at each of the four corners of this board. Each child holds a string that can be pulled to move the marking pen in the center. As Madsen (1967) and his colleagues have structured the game, the children are first placed in a cooperative reward structure. They must move the pen through the four target circles in sequence to be rewarded. On the next series of trials, each child receives a reward only when the pen moves through his or her own designated target circle. Even when the instructions are changed in this way, cooperation is still the best strategy because, if the children pull against one another at cross-purposes, chances are that no one will receive many prizes. What do you think children actually do?

Three groups of Mexican children—middle-class urban, poor rural, and poor urban children—played the game in one study (Madsen, 1967). Although all groups cooperated on the first task, middle-class urban children became highly competitive when the instructions were altered and, as a result, did not reap as many benefits as did the rural and urban poor children who continued to use a cooperative strategy. Madsen attributed these differences to subcultural background, noting that the rural and urban poor children had learned to work together for family survival and to avoid greedy, competitive behavior, whereas the middle-class urban children were exposed to parental models who competed in business.

When playing Madsen's game, Israeli children from a communal *kibbutz* were more cooperative than urban Israeli children brought up in a more achievement-oriented subculture (Shapira & Madsen, 1969), and Blackfoot Indian children were more cooperative than non-Indian Canadian children (A. G. Miller & Thomas, 1972). In many of these studies, the more cooperative children appeared to slow down, as though they were avoiding competition. In fact, among some Indian tribes that attach great value to group cooperation, children may hesitate to start a race, knowing that the winner will be ridiculed by other children (Erikson, 1963). Middle-class children in the United States, by contrast, have learned competition so well and value it so highly that they compete even when cooperation is the more "rational" strategy, a trend that becomes stronger with age (Madsen, 1967, 1971; Madsen & Shapira, 1970).

In part, then, cooperative and competitive motives develop as the child's intellectual and social skills develop. However, the acquisition of a preference for one behavior over the other in a given situation may depend on the culture or subculture in which a child grows up—or, more precisely, on the values transmitted by parents and other adults. In some societies, such as the Sioux tribes, cooperation is so highly valued that competitive motives are rarely expressed. On the other hand, we must wonder whether mainstream society in the United States emphasizes competitive motives so heavily that cooperative behaviors receive too little exercise.

III. Helping behavior: From handouts to heroism

If it is often difficult to induce people to cooperate for mutual benefit, we might guess that it is even harder to make them work for another person's benefit—to engage in helping behavior. After examining situational factors that influence helping behavior, we will consider the psychological states and traits of the potential helper. Finally, we will search for characteristics of the recipient of help that elicit helping behavior and conclude with a more general look at explanations of helping behavior.

A. Sizing up the situation

Any of us may find ourselves in a situation that calls for giving the time of day, returning a lost wallet, donating to charity, or jumping into a lake to rescue a drowning swimmer. How does the potential helper size up each situation and decide whether or not to help? Latané and Darley (1970) developed a five-stage model for analyzing behavior in emergencies, a model that appears to be applicable in a variety of nonemergency situations as well (see Figure 9-4).

This model may sound too "cold and calculating" if it is taken literally as a sequential decision-making process. Nonetheless, its elements—noticing the event, interpreting it, determining personal responsibility, choosing a form of assistance, and implementing that assistance —must be present in some form for helping to occur.

Figure 9-4
Deciding to intervene in an emergency. The New York City workman pictured above is studiously ignoring a mugging only a few paces away. Why doesn't he help? What would you do if you walked around the corner and witnessed this scene? As Latané and Darley (1970) see it, there are five critical steps in the intervention process: (1) *Notice that something is happening.* Perhaps the workman does not even notice the mugging. If you are hurrying to a job interview or are distracted by a bus screeching to a halt across the street, you may not notice either. But if you do see the two men, you are ready for the next step. (2) *Interpret the situation as one in which help is needed.* Like the workman, your interpretation of the scene depends on how many and what types of cues

are available, how many of them you process, and how you read them. You may decide that the incident is just a friendly skirmish, or, if you are a drama student, you may perceive it as an act in a play. But if the cues are unambiguous—if the victim bleeds or cries out—you are more likely to think "Wow, he needs help" and go on to Step 3. (3) *Assume personal responsibility.* Even if the workman interprets the incident as an emergency, he may feel that it is none of his business. Similarly, you may decide that the policeman across the street is more responsible than you are, or that the victim probably deserves all he gets, or that you are not willing to risk anything for a total stranger. In considering the costs and rewards of intervening, the size and strength of the mugger might figure strongly in your calculations. If your analysis of the situation and your motives prompt you to assume personal responsibility for intervening, you are ready for the next step. (4) *Choose a form of assistance.* Here again, costs and rewards must be calculated—this time, the costs and rewards of alternative helping responses. Should you hit the mugger over the head with one of the workman's buckets? Such direct intervention may mean embarrassment and even injury. Should you call the police? That may take too much time to be effective. The intervention process may break down at this point if you are so distressed that you cannot settle on a course of action. If you can decide, however, you are almost ready to act. (5) *Implement the assistance.* Still more decisions are required if you reach this final step: Where should you grab the mugger—the neck or the arms? What should you shout—"Police!" or "Freeze!"? Stress may nullify all the decisions you made before this point if you cannot effectively execute a helping behavior. (Photo by Catharine Ursillo/Nancy Palmer.)

Muggings, car accidents, and tornadoes are all examples of emergencies. Latané and Darley (1970) claimed that the first characteristic of an emergency is the threat or actuality of harm. Not only are there potential or actual costs to the helper, but there are few rewards, since the best outcome is usually just a return to normality. Although we are very likely to notice an emergency, the high costs and low rewards of intervening may influence our interpretation of the situation and, most importantly, our decision on whether or not to assume personal responsibility.

An emergency is also a rare event, meaning that most people have no experience on which to draw in selecting and implementing a course of action. Moreover, emergencies differ from one another, again implying that witnesses are not armed with plans of action. Also, emergencies offer little time for contemplation and consultation. Finally, they require instant action, produc-

ing a great deal of stress, which may interfere with efficient decision making and action. Emergencies, then, are dangerous, unusual, unique, unforeseen, and pressing. These characteristics can cause any number of breakdowns in the intervention process.

While people often "rise to the occasion" and help very effectively in crises, the rate of helping in emergencies is generally lower than that in more mundane situations. Consider this nonemergency: you are walking down a street and a man approaching you on crutches drops a book, apparently unaware that he has done so. The event is easily noticed and easily interpreted as one requiring help, particularly since crutches signal dependency. You readily assume personal responsibility, because you are the only person on the street; if you do not help, no one else will. Moreover, the costs of helping are minimal, since picking up a book is a well-learned and painless form of assistance. At each step, the decision to help is relatively easy to make—easier, in fact, than walking by and feeling like a moral midget for the rest of the day. Given the characteristics of this situation, it is not surprising that 100% of the subjects in one study rendered aid (F. W. Schneider, 1973).

Consider some minor variations, however. If the man were not on crutches, passersby might interpret the situation as one the victim is perfectly capable of handling himself. A man without crutches would do well to make the situation less ambiguous by saying "I dropped my book. Would you mind picking it up?" Still, however, the passerby might not perceive the need for help ("What's wrong with you, fella, that you can't pick it up?"). The victim would elicit still more help if he added "I just had a hernia operation," indicating that the need is a legitimate one calling for action, and placing responsibility squarely on the shoulders of the passerby.

Now suppose strangers approach you on the street and ask for each of the following: the time, directions to a well-known place, change for a quarter, your name, or a dime. Which requests would you be most hesitant to honor? Latané and Darley (1970) asked people in New York City to comply with these requests and obtained the response rates shown in Table 9-1.

People were fairly willing to provide these types of help, but they were significantly less likely to give their names or hand over dimes than they were to honor the other requests. Why? Perhaps because of slightly higher costs. Giving one's name to a stranger posed a threat; many of the subjects were surprised, asked why the experimenter wanted to know, and usually gave only their first names. Giving away a dime involved a small financial cost to the actor. However, it must be noted that the requester gave no reason for the request. Elaborating their requests for help, strangers collected even more dimes (1) when they stated their names first and then made the request (49% response); (2) when they requested the dime and added that they needed it to make a phone call (64%); and (3) when they explained that their wallets had been stolen (72%). Altogether, these findings suggest that people are very responsive to requests for low-cost help, particularly if they are given a plausible explanation.

Even when the need is clearly stated in a series of requests, however, the potential helper considers the costs of complying with each request. In a study by Suedfeld, Bochner, and Wnek (1972), male participants in a peace demonstration were approached by a young woman who stated that her male friend was feeling ill.

Table 9-1
Frequency of response to different requests

	Number Asked	Percentage Helping
"Excuse me, I wonder if you could . . .		
a. tell me what time it is?"	92	85
b. tell me how to get to Times Square?"	90	84
c. give me change for a quarter?"	90	73
d. tell me what your name is?"	277	39
e. give me a dime?"	284	34

From *The Unresponsive Bystander: Why Doesn't He Help?*, by B. Latané and J. M. Darley. Copyright 1970. Reprinted by permission of Prentice-Hall, Inc., Englewood Cliffs, New Jersey.

All 80 subjects followed the woman to her sick friend and 79 agreed to help move him out of the way. While a large majority (66%) agreed to help carry him to a first-aid station, only 19% agreed to help when they learned that he preferred to go to his apartment seven miles away, and only 11% offered money when the woman finally asked for bus fare to get there. As the cost of helping, in terms of time or money, increased, helping behavior decreased.

Although we have by no means said all that can be said about situational factors, we have introduced a five-stage model of the intervention process that will permit us to analyze a variety of personal and situational factors influencing decisions by a potential helper. The ambiguity of a situation—as it is affected by the nature of the need, the legitimacy of the need, and the manner in which it is transmitted to the helper —is an important consideration. And the perceived costs and rewards of helping or failing to help will be a recurring theme in the analysis of helping behavior.

B. The influence of other people

At the heart of social psychology is the truth that people influence one another. If you witness a car accident along with others, the other witnesses become part of the situation from your perspective. They can serve as a source of reinforcement or punishment, perhaps approving you if you act, perhaps scorning you for doing so. They can demonstrate or model helping behavior. Or they can display behavior that is unresponsive, influencing you in still another way. The first two types of influence—reinforcement and modeling—account for much human behavior and learning. The last type of influence— termed the "bystander effect"—has special implications for helping behavior and suggests why 38 witnesses did not act while Kitty Genovese was slain.

Reinforcement. A simple way to increase the strength of almost any behavior is to follow it by positive consequences. As we have already seen, helping may be intrinsically rewarding, especially when the capacity for empathy is well developed. But helping behavior can be given an extra boost if it is followed by external rewards (M. K. Moss & Page, 1972; Weiss, Buchanan, Altstatt, & Lombardo, 1971). Fischer (1963), for example, demonstrated that 4-year-old children were more likely to share marbles with another child if they were rewarded with bubble gum.

If helping has always been rewarding, a person will become more helpful over a lifetime; however, if most attempts to help have been fiascos, a person may hesitate to risk further pain and embarrassment. On the main street of Dayton, Ohio, females stopped passersby and asked for directions (M. K. Moss & Page, 1972). The direction giver was either positively rewarded with a cheerful thanks, responded to neutrally ("Okay"), or cut off with a negative statement ("I can't understand what you're saying; never mind, I'll ask someone else"). Shortly thereafter, a second confederate dropped a bag, providing an opportunity for the subject to initiate help. Negative consequences for the first helping reaction led to less helping in the second situation. Subjects in this group were less helpful than control subjects who had no prior encounter. The mild reward for helping did not significantly increase helping rates in the second encounter.

Reinforcement principles aid in understanding how children learn to help. Helping is made profitable for children if they receive material or social rewards after sharing or helping; they also can develop the ability to experience the emotions of others vicariously and to act to increase the joy and reduce the distress of others. Reinforcement principles are also useful in increasing the rates of helping among adults, but they do not quite explain the heroic altruist's immense sacrifices for others.

Modeling. A second proven method of teaching or eliciting a behavior is to model it, allowing the learner to see the behavior and, better yet, see positive consequences following it (White, 1972). When the collector for the United Fund calls, you may be more likely to contribute if you have already seen your friends do so and know that they have the stickers on their doors and the virtuous feelings to prove it. Modeling effects have been demonstrated in many studies of helping behavior, but how modeling works—that is, the nature of the mediating processes—is not always clear (Aderman & Berkowitz, 1970). A model can remind the observer of what is proper or appropriate in a situation, show the observer how to perform a helpful act, reduce the inhibitions against acting, and/or cue the observer to the consequences of a helpful act.

Bryan and Test (1967) demonstrated that simply watching someone else change a flat tire or donate to the Salvation Army makes one more likely to help. But sometimes models work in strange ways, as Macaulay (1970) observed. Upon approaching a Santa Claus bell ringing for needy children in the Christmas season, a middle-aged woman (the model) either contributed some money along with some kind words about giving or said rather rudely that she did not wish to donate and walked on. Donation rates were recorded immediately after the model had acted charitably or uncharitably and in control periods. The model who donated significantly increased the rate of donation over the rate in the control periods. Surprisingly, the model who refused also increased subsequent donations, though less dramatically. As Macaulay suggested, this "Scrooge" figure may have had a "boomerang effect," reminding others of what a proper response really constituted. Macaulay's research also suggested that someone who gives to a cause or even approaches a solicitor may "break the ice," lowering the restraints against acting that others may feel as they pass by.

Most research on modeling effects has concluded that similarity between model and observer and the consequences of the model's act affect the observer's actions. Both effects were demonstrated in an ingenious study by Hornstein, Fisch, and Holmes (1968), which is described in Figure 9-5.

Figure 9-5
What becomes of lost wallets?

You pick up an envelope containing a wallet from the sidewalk. Wrapped around the wallet is a letter from someone who had apparently found the wallet and had meant to mail it to its owner but had himself then lost it. The letter writer, who becomes a model of helping behavior for you, may influence your behavior.

When Hornstein, Fisch, and Holmes (1968) arranged this incident, some subjects saw a letter written in standard English (similar model), whereas others read a letter that was, while clearly written, evidently penned by a foreigner (dissimilar model) with a poor command of English ("I am visit your country finding your ways not familiar and strange"). In addition, the apparent consequences of helping for both models were varied. Models either wrote that it was a pleasure to help (positive condition), said nothing about their reactions (neutral condition), or said that they had been inconvenienced and annoyed by the whole episode (negative condition).

Overall, pedestrians were somewhat more likely to help when the model was perceived as similar to themselves, but the more provocative findings concerned the consequences of the model's act. When the model was a foreigner, his reaction—positive, neutral, or negative—did not significantly affect the rate of return of wallets; approximately one-third of the subjects returned the wallet intact. However, when the model was similar to the subject, consequences for the model mattered a great deal: 70% of those in the positive condition and 60% of those in the neutral condition returned the wallet, while only 10% of those who read of the model's annoyance did so. When it seems appropriate to compare yourself with someone serving as a model of helping behavior, the consequences of his or her behavior will have a more powerful effect on your own behavior than will the consequences for a dissimilar model.

3probabilities of pro-social behavior.

(1) In general, then, observing another person behave prosocially makes it more probable that you will act prosocially. (2) Under certain conditions, an antisocial model may even remind you of socially acceptable behavior and increase your tendency to help. (3) People are generally more influenced by models who are similar to themselves and who reap positive consequences as a result of their actions.

What do these modeling effects suggest to parents attempting to make their children more helpful? Must a parent set a glowing example, or is it enough to instruct children to be helpful? What if there is a discrepancy between words and deeds, between preaching and practice?

Grusec and Skubiski (1970) of the University of Toronto had elementary school children play a game to see if they would donate part of their winnings to charity. Some children saw an adult model donate half of his or her winnings to charity, others heard the model advocate donating to charity, and still others were not exposed to a model. Actions spoke louder than words—the modeling of donating behavior produced larger contributions than did verbal exhortations to donate. In fact, only when the child was a girl and when the model had established a warm relationship with her beforehand was preaching more effective than no model at all.

To determine the effects of hypocrisy—a contradiction between word and deed—Bryan and Walbek (1970a, 1970b) conducted a series of experiments in which children observed models who either donated or refused to do so, while either delivering a statement unrelated to charity, preaching charity, or preaching greed. The most powerful influence on children's donations was *what the model did.* If the model preached one thing and practiced another, it was the behavior that was imitated.

However, words were not entirely lost on the children. Verbal modeling influenced the children's evaluations of the model and their own verbalizations when they were asked to tape a message for the next player. Any statement about charity by a model—whether it expressed charitable or greedy sentiments—tended to elicit charitable statements from the children, whereas the model's behavior had little influence on children's preachings. Furthermore, recent research suggests that preaching charity increases children's donations if it is strongly stated and mentions reasons for giving (J. P. Anderson & Perlman, 1973; Midlarsky & Bryan, 1972). However, it is still most effective to practice what you preach.

The bystander effect. It is logical to expect that the more people who witness an emergency, the more likely it is that at least one witness will provide aid. This is one reason that New Yorkers were so shocked by the complete failure of 38 witnesses to help Kitty Genovese. In view of the fact that watching someone else help makes us more likely to help, and in view of the desire of most of us to "look good" when others are watching, we might be even more convinced that there is "safety in numbers." But the real situation is far more complex.

Bibb Latané and John Darley actually hypothesized that the presence of other bystanders *decreases* the probability of helping behavior by an individual witness. (at times) In one of their first studies, male college students who were completing questionnaires were exposed to pungent smoke puffing through a vent into the testing room (Latané & Darley, 1968). Subjects were either alone, with two other "naïve" subjects, or with two passive confederates of the experimenter, who noticed the smoke but shrugged and continued writing. Being with two deliberately stoic others considerably reduced the subject's likelihood of reporting the smoke, but even three naïve witnesses together were less likely to act than was a single subject. This study provided initial evidence that people are less likely to help when they are in the presence of others than when they are alone—the phenomenon called the *bystander effect.* However, as Latané and Darley noted, the puffing smoke—at least at first—was not clearly an emergency, and subjects who remained seated, coughing and rubbing their eyes, may have misguidedly wanted to appear brave. In the presence of others, they may have thought "Well, if you can take it, so can I."

Consequently, a study was devised in which the emergency was less ambiguous and did not threaten the subjects themselves. Latané and Rodin (1969) staged an incident in which subjects working on questionnaires heard a crash, a scream, and words of anguish ("Oh, my God, my foot") from an adjoining room where the woman who had given them their instructions had just gone. Subjects were alone, with a passive confederate, with another naïve subject unfamiliar to them, or with a close friend. Again, there was little safety in numbers: 70% of those who were alone helped the woman, but only 40% of the pairs of strangers and 7% of the subjects coupled with a passive confederate did so. Help was provided by 70% of the pairs of friends. Clearly the victim was not safe in the hands of pairs of strangers and subjects paired with a deliberately passive witness. In the smoke study and in this one, the presence of others, particularly passive others, may have made subjects less likely to interpret an event as an emergency requiring action.

Latané and Darley (1970) designed another emergency situation to see if the presence of others could cause a different kind of breakdown in intervention—at the point at which a bystander decides whether or not to assume personal responsibility. This study was discussed in Chapter 2; as you may recall, students were assigned to individual testing rooms equipped with an intercom system to discuss personal problems in an urban setting. In his first turn at speaking, the victim-to-be mentioned that one of his problems was that he suffered seizures; in his second round, he began to stutter, said he felt a seizure coming on, and begged for help as he became more and more incoherent. Some subjects were led to believe that they were the only ones hearing the victim, others that there was one other

listener, and still others that there were four other listeners in separate rooms.

The results of this study (discussed in detail in Chapter 2) provide still more evidence of the bystander effect, suggesting that even when the emergency is unambiguous, the presence of others interferes with helping by reducing the probability that any single witness will accept responsibility.

Latané, Darley, and others have provided a great deal of evidence of the so-called bystander effect in emergencies. Of course, these findings pertain to an individual's likelihood of acting; there is still some safety in numbers in the sense that the larger a group of witnesses, the more likely it is that at least one hero will be present. Still, a person in a group, while noticing events, is less likely than a person who is alone to interpret them as situations calling for helping behavior. This *social influence* may exist because people look to others to decide how they should interpret a situation. The apparent indifference or coolness of group members while they are trying to read cues in the situation may foster the conclusion by each that nothing is seriously wrong. Moreover, even if people conclude that something is wrong, they may fail to act because of a *diffusion of responsibility*, which may make an individual witness less likely to accept *personal* responsibility for helping.

However, the bystander effect has not been observed in all studies, which suggests that it occurs only under some conditions and that there are ways to prevent it.[2] Taking the Kitty Geno-

---

[2]For example, S. H. Schwartz and Clausen (1970), in a study of reactions to seizures, found that the bystander effect applied only to females and to indirect rather than direct aid. And I. M. Piliavin, Rodin, and Piliavin (1969) found that large groups of subway passengers watching a man stagger and collapse were not subject to a bystander effect. Interestingly, young elementary school children appear to be immune to the bystander effect. In fact, the presence of another child may reduce stress caused by an emergency and lower a child's inhibitions against acting. Staub (1970) found that pairs of young children were more helpful than single bystanders.

vese incident as an example of the bystander effect, we can try to identify elements in that situation that produced a dramatic failure to help and to imagine a different outcome given different circumstances.

A study by Bickman (1972) offers some guidance in this regard. Female students heard via intercom "another subject" declare that something had fallen from a bookcase in her testing room, get up from her chair, and then cry out "It's falling on me," followed by a scream and a loud crash. A confederate then interpreted the event over the intercom as either a certain emergency, a possible emergency, or no emergency at all. This other "bystander" was either able to help (was in the same building as the victim and subject) or unable to help (was located in a distant building). The more the interpretation by another witness indicated that an emergency was taking place, the more often subjects stated afterwards that they thought the victim needed help and the faster they actually provided help. Furthermore, subjects responded faster when they thought the other bystander could not easily assume responsibility for acting.

The reactions of other bystanders are simply a subset of the situational cues that a person must process and interpret. As already noted, the bystander effect is diminished if friends rather than strangers witness an event, perhaps because friends are more likely to see behind each other's initial hesitancy and coolness (Latané & Rodin, 1969). Furthermore, just as people are influenced by the helping behavior of a model similar to themselves, they may be likely to *fail* to help when they perceive a nonreactive bystander as similar to themselves (R. E. Smith, Smythe, & Lien, 1972). Moreover, it appears to be important for witnesses to actually observe each other's reactions if alarm is likely to be registered. J. M. Darley, Teger, and Lewis (1973) found that naïve subjects who were facing each other were as likely to respond to an emergency in an adjoining room as were subjects alone when the emergency occurred, but pairs of subjects seated so that they could not read each other's faces for cues were much less helpful. *they can't ignore it looking into each other eyes.*

Judging from this information, anything that makes a situation less ambiguous may dampen the "unresponsive-bystander effect." R. D. Clark and Word (1972) obtained 100% rates of helping from groups of bystanders when a maintenance man fell and cried out in pain in the next room. The presence of others inhibited helping only when the emergency was more ambiguous (when the fall but not the cry was heard). These researchers argued that in the Latané and Rodin (1969) experiment helping rates were low because the situation was tape recorded and ambiguous. They also pointed to lack of ambiguity to account for high helping rates in a study by I. M. Piliavin, Rodin, and Piliavin (1969), where larger groups actually responded faster than smaller groups when a man collapsed on a subway car. In this situation, the subjects could directly see the emergency (rather than overhearing it from another room), could see for themselves what other witnesses were doing or not doing, and had no way to escape the situation. Subsequent research by R. D. Clark and Word (1974) also pointed to the role of ambiguity in reducing helping rates.

Assuming that bystanders interpret an event as an emergency, acceptance of personal responsibility is more likely if a witness has a special bond or commitment to the victim (Geer & Jarmecky, 1973; Korte, 1969; Moriarty, 1975; Tilker, 1970). Furthermore, if a bystander feels more competent to deal with the emergency than other witnesses, he or she is more likely to accept personal responsibility (Korte, 1971). For example, in the study by Bickman (1972) subjects were more helpful if they thought another witness was far away from the emergency. A. S. Ross (1971) found that subjects helped more when the other bystander was a young child than they did when the other was an equally competent adult. On the other hand, if you know that another witness is a medical student who works in an emergency room, you may be less likely to assume responsi- *of course* bility, deferring to his expertise (Schwartz & Clausen, 1970).

To summarize, the social-influence process by which other bystanders inhibit helping behavior can be countered if (1) someone in the group voices the opinion that an emergency is occurring; (2) the bystanders are friends sensitive to each other's reactions; (3) a nonreactive bystander is perceived as dissimilar to the self; (4) bystanders can see each other and pick up signals of alarm; and (5) the incident is difficult to interpret as anything other than an emergency. Bystanders in groups are more likely to assume personal responsibility if they have some special bond of responsibility to the victim or feel more competent to act than other bystanders.

How does this information help us understand the Kitty Genovese slaying? First, the 38 witnesses were subject to the kind of social influence that Latané and Darley described; that is, it was not just a case of "bystander apathy." Since the street was dark, there was room, at least initially, for alternate interpretations of the situation (for example, as a lover's quarrel). More importantly, witnesses could not see each other, and with no cues to the contrary, they may have assumed that others were not interpreting the event as an emergency. In addition, responsibility was diffused. Although some bystanders may have known each other and even Ms. Genovese, no witness felt singled out for responsibility. Each may have assumed that someone else had already phoned the police or that someone else would rush into the street. There are limits to the bystander effect and ways to reduce its power; many studies underscore people's willingness to get involved and provide help. However, the Kitty Genovese incident can play itself out time and again if the conditions are right.

C. Psychological states and helping

With so many situational factors influencing helping behavior, we begin to wonder if the characteristics of potential helpers matter much.

Do some people possess personality characteristics that make them more likely to aid others? Before searching for such personality traits, we will consider the effects of more fleeting moods and feelings—psychological states.

Suppose you have had a very good day, with money, grades, and love all coming your way at once. Do you want to spread happiness throughout the world, or do you jealously guard and savor your good feelings, refusing to let anyone spoil your good mood? A variety of moods and feelings affect helping behavior: (1) prior success and failure; (2) self-concern, as when you think you are being evaluated or are in a hurry; (3) good moods caused by something other than success; and (4) feelings resulting from harming someone or witnessing harm being performed.

Success and failure. Isen (1970) administered a battery of tests to teachers and college students, telling some that they had scored very well, others that they had performed poorly, and still others nothing at all. A fourth group was spared from taking the tests. The successful subjects became more helpful than the other groups, donating more to a school fund and more often helping a woman struggling with an armful of books. Subjects who thought they had failed were no less helpful than those who received no feedback. Isen therefore spoke of a "warm glow of success" which makes people more likely to provide help.

Self-concern. What if you have not exactly failed in an important area of life, but failure is a distinct possibility? Self-concern—whether it is over final grades, unexplained headaches, or the fear of losing a lover—may interfere with the ability to empathize with others, or it may create a bad mood that interferes with helping behavior.

In several studies reported by Berkowitz (1972), self-concern lowered the rate and amount of helping behavior. Male college students who had just taken a test of "supervisory ability" were less helpful when asked by the experimenter to help score data than were subjects who had taken a less important test. Females were apparently more self-concerned and less helpful when they thought their "social sensitivity" was being assessed and were waiting impatiently for the verdict. For both sexes, concern about being evaluated in a traditionally important area of competence interfered with helping behavior.

Even being in a hurry for an appointment may make one too preoccupied to provide help. Darley and Batson (1973) induced seminary students to think either that they were already quite late, that they would arrive just in time, or that they would have time to spare as they left for a speaking engagement. The percentages of subjects in these three groups who stopped to help a man slumped in an alley were 10%, 45%, and 63%, respectively. In fact, even subjects scheduled to speak about the parable of the Good Samaritan were less likely to help when they were in a hurry. *Again not long tested.*

Although most evidence suggests that self-concern interferes with concern for others, the self-concerned person may occasionally be more helpful if helping appears to be a way to gain approval, eliminate self-doubt, or repair one's image (Hildebrand & Berkowitz, reported by Berkowitz, 1972; Isen, Horn, & Rosenhan, 1973).

Good moods. Succeeding on a task increases helping behavior, but why? Possibly success only creates a feeling of happiness, in which case happiness rather than success is essential to the formula.

Isen and Levin (1972) set out to produce good moods that had nothing to do with success. In their first attempt, a confederate passed out free cookies to students in certain rows of library carrels. A second confederate later asked both students who had received cookies and students who had not to volunteer for an experiment that required either aiding or distracting subjects whose creativity under pressure would be tested. Interestingly, beneficiaries of cookies were more willing than control subjects to help future subjects but less willing to distract them, suggesting that the good moods induced by cookies did not lead to compliance with just any request.

It can be argued, however, that this was just another demonstration of the modeling effect, with the cookie distributor modeling helping behavior. Therefore, in their second study, Isen and Levin arranged for some subjects to find a dime in the coin return of a pay phone. As predicted, people made happy by the seemingly small good fortune of a free dime were more likely to help a woman who dropped a pile of papers than were those who found no dimes. Here the subjects were exposed to no model of helping behavior and helped spontaneously rather than complying with a request.

Perhaps we could still argue that subjects got something for nothing and were prompted to restore balance in the world by giving of themselves. However, even experiences like reading aloud statements expressing elation or recalling pleasant events from one's childhood can increase the rate of helping (Aderman, 1972; B. S. Moore, Underwood, & Rosenhan, 1973). Good moods—for some unexplained reason—consistently produce helpful behavior in a variety of circumstances.

Reactions to harm. When you injure someone, you are often motivated to make amends by doing something positive for the victim. Although inducing people to harm one another holds little promise as a way to make the world more prosocial, studying the relationship between harming and helping contributes to our understanding of helping behavior.

Carlsmith and Gross (1969) placed subjects in the role of teacher and required them to administer either shocks or harmless buzzes when a "learner" erred. When the learner later asked subjects to help phone people for a "Save the Redwoods" campaign, 75% of those who had administered shocks, but only 25% of those who had administered buzzes, agreed to help.

Simply witnessing harm being inflicted also can motivate helping behavior (Rawlings, 1970). Perhaps the first explanation that comes to your mind is that a harm doer feels guilty. However, it is not so easy to attribute guilt to someone who simply witnesses injury, unless we argue that most people carry burdens of guilt for past sins and that witnessing a harmful act activates this guilt. Perhaps a witness feels sympathy for the victim.

Konečni (1972) attempted to pit alternative explanations against one another. The behavior of interest was picking up computer cards dropped on the street by an experimenter. The incident unfolded in four different ways: (1) control—the experimenter simply dropped the cards near the subject and said "Please don't step on them"; (2) restitution—the experimenter brushed against the subject's arm, making it appear that the subject had been responsible for the "accident"; (3) sympathy—a confederate bumped into the experimenter, causing the "accident," and walked away as the subject watched; and (4) generalized guilt—the subject apparently caused a confederate to drop his books, was blamed, was not allowed to help, and then met the experimenter who dropped his computer cards.

The highest rate of helping (64%) occurred in the sympathy condition, in which subjects witnessed harm being done. When the subject had caused the injury and could make a direct compensation, and when the subject had injured one party and had the opportunity to reduce guilt by helping still another party, the helping rate (39% and 42%, respectively) was still higher than it was in the control condition (16%).

Konečni's study supported both guilt and sympathy explanations, but perhaps what we are calling guilt or sympathy actually boils down to a negative mood that can be escaped by performing a helpful act but that can be reduced by other means as well. For example, if people who have inflicted or have witnessed harm receive an unexpected monetary reward or social approval, they are less helpful than subjects who are left in a bad mood (Cialdini, Darby, & Vincent, 1973; McMillen, 1971). While this may seem to contradict the conclusion that good moods increase helping behavior, helping sometimes offers people a means of restoring their images and erasing bad moods.

Helping is clearly not the only response to witnessing or perpetrating an injury. As we saw in Chapter 3, M. J. Lerner (1970) has completed a series of studies that suggest that most people want to believe that the world is just, that people "get what they deserve, or rather, deserve what they get" (p. 207). Curiously enough, this *belief in a just world* may lead people to think less of a perfectly innocent victim. People can either swallow the bitter pill of injustice, or they can downgrade an innocent victim to convince themselves that the suffering was deserved after all.

According to Walster, Berscheid, and Walster (1970), harmdoers or witnesses of harm have several options. They can actually restore balance in the world by compensating the victim, sacrificing something in an altruistic act, or punishing themselves. But they can also distort reality and avoid losing anything—by derogating the victim ("That fool deserved it"), by denying responsibility ("It wasn't really my fault"), or by minimizing the suffering ("It really didn't hurt all that much").

On the basis of several studies, Walster, Berscheid, and Walster (1970) suggested that whether a person attempts to help a victim depends on the credibility of any rationalizations that might justify the harm and the adequacy of available means of compensation. When we can come up with a plausible justification of the harm done, we are less likely to compensate the victim. Furthermore, we usually do not like to overcompensate someone, nor do we like to be in a position where nothing we can offer in repayment will be enough (Berscheid & Walster, 1967). This line of thinking follows from **equity theory** (J. Adams, 1965), which is described in Figure 9-6.

As we have seen, the effects of psychological states on helping behavior are complex. Success, feelings of competence, and good moods generally increase the rate of helping behavior. Failure, feelings of incompetence, self-concern, and bad moods generally do not do so, unless helping is perceived as a ready means of bolstering one's ego or repairing one's image in some-

Figure 9-6

Equity theory and helping. Equity theory states that we attempt to maintain a balance in interpersonal relationships between what we give and receive and what other parties give and receive. When one group victimizes another, inequity is produced, usually causing distress in both groups. But what motivates harmdoers to restore equity so that ratios of outcomes to inputs are equal in the relationship? In an elaboration of equity theory, Walster, Berscheid, and Walster (1970) offer good advice to victims who want compensation. To begin with, Indian leaders should avoid exaggerating their suffering and making impossible demands, for harmdoers are more likely to offer compensation when they think that it will restore equity than when they feel there is no way they can balance the scales. Indian leaders might also try to discredit any justifications that would allow the harmdoer to restore equity psychologically without really doing anything helpful for Indians. For example, they might make it harder for the government officials to deny personal responsibility for taking land years ago by emphasizing modern cases of injustice. If the victims do not receive voluntary compensation, they sometimes resort to destruction and violence, perhaps figuring that if they cannot win they will restore equity by making their victimizers lose. Equity theory is applicable not only to relationships between harmdoers and victims and to helping behavior more generally, but also to the whole range of interpersonal behavior. (Photo by Ilka Hartmann/Jeroboam Inc.)

helping behavior different from love in motive and type.

one else's eyes. Feelings aroused by inflicting harm often prompt people to help their victims or even third parties. Witnessing harm may produce sympathy or a feeling that the world is unjust and motivate helping behavior. However, people can justify harm done by themselves or others by derogating the victim, denying responsibility, or minimizing the extent of suffering—in which cases, helpful behavior is not the outcome. Knowledge of a person's psychological state proves very useful in predicting helping behavior.

D. Finding the Good Samaritan: Background and personality

We have identified factors that make most people more or less helpful than usual. But aren't some people consistently more helpful than others? For instance, Mahatma Gandhi renounced his titles and lived in poverty to train young Indian freedom fighters in passive resistance. He suffered imprisonment, long fasts, and finally assassination in the long struggle for Indian independence and unity. Albert Schweitzer left a successful career in the ministry to earn a medical degree and devote his life to saving lives in Central Africa (see Vonhoff, 1971, for brief sketches of noted helpers throughout history). Surely these two men would be the first to return a lost wallet, pick up a book, or lend a stranger a dime. On the other hand, most of us have encountered people who almost literally will not give us the time of day unless there is "some percentage in it."

Several studies (Latané & Darley, 1970; Staub, 1971; Yakimovich & Saltz, 1971) have attempted to identify background and personality variables that would predict response to a victim of a seizure, a serious fall, or another emergency. None of several standard paper-and-pencil tests—measuring authoritarianism, alienation, trustworthiness, Machiavellianism, need for approval, or social responsibility—predicted helping behavior. Of the background variables considered by Latané and Darley (1970)—for exam-

ple, father's occupation, church attendance, and number of siblings—only size of hometown predicted helping behavior, with subjects who grew up in small towns being somewhat more likely to help than those who grew up in larger cities or towns. This finding has been replicated: subjects from small towns and rural areas were more likely to report shoplifters than were those from large cities (Gelfand, Hartmann, Walder, & Page, 1973), and residents of Midwestern cities and small towns were more compliant with small requests than were New York City residents (Merrens, 1973).

A person's background—particularly his or her family life—may influence helpfulness in another way. London (1970) reported on interviews with people who had rescued Jews from the Nazis. The rescuers almost always had a love of adventure and were often socially marginal people (who perhaps had less to lose by their nonconformity to Nazi authority). Most interestingly, almost all identified strongly with at least one parent who had high moral standards and perhaps served as a model of altruism. This theme of identification with a moral parent was echoed by Rosenhan (1970), who conducted interviews with civil rights workers in the early 1960's. Workers who were fully committed to the cause—but not those who merely dabbled at it—often indicated that they had a close relationship with at least one parent, and that that parent had at one time been committed to an altruistic cause.

What other background variables help us understand prosocial behavior? Taking the bulk of studies into account, there is no firm evidence that men and women differ in helpfulness; the sex differences that have been reported are inconsistent (Ehlert, Ehlert, & Merrens, 1973; Gross, 1972; D. L. Krebs, 1970). Nor is social class clearly related to helping behavior. Personality variables such as the belief that one's fate lies within one's own control, mature moral judgment, need for social approval or self-esteem, and the tendency to ascribe responsibility for

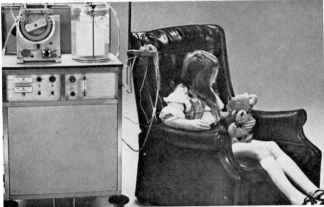

Being attached to a kidney machine is no way to spend a childhood.

When a child's kidneys fail, she can be kept alive by spending 6 hours a day 3 days a week attached to a Kidney Machine. That's no way to spend a childhood.

There are more than 13,000 men, women and children whose lives depend upon the Kidney Machine.

Their only hope for having somewhat of a normal life is a kidney transplant. Kidney patients can spend five or more years connected to the Kidney Machine... waiting, because compatible donors are few and rare. In too many cases, the machine outlives the patient.

We need a cure.

KF

Support The National Kidney Foundation
Box 353, New York, N.Y. 10016

This ad was created for the National Kidney Foundation by Davis Fried Krieger Inc. of New York City, as a public service. It is reproduced in 100 screen for magazine use.

Figure 9-7
How do advertisements for charity work? Do you feel sympathy for this girl because her childhood is not what it should be? Do you feel guilty because you never had to depend on a kidney machine for survival or because you have not supported the Kidney Foundation? Both sympathy and guilt can motivate helping behavior. Then again, this advertisement may disturb your belief in a just world. While you may then try to make the world just again by donating, you may also decide that the girl deserves her fate. The relationship between harm and helping is complex. (Courtesy of the National Kidney Foundation.)

others' welfare to oneself have predicted helping behavior in one or more studies (Schwartz & Clausen, 1970; Satow, 1973; Michelini, Wilson, & Messé, 1973; Staub, 1974), but the evidence is not strong enough that we can use these characteristics to separate the Good Samaritans from the bulk of humanity. Even the factors we have identified here—a small-town upbringing and exposure to an altruistic parental model—are relatively weak predictors of helping behavior. In short, while some researchers would disagree (Huston, 1974b; Huston & Korte, 1976; Severy & Ashton, 1973), the search for the stable personality traits and background characteristics of helpful people has fallen far short of profiling the Good Samaritan.

Some of the snags in this search were pointed out by Gergen, Gergen, and Meter (1972, 1977), who gave a battery of personality tests to 72 college students and then noted their responses to five different requests for help from the psychology department. Although several re-

strong moral upbringing can many times have the opposite effect & children rebel.

lationships between personality scores and volunteering were significant, a trait often predicted one type of helping but failed to predict, or was even negatively associated with, another. To make matters more confusing, relationships that held for male students rarely held for female students, and vice versa. The researchers were forced to conclude that different types of students were looking for different types of payoffs by volunteering as they did.

The point Gergen's study makes so forcefully is that the characteristics of the situation and of the request for help interact in complex ways with personal characteristics. People who return lost wallets probably do not have the same personality traits as those who rush into burning buildings. Even in a single situation, potential helpers may differ in their perceptions of what is happening and what should be done. And finally, emergencies, which call for quick decisions under stress, may leave very little room for personality variables to operate.

The individual's background and personality are bound to influence how he or she interprets a situation and responds to it, but these influences will not become apparent if we continue to look for personal characteristics that magically predict behavior in *all* situations. A more fruitful approach is to begin with a careful analysis of various situations. Then for any one class of situations we may be able to identify the personal factors that make a difference, fully realizing that these will probably not be the same factors as those that matter in another type of situation. For the present, the personality of the Good Samaritan must remain an enigma.

E. People who need people: The recipients of help

Having devoted so much attention to helpers, it seems only fair to give the recipients of help equal time. Who receives help? As you might expect, we are unlikely to identify characteristics that elicit help in *all* situations. Charac-

teristics of the potential helper and characteristics of the potential recipient of help must be considered together, because the characteristics of the recipient are situational cues that a potential helper reads and interprets. Thus our attention to the recipient of help will shed still more light on the determinants of helping behavior.

Dependency. By its very nature, helping is a response to a person in need, but the nature of the recipient's dependency influences the rate of helping behavior. Dependency can be a stable characteristic of a person (for example, a mentally retarded child or a paraplegic) that elicits helpful behavior from almost everyone; it can be a function of a relationship between two people (for example, between parent and child or between bus driver and passenger); or it can result from a temporary plight (for example, a sprained ankle). Dependency can seem to be caused by forces outside one's control, as when one is struck by a falling beam, or may be attributable to one's own actions, as when a person is debilitated by an overdose of heroin. Dependency can also be more or less legitimate (for example, wanting someone to drive you to the hospital versus wanting someone to drive you to the race track).

In a variety of studies, Berkowitz and his colleagues demonstrated that if dependency is introduced into the relationship between two people, helping behavior will follow. Typically, the subject was assigned the role of "worker," and his or her supervisor's rewards depended either heavily or very little on the worker's productivity. Subjects worked harder when the supervisor depended on their performance, even if it was arranged that the supervisor would not hear of the worker's effort until much later (Berkowitz & Daniels, 1963).

Potential helpers also weigh the legitimacy of a recipient's dependency. Imagine how you would react if a woman approached you in the supermarket and asked for ten cents to buy milk. Then imagine the same woman asking for a dime for frozen cookie dough. When Bickman and Kamzan (1973) arranged these two situations, 58% of the shoppers contributed for milk, while only 36% contributed for cookie dough. The more legitimate the need, the more help will be received.

Potential helpers also react to the source of dependency. Suppose that a man collapses on the subway, either carrying a cane and appearing ill, or carrying a bottle and smelling of liquor. I. M. Piliavin, Rodin, and Piliavin (1969) found that groups of bystanders were less likely and slower to help the drunk than to help the sick man—possibly because the drunk could be blamed for his dependency. Contributors to charitable causes may be more likely to help a victim of child abuse than to help people whose dependency is attributable to personal weakness or immorality (Bryan & Davenport, 1968).

However, even if a person's dependency is legitimate, and even if it appears to be no fault of the victim, potential helpers consider the costs of helping. This may explain why J. A. Piliavin and Piliavin (1972), in another staging of collapses on subway cars, found that a victim who bled from the mouth (a dark red liquid did the trick) was helped less often, less speedily, and more indirectly than a "clean" victim. Abhorrence of the sight of blood and the greater risks of helping the clearly dependent bloody victim may have caused bystanders to think twice about their personal responsibilities.

In a realistic study in shoe stores, dependency and cost were both manipulated (Schaps, 1972). Salesmen had to serve either a dependent customer who limped in with a broken heel or a "normal" customer. The cost of devoting a great deal of time to these customers was either low—because the store was almost empty—or high—because the store was busy and the salesman risked losing valuable business with other customers. When the costs of helping were low, the dependent customer received more service, but when the costs were high, the dependent woman actually received somewhat less service

than the normal one. Thus when the costs of helping escalate—because of blood and gore or a threat to one's earning power—even the most dependent persons may not elicit the helping behavior to which they seem entitled. (Selfishness.)

Friends, relatives, and attractive people. Relationships between friends or relatives imply mutual dependency and an obligation to help. Naturalistic studies of such disasters as tornadoes indicate that people tend to help members of their families first, then friends and neighbors, and finally strangers in the stricken area (Form & Nosow, 1958). The victims seem to prefer it that way, too, perhaps because they know they can ① repay help from family and close friends. They may be wary of dealing with organizations such as the Red Cross or accepting help from strangers (Taylor, Zurcher, & Key, 1970).

In one study, children tended to give the more attractive of two toys to a strange child rather than to a friend because, as they explained later, they hoped to make a new friend (B. A. Wright, 1942). More generally, though, even a brief acquaintance with someone increases the rate of helping (Latané & Darley, 1970; Liebhart, 1972).

Similarly, the attractiveness of a recipient of help increases the rate of helping (L. R. Daniels & Berkowitz, 1963; Gross, Wallston, & Piliavin, 1975). However, it may have occurred to you that the cues of dependency may reduce a person's attractiveness. Pomazal and Clore (1973) reported some provocative findings on this point. In one part of their study, males and females, some wearing a knee brace and arm sling, tried to hitchhike. Hitchhikers with the brace and sling received significantly fewer ride offers than did their physically intact counterparts. This was especially true for female victims, with the nondisabled female receiving help from 26% of the motorists (mostly males) and the disabled one receiving ride offers from 12%. The nondisabled female was also the target of considerably more flirting. Pomazal and Clore suspected that the

① not real love, because they need real help, and not just sympathy.

motives of these chivalrous male helpers were not altogether altruistic. When you are hitchhiking, attractiveness may get you everywhere.

Similarity of helper and recipient. The fact that people tend to help those who are attractive suggests that people may be especially helpful to those who are similar to themselves in dress, ideology, race, and nationality. This is often the case. For example, Emswiller, Deaux, and Willits (1971) reported that "hippie" and "straight" subjects were more likely to give dimes to those who resembled them in appearance than to dissimilar solicitors. Similarly, people tend to help those who share their ideological or political beliefs. When Nixon workers and McGovern workers dropped their campaign literature near the voting polls in 1972, they were helped 71% of the time if their preference was congruent with that of the voter (as determined by an interview after the incident) and 46% of the time if the beliefs were incongruent (Karabenick, Lerner, & Beecher, 1973).

Likewise, people tend to be most helpful to members of their own ethnic group, though the effects are not dramatic (Wispé & Freshley, 1971). Using the "wrong number technique," Gaertner and Bickman (1971) exposed subjects to either a Black voice or a White voice asking for help in calling a garage (the victim was stranded on a highway and had used his last dime to call the wrong number). While Blacks helped Whites and Blacks equally, Whites were more likely to help members of their own race. However, Bickman and Kamzan (1973) reported that White females were just as likely to give dimes to Black females as to White females.

It is not clear that people always help their compatriots more than they help foreigners, either. The major study done by R. E. Feldman (1968) in Boston, Athens, and Paris (reported in more detail in Chapter 3) produced mixed results for such behaviors as giving directions, mailing unstamped letters, and returning overpayments for goods in stores. Citizens were generally more helpful to compatriots, but not in all situations studied.

Who, then, elicits helping behavior? First, the people who receive help almost always signal to potential helpers that they are dependent. When the potential helper perceives that the need is legitimate and is no fault of the victim, he or she is more likely to help, unless the costs of helping a highly dependent other are prohibitive. When the helper and recipient are bound by kinship or friendship, or by any special relationship that makes one person dependent on another, help is usually more likely. Furthermore, the attractiveness of the recipient—which may be a function of his or her similarity to the potential helper in dress, ideology, race, or nationality—often elicits helping behavior. Recently, several researchers have taken a broader interest in the recipients of help, studying variables that determine whether or not people seek help in the first place and how they react to help received (Gross, Wallston, & Piliavin, in press).

F. Explanations of helping behavior

We have seen that helping behavior is influenced by a host of situational and personal variables, but have still not approached a full understanding of helping. Some theorists have argued that we can understand helping behavior by referring to norms—socially defined expectations about what is appropriate behavior. Two norms—the norm of social responsibility and the norm of reciprocity—are particularly relevant. However, others have argued that normative explanations are unsatisfactory and that we can understand helping behavior best by analyzing the costs and rewards of helping. We will look briefly at these two ways of integrating research findings.

Norms and helping. The norm of *social responsibility* states that we should help those who need it. Is this only an ideal toward which we strive, or is it an accurate summary of behavior? We have seen that people are indeed likely to help those who appear dependent on them, but we have noticed that helpers consider the legitimacy and origin of dependency as well as the risks involved in helping a dependent person. More importantly, agreement with the norm of social responsibility does not automatically produce helpful behavior. In a summary of research on helping behavior in children, Bryan (1972) noted that most elementary school children believe that it is good to help the needy. But reminding children of the norm is not sufficient to elicit helping behavior, for children, like adults, are able to live with contradictions between their verbal endorsements of the norm and their actual behavior (Bryan & London, 1970). *(they do it, but whether they are able to love it)*

If the norm of social responsibility is to have any explanatory value, a person's belief in the norm must be measured in advance, and the conditions under which the norm influences behavior must be specified. A step in this direction was taken by S. H. Schwartz (1973), who found that personal norms did influence the rate at which people donated bone marrow. But even Schwartz admitted that personal norms are only one of many determinants of helping behavior, and Leonard Berkowitz (1972), after years of research on the norm of social responsibility, concluded that it was a relatively weak determinant of behavior. The norm of social responsibility may be more an ideal than an accurate generalization about human behavior, since so many factors make us less than willing to help in situations that should be expected to elicit socially responsible behavior (Teger, 1970).

The norm of *reciprocity* holds somewhat more promise. As conceptualized by Gouldner (1960), it states that people should help those who have helped them, and that people should not injure those who have helped them. Gouldner argued that the norm of reciprocity is universal and essential in maintaining stable relationships among people in society. The only people exempt from the requirement to reciprocate help are the dependent—young children, the aged, or the sick—the very people whom the norm of social responsibility tells us to help.

Perhaps the greatest testimony to the strength of the reciprocity norm is the fact that gifts and other forms of help can be used to control and dominate others. A corporate executive may contribute to a political campaign, not out of the goodness of his heart, but to create a debt that must be paid off. Prison inmates may attempt to "buy" newcomers:

> Aggressive inmates will go to extraordinary lengths to place gifts in the cells of inmates they have selected for personal domination. These intended victims, in order to escape the threatened bondage, must find the owner and insist that the gifts be taken back [McCorkle & Korn, 1954, p. 90].

(in another story.) No wonder people sometimes bite the hands that feed them. When someone does a favor, the obligation to reciprocate may make us uncomfortable. As Jack Brehm (1966) explains it, we experience *psychological reactance*, a motivation to reestablish freedom of behavior when our options are reduced. In a study by Brehm and Cole (1966), male college students who arrived to take part in a research project found a note on the door telling them to wait outside. A confederate, supposedly another subject, asked the experimenter if he could leave for a few minutes. While the confederate was gone, the subject was told that he would be rating his first impressions of the confederate, either for an important research grant awarded to a "Dr. Terrell," or for a student's class research project. The hypothesis was that subjects in the "High Importance" condition (Dr. Terrell's grant) would be more motivated than those in the "Low Importance" condition (class project) to stay clear of obligations to the confederate and would be more likely to experience psychological reactance following a favor.

When the confederate returned, half the subjects received a free soft drink from him, while the other half received no favor. After the first impressions were recorded, the experimenter gave the subject an opportunity to do a favor for the confederate by asking "Will one of you stack these into ten piles of five for me?" and placing a stack of papers in front of the confederate.

Approximately half the subjects in the "no favor" condition helped the confederate stack papers. When subjects had received a favor and had little reason to avoid obligation to the confederate, 14 out of 15 subjects stacked papers. However, when it was important to maintain behavioral freedom for the important research project, 13 of 15 subjects did *not* help, even though the confederate had just done them a favor. The concept of reactance helps to explain why, despite the power of the norm of reciprocity, we do not always appreciate and attempt to help someone who has done us a favor.

In fact, by determining when the norm of reciprocity fails to operate, we get a better understanding of when help is not appreciated. For example, reciprocity is less likely when the original donor appears to have given away a relatively *small* percentage of his or her total holdings (Pruitt, 1968). People reciprocate less when a favor appears to have been accidental rather than intentional (Greenberg & Frisch, 1972) or when it appears to have been required rather than voluntary (Goranson & Berkowitz, 1966). Finally, a favor that seems motivated by selfishness is less appreciated than one motivated by altruism (Tesser, Gatewood, & Driver, 1968).

We have noted exceptions to both the norm of social responsibility and the norm of reciprocity, although the latter appears to be a more accurate description of typical human behavior. The two normative explanations taken together still leave something to be desired, as noted by critics (Krebs, 1970; Latané & Darley, 1970; Schwartz, 1973). First, norms are so general that they may not tell us what to do in specific situations that differ drastically from one another. Second, if most people in society subscribe to such norms, how can norms explain individual differences in helping behavior? Third, two conflicting norms may seem equally applicable in a situation. For

example, the norm of social responsibility is contradicted by a norm that says "Don't meddle in other people's affairs." Fourth, unless the conditions that activate a norm are specified in advance, we are left in the position of arguing circularly that the norm must have been operating because helping behavior occurred. Finally, researchers can sometimes identify alternative explanations that make invoking a normative explanation unnecessary (Gross & Latané, 1974). This is not to say that we should drop the word "norm" from our vocabularies. However, it may be more useful to focus on the costs and rewards to potential helpers.

The costs and rewards of helping. Whatever their normative beliefs, people are generally motivated to increase the rewards and decrease the costs of their actions. We have already seen that external rewards—money or praise—increase the rate of helping behavior. Furthermore, as children learn to associate their own pain and pleasure with that of other people, their empathic feelings can serve as sources of reward and punishment. Acting in accordance with a well-accepted norm may be rewarding because it leads to social approval and is consistent with our belief that we are helpful people.

Increasing the costs of helping reduces the likelihood that help will be forthcoming. For example, we have seen that requests for dimes are less well received than requests for the time of day, that bloody victims are helped less frequently than "clean" victims, and that customers are helped less when the store is busy than when it is almost empty. The bystander effect may occur, in part, because when responsibility is diffused among several people, the costs of *failing* to help are reduced. Perhaps even the facilitating effects of good moods on helping behavior can be understood through cost-reward analysis. The person who is in a good mood may be more willing than the person in a bad mood to accept potential costs because he or she is already "ahead of the game" and can better afford losses.

Since the potential helper is faced with two alternative actions—helping or not helping—it is essential to consider not only the rewards and costs of helping but also the rewards and costs of *not* helping. J. A. Piliavin and Piliavin (1973) have set forth a cost-reward analysis of helping; our analysis here shares some features with theirs. An accounting of costs and rewards might take the form of the monologue in Figure 9-8. Obviously, the human species is not the rational animal portrayed in this example. A potential helper is unlikely to coldly calculate all costs and rewards, particularly in an emergency calling for a quick decision under stress. However, researchers can use such analyses to predict the probability of helping behavior when potential costs and rewards are varied. Perhaps the greatest strength of a cost-reward analysis is that it allows us to enter both situational and personal variables into our equations.

Figure 9-8
The mind of the rational helper: Cost-reward analysis. (Photo by Jim Pinckney.)

Old man, I see you slumped in the gutter, looking half dead. I realize that you need help. Will I be the one?

*   *   *

What will it cost me if I help? Maybe you're drunk and will slobber all over me. Maybe you'll get surly. What if I make things worse and am held liable? Call that 10 cost points.

*   *   *

Besides, if I just pass by, I'll be on time for my job interview and will probably get the position. Rewarding indeed—at least 5 reward points, which I'll lose if I help.

*   *   *

Then again, maybe there's something in it for me if I help. I feel for you, old man, and I can imagine your joy if I help. I like to think of myself as a helpful person. Maybe the job interviewer will be snowed when I explain why I was late. Actually, this may get me the Student Association award for community service. I know my friends will think well of me if I help. That adds up to 6 reward points.

*   *   *

It's going to hurt me some if I don't help, too. Maybe somebody I know will see me callously walk by and tell everyone. I'll feel guilty, I know; I'll wonder if I killed you, old man. Those costs are worth 3 points.

*   *   *

Time for the final tally. It will cost me 10 points to help, and I'll also lose 5 points I could have if I walk by. The total cost is 15 points. Helping is worth 6 reward points to me, and I'll avoid the 3-point cost of failing to help. The total reward value is 9 points.

*   *   *

Goodbye, old man. Perhaps when I'm in a better mood.

Although a cost-reward analysis is extremely useful in understanding helping behavior, it must be used judiciously. As was the case with normative explanations, it is tempting to explain behavior after the fact—for example, by saying "Those bystanders did not help so the costs of helping must have been high." The researcher must specify in advance factors associated with high and low cost and *then* determine whether helping rates fall as costs of helping escalate. When Bloom and Clark (in press) tested the Piliavin and Piliavin model in this way, cost factors were not related to helping. This failure to confirm the model underscores the need for further tests. Finally, different types of rewards and costs must be examined, especially since we know that different people are rewarded and punished by different things. Cost-reward analysis has not successfully explained heroic altruism, in which the costs are immense and the rewards few. Unless the cost-reward analyst can uncover hidden rewards for altruism, the altruist will continue to baffle us. *not even for the good feeling but even when we are nervous & don't want to - we love because we have a concern for them as people.*

IV. Toward a prosocial society

Can knowledge of cooperation and helping behavior be used to strengthen prosocial tendencies? Looking toward the future, we will consider briefly the goals of teaching prosocial behavior to children, raising funds for charitable causes, increasing the responsiveness of the helping professions, countering the dampening effects of urban life on prosocial behavior, and legislating a prosocial society.

A. Teaching cooperation and helping to children

United States society places a greater emphasis on competition than many other societies do. Although competitive free enterprise may be a key to the economic success of the United States, Americans may be neglecting the development of prosocial behavior by continually stimulating children to excel over others. *If* the goal is to increase prosocial behavior, there is perhaps no more superbly crafted educational system for doing so than that of the USSR.

As described by Urie Bronfenbrenner (1970), the Soviet system stresses character education, an area that is clearly subordinated to academics and athletics in the United States and Canada. Preschool children are taught to share belongings and play cooperatively, often with specially designed toys that require the efforts

of two or more children. In youth organizations and groupings within schools, children cooperate within groups while competing with other groups. Rather than singling out individual achievers, teachers reward the achievements of rows, classes, and schools. As a result, group members monitor, censure, and help each other to improve the group's standing. Moreover, older children become big sisters and brothers to younger students, looking out for their safety, playing with them, and teaching them new skills.

Bronfenbrenner observed very little emphasis on cooperation and social responsibility in the United States. He argued that if we want children to act prosocially, we must give them real responsibility for the welfare of others. Although many people would hesitate to accept a system that so thoroughly subordinates individual goals to group or state goals, we can learn a great deal from observing the techniques the Soviets use to foster prosocial behavior.

B. Alms for the poor: Enlisting support for charities

Charity is big business in the United States and Canada, as evidenced by the efforts of Madison Avenue advertising agencies to sell diseases as if they were laundry soaps (see Rosenbaum, 1974). Competing charitable organizations bombard us with posters, literature, commercials, and telethons, appealing to our sympathy, guilt, and desire for a just world.

However, as we have seen, appeals to norms of social responsibility are not notably effective. A better strategy is to reduce the costs of donating and increase the rewards; hence, fund raisers make it easy for us to give at the office, allow us to pay on time installments, and highlight the fact that donations are tax-deductible. Door-to-door fund raisers make use of sound social-psychological principles. For example, a recent drive for multiple sclerosis sent only 12-year-olds to collect money—presumably because they are young enough to look dependent on us, but old enough to handle our money. It is no accident that volunteers are recruited to solicit money from their immediate neighbors. The potential donor, susceptible to modeling, may think "The Joneses are behind this cause, and look how rewarding it has been for them," or may fear rejection if he or she appears uncharitable. The fund raiser may also help the cause by putting the potential donor in a good mood, either by being friendly and complimentary or by distributing small gifts.

Finally, creative fund raisers may benefit from the well-documented "foot-in-the-door" technique discussed in Chapters 4 and 19 of this book (J. L. Freedman & Fraser, 1966). In a fund drive for the Cancer Society, asking people to comply with a painless prior request—wearing a pin publicizing the campaign—increased the rate of subsequent donation (Pliner, Hart, Kohl, & Saari, 1974). A small prior commitment may lead people to perceive themselves as more committed to the cause. Alternatively, it appears that making a very large request and then presenting the "real" request is even more effective than the foot-in-the-door technique, for then the fund raiser must be compensated for having "backed down" (Cialdini, 1975).

Straightforward appeals to a sense of social responsibility are likely to become less effective in a society increasingly pressed by so many needs and worthy causes. Fund raisers will need to become even more ingenious in the future to motivate charitable behavior.

C. Helping in the helping professions

As the population increases, the life span lengthens, and resources grow scarcer, social services will continue to expand in the United States and Canada; hence, more and more of us will find ourselves in salaried helping roles (Danish, 1974; Danish & Hauer, 1973). However, serving as a helper within a large bureaucracy is far more complicated than helping friends and neighbors in need, the mode of social service in earlier times. There are immense problems in informing people of services to which they are entitled, linking them with the appropriate agencies, inducing them to use such agencies, and seeing that their needs are actually met.

One of the most important tasks is to alter the nature of the relationship between helper and client so that recipients of bureaucratic help are not made to feel uncomfortably dependent and, as a result, resentful of the aid giver. Drawing on research (Alger & Rusk, 1955; Gross, Piliavin, Wallston, & Broll, 1972), we might train helping professionals to understand their clients and avoid condescending attitudes (Haggstrom, 1964). Or we might restructure the ways in which aid is given to reduce the likelihood that the recipient will experience a threat to self-esteem (Fisher & Nadler, 1974) or to behavioral freedom (Greenberg & Shapiro, 1971). One increasingly used remedy is to employ paraprofessionals from the local area to bridge the gap between the client and the service agency and to provide a more personal and continuing helping relationship (Sahlein, 1973).

Still another challenge is to alter the incentives available to the helping professional. A client may receive better service from a professional paid on a fee-for-service basis than from the same professional paid a flat salary, perhaps because salaried helpers are not motivated to go beyond the call of duty (Deniels, 1969). Moreover, criteria for advancement may inhibit helping responses. For example, in vocational-rehabilitation agencies, counselors are generally rated according to the number of cases that they close as successfully rehabilitated. With a limited budget to distribute among clients, the counselor is tempted to accept clients with minor problems that can be quickly and inexpensively solved (for example, by purchasing a new pair of glasses) rather than tackling "hard" cases such as a severely mentally retarded worker who may require months of costly training in order to gain employment. Perhaps in the future salary and promotion will be used more directly as rewards for competent, creative, and well-received help.

D. Urban life and prosocial behavior

Knowing that people who live in large cities are often less prosocial than their country cousins is cause for some alarm, since the megalopolis is here to stay. Latané and Darley (1970) suggested that we can explain the behavior of city dwellers who do not get involved by pointing to situational factors. When an emergency occurs in the city, many bystanders are present, they do not know each other or the victim, and they are often unfamiliar with the locale and where to go for help.

Stanley Milgram (1970) offered another explanation for the lower rate of prosocial behavior in cities by suggesting that urbanites experience a kind of sensory and cognitive "overload." As a result, they must be selective—by shutting off some sources of stimulation entirely (for example, by getting an unlisted phone number), giving less attention to each input (for example, by serving customers in a brusque manner), and setting priorities (for example, by helping friends but not drunk strangers). These adaptations are necessary, Milgram argued, if the urbanite is to avoid being psychologically crushed by the demands of city life. What may appear to be callous disregard for others is, for the urbanite, a strategy for coping with the exigencies of city life.

Milgram's overload theory was supported by a study in which college students had to listen for numbers read orally and proofread a text in the presence of distracting background noise (Sherrod & Downs, 1974). Subjects who experienced stimulus overload were less helpful when a confederate later asked them to work math problems than were those who had not experienced the distracting noise while completing the tasks. However, if subjects were told that they could control the irritating noise, even if they

did not actually turn it off, the effects of stimulus overload were lessened.

Perhaps there are ways to increase the urbanite's sense of control over his or her environment. One trend that has been noted in some cities develops a sense of community control by localizing schools, human-service agencies, and governmental structures in small geographical areas or neighborhoods. Not only can neighborhood organizations convert strangers to acquaintances and friends, but they can foster a sense of common purpose and cooperation. This is by no means a full solution, but it suggests a workable strategy: change the urban environment to increase the prosocial behavior of its inhabitants.

E. Legislating a prosocial society

At present, U. S. law is quick to define and punish antisocial behavior, but less concerned with rewarding prosocial conduct (J. A. Kaplan, 1972; J. A. Kaplan, 1977). However, our system can punish failure to help in apprehending a criminal and can hold bystanders accountable if they have a special relationship to the victim (for example, father to son or doctor to patient), if they are responsible, even accidentally, for the plight of the victim, or if they actually worsen a victim's plight by intervening. Some countries, such as the Netherlands and the Soviet Union, punish a variety of failures to help (*Time*, December 27, 1971).

A more popular solution is to reduce the costs of helping. For instance, "Secret Witness" programs permit a person to call anonymously to report information about a crime, thus avoiding the fear of retaliation by the criminal and the time and effort involved in bouts with red tape. "Good Samaritan" laws have been passed to protect doctors from liability for all but the grossest negligence when they stop on the road to help injured motorists (Ratcliffe, 1966).

It is also simple to provide rewards for prosocial behavior. We still see offers of rewards on posters in the post office; Secret Witnesses are offered rewards for useful information; and organizations such as the Carnegie Foundation award medals for heroic altruism. Although new laws do not always change the hearts of men and women, the legal system can foster prosocial behavior by altering cost-reward structures.

Can never change hearts of men

V. Summary

Prosocial behavior—behavior that has positive social consequences—occurs when two or more people cooperate for mutual benefit or when one person helps another by doing a favor, donating resources, or intervening in an emergency. Altruism is a special form of helping that is voluntary, costly, and motivated by something other than the anticipation of reward.

Cooperation is typically contrasted with competition. We refer to cooperative or competitive or individualistic reward structures and distinguish the structure of a situation from an individual's motives—cooperative, competitive, or individualistic. Research using laboratory games tells us that we are more likely to cooperate with another person if the other person matches our choices tit-for-tat, if we can communicate, and if we come to the situation with attitudes and motives conducive to cooperation. In field situations, cooperative reward structures within groups often produce higher group cohesiveness, greater satisfaction, and more productivity than do competitive reward structures. Young children acquire the cognitive ability to cooperate and compete; then the values of their culture or subculture influence whether they prefer to cooperate or compete in given situations.

Helping behavior is also influenced by both situational and personal factors. In order to help, one must notice an event, interpret it as one requiring help, assume personal responsibility for acting, choose a form of assistance, and implement that assistance. Some situations, especially those that are unambiguous and do not pose a costly threat to the potential helper, elicit higher rates of helping behavior than others.

Another important aspect of the situation is the presence and behavior of other people. Being reinforced by others for helping, or seeing someone else help, increases rates of helping. However, as the bystander effect indicates, people are often less likely to help when they are with others than when they are alone. This is so because of a social-influence process that makes witnesses less likely to interpret an event as an emergency and because of a diffusion of responsibility that makes witnesses less likely to accept personal responsibility for acting.

& influence of others or you

The psychological state of the potential helper is also important. Success and good moods generally increase the rate of helping, while failure and bad moods typically inhibit helping. Feelings of sympathy or guilt, or a sense that the world is no longer just, occurring after one inflicts or witnesses harm, may also motivate helping behavior, although sometimes people justify the harm rather than help. Researchers have had difficulty identifying more enduring personality traits and background characteristics of helpful people, although people from small towns and people who have been exposed to altruistic parents seem more helpful. Whatever their personal characteristics, people most often help those who are dependent, especially when the need is legitimate and is no fault of the victim. They also tend to be more helpful to friends, relatives, and people who are attractive or similar to themselves.

Helping behavior has been explained by reference to norms or standards of behavior. The norm of social responsibility, which says that we help those who need help, is more an ideal than an accurate description of typical behavior. The norm of reciprocity, which states that people help, or at least do not injure, those who have helped them is a more powerful norm. In fact, it explains why people often feel that their behavioral freedom is threatened when they feel obligated to return a favor.

psychology as descriptive

Since all normative explanations are subject to criticism, it appears more fruitful to consider the costs and rewards of helping or not helping. People are generally more helpful if helping behavior is rewarded and less helpful if they must sacrifice a great deal by helping.

Knowledge of the dynamics of prosocial behavior can help us to build a more prosocial world, particularly if we change situations—for example, by altering reward structures to encourage cooperation among children, using social-psychological techniques to elicit donations, changing aspects of the urban environment that inhibit prosocial behavior, and drafting legislation to reduce the costs and increase the rewards of prosocial behavior.

doesn't change their motives and desires though.

PART 4
ATTITUDES AND ATTITUDE CHANGE

I Have A Dream...
ONE AMERICA

I. The nature of attitudes
   A. Definitions of attitude
   B. Components of attitudes
   C. Simple versus complex attitudes

II. Distinctions among terms: Prejudice, discrimination, and racism

III. The costs and extent of prejudice, discrimination, and racism
   A. The costs of prejudice, discrimination, and racism
   B. Is prejudice universal?

IV. The causes of prejudice and discrimination
   A. Historical emphasis and economic emphasis
   B. Sociocultural emphasis
   C. Situational emphasis
   D. Psychodynamic emphasis
   E. Phenomenological emphasis
   F. Emphasis on earned reputation

V. Social distance: A result of perceived dissimilarity in beliefs?

VI. Attitudes as predictors of behavior
   A. Are attitudes predispositions to action?
   B. Why don't attitudes predict behavior more consistently?
   C. Attitudes and behavior—Mutual cause and effect

VII. Summary

314

Attitudes and behavior: Prejudice and discrimination 10

You're going to find racism everyplace. In fact, I have never lived a day in my life that in some way—some small way, somewhere—someone didn't remind me that I'm Black.

Henry Aaron

With this chapter, we begin the exploration of a different aspect of social psychology, the study of attitudes and attitude change. The construct *attitude* has been a central one; more than 40 years ago Gordon Allport (1935) described it as the major "building block in the edifice of social psychology." This chapter, in particular, seeks to answer questions about the nature of attitudes and of such phenomena as prejudice and discrimination. Is prejudice universal? If not, what are its causes? For purposes of example, three all-too-usual events are presented that demonstrate the types of prejudiced attitudes and discriminatory behavior in our society.

Marilyn McKinney, an elementary school teacher from Salem, Oregon, arrives in Honolulu with plans to attend the summer session at the University of Hawaii. She begins searching newspaper want ads for a room to rent. She notices that many ads include the phrase "A.J.A.'s only." Upon learning that this means Japanese-Americans (Americans of Japanese Ancestry), she is outraged. She calls on one of the landlords who placed such an ad and discovers that he and his wife speak only Japanese. She now does not know whether to be outraged or not.

Aloysius Maloney has grown up in Grates Cove, C.B., Newfoundland, one of the many poor fishing villages of the province. His father was a fisherman who was lost at sea during a storm. His mother receives only a small welfare check in addition to the family allowance for the family's livelihood. Aloysius is very intelligent and desperately wants to go to a university on the mainland. But a university admissions officer tells him that he can't be admitted to the university because the academic quality of his school is so low. "Everyone knows that Newfoundland's schools are so inferior that no one from that province could survive in college," he is told.

Mrs. Patricia Wilson has just completed a Ph.D. in history and is seeking a college teaching position somewhere in the Chicago area. Her husband works for a nationwide company there; it is possible that he may be transferred to another city in the future. Despite her strong credentials and the fact that there are several openings in the area, she gets no job offers. She learns that many department chairpersons believe that hiring females is risky because of their child-bearing propensities, their domestic responsibilities, and the likelihood that they will follow their husbands elsewhere.

Do these examples reflect prejudice? Discrimination? Both? Neither? We will provide answers in the subsequent sections of this chapter that deal with the causes, costs, and correlates

315

of prejudice and discrimination in our society. First, however, since prejudice is an attitude, we need to explore the nature of attitudes in general.

I. The nature of attitudes

A. Definitions of attitude

An attitude may be defined as a "positive or negative affective reaction toward a denotable abstract or concrete object or proposition" (Bruvold, 1970, p. 11). The number of attitudes is almost infinite; an attitude exists within a person in regard to every object, topic, concept, or human being that the person encounters. We may have attitudes toward miniskirts and mustaches, well-done steaks and extra-dry martinis, the Chicago Cubs and the Chicago mayor. Attitudes differ from values, which are broader and more abstract. Values also lack an object, whereas attitudes *always have an object or topic.* "Bravery" or "social service" or "beauty" may be values for a person; they serve as criteria for judgments or as abstract standards for decision making, through which the individual develops attitudes (Rokeach, 1973). For example, a woman's attitude toward an aesthetically pleasing building to which access is limited may be influenced by the degree to which "beauty" is an abstract value for her. If "beauty" is a strong value for her, having to walk up ten steps to the building's entrance may not detract from her positive attitude toward the building as a place to work.

An attitude, like most variables of central interest to social psychology, is not an observable entity. Rather, it is an underlying construct whose nature must be inferred. (See Figure 10-1 for a description of methods to measure attitudes.) Attitudes possess three central characteristics: they always have an *object;* they are usually *evaluative;* and they are considered relatively *enduring.* Consider the statement: "I approve of our country's leader in everything he

is doing." The statement reflects an attitude in that it expresses an evaluation ("approve of") and it deals with an object ("our country's leader"). Although we cannot judge its transiency, we will assume (since it is so broad) that the statement is relatively enduring. But what if the statement had been, instead: "I approve of the President's position on tax reform"? The statement would still involve an attitude, although the assumption of its enduring nature might be more tenuous. The more specific the object or issue, the more likely it is that the attitude is susceptible to change. The person making the second statement might be persuaded to reject the President's tax policy, but his or her overall favorable evaluation of the President could remain consistent.

Figure 10-1
Methods of measuring attitudes

There are several methods used to measure social attitudes:

1. The Thurstone method of equal-appearing intervals

The goal is to construct a scale marked off in equal units. A Thurstone scale is composed of about 20 statements that are spread out along a continuum from very favorable to very unfavorable attitudes toward the object. A Thurstone scale is conceptualized as follows:

Extremely unfavorable — Extremely favorable
0 1 2 3 4 5 6 7 8 9 10 11

Statements are assigned scale values on the basis of how favorable or unfavorable are the ratings given them. For example, if we were constructing a scale to measure attitudes toward North American Indians, we would select for the Thurstone scale a collection of items that covered the continuum from one extreme to the other. A statement with a scale value close to 11.0 might be: "I would rather see the White people lose their position in this country than keep it at the expense of the Indians." A statement with a scale value close to 0 would be: "I consider that the Indian is only fit to do the dirty work of the White community." When the Thurstone scale composed of about 20 statements is given to subjects, they indicate only those statements with which they agree. The median of those scale values is their score.

2. The Likert method of summated ratings

Here there is no effort to find statements that are distributed evenly along a continuum. Rather, only statements that are definitely favorable or unfavorable to the object are used. The subjects indicate their degree of agreement or disagreement with each statement. An example is the following:

"The policy of encouraging Indians to remain on reservations should be terminated immediately."

Strongly disapprove	Disapprove	Undecided	Approve	Strongly approve
(1)	(2)	(3)	(4)	(5)

In constructing a scale according to the method of summated ratings, an item analysis is done. Only those items that show a substantial correlation with the total score are retained for the final form of the scale.

3. The Guttman method of cumulative scaling

Here the goal is to construct a single dimension, such that it is possible to arrange all the responses of any number of subjects into a pattern like the following:

If the person's score is:	The subject said "yes" to item:			The subject said "no" to item:		
	1	*2*	*3*	*3*	*2*	*1*
3	x	x	x			
2		x	x	x		
1			x	x	x	
0				x	x	x

4. The semantic differential (Osgood, Suci, and Tannenbaum)

The original purpose of this method was to measure the meaning of an object to an individual. It may also be thought of as an attitude scale. The subject is asked to rate a given concept (such as "North American Indian") on a series of seven-point, bipolar rating scales. Any concept—a person, a political issue, a work of art, a group, or anything else—can be rated. The usual format is as follows, with the person placing an X indicating his or her rating on each bipolar dimension:

North American Indian

Fair	—	—	—	—	—	—	—	Unfair
Large	—	—	—	—	—	—	—	Small
Clean	—	—	—	—	—	—	—	Dirty
Bad	—	—	—	—	—	—	—	Good
Valuable	—	—	—	—	—	—	—	Worthless
Light	—	—	—	—	—	—	—	Heavy
Active	—	—	—	—	—	—	—	Passive
Cold	—	—	—	—	—	—	—	Hot
Fast	—	—	—	—	—	—	—	Slow

The semantic differential can be used to determine whether the individual's responses to two concepts are alike or different. Its original purpose was to determine the "semantic meaning" of the ratings; that is, what factors are represented in the ratings.

A fourth characteristic is often included in the definition of an attitude: a *predisposition toward action*, or "a state of readiness for motive arousal" (Newcomb, Turner, & Converse, 1965, p. 40). Krech, Crutchfield, and Ballachey (1962, p. 152) define an attitude as "an enduring system of positive or negative evaluations, emotional feelings, and pro and con *action tendencies* with respect to a social object" (italics added). And Rokeach (1968), in an influential formulation, advances a similar orientation, stating that an attitude is "a relatively enduring organization of beliefs around an object or situation predisposing one to respond in some preferential manner" (p. 112). Rokeach's inclusion of "preferential manner" may be too limiting and directional, but the basic assumption that attitudes are predispositions for behavior is clear in all these statements.

When *readiness to respond* is included in the definition, it is assumed that attitudes influence concomitant or future behavior toward the object. If we know how a person feels toward Gerald Ford, we should be able to predict how that person will behave when Ford appears in town or when Ford's name appears in the voting booth. Predictions based on such knowledge are often correct, but the relationship between attitudes and behavior is not always clear-cut. In the 1968 U.S. election, as an example, many union members were most sympathetic to presidential candidate George Wallace but ended up voting for Hubert Humphrey. Likewise, in 1975 many U.S. citizens who would deny they held any racial prejudice still were quite hostile to the government's admission of 130,000 South Vietnamese refugees to the United States.

The relationship between attitudes and behavior is currently being scrutinized and reformulated. It may well be, as Daryl Bem (1970) postulates, that in many instances one's behavior determines one's attitude, rather than the reverse. We will consider this issue in detail later in the chapter. At this point, we wish to deemphasize the notion that a "predisposition to action" is a pivotal part of an attitude and to recognize that attitudes serve as ways for us to organize and categorize the information and feelings we possess about a number of topics.

B. Components of attitudes

The concept of *attitude* is a broad one; and, not surprisingly, attitude theorists have proposed that there are separable components of the attitude concept. Historical traditions also make a contribution here. For example, the proposition that people may take three existential stances in regard to the human condition—knowing, feeling, and acting—has been advanced by philosophers throughout history (McGuire, 1969). These three stances are reflected by the three components of the most frequent conceptualization of an attitude—the cognitive, the affective, and the conative components (Insko & Schopler, 1967; Sheth, 1973). These components are described in Figure 10-2.

We shall be interested in discovering the interrelationships of the three components described in Figure 10-2. Is each component unique, or are all three aspects of the same phenomenon? The answer to this question has implications for a theory of prejudice, because *prejudice is an attitude.* Let us review examples from the available literature on prejudice.

The question of whether prejudice is a psychological unity has been attacked most directly by D. T. Campbell (1947) and by Woodmansee and Cook (1967). Campbell constructed brief scales to tap each of five attitudinal components: social distance, blaming minorities, beliefs about a group's capability or intelligence, beliefs about a group's morality, and affection for a group. College and high school students gave their reactions to five ethnic groups (Blacks, Jews, Japanese, Mexicans, and English). Intercorrelations among the five attitudinal components for a particular ethnic group were greater than correlations between groups for a particular component. That is, there was more similarity between *beliefs about the morality of Japanese* and *affection for Japanese* than there was between *affection for Japanese* and *affection for Blacks.* Thus, on the basis of Campbell's study, the dimensionalization of prejudice into components seemed rather fruitless because the *different* attitudinal components for a particular minority group elicited such *similarity* of response. But the correlations may be spuriously high here, as the method of measurement was identical from scale to scale. By that we mean that all of Campbell's scales used the same format, and this common response format may have been a contributing source of the high correlations between scales. In fact, Campbell himself, at a later and wiser time (D. T. Campbell & Fiske, 1959), pointed out the misleading nature of high correlations that occur when the method similarities and content similarities are not kept separate.

Figure 10-2
The components of an attitude

Cognitive
Affective = *Attitude*
Conative

The *cognitive* component of an attitude includes the beliefs, the perceptions, and the information one has about the attitude object (Harding, Kutner, Proshansky, & Chein, 1969). Beliefs that women are more intuitive than men, that all welfare recipients are lazy, and that Republicans are unconcerned with the "little man" all represent the cognitive aspect of attitudes toward their respective objects. Stereotypes—simple, overgeneralized, inaccurate or partially inaccurate beliefs—are parts of the cognitive component. The cognitive component is fact oriented, but it cannot be entirely separated from evaluation. Most beliefs and most stereotypes about minority groups, for example, are not based entirely on facts or objective observation. As a matter of fact, a person may hold two cognitions about one group that are contradictory; for example, the same person may believe both that "Jews are too seclusive and clannish" and that "Jews are always trying to intrude where they don't belong" (Adorno, Frenkel-Brunswik, Levinson, & Sanford, 1950; D. T. Campbell, 1947).

The *affective* component of an attitude, in contrast to the cognitive one, refers to the emotional feelings about, or the liking or disliking of, the attitude object. Positive feelings might include respect, liking, and sympathy; negative feelings might be contempt, fear, and revulsion. Of the three components, the affective is probably the most central aspect of an attitude.

The *conative* component refers to one's policy orientation toward the attitude object, or one's stance "about the way in which persons [or attitude objects] should be treated in specific social contexts" (Harding et al., 1954, p. 1027). The conative component emphasizes how the respondent would respond. For example, would the respondent vote for legalized abortions? Would he eliminate housing covenants that lead to racially segregated neighborhoods?

In the second major investigation of the psychological unity of prejudice, Woodmansee and Cook (1967) made a detailed attempt to delineate the dimensions of attitudes. Their specific goal was to construct a set of scales that would measure the dimensions of the attitudes of White United States citizens toward Blacks. After an extended procedure of item selection, analysis, refinement, and further analysis, the researchers identified 11 item clusters that were internally consistent but generally separable from one another. Each of these clusters of items was made into a scale and was validated by demonstrating that members of pro-Black criterion groups (such as the NAACP) responded to the scale differently than members of right-wing political groups or racially segregated fraternities and sororities. Table 10-1 lists the 11 clusters or scales, with a sample item from each scale. The dimensions represented here certainly do not fit the three-component conception of racial attitudes reviewed in Figure 10-2. Rather, five of the dimensions are issue oriented and consist of both cognitive and conative elements. Another couple of dimensions are concerned with acceptance of Blacks and are basically affective in nature. The remaining dimensions also contain combinations of cognitive, affective, and conative aspects.

On the basis of the Woodmansee and Cook study, we are tempted to conclude that there is a more detailed set of factors than the cognitive-affective-conative trichotomy in measuring attitudes toward a specific minority group. Yet further work needs to be done because the output of factors is so dependent on the type of statistical analysis used. Woodmansee and Cook, in using highly specific analyses, made it quite likely that the resultant structure would be a complex one (D. B. Gray & Revelle, 1972).

In general, relationships between affective and conative components are higher than between either of these and the cognitive component; in other words, there is more similarity between one's feelings and one's policy orientation than there is between one's feelings and one's beliefs or between one's policy orientation

Table 10-1
Dimensions and scales of attitudes toward Blacks identified in
Woodmansee-Cook study

1. *Integration-segregation policy,* defined as the respondent's position on the propriety of racial segregation and integration.
   Sample item: "The Negro should be afforded equal rights through integration."

2. *Acceptance in close personal relationships,* or the extent of personal willingness to recognize, live near, or be associated with Negroes.
   Sample item: "I would not take a Negro to eat with me in a restaurant where I was well known."

3. *Negro inferiority,* or assertions which imply or directly state that Negroes are inferior to whites in terms of motivation, character, personal goals, and social traits.
   Sample item: "Many Negroes should receive a better education than they are now getting, but the emphasis should be on training them for jobs rather than preparing them for college."

4. *Negro superiority,* or attributing to Negroes personal characteristics which make them superior to whites.
   Sample item: "I think that the Negroes have a kind of quiet courage which few whites have."

5. *Ease in interracial contacts,* or social ease in interracial situations in which a majority of whites probably would feel self-conscious or uncomfortable.
   Sample item: "I would probably feel somewhat self-conscious dancing with a Negro in a public place."

6. *Derogatory beliefs,* or a characterization of at least some Negroes as being prone to a variety of relatively minor shortcomings. These items, for the most part, are essentially true and reasonable statements of everyday fact, but in tone they may be taken as subtly degrading and derogatory judgments against Negroes in general.
   Sample item: "Some Negroes are so touchy about getting their rights that it is difficult to get along with them."

7. *Local autonomy,* or a pitting of the policy-making prerogatives of "outsiders" to guarantee the Negro's civil rights.
   Sample item: "Even though we all adopt racial integration sooner or later, the people of each community should be allowed to decide when they are ready for it."

8. *Private rights,* or attitudes regarding the individual rights of businessmen, club members, landlords, and the like, who oppose integration on the basis of their individual rights of free association or choice of clients.
   Sample item: "A hotel owner ought to have the right to decide for himself whether he is going to rent rooms to Negro guests."

9. *Acceptance in status-superior relationships,* or reaction to Negroes in positions where they are in authority or are socially superior to whites.
   Sample item: "If I were being interviewed for a job, I would not mind at all being evaluated by a Negro personnel director."

10. *Sympathetic identification with the underdog,* a measure developed by Schuman and Harding (1963) which consists of brief stories in which a Negro is exposed to an act of prejudice or discrimination. The respondent is offered a choice of four possible reactions the Negro might have in the situation. The alternative which attributes anger, frustration, sadness, or resentment to the Negro is the "sympathetic" response; all others are nonsympathetic.
    Sample item: "A colored couple is out for a drive in the country, and they pass a fine private club. The club has a sign out front describing the advantages of membership in the club, and at the bottom it says 'membership reserved for whites only.' How do you think the

colored couple is likely to react to this? (a) It makes them unhappy to realize that they are not wanted in the club; (b) They might think that they could easily join a colored club with twice the advantages of the club they are passing; (c) It is hard for a white person to know for certain just how colored people react to a sign of this sort; or (d) They may read the sign quickly, but probably wouldn't think much of it for very long."

11. *Gradualism*, or attitudes about how rapidly the process of integration should take place.
    Sample item: "Gradual desegregation is a mistake because it just gives people a chance to cause further delay."

---

and one's beliefs. The disparity between cognitive beliefs and feelings is often demonstrated in the following way. On a set of trait rating scales, a White person rates the characteristics of Blacks just as favorably as he does those of Whites; the White respondent possesses no tendency to say that Blacks are lazier, more stupid, dirtier, less mannered, or ruder than Whites. Yet on measures of the affective component, the White respondent expresses frequent dislike and rejection of Blacks. It is as if the White person says: "I feel negatively toward Blacks, even though I cannot defend it on the basis of a belief in racial differences" (J. H. Mann, 1960; Wrightsman, 1962a).

C. Simple versus complex attitudes

Beyond the breakdown of attitudes into components, another issue in attitude theory has practical implications. This issue deals with whether any given attitude is simple or complex.

If we ask people to react to a particular attitude object, the diversity of responses and, particularly, the differences in specificity of attitude may be seen. In response to the question "What is your attitude toward Elizabeth Taylor?" one individual might respond "She's fantastic!" Another person may answer "I can't stand her!" If the response ends there, we are forced to conclude that the attitudes being expressed are highly *simplex*, in the sense that they are undifferentiated, lacking in qualifications or elaborations, and largely evaluative. Consider, however, the following response: "I believe that Elizabeth Taylor is potentially a beautiful woman but she's

gotten too fat. Most people say she is pretty immoral, and maybe I would too, but I like her candor and her rejection of phoniness. She's a so-so actress, I guess: I liked her in *Virginia Woolf,* but in her latest movie she was pretty bad. She really can't be blamed for her breakup with Richard Burton . . ." and so on. A salient aspect of this expressed attitude is its *complexity*. It is complex (1) because it contains many elements and (2) because the elements are often not congenial with one another.

An important feature of attitudes is their simplicity or complexity. As is shown in the example in the previous paragraph, the complexity of an attitude is reflected in the richness of ideational content and in the number of reactions the person has to the object (W. A. Scott, 1968, p. 207). Krech et al. (1962, pp. 38–40) have identified three characteristics of attitudes relevant to their complexity. First, attitudes may differ in their degree of *multiplexity*. The number and variety of cognitions (specific elements) incorporated in one's attitude toward an object define the attitude's multiplexity. Second, an attitude may vary in its *consonance*, or the degree to which the elements within the attitude are consistent or harmonious with one another. If the attitude is simplistic, the issue of consonance is not relevant. Multiplex attitudes, however, can be either more or less consonant. The elements of a multiplex attitude can be harmonious and fitting (Krech et al., 1962, p. 38). Suppose a respondent sees Elizabeth Taylor as "a beautiful woman, a talented actress, and a person whose morals are admirable because they reflect the goal of being a free person, not constrained by the conventionalities of society." While this attitude is relatively multiplex, its elements are quite consonant with one another. Other multiplex attitudes reflect elements that are not harmonious with each other and lack *cognitive consonance*. A multiplex attitude that lacks cognitive consonance is not by any means a faulty one; in fact, it often reflects an intelligent and mature response to an attitude object that is itself complex and possibly not well-integrated. Figure 10-3 reflects an example of this, using an attitude object quite salient in the minds of social psychologists.

The third characteristic of attitudes is their *relatedness* or *interconnectedness,* a quality that deals with a person's attitudes about two or more attitude objects. One man's attitude toward Elizabeth Taylor may be a part of his general framework—perhaps a highly moralistic one—from which he also derives reactions to many other attitude objects. If he views Elizabeth Taylor as immoral, it is possible that his attitudes toward such diverse objects as hippies, politicians, and the police may also be evaluated within the same basic moralistic orientation. If a person's attitudes toward different objects are harmonious and consistent, we say they are related; they show an *interconnectedness* (Krech et al., 1962). Thus, in contrast to multiplexity and consonance, interconnectedness deals with relationships among *different attitudes* in the same person. If the person's attitudes toward different basic objects of importance are consistent, an ideology exists.

II. Distinctions among terms: Prejudice, discrimination, and racism

With this description of the nature of attitudes behind us, we now focus on attitudes toward minority groups. Two terms that are often used interchangeably, *prejudice* and *discrimination,* are actually different concepts. **Prejudice** refers to an attitude; **discrimination** refers to behavior. (See Figure 10-4.) *Racism* is harder to define; a

Figure 10-3
Social psychologists' attitudes toward U. S. Senator William Proxmire: Multiplex and lacking cognitive consonance. We asked some social psychologists to describe their reactions to U. S. Senator Proxmire, because we know that many admire him for his positions on several issues (especially cutting military spending) but that they are concerned about his apparent vendetta against social-psychological research funding by the U. S. National Science Foundation. Their responses reflect these multiplex attitudes: (1) "I thought he was bright until he attacked the NSF [National Science Foundation] research." (2) "I don't know how to respond to someone who jogs to his office and keeps in shape but also is so vain as to get a hair transplant." (3) "Proxmire has alerted us to the waste in spending for military 'defense,' but maybe it was just to get publicity. I thought his attack on the Walster and Berscheid love research was for that reason." (Photo courtesy of Senator Proxmire.)

booklet issued by the U.S. Commission on Civil Rights and entitled *Racism in America and How to Combat It* defines *racism* as "any attitude, action, or institutional structure which subordinates a person because of his or her color" (page 1). This

Figure 10-4
Reactions to prejudice or discrimination? *Prejudice* refers to attitudes; behavior that denies access or opportunities on the basis of a person's race or religion is *discrimination*. (Photo by Lloyd Eby/Freelance Photographers Guild.)

definition includes both prejudice and discrimination in racism. Carmichael and Hamilton, in their useful *Black Power* (1967), define racism as "the predication of decisions and policies on considerations of race for the purpose of *subordinating* a racial group and maintaining control over that group" (1967, p. 3). Racism may be either individual or institutionalized.

The social psychologist defines prejudice as an unjustified evaluative reaction to a member of a racial, ethnic, or other minority group that occurs because of the object's membership in that group. The definition implies that the same evaluative attitude is held by the prejudiced per-

son toward the minority group as a whole. A prejudice may be unjustified for several reasons: because it involves prejudgment, because it is illogical, because it is derived from hearsay or from a racist institution, or because it leads one to overcategorize and treat individuals on the basis of a group affiliation. We define a prejudiced attitude as either favorable or unfavorable, either positive or negative, while recognizing that a negative orientation is more frequently the case. We should look at the implications of this definition.

First, prejudice derives from one's attitudes toward groups. If we could so individualize our responses to others that we had no general attitude about Blacks as a race, welfare recipients as a class, or women as a sex, we would be on the way to avoiding the development of any prejudices. But most people cannot do this; they need to make conclusions about an entire group on the basis of exposure to a few members of that group. Many people have attitudes toward rabbis, or Rhodesians, or railroad conductors, even though they have never met a single one. Attitudes may evolve entirely on the basis of impressions formed while watching television, listening to an acquaintance, or reading a magazine. Regardless of the source, a group-based attitude seems inevitable. Ironically, grouping, or categorization, is a mature step in the development of a child's thinking; he or she is rewarded for being able to see that, for example, "This animal is like that one but dissimilar to the one way over there." Children are considered more intelligent when they can extract a general concept from a mass of objects. Once such concept formation is developed, its effects may become reversed. A prejudice may be formed when a person observes (accurately or inaccurately) a few discrete characteristics of several members of the same group. A man may note that his wife jumps to conclusions on the basis of limited information and that his (female) secretary also jumps to conclusions with little information. Upon recognition that they are both members of the same group, the man may generalize his impressions to the whole group or class ("Have you noticed, Fred, how all women will jump to a conclusion so easily?") and to other individual members of the class ("Now that you mention it, Bob, Nancy is like that, too"). Not all prejudiced attitudes are formed in this fashion, but categorical generalizations about a group as a whole, based on few instances, are a part of prejudice.

The social psychologist's definition of prejudice assumes the existence of *overcategorization*. A prejudiced person may think each and every member of a negatively evaluated group is bad in all respects, simply by reason of membership in that group. Likewise, if a group is favored, each of its members can do no wrong. Allport has stated that "given a thimbleful of facts we rush to make generalizations as large as a tub" (1954, p. 9). The most deleterious aspect of prejudice may be its overlooking the diversity present in each group of human beings. The principle of variability in our assumptions about human nature, discussed in Chapter 3, is a healthy antidote to the overcategorization that is a part of prejudice.

Seemingly, prejudices imply prejudgment; as we saw in Chapter 3, we can form impressions of a man before knowing anything more specific about him than that he belongs to a certain church or race or occupational group. Even a person's first name evokes from us certain stereotyped descriptions of that person. (See Figure 10-5 for examples.) Since we must often make decisions before all the information is in, we prejudge. According to Allport, a prejudgment becomes a prejudice only if it cannot be revised in the light of new information. If one becomes emotionally involved in one's prejudgments, so that they cannot be altered upon exposure to more extensive information, then one's prejudgments have become prejudices.

It is important to distinguish between discrimination and prejudice. Acts that accept one person or reject another solely on the basis of their membership in different groups constitute *discrimination*. The acts of rejection can be ones of aggression and hostility or of avoidance and withdrawal. Many times discrimination goes hand-in-hand with prejudice, but not always. On the one hand, a person may have prejudiced attitudes and yet not be discriminatory in his or her behavior. (A college student who intensely dislikes Jews may not object when a Jew is assigned as his dormitory roommate.) On the other hand, a person may be unprejudiced in his or her attitudes and yet discriminatory in behavior. (Taxicab drivers—some of whom may be Blacks—may refuse to pick up Black passengers because of orders from the owner of the taxi company.)

If we return to the three episodes presented at the beginning of this chapter and again ask if each instance reflects prejudice, discrimination, both, or neither, our answer should be "discrimination" in each case. In each episode, an undesirable action is taken against the person on the basis of his or her membership in a group, rather than as a result of any qualities he or she possesses as an individual. The action may be rationalized or justified by the action-taker, but it is still an example of discrimination.

Figure 10-5
Do names evoke stereotypes?

There is a dialogue between Humpty Dumpty and Alice in Lewis Carroll's *Through the Looking Glass*, as follows:

"*Must* a name mean something?" Alice asks doubtfully.

"Of course it must," Humpty Dumpty said. . . . "My name means the shape I am. . . . With a name like yours, you might be any shape, almost."

One's name does make a difference; when we hear someone's name—particularly if it is unusual—we are likely to form an image of that person. It is obvious that extreme names make a difference—names like Tonsillitis Jackson or Sports Model Higginbottom. (Kibler and Harari, 1974, tell us that these are real people's names.)

Some documented effects of naming, reviewed by Kibler and Harari (1974), include the following:

1. *Elmer* suggests a boy from the country, while *John* and *Robert* are seen as "real boys" (Eagleson & Clifford, 1945).

2. *Gordon* is associated with "hardworking" and "successful" and *Louise* with "pretty" (Winsome, 1973).

3. Common male first names are evaluated by others more positively than are uncommon ones (Lawson, 1971).

4. Even as early as the third grade, children associate certain stereotyped behaviors with certain names (Bruning & Husa, 1972), and the popularity of children is related to the social desirability of their first names (McDavid & Harari, 1966).

5. Teachers give essays supposedly written by boys with socially desirable names better grades than essays supposedly written by boys with undesirable names (Harari & McDavid, 1973). With girls' names this difference was not as clear-cut.

6. Male psychiatric patients with unique first names like *Oder* and *Lethal* were more psychotic than a matched group of clinic cases with popular names (Hartman, Nicolay, & Hurley, 1968).

7. There are ethnic differences in the social desirability of some first names. Garwood and McDavid (1974) report that Black teachers view *Harold* and *Stanley* as desirable names, whereas White teachers rate these names as connoting inactivity, weakness, badness, and femininity.

It is clear that stereotypes of first names and the expectations created by these stereotypes affect our behavior.

III. The costs and extent of prejudice, discrimination, and racism

A. The costs of prejudice, discrimination, and racism

Prejudice, racism, and discrimination have tragic and costly effects on both their perpetrators and their recipients. The man who castigates minority-group members thereby assuages his guilt over his failure to remedy their plight. If a woman convinces herself that most North American Indians are really drunkards, it is easier for her to avoid making sacrifices to help them.

The act of stereotyping may be a self-fulfilling prophecy in that it justifies actions that effectively restrict Indians to a captive group. For example, Chance (1965) reports that the St. James Cree act more "Indian"—that is, according to the stereotype—when they are in town than when they are in their own village (cited in Trimble, 1974b). The costs of racism go beyond such matters as the inconvenience or inadequacies of a separate school system or other segregated facilities to much more important costs—those involving aspirations and outcomes and physical and psychological health. (See Figure 10-6.) Not only do members of minority groups suffer prejudice and discrimination, but they also come to adopt the beliefs about themselves that are held by the majority group. For example, Trimble (1968) reports that both North American Indians and non-Indians agreed on what words were descriptive of Indians; the two groups equally selected such words as "lazy," "drunkards," "superstitious," and "quiet." (However, in a follow-up study done more recently, Trimble, 1974a, still found agreement, but he also found Indians describing themselves as "proud," "militant," "aggressive," and "strong.") According to Gurin, Gurin, Lao, and Beattie (1969) many Black college students blame the Blacks' problems on their personal inadequacies rather than on the social system in which they live. Such negative self-evaluations must be modified before Blacks can develop pride (Maykovich, 1972; Vontress, 1974).

Extreme acts of discrimination can eliminate a minority group from the face of the earth. The number of native North Americans has dropped from an estimated 3 million to 600,000. Indian tribes saw the massacres by the United States army in the last century systematically destroy their leadership, and Indian groups have not overcome the toll of this planned eradication. At present, the average life expectancy of the Indian is 44 years, compared with 71 years for White citizens of the United States and Canada. The average number of years of schooling for Indians is five and one-half years, which is less than the average for Blacks or Mexican-

Americans. The *quality* of education given Indians may be an even greater tragedy. In the Blackfoot school district of Idaho, three-fourths of the elementary school students are Indians; yet in the late 1960s every teacher was White. Nothing of the Indian culture was taught. When Senator Robert Kennedy visited one of these schools in 1968 and asked if there were any library books on the Indian culture, he was shown *Captive of the Delawares*, which has on its cover a picture of a White child being scalped by an Indian! On almost every measure of impoverishment and deprivation—economic, physical, social, and educational—the Indian is worse off than any other minority group in Canada and the United States (Trimble, 1972). Soon the native North American

Figure 10-6

Asian Americans—A discriminated-against group. We may not always think of U. S. and Canadian citizens of Asian ancestry (Chinese, Japanese, Filipinos, Koreans, and others) as an *oppressed* minority. In fact, Sue, Sue, and Sue (1975)—three Chinese-American brothers and psychologists—report the case of one Japanese-American student applying for graduate school who was told that, in order to qualify for a special program as a minority-group member, he would have to show that he came from a disadvantaged background. While on many measures the *average* for such groups is similar to the majority group in the U. S. and Canada, there still remain in most "Chinatowns" and "Little Tokyos" the problems of poverty, unemployment, mental illness, and other responses to racial discrimination. (Photo by Kent Reno/Jeroboam Inc.)

may disappear as an entity unless changes are instituted.

The advocacy of *sexism*, or prejudice and discrimination against one sex (usually the female), is also costly to our society. (See Figure 10-7 for one example.) Unlike the racial minorities, women have diminishing influence on college campuses; presently, a smaller percentage of new Ph.D.'s are women than was the case 50 years ago (Astin, 1969; Bachtold & Werner, 1970). Perhaps this decrease stems from the discouragement many females receive when they apply for graduate work. Ann S. Harris reports the following responses given by male faculty members to female applicants for doctoral work: "You're so cute, I can't see you as a professor of anything"; "Any woman who has got this far has got to be a kook. There are already too many women in this department"; "I know you're competent and your thesis advisor knows you're competent. The question in our minds is are you really serious about what you're doing?" and, "Why don't you find a rich husband and give this all up?" (A. S. Harris, 1970, p. 285).

In light of these remarks, it is not surprising to find reports (A. S. Harris, 1970; Keiffer & Cullen, 1969) of more demanding admission standards in undergraduate colleges and graduate schools for female applicants than for males. And even after women have survived this elimination process, business and industry are less willing to employ or to continue training women for executive positions (Goldsmith, 1970; B. Rosen & Jerdee, 1974a, 1974b). It has been shown (Fidell, 1970) that university department chairmen favor hiring men rather than women as faculty members, when their credentials are identical. And the term "chairmen," rather than "chairpersons," appears to be correct: while 23.5% of the members of the American Psychological Association are female, only eight women are among the heads of the 333 graduate psychology departments in the United States (Kimmel, 1974). Women are more likely to be employed in small colleges, to be lower in academic rank, and to be underpaid (Joesting, 1974). For example, academic women's salaries averaged, as of 1974, 83.2% of men's salaries, and only 27% of women had tenure, compared to 57% of men (National Center for Educational Statistics, 1975).

B. Is prejudice universal?

One theme of the present book is the necessity of making assumptions about people in general. Because people account for so much of our environment, we expect them to behave in predictable ways. We subdivide assumptions about people into assumptions about more specific groups; for example, "Men do not cry," "Basketball players are smarter than football players," or "People who look you in the eye are telling you the truth." (These assumptions qualify as stereotypes when they are factually incorrect, illogical, and rigid.) The function of our assumptions is to permit us to operate more efficiently in our interpersonal world.

Forming assumptions about specific groups occurs in every society—with the possible exception of a few remote societies that possess few members and undiversified sex roles. In this sense, prejudice may be considered virtually universal, if we adhere to our definition of prejudice as an unjustified evaluative attitude about a person on the basis of his or her membership in a group. A consideration of prejudiced relationships in the United States, Canada, and other countries may be illuminating, however, particularly in regard to causes of the intensity of prejudice. Some relevant principles and their illustrations will be presented in the following paragraphs.

When two or more racial or religious groups occupy the same territory, the degree of prejudice and discrimination expressed is a function of the relative population sizes of the groups (Blalock, 1957). If very small numbers of the minority group are present, discrimination against that group is less manifest. Though this statement is quite obvious, its ramifications are important to consider. For example, in the United

Figure 10-7

Are women discriminated against as therapy patients? Traditional sex-role
stereotypes influence conceptions of mental health (Broverman, Broverman,
Clarkson, Rosenkrantz, & Vogel, 1970); that is, the ideal woman is seen as "an
affiliative, nurturant, sensuous playmate who clings to the strong supporting
male" (Neulinger, 1968, p. 554). Does this mean that psychotherapists evaluate
female patients on the basis of stereotyped sex roles? Is a female patient who
acts in an unconventional manner judged less favorably by psychotherapists?
There have been well-publicized claims to this effect (see Chesler, 1972). The
evidence indicates that bias may be limited to certain types of women. For
example, Abramowitz, Abramowitz, Jackson, and Gomes (1973) asked
psychotherapists to rate male and female therapy patients who were politically
active as liberals or conservatives. In general, the psychotherapists rated the level
of adjustment of males and females as similar. However, greater maladjustment
was ascribed, by those therapists who were politically conservative, to females
who were liberal than to conservative females. For those therapists, commitment
to the vocal political left may have been seen as less appropriate in the female
than in the male student, leading to a bias against such clients (Gomes &
Abramowitz, 1974). (Photo by Jim Pinckney.)

States, White Southerners have always expressed more intense anti-Black attitudes than have White persons from other regions. Although there are several plausible reasons for this difference, one reason is that, in the past, Blacks have accounted for greater percentages of the population in Southern communities than elsewhere. Recent migrations of Blacks to other parts of the United States have altered the regional imbalance in anti-Black attitudes. Also, Southerners as a group express less anti-Jewish prejudice than do Easterners; and, in fact, few Jewish-Americans live in the South. The South and the Far West are the least anti-Semitic regions of the United States (Pettigrew, 1959; Prothro, 1952).

If degree of prejudice is a function of the percentage of population of minority groups, one might be tempted to seek a magic ratio that is most nearly ideal for the harmonious coexistence of different ethnic groups within a school. Would it be best, for example, to have 10%, 20%, or 30% Blacks in an ideally desegregated school? But the fact is that there is no ideal percentage. There is no guarantee that intergroup relations will be more harmonious if the ratio is 80:20 instead of, for example, 50:50. Other factors—such as the past history of relationships in the community, the speed of social change, the role of community leaders—are much more important than the percentage of ethnic-group members.[1]

When a powerful group is in the minority and the maligned group is actually larger in numbers but lacking in power, the almost inevitable result is prejudice and discrimination directed toward the less powerful group. This phenomenon is seen in Northern Ireland, where

Protestant-Catholic tensions run high.[2] Although the Protestants outnumber the Catholics two to one in Northern Ireland, in the city of Londonderry some 60% of the city's 56,000 people are Catholics. More anti-Catholic discrimination exists here. Until the British government intervened in 1969, the Protestant minority controlled the city council by means such as gerrymandering election precincts and giving every employer (the business-ownership class is mostly Protestant) six or more extra votes on election day. Jobs and housing are scarce; as much as 90% of the city's public housing is allocated to Protestants. In other areas of Northern Ireland, where the Catholic percentages are lower, repressive measures are less blatant.

In the Republic of South Africa, 3.5 million Europeans live in fear of and domination over 12.7 million Africans. The ratio in neighboring Rhodesia is even greater. In South Africa segregation of the races is virtually total. Mixed marriages are not just illegal; they are punishable. Africans may not stay overnight in White areas; even park benches, drive-in theaters, and post office windows are segregated. Africans are not allowed to hold meetings or to form political parties; they are jailed if they cannot produce their pass permits on demand. The policy of *apartheid*, or racial separation, has been extended in South Africa to the development of separate territories, called Bantustans, where the Africans are forced to live.[3] Although it is claimed that the Africans will have total sovereignty over these areas, that is small comfort, because the

[1]It has been proposed that a certain percentage of Blacks in a school is a "tipping point," causing a mass exodus of Whites. But research in the Baltimore city schools by Stinchcombe, McDill, and Walker (1969) indicates there is no "tipping point." Once a school was desegregated in Baltimore, the percentage of Whites leaving was rather consistent, regardless of whether 10%, 50%, or 70% of the students were Blacks.

[2]Northern Ireland is a useful example of the fact that two groups can be prejudiced and hostile toward each other even when no physically distinguishable characteristics exist (Klineberg, 1971).

[3]It may be sadly noted that the South African and Rhodesian governments are almost 100 years behind the United States and Canadian governments in establishing a policy of separate reservations for native groups. The U.S. Congress passed the General Allotment Act, which set up Indian reservations, in 1887. Canada created similar reservations as the various territories joined the Confederation.

Bantustans are located in largely undesirable, unoccupied lands that the Whites are willing to give up anyway. The Whites in power in Rhodesia likewise are developing separate areas for the Africans.

The case of the Republic of South Africa is extreme because the Nationalist Party (which has been in control since 1948) has been increasing its domination, belligerence, and punitive tendencies. There are a few newspapers that present an antigovernment view, but the government effectively suppresses news. For example, it was not until 1975 that the government permitted any television in South Africa. Still fearing its "unwholesome influence," the authorities even now allow it to be shown only two hours per night, and its content is heavily restricted. The South African government also maintains a Publications Control Board that censors or bans any publication or movie dealing "improperly" with any of 45 topics. *Newsweek* (February 22, 1971) reported that after this board had censored the U.S. film *M*A*S*H*, only about 25 minutes of the original two hours remained.

Canadians have generally prided themselves on the description of their society as a "mosaic" rather than a "melting pot," a term often used to describe the United States. However, the ideal mosaic, with its implications of equality for all, has been more aptly described by J. A. Porter (1965) as "the vertical mosaic." At the top of the "pecking order," be it in business, industry, academia, or the military, are the White Anglo-Saxon Protestants. Traditional prejudices and discrimination, whether against the French Canadians of Quebec, the Italian community of Toronto, the Métis of Manitoba, or the Chinese community of Vancouver, have resulted in the WASPs gaining a disproportionately large share of the power and wealth. In recent years, as indicated by the government's recent "Green Paper" on immigration, new prejudices have developed against Blacks from the U.S. and West Indies and against Asians and Vietnamese. Concern has also developed over the excessive U.S.

influence on Canadian culture, and "anti-Americanism" is popular on many campuses (perhaps rightly so, some would say, since many departments are composed of more than 50% U.S. citizens, while Canadians cannot find jobs). Although Pierre Trudeau's "Just Society" has not yet been realized, it is an ideal probably desired by the vast majority of Canadians.

In both the United States and Canada, government officials and the mass media can play on the fears of the citizenry in order to increase prejudice and discrimination. Shortly after the Japanese attack on Pearl Harbor on December 7, 1941, pressure mounted to evacuate Japanese-Americans from the West Coast and to restrict them to internment camps, "so they could not commit espionage or sabotage." Both the mass media and government officials (including Earl Warren, who was then Attorney General of California) insisted that these Japanese-Americans, two-thirds of whom were U. S. citizens, were a threat to the country's security. So, early in 1942, more than 110,000 Japanese-Americans were removed to ten hastily constructed camps inland, where they were detained for three years. The crowded, makeshift, unsanitary nature of these camps not only destroyed family pride but broke the vital link with the past that kept families together and preserved a sense of Japanese culture even in California (Houston & Houston, 1973). These Japanese-Americans also lost an estimated $400 million in confiscated property. After World War II, the United States government begrudgingly settled their property claims, usually paying at the rate of ten cents for each dollar of evaluation. The last claim was not settled until 1967. This internment, without benefit of trial,[4] occurred despite the fact that not a single Japanese-American was convicted of

---

[4]The Supreme Court, in acting on the last claims of Japanese-Americans in 1967, failed to act on the legality of the government's internment without benefit of charges or trial. Apparently, the alternative still exists should the government choose to use it.

spying or otherwise aiding the enemy during the war, and many Japanese-American soldiers served with distinction in the all-Nisei (second-generation American) 442nd Regimental Combat team (Bosworth, 1968).

The experiences of Japanese-Canadians were not all that different from those of their U.S. relatives. Public fears of espionage and sabotage, again played up by the mass media and public officials, resulted in the Canadian government's removing most Japanese-Canadians from Vancouver to "settlements" in the interior of British Columbia.

The mass media can promote socially undesirable racial prejudice in other ways; many newspapers continue to identify Blacks or Indians or Puerto Ricans by race when they have committed a crime, even if the racial identification does not facilitate capturing the lawbreaker. When a White child sees Blacks identified as criminals on the television news report but is never informed of Black accomplishments, a stereotype almost inevitably results. One of the values of the *Sesame Street* program on educational television is that several races are portrayed in a positive manner.

Likewise, economic factors may serve either to encourage or to reduce discrimination. For instance, if one group seeks the goals (employment, unionization) that another group controls, and if only one group can achieve those goals, prejudice and conflict result. Historically, the immigration of large masses seeking employment—such as the Vietnamese refugees in the middle of this decade—has threatened the indigenous working force and has led to prejudice and discrimination toward the newcomers. Today rigid rules still exist for qualifying as an apprentice in a skilled-trades union; often only those who are related to a current union member will be accepted as apprentices. Such acts are discriminatory practices set up to protect the worker from the infiltration of immigrants, Blacks, and women.

In contrast, economic factors can also *over-come* discrimination. One reason for the emergence of Blacks in television advertising in the United States is the large market made up by the 25,000,000 people of the Black community. Likewise, businesses cannot exercise discriminatory practices in the face of an economic boycott by potential customers. The power of such boycotts was shown when many lunchcounters, stores, and movies in the U.S. South desegregated prior to the Civil Rights Act of 1965.

To conclude that prejudice is universal is to dampen hopes for a future society in which all persons are accepted equally. Still, a great deal of evidence points to the conclusion that prejudice, in some form, has always existed in competitive societies and will continue to exist as long as differences between groups of people are accentuated. Even areas that are considered cultural melting pots, such as Brazil and Hawaii, show degrees of discrimination against certain social classes or races. Certainly the extent of prejudice may be reduced, but it is a phenomenon that may be with us for some time.[5]

Even though prejudices remain, discrimination may be reduced through legal processes,

[5]Karlins, Coffman, and Walters (1969), in comparing the stereotypes of ethnic groups held by three generations of Princeton students, found that more recent students protest more often about the requirement of assigning trait names to any ethnic or racial group. Many students still comply, however. In 1967, these investigators gave the current Princeton undergraduates the same task that Katz and Braly had administered to Princeton students in the mid-1930s and that Gilbert had given in 1951. The study provides little hope that negative stereotypes will gradually fade from existence. The 1951 group was less uniform in the traits its members assigned to racial groups, but the 1967 group showed almost as much agreement over the traits it assigned as the original 1937 group. The earlier stereotypes had been replaced with others. In 1967, Blacks were no longer rated as *superstitious* but were considered *musical*. The extent of agreement among 1967 students' ratings was high. Research in the early 1970s indicated that the degree to which White college students agree with the predominant White view of Blacks is significantly related to the extent of Whites' negative racial attitudes. That is, the more racially prejudiced Whites show greater agreement with the societal view of Blacks (Brigham, 1971b).

education, and government action. (We consider these procedures further in Chapter 12.)

IV. The causes of prejudice and discrimination

Many theories about the causes of prejudice have been advanced. Gordon Allport's readable book *The Nature of Prejudice* (1954) outlines these theories, which are also represented in Figure 10-8. We will discuss each theory in turn, but first we need to recognize that two levels of analysis have been used—the societal and the individual (Ashmore, 1970). The societal explanations are concerned with situational effects on prejudice in given societies, social systems, and

groups. The individual level of analysis asks why one person is more prejudiced than another.

A. Historical emphasis and economic emphasis

The historian reminds us that the causes of prejudice cannot be fully understood without studying the historical background of the relevant conflicts. At the societal level of analysis, it is a sad fact that most prejudices toward minority groups have a long history in the United States. Allport points out that anti-Black prejudice, for example, has its roots in slavery and the slaveowner's treatment of Black families, in the exploitation of Blacks by carpetbaggers, and in the failure of Reconstruction in the U.S. South after the Civil War.

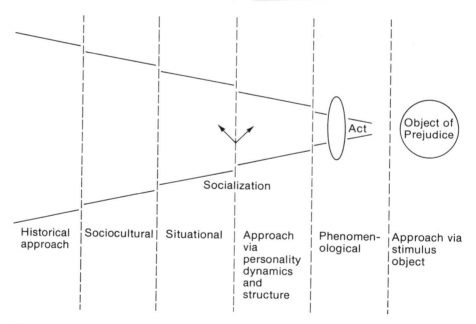

Figure 10-8
Theoretical and methodological approaches to the study of the causes of prejudice. (Adapted from "Prejudice: A Problem in Psychological and Social Causation," by G. W. Allport, *Journal of Social Issues*, Supplement Series No. 4, 1950. Copyright 1950 by the Society for the Study of Social Issues. Reprinted by permission.)

Certain historically oriented theories of prejudice emphasize economic factors. For example, advocates of the theories of Karl Marx see prejudice as a way of letting the rulers exploit the laboring class. As O. C. Cox has stated, "Race prejudice is a social attitude propagated among the public by an exploiting class for the purpose of stigmatizing some group as inferior so that the exploitation of either the group itself or its resources may both be justified" (1948, p. 393). Treatment of Black slaves before the U.S. Civil War, of Oriental immigrants in California 80 years ago, and of Chinese laborers brought in to build the Canadian Pacific Railroad all are examples of the haves vilifying the have-nots. We saw in Chapter 3 that the response of *blaming the victim* is a strong one; the act of oppression leads to reactions which, in effect, "prove" that such oppressive acts were warranted.

Attempts were made to justify colonialism, which arose from economic and other national needs in the 18th and 19th centuries, on the basis of assumptions that colonial peoples were "a lower form of the species" or "the White man's burden" to be borne magnanimously. In actuality, colonialism provided European nations with cheap sources of materials and captive markets for goods. We may wonder, as Blauner (1969) does, what the outcome will be as poorly educated Blacks become economically dispensable in a society in which their unskilled labor is replaced by automation.

Economic exploitation is not only of historical interest. Women are denied education and career opportunities, thus permitting their "employment" as housewives. Kenneth B. Clark (1965) has shown how the political, economic, and social structure of Harlem is in many ways that of a colony, and third-party candidate Eugene McCarthy referred to Black Americans as a colonized people during his 1976 U.S. presidential campaign. Economic exploitation is still rationalized, as unskilled workers are paid less than a living wage. ("Pay 'em more and they'd waste it away.") Contrary to this assumption about the nature of the masses, however, recent studies indicate that when families on welfare are given increased payments, they tend to spend the extra money on necessary items, rather than on unessentials or frivolities (Goodwin, 1972).

Despite its usefulness in the understanding of prejudice against some minority groups, the historical approach does not provide an inclusive answer to the question of the causes of prejudice. It does not explain why some people in power are more prejudiced than others, or why some groups are the object of prejudice more than others. Why does one child in a family grow up to be a bigot while another heads the local Urban League? The economic-exploitation theory does not explain why certain immigrant groups that came to North America were exploited without suffering the degree of prejudice that Blacks and Jews have received. In the U.S. South, White sharecroppers are exploited by the ownership class to the same degree as Black sharecroppers, yet they have not been harassed by lynch mobs or arsonists.

B. Sociocultural emphasis

Sociologists and anthropologists emphasize sociocultural factors as determinants of prejudice, discrimination, racism, and intergroup conflict. Among these sociocultural factors are (1) the phenomena of increased urbanization, mechanization, and complexity; (2) the upward mobility of certain groups; (3) the increased emphasis on competence and training, the scarcity of jobs, and the competition to get them; (4) the increased population in the face of a limited amount of usable land and lack of adequate housing; (5) an inability to develop internal standards, leading to reliance on others (individuals, organizations, the mass media, or advertising) and a conforming type of behavior; and (6) changes in the role and function of the family, with concomitant changes in standards of morality.

The overt racism demonstrated in the early 1970s by members of the English working class may reflect the threat to full employment posed by the influx of large numbers of Pakistanis, Indians, and West Indians (Esman, 1970). The covert racism of the Canadian government's "Green Paper" on immigration undoubtedly reflects the concern of many White Canadians over the perceived threat to the "stability" of Canadian society posed by the increased numbers of "nontraditional" immigrants, such as Blacks from the United States and the Caribbean and Orientals from Vietnam.

Increased urbanization can also be considered a cause of prejudice against ethnic groups. G. Watson (1947) found that many of his subjects became more anti-Semitic after they had moved to the New York City area. In the big city, depersonalization is the rule; the New York subway rider rarely sees the same commuters from one day to the next. Urban life also pushes and shoves, crushes and destroys.

Also, the masses in the city follow the conventions of the times. Material values are emphasized, and the poor are looked upon with contempt because they have not reached the level of material existence prescribed by the sociocultural conventions (Herzog, 1970; J. H. Peterson, 1967). But even as we submit to the pressure of materialistic values, we despise the city that promotes them. Urban traits—dishonesty, deceit, ambitiousness, vulgarity, loudness—were, several decades ago, exemplified in the stereotype of the Jew. The late sociologist Arnold Rose believed that "the Jews are hated . . . primarily because they serve as a symbol of city life" (1948, p. 374). More recently, Blacks and Puerto Ricans have been the recipients of the blame for urban "crime in the streets."

The sociocultural emphasis is a logical explanation of prejudices toward urbanized minority groups as well as toward groups that have not accepted White middle-class values. But it does not explain the hostility toward hardworking Japanese-American and Japanese-Canadian farmers during World War II, or the fact that farm dwellers—isolated from the depersonalized, pulverizing city—are as prejudiced as city dwellers.

C. Situational emphasis

Let us now turn to explanations that operate at the individual level. The first of these is the situational emphasis. Allport derives the situational emphasis by subtracting the historical background from the sociocultural approach. The situational emphasis is oriented toward the present; it states that prejudice is caused by current forces in the environment. The atmosphere in which children grow up influences their beliefs and behaviors; if their parents, teachers, and peers express prejudiced attitudes and act in discriminatory ways, they are likely to learn these responses and adopt them as their own. The norms of many groups may implicitly or explicitly teach prejudice to children who grow up within those groups. Imitation of parents, older children, and other models is one vehicle for the transmission of prejudiced beliefs. Conformity to others is a strong influence, according to theories that blame the situation for the development of prejudice in a person. As Schellenberg (1974) indicates, we gain social approval by conforming to the opinions about national groups held by our friends and associates.

Changes over time in specific stereotypes of racial or national groups often reflect this situational emphasis. During World War II, U.S. and Canadian citizens were exposed to government propaganda, leading to adoption of negative stereotypes of Japanese and Germans and to favorable stereotypes of allies of the United States and Canada, including the Russians. Early in the war most U.S. citizens described the Russians as *hardworking* and *brave*. In 1948, as postwar conflicts between the two great powers emerged, the stereotypes were quite different, as Table 10-2 indicates. While *hardworking* was still seen as an appropriate description, more people in the United States believed Russians were *cruel*. In a world where the Soviet Union was no longer an ally but a competitor, assumptions about the nature of Russians changed. At present a different change is taking place in regard to the assumptions about mainland Chinese held by many U.S. citizens.

Table 10-2
Percent of American respondents who agreed that the following adjectives described the Russians

Adjective	Percent Agreeing	
	In 1942	In 1948
Hardworking	61	49
Intelligent	16	12
Practical	18	13
Conceited	3	28
Cruel	9	50
Brave	48	28
Progressive	24	15

From *How Nations See Each Other*, by W. Buchanan and H. Cantril. Copyright 1953 by the University of Illinois Press. Reprinted by permission.

D. Psychodynamic emphasis

Directly opposed to the situational emphasis is one that sees prejudice as a result of the prejudiced person's conflicts and maladjustments. Here, we find theories that are essentially psychological, in contrast to the historical, economic, and sociological emphases of previous approaches.

Two types of *psychodynamic* theories of prejudice are useful. One of these assumes that prejudice is rooted in the human condition, because **frustration** is inevitable in human life. Frustration and deprivation lead to hostile impulses, "which if not controlled are likely to discharge against ethnic minorities" (Allport, 1954, p. 209). Displacement of hostility upon less powerful groups, or **scapegoating,** is a result of frustration when the source of the frustration is not available for attack or is not attackable for other reasons. Lynching of Blacks, burning of synagogues, and other assaults on representatives of minority groups are instances of such behavior. (See Figure 10-9.)

Ashmore (1970) reviews evidence for a frustration theory of prejudice, finding some studies that demonstrate scapegoating but others that do not. For example, Allport and Kramer (1946) report that among Catholic students, those who complained of being discriminated against because they were Catholic were more anti-Black and anti-Semitic than were other Catholic students. However, children with highly punitive parents (as measured by the children's ratings) are not more prejudiced toward minority groups than are children with less punitive parents (R. Epstein & Komorita, 1965a, 1965b, 1966). In evaluating frustration theories, Feshbach and Singer (1957) make a very useful distinction between shared threats and personal threats. A shared threat, such as the possibility that one's community might be hit by a hurricane, has the effect of bringing people together; such a threat has been found to reduce anti-Black prejudice. But a personal threat has, as frustration theory would predict, an escalating effect on prejudice.

The approach represented by psychoanalytic theory is a related notion that emphasizes the unconscious processes that influence the development of prejudice. This theory notes that prejudice may serve the unconscious in a variety of ways; it may cover up severe inferiority feelings, help resolve guilt feelings, and act as a displacement of frustration. For example, George Wallace's campaign for the 1976 Democratic party nomination for U.S. President was partly directed toward middle-class White voters who were threatened by the fact that Blacks were moving up the socioeconomic ladder, while they were not.

Within the psychodynamic emphasis, a second approach focuses on the development of prejudice only in people who have a *personality defect* or *weak character structure*. This approach does not accept prejudice as normal; it postulates that prejudice is the result of the strong anxieties and insecurities of neurotic persons. A similar approach derives from authoritarianism, which conceptualizes prejudice as a function of the antidemocratic orientation of certain people. This antidemocratic or authoritarian ideology includes extreme conservatism and ethnocentrism in addition to prejudice; it is the subject of Chapter 18 of this text.

As Pettigrew (1961) shows, each of these explanations of prejudice within the psychodynamic approach represents an *externalization process*, in which people apply their ways of dealing with personal problems to the structuring of outside events. But there exist prejudiced persons to whom the psychodynamic emphasis does not apply. It is a particularly inadequate explanation in cases in which prejudice pervades the entire environment.

E. Phenomenological emphasis

The phenomenological emphasis advances the interesting notion that what should be studied is not the objective world, but the individual's perception of the world. A person's perceptions create his prejudices; if he perceives members of a minority group as hostile or threatening, he responds to them aggressively. Genuinely conciliatory behavior on the part of the Black Panthers, for example, is irrelevant if White policemen are convinced that the Panthers are out to get them.

Figure 10-9
Reactions to school busing for purposes of school desegregation in the United States. In the mid-1970s, protests about school desegregation in the U.S. had moved from the South to the North. Particularly violent was the response in Boston to crosstown busing for purposes of achieving racial desegregation. Boston is divided into separate ethnically homogeneous neighborhoods protective of their schools. Even an appearance by Senator Edward Kennedy at a protest meeting—asking for calm and reason—led to shoving and egg throwing. (Photo by Peter Southwick.)

With the phenomenological emphasis we have reached the immediate level of causation as represented in Figure 10-8. But our survey of approaches is not complete until we consider the stimulus object of prejudice itself.

F. Emphasis on earned reputation

All the previous approaches have localized the source of prejudice in the observer. They have failed to consider that minority groups, by their behavior or characteristics, may precipitate the negative feelings. that are directed toward them. The *earned-reputation* theory postulates that minority groups possess characteristics that provoke dislike and hostility. Daniel P. Moynihan, when urban affairs advisor to President Nixon, in one of his incendiary memos exemplified a belief that White persons may have some good reasons for their negative attitudes toward lower-class Blacks. Moynihan wrote "It is the existence of this lower class with its high rates of crime, dependency, and general disorderliness, that causes nearby Whites . . . to fear Negroes and to seek by various ways to avoid and constrain them" (quoted in "Moynihan's Memo Fever," *Time*, March 23, 1970, pp. 15–16). Likewise, in his controversial book *The Unheavenly City* (1970), political scientist Edward C. Banfield concluded that lower-class Blacks remain trapped in their ghettos because they do not possess the skills necessary to escape. *Tally's Corner.*

These viewpoints to the contrary, *few* social scientists believe that the characteristics of the minority group are a major cause of the hostile attitudes toward them. In fact, some social scientists prefer to assume that there are no real differences between racial or ethnic groups. While such a stance is well-meaning, it fails to deal with the crux of racial relationships—the actual disparities that are present (J. M. Jones, 1972).

There is increasing evidence, however, that the earned-reputation theory may contain some truth. For example, Triandis and Vassiliou conclude "The present data [from Greek and United States subjects] suggest that there is a 'kernel

of truth' in most stereotypes *when they are elicited from people who have firsthand knowledge of the group being stereotyped"* (1967, p. 324; italics in original). A careful review by Brigham (1971a) concludes that ethnic stereotypes can have a "kernel of truth" in the sense that different groups of responders agree on which traits identify a particular object group. But often we do not know whether or not the object group actually possesses those traits. Agreement on the negative characteristics of a group is not the same as proof, no matter how many persons agree.

None of these theories of the causes of prejudice is sufficient to explain every case; a phenomenon as pervasive as prejudice has many sources. A specific person's prejudice against some group may develop out of both what he has learned from his environment and his personal frustrations. Thus, we must acknowledge the multiple causation of prejudice, while realizing that attempts to identify specific causes for individual cases of prejudice are helpful. For example, in seeking ways to change attitudes, we must keep in mind that the task may require different emphases if the causes of prejudice are different. Changing a prejudice that stems from growing up in an environment that teaches the prejudice calls for reeducation; changing a prejudice that results from personal frustrations or hostilities requires perhaps deeper-reaching therapeutic devices.

V. Social distance: A result of perceived dissimilarity in beliefs?

Another way of looking at the causes of prejudice is to examine the reasons for a person's preference for remaining segregated from members of another group. The term **social distance** is used to refer to a person's acceptable degree of relationship with members of a given group (Westie, 1953). Social distance is usually measured by asking whether the person would accept members of group X as close friends, invite them to a party, let them live in his or her neighborhood, vote for one of them, and so on.

In recent years a controversy has developed among social psychologists: if a White rejects Blacks, does this rejection occur because the White assumes that Blacks hold different values or because of more blatant racial reasons? Does racial prejudice stem from an expectation that the other racial group is different? In *The Open and Closed Mind* (1960), social psychologist Milton Rokeach has argued that prejudice or rejection may be largely a result of a perceived dissimilarity in values. Rokeach argues that if a White person rejects Blacks, he or she does not do so on the basis of their being Black per se, but because he or she sees Blacks as possessing different values, habits, and life-styles than Whites. Rokeach, Smith, and Evans (1960) designed two studies in which subjects indicated how friendly they would feel toward a variety of persons who differed in racial and religious backgrounds and in beliefs on important issues. It was found that friendship was based much more on congruence of beliefs between the subject and the stimulus person than on racial or religious similarity.

Harry Triandis, another social psychologist, has argued, however, that people do reject other individuals because of their race per se. He stated "People do not exclude other people from their neighborhood, for instance, because the other people have different [values], but they do exclude them because they are Negroes" (1961, p. 186). Triandis reported results contrary to Rokeach's findings, using more behaviorally oriented questions than Rokeach's single friendship question.

Using as their subjects 44 White ninth graders in the San Francisco Bay area, D. D. Stein, Hardyck, and Smith (1965; see also D. D. Stein, 1966) designed a study that attempted to reconcile these findings. The researchers presented each subject a task by which to determine whether the subject's preferences were based on similarity in race, similarity in values, or both. The task was to decide how much they would

like another teenager as a companion; different teenagers responded to a "stimulus person" who was Black or White and similar to or different from themselves. Stein and associates found that difference in values accounted for much more rejection of Blacks than did race. But race did have an effect on the most intimate activities ("invite home to dinner," "live in same apartment house," and "date my sister").

These results confirm Rokeach's (1960) contention that rejection of others occurs largely because the others are believed to be different. At the same time, Stein et al. showed that Triandis (1961) was correct in his statement that Blacks are often excluded simply because they are Blacks, even if they possess values like one's own. The latter phenomenon does occur, but it is less likely to happen if the White person can be shown that the Black is basically similar to himself in beliefs and values.

Further extensions of this topic indicate the complexities involved. (See Figure 10-10 for one.) For example, Triandis and Davis (1965) were dissatisfied with earlier studies because they believed that prejudice had not been effectively measured. To assess social distance (or, in general terms, prejudice), Stein et al. had asked subjects how friendly they would feel toward stimulus persons. Moreover, the subjects were asked whether they would be willing to participate with each of these persons in 11 different social situations, which were all pleasant, positive behaviors. Triandis and Davis argued that prejudice involves negative behaviors as well as the lack of positive behaviors; therefore, they built into their study measures that could more pointedly reflect active rejection, rather than simply lack of acceptance.

Triandis and Davis used eight different stimulus persons—all possible combinations of White, Black, male, and female persons with attitudes for or against civil rights. The subjects (undergraduates at the University of Illinois) were asked to rate each of the eight stimulus persons on a series of concepts and behaviors (such as "good/bad," "clean/dirty," "would exclude from my neighborhood," and "would eat with").

Figure 10-10

How generalizable is a conclusion that similar beliefs are more important than race? Does this conclusion, based on the responses of 44 ninth graders in California, hold for subjects of other ages in other parts of the country? The answer, so far at least, is usually "yes." Stein (1966) repeated his procedures with 630 ninth-grade students in the Northeastern part of the United States. Once again the similarity and/or dissimilarity of values was found to be the primary determinant of the attitudes of White students. As concerns regional differences, one might expect that in the U.S. South race per se would be a more powerful determinant than elsewhere. In the original study Rokeach et al. (1960) found that White college students in both the North and the South were more accepting of Blacks whose beliefs agreed with theirs than they were of Whites who disagreed with them. (The Southern sample was from Houston, Texas.) C. R. Smith, Williams, and Willis (1967) extended this study and asked six samples ($N = 307$) of White and Black students from Northern, border, and Southern states to react to stimulus persons who varied in race, sex, and values. For all samples except one, similarity in belief was a more important determinant of acceptance than was similarity in race or sex. In the sample of Southern Whites (college students in Louisiana), the race of the stimulus person was a slightly more important determinant than was similarity in values. For six of eight issues, the majority of the subjects in the sample of Southern Whites favored Whites who had dissimilar values over Blacks who had similar values—although five of these six differences were slight. The sixth issue, where the difference was greatest, dealt with interracial fraternities and sororities. Two studies using teenagers in the South have been completed, one in North Carolina (Insko & Robinson, 1967) and one in Tennessee (Wrightsman, Baxter, & Jackson, 1967). Both studies confirm that, for these Southern teenagers, perceived similarity of values is a greater determinant of friendship than is similarity of race. (Photo by Suzanne Arms/Jeroboam Inc.)

Triandis and Davis used a multidimensional view that conceptualized prejudice as being made up of several factors. (These factors are described in Table 10-3.) The relative impact of race, sex, and values is different from one factor to another. For example, similarity of values is a more important determinant than race of formal social rejection, but race is a more important factor in friendship rejection. Race is second only to sex in the case of marital rejection and is the most important determinant of social distance and subordination. Thus, similarity in race appears to be a more important determinant of one's choices for intimate behaviors, while similarity of values is an important determinant for less intimate behaviors.

A second benefit of the Triandis-Davis approach is the notion that different types of subjects weigh race and values (or beliefs) in different ways when responding to a particular social encounter. By factoring the subjects' responses to many types of information—that is, separating out the various contributing factors—Triandis and Davis identified two types of prejudiced subjects. One type, called *conventionally prejudiced*, possessed interracial prejudice. The second type, called *belief prejudiced*, responded more

to the values of the stimulus persons and rejected stimulus persons (regardless of race) who favored civil rights legislation. This is a useful finding, since subjects were typed by measures largely independent of their ratings.

Triandis and Davis conclude that in the case of intimate behaviors, the race of the other person is a determinant for most subjects. Blacks are rejected even if they are known to be similar to oneself. In the case of less intimate behaviors, people are rejected if their beliefs and values are different, regardless of their race. These findings are in general agreement with those of Stein et al., the major discrepancy being the latter's conclusion that values or beliefs are equally important throughout the social-distance scale. Nonetheless, all these studies have one thing in common—they may be criticized because they are paper-and-pencil measures of abstract situations. There is no guarantee that the White student who says that he or she prefers a Black with similar values over a White with dissimilar values will associate with Blacks (D. O. Sears & Abeles, 1969). Because of these limitations, later studies by Rokeach (Rokeach, 1968; Rokeach & Mezei, 1966), which tested race versus values in real-life situations, take on additional signifi-

---

Table 10-3
Five prejudice factors derived by Triandis and Davis

Factor I. Formal Social Acceptance with Superordination versus Formal Social Rejection, defined by high loadings on items such as "I would admire the idea of," "I would admire the character of," "I would obey," "I would cooperate in a political campaign with."

Factor II. Marital Acceptance versus Marital Rejection, defined by high loadings on "I would marry," "I would date," "I would fall in love with," and so on.

Factor III. Friendship Acceptance versus Friendship Rejection, defined by high loadings on "I would accept as an intimate friend," "I would eat with," "I would gossip with," and so on.

Factor IV. Social Distance, defined by high loadings on items such as "I would exclude from the neighborhood," "I would prohibit admission to my club," "I would not accept as a close kin by marriage."

Factor V. Subordination, defined by high loadings on items such as "I would obey," "I would not treat as a subordinate," "I would be commanded by."

From "Race and Belief as Determinants of Behavioral Intention," by H. C. Triandis and E. Davis, *Journal of Personality and Social Psychology*, 1965, 2, 715–725. Copyright 1965 by the American Psychological Association. Reprinted by permission.

cance. Two of these field studies were done on a university campus, with undergraduates as subjects, while the third was done in a state employment service, using as subjects men who were seeking employment.

The procedure in all three studies was the same: a naïve subject (a male undergraduate or a man seeking work) met with four strangers (accomplices of the experimenter) and participated in a group discussion about an important or relevant topic. (In the study at the employment office, the men were under the impression that this discussion was a part of the normal application procedure.) In all cases, two of the accomplices were Blacks and two were Whites. One White and one Black agreed with the subject; one White and one Black disagreed. The subject then had to choose which two of the four accomplices he would prefer to be with at a coffee break (for college students) or which two he would prefer to work with (for men seeking employment). *regardless of color.*

In all three studies, the two persons who held the same beliefs or values as the subject were chosen much more frequently. In combining the three studies, we find that 47 of the 118 subjects chose the two men whose beliefs were most similar to theirs, while only seven subjects chose the two men of the same race. This result was most frequent in the employment office study; of 50 subjects, 30 chose the two men with similar beliefs, while only two chose men of the same race. Similarity of beliefs or values was, in these studies, a more powerful determinant of interpersonal choice than similarity of race. Using group discussions of the Reserve Officers Training Corps (ROTC), Hendrick, Stikes, Murray, and Puthoff (1973) found even stronger results favoring belief similarity over racial similarity (see also Hendrick, 1974a). It would be useful to extend this technique to choices of behaviors more intimate than drinking coffee or working together.

Similarity in race has also been matched with *competence* in order to determine the importance of each in determining reactions to coworkers. In other words, would a White person working on a group task prefer to have as a fellow worker a more competent Black or a less competent White? Using all-White groups in a laboratory task, Fromkin, Klimoski, and Flanagan (1972) found that members of previously successful groups chose new group members largely on the basis of their competency on the task (and not on the basis of race). But in groups that had been unsuccessful in the past, new colleagues were chosen on the basis of race more than on competency. In these groups, less competent Blacks were preferred as much as very competent ones, and Blacks were preferred over Whites. Perhaps these groups saw any change in racial composition as a change for the better.

Although the preceding results are encouraging, they do not ensure that simply bringing together Whites and Blacks with similar values will bring about social acceptance. As Triandis (1961) and Stein et al. (1965) point out, in the majority of instances of racial discrimination, the White person does not inquire into the beliefs and values of the Black to determine whether they are congruent or incongruent with her or his own.[6] Rather, the typical White person, with no further information, makes the assumption that the Black's values are different (Stein et al., 1965; Byrne & Wong, 1962). In fact, a highly racist White person may *want* to believe that Blacks have different values from his or her own; such beliefs serve as a justification for the White person's prejudice and discrimination. Indeed, Byrne and Wong (1962) found that strongly anti-Black subjects assumed more dissimilarity than did less prejudiced subjects.

---

[6]In actuality, the White may not elicit even one area of similarity between himself and the Black. It should be recognized that in the majority of studies reviewed here, between 10 and 20 statements of belief similarity were used. In other words, the manipulations of *race* and *belief similarity* may not have been of the same magnitude (Ashmore, 1970). In fact, Triandis (1961), found that when belief similarity was introduced through one sentence only, race was a stronger determinant. A study that manipulated race and belief similarity by having subjects watch videotapes (Hendrick, Bixenstine, & Hawkins, 1971) found strong effects from belief similarity but weak effects from race similarity.

Thus, those responsible for desegregating schools, offices, and unions need to introduce procedures by which Whites can learn that many of their Black colleagues possess the same aspirations and values that they do. Our avoidance of others of a different race may be reduced when we come to realize that their differences from us are only skin deep.

VI. Attitudes as predictors of behavior

A. Are attitudes predispositions to action?

As we have indicated, no concept is more central to social psychology than the concept of *attitude*. But why study attitudes? Why invest all this energy in the study of a hypothetical, underlying construct? Social psychologists may offer two reasons: First, attitudes are presumed to be related to a variety of behaviors and actions. Second, attitudes—as a construct—are worthy of study for their own sake (Kelman, 1974).

Many definitions propose that an attitude is a predisposition to behave, that it is a cause of behavior. Students of attitude change make this assumption; A. R. Cohen, for example, has written

> Most of the investigators whose work we have examined make the broad psychological assumption that since attitudes are evaluative predispositions, they have consequences for the way people act toward others, for the program they actually undertake, and for the manner in which they carry them out. Thus attitudes are always seen as precursors of behavior, as determinants of how a person will actually behave in his daily affairs [1964, pp. 137–138].

Currently the assumption that attitudes are important is being challenged. In psychotherapy the heightened interest in behavior modification reflects a belief that underlying dispositions such

as attitudes, values, and motives are irrelevant in the task of changing behavior. Beyond that, several reviews that appeared about the same time (Kiesler, Collins, & Miller, 1969; Wicker, 1969a; Brigham, 1971a) showed that there was no one-to-one correspondence between expressed attitude and subsequent behavior.

You will recall that at the beginning of this chapter we quoted Gordon Allport's statement that the concept of *attitude* is the "primary building stone in the edifice of social psychology." What if attitudes have nothing to do with determining behavior? "That's the way the edifice crumbles," the critics might say. Should we discard the attitude concept? Before doing so, we need to look carefully at the evidence. Is there a relationship between one's attitudes and one's behavior?

Unfortunately, the picture is not at all consistent. Some attitude constructs frequently predict behavior. For example, authoritarian attitudes are related to behavior in a variety of settings (Izzett, 1971; H. Smith & Rosen, 1958; Martin & Westie, 1959). Subjects who are high scorers on the California F scale (an attitude measure) are more likely to vote for conservative political candidates, to raise their children in a traditional, authoritarian manner, to prefer more regimented and less democratic leadership on their job, and to perceive others as having the same feelings as themselves. However, when we turn to the topics of prejudice, discrimination, and racism, some studies appear to show little consistency between attitudes and behavior. The classic study used by critics as "evidence" for inconsistency was done by Richard LaPiere, back in 1934. At that time there were strong feelings against Orientals in the United States, particularly along the West Coast. LaPiere, a highly mobile sociologist, took a Chinese couple on a three-month automobile trip—twice across the United States and up and down the West Coast. The three stopped at 250 hotels and restaurants and only once were refused service. Later LaPiere wrote each of these places, asking if they would accept Chinese patrons. Only about one-half of the proprietors bothered to answer; but, of these, 90% indicated that they would not serve Chinese! La-Piere's study has generally been interpreted as an indication that prejudiced attitudes (either the failure to respond or a negative response to the letter) do not predict the extent of actual discriminatory behavior (refusal to serve Chinese patrons). ↓ criticisms of ↑

But there are a number of justified criticisms of such a conclusion. First, we do not even know whether the person who admitted the Chinese couple was also the person who answered the letter (Triandis, 1971). Second, we should question whether the LaPiere study was even tapping prejudice; instead, we believe his study related two types of role behavior. Dillehay has written eloquently on this view: "the LaPiere [study] compared role behavior of one kind with role behavior of another kind, probably entailing a different actor. There is no measure of attitude at all. What connects these behaviors is plainly seen when we note that the unit sampled is suprapersonal, the establishment rather than the individual" (Dillehay, 1973, p. 888).

Another way of explaining the discrepancies in LaPiere's study uses a *threshold analysis*. In this approach D. T. Campbell (1963) proposed that an attitude may serve as a mediator for both verbal responses and behavioral responses. *But*, as Wicker has stated, "the way the attitude is manifested may depend upon certain situational pressures" (1969a, p. 44). A restaurant proprietor's attitude may be anti-Black, but it may be harder for him or her to refuse a Black couple who actually appears at the restaurant entrance than to refuse a telephone request for a reservation. The inconsistency in LaPiere's findings is removed through the concept of thresholds or hurdles. According to Campbell, LaPiere's findings indicate that the majority of restaurant and hotel managers who accepted the Chinese couple but refused the mailed request possess moderate levels of prejudice—enough to get over one hurdle (mailed request) but not enough to get over the other (face-to-face confrontation). While the notion is an intriguing one, it has problems;

Wicker reports one study (Linn, 1965) in which there was more rejection of minority-group members in a face-to-face situation than there was symbolic rejection. Apparently the hurdles were reversed.

Thus we are less than eager to accept LaPiere's study as a prototype. Nor are we willing to accept the results of a similar, later study as showing the lack of a relationship between attitudes and behavior. Kutner, Wilkins, and Yarrow (1952), using a procedure similar to LaPiere's but employing one Black and two White females in the Northeastern part of the United States, obtained similar results. In each of 11 restaurants the Black woman was admitted and the service was described as "exemplary." But when letters were sent later asking for reservations for an interracial party, no replies were received. Subsequent telephone calls elicited a grudging reservation from five restaurants and a refusal from six. When control calls were made to each of these restaurants—calls that did not mention the race of the guests—10 of the 11 restaurants immediately accepted the reservations. Again, behavior toward an individual minority-group member who was physically present was inconsistent with behavior in response to a written request, but *attitudes* were not really assessed (Dillehay, 1973).

More recent studies have related the responses on paper-and-pencil measures of prejudice to actual behavior in an interracial situation. For example, J. A. Green (1968) posed as a representative of a publishing firm and told students at the University of Colorado that his company needed to take photographs to be included in new textbooks. Subjects were shown the poses that were planned for the photographs; these poses always included two persons, but they varied in intimacy, ranging from "equality in a public situation" to "a fairly intimate heterosexual relationship." For each pose there was one version in which both figures were White, and another version in which one figure was a Black, one White. Subjects were asked to indicate how willing they were to pose; if they were willing, they were instructed to sign a "photograph release form." (The willingness of subjects to pose in photographs with Blacks, as a measure of behavior, was apparently developed by deFleur and Westie, 1958.) One other variable was manipulated in Green's study—the release forms differed in specifications for subsequent uses of the photographs. In one case, the photographs would be used only in a Peace Corps textbook in underdeveloped countries miles and miles away from the United States; in another case they were to be used in a popular magazine article dealing with U.S. Peace Corps textbooks. The dependent variable was the extent to which the subject's response to all-White and White-Black versions of the poses differed. A week later all subjects completed the racial attitude scale developed by Woodmansee and Cook. The behavioral responses were compared for subjects who, according to the attitude scale, were either moderately favorable toward Blacks or moderately unfavorable. The results indicated that the paper-and-pencil measure of attitude was related to behavior on the photograph release form; subjects with favorable attitudes were more willing to be photographed with Blacks than were subjects with unfavorable attitudes. The correlation between attitudes and the acceptability of the behavioral index was +.43.

Participation in a civil-rights discussion was related to attitudes toward Blacks in a study by Fendrich (1967). Subjects individually completed a scale of attitudes toward Blacks and a measure of "commitment" or willingness to interact with Blacks. They also indicated whether or not they would be "willing to attend small group discussions with members of the NAACP that were scheduled in the near future" (1967, p. 352). Subjects were subsequently contacted and invited to a meeting. If they attended the meeting, they were asked at the end of the discussion to sign up for work on civil-rights projects. Thus a behavioral measure was available, which included four points: unwillingness to attend meetings, expressed willingness but failure to attend, atten-

dance only, and attendance plus signing up for further activities. Fendrich reports that when subjects indicated their degree of commitment before completing the attitude scale, there was a strong relationship between the subject's attitude and the degree of willingness to participate in civil-rights discussions. As Wicker (1969a) indicates, however, there are limitations in Fendrich's study—first, the attitude scale, commitment measure, and initial reaction to attending the NAACP discussion were all collected individually and at the same time. Second, pressures toward social desirability might have been a factor. And third, it is unclear whether the initial interviewer was the person who later contacted the subject and led the discussion group. However, the results of these studies by Green and Fendrich are typical of those relating a paper-and-pencil measure of attitude to behavior; they find that a substantial relationship exists.

More recent studies using behaviors in a real-life context are not consistent with these. For example, in a study also described in Chapter 4, Weitz (1972) simulated an interracial encounter in which White subjects (summer-school students at Harvard University) expected to interact with a Black or a White. Weitz obtained both attitudes (through the use of paper-and-pencil measures) and behaviors (including how close the subject sat to a Black and the intimacy of working tasks selected); in addition, she had the voice tone of subjects rated. Each subject was told to read instructions to the other participant, who was either Black or White. Weitz found that whereas the attitude responses indicated friendliness, the behavioral responses reflected rejection of Blacks. In fact, there was a *negative* correlation between the friendliness of the subject's attitude and his voice tone and behavior toward the Black. Weitz concludes: "It appears that these subjects [those with the *most* extreme favorable attitudes] were repressing negative or conflictive affect toward Blacks by overreacting in the positive direction on the verbal measure—the 'doth protest too much' syndrome" (1972, p. 17).

An implication of Weitz's study is that some people with liberal attitudes in regard to racial acceptance do not show such acceptance in their behavior. Apparently a self-concept of being unprejudiced is important for many people; they have to dissociate their negative feelings toward minority groups from their self-image (Gaertner, 1974). They develop "racially appropriate" responses; they misperceive others. Kovel called this type of person an *aversive racist*, "the type who believes in white race superiority and is more or less aware of it but does nothing about it. An intrapsychic battle goes on between these sentiments and a conscience which seeks to repudiate them, or at least to prevent the person from acting wrongly upon them" (Kovel, 1970, p. 54).

It follows that the aversive racist tries to avoid contact with minority group members, but when contact is unavoidable, his or her manner is—like that of some of Weitz's subjects—polite, correct, but cold (Gaertner, 1974). Some aversive racists may even engage in efforts to improve the condition of the minorities—after all, they see themselves as liberals—but such efforts at reform are impersonal, remote actions that preclude contacting Blacks intimately.

Evidence for Kovel's analysis comes from a field study by Gaertner (1973) that assessed the likelihood of White liberals and White conservatives helping a Black or White person. See Figure 10-11 for the description and findings of this study.

B. Why don't attitudes predict behavior more consistently?

There are two distinguishable reasons why the relationship between attitudes and behavior is not always strong or even consistent. The first of these assumes that such a relationship does exist but is watered down by other factors. The second explanation rejects the very existence of the traditional relationship. We shall consider these explanations in order.

The "watered down" theory. If the subsequent notions hold true, it may be possible that in a controlled situation attitudes will not predispose behavior. In other words, because of these factors, the relationship between attitudes and behavior will be watered down.

1. A person's responses to general objects may vary from his or her responses to specific objects. The purpose of an attitude scale is to measure attitudes toward a minority group. Thus, the object is highly general. Behavioral measures, however, often deal with reactions to a specific person who is a member of that group. It may be "unlikely that the subject's beliefs about [or actions toward] the particular Negroes he comes into contact with are similar to his beliefs about Negroes in general" (Fishbein, 1966, p. 206). For example, inconsistencies or stimulus dissimilarities between a restaurant proprietor's stereotype of Chinese and a Chinese couple's actual appearance in the restaurant may have contributed to LaPiere's finding.

2. Behavior is complex and multidetermined. Suppose an elderly man tells his friend that "the less contact he has with Blacks the better" and then boards a bus. Noting that all the seats but one are occupied, the man takes the available one—next to a Black. We cannot conclude that his verbal statement is false just because his choice of seats has repudiated it. Rather, we must recognize that even the apparently simple action of taking a seat is multi-determined. While it may be upsetting for the old man to sit next to a Black, his feet may hurt him so much that sitting under any conditions is more tolerable than standing. On this point Norman Weissberg has written "An attitude, no matter how conceived, is simply one of the terms in the complex regression equation we use to predict behavior; we cannot expect it to do too much. I think we must take seriously Lewin's formula that Behavior = f (Person, Environment). If the latent variable [attitude] is conceived inside [the person] one still needs to know the specific nature of the environment, the form

purpose of attitude scale.

Figure 10-11
Liberals and conservatives—Who helps Blacks more?

Social psychologist Samuel L. Gaertner (1973) tested the relationship between attitudes and behavior among members of the Liberal and Conservative parties in New York State. Each person received an apparent wrong-number telephone call, which quickly developed into a request for assistance. The caller, who was clearly identifiable by his voice characteristics as being either Black or White, explained that he was trying to reach his mechanic from a public phone booth located on the parkway, because his car had broken down. The caller further reported that he had no more change with which to make another phone call to the garage. Could the other person call his garage for him?

If the subject agreed to help, the caller gave him the phone number of the garage to call. If the subject refused to help or hung up after the caller stated "That was my last dime," a *No-Help* response was recorded. If the subject hung up before the word *dime* was said, a *Premature Hang-Up* response was scored and treated as a separate category from *Helping* and *No-Helping* responses.

If we exclude the category of *Premature Hang-Ups* from the results, we find that Conservative Party members discriminated against the Black victim to a greater extent than Liberal Party members did, in a sense. Conservatives were more likely than Liberals to help a White caller (92% versus 76%), but *both groups* were less responsive to Black callers (about 65% of Conservatives and 64% of Liberals helped). Using the greater difference in response rates of conservatives, Gaertner (1973) concluded that in a situation in which help had been solicited, "Conservatives discriminated against Blacks to a greater extent than Liberals did, supporting previous findings that political and economic conservatism is positively related to more extreme anti-Black attitudes" (1973, p. 339). But he also notes that this occurred only when the subjects obtained enough information to realize that their assistance was being requested. Actually, a number of respondents hung up before that, and significantly more Liberals than Conservatives hung up on the Black caller (17% versus 8%).

Thus the usual claim that Liberals harbor less anti-Black sentiment than Conservatives is not wholly supported. In fact, consistent with the concept of aversive racism, Gaertner suggests that the anti-Black attitudes of liberals differ qualitatively rather than quantitatively from the racial attitudes of conservatives. It is in situations in which there are few norms to guide behavior—such as hanging up after informing a caller of his wrong number—that the aversive-racist feelings lead to discriminatory behavior.

of the function relating P and E, and their interactions with the one under consideration before one can accurately predict behavior" (1965, p. 424). In addition, the reliability of behavioral measures is often unknown. Strenuous efforts to develop reliable measures of attitudes are wasted if they are used in conjunction with crude and unreliable measures of behavior. Note that, in the example, the old man has only two possible choices (unless he decides to wait for the next bus): he can either stand or he can sit next to a Black. If he is forced to choose on repeated trips, how consistent will his responses be? Per-

haps, if his strong anti-Black attitudes are a determinant, he will quit taking that particular bus. In short, one-shot measures of behavior do not give us much information.

3. Among the complex determinants of behavior are more than one attitude. The relationship between behavior and a single attitude may appear inconsistent because other attitudes have greater influence (Wicker, 1969a; Cook & Selltiz, 1964). In one study, Insko and Schopler (1967) used a person whose attitudes were favorable to the civil-rights movement but who refused to contribute money to the movement. Perhaps this

person has stronger attitudes about caring for the needs of his or her family, maintaining a good credit rating, and the like. Understanding the competing role of different attitude domains may facilitate future prediction of behavior. Other personal characteristics, such as motives, interests, abilities, and activity levels, also influence behavior.

4. Situational factors also influence behavior. A direct relationship between an attitude and behavior may be possible only when situational conditions permit. An excellent example of this was described in Chapter 4, regarding Machiavellianism. We might initially expect that the behavior of highly Machiavellian subjects would be different from the behavior of subjects with less Machiavellian attitudes in *any* competitive interpersonal situation. But Christie and Geis (1970) found that this was not the case. A careful taxonomy of the interpersonal situations in 50 studies enabled Christie and Geis to specify with a high degree of accuracy those situations in which the attitude-behavior relationship would be significant. For example, if opportunities to communicate in a competitive task were limited to binary choices and no superfluous conversation was allowed, highly Machiavellian subjects were no more successful in the task than those low in Machiavellianism. But when the latitude for communication was broader, high Machiavellians improvised more and behaved more successfully—that is, won more money, achieved higher scores, and so on.

All these reasons tend to diminish the obtained relationship between attitudes and behavior. But they do not mean that we should accept a claim that there is no relationship between attitudes and behavior or throw up our hands in despair over the task of predicting behavior on the basis of internal states. Instead we should seek explanations that take into account the complexities of the relationship. Icek Ajzen and Martin Fishbein (1969, 1970, 1972; Fishbein & Ajzen, 1975) have done so, using a model in which the person's attitude toward the act and his or her

normative beliefs about the desirability of the act become predictors of the person's behavior (actually of the behavioral intention). Allan Wicker (1971) has chosen to focus on other variables that may strengthen the attitude-behavior relationship, specifically the person's perceptions of the consequences of his or her act.

Rejections of the traditional relationship: Cognitive dissonance and self-perception. Daryl Bem (1967, 1970, 1972b) has proposed the radical idea that behavior causes attitudes. There are antecedents to this notion in the theory of cognitive dissonance (Festinger, 1957), which deals with cases in which a person recognizes that two of his or her attitudes and/or behaviors are in conflict. If the individual believes that cigarette smoking causes cancer and yet smokes three packs a day, cognitive dissonance exists. If a man considers himself a thoughtful person and then forgets his fiancée's birthday, he seeks to resolve the contradiction. An essential aspect of cognitive-dissonance theory is its prediction that a person is motivated to remove any dissonance that exists as a result of conflicting attitudes or behaviors.

As we shall see in the next chapter, a nonobvious quality of cognitive-dissonance theory has attracted to it a number of social psychologists. An obvious prediction would be that the greater the reward for advocating a public position that contradicts one's private attitude, the more change there will be toward the public position. But in a number of studies, greater shifts in attitude toward a public position occurred when the rewards were *less*. Thus, cognitive-dissonance theory says that under certain conditions, public behavior causes shifts in private attitudes. Choosing to sit next to a Black on the bus every day may actually cause our foot-weary old man's prejudice to decrease.

As indicated, Daryl Bem has proposed an even more radical notion in his self-perception theory: attitudes do not cause behavior—behavior causes attitudes. As Bem sees it, the most important cues we get about the internal states of other people come from observing their behavior. We judge the feelings of others on the basis of their actions. It is the same with ourselves; to Bem, we infer our own attitudes about an object from the way we behave toward it. We do not eat brown bread because we like it; rather, we like it because we eat it.

A commercial on television has someone proclaiming "I hate Listerine but I use it!" Since this seems to contradict Bem's theory, perhaps we should examine the evidence for his notion. Bandler, Madaras, and Bem (1968) hired volunteer subjects to undergo a series of electric shocks. Before administering some shocks, the experimenters told the subject that they preferred him to escape the shock—in other words, the experimenters wanted the subject to terminate the shock after it came on. Other subjects were told that the experimenters preferred them to endure the shock to its end. However, it was emphasized that on every trial the subject's choice to endure or escape the shock was his own decision, regardless of the experimenters' preferences. After each shock, subjects rated the degree of discomfort on a 7-point scale; although they did not know it, all shocks were actually of equal intensity. Bem (1970, 1972b) concluded that the results supported self-perception theory: shocks were rated significantly more uncomfortable when the subject escaped them than when he endured them. In other words, the behavior of terminating or enduring shocks caused the perception of the intensity of the shock.

C. Attitudes and behavior— Mutual cause and effect

Cognitive-dissonance and self-perception theories have added a healthy impetus to a needed reconsideration of the relationship between attitudes and behavior. It may be, as these theories claim, that behavior changes or even forms attitudes. But observations of behavior are not the sole cues to self-knowledge; internal factors also make a contribution (deCharms, 1968;

R. Jones, 1970), and prior attitudes may predispose behavior. There is no reason why the process cannot be one in which attitudes and behaviors have effects on one another. In the case of mutual cause and effect, the definition of attitudes as predispositions to behavior is too limited. Attitudes are also dependent variables that are important to study for their own sake.

VII. Summary

An attitude is not observable but, rather, acts as an underlying construct. Its essential characteristics are that it has an object, is evaluative, and is relatively enduring. Attitudes may differ in regard to the degree of their complexity. Highly simplex attitudes are undifferentiated, lacking in qualifications, and largely evaluative. Complex attitudes contain many elements, which may or may not be consonant with each other.

Prejudice refers to an attitude; *discrimination* refers to behavior. Prejudice is defined as an evaluative attitude about a member of a racial, ethnic, or other group that results from the object's membership in that group.

Prejudice may well be universal in the sense that in competitive societies distinctions between groups will always be made on the basis of some characteristics. However, the extent of socially undesirable discrimination can be reduced greatly, and socially undesirable aspects of prejudice can be reduced significantly.

Theories about the causes of prejudice make a distinction between the prejudice existing in the society at large and the degree of prejudice held by different individuals. The *historical emphasis* hypothesizes that prejudice is often a result of traditions and relationships that have existed for generations. Economic exploitation of less powerful racial and ethnic groups is advanced as one cause of prejudice.

Sociologists and anthropologists emphasize *sociocultural factors* as causes of prejudice. Among these are increased urbanization, the competition for scarce jobs, and changes in the functions of the family.

The *situational emphasis* states that prejudice is caused by current forces in the environment.

Psychodynamic theories of the causes of prejudice posit that it results from personal conflicts and maladjustments within the prejudiced person. Among specific factors are low frustration tolerance, authoritarianism, and personality deficit.

The *phenomenological emphasis* argues that a person's perceptions of his environment are of crucial importance in understanding his behavior.

With regard to interpersonal contact in less intimate social situations, most persons prefer to be with those who possess similar values, regardless of race. In more intimate social situations, such as dating or dining together, both racial similarity and similarity in values have an influence on a person's choice of companions.

An attitude may be a predisposition to behavior, but behaviors can also influence attitudes.

I. Attitude change and nonchange
II. Stimulus-response and reinforcement theories of attitude change
   A. Basic position
   B. Assumptions about human nature
   C. Representative research
   D. Applications of stimulus-response and reinforcement theories to attitude-change procedures

III. The social-judgment theory of attitude change
   A. Basic concepts in assimilation-contrast theory
   B. Assumptions about human nature
   C. Representative research
   D. Applications of the assimilation-contrast theory to attitude-change procedures

IV. Consistency theories of attitude change
   A. Heider's balance theory
   B. Osgood and Tannenbaum's congruity theory
   C. Festinger's cognitive-dissonance theory
   D. Reactance theory: The "the-grass-is-always-greener-on-the-other-side-of-the-fence" phenomenon
   E. Explaining attitude change through each consistency theory
   F. Assumptions about human nature
   G. Representative research
   H. Applications of consistency theories to attitude-change procedures

V. Self-perception theory
   A. Basic perspective
   B. Assumptions about human nature
   C. Representative research
   D. Applications of self-perception theory to attitude-change procedures

VI. Functional theories of attitude change
   A. Applications of the theory to attitude-change procedures
   B. Assumptions about human nature
   C. Representative research
   D. Evaluation

VII. The future of theories of attitude change
VIII. Summary

Theories of attitude change

11

In a *Peanuts* cartoon of several years ago, a little boy is sitting on a stoop next to a little girl. "Wouldn't you like to have your life to live over, knowing what you know now?" he asks her. After thinking it over, she replies "What do I know now?"

The need to understand how attitudes are formed and changed reflects what has recently been a major preoccupation of social psychologists. A knowledgable commentator on the field, William McGuire (1966), has estimated that one-fourth of the material in social-psychology textbooks deals with attitudes and attitude change. But this preoccupation of social psychologists can be justified by looking at the all-too-abundant attempts that are made to change our attitudes.

Consider, for example, a few brief moments in the life of a young woman named Joan O'Malley. It is a dreary Monday morning. Joan drags herself out of bed and flips on the television. She hopes the early morning program will provide some entertaining piece of news to share with everybody at the office. Instead, a commercial praises a new hair rinse that will transform one into the essence of charm, popularity, and sexuality. That's the last thing she needs, Joan thinks—to heighten her "sexuality." The phone jangles—it is Ernie, still trying to convince her to go away with him for the weekend. But Joan is resistant; she has never done that before. She finally terminates the conversation by telling him that she will see him at lunch and discuss it

further then. She sighs for a moment, then quickly prepares her breakfast, swallows her soggy cornflakes, and scans the front page of the newspaper. The headlines tell of efforts to stop the President from vetoing an appropriation for new jobs. Joan wonders whether the President will be affected. As she leaves for work, her mail arrives, but it is nothing but some throwaway ads.

If Joan O'Malley had nothing else to do all day, she might be able to keep an accurate count of the number of efforts made to change her attitudes or behavior. On this dreary morning, she has already been inundated by advertisements emanating from several media—even including the cereal box! It certainly seems to her that every story in the newspaper is concerned with changing attitudes or behavior—whether it be about pressures on the President, a local lawsuit to bring about further school desegregation, or Arab terrorists' threats to destroy a hijacked plane unless their demands are met. And then there is always Ernie and his constant efforts.

When we consider these events as typical of the ever-present assaults upon our sensibilities, it is no wonder that social psychologists

351

have taken an inordinate interest in attitude change. Especially during the 1960s, theories of attitude change proliferated, and several long and detailed books appeared, some of which dealt with only one theory (for example, S. Feldman, 1966; Abelson, Aronson, McGuire, Newcomb, Rosenberg, and Tannenbaum, 1968).

Despite the information overkill provided us by these books and hundreds of research articles, we are still a long way from understanding the dynamics of attitude change. There are a number of theories of how attitude change takes place, but each theory has a different focus and hence explains only certain cases of attitude change. It may well be, as Zimbardo and Ebbesen claim, that theorists and researchers studying attitude change are not primarily concerned with changing attitudes. Rather, perhaps their major interest is in "using the attitude change paradigm to study basic psychological processes and the operation of theoretically relevant variables" (1969, p. v).

It is also true that much of our knowledge of attitude change stems from studies done outside the framework of *any* theory. For example, if a company hires a new employee who is very anti-Black, we know what working conditions can be used to change this employee's attitude. We can specify five different aspects of his or her job that are likely to bring about favorable change. The fact that this knowledge has been gleaned largely from field observations rather than theory-testing investigations does not make it useless. Yet the area of attitude change has a rather schizoid character. On one side, there are the theories and laboratory research; on the other side are programs of field research on real-world topics, such as the effects of advertising, propaganda, and attempts to reduce prejudice or pollution. Because of this division, and because of the vast importance of the issue, we shall devote two chapters to attitude change. (Chapter 4, on impression management; Chapter 8, on moral judgments and behavior; Chapter 10, on attitudes and behavior; Chapter 13, on changing social institutions; Chapter 19, on conformity;

and Chapter 20, on leadership, are also relevant to attitude change.) In the present chapter, we shall compare theories and explore how each theory would try to bring about change in the same real-world situation. Because each major theory makes different assumptions and emphasizes different aspects of the process of attitude change, we shall describe the basic concepts and typical research of each theory before examining its application to an actual situation.

The theories to be described may be related to the five basic orientations presented in Chapter 1. The first, *stimulus-response and reinforcement theory*, is of course a reflection of the orientation also bearing that name. The second and third, the *social-judgment theory* and *consistency theory*, are outgrowths of Gestalt theory and field theory. The fourth, *self-perception theory*, is a radical-behaviorist or Skinnerian response to consistency theory; that is, it emphasizes the conceptualization that behavior change is an impetus to attitude change, rather than the reverse. The fifth theory of attitude change, *functional theory*, is an eclectic one, although it draws mainly upon psychoanalytic theory and other orientations that emphasize personal needs.

I. Attitude change and nonchange

We are all like Joan O'Malley, in that we are all constantly bombarded with appeals to change our attitudes. Any adequate theory of attitude change should be able to predict which attitudes will *not* change in response to a particular appeal. In other words, the theory must deal with failures to change as well as with change. Any adequate theory of attitude change also needs to possess theoretical constructs that can be translated into clear operational terms. As an example, suppose that our task is to reduce the degree of prejudice expressed by college-aged White persons who are strongly anti-Black. Let us assume that each of a group of prejudiced White males has been hired for the summer to work for pay on a science project. Unbeknown to the prejudiced Whites, each will be working in a small group composed of himself, one other White person who is unprejudiced, and one Black. How should we construct the task and the work environment in order to bring about the desired reduction in prejudice? Can the experimenter make any effective variations at all, if the work environment does not meet the needs of the prejudiced White?

Attitude change may also occur without the presence of any deliberate attempts to bring about a change. For example, as we saw in Chapter 3 in regard to philosophies of human nature, exposure to new knowledge about the world or specific persons may cause us to change our attitudes. Does the knowledge that a famous professional football player has been arrested for exposing himself in front of little girls decrease our adoration of him? When the wife of the President of the United States says she would not be surprised if her daughter were to have a premarital affair, do some of her supporters abandon their allegiance? Any adequate attitude-change theory should be able to predict how individuals' attitudes about an attitude object are changed (or not changed) as a result of gaining new information about that attitude object.

Attitude-change theories reflect assumptions about human nature. By specifying how they propose the process of change occurs, they are forced to make certain decisions about the human condition. Do people have a strong need to make their separate attitudes consistent with each other? Does a person's attitude change only if the new attitude is more personally profitable? Or may we think of attitudes as secondary to behavior, in that we use our behavior as a guide to what our attitudes are and change our attitudes so that they are congruent with our behavior? By looking at the assumptions held by each theory, we can compare each with our own conceptions of human nature and with the information we have about human behavior. Bearing these considerations in mind, let us examine the first type of attitude-change theory.

Figure 11-1
We are all constantly bombarded with attempts to change our attitudes. (Photos by Jim Pinckney.)

II. Stimulus-response and reinforcement theories of attitude change

A. Basic position

As indicated in Chapter 1, stimulus-response theory focuses on the relationship of specific stimuli and responses to them. Behavior is analyzed by being broken down into units of habits and other separable responses. A response is more likely to be made again if it is reinforced (rewarded). It follows from this analysis that a stimulus-response theory of attitude change should place great emphasis on the characteristics of the communications (messages, appeals, and so on) that attempt to change our attitudes.

As a matter of fact, the stimulus-response approach does place greater emphasis on the **stimulus** qualities of a communication than do other theories. The characteristics of the communicator (the source) and of the audience are considered as well as the content of a communication. One of the contemporary applications of this approach to attitude change derives from the Yale University Communication Research Program, where, during the 1950s, Carl Hovland and his colleagues sought to quantify the stimulus and response characteristics of each communication situation.

For example, Hovland, Janis, and Kelley (1953) postulated that the process of attitude change resembled the process of learning, and that the principles applicable to acquiring verbal and motor skills could also be used to understand attitude formation and change. In the learning of new attitudes three variables are hence important: *attention, comprehension,* and *acceptance.* (The relationship of these processes is illustrated in Figure 11-2.) Before an appeal or a communication can bring about attitude change, it must be noticed or attended to. But even when the appeal *is* noticed, it may not be effective. For example, the recipient may be unable to comprehend or assimilate the communication. Thus, efforts must be made to make sure the message has been correctly comprehended. A third step, acceptance, must be achieved before attitude change can take place. The degree of acceptance is related to the incentives; to quote Insko, "The persuasive communications may provide incentives in the form of arguments or reasons why the advocated point of view should be accepted, or the persuasive communication may arouse expectations of phenomena that are reinforcing (incentives) or that in the past have been associated

[margin note: any event (internal or external) that brings about a change in behavior.]

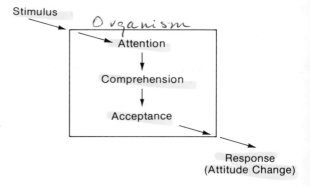

Figure 11-2
Steps in the attitude-change process, according to the Hovland-Janis-Kelley model

with reinforcement" (1967, p. 14).[1] More than any other approach, the stimulus-response and reinforcement theories see as basic this assumption that *attitudes are changed only if the incentives for making a new response are greater than the incentives for making the old response.*

A major contribution of stimulus-response and reinforcement theories is the specification of aspects that may influence the acceptance of the persuasive communication. These aspects include (1) the communication stimuli (its content, its arguments or appeals), (2) the characteristics of the source, and (3) the setting in which the person is exposed to the communication—"including, for example, the way in which other members of the audience respond" (Kiesler, Collins, & Miller, 1969, p. 106). This analysis has led to the following types of research questions:

1. How does the source of the persuasive communication affect attitude change? For example, if the source is highly believable or authoritative, is there more attitude change than if the source is untrustworthy?

---

[1]From *Theories of Attitude Change,* by C. A. Insko. Copyright 1967. This and all other quotes from this source are reprinted by permission of Prentice-Hall, Inc., Englewood Cliffs, New Jersey.

2. If a salesman is trying to convince you to adopt his point of view, should he review both sides or present only his own side of an argument?

3. Does the order of presentation make any difference? For example, if I am required to present both sides of an argument to you, should I present the side I am advocating at the beginning or save it for last? (This is known as the primacy-recency issue.)

The Yale Communication Research Program generated a great deal of research on these aspects of a persuasive communication; we shall describe the findings in Chapter 12, when we deal with the outcomes of attempts to change attitudes.

B. Assumptions about human nature

It has become fashionable to state that stimulus-response and reinforcement theories assume that humans respond to stimuli in a rather passive, robot-like fashion. A careful reading would indicate, however, that such a notion does not represent S-R theory fairly. For example, the Yale Communication Research Program recognized that the recipient must attend to and comprehend a stimulus before his or her attitude can be changed by it. While it is true that researchers using the S-R approach have primarily been interested in aspects of the stimulus and the communicator, they also recognize that the recipient's characteristics can influence the extent of attitude change. Contemporary S-R theories are more often S-O-R theories, in that they recognize the place of the *organism* that intervenes between stimulus and response.

Basic to S-R and reinforcement approaches is the notion that incentives for change must be stronger than incentives for maintaining the status quo. Behind this notion may be a recognition of each person's *individuality*, in the sense that to predict the person's response, his or her past

history of reinforcements must be understood and accounted for. Beyond this, there is an assumption that if the past history of reinforcements is known by the communicator, it can be used to manipulate the recipient's attitudes. Reinforcement theorists claim that if they had enough information about the recipients and if they had the resources at hand, they could bring about attitude change in every recipient through the same general techniques.

C. Representative research

Research employing reinforcement approaches to attitude change has been frequent and varied. In exploring aspects of communication, this approach has studied the effect of *verbal reinforcement* on attitude change. A typical study in that genre will be reviewed here.

In ordinary conversation, expressions of some of our most heartfelt attitudes fall on deaf ears. When we express other attitudes, they evoke an enthusiastic response from our listeners, such as "You're so right!" or "I wish I'd said that!" Are those statements that are verbally reinforced more likely to be made in the future? Does a positive reaction from others tend to entrench a statement in our repertory of beliefs?

Insko (1965) set out to determine if the attitudes of students at the University of Hawaii could be modified by verbal reinforcement during a telephone conversation. Students were phoned by an interviewer who sought their opinions about Aloha Week (a set of festivities held every fall in Honolulu). The interviewer asked the student a number of questions and responded with "Good" to certain answers; by this means verbal conditioning was instituted. Previous studies have shown that if certain types of statements are verbally reinforced with a response such as "Good," the subject will make these statements more often in the future. Insko wanted to discover whether such verbal reinforcement on the telephone would have any significant effect on attitudes. Approximately one week after the telephone calls, the same students completed a Local Issues Questionnaire in their class. About two-thirds of the way through the questionnaire, they responded to an item asking for their opinions about a springtime Aloha Week. Students who had been verbally reinforced by telephone for their favorable attitudes expressed higher degrees of favorable attitudes than did control subjects. The effect of the verbal reinforcement was thus manifested in another setting a whole week later.

Verbal reinforcement has been used to modify such phenomena as wearing clothes of certain colors (Calvin, 1962), the expressing of prejudiced attitudes (Mitnick & McGinnies, 1958), adhering to certain philosophies of education (Hildum & Brown, 1956), and holding certain attitudes toward capital punishment (Ekman, 1958). In such cases, reinforcement of certain attitudes enhances the future expression of such attitudes. There are, however, limitations to such a conclusion. First of all, the verbal-reinforcement procedure causes the respondent to accentuate his or her previously held attitudes and behavior and does not concentrate on *reversing* the direction of attitudes. Second, most of the attitudes studied have been rather peripheral for the person and are not deeply held. Most University of Hawaii students are indifferent as to whether Aloha Week is held once a year, once a month, or once a century. Moreover, changes even in one's attitude toward capital punishment may occur without much investment on the part of the changer. A third limitation is that the nature of the reinforcement is unclear. Why does a verbal response such as "Good" lead to change in expressed attitudes? As Insko has stated:

> One of the least convincing aspects of reinforcement theory has to do with the explanation of how a persuasive communication supplies reinforcement for acceptance of an advocated point of view. It can be asserted that much acceptance is dependent upon the communication's arousing expectations of possible future reinforcements as a consequence of conformity to the recommended point of view, but, in general, this is not very convincing [1967, p. 63].

A fourth concern questions whether reinforcement is indeed the cause of the change in attitudes. It may be that demand characteristics were operating on the subjects in Insko's study; subjects may have expressed more favorable attitudes toward Aloha Week on the Local Issues Questionnaire because they felt they were "supposed to" rather than because any true shift in attitude had occurred (M.M. Page, 1969, 1971, 1974).

D. Applications of stimulus-response and reinforcement theories to attitude-change procedures

Consider our previous example of the strongly prejudiced male college student who will be working with a Black during the summer. What procedures would reinforcement theory advocate to reduce his prejudice? First, any expressions of acceptance by the White toward the Black should be positively reinforced. If the White student should happen to compliment the Black regarding his clothes or task skills, the other White staff members should verbally reinforce the prejudiced White for making such compliments. Also, expressions of interest or friendship and more subtle, positive responses toward the Black by the prejudiced White should elicit attention and appreciation from both of the other staff members. Verbal-conditioning research has led to increased recognition of the subtle nature of verbal reinforcement. Even nonverbal responses—a smile, an intense concentration on what the speaker is saying—are reinforcing.

Second, it must be remembered that the nature of the attitude-change process includes the three steps of attention, comprehension, and acceptance. To achieve attention, the preju-diced White must listen to what the Black is saying. One cannot simply bring the two to-gether and assume that the White will attend to anything the Black says or notice anything he does. The task should be structured so that the prejudiced White understands that paying atten-tion to the Black will be beneficial. Each member of the group might be told that he will eventually have to switch jobs with another group member. Therefore, each will benefit from paying atten-tion to what the other is doing or saying.

Next, comprehension must be achieved be-fore attitude change can occur. The elements of the situation must be understood accurately. How may we ensure that the content of the atti-tude-change attempts is comprehended? The prejudiced White may be required, as part of his job, to meet in sessions with the other White group member, while the Black group member is absent. These sessions may permit the other White, who is a confederate of the experimenter, to determine if the prejudiced White has under-stood the communications involved in the at-tempt to change attitudes. Most likely, the preju-diced White has misperceived previous discus-sions and statements. As prejudice may often develop from unmet needs or personal malad-justments, the prejudiced White is likely to twist what he hears to fit his own expectations and stereotypes. The "message" may never pass ac-curately beyond the comprehension stage, and any opportunity for the desired attitude change will be thwarted—unless checks on comprehen-sion are made and remediation is instituted.

The last step in the process of attitude change is acceptance of the content of the com-munication. Here, the concept of incentives is important. The prejudiced person must become motivated to make a new response; the appropri-ate incentives to bring this about must be iden-tified and used. The incentive for one person may be social acceptance; for another, money. Theory is of little help at this point, but the rein-forcement theorist would still emphasize that, if all these steps are achieved, attitude change is more likely to occur.

Once the prejudiced White has accepted the Black, the stimulus-response theorist would seek **stimulus generalization**—or the acceptance by the prejudiced White of Blacks in general. If verbal conditioning has been effective in es-tablishing a new response (attitude) toward the Black participant, the laws of learning predict that such stimulus generalization will take place.

but still is not real love for the Black person.

III. The social-judgment theory of attitude change

When we attempt to change a person's atti-tude, we need to consider just what the person's present attitude is. We may make the mistake of advocating too great a change, thereby causing the person to reject our appeal. But a moderate change in the person's attitude may be quite fea-sible, if we know the limits of the person's ac-ceptable attitudes. For example, a student, asked if college tuition should be raised, may say no. It would appear that his or her attitude is against *any* increase. But the student might accept a mod-est increase, although he or she would reject a large one (Rhine & Severance, 1970). Such a con-ception reflects what is called the *social-judgment theory* of attitude change.

In contrast to other approaches, the social-judgment theory of attitude change draws—in a general way—upon the principles of psychophy-sics (Eiser & Stroebe, 1972). Within this context there are two major approaches: The first is the assimilation-contrast theory, developed by M. Sherif and Hovland (1961) and revised by C. W. Sherif, M. Sherif, and Nebergall (1965) and by Hovland, Harvey, and Sherif (1957). The sec-ond is the adaptation-level theory, developed by Helson (1959, 1964; see also Appley, 1971). The assimilation-contrast theory will be examined here as an example of a social-judgment ap-proach to attitude change.

A. Basic concepts in assimilation-contrast theory

The formation of reference scales, anchors, contrast, assimilation, latitudes of acceptance and rejection, and involvement are concepts that are central to the assimilation-contrast theory of Sherif and Hovland. We consider the place of each of these in the following paragraphs.

Formation of reference scales. When a person is presented with a number of stimuli, he or she will usually form a *reference scale*, by which the person can place these stimuli along one or more dimensions. If you are going to buy a new car, you may look at and test drive five or six cars at different dealers. These cars doubtless differ in price, make, color, horsepower, maneuverability, and numerous other characteristics. You probably find yourself ordering the cars along reference scales that reflect the dimensions of greatest interest to you. You may like the gasoline economy of one car and the smooth ride of another, but you eventually establish one grand scale of relative preferences that combines all the dimensions in some way that is satisfactory to you.

Sherif and Hovland note that many stimuli do exist along a well-ordered dimension that can be agreed upon by all. Judgments of weights can be placed in order, and the order can be agreed upon by every judge—if the differences are great enough. Many social stimuli—nominees for "Best teacher on campus," for example—result in the formation of a reference scale even if the stimuli do not possess any objective order. Since such stimuli lack the objective standards of weight judgments, they are more susceptible to social influence or other considerations. You may like the "Best teacher" nominee from your own field. Your reaction to a particular car may be influenced by the fact that your good friends blanch at its color or admire its acceleration.

Anchors. Anchors often serve as the end points in a series of stimuli. For example, a prejudiced man may be willing to work on a job "with Blacks" if it means that there are two or three Blacks in a factory employing a thousand people. But if he were paired with a Black to work together closely every day, he might refuse the job. We could think of job offers that varied the intimacy of contact with Blacks as different attitude stimuli. The anchors, such as those proposed here, exert relatively greater influence on the determination of judgments than do other stimuli (Insko, 1967).

The presence of an anchor may influence judgments of other stimuli. For example, looking at Miss America or at a dream car may cause a young man to judge that his realistic alternatives to each of these stimulus objects is less attractive than he thought before. Likewise, if the young man has been without a car or a woman friend for several years, any alternative looks better than it would have otherwise.

Such anchors serve as particularly potent reference points when (1) the person has little past experience with the particular reference scale, (2) the potential range of stimuli is unknown, and (3) no explicit standards for reference are provided (Kiesler et al., 1969). Anchors are relevant to the understanding of attitude change because an attitude may be regarded as an internal anchor, and a persuasive communication may be thought of as an external anchor (Insko, 1967). Thus, the attitude-change process, in the view of Sherif and Hovland, confronts two anchors that mark the limits, between which there is a discrepancy in attitudes.

Contrast and assimilation. Contrast is a shift of an attitude away from an anchor; *assimilation* is a shift in attitude toward an anchor. When an anchor is at an extreme position—beyond the end of a series of stimuli—contrast is present. When the anchor is closer to one end of the series of stimuli, assimilation results. (See Figure 11-3 for illustration.) Insko has summarized the implications of this process as follows:

> Thus according to assimilation-contrast theory, a primary factor affecting the influence of a

persuasive communication upon attitude and opinion change is the degree of discrepancy between the position of the communication (external anchor) and the recipient's attitude or opinion (internal anchor). If the communication advocates a position that is not too discrepant from that held by the communication recipient, assimilation will result; i.e., the individual will perceive the communication as advocating a less extreme position, will favorably evaluate the communication, and will be strongly influenced. If the communication advocates a position that is highly discrepant from that held by the communication recipient, contrast will result; i.e., the individual will perceive the communication as advocating a more extreme position, will unfavorably evaluate the communication, and will be either minimally positively influenced or negatively influenced [1967, p. 67].

According to Sherif and Hovland, Insko's account is oversimplified, in that it fails to recognize the role of *latitudes of acceptance.* The important discrepancy is not the discrepancy between the communication and the attitude but the one between the communication and the latitude of acceptance. When we know a person's latitude of acceptance, we can more accurately predict the person's susceptibility to attitude change (Atkins, Deaux, & Bieri, 1967; Eagly & Telaak, 1972).

Latitudes of acceptance and rejection. According to the social-judgment theory, a person's attitude is not a single point but rather a band of acceptable positions—a latitude of acceptance. The *latitude of rejection* includes all those elements that the person finds unacceptable. (Elements could be "Best Teacher" nominees, makes of cars, or degrees of contact with Blacks, depending on the attitude under study.) An area of neutrality exists between these two bands.

Involvement. We all recognize that we are more ego involved in some of our attitudes than in others; we care deeply about some matters and care less about others. Social-judgment theory states that the size of the latitude of rejec-

tion is an indication of the amount of ego involvement in the issue (Granberg & Steele, 1974). With more ego-involving attitudes, the latitude of rejection increases in size and the latitude of noncommitment gets smaller (C. W. Sherif et al., 1965).

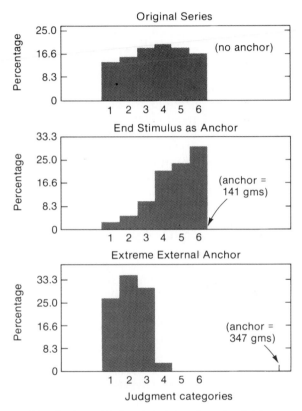

Distribution of judgments for series of weights without anchor (top) and with anchors at two distances above original series.

Figure 11-3

Judgments of weights and position of anchor. (Adapted from Sherif, Taub, & Hovland, "Assimilation and Contrast Effects of Anchoring Stimuli on Judgments," *Journal of Experimental Psychology,* 1958, 55, 150–155. Copyright 1958 by the American Psychological Association. Used by permission.)

B. Assumptions about human nature

Compared to every other theory, social-judgment theory appears to assume that more precise attitudes are held. That is, the theory holds that each person *localizes* his or her attitude at some point along a scale that includes areas of acceptance and rejection. It assumes that for each attitude we develop anchors and a degree of intensity, and hence the potential positive or negative effects of each persuasive communication can be determined. Social-judgment theory sees the human as a cognitive being, in the sense that people know what their attitudes are, where they stand along a continuum, which other attitudes they would accept, and which they would reject.

Some attitude theorists reject the notion that attitudes are precisely known or measured or can be located within latitudes of acceptance and rejection by the possessor. Abelson (1968), for example, has proposed that most people possess *opinion molecules* for most attitudes. An opinion molecule is composed of (1) a belief or fact, (2) an attitude, and (3) the perception that the attitude is socially supported. Abelson offers the following as an example of an opinion molecule: "It's a fact that when my uncle Charlie had back trouble, he was cured by a chiropractor (fact). You know, I feel that chiropractors have been sneered at too much (attitude), and I'm not ashamed to say so because I know a lot of people who feel the same way (social support)" (cited in Bem, 1970, p. 38). Opinion molecules are isolated units that serve our needs to make conversation. As such, they have little need to be precise or logical.

C. Representative research

Research done within the framework of assimilation-contrast theory has concentrated on two questions: (1) How much is attitude change influenced by the discrepancy between the communication and the recipient's position? (2) What are the effects of the latitudes of acceptance and rejection?

Effects of the discrepancy between the communication and the position of the recipient. Research on such discrepancies faces many problems. First, when experimenters vary the discrepancy between a communication and a person's position, the recipient's initial position often gets manipulated too. That is, in order to get greater discrepancies, more extreme initial attitudes may be used. Second, there is the problem of regression toward the mean. If a persuasive communication is located near the mean of possible initial positions, most persons with extreme attitudes are likely to move toward the mean on retesting. Thus, what appears to be a result of exposure to a communication may simply be an effect of this statistical artifact. A third problem is the previously mentioned possibility that persons with extreme initial positions are likely to be more ego-involved with their positions (Tittler, 1967) and, hence, have smaller latitudes of acceptance (Markley, 1971, 1972; C. W. Sherif, 1972). A fourth problem is that the entire possible range of discrepancies is not covered in all studies. Recent research is beginning to take these problems into account (C. W. Sherif, Kelly, Rodgers, Sarup, & Tittler, 1973).

A well-designed study on this topic was carried out by Bochner and Insko (1966), who examined attitudes toward amounts of sleep. What is an appropriate amount of sleep per night for the average adult? Bochner and Insko presented subjects with a three-page essay advocating that—for reasons of health and efficiency—people should reduce the number of hours they sleep each night. (It had been determined earlier that subjects in this study generally advocated about eight hours' sleep. Actually, the mean was 7.89 hours, with a standard deviation of 1.05 hours.)

One of the independent variables manipulated in Bochner and Insko's study was the degree of discrepancy between the communication's recommended amount of sleep and the subject's advocated position. This variable was manipulated by selecting subjects who had advocated eight hours' sleep and presenting different subsets of these subjects with different recommended amounts. Nine different amounts were used, from zero to eight hours per night. The recommendation of zero hours of sleep per night is farfetched, but in the present context it represents an absolute extreme point.

The degree of credibility (high versus moderate) of the communicator or source was another independent variable manipulated in Bochner and Insko's study. Half of the subjects were told that the essay on sleep had been prepared by "Sir John Eccles, Nobel prize–winning physiologist"—a highly credible source. The other half of the subjects were told that the source was "Mr. Harry J. Olsen, director of the Fort Worth YMCA"—a moderately credible source. (Data collected from a sample of the subjects indicated that the subjects did rate the physiologist as a significantly more credible source for this issue.)

Subjects' responses to these manipulations were elicited in three ways: (1) After they had read the essay, they were asked their opinion regarding the desired number of hours of sleep. (They could choose anywhere from "no sleep at all" to "ten hours per night.") (2) They were asked to evaluate the communication. (Was it "relevant," "logical," "easy to understand"?) (3) They were asked to evaluate the source. (Was he "competent," "trustworthy," "credible"?)

The effects of the variations on attitude change are reflected in Figure 11-4. Advocating smaller numbers of hours of sleep slightly changed the subject's expressed attitude—up to a point. For example, if eight hours had been advocated, the average subject chose approximately seven and one-half hours as desirable; when five hours were recommended, the subject chose a little less than seven hours. When two hours were recommended, the subject chose about six and one-half hours; but when zero hours were advocated, there was a reversal in the trend, and the average response was back to seven hours. Thus, when both conditions of source credibility are combined, there is a curvilinear reaction (though not a statistically signif-

icant one). So Bochner and Insko's study does not clearly confirm an assimilation-contrast theory of attitude change. As can be seen in Figure 11-4, when the source was highly credible, the discrepant communication was more effective in changing attitudes. That is, there was a significant interaction between source credibility and discrepancy.

Results for the other two dependent variables indicated (1) the greater the discrepancy between the subject's initial position and the position advocated by the source, the greater the subject disparaged the communication; and (2) when the YMCA director was the source and the number of hours of sleep advocated was very small, he was greatly disparaged. Such a trend was not true when the Nobel prize-winning physiologist was the source.

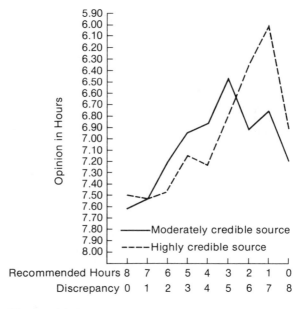

Figure 11-4

Effects of credibility of source and discrepancy of advocated position on attitude change. (From Bochner & Insko, "Communicator Discrepancy, Source Credibility, and Opinion Change," *Journal of Personality and Social Psychology*, 1966, 4, 618, Fig. 1. Copyright 1966 by the American Psychological Association. Used by permission.)

The effects of latitudes of acceptance and rejection.
Norman Miller (1965) used an elaborate manipulation with high school students to bring about ego involvement with their attitudes toward the amount of mathematics and science in the curriculum or with their attitudes toward fluoridation of public drinking water. The manipulation employed four aspects: (1) the importance of the issue was stressed; (2) social support was provided for the students' attitudes; (3) they were asked to provide reasons in support of their own attitudes; and (4) they distributed literature in support of their attitudes. The manipulation of degree of ego involvement had no great effect on the latitudes of acceptance or rejection regarding science and mathematics in the curriculum. Miller's study is damaging evidence against one of the most basic postulates of Sherif's assimilation-contrast theory.

The theory predicts that if the content of a persuasive communication is within the person's latitude of acceptance, there will be attitude change in the direction of the message content. But if the message advocates a position within the latitude of rejection, there will be either no change or a boomerang effect. While some early research (Atkins, Deaux, & Bieri, 1967; P. D. Peterson & Koulack, 1969) indicated support for this hypothesis, a later study has found that persons with a wide latitude of acceptance on a topic show greater attitude change than do people with narrow latitudes of acceptance, *even when the message advocates a position in the latitude of rejection* (Eagly & Telaak, 1972). Table 11-1 reproduces some of the materials used by Eagly and Telaak; note that the second persuasive message is an extreme one, a message that would certainly be in the latitude of rejection for persons favoring birth control. (In fact, it was so for all but 2 of the 124 University of Massachusetts students who served as subjects.) Eagly and Telaak found that persons with wide latitudes of acceptance on this issue changed their attitude in the direction of the persuasive communication, while persons with narrow or moderate latitudes of acceptance did not. It does not seem, based on these findings, that assimilation and contrast play a

role in determining our reaction to messages that are discrepant with our present attitude.

D. Applications of the assimilation-contrast theory to attitude-change procedures

As Insko (1967) indicates, applying principles of social judgment to attitude change is an intriguing possibility. We recognize that all judgments, including attitudes toward people, are made within the context of other judgments. Also, reactions to most stimuli are influenced by the nature of the immediately preceding stimuli. However, the assimilation-contrast approach appears weak in several ways. The ways that different constructs might influence each other cannot be spelled out. Insko (1967) guesses that one's perception of where a communication resides influences the evaluation given to the communication, which in turn causes attitude change. Empirical tests of the theory have found that some of its predictions are not borne out. For instance, one study (Norman Miller, 1965) showed that ego involvement does not seem to reduce the latitude of acceptance.

Despite these important limitations, we may attempt to apply the general thrust of the assimilation-contrast theory to our example of the real-life task of constructing a working situation that would facilitate a change of attitude toward Blacks. Basic to this approach would be factors such as the specification of anchors, latitudes of acceptance and rejection, and degree of ego involvement. If the assimilation-contrast theory has any validity the following guidelines would be applied:

1. The attitudes of the prejudiced White are more likely to change in the desired direction if the messages of the persuasive communications are within the subject's latitude of acceptance. Therefore, the limits of acceptance must first be determined—perhaps by questioning the subject outside of the work situation.

2. If the messages directed toward the subject fall within his latitude of rejection, the messages are very unlikely to have the desired ef-

fects. In fact, they are likely to reinforce his initial stand or even produce boomerang effects—that is, make him *more* prejudiced.

3. If the anti-Black White subject is quite ego involved in his attitude toward Blacks, his latitude of acceptance of favorable statements about Blacks is more limited. Therefore, the in-

novator of change must be particularly sensitive to this restricted range, making sure that the persuasive communications fall within the latitude of acceptance.

4. The greater the discrepancy between the persuasive communication and the position of the subject—as long as the communication is

---

Table 11-1
Sample persuasive messages and sample items for assessing the subject's own position and latitude width

Sample Persuasive Messages	*Scale Value**
An individual's sexual activity is his or her own business. The definition of morality is defined by young people today in such different ways than that of their parents, and their behavior would be no different with or without birth control products. Because this decision is such a personal thing and cannot be dictated by others, birth control products, including the pill, should be made available to people of reasonable age. In spite of the fact that our liberal society should protect the individual's rights to make such crucial decisions for himself, we cannot and should not condone birth control for youngsters. Therefore the question of birth control should be an individual decision, with such products available to young adults of reasonable age because their sexual behavior would be no different with or without artificial birth control.	3.00
Birth control is unnatural and should not be practiced. If we were meant to practice birth control we would have a built-in system to take care of such things. The world has done quite all right up to now. When you stop to think how beautiful nature is you realize birth control has no place in it. Man and woman love each other and in the process of expressing this love they create another human being who is a combination of both of them. The man protects the woman and the woman protects the unborn child. Nature has the whole thing arranged so beautifully and birth control has no place in it. Birth control in any way is unnatural and should not be practiced. If man wants to live a rich and full and beautiful life as nature intended, he should not use such artificial devices.	9.50

Sample Items	
Birth control devices should be available to everyone, and the government and public welfare agencies should encourage the use of such devices.	1.81
To curtail indiscriminate premarital sex, birth control products should be distributed by doctors to married people only.	5.78
All birth control devices should be illegal and the government should prevent them from being manufactured.	10.25

*On an 11-point scale on which 1 is the favorable and 11 the unfavorable pole.

within the acceptance limits—the more shift in the subject's position. (However, the assimilation-contrast theory does not consider individual differences in breadth of acceptance. What if our subject's latitude of acceptance is so narrow that he can only tolerate attitude positions very close to his own? There is very little opportunity for change if such conditions exist. Assimilation-contrast theory certainly dampens our optimism about achieving great changes in intensely held attitudes.)

5. The concept of anchors may be applied by considering a list of interracial behaviors that could be given to the subject. For example, he might be working in an interracial group with two Black males instead of one, or the group might be composed of himself and two Black females, or the group might be located on a predominantly Black campus. When such possibilities serve as anchors, the subject's reaction to his present situation may show greater tolerance than it would have in the absence of such anchors.

Clearly such applications must be spelled out in more detail to be of any real use—and even after that they may still prove unworkable. The main attraction of assimilation-contrast theory is its recognition of an optimum distance between the subject's attitude position and the position of the persuasive communication. If the communication is closer than this optimum point, it is less likely to move the person. If the communication is too far beyond the optimum point, it is tuned out by the subject.

IV. Consistency theories of attitude change

Perhaps attitude change results from an individual's awareness that his or her attitudes and actions are inconsistent. A man may observe himself doing things that violate some of his attitudes. The consistency approach sees this incongruity as a primary determinant of attitude change. Several consistency theories may be differentiated. Heider's balance theory has stimulated more recent developments—including Osgood and Tannenbaum's congruity theory, Brehm's reactance theory, and Festinger's cognitive-dissonance theory.

Before describing these different approaches, we need to consider how all consistency theories are similar. Each assumes that the attitude-change process is one of rationalization and that people are motivated to be and to appear consistent (Zajonc, 1960). Each theory holds that a person's awareness of his or her own inconsistency is something that cannot be tolerated. This assumption will be evaluated after the theories are described.

A. Heider's balance theory

Fritz Heider (1946, 1958) has developed conceptions about the ways people view their relationships with other people and with their environment. For simplicity, Heider has limited his analysis to two persons (P and O) and to one other entity (X), which could be an idea, a person, a thing, or an attitude object. The person P is the focus of the analysis, while O represents some other person. Heider's goal was to discover how the relationships among P, O, and X are organized in P's cognitive structure. We will concentrate our review here on one kind of relationship—the liking relationship. Heider proposed that the relationships among P, O, and X may be either balanced or unbalanced. Consider the following: P, who has spent all summer as a volunteer worker for the Republican presidential candidate, enters the state university as a freshman in the fall. He is assigned Professor O as a faculty advisor. When P meets O to plan a first-semester schedule, P observes that O is wearing a campaign button for the Democratic candidate. Will P like O? Will P think much of O's recommendations about courses to take? Will P want to take a course from O? Probably not—because P does not feel comfortable in unbalanced relationships. For example, if we let X stand for the Democratic party candidate, a balanced state exists when P likes O, P likes X, and O likes X. The only way a balanced state can exist within P's cognitive structure—as long as P dislikes X—is for P to dislike O. P can say, in effect, "Professor O is no good, which fits because he's a big supporter of candidate X."

Heider proposed that balanced states exist either when all three relations are positive (as in liking) or when two relations are negative (disliking) and one is positive. The preceding example fits the latter possibility. Of course, if P had found that his advisor was a Republican supporter and if P had come to like O, then balance theory would describe the relationship as P likes O, P likes X, and O likes X. Figure 11-5 represents the possible balanced and unbalanced states. As can be seen, unbalanced states do occur; people do like other people who differ in their attitudes toward important things. The reverse situation is also possible: you may discover that someone you hate intensely likes the same rather obscure art works that you do. What do we do about such states? Heider proposes that such unbalanced states produce tension and generate forces to achieve or restore balance.

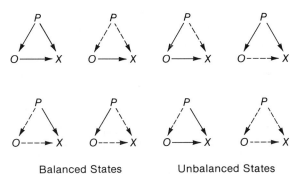

Balanced States   Unbalanced States

Figure 11-5
Examples of balanced and unbalanced states according to Heider's definition of balance. Solid lines represent positive and broken lines negative relations. (Adapted from Zajonc, 1960, Figure 1. Reprinted with permission of the publisher; copyright 1960, Columbia University Press.)

Heider's approach, then, is a highly simplified one (R. H. Willis & Burgess, 1974). Indeed, its greatest fault may be that it's too simplified, for the approach fails to consider degrees of liking. At the same time, it is capable of accounting for a wide variety of phenomena, including interpersonal attraction and verbal reinforcement of attitudes (Insko, Songer, & McGarvey, 1974).

B. Osgood and Tannenbaum's congruity theory

The congruity theory of Osgood and Tannenbaum (1955) is an extension of the balance notion. It is especially concerned with the direction of attitude change. The principle of congruity "holds that when change in evaluation or attitude occurs it always occurs in the direction of increased congruity with the prevailing frame of reference" (Zajonc, 1960, p. 286). People's attitudes change in the direction of reducing inconsistency or ambiguity.

The congruity theory has been particularly concerned with the source of a communication, the content of a communication, and the reaction of the recipient to each of these. Let us use an example from Chapter 10. Professor Jones thinks positively of U.S. Senator Proxmire (+) and also believes the National Science Foundation is a valuable institution (+). If Senator Proxmire were to praise the National Science Foundation, congruity would exist in Professor Jones's cognitive system (a + is affirmative toward a +). But when Senator Proxmire castigates the NSF for its support of social-science research, an inconsistency arises for Professor Jones. The pairing of a positive source and a negatively evaluated communication creates incongruity (a + is negative about a +). Incongruity is defined as existing when the evaluations (or attitudes) toward the source and the object are similar and the assertion is negative (as in this case), or when the evaluations of the source and object are dissimilar and the assertion is positive. According to the theory, in cases of incongruity, there is pressure to change one's attitudes about either the source or the object of the assertion in the direction of increased congruity. Congruity theorists have gone even farther with this approach, by specifying degrees of evaluation of each source and object. For example, if Professor Jones is strongly favorable toward Senator Proxmire (+3) and mildly favorable toward the National Science Foundation (+1), the senator's attack against the NSF will lead to a shift in Professor Jones's cognitive structure—toward both the source and the object. Probably more change will occur in the mildly held attitude concerning the National Science Foundation.

C. Festinger's cognitive-dissonance theory

Cognitive dissonance exists when a person possesses two **cognitions,** one of which is contradictory to the other (Festinger, 1957). Two terms here require clarification. The term **cognitions** refers to thoughts, attitudes, beliefs, and also behaviors of which the person is cognitively aware. The following statements are cognitions: "I am a thoughtful person"; "I believe that schools are repressive institutions"; "I forgot my wife's birthday"; "It is a nice day today." In saying that one cognition contradicts the other, Festinger means that if cognition A implies the presence of cognition B, then it is dissonant to hold cognition A and the opposite of cognition B at the same time. For example, if I hold the cognition that "I am a thoughtful person" and if I realize that I have forgotten my wife's birthday, dissonance is created. Or, to use a hackneyed example, if I know that cigarette smoking causes lung cancer, it is dissonant for me to smoke three packs a day (assuming that I want to live a long, healthy life).

A basic assumption of the theory is that a state of dissonance motivates the person to reduce or eliminate the dissonance. The presence of dissonance is so psychologically unpleasant that the person subsequently seeks to avoid such situations. The theory demonstrates a precision that is lacking in previous consistency approaches because it specifies the amount of dissonance aroused. The level of dissonance activat-

ed is a function of (1) the ratio of dissonant to consonant cognitions and (2) the importance of each cognition to the person (Sherwood, Barron, & Fitch, 1969). The relationship is expressed in the following formula:

$$\text{Dissonance} = \frac{\text{Importance} \times \text{Number of dissonant cognitions}}{\text{Importance} \times \text{Number of consonant cognitions}}$$

Thus, the magnitude of dissonance increases as the number or importance of dissonant cognitions increases relative to the number or importance of consonant cognitions.

How is dissonance reduced? One method is to decrease the number or importance of the dissonant elements. If a man has forgotten his wife's birthday, he may devalue the importance of the occasion; he may convince himself that celebrating birthdays is meaningless, or that his wife would just as soon not be reminded that she is yet another year older. Or the man may increase the number or importance of the consonant cognitions; he may engage in a number of activities—bringing her a gift he knows she would like, bringing her breakfast in bed—to convince *himself* of his thoughtfulness.

A third way of reducing dissonance is, of course, to change one of the dissonant elements so it is no longer inconsistent with the other cognitions. The man may conclude that he is not so thoughtful as he had assumed he was. Which elements change in the equation depend on its specific ingredients. If the dissonance occurs between one's attitude and one's behavior, either might be modifiable. The important point is that according to the theory, the person is motivated to reduce or eliminate the cognitive dissonance.

D. Reactance theory: The "the-grass-is-always-greener-on-the-other-side-of-the-fence" phenomenon

Social observer L. Rust Hills (1973), writing on the rules of social life in the contemporary United States, concludes that there are three "social cruel rules," one of which is the following: "(a) Whenever you really feel like going out you don't have an invitation; and in converse: (b) whenever you are invited to go out, you feel like staying at home" (p. 15). A similar phenomenon has been identified; the very fact that we are restricted from doing something may cause us to develop a more favorable attitude toward it. Social psychologists label this phenomenon *psychological reactance.*

Social psychologist Jack W. Brehm (1966, 1972) has proposed that the concept of reactance, an outgrowth of cognitive-dissonance theory, may explain the attitude change that takes place toward certain objects or activities under certain conditions. Brehm uses the following example:

> Picture Mr. John Smith, who normally plays golf on Sunday afternoons, although occasionally he spends Sunday afternoon watching television or puttering around his workshop. The important point is that Smith always spends Sunday afternoon doing whichever of these three things he prefers; he is free to choose which he will do. Now consider a specific Sunday morning on which Smith's wife announces that Smith will have to play golf that afternoon since she has invited several of her ladyfriends to the house for a party. Mr. Smith's freedom is threatened with reduction in several ways: (1) he cannot watch television, (2) he cannot putter in the workshop, and (3) he must (Mrs. Smith says) play golf [1966, p. 2].

Reactance theory concerns itself with situations in which one's freedom of choice is threatened. According to the theory, if a person's freedom of choice is restricted, he or she will be motivated to reestablish the freedom that has been lost or threatened (Worchel & Brehm, 1971). More relevant to the present context, if a formerly available activity is restricted, it becomes more desirable and attractive. Attitudes toward an object become more favorable if the opportunity to obtain that object is suddenly restricted (Sensenig & Brehm, 1968). In fact, if a person even sees another person's freedom being restricted, the observer will experience reactance (Andreoli, Worchel, & Folger, 1974).

Reactance theory can be applied to questions about the availability of pornography, discussed in Chapter 6. According to the theory, material that is restricted or censored would take on a greater appeal (Fromkin & Brock, 1973); in fact, Worchel and Arnold (in press) found that censorship of a message caused the potential audience to change their attitudes in the direction of the position advocated by the communication, as well as to develop greater desire to hear the communication. One interpretation (Ashmore, Ramchandra, & Jones, 1971) is that the potential audience felt that the censor was threatening their freedom to hold the attitude advocated by the censored message.

E. Explaining attitude change through each consistency theory

Jerry, a college student, meets Ingrid, is attracted to her, and asks her for a date. At first, Jerry feels that Ingrid is an ideal companion. But then she mentions that she is a member of a certain ethnic group—to be completely fictitious, let us call her a Danirean (see Hartley, 1946)—and all his life Jerry has been taught that Danireans are despicable. Such a romantic difficulty is nothing new, of course; it has served as a basic conflict for a number of literary works—including *Romeo and Juliet, West Side Story,* and, to a small degree, *Love Story.* How would each consistency theory conceptualize this dilemma? Each assumes that, because the conflict is unpleasant to Jerry, he will resolve it. Each theory also attempts to state how attitude change might occur and whether it will do so.

Heider's balance theory would represent the above situation as follows: P = Jerry, O = Ingrid, and X = Danireans. Here, P likes O; P dislikes X; and O likes X. Jerry's state is unbalanced, and, according to Heider's theory, he will seek to restore balance. Balance could be achieved if Jerry decided to dislike Ingrid rather than like her, or if he decided to like Danireans rather than dislike them. Balance theory also implies other possible ways of resolving unbalance, such as differentiation, misperception, or forgetting. For example, Jerry could differentiate between good Danireans, like Ingrid, and bad ones, like all the rest.

Osgood and Tannenbaum's principle of congruity asserts that resolving discrepant attitudes always occurs in the direction of greater congruity with the prevailing frame of reference. This approach emphasizes the source (Ingrid), the object (Danireans), and the assertion of the source about the object ("I am a Danirean and proud to be one"). Incongruity exists here because the positively evaluated source makes an assertion in favor of a negatively evaluated object. Like balance theory, the principle of congruity predicts a change of attitude toward the source, the object, or both. The relevant research data indicate that Jerry's reaction would be both to like Ingrid somewhat less and to dislike Danireans somewhat less.

The principle of congruity also considers another way of resolving incongruities. Instead of attitude change, one can refuse to believe that the assertion of the source is true. In other words, when Ingrid says she is a Danirean, Jerry might respond "You must be kidding!" Such incredulity could not be maintained for long in face-to-face situations. Incredulity is a more frequent resolution in experimental studies that attribute assertions (correctly or incorrectly) to well-known sources. The subject in such an experiment might respond "I just don't believe that Senator Proxmire (or Ann Landers or Walter Cronkite) said that!" The principle of congruity offers more precise predictions about attitude change than does balance theory (Zajonc, 1960), for it specifies degree of change, rather than merely the direction. Yet both theories are rather restrictive in that they assume that the person will work within the number of elements available.

Festinger's theory of cognitive dissonance offers both something more and something less than the preceding consistency theories. For one, a great deal more research has been done on cognitive dissonance than on the other approaches. Also, cognitive dissonance emphasizes the motivating aspect of dissonance or incongru-

ity. It implies that, as a result of the dissonant "Ingrid the Danirean" episode, Jerry will avoid similar possibilities in the future. Realizing his strong negative feelings toward Danireans, Jerry will determine whether a girl is a Danirean before he becomes emotionally involved with her. The preceding consistency theories do not propose these generalized motivating effects of incongruous relationships. In dealing with the resolution of present inconsistency, balance theory and congruity theory have less to say about future behavior than does cognitive-dissonance theory.

The theory of cognitive dissonance, however, is often less specific than congruity theory when prescribing ways of resolving dissonance. In the case of Jerry and Ingrid, the two dissonant cognitions would be (1) all Danireans are despicable and (2) Ingrid, a Danirean, is wonderful. Jerry would be motivated to resolve this dissonance, and one method would be for him to seek out information that would reduce the dissonance. Jerry might read travel books or materials published by the Danirean Tourist Service that picture Danireans as smiling, friendly people, living in a pleasant country. Or Jerry might try (unconsciously, perhaps) to annoy Ingrid, causing her to present a less attractive side of her personality. Either of these types of information could reduce dissonance.

The applications of reactance theory to this case are more limited. If, for example, Jerry's parents restricted him from seeing Ingrid because of their hostile feelings toward Danireans, Ingrid—according to reactance theory—would become all the more attractive to Jerry. This proposition—called the "Romeo and Juliet effect"—has been put to an empirical test, the results of which were presented in Chapter 5.

F. Assumptions about human nature

The *consistency theories* explicitly assume that human nature is rational—that holding conflicting attitudes is intolerable to people and hence stimulates them to change. This general approach monopolized thinking about attitude change during the 1960s; for example, in 1966 Albert Pepitone wrote that "there is no question but that theoretical social psychology is today fairly dominated by hypotheses and experiments derived from these models" (p. 257). Reactance theory adds a further assumption that people are motivated to restore a state of personal freedom of choice.

As indicated earlier, the limits of consistency theories are beginning to appear. A whole-sale assumption that people are always rational and forever abhor inconsistency has been rejected in favor of the notion that at least *some* people *sometimes* act in such a way as to minimize inconsistencies. But on other occasions people can live with their inconsistencies quite well, and seeking consistency may be a relatively unimportant motive compared with motives of seeking novelty, complexity, approval, achievement, or power (J. I. Shaw & Skolnick, 1973). (See Figure 11-6 for an intriguing example.)

Figure 11-6

Dissonant attitudes and behavior, or "Politics makes strange bedfellows." On July 4, 1973, Senator Edward Kennedy appeared on a platform in Decatur, Alabama, with Governor George Wallace. As the photograph shows, all appeared to be sweetness and light. Five years before, Kennedy had said the following about Wallace: "My brothers believed in the dignity of man. How can those who stood with them support a man whose agents used cattle prods and dogs against human beings in Alabama?" How would cognitive-dissonance theory explain this contradiction? How would a politician explain it? Would Kennedy's public embracing of Wallace change his own attitude toward Wallace? Or vice versa? (Photo by Ken Regan/Camera 5.)

G. Representative research

Although each consistency approach has been subject to some empirical tests, more than 500 studies have been completed within the cognitive-dissonance framework alone. These studies may be grouped in three major categories. The first includes those studies that emphasize conditions in which conflicting cognitions exist. The second category of studies focuses on the state of uneasiness after a decision has been made—when, for example, one asks oneself whether the choice just made was the correct one. According to the theory, any time one chooses between two attractive options, *postdecision dissonance* exists, and one seeks out behaviors that support the correctness of the choice made. (See Figure 11-7 for one example.) Early research has confirmed such an explanation. For example, persons who have recently purchased new cars are more likely to read magazine advertisements for that make of car than for any other make—apparently in an attempt to reduce dissonance over their decision (Ehrlich, Guttman, Schönbach, & Mills, 1957). Likewise, those persons who go through a severe initiation to gain membership to a group value the group membership more highly than those who go through milder initiation rites (Aronson & Mills, 1959). However, more recent research on *selective exposure* indicates no consistent support for a conclusion that people are more attracted to information that is congenial with their own decisions (S. Rosen, 1961; Feather, 1963; J. Freedman & Sears, 1965). Mediating variables, such as an ability to adapt to incongruities, may explain conflicting findings (Driver, Streufert, & Nataupsky, 1969).

The third group of studies falling within the cognitive-dissonance framework concentrates on the dissonance resulting when a person has been forced to take a public position contrary to his or her private attitude. The theory proposes that this conflict leads to change (usually in the private attitude). It also makes the controversial prediction that the less a person is *induced* to advocate a public position violating his

or her private attitude, the more the person will shift in private attitude. The original study to test this proposition (Festinger & Carlsmith, 1959) paid male subjects either $1 or $20 to lie to another student. After participating for one hour in a series of dull, meaningless tasks (for example, putting 12 spools in a tray, emptying the tray, and refilling it, time and time again), the subject was paid to tell a prospective subject that the experiment was interesting, educational, and worthwhile. Later, under the guise of a survey unrelated to the experiment, each subject who lied for either $1 or $20 answered a questionnaire about his private attitudes toward the experiment. Festinger and Carlsmith found that subjects who had been paid only $1 rated the experimental tasks as more enjoyable (mean of $+1.35$ on a scale of -5 to $+5$) than did the subjects who were paid $20 (mean = -0.05) or the control subjects (mean = -0.45). Thus, when one's morality is compromised for only a small payment, his dissonance is increased. The way the subject reduces dissonance is by convincing himself that the public statement he made is an accurate one.

Not everyone has accepted this conclusion. The methodology of cognitive-dissonance studies, particularly those that involve deception, has been severely criticized. Questions have been raised about the accuracy of the results (Chapanis & Chapanis, 1964), since in many of the studies a sizeable percentage of the potential subjects saw through the deception used in the experiment. In Festinger and Carlsmith's study, 11 of the 71 potential subjects could not be used in the analysis.

Moreover, critics have questioned the plausibility of some of the manipulations. Are subjects suspicious when they are paid $20 for a few minutes of their time plus a commitment to serve as a retainer for any vague future time? Rosenberg has argued that paying large monetary rewards in cognitive-dissonance experiments has led to an increase in the subject's **evaluation apprehension,** defined as "an active, anxiety-toned concern that he win a positive evalua-

Figure 11-7

Postdecision dissonance reduction at post time. "Put your money where your mouth is" was an admonition followed by researchers Robert Knox and James Inkster (1968), who were not content to test cognitive-dissonance theory only under artificial, laboratory conditions. The researchers went to a local racetrack and interviewed bettors at the $2 window about the chances of their horse's winning. Some subjects were interviewed as they stood in line at the window, waiting to place their bets. On a seven-point scale of chances to win, these soon-to-be-bettors averaged a response of 3.48, or a little better than "fair" chances of winning. Other subjects were interviewed right *after* they had placed their bet. Their average confidence rating was 4.81, or a "good" chance of winning. The difference was statistically significant, implying that the actual act of committing oneself by placing the bet creates dissonance, and hence the dissonance-reducing rating of greater confidence in one's choice. (Photo by Joe Alai/Freelance Photographers Guild.)

tion from the experimenter, or at least that he provide no grounds for a negative one" (M. J. Rosenberg, 1965, p. 29). Such apprehension might cause the subject with the $20 payment to resist admitting his or her change in private opinion. To clarify this point, Rosenberg designed and executed a cognitive-dissonance study in which the advocacy of a counterattitudinal public position and the measurement of it were more widely separated than in Festinger and Carlsmith's study. Rosenberg found that the greater the reward for lying, the greater the change in attitude—the precise opposite of Festinger and Carlsmith's finding. Rosenberg concluded that reinforcement theory does a better job than cognitive-dissonance theory in explaining the results of studies in which persons publicly advocate a position counter to their attitudes.

Tedeschi, Schlenker, and Bonoma (1971) seek to explain the findings of dissonance studies by relying on the concept of *impression formation*. When a person is forced to do something contradictory to his or her attitudes, they reason, the person is quite concerned with the impressions formed by observers. The person makes an effort to present an image of one who is consistent, rational, and predictable (Schlenker, 1973).

In an attempt to resolve the conflicting findings, Carlsmith, Collins, and Helmreich (1966) proposed that the extent to which the subject must convince other people of the desirability of his or her public position is crucial. These authors predicted that if, in a face-to-face confrontation, a subject has to present a position that is in opposition to his or her privately held attitude, a smaller payment will lead to greater change in private attitude. To the contrary, if the subject has to express a counterattitudinal position anonymously in writing (to be seen only by the experimenter), the more he or she is paid, the more the subject's private attitude will change. Both these expectations were confirmed (Carlsmith, Collins, & Helmreich, 1966), indicating that both cognitive-dissonance theory and reinforcement theory make accurate predictions under certain conditions.

Perhaps the difference between public and private behavior results from a greater commitment to counterattitudinal behavior in a public situation. For example, it has been found that when the subject is unable to disassociate himself publicly from his behavior, he changes his attitude more if he is paid less (Frey & Irle, 1972). In a somewhat different interpretation, Collins (1969) has proposed that when a person has to express a public opinion counter to his or her private attitude, the adverse consequences may cause more attitude change when there is a smaller reward than when there is a larger one. Attribution theory (see Chapter 3) may also explain the relationship, as stated by Collins:

> An individual makes a counter-attitudinal statement. Then he is faced with an attributional problem—should he attribute the statement to some force within himself, i.e., is the statement a reflection of his own attitude? If this is the case, he may want to change his previous attitude to be consistent with his current overt statement. Alternately, he may attribute the overt statement to some external force in the environment. In this case he does not need to make an adjustment (i.e., no attitude change) because the externally induced overt statement is irrelevant to his own, internal attitude [1969, p. 310].

(This last interpretation reminds us of D. J. Bem's (1965, 1970, 1972) self-perception theory of attitude formation to be described in the next section of this chapter.)

More recent research clarifies the reaction to forced compliance. Several studies (Collins & Hoyt, 1972; Hoyt, Henley, & Collins, 1972; B. J. Calder, Ross, & Insko, 1973) had subjects write essays in conflict with their previously expressed attitudes with several degrees of possible consequences. This act caused some subjects to change their private attitudes to be more consistent with what they had said in their essays, but only those subjects who were paid small amounts and who were aware that they were responsible if their essay writing had any serious consequences.

After Festinger and Carlsmith's (1959) original study of forced compliance for $1 or $20, the number of studies on the phenomenon increased yearly for a decade. Many variations of the procedure, in a variety of settings, and with a variety of reactions from an audience (Goethals & Cooper, 1972), have been employed. Reviewing this mass of research, C. A. Kiesler and Munson (1975) conclude that the most reasonable current statement of the conditions under which dissonance and a change in attitude occur is the following: "A person will experience and reduce dissonance if he performs an act inconsistent with his beliefs and if the act has aversive consequences for the person or others, and if the person perceives that he bears some personal responsibility for the act" (1975, p. 424).

It has been suggested that an adequate attitude-change theory must explain not only purposeful attempts to change attitude but also cases in which unplanned events present new information discrepant with a person's previous attitudes toward the object. For example, how did supporters of Edward Kennedy react to the incident on Chappaquiddick Island in July, 1969? The facts of the case were as follows: Senator Kennedy and a female staff worker, Ms. Mary Jo Kopechne, were returning to Martha's Vineyard in a car driven by the senator. After taking a wrong turn onto a country road, Kennedy drove off a bridge into about ten feet of water. Senator Kennedy rescued himself, but the young woman drowned. Even though the accident apparently happened at about 11:15 P.M., Senator Kennedy did not report it until about 10 A.M. the following day. He claimed he had made several unsuccessful attempts to locate and rescue Ms. Kopechne immediately after he escaped from the submerged car. He attributed his delay in informing the police to his state of shock and exhaustion. The senator was later tried for leaving the scene of an accident; he pleaded guilty and received a two-month suspended sentence. After the trial he asked the voters of Massachusetts to judge whether he should retain his Senate seat. Their response was favorable, and he did so. A year later he successfully ran for reelection.

Any of the consistency theories described here would predict that persons who held Senator Kennedy in high regard would experience some degree of cognitive inconsistency. The highly esteemed senator had committed an apparently undesirable act. This inconsistency could be resolved in two ways: the person's regard for Kennedy could diminish, or he could maintain his regard for Kennedy by interpreting the case in such a way as to make Kennedy less guilty.

Silverman (1971) has investigated the ways Kennedy supporters responded to the Chappaquiddick incident. Approximately three weeks after the incident, Silverman tabulated the reactions of 102 persons at the University of Florida. The questions he posed are listed in Table 11-2. Instead of the usual sample of college sophomores, Silverman chose mostly faculty members and graduate students as subjects because he wanted persons who had held favorable attitudes toward Senator Kennedy prior to the incident. Of the 102 respondents, 84 (82%) reported that their attitudes toward Senator Kennedy before the incident were very or moderately favorable. (As an aside, we may note that it would have been better to assess these attitudes before the Chappaquiddick incident, but of course Silverman could not have had the prescience to know that the incident would occur. One limitation of studies using naturally occurring events such as this one is the inability to anticipate such events.) The 84 subjects who retrospectively reported that they were pro-Kennedy before the incident are of main concern in the subsequent discussion. Of these, 49 (58%) maintained very favorable or moderately favorable attitudes at the time of the interview—three weeks after the incident. These respondents are referred to as the nonchangers. Thirty-three (39%) reported that their attitudes had changed to moderately unfavorable or quite unfavorable; these respondents Silverman labeled the changers. Two subjects who shifted to no opinion were not used in further analyses.

Thus, Silverman had two groups of initially pro-Kennedy subjects whose postincident attitudes were different. Consistency theory would predict that these two groups of subjects would answer the questions from the interview in different ways. For example, in response to Item 10 in Table 11-2, the nonchangers should reject the possibility that the senator might have been aware that he was sacrificing the young woman's life in not reporting the accident as soon as possible. In actuality, this is what happened: 80% of the nonchangers, compared to 42% of the changers, answered "definitely not" to Item 10 in Table 11-2. Likewise, in connection with Item 8 of Table 11-2, if a person had maintained his pro-Kennedy attitude, he should be more enthusiastic about Ted Kennedy's keeping his Senate seat and seeking reelection. The data do not indicate the intensity of the response but report

---

Table 11-2
Silverman's questionnaire about reactions to Senator Kennedy's accident

Questionnaire items, in the order given, are presented below.

1. To what extent have you been following the details of Senator Kennedy's recent automobile accident in the various news media? (Alternative responses were *as fully as possible, moderately,* and *little or not at all.*)

2. Prior to the events of the accident, what was your opinion of Senator Kennedy as a person (rather than as a political figure)?

3. What is your present opinion of Senator Kennedy as a person?

4. Prior to the events of the accident, what was your opinion of Senator Kennedy as a political figure and potential president?

5. What is your present opinion of Senator Kennedy as a political figure and potential president? (Alternative responses for items 2–5 were *very high, moderately high, moderately low, very low,* and *no opinion.*)

6. Do you believe that the action taken against Senator Kennedy by the local law-enforcement agencies and courts (2-month suspended sentence for leaving the scene of an accident) was: (Responses were *too severe, fair and just, too lenient,* and *far too lenient.*)

7. Given the same circumstances and events, do you believe that a private citizen would have been treated: (Responses were *more leniently, the same, more severely, far more severely.*)

8. Considering the events concerning the accident, do you believe that it was proper for Senator Kennedy to keep his seat in the Senate and to announce his intention to run again in 1970? (Responses were *yes, no, undecided.*)

9. Do you believe that if Senator Kennedy had taken other action than he did immediately after the accident, the girl's life may have been saved?

10. Do you believe that Senator Kennedy was aware that he was possibly sacrificing the girl's life in not reporting the accident as soon as possible?

11. Do you believe that Senator Kennedy's delay in reporting the accident immediately was based at all on his concern for his reputation? (Responses for Items 9–11 were *definitely not, possibly yes, probably yes, definitely yes.*)

The 12th item was open-ended and stated "Please write below, in as much detail as possible, your own opinions about why Senator Kennedy delayed about 10 hours in reporting the accident to the police."

Table 11-2 and Table 11-3 are from "On the Resolution and Tolerance of Cognitive Inconsistency in a Natural-Occurring Event," by I. Silverman, *Journal of Personality and Social Psychology,* 1971, *17,* 171–178. Copyright 1970 by the American Psychological Association. Reprinted by permission.

that 98% of the nonchangers, compared with 73% of the changers, advocated Kennedy's remaining in office; the difference in percentages is statistically significant, indicating that it was unlikely to have occurred by chance.

Silverman included Item 12 on Table 11-2, the open-ended question, so that respondents could furnish their own opinions about why Kennedy delayed reporting the incident. Table 11-3 presents the types of reasons given, as well as the frequencies and percentages of nonchangers and changers indicating each type of reason. As shown in Table 11-3, Silverman ordered these reasons according to how morally incriminating they were, moving from less morally incriminating ("no opinion") to most incriminating ("to try to cover up"). Note in Table 11-3 that there is further evidence supporting the consistency theory: those respondents maintaining their pro-Kennedy attitudes gave less incriminating reasons for his delay, whereas changers saw more incriminating and reprehensible factors as the true reasons for delay.

Consistency theory also serves as an explanation of reactions to three more recent highly publicized happenings. After U.S. Senator Thomas Eagleton was replaced as the 1972 Democratic party nominee for vice-president, MacDonald and Majumder (1973) surveyed the reactions of respondents. Those whose attitudes toward Senator Eagleton had initially been positive but became negative after learning of his treatments for mental disorders tended to hold beliefs about the incident that were in keeping with their changed attitudes. For example, they were more likely to believe that the publicity about Eagleton's nervous breakdown would hurt the Democratic ticket in the election. Those respondents who maintained a favorable attitude toward Senator Eagleton held beliefs about his dismissal that permitted them to keep their positive feelings. Positive or negative reactions to the resignation of Vice-President Agnew and his pleading "no contest" to charges of income tax evasion were also related to former attitudes to him (Cozby, 1974).

More recently, Bishop (1975) has studied the role of cognitive consistency and inconsistency in relation to reactions to the Watergate break-in. He surveyed respondents in November 1973—before the full disclosure of Nixon's involvement. Using the technique employed by Silverman (1971), Bishop constructed a typology of attitude-changers. Those subjects who maintained their positive attitudes to President Nixon even after knowing about the Watergate break-in were classified *positive nonchangers*. Those who shifted from positive to negative attitudes toward

---

Table 11-3

Frequencies and percentages of nonchangers and changers in Silverman's study giving various reasons "why Senator Kennedy delayed"

Category	Nonchangers	Changers
No opinion	11 (22%)	4 (12%)
Shock (disorientation, concussion, exhaustion, panic)	18 (37%)	12 (36%)
Upon advice (or to seek advice from friends, associates, lawyers, family)	7 (14%)	3 (9%)
Confusion (to organize thoughts, plan course of action)	10 (20%)	5 (15%)
Fear (or concern for reputation, political future, marriage, jail)	19 (39%)	19 (58%)
Intoxication (to reduce blood alcohol and avoid incrimination)	5 (10%)	8 (24%)
To try to cover up (develop an alibi, conceal facts of event, find someone to stand in as the guilty party)	12 (24%)	11 (33%)

President Nixon were called *positive-negative changers*, while those who maintained their negative attitudes were called *negative nonchangers*. Table 11-4 reflects reactions to Watergate by these three types, also divided by their voting for Nixon or McGovern. The news about Watergate had the most effect on those who had voted for Nixon in the 1972 election. Among these, the respondents whose attitudes had changed had adopted beliefs about the Watergate affair that were congruent with their changed opinions. (Similar findings are reported by J. B. Garrett and Wallace, 1975, in another study of reactions to Watergate.)

Table 11-4

Relationships, in percent, between attitude change and Watergate-related items, controlled on 1972 vote

Watergate-Related Items	Voted for Nixon		Would Have Voted for Nixon		Voted or Would Have Voted for McGovern†
	Positive Nonchangers (N = 33–34)	Pos.-Neg. Changers (N = 27–29)	Positive Nonchangers (N = 22–24)	Pos.-Neg. Changers (N = 19–21)	(N = 117–121)
In general, how much attention have you paid to the events of Watergate this year?					
A good deal	26	55	29	38	58
Some	56	42	42	43	38
Not much	18	3	29	19	4
In general, how fair would you say the press and other news media have been in their treatment of President Nixon in the Watergate affair?					
Very fair	3	28	4	24	47
Somewhat fair	50	62	58	76	50
Not at all fair	47	10	38	0	3
Given the same circumstances and events of Watergate, how do you think the press and other news media would treat Edward (Ted) Kennedy if he were President?					
Far more leniently	25	10	17	0	1
Somewhat more leniently	41	25	48	52	30
The same	23	36	22	33	53
Somewhat more severely	12	18	13	5	12
Far more severely	0	11	0	10	4
How much, if at all, do you think the Watergate affair has reduced *confidence in President Nixon* among the general public?					
A great deal	76	100	63	95	88
Somewhat	24	0	37	5	11
Not at all	0	0	0	0	1
How much, if at all, do you think the Watergate affair has reduced respect for the *office of the presidency* among the general public?					
A great deal	29	21	25	29	37
Somewhat	44	52	62	57	50
Not at all	27	17	13	14	13

To what degree, if at all, has the Watergate affair reduced your *confidence in the federal government as an institution?**

A great deal	9	28	17	24	30
Somewhat	47	55	46	62	49
Not at all	44	17	37	14	21

Which one of the following two statements comes closer to your general point of view about Watergate?*

It's just politics—the kind of thing that both parties engage in.	79	21	71	19	14
It's a very serious matter because it reveals corruption in the Nixon administration.	21	79	29	81	86

Which one of the following four statements concerning President Nixon's connection with the Watergate affair comes closest to your own point of view?*

President Nixon planned the Watergate bugging from the beginning.	0	3	0	0	8
President Nixon did not plan the bugging but knew about it before it took place.	9	35	27	33	51
President Nixon found out about the bugging after it occurred but tried to cover it up.	68	59	55	62	40
President Nixon had no knowledge of the bugging and spoke up as soon as he learned about it.	23	3	18	5	1

All things considered, do you think it would be in the best interests of the country for President Nixon to resign?

Yes	6	29	4	26	76
No	94	71	96	74	24

If President Nixon does not resign, do you think he should be impeached and compelled to leave the presidency, or not?*

Should be impeached	0	33	0	43	71
Should not be impeached	100	67	100	57	29

In general, do you believe that most people who favor impeachment of President Nixon are politically biased in their intentions or not?

Definitely not	0	3	0	9	7
Probably not	9	38	13	24	39
Uncertain	12	17	25	38	26
Probably yes	67	42	54	29	27
Definitely yes	12	0	8	0	1

Note.—Number of subjects varied slightly from item to item due to missing data. Total percentages for each item were rounded to 100 within each subgroup.

*Adopted from *The Gallup Opinion Index*, Report No. 99, September, 1973. The remaining items were modeled, in part, upon those used by Silverman (1971) and MacDonald and Majumder (1973).

†Ninety-nine (82%) of the 121 McGovern subjects were classified as negative nonchangers; 19 (16%), positive-negative changers; and 3 (2%), positive nonchangers.

Reprinted with permission of the author and publisher from "Resolution and Tolerance of Cognitive Inconsistency in a Field Situation: Change in Attitude and Beliefs Following the Watergate Affair," by G. F. Bishop, *Psychological Reports*, 1975, 36, 747–753.

While the overall results of Silverman's and Bishop's studies support consistency theory, it should be noted that the responses were by no means unanimous. Consider those subjects who maintained their pro-Kennedy attitude. Consistency theory would predict that such persons would give Kennedy the benefit of the doubt when interpreting his behavior. But of these consistently pro-Kennedy persons, 63% admitted the possibility or probability that Ms. Kopechne's life could have been saved if Kennedy had not delayed; 20% admitted the possibility that Kennedy was aware of this when he did delay; and 64% thought that his delay was at least partially the result of his concern for his reputation.

Likewise, in Bishop's study, responses were not unanimous for most questions. For example, of those Nixon voters who remained positive toward him, 6% still felt he should resign (in November 1973) and 21% felt that the Watergate affair reflected corruption in his administration.

These pro-Kennedy and pro-Nixon subjects did not act in completely consistent ways, and their reactions have caused social psychologists to reevaluate the breadth of the applicability of consistency theory (McNeel & Messick, 1970). For example, K. O. Price, Harburg, and Newcomb (1966) asked subjects their reaction to the case in which person P disliked person O, and both P and O disliked object X. Only 17% of the subjects felt uneasy or negative about such a relationship. A statement by Freedman seems an appropriate way to describe some respondents of studies such as these:

> It seems that people are not usually looking for inconsistencies among their cognitions, do not notice that many of them exist, and therefore do not act on them. This lack of concern with inconsistencies is, I believe, because it is not a very important consideration for most people in most circumstances. And when they do notice inconsistencies, people seem to endure them without being particularly troubled [1968, p. 502].

Further research is necessary to determine whether—as Freedman believes—inconsistency is not a problem "for most people in most circumstances." Certainly inconsistency is not a problem for some (Touhey, 1973).

H. Applications of consistency theories to attitude-change procedures

Brehm and Cohen (1962) have applied consistency theories (specifically cognitive-dissonance theory) to the task of desegregation and integration. They propose that most anti-Black White persons who interact closely with a Black will experience dissonance arousal as their anti-Black attitudes will seem discrepant with their behavior. Dissonance will be particularly increased if this behavioral commitment is irrevocable. As dissonance is unpleasant, efforts will be made by the prejudiced Whites to bring their attitudes closer together. As Brehm and Cohen have stated:

> In effect, we expect that, among other things, the dissonance-reduction process should result in a more favorable perception of the social climate shared with the Negroes and a change toward more favorable attitudes toward Negroes. Thus, everything else being equal, commitment to an irrevocable interracial policy should result in at least some change in attitudes toward the Negroes: Forcing a person to behave in a fashion discrepant from what he believes can result in a change in private opinion [1962, p. 272].

Some of the factors controlling the magnitude of dissonance experienced and the consequent magnitude of attitude change include the extent of contact with a Black, the extent of freedom of choice, and the initial attitude position. The greater the contact (in terms of proximity, intimacy, frequency, or duration), the greater the dissonance and the greater the efforts to reduce dissonance. As concerns the extent of freedom of choice, Brehm and Cohen have proposed that the more a person is compelled to make a commitment, the less the amount of dissonance created if he or she succumbs and, hence, the less the attitude change. To facilitate attitude change, the individual must be given some choice in interacting with Blacks. However, if he behaves inconsistently with his anti-Black attitude, he should not be given a chance to disclaim his action, for such a disclaimer reduces dissonance and creates less need to change the original attitude (Helmreich & Collins, 1968; J. Harvey & Mills, 1971). Finally, the more unfavorable the initial attitude position of an anti-Black White, the more the White's attitude should change in a favorable direction—assuming that the White has, through the exercise of choice, become committed to interaction with Blacks.

However, those who wish to apply a cognitive-dissonance model to such a situation must be careful in trying to force compliance. If persons refuse to act in ways inconsistent with their prejudiced attitudes, their attitudes may become even more extremely negative than before (Darley & Cooper, 1972; C. A. Kiesler, 1971).

The consistency theorist would try to marshal an attractive situation that the anti-Black White person enters into of his own free will. Once the White finds himself in the situation and committed to making his work a success, he should be oriented toward the discrepancy between his attitudes and his present behavior. The attitude will shift, being more amenable to change than the behavior.

V. Self-perception theory

A. Basic perspective

As we indicated in Chapter 10, Daryl Bem's self-perception theory proposes that people come to "know" their attitudes and other internal states partially by inferring them from observations of their own overt behavior (D. J. Bem, 1972b). That is, self-perception theory argues that, in at least some cases, we form an attitude *after* behavior occurs; the attitude does not determine the behavior.

Perhaps we can illustrate the self-perception perspective by looking at how it would reinterpret the findings of Festinger and Carlsmith's (1959) study (described in Section IV) in which undergraduates were paid $1 or $20 to tell someone else that a boring experiment was enjoyable and interesting. You will recall that Festinger and Carlsmith found that subjects who had been paid only $1 were more likely, later on, to express a private attitude more in keeping with what they had said publicly. The researchers interpreted the findings as reflecting the operation of cognitive-dissonance theory; that is, having told a lie about the nature of the experiment and having done it for only $1 had created a dissonance between their earlier attitude and their behavior. The way they reduced this dissonance was to change their private attitude to be more in keeping with what they had said. According to cognitive-dissonance theory, the subjects paid $20 would not have as much dissonance—they could say to themselves "For $20 I'll say something I don't believe." Hence the $20 subjects should not—and did not—change their private attitudes.

Self-perception theory would interpret these results by considering the viewpoint of an outside observer who hears the subject make favorable statements about the experiment to another student, and who further knows that the subject was paid either $1 or $20 to do so. Bem writes:

> This hypothetical observer is then asked to state the actual attitude of the individual he has heard. If the observer had seen an individual making such statements for little compensation ($1), he can rule out financial incentive as a motivating factor and infer something about the individual's attitudes. He can use an implicit self-selection rule and ask: "What must this man's attitude be if he is willing to behave in this fashion in this situation?" Accordingly, he can conclude that the individual holds an attitude consistent with the view that is expressed in the behavior: He must have actually enjoyed the tasks. On the other hand, if an observer sees an individual making such statements for a large compensation (e.g., $20), he can infer

little or nothing about the actual attitude of that individual, because such an incentive appears sufficient to evoke the behavior regardless of the individual's private views. The subject paid $20 is not credible in the sense that his behavior cannot be used as a guide for inferring his private views [1972b, p. 7].

Self-perception theory proposes that participants in Festinger and Carlsmith's experiment behaved just like this hypothetical observer. They considered their own behavior and implicitly asked themselves: "What must my attitude be if I am willing to behave in this fashion in this situation?" Their final attitudes are self-attributions based on their behavior and the apparent compensation for it.

How, then, do attitudes change? They change to become consistent with behaviors and the settings in which the behaviors occur. Self-perception theorists would advise the would-be persuader, propagandist, or advertiser "Get people to behave the way you want them to—and control their circumstances—and the attitudes will take care of themselves."

B. Assumptions about human nature

The self-perception approach shares with the consistency theories a very general assumption that human nature is *rational.* However, in the present approach, rationality is reflected in the search for self-understanding rather than in a strain toward consistency. That is, the self-perception theorist assumes that people want to understand their own behaviors and hence make attributions about their values, attitudes, and emotional states on the basis of their behaviors and the circumstances in which their behaviors occur. In the early 1970s Bem characterized the difference in assumptions as follows:

> During the Sixties, it will be recalled, all thinking beings were characterized by chronic drives toward consistency and uncertainty reduction, vigilant forces which coaxed us all toward cog-

nitive quiescence. Our affects, cognitions, and behaviors were held in homeostatic harmony, and our "evaluative needs" initiated emergency information searches whenever any internal state broke through threshold without clear identification or certified cause. In contrast, we are emerging into the Seventies as less driven, more contemplative creatures, thoughtful men and women whose only motivation is the willingness to answer the question, "How do you feel?" as honestly and carefully as possible after calmly surveying the available internal and external evidence [1972, pp. 42–43].

C. Representative research

Self-perception theory has offered a reinterpretation of many of the attitude-change findings generated by cognitive-dissonance theory (Kleinke, 1975a). Therefore, in discussing examples of its "representative research," we have isolated several studies (D. Green, 1974; M. Ross & Shulman, 1973; Snyder & Ebbesen, 1972; Shaffer, 1975) that attempt to serve as "crucial tests" of predictions of the two theories. That is, these studies note that cognitive-dissonance and self-perception theories make conflicting predictions about the outcomes of the same manipulations.

One means to test the predictions of the two theories is to examine the role that the *salience* of initial attitudes plays in each theory (D. J. Bem & McConnell, 1970). According to cognitive-dissonance theory (Festinger, 1957; Zimbardo, 1969), the more salient the initial attitudes, the more dissonance is created. Reminding a person that his actions are contradictory to his beliefs should cause more dissonance and hence greater resolution of the dissonance; cognitive-dissonance theory would predict that when so reminded, the person would be *more* likely to change his attitudes to conform with his public behavior.

In contrast, self-perception theory proposes that people infer their attitudes from their behavior, but only "to the extent that information from internal cues is weak, ambiguous or uninterpretable" (D. J. Bem & McConnell, 1970, p. 23). In a forced-compliance situation such as the one we are discussing, those internal cues that are important to the subject are his or her initial attitude, his or her behavior, and the surrounding circumstances. Ordinarily the behavior and its circumstances should be most important, but when the cue of the initial attitude is highlighted, there should be less attitude change, because the subject remembers what it was and uses it as a cue for his present attitude (Snyder & Ebbesen, 1972). Thus, according to this interpretation of self-perception theory, the two theories make completely opposite predictions as to the effect of salience of initial attitudes on later attitudes, in the case in which the person acts in a way inconsistent with his or her initial attitude.

Two studies (M. Ross & Shulman, 1973; Snyder & Ebbesen, 1972) tested these two theories, using the same general procedures. College students were induced to choose to write an essay opposing student control over the university curriculum (the students were in favor of student control, so the essays they wrote contradicted their attitudes). At a later time the subjects again indicated their attitudes on the issue. It was assumed that the action of advocating a contrary position would change their attitudes. But some subjects were reminded of their initial attitudes, while others were not; this was the *salience* manipulation. In essence, the study by Snyder and Ebbesen obtained findings that, in some cases, provided confirmation for predictions from self-perception theory; specifically, making the prior attitude salient meant that the final attitude was closer to the initial attitude. (There were additional findings that Snyder and Ebbesen concluded are not predicted by either theory.)

But Ross and Shulman's experiment obtained solid support only for predictions stemming from dissonance theory; those subjects who reexamined their initial responses changed their attitudes more than did subjects who were not given a second look at their initial attitudes.

What are we to do when two studies set forth to compare theories with the same experi-

mental procedure and yet produce conflicting findings? One response might be to question whether there can be any single "crucial" test, when so many of the theories in social psychology are not clearly enough stated to be tested (Greenwald, 1975). But there is another reason why the results of the two studies were inconsistent: at a procedural level they used different operations to manipulate salience. While in some ways the subjects and procedures were quite similar, there were three differences that are quite important:

1. *Time interval.* Subjects in Snyder and Ebbesen's study completed all materials in one session. Counterattitudinal essays were written immediately after the subjects completed the initial attitude scale. In contrast, Ross and Shulman's subjects participated in two sessions, the first being devoted to the initial completion of attitudes and the second to the forced choice of the counterattitudinal-essay–writing condition, the actual essay writing, the manipulation of salience, and the final attitude questionnaire. There is no explicit statement by Ross and Shulman of the interval, but it may have been one week; instructions to subjects at the second session say "This week we are collecting arguments. . . ."

It is true that both studies place the salience manipulation in the same time period as the counterattitudinal-essay–writing task. But how much effect does the separation of these from the expression of initial attitude have? Perhaps none, but it would seem that the procedures should be similar before the two studies are judged as comparable.

2. *Manipulation of salience.* The two studies used different procedures to vary the salience of writing the counterattitudinal essay. Snyder and Ebbesen asked their subjects in the high-salience condition to "take a few minutes to think about and organize your thoughts and views on the issues of student control" (p. 506). (The actual time given for this is not indicated in the report.) Subjects in the low-salience condition were not given these instructions.

Ross and Shulman had a qualitatively different manipulation of salience. Their subjects either reexamined (for high salience) or did not reexamine (for low salience) the responses they had expressed on the questionnaire at the earlier session. (Ross and Shulman refer to these as reinstatement and nonreinstatement conditions.)

3. Timing of salience manipulation. As the above may imply, Snyder and Ebbesen manipulated salience *prior* to the essay writing. Ross and Shulman manipulated it *after* the essays were written.

It would seem that these considerable variations in experimental procedures (particularly the last two) are central to the different findings in the two studies. Despite Ross and Shulman's claims that the experimenters would not view the final attitude responses, it seems to us that their procedure "loaded the dice" for dissonance theory by placing the elicitation of the final attitude directly after the manipulation of salience. "Loaded the dice" may be too strong, but it is certainly true that the experimental procedures of the two studies are quite dissimilar. In effect, Ross and Shulman's action counterbalanced their procedure of separating the experiment into two sessions.

The goal of developing "crucial tests" of competing theories is a distant one as long as the ground rules for operationalization in social psychology remain vague; Greenwald (1975) notes that there is no standard operation for rendering an attitude salient. Nor do there appear to be agreed-upon rules for going about replications, as is evidenced by the way that the ambiguous term "conceptual replication" has crept into social psychologists' vocabulary.

D. Applications of self-perception theory to attitude-change procedures

In constructing a situation designed to reduce anti-Black attitudes, the self-perception theorist would probably recommend procedures identical to those proposed by the consistency theorist in Section IV-H. However, the interpretation of the processes would be different. An important goal in the self-perception approach would be to create a situation in which the person's internal cues (anti-Black attitudes, feelings of discomfort in the presence of Blacks, and so on) would be minimized, for it is in this approach that behavior and the circumstances in which it occurs are thought to be predominant.

VI. Functional theories of attitude change

The basic proposition of a functional theory of attitude change is a simple one: people hold attitudes that fit their needs; in order to change their attitudes, we must determine what these needs are. The functional approach is a phenomenological one; it maintains that a stimulus (for example, a television commerical, a new piece of information, an interracial contact) can be understood only within the context of the perceiver's needs and personality.

Two rather similar functional theories have been developed, one by D. Katz (1960, 1968; Katz & Stotland, 1959) and one by M. B. Smith, Bruner, and White (1956). Each theory proposes a list of functions that attitudes serve. The two theories have some differences, but Kiesler, Collins, and Miller (1969) have helpfully synthesized the functions of each, as shown in Table 11-5. We will describe each general function, drawing heavily on the analysis of Kiesler and his associates.

1. First, attitudes serve an instrumental, adjustive, or utilitarian function. According to Katz, a person develops a positive attitude toward those objects that are useful in meeting his or her needs. If an object (or other person) thwarts the person's needs, he or she develops a negative attitude toward that object or person.

2. Second, attitudes serve an ego-defensive or externalizing function. Here Katz's functional

Table 11-5
The functions of attitudes

Katz	Smith, Bruner, and White
Types:	
1. Instrumental, adjustive, utilitarian	Social adjustment
2. Ego defense	Externalization
3. Knowledge	Object appraisal
4. Value expressive	Quality of expressiveness

From *Attitude Change: A Critical Analysis of Theoretical Approaches,* by C. A. Kiesler, B. E. Collins, and N. Miller. Copyright 1969 by John Wiley & Sons, Inc. Reprinted by permission.

theory is influenced by psychoanalytic considerations. An attitude may develop or change in order to protect a person "from acknowledging the basic truths about himself or the harsh realities in his external world" (D. Katz, 1960, p. 170). For example, derogatory attitudes toward outgroups and minority groups may serve as a means of convincing oneself of one's own importance. Without utilizing psychoanalytic supports, Smith, Bruner, and White see attitudes as functioning in a similar way, permitting the externalizing of reactions.

3. The knowledge function, or object appraisal, is a third function of attitudes. Attitudes may develop or change in order to "give meaning to what would otherwise be an unorganized chaotic universe" (D. Katz, 1960, p. 175). Particularly, this will happen when a problem cannot be solved without the information associated with the attitude. M. B. Smith, Bruner, and White see attitudes as a "ready aid in 'sizing up' objects and events in the environment from the point of view of one's major interests and going concerns" (1956, p. 41). Thus, categorizing objects or events is done more efficiently, and time is not spent in figuring out afresh how one should respond. Object appraisal, then, "stresses the role that gathering information plays in the day-to-day adaptive activities of the individual" (Kiesler et al., 1969, p. 315).

4. Value expression is a fourth function of attitudes. According to Katz, people gain satisfaction from expressing themselves through their attitudes. Beyond this, their expression of attitudes helps them form their own self-concepts. Smith, Bruner, and White diverge most widely from Katz at this point. To them, the expressive nature of attitudes does not mean that any need for expression exists but rather that a person's attitudes "reflect the deeper-lying pattern of his or her life" (M. B. Smith et al., 1956, p. 38).

A. Applications of the theory to attitude-change procedure

Consider the causes of prejudice described in Chapter 10. The person chosen for the summer project may have expressed anti-Black attitudes because he was exposed to such attitudes in his environment and learned them from his family and friends. On the other hand, his prejudice may reflect a deep-seated personality maladjustment. That is, his internal feelings of personal worthlessness may be so threatening to him that he defends against them by disparaging Blacks, Chicanos, or other vulnerable groups. A functional theory proposes that the techniques of attitude change most effective for one type of prejudice would not be best for the other.

Thus, functional theory would first seek to determine what needs were being met by the White's anti-Black attitudes. A series of projective tests or clinical interviews would probably be used to try to make this determination; the actual procedures used are not mentioned by the theory.

If the person seems to be anti-Black because of the environment in which he has grown up, the attitude-change process should be based upon the dissemination of new information and the use of social pressure and reeducation. In other words, the task is to create a new environment, in which new information about Blacks is transmitted to the subject. Previous attitudes and behaviors may have served a need to be socially accepted; thus, the subject must be shown that new attitudes toward Blacks must be developed to be accepted by the present group.

But if his anti-Black attitudes serve other needs, such as the need to fend off fears of personal inferiority, a deluge of information will have little effect. In this case, therapeutic devices such as catharsis and developing insight into the ego-defensive function served by the attitude might be more beneficial.

B. Assumptions about human nature

We can be brief here. The *functional theory* emphasizes the individual differences in human nature. To change another's attitude, we must first recognize his or her nature and needs. By knowing the idiosyncratic needs his or her attitudes serve, we are directed toward ways to change those attitudes. The functional theory reflects assumptions about the complexity and variability of human nature.

C. Representative research

As Kiesler and associates (1969) point out, a straightforward test of functional theory would be to select two subjects whose attitudes are similar but based on different needs and then to determine the effectiveness of various kinds of attitude-change techniques on both subjects. Since Katz's functional theory has been tested by limited research, an early study by McClintock (1958) will be described as an example of the approach.

McClintock (1958) presented two types of persuasive appeals to classes in two colleges. He proposed that among all the subjects receiving an *interpretational* appeal, those whose attitudes served an ego-defensive need would show the most attitude change. In contrast, McClintock predicted that an *informational* appeal would bring about no attitude change in subjects whose attitudes served these ego-defensive needs. Almost opposite effects were expected with subjects whose attitudes served to meet conformity needs; that is, an informational appeal would be more effective with them than the interpretational appeal. This expectation of an interaction between type of persuasive argument and type of subject is characteristic of the functional approach.

Three types of persuasive communications were used by McClintock to try to change levels of prejudice: (1) an informational message (actually an exploration of the cultural relativism argument), (2) an interpersonal message (which used a case study and analysis to show that unhealthy psychodynamics can lead to prejudice), and (3) an ethnocentric message (which implied that recipients of the message should become more prejudiced). The subjects' degree of conformity needs and ego defensiveness were assessed by subscales from the California F scale (see Chapter 18).

Despite the rather unclear manipulations of persuasive messages and the brief measuring instruments, one of the two hypotheses was confirmed. Among subjects who read the informational message, 67% of those high in conformity needs changed their attitudes in the desired direction, while only 29% of those low in conformity needs did so. In contrast, the informational appeal had opposite effects on ego-defensive subjects. Only 4% of the ego-defensive subjects changed their attitudes; the rest of these subjects did not respond to the informational appeal. Thus, the informational appeal was shown to be most effective with subjects high in conformity needs.

When presented with the interpretational message, subjects with high ego-defense needs did not change as much as those whose needs were moderate or low; 53% of highs, 95% of mediums, and 75% of lows changed their attitudes in the desired direction. Degree of conformity needs had no relationship to the extent of change resulting from exposure to the interpretational message. We might expect that the interpretational message would have the greatest influence on highly ego-involved subjects, but Katz argues that these people are too defensive and rigid to make any changes. He believes that the important comparison is betweeen the moderate and the low ego-defensive subjects. Among these subjects, a significantly greater percentage of the moderately ego-involved recipients changed than did the less ego-involved (95% versus 75%). Thus, tentative evidence is presented for a basic postulate of the functional theory: that the effect of a persuasive communication is partially influenced by the functions that attitudes serve in the recipient.

The empirical base of functional theory remains, however, quite shaky. Replications of McClintock's procedure (D. Katz, Sarnoff, & McClintock, 1956; Stotland, Katz, & Patchen, 1959) produce inconsistent or conflicting results. In response to an interpretational appeal, subjects lowest in ego defensiveness were found to change as much as or more than moderately defensive subjects. In addition, these groups of subjects may well have differed in degree of prejudice as well as amount of ego defense and conformity, and, as Kiesler and his associates (1969) indicate, the differences in attitude change might be most easily explained by considering the discrepancy between the advocated position and the recipient's own position.

More recently, P. W. Smith and Brigham (1972) attempted to change the attitudes expressed by college students regarding socialized medicine by using different combinations of separate appeals that were designed to tap the knowledge, value-expressive, and instrumental (or social-adjustment) functions. However, *none* of seven combinations of appeals was effective in changing expressed attitudes. It may be that the issue of socialized medicine is of only slight importance to the students who participated in Smith and Brigham's project. Yet the study again reflects the problem of being able to identify and measure the functions that attitudes serve for individuals.

D. Evaluation

A functional theory of attitudes is appealing to anyone who recognizes that attitude change is a function of the stimulus and the perceiver. More than any other approach, this one recognizes individual differences in the reactions to any given persuasive communication, and for that reason it should not be dismissed lightly. But the development of the theory is hampered by a lack of adequate measures of the needs that the attitudes serve. Other theoretical approaches are content to measure attitudes and their changes. In itself this is a challenging task. Functional theory says that we must know what function the attitude serves for the individual, and we must be able to measure the attitude. Until such measurements are better developed, we must regretfully conclude that the theory has little practical use.

VII. The future of theories of attitude change

In the 1960s theories of attitude change—especially cognitive-dissonance theory—dominated the research efforts of many social psychologists. But even during that decade there were concerns expressed about the future—hopes that "the spectacular though currently unrealized promise of dissonance theory does not go the way of the brontosaurus" (D. O. Sears & Abeles, 1969, p. 279). In the 1970s the sheer amount of research published on dissonance theory decreased rapidly, reflecting the fact that the theory, if not in the brontosaurus category, is certainly on the endangered-species list (C. A. Kiesler & Munson, 1975).

In general, interest in theories of attitude change has subsided, perhaps partly because of the dissatisfactions with the concept of *attitude* we discussed in Chapter 10 and partly because of criticisms over deductive theory and use of laboratory experimentation. We are in a period of change right now. Social psychologists are still committed to seeking an understanding of change through the use of some theory, but the current shift demands new theories and new approaches. We agree with Kiesler and Munson that "attitude change is not the thriving field it once was and will be again" (1975, p. 443).

VIII. Summary

Five different theories of attitude change are stimulus-response and reinforcement theory, social-judgment theory, consistency theory, self-perception theory, and functional theory. An adequate theory of attitude change must be able to predict and explain cases in which attitudes do not change as well as instances in which they do.

The Yale University Communication Research Program emphasized that in the learning of a new attitude three variables are important: *attention, comprehension,* and *acceptance.*

More than any other approach, the *stimulus-response* and *reinforcement* theories make the assumption that attitudes are changed only if the incentives for making a new response are greater than the incentives for maintaining the old response. The intensity with which some attitudes are held may be increased through the use of verbal-conditioning procedures.

Two examples of a *social-judgment theory* of attitude change are Sherif and Hovland's *assimilation-contrast theory* and Helson's *adaptation-level theory*. Assimilation-contrast theory conceptualizes attitudes along a reference scale. Within this scale there is an area called the latitude of acceptance, of which the boundaries are the limits of the attitude statements with which the respondent would agree. Attempts to shift attitudes must pose new positions that are within this latitude of acceptance. According to assimilation-contrast theory, the stronger the person's degree of ego-involvement with an attitude object, the narrower his latitude of acceptance and the broader his latitude of rejection. Little solid evidence exists for the acceptance of an assimilation-contrast theory of attitude change.

The *consistency theories* of attitude change include Heider's *balance theory*, Osgood and Tannenbaum's *congruity theory*, Festinger's *cognitive-dissonance theory*, and Brehm's *reactance theory*. Common to these is an assumption that people change their attitudes in the direction of removing inconsistencies between conflicting attitudes or behaviors. Of all the consistency approaches, cognitive-dissonance theory has stimulated the most research and controversy. Cognitive dissonance is said to exist when a person possesses two cognitions, one of which is contradictory to the other.

The research evidence for the validity of a consistency theory is itself inconsistent. While some people on some occasions change their attitudes in order to achieve greater consistency, other people either do not notice their inconsistencies or manage to endure them.

Bem's *self-perception theory* offers a completely different explanation of attitude change. It proposes that people observe their own behavior and then change their attitudes so as to be consistent with their behavior.

The basic proposition of the *functional theory* of attitude change is that people hold attitudes that fit their needs. In order to change their attitudes, we must determine what these needs are. Among the functions that attitudes may serve are (1) the instrumental, adjustive, or utilitarian function; (2) the ego-defensive or externalization function; (3) the knowledge or object-appraisal function; and (4) the value-expressing function.

Each attitude-change theory possesses its own assumptions about human nature.

I. What causes attitudes to change?
   A. Types of events
   B. Personality and response to persuasive communications

II. Effects of components of the persuasive communication
   A. The source
   B. One-sided versus two-sided presentations
   C. Order of presentation

III. Reducing prejudice: The contact hypothesis
IV. Factors facilitating change in face-to-face contact
   A. Characteristics of the individuals in contact
   B. Characteristics of the situation

V. Bringing the beneficial factors together: Stuart Cook's study
   A. Assumptions
   B. Procedure
   C. Results

VI. Why do some people change their attitudes when others do not?
VII. Summary

Attitude change: Outcomes

12

Nanin, a Japanese Zen master during the Meiji era, received a university professor who came to inquire about Zen. As Nanin served tea, he poured the visitor's cup full, and then kept pouring. The professor watched the overflow until he could no longer restrain himself, shouting "It is overfull; no more will go in!" "Like this cup," Nanin said, "you are full of your own opinions and speculation. How can I show you Zen unless you first empty your cup?"

As shown in Chapter 11, there is no shortage of theories on the nature of attitude change. But changes in attitude can also be studied by looking at, and seeking explanations for, patterns of actions and behaviors. Stuart W. Cook refers to this approach as one that uses *event* theories, rather than the *process* theories that we described in Chapter 11. Event theories include hypotheses that seek to explain recurring patterns of events. For example, are we more likely to change our attitudes if an expert or authority, rather than a friend, tries to persuade us to change? Are rational, fact-filled communications more persuasive than emotional ones? You can see from these questions that event theories attempt to isolate factors that may influence changes in attitude or behavior. In the present chapter we identify some of those factors and describe their effects. Then we consider the use of event theories to explain changes in attitudes that are negative toward minority groups. A major portion of the chapter is devoted to a study that seeks to change prejudiced attitudes in a controlled, yet natural, setting.

I. What causes attitudes to change?

To explain attitude change through an event approach, we need first a classification of types of events. Such a classification helps us understand the multitude of possible influences.

A. Types of events

1. Events within the person. An attitude may change because of the personality of the person holding the attitude. Individuals may seek to achieve certain states that lead to attitude change; for example, seeking to satisfy a need for social approval may lead to the development of attitudes that are congruent with those of persons whom we revere or serve. People may decide to change their own attitudes or behaviors because they consider them unsatisfactory. New Year's resolutions may reflect such decisions, although for most of us they are rather ineffective. (See

Figure 12-1.) We shall consider these within-the-person events in more detail later in this section.

2. Events associated with a communication that attempts to change attitudes. We may think of persuasive communications—such as television commercials, ministers' sermons, or pep talks from coaches, teachers, and employers—as containing a number of qualities. The *content* of the persuasive communication is, of course, important, but so may be the *source*. Who is telling us what to believe? Is he or she believable and trustworthy (a *credible source*)?

Figure 12-1

New Year's resolutions as instigators of change. Traditionally New Year's is a time for making resolutions to change one's own attitudes and behavior. How effective are such pledges? Marlatt and Kaplan (1972) questioned 382 of their students at the University of Wisconsin and found that 135 of them had made an average of 2.9 resolutions each on New Year's. (The remaining 247 had made none at all.) The most frequent resolutions included vows to lose weight, reduce smoking, be friendlier, date more, get along with parents better, raise one's grade-point average, and lift weights.

Marlatt and Kaplan chose resolutions to lose weight as the ones to follow up, since they were frequent ($N = 52$) and their effectiveness could be measured. These 52 students were asked to report weekly for a weigh-in after their resolution. The outcome, sad to report, was that no significant loss in weight was recorded, and some resolvers gained weight.

Other qualities of the communication may also be important—its tone, for example: is it more effective to be extreme, or to moderate the tone? Does the communication present only one side of an issue or both sides? If the latter, does the communicator put his position first or last (the primacy-versus-recency question discussed in Chapter 3)? All these potential influences have been investigated by social psychologists; their effects are described in Section II of this chapter.

3. Events associated with the setting in which the attempt to change an attitude occurs. The most persuasive communication in the world may literally fall on deaf ears if it is presented in the middle of a superloud rock concert. On the other hand, attempts to persuade may be more effective if presented with a background of pleasant stimulation. For example, several studies (Janis, Kaye, & Kirschner, 1965; Dabbs & Janis, 1965) found greater acceptance of a persuasive communication if the person ate as he read the message; the researchers ascribed this outcome to a momentary mood of compliance created by the pleasant activity of eating. A similar effect was found when subjects listened to folk songs that advocated certain positions (such as "Who Killed Davey Moore" by Pete Seeger, the story of a boxer who died in a fight and a plea for the abolition of boxing). Some subjects heard guitar accompaniment when the song was spoken or sung; others did not. The presence of the musical accompaniment facilitated acceptance of the message (Galizio & Hendrick, 1972).

Distracting aspects of the situation in which the persuasive communication occurs may either heighten attitude change or reduce its likelihood. For instance, distraction may prevent the recipient from developing counterarguments, thus leading to greater change (Osterhouse & Brock, 1970). On the other hand, as we noted in the section on S-R theory in Chapter 11, a person must attend to and comprehend a message before it can make a difference, and distracting aspects of the situation may prevent the recipient of the communication from doing so (R. S. Baron, Baron, & Miller, 1973).

The setting often includes the presence of other people, who can influence both private attitudes and public behavior. Because there has been a great deal of study on how much the responses of others can change our responses, we shall defer discussion of this topic to Chapter 19, on conformity.

B. Personality and response to persuasive communications

Are there people who, by the nature of their personalities, are more responsive than others to *any* attempt to change their attitudes, regardless of its content or the setting? Conversely, are there people who maintain resistance to efforts, even the best designed and most appropriate ones, to make them change? The answer is yes, to a slight degree (McGuire, 1968a, 1968b). There are a few people for whom the intrapersonal factors are so overriding that they determine, by themselves, whether or not there will be acceptance of virtually any persuasive communication. (See also Figure 12-2.) However, in a vast majority of cases the personality of the recipient *interacts* with other factors, such as those described above, to determine whether attitude change takes place or not.

Among the characteristics of personality that seem influential in affecting response to persuasive attempts are *self-confidence* and the *need for social approval.* Common sense would predict that the less self-confidence one possesses, the greater one's susceptibility to persuasion by others. There is some evidence to support such an assumption (Janis & Field, 1959). But among people lacking self-confidence a different reaction also may occur: they may become quite defensive and hence fail to act (Barach, 1969; Bauer, 1970) or they may even change their opinions in the direction *opposite* to that advocated (D. F. Cox & Bauer, 1964).

It appears that persons lacking self-confidence are often motivated to avoid making mistakes (Barach, 1974); depending on the circumstances, this motivation leads those lacking self-esteem sometimes to go along if that seems

Figure 12-2
Brainwashing and
persuasive communications
directed toward prisoners
of war. Many of the
"confessions" signed by
U. S. prisoners of war during
the Korean War and the
Vietnam War reflected only
a change in behavior, with
no change in attitude.
Likewise, Commander
Lloyd Bucher of the captured
U. S. ship *Pueblo* signed a
false confession rather than
see his men shot one by one
before his eyes. But some
POWs have undergone
changes in attitude as a
result of the highly
persuasive efforts of their
captors. (Photo by D.E.F.A.)

safest, or to resist if there are safe alternatives available. McGuire (1972) has concluded that the non-linear relationship between self-confidence and persuasibility is a result of two phenomena: (1) our ability to resist persuasive pressure increases with our degree of self-confidence, and (2) our openness to and ability to comprehend persuasive stimuli—and hence, perhaps, to respond—also increase with self-confidence.

It seems likely that persons who possess a strong *need for social approval* would be more accepting than others of persuasive communications. This is true, to a degree, according to a carefully done study of responses of junior-high-school students to appeals for better dental hygiene practices (Rozelle, Evans, Lasater, Dembroski, & Allen, 1973). Even though Crowne and Marlowe presented findings that indicate that those persons with a relatively high need for social approval are "more responsive than lows to perceived situational demands and are more likely to respond affirmatively to social influence" (1964, p. 84), Rozelle and his colleagues found that even the message based on the person's need for social approval (it emphasized the outcome

of "popularity") had little effect on the students' actual behavior. However, people with greater needs for social approval reported greater *intentions* to behave in the prescribed fashion. Once again we see the lack of consistency between intrapersonal characteristics such as attitudes (or, in this case, intentions) and behavior, as discussed in Chapter 10. In the present context, this finding reminds us of the interrelationship of events described earlier: that personality characteristics may interact with other events in determining acceptance or rejection of a persuasive communication.

II. Effects of components of the persuasive communication

We have seen that whether or not a persuasive communication has its intended effects depends to some degree on the personality of the recipient. Certainly components of the message itself should also be influential. In this section we consider the source of the message, the effects of one-sided versus two-sided communications, the order of presentation, and the extremity of the content.

A. The source

Who says something to you influences your reactions to *what* is said. In studying the effects of the spokesperson, or *source*, social psychologists have most frequently varied the *credibility* of the source. The study in Chapter 11 by Bochner and Insko that advocated different amounts of sleep is an example of this technique, because the advocacy speech was presented by either a Nobel prize–winning scientist or a YMCA director. As used in most research, *credibility* refers primarily to trustworthiness, believability, and expertise (Schweitzer & Ginsburg, 1966; R. G. Smith, 1973). Often, objectivity or impartiality is also included. Of course, just how credible a source is may depend on the point of view of the recipient (Rosnow & Robinson, 1967); usually judges are among those used as highly credible sources, but a particular person may have reason to distrust any statement made by a judge.

In general, there will be more attitude change in the desired direction if the communicator has high credibility than if he or she has low credibility (Hovland & Weiss, 1951; Karlins & Abelson, 1970). But there are qualifications to this conclusion:

1. The personality and attitudes of the recipient can interact with the credibility of the source. For example, sources who are authorities are likely to have more effect on recipients in general, but they are especially influential for recipients who are quite dogmatic (J. Harvey & Hays, 1972). (The concept of **dogmatism** is discussed extensively in Chapter 18.)

One's locus of control (see Chapter 3) can also interact with source credibility. Ritchie and Phares (1969) predicted that recipients whose locus of control was external would perceive sources who were low in credibility as unlikely sources of reinforcement and hence would be more persuaded by sources high in credibility.

Those recipients who believed that they possessed internal locus of control should be influenced equally by low- and high-credibility persuaders. And recipients high in internal locus of control should change attitudes less than those with external beliefs. All three hypotheses were confirmed. More recently, McGinnies and Ward (1974) found the same relationships in United States subjects, but not in those in Australia.

2. If recipients are not receptive to a communication—if they lack motivation to attend to it—highly credible sources are no more influential than distrusted ones (Brock & Becker, 1965; Jellison, 1970).

3. The nature of the communication may interact with the credibility of the source to "dampen" the effect. This explains why in some cases the less credible source was just as persuasive as the more credible one. For example, in a classic study 25 years ago, Hovland and Weiss (1951) presented a communication stating that there would be a decrease in the number of movie theaters in the United States. This message was attributed either to *Fortune* magazine (highly credible) or to a gossip columnist (low in credibility). In this study, the "low-credibility" source was actually somewhat more effective in changing attitudes. Walster, Aronson, and Abrahams (1966), in explaining these results, suggested that the gossip columnist, although perhaps considered to be usually unreliable, may have been more effective here because she was seen as arguing *against her own best interests*. These researchers then conducted two experiments that confirmed such an interpretation. That is, when a communicator's vested interest was quite apparent, he or she was more influential when arguing for a position that contradicted his or her own best interests than when advocating a position congenial to his or her own best interests.

As McGarry and Hendrick indicate, "the effects of credibility on persuasion cannot be adequately viewed as a simple function of general expertness and trustworthiness" (1975, p. 1). The relationship is more complex, with such factors as the audience's motivation, their perceptions of the source's self-interest, and their perceptions of how much the source likes them (J. Mills, 1966) all contributing to the outcome.

Characteristics of the source other than credibility are also influential. For example, the *race* of the source can influence attitude change in those recipients who are prejudiced against that race (Aronson & Golden, 1962). Communicators who are physically attractive seem to be more effective (Mills & Aronson, 1965; Snyder & Rothbart, 1971), even when they are not judged as more credible. Thus, the use of movie stars and other beautiful people in TV commercials seems to have some empirical support.

B. One-sided versus two-sided presentations

Imagine that you have the task of presenting a persuasive message with the goal of changing someone else's attitude. You know the arguments for what you are advocating, but you are also aware that there is an opposing point of view. Should you present only your side, or should you acknowledge and attempt to refute the opposing viewpoint?

In answering this question, we again see how different factors interact to influence the outcome (McGinnies, 1966; Rosnow, 1968). As Karlins and Abelson put it,

> When the audience is generally friendly, or when your position is the only one that will be presented, or when you want immediate, though temporary, opinion change, present one side of the argument. [But when] the audience initially disagrees with you, or when it is probable that the audience will hear the other side from someone else, present both sides of the argument [1970, p. 22].

C. Order of presentation

If we grant that there are occasions when it is most effective to present both sides in a persuasive message, which side should be presented first for maximum impact? Here we face the question of **primacy** versus **recency** effects,

also discussed in regard to impression formation in Chapter 3. As in the case of forming first impressions, it is unclear whether the first or last information presented is most effective in changing an attitude. Fifty years ago Lund (1925) formulated a "law of primacy in persuasion" because he found that the side of an argument that was presented last changed attitudes somewhat, but not as much as the initial message did. But Hovland and Mandell (1952), who conducted their experiment in a different way, obtained results that supported the power of recency. Since then, further research (Lana, 1963a, 1963b, 1964a, 1964b; Insko, 1964; Rosnow, 1966; Crano, 1973; W. Wilson & Miller, 1968) has led to the conclusion that a number of variables help determine whether the side presented first or that presented last will be the more persuasive. One of the most thorough summaries is offered by Rosnow and Robinson:

> Instead of a general "law" of primacy, or recency, we have today an assortment of miscellaneous variables, some of which tend to produce primacy, ... others of which, to produce recency. ... Still others produce either order effect, depending on their utilization or temporal placement in a two-sided communication .... Nonsalient, controversial topics, interesting subject matter, and highly familiar issues tend toward primacy. Salient topics, uninteresting subject matter, and moderately unfamiliar issues tend to yield recency [1967, p. 89].

III. Reducing prejudice: The contact hypothesis

Antagonisms between racial, religious, or ethnic groups are characteristic of many nations. But expressions of prejudice and hostility can be reduced and controlled; Chapter 11 described methods that would be in keeping with various attitude-change theories. Later in this chapter a major intervention directed toward prejudice reduction will be explored, but before that we shall consider what influences the desired changes to occur.

Many people have made the optimistic assumption that if two racial or religious groups could be brought together, the hostility, antagonism, and prejudice often expressed by each toward the other would erode, and favorable attitudes would develop. This, in essence, is the *intergroup contact hypothesis.* Quite obviously, this hypothesis must be qualified before it can be considered valid. For example, French Canadians moving into "English" schools, Catholics and Protestants warring over the same streets in Northern Ireland, and hippies and police officers playing together in softball games are events that show how intergroup contact can have either beneficial or deleterious outcomes. Mere frequency of contact is of no import; the nature of the contact—as will be spelled out subsequently —is the determinant.

Despite this need for qualification, the contact hypothesis has the merit of recognizing that attempts to change prejudice without intergroup contact are doomed to fail. For example, programs that introduce new information about a minority group through lectures, films, and written materials have had no long-term effects on prejudiced attitudes (G. Watson, 1947; Williams, 1947). Attitude change cannot take place without some interaction between the prejudiced person and the minority group. Apparently personal association and involvement are the keys to success in changing attitudes (D. L. Robinson & O'Connor, 1974).

IV. Factors facilitating change in face-to-face contact

If certain conditions exist, then even involuntary contact between a prejudiced person and a member of a disliked group may have beneficial outcomes. Numerous studies done in field settings in the United States have clarified these conditions, which may be placed in two categories: (1) characteristics of the individuals who are in contact and (2) characteristics of the contact situation (S. W. Cook, 1970).

A. Characteristics of the individuals in contact

As indicated in Chapter 10, prejudice does not serve the same function for all persons with the same negative attitudes toward a minority group. The *causes* of a person's prejudice determine the degree to which that person might change. As Amir has indicated, "Certain personalities . . . will not be affected positively by interracial contact. Their inner security and their personal disorder will not permit them to benefit from the contact with a group against whom they are prejudiced because they will always need a scapegoat" (1969, p. 335). Mussen (1953) brought White and Black boys together for a four-week summer camp. As a group, the White boys' level of prejudice was the same after the camp as before. Some White boys became less prejudiced as a result of the experience; however, some became *more* prejudiced. The boys who became more anti-Black exhibited test responses that showed greater aggressive feelings and greater needs to defy authority.

The *intensity of the attitude* held by the prejudiced person can also influence the degree of attitude change. Again, an interaction effect occurs: that is, after contact, a group may appear to be just as prejudiced as before, when in reality some of its members have become less prejudiced and others have become more so. S. W. Cook (1957) has cited a study by Taylor on how Whites react to Blacks living in houses on the same block. Those Whites who had been favorable to Blacks before the first Black family moved in became even more favorable after Blacks had been living nearby for several weeks. Whites who had initially been against the idea of residential desegregation were even more negative after desegregation occurred. In many cases, contact intensifies whatever initial attitude one possesses.

396   Chapter Twelve

B. Characteristics of the situation

S. W. Cook has described five characteristics of the contact situation. Attitude change is facilitated when favorable conditions exist in all five aspects of the situation.

1. The potential for acquaintance. A person can have daily contact with another person over a number of years and yet not get to know that person as an individual. Our contacts with janitors, letter carriers, and cashiers are often examples of this. Such brief, superficial, role-oriented contacts do nothing to facilitate knowing the other person. If we can come to know people *as individuals,* learning their aspirations, their fears, their likes and dislikes, some attitude change may result. In big cities, apartment dwellers may know little about the family in the next apartment. Attitudes toward neighbors may be neutral or negative. But when Black and White housewives living in the same apartment building are brought together and have a chance to get to know each other as individual persons, attitude change in the direction of greater acceptance is the typical result (Deutsch & Collins, 1951; Wilner, Walkley, & Cook, 1955).

2. The relative status of the participants in a contact situation. Somewhat related to the preceding situational characteristic is the aspect of status. Beneficial attitude change is more likely if the minority-group member has the same status as the prejudiced person. If the minority-group member has either a lower status *or* a higher status, the interaction is likely to be role oriented, with less opportunity for authentic relationships between the participants.

3. The nature of the social norm concerning contact of one group with another. In some situations, the persons involved may feel that a friendly association is appropriate; in such cases, beneficial attitude change is more likely to result. Less attitude change results when the people involved have no expectation of a social relationship, as in business contacts.

Social norms are often reflected in the pronouncements of public officials. The school principal who tells irate parents "I don't like school desegregation either, but I have to enforce it" creates a social norm that discourages much change in attitudes towards Blacks, Puerto Ricans, or Chicanos. If the principal acts in compliance with the law and keeps quiet about his or her negative attitudes, there is greater chance that parents will comply with new policies and perhaps eventually come to accept their merit.

4. The presence of a cooperative reward structure rather than a competitive one. Reward structures often go hand-in-hand with social norms, but the two can also be unrelated. Norms for superficial congeniality may exist within a situation that also puts the White person in competition with the Black. To facilitate beneficial attitude change a different situation is necessary. There must be mutual interdependence, and the reward structure should be cooperative—that is, task goals for the White person should be attainable only when and if the Black person achieves his or her goals.

There is a great deal of recent evidence for the power of a cooperative orientation to reduce interracial tensions (Weigel, Wiser, & Cook, 1975; DeVries & Slavin, 1975). One impressive example is the project of Elliot Aronson and his colleagues (Aronson, Blaney, Sikes, Stephan, & Snapp, 1975; Aronson, Blaney, & Stephan, 1975). These social psychologists responded to a "crisis call" from the Austin, Texas, public-school system resulting from increased hostility between racially mixed groups of elementary-school children.

Aronson and his colleagues believe that most classrooms are arenas for competition rather than cooperation. The intense competition simply exacerbates tensions between children who come from different parts of town, "look different," and "talk different." In Aronson's project, fifth- and sixth-grade teachers were trained in the development of cooperative work groups for their students. Each child was assigned a small part of the lesson; only he or she "owned" that part of the lesson for the day. Each child then communicated his or her information in a process that resembled the assembling of a jigsaw puzzle. The procedure led to some dramatic changes in behavior:

> The children quickly learned that the only way they could learn the whole lesson (and do well on an upcoming exam) was to cooperate with the students in the group by listening attentively and helping each of them teach (by asking good questions, etc.). This required an entirely different set of behaviors than what was functional in a competitive situation. It usually required about one week for students to realize that the usual kinds of put-downs and insults were no longer functional [Aronson, Blaney, & Stephan, 1975, p. 2].

Such general procedures, emphasizing working toward common goals and requiring mutual interdependence among group members, have the effects of increasing attraction toward members of other racial groups and reducing interracial conflict in the classroom.

5. *The characteristics of the individuals who are in contact.* Particularly beneficial to favorable attitude change are contacts in which the participating minority-group members differ from commonly held, unflattering stereotypes of their group. (Contact with minority-group members who are of lesser status or accomplishment may support preexisting prejudices.) Interacting and working with a Black who is hardworking, bright, restrained, and not particularly musical or religious may be the stimulus for attitude change. It is also helpful if the member of the minority group resembles the majority-group member in regard to background, interests, and personality. The prejudiced White who realizes that his or her Black coworker is similar to him or her may be able to discard a stereotyped image of Blacks (Blanchard, Weigel, & Cook, 1974).

When a task brings different kinds of people together and places them in a situation in which their contacts are impersonal, the contacts probably will not lead to greater acceptance of the minority-group member by the White. Consider the desegregation of a public school in the United States. The school board may comply with a court order to desegregate but also convey its displeasure to the children and their parents. Black children may be bused from a different part of town, reifying their different status in the eyes of the White children. When such conditions prevail, school desegregation can lead to increased rejection of Blacks by Whites. (For an example, see Webster's 1961 study of the desegregation of a school in the San Francisco Bay Area.)

However, school authorities can do much to create conditions favorable to a desirable change in attitudes. When a school must change the racial composition of its student body, an implementation of the five conditions described here should influence the success of the change. Situations in which Blacks and Whites must work together to achieve a group goal should be sought. Examples of superordinate goals are building a new playground and seeking an all-city sportsmanship trophy.

V. Bringing the beneficial factors together: Stuart Cook's study

Stuart W. Cook (1964, 1970, 1971) has created an experimental situation with which to test the validity of the contact hypothesis. The goal of this ten-year project was to determine what happens to prejudiced attitudes when all the beneficial aspects of interracial contact are mobilized in the same situation. In this well-executed attempt to bring about a reduction in prejudice, anti-Black White subjects were involuntarily placed in contact with a Black. The assumptions, procedures, and results of Cook's project were as follows.

A. Assumptions

Cook (1964) recognized that involuntary interracial contact is a way of life in the contemporary United States. Even the most prejudiced

White persons—those who try to avoid contact with those different from themselves—must interact with persons of other races in a variety of settings, such as school, the military, or a job. The possibility of attitude change's taking place during the course of such involuntary social contact provided a potentially fruitful area of study.

Cook assumed that a reasonable delineation of the significant factors in the contact experience could be made on the basis of field studies from the past. (These factors were reviewed in Section IV.) Cook attempted to recreate the unintended interracial contact in a setting in which each potentially important factor could be controlled. The contact situation as it usually occurs in the field is often too complex to provide much understanding of why attitude change does or does not occur. Cook assumed that a laboratory setting could be created that would open the way to a more controlled analysis of the determinants of attitude change than had been permitted by field studies.

Cook also assumed that such a study would contribute to a better understanding of attitude-change theory. For example, the functional theory of attitude change could be verified if varying different factors of the contact experience produced changes in different types of subjects. Cook wrote that if analysis should

> show that change is strongly associated with the operation of situational norms regarding intergroup relations this would suggest that the change may be understood in terms of an affiliative (or security) need, e.g., the adoption of beliefs and feelings which bring a sense of identification with or acceptance by respected peers. A quite different implication would be suggested, however, by the discovery that change was most evident when the contact situation was characterized by cooperative interdependence in the achievement of shared goals and rewards. Here the process indicated would start with the generation of feelings of satisfaction and pleasure; such feelings would be associated with the participant from the disliked social group and gradually generalize to the group itself [1964, p. 6].

B. Procedure

Cook's study was carried out in a large city in the Southern part of the United States that contained several colleges. The study consisted of three stages, which used the same subjects but took place on two different college campuses. Potential subjects for the study came from four of the city's predominantly White colleges—all of which were within two miles of each other. The first stage of the study involved paid participation as a subject in a project for the "Institute for Test Development" at "Biltmore University" (not the true name of the university). The second stage took place at another local college, where the subjects worked for two hours a day for a month in a group project. This group project was designed to appear quite unrelated to the test development project; it was a different activity carried out at a different college by a different staff. The third stage of the study involved a retesting of the subject by the "Institute for Test Development" at "Biltmore University." Each of the three stages in the total project was separated from the next by two or more months.

Stage one: Pretesting. Because the staff members who would supervise the stage-two group project were both female, it was initially decided to seek only females as subjects for the project. The bogus "Institute for Test Development" recruited subjects by advertising in student newspapers. The sample who appeared probably had a high number of people who were curious or insecure in the sense that they welcomed the opportunity to get feedback about themselves. Thus we cannot consider it a representative sample of female undergraduates at these colleges.

The subjects were told that the institute was developing new tests and that one of its concerns was the test-retest reliability of its measures. At the first test session subjects were informed that because of this interest in reliability, they would be retested several months later, again for pay. This device prepared them for stage three of Cook's project, retesting after the interracial contact.

Stage two: Interracial contact. Among the 20 or so subjects in each testing series, usually between 3 and 8 subjects had scores on the prejudice measures that were extreme enough to qualify them for the second stage of the project. Cook sought only *clearly* anti-Black subjects for the interracial-contact situation—that is, only those whose scores were in the top third on prejudice on each of three basic prejudice measures.

Anywhere from a few days up to several months after the first testing, a highly prejudiced subject received a phone call from a faculty member at "St. George's College" (not the true name of the college), inviting her to apply for part-time work on a group project. The job would take two hours a day and last a month. The faculty member then went on to describe briefly a management task called the Railroad Game (B. T. Jensen & Terebinski, 1963). The faculty member explained that the task was being tried out as one of several tasks being evaluated by the government for the purpose of training groups of strangers to work together. The findings of the local study would be of value in understanding how crews at isolated bases might work together.

If a potential subject expressed interest, an appointment was arranged at "St. George's College." There followed three appointments during which the subject was interviewed, tested for suitability for the job, and given some training in the Railroad Game. She was then pronounced as suitable by the supervisor (though there never had been any doubt), and she signed a contract agreeing to work two hours a day for a month with the understanding that she would be paid nothing unless she completed the month's work. The purpose of these devices was to discourage the prejudiced subject from withdrawing from the project when she discovered that it was an interracial one. During the training, no reference was made to the fact that one of the other two crew members would be Black—any questions

from the subject about the other two crew members on the Railroad Game were answered by saying "You wouldn't know them; they're girls from two other colleges here." At one point during the training the supervisor introduced her helper, a Black female college student, but the subject could perceive the helper's position as subordinate and rather detached.

All these heavy-handed procedures were undertaken because the subjects were, in their expressed attitudes, so anti-Black that Cook questioned whether they would go through with the job when it was revealed that they would be working closely with a Black. On a sentence-completion task in stage one, many of these subjects had responded that they would either quit, move, or seek a transfer if put on a job with a Black. (Other typical responses are found in Table 12-1.) Additionally, the project was begun in 1961, when it was very unusual for Southern Blacks and Whites to be working together or eating together under conditions of equal status.

The group's task in the Railroad Game was to operate a railroad system composed of ten stations, six lines, and 500 freight cars of six different types. It took the group some time to

---

Table 12-1
Responses of prejudiced Whites to sentence-completion test

---

1. If they began admitting Negroes to the club to which I belong, I would . . .
   "drop out."
   "find another club."
   "stop it."
2. If my boss began hiring many Negroes, I would . . .
   "quit right away."
   "tell him to hire Whites or I'd leave."
   "not like it at all."
3. If someone at my church suggested inviting the Young People's group at a Negro church to a joint supper meeting, I would . . .
   "vote against it."
   "feel uncomfortable."
   "throw up."

learn how to operate the system efficiently. One reason was that much information had to be acquired; a second, that they had to learn how to maintain a distribution of cars—appropriate for upcoming shipping orders—at different stations. When requests were received to ship merchandise of specified types from one station to another, the group was to make a decision as to which route to follow and what types of cars to use. These decisions were then telephoned by the crew to the supervisor and her helper who were located behind a screen in another part of the workroom. (See Figure 12-3.) The helper maintained a computer system, which furnished the crew with the official records of the dispersion of cars, profits earned, losses and penalties incurred, and the like.

As used in Cook's project, the Railroad Game lasted 40 "days"—a day covering about 30 to 40 minutes. An experimental session was composed of two such "days" separated by a 30-minute break. The purpose of the break was explained to the subject as giving the supervisor and her helper time to prepare materials; in actuality, it was used for other purposes to be explained subsequently.

On the first session of the month-long job, the prejudiced subject met with the other two crew members for the first time. Both were female students at a local college. One crew member, given the dispatcher's job, was White. The other, the accountant, was Black. Both were to act as though they were novices to the situation, but in fact both were confederates of the experimenter. The supervisor (who was a White in her 30s) briefly reviewed the task and mentioned the crew's opportunity to make bonus money by outdoing the performance of earlier crews. After answering questions, the supervisor gave the crew their first day's shipping orders and retired behind the screen. The crew, all seated at the same table, could communicate directly with each other but could talk to the supervisor and her helper only by telephone. (See layout in Figure 12-3.)

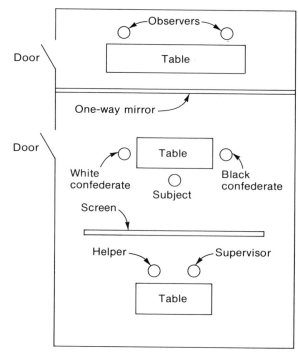

Figure 12-3
Layout of the "Railroad Game" workroom

After 30 minutes of running the railroad, plus overtime if the crew wished to use it to complete the "day's" orders, there was a 30-minute lunch break. Food ordered at the beginning of the session was brought in by the supervisor and her helper, who then departed. The crew distributed the food and retained their same seating locations for lunch. Conversations during the early sessions concentrated on the Railroad Game and getting to know each other. The true purpose of this lunch break was to create a situation that fulfilled the beneficial characteristics described in Section IV of this chapter. It may be helpful to review these to see how their requirements were met in this situation.

1. The *acquaintance potential* was facilitated by the conversation of the confederates. The Black confederate brought to each lunch-break

conversation facts about herself, her family, her future plans and aspirations, and such personal information as her preferences, tastes, apprehensions, and disappointments. Sometimes facts were volunteered; sometimes they were evoked by preplanned questions from the White confederate. Questions directed to the Black by the subject (if they occurred) also provided opportunities for the dissemination of information. Observers behind a one-way mirror kept a frequency tabulation of the amount of personal information brought out by each confederate; this procedure served as a check so that the amount of personal information could be roughly equated from one subject to another.

2. In compliance with the second factor, *relative status of the participants*, the Black confederate was defined by the situation as being of equal status with the other two crew members. Her job responsibilities and authority were equal to theirs. Built into the procedure was a rotation of crew assignments, which reinforced the equality of status for the three participants.

3. The third factor, *social norms regarding contact between groups*, was handled by making it clear to all participants that the situation favored acceptance of Blacks. The White supervisor had a Black helper to whom she allocated a great deal of responsibility. The Black crew member was treated the same as the Whites. Beyond this expression by the institutionalized structure, other ways of communicating a favorable norm were utilized. With time, the White confederate increasingly expressed sympathy with the Black and disapproval of segregation.

4. The *presence of a cooperative reward structure* was achieved through the structure of the Railroad Game. The subject was involved in efforts to achieve a goal in common with the Black participant. For instance, if the group did well, a bonus was paid to each group member. Thus, the situation avoided a reward structure in which participants work individually toward mutually exclusive goals. In addition, the Railroad Game procedure led to close interaction and mutual

assistance between the prejudiced White person and the Black, especially when these participants were paired as the dispatcher and the status keeper. The two, together with the White confederate, shared reverses as well as successes day by day for 20 calendar days. Moreover, the rotation of crew assignments put the prejudiced White person in a position of both teaching the Black and being taught by her.

5. The *characteristics of the individuals in contact* were also considered. The Black confederate was selected and presented throughout as being personable, able, ambitious, and self-respecting. Care was taken to see that the Black did her Railroad Game tasks well. Thus, the Black participant was quite a different person from the stereotyped one expected by the prejudiced White.

Additionally, the Black confederate presented information about the injustices and indignities she had suffered as a result of racial discrimination. On 10 of the 20 calendar days in which the crew was together, their conversations were preplanned, eventually leading to a discussion of race relations. For example, an early conversation topic was shopping for clothing. In a briefing session, the Black confederate and the White confederate were trained to put across particular points regarding discrimination against Blacks by downtown department stores. (For example, in the early 1960s department stores in the South would not permit a Black to try on clothes at the store. Instead, the store would deliver clothes to the Black's home, where they could be tried on without the knowledge of Whites.) During the lunch-break conversation, after some general trading of experiences, the White confederate would ask the Black a question regarding the matter of segregation in the sales practices of department stores. The race-relations aspect of the discussion lent itself to a review of injustices and indignities suffered by the Black participant or by persons she knew.

As the month-long contact experience continued, the White confederate became more openly upset about the ways in which Blacks were being persecuted in United States society. However, the confederate avoided asking the subject to agree with this opinion. If subjects were put on the spot by such questioning, they probably would have become defensive about their prejudiced attitudes and hence more rigidified in these attitudes.

On the final calendar day of the Railroad Game, the last half-hour was devoted to a questionnaire that was filled out by each crew member in a separate room. The subject was told that the purpose of this procedure was to evaluate the Railroad Game as a potential training task. Included were several open-ended questions about the other crew members, but the topic of race was not mentioned. Although the subject's answers to these questions might have revealed her reactions to the confederates, Cook did not use them as a measure of attitude change, as he was interested in whether there were changes in attitude toward Blacks as a group.

The week after the completion of the Railroad Game the subject was provided with an additional experience that was designed to encourage generalization from the single Black to other Blacks. (Finding a modification of feelings and behavior toward a specified Black participant without an accompanying generalization to Blacks as a group would not have been surprising.) The additional experience was a series of five interviews with other college women. These interviews were carried out by the subject as a basis for rating persons who were presented as potential participants in the next Railroad Game. Of the five persons interviewed by the subject, two were Blacks and three were Whites.

Stage three: Retesting of attitudes. Between one and three months after the termination of the part-time job at "St. George's College," each subject received a letter from the "Institute for Test Development" at "Biltmore University." The letter was a reminder to the subject that there would be an opportunity to serve as a paid sub-

ject for additional tests. Each subject was scheduled to retake most of the original tests, including the tests measuring attitudes. The obtained changes in attitude on the measures of prejudice were used as indicators of the effectiveness of the attitude-change intervention.

C. Results

The outcomes of this project can be described at three levels: *anecdotal* evidence for changes in behavior and attitudes toward the Black participant, *objective* evidence for changes toward that specific Black, and differences in response to the measures of attitudes toward Blacks *in general*.

Anecdotal evidence. It should be remembered that not only had the prejudiced Whites in this project had little or no previous contact with Blacks, but most of them, in completing their paper-and-pencil tests, had also expressed strong personal rejection of Blacks. At the beginning of the project the idea of eating with a Black was probably unpleasant to every one of the prejudiced Whites.

In light of such factors, consider what happened during a lunch break late in the month of one crew. As usual, the crew members had ordered their lunches before the first "day" of the game; the food was to be delivered from the college snack bar before the lunch break. One high point of this procedure was anticipating what type of pie the snack bar was offering that day. On this day the subject decided to forgo a piece of pie, but the Black confederate ordered one. When the lunches arrived, the crew discovered that blackberry pie was being served—the subject's favorite. As the Black confederate ate her pie, the subject kept turning her eyes to the pie as if hypnotized. Finally, after the Black confederate cast aside her half-eaten pie, the subject turned to her and said "Betty Jean, would you mind if I ate the rest of your pie?" Surely, had the prejudiced White been told one month before that she would soon be eating a Black person's leftovers, the suggestion would have been met with ridicule.

Numerous other anecdotal examples showed changes in the behavior of prejudiced Whites toward Blacks. One subject hitched a ride downtown with the Black confederate because it would save her bus fare. Other subjects were visibly influenced by the content of the lunchtime conversations and were particularly touched by the Black confederate's recounting of indignities she had suffered. The conversations presented opportunities for relearning for many of the prejudiced Whites; they had never realized, for example, that Blacks traveling across the South in the early 1960s could never be sure whether they could use the rest rooms at gasoline stations. The Whites did not know that the textbooks in all-Black high schools were outdated hand-me-downs from White schools or that many Blacks had struggled to complete college and then found that the only jobs available to them were as porters or maids. Such new information seemed to create discomfort in the White subjects. The communications that took place during the lunch breaks served to focus the attention of the subjects—a necessary factor in the attitude-change model advanced by the Yale Communication Research Program (presented in Chapter 11).

Objective changes in behavior toward the Black participant. When the three participants were introduced at the beginning of the month-long project, the prejudiced White typically treated the Black with deliberate neglect. The White subject would direct her questions and comments almost entirely to the other White and very rarely turn her head toward the Black. The seating arrangement illustrated in Figure 12-3 was designed to permit observers behind a one-way mirror to tally the number of times the subject directed comments toward each of the other two participants. In most cases, the subject shifted during the month from a pattern of directing comments solely toward the other White to a pattern that included the Black in a significant number of interactions. Toward the end of the project approximately 60% of the prejudiced subject's comments were directed toward the White and 40% toward the Black (disregarding comments directed toward both).

Likewise, there were great changes in extent of physical contact over the month's time. At the beginning of the project, the typical prejudiced White resolutely avoided contact with the Black. As time went on, the White subject was less apprehensive about leaning her arm against the Black's to pick up a new order or to examine a bracelet. At the end of the project, some subjects sought opportunities to keep the Black as a friend, suggesting that they go shopping or double-date. All these occurrences indicate strong changes in many of the prejudiced White subjects toward a specific Black. The remaining question was whether or not the changes were generalized to all Blacks.

Changes in responses to attitude measures. All of the subjects were retested sometime between one and nine months after they had completed the Railroad Game. Changes in their prejudice scores were compared with the changes in control subjects who did not participate in the Railroad Game. These control subjects were initially as anti-Black as the experimental subjects, and the time intervals between testings were about the same. However, the experimentals and the controls were not randomly divided into those two groups. Rather, the controls were those test subjects who had negative attitudes but had *turned down* the opportunity to participate in the Railroad Game. It would have been better to choose the control subjects from a group that had expressed interest in the Railroad Game but had not been used, but there were not enough prejudiced test subjects to implement that procedure.

For the first 23 Railroad Game subjects three measures of attitude were basic. One measure used was the School Segregation scale by Komorita (1963), which deals with desegregation policy with an emphasis on school desegregation. It is a Likert-type scale made up of 67 items to which respondents indicate their degrees of agreement or disagreement. A second measure used was Westie's Summated Difference scale (Westie, 1953); it is a social-distance scale covering the topics of residential desegregation, community leadership, personal relationships, and physical contact. Scores on it are derived from the differences in the person's acceptance of Whites and of Blacks with the same occupations. The third measure used was the sentence-completion test described previously, items from which are given in Table 12-1. This set of 10 items, developed by Getzels and Walsh (1958), requires the subject to complete statements dealing with their reaction to interracial situations. The 10 items are imbedded in a set of 100 items dealing with a variety of issues.

The amount of change in each subject was assessed by using the standard deviation, a measure of dispersion in the scores for a group. The standard deviation of a group of subjects for each of the three tests was determined after administering each test to students from three local colleges. Then the amount of change for each subject on each test could be expressed in terms of the standard deviation. A standard deviation is expressed by a number of points; if the group's scores are distributed in a normal fashion, with most of the scores toward the middle and fewer and fewer toward each extreme, there will be about six standard deviations within the set of scores. Thus, if a person's score shifts three standard deviations, her new score is halfway across the distribution from her old score. This would be considered a large shift in score. (It would be equivalent to an IQ score's changing from 70 to 115, or from 95 to 140.) A change in score equal to one standard deviation is generally regarded as an important change. This was the criterion used by Cook.

Eight of 23 subjects in the first project (35%) changed in the direction of less negative attitudes toward Blacks. (Of these, 7 changed by more than one standard deviation, ranging from

1.1 to 2.9; the remaining subject was just below the criterion point, with a change of .84 of a standard deviation.) Among the group of 23 female controls, none averaged a change of one standard deviation, although 2 were close, changing .91 and .90 of a standard deviation. Some subjects' attitudes were more negative on retesting. Among the experimental subjects, 1 changed an average of .82 of a standard deviation in a negative direction after participating in the Railroad Game. This same degree of negative change was found in 2 control subjects (.76 and .73), even though they had not participated in the intervention procedure.

A more substantial feeling for the degree of change can be gained by looking at the kinds of changes in specific subjects. Cook's descriptions of three of these subjects are presented in Figure 12-4.

A similar pattern is indicated by the second series of subjects, who participated in the project three years later. Significantly more Railroad Game subjects than control subjects had changed their attitude in the desired direction by the time of retesting. Once again, in the second series, the percentage of experimental subjects who changed one standard deviation or more was between 35 and 40%. About 40% retained essentially the same attitudes, and approximately 20% became even more prejudiced in their attitudes toward Blacks.

What are we to make of these results? In one sense, the findings provide some hope that prejudiced attitudes can, indeed, be changed. Although it is impossible to compare the extent of changes directly with changes observed in earlier field studies, Cook believes that the number and the degree of changes here are at least as great as the changes recorded in field studies. Moreover, Cook's results were achieved after only 40 hours of actual contact, whereas most field studies operate over a much longer time span (Cook, 1970).

In several ways, however, the results are not very satisfactory. For example, we cannot know whether those subjects who changed will

Figure 12-4

Types of attitude change resulting from interracial contact in the Railroad Game study

Stuart W. Cook has described the types of change shown by subjects after their month-long interracial contact. Three cases are presented below:

The first had initially rejected the idea of having Negroes on her city council or heading her community chest drive. She balked at sharing restrooms and beauty parlors with them. She was averse to the idea that she might exchange social visits with Negroes or have them as dinner guests. All of these relationships she accepted at the time of the posttest.

The second had endorsed complete residential segregation but after the experiment said she would welcome Negroes in her part of town. She came to accept them in leadership positions from which earlier she wished to exclude them. She made the same change with respect to exchanging social visits with Negroes and sharing with them beauty parlors, rest rooms, and dressing rooms in department stores.

The third subject made similar changes. She abandoned her former endorsement of residential segregation, accepting Negroes as next-door neighbors. She moved entirely away from rejecting the idea of potential physical contact with Negroes in beauty parlors, rest rooms, and dressing rooms. She came to accept them as social visitors and dinner guests.

From "Motives in a Conceptual Analysis of Attitude-Related Behavior," by S. W. Cook, *Nebraska Symposium on Motivation, 1969.* Copyright 1970 by the University of Nebraska Press. Reprinted by permission.

retain their less negative attitudes. Though Cook's procedure is highly commendable in that retesting was delayed for at least one month after the contact experience, one cannot know whether the changed attitudes will endure for extended periods. Quite possibly, when a subject who has changed her attitudes returns to a situation in which prejudices are expressed, she will revert to her initial negative position. The problems

of retesting the subjects every six months or so for an indefinite period of time are obvious. (To complete the first retesting Cook had to locate two Railroad Game subjects who had moved 200 or 300 miles away.) Future research should build on Cook's study, following up over a long period of time those persons who participated in involuntary interracial-contact situations.

Another reason for dissatisfaction with Cook's findings is the limited percentage of persons who changed. If 40% of the subjects developed less negative attitudes as a result of contact, why did not all the subjects change in this direction? Why did some become more negative? Cook has pointed out that perhaps some persons are more resistant to attitude change because of factors in their personal makeup. Clearly, intrapersonal factors are involved in producing attitude change in some persons but not in others. To gain greater understanding of the intrapersonal attributes related to change, a comparison was made between subjects whose attitudes changed and subjects whose attitudes did not change. The results of this analysis are described in the next section.

VI. Why do some people change their attitudes when others do not?

Let us consider the intrapersonal characteristics that would make a prejudiced White person more susceptible to change under the conditions of the Railroad Game study. Two constructs can be used in the way of an explanation: *self-concept* and *assumptions about people in general.* A person who is dissatisfied with his or her self-concept may be more susceptible to change than someone who is happy or complacent about his or her present state of being. Thus, a negative self-concept may facilitate or instigate change. A second factor is also needed if change is to take place. The prejudiced White person must be willing to listen to and trust other people, who serve as the agents of change. That is, if a prejudiced White person holds favorable assumptions about other people, then that person will accept what others say or do as genuine, correct, and well advised. But if a person has unfavorable assumptions about people in general—if he or she disparages or distrusts what other people say or do—then that person is not likely to be influenced by communications aimed toward her or him. Even a very negative self-concept will not facilitate attitude change in the Railroad Game situation, if the subject distrusts the other people involved.

To test this minitheory, 10 Railroad Game subjects who became more favorable in their racial attitudes were compared with the 13 subjects who did not become more favorable. These two groups were called the positive changers and the nonchangers (although the nonchangers actually included one subject who became more negative in her racial attitudes). Responses to the 15-hour battery of tests were used to compare these two groups of subjects (Wrightsman & Cook, 1965; Cook & Wrightsman, 1967). From this battery, 78 different measures were available. They were statistically analyzed to see which ones clustered together or were measuring the same general construct. (This procedure is called *factor analysis*.) The 11 factors that emerged from this procedure are listed in Table 12-2. It is important to recognize that these factors are abstractions, which represent what is common to a variety of measures. The names of the factors are assigned by the researchers doing the analysis and are based on their judgment of what is common to those measures that are highly related to a particular factor. For example, Factor 1 in Table 12-2 is called *rigidity*. The results of the factor analysis showed that the following tests are highly related to the rigidity factor: Gough Sanford Rigidity scale, Wesley Rigidity scale, Independence of Judgment measure on Welsh Figure Preference Test (on this test a low score indicated rigidity), Rehfisch Rigidity scale, Rokeach's Dogmatism scale, and so on. Considering the content of these tests and their high relationship to Factor 1, we

can see why the word *rigidity* was used to indicate what was being measured *in common* by all these scales.

Table 12-2
Results of factor analysis

Factor Number	Title Given to Factor
1	Rigidity
2	Hostility and Anxiety
3	Anti-Negro Attitudes
4	Aptitudes and Abilities
5	Positive Attitudes toward People
6	Sociability
7	Tolerance for Unpleasantness
8	Negativism about Self
9	Attitudes toward Teaching
10	Positive Response Set
11	Residual Factor

Adapted from "The Factorial Structure of 'Positive Attitudes toward People,'" by S. W. Cook and L. S. Wrightsman. Symposium paper presented at the meeting of the Southeastern Psychological Association, Atlanta, April 1967. Used by permission of the authors.

Table 12-2 shows that the factors together cover a wide range of intrapersonal characteristics. There are personality characteristics (Factors 1, 2, 6, 7, and 8), racial attitudes (Factor 3), and other attitudes (Factors 5 and 9); and there is a factor representing the aptitude and ability measures used in the battery (Factor 4). The last two factors in the analysis represent only the variance that remained after the preceding nine factors extracted what was common to each of the measures. In other words, Factors 10 and 11 are of little importance.

Each of the 11 factors can be considered as composite scores, and a composite score on each factor can be obtained for each subject. Thus we now have, for each of the 10 positive changers and each of the 13 nonchangers, a composite score on each of the 11 factors. The two groups of subjects may now be compared on each factor. The question to be asked is: do the positive changers, as a group, significantly differ from the nonchangers in their average score on any of the factors? The mean scores for each group are reported in Table 12-3. First of all, let us note some of the factors for which there is no difference in initial score between the positive changers and the nonchangers. For example, those prejudiced Whites whose attitudes changed after the Railroad Game experience were no more and no less rigid than were the prejudiced participants whose attitudes did not change (Factor 1). Positive changers were no more or less hostile or anxious than the nonchangers (Factor 2). Surprisingly, their initial anti-Black attitudes were no less intense or extreme than those of the nonchangers. Other factors on which the positive changers and the non-changers did not differ in average score are indicated as nonsignificant in Table 12-3.

As shown in Table 12-3, Factors 5, 7, and 8 had a significant p value. For example, for Factor 5 (positive attitudes toward people) the p value was .01, which shows that on this factor the average scores for the two groups were significantly different; in only 1 comparison out of 100 (that is, .01) could a difference in means as large as this have occurred by chance, or coincidence. The significance level for the other two (Factors 7 and 8) is not as extreme, but in each case the level of significance is great enough to permit a conclusion that the two groups are truly different in average score. Let us consider each of these three factors in turn.

Factor 5 (positive attitudes toward people) includes high loadings from the following measures: Philosophies of Human Nature scale, Machiavellianism scale (negative loading), Anomie

Table 12-3

A comparison of factor scores of subjects whose attitudes changed favorably versus subjects whose attitudes did not change favorably

Factor Number	Factor Title	Mean Factor Scores		p Value of Difference between Means
		Positive Changers (N = 10)	Nonchangers (N = 13)	
1	Rigidity	+3.23	+3.72	N.S.
2	Hostility and Anxiety	+1.13	+2.26	N.S.
3	Anti-Negro Attitudes	+7.75	+7.27	N.S.
4	Aptitudes and Abilities	−1.26	−2.82	N.S.
5	Positive Attitudes toward People	+3.68	−4.46	.01
6	Sociability	−0.58	+0.06	N.S.
7	Tolerance for Unpleasantness	−0.54	+0.95	.025
8	Negativism about Self	+0.46	−1.17	.025
9	Attitudes toward Teaching	+0.95	+0.08	N.S.
10	Positive Response Set	+1.52	+0.94	N.S.
11	Residual	+0.72	+1.27	N.S.

Note: N.S. = Nonsignificant difference. (Adapted from "Factor Analysis and Attitude Change," by L.S. Wrightsman and S.W. Cook. Paper presented at the meeting of the Southeastern Psychological Association, Atlanta, April 1965. Used by permission of the authors.)

scale (negative loading), faith in people, and Edwards' Social Desirability scale. Thus, Factor 5 definitely represents an accumulation of variables that are concerned with attitudes toward people in general. One aspect of **anomie,** for example, is a belief that other people are uninterested and unsympathetic. The Machiavellianism scale (see Chapter 4) indicates a cynical belief about others. The Philosophies of Human Nature scale (as described in Chapter 3) provides a measure of one's general positive or negative attitude toward human nature. A positive score on this factor means that the subject is un-Machiavellian and believes people in general are good, trustworthy, unselfish, and not alienated. As shown in Table 12-3, the mean of the positive changers was +3.68 (a positive value), while the mean of the nonchangers was −4.46, indicating that the nonchangers as a group did not see human nature as good, trustworthy, and so on. In fact, 11 of the 13 nonchangers were below the neutral point on this factor, while only 2 of the positive changers were below neutral (and then only barely). These findings confirm the notion that subjects who enter an experience of interracial contact with cynical, distrusting attitudes toward human nature are unlikely to change in the direction of more favorable interracial attitudes.

Factor 7 (tolerance for unpleasantness) is not an easily labeled factor, because the measures contributing to it do not seem to be conceptually similar. Positive scores on the factor apparently mean that the persons have little need for social approval and are rather escapist in their thought patterns. Table 12-3 points out that this description fits the nonchangers more than the positive changers—a result that is in line with the expectations of the minitheory.

People with positive scores on Factor 8 (negativism about self) are dissatisfied with their self-concepts. They have indicated a relatively large discrepancy between the way they are and the way they would like to be. Additionally, test loadings on Factor 8 indicate that persons scoring positively on this factor are pessimistic about their personal future and are dependent on others. Table 12-3 reflects that the positive changers are, as a group, above the mean on this factor, while the group of nonchangers lacks such negativism toward themselves. Thus, the second aspect of the minitheory is confirmed.

There is some evidence then that a situation that is carefully designed to reduce the amount of prejudice directed toward a minority group will succeed only in some cases. One determinant of success resides within the participants: their self-evaluations and their expectations about other people are important.

VII. Summary

We can learn about determinants of attitude change by looking at the patterns of events that lead to change or nonchange. In classifying events, we note that there are (1) events within the person (such as personality, self-confidence, or need for social approval), (2) events associated with the persuasive communication, and (3) events associated with the setting in which the attempt to change an attitude occurs.

The source of a persuasive communication has an effect on whether it is accepted or not. Generally, those messages attributed to sources who are highly credible (expert, trustworthy, believable) are more likely to be effective. However, the perceived self-interest of the source interacts with the source's credibility to influence degree of acceptance.

The effect of one-sided versus two-sided persuasive communications depends on the friendliness of the audience and the desires for temporary versus relatively permanent change. Order of presentation (the primacy-recency issue) also has complex effects. Presentation of one's own viewpoint at the beginning of a message is most effective when the topic is one of interest to the audience or is a controversial one with which the audience has little involvement.

Any change in interracial attitudes is unlikely to occur from interventions such as lectures, films, and other procedures that do not bring groups into contact with one another. The hypothesis of interracial contact specifies certain aspects of the contact situation that facilitate favorable attitude change.

When a prejudiced person is involuntarily placed in contact with a minority-group member, there is greater likelihood that his or her attitude will become less negative if (1) there is opportunity to know the other person as an individual, (2) the relative status of the participants is equal, (3) the norms favor acceptance, and (4) the reward structure of the task is cooperative rather than competitive.

Not all interracial contacts lead to a reduction in prejudice or hostility. Stuart Cook's laboratory approach has shown that when the above beneficial conditions are brought together in one situation and the anti-Black subject is exposed to a month-long interracial work experience, her attitude toward Blacks becomes significantly less negative in about 40% of the cases.

The intrapersonal characteristics that facilitate a reduction in prejudice in the above situation included a negative self-concept and positive attitude toward people in general.

I. Pure science or applied science—Or both?
   A. The dialogue between Kenneth Ring and William McGuire
   B. Bringing divergent viewpoints together

II. Kurt Lewin and action research
   A. The importance of testing theories in field settings
   B. The nature of action research
   C. Action research and planned change

III. Social psychologists as change agents
   A. Strategies for bringing about change in institutions
   B. Interrelationships among strategies

IV. "Unplanned" social change
   A. Defining social change
   B. The measurement of social change
   C. Social movements as predictors of social change

V. Examples of social change
   A. Technology and its effects on attitudes toward work
   B. Changing attitudes toward authority

VI. Youth and social change
   A. The generation gap—Myth or fact?

VII. "Future shock" and the usefulness of utopias
VIII. Summary

Changing society and its institutions 13

It was the best of times, it was the worst of times, it was the age of wisdom, it was the age of foolishness, it was the epoch of belief, it was the epoch of incredulity, it was the season of Light, it was the season of Darkness, it was the spring of hope, it was the winter of despair, we had everything before us, we had nothing before us. . . .

Charles Dickens (A Tale of Two Cities)

What Charles Dickens wrote about the period of the French Revolution applies as well to today. In *Future Shock,* Alvin Toffler (1970) describes our present state as "the dizzying disorientation brought on by the premature arrival of the future." And if it is true that the future has become the present, it is a present full of pessimism, doubt, lack of confidence, and diminished vision.

This chapter, like the previous two, is concerned with changes in attitudes and behavior. However, its orientation is different. First, we ask how social psychologists can apply their knowledge, if they can, in order to bring about changes in groups, institutions, and society at large. In doing so, we consider different viewpoints regarding the responsibilities of social psychologists to the society in which they and we live. Then we look at the phenomenon of social change and some of its effects on such matters

Portions of this chapter are revisions of material in Chapter 12, The Nature of Social Change, by Norma J. Baker, and Chapter 20, Community Applications of Social Psychology, by Carl E. Young, in the first edition of this book.

as attitudes toward work, attitudes toward authority, and the generation gap.

One of the most potentially important documents of the last decade was a report from the United States National Science Foundation titled *Knowledge into Action: Improving the Nation's Use of the Social Sciences* (1969). In emphasizing our critical need to apply the knowledge we have, the authors state that our society requires the best advice that its social scientists can muster. It needs that help now. While affirming that more research is needed, the authors contend that further delay in applying our knowledge to existing social problems would be both unethical and disastrous.

In his presidential address to the American Psychological Association, George A. Miller urged an extension of this viewpoint. He said "I can imagine nothing we could do that would be more relevant to human welfare, and nothing that could pose a greater challenge to the next generation of psychologists, than to discover how best to give psychology away" (1969, p. 21). Miller, reflecting a theme of this book, notes that each of us makes assumptions about

411

human nature. All people routinely "practice psychology" as they attempt to cope with the problems of their everyday lives. But, states Miller, they could practice it better if they knew which assumptions were scientifically verified—if the valid principles of psychology were "given away" to them. For some social psychologists—including the authors of this book—Miller's words served as a beacon: this textbook has as its goal helping students to use knowledge in their everyday interpersonal behavior.

But the fact that we possess knowledge does not necessarily mean that we will apply this knowledge. Examples to the contrary are numerous and often ironic—such as a professor's spending an entire class session lecturing on the necessity of using group discussion in classroom teaching! In reality, some scientists may *fail* to apply what they know to social problems (1) because they do not want to do so, (2) because they do not believe there is enough knowledge to be applied with confidence, (3) because the idea or need to do so has never really occurred to them, or (4) because they do not know how to apply what they know. Two of the aims of this chapter, therefore, are to encourage you to apply the social psychology that you now know and to expose you to some of the ways in which it has already been applied.

I. Pure science or applied science—Or both?

The idea of social scientists' applying their knowledge to the solution of social problems seems quite sensible. You may be surprised, however, to learn that many social psychologists have not systematically tried to put their findings to any practical use. Moreover, much debate and controversy rage about whether social psychologists *should* become involved in applied research, much less in social intervention. On the one hand, basic research scientists have felt that it is not part of their role as scientists to point out

the practical value of their findings. In fact, some have held that "the pursuit of scientific knowledge is a good activity in its own right, and even better since scientific knowledge is an absolute good apart from its consequences" (Baumrin, 1970, p. 74). This position has been commonly referred to as *knowledge for knowledge's sake.* Applied scientists, on the other hand, advocate that science study human problems in order to work out solutions as well as to determine what the consequences of any action would be. The issues involved in this controversy between applied science and basic research are very important, since they directly influence not only the ways in which social psychologists become involved in solving real-world problems but also the general direction of future developments in social psychology.

A. The dialogue between Kenneth Ring and William McGuire

Kenneth Ring and William McGuire are social psychologists who are attempting to influence the future development of social psychology in different ways. Their respective positions exemplify some of the agreements and disagreements that currently exist among social scientists on issues such as laboratory versus field investigations, the need for theory building, and the place of social action.

Ring's radical social psychology. Kenneth Ring (1967, 1971) has been an advocate of the applied, or social-action, position. Ring contends that basic and applied research have been spreading apart in the last two decades and that basic research has enjoyed much more popularity and prestige than applied research. Ring believes that both these trends are undesirable. He feels that basic researchers have largely avoided problems of broad social significance and have tended to study behavioral phenomena in a manner analogous to the development of fashion fads: that is, they have proceeded from less flamboyant research topics to more flamboyant ones. There has been much pioneering but little settling; rather than following up a new area of research and testing its applications, the social psychologist has sought other new areas to develop. (See Figure 13-1.) In like manner, M. Sherif (1970) has objected to the uneven development of social-psychological knowledge; he sees researchers in general as rugged individualists who pursue their own exotic interests.

Ring notes that much laboratory research in social psychology has had a fun-and-games approach. While it may be entertaining to read about college males sucking on pacifiers or college females being approached by a handsome stranger seeking a date, such studies neither educate us about the social-psychological nature of social problems nor give us a means by which to attack these problems. Ring claims that the result of the faddish and fun-and-games nature of much of our research is that social psychologists have tended to learn more and more about less and less important matters.

Furthermore, Ring argues, social-science research is seldom value free; each of us has to choose sides. "One can, unthinkingly or through choice, ally oneself with the institutional forces which support professional psychology. Or, one may choose to side not with the powerful but with the weak" (1971, p. 5). By siding with the weaker, less organized segments of society, the radical social psychologist takes on both a research task and a political task. The research task is to study how selected institutions operate in reference to the weak and how they affect the weak. An analogy to Ring's proposed research task would be the work of Ralph Nader and his "raiders" on behalf of the average consumer. Ring's three research components—description, analysis, and criticism—would be utilized to identify needed changes in government, schools, the military, and other institutions.

Ring's second task, the political task, would be to assure that the research is used to bring

about the recommended institutional changes. This might involve publicity, lobbying, organizing special-interest groups, and other forms of constructive social action. Ring refers to this combination of advocacy research and partisan social action as "the psychology of the left." He sees it as a plausible stance for social psychologists, since—like other academics—they are frequently political liberals or to the left of liberalism.

The radical social psychologist in action. The work of social psychologist Hannah Levin (1970) exemplifies Ring's "New Left" position. While working as a consultant to a community health center, Levin was dismayed by the fact that the people who lived near the health center had little or no say in its operation. The health authorities told the people that they could have an advisory board, but those who administered the actual health program would have to be physicians. However, the people wanted the operating policies to be determined by the local residents. In the confrontation that followed, Levin became a professional advocate for the people. Levin and the people's group were informed that they could advise, or even participate, but not control. The health authorities were unable to see the difference between participation and control. According to Levin, the people's retort was "If you don't see any real difference between participation and control, then you can participate and the community will control!" (1970, p. 123). Levin found that her arguments on behalf of the people motivated many of them to action. She gave the people a new confidence that eventually enabled them to establish influence over the policies of the health center. One outcome of community control was a shift in priorities from programs that emphasized suicidal and acutely disturbed patients to programs that emphasized youth. The people in the community declared that it was irresponsible to ignore the many health needs of schoolchildren for the sake of a "few suicides" and "psychotics."

Figure 13-1
Plenty of pioneers but few settlers. In the early 1960s the world was stunned
by Stanley Milgram's discovery that, in a majority of cases, normal adult men
would obey an experimenter who told them to administer extremely strong
(450-volt) electric shocks to another person. (Milgram's work on obedience is
described in detail in Chapter 18.) This study is a good example of pioneering
without settling. Even though it became an instant classic, only a few more
studies on the topic were conducted by Milgram or other researchers. While
newspapers reported Lt. Calley's obedience at My Lai and that of Nixon's staff,
social psychologists made only negligible efforts to observe and document the
extent of obedience in either the military or the civilian world. (Photos copyright
1965 by Stanley Milgram. From the film *Obedience*, distributed by the New York
University Film Library.)

McGuire's position. Shortly after Ring's first article appeared, William McGuire wrote two responses (1967a, 1967b) that were, at that time, typical of social psychology's mainstream position with regard to basic research. McGuire disagreed with the claim that basic and applied research would continue as quite separate entities in the future. He foresaw a merger of sorts—"a 'best of both worlds' solution in which we shall be doing theory-oriented research in natural settings" (1967a, p. 125). He assumed, and rightly so, that a theory that has been tested in a community setting is much more likely to prove relevant in solving problems in the real world than a theory tested in a laboratory. McGuire noted that the important scientific term *experiment* has unfortunately become equated with manipulative research in a laboratory setting; such a connotation of the term is overly restrictive. Instead, *experiment* should suggest its dictionary meaning of *to test* or *to try.* This broader definition allows for many alternatives to laboratory research, such as longitudinal studies, observational research, and the use of national-survey samples.

In a more recent position paper, McGuire (1973) has described these alternatives in more detail. The assumptions they reflect about the nature of social phenomena are different from those of the traditional experimental method that varies one or two independent variables while "controlling" all others. Yet, while McGuire is among those at the forefront in advocating the adoption of creative hypothesis-generating and hypothesis-testing procedures, he remains committed to the production of research-based knowledge as the function of the social psychologist.

McGuire disagrees with Ring on two main points. First, McGuire believes that a researcher's basic responsibility is theory building; he would agree with Kurt Lewin's dictum "Nothing is so practical as a good theory." McGuire believes that a theory should be tested in the laboratory and the real world—as was done with Darley and Latané's theory of diffusion of responsibility as an explanation of the responses to the attack on Kitty Genovese. But McGuire does not believe that scientists should be *obligated* to apply their findings to real-world problems. McGuire also disagrees with Ring's assertion that much laboratory research has taken a fun-and-games approach. McGuire's position is analogous to the biblical dictum "Judge not that ye be not judged."

We agree with McGuire's belief that in the long run basic, theory-oriented research will lead to more useful contributions to the field of social psychology than will action-oriented research (1967b, p. 20). Along with both Ring and McGuire, we seek more research in natural settings. In advocating the difficult task of doing theory-oriented research in real-life settings, we also recognize the possibility that our immediate problems may well get completely out of hand while society waits for natural returns on social psychology's theory investments. Our response is a calculated risk.

B. Bringing divergent viewpoints together

An important point on which Ring and McGuire agree is that social psychologists need to study more diverse populations in more depth than has been done in the past (Lehmann, 1971). The quip that psychology is the science of white rats and college sophomores has had its element of truth (Rosnow, 1970). At least one reason is that the very nature of laboratory research has required large numbers of easily available subjects. Other populations of subjects have been studied, but not very often or on many different variables (Higbee & Wells, 1972; Higbee, 1975). The problem with using restricted types of samples, of course, is one of generalization. For example, do college sophomores really behave enough like bureaucrats or grocery clerks or migrant workers to allow the research findings on the college population to be applied to these other populations? At this time, our limited evidence discourages such generalizations (Oakes, 1972). Indeed, the conclusions drawn from volunteer samples of college sophomores are not even applicable to *all* college sophomores.

II. Kurt Lewin and action research

One of the first social psychologists to address the issues raised by both Ring and McGuire was Kurt Lewin. In the 1930s and 1940s, Lewin was very much concerned about the need to build theories on the basis of field research whenever possible. As indicated in Chapter 1, he originated the term **field theory,** the central tenet of which is that behavior must always be viewed in relation to the environment. Although investigations using laboratory **simulations** of human environments are informative, the study of human behavior in its natural environment can be even more useful. Moreover, theories that have been tested in the laboratory need to be validated in the community and in other naturalistic settings.

A. The importance of testing theories in field settings

The important relationship between laboratory research and field research is exemplified in the study of the effects on aggression of viewing violence. In Chapter 7, we described early studies on the effects when children watched a film of another person or cartoon figure acting violently. These laboratory studies tended to support the contention that observing violence breeds violence. However, one later study on the effects of television viewing in natural settings indicated that viewing aggressive behaviors may actually reduce the degree of aggression expressed by children (Feshbach & Singer, 1970). Although this study was not meant to challenge laboratory investigations, the inconsistent conclusions should cause all of us to invest more research energy in questioning and testing our hypotheses and theories in natural field settings

(Lehmann, 1971). Another example of this need is reflected in Figure 13-2.

B. The nature of action research

Although Kurt Lewin was interested in the development of theories, he was also interested in *doing* something with them. "Research that produces nothing but books will not suffice," he stated (Lewin, 1948a, p. 203). He would have agreed with Ring's position that social psychologists should bring their research and interpersonal skills to bear on social problems. Lewin tried to resolve such social conflicts as marital frictions, management-worker disputes, and the psychosociological problems of minority groups. Describing his work in these areas as **action research,** Lewin noted that community organizations and agencies that are concerned with eliminating and preventing social problems are often unsuccessful, no matter how hard they seem to try. His goal was to transform such goodwill into organized, efficient action by helping community groups answer three questions: What is the present situation? What are the dangers? And, most important of all, what shall be done? To Lewin, action research consists of "analysis, fact-finding or evaluation; and then a repetition of this whole circle of activities; indeed, a spiral of such circles" (N. Sanford, 1970, p. 4). In short, the action researcher obtains data about an organization, feeds these data into the organization, measures the change that occurs, and then repeats the process.

C. Action research and planned change

In discussing this intervention process, Lewin was careful to point out that feeding data back into the organization was seldom sufficient to bring about the desired change. The other necessary ingredient was knowledge of and training in group dynamics. (This point will be discussed subsequently.) Because of his belief in the importance of group dynamics, Lewin helped

Figure 13-2
Consistencies between the laboratory and the field. The important relationship
between laboratory research and community (field or naturalistic) research is
exemplified in the work of Roger Barker, the social psychologist who founded
ecological psychology. While studying under Lewin, Barker participated in an
investigation of the relationship between frustration and aggression in young
children (Barker, Dembo, & Lewin, 1941). Ironically, Lewin, the field theorist,
and Barker, the subsequent ecological psychologist, carried out this early work
in a laboratory setting! In the study, children were allowed to play with some
toys in an experimental playroom. After playing with these toys for 30 minutes,
they were exposed to new and more desirable toys and then were allowed to
play with any toys (new or old) they wished. The children were then given their
original toys but were separated from the newer and more desirable toys by
a wire mesh. Under these frustrating conditions, the children exhibited a number
of regressive behaviors, and their play became less and less constructive. This
laboratory study was replicated successfully by others and became a
fundamental part of the social-psychological literature. More than 20 years later,
Fawl (1963), a student of Barker's, decided to replicate the study using specimen
records of children's everyday behaviors. Fawl reported "The results . . . were
surprising in two respects. First, even with a liberal interpretation of frustration
fewer incidents were detected than we expected. . . . Second, . . . meaningful
relationships could not be found between frustration . . . and consequent
behavior such as . . . regression . . . and other theoretically meaningful
behavioral manifestations" (1963, p. 99). In brief, frustration was rare in the
ordinary behaviors of the children; and, when it did occur, the phenomenon
did not conform to the prediction of the original study. The natural setting made
a difference. (Photo by Jim Pinckney.)

found the Research Center for Group Dynamics (now the Institute for Social Research at the University of Michigan) for the purpose of integrating research, training, and action. He was also instrumental in founding the National Training Laboratory in Group Development (now called the NTL Center for Applied Behavioral Science). This institution was established "as a training center for teams which would take leadership in action-training-research projects in the fields of education, industry, government, social work, labor, religious work, volunteer organizations, and community life" (R. Lippitt, 1949, p. 262). In summary, Lewin has greatly influenced the applications of social psychology, and his influence is especially evident in the psychology of planned change.

III. Social psychologists as change agents

In applying social psychology to real-life problems, the goal is to promote change in a predictable manner. People such as Martin Luther King, Ralph Nader, Karl Marx, and Cesar Chavez have used different means in order to change society. Yet each sought or seeks to be able to predict and control the consequences of his intended changes. Predictability is very important, since the very act of instituting change may cause unanticipated side effects that outweigh any advantages. The use of DDT is a classic example. Although DDT was originally seen as the restorer of ecological imbalances, its massive usage has precipitated an ecological disaster endangering wildlife, fish, and human existence. Likewise, crosstown busing of Black children was instituted to improve their school achievement, but an unanticipated side effect was the extremely hostile response by certain groups of White parents to this type of school integration. Because of the complex nature of planned change, groups of social scientists (many of whom were trained as social psychologists under Kurt Lewin) have

devoted much study to the planning and application of change methods and have become known as *change agents* (R. Lippitt, Watson, & Westley, 1958; Bennis, Benne, & Chin, 1968).

One goal of change agents is to help us in moving from an industrial society to what is being called a *post-industrialized* society, in which self-actualization and sharing are emphasized, rather than achievement and competition. Institutions—businesses, schools, government, the military—must be reoriented so that they are capable of adapting to new values, practices, and philosophies (G. L. Lippitt, 1974). Some of the changes in emphasis as we move toward post-industrialism are listed in Table 13-1.

A. Strategies for bringing about change in institutions

The general goal of the change agents is to develop strategies for bringing about change. These strategies have been divided into three major types: (1) empirical-rational strategy, (2) normative-reeducative strategy, and (3) power-coercive strategy. Since each operates from a different set of assumptions about human nature, these strategies will be discussed separately, and a case history illustrating each one will be cited.

The empirical-rational strategy. This strategy assumes that people are rational and that they will act on the basis of the best information available. Therefore, in order to improve people's ability to make decisions, one need only present them with the facts. The **empirical-rational strategy** clearly is congenial with North American values, such as willpower and educability. Because of our belief in this strategy, we maintain public schools, write letters to our legislators, read newspapers regularly, and give money for cancer research. Of course, there are limits to how much we accept this strategy. That is, we also smoke, drive at excessive speeds, refuse to exercise, and often pick a new car by kicking

Table 13-1
Changes in emphasis in the transition to postindustrialism

Type of Change	From	Toward
Cultural values	Achievement	Self-actualization
	Self-control	Self-expression
	Independence	Interdependence
	Endurance of distress	Capacity for joy
Organizational philosophies	Mechanistic forms	Organic forms
	Competitive relations	Collaborative relations
	Separate objectives	Linked objectives
	Own resources regarded as owned absolutely	Own resources regarded also as society's
Organizational practices	Responsive to crisis	Anticipative of crisis
	Specific measures	Comprehensive measures
	Requiring consent	Requiring participation
	Short planning horizon	Long planning horizon
	Damping conflict	Confronting conflict
	Detailed central control	Generalized central control
	Small local units	Enlarged local units
	Standardized administration	Innovative administration
	Separate services	Coordinated services

Adapted from "Between Cultures: The Current Crisis of Transition," by C. R. Price. In W. Schmidt (Ed.), *Organizational Frontiers and Human Values.* Reprinted by permission of the author.

its tires and slamming its doors instead of consulting *Consumer Reports* or *Canadian Consumer.* In short, we often act irrationally; hard facts have limited power to change behavior.

Another example of the limits of the empirical-rational strategy is reflected in the publication of the Pentagon Papers. When Daniel Ellsberg removed these from the U. S. Department of Defense files and disseminated them, he thought his act would put an end to United States participation in the Vietnam War. Senator Mike Gravel, who later read the Pentagon Papers into his subcommittee records, shared this hope. In the introduction to a book that reprinted them, he wrote "Had the true facts been made known earlier, the war would long ago have ended." Both men were apparently convinced that an in-

formed public was all that was necessary to compel the government to end an immoral war (Koning, 1972). Yet the publishing of this information did not stop the war, or even change the way the U. S. government presented information about the war to the public.

The professional role demanded by the empirical-rational strategy has been described as that of an *analyst* (Vollmer, 1970)—that is, one who tries objectively to diagnose a problem and to bring appropriate data to bear on its solution. There has probably been more demand for the analyst role than any other; moreover, this role has been popular among social psychologists. Social-psychological research, for example, has been consistently funded within the framework of the empirical-rational theory. Since state, provincial, and local governments seldom have large research staffs within any one program area, they are very dependent on data gathered by outside researchers. One could easily argue that all governmental research is based on the empirical-rational strategy. That is, government agencies fund research that will produce facts, which can then be disseminated for the purpose of effecting change. For example, the National Institute of Mental Health has funded studies of the ways of coping with emotional reactions to national disasters (Kafrissen, Heffron, & Zusman, 1975). The case history described in Figure 13-3 illustrates the analyst's role of producing facts.

The empirical-rational strategy is limited in that no guarantee exists as to what kind of people will read the information or put it to use. *The Report of the National Advisory Commission on Civil Disorders* that resulted from President Johnson's directive could have been one of the most important research documents of this century. Unfortunately, we can document few, if any, positive changes that have occurred as a result of the commission's report. Even though it was received with acclaim, its diagnosis and recommendations were directed to a public that was unprepared to process its data or take action. An even more extreme example of the limitations of the empirical-rational strategy is the outcome of the work of the Federal Commission on Obscenity and Pornography, appointed by President Johnson in 1968. It is difficult to imagine a more extreme and massive reaction to data than that which was generated by this commission's report in the fall of 1970. The President of the United States at that time, Richard Nixon, renounced many of the conclusions of the report before it was even published! Moreover, several U.S. legislators denounced the report on nationwide television, although these legislators admitted that neither they nor their staffs had read it! Obviously, the empirical-rational strategy is insufficient—in and of itself—to promote extensive change.

The normative-reeducative strategy. A second strategy for social change is based on different assumptions about human nature. The **normative-reeducative strategy** assumes that people are intelligent and rational, but it also assumes that they are bound up in their own particular culture. As a result, they have definite behavioral responses and patterns that are based on attitudes, values, traditions, and relationships with others. Before trying to change a person, group, or community, these cultural or normative determinants must be taken into account.

A humorous example is provided by the Shoshoni Indians of Nevada. "When horses were introduced into the Shoshoni culture, the Indians knew what to do with them. The Shoshonis had previous experience with horses; they had stolen horses for food. So, when Indian agents gave them horses for transportation, they readily accepted them. But they ate them" (E. M. Rogers, 1962).

As mentioned earlier, Kurt Lewin was one of the first to address systematically the issue of using the normative-reeducative strategy in resolving social conflicts (Lewin, 1948a). His emphasis was on reeducating groups through professional participation in the groups. In the U.S. the Peace Corps and VISTA and in Canada the Company of Young Canadians have adopted this strategy in their programs. Volunteers are sent to participate in the life of a culture and to find ways to improve life-styles within the range of the existing norms (W. W. Biddle & Biddle, 1965). Figure 13-5 reports a case history that illustrates the normative-reeducative strategy reflected in many police-training programs.

The power-coercive strategy. This strategy differs from the first two in its use of power. The **power-coercive strategy** is based on political, economic, and social uses of power that have been both popular and effective in bringing about change. Federal legislation on civil rights has moved integration forward in the United States and has promoted bilingualism in Canada; labor strikes have affected economic policies; and boycotts have changed discriminatory hiring practices. Similarly, Martin Luther King, Cesar

Figure 13-3
A case study of use of the empirical-rational strategy. The summer of 1967 was
the period of the most intense internal conflict in the United States since the
Civil War. Civil disorders occurred in Newark, Detroit, Cleveland, and a host
of other cities. On July 28, 1967, President Johnson appointed a prestigious
commission under the leadership of Otto Kerner, then governor of Illinois, and
directed this commission to answer three basic questions: What happened? Why
did it happen? What can be done to keep it from happening again? Since many
of the participants in the civil disorders were students, the commission became
interested in whether similarities existed between disorders in the cities and
disorders on college campuses. In light of the more than 130 disruptions on
college campuses in 1967, it was decided that the first three of these disorders
should be investigated. The social scientists who participated in the research
on these three campuses fulfilled the analyst role. They provided nonpartisan,
descriptive, analytic reports, which demonstrated (1) that the disorders were
spontaneous and followed the presence of police on the campuses, (2) that the
most active participants were usually nonstudents, (3) that there was no
underlying conspiracy (communist or otherwise), and (4) that the students and
administrators were able to achieve and maintain a high degree of internal
control. Thus, the social scientists provided the information needed by
government leaders to combat rumors, to reduce tensions, and to promote a
better understanding of the so-called "violent revolution" that some believed
to be taking place on college campuses (Newbrough, 1968). (Wide World Photos.)

Chavez, Saul Alinsky, and the Berrigan brothers became famous for their power-coercive strategies in their quests for constructive change (Sharp, 1970, 1971). In employing power-coercive methods, change agents have been primarily concerned with nonviolent strategies of change and have been opposed to violent means (destruction of property, the use of firearms in quelling rioters, and the like). There are at least two general reasons for the change agents' opposition to violent strategies. One is that they believe that having to use violence means denying human worth. These change agents believe that change is always possible through nonviolent strategies and that even the most favorable short-term outcome does not justify using violent methods. As Fairweather puts it, "the means for creating social change should be compatible with the goals of that change" (1972, p. 3).

Figure 13-4
Social change can be implemented. Peace Corps volunteers serve as a means of changing societies. (Photo courtesy of the Peace Corps.)

A second reason why these change agents prefer nonviolent strategies is that they are very much concerned with planned change; violent strategies introduce much more *unpredictability* into a social system than do nonviolent approaches (Fairweather, 1972). Predictability, as used in this context, refers to (1) whether one accomplishes one's desired goals, (2) how long one's accomplishments last, and (3) whether any unanticipated, negative side effects result. When evaluated according to these three criteria, nonviolent strategies are found to be much more effective across time in establishing planned change throughout a broad social system. For these reasons and many others, *most* social psychologists have been concerned with the reduction of violence, not with its promotion. (See also Figure 13-6.)

It should be acknowledged that not all social psychologists agree. William Gamson (1974, 1975) concluded that violence was often a successful tactic when used by groups that possess a sense of confidence and a rising sense of power. Gamson's conclusion is based on his analysis of the outcomes of a sample of 53 groups that sought change in the United States during the last 80 years. Gamson's advocacy of violence as a successful tactic is qualified, however. He finds it to be used successfully when it is a secondary tactic, backing up primary nonviolent power-coercive strategies such as strikes, bargaining, and propaganda. He says "Violence, in short, is the spice of protest, not the meat and potatoes" (1974, p. 39). He also notes that strictly revolutionary groups were not successful.

It seems clear that revolution and other violent strategies usually fail because they do not build a flexible, renewing process of change into the target system. Instead, they cause rigidity. Once force has been used, the target system attempts to strengthen its defenses, to contain the force, and ultimately to destroy the force. Further change requires additional force, and the phenomenon recycles and escalates. In the law-enforcement-training programs mentioned in Figure 13-5, teaching may focus upon the escalating

Figure 13-5
A case study of normative-reeducative strategy: Police training. Prior to the 1960s, relatively little attention had been given to law enforcement as a nationwide issue. But civil-rights demonstrations, campus disorders, and the riot during the 1968 Democratic party convention in Chicago all directed attention to the actions of police. Police brutality became a public issue. Both demonstrators and police were mishandled and killed.

Social scientists, working as analysts, probed the complexities of law enforcement and facilitated new understanding of police work. Time-and-motion studies revealed that less than 20% of police working hours were spent in law-enforcement activities. As society became more depersonalized and bureaucratic, police began spending more and more of their time in a wide range of social-service activities. Bard (1970) has referred to the New York City police as a "human resource agency without parallel" and has pointed out that "maintaining order and providing interpersonal service—not law enforcement and crime suppression—are what modern police work is all about" (p. 129). Social scientists rediscovered what the police already knew—that crime in the streets is much less common than crime *off* the streets. Also, violent crimes more often occur among people who know each other or who are related to one another than among people who are strangers. One of the highest personal-risk situations for police is handling family disputes (Driscoll, Meyer, & Schanie, 1973). In brief, the police were being trained in traditional law enforcement or property watching, but were being called upon to serve a wide range of social-service functions (Flynn & Peterson, 1972).

Given the complexities of the law-enforcement system, simply publishing the findings on police activities would have had little effect, by itself, in bringing about change within the system, for law enforcement, like any other institution or subculture, has its own customs and mores and has established defenses against changes in its traditions (Neff, 1974). Therefore, social scientists adopted the *normative-reeducative strategy* for working with police. They began riding in patrol cars, observing training programs, and generally acquainting themselves with the norms of law enforcement (Beilin, 1974; Peterson, 1974). The actual entry into the system was slow. Social psychologists first performed specific services for the police such as improving selection procedures for new recruits. Next came lectures and sensitivity training that dealt with such matters as the emotionally disturbed, ways to deal with aggression, and the general area of interpersonal relations (Diamond & Lobitz, 1973; Fromkin, Brandt, King, Sherwood, & Fisher, 1974). Gradually, the social scientists became more involved in all aspects of police training—and more acceptable in the eyes of the police (Brodsky, 1974; Carlson, Thayer, & Germann, 1971).

The normative-reeducative process moves slowly, since it is founded on change through mutual collaboration and understanding in diagnosing and organizing intervention. But there have been payoffs. Bard (1970) has trained a special squad of patrolmen in the use of mediation and referral in handling domestic disturbances. This project has been very successful in preventing homicides, reducing the number of assaults, reducing the number of arrests, and preventing injury to patrolmen. A central characteristic of this approach has been the predictability of change, which has been in the desired direction and has been approved by both the change agents and the police. (Photo by Peter Range/Time-Life Picture Agency.)

nature of force. If a policeman enters a setting with a drawn gun, the actors in the setting will gear their emotions and actions to the standard of force represented by the gun. (The Berkowitz studies of aggressive cues in Chapter 7 show that this principle operates in a well-controlled situation.) Any spontaneous precipitating event will be handled at that level. Needless to say, it is a high-risk situation. Conversely, if a policeman enters a setting in a calm, confident manner and with no external signs of force, a different standard is established. One often hears the axiom in police training that holstered guns can be drawn, but drawn guns can never be holstered. It is a good generalizable rule in the implementing of all power-coercive strategies.

Nonviolent power-coercive methods have brought about much planned social change in the last decade. Civil rights demonstrations clearly speeded racial integration. Separatist demonstrations illuminated the grievances of French Canada. The antiwar movements in the early 1970s played an important role in the increased withdrawal of United States troops from Vietnam. Student demonstrations on college campuses helped produce changes in such diverse areas as dorm hours, student participation in college administration, dress codes, and course offerings. Moreover, demonstrations on one campus often led to positive changes on another campus. Of course, the converse of this situation also happened; demonstrations on one campus produced negative changes on another campus. The result of the Kent State incident at some

state schools was an increase in the campus security force, a restriction on even peaceful forms of protest, and a decrease in state funds for higher education.

Figure 13-6
Do war and revolution usually succeed in bringing about change?

Some social activists and students of society believe that violent actions such as riots, revolutions, and wars are the only viable means of creating social change (Bienen, 1968). Early U. S. President Thomas Jefferson is even reputed to have said that a country should have a revolution every few years in order to create necessary reforms. More recently Mao Tse-tung has stated that continuous revolution is the only way a society can successfully change when change is needed (Fairweather, 1972).

Yet there are severe problems in such conclusions. The text discusses some of the limitations in the use of violent power-coercive strategies. Beyond these, an overturning of the social order by violent means often does not produce the anticipated new life-style. As Fairweather states, "In these situations the idealists who originally plan the action are often replaced by self-serving egocentric persons whose main purpose . . . is to seek power and domination over others. . . . Sometimes they do not share in the goals of the intellectual rebels whose idealism and dissatisfaction with injustice created the activity in the first place" (1972, p. 4).

The last decade also saw an increased use of legal sanctions. Ralph Nader and his "raiders" elicited many changes in federal laws concerning automobiles, drugs, and many other matters. Court injunctions were commonly used by citizen groups in their fights against city hall, and court decisions caused changes in everything from the busing of children to the drafting of college athletes by professional teams. In brief, the legal system has continued to be a major mechanism for social change. One of the more interesting aspects of the power-coercive strategy is that it can take many forms. The case history described in Figure 13-7 summarizes an unusually innovative approach to problem resolution by one of the masters of the power-coercive strategy.

Nevertheless, power-coercive strategies are seldom sufficient change methods in and of themselves. Even though the passage of fair-housing codes represented considerable political-legal leverage toward attaining neighborhood integration, these codes by no means assured real integration. The power-coercive approach must be coupled with the normative-reeducative approach to maximize change. A tongue-in-cheek example of this combination is provided in Figure 13-8. Legal sanctions establish the letter of the law, but normative-reeducative strategies foster the spirit of the law. It is one thing to declare that change must take place; it is quite another to build the social machinery, attitudes, and relationships that will actually produce this change with a minimum of disruption.

B. Interrelationships among strategies

In the preceding review, each strategy of change was described as if it were somehow pure or separate from the others; of course, it seldom is. In most social-change endeavors, there will be occasion to use all three of these strategies in various ways at various times. Indeed, it is most difficult to use only one strategy. For exam-

Figure 13-7
Saul Alinsky: The employment of power-coercive strategy. The late Saul Alinsky was one of the foremost organizers of community-action groups; he trained such minority-group leaders as Cesar Chavez, who organized California's agricultural workers and then precipitated a national consumer boycott against California grapes. Alinsky was a proponent of the power-coercive strategy and used this strategy in quite different ways. One of the more novel uses of this approach was his Rochester, New York, battle with Eastman Kodak. Following a Rochester race riot that was partially due to a conflict over Kodak's inadequate training and job programs for Blacks, the local churches invited Alinsky to work in their Black ghetto. He accepted and soon founded a community-action group called FIGHT (Freedom, Integration, God, Honor, Today). Instead of depending on community-action tactics such as picketing and demonstrating, FIGHT began soliciting stock proxies from churches, individuals, and organizations as a direct power challenge to Kodak's policies. Enough proxies were turned over to FIGHT to enable the group to force Kodak to improve its policies concerning minority groups (see Alinsky, 1971). (United Press International Photo.)

ple, the name of a well-known and respected researcher, when attached to an article in a prestigious journal, represents considerable political influence and power within the social-psychological profession with respect to the topic in question—even though the article may have been written exclusively as an empirical-rational statement. The empirical-rational testimony of a social psychologist before a congressional or parliamentary investigating subcommittee represents

---

Figure 13-8

Moses replying to God: Which type of strategy?

The late Saul Alinsky believed that change strategies were nothing new. While the following example may be offensive to some, it reflects Alinsky's tendency to treat nothing as sacred. In it he interprets the biblical confrontation between Moses and the Lord (Exodus 32: 7–14):

> The episode between Moses and God, when the Jews had begun to worship the Golden Calf, is revealing. Moses did not try to communicate with God in terms of mercy or justice when God was angry and wanted to destroy the Jews; he moved in on a top value and outmaneuvered God. It is only when the other party is concerned or feels threatened that he will listen—in the arena of action, a threat or a crisis becomes almost a precondition to communication.
>
> A great organizer, like Moses, never loses his cool as a lesser man might have done when God said: "Go, get thee down; *thy* people, whom *thou* hast brought out of the land of Egypt hath sinned." At that point, if Moses had dropped his cool in any way, one would have expected him to reply, "Where do you get off with all that stuff about *my* people whom *I* brought out of the land of Egypt . . . I was just taking a walk through the desert and who started that bush burning, and who told me to get over to Egypt, and who told me to get those people out of slavery, and who pulled all the power plays, and all the plagues, and who split the Red Sea, and who put a pillar of clouds up in the sky, and now all of a sudden they become *my* people."
>
> But Moses kept his cool, and he knew that the most important center of his attack would have to be on what he judged to be God's prime value. As Moses read it, it was that God wanted to be No. 1. All through the Old Testament one bumps into "there shall be no other Gods before me," "Thou shalt not worship false gods," "I am a jealous and vindictive God," "Thou shalt not use the Lord's name in vain." And so it goes, on and on, including the first part of the Ten Commandments.
>
> Knowing this, Moses took off on his attack. He began arguing and telling God to cool it. (At this point, trying to figure out Moses' motivations, one would wonder whether it was because he was loyal to his own people, or felt sorry for them, or whether he just didn't want the job of breeding a whole new people, because after all he was pushing 120 and that's asking a lot.) At any rate, he began to negotiate, saying, "Look, God, you're God. You're holding all the cards. Whatever you want to do you can do and nobody can stop you. But you know, God, you just can't scratch that deal you've got with these people—you remember, the Covenant—in which you promised them not only to take them out of slavery but that they would practically inherit the earth. Yeah, I know, you're going to tell me that they broke their end of it so all bets are off. But it isn't that easy. You're in a spot. The news of this deal has leaked out all over the joint. The Egyptians, Philistines, Canaanites, *everybody* knows about it. But, as I said before, you're God. Go ahead and knock them off. What do you care if people are going to say, 'There goes God. You can't believe anything he tells you. You can't make a deal with him. His word isn't even worth the stone it's written on.' But after all, you're God and I suppose you can handle it."
>
> And the Lord was appeased from doing the evil which he had spoken against his people.

From *Rules for Radicals*, by S. D. Alinsky. Copyright © 1971 by Saul D. Alinsky. Reprinted by permission of Random House, Inc.

considerable political leverage, for knowledge *is* power. The very fact that a social scientist agrees to undertake a normative-reeducative approach to some problem is a direct admission of the power of this individual with respect to that particular problem. Moreover, the normative-reeducative strategy depends on the empirical-rational method for its content; otherwise one would have nothing about which to educate another person.

One reason for emphasizing these interrelationships is that they are almost always more obvious in the abstract than they are during the process of implementation. And one sure way to abort a change agent's strategy is to fail to consider the fact that the change agent may be perceived by others as using some *other* strategy. That is, others may perceive a normative-reeducative process as a threat to their own power base (power-coercive); to be successful, change agents must take these perceptions into account.

IV. "Unplanned" social change

Not all change is planned change. There are alterations taking place in our values, interpersonal behavior, and social institutions that occur as a result of the development of technology, the breakup of the extended family, changes in the nature of work, and other social and economic developments. These may appear to be autonomous, unplanned changes (as opposed to those planned interventions described earlier in the chapter). Yet they should not be seen as *uncaused*; they happen for reasons that can be discerned through careful study and are therefore also the concern of social psychology.

Such changes in values, institutions, and social behavior are not easily classified as either independent or dependent variables. One development can be both. For example, outbreaks of protest by college students can be viewed as the outgrowth of certain changes in the students' value systems, interwoven with their heightened awareness of civil rights; according to this view, protest is a *dependent* variable. But student unrest can also be seen as an *independent* variable that elicits long-term changes in the very structure of higher education, such as the placement of students in important policy-making groups, including curriculum committees and boards of trustees.

Pizer and Travers (1975) propose that social psychology can help us to understand and promote social change in three ways:

1. Social psychology can help us discern the *need* for change by documenting the kinds of social and psychological problems that exist for individuals and groups as a result of existing conditions. For example, the research of social psychologists Kenneth and Mamie Clark (1947, 1950) was a factor in the U.S. Supreme Court decision of 1954 making public-school segregation illegal. (The Clarks' research showed that Black children were emotionally distraught as a result of their separation from other racial groups.)

2. Social psychology "can help us estimate both the costs and benefits of alternative kinds of change" (Pizer & Travers, 1975, p. 3). A recent subject of controversy has been the desirability of community control of the schools. Social psychologists, by comparing conditions in community-controlled and other schools, can help the citizenry and school authorities know what the effects of each are.

3. Social psychology can provide a *means* for change. As the earlier sections of this chapter indicated, many obstacles to change are social psychological in nature. By offering appropriate intervention techniques and by training change agents, social psychology can help us adapt to change.

A. Defining social change

Both order and change are significant components of human social existence. The repetitive character of many aspects of social behavior gives human life a degree of predictability; yet change and uncertainty are universal (New-brough, 1973). How, then, can social change be defined in any distinguishing way? W. Moore (1967, 1968) described social change as occurring when *change permeates a whole system*, rather than when it appears only in sequences of actions that make up a system. Moore has defined social change as "the significant alteration of social structures . . . including consequences and manifestations of such structures embodied in norms . . ., values, and cultural products and symbols" (1967, p. 3). Structures, in this context, refer to patterns of social action and interaction; voting on election day as a means of naming a new president or prime minister is a structure. Norms refer to rules of conduct; it is normative to vote, to have one's vote counted accurately, and to have the candidate with the most votes be named president—or, in Canada, to have the leader of the party with the most seats becoming prime minister. Social change, then, means that there are changes in the boundaries of the social system, in the prescription for action, and in the relation of the particular system to its environment. For example, the transfer of the control of government from one party to another does *not* represent a social change, because it does not go beyond the boundaries of our norms and patterns of social action. But if the incumbent president or prime minister assumed dictatorial control, the system would have been altered, and social change would have occurred.

B. The measurement of social change

A major difficulty in detection and measurement of social change is that change takes place across time, and time for observation is limited, especially for a single investigator. (See Figure 13-9.) W. Moore (1963) suggests that the sense of time and the perception of change are inextricably linked in human experience. One cannot think about change without including the concept of time and having some sense of time's passing. And if change is viewed as continuous,

something more than the mere difference between before and after—in other words, the *rate* of transformation—becomes important. We may then think of the rate of social change as a fractional value, with time as the denominator, and the number of events that are to be observed or measured as the numerator (W. Moore, 1963). On the basis of such an analysis, the 20th century is generally described as a period of rapid and radical social change, with the rate of change having accelerated increasingly in the last two decades. If the time since World War II serves as the denominator, the numerator would include such events as nuclear warfare, mass use of television, space travel, the population explosion, the breakdown of cities, awareness of destruction of the natural environment, the civil-rights revolution, the coming of the computer, large-scale famine, energy shortages, and the birth-control pill. U.S. and Canadian citizens born even as recently as 25 years ago may well feel that the world into which they were born has virtually dropped from under them, while a new world is being built around them.

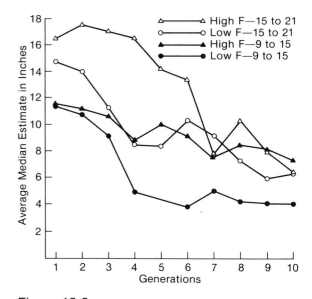

Figure 13-9
Can social change be studied in the laboratory? It might seem impossible to study something as

massive and multidimensional as social change in a laboratory setting. However, Jacobs and Campbell (1961) developed a clever way of studying the transmission of norms through several miniature "generations" of a laboratory society. They used the **autokinetic effect**—the illusion that a stationary light in a darkened room is moving. As Chapter 19 indicates, subjects' estimates of the direction and movement of the light are influenced by the reports of other observers. Although subjects usually see the light move from 1 to 5 inches, Jacobs and Campbell used confederates to establish "cultural norms" of 15 or 16 inches' movement. The maintenance, change, and transmission of the norms were studied over 11 "generations" of the group, by gradually replacing confederates and subjects with new, naïve subjects. Results indicated that adherence to the arbitrary norm declined almost immediately after all the confederates had been replaced; by the sixth generation, these contrived norms had just about disappeared. But perhaps this occurred because the contrived norms were so different from the usual response. For example, MacNeil (1965) found that contrived norms only moderately different from subjects' individual responses declined slowly.

Thus it may be that people accept norms that differ from physical reality and that under certain conditions such norms may remain for rather extended periods. Montgomery, Hinkle, and Enzie (1976) noted the view (held by Hagen, 1962, among others) that social change occurs more slowly in highly authoritarian societies than in less authoritarian ones. The researchers placed subjects who scored high or low on the California F scale measure of authoritarianism in the autokinetic setting, with confederates who made estimates of light movement that were either moderately deviant (9–15 inches) or extremely deviant (15–21 inches). Ten "generations" of the group were used, with new subjects replacing old ones at each generation. All confederates were removed by the fourth generation. The figure shows that changes in the responses were more rapid in groups of less authoritarian subjects; that is, high-F "societies" perpetuated responses closer to the original arbitrary norms, including those (15–21 inches) extremely deviant from their own judgments. Even by Generation 10, highly authoritarian groups were reporting the light to move almost 8 inches. (Graph from "Arbitrary Norms and Social Change in High and Low Authoritarian Societies," by R. L. Montgomery, S. W. Hinkle, and R. F. Enzie, *Journal of Personality and Social Psychology,* 1976, *33*(6), 698–708. Copyright 1976 by the American Psychological Association. Reprinted by permission.)

Another difficulty in making quantitative predictions regarding the direction of social change is that there is no adequate knowledge of the present status. It is difficult to predict where we are going when we do not know where we are. Some improvements in the collection and analysis of information about social conditions, the quality of life, and social change have been made by the U.S. federal government with the recent emphasis on social accounting and social reporting. In 1969 the U.S. Department of Health, Education and Welfare released a publication entitled *Toward a Social Report.* Separate chapters of the report dealt with health and illness; social mobility; the physical environment; income and poverty; public order and safety; learning, science, and art; and participation and alienation. For each of these areas, the report advocated the development of **social indicators**—descriptive statistics about U.S. society that facilitate concise, comprehensive, and balanced judgments about the quality of U.S. social existence (Bauer, 1966). Social indicators are direct measures of welfare. They are subject to the interpretation that people are better off if each or any indicator changes in the right direction while other things remain equal. Only measures that are employed repeatedly and at regular intervals are to be properly considered indicators; in other words, social indicators are time series that allow comparisons over an extended period and that permit us to grasp long-term trends as well as unusually sharp fluctuations in rates (Sheldon & Freeman, 1970). The major usefulness of social indicators is that they enable us to anticipate the consequences of rapid technological change and the second-order effects of changes in beliefs and values. (Figure 13-10 provides a description of some of the pitfalls of interpretation of social indicators.)

Although gaps in knowledge exist and all change is relative, there are many examples that justify the assumption that the rate of change

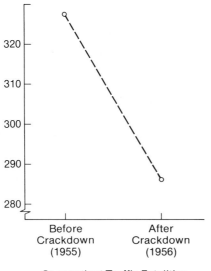

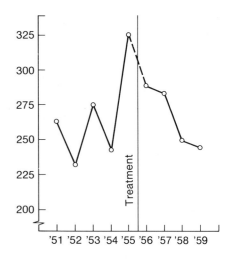

Connecticut Traffic Fatalities

Connecticut Traffic Fatalities

Figure 13-10

Reforms as experiments. Donald T. Campbell, distinguished social scientist, makes a strong appeal for an experimental approach to social reform. What is needed, he feels, is an approach by which we can try out new programs designed to cure specific social problems, learn whether or not these programs are effective, and retain, imitate, modify, or discard these programs on the basis of effectiveness. Campbell calls for an understanding of the political implications of the public use of data as social indicators. He presents several research designs for evaluating specific programs of social amelioration. One of these is the interrupted time-series design. A convenient illustration comes from the 1955 Connecticut crackdown on speeding. After a record high of traffic fatalities in 1955, the governor instituted an unprecedentedly severe crackdown on speeding. At the end of one year of such enforcement, there had been 284 traffic deaths as compared with 324 the year before. These results are shown in the left-hand graph above, with a deliberate effort to make them look impressive. The right-hand graph includes the same data as the graph to the left, except that it is presented as part of an extended time series. Campbell acknowledges that the crackdown did have some beneficial effects, but he advocates the exploration of as many rival hypotheses as possible to explain the decline in traffic fatalities from 1955 to 1956. For example, 1956 might have been a particularly dry year, with fewer accidents due to rain or snow. There might have been a dramatic increase in use of seat belts. At least part of the 1956 drop is the product of the 1955 extremity. (It is probable that the unusually high rate in 1955 caused the crackdown, rather than, or in addition to, the crackdown's causing the 1956 drop.) Campbell asks for a public demand for hardheaded evaluation and for education about the problems and possibilities involved in the use of socially relevant data. (Adapted from "Reforms as Experiments," by D. T. Campbell, *American Psychologist*, 1969, 24(4), 409–429. Copyright 1969 by the American Psychological Association. Used by permission.)

is accelerating. Toffler (1970) has described a few of these factors.

Rapid urbanization. In 1850 only 4 cities on the earth had a population of 1 million or more. By 1900 the number had increased to 19; by 1960 there were 141 such cities. Today, the urban population of the world is climbing at a rate of 6.5% per year.

The heightened pace of invention. For a group of appliances introduced in the United States and Canada before 1920—including the vacuum cleaner, the electric range, and the refrigerator—the average span between introduction and peak production was 34 years. But for a group that appeared between 1939 and 1959—including the electric frying pan, television receivers, and washer-dryer combinations—the span was only 8 years. The lag had shrunk by more than 76%. New machines or techniques represent not merely a product but a source of fresh creative ideas.

The knowledge explosion. Prior to the year 1500, Europe was producing books at a rate of about 1000 titles per year. Today the United States government alone generates 100,000 reports each year, plus 450,000 articles, books, and papers. The computer, which appeared around 1950, is a major force behind the latest acceleration in the acquisition of knowledge.

Such a rapid accumulation of materials in the world around us means that there is an increase in the number of choices we are forced to make. It also means more switching back and forth from one choice point to another and less time for extended attention to any one situation. In addition, rising rates of change compel us to cope with more and more situations to which previous personal experience does not apply.

C. Social movements as
    predictors of
    social change

Perhaps one of the best indicators of the direction of social change is the **social movement,** which also draws attention to significant

social problems. Social movements are forms of collective behavior that aim at change in the world. Psychologically defined, a social movement represents an effort by a large number of people to solve collectively a problem that they have in common (Milgram & Toch, 1969).

At various times and under various conditions the legitimacy of a society's customary institutions or values (such as the family or sexual relationships) may be questioned by different parts of the society. New arrangements are advocated. But the demand for change may meet with resistance from the advocates of the old habits. In that case, groups face each other in some form of conflict. A social movement, therefore, is not the unnoticed accumulation of many unrecognized changes. Rather, it is an explicit and conscious indictment of all or part of the social order, together with a conscious demand for change. It has an ideological component: a set of ideas that specify discontents, prescribe solutions, and justify change (Gusfield, 1968; Oberschall, 1973). M. Sherif (1970) has listed six factors that characterize social movements and countermovements; they are described in Figure 13-11.

In regard to the course of social movements, Toch has written that

> if and when a social movement becomes dominant in a society, its victory makes it vulnerable to two forms of self-destruction. If the movement persists in playing a protest role, the inappropriateness of this stance invites loss of membership. If, as is more usual, the movement proceeds to consolidate its new power, it risks becoming absorbed in the effort. . . . The movement may lose its original identity and become blind to developing needs. In due time, it may have to suppress the manifestations of discontent of new underprivileged groups [1965, p. 228].

An example of the latter course was what happened to Martin Luther King's nonviolent civil-rights movement. As some of the original goals of gaining equal rights and justice for Blacks were attained, the movement directed its momentum toward more diffuse objectives, such as the withdrawal of military troops from Vietnam and improving the plight of the poor—both Black and White. Such absorption in broader objectives caused many Blacks to believe that the movement had lost sight of their cause. Feeling that nonviolence had not succeeded, some of the Black groups became militant and advocated violent means of attaining their goals.

Figure 13-11
Characteristics of social movements

The following six characteristics are reflected in social movements and countermovements, according to social psychologist Muzafer Sherif (1970):

1. A social movement is a formative pattern of attempts at change; it develops in phases over time.

2. A social movement is initiated through interaction among people prompted by a motivational base fed by persisting social problems. Sherif uses the phrase *motivational base* in a generic sense. It may consist of material destitution, such as hunger and miserable living conditions, or it may consist of the desperation that results from being the victim of racism or exploitation. The motivational base may reflect the experience of **relative deprivation.**

3. A social movement develops through the declaration of complaints and the formulation and proclamation of a platform or ideology, which implies organization.

4. A social movement is carried out by those directly affected by the desired change and by others who throw in their lot with them.

5. The purpose of a social movement is to bring about evolutionary or revolutionary changes or to suppress changes (in the case of countermovements).

6. Efforts to effect change are made through appeals to the public, slogans, agitations, episodes of collective action, and encounters with the opposition (strikes, rallies, resistance, boycotts, demonstrations, riots, insurrection, and the like).

V. Examples of social change

In attempting to assess the direction of social change, we shall look at changes in attitudes

and values that serve as indicators of the direction of social change. In this section, we shall describe two of these—technology and its effects on attitudes toward work, and changing attitudes toward religious and moral authority. In each case these changing attitudes may be viewed as both dependent variables and independent variables, as both the consequences of previous social change and as potential sources of future change.

A. Technology and its effects on attitudes toward work

The United States and, to a lesser extent, Canada have always nurtured a cult of progress and a set of beliefs and attitudes that define what has been called "an American way" of looking at life. The component attitudes of this ideology include optimism, an orientation to the future rather than to the past, a positive view of change, and a preference for new ideas over old ones (McGee, 1962). "Old-fashioned" has become an invidious epithet, and "newness" has been valued in and for itself. The technology that makes progress possible was for a long time accepted without full consideration of its side effects. Recently, however, the notion that technological progress is synonymous with public benefit has been seriously questioned (Teich, 1972). At times the negative consequences of a new technique or device become so overwhelmingly evident they cannot be ignored. The advent of offshore oil drilling was probably viewed as progress. However, when a leak occurred and the oil collected on the beaches and destroyed much marine and shore life, national concern was aroused. Destruction of our environment was the price of the so-called progress. Figure 13-12 demonstrates another example of how a technological "advance" is made at the risk of great dangers to our environment.

Perhaps the price of progress is too great. Fundamental questions for the 1970s are: How can we make sure that our enormously complex technology remains our servant? Will life be enlarged in the technological society, bringing a new and generous vision of what is humanly possible (Ferkiss, 1969), or will life narrow down to a struggle to escape uncertainty?

Figure 13-12
Technological "advance"—at what cost? In 1956 the largest tanker afloat carried 45,000 tons of crude oil. Our need for oil is much more urgent now, so technological "improvements" have occurred. Today the largest tanker carries 476,292 tons and there is talk of building one huge enough to carry 1.25 million tons. The larger the tanker, the cheaper the price per ton for carrying oil. To those in charge of building and using oil tankers, the formula *bigger = cheaper = better* is axiomatic. Tankers are designed to be written off in ten years; they are constructed quickly and cheaply. They contain only one boiler (the *Queen Mary* had 27), with much greater risk of breakdowns or breakups (and hence oil spills). They also have only one engine rather than two, reducing maneuverability. Their braking power is such that it requires three *miles* to bring a tanker traveling at 16 knots to rest.

Because of these slipshod procedures and for other reasons, as much as 6 million tons of oil is let loose on the sea every year, poisoning marine organisms and ruining our beaches. Is it any wonder that British Columbians oppose the shipping of Alaskan oil along the coast of British Columbia to the northwestern part of the United States? (Source: N. Mostert, *Supership.* New York: Knopf, 1974; photo courtesy of Time-Life Picture Agency.)

Of more specific interest to the student of social psychology are the effects of the technological revolution on changes in attitudes and values (Mesthene, 1972). The specific area we shall examine here is technology's effects on attitudes toward work.

The side effects of cybernetics threaten to reorganize the nature of economic and social life. These effects throw into question the long-held "Protestant Ethic" position that if one works hard, life's rewards will come without fail. In the Protestant tradition, the goal is people who are not distracted by activities unrelated to their work, who postpone all possible benefits of prestige for the future, who conserve their assets and belongings for a time of need for themselves and their families, and who use their wealth to extend economic enterprise—even if to do so requires self-denial in the present. This Protestant tradition of asceticism, self-denial, and hard work was skillfully related to the spirit of capitalism by Max Weber (1930), who called it the Protestant Ethic.

During the years when Canada and the United States were assimilating waves of immigrants, the spirit of the Protestant Ethic encouraged many groups to expend extra energy to create their niche in the culture of the dominant group. The pattern in which each new group has come in at the bottom and worked hard to move upward has been a major source of energy and innovation in U.S. and Canadian society (Hodgkinson, 1967). But in this century the major industrial change has been a turning from the production of goods to the production of services. At the turn of the century, about three-fourths of the people in the labor force worked at producing physical goods, but in 1960 the majority of the people in the labor force were engaged in service occupations. Heavy manual labor has given way to machine production, a change that has freed a large portion of the labor force for work in service industries.

U.S. Department of Labor statistics indicate that the proportion of the total population included in the labor force is about 60% and that this percentage was fairly stable through the

1950s and 1960s. But the length of the work week has been greatly reduced. The standard work week in 1900 was 54 to 60 hours or more; a person steadily employed in a manufacturing plant thus worked about 3000 hours per year. More recently such a worker averages fewer than 40 hours a week and receives a paid vacation, putting in only about 2000 hours a year (Mack, 1967).

Along with such changes in the pattern of work, there is evidence that the Protestant Ethic is a declining force in the United States and Canadian core culture. Boguslaw describes current technological developments as the "utopian renaissance," which has as one of its proclaimed goals the abolition of hard labor.

> The workaday new utopians seem to have turned Max Weber's Ethic on its head to read "Hard work is simply a temporarily unautomated task. It is a necessary evil until we get a piece of gear, or a computer large enough, or a program checked out well enough to do the job economically. Until then, you working stiffs can hang around—but, for the long run, we really don't either want you or need you" [Boguslaw, 1965, p. 25].

The decline of the Protestant Ethic is documented by Kluckhohn (1958) as both a rise in the value placed upon being, as opposed to doing, and an increased interest in present-time orientation and a decreased interest in the future. Advertisements tell us to live for today; installment plans and charge accounts make it possible. The consumer role in North American culture is basically hedonistic and oriented toward the present. By spending, we are told, we are helping the economy. The following statement, made quite seriously by a college student in the 1960s, would probably irritate someone who grew up in the 1930s:

> I'm not money-mad by any means, but I'd like enough to buy a house, and have transportation, and of course good clothes for the family. Plus entertainments: I'd like to be able to see the good plays and movies. And I suppose I'd want a trip every year; visit around in the big urban

areas, you know, Berlin, Paris, Rome. I can't set any exact amount I'd like to make, so long as it's enough for the *necessities* of life [quoted in Hodgkinson, 1967, p. 126].

At the present time the whole system of values that goes with the work ethic seems to be in a state of flux. Reducing the work week does not reduce the worker's hunger for more money and goods, so that one major consequence of the six-hour day or the four-day week is the move toward moonlighting, or taking second jobs. Paradoxically, leisure may become a significant social problem in the future. Possibly, if larger amounts of leisure actually develop, some of the more subtle meanings of work will also become more apparent. Instead of viewing material reward as the primary purpose for work, more people may see work as a means of helping others, an antidote to boredom, a factor in self-esteem, and/or a creative activity (W. Neff, 1968). Until now, these meanings have been largely overshadowed by monetary motives.

B. Changing attitudes toward authority

Another indicator of rapid change is the open challenge to institutionalized authority. In the past decade open rebellion has appeared in the Roman Catholic and Episcopal (Anglican) churches, and such phenomena as the radical death-of-God theology, the new morality, and an increasing use of civil disobedience of laws perceived as unjust have emerged. Each of these may be seen as a symbol of defiance of traditional norms.

Many of the changes in religious and moral attitudes appear to reflect a move toward greater reliance on the individual and resistance to any fixed authority that prescribes codes of conduct. Some critics believe these changes are leading us toward a valueless society in which anarchy may soon prevail. A more hopeful assessment is that we are in the midst of a struggle toward greater enlightenment about the nature of morality and authentic participation in the decisions affecting all aspects of our life. In the Kohlberg frame of reference (see Chapter 8, on moral behavior and development), this could mean that greater numbers of people are moving toward the principled level of moral judgment. Autonomous moral principles have validity and application apart from the authority of the groups or persons who hold them and apart from the individual's identification with those persons or groups (Kohlberg, 1970).

VI. Youth and social change

Social change subjects different age groups to different amounts of stress. Most affected are youths in the process of making a lifelong commitment to the future. The young, who have outlived the social definitions of childhood but who are not yet fully located in the world of adult commitments and roles, are most torn between the pulls of the past and the future. Keniston (1970), who describes youth as a new stage produced by recent historical and social conditions (see Figure 13-13), discusses alternative responses that may characterize the reactions of youth to rapid social change. Two of these alternatives are activism and alienation.

Several investigations have distinguished between activists and alienated, apolitical youth (Block, Haan, & Smith, 1968; Flacks, 1967; Keniston, 1967; W. Watts, Lynch, & Whittaker, 1969). Though both activists and alienated youth reject many values and norms of contemporary society, the two groups can be clearly differentiated. The activists express their dissent through direct confrontation; the alienated react by withdrawing from conventional society. Whereas the activist is politically optimistic and socially concerned, the culturally alienated youth is too pessimistic and too firmly opposed to the system to demonstrate his or her disapproval in any organized public way. Keniston (1965) found that a primary variable in the alienation syndrome was distrust —or, in our terms, an assumption that human nature is untrustworthy. Any kind of positive commitment is rejected by the alienated youth. Given the unpredictability of the future, long-

range ethical idealism is considered to be impossible, and the present becomes overwhelmingly important. Rejecting the traditional North American values of monetary success, rigid self-control, and competitive achievement, the alienated person maintains that passion, feeling, and awareness are the most reliable forces at our disposal. For the alienated, the primary objective in life is to attain and maintain openness to experience, contact with the world, and spontaneity of feeling. Anything that might fetter or restrain responsiveness and openness is opposed.

Figure 13-13
Youth: A "new" stage of life. Kenneth Keniston, author of *Young Radicals* and *The Uncommitted*, proposes that we are witnessing today the emergence on a mass scale of a previously unrecognized stage

of life, a stage that intervenes between adolescence and adulthood. He calls this stage *youth*, assigning a new and specific meaning to this familiar term.

A central conscious issue during youth is the tension between self and society. Whereas adolescents are struggling to define who they are, youths begin to sense who they are and thus to recognize the possibility of conflict and disparity between their emerging selfhood and the social order. In youth, pervasive ambivalence toward both self and society is the rule. This ambivalence is not the same as a definitive rejection of society, nor does it necessarily lead to political activism. For ambivalence may also entail intense self-rejection, including major efforts at self-transformation such as monasticism, meditation, psychoanalysis, prayer, or the use of hallucinogenic drugs. In youth the ambivalent conflicts between the maintenance of personal integrity and the achievement of effectiveness in society are fully experienced for the first time.

The central developmental possibilities of youth are defined as *individuation* and *alienation*. The meaning of *individuation* may be clarified by considering the special dangers of youth, which can be defined as extremes of alienation, whether from self or from society. At one extreme is that total alienation from self that involves abject submission to society—"joining the rat race" or "selling out." Society is affirmed but selfhood denied. The other extreme is a total alienation from society that leads not so much to the rejection of society as to ignoring, denying, or blocking out its existence. Here the integrity of self is purchased at the price of a determined denial of social reality and the loss of social effectiveness (Keniston, 1970). (Photo by Holly R Johnson.)

A. The generation gap— Myth or fact?

Alienated youth distrust those who are older as well as generalized authority; a popular slogan in the early 1970s was "Don't trust anyone over 30." Does this position reflect an increased generation gap?

Conflict between the generations is nothing new. Consider the statement "Our youth today love luxury. They have bad manners, contempt for authority, disrespect for older people. Children nowadays are tyrants. They contradict their parents, gobble their food, and tyrannize their teachers." That statement was uttered by Socrates, in the fifth century before Christ. But so much is currently being said about the generation gap that it seems appropriate to examine the notion in this discussion of social change.

Many adults feel certain that today's alienated young are not just the modern equivalent of the goldfish-swallowing students of the 1930s. But there is a question as to how serious the alienation really is. Is there really a generation gap? Roszak (1969) and M. Mead (1970) say yes. Adelson (1970) says no. P. Slater (1970) says yes, but he also says that there is, in fact, too much conformity to obsolete parental values. We shall now turn to an examination of some of these contrasting interpretations of the phenomenon commonly labeled the generation gap, before seeking some resolution of the controversy.

1. The rise of a counterculture. Roszak (1969) argues that the revolt of the young is serious, important, and redemptive. According to Roszak, the young today are forming a culture so radically unaffiliated with the mainstream of our society that to many people it scarcely appears to be a culture at all. The source of their revolt is the dehumanization brought about by Western technological civilization. Roszak defines *technocracy* as the social form in which an industrial society reaches the peak of its organizational integration. In a technocracy, nothing is any longer small or simple or readily apparent to the nontechnical person. The scale and intricacy of all human activities transcend the competence of the amateur citizen and demand the attention of specially trained experts. Today's polarization, then, has the technical-bureaucratic organization of economic and political life on one side, while on the other side is the counterculture—the radical-anarchic, romantic-religious, protest-withdrawal tendencies of the young.

A difficulty in Roszak's interpretation of the rise of the counterculture, however, is that he sees it as a revolution of the repressed against the system that represses them. But, in fact, the revolt of the young occurs not among those who are most oppressed or repressed, nor among those who bear the greatest responsibility to the technocracy. The counterculture is in fact a subculture of middle-class White youth. Indeed, the counterculture includes really only that minority of the young who are so securely in the technocratic society that they can afford to demand something more of life than security, affluence, and the prospect of political power. The counterculture arises, then, not because the young today are more repressed but because they are so little repressed that they can raise their sights. As Keniston has stated,

> The counterculture may replace the barbecue pit with the hippie pad, family togetherness with the encounter group, and the suburban coffee hour with the commune, but the focus is still on the private world instead of on the social and political scene where it should be. . . . If American technocracy is the thesis, Roszak admirably defines the antithesis. We still await the synthesis [1969, p. 9].

Similar to Roszak's sympathetic view of the counterculture is the "Consciousness III" classification of Charles Reich in *The Greening of America* (1970). Reich defined three categories of people—Consciousness I, II, and III—each representing a stage in American life. Consciousness III people were seen as the hope of the present and the wave of the future: "The Consciousness III person, no matter how young and inexperienced, seems to possess an extraordinary 'new knowledge'. . . . He does not 'know' the facts, but he still 'knows' the truth that seems hidden from others." Reich's mystical view of the youth revolution is subject to the same criticism that Keniston makes of Roszak's interpretation of the counterculture: the question of how society is to deal with its own problems is avoided, as if it is an insignificant or irrelevant issue.

2. Toward a prefigurative culture? Another view of the generation gap is embodied in anthropological terms by Margaret Mead, who sees a deep, new, unprecedented, worldwide gulf between the young and the old. Mead, who has been studying patterns of child rearing across cultures for many years, expects that the future will radically depart from the present. Within the two decades from 1940 to 1960, events occurred that irrevocably altered our relationships to other people and to the natural world. Mead sees the events and discoveries of this time as bringing about a drastic, irreversible division between the generations. She states: "Even very recently, the elders could say: 'You know, I have been young and *you* have never been old.' But today's young people can reply: 'You never have been young in the world I am young in, and you never can be'" (1970, p. 63).

Mead's view of the dichotomy between the perceptions of the young and those of their parents is contradicted by evidence reported by Adelson, discussed in the next section. Mead's standpoint also differs from research findings on the similarities between the values of student activists and those of their parents. But her emphasis is on the speed and dimensions of change in the modern world. She distinguishes three different kinds of culture: **postfigurative culture,** in which children learn primarily from their forebears; **cofigurative culture,** in which both children and adults learn from their peers; and **prefigurative culture,** in which adults learn from their children. Mead sees a prefigurative culture developing, in which the child will have to serve as scout; the child will pose the questions, and it will be the task of his or her elders to teach the child "how to learn" rather than "what to learn." The older generation—those born before 1940—is "strangely isolated," according to Mead. It has witnessed such massive and rapid change that it cannot communicate its experiences to its successors. Meanwhile, the young are "at home" in this time. Satellites are familiar in their skies. They have never known a time when war did not threaten annihilation. When they are given the facts, they can understand immediately that continued pollution of the air and water and soil will soon make the planet uninhabitable. Like the first generation born in a new country, they only halfway comprehend their parents' talk about the past. Mead's views are reminiscent of I. Child's (1943) descriptions of the dilemma of second-generation Italians in a New England community. They were "marginal people," experiencing strong pulls between being Italian and being American and finding themselves unable to belong to either group.

Mead optimistically believes that the gap between the generations can be taken as a guide to the future. Although this guide is somewhat vague, she thinks it is possible to change into a prefigurative culture consciously, delightedly, and industriously, rearing unknown children for an unknown world. The nature of the direct participation of the young of which Mead speaks may be inferred from this comment by a participant (then a college senior) in a panel discussion of the generation gap:

> Starting in the late 50s you made a demand from us. You said expand your mind and think. We've got to fight the Russians because there's a technological race on. We capitulated and we expanded our minds. Now you've got a lot of people who can think; you've got a lot of people who have been through a system who have learned how to think. Now we're saying we want to use this knowledge with experience. You're saying, not yet, you're too young. I think we're just as old as you mentally, and if you give us time, and if you give us the room to experiment, to use this knowledge, you could have a beautiful thing [quoted in *Religious Education*, 1970, 65, 104].

Additional support for the idea of an unprecedented generation gap is given by those who examine current art forms. The music, art, theater, and literature of youth provide clues to the themes of alienation (Reichart, 1969; Friedenberg, 1969).

3. Is the gap more ideological than generational? Despite the popularity of the idea of an unprecedented conflict between the generations, there is some evidence that refutes the idea. Quite clearly, whether one perceives a generation gap depends on the specific issues one is talking about

(Bengston, Furlong, & Laufer, 1974). If the issue is whether there is a fundamental lack of articulation between the generations, then the answer is decisively no (Adelson, 1970, p. 35). In contrast to the notion that there is an extensive degree of alienation between parents and their children, Adelson concludes that there are few signs of serious conflict between adolescents in the United States and their parents. Douvan and Adelson (1966) studied 3000 young people, ages 12 to 18, from all regions of the United States and all socioeconomic levels and found that usually the relationships between youth and their parents were amiable. So did Bengston (1971), who collected data from more than 500 students enrolled in three southern-California colleges. About 80% of the students reported generally close and friendly relationships with their parents: 79% felt somewhat close or very close; 81% regarded communication as good; and 78% felt their parents understood them all or most of the time.

Lubell (1968) asked 350 White students and more than 100 Black students at 28 campuses in 14 states to compare themselves with their parents. Interview questions concerned upbringing, drug use, premarital sex, religious beliefs, career choices, economic thinking, and attitudes toward the draft, war, and politics. Lubell reports that only about 10% of the students he interviewed were in serious discord with their parents, and in most of these cases there was a long history of family tension. Similar findings by K. Cross (1968) indicate a striking similarity between the opinions of students and their perceptions of their parents' opinions. Adelson (1970) examined the areas of politics and values and found further arguments that the gap is ideological rather than generational.

An analysis of the 1968 U.S. election was made by the University of Michigan's Survey Research Center. It was based on 1600 interviews with a representative national sample of voters. Outside the southern part of the U.S., George Wallace drew proportionately more votes from younger voters than from older voters. This fact contrasts with the tendency to identify the young with leftist ideology and militancy. The radical activists are for the most part children of radical or liberal parents (Starr, 1974).

In connection with the issue of values, *Fortune* magazine polled a representative sample of 18- to 24-year-olds in the U.S., dividing them into a noncollege group (vocationally oriented) and a so-called "forerunner" group (students interested in education for self-discovery and majoring in humanities and social sciences). The "forerunners" were more liberal politically, less traditional in values, and less enchanted with business careers. But no generation gap was revealed.

According to Adelson's argument, there has been too much generalization from a narrow segment of the young to the entire younger generation. Adelson finds that a relatively small proportion of the young are in severe conflict with the values of their parents. He sees more evidence for describing what is happening as an ideological conflict that cuts across generational lines. The polarization is the result not of age but of differing ideologies. Adelson's findings tend to support the findings of similarities between the values of student activists and the values of their parents. The evidence does not completely shatter the notion of an unprecedented generation gap, but it does indicate that the conflict between children and their own parents is not as sharp as is popularly believed. The gap certainly exists, but it cannot be attributed entirely to conflict between the generations.

How may we resolve these differing opinions? Thomas (1974), after a careful analysis of these and other studies, notes that those observers, such as Roszak, Slater, Reich, and Mead, who argue that a new youth culture is emerging focus on *values*. They say that a generation gap exists because of differences in values, or broad orientations such as those presented in Table 13-2. Sociologist Philip Slater, who believes today's youth have formed a new culture, states:

> There are an almost infinite number of polarities by means of which one can differentiate between the two cultures. The old culture, when forced to choose, tends to give preference to property rights over personal rights, techno-

logical requirements over human needs, competition over cooperation, violence over sexuality, concentration over distribution, the producer over the consumer, means over ends, secrecy over openness, social forms over personal expression, striving over gratification, Oedipal love over communal love, and so on. The new counterculture tends to reverse all these priorities [1970, p. 100].

Note that these are basic, broad values. In contrast, those researchers and observers who conclude there is little evidence for a generation gap rely on a more specific level, that of attitudes. For example, in a study briefly described in Chapter 2, Yankelovich (1974) conducted a survey for CBS News that surveyed young adults and their parents on what are called "cleavage issues." These are ones on which there is public controversy—for example, sex, drugs, and politics. Yankelovich asked about opinions and beliefs; on all but a small minority of the questions there was striking similarity in the responses of parents and their offspring (Thomas, 1974).

If Thomas's analysis is correct—and there seems to be no reason to doubt it—the question then becomes which is more important, values or opinions and beliefs? Responses to that question could generate another controversy, but we ourselves place emphasis on the values. It is from this emphasis that many of our attitudes stem. A generational difference does appear to be developing. Confusion on the part of middle-aged parents trying to understand their college-aged youth will probably increase in the next decade; in fact, Roszak predicts that the counterculture will reach its peak when the present generation of 11- and 12-year-olds reach their 20s—about the year 1984. "Future shock" is thus increasing.

VII. "Future shock" and the usefulness of utopias

A contemporary television commercial asks "How can you plan for the future when the present is changing so fast?" **Future shock** is a

Table 13-2
Value orientations of traditional middle-class cultures and the current youth culture

Dimension	Culture	
	Traditional Middle-Class	Current Youth
Time	Future	Present
Activity	Doing	Being
Person-nature	People over nature	People in harmony with nature
Basic human nature	Neutral (neither good nor bad)	Good
Relational	Individualistic	Collateral

Adapted from "Generational Discontinuity in Beliefs: An Exploration of the Generation Gap," by L. E. Thomas, *Journal of Social Issues*, 1974, *30*(3), 1–22. Copyright 1974 by the Society for the Psychological Study of Social Issues. Used by permission.

recent phrase that is now a part of our language. Alvin Toffler (1970), who coined the phrase, defines it as what happens to ordinary people when they are overwhelmed by an accelerating rate of change. More than an arresting phrase, future shock may prove to be the most obstinate and debilitating social problem of the future. Its symptoms range from confusion, anxiety, and hostility to physical illness, seemingly senseless violence, and self-destructive apathy. Victims of future shock feel continuously harassed and hence attempt to reduce the number of changes they must come to terms with and the number of decisions they must make (Toffler, 1970).

A helpful way to grasp the implications of future shock is to look at a parallel term, *culture shock*. Novice world travelers experience culture shock when they find themselves in a totally new environment, cut off from the meaning of events around them and without familiar psychological cues. Many North Americans have felt such disorientation and frustration when placed in a foreign culture. But such travelers have the com-

forting knowledge that they can go back to the culture that they left behind. Future shock may be viewed as culture shock in one's own society, arising when a new culture is superimposed upon an old one. For the victim of future shock, however, there is little likelihood of returning to the familiarity that was left behind.

How will we be able to cope with the dizzying rate of change? How can we prepare for the future? For example, already one out of every five citizens of the United States changes residence during an average year; in the future this rate will increase. What effects does this constant moving have on family stability, on interpersonal relationships, on self-identity? Should the government and social psychologists combine to develop reception centers to help us "nomads" feel more comfortable and at home in an initially strange setting (Morgan, 1974)? Toffler (1970) says every society faces not merely a succession of probable futures but an array of possible futures and a conflict over preferable futures. "The management of change is the effort to convert certain possibles into probables, in pursuit of agreed-on preferables. Determining the probable calls for a *science* of futurism. Delineating the possible calls for an *art* of futurism. Defining the preferable calls for a *politics* of futurism" (Toffler, 1970, p. 407).

There has been a sudden proliferation of organizations devoted to the study of the future. Some of these future-oriented groups include the World Future Society and the Institute for the Future, which investigate the probable social and cultural effects of advanced communications technology; an academic study group called the Commission on the Year 2000; and the Harvard Program on Technology and Society, which is concerned with social problems likely to arise from biomedical advances. In the very attempt to forecast the future, the thinkers in these organizations may be altering it, in that their forecasts can become either self-fulfilling or self-defeating prophecies. Nevertheless, predictions of what lies ahead may help clarify goals and provide alternative policies.

As long as people have thought and dreamed, there have been utopian thinkers, who shared their dreams about alternative futures. In works from Plato's *Republic* to Skinner's *Walden Two*, men and women have tried to define possible futures. Some of the best-known utopias in literature are succinctly described by Grossack and Gardner (1970) in Table 13-3. Most traditional utopias picture simple and static societies that have withdrawn from the complex industrialized world. For example, Skinner's *Walden Two* (1948), applying the principles of behavioristic psychology, depicts a preindustrial way of life, based on farming and handicrafts. (See Chapter 17 for a description of Twin Oaks, a contemporary commune based on *Walden Two*.) Although Huxley's *Brave New World* and Orwell's *1984* emphasize high technology and sophisticated machines, these books deliberately simplify social and cultural relationships. The classical utopians believed that societies could be built that would be free from human imperfections. They wanted to escape from the problematic world in which they existed to a world that would be happier, more just, and more prosperous. The focus, though, was on people.

Boguslaw (1965) describes the new utopians as the system designers—the computer manufacturer, the operations researcher, the computer programmer, the data-processing specialist. These, according to Boguslaw, are the social engineers of our times—the difference between them and the classical utopians being that the new utopians are concerned with nonpeople, or human surrogates. The new utopians plan with computer hardware, system procedures, functional analyses, and heuristics. Their impatience with human error serves to unify them, and they are separated from the classical system designers by the fact that they are not humanitarians. Their dominant orientation can best be described as efficiency.

Toffler says that we now need a revolutionary approach to creating utopias, which would look forward to postindustrialism, rather than backward to simpler societies. Toffler suggests that this could be done by a group of expert behavioral scientists, working together long enough to devise a set of well-defined values on which a truly postindustrial, utopian society might be based. Such a group would explore issues such as the structure of the family, the economy, law, religion, sexual practices, the youth culture, music, art, the sense of time, and psychological problems of the future society. Meanwhile, other groups could be at work on counterutopias. Filmmakers and fiction writers, working closely with social psychologists, could prepare creative works about the lives of individuals in the imagined society. Through television, books, plays, and films, large numbers of people could be educated to the costs and benefits of various proposed utopias. There might then emerge groups willing to subject utopian ideas to empirical test. The last decade has seen the development of several thousands of communes in the United States, Canada, and Japan. (See Chapter 17 for a description of the social psychology of communes.) Many young people, in their dissatisfaction with industrialism, are experimenting with new social arrangements, from group marriage to communal farms. But most of these endeavors reveal a powerful desire to return to the past. Society would be better served by utopian experiments based on postindustrial rather than preindustrial forms.

One reason why some of the earlier utopias failed was that they severed connections between their brave new systems and the power struc-

Table 13-3
Utopias presented in Western literature

Author	Time	Work	Brief Description
Plato	4th century B.C.	The Republic	Plato envisioned an ideal society with a hierarchy of classes, each having its particular obligations. Philosophers would rule, poets would be excluded.
Sir Thomas More	1516	Utopia	In coining the word "Utopia," More anticipated an order in which natural virtues would be unhindered.
Sir Francis Bacon	1627	The New Atlantis	Bacon placed primary emphasis on technological productivity.
Edward Bellamy	1888	Looking Backward	Bellamy's utopia was a socialist work, containing scathing critiques of his contemporary world. The work sold tremendously in the United States.
H. G. Wells	1905	A Modern Utopia	In this work Wells describes a future paradise; in others he outlined the destruction of the world.
Aldous Huxley	1932	Brave New World	A satirical account of a frightening future world in which individuality is sacrificed for the community ideals. Human beings are produced in test tubes and graded according to intelligence.
George Orwell	1948	1984	Orwell predicted the rise of Big Brother and the loss of freedom in this negative utopian prediction. Three world powers exist, two of which are always warring against the third.
B. F. Skinner	1948	Walden Two	Skinner applied the principles of learning theory in an effort to produce a population rich in idealism and devoid of negative impulses.

From Man and Men: Social Psychology as Social Science, by M. M. Grossack and H. Gardner. Copyright 1970 by International Textbook Co., Scranton, Pa. Reprinted by permission.

tures of their times. The usefulness of utopias may not necessarily be in the full realization of any one design, but in the expansion of alternatives for the future. Wide dissemination of utopian and counterutopian concepts may help us become more aware of our present options. Utopian plans stem from the desire to extend human mastery over nature and over ourselves. At the same time, the greatest threat of the present utopian renaissance may be its potential for extending the control of some humans over others (Boguslaw, 1965, p. 204). But perhaps, through its analyses of utopias and counterutopias, social psychology may serve to free humanity, rather than to control it, as some psychologists would prefer (Skinner, 1971).

VIII. Summary

It is essential that social-psychological knowledge be applied so that we can remedy the social problems and understand the social change that we encounter in everyday life. In fact, an important aspect of social psychology is its concern with problems that are relevant to our society and to each of us as social beings. The methodology of social psychology permits the study and understanding of complex social phenomena, but despite this, many social researchers have not been interested in the real-world applicability of their research findings.

Radical social psychologists propose a new role for their discipline, one that combines research and political activities. The political task is to see that research is applied in bringing about recommended institutional changes.

A mainstream position in social psychology maintains the view that the function of the social psychologist is to generate new knowledge, which may or may not be applied to social problems. However, it advocates that more theory-oriented research be done in natural settings. Those with this viewpoint believe that, in the long run, more useful contributions to social psychology will come from theory-based research than from atheoretical, applied work.

Field theory, developed by Kurt Lewin, proposed that human behavior must always be viewed in relation to its environment. Studies done in laboratory settings occasionally lead to findings that are contradictory to similar studies done in natural settings. Both settings must be used as we search for useful knowledge. The field of *action research* brings theory, knowledge, and skills together to understand and solve social problems. Its goal is planned social change.

Three strategies for planned change are the empirical-rational strategy, the normative-reeducative strategy, and the power-coercive strategy.

The *empirical-rational strategy* assumes that people will act in response to the best information available to them. The goal of this strategy is thus to provide facts that can be disseminated in order to bring about change.

The *normative-reeducative strategy* assumes that our behavior is based on our attitudes, values, and relationships with others. People are products of their culture, and these determinants must be recognized in any strategy of change.

The *power-coercive strategy* utilizes pressures—political, social, or economic—to bring about desired social change. Either violent or nonviolent kinds of power-coercive strategy may be used.

The study of "unplanned" social change is also quite relevant to social psychology. More research is needed on the social-psychological consequences of rapid social change, which involves significant alterations of patterns of social action and interaction. These changes are reflected in norms, values, and cultural products and symbols.

The rate of social change can be measured by picturing a fraction, the denominator of which is time and the numerator of which is the number of events to be observed. Presumably, these events would have the potential for altering the social system. Social movements, as forms of collective behavior aimed toward change, are useful indicators of the directions of social change.

Technological developments have led to changing attitudes toward work. The Protestant

Ethic is a declining force in United States core culture. Changing attitudes toward authority are reflected in changes in religion and morality; they may be interpreted as a move toward greater individual freedom and less reliance on fixed authority.

Highly visible groups of culturally alienated youth have led many to believe that there is an intensified conflict between the generations. Contrasting interpretations of the generation gap suggest (1) that the present gap is unprecedented and radically different from previous genera-tional conflict, or (2) that the values of today's youth are very similar to those of their parents. It appears that at the level of broad values, there are generational differences, but that the more specific beliefs and opinions of parents and their offspring are quite similar.

Utopian planning is useful in increasing the options that are available to us. The direction of utopian designs should be toward providing greater freedom for us to make our own choices. As social psychologists, we seek to design and implement such utopias.

PART 5
GROUP
DIFFERENCES

I. The question of heredity versus environment
   A. The biological basis of sex differences
   B. Socialization of sex roles
   C. Interaction and overlap
   D. Theories about women and men

II. Sex differences in aptitude and personality
   A. Intelligence
   B. Conformity
   C. Achievement
   D. Masculinity, femininity, and androgyny

III. Perceptions of sex differences: The eye of the beholder
   A. Stereotypes
   B. Evaluating the performances of men and women
   C. Self-evaluation by men and women

IV. Equality and the future
   A. Equality in employment
   B. Sex roles in the future

V. Summary

446

The social psychology of sex roles

by Kay Deaux

14

I deny that any one knows, or can know, the nature of the two sexes, as long as they have only been seen in their present relation to one another.
John Stuart Mlll

The rising of us women means the rising of us all.
From "Bread and Roses,"
1920s suffrage song

One of the major social and political developments of the 1970s has been the movement for equality of the sexes, a blanket term encompassing women's liberation, men's liberation, and a host of related concerns. New legal requirements, spawned by the U. S. Civil Rights Act of 1964, Title IX of the U. S. Education Act Amendments of 1972, and the Canadian Bill of Rights, have forced changes in many of the customary social practices in the United States and Canada. Similar developments have occurred in other countries. In Europe, Sweden has set the pace with governmental support of equality between the sexes in both occupation and education. Even the most traditional societies have experienced growing pressures for a more active role for women. The effects of these pressures and policies have already been great. Large corporations, such as the American Telephone & Telegraph Company, have been ordered to pay millions of dollars to compensate workers for proven discrimination. Universities have been threatened with a withdrawal of federal research funds be-cause of alleged inequities between the sexes in respect to promotion practices. Public schools have been required to offer home-economics courses for boys and shop-mechanics courses for girls.

As in the case of any social change, such momentous alterations have not been made without resistance. Little League baseball coaches argued that girls shouldn't play, saying that it wouldn't be proper to pat girls on the rear end as coaches naturally do to boys. The courts, however, ruled in favor of equality and against this particular form of propriety. On another level, opponents of the Equal Rights Amendment to the U. S. Constitution have claimed that women have the right to be financially supported by their husbands and that changes in legal requirements will ruin the family, marriage, and the future of children.

Underlying these arguments is a basic question: *what is the nature of men and women?* Throughout this text, we have been concerned with the assumptions that are made about the nature of people in general. Here we are concerned with a more specific set of assumptions concerning the nature of women and men. How similar are men and women? Are the differences between them mostly innate, or are they learned in the process of socialization?

For some time, social psychologists were content to ignore these questions, leaving their investigation to biologists or to more clinically oriented psychologists. More recently, it has become evident that many social behaviors are affected by such **demographic** variables as sex, race, and social class, and it is often difficult to explain social behaviors without reference to these factors. Furthermore, the impact of the Women's Movement represents a basic case study in social change, and this topic is well within the province of social psychologists.

In this chapter, we will explore the question of what men and women are like. We will look at the evidence for similarities and differences between women and men, as well as the beliefs that exist about those similarities and differences. In addition, we will consider the effects that these beliefs have on social interaction between the sexes. Finally, we will look at the question of change in the future.

I. The question of heredity versus environment

A. The biological basis of sex differences

Certainly no one would argue that there are not biological differences between males and females. It is quite apparent to all of us that in respect to body build and sexual characteristics, for example, men and women are not exactly the same creature. Furthermore, we know that there are groups of sex-related hormones that are distributed unevenly among males and females. Males have a relatively higher proportion of a class of hormones called androgens, while fe-

males have a higher proportion of estrogens. Studies using animals as subjects (Beach, 1965) have shown that tampering with the hormonal balance of infants (for example, injecting young female rats less than three days old with the male hormone *testosterone*, or castrating equally young male rats and thereby preventing the production of testosterone) will alter the sexual behavior of the adult rat, causing a female-like receptive behavior in the castrated male and mounting behavior in the testosterone-treated female rat. Among humans, however, we know less about the influence of androgens and estrogens on sex-related behaviors, although it is clear that estrogens do play a role in the menstruation and lactation of adult women.

Even less is known about the possible influence of sex-related hormones on those behaviors that are not linked to sexual and reproductive functions. Do these hormones influence the cognitive abilities of men and women? Are traits such as aggressiveness and dependence linked to the sex hormones? These questions must be answered affirmatively to support an argument for biological differences in the behavior of men and women.

To substantiate a position that sex differences in a given characteristic are biological in origin, we must satisfy four conditions. These four conditions are (1) that the characteristic occurs in one sex when the child is very young; (2) that the characteristic is more typical of one sex than the other in nearly every society; (3) that it is more prevalent in one sex in other primate species; and (4) that its presence is consistent with hormonal findings. By these criteria, **aggressiveness** seems to be a likely candidate in the search for biological differences between men and women. Differences between males and females in observed aggressiveness—at both adolescent and adult ages—consistently favor the male in nearly all societies (Maccoby & Jacklin, 1974a, 1974b; D'Andrade, 1966; Whiting & Edwards, 1973). Studies of primates have revealed the same pattern of greater male aggressiveness, and hormonal treatment of animals also supports

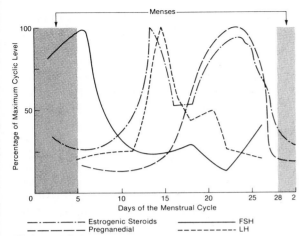

—·—·—·— Estrogenic Steroids   ——————— FSH
————— Pregnanedial   ---------- LH

Figure 14-1

The relationship between the menstrual cycle and mood. Some investigators have suggested that there is a strong connection between a woman's mood and the phase of the menstrual cycle she is in (Bardwick, 1971; Ivey & Bardwick, 1968). These authors report that when women are in midcycle (the ovulation phase) and estrogen is high, they will show a greater degree of self-esteem and low level of negative emotions. In contrast, the period immediately preceding menstruation is thought to be characterized by anxiety, hostility, and depression.

While there is no doubt that women do experience physiological changes associated with cycles of hormone production (see graph), it is not at all clear what effect these hormonal changes have on women's behavior. In fact, most studies have indicated few or no consistent effects on performance (Southam & Gonzaga, 1965; Parlee, 1973; Zimmerman & Parlee, 1973), despite the widespread belief that women cannot work well at "that time of the month."

One recent study suggests the intriguing possibility that women may actually perform *better* during the menstrual period (Rodin, 1974). According to Rodin's results, a woman who initially performs poorly and can blame the failure on her physical state, rather than on any lack of ability, will show better performance on a subsequent test than the woman who does not have the same explanation available for her failure. (From *Psychology of Women: A Study of Bio-Cultural Conflicts* (1971) by J. M. Bardwick. After Schwartz, 1968. By permission of Harper & Row, Publishers.)

the argument. Even among humans, there is some evidence that unusually high levels of male hormone in young girls (as a result of drugs taken by the mother during pregnancy) will result in more aggressive, rough-and-tumble play by these "androgenized" girls (Money & Ehrhardt, 1972). Thus we can conclude with some degree of confidence that aggressiveness is, at least in part, biologically determined.

Other theorists have suggested that men and women also differ in cognitive abilities, such as learning and problem-solving, as a result of physiological and hormonal differences. Perhaps the most widely known example of this viewpoint is the theory formulated by D. M. Broverman, Klaiber, Kobayashi, and Vogel (1968). These researchers suggest that men and women excel on different kinds of tasks. In their view, women surpass men on simple tasks that require rote learning and quick reaction time, such as identifying colors as quickly as possible. Men, in contrast, are seen as excelling in more complex behaviors that require cognitive mediation—for example, learning to discriminate between two stimuli or solving a novel jigsaw puzzle.[1] The reason for these differences, Broverman and his colleagues suggest, is a difference in the balance of androgens and estrogens in men and women, which favors an activating or inhibiting process in the nervous system. Inhibiting systems allow for the delay of immediate responses, a process required in complex problem-solving; activating systems facilitate an immediate, reflex response. Thus, according to the theory of Broverman et al., men and women are psychologically different as a result of basic biological differences.

Unfortunately for Broverman and his colleagues, however, there is a considerable amount of evidence that contradicts, or at least fails to support, their position. First of all, their research

[1]It is interesting to note that this suggested difference between men and women is very similar to the Type I/Type II learning distinction that Arthur Jensen and proponents of a biological position use to explain racial differences in intelligence (see Chapter 15).

does not itself present the kinds of evidence required by the four criteria we noted previously; that is, the results needed to argue strongly for a biological difference between the sexes are not present. Furthermore, a number of researchers have criticized many of the assumptions that Broverman and his colleagues make (Parlee, 1972; Maccoby & Jacklin, 1974a; Nisbet & Temoshok, 1976). These critics point to at least two weak links in the Broverman hypothesis. First of all, thorough reviews of task performance have indicated that the simple categorization that Broverman uses does not parallel known sex differences. Men excel or are no different from women on *some kinds* of simple, repetitive tasks, and women are equal to or better than men on *some kinds* of more complex tasks. A second criticism deals with the physiological mechanisms that are assumed in the Broverman hypothesis. A thorough review of the relevant literature indicates little evidence that androgens and estrogens affect the activating and inhibiting systems in the way suggested by the theory. There may in fact be differences in cognitive abilities between men and women, resulting from hormonal and physiological differences. At the present time, however, the evidence we have does not support such differences.[2]

To summarize the biological viewpoint, we can say with certainty that some anatomical and hormonal differences between the sexes do exist. Do these differences affect any behavioral or psychological characteristics of men and women? Only in the case of aggressiveness is the evidence

at all convincing. For other traits and behaviors, the evidence is much less substantial. And even if there are biological origins for some sex differences, we must still consider the extent to which these differences may be modified by experience. What role does socialization play in the creation or modification of sex differences?

B. Socialization of sex roles

No child grows up in a total vacuum. From birth on, the infant is surrounded by a variety of people and events that shape its perception of the world. The process by which the individual becomes aware of and incorporates the values of his or her society is generally referred to as the socialization process. Parents or parent substitutes are usually the most important figures in the child's early life; later, teachers, peers, and the mass media provide the child with additional information about the society's values and customs. **Sex-role socialization** refers to those specific events that teach children what is appropriate for a male and a female in their society. While we are far from understanding all the complexities of this socialization process, it is evident that boys and girls do learn different behaviors in the process.

Many of these socialization practices are quite consistent over a wide variety of societies. Barry, Bacon, and Child (1957) examined sex-role socialization practices in 110 different societies. While few differences were found in the attention given to infants in these societies, older boys and girls were socialized quite differently. Some of these differences are shown in Table 14-1.

Among the societies studied, Barry and his colleagues found that achievement and self-reliant behavior were almost never encouraged in young girls, while parents appeared to stress these behaviors for boys. In contrast, girls were often encouraged to be nurturant, while none of the societies stressed nurturance for boys. Other behaviors showed less emphatic differences in

---

[2]History shows that scientists have often been too eager to explain sex differences in biological terms. In surveying the early research on sex differences and brain functions, Shields (1974) presents an illustrative example. As theories of the functions of particular brain areas changed, so did conclusions about male or female superiority in that particular area. When frontal lobes were believed to be the seat of intelligence, for example, males were believed to have more well-developed frontal lobes. However, as research pointed to the importance of parietal lobes, investigators then concluded that men had larger parietal lobes, while women were accorded greater frontal-lobe development.

Table 14-1
Observations of sex differences in socialization practices

Observed Behavior	Percentage of Societies with Evidence of Sex Differences in Direction of:		
	Girls	Boys	Neither
Nurturance	82%	0%	18%
Obedience	35%	3%	62%
Responsibility	61%	11%	28%
Achievement	3%	87%	10%
Self-reliance	0%	85%	15%

Barry, Bacon, and Child (1957) analyzed previously collected ethnographic reports of 110 different societies, most of which were essentially illiterate. Their unit of analysis was the society itself; in other words, if the reports indicated that the society in general seemed to encourage achievement in boys, that society was categorized accordingly. In many cases, the ethnographic reports did not contain information on all of the socialization practices in which the authors were interested. Thus the number of societies on which the above percentages are based ranges from 31 (in the case of achievement) to 82 (for self-reliance). Notice the tendencies to socialize boys and girls differently; for example, most societies encourage the development of nurturance in girls but not in boys.

Adapted from "A Cross-Cultural Survey of Some Sex Differences in Socialization," by H. Barry III, M. K. Bacon, and I. L. Child, *Journal of Abnormal and Social Psychology*, 1957, 55, 327–332. Copyright 1957 by the American Psychological Association. Used by permission.

socialization. In the majority of societies, for example, obedience was not stressed for either boys or girls. When obedience was an issue, however, the pressure was directed toward girls.

Although these results suggest a high degree of consistency among societies, Barry et al. (1957) also attempted to explain why some societies were more **sex-typed** than others. Two conditions appeared to be important among the societies studied: (1) sex differentiation was more common in societies that depended on physical strength—for example, where the hunting of large animals was important; and (2) sex differentiation was more common in societies that consisted of large cooperative family groups rather than of more isolated nuclear families. As the needs and customs of a society change, we

find that sex-role socialization patterns change as well. Draper (in press) has studied the !Kung people, who live in the Kalahari Desert of South Africa. This group of people has recently shifted from a nomadic existence to a more sedentary, agrarian way of life. Whereas, before, the men and women contributed equally to small-game hunting and food gathering, both adults and children now have more distinct roles. Men leave the villages to raise crops and care for cattle, while women remain in the villages and tend to the immediate needs for food and shelter. Observers have noted different socialization pressures on the young boys and girls that reflect the different activities of the adults.

Whiting and Edwards (1973) have also observed differences in sex-role socialization that appear to be related to the needs of the society. In one African tribe, for example, a shortage of young girls resulted in the assignment of child-caring duties to a large number of young boys. The boys in this society became less aggressive and less dominant than young boys in otherwise similar societies. In summary, there is a considerable body of evidence suggesting that the degree to which boys and girls are socialized to different forms of behavior can vary widely.

But what about our own society? In the United States, Canada, and most other Western, industrialized societies, physical strength is no longer terribly important, and the nuclear family is by far the most common living arrangement. Therefore, on the basis of the cross-cultural data just discussed, we should expect fewer differences in the socialization of boys and girls. Whiting and Edwards (1973) present some evidence that this is true. Observation of a group of children in New England showed that boys and girls were more similar to each other than were boys and girls in the other societies they studied (which included those of Mexico, India, and Africa). Yet, although the pressures toward sex-typed socialization may be less, there is still plenty of evidence that Western parents do not treat boys and girls exactly the same. Sears, Maccoby, and Levin (1957) found that mothers allowed boys much more expression of aggressiveness toward both parents and peers. There was also evidence indicating that girls were more often praised for good behavior than were boys.[3] While pressures toward differentiation by parents may not be as strong in industrialized societies as in others, they still exist.

---

[3]Research on socialization practices has tended to concentrate on the mother, in part because mothers have traditionally had more contact with the children. However, investigations that have considered both parents reveal some complexities. Rothbart and Maccoby (1966) found that while mothers were more accepting of both aggressive and dependent behavior in a boy child, fathers were more tolerant of these behaviors in a girl. With growing emphasis on the father's role in child rearing, we might expect future research to reveal new facts about the socialization process.

As every parent knows, children learn the values of their society from other sources as well as parents. The mass media, for example, present children with innumerable examples of what life is supposedly like. Consider the boy who watches *All in the Family*, who gradually incorporates "Stifle yourself" as part of his vocabulary; consider the young girl who, after watching Cher, begins to raid her mother's makeup kit. These examples are cases of **modeling,** or observational learning, which is defined as "the tendency for a person to reproduce the actions, attitudes, and emotional responses exhibited by real-life or symbolic models" (W. Mischel, 1966, p. 57). Modeling is learning that takes place without direct reinforcement. In other words, from simple observation, without direct praise or chiding from a parent, the child can learn sex-typed behaviors—and a wide variety of other behaviors too.

The enormous role of television in a child's daily life has been well established: the average child watches TV for approximately 33 hours a week and by the age of 18 will have been in front of a television set for a considerably greater amount of time than he or she will have spent in school (A. H. Stein & Friedrich, 1971). While the controversy concerning television's role in encouraging aggression and violence has received much attention (see Chapter 7), it is only more recently that social psychologists have begun to consider the effect of television on the development of sex roles and sex stereotypes. The popular children's program *Sesame Street*, which first was criticized for presenting Blacks and other ethnic groups in a stereotyped fashion, was later accused of limiting women to supportive and peripheral roles. Commercials have been subject to scrutiny as well. In an important study, L. Z. McArthur and Resko (in press) analyzed the content of approximately 200 television commercials for evidence of sex-role stereotyping. Not only were significantly more men than women shown in these commercials, but the actions and roles of the two sexes differed considerably. The male figure in the commercial was most frequently shown as an authority figure or expert on the advertised product; the woman was most often depicted as the willing user of the product. Even for products such as laundry detergents, with which women are probably more familiar, the male expert generally prevailed. (See Figure 14-2.)

McArthur and Resko also considered what rewards the potential users were promised for using particular products. Again differences appeared: men are rewarded with social and career advancement, while women are promised the approval of family, husband, or male friend. It seems clear that the avid television watcher is presented with quite different pictures of the goals of adult men and women.

Children's books have also been scrutinized in recent years, and again there is evidence that the images presented of men and women are different (Oliver, 1974; Weitzman, Eifler, Hokada, & Ross, 1972; *Women on Words and Images,* 1972; I. L. Child, Potter, & Levine, 1946). Far more books feature boys or men as the central characters, and generally the males are described as doing more things. For example, in a sample of 130 children's books, adult males were shown in 146 different occupations, while adult females were shown in only 26 different jobs (*Women on Words and Images,* 1972). As we saw in Chapter 2, boys and girls are also described differently. Girls are more often shown as lacking ability and as needing help and protection; boys are seen taking action in emergencies and making decisions. Girls sit quietly; boys actively explore.

Even the toys that are available for children show the pervasive assumptions that society makes about sex roles. Pictures illustrating the use of toys show mothers as spectators and fathers as participants. A greater variety of toys are recommended for boys than for girls, and, in general, the more complex the toy, the more likely it is that a boy will be shown using it (Lever & Goodman, 1972).

It seems very clear that the media depict men and women differently. And it has been shown that children as young as 3 or 4 years

have already learned the sex-role stereotypes (Flerx & Rogers, 1975). Yet despite the abundant evidence for differences in the presented images, research has not yet established a definite link between sex-typed models and the actual behavior of children. More general studies of modeling certainly give us a basis for predicting such effects, but research must be done to show how strong these effects are.

Of course, many of the more blatant differences in treatment are beginning to disappear, through the influence of groups concerned with eliminating sex discrimination. Still, the pervasiveness of the stereotyped presentations is remarkable, and underlines the extent to which cultural norms play a part in our experience.

Figure 14-2
Men and women as pictured in TV commercials.

C. Interaction and overlap

In the preceding pages we have shown the potential influence of both heredity and environment on current sex differences. Yet while advocates of each position can muster considerable support for their explanations of sex differences, a full understanding will probably include features of both positions. Sex differences and sex roles are the result of an interaction between genetics and experience. The question really is not "Which?" but rather "How do these two factors interact?"

To gain some understanding of the complexity of this subject, consider some data from a study of very young human infants. H. A. Moss (1967) observed mother-infant interactions, and found that while mothers were more likely to relate to boys by *touch* or through *physical stimulation*, they were more likely to *imitate* vocal behavior of girls and give girls other forms of *verbal stimulation*. Is an environmental or biological explanation more appropriate? Certainly the evidence suggests that mothers are treating boy and girl infants differently, and we could speculate that the children would learn that there are different ways to get attention. Girls might learn to be more vocal, while boys might learn to be more physical. On the other side, the **hereditarians** have argued that there are innate differences between boys and girls reflected in both these maternal behaviors: infant males show higher activity levels, and females show earlier vocalization and use of language (Bardwick, 1971). Perhaps parents act differently toward boys and girls because the boys and girls treat their parents differently (see Figure 14-3).

This example should show why simple answers are not the best answers. Biologically, males and females are in some ways different, and research is only beginning to discover how the basic hormonal differences may affect other behaviors. Imposed on these biological differences are very different socialization pressures; the interaction of these causes males and females to follow different paths in their development.

"LOOK HOW WELL I HAVE MY MOTHER CONDITIONED— EVERY TIME I SAY HER NAME, SHE COMES RUNNING TO CUDDLE ME."

Figure 14-3
Are parents or children giving reinforcements?

Before leaving this discussion, we should consider two additional points. First of all, socialization practices can differ widely. While we have seen that a large number of societies show some consensus in sex-role training, there are also many differences, usually corresponding to the particular requirements of a society. Even within a single country, there are many differences among various social classes and among people of different ethnic origins. In the United States, for example, sex-role stereotypes are more pronounced among the working class than they are among the upper class. Families in which both parents work (or where only the mother works) provide different experiences for children than do the more traditionally patterned families (Baruch, 1972; Almquist & Angrist,

1971). Socialization is a very complex and varied process.

A second point we wish to emphasize is that when we talk about sex *differences*, this does not mean that men and women are completely different from each other. Not all men are aggressive and not all women are dependent. Most cases of sex differences are simply a matter of averages: for example, on the average, men show more physical aggression than women. Yet, on most characteristics for which sex differences have been found, the distributions overlap (see Figure 14-4). If you were studying aggressive behavior in young children, you would find many little girls who were potential sluggers and many young boys who tended to shy away from physical confrontation. In fact, most behaviors would show that the differences within one sex (for

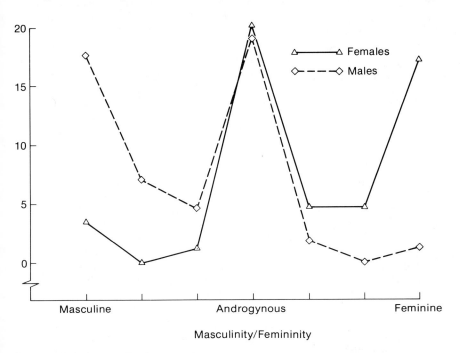

Figure 14-4

The concept of overlap. On nearly every dimension on which men and women are compared, overlapping distributions are found. In other words, the differences between women and men are relative, not absolute. The figure above is an illustration of this overlap, using data obtained on measures of masculinity and femininity. (See pages 461–463 for a discussion of masculinity, femininity, and androgyny.) While women, as you might expect, more often score high on the feminine end of the scale, many women score in the midrange and some lie at the masculine pole. Conversely, many men are rated highly masculine, but others range toward the feminine end of the scale. Other behaviors that social scientists study often show even greater overlap between men and women, despite the fact that statistical tests may show the average scores to be significantly different.

example, the difference between the most aggressive and the least aggressive boy) are far greater than the differences between sexes. It will be important to remember these points in the following discussion of observed sex differences.

D. Theories about women and men

As evidenced in the preceding sections, there are no definitive answers to the questions of why men and women differ when they do. Yet many of the observations and experimental findings have been used to support various theories of sex-role development. Let us briefly consider how some of the theories in social psychology can be applied to the question of sex-role development.

1. Psychoanalytic theory has been quite explicit in describing a process of sex-role development (S. Freud, 1927, 1932, 1933). For Freud, and many subsequent adherents of psychoanalytic theory, the crucial distinctions between women and men are a consequence of different experiences in the Oedipal stage of development. These theorists assume that because women lack a penis, they can never fully resolve childhood conflicts that are based on penis envy. The woman's desire for the male organ can be satisfied only by giving birth to a male child, and until this event occurs, unresolved conflicts in the woman continue to sap her energy. As a result, the woman is a more passive individual than the male, who has this organ and can resolve the Oedipal conflicts.

Later psychoanalysts, such as Karen Horney (1924, 1926) and Erik Erikson (1964a), have been less willing to accept penis envy as the only determinant of sex differences. For both writers, the woman's uterus and her potential for giving birth are considered important in explaining sex differences. However, Horney and Erikson continue to stress the importance of anatomical factors and psychosexual stages in the personality development of men and women. Conflicts and events inherent in the child's psychosexual development make adult sex differences an inevitable outcome.

2. S-R theorists have also been active in explaining the development of sex-role behavior in terms of their theoretical assumptions. In some instances, the discussions have focused on specific reinforcements that parents give to boys and girls for acting in sex-appropriate ways. For example, a parent might hug and kiss a little girl when she wore a pretty dress, or praise a young boy when he won a fight with a neighbor child.

Far more extensive, however, has been the use of social-learning theory to explain sex-role development (see, for example, W. Mischel, 1966). According to this position, children learn most sex-role behaviors through observation. By watching parents, peers, and various forms of media, children learn the behaviors that are appropriate for men and women, and they then adopt these behaviors. Reinforcement is not necessary; a child needs only to observe a model performing the specific behavior. As we have seen, the media in particular provide numerous examples of specific sex-role behavior, and it is quite possible that sex-role development is influenced by these examples. Social-learning theorists would also argue that if the models that children observed did not show pronounced sex-role behaviors, sex differences would be much less common than they are today.

3. Although role theory has not been as explicit as the psychoanalytic and S-R theories in explaining the development of sex-role behaviors, this theory has often been used to describe differences between women and men. According to this theoretical viewpoint, sex is an ascribed role, and a given society will define particular behaviors that are appropriate for persons occupying that role. Herding cattle, for example, might be considered a function of the male role, while tending a garden might be considered an appropriate aspect of the female role. To the extent that men and women adopt the behaviors that have been defined as parts of the male and female roles, the assumptions of role theory can be applied.

Yet while role theory may be easily applied to sex differences, it is somewhat unsatisfying in providing an explanation for the variations in the behavior of women and men. As we have pointed out, not all men act the same, nor do all women. Role theory gives us little basis for explaining these variations, despite its easy applicability to general cases.

4. Field theory and Gestalt theories have been less frequently applied to explanations of sex differences. Field theory, in its strong present orientation, speaks little to the development of sex differences. Instead, this theoretical approach would point to pressures and forces in the current situation. For example, an individual's present feelings about himself or herself (perhaps influenced by past experience) would be the basis of divergent behaviors by men and women. Field theory would also emphasize the importance of environmental pressures that provide different outlets for men and women in our society. In its general assumptions that both person and situation are important in understanding human behavior, field theory can be easily applied to the behavior of women and men. In specifics, however, the approach does not offer a well-developed framework.

Gestalt approaches can also be applied to the issue of sex differences, but again only in a general way. The Gestalt stress on the importance of perceptions of events emphasizes how others evaluate women and men; as we shall see later, these perceptions can be quite different for the two sexes. In terms of the specific development of sex-role behavior, though, Gestalt theory has not been an active influence.

II. Sex differences in aptitude and personality

Each of the theories discussed has a distinct viewpoint on why sex differences develop. In this section, we will look at what some of those differences are. How do the average man and the average woman differ in aptitude and personality?

A. Intelligence

A question that has frequently been posed by social psychologists, philosophers, and even comedians is "Who's smarter, men or women?" You might think that it would be a simple matter to compare the scores of men and women on a standard measure such as the Stanford-Binet Tests of Intelligence and come up with an answer. The method that was used to construct this test, however, prohibits an answer. The designers of the Stanford-Binet Tests, Terman and Merrill (1937), were faced with the problem that females and males did differ in the correctness of their answers to some of the possible test items. To resolve this problem, the test constructors made the assumption that men and women do not differ in innate intelligence and that sex differences in scores on particular items simply reflected differences in experience (McNemar, 1942). Consequently, items that tended to produce large differences between the sexes were eliminated from the final version of the test. The result of this procedure is that males and females will on the average obtain nearly identical scores on the Stanford-Binet measure of intelligence.[4] The construction of most other intelligence tests has been based on similar procedures.

Because general measures of intelligence cannot reveal any differences between men and women, investigators have turned their consideration to more specific measures of ability and to achievement. In many cases, sex differences have been found. Girls are generally better at academic achievement; they get better grades than boys throughout grade school, high school,

[4]It is interesting to note that when children are tested for intelligence again in adulthood, and these adult scores are compared to the earlier ones, men show a greater increase in measured intelligence than do women (E. C. Lewis, 1968). These differences are probably explained by different socialization pressures, which in the case of women may discourage intellectual pursuits.

and college (Sherman, 1971). Girls also tend to outscore boys on tests of verbal ability, while boys are the higher scorers on tests of mechanical aptitude (Garai & Scheinfeld, 1968; Tyler, 1965; Maccoby & Jacklin, 1974a). From adolescence on, males consistently do better on tests of spatial ability that call for both visual and analytic skills (Maccoby & Jacklin, 1974a). This list of differences could be much longer, but the areas mentioned should give some idea of the range of aptitudes in which differences are found. One point that should be stressed in considering these patterns is that in many cases the differences between boys and girls do not appear until adolescence. In grade school, for example, there are few sex differences in mechanical or spatial ability. Thus, socialization may play an important role in the development of some of these abilities.

B. Conformity

One of the most frequently cited personality characteristics that shows sex differences is conformity. In what social psychologists call the "Asch situation" (described in Chapter 19), individuals are asked to make judgments about the lengths of lines, after hearing several others agree on one response (which is in fact incorrect). Whether the group is grade-school children, college students, or adults, females show greater conformity to the group judgment than do males. In a similar vein, Janis and Field (1959) reported that women were more susceptible to persuasive communications than were men. Yet despite a rather consistent pattern of results showing greater female conformity, questions have recently been raised.

Sistrunk and McDavid (1971) suggested that perhaps women conform more *only in situations that are unfamiliar to them.* Since the majority of conformity situations have used stimulus material that requires spatial-perceptual judgments (and, as we pointed out earlier, these are areas in which men excel), maybe the question of which sex conforms more has not been given a fair test. To answer this question, Sistrunk and

McDavid devised a large number of items that could be sorted reliably into three groups: one set with which men were more familiar, one set with which women were more familiar, and one set with which men and women were equally familiar. They then presented subjects with statements indicating the percentage of people who agreed with each statement and asked subjects to indicate their own opinion. The more that a subject agreed with the fictitious consensus, the more conformity was indicated. The results of this experiment (shown in Figure 14-5) suggest that men and women don't really differ in the amount of conformity they will show when they are equally familiar with the topic. When either sex is unfamiliar with the subject (men on "feminine" topics and women on "masculine" topics), there is likely to be some conformity. One implication of this study is the importance of *considering situations* before claiming that men and women are basically different in some characteristics. As we will see in other research, these situational factors can be very important.

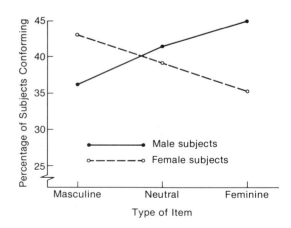

Figure 14-5
Sex differences in conformity behavior are related to the content of the items. (Adapted from "Sex Variables in Conforming Behavior," by F. Sistrunk and J. W. McDavid, *Journal of Personality and Social Psychology,* 1971, *17,* 200–207. Copyright 1971 by the American Psychological Association. Used by permission.)

C. Achievement

A basic definition of achievement motivation is a striving for success in competition with some standard of excellence. Particularly in Western society, achievement behavior is pervasive, and social psychologists have conducted extensive research in an attempt to understand the nature of *man's* strivings for excellence. And *man* is quite appropriate in this context, because almost none of the early research dealt with women. The reason for this disregard was quite simple: predictions made from the theory did not hold for women, and so investigators chose to ignore them.[5]

After some period of neglect, a number of investigators began to consider female achievement. Some have suggested that women are motivated more to affiliate than to achieve (L.W. Hoffman, 1972). Women are described as seeking social approval rather than exhibiting an internally based striving for standards of excellence. An alternative point of view offered by A. H. Stein and Bailey (1973) is that women and men are equally concerned with achievement, but the areas in which women choose to excel are different. Women in general may find it important to achieve in the areas of homemaking, cooking, and more traditional female occupations such as nursing and elementary education, but their concerns for doing well are motivated by achievement rather than affiliation. While this latter interpretation offers some promise for understanding the achievement behavior of women, we still have the question of why men and women choose different areas in which to excel. Are women afraid they would fail if they attempted more traditionally masculine activities? Actually there is some evidence that women are more concerned about failure than men are and

are less likely to risk the possibility of a failure (Stein & Bailey, 1973). Yet a more recent hypothesis is that women are also more afraid of success than men are.

Why would anyone be afraid of success? To understand this interpretation, let us first consider the definition of a **motive to avoid success.** Matina Horner, who developed thought about this concept, states that fear of success is a "latent, stable personality disposition acquired early in life in conjunction with standards of sex-role identity" (Horner, 1972, p. 159). She further explains that most women have this "disposition to become anxious about achieving success because they expect negative consequences" (p. 159). In other words, Horner suggests that women learn to believe that if they are successful, they will not get a payoff. Instead, negative consequences such as loss of femininity, lack of dates, and unpopularity may result. While men may also show evidence of a fear of success,[6] Horner's results suggest that the motive is much more common among women.

To measure the existence of this motive, Horner provided subjects with a single sentence and asked them to write a related story. In one case the sentence was "After first-term finals, Anne finds herself at the top of her medical school class," while a parallel version used *John* instead of *Anne.* Some typical stories that were scored as showing either presence or absence of fear of success are shown in Table 14-2. Horner originally reported that in response to these cues, 65% of the women who were tested showed evidence of fear of success, while only 10% of the men scored that way. Later research, however, shows that age, geographical location, and type of university may affect these percentages.

The concept of fear of success has proved to be a popular one and has been used in many

[5]Psychologists have recently been made aware of their tendency to study men more often than women (Holmes & Jorgensen, 1971). Perhaps even more revealing is the fact that authors will more often generalize their findings to human beings as a whole when they have used male subjects than when they have used female subjects (Dan & Beekman, 1972).

[6]Stories by men that are scored as showing fear of success tend to have different themes. Men tend to question the value of success and the importance of wealth and status, rather than fear social rejection (Hoffman, 1974; Horner, 1972; Monahan, Kuhn, & Shaver, 1974).

Table 14-2
Measuring fear of success

Examples of Stories Indicating Fear of Success

Anne doesn't want to be number one in her class. She feels she shouldn't rank so high because of social reasons. She drops down to ninth in the class and then marries the boy who graduates number one.

Anne is a code name for a nonexistent person created by a group of med students. They take turns taking exams and writing papers for Anne.

Her classmates are so disgusted with her behavior that they jump on her body and beat her. She is maimed for life.

Examples of Stories Not Indicating Fear of Success

John is a conscientious young man who worked hard. He is very pleased with himself. He is thinking that he must not let up now, but must work even harder than he did before. While others with good marks sluff off, John continues working hard and eventually graduates at the top of his class.

John is very pleased with himself, and he realizes that all his efforts have been rewarded. He is thinking of his girl, Cheri, whom he will marry at the end of med school. He realizes he can give her all the things she desires after he becomes established. He will go on in med school making good grades and be successful in the long run.

Table adapted from Bardwick, Douvan, Horner, and Gutmann (1970).

situations to explain the reluctance of women to strive for achievement as strongly as men seem to do. At the same time, many people have questioned the concept, and later research has suggested a number of qualifications to the original idea (Alper, 1974; Spence, 1974; Tresemer, 1974).

Several researchers, including Feather (1975) and Monahan, Kuhn, and Shaver (1974), have suggested that fear-of-success stories might be reflecting only the stereotypes that people in general hold of women, and not the female respondent's own motive. Thus if you were asked

to complete the story about Anne in medical school, you might write a story reflecting what you thought an "average Anne" would do, rather than what you yourself would do. To look at this possibility, Monahan, Kuhn, and Shaver asked both male and female subjects to fill out stories about Anne and John. They reasoned that if fear of success were a cultural stereotype for women, then both males and females would write more fear-of-success stories to the Anne sentence than to the John sentence. On the other hand, if an individual motive is the cause, females would tell more fear-of-success stories to both the Anne and the John lead than would males. The results of this study suggest that stereotypes are a better explanation. When the sentence described John in medical school, 21% of the male subjects and 30% of the female subjects wrote stories indicating a fear of success. For Anne in medical school, the percentages of fear stories were 68% among males and 51% among females. Both males and females seemed to view Anne as more likely to fear success than John, but males and females themselves did not differ in the frequency of these stories.

Critics of fear of success as a general motive have also pointed to the importance of situational factors. They argue that it is not success as such that is critical, but rather *the consequences of success.* Further, they point out that the consequences of success can vary, depending on the person and the situation. For example, what if you ask people to write a story about an Anne who is doing well in her nursing course, or her program in elementary education? Because these occupations are traditionally feminine, you would not expect negative consequences for a woman who does well. And that's exactly what happens: fear-of-success stories are much less frequent (Alper, 1974). On the other hand, what happens if John is described as being at the top of his nursing-school class? In this instance, much more fear of success is indicated for John than for a similar Anne (Cherry & Deaux, 1975). Studies such as these suggest that fear of success may be not a general motive but a reaction to the particular consequences that can be expected from particular situations. In some situations, men can expect negative consequences for success. The masculinity of a male nurse may be questioned in the same way as the femininity of a female doctor. The stereotypes that the society holds concerning appropriate behavior for males and females will affect the "fear of success."

It may still be true, of course, that there are more situations in which women have reason to expect negative consequences for success than there are for men. Many people assume, for example, that in a dating couple, the man should be the smarter of the two, and there are many stories of women representing themselves as having lower grades than they actually have in order to avoid scaring off a prospective husband (Komarovsky, 1959). Horner originally showed that women who scored high on her fear-of-success measure were reluctant to perform when in competition with a male. We can assume that in this case the women assumed that doing better than the man would result in some form of negative consequences, such as social rejection. But what if the woman realizes that acceptance will come only if she does succeed in a situation? Two recent studies (Fisher, O'Neal, & McDonald, 1974; Jellison, Jackson-White, & Bruder, 1974) have shown that in such cases women will choose to succeed. In the study by Fisher et al., women first competed with another person and either succeeded or failed, after which they heard the other person evaluate them either favorably or unfavorably. Women who heard the male coworker accept them following their success, or reject them following failure, performed better than their male coworker on a second task. In contrast, those women who had been rejected after succeeding or accepted after failing showed a lower level of performance in the second competitive situation.

In conclusion, while there is some evidence that men and women do differ in the degree to which fear of success is a motivator, the situation

seems to be the important factor. It is the *consequences of success*, and not *success per se*, that women (and men) fear, and when negative consequences are not anticipated, fear of success disappears as well.

D. Masculinity, femininity, and androgyny

In the preceding discussion, we have been talking about the personality traits of men and women. The distinction between males and females has been biologically based, and for most of us this split is an obvious one. In contrast, *masculinity* and *femininity* are psychological concepts. Masculinity generally indicates a set of interests and behaviors such as independence, preference for active sports, and lack of emotionality. Femininity can include such characteristics as submissiveness, preference for cooking and sewing, and emotional responsiveness. When considering masculinity and femininity as psychological concepts, we can compare males and females on this trait in much the same way as on conformity, achievement, or other psychological characteristics.

It is probably no surprise to learn that, in general, males are more masculine and females more feminine—though these are overlapping distributions, as in the case of other personality traits discussed earlier. While some people mistakenly assume that masculinity and femininity are innate qualities of maleness and femaleness, actual measures of masculinity and femininity are much more empirically based. Often scales are based on particular interests that are commonly endorsed by one sex or the other, at a particular place and a particular time in history. For example, a typical item might be "I like to repair mechanical things." If more men tended to agree with this statement than women, it would be scored as indicating masculinity. Scoring an item this way does not require the assumption that biological differences are a cause;

instead the item merely reflects cultural norms, which could be entirely a product of socialization. In fact, most items on these scales seem to reflect a very high degree of specific socialization experience by men and women.

While a number of measures of masculinity and femininity have been devised, virtually all of these scales have made two general assumptions: that masculinity-femininity is a single dimension and that being masculine is the opposite of being feminine (see Constantinople, 1973, for a more elaborate discussion). In most cases, if an individual endorses an item indicating masculine interests, there is a simultaneous nonendorsement of feminine interests. For example, you might be given the choice between "I like to cook" and "I like to climb mountains." Other tests might allow you to agree with both statements, but would give you a $+1$ for mountain-climbing and a -1 for cooking, yielding a single score that would fall someplace between very masculine (high positive scores) and very feminine (high negative scores). Some masculinity-femininity scales use personality traits rather than interests, but the scoring principles are the same. Endorsement of "assertive," for example, would be scored as indicating masculinity, while "passive" would be a point for femininity.

Many investigators have begun to question the assumption of a single dimension. Sandra Bem (1975) has recently developed a new type of scale that considers masculinity and femininity as *two separate dimensions*. Bem offers the concept of **androgyny** to label the possession of approximately equal portions of masculine and feminine characteristics. A person who indicates that he or she has a high number of masculine traits (for example, aggressiveness, competitiveness, self-reliance) and a low number of feminine traits (for example, affection, sympathy, shyness) would be considered a "masculine sex-typed" individual. A person with a high number of feminine characteristics and a low endorsement of masculine characteristics would be "feminine sex-typed." In addition to these fairly tradi-

tional classifications, Bem offers *androgyny*. Androgynous individuals would be those persons who considered themselves to have an equal number of masculine characteristics and feminine characteristics. For example, a person might see himself or herself as independent, willing to take a stand, ambitious, cheerful, understanding, and warm. Such a person would have a balance between masculine and feminine characteristics.

Bem's value position on this issue is clear. She argues that the most well-developed individual is the one who combines the best of both worlds and who can therefore respond to a greater variety of situations with the appropriate behavior. Whereas the masculine–sex-typed person may function well only in those situations calling for initiative and independence, and a feminine–sex-typed person may function best in situations calling for warmth and expressiveness, the androgynous individual should be able to handle both situations equally well. Thus, Bem argues, androgynous people are basically more adaptive to their environment.

Is there any evidence for this contention? Because the concept is a new one, it is a little early to tell. Bem (1975) has, however, provided at least one successful test of her notion in a conformity study. Using equal numbers of males and females who scored masculine, feminine, and androgynous, Bem relied on earlier findings suggesting that males conform less than females and predicted that both males and females who scored as feminine would be more likely to yield to conformity pressure than would either masculine- or androgynous-scoring individuals. The results confirmed her prediction.

Using a similar concept of androgyny, Spence, Helmreich, and Stapp (1975) have found that those individuals who possess high degrees of both masculine and feminine characteristics possess more self-esteem than do more traditionally sex-typed individuals. Thus, while the evidence is still sparse, there seems to be some support for a concept of the androgynous individual who, whether male or female, is able to incorporate the best of both masculine and feminine traits.

III. Perceptions of sex differences: The eye of the beholder

In the preceding section, we have looked at some of the ways in which men and women differ. While differences do exist, it should be clear by now that these differences are not absolute. In many cases the differences are small and the distributions are overlapping; in other cases differences emerge only in very specific situations; and in still other cases there are no differences at all. Yet often what people *believe to be true* may be just as important as, or even more important than, what actually is true. In this section we will consider what people in general think about men and women and how these perceptions may affect behavior.

A. Stereotypes

It will probably come as no surprise that people tend to have stereotyped views of men and women. Just as people tend to associate a specific set of characteristics with certain racial, religious, and ethnic groups (see Chapter 10), so men and women as groups are endowed with certain stereotyped traits. In some cases these stereotypes appear to reflect a kernel of truth. For instance, people generally assume that men are more aggressive than women, and there is considerable evidence to substantiate this belief. (However, as pointed out before, not all men are more aggressive than all women, and so the stereotyped assumption will still be inaccurate in many instances.) In other cases the stereotyped beliefs of what men and women are like seem to have little basis in objective findings (Unger & Siiter, 1974). Yet the beliefs persist and can

influence many forms of behavior (Neufeld, Langmeyer, & Seeman, 1974).

Many researchers have asked groups of people to describe what the average man and the average woman are like, and they have found that there is a surprisingly high degree of consensus as to which traits are typical of each sex (L. J. Ellis & Bentler, 1973; Frieze, 1974; Rosenkrantz, Vogel, Bee, Broverman, & Broverman, 1968). Frequently the ascribed characteristics fall into two general groups: one collection of traits representing competence and independence and a second group centering around warmth and expressiveness (I. K. Broverman, Vogel, Broverman, Clarkson, & Rosenkrantz, 1972). Males are generally seen as embodying the competence cluster, while women are seen as characterized by the expressive cluster.

Table 14-3 lists some of the adjectives most frequently associated with males and females. While it might be argued that these two patterns are simply different, but do not represent more or less favorable impressions, other evidence suggests that the picture is not so optimistic. For example, studies of stereotyping generally find that many more of the characteristics that our society values are associated with men than with women. Perhaps even more indicative of the rather negative stereotype associated with women is a study by I. K. Broverman and her colleagues (I. K. Broverman, Broverman, Clarkson, Rosenkrantz, & Vogel, 1970). The authors asked 79 practicing mental-health clinicians (clinical psychologists, psychiatrists, and social workers) to describe the characteristics of one of three types of persons: a normal adult male, a normal adult female, and a normal adult person with sex unspecified. The clinicians were asked to characterize the healthy, mature, socially competent person in each category. The results, not particularly encouraging if sexual equality is our goal, were quite clear-cut. Both male and female clinicians saw the healthy adult male and the healthy adult person as nearly synonymous; the healthy adult female, in contrast, was signifi-

Table 14-3
Stereotypic items typically used to describe males and females

Competency Cluster

Feminine	Masculine
Not at all aggressive	Very aggressive
Not at all independent	Very independent
Very submissive	Very dominant
Not at all competitive	Very competitive
Very passive	Very active
Has difficulty making decisions	Can make decisions easily
Not at all ambitious	Very ambitious

Warmth-Expressive Cluster

Feminine	Masculine
Very tactful	Very blunt
Very quiet	Very loud
Very aware of feelings of others	Not at all aware of feelings of others
Very strong need for security	Very little need for security
Easily expresses tender feelings	Does not express tender feelings at all easily

Adapted from "Sex-Role Stereotypes: A Current Appraisal," by I. K. Broverman, S. R. Vogel, D. M. Broverman, F. E. Clarkson, and P. S. Rosenkrantz, *Journal of Social Issues,* 1972, *28*(2), 59–78. Copyright 1972 by the Society for the Psychological Study of Social Issues. Used by permission.

cantly different from the healthy adult person. For example, both the healthy adult person and the healthy adult male were described by adjectives from the competency cluster, such as *independent, active,* and *competitive,* and in nearly every case the healthy adult woman was seen as possessing far less of each characteristic. In contrast, the healthy woman was viewed as more submissive, more concerned about her appearance, and more excitable in minor crises, a set of characteristics not attached to either the healthy adult or the healthy man.

At least two points are clear from the research on sex-role stereotypes: first, the stereotypes are pervasive and exist among a wide variety of populations—clinicians, college students, older adults, and children (Abramowitz, Abramowitz, Jackson, & Gomes, 1973). Second, these stereotypes are held by men and women alike, suggesting that they are a cultural rather than a male **chauvinist** phenomenon.

While the existence of less favorable attitudes towards women has an impact in its own right, it is also important to consider the effect that these stereotypes have on other judgments. As we shall see, beliefs about what men and women are like can have the effect of a **self-fulfilling prophecy.** If women are assumed to be less competent, for example, their performance may be judged as less successful than it actually is. Or if women are assumed to be less competent, they may be given less opportunity to assert themselves (with the result that they may be viewed as less assertive!). Beliefs can influence behavior, and the results can be quite detrimental for the less favorably viewed female.

B. Evaluating the performances of men and women

One of the first attempts to learn whether women are judged differently than men in a performance situation was made by P. Goldberg (1968), who asked female college students to judge the quality of several professional articles. Each article had two versions, which were identical in every respect except for the sex of the author, as indicated by the author's name. Goldberg's results showed that respondents rated an article purportedly written by "John McKay" as substantially better than one written by "Joan McKay," despite the fact that the articles were actually identical. These results were true whether the articles were about more "masculine" topics, such as architecture, or "feminine" topics, such as dietetics. Although this study has been replicated with similar outcomes for both male and female subjects (Bem & Bem, 1970), a more recent study suggests that, at least among college students, times may be changing. H. Mischel (1974) found that while high school students continue to favor male authors, college students show bias only when articles are on typically masculine topics, such as law and city planning. Female authors are given the edge on topics such as dietetics. Mischel continued this investigation in Israel, where there is less sex-role socialization than in the United States, and found that Israeli students do not show bias in favor of either sex when judging the quality of articles.

Even within a society where biased evaluations persist, there are factors that can modify the judgments. One such factor is an authority's approval of the work in question. Pheterson, Kiesler, and Goldberg (1971) asked subjects to evaluate the artistic merit of a painting done by either a male or a female artist. In some cases, the painting was described as an entry in a local art contest, while in other cases the subjects were told that the painting had been declared the winner of the contest. When told that the painting was merely an entry, people showed the predict-

able tendency to evaluate the male artist more favorably. Yet when the painting had been declared a winner, the female artist was considered as good as the male artist.

This tendency to upgrade the evaluation of the woman when there is incontrovertible evidence that the work is good has been found in other situations as well. Using a rather unusual situation, Taynor and Deaux (1975) presented subjects with a description of an individual (either a woman or a man) behaving effectively in an emergency situation. In the story, subjects learned that the principal character had been robbed by a gunman but was able to follow the thief as he escaped and report an accurate description of the thief and his getaway to the police. Because of this person's quick thinking, the police were able to apprehend the gunman quickly, and they commended the person for his or her actions. Subjects reading this vignette were asked how deserving the male or female character was. The results clearly showed that in this particular situation a woman was considered more deserving of a reward than was a man. Apparently, because of the prevailing assumption that a woman is unable to perform as well as a man, evidence that undeniably shows a woman excelling can cause her to be overrewarded.[7]

While this evidence provides a more optimistic note within the rather bleak general picture of female performance being underevaluated, it is still true that in many common situations, such definitive judgments of accomplishment are not present. Faced with a more ambiguous criterion for success, the observer (whether male or female) will still tend to assume that the man's performance is better.

---

[7]Unfortunately, men may not get the same benefits. In a later study by the same authors, men who excelled in a more feminine situation involving handling a young child were not overrewarded for their performance (Taynor & Deaux, 1975). Perhaps it is assumed that men should be able to do feminine jobs well, and thus there is no call for excess reward.

Not only do we evaluate a woman's performance less favorably in most situations, but we also find different reasons for that performance. As discussed in Chapter 3, people often make attributions as they try to find explanations for events that occur around them. These attributions may be accurate or inaccurate, but they provide a sense of understanding. In judging a person's performance, for example, it is possible to assume that the individual was responsible for the outcome (it was his or her *ability* or *effort* that made an event happen) or that some factors external to the individual were responsible (the task was so easy that anyone would have succeeded, or good luck was the cause). These judgments can be extremely important, because they may influence the expectations that will be held for an individual. If a person is viewed as able, he or she will be expected to succeed again in the future. On the other hand, if luck is considered the cause, there is no reason to expect that person to succeed again, since luck will not continue indefinitely.

Deaux and Emswiller (1974) predicted that evaluations of male and female performance would show these different explanatory tendencies. Students were asked to listen to the performance of either a male or a female student performing a perception task which involved recognizing a number of masculine objects, such as a tire wrench and a Phillips screwdriver. After hearing that the other student performed the task quite well, subjects were asked to judge the reasons for that performance. As predicted, the male's performance was explained by the skill of the performer, while a female's equivalent performance was considered to be more a matter of luck.[8] Women didn't get the same benefit of

the doubt on a feminine task, when the objects included colanders and double boilers. Men and women were actually rated equally in this situation, though both were seen as having less ability than men on the masculine task. Even though the objective evidence was the same, it seems that judges combined this information with their own stereotypes and produced different explanations for the male and female performance (Feather & Simon, 1975).

In some situations, of course, it would be very difficult for any rational observer to use luck as an explanation. Feldman-Summers and Kiesler (1974) provided subjects with descriptions of a physician who had established a tremendously successful practice after several years of work. Subjects were asked to consider the reasons for the success of the physician, who was identified as either a male or a female. In this case, it seems unlikely that anyone would say luck was a major cause for either a male's or a female's success, and in fact luck was rarely used by judges to explain the successful career. As an alternative, subjects felt that the woman had tried harder than the man to reach the same place; a tendency persisted for males to be viewed as having more ability than females (though male subjects were the prime users of this explanation). These results are a little more encouraging for proponents of equality. The woman's success is not considered to be due to external factors, but is credited to her own effort. Nevertheless, innate ability still seems to be the province of males, and for a female to do as well, she, like Avis, must try harder.

C. Self-evaluation by men and women

Not only do observers give different reasons for the successes of male and female target persons, but males and females do it for themselves as well. A number of studies have shown that when a male and a female are asked to pro-

---

[8]A young woman writing a letter to the editors of *Ms.* Magazine expressed an awareness of these luck attributions when she complained "In my high school automechanics class, if I do something right, it's called luck; if I do something wrong, I am suddenly representing my sex" (S. Gordon, 1973).

vide reasons for their own successful performance, they show variations in judgment much like those of observers. In a typical study, male and female college students are asked to solve a series of anagrams. After performing this task, each student is asked to evaluate his or her performance and the causes for that performance. In such situations, it is far more common for the female to explain her performance on the basis of luck, whether the outcome was a good or a bad one. Men, on the other hand, are much more likely to claim that ability was responsible for their success (Deaux & Farris, 1974; Feather, 1969; Frieze, Hanusa, Fisher, & McHugh, in press; McMahon, 1971).

These tendencies to prefer either luck or ability explanations extend even to the preferences that men and women will show for different kinds of games. Deaux, White, & Farris (1976) observed large numbers of men and women who played games at county fairs. Games at the fairs could be categorized as requiring some ability (for example, ring toss) or as totally determined by luck (for example, bingo). These observers found that substantially more men than women were playing games requiring skill. In a laboratory analogue of their fair setting, the same authors found that when given a choice between a game described as requiring ability and another game described as determined wholly by luck (but in fact identical with the first), males showed an overwhelming preference for the supposedly skill-oriented game, whereas females more frequently chose the game of luck.

In summary, it is clear that the personality characteristics of men and women are assumed to be quite different. Perhaps as a consequence of these beliefs, the performances of men and women are evaluated differently, with the man more likely to be judged superior. Beyond this, even the reasons for success are assumed to be different for men than for women. While certain factors can modify these judgments toward a more nearly equal base, the norm is for unequal judgments. And in an even more telling demonstration of the pervasiveness of cultural norms and beliefs, men and women show the same differences in explaining their own performances that neutral observers do.

IV. Equality and the future

Within the past decade or two, the Women's Movement has resurfaced in the United States and throughout the world and is now more widespread than earlier movements involving Blacks, Chicanos, and the young. Hundreds of groups and organizations contribute to what is collectively called the Women's Movement. While the goals and programs of the groups vary, there are a number of issues that are common to the majority. If their goals are realized, many of the stereotypes of males and females that have been discussed in this chapter may change.

What are the goals of the various organizations? Does the evidence provided by social-psychological research offer any understanding of these goals? Can we predict what impact the Women's Movement will have? These questions form the basis of this section.

A. Equality in employment

Common to most groups in the Women's Movement is a demand for equal pay. Most statistics indicate that the full-time working woman has a salary equal to approximately 60% of the salary of the full-time working man. At the most basic level, the movement contends that people who occupy the same job position should receive the same salary. Beyond this goal, advocates of equality argue that both women and men should be given the opportunity to pursue any of the jobs that society has to offer. In other words, not only should a female on an assembly line make the same pay that a male assembly line worker with equivalent experience and responsibility does, but she should also be given equal opportunities for promotion to foreman, plant manager, and other high administrative positions.

The statistics clearly support the argument that few women occupy these higher-level positions, but it is somewhat difficult to label the causes. There is no doubt that discrimination exists on the part of many employers. Title VII of the 1964 Civil Rights Act prohibits discrimination on the basis of sex, as well as race, reli-

gion, and ethnic origin, and hundreds of organizations have faced lawsuits by women who have claimed discrimination. Many of these claims have been successful, and organizations have been faced with multimillion-dollar settlements of back pay and salary increases to correct the proven discrimination. In more hypothetical situations, social psychologists have also documented the existence of bias in hiring decisions. Fidell (1970) sent a number of academic résumés to chairmen (while "chairpersons" might be prefer-

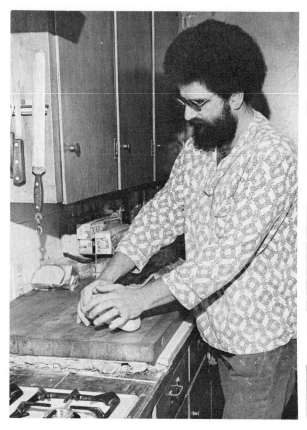 

Figure 14-6
Occupations of the future. Sheldon Schachter, a California househusband, baking bread for his family, and Sue Newman, a Florida plumber, at work. (Left: Monterey Peninsula Herald photo by Bob Fish; right: Wide World Photos.)

able, vitually all psychology-department heads are male) of major-university psychology departments in the United States and asked each chairman to evaluate the person as a potential professor in that department. Two forms that were identical except for the sex of the applicant were used, each going to half the selected chairmen. The results of this study showed that men were generally offered a higher position than were women (that is, associate professor rather than assistant professor), despite the equality of the backgrounds.[9]

Dipboye, Fromkin, and Wiback (1975) asked college recruiters from major organizations to rate the desirability of hiring a number of potential candidates who varied in both sex and competence. While the academic qualifications of the potential candidate were clearly the most important factor in the recruiters' decisions, sex again had an effect. Recruiters showed a significant preference for the male candidate over the equally qualified female candidate. In another simulated hiring study, Terborg and Ilgen (1975) found that women were hired as often as men but were offered lower starting salaries.

As laws prohibiting discrimination become more widely enforced, some of the more blatant cases of bias will probably be eliminated. At a more subtle level, however, discrimination may continue much longer. Let us consider three sets of circumstances that may perpetuate inequality, using evidence from both research and actual experience.

1. Evaluation and promotion differences. In many job situations, the criteria for success are ambiguous. Subjective individual judgments may determine how an employee is evaluated and what promotions are awarded. The research has suggested that people tend to evaluate a man more favorably even when his performance is identical

to a woman's (Rosen & Jerdee, 1974a, 1974b, 1974c; E. A. Shaw, 1972). V. E. Schein (1973) has shown that middle-level managers in organizations tend to have the same stereotypes that we have seen. In this instance, managers viewed the typical male and the successful manager as quite similar, and both views differed from the picture of the average female. Furthermore, if employers view men's and women's performances as caused by different factors (as the Deaux and Emswiller study would suggest), then the employers may have higher expectations for the male than for the female. The person who has more ability (the man) presumably has more chance of future success than the one who was simply lucky or who worked particularly hard on one occasion in order to achieve (the woman). In support of this suggestion, Terborg and Ilgen (1975) found that simulated employers were more likely to assign women to routine tasks and men to challenging tasks, despite the fact that the two had been hired at the same job level. As long as the stereotypes of differences between males and females persist, it seems likely that subtle and perhaps unconscious discrimination will occur.

2. Occupational status. While comparison of responsibilities within a given job setting can provide some difficulty, it is even harder to compare responsibilities when the jobs are widely different. Within the telephone companies, for example, corporate defenders have argued that the equipment installation and maintenance positions demand far more skill and responsibility than do operator positions, thus justifying the pay differential. Not surprisingly, operators disagree, arguing that their job requires different kinds of skills, but skills nonetheless. It is a difficult argument to resolve.

Salary levels frequently relate to the prestige levels that are associated with the occupations. Part of the explanation for the average salary differences between men and women is that occupations with higher prestige ratings generally

[9]Lest one infer that only psychologists are biased, it should be mentioned that A. Y. Lewin and Duchan (1971) found similar results in physics departments.

have a higher percentage of men in a given field (Bose, 1973).[10] From one vantage point, this difference doesn't seem unreasonable. Men pursue advanced education more often than women and then enter professions requiring this advanced education. Occupations requiring less training will more often be held by women. Do these differences in occupation suggest evidence of discrimination? Probably not. But recent evidence by Touhey (1974a, 1974b) suggests that occupational prestige is influenced not only by the qualifications required but by the sex of the typical occupant as well. To demonstrate this bias, Touhey presented subjects with descriptions of several traditional masculine occupations (for example, lawyer, college professor, architect) and asked subjects to rate the prestige of each occupation. In half the cases, the job description prepared by Touhey pointed out that *an increasing number of women* were expected to enter the field within the next 25 years, while in the other half of the cases the percentage of the men was expected to *remain stable*. Without exception, occupations were given lower prestige ratings when the percentage of women in them was expected to increase. Touhey then in effect reversed the labels; he conducted a similar experiment using traditionally *female* occupations (for example, kindergarten teacher, registered nurse, librarian) and describing the percentage of *men* in the job as stable or increasing. The exact reverse occurred. Jobs that more men were expected to

enter showed an increase in prestige. These results are illustrated in Figure 14-7.

If this judgment process is reflected in actual occupational settings, then we might expect to see a continued salary disparity between men and women as long as the sexes are attracted toward different kinds of jobs.

3. Self-discrimination. A third factor that may lead to unequal opportunities for women and men is the attitudes of women themselves (O'Leary, 1974). If opportunities are presented but women fail to take advantage of them, the statistics will continue to be lopsided. Some evidence that women may not maximize their opportunities is shown in reactions to the Bell Telephone judgment. When Bell Telephone opened up all of its positions to both sexes, the percentage of men operators increased significantly, while the percentage of women in installation jobs showed a much less dramatic upturn (Boehm, 1974).

We have seen that women are less likely to claim ability as a cause of their success, and in general they have lower expectations for themselves than men do on similar tasks. Claiming luck as an explanation for anagram performance is a fairly restricted example, yet it may be indicative of a much broader process by which females deny themselves opportunities and fail to take credit for genuine accomplishments, thus maintaining the self-fulfilling prophecy.

B. Sex roles in the future

The potential effects of the Women's Movement reach far beyond the employment area, and it is difficult to predict how extensive the changes might eventually be. One of the broadest goals of both women's- and men's-liberation groups is a change in the basic sex-role concepts that exist in our present society. To the extent that such concepts are based on socialization rather than heredity, such changes are clearly

---

[10]In her study of the prestige ratings of occupations, Bose included both housewife and househusband among the more traditional occupations. On a scale of 0 to 100, housewife was rated 51.0, while househusband earned only a 14.5 rating from a sample of Baltimore citizens. Bose suggests that one factor inhibiting some women from entering the job market is the trade-off value. Nearly all traditional female occupations are ranked lower in prestige than housewife. For men, in contrast, almost any occupation is viewed more favorably than househusband. Proponents of alternative patterns of marriage, in which the man stays home and tends house while the woman works, will have to contend with the status loss for the husband that currently exists.

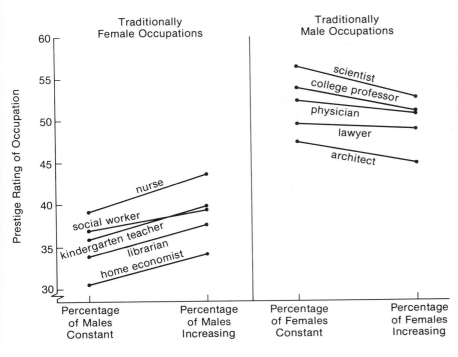

Figure 14-7

Prestige ratings of occupations are dependent on the percentages of males or females who engage in those occupations. Adapted from data presented in Touhey (1974a, 1974b).

possible. In 1869, John Stuart Mill wrote that no one could know the true nature of the sexes as long as they were seen only in the existing context. More than 100 years after that statement, we have perhaps more clues, but as yet no final answers.

Considering the evidence presented earlier on biological and environmental determinants of sex-role behavior, we believe that a substantial portion of our accepted sex-role stereotypes are in fact based on social and cultural learning. Many of these traditional patterns of behavior are changing. Within the family setting, many couples are beginning to experiment with new forms of dividing responsibility. In some homes, women are the wage earners and men tend the house. Even more frequently, husbands and wives both work and both share household duties as well. Efforts are being made to eliminate biased presentations of men and women on television, in books, and in advertisements.

Schools have been required to open all activities to both boys and girls, in sports and in classrooms; shop and home economics courses are no longer offered to one sex only. To the extent that differences between males and females are affected by such socialization practices, we can expect the norms to change.

Thus many of the differences between men and women that have been discussed in this chapter may not exist 25 years from now. Women may show as much (or as little) striving for achievement as do men, and men may be able to express emotions as readily as women. It is likely that the psychologically androgynous individual will become somewhat more common, incorporating characteristics previously assumed to be both masculine and feminine. These are big questions, and in many ways we can consider that we are living in the midst of a large-scale social experiment. The final outcome of this experiment is yet to come.

Figure 14-8
Advocates of changes in sex-role stereotypes believe that "person" is more important than "male" or "female." Boys and girls, they argue, should be free to choose from a variety of alternatives; their choices should not be limited by sex. (Copyright 1973 by G. B. Trudeau/Distributed by Universal Press Syndicate.)

V. Summary

In the past decade or so, a number of social, political and economic changes have occurred that relate to the issue of sex roles. Support for both heredity and environment arguments on the nature of men and women can be found. Biologically, there are differences between men and women, and, while the influence of hormones on behavior is only minimally understood, there is evidence that traits such as aggressiveness may be in part genetically determined. On the side of socialization, it has been shown that parents treat boys and girls differently, in ways appropriate to sex-role stereotypes. Media also play a part in presenting different activities as appropriate for boys and girls and men and women. The best answer for the heredity-environment argument is that the two factors interact.

While differences between men and women have not been found in general intelligence, certain specific areas such as spatial ability and verbal ability do show differences, particularly as children reach adolescence. Men and

women also differ on some personality traits, although there is always an overlap rather than a complete difference between the sexes. Research on need for achievement has shown differences between men and women. Some authors have suggested that women are less motivated to achieve, while others argue that men and women simply differ in the situations in which achievement needs are exercised. Another possibility is that women hesitate to achieve because they fear negative consequences for success, such as social rejection. Men may also have reason to fear negative consequences in some achievement situations.

Masculinity and femininity are psychological concepts representing typical male and female interests. A psychological form of androgyny has recently been presented as a concept that can be applied to people who possess both masculine and feminine characteristics, and it is suggested that these people may be more adaptable to their environment than the traditionally sex-typed individual.

Stereotypes of men and women show much sharper differences than actually exist. Men are generally seen as more competent and women as more expressive, but overall the stereotyping process favors men. Judgments of male and female performance also differ, and unless an expert opinion is presented, men will be usually judged as superior to women. The explanations given for a man's and a woman's success also differ in favor of the man. Men and women themselves show the same differences in judging their own performances.

The impact of the movement for equality between women and men is causing changes in many segments of society. Although more overt forms of discrimination are legally prohibited, several more subtle factors may perpetuate discrimination in the employment sector. Among these are a tendency to devalue women's performance, a bias in favor of jobs held mainly by men, and a tendency of women to devalue themselves.

I. The concept of race
   A. The technical definitions of race
   B. The popular definition
   C. Implications for the study of racial similarities and differences

II. Racial differences in intelligence-test scores

III. Interpretations of the findings
   A. Heredity as an explanation
   B. Evaluating the hereditarian arguments
   C. Arthur Jensen's viewpoint
   D. Environmental deprivation
   E. Intelligence as culturally defined
   F. Characteristics of the testing situation
   G. The Black personality and self-concept

IV. Comparisons between Whites and races other than Black

V. Social-class similarities and differences
   A. Definitions and measurement of social class
   B. Differences in children
   C. Occupational groups and IQ

VI. The interpretation of social-class differences in intelligence
   A. Heredity
   B. Environment
   C. Motivation and personality factors in the testing situation

VII. A study of race and social class varied concurrently

VIII. Expectations for the future and a final caution

IX. Summary

Similarities and differences among races and social classes

15

The less intelligent the White man is, the more stupid he thinks the Black.

Andre Gide

In the year 1909, William Howard Taft, the newly inaugurated President of the United States, made the following statement to a group of Black college students in Charlotte, North Carolina: "Your race is adapted to be a race of farmers, first, last and for all times" (quoted in Logan, 1957, p. 66). In the 70 years since Taft's erroneous prediction, Blacks and members of other minority groups have shown that they possess the ability to succeed in any endeavor requiring high degrees of motivation and intelligence. Yet there remain those—some demagogues, some social scientists—who believe that important racial differences exist. The possibility of racial differences in intelligence remains a controversial question, both academically and practically. Do races differ in intelligence? Or are the similarities between races more important than any potential differences? What is a *race*, anyway? What contributes to the determination of differences in IQ? The answers to these and other questions will be pursued in this chapter.

First, we will draw some conclusions about similarities and differences between races and between social classes. As we seek to understand the causes of any group differences in abilities and personality, we will dissect the concepts of **race** and **social class.**

I. The concept of race

Since the beginning of recorded history, people have made comparisons between their own group and others (Gossett, 1963). In almost all cases, the foreign "race" was seen as inferior. Aristotle, for example, believed that Greece's benign climate enabled the Greeks to develop physical and mental characteristics that were superior to those of other Europeans. In such comparisons, the term *race* seemingly stands for "any group that is different in any way." The conception of race as being based on skin color seems rather recent. Thus we must question what constitutes a race. Would Aristotle's Greeks and, for example, Northern Europeans constitute different races?

The answer to that straightforward question is complex, because there remain, even today, so many meanings for the term *race*. In an attempt to simplify we will divide the multitude of definitions into two types: *technical* definitions and *popular* definitions. Technical definitions are those used by geneticists and anthropologists who study races; popular definitions reflect the ways that people in general label someone's race.

475

A. The technical definitions of race

What do scientists mean by the term *race?* In essence, they define a race as a population of people who live close together geographically and who intermarry. Throughout the period of scientific study of races, scientists have used different means to separate these populations that intermarry and hence maintain some degree of similarity within each population. For instance, classifications of race some 200 years ago were usually based on differences in skin color alone. In 1735 Carolus Linnaeus described all humans as of one species—a controversial position at that time!—and then divided that species into four skin-color varieties. Linnaeus ascribed different mental characteristics to each variety; not surprisingly, he considered Europeans to be "lively" and "inventive."

About 100 years ago, scientists seeking definitions of *race* rejected Linnaeus's use of skin color as a *sole* determinant and began to utilize a number of observable physical characteristics—head shape, various facial features, body physique, hair color, and hair texture—as well as skin color. Note that such a classification system avoids the use of *nonbiological* attributes (particularly common cultural background) in defining race. Groups differing in culture, customs, and languages—but not in biological or physical characteristics—are now called **ethnic groups;** they are not considered different races, even though Italians, Irish, Nordics, Slavs, and others have been called "races" at one time or another.

The above approach, using a combination of surface physical characteristics, reflects one technical definition that is called the *physical* definition of race. Although it is a scientifically acceptable definition, it suffers the handicap of being based on **phenotypes** (surface characteristics) rather than **genotypes** (underlying characteristics). The most recent definition of *race* uses underlying characteristics as its building blocks. This *genetic* approach makes the following assumptions (summarized from Dunn & Dobzhansky, 1952): First, groups of people differ not only in the observable characteristics of physical appearance, but also in characteristics such as blood type and susceptibility to certain diseases. Examples of the latter include sickle-cell anemia and Tay-Sachs disease (Ginsburg & Laughlin, 1968). Second, each of these characteristics is determined by genes (usually many genes have a role in the determination of each characteristic). Third, groups of people differ in their genetic makeup, and certain groups of people can be distinguished on the basis of the degree to which they possess certain genes. According to this genetic approach, then, races are defined as "populations which differ in the frequencies of some gene or genes" (Dunn & Dobzhansky, 1952, p. 118).

Genetic analysis has been most thoroughly applied in the case of blood types, as may be seen in Figure 15-1. Further efforts at genetic analysis may be expected in the future. Yet even though this genetic approach to the classification of races is refreshing in its promise of objectivity and precision, its complexity is frustrating. It delineates and identifies a large number of races. Moreover, races, defined genetically, differ in only a relative way (B. Glass, 1968). That is, the genetic constituencies of two different races are highly similar; the differences in many cases are only of proportions of particular characteristics, rather than of presence or absence (C. Jorgensen, 1975). For example, on the basis of an analysis of human proteins, Cavalli-Sforza (1974) has concluded that the genetic differences between races are not as great as the differences in their appearance would imply. We can say very little about a person's race simply from knowing that he or she has Type O blood. At the same time, the significant differences in genetic compositions of different racial populations indicate that the concept of race is a viable one—even though it is exceedingly difficult to pin down.

The emphasis on genetic differences between races has implications for adaptation and

Figure 15-1
The genetic analysis of races through blood types

The analysis of blood types reflects both similarities and differences between racial groups. The blood of every human being in the world is one of four types —A, B, AB, or O—but the proportions of each type differ markedly in different populations. Type O is one of the most common types among Caucasians in Western Europe, Canada, and the United States; for example, in a group of 422 Londoners, 47.9% had Type O; 42.4% had Type A; 8.3% Type B; and 1.4%, Type AB. The percentage of the population having Type O drops steadily as one moves east across Europe and Asia; in a group of 1000 Chinese in Peking, only 30.7% had Type O. The most frequent type among these Chinese is Type B (34.2%). Type B is completely absent in most North American Indian tribes and also in Australian aborigines. There are also large differences in proportions within specific European groups and within African populations.

change; it is now believed that races are products of selective survival and breeding and are affected by environmental, economic, and political constancies and changes. For example, changes in the physical environment from hot to cold, from wet to dry, from absence to presence of disease, can force changes in the genetic basis of a race. Political changes resulting from the introduction of new trade routes or conquest of a new territory or genocide of a population through warfare can change the genetic constituencies of races (C. Jorgensen, 1975). Such a conception has significance for notions about racial similarities and differences in intelligence. Within a particular society, such as in the United States or Canada, the environment facing persons of different races is essentially the same. Hence in most societies the environmental influences should lead to greater *similarities* between racial groups in respect to genetic selection.

In the future, there will probably be increased efforts to measure genetic similarities and differences among populations. But we should acknowledge that not all workers in the field accept the genetic definition of race given above. Geneticists and physical anthropologists use this definition more than do social anthropologists or sociologists. The latter usually prefer a classification based on a compendium of physical characteristics. In summary, both the geneticist's and the sociologist's definitions are acceptable technical definitions of race.

But is it desirable to retain the term at all? Anthropologist M. F. Ashley Montagu (1957, 1964) wants to remove the term *race* from the English language. He believes the label has caused a divisive, prejudicial orientation toward people. We worry about this; for example, do social scientists, by studying racial "differences" so extensively, help perpetuate a society that focuses on one's race as a primary attribute?

Yet we believe that the term *race* is necessary. We need some term to account for the "local genetic differences between population groups which are only partially isolated from each other and continue to exchange genes but also to maintain some obvious differences" (Ginsburg & Laughlin, 1968, p. 27). We agree with those anthropologists (Washburn, 1964; Kilham & Klopfer, 1968) who favor continued use of the term as long as it has biological meaning. At any rate, adherents of both of the acceptable technical definitions of race would agree that the popular definition of race—which will be considered next —is oversimplified and misleading.

B. The popular definition

The definition given by people in general for the term *race* is vastly different from the acceptable technical definitions. In the United States, a person's racial classification is often self-determined, although influenced by family tradition, custom, and law. Most often, it is based only on skin color. In certain states laws assign one's racial classification on the basis of the race of one's ancestors. For example, if one or more of a person's great-grandparents were "Negro," the state classifies that person also as Negro.[1] In addition, the popular definition of race includes only six classifications: White (or Caucasian), Black, native American (Indian), Oriental, Asian Indian, and Brown (or Melanesian). These roughly correspond to the geographic groupings that are now considered to be too simplified.

A vital aspect of the popular definition is its all-or-none character. According to its approach, a person is clearly a Black, a White, or an Oriental. With a few exceptions (mulattoes, Creoles, Métis), the hybridization of races is denied, at least in the United States and Canada. Yet it is estimated that between 20 and 30% of the total genetic background of those United States residents classified as Black is Caucasian in origin[2] (P.F. Roberts, 1955; B. Glass & Li, 1953; Reed, 1969) and that no less than 70% of all the U. S. residents classified as Blacks have some Caucasian genetic background. This would further imply that a few Blacks living in the United States have an *almost pure* Caucasian ancestry and that most have *some* Caucasian ancestry.

For the same reason (intermarriage or interbreeding), some Whites in the United States (as defined by skin color) possess some Black ancestry. The precise extent is difficult to pinpoint; Stuckert (1964) estimates that approximately 20% of United States Whites have some Black genetic background. These estimates

should further emphasize to all of us that different "races" in the United States, Canada, and other cosmopolitan countries possess considerable *similarities*, not only in their environment but *even in their genetic makeup.*

But although many citizens of the United States and Canada are of racially mixed backgrounds, the popular definition denies this fact by putting people into literally Black-or-White categories. The popular definition has great difficulty with persons whose skin color and other characteristics are not clearly those of one race. The fact that some United States citizens are difficult to categorize according to the popular classifications of race is evidenced by estimates that from 2500 to 25,000 persons have passed from the Black subculture into the White subculture each year (Hart, 1921; C. B. Day, 1932; McKinney, 1937; Burma, 1946; Davie, 1949).

C. Implications for the study of racial similarities and differences

Research methodology that studies social-psychological similarities and differences *should* be based on the technical definitions of race. But, instead, almost every researcher has used the popular definition; group comparisons have been made after individuals have been assigned to one "race" or another by simply looking at them or by using a self-labeling procedure (Schoenfeld, 1974). Only the rarest study seeks out genealogical data in order to classify subjects. Fried (1968) concludes that the use of the popular definition by researchers converts the issue of racial differences into a pseudoproblem. While his viewpoint is tempting, we believe we must report and interpret whatever data we have. At the same time, we recognize that the comparisons that we will discuss are among groups that are not pure (that is, separable) in genetic background or in physical appearance.

Despite these limitations, some social scientists have concluded that Blacks are innately

---

[1]Plessy, the Negro whose court action led to the *Plessy v. Ferguson* (1896) decision by the U.S. Supreme Court, protested having to sit in a separate railroad car because of his race. Seven of his eight great-grandparents had been White. The original Supreme Court decision was overturned by the 1954 desegregation decision (Logan, 1957).

[2]The most recent of these estimates (Reed, 1969) uses not only ABO blood-type frequencies but also the presence of the Fy^a gene of the Duffy blood system. This gene is practically nonexistent in contemporary African populations. On the basis of its frequency, Reed estimates that about 22% of the genetic background of U.S. Blacks, as a group, is of Caucasian origin.

inferior mentally to Caucasians. (In fact, this was the dominant view of social scientists 75 years ago.) Some advocates of inherent differences in mental or physical ability are motivated by a commitment to racial segregation, but there are also behavioral scientists who, while free of any desire for the separation of races, believe that the evidence indicates that an innate difference between races does exist. The publications of the International Association for the Advancement of Ethnology and Eugenics are examples of this viewpoint. In recent years, the public press has given much attention to the views of Arthur Jensen, a psychologist who believes that heredity accounts for about 80% of the IQ differences among individuals and that innate differences may exist between Blacks and Caucasians. While we conclude that Jensen's conclusions are incorrectly derived, we believe that his position needs to be analyzed. We analyze it in Section III of this chapter.

In contrast to Jensen, there are behavioral scientists who believe, on the basis of their reading of the evidence, that any differences in ability between races can be explained by factors other than hereditary differences. The heavily publicized Moynihan Report (U.S. Department of Labor, 1965) states "There is absolutely no question of any genetic differential [between Negroes and Whites]. Intelligence potential is distributed among Negro infants in the same proportion and pattern as among Icelanders or Chinese or any other group." Likewise, the 1964 UNESCO statement "Biological Aspects of Race" (printed in UNESCO, 1965, p. 2) reported "The peoples of the world today appear to possess equal biological potentialities for attaining any civilizational level."

In the face of these contrasting conclusions, the reader should avoid forming a conclusion about the possibility of innate differences until reading the subsequent sections, in which data supporting conflicting viewpoints are presented and evaluated. First, IQ differences between Blacks and Whites will be examined, since this is the most frequently researched comparison.

II. Racial differences in intelligence-test scores

Alfred Binet developed the first IQ test in France in 1905 in order to provide an accurate and standardized way of determining whether or not a child had enough mental ability to learn in school. Binet wished to develop a test that was fair to children of different educational and cultural backgrounds. This goal is as elusive today as it was then; the materials used in IQ tests inevitably reflect the background of the test maker. Yet the tests continue to be given to test takers with different backgrounds, and their results continue to be interpreted as reflecting differences in ability rather than past experience.

Reviews of the numerous studies comparing the performances of Blacks and Whites on intelligence tests draw similar conclusions about the extent of differences.[3] Black groups average 10 to 20 points below White groups in measured IQ. Only rarely has a study found the average Black IQ score to be as high as 100. However, in all studies, the IQ scores of some Blacks are above the population average of 100. This statistic (the percent of overlap) ranged from 1 to 50%—in other words, in different comparisons, anywhere from 1 to 50% of Black subjects scored above the average score of White subjects. Unfortunately, the importance of the fact that a sizeable proportion of Blacks exceed the White's average IQ score is usually overlooked by both researchers and people in general. For example,

[3]The reviews by Tyler (1965), by Dreger and Miller (1960, 1968), and by K. S. Miller and Dreger (1973) are perhaps the best combinations of objectivity and thoroughness. Pettigrew's review (1964, Chap. 5) concludes that environmental deprivation can account for racial differences. Earlier works include the comprehensive review by Shuey (1966), which includes more than 200 references, but Shuey has been criticized for her polemic attitude and lack of objectivity (Dreger & Miller, 1960; Pettigrew, 1964). Another frequent reviewer of the issue is Henry E. Garrett (1960, 1962, 1964, 1965, 1969), but many of his statements and activities (one of which is going on a speaking tour sponsored by the White Citizens Council) cause us to question his objectivity.

there are instances of individual Black children —apparently free of mixed ancestry—whose mental development reaches levels equal to those of the most superior Whites. Witty (Witty & Jenkins, 1935; Theman & Witty, 1943) reported the case of a 9-year-old Black girl in the United States with an IQ of 200. As Schoenfeld (1974) notes, we are a society that dotes on differences among people. Regardless, the high degree of overlap between scores of different racial groups should remind us of their essential similarities.

Also consistent is the finding that the IQ differences between groups of younger persons are very much less than differences between groups of older persons. The apparent deterioration of Black IQs with increasing age is characteristic of all groups—regardless of their race —that have not received adequate stimulation from the environment. The reviews indicate that differences between Blacks and Whites appear regardless of the type of test used—group versus individual, verbal versus performance, or traditional versus **culture-free** test. (Culture-free tests attempt to use materials that are uninfluenced by the environment in which the test taker lives; we doubt that it is possible to construct such a test.) A common supposition that the performance of Blacks is closer to that of Whites on nonverbal tests is not upheld. In many comparisons, the opposite obtains; differences between Blacks and Whites on perceptual and other nonverbal tests are often greater than the differences on verbal tests.

The most extensive testing of mental ability took place during the two world wars, when more than 20 million men in the United States were evaluated to determine their readiness for military training. Test-score differences between racial groups were found. Using the U. S. Army Alpha Test of mental ability with World War I recruits, Yerkes (1921) found that only about 9% of the Black men scored above the average for White men. However, for Black men living in the Northern part of the United States, the percentage of scores exceeding the average White score was higher—29 percent. This indicates a

regional difference for Blacks; there was also one for Whites. Using a selection of states, Klineberg (1944) showed that the average Army Alpha performance of Black recruits from four Northern states was better than the average performance of White recruits from four Southern states. The median Army Alpha scores (not to be confused with IQ scores) for Blacks were: Pennsylvania, 42.0; New York, 45.0; Illinois, 47.3; and Ohio, 49.5. The median scores for Whites from the four Southern states were: Mississippi, 41.2; Kentucky, 41.5; Arkansas, 41.6; and Georgia, 42.1. Thus Klineberg, by selecting the four states where Blacks did best and the four states where Whites did poorest, argued that the quality of environment plays a role in the determination of performance on a test of mental ability. However, Whites from each state listed did better than Blacks from the same state. In fact, Garrett (1945) found, after studying these data, that Blacks scored about as far below Whites in the four Northern states as they did in the country as a whole. Thus, as Alper and Boring (1944) conclude, there are two consistent findings in the Army Alpha data—regional differences and racial differences.

The advantage of Northern Blacks over Southern Whites found in World War I did not hold in World War II comparisons. Blacks from the New England states performed better than Blacks from any other geographical area. But the percentage of New England Blacks receiving above-average AGCT scores (Grades I and II) was 8.9%, while 20.8% of the Whites from the Southwest (their weakest area) placed in Grades I and II (Davenport, 1946).

It is pointless to document further the consistent finding of differences in measured IQs of Blacks and Whites. The fact that such differences in test scores occur is agreed upon both by those who believe there are innate racial differences (the hereditarians) and by those who believe the best explanation rests upon environmental handicaps (environmentalists). The controversy centers on the causes—and hence the importance—of these test-score differences. Additionally, as we will see in the next paragraphs, some social psychologists emphasize a distinction between differences in *test scores* and differences in *underlying intelligence*.

III. Interpretations of the findings

As indicated, hereditarians and environmentalists have widely disparate explanations for the consistent differences between Blacks and Whites in IQ scores. In addition to broad causes such as heredity and environment, more specific factors—such as the characteristics of the testing situation, the motivation of the test taker, and the appropriateness of the test—must be considered when attempting to explain racial differences. G. S. Lesser, Fifer, and Clark (1965) have provided a list of the possible specific influences, which is abstracted in Table 15-1. These proximal causes emphasize a distinction that should always be kept in mind—the distinction between IQ scores and intelligence as an underlying concept. All the studies use IQ scores and infer from these scores conclusions about levels of intelligence. But the proximal causes—such as degree of rapport between tester and subject—may influence measured IQ scores and not the underlying concept of intelligence. To summarize, IQ-test performance and intelligence *are not the same thing. Many determinants in addition to one's level of intelligence affect the score one receives on an IQ test.*

Let us consider these possible influences in some detail. We shall then present an answer to the basic question: Can any of the difference in tested IQs between Blacks and Whites be attributed to innate differences between these two groups?

A. Heredity as an explanation

As an explanation of racial differences, heredity has had a long history. Around the year 1900, the dominant viewpoint of social scientists

Table 15-1
Possible influences on test performance

I. Variables of background and environment
   A. Cultural background (racial or ethnic group)
   B. Family characteristics
   C. Formal school training
   D. Experience with similar tests
   E. General health and special handicaps (for example, impaired sight, hearing, or coordination, emotional disturbance, and the like)
   F. Age
II. Personality and motivational variables
   A. Persuasibility or responsiveness to examiner
   B. Interest in test problems
   C. Effort and persistence
   D. Anxiety level
   E. Achievement motivation
III. Characteristics of the testing situation
   A. Perceived importance of the test
   B. Expectations of success or failure
   C. Temporary physical conditions (fatigue, transient respiratory or digestive ailments, or other temporary indispositions)
   D. Interference from the testing environment
   E. Influence of the tester
IV. Test demands
   A. Specific abilities required
   B. Speed of response required

Adapted from "Mental Abilities of Children from Different Social-Class and Cultural Groups," by G. S. Lesser, G. Fifer, and D. H. Clark, *Monographs of the Society for Research in Child Development*, 1965, 30(4), 1–115. Copyright 1965 by The Society for Research in Child Development, Inc. Used by permission.

was that the development of mental ability in Blacks stopped at an earlier age than that of Whites. Since that time, however, there has been an increasing reluctance on the part of behavioral scientists to posit innate differences as a sole, or even major, explanation of racial differences. For example, even the highly publicized—and often misrepresented—view of Arthur Jensen (1969b, 1969c, 1969d) emphasizes that genetic factors may play a role *but also recognizes the presence of environmental factors.*

The following list presents the basic arguments for a belief in hereditary racial differences in intelligence. We will evaluate each of these in the next section.

1. The failure (as claimed by some) of the Black race to produce a civilization as well-developed as those of other races indicates to hereditarians the presence of an inherent racial difference in mental abilities.

2. The Black fails to perform as well as the White in situations in which—the hereditarians claim—the Black person's past environment is no different from the White's.

3. There was a lack of improvement in the test scores of Black recruits, relative to Whites, during the time period between World War I and World War II. This argument is based on the assumption that the Black's environment and educational opportunities increased more during this period than did those of Whites. Anastasi and D'Angelo, for example, state: "Insofar as socioeconomic conditions have improved for Negroes over the past two or three decades [1925–1950], it might be expected that their test performance would also rise" (1952, p. 157).

4. A relationship exists between skin pigmentation among Blacks (as an indication of racial purity) and levels of intelligence. Hereditarians have claimed that darker-skinned Blacks have lower IQs. Tanser (1939) found skin-color differences correlated with the performance of Blacks, with those of darker skin pigmentation having lower scores. Ferguson (1919) separated World War I recruits at Camp Lee, Virginia, into darker-skinned and lighter-skinned groups. The median Army Alpha score for the lighter-skinned group was 51; for the darker, it was 40. Almost all the men were from the same state, Virginia. J. Peterson and Lanier (1929) reported similar differences in Southern Black children but not in Northern Black children. Klineberg (1935) found no relationship in his New York City sample.

Several studies have considered skin pigmentation in other groups. Using native North Americans as subjects, Garth, Schuelke, and Abell (1927) concluded that the more impure the Indian's racial background, the higher his IQ. In the only recent study on this topic, R. F. Green (1972) compared the IQ scores of Puerto Rican natives who had been separated into five groupings on the basis of their skin color. While the two darkest groups had lower average IQ scores, they also had less education.

5. There is a demonstrable difference in developmental rates between Black infants in Africa and White infants in the United States and Europe (Dasen, 1973). Geber and Dean (1957a, 1957b) tested the developmental rates of 107 Black infants born in a hospital in Uganda, East Africa, in 1956. During the first week of life almost all the children were found to be more advanced than European children of the same age. When drawn to a sitting position, 90 of the 107 babies could prevent their heads from falling back, whereas head control usually does not occur in European children until the 8th to 12th week. A baby 48 hours old was shown lying on his stomach and raising his chin from the table. Dasen (1973, 1974) reports similar trends in Baoulé infants of Nigeria, West Africa. (Twelve other studies on this topic—ten of which find similar results—are critically reviewed by N. Warren, 1972.) This precocity was generally lost by the third year, and after that time the developmental rate of the African children remained lower than that of most European children (Geber, 1956).

B. Evaluating the hereditarian arguments

Of the five hereditarian arguments listed above, we believe that the first cannot be evaluated objectively for two reasons. First, we have no detailed or accurate information about Negro civilizations in the African past. There are some indications that civilizations in Ethiopia, central

Africa, and West Africa were highly developed both before Christ and during the period A.D. 600-1200 (Du Bois, 1947). Second, a conclusion about the relative success of different civilizations involves a value judgment. Dominant societies in North America, Western Europe, Australia, and Japan value verbal skills and technological development—perhaps at the sacrifice of authentic human relationships. But does this mean that such societies or civilizations are more advanced than ones with no written language but with highly developed art forms or family relationships? Surely we cannot make such an assumption.

The second hereditarian argument assumes that the past environments of Blacks and Whites can be equated statistically, by comparing Blacks with only those Whites whose levels of education and quality of environments are similar to those of the Blacks. Such an approach is only an *indirect test* of the influence of heredity, in that it proposes that if the tested IQs of Blacks are lower than those of Whites whose environments are the same, then heredity accounts for the test-score difference. Four studies are usually offered by hereditarians as tests of this assumption of equated environments. Let us consider the adequacy of one, by Bruce, as an example.

Bruce (1940) tested Black and White children in a backward area in rural Virginia and attempted to equate the socioeconomic status of the children by using the Sims Score Card, a method of evaluating family economic level. Forty-nine Black and 49 White children were paired, and differences in mean IQ were found. Three tests were used. The Kuhlmann-Anderson test produced means of 83 for Whites and 73 for Blacks; the Arthur test had a mean of 89 for Whites and 77 for Blacks; and the Stanford-Binet test produced means of 86 for Whites and 77 for Blacks.

There are problems, however, with Bruce's study. First, the author admits that the Sims Score Card does not discriminate adequately at the lower socioeconomic level, where these chil-

dren were. The two groups might have differed in socioeconomic status yet have been completely equated on the score card, because of the crude nature of the measuring instrument. Second, though Bruce was "inclined to believe that there is an innate difference between the particular White and Negro groups studied" (p. 97), she pointed out that the two groups were not completely equal in the Sims score, the Black families being lower. Third, the White and Black children were from different schools; the schools in Virginia were racially segregated at that time, and there is no evidence that the quality of instruction and facilities and the availability of materials were the same. Our best guess is that the White school was better equipped. Fourth, even if the objective indices (Sims Score Card, school facilities, and the like) had been equal, we certainly question whether there was true equality between the races in rural Virginia 40 years ago. The sheer fact of being Black was a stigma and a restriction and, hence, an environmental handicap. Bruce's study fails to qualify as a test of equated environments for these reasons.

The third hereditarian argument found no reduction in the amount of difference between Black and White IQ scores from the time of testings in World War I to testings in World War II. This gap persisted despite a presumed improvement in the Blacks' environment in the intervening quarter of a century. But, even though the Blacks' environment may have improved substantially during that period, the degree of improvement may not have been any greater than that experienced by Whites. For example, income differentials between Whites and Blacks have remained relatively stable over a period of years, with the average Black income staying at about 55% of the average White income (Farley & Hermalin, 1972). Such relationships weaken the thrust of this type of hereditarian argument.

The fourth hereditarian argument, the relationship of skin color to level of intelligence, could be a function of either environment or heredity or both. For example, R. F. Green's (1972) analysis of Puerto Ricans' IQ scores indicates that those adults with darker skins also had less education. During the first half of this century, when most of the studies based on skin pigmentation were done, lighter-skinned Blacks in the United States had greater access to cultural opportunities and were rejected less than were darker-skinned Blacks. During that period, also, there was a great deal of prejudice against darker-skinned Blacks by other Blacks.

Another reason to be skeptical of the hereditarian claim is that classification by skin color (which usually is done subjectively) is not always an accurate indicator of the percentage of White ancestry. We agree with Tyler (1965), certainly one of the most objective reviewers, who believes it is best not to draw any conclusion about the possible hereditary causes of skin-shading differences in IQ score.

Looking critically at the fifth argument of the hereditarians, we conclude that different developmental rates in African infants may or may not imply differences in intelligence. Apparently —on the basis of Geber's testings and the observations by Ainsworth (1967) of 27 Ganda infants—newborn babies in these environments are more advanced in sensorimotor development than are newborn European or United States children. Every one of the babies under 6 months of age had Gesell Developmental Quotients of 100 or better, and 95% of the infants tested between the ages of 6 and 9 months were above the European average. (Geber used a Gesell test standardized on French children.) These differences occurred on Language Development items as well as in other parts of the test. For African children of 2 years of age, the superiority to European norms was less marked, and the 3-year-old African children characteristically had DQs below the European norm.

But the quality of research done in the dozen or so studies of African precocity reviewed by N. Warren (1972) is generally not good. Samples of children are often drawn casually, statistical significance tests are often not reported, and there is some question about the subjectivity involved in the administration and scoring of the Gesell scales.

These findings could imply either hereditary or environmental causes. Some believers in innate differences point out that *across* species a more rapid early developmental rate (or, in other words, a less prolonged infancy) is associated with a lower ceiling on development. For example, at birth gorillas are more developed than are chimpanzees, and chimpanzees are more developed than human beings. The human species, however, reaches the highest mental abilities as an adult, followed by the chimpanzee and then the gorilla. Such a relationship occurring *across* species cannot be applied to subgroups *within* a species, however. There is no justification in concluding that the ceiling on sensorimotor level or language capacity of Ganda children is less than that of Europeans merely because of the African child's more rapid development in infancy.

Ainsworth recognizes that the developmental rates of the Ganda child have a relevance to the question of innate racial differences that is "all too painfully evident" (1967, p. 330). However, Ainsworth, as well as Geber, believes that child-care practices, rather than innate differences, are most influential in accounting for the accelerated development of African infants. Geber particularly emphasized the close contact between mother and infant during the child's first year, breast feeding on demand, and the mother's method of carrying the infant. Ainsworth added such observations as the absence of confinement, frequent parental handling, and particularly the fact that the Ganda baby is often held in a standing position from an early age. Such explanations may, of course, be validated by observations of child care in other societies and by determining relationships between the mother's behavior and developmental quotients in children in a given society.

But how do we explain the extreme slowing down of developmental rates in older African children? Geber and Ainsworth believe that this deceleration comes from the frequently abrupt reduction in mother-child interaction as the child gets older and as new siblings appear. Ganda mothers have an "all-absorbing preoccupation with the infant" (Ainsworth, 1967, p. 329); older children receive no stimulation from the mother, have no toys or organized play activities, and may even be removed from the mother and given to an aunt or grandmother to rear. Likewise, in a review of psychomotor development of infants, Werner (1972) concludes that racial differences interact with the kind of stimulation from the mother and the infant's nutrition to determine changes in the developmental rate. However, such an explanation (based on a feast-or-famine type of child care and stimulation) does not seem completely adequate. Although these child-care practices may indeed constitute a contributing factor, this explanation completely fails to account for differences in behaviors during the first week of life.

Much more work needs to be done before factors of individual experience or infant stimulation can be accepted as the major determinants of mental development (Warren, 1972). The Uganda results have not been confirmed in some United States studies. For example, C. E. Walters (1967), using 108 U.S. infants who were classified as either White or Black on the basis of the popular definition of race, found the developmental rates of the two groups to be very similar. The 51 Black and 51 White babies were equated for socioeconomic status and were administered the Gesell Developmental schedules at 12, 24, and 36 weeks of age. The only significant difference was in motor behaviors at 12 weeks of age, favoring the Black infants. In light of the African research, the general lack of differences may be a result either of similar child-rearing practices by Black and White mothers in the United States or of the racially impure nature of both groups.

C. Arthur Jensen's viewpoint

Claims of innate racial differences in mental ability received a second wind from the research and writings of Arthur Jensen, an educational psychologist at the University of California at Berkeley. Jensen's conclusions[4] need to be studied at length—both because the findings are detailed and because they have served as ammunition for racial segregationists.

Jensen's basic hypothesis is that individual differences in intelligence, as measured by IQ tests, are "predominantly attributable to genetic differences, with environmental factors contributing a minor portion of the variance among individuals in IQ" (1969c, p. 4). His conclusions are based partly on correlations between the IQs of pairs of subjects with various degrees of hereditary relationships (identical twins reared together, identical twins reared apart, fraternal twins, siblings reared together or apart, a parent and child, a grandparent and grandchild, and so on). Mainly these data come from Burt (1955, 1958), who drew samples of many kinship relationships from the school population of London, England. For many years Burt's data were accepted as "gospel." But recently Leon Kamin's (1974) brilliant analysis of Burt's research documents the following limitations in this oft-cited work: (1) Burt is quite unspecific about what mental ability tests were given to the children and whether the tests were standardized; (2) Burt himself acknowledges in his notes that his tests were of low reliability; (3) the sex and age of the subjects is often unreported; and (4) Burt uses vague "adjusted measures," rather than raw scores, in his statistical analysis. These inadequacies, along with the numerous inconsistencies in different articles *by Burt reporting his own data* have

---

[4]Jensen's original article (1969b) was the longest ever published in the *Harvard Educational Review.* A U.S. congressman has had the entire article placed in the *Congressional Record.* A summary of the original article may be found in the October 1969 issue of *Psychology Today* (Jensen, 1969c). Jensen's rebuttal to numerous critics (see Spring, 1969, issue of *HER*) can be found in the Summer 1969 issue of the *Harvard Educational Review* (1969d) or in *Psychology Today* (1973). Those readers who did not already know that scientists are human and can engage in such human actions as indignation, vindictiveness, and name-calling may wish to consult the prolonged exchange between Alfert and Jensen in the Autumn 1969 issue of the *Journal of Social Issues* (Alfert, 1969a, 1969b; Jensen, 1969a, 1969e).

forced even Jensen (1974) to question their accuracy. Yet in his earlier, highly publicized article, Jensen had relied on Burt's data on the measurement of the **heritability** of IQ. This concept is central in Jensen's speculations about possible racial differences in intelligence. In Figure 15-2 we describe and evaluate this concept of *heritability*.

Figure 15-2
Heritability: What is it and what difference does it make?

In arguing for the possibility of genetic determinants of intelligence, Arthur Jensen uses the concept of heritability, or the proportion of the total variation in some characteristic (such as intelligence) among people within a given population that can be attributed to genetic factors (Jensen, 1973c). The rest of the variation is attributed to the environment or to interactions between the environment and heredity. Analyses of the correlations developed by Burt (1955, 1958) and others for persons with various family relationships (identical twins, fraternal twins, siblings, parents, and children) are *interpreted* by Jensen to indicate that Caucasian populations show strong heritability coefficients. Some of these correlations are presented here:

	N	Group test IQ	Arithmetic or other achievement test	Height	Weight
Identical twins reared together	83	.904	.862	.957	.932
Identical twins reared apart	21	.771	.723	.951	.897
Fraternal twins reared together	172	.542	.748	.472	.586
Siblings reared together	853	.515	.769	.503	.568
Siblings reared apart	131	.441	.563	.536	.427

(Data from Burt, 1955 and 1958, as corrected and reported by Jensen, 1974, pp. 9, 11, 13, 19, and 21.)

Note that the greater the genetic similarity, the higher the correlation between the IQs of the two persons. Through a statistical process Jensen derives a heritability coefficient for this group of people and concludes that "genetic factors are about twice as important as environmental factors as a cause of IQ differences among individuals" (1973b, p. 81). Jensen assumes—based on what he admits was limited information—that Black populations would possess similar heritability coefficients. It should be noted, though, that the heritability coefficient for any group will be influenced by just how much difference exists in the environments of the different group members. The more environmental diversity, the lower the heritability coefficient. In a case (theoretical, of course) in which everyone's environment was the same, the heritability coefficient would be 100%, because genetic differences between group members would be the only cause of IQ differences.

But what implications for differences *between* racial populations stem from the proposed heritability rates *within* different racial populations? Jensen responds:

> The fact that IQ is highly heritable within the White and probably the Black population does not by itself constitute formal proof that the difference between the populations is genetic, either in whole or in part. However, the fact of substantial heritability of IQ within the population does increase the *a priori* probability that the population difference is partly attributable to genetic factors [1973c, p. 81].

There are two problems with Jensen's interpretations. First, more recent research (Scarr-Salapatek, 1971a, 1971b) has provided us with heritability coefficients for other groups. Scarr-Salapatek found that in lower-class White and Black populations, the heritability coefficients were lower (.50 to .60) than those for her middle-class samples or those reported by Jensen. (Recall that Jensen's estimate was a heritability coefficient of .80.) The important matter is that differences in environment between two lower-class children or two Black children have more effect on differences in IQ than they do on the IQs of two White middle-class children. Improving the quality of their environments would have the effect of increasing the heritability of intelligence in Black and lower-class groups, but it would increase their average IQs, also.

There are many limitations to the heritability concept (Layzer, 1974) and many problems in comparing correlation coefficients and thereby deriving conclusions about how much heredity contributes to differences in IQ (Weizmann, 1971). Scarr-Salapatek's analyses have not gone without challenge (Dawes, 1972; Willerman, 1972; Allen & Pettigrew, 1973; Erlenmeyer-Kimling & Stern, 1973).

The second difficulty with Jensen's conclusion derives from the use of correlations between IQ scores of family members for the "raw data" from which to derive heritability coefficients. There is great variation from study to study in regard to what the actual correlation is, for example, between pairs of identical twins. Part of the problem is ambiguities, omissions, errors, and inconsistencies in Burt's reports of his own studies (Jensen, 1974, tries to pull these together and correct errors) but beyond that the correlations are bound to differ in response to type of sample used. For example, Kamin (1974) reports the IQ correlations for separated identical twins in four different studies to range from .86 to .62. Additionally, the heritability formula fails to take into account the greater similarity in the environments of identical twins than of fraternal twins or of two siblings born at different times (Schwartz & Schwartz, 1974). Identical twins are of the same sex, are often dressed the same, given the same toys, and treated alike, and to use differences between identicals and fraternals as reflecting effects of heredity alone is misleading.

In summary, the concept of heritability seems to us to be of no value when seeking the causes of IQ differences between groups. Flaschman and Weinrub (1974) pose a hypothetical example that makes the point:

Take 100 sets of newborn identical twins ... split each pair of twins so that we have two groups, A and B, of 100 unrelated babies each. Raise Group A in the best environment money can buy—good food, books, sensory stimulation, attention, etc. Raise Group B in a poor environment—poor clothing and housing, a near-starvation diet, rats, and other conditions which poor working-class chil-

dren are subjected to. Suppose after five or six years, we give IQ tests to both groups and find that children in Group A have an average IQ of 120, those in Group B 60. Further, we can imagine that we can measure the heritability of IQ in each group, and let us say, for the sake of argument that in both Groups A and B the heritability *for that group* is 100% (that is, any variation is genetic since all were treated exactly the same in each group). Does this mean that the IQ differences between the groups is genetic? No, it can't because the individuals in Group B are genetically identical to those in Group A. The flaw in this reasoning is that we measure the heritability within each group, but not for the sum of the two groups— everyone in both A and B [Flaschman & Weinrub, 1974, p. 22; italics in original].

When it comes to racial differences in intelligence, Jensen does not dispute that environmental factors play a part in the obtained differences. He writes "No one, to my knowledge, questions the role of environmental factors, including influences from past history, in determining at least some of the variance between racial groups in standard measures of intelligence, school performance, and occupational status" (Jensen, 1969b, pp. 79–80). But Jensen also advocates consideration of an influence from hereditary factors: "The possible importance of genetic factors in racial behavioral differences has been greatly ignored, almost to the point of being a tabooed subject" (1969b, p. 80). Reasons for a possible hereditary influence upon intelligence include four elements, in Jensen's view.

1. Jensen first mentions genetic differences between racial groups. "The existence of genetically derived differences between racial groups (or 'breeding populations') is found in virtually every anatomical, physiological, and biochemical comparison one can make between representative samples of identifiable racial groups" (Jensen, 1969b, p. 80). Differences between races exist in regard to physical structure and athletic abilities as well (Cobb, 1934, 1936). A sidelight of this difference is found in Morgan Worthy's

research on racial differences in response (see Figure 15-3).

2. The sheer difference, consistent in so many studies, between Black and White test per-

formances—or between the performances of Blacks and those of other culturally disadvantaged minorities—leads Jensen, being the strong hereditarian that he is, to hypothesize (not

Figure 15-3
Are there racial differences in athletic performance? Why are there so few Black quarterbacks, baseball pitchers, and golfers in professional sports? We believe it is simply a matter of prejudice against Blacks plus lack of opportunity to develop. Pitchers and quarterbacks are prestige positions; to some extent they have been "reserved" for Whites. But Morgan Worthy, a psychologist at Georgia State University, believes there is a different reason. Worthy (1971, 1974a, 1974b) notes that within a professional sport, Blacks are *over*represented at some positions and *under*represented at others. For example, many defensive backs in football are Blacks; many outfielders in professional baseball are Blacks. Worthy (Worthy & Markle, 1970) reports evidence that White athletes excel at self-paced sports activities, whereas Blacks excel in reactive activities. Golf is self-paced, in that the golfer initiates action when he or she chooses; pitching in baseball would also reflect a self-paced response. But hitting is reactive; the individual must respond to actions of others or changes in the stimulus situation. But the differences in task responses are also found between Whites with different eye colors (Worthy, 1971). Worthy finds that White persons with dark eyes tend to perform better "in tasks that require sensitivity, speed, and reactive responses; light-eyed organisms tend to specialize in tasks that require hesitation, inhibition, and self-paced responses" (Worthy, 1974a, p. 2). Eye color, rather than race *per se*, appears to be the determining variable. Worthy's early work—which made racial comparisons—may have been another example of race's being invoked as an explanation when something else was actually operating. (Photos courtesy of New York Mets, Cincinnati Reds.)

to conclude) that hereditary factors may be part of the reason for the differences in test performance.

3. Jensen apparently accepts the studies of Bruce, Tanser, and others as successful attempts to "equate environments." Jensen concludes "No one has yet produced any evidence based on a properly controlled study to show that representative samples of Negro and White children can be equalized in intellectual ability through statistical control of environment and education" (1969b, pp. 82–83). Although that sentence can be read in several ways, Jensen seemingly accepts the equated-environment studies as definitive.[5]

4. Jensen also cites the work of Geber (1956) on the precocity of African infants and various physiological differences between races. However, Geber's work has been severely criticized by N. Warren (1972) for improper methodology and failure to report findings in detail.

Despite detailed listing of considerations that led to his conclusion, Jensen overlooks several important points. First, he fails to consider the absence of pure races in the United States. His term *breeding populations* ignores the extensive racial mixing in the United States in both past and present (Alfert, 1969a, p. 207).[6] Second, Jensen criticizes others for assuming that a score on an IQ test represents one's level of intelligence, yet he himself takes racial differences in obtained IQ's and calls these pure indications of differences in intelligence. Jensen assumes that the obtained IQ score and rate of mental development are equivalent. Third, Jensen fails to recognize the role of proximal factors, such as motivation in the testing situation or the race of the

examiner, which may make a Black subject's test score an invalid indication of his level of intelligence. (A statement by the Council of the Society for the Psychological Study of Social Issues, 1969, contains these criticisms and the Council's reaction to the publicity generated by Jensen's article.)

Jensen claims that environmental deprivation is not enough to explain the observed differences between racial groups; we maintain that his claim is not proven. What researcher has the tools to measure the effects of a society that denies the Black child access to much of his world and that constantly reminds him of his inferior status? Clearly, environmental deprivation plays a role in mental development; whether there are underlying genetic differences is, in our judgment, not presently a testable matter.[7]

If there are innate racial differences in mental ability between Blacks and Whites in the United States and Canada, the differences are probably slight. Even the obtained differences in test scores are relatively unimportant when one considers the overlap between groups. Hicks and Pellegrini (1966) have reviewed 27 studies and have estimated that knowing a person's race reduces by only 6% the uncertainty in estimating his or her IQ score. The obtained differences are so small that classification of persons into mental ability groups on the basis of race would not be useful when the children come from reasonably similar backgrounds. Jensen (1969b, p. 78) acknowledges this conclusion.

D. Environmental deprivation

The fact that the average Black living in the United States has an economically poorer environment than the average White is so manifestly apparent it may be accepted without docu-

---

[5]Jensen (1969c) states that there have been 43 studies that attempt to equate environments. One not listed by him (Tulkin, 1968) controlled both socioeconomic status and family characteristics. No significant Black-White IQ differences were found by Tulkin for the upper-class group, but there were differences in the lower-class group.

[6]In response to this criticism, hereditarians could argue that the observed difference of 15 points in average IQ between racial groups underestimates, rather than overestimates, the true difference between hypothetically pure groups.

[7]Jensen himself recognizes the lack of adequate tools. In an interview for *Life* magazine, (Neary, 1970), Jensen is quoted as saying "The ideal experiment would be to take a fertilized ovum, both parents Negro, and implant it into a White mother and have that child brought up in a society where there's no prejudice against skin color" (p. 65).

Figure 15-4

Do such people as Shockley and Jensen have a right to speak? William
Shockley, a Stanford physicist who shared a Nobel prize in 1956 for his role
in inventing the transistor, believes that Blacks are genetically inferior to Whites.
Shockley has had no training in psychology or genetics, but his eminence as
a Nobel-prize winner has given him a forum to advocate his proposal that the
U.S. government pay less intelligent people to undergo voluntary sterilization
before having any children. Shockley has spoken or attempted to speak on
several college campuses. The photograph shows a protest of his speech at
Princeton University (Boeth, 1973). It should be noted that both Blacks and
Whites have demonstrated against giving him a public forum.

   Also, Arthur Jensen's attempts to speak at several public or professional
meetings have been interrupted by hecklers or disrupted by members of the
audience who took over the lectern. These reactions reflect a position that the
academic community cannot become a vehicle for disseminating Shockley's
hypotheses and policy suggestions, because they reflect a threat of genocide like
the Nazi Germans' extermination of Jews during World War II.

   On the other side are those who, while equally opposed to Shockley's
position, contend that the rights provided in the First Amendment to the
Constitution must be maintained (Bristow, 1973). The First Amendment gives
all of us the right to espouse our ideas wherever we can develop an audience.
These advocates of free speech also believe that Shockley's ideas, if given a
public hearing and screening, will collapse under their own invalidity (Bristow,
1973). By critically discussing the positions of advocates of racial differences
even while we disagree with them, we affirm a belief that such speculations
need to be aired, even when their implications may run counter to accepted
values in our society. Our goal is to interpret such speculations as Jensen's and
Shockley's so that we can make informed reactions to them. (United Press
International Photos.)

mentation. Pettigrew's (1964) comprehensive book is an excellent source of facts, however, indicating that among Black people's burdens are high unemployment rates, poor health, low incomes, less education, poor housing, and many other factors—all of which combine to lead to a shorter life expectancy, higher susceptibility to certain diseases (such as tuberculosis), and greater incidence of psychosis (but not neurosis).[8] Certainly such severe environmental limitations might affect performance on intelligence tests (Eichenwald & Fry, 1969); the question is: do they?

One method of testing the effects of environment on the performance of Blacks is to place Black children in different environments from those they have had in the past. In doing so, the researchers assume that these new environments are better, more stimulating, and more growth-oriented, although such evaluations reflect value judgments as to what is "good." For example, it is assumed that because of better schools and other factors, there are regional differences in quality of environments. The Army Alpha studies of World War I recruits concluded that Northerners of each race scored consistently higher than Southerners of the same race. Peterson and Lanier (1929) found similar differences for schoolchildren; Black schoolchildren living in New York or Chicago scored significantly higher on several intelligence tests than Black children living in Nashville. These regional differences in

IQ score may have resulted from what the researchers consider to be greater educational opportunities and cultural benefits in the North than in the South. Some evidence for the validity of this assumption is the correlation of +.77 (found by H. B. Alexander in 1922) between the per capita expenditure for education in each state and the average Army Alpha score for military recruits from that state. If it can be shown that the IQs of Black children improve when they move from a less stimulating environment (the South) to a more stimulating one (the North), then we may conclude that environmental handicaps serve as an explanation for differences between Blacks and Whites. Several studies have done just that—comparing Northern-born Black children with Black children who migrated to the North. These studies, done by Lee (1951) and by Klineberg (1935), consistently correlated increases in IQ score with increases in length of exposure to the schools in the North.

More recent tests of the effects of environmental change have also produced positive results. In many of these studies, children from poorer backgrounds have been placed in special kindergartens, in which the researchers have created what they consider to be a more stimulating environment. The Early Training Project (S. W. Gray, 1969; S. W. Gray & Klaus, 1965, 1970; Klaus & Gray, 1965, 1968) was an attempt to offset the progressive retardation of mental development in young, Black children from poor families. The program offered a ten-week summer session in which a group of 20 children was given what the researchers considered an enriched environment and a great deal of reinforcement. Throughout the year, a home visitor provided each child with new educational materials and encouraged parents and children to participate in activities together. Careful attention was given to establishing adequate control groups, both within and away from the small city in the Southern part of the United States where the project was based. Although the primary purpose of the project was not to change IQ scores per se, measures on the Stanford-Binet Test of

---

[8]The Equality of Educational Opportunity study, or "Coleman Report" (J. Coleman, Campbell, Hobson, McPartland, Mood, Weinfeld, & York, 1966), documents the inferior education given to Black schoolchildren in the United States. Sponsored by the U.S. Office of Education, the Coleman report collected diverse types of information about U.S. schoolchildren—their levels of achievement and ability, their attitudes, their teachers' credentials, the facilities in their schools, the number of students per classroom, and so on. One of the report's important findings was the reaction of Black students to a measure of *internal locus of control* (see Chapter 3). The Coleman Report found that Black schoolchildren believed that they had less internal control than White children had. Also, those Black children with higher internal-control scores had higher achievement scores.

Intelligence indicated that the progressive retardation commonly found among lower-class Black children in the South was arrested, while the control groups continued to show diminishing scores. The mean IQs for the two experimental groups showed a gain of seven points over a two-and-a-half-year period, while the two control groups had average losses of four to six points. Even after their fourth year in school, IQ differences between experimental and control groups were significant (S. W. Gray & Klaus, 1970).

In summary, when the environmental conditions of Blacks are improved, their IQs increase. The increased IQs are close to the average score of 100 and are probably not much different from those of Whites in the same environment. The nature of their environments may account for a very large part of the difference between Blacks and Whites; however, we cannot say whether it alone accounts for all of the difference.

E. Intelligence as culturally defined

Intelligence is, to a large degree, a culturally defined concept. Each society determines what is intelligent behavior in that society. For instance, the Wechsler test asks "If you were lost in a forest in the daytime how would you go about finding your way out?" In our society there are certain acceptable (in other words, intelligent) and unacceptable (unintelligent) answers. In a society where the way of life is different, other types of answers might be more sensible and hence would be considered more "intelligent." We must always be careful not to assume that an intelligent response to the demands of *our* environment is necessarily the same as an intelligent response to the demands of other environments and other societies. IQ tests, because they inevitably use materials common to a particular society, are improperly and unfairly used when given to persons with a different cultural background (Mercer, 1972).

Another factor to be kept in mind is that each society tends to develop its own values and skills. The White, Western European/North American civilization is a highly verbal one. Hence, our methods of measuring intelligence are largely verbal. Because of our **ethnocentrism,** we are tempted to assume that a society that has never produced a written language (as was the case in the Hawaiian Islands and in many African tribes) is unable to produce intelligent people. This is a dangerous assumption, because it is based on a value judgment; it implies that what our society emphasizes is, by its very nature, the important determinant of intelligent behavior. Arnold Toynbee (1948), the author of a monumental study of the history of civilization, stated "When we classify Mankind by colour the only one of the primary races . . . which has not made a creative contribution to any one of our twenty-one civilizations is the Black Race" (p. 233). But Toynbee's selection of what constitutes a "creative contribution" must be seen as a value judgment. Other societies have undoubtedly been creative in other ways—in the development of nonverbal means of communication, authentic human relationships, complex religious views, art forms, and so on. It is also difficult to compare civilizations in widely different areas of the world with regard to their relative success in adapting to their environment. The respective environments are simply too diverse.

This conclusion implies that whites are ethnocentric when they label Blacks, native North Americans, or other groups as "culturally deprived" or "culturally disadvantaged." These minority groups certainly have rich cultural heritages; however, they are different from the White Western European one. They may well be heritages that do not prepare children for the demands of tests and curricula designed for middle-class Whites.

An excellent example of such *cultural relativism* is DuBois's (1939) study of the intelligence of Pueblo Indian children in New Mexico. DuBois carefully constructed and validated a Draw-a-Horse test; in doing so, he followed the procedures that had been used in the construction of the Goodenough Draw-a-Man test of intelligence. When both tests were administered to groups of White and Indian children, the Whites did better on the Draw-a-Man test, and the Indians did better on the Draw-a-Horse test. On the latter test, the mean "IQ" for the 11-year-old White boys was 74. Thus, it can be shown that each society has chosen to emphasize different skills and different types of intelligent behavior. (See also Figures 15-5 and 15-6.)

Figure 15-5

"Conceptual intelligence" in the United States and "spatial intelligence" in Liberia. The work of Gay and Cole (1967) on the teaching of mathematics to Kpelle children and adults provides a demonstration of cultural definitions of intelligence. The Kpelle are a rather un-Westernized tribe in Liberia. They have great difficulty in forming the concepts of color and shape when they are given square or triangular cards of red or green. Most of them take abnormally long periods of time to sort eight such cards into two piles, while Peace Corps volunteers in training for service in Liberia do the sorting correctly without hesitation. One may quickly conclude that the Kpelle lack conceptual ability and hence are "less intelligent." But consider a second task. A bowl of uncooked rice is passed around the room and the person is asked "How many measuring cups of rice do you think are in it?" (Gay & Cole, 1967, p. 1). The estimates of 60 Peace Corps volunteers were between 6 and 20 cups, with an average of around 12. In fact, there were exactly 9 cups in the bowl, so the average error of the Peace Corps trainees was about 35%. When 20 illiterate Kpelle adults were asked the same question, the average estimate was just under 9 cups, an underestimate of 8%. Thus, the Kpelle excel on a measure of spatial ability (a part of intelligence) and a task that is related to their ability to adapt to their own environment. (Photo courtesy of the Peace Corps.)

Figure 15-6
Try the Chitling Test

Black sociologist Adrian Dove was well aware of the culture biases of the usual IQ tests when he constructed the Dove Counterbalance General Intelligence Test (the Chitling Test). He described his test for ghetto Black children as "a half-serious idea to show that we're just not talking the same language." Here is a sampling of the 30 items. How "culturally deprived" is the White middle-class child when the tables are turned?

1. A "handkerchief head" is: (a) a cool cat, (b) a porter, (c) an Uncle Tom, (d) a hoddi, (e) a preacher.
2. Which word is most out of place here? (a) splib, (b) blood, (c) gray, (d) spook, (e) Black.
3. A "gas head" is a person who has a: (a) fast-moving car, (b) stable of "lace," (c) "process," (d) habit of stealing cars, (e) long jail record for arson.
4. "Bo Diddley" is a: (a) game for children, (b) down-home cheap wine, (c) down-home singer, (d) new dance, (e) Moejoe call.
5. If a pimp is up tight with a woman who gets state aid, what does he mean when he talks about

"Mother's Day"? (a) second Sunday in May, (b) third Sunday in June, (c) first of every month, (d) none of these, (e) first and fifteenth of every month.

6. If a man is called a "blood," then he is a: (a) fighter, (b) Mexican-American, (c) Negro, (d) hungry hemophile, (e) Redman or Indian.

7. What are the "Dixie Hummingbirds"? (a) part of the KKK, (b) a swamp disease, (c) a modern gospel group, (d) a Mississippi Negro paramilitary group, (e) deacons.

8. T-Bone Walker got famous for playing what? (a) trombone, (b) piano, (c) "T-flute," (d) guitar, (e) "hambone."

Those who are not "culturally deprived" will recognize that the correct answers are: (1) c, (2) c, (3) c, (4) c, (5) e, (6) c, (7) c, and (8) d. (From "Taking the Chitling Test," *Newsweek*, July 15, 1968, Vol. 72, pp. 51–52. Copyright Newsweek, Inc., 1968.)

F. Characteristics of the testing situation

In addition to the distal factors of heredity and environment, more proximal factors (many listed in Table 15-1) may account for racial differences in tested IQ scores. We must recognize that not all persons taking an intelligence test enter the testing situation with the same type or degree of motivation. There may be factors in the testing situation that would cause a Black's response to differ from that of a White. Several reports (Mussen, 1953; B. C. Rosen & D'Andrade, 1959; Merbaum, 1960) indicate that economically deprived Southern U.S. Black children show less concern for achievement and excellence of performance than do economically deprived Southern U.S. White children. Irwin Katz's (1964) comprehensive review proposed that Black behavior in a testing situation may be a function of "(a) social threat; i.e., Negroes were fearful of instigating White hostility through greater assertiveness, (b) low task motivation in confrontation with White achievement standards . . . , (c) failure threat" (p. 391). A series of studies (I. Katz & Benjamin, 1960; I. Katz & Cohen, 1962; I. Katz,

Epps, & Axelson, 1964; I. Katz & Greenbaum, 1963; I. Katz, Henchy, & Allen, 1968; I. Katz, 1967) has shown that the performance of Black college students in standard testing and laboratory situations is influenced by such factors as the race of the experimenter, the presence of other subjects of the same or another race, the nature of the task, the nature of the instructions, and the personality characteristics of the subjects. Such findings have been shown in both the Northern and Southern United States, and they apply to young subjects as well as to college students. For example, using Northern Blacks of ages 7 to 10, Katz, Henchy, and Allen (1968) found significantly better performances on a verbal-learning task when a Black experimenter was present than when a White experimenter was used.

Several studies have indicated that the performance of Black children deteriorates when tested by White examiners. Pasamanick and Knobloch (1955) concluded that the poor language scores of 2-year-old Black children were caused by an inhibition about being tested by a White examiner. Shuey (1966), however, after reviewing a large number of studies using Black examiners, concluded that the results are similar to those of studies using White examiners, and hence the race of the examiner has no effect. (This is a conclusion in keeping with Shuey's acceptance of innate racial differences.)

Until the last two decades, few studies had used both Black and White examiners to test the same children. Forrester and Klaus (1964) did, using as subjects 24 Black children, aged 5 and 6. The tests used were Forms L and M of the 1937 Stanford-Binet, and the testing was done by two equally trained Southern female examiners. The children were randomly assigned to four groups, and each group was given both test forms, with the order of test administration and the race of the examiner counterbalanced. The mean score when the children were examined by the Black was 105.7; when the White examiner was used, the mean was 101.9—a statistically significant difference. The race of the examiner did make a difference, although the results of this study could possibly be accounted for by differential skill of the examiners rather than by differences in race. Not all recent studies indicate significant effects resulting from the race of the examiner (see Tanner and Catron, 1971). Nevertheless, Forrester and Klaus's study should serve to caution us against accepting unquestioningly the validity of IQ scores of young southern Black children who have been tested by Whites.

It is possible that Black test takers in less well-designed testing situations using White examiners suffer even more than those in carefully controlled situations. Some White examiners may begin the testing of a Black child with unverbalized expectations of an indifferent performance. This leads to a decreased rapport between subject and tester, a failure on the tester's part to try to understand dialect, less probing, and hence a lower score; it is a neat example of a self-fulfilling prophecy, similar to the phenomenon found in teachers by R. Rosenthal and Jacobson (1968) (see Chapter 2).

G. The Black personality and self-concept

There is ample speculation that Blacks in the United States have borne a disfigured personality, a "mark of oppression" (Kardiner & Ovesey, 1951; Karon, 1958) that "represents the emotional wound of living in a White world of prejudice and discrimination" (I. Katz, 1969, p. 15). Black children appear to value the opinions of Whites more than those of other Blacks (Cantor, 1975). They often disparage their own race, learn the negative stereotypes about themselves that are held by Whites, and blame their own kind—rather than society at large—for the inferior status of their group (Gurin, Gurin, Lao, & Beattie, 1969).

Yet it should be noted that these findings and conclusions about Blacks' having a poor self-concept have been offered by *White* researchers. They have been criticized (Nobles, 1973) for failing to recognize that Blacks have a different perspective on the self, stemming from their African background. Some non-Wes-

tern world views, including the African, believe that the self comes into existence *as a consequence of the group* (Abrahams, 1962; Mbiti, 1970). One's identity is a group's identity; "I am because *we* are" (Nobles, 1973, pp. 23–24).

The dangers of applying a White orientation to a different group must always be recognized. Nevertheless, several recent interventions have sought to increase the degree of self-esteem held by Black schoolchildren and college students (Daly, 1974; N. W. Brown & Renz, 1973).

IV. Comparisons between Whites and races other than Black

Studies of differences between Whites and native North Americans or between Whites and Orientals suffer from many methodological problems. Among the Dakota Indians, for example, it is considered bad form to answer a question in the presence of someone else who does not know the answer (Klineberg, 1935). The effects of such cultural norms on IQ-test performance should be apparent. Moreover, Indian tribes have their own cultures and differ from one another in degrees of contact with non-Indian groups (Wrench, 1969).

After reviewing the available literature on differences between Whites and native North Americans, Tyler (1965) concludes "The only general statement that was warranted is that Indians as a group average considerably lower than Whites on standard intelligence tests" (p. 325). But Indian performance is better on nonverbal than on verbal measures of intelligence—a finding that does not apply to Blacks. Rohrer (1942) was able to test the intelligence of the Osage Indians, who had not suffered physical deprivation and isolation to the degree that most tribes had. He found average IQs of 100 and 104 on the two tests he used. The overlap between Indian and White scores is such that race cannot be used to assign classifications of ability.

Research on Chinese-Americans and Japanese-Americans is fraught with even greater difficulties, because Chinese and Japanese who have emigrated to the United States do not constitute a random sample of their compatriots. (Of course that could be said of the English and French who came earlier, too.) In contrast to other minority racial groups, the typical performance of Oriental children in the United States is often equal to or better than that of White children. Pintner (1931) reported average Binet IQs of 85 to 98, with averages above 100 on performance tests. Several investigators (Anastasi, 1958; Darsie, 1926; Sandiford & Kerr, 1926) have speculated that the superior performance of Oriental children may be attributable to a factor of *selective migration*; perhaps only the more able, intelligent families emigrated from the Orient to North America. Evidence for or against such a supposition is hard to obtain.

Hawaii offers a fertile area for the study of racial similarities and differences, as most of the Oriental, Caucasian, and Polynesian groups who live there possess similar cultural opportunities and socioeconomic status. (The latter statement is not true for the Hawaiian and Filipino groups in Hawaii, who are generally lower in status; but the Chinese, Japanese, Korean, and Caucasian groups have, in recent years, been reasonably equivalent in status.) However, findings on racial comparisons of schoolchildren in Hawaii are limited because studies have been made only on the children in the public schools (Livesay, 1942, 1944; S. Smith, 1942; L. H. Stewart, Dole, & Harris, 1967). There is a large enrollment of children in private schools, some of which siphon off the more talented students, and the percentages of children from the diverse racial groups attending these private schools vary.

V. Social-class similarities and differences

Although it is sometimes claimed that the United States and Canada are classless societies, it is evident that within North American life certain types of people are grouped together (and apart from others) on the basis of interests, education, income, values, and other socioeconomic variables. These groupings, though not always clear-cut, are important enough to be studied in their own right and are called social classes. We need now to investigate the findings pertinent to social-class similarities and differences in intelligence, personality, and motivation.

A. Definitions and measurement of social class

A review of different definitions of social class (Krech, Crutchfield, & Ballachey, 1962) indicates that three methods are used to define the term:

1. The objective method. This approach measures social class by "objective characteristics [that] are likely to discriminate most sharply among the different patterns of social behavior which [the social scientist] conceives as class behaviors" (p. 313). The objective characteristics most frequently used are amount and source of income, amount of education, type of occupation, and type and location of housing.

2. The subjective method. This approach defines social class "in terms of how the members of the community *see themselves* in the status hierarchy" (p. 313).

3. The reputational method. This approach defines social class "in terms of how the members of a community place *each other* in the status system of the community" (p. 315). In conjunction with this approach, a number of surveys show that respondents make a clear-cut and consistent ranking of the socioeconomic status of various occupations. Table 15-2 presents one ranking —an updating of the North-Hatt Occupational Prestige scale by Hodge, Siegel, and Rossi (1964), based on the responses of a national sample of adults.

Most of the research on social-class factors in intelligence has used the objective method to define social class, while recognizing that there is a moderate to high degree of agreement among the methods in classifying a particular individual. Unfortunately, many researchers are not very explicit about their particular measures, and at least some use very rough estimates of social class (such as neighborhood of residence). It is impossible to be confident that the "middle class" of one study is equivalent to the "middle class" of another. All we can do is use the class designation, knowing that we have a rough distinction between two groups—one higher in socioeconomic status than the other.

Table 15-2
Occupational prestige rankings in 1964

	Rank	Occupation	Prestige Score		Rank	Occupation	Prestige Score
	1	U.S. Supreme Court Justice	94		31.5	Owner of a factory that employs about 100 people	80
	2	Physician	93	Tied	31.5	Building contractor	80
Tied	3.5	Nuclear physicist	92		34.5	Artist who paints pictures that are exhibited in galleries	78
	3.5	Scientist	92		34.5	Musician in symphony orchestra	78
Tied	5.5	Government scientist	91	Tied	34.5	Author of novels	78
	5.5	State governor	91		34.5	Economist	78
	8	Cabinet member (U.S. federal government)	90		37	Official of an international labor union	77
Tied	8	College professor	90		39	Railroad engineer	76
	8	U.S. Representative in Congress	90	Tied	39	Electrician	76
	11	Chemist	89		39	County agricultural agent	76
Tied	11	Lawyer	89	Tied	41.5	Owner-operator of a printing shop	75
	11	Diplomat in U.S. Foreign Service	89		41.5	Trained machinist	75
	14	Dentist	88		44	Farm owner and operator	74
Tied	14	Architect	88	Tied	44	Undertaker	74
	14	County judge	88		44	Welfare worker for city government	74
	17.5	Psychologist	87		46	Newspaper columnist	73
Tied	17.5	Minister	87		47	Policeman	72
	17.5	Member of the board of directors of a large corporation	87		48	Reporter on a daily newspaper	71
	21.5	Priest	86	Tied	49.5	Radio announcer	70
	21.5	Head of a department in a state government	86		49.5	Bookkeeper	70
Tied	21.5	Civil engineer	86		51.5	Tenant farmer (one who owns livestock and machinery and manages the farm)	69
	21.5	Airline pilot	86	Tied	51.5	Insurance agent	69
Tied	24.5	Banker	85		53	Carpenter	68
	24.5	Biologist	85				
	26	Sociologist	83				
Tied	27.5	Instructor in public schools	82				
	27.5	Captain in U.S. Army	82				
Tied	29.5	Public-school teacher	81				
	29.5	Accountant for a large business	81				

	Rank	Occupation	Prestige Score		Rank	Occupation	Prestige Score
Tied	54.5	Manager of a small store in a city	67	Tied	72.5	Lumberjack	55
	54.5	Local official of a labor union	67		72.5	Restaurant cook	55
					74	Singer in a nightclub	54
Tied	57	Mail carrier	66		75	Filling-station attendant	51
	57	Railroad conductor	66		77.5	Dockworker	50
	57	Traveling salesman for a wholesale concern	66	Tied	77.5	Railroad section hand	50
	59	Plumber	65		77.5	Night watchman	50
	60	Automobile repairman	64		77.5	Coal miner	50
	62.5	Playground director	63	Tied	80.5	Restaurant waiter	49
Tied	62.5	Barber	63		80.5	Taxi driver	49
	62.5	Machine operator in a factory	63		83	Farmhand	48
	62.5	Owner-operator of a lunch stand	63	Tied	83	Janitor	48
Tied	65.5	Corporal in U.S. Army	62		83	Bartender	48
	65.5	Garage mechanic	62		85	Clothes presser in a laundry	45
	67	Truck driver	59		86	Soda-fountain clerk	44
	68	Fisherman who owns his own boat	58		87	Sharecropper (one who owns no livestock or equipment and does not manage farm)	42
Tied	70	Clerk in a store	56		88	Garbage collector	39
	70	Milk route man	56		89	Streetsweeper	36
	70	Streetcar motorman	56		90	Shoeshiner	34

B. Differences in children

Reviewing the large number of studies on social-class differences leads us to a general conclusion that the average intelligence-test performance of children from upper-class and middle-class families exceeds that of children from lower-class families. Such differences exist in almost all the studies, regardless of the tests and groups used. (Tests that attempt to be **culture free** produce fewer differences, but there is less evidence for the validity of this type of test.) After a comprehensive review, Tyler (1965) stated "From the early days of the intelligence-testing movement to the present, one investigator after another has reported consistent differences between the average IQs of groups at different socioeconomic levels" (p. 333). The massive Coleman Study (Coleman et al., 1966) found that children of lower socioeconomic status scored below the national averages on both verbal and nonverbal tests at all grades tested (grades 1, 3, 6, 9, and 12).

Using the father's occupation as an index of a child's social class, McNemar (1942) analyzed the standardization data for the 1937 revision of the Stanford-Binet and found the following mean IQs: professional, 115.9; managerial, 112.1; clerical, skilled trades, and small business, 107.7; farm owners, 94.8; semiskilled workers, 104.7; slightly skilled, 98.5; day laborers, 96.1. Thus, the difference between children with fathers in the highest and lowest occupational groups averaged almost 20 points. Those differences are as great for children aged 2½ to 5 as they are for teenagers. Similar findings occur on the Wechsler Intelligence Scale for Children (Seashore, Wesman, & Doppelt, 1950), which shows a mean IQ of 110.9 for children with professional or managerial fathers and a mean of 94.6 for children with rural or urban laborers or farm foremen as fathers. Here the difference is about 15 points. Differences of such magnitudes are also found in other societies and countries, including Scotland (Scottish Council for Research in Education, 1953), France (Heuyer et al., 1950), and Hawaii (Livesay, 1944). Such differences also occur within the Black U.S. population (Horton & Crump, 1962).

More recently, attention has been focused on the interaction of intelligence, motivation, and personality in specific groups differing in social class. For example, Epps (1969) measured the ability, achievement, and personality of Black high school students in the Northern and Southern U.S. Social class was assessed on the basis of the father's occupation and the mother's educational level. In all four groups (classified by sex and region) middle-class students had higher vocabulary scores than lower-class students. The correlation coefficients were all small (+.18 to +.25) but statistically significant. Of more importance is Epps's finding that social class was more strongly related to the student's "amount of expected future education" than to any other measure in the study (which included, in addition to those previously mentioned, measures of self-concept, test anxiety, self-esteem, and conformity).

C. Occupational groups and IQ

Differences in social-class level are also related to the tested IQ scores of adults. In both world wars, data from military recruits have been used to show variance in test scores according to occupation (Yerkes, 1921; Fryer, 1922; T. W. Harrell & Harrell, 1945; N. Stewart, 1947). In World War I, the highest Army Alpha means for U.S. enlisted men were obtained by engineers and accountants; in World War II, accountants,

lawyers, and engineers were highest. (Some high-ranking occupations, such as medical doctors, were not included because most of these men were commissioned officers.) In World War I the groups with the lowest average scores were miners, farm workers, and unskilled laborers; in World War II the same groups, plus the teamsters, were lowest. Such differences among occupational groups have also been found among military recruits in Sweden (Carlsson, 1955), employed adults in New York City (Simon & Leavitt, 1950), and employees of a large company in Great Britain (Foulds & Raven, 1948).

VI. The interpretation of social-class differences in intelligence

Everyone agrees that there are social-class differences in average IQ scores. Controversy centers around the causes for these differences. We will consider three possible causes: heredity, environment, and motivational and personality factors in the testing situation.

A. Heredity

Since 1870, when Sir Francis Galton's *Hereditary Genius* (1952) was first published, it has been shown that the offspring of more prominent families are more successful than other children. The hereditarian position claims that more intelligent people have more natural ability and hence have gravitated to positions of eminence. Anastasi (1958) has summarized this position: "The more intelligent individuals would gradually work their way up to the more demanding but more desirable positions, each person tending eventually to 'find his level.' Since intellectually superior parents tend to have intellectually superior offspring, the children in the higher social strata would be more intelligent, on the whole, than those from the lower social levels" (p. 521). The fact that social-class differences in tested IQs are just as great in young children (ages 2½ to 5) as they are among adolescents (ages 13 to 17) is sometimes used to buttress this hereditarian argument. It says, in effect, that despite continued differences in environment, social-class differences in tested IQ do not increase with age; therefore, the differences must not be due to environment at all, but must be caused by another factor—namely, heredity.

His strong belief in the power of heredity in determining one's level of intelligence has caused one psychologist, Richard Herrnstein (1971, 1973), to challenge a policy of zero population growth. Herrnstein makes the assumption that brighter, better-educated people would be more likely to limit voluntarily the number of children they have, thus indirectly enabling the percentage of offspring from less-educated families gradually to increase. If Herrnstein's assumption is correct and if one's genetic background does influence one's level of intelligence, the outcome would be to lower the average level of intelligence in the country. The policy implication of Herrnstein's position is that the higher one's intelligence, the greater one's obligation to breed, so that the average level of intelligence of the human species will be maintained or even increased (P. R. Ehrlich & Holdren, 1971). We believe there is no solid basis for Herrnstein's conclusions and recommendations.

There are two general limitations on the conclusion that social-class differences are primarily a result of heredity. First, all the findings reported so far in this section do not preclude the possibility that social-class differences in the early environment could have played a role. We discuss the effects of prenatal, perinatal, and early postnatal factors in the next section. Second, there are studies demonstrating that continuing to live in a poor environment leads to decreases in tested IQ as children get older (R. L. Green, 1965). Asher (1935) found that children growing up in isolated Kentucky mountain areas had a median IQ of 83.5 at age 7 and a median IQ of 60.6 at age 15. Asher attributed this huge decline to the limited social and material environment. L. R. Wheeler (1942) and Klaus and Gray (1968) also report a deterioration of IQ scores in a prolonged economically limited envi-

ronment. The devastating degree to which differences in environment affect tested IQ levels causes us to question any conclusion that heredity is all-powerful.

Nevertheless, Arthur Jensen (1968a, 1968b) has postulated that hereditary differences combine with environmental factors to affect social-class differences in intelligence. Jensen makes a distinction between Level I and Level II abilities. Level I, called *learning ability*, is assessed by rote-learning tasks, short-term-memory measures, free recall of briefly presented sets of familiar objects, and serial-learning tasks. Level II, or *intelligence*, is defined by Jensen in terms of the traditional scholastic-aptitude measures, involving vocabulary, reasoning, numerical series, and the like. Jensen repeats the common observation that lower-class children with IQs of 60 to 80 "appear to be much brighter socially, on the playground, and in generally nonscholastic types of behavior than their middle or upper-middle [class] counterparts in the same range of IQ" (1968a, p. 3). Jensen then hypothesizes that children from the two social classes do not differ in Level I abilities but do differ in Level II abilities. The data, collected on both Black and White preschool children aged 4 to 6, confirm this hypothesis. Figure 15-7 represents the relationship. Children differing in social class and in intelligence (Level II) do not differ in learning ability (Level I). The study concludes that the acquisition of learning abilities is necessary but not sufficient for the development of abilities measured by standard intelligence tests. Jensen believes that hereditary factors play a larger role in determining intelligence than in determining learning ability.

B. Environment

Environment is a many-faceted phenomenon. Consider the differences between the environments of two 8-year-old girls, both living in the same part of the United States. One lives in a prosperous suburb, while the other lives in an inner-city slum. (See Figure 15-8.) Their environments have differed markedly almost from

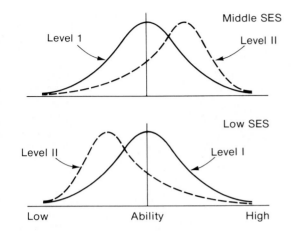

Figure 15-7
Hypothetical distributions of Level I (solid line) and
Level II (broken line) abilities in middle-class (upper
curves) and culturally disadvantaged (lower curves)
populations. (From "Patterns of Mental Ability and
Socioeconomic Status," by A. R. Jensen. Paper
presented at the Annual Meeting of the National
Academy of Sciences, Washington, D.C., April 24,
1968. Reprinted by permission of the author.)

the moment each was conceived. Probably the
mother of the child in the slums received less
extensive medical care, was less healthy, and ate
a less adequate diet while pregnant than the
mother living in the suburbs. After birth, the
slum child probably grew up in an unhealthful
environment, had fewer visits to the doctor, and
got poorer dental care than the other child. She
was probably denied the benefits of a nursery
school and possibly a kindergarten, both of
which were provided her well-to-do comparison.
Most likely, the inner-city public school is older
and has fewer up-to-date instructional materials
and a greater teacher turnover than the suburban
school. The slum child's opportunities to travel,
even within the city, are also limited.

Just how much do these numerous environmental differences affect mental development?
Contemporary thinking sees environmental factors as playing a large part in the determination
of intelligence. Intelligence is seen as "an epigen-

etic phenomenon, being limited by the structure
of the nervous system, which is, in its broad
limits, genetically determined, but free to vary
within these limits according to the adequacy of
the environment during development" (Haywood, 1967). We should look then at specific
aspects of the environment that may help determine how close a child's intelligence comes to
these limits.

Prenatal environment. We are aware that poor
nutrition in a pregnant woman can affect the
physical state of her offspring; for example,
Naeye, Diener, and Dellinger (1969) report that
the newborns of poor mothers were 15% smaller
than normal. Likewise, inadequate nutrition during pregnancy or the child's infancy can impair
the child's mental development (Eichenwald &
Fry, 1969; Kaplan, 1972). Harrell, Woodyard, and
Gates (1956) have shown that if one supplements
the diets of pregnant women with iron and with
vitamin-B complex, their offspring will have
higher IQs than the offspring of unfortified control subjects. At age 3, the mean difference in
the two groups of children was five IQ points;
at age 4 the difference had increased to eight
points. (The effect occurred only in children
whose mothers had had an extremely inadequate
diet.) Such IQ differences could be the result of
other maternal differences deriving from the fact
that the experimental-group mothers felt "special" as a result of being in the study. As it
stands, however, the study indicates that changes
in the prenatal environment may influence mental development.

Perinatal environment. Premature births, com-
plications during pregnancy and delivery, and
birth injuries are all apparently more probable
in the lower class than in the middle class (Rider,
Taback, & Knobloch, 1955; Pasamanick & Knobloch, 1960; Pettigrew, 1964). The mental abilities
of the child who survives such traumas may very
well be affected.

Early postnatal environment. The environment
during the first five years of life has always been

Figure 15-8
The nature of environmental stimulation for children growing up in the same region can vary tremendously. (Photos by Jim Pinckney.)

considered crucial. In the past two decades new theories about the effects of stimulation during infancy and early childhood have been advanced that place even greater emphasis on this period of life (Eichenwald & Fry, 1969; Korner, 1973).

Hebb (1949), for example, explored the role of *cell assemblies* of the brain in information processing. Cell assemblies grow and develop as a result of repeated sensory stimulation and later combine to form *phase sequences,* which permit the person to respond adequately to the outside world. The greater the number of these phase sequences, the greater the ability to adapt and learn. Research with animal subjects indicates that such matters as early stimulation or less restriction have effects on the rapidity of physiological growth. Specific changes have been found in adult weight and skeletal length (S. Levine, 1959), age at which adult EEG pattern emerges (Meier, 1961), and early sexual development (Morton, Denenberg, & Zarrow, 1963). As S. W. Gray (1962) indicates, one may question just how relevant animal studies on extreme restriction are

to human cultural "deprivation." It may be, however, that children of different social-class levels differ in the amount or type of sensory stimulation received in the first few years of life, leading eventually to IQ differences. Gray (1962) believes that the difference in absolute amounts of stimulation received by children of different social classes is probably not great, but there does exist a social-class difference in the range and variety of the stimuli and in the order of presentation of stimuli. (The middle-class parent, for example, is more interested than the lower-class parent in choosing toys that increase mental development—that is, lead to higher scores on IQ tests.)

J. McV. Hunt (1961, 1962) extended the usefulness of Hebb's concepts by combining them with information theory to emphasize the importance of the growing child's experience of the development of his or her own intelligence. Beginning at infancy, the child is stimulated by many objects. As his or her senses receive a variety of stimuli, they become more and more developed; perceptions are selected and refined. Yet children do not all develop in the same manner. As B. S. Bloom, Davis, and Hess have stated,

> Perceptual development is stimulated by environments which are rich in the range of experiences available; which make use of games, toys, and many objects for manipulation; and in which there is frequent interaction between the child and adults at meals, playtimes, and throughout the day.... The typical middle-class home provides a very complex environment for the child's early perceptual development, and this gives these children some advantage in the early years of school [1965, p. 12].

Hess and his associates (R. D. Hess, 1964; R. D. Hess & Shipman, 1965; Shipman & Hess, 1965) have investigated specific social-class differences that might explain IQ deficits in lower-class children. They have determined specific social-class differences in mother-child verbal interactions and how these interactions affect the child's cognitive development.

Attempts at intervention. Several recent attempts to alter the environment of lower-class children exemplify another demonstration of the role of environment in determining social-class differences in IQ scores. The Early Training Project in Tennessee (S. W. Gray & Klaus, 1965; S. W. Gray, 1969; Klaus & Gray, 1965, 1968) placed lower-class children in a ten-week preschool for either two or three summers. The children were usually 4, 5, or 6 years of age when they first participated. One experimental group attended the three summers before entering the first grade; the other attended for two summers immediately prior to entering the first grade. The experiences in the preschool were designed to stimulate the development of perceptual skills, aptitudes, language, and interest in school-related activities. In addition, during the school year, a visitor called on each child's family to encourage the use of new and different materials and to help develop greater verbal interaction in the family. The progress of the children was compared with that of two matched control groups, one of which was composed of children in the same city and one of which included children from a nearby city. Both control groups had a progressive deterioration of IQ scores over two and one-half years (averaging four to six points), while the experimental groups showed increases of five to ten points. The three-year group showed more improvement than the two-year group. Although later follow-up testing indicated some shrinkage in the extent of these IQ differences after the intervening period had ended, the early results (over a 27-month period) indicated that changes in environment produce significant changes in test performance. The differences between experimental and control groups were also found on reading-readiness tests given in the first grade. Differences in IQ were still present after the children had completed the fourth grade, although at that time there were no significant differences between experimental and control children on achievement tests or language tests (S. W. Gray & Klaus, 1970).

A different program of intervention developed by Bereiter and Engelmann (1966) has led to similar results—changes in IQs of lower-class children of about seven points on the average, over a six-month period. However, the intervention here was specifically limited to academic materials, as compared to the broader activities of the Early Training Project. Using a Bereiter-Engelmann type of intervention with children from economically depressed areas of Champaign, Illinois, Karnes (1969) has increased IQs by 14 points.[9]

The recent project claiming the greatest improvement in IQs through intervention in the environments of poor children is the "Milwaukee Project" (Heber & Garber, 1970). Certain infants

---

[9]Special intervention programs such as those described here have had greater success in changing IQ levels than has the Head Start Program. The Head Start Program suffered from too wide a variety of purposes (assessment and treatment of physical and emotional deficiencies as well as mental) and too hasty an implementation. However, in some cases it has changed children's performance on ability and achievement tests (Seidel, Barkley, & Stith, 1967).

born in the slums were selected to receive a structured program of sensory and language stimulation, in an effort to increase achievement motivation, problem-solving skills, and language development. Reports in the popular press claim increases in IQ scores of 30 points! Yet there has been no detailed published report of the procedures and findings of this study, and we must remain skeptical of its true value (E. B. Page, 1972).

C. Motivation and personality factors in the testing situation

The effects of motivation and personality on class differences in tested performance need to be examined. One of the basic beliefs held by the core of the middle class (Gruen, 1964) is that education is the portal to success. Hence the standard middle-class reaction to a testing situation is to respond with energy and effort (if not eagerness), regardless of the apparent validity or importance of the test (Wrightsman, 1960a, 1962b). This happens because the middle-class person believes to a greater degree than others do that the results of testing are an indication of educability and of the possibilities of success and achievement.

Members of the lower class adhere less adamantly to these values. R. Bell (1964) described examples of the *value stretch* present in the lower class. Some lower-class parents do have high educational aspirations for their children; at the same time, they think that 19 or 20 is a good age for their children to get married and that four or five children is a nice-sized family. Such choices are not consistent with the achievement of a college education.

Similarly, there is evidence (Rosenhan, 1966) that lower-class children are more uncomfortable and alienated than are middle-class children in such middle-class encounters as school and testing situations. Rosenhan hypothesized that as a consequence of the lower-class child's greater alienation, receiving approval would fa-

cilitate the performance of lower-class children more than that of middle-class children. Rosenhan verified his hypothesis, using a binary-choice task that probably had a strong aptitude component. Within the lower class, there were no significant differences in performance between Blacks and Whites. This indicates, in Rosenhan's judgment, that "for young children social-class differences are more potent determiners of behavior than are racial differences" (Rosenhan, 1966, p. 253). We cannot assume that lower-class children enter a testing situation with the same motivations as those of middle-class children. The performance of lower-class children in the situation may therefore misrepresent their true level of capability.

VII. A study of race and social class varied concurrently

What are the relative effects of race and social class? One of the few studies that looks at the effects of race and social class in the same children was reported by Lesser, Fifer, and Clark (1965). In a carefully designed study, 320 first-grade children in New York City were tested, with equal numbers from Puerto Rican, Chinese, Jewish, and Black ethnic groups. No attempt was made to determine the racial purity of each subject. Each ethnic group was composed of 40 boys and 40 girls, half of whom were from lower-class families and half of whom were from middle-class families. (Social class was measured by use of a variant of the Index of Status Characteristics, developed by Warner, Meeker, and Eells, 1949.) Four different types of tests were used—verbal ability, number facility, space conceptualization, and reasoning—in order to study patterns of abilities in the different groups.[10] All children were

---

[10]The tests were modifications of the Hunter College Aptitude Scales for Gifted Children (F. B. Davis, Lesser, & French, 1960). Unfortunately, this test is neither well known nor widely used.

tested individually by a trained examiner of their own ethnic group, in their own classroom. The language spoken by the examiner (English, Chinese, Yiddish, or Spanish) was the same as that spoken predominantly in the child's home. The mean scores (actually normalized standard scores with a mean of 50 and a standard deviation of 10) are presented in Table 15-3.

There are provocative findings about the interrelationships of race, ethnicity, and social class in the tabled averages. For example, social class clearly affects the level of scores: in each of the four ethnic groups, middle-class children performed significantly better than lower-class children in each of the four types of ability. Differences are almost uniform. The performance of Blacks shows a greater separation between classes than any other racial or ethnic group. The authors recognize that this may be partly a function of the children of New York City but feel the data "still suggest the strong possibility that a social-class difference will more strongly affect one's intellectual performance if he is a Negro than if he is Chinese" (D. H. Clark, Lesser, & Fifer, 1964, p. 5).

Yet the pattern of scores is much more affected by ethnicity and race than by social class. Jewish children of both classes did their best on the verbal test, while Chinese children of both classes performed better on each of the other three tests than on the verbal measure. Black children consistently did better on verbal than on numerical tests. As Anastasi (1958) predicted, "Each [group] fosters the development of a different *pattern* of abilities" (p. 563).

There are clear-cut differences among the ethnic groups in performance. Jewish and Chinese groups generally performed better than Black and Puerto Rican children. On the verbal test the rank order is Jewish, Chinese, Black, and Puerto Rican, while on the spatial tests the rank ordering is Chinese, Jewish, Puerto Rican, and Black. The direction of some ethnic-group differences depends on the type of ability measured.

A replication of this study (Stodolsky & Lesser, 1967) was conducted in Boston, using first graders from middle-class and lower-class families of Chinese, Black, and Irish-Catholic backgrounds. Results for the Chinese and Black children in Boston strongly resembled the results for

Table 15-3
Four ethnic groups by social class—Table of means*

Group	N	Class	Verbal	Reasoning	Numerical	Spatial
Jewish	40	Middle Class	62.6	56.7	59.2	56.5
	40	Lower Class	54.7	48.5	50.2	47.0
Chinese	40	Middle Class	51.2	55.9	56.0	56.7
	40	Lower Class	45.2	51.8	51.8	52.0
Negro	40	Middle Class	55.8	53.9	51.2	52.9
	40	Lower Class	44.0	41.5	39.6	40.1
Puerto Rican	40	Middle Class	47.3	48.7	49.2	49.4
	40	Lower Class	39.3	42.5	42.9	45.3

*Normalized standard scores on total groups for each test: $\overline{X} = 50$; SD = 10.

Adapted from "Mental Abilities of Young Children from Different Cultural and Social-Class Backgrounds," by D. H. Clark, G. S. Lesser, and G. Fifer. Paper presented at the meeting of the American Psychological Association, Los Angeles, September 1964. Used by permission.

these two groups in New York City. However, scores for the Irish-Catholic children demonstrated neither a distinctive ethnic-group pattern nor the usual similarity between patterns for middle-class and lower-class children from the same ethnic group.

VIII. Expectations for the future and a final caution

Conceptions of *social class* and *cultural disadvantage* are becoming increasingly unsatisfactory to many workers in the field, because of the broad nature and implied value judgments of these terms. More precise and less evaluative definitions of environments are being advocated. B. S. Bloom (1964) has reviewed attempts to measure the quality of environments and concluded that the dearth of adequate measures has led to an underemphasis on the role of environments in research and prediction. Among the characteristics of the environment that may be influen-

tial are communication and interaction with adults, motivation to understand one's environment or to achieve, types of incentives, and the availability of adult role models (Bloom, 1964, p. 188).

A more refined analysis of the environment comes from a dissertation by Wolf (1963), who proposed 13 environmental process variables that may influence the development of intelligence. These variables are listed in Table 15-4. In regard to each of these, a child's environment can be considered adequate or deprived. A *deprivation index* may be developed, based on the extent of inadequacy in regard to each of these characteristics, and this deprivation index may serve as a more precise measure of the quality of environment than does the usual measure of social class.

Wolf, in fact, found it more precise. He interviewed the mothers of 60 fifth-grade students in order to rate each child's environment on each of the 13 process variables. The multiple correlation of +.76 between these ratings and the children's IQs (on a Henmon-Nelson group

---

Table 15-4
Environmental process variables

A. Press for Achievement Motivation
  1. Nature of intellectual expectations of the child
  2. Nature of intellectual aspirations for the child
  3. Amount of information about child's intellectual development
  4. Nature of rewards for intellectual development
B. Press for Language Development
  5. Emphasis on use of language in a variety of situations
  6. Opportunities provided for enlarging vocabulary
  7. Emphasis on correctness of usage
  8. Quality of language models available
C. Provision for General Learning
  9. Opportunities provided for learning in the home
  10. Opportunities provided for learning outside the home (excluding school)
  11. Availability of learning supplies
  12. Availability of books (including reference works), periodicals, and library facilities
  13. Nature and amount of assistance provided to facilitate learning in a variety of situations

---

Adapted from "The Identification and Measurement of Environmental Process Variables Related to Intelligence," by R. M. Wolf. Unpublished doctoral dissertation, University of Chicago, 1963.

test) compares favorably with the correlations of approximately +.40 between IQ and measures of social class (such as parent's education or social status). Davé (1963) has found similar improvements in the prediction of school achievement using a conception of environmental deprivation. Bloom believes Wolf's and Davé's findings show that the influential factors are not the social-class characteristics of the parents but, rather, what the parents actually do in the home.

The nature of *overlap* is just as important in understanding social-class similarities as it is in understanding racial similarities. Although the differences in average score are large, two different social-class groups may resemble each other greatly in spread of scores. The highest and lowest IQs obtained in one group are likely to be quite similar to those of another group, even though the means may differ by 15 points or more. As an example, we may look at the studies using military recruits, which found significant test-score differences between occupational groups. The occupational group with the highest mean AGCT was the accountant group (mean = 128.1), but the range for these 172 men was 94–157 (T. W. Harrell & Harrell, 1945). The 289 electricians, whose mean AGCT score of 109.0 placed them toward the middle of the occupational hierarchy, had a range of 64–149. Thus, the highest score achieved by an electrician was only 8 points lower than the highest score of an accountant. Even the group with the lowest mean, the teamsters, had a range of 46–145. In short, we should never judge a person's level of intelligence simply on the basis of his or her occupation or social class. While these factors do produce average differences in groups, the use of a person's social class, race, or occupation as an indication of his or her ability level is unwarranted.

IX. Summary

The construct of race is technically defined either in terms of frequency of one or more genes possessed by a population (the definition preferred by geneticists and physical anthropologists) or in terms of certain physical characteristics (the definition preferred by social anthropologists and sociologists). The popular definition of race—based on skin color, self-determination, tradition, custom, and law—is vastly oversimplified, especially in its all-or-nothing character. Demonstrated race differences in tested intelligence are discussed in terms of the popular definition only because it is the one that the researchers have used.

Data derived from the U.S. Army Alpha test in World War I showed both racial and regional differences in tested intelligence. Northern Blacks performed better than southern Whites, but northern Whites performed better than northern Blacks.

The existence of differences in IQ test scores of Blacks and Whites is well documented. The controversy centers on the relationship of hereditary and environmental factors as causal agents. In our society, where racial discrimination takes varied and subtle forms, there have as yet been no adequate studies to determine whether racial differences in intelligence persist when no environmental handicaps exist.

The small differences between Blacks and Whites in tested intellectual ability and the large overlap of scores makes classification of persons into mental-ability groups on the basis of race (especially when social-class backgrounds are similar) an essentially useless exercise.

Both natural observation and intervention studies have shown that improving environmental conditions improves IQ scores. Factors such as the race of the examiner, motivation and personality of the test taker, and cultural appropriateness of the test have also been shown to affect test scores—usually to the advantage of middle-class White subjects and to the disadvantage of persons from minority groups and lower-class backgrounds.

Research findings are consistent in showing that the tested performance of children from upper- and middle-class families exceeds that of children from lower-class families. Studies of interaction of intelligence with motivation and personality within social-class groups indicate that the values and aspirations of lower-class children tend to perpetuate their position in the society.

Environmental factors, which start at the moment of conception, may determine how closely one's level of intelligence approaches the genetically predetermined limit of one's abilities. The "cultural-deprivation" hypothesis emphasizes differences in early socialization, a develop-

ing personality deficit, and a felt lack of control over one's own environment.

The concept of overlap is also important when considering social-class differences in intelligence. The spread of scores for two different classes may be very similar, and to attempt to use social class as an indication of ability is not justifiable.

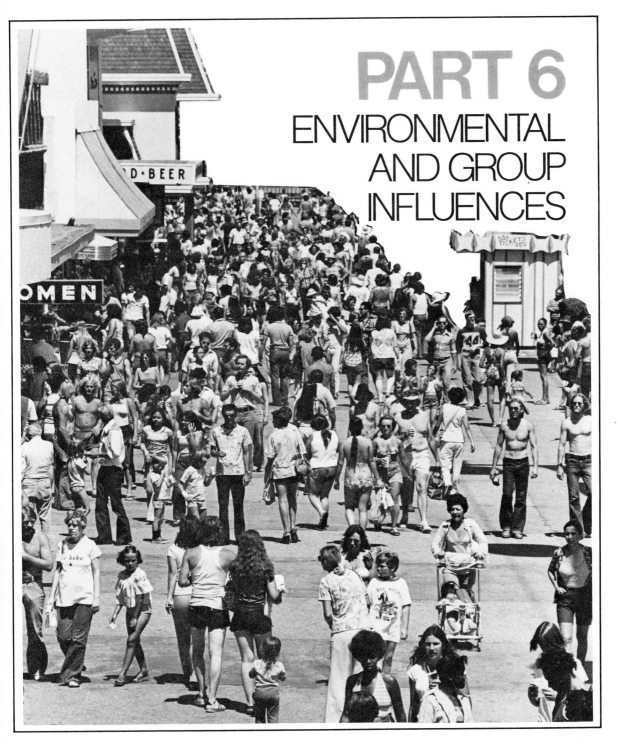

PART 6
ENVIRONMENTAL AND GROUP INFLUENCES

I. Personal space and interpersonal distance
  A. Interpersonal distance, liking, and friendship
  B. Effects of the situation
  C. Individual differences in interpersonal distance
  D. Deviations from interpersonal-distance norms
  E. Compensation for intrusion
  F. Seating patterns and social interaction

II. Territorial behavior
  A. The concept of territoriality
  B. Public territories and their defense
  C. Territoriality in confined groups
  D. Interactions in primary territories

III. Environmental determination—Effects of physical arrangements on interactions
  A. Who interacts with whom?
  B. How does the setting affect the interaction process?

IV. Crowding: Too many people, not enough space
  A. High density versus crowding
  B. Density and social pathology
  C. Crowding in the laboratory
  D. Naturalistic studies of crowding
  E. Putting the pieces together: Models of crowding

V. Summary

Interpersonal behavior and the physical environment

16

by Eric Sundstrom

We shape our buildings, and afterwards our buildings shape us.
Winston Churchill

. . . arrangements of furniture and accessory objects . . . designate and control the "where" and the "how" of interaction.
J. Ruesch and W. Kees

Social psychologists are becoming increasingly aware that physical surroundings can have a powerful impact on social behavior. They are beginning to pose many questions—for example,

What are the effects of high population density?

How do variations in architecture affect social behavior?

How do people space themselves in conversations?

To what extent do humans exhibit territorial behaviors like those observed in nonhumans?

What are the effects of heat, noise, and other stressful conditions on social behavior?

This chapter examines these and other questions concerning physical settings and interpersonal interaction. We focus primarily on human-made structures such as buildings, rooms, partitions, and furniture arrangements.

Broadly speaking, this chapter reflects common concerns of social psychology and an emerging *environmental psychology* (see Craik, 1973; Ittelson, Proshansky, Rivlin, & Winkel, 1974; Wohlwill, 1970). *Environment* means the total milieu an individual occupies, including social norms, cultural traditions, and interpersonal relationships (K. Lewin, 1954). Physical features represent only a part of the complexity of an environment—but for environmental psychology they are the central focus (see Proshansky, Ittelson, & Rivlin, 1976). This chapter emphasizes **proxemics** (E. T. Hall, 1966; Ittleson et al., 1974), which is the study of spatial behavior, including distances between people, effects of seating arrangements, choices of physical location, and other responses related to interpersonal interaction.[1]

Consistent with an **ecological perspective** (see Chapter 1), our discussion assumes a mutual relationship between person and setting. The physical environment affects interpersonal be-

[1]Research and theory on *environmental perception and cognition* appear in Ittelson (1973) and Downs and Stea (1973). For *architectural applications*, see Lang, Burnette, Moleski, and Vachon (1974). An orientation to *urban problems* is presented in Michelson (1970).

511

havior by limiting a person's behavioral choices (see Proshansky, Ittelson, & Rivlin, 1970b). But within those limits, individuals actively use their settings to meet their goals. These points are illustrated in a disturbing example: the Pruitt-Igoe housing project (see Figure 16-1). Built in 1955 in St. Louis, Missouri, this urban-renewal project created 33 high-rise apartment buildings, each 11 stories tall, available as housing for low-income families (Newman, 1973). The buildings were placed on open grounds; there were about 50 dwelling units per acre. In all, there were 2764 attractive but austere apartments. But despite optimistic publicity, the project was a miserable failure. After two to three years the buildings were physical wrecks, with broken windows, cluttered hallways, urine-stained stairwells, and other signs of neglect and decay. The buildings harbored criminals and juvenile delinquents; vacancy rates rose to about 70%. The project was so unsuccessful that in 1976 the city contracted to tear down the last of the buildings. Research done after the fact suggested that the project failed in part because the design of the buildings prevented residents from interacting with each other as they had in the slum tenancies. When slum residents lived in two- and three-story buildings, they could easily supervise their children playing in the streets below. The height of the Pruitt-Igoe buildings discouraged such supervision and provided stairwells where mischievous children could avoid being seen. Slum tenants had also spent a great deal of time talking with neighbors—on porches, across back fences, in alleys, and in other places

Figure 16-1

The Pruitt-Igoe housing project in St. Louis provided modern apartments for low-income families—but the high-rise buildings were plagued with vacancy and vandalism. The apartments seemed to discourage residents from continuing their previous habits of interpersonal interaction. The few spaces designed for informal interactions, such as the galleries pictured on the left, were dissociated from the apartments. The open doors lead to what were laundry rooms. (Photos reprinted with permission of Macmillan Publishing Company, Inc., and The Architectural Press, Ltd., London, from *Defensible Space*, by O. Newman. Copyright © 1972, 1973 by Oscar Newman.)

near their residences. The Pruitt-Igoe buildings had bare, narrow corridors; there were few places near the apartments for informal interaction. As a consequence, Pruitt-Igoe residents reported feelings of isolation (Yancey, 1971).

Because of the give-and-take relationship between people and environments, this chapter is organized around two questions: (1) How do we use our physical surroundings as we interact? (2) How does a physical setting influence interpersonal behavior? As we examine these questions, one assumption about human nature recurs again and again: human transactions with settings and with people follow a *homeostatic principle*. That is, people seem to seek an optimal amount of stimulation from the environment—not too much and not too little (Helson, 1964; Wohlwill, 1974). In an experiment that illustrates the principle, people indicated their preferences among pictures of landscapes and urban areas that varied in complexity. They preferred moderately complex pictures over simple or extremely complex ones (Wohlwill, 1968). A similar process applies to social interaction. People seem to seek optimal amounts of psychological closeness to others and interaction with others (Altman, 1975; Argyle & Dean, 1965; Wohlwill, 1974). What is optimal depends on a variety of things, but when people experience too much or too little of the contact they desire with others, they feel uncomfortable. People actively attempt to achieve their desired level of social interaction by the ways they locate themselves in their settings and the ways they use and arrange their settings. For example, the residents of Pruitt-Igoe felt isolated—they achieved too little interaction with neighbors. Hence, many moved someplace else.

We turn first to the question of individual use of physical settings in regulating interactions. We approach it by examining two concepts: (1) **personal space,** which refers to our optimal physical distance from other people within a setting, and (2) **territoriality,** which refers to our use and control of places.

I. Personal space and interpersonal distance

According to Robert Sommer, a pioneer in research on physical settings, *personal space* is:

> an area with invisible boundaries surrounding a person's body into which intruders may not come. Like the porcupines in Schopenhauer's fable, people like to be close enough to obtain warmth and comradeship, but far enough away to avoid pricking one another [1969, p. 26].

Research on personal space explores two questions: (1) What factors affect interpersonal distance? (2) What happens when people do not achieve the spacing they desire?

Some of the most influential observations concerning interpersonal distance were made by an anthropologist, Edward Hall (1959, 1963, 1966). He described a typical scene as two people talk:

> If one person gets too close, the reaction is instantaneous and automatic—the other person backs up . . . I have observed an American backing up the entire length of a corridor while a foreigner whom he considers pushy tries to catch up with him [1959, p. 160].

Hall observed that Latin Americans and Arabs seem to prefer closer proximity and more touching than North Americans, while the English seem to prefer larger distances.[2] Because physical closeness signifies friendliness, Hall noted that members of different societies might misunderstand one another. A Latin American may think a Canadian is cold and withdrawn, while the Canadian sees aggressiveness and intrusiveness in the Latin American's actions. Actually, both people are trying to find a comfortable distance.

In an attempt to summarize the meanings of different interpersonal distances in the United

---

[2]Reviews of cross-cultural differences appear in Altman (1975) and in Evans and Howard (1973).

States, Hall (1966) proposed a series of *distance zones* for different kinds of interactions (see Figure 16-2). The closest zone, called the *intimate zone*, ranges from touching to 1½ feet (about ½ meter). This distance is for encounters such as "love-making and wrestling, comforting and protecting" (p. 177). In the intimate zone

> the presence of the other person is unmistakable . . . because of greatly stepped-up sensory inputs. Sight (often distorted), olfaction, heat from the other person's body, sound, smell, and the feel of the breath all combine to signal unmistakable involvement with another body [p. 116].

Cues are thus exchanged through several sense modalities at close distances. Distance regulates the degree of mutual stimulation between people; the closer they are, the more cues they exchange.

Hall noted that close proximity is sometimes forced on us at times when we do not want intimate contact—for example, on a crowded subway platform. We may feel uncomfortable, stand rigidly with our arms at our sides, and gaze into space in an attempt to minimize such a deviation from distance norms.

A second zone, the *personal-distance zone*, extends from 1½ to 4 feet (about ½ to 1¼ meters) and refers to the "protective sphere or bubble" a person maintains around himself or herself. Close distances within this zone are usually reserved for close friends or intimates. Larger dis-

Figure 16-2
Edward Hall (1966) observed that interaction distances depend on the situation and the interpersonal relationship. *Intimate* distance (touching to 18 inches) is pictured at the left. *Personal* distance (1½ to 4 feet) is for everyday interactions among friends or acquaintances. *Social* distance (4 to 12 feet) occurs when people talk about formal or business matters. *Public* distance (12 to 25 feet), shown at the left, is for public addresses. (Photos by Jim Pinckney.)

tances (2½ to 4 feet) are for everyday conversations.

The *social zone* ranges from 4 to 12 feet (about 1¼ to 3½ meters) and is used for business interactions. Voices remain at normal levels, audible at 20 feet. You might expect two office workers, a customer and a sales clerk, or a teacher and student to use the social distance.

Finally, Hall (1966) defined a *public zone* between 12 and 25 feet (about 3½ to 7½ meters) for formal interactions, conversations with important figures, or public addresses. These four distances—intimate, personal, social, and public—each reflect a different interpersonal situation, defined by the formality of the interaction and by the relationship of the interacting pair. The distances also involve varying degrees of sensory stimulation; the greater the proximity, the greater the sensory exchange. We can summarize by saying that interpersonal distance serves two functions: (1) communication about interpersonal relationships and (2) regulation of sensory input. These two features of distance reflect the *immediacy* between people (Mehrabian, 1972), or their psychological closeness. But what factors affect the distances people choose? The following sections discuss three such factors: (1) liking, (2) the situation, and (3) individual characteristics.

A. Interpersonal distance, liking, and friendship

Hall's distance zones must be regarded as tentative, pending further research. However, his observation that friends or relatives adopt closer distances than strangers has received good empirical support. For example, in a field study on distance and interpersonal relationships, F. N. Willis (1966) asked students on a college campus to begin a conversation with either an acquaintance they did not know by name, a friend, or a close friend. As soon as a subject began to talk, an observer measured the face-to-face distance between the two persons with a tape measure. Results indicated that women adopted smaller

distances with close friends than men did, and men tended to keep about the same approach distance regardless of the relationship. Women displayed smaller conversation distances with close friends than with others; men's distances tended to be relatively unresponsive to the nature of the relationship.

Closer distance between friends is not limited to one side of the Atlantic, as Heshka and Nelson (1972) found in a similar study in London. They photographed pairs of conversing adults and asked them to describe their relationship. Strangers stood farther apart than acquaintances, good friends, or relatives. But the differences in distances as a function of relationship occurred with male-female pairs and female-female pairs, not with male-male pairs. A field study in South Africa reported similar findings (D. J. A. Edwards, 1972). There is also evidence (reviewed by Sundstrom & Altman, 1976) that people place miniature figures described as friends closer together than figures described as strangers. In summary, it appears that friends prefer closer proximity than strangers or acquaintances, provided one or both of them is female.

Proximity also seems to signal *liking*. For example, Byrne, Ervin, and Lamberth (1970) formed couples of male and female students for a study of "computer dating." Couples had either similar or dissimilar attitudes, as they soon discovered when they went on a short "Coke date." Those with similar attitudes liked each other better, consistent with the similarity-attraction hypothesis described in Chapter 5. While couples stood in front of the experimenter's desk for an interview, he surreptitiously recorded their distance from each other. As expected, the more the partners liked each other, the closer they stood. In another study, junior high school students who reported liking one another sat closer together (Aiello & Cooper, 1972). In an experimental test of the idea that proximity signals liking, Rosenfeld (1965) asked students to talk with another person, actually a confederate. Subjects were to "appear friendly" and seek approval, or to avoid being friendly. Approval-seeking subjects put their chairs an average of 4.75 feet from the confederate, compared with 7.34 feet for the approval-avoiding subjects. Other role-playing studies report similar findings (Mehrabian, 1968a, 1968b). While these subjects may have reacted more extremely in the laboratory than in everyday conversation, their responses do suggest that proximity reflects degree of liking.

B. Effects of the situation

Although we note few research findings on the effects of situations on interpersonal distance, common sense tells us they are important. For example, formal occasions such as receptions and ceremonies may call for relatively large distances (Hall, 1966; Little, 1965). Similarly, the *intimacy* of a pair's conversation topic may influence their distance—they may move closer and speak softly to avoid being overheard. The size of the room can also be important; for example, people in a crowded bar may be forced to sit closer to others than they like. However, we have evidence that people in a corner of a room prefer larger distances than do people in the center of a room (Dabbs, Fuller, & Carr, 1973).

Another situational feature that seems to influence distance is whether two people are seated or standing. Sommer (1962) asked pairs of subjects to sit and talk in a room that contained two pairs of facing chairs placed so that they formed the corners of a rectangle. Side-by-side and face-to-face distances varied from one to five feet. Subjects generally chose face-to-face seating, but when the facing chairs were less than three feet apart subjects usually sat beside one another. The closest comfortable face-to-face distance allowed about 5½ feet from face to face. Subjects also chose adjacent seating if the side-by-side distance was smaller than the face-to-face distance. From this study, we can tentatively conclude that comfortable seated distance is around five to six feet for face-to-face conversa-

tions, and somewhat less for side-by-side arrangements.

C. Individual differences in interpersonal distance

We have seen that males prefer larger interpersonal distances than females (F. N. Willis, 1966). People also tend to stay farther away from males than from females (Altman, 1975). In studies of conversation, female-female pairs adopt closer positions than male-male pairs (D. J. A. Edwards, 1972; Mehrabian & Diamond, 1971b). Interpersonal distance also varies with age; children have small personal space zones that increase up until their teens (Aiello & Aiello, 1974; G. H. Price & Dabbs, 1974).

Personality dispositions toward large psychological distances from others seem to involve large physical distances as well, though the evidence is not completely consistent. For example, *introversion* has been associated with large physical distances (M. Cook, 1970; Leipold, 1963; Patterson & Holmes, 1966; Patterson & Sechrest, 1970), but some researchers have not found the relationship (Meisels & Canter, 1970; E. Porter, Argyle, and Salter, 1970). Also, several researchers have found high amounts of *anxiety* associated with large interpersonal distances (Bailey, Hartnett, & Gibson, 1972; Luft, 1966; Patterson, 1973b).

As you might expect, personality disorder tends to be accompanied by abnormal patterns of interpersonal distance. For example, Horowitz, Duff, and Stratton (1964) reported that hospitalized schizophrenics preferred larger personal-space zones than nonpatients, although the schizophrenics showed greater variability in required distances than nonpatients. There is also evidence indicating that individuals have larger personal-space requirements when with someone who has a visible handicap or an alleged personality problem (Kleck, Buck, Goller, London, Pfeiffer, & Vukcevic, 1968; Worthington, 1974).

Individual differences also stem from a person's *subculture*. Within the U.S., researchers have compared Whites with Blacks, Puerto Ricans, Chicanos, and other groups. Although many group differences have emerged, they have been inconsistent—sometimes pairs of Blacks have shown larger distances than pairs of Whites, sometimes smaller, depending on age, sex, and setting (Altman, 1975). One explanation of subcultural differences in distance is based on *socioeconomic status:* members of some ethnic groups are poor and live in crowded conditions; by adapting to such conditions, they may become accustomed to high levels of interpersonal stimulation and prefer smaller distances. A naturalistic study on this idea (Scherer, 1974) observed first- through fourth-grade children on a school playground and recorded their conversation distances. There were no differences between Black and White children from low socioeconomic-status groups, but both Black and White middle-class children showed larger distances than the poorer children (although only the difference for the middle-class Whites was significant). These findings suggest that we can better understand subcultural differences in interpersonal distance by recognizing the effects of socioeconomic differences.

In summary, we can say that the optimal distance between two people depends on their relationship, the degree of liking, the situation, and individual and socioeconomic differences. These factors, in effect, set *norms* regarding "proper" distance. The next question is, what happens when distance norms are violated?

D. Deviations from interpersonal-distance norms

A violation of distance norms occurs when people space themselves closer or farther apart than their situation dictates. It would be a norm violation to sit only six inches away from someone on a bench at a bus stop unless conditions were crowded; it would be impolite to talk with a friend from ten feet when it is possible to get closer.

Research on violation of space norms has concentrated on two situations: (1) In *personal-space invasions* an experimenter deliberately sits or stands inappropriately close to a stranger without saying anything, usually in an uncrowded situation. (2) In what we shall call an *intrusion,* two people are talking and one adopts an uncomfortably close position. The difference is that in the personal-space invasion, the invader has no apparent intention of talking with the subject.

1. Reactions to personal-space invasions. Felipe and Sommer (1966) conducted an experiment in which subjects were female university students studying alone in a library at rectangular tables (four chairs on each side). In an "invasion," a female experimenter sat in the chair immediately beside the subject, leaving a shoulder-to-shoulder distance of 12 inches. Recall that the intimate-distance zone is about 18 inches, so this is highly irregular behavior for a stranger. If the subject moved away, the invader moved to maintain the original distance. Students who were not "invaded" served as a control group. "Invaded" subjects left their chairs more quickly; after 30 minutes only 30% of the "invaded" group remained, compared with 87% of the control subjects. Besides leaving the scene, "invaded" subjects showed signs of discomfort.

> Frequently an S [subject] drew in her arm and head, turned away from E [the experimenter] exposing her shoulder and back, with her elbow on the table, her face resting on her hand. The victims used objects including books, notebooks, purses, and coats as barriers [Felipe & Sommer, 1966, p. 213].

Besides reacting to invasions with signs of discomfort (Patterson, Mullens, & Romano, 1971), people may simply "freeze" or decrease motor activities (Mahoney, 1974). These reactions might have been expected, as the invader violated spatial norms with no apparent reason.

Other studies of personal-space invasion suggest that under some conditions, male invaders generate faster flight than female invaders (Dabbs, 1972); well-dressed invaders produce faster flight than casually dressed ones (Barash,

1973); females react more negatively to side-by-side invasions, whereas males react more negatively to face-to-face invasions (J. D. Fisher & Byrne, 1975).

Other evidence indicates that people tend to avoid invading the personal space of others if they possibly can. For example, when someone is standing a foot away from a water fountain, people use it less frequently than if someone is standing five feet away (Barefoot, Hoople, & McClay, 1972; Baum, Riess, & O'Hara, 1974). Invasions are apparently uncomfortable not only for the recipient but for the invader as well.

2. Reactions to intrusion. As you might expect, intrusions during conversation make people uncomfortable, and they try to increase the physical or psychological distance. But flight is unlikely. In one experiment, subjects worked on a projective test, seated beside an experimenter who either adopted a comfortable distance or sat only six inches away. Test scores showed more anxiety at six inches (J. C. Baxter & Deanovich, 1970). Another experiment found evidence of physiological arousal at close proximity (McBride, King, & James, 1965). There is also evidence that an intrusion by a dissimilar person is more distressing than an intrusion by someone with similar views (Fisher, 1974). Another experiment asked students to stand and talk with an accomplice who maintained a distance of either 34 or 22 inches. At the close proximity, subjects backed away—10 inches in six minutes, compared with 2 inches starting at the moderate distance (McDowell, 1972). Instead of leaving the scene, these subjects simply compensated for the intrusion by adjusting their distance, like the diplomat from England talking to the diplomat from Latin America (Hall, 1959).

E. Compensation for intrusion

We have seen that the optimal distance between people depends on their relationship. Deviations from optimal distance are uncomfortable, and people attempt to compensate. In other words, distance operates on a *homeostatic principle.* A theory based on this principle (Argyle & Dean, 1965) proposed that the psychological closeness or intimacy between two people is indicated by proximity, eye contact, intimate topics of conversation, and smiling. Other signs of closeness include facing others directly (direct body orientation) and leaning toward them. Together, these *immediacy behaviors* regulate the mutual sensory stimulation between two persons and indicate a positive attitude (Mehrabian, 1972, p. 6).

According to Argyle and Dean's theory, as two people talk they maintain what they judge to be an appropriate level of intimacy by monitoring and adjusting signals of closeness. The theory predicts that when one cue reflects greater intimacy than actually characterizes the relationship, other cues are reduced. For example, when people are physically too close, they decrease their eye contact. In a test of this prediction, subjects talked with a confederate at varying distances in a room where the conversation could be observed through a one-way mirror. Their chairs were placed at a 90° angle next to a rectangular table; chairs were two, six, or ten feet apart. Observers behind the one-way mirror looked over the confederate's shoulder to record the amount of eye contact as the confederate and subject talked for three minutes at each distance. Results (shown in Figure 16-3) indicate less eye contact at two feet than at six or ten feet, measured in both total duration and average length of each glance. The effect of closeness was most pronounced in male-female pairs.[3]

---

[3]Argyle and Dean's experiment has been replicated (Argyle & Ingham, 1972; Goldberg, Kiesler, & Collins, 1969), but it has been criticized on methodological grounds. One experiment (Stephenson & Rutter, 1970) found that when observers record the presence of eye contact, they are more likely to mistakenly record eye contact as distance increases. Aiello (1972) corrected the flaw in Argyle and Dean's method, and found the predicted inverse relationship between distance and eye contact only for males. Females tended to show high levels of eye contact at intermediate distance (six feet) and low levels at either close or far distances, suggesting that their optimal level of contact is closer than the optimal level for males.

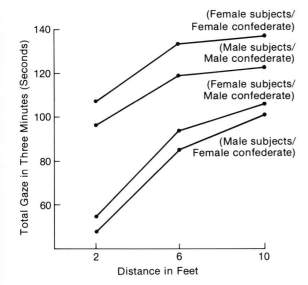

Figure 16-3
Relationship between eye contact and distance (from Argyle & Dean, 1965, p. 300). At close proximity, subjects spent less time in eye contact, illustrating the homeostatic model of interpersonal distance: when people find themselves too close, they compensate by reducing other signals of immediacy, such as eye contact and directness of body orientation. (From "Eye-Contact, Distance and Affiliation," by M. Argyle and J. Dean, *Sociometry*, 1965, *28*, 289–304. Copyright 1965 by the American Sociological Association. Reprinted by permission.)

These results support the idea that people regulate their psychological closeness to attain an optimal level of *immediacy* with another person—an idea that stimulated considerable research by social psychologists. A review of this work (Patterson, 1973a) found moderate support for the proposed relationship between distance and eye contact; other recent research provides additional support (Argyle & Ingham, 1972; Patterson 1973b; Russo, 1975). Three out of four studies reported that subjects compensated for close proximity by leaning backward. And all 11 of the studies that reported data on distance and body orientation found that close prox-

imity was associated with indirect body orientation (see also Patterson, 1973b). The basic principle seems to have good empirical support; people regulate their degree of immediacy, and if one cue indicates too much closeness, others are adjusted.

We also have evidence that an excessively *large* distance is uncomfortable. When subjects are shown pictures of people talking at different distances, they rate the largest distances as most uncomfortable (Dinges & Oetting, 1972; Haase, 1970).

In summary, the concept of a *homeostatic mechanism* seems to explain the data on intrusion and compensation. People seem to seek an *optimal interpersonal distance*, characterized by a desirable degree of psychological closeness. When people are too close, they are uncomfortable and adjust their distance—or they adjust some other indicator of immediacy such as body orientation or eye contact. Optimal distance seems to be small for friends (smaller if one or both are female), and may shrink or expand depending on the situation, the topic of conversation, and other factors. However, in *personal-space invasions*, where the invader does not talk with the recipient, such compensation for invasions may not be effective in reducing discomfort; the typical reaction is flight. Here we see a failure of the homeostatic mechanism, perhaps brought on by the unpredictability of a person who voicelessly violates spatial norms with no apparent reason (see Figure 16-4).

F. Seating patterns and social interaction

Just as interpersonal distance regulates the psychological closeness between people, so does their choice of seating arrangements. A personnel interviewer talking to a prospective employee may sit behind a desk, controlling their distance, their body orientation, and the presence of barriers between them.

In an attempt to discover where people sit during conversations, Sommer (1959) observed

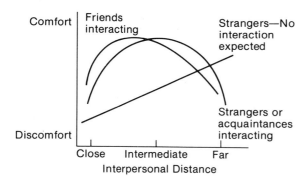

Figure 16-4
Comfort and discomfort as a function of
interpersonal distance and the interaction situation.
For conversation with strangers or acquaintances,
there is an *optimal distance*; deviations from it may
produce discomfort. For interacting friends, the
optimal distance appears to be smaller. Other factors
can also influence the optimal distance if the pair
contains one or more females. The situation in which
strangers do not expect to interact represents a
personal-space invasion, which produces extreme
discomfort and eventual flight. (From "Personal
Space and Interpersonal Relationships: Research
Review and Theoretical Model," by E. Sundstrom
and I. Altman, *Human Ecology*, 1976, 4, 47–67.
Copyright 1976 by Plenum Publishing Corporation,
Inc. Reprinted by permission.)

hospital staff members at a hospital cafeteria as
they ate lunch at rectangular tables. Among pairs
who were talking, 73% sat in neighboring chairs,
most of them in corner-to-corner arrangements,
at a 90° angle. When Sommer later asked pairs
of people to discuss an assigned topic, most
chose the corner-to-corner arrangement, perhaps
because the 90° seating allows a choice of
whether or not to make eye-contact.

Another question concerns the seating positions for specific *kinds* of interactions. Sommer
(1965) asked psychology students to fill out a
questionnaire on seating arrangements at a rectangular table for four kinds of interpersonal
behavior: casual *conversation*; *cooperation* on the
same task; *coaction*, or working on different tasks;

and *competition*, or working on the same task with
the goal of outperforming the other person. Subjects again preferred 90° seating for conversation. They preferred side-by-side arrangements
for cooperation, distant but nonfacing seats for
coaction, and face-to-face seating for competition
(see also Cook, 1970). Other research shows that
when a person wants privacy in a public place,
he or she faces away from others and maximizes
the distance from them (Sommer, 1969). In general, it seems that people regulate their seating
patterns in accordance with the kind of interaction they desire.

Seating arrangements may be associated
with leadership in a group. According to a prevalent cultural norm, leaders usually sit at the
"head" of a table. For example, when corporate
boards of directors meet at rectangular or oblong
tables, the chairperson of the board often sits
at one end. But why should leaders or dominant
individuals choose such a position? In one early
study, people in a group directed their comments
to others who were most visible to them—those
directly across the table (Steinzor, 1950). Because
the person at the end of a table is most visible
to everyone in the group, he or she should participate in more interactions than other group
members; and high participation seems to be associated with leadership (see Chapter 20). It appears that (1) sitting at the head of a table predis-
poses a person toward leadership, and (2) a person who wants to achieve leadership in a group
ought to sit at the head of the table.

In a simulation study related to these ideas,
Strodtbeck and Hook (1961) used 12-person jury
deliberations, and asked subjects to elect forepersons. The "juries" sat at rectangular tables with
five chairs on each long side and one at each
end. Subjects at the ends of the table were elected
more often than occupants of other positions.
Furthermore, people in end positions were rated
more influential, and participated more in group
discussions. Altemeyer and Jones (1972) reported
similar results in another study of group discussions. We do not know if dominant people chose

end positions or the end positions facilitate leadership. But it appears that the choice of seating position is associated with leadership.

The idea that we address those whom we face directly in group discussions also applies in the classroom. Sommer (1967) observed students in seminars; those facing the instructor participated in class discussion more than other students. Similarly, in rooms with chairs arranged in fixed rows, students in the front rows and in the middle sections of the classroom participated most (see Figure 16-5). More recently, Sommer (1974) found that students' grades in a class followed a similar pattern: the best-performing students sat in the front and middle sections of the room. We can explain such data two ways: (1) students directly facing the instructor are relatively likely to participate, and (2) students who do well in a class may choose "high participation" seats. Not only do we use our locations within a setting to regulate interactions, but to some extent our locations may influence our behavior. (We take up the issue of environmental influences on behavior in a later section.) Next we turn to another facet of our use of physical settings to regulate interaction: territoriality.

II. Territorial behavior

You are probably familiar with signs that say "no trespassing" or "private—keep out." Even in an unpopulated area you might hesitate to pass a "private property" sign and walk onto someone else's land. Signs represent just one way to mark *territories*, or geographical areas and physical places that people think of as "theirs." In contrast to personal space, *territories* refers to fixed geographical regions, not to the distance between individuals. (Personal space may be seen as a kind of portable territory.) In this section, we examine the concept of territoriality as it originated in studies of nonhuman species and as it applies to human behavior.

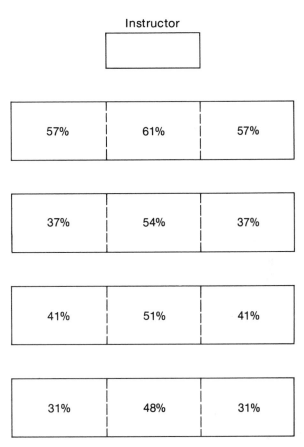

Figure 16-5
Classroom participation as a function of seating positions (from Sommer, 1967, p. 500). Note that students who tended to participate most were seated in the front row or in the center sections of the room. These students were relatively likely to make eye contact with the instructor. Students who sit in these seats may also obtain better grades (Sommer, 1974), but we do not know whether students who want to participate choose their seats in areas of high participation or whether the seating position influences participation. (Reproduced by special permission from "Classroom Ecology," by R. Sommer, *Journal of Applied Behavioral Science*, 1967, 3(4), 489-503. Copyright 1967 by NTL Institute Publications.)

A. The concept of territoriality

1. Territories among nonhumans. In ethologists' terms (for example, E. Howard, 1920), a *territory* is a specific geographical region that an animal marks with calls, scents, or other signs. The animal uses its territory as a nesting place and base for hunting or foraging. If an animal of the same species intrudes, a conflict may ensue, along with threatening gestures or a fight. The intruder usually retreats (Carpenter, 1958). However, as you read in Chapter 7, not all species are territorial, and not all territorial species follow the same instinctive patterns of behavior.

An example of a territorial species is the stickleback, a small freshwater fish of Europe. A famous ethologist, Niko Tinbergen (1952), described its behavior. Every spring the male establishes a circle-shaped territory on the bottom of a pond. He drives off all intruders as he builds a nest; his nondescript gray coloring changes; red and blue markings signal his readiness for mating. When a female stickleback passes, swollen with eggs, the male attracts her to the nest through a ritualized mating ceremony. He nudges at her, and she eventually deposits her eggs in the nest; the male fertilizes them and drives her away. He remains with the nest, defending the eggs until they hatch and protecting the young fish until they can fend for themselves. The male stickleback's territory is seasonal. Other species, including some primates, rove over a *home range*, nesting in different locations within an area with more or less definite boundaries. For example, howler monkeys travel in troops over home ranges of several acres. When troops meet, they howl (these monkeys have a formidable howl!) until one troop retreats (Carpenter, 1934).

Territoriality apparently serves a variety of survival functions for a species. For example, territoriality produces an even dispersion of animals over a habitat, which ensures that it is not overgrazed or overhunted. Carpenter (1958) listed 32 functions of territoriality associated with such things as nesting, caring for the young, feeding, and propagation. Several writers also observed links between territoriality and social organization (Leyhausen, 1965; Sommer, 1969; Wynne-Edwards, 1962). For example, as was noted in Chapter 7, territoriality serves to keep solitary animals separated from one another so that aggression is minimized. In some species, dominant animals have relatively large territories; dominant males also have greater access to females. Such an allocation of resources ensures reproduction of the fittest animals. Leyhausen (1965) observed that domestic cats have territories *and* home ranges. When two cats meet outside their territories, the lower-ranked animal tends to retreat, usually without a fight. An animal within its own territory, however, nearly always drives away other animals, even those higher in the dominance hierarchy. Such *territorial dominance* allows even a low-ranked animal to maintain a territory, although it will have only limited access to other areas. Territoriality and dominance can thus provide complementary bases for social organization.

Some writers with an ethological orientation (Ardrey, 1966; Lorenz, 1966) suggest that humans, like many other species, are territorial, and that part of human aggressiveness stems from responses to invasion of territories. But while humans do seem to form attachments to places, we think that direct generalization from nonhuman territoriality to human behavior is inappropriate for several reasons (Sundstrom & Altman, 1972): (1) While nonhuman territoriality is highly *stereotypic*, humans show variability in their use of space, suggesting that for them it is learned behavior. (2) Overt hostility in response to invasion of territory appears infrequent among humans—instead, they react to intrusion with verbal exchanges, nonverbal gestures such as staring out of a window at intruders in a yard, and even recourse to legal authority. (3) Territories supply biological necessities for nonhuman animals, whereas humans claim spaces for recreation and vocation as well. (4) Nonhuman animals typically have a single territory at a given time, whereas humans often maintain territories in different places (for example, home and office). (5) Although many other animals show exclusive use of spaces, humans take turns using such places as restaurant tables and public restrooms. Furthermore, if humans are territorial, they are unique in their habit of routinely entertaining visitors without hostilities (Edney, 1974). We clearly cannot take for granted that observations of nonhuman territoriality generalize to humans. However, the territory concept provides many hypotheses regarding human use of space.

2. Human territorial behavior. Our use of physical settings is complex; we own or rent homes or apartments, we work in prescribed places at offices or factories, we temporarily use tables at restaurants and libraries, and so on. Some theorists (Goffman, 1971; Lyman & Scott, 1967) have suggested that humans have different kinds of territories; for example, Altman (1975) distinguishes three types of territories: primary, secondary, and public. **Primary territories** are "owned and exclusively used by individuals or groups, are clearly identified as theirs, are controlled on a relatively permanent basis, and are central to the day to day lives of the occupants" (p. 112). Examples of primary territories include homes, apartments, dormitory rooms, and sometimes offices. (Offices may not always qualify as territories—Sommer [1974] noted that some companies forbid employees to decorate their offices with furniture, pictures, rugs, drapes, or other personal items.)

Among the distinguishing features of primary territories are *centrality* to a person's life and relatively *long-term* usage. Primary territories also tend to be filled with objects, decorated, and *personalized* by the occupants—they may be central to a person's identity. In primary territories people have a high degree of *control* over access by others, and visits from others without permission are serious affronts, if not offenses against the law.

Secondary territories are "less central, pervasive, and exclusive, and the term parallels the distinction between primary and secondary groups" (Altman, 1975, p. 114). Secondary territories are used regularly by a specific group of people, who have only limited control over access to the place by others. One example is the neighborhood bar, where regular users sometimes glare at "outsiders" and make hostile remarks (Cavan, 1963). Other examples include country clubs, small coffee shops, neighborhood churches, and classrooms. A distinguishing feature of a secondary territory is the ability of regular users to distinguish outsiders.

Public territories are established in spaces available to many people on a temporary basis, such as tables at libraries, spaces on benches, chairs in coffee shops, and seats on cross-country buses. Such areas "are open to all, but certain images and expectations of appropriate behavior" modify freedom of action and determine who can use these places (Lyman & Scott, 1967, p. 237). For example, restaurant managers typically do not allow brown bag lunches; some restaurants refuse to serve men unless they are wearing coats and ties.

Another kind of territory is an **interaction territory,** or group space,[4] the area around two or more people as they talk. Analogous to "personal space," these areas are like bubbles around groups that last as long as conversation continues.

Research on group spaces (Cheyne & Efran, 1972; Efran & Cheyne, 1972, 1973, 1974; Knowles, 1972, 1973) suggests the following: (1) Groups actively maintain the boundaries of their group spaces against intrusion by outsiders. (2) People are reluctant to invade a group space; if

[4]Lyman and Scott (1967) defined *interactional territory* as a kind of territory. Altman (1975) also categorized it as a territory but sometimes referred to it as a group personal space. Because the concept is not tied to a specific region but instead refers to the arrangement of a group of people, we prefer the term *group space*.

they do intrude, they show signs of discomfort and submissiveness. (3) The "permeability" of a group space depends on several factors; for example, the likelihood of intrusion decreases as group size and status increase, and male-female pairs are less likely to be invaded than same-sex pairs.

We can say that *human territoriality* is characterized by *the perception that a specific area or space is under the control of its occupants*. The space may be used on a long-term basis or very briefly; it may be personalized or free from identifying objects; its boundaries may be marked by walls and doors or by tacit agreement; and it may be used often or infrequently. The amount of control an occupant has depends on many factors, especially ownership and accessibility to others.[5]

The functions of human territoriality appear as complex as its definition. Two have been suggested: (1) control over interactions (Altman, 1975) and (2) organization of interpersonal behavior (Edney, 1976). We shall examine each in turn.

According to a theory proposed by Irwin Altman (1975), territorial behavior is one of several mechanisms by which people attain an optimal amount of *privacy*, defined as "selective control of access to the self or one's group" by other people (p. 18). Privacy includes our control over *inputs* from others—such as seeing them, hearing their voices, or hearing their activities—and over our *outputs*, or the information we transmit or leak to others.[6] Territoriality helps to maintain control over interactions—or privacy—through use of physical barriers such as doors and curtains (see Figure 16-6); through symbolic barriers such as "keep out" signs; and through tacit, shared agreements about a per-

"HELLO, I'M TAKING A POLL ON HOW PEOPLE FEEL ABOUT INVASION OF THEIR PRIVACY..."

Figure 16-6
Dunagin's People, by Ralph Dunagin, courtesy of Field Newspaper Syndicate.

son's or group's right to a place. For example, professors can open or close the doors of their offices depending upon their desire for privacy, and they may use a "faculty" washroom designated with a sign.

The idea that territorial behavior assists in maintaining desired privacy supports our assumption about the homeostatic nature of human interaction, which is based on the idea that at any given time we seek an optimal level of social stimulation. Altman described the process this way:

> If I desire a lot of interaction with another person and get only a little then I feel lonely, isolated or cut off. And if I actually receive more

---

[5]We are territorial about objects, people, and even ideas (Altman, 1975).

[6]One intriguing aspect of privacy concerns the collection of personal data by government agencies and private credit bureaus. Such intelligence activities can abridge our ability to control the transmission and use of information about ourselves, reducing our privacy (see Chapter 18).

interaction than I originally desired then I feel intruded upon, crowded, or overloaded. But what is too much, too little, or ideal shifts with time and circumstances. What is too much interaction for one situation may be too little for another, so what is optimum depends on where one is on the continuum of desired privacy. If I want to be alone a colleague who comes into my office and talks for fifteen minutes is intruding and staying too long. If I want to interact with others, then the same fifteen minute conversation may be far too brief [1975, p. 25].

This is a *dynamic* homeostatic model—it assumes that our optimal level of social stimulation changes from time to time, depending on both our recent experience and our personality. Altman holds that whenever we desire more or less privacy than we currently experience, our response is to use privacy-regulation mechanisms such as territoriality (or personal space).

Different types of territory allow varying degrees of control and privacy. The primary territory, of course, provides the greatest opportunity for regulation of interaction—in our homes we can retreat to a room to be alone, or invite guests when interaction is desired. In secondary territories control is based less on physical boundaries and more on symbolic boundaries and tacit agreements. For example, a whole neighborhood may know without the benefit of locked doors that Clancy's Bar "belongs" to a group of construction workers and that outsiders are unwelcome. Finally, *public territories* allow only minimal control; people often must regulate immediacy behaviors, such as distance, body orientation, or eye contact to achieve their desired privacy. For example, a student sitting at a library table might face a wall to avoid distractions. In short, territoriality helps people to regulate with whom they interact and for how long, and therefore to achieve their desired level of social interaction.

A second function of territoriality is to *organize* interpersonal interaction (Edney, 1976). Our community life links role expectations to certain places. For example, the roles of teacher and student are carried out in classrooms; the roles of proprietor and customer are enacted in stores, restaurants, and other businesses (see Barker, 1968). According to Edney, "this provides order to human interaction by making more predictable what kinds of behavior will happen where" (1976, p. 38). Within families or small groups, territoriality may take the form of relatively exclusive use of certain places by certain people. For example, two college roommates may decide quickly which desk belongs to which roommate. Such organization will add predictability to their use of the room and head off conflicts.

One implication of the territory-as-organizer idea is that our conflicts about places represent either (1) misunderstandings about the territorial norms under which a certain place is used or (2) deliberate violation of norms. A couple picnicking on a farmer's unfenced hayfield may not realize they are encroaching, but to the farmer they are intruders. On the other hand, the couple may have deliberately ignored a "keep out" sign. In either case conflict probably arises. We might view any conflict over space as a breakdown in the territorial organization of interpersonal behavior (Edney, 1976).

Research on human territorial behavior has emphasized different functions in different settings. Studies of public territory, especially in libraries, have focused on the regulation of interpersonal interaction. Studies of confined groups such as prison inmates have focused on the organizing function of territoriality. A few studies devoted to primary territories, such as dormitory rooms and single-family homes, have investigated the control function.

B. Public territories and their defense

To avoid interaction with others in public places, we tend to maximize our distance and face away from them. For example, Sommer

(1966) observed that the majority of students entering a library alone either sat by themselves (64%) or took chairs at tables with other students and sat diagonally across from them (26%). Only 10% sat directly across from or beside another student. Observations in another library also showed that students maximized their distance from others, and from the belongings of others as well. Furthermore, they stayed longest at tables where no other person was seated (F. D. Becker, 1973).

Another method of achieving desired degrees of privacy in public places is to defend an area actively, by occupying as much space as possible. In a questionnaire study that explored this idea, students were shown diagrams of six-chair library tables and asked one of two questions: (1) "If you wanted to be as far as possible from the distraction of other people, where would you sit at the table?" (2) "If you wanted to have the table to yourself, where would you sit to discourage anyone else from occupying it?" Underlying these questions were two tactics for obtaining privacy: avoidance of other people (retreat) and attempts at keeping others away (active defense). The overwhelming majority of "retreat" subjects chose end chairs, while students who wanted to keep others away chose center chairs. Another version of the questionnaire pictured an entire room, with four tables and a door. Most "retreat" subjects chose seats next to the wall. In general, students chose seats facing away from the door at tables in the rear of the room, perhaps to minimize distractions (Sommer & Becker, 1969).

A person's perceived control over a public territory depends partly on the length of time he or she has spent there. This point is illustrated in an informal experiment in a campus snack bar, where a confederate approached people who had been seated for varying lengths of time at their chairs and said "Excuse me, but you are sitting in my seat." Those who had been seated for only a few minutes tended to leave apologetically. But those who had been seated for longer

periods resisted the attempted intrusion. One person who had been there for 25 minutes refused to move (Sommer, 1969). "Tenure" seemed to impart a stronger territorial orientation. Another naturalistic study reported that the longer a party of people had been on a beach, the larger the circular area they viewed as "theirs" (Edney & Jordan-Edney, 1974).

Sometimes we attempt to reserve public territories in our absence by leaving belongings as **markers.** In the same campus snack bar (Sommer, 1969) an experimenter left a newspaper, a paperback, or a sweater on the back of a chair. In 22 trials conducted in uncrowded conditions (less than one-fourth of the chairs filled), people sat in "marked" chairs on only 3 trials. Apparently, markers effectively reserved space.

To examine the efficacy of markers in a setting with high population density, another experiment was conducted in a heavily used study hall (Sommer & Becker, 1969). Five different markers were used: a sportcoat with a textbook and notebook; a sportcoat; a textbook and notebook; a neat stack of four journals; and four scattered journals. Each marker was used on just one chair each evening. An unmarked chair served as a control. For 25 evenings an observer recorded how long it took before the marked and control chairs were occupied. As shown in Table 16-1, the combination of a sportcoat, textbook, and notebook was consistently an effective marker in a hall where an unmarked chair remained unoccupied for an average of 20 minutes. Apparently, personal objects can be used to reserve territories in public areas even where space is in high demand.

Sommer and Becker (1969) also noticed that when someone considered using a marked chair, he or she usually asked a neighbor if the chair was taken. In a series of experiments on "the good neighbor," a confederate sat at the same table with another student with one empty seat between them, and then left a stack of paperbacks as a marker. A second confederate approached the marked space. Neighbors did not

Table 16-1
Number of occupants and length of occupancy in "marked" and "unmarked"
chairs in a study hall (after Sommer & Becker, 1969; Sommer, 1969)

Type of Marker	Proportion of Trials in which the Chair Was Taken	Average Number of Minutes before Chair Was Occupied
Sportcoat, textbook, and notebook	0/5	n. a.*
Sportcoat	1/5	n. a.*
Text and notebook	1/5	n. a.*
Four neatly stacked journals	3/5	77
Four scattered journals	5/5	32
Unmarked chair	25/25	20

*n. a. = not applicable.

actively defend the space. But when the would-be intruder *asked* whether the seat was taken, the neighbor did defend it, especially if its occupant had been there for an hour (compared with 15 minutes). A similar study reported that neighbors sometimes, but not always, placed their own belongings in areas they had been asked to save (Hoppe, Greene, & Kenny, 1972). We may conclude that the recognition of public territories impels neighbors to act as defenders in only a limited way.

When someone deliberately violates the norms regarding public territories and occupies a marked area, reactions seldom seem to include confrontation. Instead, another place may be selected (Becker & Mayo, 1971). Unwillingness to reassert control over a public territory may reflect the tentative nature of our claims to such places.

C. Territoriality in confined groups

Perhaps because of their accessibility to observation by psychologists, such populations as military personnel, mental patients, juvenile of-

fenders, and prisoners often serve as subjects for naturalistic studies of territoriality. These groups live in settings with few physical separations between individuals, bringing into sharp focus the operation of territorial behavior as an organizer of social interaction. A sociologist who posed as a staff member at a mental hospital observed that patients established *personal territories*, or spaces "where an individual develops some comforts, control, and tacit rights he shares with no other patients except by his own invitation" (Goffman, 1961, p. 243). He added:

> Patients who had been on a given ward for several months tended to develop personal territories in the day room, at least to the degree that some inmates developed favorite sitting or standing places and would make some effort to dislodge anybody who usurped them [p. 244].

Even in the restrictive setting of a mental ward, patients tried to maintain some semblance of a primary territory.

As you might expect from studies of nonhumans, territoriality in confined groups is related to group **dominance hierarchies.** For example, Esser, Chamberlain, Chapple, and Kline (1964) observed 22 male mental patients in a closed ward and recorded patients' locations each half-hour during the day. Patients were ranked in terms of their frequency of social interactions; an "interactional hierarchy" was used to approximate the group dominance hierarchy. Territory was defined as a space where a patient was found 25% of the time. Results showed that only the lowest-ranked two-thirds of the group had territories. The "dominant" patients who interacted frequently tended to move freely around the ward; the less sociable ones tended to restrict their locations to a few specific spots. On the other hand, a similar study of a group of juvenile delinquents found that boys *highest* in the dominance hierarchy were most territorial (Esser, 1973). How can we reconcile these contradictory findings? One explanation is that some group settings have a few desirable places, such as private rooms in a boys' home. Here we might expect dominant group members to make frequent use of the desirable places and to be territorial. But in a stark and uniform setting we might expect dominant members of a group to take over large *quantities* of space. Thus, the prerogatives of power may include either the use of desirable territory or mobility, depending on the setting. Consistent with this idea, an observational study of 45 male prison inmates found that highly dominant group members were most mobile *and* had the most desirable bunks as "territories" (Austin & Bates, 1974).

Relationships between dominance and territoriality may also involve changes in territorial behavior during disruptions in a group. This point was illustrated in a ten-week observational study of a group of juvenile offenders confined to a residential cottage (Sundstrom & Altman, 1974). The boys' locations were periodically recorded on cottage maps, and they ranked one another on dominance. They also rated areas of the cottage in terms of desirability; highly valued areas included the front row of TV chairs, seclud-

ed bedrooms, the pool table, and the Ping-Pong table. Undesirable places included hallways, dormitory bunks near the door, and the restroom. Observations of their locations revealed that during the first five weeks, highly dominant boys were most territorial, and used the desirable space more often than other group members. Then a change in the composition of the group occurred—two highly dominant boys were removed, and two new, highly dominant boys replaced them. During the two weeks after the change, territorial behavior of the whole group dropped—the boys tended to use many areas instead of restricting their locations. The tendency for dominant boys to use desirable places disappeared. Cottage supervisors reported a 50% increase in aggressive behaviors.

Territorial behavior increased again during the last three weeks of observation, and aggressive behavior subsided. But the dominant boys did not become more territorial, nor did they establish the habits of the previous dominant boys of using desirable space. Thus, in contrast to the stable first period, there was a slight inverse relationship between territorial behavior and dominance. These findings illustrate the close link between territoriality and social organization in confined groups: a smoothly functioning group has an orderly territorial system, and disruptions may be associated with a breakdown in the territorial system. Studies of sailors (Altman, Taylor, & Wheeler, 1971), families (Altman, Nelson, & Lett, 1972), and couples (Rosenblatt & Stevenson, 1973) also suggest that territorial organization is important for groups who share living quarters.

D. Interactions in primary territories

Possibly the best human analogue of a territory is the single-family residence, where occupants exercise considerable control. As in nonhuman species (Leyhausen, 1965), a kind of *territorial dominance* has been reported, in which people tend to dominate interactions in their own residences. A physician (A. D. Coleman, 1968) noticed that many of his patients appeared weak and submissive in his office. But when he called at patients' homes, they were confident and dominant. Another researcher (Martindale, 1971) tested this idea experimentally in a college dormitory. Pairs of students took the roles of prosecutor and defense attorney to debate about the appropriate jail sentence for a fictional criminal. Each debate took place in one student's room; the other was a visitor. Students in their own rooms argued more persuasively and spent more time talking than the visitors. A similar experiment (Conroy & Sundstrom, 1975) found parallel results using a cooperative task, but only for students with dissimilar attitudes about their task. Another study (Edney, 1975) reported that a visitor to a dormitory room rated the resident as more "at home" than the resident rated the visitor. Just being in our own residence seems to provide a psychological advantage, implying a tacit recognition of our control in a primary territory.

The territorial-dominance effect seems applicable to sports, in comparing home games with on-the-road games. We could even consider a basketball team's home court a primary territory, because of the frequency and exclusiveness of the team's practices and games there and their control over the access of others to the court. Out of curiosity, Altman (1975) counted the number of games won and lost by University of Utah basketball and football teams during 1971, 1972, and 1973. As shown in Table 16-2, both teams won more games at home than on the road. (Of course, the advantage to the home team may have been its familiarity with the court as well as the visitors' recognition of its preeminence.)

Another aspect of control in primary territories is maintenance of territorial boundaries. An investigation of single-family dwellings found that residents of houses with clearly marked boundaries (for example "no trespassing" signs or barriers such as hedges) had lived in their houses longer and intended to stay longer than neighbors who had no such boundary markers. Moreover, residents of marked houses answered their doors faster, perhaps because of greater surveillance of boundaries among relatively permanent residents (Edney, 1972).

Table 16-2

Proportion of home and away games won by University of Utah football and basketball teams, 1971–73 (after Altman, 1975)

Location of Game	Year			Total	Percentages Won
	1971	1972	1973		
Basketball					
Home	10/14	6/16	14/15	30/45	67%
Away	3/11	2/11	3/9	8/31	26%
Football					
Home	1/5	4/4	4/5	9/14	64%
Away	3/6	2/6	3/7	8/19	42%

Apartment-dwellers may have more difficulty in maintaining their territorial boundaries. Oscar Newman (1973) found that robberies became much more frequent as building height increased (see Figure 16-7). He theorized that high-rise apartment buildings harbor criminal

activity in part because (1) residents cannot tell other residents apart from visitors and neither recognize nor challenge them; (2) some apartments lack boundaries that demarcate adjacent "zones of influence" (or secondary territories); and (3) many apartment buildings make surveillance of entrances very difficult. Newman compared two neighboring housing projects in New York City; these had virtually identical population densities. However, one project (Brownsville) had what Newman called "defensible space." Its low, three-to-six-story buildings provided ample opportunities for surveillance both within and outside the buildings, and had adjacent, demarcated zones outdoors. The high-rise buildings of the other project (Van Dyke) contained about twice as many families per building as the smaller Brownsville buildings and had no surrounding demarcated zones. Rates of crime were about twice as high in the high-rise project. We see here a failure to establish territorial boundaries, because of the architecture of the buildings.

In summary, human territoriality is quite complex. Our use of spaces allows regulation and organization of interpersonal activities in a variety of settings. But the usefulness of a physical setting for regulation of our interactions depends on its physical characteristics, as we shall see in the next section.

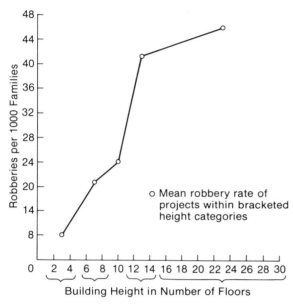

Figure 16-7

Mean rate of robberies per 1000 families in New York apartment buildings in 1969 as a function of building height (from Newman, 1973, p. 29). Note that many more robberies occur in buildings with 12 or more stories. One explanation is that high-rise dwellers cannot tell neighbors from intruders. Another possibility is that high-rise buildings allow less surveillance over space outside the apartments, such as lobbies and stairwells. According to Newman (1973), buildings with "defensible space" provide opportunities for residents to identify and monitor visitors. (Reprinted with permission of Macmillan Publishing Company, Inc., and The Architectural Press, Ltd., London, from *Defensible Space*, by O. Newman. Copyright © 1972, 1973 by Oscar Newman.)

III. Environmental determination— Effects of physical arrangements on interactions

If we think of the physical environment as a collection of factors that affect interpersonal behavior—as a source of *independent variables*—we can pose two questions: (1) How does the setting affect who interacts with whom? (2) How does the environment influence the way interactions are conducted? Consider the example of students living in a dormitory. The arrangement of the foyer, lounge, elevators or stairs, corridors, and rooms may help determine whom a student sees in his or her everyday activities—that is, *who* interacts. There is evidence that students living in dormitories form friendships on the basis of the proximity of their rooms (Menne & Sinnett, 1971). And there are many ways the architecture can affect *how* the students interact. For example, rooms may have built-in bunks and desks so situated that when three people try to sit and talk, they are crowded and uncomfortable. In addition, the environment can *indirectly* affect interactions through conditions that affect peoples' emotional states. For example, there is evidence that unpredictable noise can lower a person's tolerance for frustration (D. C. Glass & Singer, 1972). On the other hand, an aesthetically pleasing setting can be relaxing and make for pleasant interactions. In short, the setting can influence who interacts, how they conduct their interactions, and how they feel as they do so.

A. Who interacts with whom?

1. Residential proximity and friendship. An early field study of a married-student housing complex investigated friendships among married couples (Festinger, Schachter, & Back, 1950). In one part of the project, called Westgate West, couples lived in two-story buildings. There were five nearly identical apartments on each floor, all with front doors facing the same direction. Couples were assigned to apartments from a waiting list as vacancies arose. The researchers asked each couple to name the three other couples they saw most often. Responses indicated that, among residents of the same floor, the closer their apartments were, the more often they mentioned one another as friends. Of all next-door neighbors who could have been mentioned, 41% were chosen. Couples mentioned only 22% of the possible choices two doors away, and fewer still of the neighbors three and four doors

away. In short, the formation of friendships was strongly related to physical proximity.

Residents of the same floor mentioned one another as friends more often than did residents of different floors, even though the distance between floors was small. In fact, the front door of the apartment directly above one of the units was actually closer than any unit on the same floor. Festinger, Schachter, and Back introduced the concept of *functional distance* to describe the extent to which the architecture determines who interacts. For example, couples on the second floors of the buildings were often friends with people on the first floors who lived next to the stairs. Close "functional proximity" implies relatively frequent opportunity to interact. We might expect frequency of interaction—and formation of friendships—to increase with physical and functional proximity, although of course other factors also influence who is chosen as a friend (see Chapter 5).

Other research also associates friendship with proximity. For example, a study of a Chicago suburb, Park Forest, reported that parties and get-togethers consisted mainly of neighbors from the same block (Whyte, 1956). Again, proximity was associated with friendship. However, these observations were based on populations with high turnover rates; many of these people had only recently established residences. If proximity helped to determine interaction patterns, it probably did so mainly during the *initial phases* of people's relationships with one another. New dormitory residents initially tend to form friendships on the basis of proximity, but they later seek out people with similar attitudes, even if those people live farther away (Newcomb, 1961). For proximity to influence long-term friendships, other conditions might also need to hold—namely, (1) homogeneity (Gans, 1970) and (2) continued necessity of mutual contact and assistance (Michelson, 1970). Recent research suggests that residential friendship patterns can be predicted from residential proximity *and* similarities in age, marital status, family size, occupation, education, and leisure activity preferences (Athanasiou & Yoshioka, 1973).

2. Barriers, partitions, and privacy. The placement of partitions and barriers within buildings can influence who sees, hears, and talks with whom. A few studies have directly examined the effects of partitions on interactions. One study compared different types of U. S. Air Force barracks buildings. In three buildings, partitions were installed so that the men's bunks were enclosed in cubicles in groups of six. Three otherwise identical barracks had no partitions and retained the usual open arrangement. Compared with those in the open arrangement, men in the cubicle arrangement reported spending more time talking with fewer individuals (Blake, Rhead, Wedge, & Mouton, 1956). Similar findings were reported in an office that used file cabinets as partitions (Gullahorn, 1952). These results are consistent with our assumption that people maintain an optimal level of social stimulation; with large numbers of interaction partners, the amount of time spent with each partner apparently decreases. We would expect that enclosure of a group would produce increased group interaction, and perhaps increased solidarity.

If anything, however, recent trends lean toward "open" work settings. Some companies have adopted a German innovation called *Buro-landschaft*, or **office landscaping** (P. Howard, 1972; Sommer, 1974). As an alternative to providing workers with individual cubicles or offices, the office landscape is a large, open area where the only divisions between work spaces are furnishings such as desks, movable screens, bookcases, blackboards, and plants (see Figure 16-8). Such office landscapes provide greater opportunities for privacy than the "bull pen" arrangement, but they offer less privacy than individual offices (Sommer, 1974).

In one study of an office landscape, two departments of a manufacturing firm simultaneously moved to new buildings, one of them

to a "landscaped" arrangement. Six months later, workers in both departments completed a questionnaire. Although workers in the office landscape reported spending more time talking, they said they cooperated less with coworkers and accomplished less. They found the landscape arrangement more noisy and distracting, and less private (Hundert & Greenfield, 1969). Other studies have reported similar findings (Brookes & Kaplan, 1972; Nemecek & Grandjean, 1973).

Another survey in an office landscape indicated that workers who were satisfied with the arrangement reported greater opportunities for contact and greater solidarity (McCarrey, Peterson, Edwards, & VonKulmiz, 1974). Those who expressed dissatisfaction with the open arrangement reported "too much noise, too many distractions, lack of ability to put sustained effort on a problem, lack of territory definition, overly great accessibility to others" (p. 402).

One important point is that the amount of privacy a person desires in an office depends on his or her task. With simple, repetitive tasks such as typing or adding figures, an open office arrangement could produce **social facilitation** (see Chapter 17), or improved task performance that occurs when other people are present. For complex tasks, private offices would allow workers control over their interactions with others, so that they could avoid interactions they found distracting.

B. How does the setting affect the interaction process?

1. Room arrangements and interaction. One source of environmental effects is the arrangement of furniture within rooms. An example occurred in a newly built geriatrics ward for women at a Saskatchewan hospital. The wardroom was cheerfully decorated and newly furnished; it was a showplace for the whole hospital. But the patients seemed depressed. They sat in the chairs staring into space; the longer they had been on

Figure 16-8
In "office landscape" arrangements, where desks are separated only by office furniture, workers have reported having less privacy and spending more time talking with others. Workers satisfied with the arrangement find opportunities for solidarity; dissatisfied workers report distractions and inability to control inputs. (Photos courtesy of Eric Sundstrom.)

the ward, the less they seemed to talk to each other. Sommer and Ross (1958) noticed that the chairs were lined up along the walls so that the patients sat side-by-side, all facing the same direction. Sommer persuaded the hospital staff to rearrange the wardroom furniture so that chairs were placed around tables instead of lined up along the walls. The patients at first resisted the change, possibly because it disrupted long-standing territorial habits. But after a few weeks the frequency of conversations had approximately doubled. Thus, a simple rearrangement of the furniture had a powerful impact on the ways these elderly women interacted. Placed in relatively direct orientation, they talked, despite previous silences.

In a more formal experiment, subjects entered a well-furnished room in pairs. They expected to listen to music and give an opinion of it. They sat in chairs oriented at 0°, 90°, or 180°, and separated by 3, 4½, 6, or 9 feet. As the subjects waited for the music to begin, they were observed through a concealed one-way mirror. Their affiliative behaviors were recorded, including total number of statements, positive verbal content, rate of verbal reinforcement, and length of pauses before speaking. Results indicated no effects of distance, but a significant positive relationship between directness of orientation and affiliative behavior scores—that is, the more directly the pairs faced, the more affiliative they were (Mehrabian & Diamond, 1971a). In a similar experiment, groups of four strangers could choose their own seating, with various distances and angles of orientation toward others. Results indicated, among other things, a positive relationship between the amount of time a pair of people spent talking and the directness of their chair orientation (Mehrabian & Diamond, 1971b). In still another experiment, members of group discussions at circular tables addressed more remarks to other members seated directly across the table than to members seated in more indirect orientations (Steinzor, 1950).

The geriatrics-ward study and subsequent studies illustrate what Osmond (1957) called **sociopetal spaces**—arrangements that bring people together—and **sociofugal spaces**—arrangements that keep people apart. A common example of sociofugal space is the typical airport waiting area, with chairs bolted to the floor in rows facing the same window overlooking the concourse (see Figure 16-9). Other sociofugal spaces include waiting rooms in hospitals, doctors' offices, employment offices, and other places where people have to wait together in relatively crowded conditions. In many cases, designers may intentionally provide sociofugal arrangements so that users of a setting can go about their business without being forced to pay attention to one another. On the other hand, people go some places, such as cocktail lounges, with the express purpose of talking. These places usually have at least partly sociopetal arrangements, with chairs arranged around tables to encourage conversation.

This research implies that furniture arrangements can affect affiliative behaviors—people may be more affiliative the more directly their seats face one another, provided that the chairs are within comfortable distance for conversation. This hypothesis can guide the planning of at least some physical settings.

2. Indirect effects of the environment on interaction. We are all aware that environmental conditions—such as heat, noise, and pollution—can lead to stress and in other ways affect our mood or arousal level. Even the aesthetic nature of a room can affect interpersonal processes, as indicated in an early experiment (Maslow & Mintz, 1956). College students were ushered into one of three roughly equal-sized rooms as part of a study that involved rating a series of photographs. The "average" room was a professor's office, well kept but obviously worked in. The "beautiful"

Figure 16-9
Sociofugal spaces, such as this airport waiting area, keep people apart and discourage interaction through the placement of chairs. *Sociopetal spaces* are those that encourage interaction.

room was carpeted, well lit, pleasantly furnished, and tastefully decorated. On the other extreme, the "ugly" room looked more like a janitor's storeroom. It had gray walls and half-covered windows with dirty shades, and it was lit by a single overhead light bulb; the walls were lined with pails, mops, and brooms; the bare floor badly needed mopping. In one of the rooms a student interviewer asked each subject to rate a series of 10 photographs of faces on dimensions such as "fatigue versus energy" and "displeasure versus well-being." Not surprisingly, the ratings were most favorable in the beautiful room and least favorable in the ugly room. The researchers also unobtrusively observed the two interviewers in the study, and found that they finished their interviews more quickly in the "ugly" room (Mintz, 1956). When asked to rate the photos themselves, unaware that they were being treated as subjects, the examiners also gave lower ratings in the "ugly" room. The importance of room characteristics is apparently not lost on business executives, clinical psychologists, and other professional people who carefully decorate their offices to achieve comfortable settings for interviews.

Other sources of indirect environmental effects include extreme temperatures and noise, both of which can be stressful. To examine the effects of high temperature on interpersonal attraction, one experiment placed groups of subjects in an environmental chamber that allowed control over temperature, humidity, and air circulation. Half the subjects worked under "normal" temperature conditions; half worked under "hot" conditions (100° F. with 60% relative humidity). Subjects performed simple tasks for 45 minutes; then, after seeing an attitude scale allegedly completed by a stranger, they indicated how much they liked this stranger. In the "hot" condition, the stranger was rated as significantly less attractive (Griffitt, 1970). A later study found similar results (Griffitt & Veitch, 1971). Thus, heat apparently can lessen interpersonal attraction, at least in a laboratory situation in which a stranger is evaluated.

Similarly, we have limited evidence that high temperatures predispose aggressiveness.[7] Goranson and King (1970) tabulated the daily temperatures for 12 days preceding riots and violent incidents in 17 U.S. cities. Compared with temperatures during previous years, there was an unusually high temperature on the day preceding the riot and on the riot day itself. In a

test of the relationship between heat and aggression, subjects were placed in either a "hot" room (80°F.) or a comfortable one and given an opportunity to "teach" another person (actually an accomplice) pairs of nonsense syllables through use of electric shocks. When the "learner" made an error, a subject could press one of ten buttons on a shock-generating "aggression machine." Before the teaching procedure, subjects were either angered by the confederate (through shocks) or not angered. Angered subjects gave more intense shocks, but subjects in the "hot" condition gave *less intense* shocks, contrary to predictions (R. A. Baron, 1972). Perhaps subjects were overcompensating for a situation they thought could heighten their aggressive impulses. (On the other hand, they could have seen through the deception in the "hot" condition and inhibited their aggressive impulses.) In a further investigation of the problem, angered subjects had an opportunity to deliver shocks in either the "hot" or the normal condition, after either seeing or not seeing an aggressive model (R. A. Baron & Lawton, 1972). Heat produced a decrease in aggression without a model, but as expected, the "hot"/aggressive-model condition produced the most intense shocks. High temperature thus *enhanced* the effects of the aggressive model. A third experiment (R. A. Baron & Bell, 1975) placed subjects in a "hot" or "cool" room after they were angered or not angered, and then showed them an aggressive model or no model. Among the nonangered subjects, heat enhanced aggression with or without the model. But the angered subjects actually showed *less* aggression in the "hot" room. As the researchers suggested, maybe the "hot/angry" group experienced intense discomfort and only wanted to leave the scene. We are left with only mixed support for the idea that heat enhances aggression.

Noise is another aversive, arousing environmental influence that can affect interpersonal behavior. You might expect it, like heat, to intensify emotional reactions and to increase the likelihood of aggression. In an experimental test of

[7]Heat and noise are two of the arousal-producing conditions that can increase the likelihood of aggression. See Chapter 7.

this idea, subjects saw aggressive or nonaggressive films; then, in a room that was either noisy or silent, they had an ostensible opportunity to shock another person. As expected, they delivered more shocks in the noisy room, and the "noise/aggressive-film" group gave more shocks than any other group (Geen & O'Neal, 1969).

Noise can have even more subtle effects, indicated in a program of research by D. C. Glass and Singer (1972, 1973). They asked subjects to work for about half an hour on tasks such as addition of numbers and verbal-reasoning problems. As the subjects worked, they heard occasional bursts of loud noise (108 decibels, like that of a riveting machine). In the "predictable-noise" condition, the noise was presented regularly every minute for nine seconds. In the "unpredictable-noise" condition, the noise occurred at random intervals for random lengths of time. Subjects in a third group, in the "controllable-noise" condition, received unpredictable noise, but were given a button they were told would stop it. They could use the button if the noise became intolerable. There was a "no-noise" control group. Dependent variables measured during the exposure to noise included physiological indicators of stress (galvanic skin response, vasoconstriction, and muscular tension) and the number of errors subjects made as they worked on a task. Results of several repetitions of the basic procedure indicated that (1) initially, subjects showed elevated physiological responses to noise, which were intensified in the unpredictable-noise condition; (2) physiological responses decreased as the experiment continued; and (3) the noise had no effect on how well subjects performed simple tasks, although it produced deficits in performance of complicated tasks. Apparently, subjects adapted under conditions involving loud, unpredictable noise. *Adaptation* is defined as "a cognitive process involving one or another mechanism designed to filter out of awareness certain aspects of the aversive event, or in some other way reappraise it as benign" (D. C. Glass & Singer, 1973, p. 181). We adapt to many aversive conditions

besides noise, such as smog, heat, and extreme humidity.

After subjects had been exposed to noise, they worked on another set of tasks. They attempted puzzles that were actually insoluble; the length of time they worked indicated their persistence, or toleration for frustration. They also proofread a manuscript. Subjects who had been exposed to unpredictable noise *and* thought they had no control over it showed less toleration for frustration and made more proofreading errors than the other groups. Thus, unpredictable, uncontrollable noise produced *negative aftereffects*,[8] even in brief laboratory experiments. Glass and Singer wrote "unpredictable and uncontrollable noise should affect aggressiveness, exploitative behavior, liking for others, and general irritability in interpersonal relations" (1972, p. 159).

The deleterious effects of aversive conditions are generally intensified when we have no control over them (Averill, 1973). As we shall see in the next section, the lack of control over interpersonal interactions can also be stressful.

IV. Crowding: Too many people, not enough space

In this section we examine what happens when too many people share a single space—how a space shortage affects people, and how they behave within their physical settings as they try to cope with the situation. This approach combines the two perspectives introduced so far: (1) human use of physical settings to control interactions and (2) the environment as a determinant of interpersonal behavior.

---

[8]Glass and Singer's original hypothesis held that "man pays a price for adaptation" (1973, p. 165), following Dubos (1965). But results of the experiments on noise showed that the negative aftereffects of noise were *independent* of the amount of physiological adaptation subjects exhibited. This finding suggests that instead of viewing the aftereffects as psychic costs of adaptation, we must think of them as effects of mere exposure to the aversive conditions.

A. High density versus crowding

Population density is the number of persons per unit of space. High population density has been associated with numerous social ills. For example, 35 articles in popular magazines published between 1960 and 1970 held that high density was linked with crime, war, alcoholism, drug addiction, poor education, family disorganization, decreased quality of life, and other social pathologies (Zlutnick & Altman, 1972). Most of the articles gave little evidence for their opinions, although research has since begun to accumulate. But before we review research findings on density, consider some examples:

> Fifty people attend a cocktail party in a three-room luxury apartment in Manhattan.
>
> Fans at a football game crowd into rows in the grandstand for the annual homecoming game.
>
> A family of migrant farmworkers composed of a couple and their four children lives for the winter in a two-room shack.
>
> A teenage boy shares a small bedroom with three younger brothers; all four sleep in bunk beds.
>
> Shoppers crowd around a bargain table at a department store.
>
> Twelve people squeeze into an elevator in an office building.

What these situations have in common is a relatively high concentration of people in a small space. But there are important differences. First, many conditions of high population density are uncomfortable, as in the department store, but there are times people actually *seek out* conditions of high density, as in parties, dances, or football games. A second difference concerns the *duration* of exposure to conditions of high density—an elevator ride, for example, is usually very brief. Third, these situations vary in the extent to which people lose control over interpersonal processes, including the amount of interaction with others, and the extent to which other people in-

terfere with ongoing activities. At parties, the presence of others does not entail an excessive amount of interaction—in fact, we go to parties because we want to be with others. But the teenage boy who shares his bedroom may not always want to talk with his brothers; their presence may even distract him from his homework.

From these examples, we see the necessity to distinguish the physical condition—high population density—from the experience of it. **Crowding** may be defined as a psychological state of stress that *sometimes* accompanies high population density (Stokols, 1972b). *Stress* is a psychological (and physiological) state that results from conditions perceived as threatening or potentially harmful (Lazarus, 1966); especially stressful are unpredictable, aversive stimuli (Averill, 1973), as we noted in the case of noise.

The definition of crowding as a form of stress underlines a second point: high density per se may not produce stress. Crowding means disturbances in a person's ability to maintain desired amounts of interaction with others (Altman, 1975; Stokols, 1972a, 1972b; Sundstrom, 1975b). For example, an elevator ride with eight people may not bring feelings of crowding unless they stare, initiate unwanted conversation, talk too loudly, smoke, or stand in the way. In terms of the homeostatic model of interaction, crowding represents a situation in which control over interpersonal interaction has broken down—the optimal amount of interaction has been exceeded, and there is no longer enough privacy (Altman, 1975).

Of course, there are many conditions in which people *seek* high density because they are not experiencing *enough* social interaction. According to one study, campers tend to shun an isolated campsite in favor of sites near others (Shafer & Burke, 1965). And certain societies, such as the !Kung Bushmen, live in extremely high densities even though there is ample room for expansion of the villages (Draper, 1973). Crowding occurs when a person desires less interaction than he or she currently experiences.

At the other extreme, *isolation* can also be stressful.

Our assumptions about the homeostatic nature of interpersonal interaction lead us to predict that crowding generates *coping behaviors* designed to reestablish control over interaction. For example, on a crowded[9] elevator, people face away from each other, look off into space and stand with their arms at their sides, avoiding any indication of psychological closeness. Similarly, a student living in a small two-bedroom apartment with four others may often retreat to the campus library. In summary, we can view crowding as a sequential process (Stokols, 1972a; Sundstrom, 1975b) that includes the following steps:

1. Conditions of high population density
2. Interpersonal disturbances, such as unwanted interaction, interference, or competition
3. Experience of crowding
4. Coping behaviors, such as withdrawal from interaction

To these, we can add one more.

5. Psychological costs derived from the effort involved in coping or from prolonged crowding

The last component provides a possible link between high population density and such social pathologies as crime and mental illness. With this framework in mind, we consider research on crowding.[10]

[9]The term *crowded* refers to a physical situation characterized by high population density (see Stokols, 1976). This is distinct from *crowding,* which is a subjective experience.

[10]An alternative conception of crowding appears in a recent book by Freedman (1975). He writes "The term *crowding* should be understood always as referring to the physical situation of high density, and not to an internal feeling" (p. 11). From our perspective, the equation of crowding with high density oversimplifies the concept of density. As we have indicated, "high density" means many different things. The aversive or pleasant nature of conditions we call high density depends on the events that occur and on the individuals who experience these events. A high-density situation may be stressful for one person but pleasurable for another. Thus, individual experience is our basis for defining *crowding.*

The earliest studies of crowding focused on the *outcomes* of high population density, as opposed to the *processes* involved (Altman, 1975). Through research on nonhumans and through sociological studies of census data, researchers have examined the relationships between density and social pathology. We shall look first at these studies, then at experimental research.

B. Density and social pathology

1. Population density in nonhumans. Perhaps the best known study of crowding in a nonhuman species is Calhoun's (1962) experiment with Norway rats. After building a colony of four connected pens that could comfortably house 48 rats, Calhoun allowed the population to increase to 80, supplied them with food and water, and sat back to observe. They eventually showed abnormalities in nest building, courting, mating, rearing of the young, and social organization. Some males became aggressive and disregarded the ritualized signals of submission that usually end a fight. Females often neglected the young, and as many as 75% of the infant rats died. Territories were disregarded or maintained through force. Autopsies revealed signs of prolonged stress, such as enlarged adrenal glands. In short, density among rats was associated with stress and many forms of social pathology. Similar findings have been reported with mice (Southwick, 1955). One experiment tested the effect of increased group size on pain-elicited aggression in deer mice. The crowded mice were more aggressive than uncrowded mice, and aggression among crowded mice increased over time (Gregor, Smith, Simons, & Parker, 1970).

Social pathologies in crowded conditions are not limited to laboratory cages. For example, a naturalistic study of Sika deer on an island off the coast of Maryland revealed that the population had grown to an unusually high density of about one deer per acre, or about 300 deer. Two years later, over half of the herd died during the winter, even though food was plentiful. Autopsies showed that their adrenal glands were enlarged, indicating prolonged stress. More deer died the next winter, and the herd stabilized at about 80 (Christian, Flyger, & Davis, 1960). A similar population decrease has been observed among crowded mice in a laboratory (Marsden, 1972). A review of research findings on effects of density on nonhumans concluded: "We seem to be left with the well-established fact that in enclosed colonies very large populations lead to social and eventually physical anomalies, including aggressiveness" (Freedman, 1972, p. 216). The critical variable in these effects seemed to be the number of animals that interacted, not just density (Freedman, 1972). While these data suggest hypotheses regarding humans, we must of course be cautious in generalizing from nonhumans to human populations.

2. Density and pathology in human populations. Early studies revealed that density (the number of persons per unit of space) was positively related to mental illness (for example, Hollingshead & Redlich, 1958; Lantz, 1953; Pollock & Furbush, 1921). Other studies related density to crime rates (for example, Lottier, 1938; C. Shaw & McKay, 1942; R. E. Watts, 1931). But this early research (reviewed by Zlutnick & Altman, 1972) overlooked the important fact that high-density areas of cities are often populated by poor people; the social pathologies associated with high density could have resulted from other stressful aspects of ghetto life. To test this idea, Winsborough (1965) examined data from Chicago; he found positive correlations between the number of persons per acre and death rates, tuberculosis, infant mortality, public assistance, and juvenile assistance. But when he statistically removed the effects of socioeconomic status and other factors (occupation, income, education, ethnicity, and housing quality), the relationship disappeared, and in some cases became negative! In light of this evidence, you might conclude that high population density among humans is just a harmless condition that accompanies the privations of poverty.

A second generation of correlational re-

search has introduced two improvements over earlier studies. First, it recognizes the complexities of the concept of *density*. We can distinguish **inside density,** the number of persons within a residence, from **outside density,** the number of persons per acre (Zlutnick & Altman, 1972). These two types of density have very different consequences. High inside density is illustrated in the example of the family of six migrant farmworkers living in a two-room house. They cannot easily separate themselves with physical barriers; when they want privacy they may be unable to obtain it. On the other hand, high outside density involves contacts with people outside one's home —on sidewalks, in grocery stores, in parks, and in other public places. You might expect situations with high inside density to be more stressful, because they allow less control over interactions (see Figure 16-10).

A second improvement in recent correlational research is its attention to socioeconomic status, ethnic background, and other factors that make it difficult to interpret correlations between density and social pathology. Recent studies have used statistical techniques to control the effects associated with these factors (Booth & Welch, 1974).

An example of the new generation of correlational studies was conducted in Honolulu. The number of persons per acre, a measure of *outside density*, was related to several types of social pathology, such as incidence of mental hospitalization and juvenile delinquency. This relationship held after effects of income and education were statistically removed (Schmitt, 1966). On the other hand, a similar study among Filipinos found that *inside density* was related to self-reports of physical symptoms independent of social class (Marsella, Escudero, & Gordon, 1970). These data suggest the presence of regional and cultural differences in outcomes of high density.

In an important study, Galle, Gove, and McPherson (1972) distinguished two measures of *inside density*—the number of persons per room within a dwelling and the number of rooms per dwelling—and two measures of *outside density*—the number of dwellings per structure and the number of structures per acre. Their correlational analysis of Chicago census data statistically controlled socioeconomic status and ethnicity. Only the number of persons per room within dwellings was significantly related to mortality, fertility, public assistance, and juvenile delinquency! These results suggest that social pathologies may be associated with a lack of physical separations between persons in their residences (Michelson, 1970).

Other evidence further underlines the importance of inside density in social pathology. One study involved census-tract data from 65 nations, including Canada and the United States, and countries in Central and South America, Europe, Africa, Asia, and Australia. After controlling for effects of socioeconomic status, results indicated a significant relationship between inside density and rates of homicide (Booth & Welch, 1973).

Similarly, a study of inside density and crime rates in the United States used data from 656 cities with populations over 25,000. Analyses of the data controlled for the effects of race, education, and income. Cities of over 100,000 were analyzed separately, because of their markedly higher crime rates. In larger cities, persons-per-room density accounted for modest increments in crimes against persons, such as murder, assault, and rape, especially when high persons-per-room density was associated with low income. In smaller cities, where high inside density is more easily avoided, the ability to predict the crime rate from the density within dwellings was weaker (Booth & Welch, 1974).

Figure 16-10

Inside density refers to the number of people who share a residence; *outside density* refers to the number of people per acre (Zlutnick & Altman, 1972). In ghetto apartments, both inside and outside densities are high. Luxury apartments may also be located in congested areas, but their inside density is usually low. Suburban single-family dwellings usually have low densities both inside and outside. The photo on the left illustrates high-outside, high-inside density, and the photo on the right shows low-outside, low-inside density. (Photos by Peter Gridley and by Flying Camera, Inc., both courtesy of Freelance Photographers Guild.)

Although the relationships between dwelling density and social pathology vary from one culture to another (see Figure 16-11), we may conclude that in the United States and many other countries there is a relationship between density within dwellings and aggression.[11] But how can we explain it? Perhaps aggression stems from "thwarted routines" and frustration in conditions of high density (Booth & Welch, 1974). To address such questions, we need to examine directly what happens when people are enclosed in a small space.

C. Crowding in the laboratory

Laboratory experiments usually last only a few hours and take place in a setting unfamiliar to the subjects. But even brief exposures to high density have noticeable effects.

In manipulating density within rooms, researchers have followed two strategies: (1) In variations of *spatial density*, room size varies while the group size remains constant. (2) Variation of *social density* involves changes in group size in a constant-sized area (McGrew, 1970). An increase in social density not only reduces the supply of space but also provides increased opportunities for interaction.

Most laboratory experiments on crowding vary spatial density, by asking groups of people to work on a task in either a large or a small room. "High density" typically means four to eight square feet per person (think of an elevator, six feet square, in which six people are seated in chairs). Not surprisingly, people find such conditions crowded, restrictive, and uncomfortable (Y. Epstein & Karlin, 1975; Griffitt & Veitch, 1971; M. Ross, Layton, Erickson, &

---

[11]Because the correlations between dwelling density and crime rates are based on *aggregate data*, we must take care in interpreting them. It is entirely possible that the people who live in crowded conditions are not always the same people who produce the high rates of crime. The only satisfactory way to resolve this problem is to examine data for each individual.

Figure 16-11

Although we have correlational evidence that social pathology is related to population density, there are important exceptions. Tokyo, for example, has more than 20,000 people per square mile—more than ten times the average density in U. S. and Canadian cities! But crime rates are remarkably low; high density seems to add vitality to the city. The relative lack of social pathology may derive from an emphasis on privacy and attention to detail in house design and from the presence of small, close-knit communities within the city (Canter & Canter, 1971). Another crowded city in which density is unrelated to social pathology is Hong Kong (Mitchell, 1971; Schmitt, 1963), where cultural mechanisms, such as a highly developed etiquette system, may help to ameliorate the effects of high density.

Schopler, 1973; Stokols, Rall, Pinner, & Schopler, 1973; Stokols & Resnick, 1975a; Sundstrom, 1975a). Furthermore, high spatial density seems to produce physiological arousal. Two experiments placed groups of six students in an extremely small room. They showed greater arousal than students in a large room (indicated by galvanic skin response). Arousal in the small room continued throughout the experiments, indicating that subjects did not show adaptation (Aiello, Epstein, & Karlin, 1975b). Recall that close proximity with others can produce evidence of arousal (McBride, King, & James, 1965), so the stress that accompanies high spatial density may derive partly from close proximity with others. Five major classes of findings have been reported in experiments on room density.

1. Sex differences in reactions to high density. All-female groups tend to react *positively* to others when room density is high, whereas all-male groups react negatively. For example, when groups of eight males or eight females worked on a task in a large or small room, the small room heightened feelings of stress, crowding, and restriction for everyone. But women saw themselves as more aggressive and made more hostile comments under conditions of low density; men rated themselves as more aggressive and made more hostile remarks under conditions of high density (Stokols et al., 1973). (Parallel findings appear in Emiley, 1975; Y. Epstein & Karlin, 1975; J. L. Freedman et al., 1972; and Ross et al., 1973. However, Marshall & Heslin, 1975, reported contrary findings.) Men also behaved more competitively under conditions of high density, whereas women showed more competition when density within rooms was low (Y. Epstein & Karlin, 1975; J. L. Freedman et al., 1972). This frequently reported sex difference agrees with studies of personal space in which men stayed farther apart than women. However, this effect does not seem to appear in mixed sex groups (J. L. Freedman et al., 1972), and it may depend on the type of task (Marshall & Heslin, 1975) and on its duration.

2. Personality and reactions to high density. As you might expect, people with large personal-space zones indicated a preference for low densities (Cozby, 1973a; Dooley, 1974). And subjects who reported an external **locus of control** (see Chapter 3) perceived a greater degree of crowding in a small room with five other people, than did subjects reporting an internal-locus-of-control orientation (Schopler & Walton, 1974).

3. Effects of the situation. You have seen that architecture can affect privacy; there is evidence that it affects crowding as well. One study asked students to place "comfortable" numbers of miniature figures in simulated rooms. Results showed that subjects were comfortable with higher densities in rooms divided by partitions (Desor, 1972). A field experiment, however, found just the opposite results. When partitions were placed in a waiting area in the California Department of Motor Vehicles, people showed *more* signs of tension than when the partitions were absent (Stokols, Smith, & Prostor, 1975).

Perhaps the partitions in this setting made people feel restricted and reduced their sense of control.

Another study using the placement of miniature figures reported that subjects were comfortable with higher densities in light-colored rooms, which were perceived as larger (Baum & Davis, 1974). A study using the same method showed that college students tolerated higher densities with acquaintances than with strangers; they preferred higher densities during recreational activities than during work; they allowed more miniature figures in rooms where occupants were described as interacting than in those whose occupants were pursuing independent activites (Cohen, Sladen, & Bennett, 1975).[12]

4. Density and performance of tasks. We have evidence that high spatial density has no direct detrimental effects on task performance, whether the task is simple or moderately complicated (J. L. Freedman, Klevansky, & Ehrlich, 1971; Ross et al., 1973; Stokols et al., 1973). In one experiment, performance of a simple task was even *enhanced* following exposure to extreme high-density conditions (Y. Epstein & Karlin, 1975). But performance of tasks under conditions of high density can be taxing. In an experiment modeled after D. C. Glass and Singer's (1972) studies on the aftereffects of noise, groups of eight subjects worked on a task in a small or large room. Subjects' perception of control was also manipulated by either telling them that they were free to leave at any time or telling them nothing. There were no effects of density on task performance. But subjects in the high-density condition who ostensibly had little control over the situation did more poorly on measures of tolerance for frustration (Sherrod, 1974). These findings underline the importance of *perceived control* over interpersonal interaction.

And we may conclude that under some conditions, uncontrollable exposure to high spa-

[12]We must consider research findings based on the placement of miniature figures to be tentative until they are confirmed by research that places subjects in actual conditions of varying densities.

tial density brings negative aftereffects, or psychological costs.

5. *Interpersonal coping behavior.* High density within a room may be stressful because of interpersonal conditions that accompany it. For example, in an experiment that varied both social density and proximity in groups of male students, excessively close seating produced reports of discomfort even with low density (Bergman, 1971). Similar results appeared in an experiment by Worchel and Teddlie (1976). Another experiment demonstrated that in a small room, a group of people expected to evaluate one another felt more crowding than a group instructed to "get acquainted" (Stokols & Resnick, 1975a). When we feel crowded, we expect attempts at regulating interpersonal interactions, or *coping behaviors.* Stokols and his colleagues (1973) found that groups of eight people in a small room laughed more often than groups in a large room; there was also more laughter when subjects worked on a competitive task than on a cooperative one. Laughter may represent an attempt at tension release.

Another experiment demonstrated that coping behavior can begin even *before* a person experiences crowding. Students entered a small room by themselves; they expected to work with either four or ten people. As they waited, two other people arrived, one at a time (actually confederates). Subjects in the waiting-for-a-crowd condition sat closer to corners of the room, looked less at the first confederate, and liked the confederates less than subjects who were not awaiting a crowd. And the subjects waiting for a crowd felt more crowded and thought the room was smaller and more stuffy. Not only did they attempt to reduce their psychological distance from others, but their perception of the physical setting was affected by the expectation that it would be crowded (Baum & Greenberg, 1975).

Do coping behaviors actually reduce stress? We have only indirect evidence related to this question (Sundstrom, 1975a). Groups of six males worked on an impression-formation task in either a large or small room, where they were observed through one-way mirrors. They talked in pairs and rated one another's personalities. The groups contained three confederates who introduced manipulations of two kinds of interpersonal disturbance. *Intrusion* involved inappropriate physical contact (knees touching) and excessive eye contact. *Goal blocking* (interference with attaining a goal) involved inattention to subjects as they talked during the impression-formation task. Subjects each talked with all three confederates. As in previous research, the small room elicited reports of crowding and discomfort. And as you might expect from the research on personal space, subjects with intrusive interaction partners looked less often at their partners' faces, especially in the small room. This response, possibly a *coping behavior*, continued over three interactions. Concurrent reports of discomfort *decreased* over time, indirectly suggesting that the coping response actually did reduce stress. Goal blocking led to a partial withdrawal from interaction, consisting of lower frequencies of looking at interaction partners' faces, less gesturing and head nodding, and less willingness to discuss personal topics. Reports of irritation concurrently *increased*, implying that partial withdrawal from interaction was ineffective in reducing the impact of goal blocking. These results suggest that if high-density conditions lead to intrusion or goal blocking, coping behaviors may reduce stress under some conditions, but not others.

D. Naturalistic studies of crowding

Many experiments on spatial density take place outside laboratories, in institutional settings such as classrooms and dormitories. Most such studies focus on interpersonal behaviors that accompany high density, including coping behaviors.

1. *Density in playrooms and classrooms.* One early experiment examined 3- to 8-year-old chil-

dren (Hutt & Vaizey, 1966). Five unacquainted children played in a rectangular room. Social density was varied by adding other children; subjects played alone, in a moderate-sized group (7 to 11), or in a large group (12 or more). Of course, the large group had the highest density (39 square feet per child). Children in the large group showed more aggressiveness and more social withdrawal than in the smaller groups.

Withdrawal may have been an attempt to regulate the amount of social interaction these children experienced. Other field studies of children have also reported withdrawal when spatial or social density within a room was high (Loo, 1972; J. L. Price, 1971; Slosnerick, 1974). Parallel findings have been reported among psychiatric patients (Ittelson, Proshansky, & Rivlin, 1972) and interacting adults (Tucker & Friedman, 1972). Under conditions of high room density, we may consider withdrawal to be a *coping response* that maintains desired amounts of social interaction.

Evidence concerning aggressiveness among children in conditions of high density is less consistent. One study varied spatial density in classrooms and observed the children's reactions. There were no differences in aggressiveness (J. L. Price, 1971). Another experiment observed a group of children in a large and a small room and found *less* aggression in the small room (Loo, 1972). A study that helps clarify these inconsistencies posited that aggression in conditions of high density stems from competition for resources, especially toys. Groups of children played in a room where the spatial density and the number of toys were varied. There was more aggression in the condition with high density and a small supply of toys, suggesting that competition and frustration underlie childrens' aggression in crowded quarters (Rohe & Patterson, 1974).

2. Residential environments and crowding. An innovation in the design of college dormitories involves suites of two or three double rooms ar-

ranged around a common lounge and bathroom. Suites are an alternative to arrangements in which many rooms open onto a single long corridor. The suite arrangement facilitates frequent contacts among a small group of students, while the corridor design allows interactions among the many residents of a corridor. Research indicates that students living in corridor arrangements report more crowding than suite residents (Baum & Valins, 1973; Valins & Baum, 1974). Corridor residents are also less likely than suite residents to form cohesive groups and to interact with others (Baum, Harpin, & Valins, 1975). Such behavior regulates the amount of interaction in which the corridor residents participate. Even when placed in a laboratory situation (Valins & Baum, 1974), corridor residents looked less at another person in a waiting room and initiated fewer conversations.[13]

The difference between corridor rooms and suites is a difference in *outside density*. Researchers have also examined reactions to variation in *inside density* in dormitories. For example, a survey showed that students living in identical trailer houses reported greater crowding as the number of students living in the same trailer increased. This trend held for students who shared a bedroom and for those who did not (Eoyang, 1974). Similar results were reported in a study of prison inmates (Paulus, Cox, McCain, & Chandler, 1975). And when Navy men were isolated in groups of two or three in large or small quarters, larger groups in crowded quarters showed greatest stress during the last days of their isolation (S. Smith & Haythorn, 1972). The potential number of interaction partners—social density—seems to be important in determining residential crowding.

---

[13]Note that this finding could be due to personality differences between students who apply for suite rooms and those who apply for corridor rooms. If so, we have differences in individual *adaptation levels* for social interaction (Helson, 1964), not a coping strategy that grows out of residential characteristics.

In a study of social density in dormitory rooms, students were randomly assigned to regular double rooms in groups of two or three. Students in groups of three reported more crowding, and women in large groups reported more crowding than men in large groups. (This finding runs counter to laboratory findings that women react more favorably than men to high density. Perhaps women's positive responses in high density are limited to the first few hours of exposure.) By the end of the semester, students in groups of three showed a decrement in performance of complicated tasks, while paired subjects showed a slight improvement. Furthermore, "tripled" women showed more health problems—physical and psychological—than the other students. And more of these women applied for changes in room assignments than did women in other groups (Aiello, Epstein, & Karlin, 1975b). Thus, crowded dormitory living had detrimental effects, especially for women.

Another study among college students demonstrated that residential crowding depends on the social atmosphere (Stokols & Resnick, 1975b). Students in a large class completed a questionnaire about their classroom and about their living arrangements. Residential crowding was strongly related to students' ratings of their social relationships in terms of trust, competition, hostility, and other factors. Furthermore, residential crowding was related to reports of crowding in the classroom! Apparently, residential crowding can generalize to other settings.

E. Putting the pieces together: Models of crowding

We return now to the idea that crowding involves a *sequential process:* high population density may produce interpersonal conditions that lead to stress, which in turn motivate coping behaviors; psychological costs may or may not follow. We can identify three models of crowding, each based on a different version of the sequence; these are the overload model, the behav-ioral-constraint model, and the ecological model (Stokols, 1976).

1. The overload model. This model assumes that crowding entails excessive *inputs*, both social and physical. The term *overload* "refers to a system's inability to process inputs from the environment because there are too many inputs to cope with, or because the successive inputs come so fast that input A cannot be processed when input B is presented" (Milgram, 1970, p. 167). This is consistent with the *homeostatic* model: crowding seems to represent, in part, an inability to control unwanted interactions with other people (Altman, 1975). Overload can stem from many conditions: (1) physical conditions such as high temperature, noise, or visually complex settings; (2) personal-space invasions, intrusions, or other nonverbal inputs from individuals who are too close; (3) unwanted conversation; (4) too many simultaneous interaction partners; or (5) prolonged interactions. In each case, we expect people to cope by attempting to reduce social input, as in the experiment where subjects looked less at intrusive interaction partners (Sundstrom, 1975a). A common response to high density within rooms seems to be *withdrawal* from interaction. We can also regulate social inputs through architectural interventions, such as closing doors (Stokols, 1976), or through such mechanisms as allocating less time to each social input, ignoring low-priority social inputs, and using screening mechanisms such as secretaries and unlisted telephones (Milgram, 1970).

Ignoring low-priority inputs is illustrated by the finding that urban residents were less likely to be altruistic than people from small towns (Milgram, 1970). One study showed that people given a large number of responsibilities were less altruistic than people with few responsibilities (Krupat & Epstein, 1973). Similarly, students in high-density dormitories were less altruistic than students living in low-density dormitories (Bickman, Teger, Gabriele, McLaughlin, Berger, & Sunday, 1974).

But what if such coping responses fail to prevent overload? We have seen that high density can produce negative aftereffects, including reduced ability to perform tasks. Prolonged high residential density has even been associated with health problems among women (Aiello et al., 1975). Although we might expect to find *adaptation*, we know little about the conditions under which it occurs.

2. The behavioral-constraint model. This model is based on the idea that in high-density conditions, other people reduce a person's behavioral choices, interfere with activities, and thwart the achievement of goals. Such restrictions can produce *psychological reactance* (see Chapter 11), along with a desire to reestablish behavioral freedom (Stokols, 1976). Here, the homeostatic principle applies to the maintenance of optimal behavioral freedom. When our freedom is restricted, we are motivated to reestablish it. In studies of adults, the mere *anticipation* of restricted freedom under conditions of high density produced reports of crowding (Schopler & Walton, 1974); a competitive situation had a similar effect (Stokols et al., 1973).

When a person's behavior is thwarted, one outcome is *frustration*, which may predispose aggression, as we saw in experiments with children. Perhaps the association of high dwelling density with crime and homicide stems from such frustration (Booth & Welch, 1973, 1974). Also, recall that conditions of arousal—or overload—can increase the likelihood of aggression (see Chapter 7).

Of course aggression is by no means the only way to cope with interference. One strategy is *coordination of activities* (Stokols, 1976)—for example, in a crowded theater lobby people simply take turns buying refreshments. Another way to cope with interference is to leave the scene. Aggressive reactions to interference may be unlikely and may represent a last resort.

3. The ecological model. This model of crowding is based on Roger Barker's (1968) concept

of a *behavior setting*, which is an identifiable place with boundaries, characteristic physical features, and stable patterns of role expectations (see Chapter 1). Examples include classrooms, grocery stores, banks, and other everyday settings. There is evidence that in **understaffed settings,** where there are fewer people than there are roles, individuals take more responsibility than they would under optimal staffing conditions. For example, Barker (1960) reported that for Rotary Clubs in eastern Kansas, attendance correlated −.44 with club size, indicating lower participation in large clubs. On the other hand, a setting is *overpopulated*[14] when there are more people than necessary to perform the requisite activities (Wicker, 1973). The ecological model holds that overpopulation of a behavior setting produces crowding (Stokols, 1976). In one experiment on overstaffing, when subjects worked in a situation in which three people were present and only two could be accommodated, they felt less needed, valuable, and important than subjects in an optimally staffed situation (Wicker & Kirmeyer, 1975). We know little about coping responses in overpopulated behavior settings. However, one possibility is that overstaffed groups divide their tasks into more specialized jobs to accommodate more people.

4. Crowding in primary and secondary environments. As we noted earlier, the experience of crowding depends on the setting. In a theory of crowding, Stokols posits that crowding is most intense and difficult to resolve in *primary environments*, or places where "an individual spends much time, relates to others on a personal basis, and engages in a wide range of personally important activities" (1976, p. 19). Examples include residences and work environments. Note that a

[14]This term is an alternative for "overmanned," which was used in Barker's original theory (1960). In developing the theory Wicker (1973; Wicker & Kirmeyer, 1975) has recognized the unintentional sexist connotation and has begun to use neutral terms.

primary environment resembles a *primary territory*, a place that is central to a person's everyday functioning (Altman, 1975). In primary settings, Stokols proposes that sources of overload, thwarting, or overstaffing are perceived as greater threats to a person's psychological security than in *secondary environments*, where "encounters with others are relatively transitory, anonymous, and inconsequential" (p. 20). Shopping centers, sidewalks, corridors in schools, and elevators are secondary environments. Note that the distinction between primary and secondary environments also roughly parallels the distinction between inside and outside density—many primary environments are dwellings or offices. Secondary environments, both indoors and outdoors, would be subject to overpopulation from high outside density. Evidence that associates homicide with high inside density (Booth & Welch, 1973) agrees with the idea that crowding is most intense in primary environments.

A second dimension of crowding is its *neutral* or *personal* nature. Stokols focuses on thwarting, or social interference, as a major antecedent of crowding. *Personal thwarting* is perceived as an intentional act by a specific person, directed personally at oneself. *Neutral thwarting* is perceived as unintentional, of diffuse origin, and not personally directed. For example, Oscar Lewis told the story of a poor family living in a one-room house from the point of view of a young girl:

> Living in one room, one must go at the same rhythm as the others, willingly or unwillingly—there is no way except to follow the wishes of the strongest ones. . . . we all had to go to bed at the same time, when my father had to get up early the next morning, the light had to be put out. Many times I wanted to draw or to read [1970, p. 267].

Although her father interfered with reading, the thwarting may be seen as neutral because she attributed his interference to influences of the environment and saw it as directed not only at

her, but at the whole family. While personal and neutral thwartings can occur in any setting, Stokols hypothesizes that in primary environments thwarting will tend to be seen as personal, and in secondary environments as neutral.

The personal-neutral distinction also applies to sources of overload: one explanation for the aversive nature of personal-space invasions in uncrowded situations is that invaders' behavior cannot be attributed to the setting (Sundstrom, 1975b). For example, when a person stands too close at an uncrowded bus stop we assume his or her rudeness is deliberate and experience more intense crowding than if the proximity was caused by congestion. In summary, crowding is intensified in primary environments and by personally directed sources of overload or interference.

The best general statement we can make about crowding is that it is highly complex, like most other phenomena we have examined. One way to summarize the findings is to imagine what combination of situational, interpersonal, and personality characteristics would produce the most intense experience of crowding (Altman, 1975). Consider the following situation: A teenage boy who prefers a large personal space lives with his family of seven in a three-room apartment in a crowded ghetto, near a noisy freeway, in a warm climate. His brother, with whom he shares a double bed, deliberately interferes whenever he tries to do schoolwork. At his crowded school the classes are large; he likes to play basketball, but there are 16 other players on the school team. Here we see three interpersonal antecedents of crowding: overload, interference, and overpopulation of behavior settings. And the resulting stress would be intensified by their occurrence in a primary setting, as well as by heat, noise, and the personal nature of his brother's interference. We might expect fatigue, frustration, and feelings of marginality. Outcomes involving aggression would not be surprising, although most evidence of such outcomes is correlational. This example is not farfetched, and it illustrates the powerful influence the physical setting can exert.

V. Summary

We assume a give-and-take relationship between persons and their physical settings—the setting can *affect* interpersonal behavior, but people actively *use* their settings as they interact. One way of using settings involves our locations within them; *personal space* refers to the physical distances between people. For any situation, each person has an *optimal distance* from others, depending on the formality of the interaction, the situation, personality characteristics, and the interpersonal relationship. Optimal distances are relatively small between females and people who like each other and in intimate interactions. Interpersonal distance seems to operate on a *homeostatic principle;* if another person is closer or farther than the optimal distance, we may feel uncomfortable and attempt to compensate, by adjusting the distance or some other signal of *immediacy* or psychological closeness, such as eye contact or directness of body orientation. Seating patterns influence interpersonal distance, directness of orientation, and the presence of barriers; people who want to talk usually adopt a 90° seating arrangement. In groups, however, people tend to address those whom they face most directly.

Territorial behavior, another way in which people use their settings, refers to the perception that a specific area or place is under the control of its occupants, and to the habitual, exclusive use of a place. Territoriality is a mechanism for maintaining an optimal amount of interaction with other people; it assists in the regulation of *privacy,* defined as the selective control over interactions. *Primary territories* are central to the lives of the occupants, used on a permanent basis, and clearly identifiable as belonging to the occupants. *Secondary territories* are areas regularly used and controlled by groups who can recognize

outsiders. *Public territories* are temporarily established in spaces open to a wide variety of users; examples include tables at libraries. Public territories can be reserved with markers. They are sometimes chosen on the basis of their distance from other people. In confined groups territorial behavior serves to organize group interactions; dominant members usually have better space and more space than less dominant members. When people are inside their territories, they seem to dominate interactions, a phenomenon called *territorial dominance.*

The physical setting can act as a determinant of interpersonal behavior by affecting who interacts with whom. When people live close to one another, they are more likely to be friends. In *office landscape* arrangements, where workers are separated only by movable office furniture, people may be unable to achieve privacy. Unless they prefer frequent social inputs, they may find the arrangement distracting. Within a room, *sociopetal* spaces bring people together and *sociofugal* spaces keep them apart; the more directly two chairs face, the more sociopetal they are.

Physical settings can also affect interactions indirectly through emotional states induced by noise or heat. High temperatures can decrease liking and increase the likelihood of an aggressive response. Noise can also increase the possibility of aggression, and although people can adapt to it, they may experience aftereffects such as decreased toleration for frustration.

Crowding is a psychological state of stress that accompanies high population density, defined as a relatively large number of persons per unit of space. *Inside density* refers to the number of persons per unit of space inside a dwelling; *outside density* refers to the number of people per acre. Correlational evidence links high inside density with crime, especially homicide. Crowding apparently operates as a sequential process: high density produces aversive interpersonal events that lead to stress. An individual attempts to reduce the stress through *coping* responses. Negative aftereffects or psychological costs may follow. According to the *overload* model, stress is brought on by excessive inputs, both physical and social. Coping responses include withdrawal from interaction and disregard of low-priority inputs. Aftereffects include impaired ability to perform tasks. According to the *behavioral-constraint* model, other people's interference with activities results in frustration. One coping response is coordination of activities with others; a less adaptive reaction is aggression. According to the *ecological model*, crowding results from the overpopulation of a behavior setting, meaning that there are more people than roles. Crowding is most intense in *primary environments*, where a person spends a great deal of time and interacts with others on a personal basis.

I. What is a group?
A. The definition of a group
B. The individualistic orientation versus the group orientation
C. Are groups "real"?

II. Do groups have effects beyond those of the individuals in them?
A. Deindividuation in groups
B. Groups versus individuals as problem solvers
C. The polarizing effects of group interaction

III. Qualities affecting the influence of groups
A. Effects of group size
B. Communication opportunities
C. Cohesiveness

IV. T-groups and encounter groups
A. Types of experiential groups
B. The effects of participation

V. Communal groups
A. Why study communes?
B. Definitions of a commune
C. Social-psychological factors that lead to a successful commune

VI. Summary

The behavior of groups 17

The problem had started outside Casey's Bar in the Mexican-American ghetto of East Los Angeles. The bar's owner, a White man named Andrew Casey, claimed that he had caught Ernesto Sanchez and two other Mexican-American youths tampering with his car in the parking lot. As the three young men tried to escape, said Casey, he fired at Sanchez with a .25-caliber pistol and hit him in the back of the head. When word spread through the Mexican-American community that Sanchez was dead, a crowd of 300 to 400 converged in front of the bar.

Among these was Steven Concepción, a college student home for the spring vacation. Steven considered himself a peaceful person; in fact he had practiced the tactics of nonviolent protest during his high school days. But as he listened to the crowd and learned that Casey had been charged only with manslaughter and freed on a $500 bond, he began to respond to the emotion of the crowd. As the crowd started to throw bricks, he began to join in, really enjoying the release of feeling expressed by every heave of a brick through the bar's massive front window.

I. What is a group?

In the above incident, our initial explanation for Steven's behavior might be that "he was influenced by the group to which he belongs." But can we call an assemblage of persons on a street corner a *group*? Doesn't a group imply some long-term relationship? While many groups do exist for an extended period of time, the *length* is not as important as the *relationship*.

A. The definition of a group

In specifying what is a group, we draw on the work of John DeLamater, who has offered a thorough critique of previous statements: "A comprehensive definition of 'group' can be formulated in terms of the following properties: interaction between individuals, perceptions of other members and the development of shared perceptions, the development of affective ties, and the development of interdependence or roles" (1974, p. 39). Note, then, that a group can be formed spontaneously, when the actions of one person begin to influence those of another and a state of dependency emerges. The passengers on Flight #391 from Dayton to St. Louis ordinarily would not constitute a group. But if the passengers were told that the plane was to make a crash landing, leading some of the passengers to start screaming or climbing over each other to get to the emergency exits, a group would have been formed, in which there was interaction, interdependence, and shared emotions.

551

Football teams, families, faculties of small colleges, and fishing crews are groups. Members of each of these entities clearly interact with and influence each other. There is a common group goal and at least some rudimentary group structure (M. E. Shaw, 1976). But groups may be composed of individuals who do not even come into close proximity with each other or see each other. The national sales manager for Marlboro cigarettes and his field representatives in each state may constitute a group; likewise, all the members of an audience at the latest Woody Allen movie constitute a group in a limited sense. (Each audience member, by his or her outward reaction to what is on the screen, may influence whether the others—who are there to have a good time—have their needs satisfied.)

Collections of individuals who are not interacting with each other are called *aggregates*. Persons standing on a street corner waiting for the light to change, members of a political party, passengers seated in the terminal waiting to board a bus—these ordinarily do not interact or share feelings to such a degree that they can influence each other. However, as the beginning vignette shows, an aggregate can quickly become a group.

B. The individualistic orientation versus the group orientation

Throughout the earlier chapters of this text, our focus has primarily been on the *individual*. We have granted—even emphasized—that individuals are influenced by a number of social considerations, including their roles and group memberships, but our assumption has been that, in the words of Steiner, "the individual is a system in his own right, functioning in the midst of other such systems" (1974, p. 95). Steiner notes that the individualistic orientation is one way of studying human social behavior, but that there is a second approach that focuses on a *group orientation*. In the latter "the individual is presumed to be an element in a larger system, a group, organization or society. . . . Consequently,

one looks for causes that are located outside the individual himself, in the collective actions of others, or in the constraints imposed by the larger system" (Steiner, 1974, p. 96).

During the 1940s and 1950s there was strong support within social psychology for a group orientation to the study of social behavior. In Chapter 13 we noted the impact of Lewinian field theory, which maintained that groups should be studied both within the confines of the laboratory and in their natural settings. During that time even the concepts of the individualistic orientation—such as attitudes, motives, and values—were viewed against a background supplied by the family, the work organization, and the community in which the individual was imbedded.

But by the later 1950s interest in groups had begun to decline (McGrath & Altman, 1966), apparently for several reasons:

1. Steiner (1974) has proposed that when society is serene—as it was in the U.S. and Canada in the Eisenhower and St. Laurent years of the 1950s—we focus our attention on either individuals or very large organizations. The small group tends to be ignored.

2. In the eyes of many social psychologists, the actual research done in group dynamics was not very satisfactory. Much of the laboratory research on "groups" seemed to violate the very definition of the term. For example, in some studies, "groups" of students would be formed on the spur of the moment and told that they either would like each other or would not. While it is true that the people in these groups did interact, the investigator was the one who specified all the roles and norms, and any affective ties that occurred were quite transitory and artificial (DeLamater, 1974). In fact, in reviewing literature on group processes during the 1960s, Helmreich, Bakeman, and Scherwitz (1973) suggested that research on groups had fallen victim to a psychological Gresham's Law by which "bad research drives out good" (Steiner, 1974).

For whatever reasons, the individualistic orientation—with its emphasis on the actions of the perceiver, on attitudes, and on our responses to cognitive dissonance—dominated social psychology in the 1960s. (But readers of previous chapters of this book already knew that!) It appears that trends are changing, though.

Steiner believes that social psychological trends lag about eight to ten years behind the times. We all agree that the late 1960s were a period of great disruptions, in which there was a vying for control and influence by different segments of society (Black Power, Quebec Separatism, student activists, the right wing, even the FBI and the CIA). It should follow from Steiner's analysis that we are beginning to witness a renascence of interest in the group orientation to the study of social behavior.

In selecting topics for study, social psychology is often accused of faddishly following what society is presently concerned about. Recent obsessions such as T-groups, sensitivity training, and Transactional Analysis may be interpreted as society's expressing impatience with the self-contained individual as the basic unit of social action. New communes are forming daily. (Both of these phenomena are considered later in this chapter.) The social psychology of the late 1970s is beginning to look a lot like an improved version of the social psychology of the later '40s.

C. Are groups "real"?

Despite the likely renascence of a group orientation in social psychology, the question remains, are groups "real"? The venerable Floyd H. Allport used to say "You can't stumble over a group." For him, groups existed only in the minds of people; they were no more than shared sets of values, ideas, thoughts, and habits that existed simultaneously in the heads of several persons.

Others have argued just as impressively that groups *are* entities and should hence be treated like any other unitary objects in our environment (Durkheim, 1898; Warriner, 1956). Such advocates renounce the suggestion that all social behaviors can be explained adequately at the in-

dividualistic level (to use Steiner's distinction); "hence any valid explanation of group processes must be at the level of the group" (M. E. Shaw, 1976, p. 12).

Do groups have effects beyond those of the individuals in them? This simple question requires a complicated answer. Before giving one, we think it is useful to consider some of the areas in which groups do have pronounced effects. While large sections of Chapters 18, 19, and 20 also are relevant to the question, in the next section of this chapter we consider specific effects: deindividuation, facilitation, problem-solving effectiveness, and polarization.

II. Do groups have effects beyond those of the individuals in them?

A. Deindividuation in groups

Under certain group conditions, people may do things that they would not do alone. Group membership may offer opportunities for **deindividuation**—a descriptive term suggested by Festinger, Pepitone, and Newcomb (1952). Deindividuation is a state of relative anonymity, in which the group member does not feel singled out or identifiable. Other things being equal, the larger the group, the more deindividuated a person can become. We saw in the beginning example how Steven lost his identity in a mob and found himself committing acts that, if isolated, he would have refrained from committing. LeBon's (1896) classic analysis of crowd behavior deals with a similar conception. LeBon postulated that persons in a mob lose their sense of responsibility and adopt the unitary consciousness of the crowd (Cannavale, Scarr, & Pepitone, 1970).

But even in small groups the degree of deindividuation can be manipulated, as Festinger, Pepitone, and Newcomb (1952) were the first to show, 25 years ago. They encouraged groups of male college students to make unfavorable and even hostile statements about their parents—feelings that students in the serene

1950s would have been reluctant to express under ordinary circumstances. Some groups of young men participated in these discussions in a regular classroom; other groups were in a semi-darkened room, where each participant wore a shapeless gray coat over his clothes. Many more critical and hostile statements were made in the latter deindividuated condition, indicating that inner restraints of the group members were reduced. Men in the deindividuated group were less able to indicate which other participant had made a specific negative statement. Interestingly, as Festinger et al. had proposed, group members rated these deindividuated groups as more attractive than the control groups. The release of restraints was an attractive option, at least for this brief time.

Despite the allure of deindividuation as an explanation for certain group behaviors, almost 15 years passed before a second study was done using deindividuation as an independent variable. J. E. Singer, Brush, and Lublin (1965) compared group members who were dressed up for the occasion with deindividuated subjects dressed in old clothes and lab coats. The deindividuated groups were again found to release more inner restraints: they used obscenity more often in group discussions of pornographic materials than did the more identifiable subjects. Singer et al. concluded that for deindividuation to be most effective, subjects must experience loss of self-consciousness and reduced feelings of distinctiveness. More recently Cannavale et al. (1970) replicated the original study by Festinger et al., using the same device to encourage criticism of parents, but using female groups, male groups, and mixed-sex groups. Results similar to those of the earlier study were found; for instance, the correlation between extent of deindividuation and lowered restraint was +.57 in the original study and +.56 for the all-male groups in the more recent study. But in all-female and mixed-sex groups, no relationship was found between deindividuation and the unleashing of restraints. The authors concluded that in these groups a high level of apprehension

about criticizing parents prevented the deindividuation phenomenon from emerging.

The phenomenon of deindividuation has received notoriety through the research program of Zimbardo (1970a, 1970b), who hypothesized that it is a "process in which a series of antecedent social conditions [lead] to changes in perception of self and others, and thereby to a lowered threshold of normally restrained behavior" (1970b, p. 251). Zimbardo recognizes that deindividuation can cause an increase in the expression of socially tolerated behaviors that we usually do not express overtly (such as intense feelings of joy, sorrow, or affection for others); however, he has chosen as his topic of study the function of deindividuation in the expression of such antisocial feelings and actions as hostility, anger, and theft. A complete description of the variables in the deindividuation process, as identified by Zimbardo, is presented in Table 17-1.

In a laboratory study, Zimbardo manipulated several of the components listed as input variables in Table 17-1 in order to produce a state of deindividuation. For example, anonymity was produced in half the subjects by dressing them in hoods, never using their names, and doing the experiment in the dark. (Several of the deindividuated subjects are pictured in Figure 17-1.) Moreover, the group's task was one in which different members shared responsibility for performing an antisocial act—giving electric shocks to a fellow college student.

A group of four subjects participated at the same time; all were female undergraduates at New York University. Subjects in the *deindividuation* condition were treated as indicated above, and subjects in the *identifiability* condition were given large name tags and were greeted individually. The latter soon got to know one another by name. All subjects were told that the experiment dealt with one's ability to make empathic judgments about another person with whom one was either actively or passively involved. Actively involved meant that the subject induced reactions in the target person; the subject could give the target person a series of strong electric shocks, then observe and rate her behavior. Subjects who were passively involved would only observe and then rate the target person. The procedure was prearranged so that every actual subject believed that she and one other subject in the group of four would administer the electric shocks. During the administration of the electric shocks and observation of the target person's reactions, all subjects were placed in separate cubicles so they would not know how the other subjects responded.

Two vastly different target persons were used. Subjects listened to five-minute tape recordings of interviews between each target person and Zimbardo, so that they were well aware of the differences between the two target per-

---

Table 17-1
Zimbardo's representation of the deindividuation process

Input Variables ⟶	*Inferred Subjective Changes* ⟶	*Output Behaviors*
A —Anonymity B —Responsibility: shared, diffused, given up C —Group size, activity D —Altered temporal perspective: present expanded, future and past distanced E —Arousal F —Sensory input overload G —Physical involvement in the act H —Reliance upon noncognitive interactions and feedback I —Novel or unstructured situation J —Altered states of consciousness, drugs, alcohol, sleep, and so on	Minimization of: 1. Self-observation-evaluation 2. Concern for social evaluation ↓ Weakening of controls based upon guilt, shame, fear, and commitment ↓ Lowered threshold for expressing inhibited behaviors	a. Behavior emitted is emotional, impulsive, irrational, regressive, with high intensity b. Not under the controlling influence of usual external discriminative stimuli c. Behavior is self-reinforcing and is intensified; amplified with repeated expressions of it d. Difficult to terminate e. Possible memory impairments; some amnesia for act f. Perceptual distortion— insensitive to incidental stimuli and to relating actions to other actors g. Hyper-responsiveness— "contagious plasticity" to behavior of proximal, active others h. Unresponsiveness to distal reference groups i. Greater liking for group or situation associated with "released" behavior j. At extreme levels, the group dissolves as its members become autistic in their impulse gratification k. Destruction of traditional forms and structures

sons. One target person was a sweet, altruistic young woman who was working with retarded children to help pay her fiancé's medical school expenses. The other target person, also a female, was obnoxious, self-centered, and negativistic. A transfer student who worked part-time as a model, this second target person said that she could not stand the Jewish students at N.Y.U. (Most of the subjects were Jewish.)

In the electric-shock portion of the experiment, each subject viewed the target person and the experimenter through a one-way mirror. The order of viewing the two target persons was counterbalanced across groups, as were the previous taped interviews. The target person appeared to be taking a verbal test but could not be heard by the subject. Each time the target person was supposedly shocked, she writhed, twisted, grimaced, and otherwise expressed pain. Subjects were given a chance to administer shocks on 20 trials, but on the tenth trial the target person reacted so strongly that her hand ripped out of the electrode strap. As she ruefully rubbed her hand, she was strapped down again, and the remaining 10 trials were completed. This

predetermined reaction divided the 20 trials into two sets, which then could be compared to see whether there was a change in the use of shock after interruption. After the 20 trials, subjects rated the target person and then repeated the whole procedure—audiotaped interview, electric shocks to the visible target person, and ratings—with the second target person.

Compliance with instructions was equally high in both conditions; both identifiable and deindividuated subjects, on the average, administered shocks on 17 of the 20 trials. But deindividuation produced shocks of greater duration. The deindividuated group gave, on the average, shocks of .90 of a second; the identifiable subjects gave shocks averaging .47 of a second. Also, as Figure 17-2 shows, there was a tendency in the deindividuated groups to shock the target person more *after* the interruption. Both the pleasant target person and the obnoxious one were given more shocks by deindividuated subjects after the electrode holder had been snapped. Do deindividuated subjects follow M. J. Lerner's (1970) "just world" hypothesis? Apparently, they assume that if the target person is suffering so

Figure 17-1
Subjects in the deindividuated condition in Zimbardo's study

much as to break the strap, she must deserve the suffering and must be given even longer shocks. In contrast to the identifiable subjects, deindividuated subjects aggressed increasingly, disregarding the characteristics of the recipient. Individuated subjects appeared to take pity on the nice young woman after the electrode strap broke but continued to increase the duration of shocks given to the obnoxious woman.

In this study, no agent of coercion was used. Each subject could choose not to administer shocks; she could assume that the other subject would carry through on the shock administration. (Subjects were told that the experimenter could not determine which subject or subjects had actually administered a shock, as the two

circuits had a common terminal.) Yet in a condition of deindividuation "these sweet, normally mild-mannered college girls shocked another girl almost every time they had an opportunity to do so, sometimes for as long as they were allowed, and it did not matter whether or not that fellow student was a nice girl who didn't deserve to be hurt" (Zimbardo, 1970b, p. 270).

Deindividuation is a phenomenon not limited to the social-psychology laboratory. Much to his credit, Zimbardo extended his observations of the process to the real world. Deindividuation is epitomized by the masses of people in large cities who intermingle without forming any real relationships. Zimbardo predicted that the anonymity and deindividuation endemic to a metropolis such as New York City facilitate the expression of antisocial acts such as theft, looting, and vandalism. With Fraser, a fellow researcher, Zimbardo bought a used car and left it on a busy street adjoining the Bronx campus of New York University. At the same time, a similar car was left on a street near the Stanford University campus in Palo Alto, California. To clearly indicate that the cars had been abandoned, the experimenters removed the license plates and raised the hoods of both cars.

The pictures in Figure 17-3 show what happened to the car left in New York. Within 26 hours it was stripped of battery, radiator, air cleaner, radio antenna, windshield wipers, side chrome, all four hubcaps, a set of jumper cables, a can of car wax, a gas can, and the one tire worth taking. All the looters were well-dressed, clean-cut Whites; in several cases the looting was a family operation, with the son aiding the father's search-and-remove operation, while the mother served as a lookout. No one ever restrained any of the looters, although passersby sometimes stopped to chat while the car was being stripped.

What happened to the car left in the suburban Palo Alto neighborhood was a complete contrast. The car was unharmed during its seven-day abandonment. In fact, one day when it rained, a passerby lowered the hood so the motor would

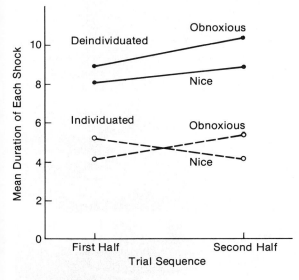

Figure 17-2
Results of the Zimbardo deindividuation experiment. Note that the mean duration of shocks given in the deindividuated condition was higher than in the individuated, identifiable condition. In the deindividuated condition the obnoxious young woman was shocked for longer periods than the nice young woman, and even longer shocks were given after the interruption resulting from the broken electrode strap.

Figure 17-3
Family fun: Stripping and looting in Fun City.

not get waterlogged! As Milgram (1970) and others have pointed out, however, the Bronx and Palo Alto environments differ in many respects in addition to population density. Further research will need to take other factors into account, as the deindividuation process is pinpointed.

On the basis of these studies and other equally provocative observations, Zimbardo concludes that for looting to be initiated, well-developed feelings of anonymity must exist, plus some minimal releaser cues. For example, it must be clear that the car has been abandoned. A minimal releaser cue may be a lack of license plates, a tire removed, or some other disabling sign. Emphasis should be put on the word *minimal.* Zimbardo reports two anecdotes that convey how readily looting may be triggered in an urbanized society.

According to one anecdote, as part of an army convoy was passing through the Bronx, an army tank stalled and was momentarily left unoccupied while its driver sought a mechanic. By the time the driver returned a few hours later, the tank had been stripped of all removable parts. According to the second anecdote, a motorist in Queens, New York, pulled his car off the highway to replace a flat tire. While the car was jacked up and the motorist was removing the tire, a stranger came up, raised the car's hood, and started to remove the battery. When the stranger was confronted, his response was "Take it easy, buddy; you can have the tires; all I want is the battery!" (Zimbardo, 1970b, p. 292).

B. Groups versus individuals as problem solvers

We have been aware for a long time that the awareness of others watching us has an impact on virtually every component of behavior. In fact the very first social-psychology experiment, conducted by Triplett in 1897, found that boys could ride a bicycle and wind a fishing reel faster when they were aware of being in the presence of others than when they were alone. For many years it was assumed that the presence of others had beneficial effects (Ickes, 1974; Crandall, 1974); in fact, Floyd Allport termed the phenomenon **social facilitation.** Much more recently Zajonc (1965) proposed—and seemingly demonstrated—that awareness of others only facilitates an individual's performance when the task to be performed is simple or well learned. That is, another's presence can *impair* one's actions when the task is difficult or not well learned (Zajonc & Sales, 1966). This conclusion has not gone unchallenged; the question is whether it is the mere presence of an audience that leads to the effects (Cottrell, Wack, Sekerak, & Rittle, 1968; Cottrell, 1972). Is it the evaluative potential of that audience that motivates the behavior "through anticipation of positive or negative outcomes in the form of praise or criticism" (Ickes, 1974, p. 3)? Research on this question continues; however, regardless of its causes, the previous work has already demonstrated the power of the presence of others on an individual's response.

However, in this section we consider a related question: Do individuals working together in a group perform more successfully or efficiently than they would working alone? We consider the effects on judgment and problem solving, relying heavily on an analysis made by Marvin E. Shaw (1976).

1. On judgments or observations. If your car is rammed from behind, is it better to have one witness or a group of onlookers if you seek accurate testimony? When we ask whether a group's performance exceeds that of individuals, we have to ask "what individuals and on what tasks?" To say the group's performance is better than that of the average individual acting alone is not impressive when we are dealing with purely physical tasks such as pulling a car out of the mud. But on mental tasks or judgments, to say that the group was better or more accurate than the most proficient individual would have been alone seems to indicate a clear-cut contribution from the group.

In attempting to deal with this problem, two approaches have been developed. The first is called the *"statisticized" group technique* (Lorge, Fox, Davitz, & Brenner, 1958). It averages the individual responses of all group members and compares the resulting figure with the average for independent, noninteracting individuals. While there is some indication that some "group" averages show more accurate judgments of weights, temperatures, and such physical phenomena (Knight, 1921; K. Gordon, 1924), this method is quite unsatisfactory. It fails to take into account the social-psychological processes in group interaction (Preston, 1938).

The second method is better, for it compares the responses of separated individuals with the response resulting from a group discussion. (This response may either be a group consensus or individual judgments made after group discussion.) A variety of judgments and observations have been applied, ranging from the number of beans in a bottle to the veracity of "testimony" about an imaginary crime (Burtt, 1920; Jenness, 1932; Marston, 1924). The comparisons indicate some group superiority, but not as much as one might expect. Shaw's conclusion seems appropriately restrained:

> In general, it appears that group judgments are seldom less accurate than the average individual judgment and are often superior. This can be accounted for by the number of judgments contributing to the estimate (Stroop, 1932), by the range of knowledge represented by the individual group members (Jenness, 1932), and by the effects of others on the less confident group members (Gurnee, 1937). It is also apparent that the kind of task may determine whether group judgment will be superior to individual judgments [1976, pp. 60–61].

Thus, when it comes to judgments, the quality of the group outcome is not always superior to that of the wisest group member. One of the reasons for this sad outcome is what Irving L. Janis (1971, 1972) calls "groupthink." This pervasive phenomenon is described in Figure 17-4.

2. On problem solving. We can see how a dominant member can cause a team or a committee to make a subjective judgment that is less than the best. But are groups better than individuals at problem-solving tasks for which there is one certifiably correct answer? A number of methodologies have been used to answer this question (M. E. Shaw, 1976):

a. Persons who have previously attacked problems separately then attempt to solve similar problems in groups. The order and problems are counterbalanced, so that a practice effect does not account for the differences.

b. Different samples of persons are used, with some of them solving puzzles separately, the others working in groups. The problems to be solved range from simple puzzles to complex syllogistic-reasoning tasks. (See Figure 17-5 for a classic example and its results.)

The evidence is consistent in a number of studies (Marjorie E. Shaw, 1932; G. B. Watson, 1928; Husband, 1940; D. W. Taylor & Faust, 1952; J. H. Davis & Restle, 1963). Shaw's summary states that "groups produce more and better solutions to problems than do individuals, although the differences in overall time required for solution are not consistently better for either individuals or groups" (M. E. Shaw, 1976, p. 64). But when the person-hours required for solution are considered, individuals have to be judged as superior.

3. "Brainstorming." About 20 years ago an advertising executive (Osborn, 1957) began to advocate "brainstorming" as a device by which groups could come up with new or creative solutions to difficult problems. The ground rules for brainstorming are the following:

a. Given a problem to solve, all group members are encouraged to express whatever solutions or ideas come to mind, regardless of how preposterous or impractical they seem.

b. All reactions are recorded.

c. No suggestion or solution can be evaluated until all ideas have been expressed. Ideal-

Figure 17-4
"Groupthink" in the White House. Social psychologist Irving L. Janis defines *groupthink* as a "mode of thinking that persons engage in when concurrence-seeking becomes so dominant in a cohesive ingroup that it tends to override realistic appraisal of realistic courses of action" (1971, p. 44). He illustrates a number of times in which groupthink dominated the group decision made by a U. S. President and his staff. President John F. Kennedy's decision to invade the Cuban Bay of Pigs is one. Realistic dissent is squashed out of a desire to maintain a cozy, "we-feeling" atmosphere. It becomes internalized; each person decides that his or her misgivings should be set aside for the benefit of group harmony. Janis notes that at the most crucial meeting about the Bay of Pigs invasion, President Kennedy called on each staff member to give his vote for or against the plan. But he did *not* call on Arthur Schlesinger, the one person there known by the President to have major misgivings. In *A Thousand Days* Schlesinger wrote "I can only explain my failure to do more than raise a few timid questions by reporting that one's impulse to blow the whistle on this nonsense was simply undone by the circumstances of the discussion." (Photo courtesy of Freelance Photographers Guild.)

ly, participants should be led to believe that no suggestions will even be evaluated at the brainstorming session.

   d. The elaboration of one person's ideas by another is not only permitted but encouraged.

Osborn claimed great success with the brainstorming procedure. Empirical evaluations have not consistently produced results that indicate brainstorming is worth its time (Bouchard, Barsaloux, & Drauden, 1974). For example, D.

Figure 17-5

Do groups solve problems better than individuals? You may recall the mental problem involving the missionaries and the cannibals. In the task, three cannibals and three missionaries must be transported across a river, in several trips, since the boat holds only two persons at a time. One of the cannibals and all three of the missionaries know how to operate the boat. The crossing must be carried out so that the cannibals on either shore never outnumber the missionaries. In a classic study Marjorie E. Shaw (1932) used puzzles and problems like this one to compare group and individual problem solving. Subjects worked either in five groups of four persons each or as individuals. In solving such problems, 5 individuals out of 63 produced correct solutions (8%), compared with 8 out of 15 groups (53%). The groups took about 1½ times as long to solve the problems, however. The cost in person-hours was thus greater in the groups. Shaw concluded that the major advantage of the group was its ability to recognize and reject incorrect solutions and suggestions. (Drawing by Sidney Harris.)

W. Taylor, Berry, and Block (1958) found that four separated individuals, operating under brainstorming instructions, produced almost twice as many ideas per unit of time as did face-to-face brainstorming groups of four persons each. This was the case also when the subjects were research scientists who had experience working together on solving problems (Dunnette, Campbell, & Jaastad, 1963). The outcome of these studies does not question the effectiveness of brainstorming per se, but whether the bringing together of individuals is an efficient way of achieving it, as Osborn claimed (Graham & Dillon, 1974).

Much of the research on brainstorming groups has been criticized because it brought together individuals who did not know each other and who were formed into "groups" briefly for the purpose of the experiment and then disbanded (Bouchard, 1972). We are aware that members of such groups might be reluctant to express some of their wild flights of fancy in front of strangers, even under ground rules that no criticism of any idea could be expressed. Such transitory groups may not be very motivated, either. On the other hand, it has been shown that training and practice can improve the performance of brainstorming groups (Parnes & Meadow, 1959; D. Cohen, Whitmyre, & Funk, 1960). Likewise, groups can be preselected to contain individuals with different skills, so that group brainstorming does not involve the mismanagement of time it is often claimed to generate (Bouchard, 1969; Heslin, 1964; R. D. Mann, 1959).

C. The polarizing effects of group interaction

The interaction between individuals is the central feature that makes the group worthy of study by social psychologists. Group discussion —often requiring a consensus decision—can change the outcomes for individuals to a degree that makes it appropriate for us to say that groups have identities of their own.

Observations of discussions by groups, as a part of their decision-making process, reveal that pressures toward uniformity occur (Festinger, 1950). In a classic study of the group problem-solving process, Schachter (1951) arranged for one member of a group to maintain a position on the discussion topic that was quite at odds with the positions of all the other group members. Reactions to this person, called a *deviate* because of his position on the issue, included a great deal of attention, at first. Other members directed more of their communications toward him than toward each other. However, after it began to be clear that his position on the topic was not going to shift, the others terminated their communications to him and concentrated on resolving their own, relatively minor, differences.

One very strong outcome of such discussions is a *polarization* of responses. That is, the consensus judgments and opinions resulting from the group participation are more extreme than the average of the separate participants beforehand. *Polarization* is operationally defined in this sense as an increase—from the initial measurement to a postdiscussion measurement—in "the proximity of the sample's average to the dominant pole or, in other words, an increase in the extent to which an attitude is dominant in a sample" (Lamm, Trommsdorff, & Rost-Schaude, 1973, p. 474).

More than a dozen experiments have produced some degree of polarization of attitudes as a result of group discussion (including Moscovici, Zavalloni, & Louis-Guérin, 1972; Gouge & Fraser, 1972; and Myers & Bishop, 1971), so we may consider it to be a very robust phenomenon. Why does it occur? Several explanations have been offered:

1. Moscovici and Zavalloni (1969) believe that group discussion leads to an enhancement of participants' involvement with the issues and their confidence that their position is the correct one.

2. Andrews and Johnson conclude that there may be a "climb-on-the-bandwagon" effect, caused by "group members discovering that

most of them are leaning in the same direction on a particular question" (1971, p. 192). This would seem to be especially likely in groups whose members anticipate having future interactions with each other in other settings.

3. It may be that those group members whose original positions are most extreme are also most forceful and vehement in arguing their position. For example, it has been found that persons with more extreme positions also have greater confidence in their position (Stroebe & Fraser, 1971).

4. Myers and Bishop (1971) offer a "mutual-reinforcement" explanation of polarization, which concludes that the dominant side of the issue takes up most of the discussion time and arguments. They found that 76% of the arguments were in support of the side that was held by most members of the sample. Thus a shift toward extremity occurs because tendencies toward accepting dominant positions are reinforced by hearing statements of attitudes similar to one's own. In his discussion of "groupthink" Janis observed that group members "show interest in facts and opinions that support their initially preferred policy and take up time in their meetings to discuss them, but they tend to ignore facts and opinions that do not support their initially preferred policy" (1972, p. 10).

For whatever reason it occurs, the polarization effect in groups is of great relevance to any society that utilizes groups to make important decisions. Figure 17-4 illustrates how it can operate in decisions involving possible wars. Juries are quite subject to polarization effects, since they are under pressure to reach a consensus. Chapter 19 will consider the polarization effect further, with respect to whether groups tend to make riskier decisions than do individuals.

III. Qualities affecting the influence of groups

Groups are no more alike than are individuals. Any discussion of the effects of groups must take into account some of their most variable and salient qualities. In this section we consider three of these: group size, communication networks, and cohesiveness.

A. Effects of group size

Even within the limits of the definition of *group* that we introduced at the beginning of this chapter, it is possible to conceive of groups ranging in size from a couple on their honeymoon to all the members of the U.S. Congress or the Canadian House of Commons. Most experimental research has concentrated, of course, on groups of a small size (that is, from three to ten people). The most frequently studied topic has been the relationship of the group's size to its performance on mental tasks.

There have been efforts (probably unwise) to specify the "ideal size" for problem-solving groups. For example, P. E. Slater (1958) concluded that groups of five were the most effective for dealing with mental tasks that involved the collection or exchange of information or making a decision based on the evaluation of that information. And Osborn (1957), the developer of brainstorming, suggested that the optimum size of such groups is between five and ten.

Such conclusions are probably oversimplifications, for several reasons. First, there are varying criteria for what is successful. Smaller groups may be more satisfying to participants because they get a chance to express their opinions fully, but the addition of a few more members may add essential skills and make for a better solution to the task, even if it hurts members' participation and morale. Second, some tasks may really require only one person, whereas other tasks can be solved only by several individuals (Hackman & Vidmar, 1972; Steiner, 1972). Third, the amount of structure in the group certainly interacts with its size (B. W. Jorgensen, 1973). While it may be that groups composed of more than five people are *less satisfying* to each group member, larger groups can be effective without any major loss of morale.

Size of the group and its effects are important in everyday life. We know that the traditional jury in England, the United States, and Canada consists of 12 persons who must come to a unanimous decision. But a number of U.S. states are experimenting—mostly on civil cases—with smaller jury sizes and majority verdicts (Kalven & Zeisel, 1966). Several other countries already use trial juries of less than 12 people (Saks & Ostrom, 1975). What are the effects of these variations on *group process* and *outcome?* Do smaller numbers of jurors spend less time in deliberation? Are smaller groups more likely to reach *guilty* verdicts? Are their verdicts less likely to be correct?

A recent study used mock juries to look at some of these contributions (J. H. Davis, Kerr, Atkin, Holt, & Meek, 1975). Juries composed of either 6 or 12 undergraduates listened to a tape recording of a trial, an abbreviated version of the transcript of an actual rape trial. The recording lasted 45 minutes. Some "juries" of subjects were instructed to come to a unanimous decision regarding guilt or innocence within 30 minutes. Others were told that their jury must reach a two-thirds-majority decision.

The 12-person and 6-person juries came to almost the same decision; 89% of the 6-person juries and 83% of the 12-person juries judged the defendant to be innocent. Similarly, those groups forced to unanimity did not make judgments very different from the two-thirds-majority groups (81% and 92%, respectively, returned a verdict of "innocent"). The major differences were in the group *process* rather than the verdict. Table 17-2 indicates that unanimous juries needed a larger number of poll votes before reaching a verdict, as well as a longer deliberation time. On the basis of this study, it would first appear that Supreme Court decisions permitting less than unanimous decisions seem safe enough. These variations appear to produce about the same outcomes with less decision time. But this is not the whole story. Further analyses by Davis and his colleagues indicated that of the 36 juries operating under the two-thirds rule, 26 had a two-thirds majority on their first poll (but did not have unanimity). Of these 26, a total of 9 juries (35%) decided *immediately* upon the majority position, and several more deliberated only

Table 17-2
Mean number of polls and mean time (in minutes) to verdict in each experimental condition in Davis et al. (1975) study

Assigned Social-Decision Scheme	Jury Size		Total
	6 Persons	12 Persons	
Unanimity			
Polls	2.39	2.89	2.64
Time	13.28	19.22	16.25
Two-thirds majority			
Polls	1.94	1.78	1.86
Time	11.83	7.61	9.72
Total			
Polls	2.17	2.33	2.25
Time	12.56	13.42	12.99

Note: N = 18 groups in each cell.

From "The Decision Processes of 6- and 12-Person Mock Juries Assigned Unanimous and Two-Thirds Majority Rules," by J. H. Davis, N. L. Kerr, R. S. Atkin, R. Holt, and D. Meek, *Journal of Personality and Social Psychology*, 1975, 32, 1–14. Copyright 1975 by the American Psychological Association. Reprinted by permission.

a short time after the first vote. The nonunanimous rule may lead to a "cursory consideration of dissenting views" (Davis, et al., 1975, p. 12).

B. Communication opportunities

Group size is meaningless if group members have difficulty in communicating with each other. Real-world groups sometimes establish restricted channels through which messages may go; members of President Nixon's Cabinet complained that they were not allowed to speak to the President directly, only to his second-level staff members (Rather & Gates, 1974). Relationships between individuals may affect communication channels; there may be two members of the church's board of deacons who "haven't spoken to each other for years." Location of some group members in a different building may inhibit communication between them. (Chapter 16 considered some of the effects of physical environment on group members' interaction.)

We refer to the prescribed patterns of communication between members as **communication networks.** Some possible networks involving three-, four-, and five-person groups are represented in Figure 17-6. Notice, for example, among the five-person networks the one called the "wheel." This type gives great control to the person in the middle; he or she can communicate with each of the other four members, but they (in *peripheral positions*) cannot communicate with each other, only with the *central person*. If such a communication network were established as the ground rules at the formation of a new group, it would not surprise us if the central-position person emerged as the leader (Hirota, 1953; M. E. Shaw, 1954; M. E. Shaw & Rothschild, 1956). In such cases, possession of information leads to power.

The "Y" and "chain" networks in Figure 17-6 also lead to a centralized organization, but the "circle" does not facilitate the emergence of any dominant leader (Leavitt, 1951). In real-life groups that have a "circle" communication net-

work (a relatively unlikely one) or a "comcon" network, in which every member is able to communicate with everyone else, it is not possible to predict which position will lead to leadership and dominance. In such an organization, the individual personalities of group members are the determining factors.

Two questions about communication networks are most important: What is their effect on productivity? Which are most satisfying to group members?

The second question can be answered simply. People prefer positions in which they have greater opportunities for communication and participation. "Silent" partners do not like to remain quiet. The central position in the "wheel," the "chain," and the "Y" is rated as a satisfying one, but the morale of persons in the peripheral positions in these networks is poor (Leavitt, 1951). Networks that permit decentralized communication lead to higher morale from persons at each position.

The efficiency of different communication networks is more dependent upon the task given to the group. Leavitt (1951) found that a centralized network—such as a "wheel" or "Y"—was most efficient in respect to the time required for the solution of a problem, the number of errors, and the number of messages. But Leavitt used a simple symbol-identification task that required only the collection and straightforward assembling of information by one person, analogous to collecting pieces of a simple jigsaw puzzle and putting them together.

Probably more in keeping with the problems faced by most groups were those of M. E. Shaw (1954), who used problems that drew on the problem-solving abilities of group members and the manipulation of information. Shaw found that the "circle" was the most efficient and the "wheel" the least efficient, as measured in time required for solution. The decentralized networks also were able to detect and correct errors more rapidly than the "wheel" or the "Y." Yet there is another side; the "wheel" groups required fewer messages before a correct solution was achieved. The difference in outcomes for simple and complex tasks is a quite consistent one, as Table 17-3 indicates, using the results of 18 studies collated by Shaw (1964).

C. Cohesiveness

The spirit of "closeness"—or lack of it—in a group can be an influential determinant of its behavior. For example, sportswriters are fond of observing that certain athletic teams have "the best material" or "personnel" but that "they just can't put it together." In such cases it is likely that an absence of closeness—or even the presence of hostilities between team members—is influential in the team's less-than-expected performance. A number of terms have been used to label this variable, including "we-feeling" and "emotional climate" (Vraa, 1974). The most frequent term is group **cohesiveness,** defined as

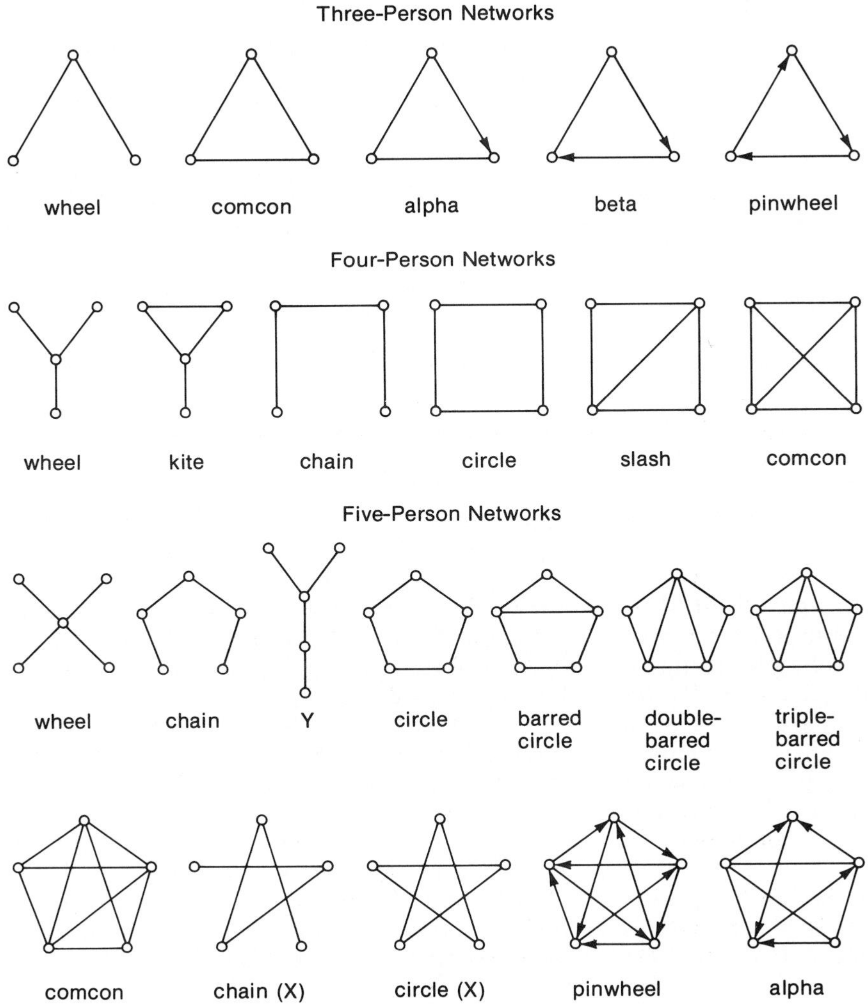

Figure 17-6
Communication networks used in experimental investigations. Dots represent positions, lines represent communication channels, and arrows indicate one-way channels. (Reprinted from Figure 1, p. 113, of Shaw, 1964.)

Table 17-3
Number of comparisons showing differences between centralized ("wheel,"
"chain," "Y") and decentralized ("circle," "comcon") networks as a function
of task complexity

	Simple Problems*	Complex Problems†	Total
Time			
Centralized faster	14	0	14
Decentralized faster	4	18	22
Messages			
Centralized sent more	0	1	1
Decentralized sent more	18	17	35
Errors			
Centralized made more	0	6	6
Decentralized made more	9	1	10
No difference	1	3	4
Satisfaction			
Centralized higher	1	1	2
Decentralized higher	7	10	17

*Simple problems: symbol-, letter-, number-, and color-identification tasks

†Complex problems: arithmetic, word-arrangement, sentence-construction, and discussion problems.

From "Communication Networks," by M. E. Shaw. In L. Berkowitz (Ed.), *Advances in Experimental Social Psychology*, Vol. 1. Copyright 1964 by Academic Press, Inc. Reprinted by permission.

"characteristic of the group in which forces acting on members to remain in the group are greater than the total forces acting on them to leave it" (J. H. Davis, 1969, p. 78). Thus groups in which the members like each other and want to remain in each other's presence are cohesive; groups in which the members are unattracted to each other or groups that are breaking up are said to be low in cohesiveness. As M. E. Shaw (1976) notes, group members who are attracted to the group work harder to achieve its goals; thus one consequence is generally higher productivity by cohesive groups.

The group's goal may not be the goal of the organization of which it is a part; studies (Schachter, Ellertson, McBride, & Gregory, 1951;

L. Berkowitz, 1954) have shown that several highly cohesive groups are more likely to agree on a goal common to all of them (J. H. Davis, 1969). The example of "groupthink" discussed in Figure 17-4 shows that there are dangers from highly cohesive groups, as well as promises of better group functioning.

One of the reasons that cohesiveness is often related to quality of task performance is the mutual availability of members. People in such groups enjoy each other and are not reluctant to involve each other in their search for solutions to tasks. But there is a danger: as J. H. Davis (1969) notes, the interaction may be so pleasurable in and of itself that less energy is devoted to completion of the group's task.

Another reason for success by cohesive groups is the greater pressures on their members toward uniformity. Back (1951) found that members of more cohesive **dyads** changed their opinions in the direction of their partner's opinions more than did members of dyads low in cohesiveness. Similar findings with larger groups have been obtained by Festinger, Gerard, Hymovitch, Kelley, and Raven (1952) and by Lott and Lott (1961).

IV. T-groups and encounter groups

In the last decade individuals have increasingly sought to improve their own skills or lifestyles through participation in groups. Two movements that reflect these needs are the sensitivity-training movement, discussed here, and the communal movement, described in the next section.

A. Types of experiential groups

T-groups (training groups), sensitivity-training groups, and encounter groups all have the same general purposes—to discover one's self and one's impact on others. We often do not realize what our actions mean to other people; the encounters offered by these groups give us feedback about how we are "coming across" to other people. This feedback, in turn, often causes us to revise our conceptions of our selves and our motives.

Experiential groups vary greatly in length of existence and activities. Weekend sessions (called "microlabs") may be contrasted with concentrated workshops lasting two or three weeks. Other T-groups may spread their activities out over a much longer period but meet only an hour each day, or three hours a week. The activities may be leaderless discussion, physical activities involving the group, or nude marathons—in fact, almost anything is fair game, as long as the group leader considers it to be of benefit for personal-

growth purposes. Techniques mushroom, and there is little agreement over desirable techniques, specific purposes, or even definitions of terms. However, there does seem to be general agreement in a distinction between the terms "T-group" and "encounter group."

"T-group" stands for *training group*. As a technique, it was originally developed by Kurt Lewin and his colleagues who, in August 1946, were leading a workshop that was exploring the use of small groups as a vehicle for personal and social change (R. Lippitt, 1949). The techniques being used were rather traditional, with sessions throughout the day. During the evenings the staff (including Lewin, Ronald Lippitt, Kenneth Benne, and Leland Bradford) would meet to discuss the daily events. One evening, to the surprise of all, three trainees appeared and wanted to listen to the staff's discussion. In an interview obtained by Back (1972), Ronald Lippitt later described what happened:

And on this particular night, three of the trainees, three school teachers who hadn't gone home that evening, stuck their heads in the door and asked if they could come in, sit and observe and listen, and Kurt [Lewin] was rather embarrassed, and we all were expecting him to say no, but he didn't, he said, "Yes, sure, come on in and sit down." And we went right ahead as though they weren't there, and pretty soon one of them was mentioned and her behavior was described and discussed, and the trainer and the researcher had somewhat different observations, perceptions of what had happened, and she became very agitated and said that wasn't the way it happened at all, and she gave her perception. And Lewin got quite excited about this additional data and put it on the board to theorize it, and later on in the evening the same thing happened in relation to one of the other two. She had a different perception on what was being described as an event in that group she was in. So Lewin was quite excited about the additional data, and the three at the end of the evening asked if they could come back again the next night, and Lewin was quite positive that they could; *we* had more doubts about it. And the next night the whole fifty were there and were every night, and so it became the most significant training event of the day as this feedback and review of process of events that had gone on during the work sessions of the day. And as Ken Benne, Lee Bradford, and I discussed this, actually it was at a hamburger joint after one of these evenings, we felt the evidence was so clear that the level of our observations of the phenomena about these sessions were a major basis for reorganizations of perceptions and attitude change and of linking up to some degree attitudes and values with intentions and behavior [Back, 1972, pp. 8–9].

T-group training is usually more oriented to development of skills in communication and leadership, whereas encounter groups focus more on personal growth. There is a cognitive Eastern–U.S. locus for the T-group movement; the headquarters of the National Training Laboratories are in bureaucratized Washington, D.C., and its summer workshops are held in Bethel, Maine.

Encounter groups are more a product of the free-wheeling style of California; not surprisingly, a headquarters of sorts for encounter-group experiences is Esalen, located in the Big Sur area of northern California. (See Figure 17-7.)

Figure 17-7
Encounter-group activities. (Photo by Hap Stewart/Jeroboam Inc.)

B. The effects of participation

What are the effects of participation in such experiential groups? They vary so much in composition and duration, in purpose and procedures, that it is hard to make any general conclusion. Certainly many participants are convinced of their benefits; some people become encounter-group "freaks," participating in a new one every weekend or as often as they can afford several hundred dollars.

Another difficulty in evaluating their effects is that little in the way of well-controlled research has been done. The problems in establishing control groups are similar to those in research on the effectiveness of psychotherapy. Changes in actual behavior are often hard to detect. Much "research" falls back on utilizing self-reports of participants as to the benefits, a procedure rife with demand characteristics. (Someone who has paid $150 for a weekend group encounter would be threatened by admitting it was a flop.)

In what is claimed to be the first well-controlled experiment on the effects of encounter groups (Lieberman, Yalom, & Miles, 1973a, 1973b), the researchers recruited 206 students at Stanford University who wanted an encounter-group experience and randomly assigned them to 17 groups, all led by experienced professionals. A total of 69 other students formed a control group; these students also wished to participate in encounters but could not because of schedule conflicts. The 17 groups included an NTL-type T-group, personal-growth-oriented encounter groups, Gestalt groups, psychodrama groups, Transactional-Analysis groups, and leaderless groups that listened to tape recordings. Each participant was evaluated three times; several weeks prior to the group experience, a week after its completion, and six to eight months later.

Immediate reactions were generally favorable; 65% felt that some positive change had taken place and that it would endure. But six months later their enthusiasm and judgments of personal benefit had waned measurably.

What about changes in behavior? Did the participants' close friends and relatives detect any changes in their behavior six months later? No, at least no more than was the case for the control subjects who did not participate in an experiential group.

Effects differed according to the type of group and the leader. Groups that had norms that encouraged moderate degrees of confrontation and emotional intensity, along with adequate amounts of support from the other participants, seemed to lead to the greatest personal growth. Likewise, leaders were most effective when they used moderate amounts of stimulation and showed high degrees of care.

Despite the lack so far of demonstrated effectiveness, many of us will be faced with the question of participation in an experiential group—if we have not already been. While such experiences may be encouraged, because they give us new knowledge about ourselves, there are also cautions to be considered. Siroka, Siroka, and Schloss advise each of us to consider the following questions before joining an experiential group:

1. What are my reasons for joining this group? What do I want and expect from the experience?

2. What is the purpose of the group? What are its stated goals?

3. Are my goals and the group's goals similar?

4. Who is the leader of this group? What is his [or her] theoretical orientation, experience and training? Can I have an interview with him [or her] before the group? (These are vital considerations. Perhaps the most serious dangers in sensitivity training result from "wild" groups, haphazardly organized and run by individuals with few personal or professional qualifications.)

5. Is there a screening process for group members?

6. Is there any provision for follow-through? Will the leader make himself [or herself] available for consultation after the group?

7. Am I hoping to resolve long-standing

emotional problems? If so, psychotherapy, not sensitivity training, may be what I need [1971, p. 170].

V. Communal groups[1]

A communal movement is emerging throughout the world. It is estimated that more than 5000 communes were established in the United States during a five-year period around 1970 (Westhues, 1972). Many people who have not joined a commune are sympathetic to the movement. At another level, social critics see the communal movement as another turn in the development of the counterculture (discussed in Chapter 13). Some see it as an outgrowth of the experiences of those persons who have attempted, futilely, to reform the existing society and its political and economic systems. Having failed to bring the operation of those systems into closer conformity with their personal values, these disaffected persons radically alter their environments and life-styles to bring these into congruence with their beliefs.

A. Why study communes?

A movement inspired by such ultimate ends is infinitely fascinating, but the question remains as to how much serious study it deserves in a social-psychology textbook (Atyas & Wrightsman, 1974). Is the communal movement a passing, doomed protest—the sincerity of its statement tragically ephemeral and irrelevant to social realities? Do communal living groups constitute a viable alternative to the prevailing modes of life in our society? Can they be a prism to break our culture-bound perceptions, valuable less as a social arrangement to be emulated than

[1]Portions of this section are drawn from a working paper by Jonatha Gibaud-Wallston and the author for a seminar on communes. David McMillan also contributed to the ideas presented here.

as a means of expanding our awareness of the capacity of individuals to adjust to extreme alterations in their life style? Or, to become cynical about it, is the establishment of communes merely a fad, dressed up ostentatiously to appear socially significant by decorative religious emblems and gaudy and ill-fitting robes of borrowed philosophies, with some support from undergarments consisting of our society's dirty linen?

These questions seek answers, as contemporary society faces the demands of new lifestyles. We believe that, by studying communal groups, we can sharpen our understanding of what social-psychological variables interact to produce a miniature society that sometimes successfully resolves the inescapable conflict between individual freedom and the welfare of the group as a whole. Thus in discussing communal groups we maintain the group orientation of this chapter, rather than focusing on the individual participant.

The task is not easy. Every commune is different, even though a meaningful grouping of types can be made. (See Table 17-4.) Problems in doing research on communal groups are manifest. Most of the speculations and pronouncements in the popular literature are based on exposure to historical records, personal chronicles, personal observations of a limited duration by outsiders, and armchair theorizing by sociologists, psychologists, and other social scientists. And we may easily understand why this is so.

While many communal groups consider the education of the public an important activity, the time and energy consumed by visitors and unassimilated persons have often caused strict limitations on when and how visiting will be allowed. Furthermore, living as a visitor with a communal group even for an extended period of time can offer only partial insights into the phenomenon. An outsider's perspective hardly approximates that of someone whose arrival may depend on the effective functioning of the group as a whole. From the researcher's viewpoint it seems quite inappropriate to administer a bunch of paper-and-pencil questionnaires to a group who are trying to carve out a new society in the middle of the woods. Even the responses to sympathetic interview questions by the commune members may be colored by group loyalty, dissonance reduction, or insufficient awareness of their own dynamics and those of the group.

Table 17-4
Types of contemporary communes

---

1. Hip-psychedelic and anarchistic communes (heavily into drugs; no consistent group goals)
2. Communes based on Skinnerian behaviorism (Twin Oaks, outside Louisa, Virginia, is the oldest example.)
3. Group-marriage communes (Harrad West, in California, is an example.)
4. Religious communes (includes both traditional ones such as Koinonia and "New Age" religious communes such as "Jesus People" groups)
5. Ideological communes (that possess a particular political or ideological viewpoint)
6. Other types, including women's communes, occupational communes, and so on

---

In addition, the extensive variety of communes (partially reflected in Table 17-4) makes generalizations from one's own experience somewhat dubious. Several other features militate against studying the responses of individuals to gain understanding of the group process: (1) the relative anonymity of people living in communes, resulting from the prevailing ethic that one should be accepted for what one is; (2) high turnover rates and mobility among members of some communes; and (3) even the sensitive reluctance of the investigator to invade the privacy of an individual for the sake of research purposes.

Finally, there is the rejection by many communal groups of the scientific method in general, and particularly of the instruments of social scientists as a means of knowing (Roszak, 1969). As Melville (1972) points out, descriptive surveys and questionnaires fail to reveal what communal life "feels like." Melville also quotes the cautionary statement made by a member of a communal group in Oregon:

> Any family, any commune, is like a Rorschach test. What you see when you come here says more about who you are than what it is. Visitors come expecting to see free, live, naked bodies, scruffy, idle, nonproductive hippies. And what they observe is some people embracing others, a few people walking around naked, and a lot of us just sitting around. But they completely miss what's really going on because they don't see what these things mean to us [1972, p. 138].

But the continuing enthusiasm of persons experimenting with communal living groups and the far-from-neutral reactions of sympathetic observers and vehement critics indicate to us that a study of communal groups lays bare some of our basic concerns about interpersonal relationships. What we may learn from such study compensates for the difficulties.

B. Definitions of a commune

When self-labeled communes can vary so much in size, purpose, and location, it is difficult to agree on a definition of them. We will review several conceptions of the term and then offer what we believe is an encompassing definition.

H. J. Cross and Pruyn provide one of the most flexible definitions: they see a commune as an "absolute alternative life style to that of the dominant culture" (1972, p. 36), different from other countercultural institutions in that it provides alternatives on a variety of dimensions rather than just one or two. Thus a group marriage is not considered to be a commune if the exchange of sexual partners is the whole extent of the couples' involvement with each other. The most typical communal characteristics Cross and Pruyn see are the sharing of work and property and the development of more intimate interpersonal relationships.

Communes have often been compared with utopian societies. Both are identifiable entities with physical and social boundaries. However, Roberts considers communes to be a subspecies of utopian communities. For him, they are experimental attempts to improve on the prevailing society, usually on the basis of some ideology. Yet they differ from utopias in several ways. Communes generally have an upper limit of membership beyond which sheer size precludes meaningful relationships; for example, whenever a Hutterite community reaches 130–150 people, it branches into two (Hostetler, 1974). (There are exceptions to the size limitations: Stephen Gaskin's "The Farm" commune now has 800 people living together in rural Tennessee and is still proselytizing.) Communes are also adamantly antibureaucratic, and they usually reject the hierarchical status present in many utopian communities.

In a very useful book, Kanter (1972) has emphasized the themes common to communes and utopian societies, including voluntary membership, a goal-directed organization, and self-established rules or laws. In both, conformity is ensured by commitment mechanisms rather than by coercion. For Kanter, matching existence to an ideal is the governing consideration in a communal group, and the "key communal arrangement [is] the sharing of resources and finances" (1972, p. 2). The needs of the group are usually set above any service to the outside environment.

Putting all these observations together, we define a commune as *a group of people who share time, space, resources, and psychic energy in an intentional effort to create an alternative experiment in intimate group living.* The inclusion of "alternative experiment" separates communes from fraternity or sorority groups, religious orders, and other groups that may share the same space and even occasionally pool their financial resources. "Intimate" also distinguishes communes from these other groups, although the inclusion of "intimate" should not be interpreted to mean that nontraditional sexual relationships are charac-

teristic of *all* communal groups. Communes may also be defined in terms of their shared values, which usually include brotherhood, trust, openness, the value of experimentation, and unity of body and mind. (See also Figure 17-8.)

C. Social-psychological factors that lead to a successful commune

Some communes do not last very long; others have been in existence for several generations (Zablocki, 1971). Can we distinguish between them on the basis of social-psychological qualities? Are there social-psychological factors that aid in successfully balancing individual and group well-being? We shall see. First, we need to discuss what "success" is for a commune.

For many observers, a commune is successful as an alternative experiment in group living if it *lasts* or if it achieves its specific goals. Group longevity, low turnover rates, and members' satisfaction are used as criteria, even though we are aware that a group's existence may continue even after its experimental values have been eroded.

R. E. Roberts (1971) suggests two alternative criteria of success: changes in the rest of society as outcomes of communal activity (such as an increased tolerance for diversity or a recognition of women's rights) and the effects of the communal group experiment on the individual. For example, even if the participants ultimately reject communal living as inconsistent with their needs, the clarification achieved by the experience may constitute one of the most important steps toward personal fulfillment in their lives. Melville (1972) also suggests that success is to be measured less by whether the commune survives than by the fate of the ideas it reflects. Provocative as well as amusing is the comment made by one ardent advocate of communal groups: "Of course communes work—I'm in my fourth" (quoted by Kanter, 1972, p. 215).

Degree of commitment to the values of the communal group is seen by Kanter as central to the group's success. She suggests that a person commits himself to the group "to the extent that he sees it as expressing or fulfilling some fundamental part of himself; . . . to the degree that he perceives no conflict between its requirements and his own needs; . . . and to the degree that he can no longer meet his needs elsewhere. When a person is committed, what he wants to do . . . is the same as what he has to do" (1972, p. 66). Thus commitment ensures the stability of the group and its ability to overcome challenges from both without and within.

Kanter believes successful communes exert social control over their members through the use of commitment mechanisms. She identifies six social-psychological processes as crucial in building commitment. Three of these involve "detaching" individuals from other allegiances and three require "attaching" the person to the group so that the person's dependence on the group is increased. Two of the processes aim for a perception of the group as providing benefits in the form of energy or resources that the person would lose if he or she were to leave the group. For instance, the process of *sacrifice* requires the

giving up of something (such as privileged or lucrative position) in order to belong to the group. The process of *investment* mandates that all group members turn over at least some of their resources to the group. For example, they might be expected to put their material possessions (money, clothes, cars, TV sets, paintings, housewares) at the disposal of the group, as well as to pledge that all subsequent income will go in the common treasury.

Two other processes have as their goals providing each group member with emotional gratification by the group as a whole and securing the loyalty of each person to the group. The first of these is *renunciation*, which necessitates "giving up competing relationships outside the communal group and individualistic, exclusive attachments within" (Kanter, 1972, p. 73). The second process is *communion*, or the development of a meaningful relatedness through the whole group.

A third set of commitment processes provides direction and purpose to the group member and involves a value orientation. *Mortification* is the term Kanter assigns to the rejection of certain elements of the person's former identity—those

Figure 17-8
Assumptions about human nature in communal groups. Most members of most communal groups share certain assumptions: that human nature is perfectible, that cooperation is natural, that individual needs and community needs can be integrated, and that there is a unity of body and mind. (Copyright 1973 by G.B. Trudeau/distributed by Universal Press Syndicate.)

that might be at variance with the group's values. The other, *transcendence*, involves finding a sense of meaning, "of rightness, certainty, and conviction" through the communal group.

Kanter suggests that if these six processes are incorporated in the organization of the commune, the group will be able to develop the commitment necessary for its survival. Many of the specific strategies Kanter detected in her analysis of 19th-century utopian communities have also been noted by observers of contemporary communes; these do seem to contribute significantly to the success or failure of these groups. The fact that similar mechanisms have been detected by experts on organizational development and small-group dynamics contributes to the validity of generalizing from the experience of communes to other facets of society.

Though differences in commitment can be seen as a variable that determines success or failure, other social-psychological factors are quite influential in communal development. One of the most commonly agreed-upon requirements is the provision for some kind of *leadership*. Many communal groups reject the status differences and implicit hierarchy in having a designated leader, but provision for someone (or ones) to establish and enforce rules and make decisions is essential. The denial of this leads to a delightful irony in Gridley Wright's depiction of his commune as leaderless: "I kind of laid down that there would be no structures" (Melville, 1972, p. 126). In contrast, Lou Gottlieb's Morningstar Ranch commune, while eschewing the status distinction, recognized the need for someone to take action, and hence rotated the leadership role, designating someone each Monday as "dictator-of-the-week" (Melville, 1972, p. 129).

Often there is a designated leader who is both a charismatic figure and the ultimate authority in the group, as in Oneida's John Humphrey Noyes or The Farm's Stephen Gaskin. A member of The Farm commune once told us that "Stephen [Gaskin] is like both the mayor and the minister of this community." In other

communes, the founder or designated leader may provide a spiritual leadership only, and leave the practical business to others. Regardless, R. E. Roberts concludes that "the price of stability in communal groups does seem to be the acceptance of some form of authority" (1971, p. 36).

While a high degree of centralized control may contribute to success—particularly in larger groups—it must not be removed or distant from group membership and subject to influence by others. Another way to say this is that there needs to be a *recognized decision-making process that incorporates the inputs of all members.* The inability of some communal groups to make decisions is one of the major sources of frustration and dissatisfaction for members. Yet it is a difficult problem to solve satisfyingly when the commune insists on consensus for action, or when the commune prizes the individual autonomy of "do your own thing." Even when there is a recognized and powerful leader, procedures must usually be instituted for group members to make decisions at some level and for the leader to explain the rationale for decisions made.

The need for a decision-making process also implies *mechanisms for resolving conflicts* between the reality of the situation and the group's ideals or values. For example, when tasks necessary for the survival of the group, such as planting vegetables or building a new cabin, become burdens for a few rather than work shared by many, what is required is a reassessment of the procedures for allocating responsibility.

Agreed-upon rules and procedures are important to the success of a commune. Although the existence of rules is entirely counter to the philosophy of many groups, failure to adhere to at least minimal rules is often cited as the source of some basic unhappiness with communal living. Clarity with respect to what the rules are and the means of enforcing them seem more important than their exact nature or their number. Rules and procedures adopted should be appropriate to the temperament of group members—homogeneity is again a factor here.

For example, one man who was quite unhappy in a rather laissez-faire commune left it to go to Twin Oaks, whose considerable structure pleases him much better. On the other hand, the work schedules and sign-up sheets of Twin Oaks were a source of irritation to another man who now lives without them in a group of people with high degrees of internal responsibility—the work gets done well and equitably without formal assignment.

Many of the modern communes meet regularly in encounter- or sensitivity-group sessions, often with the assistance of a trained professional, to deal with interpersonal issues. Some of the 19th-century utopias met this need by the institution of "mutual criticism," in which the entire community or a board of about 12 persons subjected all members—often at their own request—to a close analysis in public of their every defect and virtue. (Contrary to what might be expected, the experience was seen as evidence of caring for the individual by the whole group, and constituted much of the mortification-transcendence process spoken of by Kanter.)

As a contemporary example, the Twin Oaks commune—the one designed to resemble B. F. Skinner's fictional "Walden Two"—uses a "bitch box" for processing complaints. Those with grievances about another member's contributions place these in the bitch box; one of the designated jobs of one of the members is to deal with these complaints by discussing them with the offending member (Kinkade, 1973). Stephen Gaskin's commune used to employ "the Monday night class" for a similar purpose. With all 500 or so commune members assembled in a barn, Gaskin would listen to the complaints of individual members and resolve them. We recall one such incident in which a man complained that he had given the farm treasurer (who happens to be a woman) some money to pay a personal bill of his but she had spent it on an emergency need for the farm. "Sometimes the group has to be served before the individual," was Gaskin's response.

Considering other social-psychological factors, we note the importance of the *prior acquaintance* between group members before they enter communal living arrangements. Some homogeneity of outlook and life-style seems essential to group success, and the best way to assure it is to have had some common experience. It is stated that one of the factors operating when a person leaves one commune to enter another is an incompatibility with members of the first group, rather than a disenchantment with communal living. The New Communities Project in Boston has attempted to get people together before they commit themselves to the same communal group, so that they can learn about each other and assess the significance of their points of difference. Similarly, the Alternatives Foundation has used a questionnaire to match prospective commune members on the basis of their views on sex, drugs, child rearing, politics, religion, and—last but not least—what absolutely "turns the person off" (R. E. Roberts, 1971).

Once the initial membership of a group is established, *procedures for admittance or exclusion of new members* seem important to the success of the group (Melville, 1972). Here again we see a conflict between the values of acceptance and openness and the often harsh realities of what can be accomplished. Those communes that attempt to be completely open to all comers usually run into troubles, such as overcrowding, limited food supplies, and/or conflicts with neighbors, local police, or public-health authorities. The resulting frustrations and privations often lead some of the founders of the commune to leave. On many occasions the newcomers do not subscribe to any of the central values of the commune—they appear to subscribe to no values at all except selfishness and sloth! But if the commune has an open admission policy and no provision for excluding or rejecting members, the group is stuck with them.

There are many examples of the perils of no policy and the responses of other communes to the problem. Morningstar Ranch lost strong members to several other communes because of its open-land policy. The difficulties involved in supporting many people on the infertile soil of New Mexico caused some of the communal groups around Taos to discourage new people from joining them. Twin Oaks allows new members, but only after they have lived there for a trial period of two months, after which the commune can say no. The Farm requires that those who wish to join have an interview with Stephen Gaskin to assure that each accepts Gaskin as his or her "Zen master and teacher."

Adherence to a specific ideology, particularly of a religious nature, seems to facilitate a high degree of commitment to the communal group. Not only does a shared ideology provide a basis for decision making, the authority of leadership, and a unique identity for the group, but it also can provide occasions for rituals and ceremonies that bring the group together in a satisfying interaction that provides justification for the privations suffered by the group.

The *provision of opportunities for privacy* is considered essential by most observers. If there are no private rooms, there must still be some means of retreat, even if only through the experience of space in the land surrounding the common buildings (Kanter, 1972; Melville, 1972; R. E. Roberts, 1971). Associated with a need for privacy is a desire to control one's own environment. Joining a communal group requires some adjustments here, as the following statement by a communard indicates:

> I learned a lot about sharing. I had lived five years in a couple and had really got into some privatistic things ... [controlling] things like always knowing what's in the refrigerator; little things that psychologically make a lot of difference. Taking control of the house and knowing what had to be done, and planning around that. At first it was difficult for me to lose that control, although it was liberating. I sometimes didn't have input into what we ate, which brought back bad memories of my parents' house. Or we would get a lot of magazines

which we would save. But in the commune that would get lost, and I had to change my feelings about those pieces of property [quoted in Kanter, Jaffe, & Weisberg, 1974, p. 5].

Factors contributing to the differentiation of the group from the larger society are seen as contributing to group success as long as they don't go too far. Thus, modes of dress and language peculiar to the group may enhance group identification, but at the cost of suspicion by neighbors or inability to communicate with the external world when such communication is necessary, as in the transaction of essential business (Kanter, 1972). Geographic isolation is mentioned by both Melville and Kanter as contributing to group success, but Roberts sees it as unrealistic and possibly self-defeating in a technological age.

Many of the social-psychological variables that might be cited as deterrents to success are, naturally enough, the reverse of variables contributing to success; others represent desirable features carried to an unhealthy extreme. Thus lack of commitment, lack of common purpose or values, and the existence of too many rules are noted by Melville, and lack or loss of leadership and absence of the means for handling internal disputes are mentioned by Roberts. But there are some deterrents to success worth special elaboration.

Melville makes the interesting comment that one of the major problems of communes is that they are "populated by the wrong people trying to do the right things" (1972, p. 236). He points out that commune members usually are ill equipped to deal with the problems of their new life-style by virtue of their affluent, middle-class training. Melville also quotes from Horace Greeley in identifying a related problem:

> A serious obstacle to the success of any socialistic experiment must always be confronted. I allude to the kinds of persons who are naturally attracted to it. Along with many noble and lofty souls, whose impulses are purely philan-

thropic, and who are willing to labor and suffer reproach for any cause that promises to benefit mankind, there throng scores of whom the world is quite worthy—the conceited, played-out, the idle, and the good-for-nothing general-ly; who, finding themselves utterly out of place and at a discount in the world as it is, rashly conclude that they are exactly fitted for the world as it ought to be [1972, pp. 49–50].

Unhappily for many of the well-intentioned, the values espoused by many communes lead them to tolerate such people rather than eject them, and their presence seriously jeopardizes the sur-vival of the commune.

VI. Summary

A *group* has the following properties: in-teraction between individuals, the development of shared perceptions, the presence of emotional ties, and the development of interdependence and roles. Collections of people not possessing these characteristics are called *aggregates.*

The study of social behavior benefits from a group orientation in addition to the individu-alistic orientation that has been the focus of much of this book. Social psychologists are be-ginning to show renewed interest in small-group phenomena.

Groups are "real" in the sense that they have effects that do not occur from an accumula-tion of their members' responses. Group discus-sion tends to polarize opinion in the direction of the majority of the individuals. Group mem-bership under conditions of anonymity can lead to *deindividuation* and many behaviors that would not ordinarily be demonstrated.

Group performance on skill tasks and problems generally exceeds that of the most skilled individual member. The evidence for the wisdom of subjective judgments made by a group is less consistent; groups can be swayed by a "groupthink" process to ignore deviant po-sitions that may turn out to be correct. Use of a group for "brainstorming" appears to be an inefficient use of time and resources.

Group productivity and morale are affected by the size of the group, its communication net-work, and its degree of cohesiveness. These vari-ables often interact.

Experiential groups or sensitivity-training groups have as their goals self-insight, personal growth, and improvement in interpersonal skills. While many participants in such groups are con-vinced of their benefits, there is little hard data supporting claims that they lead to long-term changes in behavior.

The study of communal groups permits a demonstration of the role that social-psychologi-cal variables play in designing a new microso-ciety. Among the factors that seem to be impor-tant in the success of a commune are provisions for rules, some specified leader or leaders, pro-cesses for decision making and conflict resolu-tion, prior acquaintance of members, cohesive-ness, and commitment to the group.

I. **Authoritarianism within the person**
   A. The genesis of the authoritarian-personality study
   B. The program of research
   C. Authoritarianism as an emerging concept
   D. The role of psychoanalytic theory in conceptualizing authoritarianism
   E. Measurement of the components of the authoritarian syndrome
   F. Evaluation of the authoritarian-personality study
   G. A related concept: Dogmatism

II. **Destructive obedience—A behavioral analogue of authoritarianism?**
   A. Obedience in the real world
   B. Milgram's laboratory studies of destructive obedience
   C. Criticisms of Milgram's study of obedience
   D. Relationship of obedience to authoritarianism and other psychological characteristics

III. **Authoritarianism in our society**
   A. Freud and Marcuse—Two views on the repressive nature of society
   B. A more optimistic view of the future of society

IV. **Authoritarianism in the future**

V. **Summary**

Authoritarianism, obedience, and repression in our society

18

The serious threat to our democracy is not the existence of foreign totalitarian states. It is the existence within our own personal attitudes and within our own institutions of conditions which have given a victory to external authority, discipline, uniformity and dependence upon The Leader in foreign countries.

John Dewey

You better watch out. The common man is standing up and someday he's going to elect a policeman President of the United States.

Eric Hoffer

Social psychology is one field of knowledge that has been quite sensitive to the contemporary concerns of the society in which it operates. During the 1930s and 1940s, many citizens in the United States and Canada grew increasingly apprehensive about the rise of authoritarianism and fascism in Europe and the repressive nature of these extreme right-wing movements. An outgrowth of these concerns was the social-psychological study of the authoritarian personality.

The social-psychological approach assumes that tendencies toward authoritarianism can develop in all individuals and that the degree of authoritarianism existing within each individual can be measured with some accuracy. Therefore, part of this chapter will be devoted to the description of authoritarianism as a personal ideology, or related set of beliefs and personality characteristics within the person that play a part in his or her behavior.

Highly authoritarian persons can demonstrate this authoritarian ideology in a variety of situations—in their preference for political candidates that reflect repressive or militaristic values, in their distrust of people who "look strange," or in their emphasis on physical punishment in responding to their children. One of the common behavioral manifestations of authoritarianism is an excessive degree of *obedience* to an authority figure—even if obedience requires hurting another person. In this chapter we describe Stanley Milgram's provocative series of studies on destructive obedience, and we report on the relationship of overly obedient behavior to authoritarianism, hostility, and moral development. Some social scientists have been quite critical of the procedures used by Milgram, because of the possible psychological harm to the subjects; these judgments will provide an occasion for examining whether there are unethical aspects to contemporary social-psychological research.

Authoritarianism is not limited to individual persons. Societies and governments exhibit it also, in varying degrees. The rise of Nazi Germany and Fascist Italy in the 1930s represented one type of authoritarian government—authoritarian in the sense that democratic elections were terminated, the behavior of individuals was restricted by the government, the mass media were used for propaganda purposes, and a nationalistic, belligerent fervor was increasingly encouraged by the government. During the period of 1968 through 1973, the governments in power in the United States and Canada engaged in activities that reflected a movement toward authoritarianism. The Central Intelligence Agency, established by the U. S. Congress to conduct foreign intelligence gathering, spied on U. S. citizens; the Royal Canadian Mounted Police had agents on Canadian campuses; the mass media were threatened with loss of their licenses if they continued to criticize the U. S. government, and

the political campaigns of nonincumbent candidates in the U. S. were sabotaged.

These or other manifestations of right-wing authoritarianism will always, in some degree, be with us. But authoritarianism can also be demonstrated through political extremism of the left wing and through efforts toward anarchy. This chapter will explore both right-wing *and* left-wing authoritarianism. We shall deal with such questions as: What leads to the development of an authoritarian society? Are people who subscribe to an extremist movement psychologically different from those who do not? What is the future of authoritarianism in the countries of North America and Western Europe?

A whole country may become more authoritarian because of the increasing complexity of its everyday life-style. As more people inhabit a given area, as food and jobs become scarcer, and as human relationships deteriorate, demands for greater governmental control lead to invasions of privacy and restrictions on the rights of citizens. Although some of the outcomes of

Figure 18-1
A trend toward
authoritarian government.
(United Press
International Photo.)

these pressures are similar to those of right-wing authoritarianism, the cause differs in that this authoritarianism is a byproduct of forces that are not always politically motivated. Both types of authoritarianism in a society will be investigated in this chapter.

I. Authoritarianism within the person

In 1936, the Institute of Social Research at the University of Frankfurt in Germany published an influential study linking personality dispositions with extremist political leanings. Further work in Germany was endangered, however, by the anti-Semitic persecutions carried out by the ruling Nazi party. Eminent German social scientists including Max Horkheimer, Herbert Marcuse, and T. W. Adorno (founders of the Frankfurt school of Marxist sociology) and Else Frenkel-Brunswik emigrated first to Geneva and then to the United States. Both Adorno, a political scientist, and Frenkel-Brunswik, a psychologist, accepted positions at the University of California at Berkeley, where they could continue their important studies on personality and politics.

A. The genesis of the authoritarian-personality study

During the early 1940s, other social psychologists at Berkeley were busy studying personality factors and morale with regard to the war. Among these were Nevitt Sanford and Daniel Levinson. With the support and encouragement of the American Jewish Committee, these social scientists collaborated with Adorno and Frenkel-Brunswik in the social-psychological study of the antidemocratic or authoritarian personality. The publication of their book, *The Authoritarian Personality*, in 1950 was truly a landmark in the history of social psychology. This huge book (990 pages) included clinical hunches, extensions of psychoanalytic theory, multiple item-analyses of various attitude scales, depth interviews, and

post hoc theory. More than 25 years later the work remains a document of contemporary interest. As we turn now to a discussion of the rationale of the study described in Adorno et al. (1950), we should be aware of distinctions among the *program of research* carried out by the directors of the study, the *concept* of authoritarianism, and the *scales* used to measure aspects of authoritarianism.

B. The program of research

The program generated by the group of California researchers was initially directed toward the concept of **anti-Semitism.** The dimensions of anti-Jewish attitudes were analyzed, and an attitude scale was devised to measure individual differences in anti-Semitic attitudes. Gradually the focus of the program shifted toward prejudice—or what the California group chose to call ethnocentrism. They preferred the latter term to *prejudice*, since *ethnocentrism* refers to a relatively consistent frame of mind—a rejection of *all* outgroups and aliens. The ethnocentric person has a dislike for anything and everything different. For example, it has been found that highly ethnocentric subjects are less likely to have foreign-made automobiles (Day & White, 1973). Prejudice, in contrast, is usually thought of as a feeling of dislike for a specific minority group; one is prejudiced against Italians, men with mustaches, or people who lisp. The emphasis on ethnocentrism reflected the California researchers' assumption that it resulted from some characteristic of the ethnocentric person rather than from the characteristics of a specific minority group. (The authors of *The Authoritarian Personality* have shown, for example, that the same person who berates the "clannishness and seclusiveness" of Jews will paradoxically agree that "Jews are always trying to intrude where they are not wanted.") These concerns about ethnocentrism eventually led the California researchers to a broader study of antidemocratic tendencies at the personality level and to the postulation of an authoritarian personality syndrome.

C. Authoritarianism as an emerging concept

The *concept* of authoritarianism emerged quite late in this program of research. In fact, the term *authoritarianism* does not appear in the index of *The Authoritarian Personality*, although *authoritarian aggression* and *authoritarian submission* do appear. **Authoritarianism** was conceptualized as a basic personality style, or syndrome of organized beliefs and symptoms. (N. Sanford, 1956, refers to it as the F-syndrome, "F" referring to fascistic.) The California group postulated nine components of authoritarianism: **conventionalism, authoritarian aggression, authoritarian submission, power and toughness, anti-intraception, superstition and stereotypy, destructiveness and cynicism, projectivity,** and overconcern with sex. Each of these components is defined, with sample items from the F scale, in Table 18-1. (It should be noted that agreement with a single item does not make one authoritarian; rather, it is a consistent authoritarian response to *many items* that reflects an authoritarian ideology.)

D. The role of psychoanalytic theory in conceptualizing authoritarianism

In developing their conceptualizations, the California group relied heuristically on the theory of psychoanalysis and Freud's concepts of the superego, the ego, and the id. (These are discussed in Chapters 1 and 8 of the present book.) In an exposition of the theory of the authoritarian personality, one of the California group, Nevitt Sanford, hypothesized that within the ethnocentric and authoritarian subject, each of these three systems has characteristic modes of functioning:

> As a first approximation, one might say that in the highly ethnocentric person the superego is strict, rigid, and relatively externalized, the id is strong, primitive, and ego-alien, while the ego is weak and can manage the superego-id conflicts only by resorting to rather desperate

defenses. But this general formulation would hold for a very large segment of the population and, thus, it is necessary to look more closely at the functioning of these parts of the person in the authoritarian syndrome [1956, p. 275].

Considering individually the constructs that entered into the theory of authoritarianism, we may say that the first three—*conventionalism, authoritarian submission,* and *authoritarian aggression*—all refer to the functioning of the superego. The emphasis is on strict demands by the superego, backed up by external reinforcements and by punishment in the name of authority figures to whom the highly authoritarian person has submitted.

Manifestations of a weak ego are reflected in the constructs of *anti-intraception, superstition and stereotypy,* and *projectivity*. As indicated in Table 18-1, anti-intraception reflects an early stage in the development of defense mechanisms that involve repression and denial. Superstition and stereotypy, by shifting responsibility onto an external world, imply that the ego has forsaken attempts to control behavior. Projectivity also reflects a relatively primitive, immature way of avoiding one's anxieties. (See also Figure 18-2.)

The dimension of *power and toughness* appears to signal a weak ego and a very conventional orientation held by the superego. This is indicated by the authoritarian person's reliance on will power—a rather unsophisticated assumption about human nature. *Destructiveness and cynicism,* as well as *sex,* reflect a rather undisguised and forceful id. From these and from further considerations of the relationship between the nine basic components of the authoritarian syndrome and the psychoanalytic structuring of personality, we begin to see the nature of the authoritarian personality. Brought up in a family with a dominant, status-oriented father and a punitive mother, the authoritarian person is punished harshly for any early disobedience. He or she soon comes to repress any "evil" thoughts and accepts what authority figures, including parents, say is right. To differ becomes too threatening; unable to face up to his or her inadequacies, the

Table 18-1
Components of authoritarianism

1. *Conventionalism.* *Rigid* adherence to and *overemphasis* on middle-class values, and overresponsiveness to contemporary *external* social pressure
   Sample item: "A person who has bad manners, habits, and breeding can hardly expect to get along with decent people."
   Sample item: "No sane, normal, decent person could ever think of hurting a close friend or relative."
2. *Authoritarian submission.* An exaggerated, emotional need to submit to others; an uncritical acceptance of a strong leader who will make the decisions
   Sample item: "Every person should have a deep faith in some supernatural force higher than himself to which he gives total allegiance and whose decisions he obeys without question."
   Sample item: "Obedience and respect for authority are the most important virtues children should learn."
3. *Authoritarian aggression.* Favoring condemnation, total rejection, stern discipline, or severe punishment as ways of dealing with people and forms of behavior that deviate from conventional values
   Sample item: "Sex crimes, such as rape and attacks on children, deserve more than mere imprisonment; such criminals ought to be publicly whipped, or worse."
   Sample item: "No insult to our honor should ever go unpunished."
4. *Anti-intraception.* Disapproval of a free emotional life, of the intellectual or theoretical, and of the impractical. Anti-intraceptive persons maintain a narrow range of consciousness; realization of their genuine feelings or self-awareness might threaten their adjustment. Hence they reject feelings, fantasies, and other subjective or "tender-minded" phenomena.
   Sample item: "When a person has a problem or worry, it is best for him not to think about it, but to keep busy with more cheerful things."
   Sample item: "There are some things too intimate and personal to talk about even with one's closest friends."
5. *Superstition and stereotypy.* Superstition implies a tendency to shift responsibility from within the individual onto outside forces beyond one's control, particularly to mystical determinants. Stereotypy is the tendency to think in rigid, oversimplified categories, in unambiguous terms of black and white, particularly in the realm of psychological or social matters.
   Sample item: "It is entirely possible that this series of wars and conflicts will be ended once and for all by a world-destroying earthquake, flood, or other catastrophe."
   Sample item: "Although many people may scoff, it may yet be shown that astrology can explain a lot of things."
6. *Power and toughness.* The aligning of oneself with power figures, thus gratifying both one's need to have power and the need to submit to power. There is a denial of personal weakness.
   Sample item: "What this country needs is fewer laws and agencies, and more courageous, tireless, devoted leaders whom the people can put their faith in."
   Sample item: "Too many people today are living in an unnatural, soft way; we should return to the fundamentals, to a more red-blooded, active way of life."
7. *Destructiveness and cynicism.* Rationalized aggression; for example, cynicism permits the authoritarian person to be aggressive because "everybody is doing it." The generalized hostility and vilification of the human by highly authoritarian persons permits them to justify their own aggressiveness.
   Sample item: "Human nature being what it is, there will always be war and conflict."
   Sample item: "Familiarity breeds contempt."
8. *Projectivity.* The disposition to believe that wild and dangerous things go on in the world. In the authoritarian personality the undesirable impulses that cannot be admitted by the conscious ego tend to be projected onto minority groups and other vulnerable objects.
   Sample item: "The sexual orgies of the old Greeks and Romans are nursery school stuff compared to some of the goings-on in this country today, even in circles where people might least expect it."
   Sample item: "Nowadays when so many different kinds of people move around so much and mix together so freely, a person has to be especially careful to protect himself against infection and disease."
9. *Sex.* Exaggerated concern with sexual goings-on and punitiveness toward violators of sex mores.
   Sample item: "Homosexuality is a particularly rotten form of delinquency and ought to be severely punished."
   Sample item: "No matter how they act on the surface, men are interested in women for only one reason."

Figure 18-2

The personalities of authoritarians, right-wingers, and superpatriots. At this point the reader may wonder whether the authoritarian person is so disturbed as to be classified mentally ill. The evidence is that mental illness and maladjustment are no more frequent among authoritarians than among other persons of equivalent age and social class (Michael, 1967). Elms (1970), for example, interviewed and gave the Rorschach inkblot test to 21 Dallas citizens who had written letters to the editor reflecting right-wing extremism; these letters had subscribed to beliefs about communistic infiltration of the government and the schools and had advocated extralegal ways to achieve right-wing political aims, such as mass arrest of demonstrators. Elms found no greater frequency of maladjustment—paranoia, hostility, or psychosis—in this group than in a group of Dallas liberals. Likewise, Chesler and Schmuck (1969), after interviewing 60 "superpatriots" in the Midwest, concluded that as a group they were generally "pleasant, considerate, and law-abiding." Observations of supporters of George Wallace, however, contradicted the conclusion that superpatriots always are law-abiding. In Davidson County, Tennessee, during the week before the 1968 presidential election, cars were observed to determine whether they had the newly required county auto-tax sticker. Cars with Wallace bumper stickers significantly less often had the sticker than did cars with Nixon stickers, Humphrey stickers, or no bumper stickers at all (Wrightsman, 1969). (Photo by Henry Warfield/Freelance Photographers Guild.)

authoritarian projects these onto other people who are less powerful—foreigners, handicapped people, and members of other races and other religions.

E. Measurement of the components of the authoritarian syndrome

In both beneficial and detrimental ways, the scales that were constructed to measure aspects of authoritarianism have had a profound effect on the development of social-psychological research. The focus on a salient social issue inspired several generations of social psychologists to immerse themselves in the study of authoritarianism. But the detailed descriptions in *The Authoritarian Personality* of the construction and refinement of those scales lent them an aura of scientific precision that, unfortunately, was misleading. We will probe both the beauty spots and the blemishes later. First, we need to list, in the order of their chronological development, the various scales used to measure the components of the authoritarian syndrome. These were (1) the A-S scale, measuring anti-Semitism; (2) the E scale, measuring ethnocentrism; (3) the P-E-C scale, measuring politico-economic conservatism, conceptualized as another aspect of authoritarianism; and (4) the F scale, measuring authoritarianism, or an antidemocratic ideology.

Each is an attitude scale that includes anywhere from 14 to 52 items. With the exception of the P-E-C scale, all the statements on a scale are worded in the same direction, so that agreement with the statement indicates an anti-Semitic or ethnocentric or authoritarian response. Only three of the P-E-C statements are worded in the opposite direction. This indelicacy of scale construction has led some researchers to claim that the scales are not measuring aspects of the authoritarian syndrome at all but rather are tapping an **acquiescent response set** (see Chapter 2). This is an important issue, since the major point of the theory has not been verified if people who get high scores are simply acquiescent

rather than authoritarian. We shall deal with this controversy in our evaluation of the authoritarian personality project.

The research of the California group—published in articles during the 1940s and in the culminating book in 1950—led to a decade (from approximately 1947 to 1957) that might be called a golden age of research on authoritarianism. During this period, Titus and Hollander reviewed 60 studies using the F scale and concluded that, through the investigation of the authoritarian personality, "the commonality of two streams of research interest was established. By applying the tools of 'depth psychology' to the study of ideology this work opened the way for a substantive integration of personality dynamics and social behavior" (1957, p. 47). This attempt to relate ideology to personality was indeed a magnificent endeavor. Let us now see how successful it was.

F. Evaluation of the authoritarian-personality study

The California group definitely succeeded in stimulating new research. Christie and Cook (1958) listed 230 references to studies on authoritarianism published through 1956. Undoubtedly, more than 230 additional studies have been published since that time. In fact, *The Authoritarian Personality* is one of the few books in social psychology that has been important enough to stimulate another book that is devoted solely to its evaluation—a volume edited by Christie and Jahoda (1954) entitled *Studies in the Scope and Method of "The Authoritarian Personality."* A later book, *Dimensions of Authoritarianism* (Kirscht & Dillehay, 1967), reviews research and theory.

One indication of the validity of any theory is the degree to which its measuring instruments allow the prediction of relationships with measures of other variables. Predicted relationships between the F scale, as a measure of authoritarianism, and other variables have frequently been confirmed. A few of these relationships are presented in the following paragraphs.

Prejudice. The California group, having hypothesized that ethnocentrism was a part of the authoritarian syndrome, subsequently tested more than 2100 subjects and found a correlation coefficient of $+.73$ between the F scale and the E scale. Numerous other studies found that the F scale correlates significantly with many different measures of prejudice. Some of these, such as the xenophobia measure of prejudice developed by D. T. Campbell and McCandless (1951), appear to be free of an acquiescent response set. Subjects who were xenophobic (likely to reject minority and foreign groups) were more authoritarian. J. G. Martin and Westie (1959), using urban adults as their sample, found that anti-Black subjects had higher F-scale scores, even when the effects of differences in religious affiliation and occupational mobility were ruled out.

Interpersonal perception. Highly authoritarian students tend to perceive others as possessing the same beliefs and attitudes that they have (Simons, 1966). Scodel and Mussen (1953) had pairs of male students (one quite authoritarian and one nonauthoritarian) discuss innocuous issues such as television and movies. Then each subject answered the F scale and the Minnesota Multiphasic Personality Inventory (MMPI) as he thought the other person would. Highly authoritarian subjects perceived the other person incorrectly; such a subject expected the other person's score to be similar to his own. Nonauthoritarian subjects were more accurate in predicting how the others would respond on both the F scale and the MMPI; on the F scale, the nonauthoritarian usually estimated his partner's score to be higher than his own but lower than it actually was.

What if the two types of students are given a "student in Communist China" as the target person and are asked to rate him? Will highly authoritarian subjects still describe his attitudes as more similar to their own? Granberg (1972) found that they did so; the authoritarian tendency to project one's own attitudes on others reaches even to members of outgroups.

Intolerance of ambiguity. In a general sense, highly authoritarian persons are made uncomfortable by situations that contain ambiguity (Zacker, 1973); in such situations they try to impose some simplified structure. Similarly, authoritarian subjects were found by Steiner and Johnson (1963) to be reluctant to believe that "good people" can possess both good and bad attributes. Such a finding would imply that the philosophies of human nature (see Chapter 3) held by authoritarian persons are absolutistic and oversimplified—that is, that authoritarians are unable to integrate diverse and conflicting characteristics into a whole impression. Other research (Wrightsman, 1974) indicates that this is the case—though not to a very great degree. For example, the correlation coefficient between F-scale scores and Complexity scores from the Philosophies of Human Nature Scale for 270 undergraduate women was $-.22$, which is significantly different from .00, but hardly a very powerful relationship. In a related fashion, Herold (1970) found little tendency for highly authoritarian respondents to attribute less complexity to others than did less authoritarian respondents.

Family ideology and child-rearing attitudes. Highly authoritarian persons tend to have a more traditional family ideology, which includes strong parental control over family decisions, clear-cut and separate roles for the mother and father, and restrictions on the rights of children to dissent. Less authoritarian subjects prefer a more democratic family structure (Levinson & Huffman, 1955).

Volunteering. R. Rosenthal and Rosnow (1969) have published a valuable review of the effects of using volunteers as subjects in psychological studies. They summarize eight studies that compare volunteers and nonvolunteers in regard to authoritarianism. The majority of these studies conclude that volunteers are less likely than nonvolunteers to be highly authoritarian. For example, Ephraim Rosen (1951) found that undergraduates who volunteered for a personality experiment were lower on the F scale than persons who chose not to volunteer. In addition, respondents who completed a mail questionnaire were found to be less authoritarian than persons who failed to return the questionnaire (Poor, 1967). These and related findings are evidence for the anti-intraceptive nature of highly authoritarian persons, who fear exposing their feelings to self-scrutiny.

Community participation. By interviewing a representative sample of adults in Philadelphia, Fillmore Sanford (1950) found that authoritarian interviewees reported less interest in political affairs, less participation in politics or community activites, and more characteristic preferences for strong leaders than did nonauthoritarians.

Preferences for U. S. president. Levels of authoritarianism are often related to political-party preferences and voting for certain candidates (Koenig, 1964; Lindgren, 1974; Poley, 1974). In the 1952 U. S. presidential nominating campaign, General Douglas MacArthur symbolized a rather militaristic and authoritarian approach to the country's problems. Highly authoritarian students were found to prefer MacArthur to other candidates for the 1952 Republican presidential nomination (O. Milton, 1952). In addition, supporters of the candidacy of Senator Barry Goldwater in 1964 had, on the average, higher F-scale scores than did supporters of President Lyndon Johnson (Higgins, 1965; Wrightsman, 1965). The latter difference was consonant with Senator Goldwater's image—at that time—as more "hawkish" than Johnson on the Vietnam War. During the 1964 campaign Goldwater advocated more frequent bombing of North Vietnam as well as other actions that would have intensified the war; it was not until after his election that President Johnson adopted these policies.

Attitudes and behavior regarding the Vietnam War, and specifically Lieutenant Calley. On October 15, 1969, a national moratorium was held to protest United States involvement in the Vietnam War. One week later Izzett (1971) gave students who had attended class that day and those who had not the California F scale and a six-item measure of attitudes toward the United States' Vietnam policies. Students who had not attended class on Moratorium Day had significantly less authoritarian attitudes; they also had stronger anti–Vietnam War attitudes than did students who attended class.

In a related study, an attitude scale toward Lieutenant Calley and the My Lai massacre was constructed by Fink (1973), who administered it along with the F scale to a group of college students. Those subjects who believed that Lieutenant Calley's actions were excusable and that he should not have been court-martialed were more authoritarian than were those who were critical of Lt. Calley's actions. As Fink notes, these results reflect how attitudes regarding the Calley/My Lai case are organized and integrated within the ideology of the respondent. Another major study of attitudes toward the My Lai case—a national survey by Kelman and Lawrence (1972a, 1972b)—did not measure authoritarianism, but one of its interpretations supports a conclusion that pro-Calley respondents are more authoritarian. Kelman and Lawrence found that defenders of Lieutenant Calley emphasized adherence to rules and to policies set by legitimate authorities. Many of these respondents felt that Calley had no choice but to obey orders and therefore was not personally responsible for the outcome of actions carried out under such instructions (Kelman, 1973).

These are only a sample of the variety of findings on the relationships between the F scale and other variables; see, for example, Figure 18-3. Much more extensive reviews may be found in Stone (1974), Kirscht and Dillehay (1967), Christie and Cook (1958), and Titus and Hollander (1957). The F scale has, in a sense, been too successful as a measuring instrument. It has produced significant relationships with the majority of measures with which it has been paired. If the F scale were measuring authoritarianism and that alone, we would have to conclude that authoritarianism is indeed a powerful variable. Yet as the significant findings accumulate, their result is a decrease in conceptual clarity and meaningfulness (Orpen & Van der Schyff, 1972). Most probably, the F scale is measuring a set of overlapping but distinctive variables, rather than one extremely powerful variable (Krug, 1961). In other words, differences between individual F-scale scores probably reflect differences in education, sophistication, and acquiescence, as well as true differences in authoritarianism.

Both the F scale and the whole research program of the California group have been severe-

Figure 18-3
Do authoritarians make successful coaches? Penman, Hastad, and Cords (1974) noted that it is traditionally assumed that the development of a winning athletic team is based on strict adherence to discipline and conformity to the coach's instructions. Would coaches who scored high on a measure of authoritarianism then have more successful teams than less authoritarian coaches? To see, Penman et al. administered a scale to 30 experienced head football coaches and 34 head basketball coaches in large high schools in Minnesota and Washington. When coaches were divided into three groups on the basis of their winning percentages over the years, those in the most successful group were found to have high authoritarianism scores.

ly criticized for a variety of reasons. The construction of the F scale possessed what might be called "birth defects" (Altemeyer, 1969), that violated sound measurement procedures. For example, as stated above, all the items are worded in the same direction, so that agreement with each statement indicates authoritarianism. Such a format encourages the confounding of authoritarianism with an acquiescent response set, or yea-saying tendency (Berkowitz & Wolkon, 1964). Thus, we can legitimately ask whether the person with a high score on the F scale is really authoritarian or simply an acquiescent type (G. D. Wilson & Nias, 1972). Some critics have concluded that scores on the F scale reflect acquiescence more than authoritarianism and that such a confusion reduces the purity and accuracy of the scale (Bass, 1955). Other critics, using different statistical techniques, have concluded that authoritarianism *is* the primary factor (Rorer, 1965). And a third group of critics argues that the acquiescent response set *should* be measured by the scales, since that phenomenon is related to authoritarian submission. A careful analysis by D. T. Campbell, Siegman, and Rees (1967) leads us to conclude that an acquiescent response set probably does contribute to F-scale scores.

Equally disturbing is the finding of a significant relationship between F-scale scores and amount of education. These relationships are negative in direction, showing that less educated persons have higher F-scale scores. Does this finding mean that education reduces authoritarianism, or that education reduces the tendency to agree with the absolutistic language of the F-scale items? (Observe the consistent, extremely moralistic style of the items in Table 18-1.) This issue has yet to be resolved.

The charges leveled at the major substantive findings of the California study are more serious. Critics have questioned whether the components of the authoritarian personality really do hang together as claimed. They have asked whether authoritarians are really more prejudiced, more ethnocentric, more intolerant of ambiguity, and more politically conservative. Indeed, some of the procedures used in the California study lead us to wonder whether the hypotheses were given a fair, unbiased test. For example, in selecting items for the F scale, the authors did not retain certain items that did not correlate with the anti-Semitism scale. Later, however, the significant correlation coefficient of +.53 (which is no surprise, considering the circumstances) was used by the California researchers as evidence that anti-Semitism and fascism are related.

A second example of an unfortunate procedure lies in the validation of the E scale, used to measure ethnocentrism. Persons who were either very highly ethnocentric or unprejudiced on the basis of their E-scale scores were interviewed intensively. The interview responses of the highly ethnocentric subjects more often included prejudiced, politically conservative, and antidemocratic remarks, as well as undue glorification of parents and unrealistically high opinions of themselves. Although these kinds of responses provide evidence that the scale score is predictive of interview behavior, the authors tell us that, prior to the interview, *the interviewers had access to detailed information on the subject's responses to the E-scale items.* Such procedures are clearly in violation of the requirement that the criterion (in this case, the interview) should be an *independent* measure of the variable under study. Quite possibly, an interviewer who knows that a subject is highly ethnocentric will probe for responses that are indicative of prejudice. (In fairness to the authors, it should be noted that one group of interviews with psychiatric patients was carried out by interviewers who were unfamiliar with the purposes of the study or with the E-scale scores of the specific interviewees. The results of this group were consistent with the results of other groups.)

Such methodological flaws are serious. Other criticisms, which will not be reviewed here, led Hyman and Sheatsley (1954) to conclude that even though the theory behind the California authoritarian personality study may be correct and provable, the methodological weaknesses of the study prevent the demonstration of this correctness. Yet the extensive research on the authoritarian personality since Hyman and Sheatsley's pronouncement leads us to conclude that the theory is valid in that it explains the behavior of *some people*. There are individuals for whom authoritarianism is a basic ideology, encompassing anti-Semitic, racist, and reactionary beliefs, as well as a general approach to the world. At the same time, there are persons who are authoritarian without being particularly prejudiced, and, more importantly, there are many individuals who are prejudiced but not authoritarian. A multidetermined theory of prejudice must always be emphasized—as it is in Chapter 10—along with the fact that authoritarianism is not a complete answer.

G. A related concept: Dogmatism

The construct of dogmatism, advanced by social psychologist Milton Rokeach, is somewhat related to authoritarianism. Dogmatism is defined by Rokeach as "(a) a relatively closed cognitive organization of beliefs and disbeliefs about reality, (b) organized around a central set of beliefs about absolute authority which, in turn, (c) provides a framework for patterns of intolerance toward others" (1960, p. 195). Thus dogmatism is characterized by both a closed-minded, rigid style and a content sympathetic to authoritarianism and intolerance.

Rokeach (1960) and other social scientists (for example, Shils, 1954) have criticized the California F scale because it measures only right-wing authoritarianism, making it deficient in balanced content. These scientists have argued that authoritarianism can be a characteristic of left-wing political ideologies such as communism as well as right-wing ideologies such as fascism. The highly authoritarian person could gravitate toward either extreme of the political scale. Rokeach advanced the concept of dogmatism as an indicator of a general kind of authoritarianism that would encompass both the extreme left and right ends of a political-belief distribution.

There are two ways of confirming these scientists' claim. One is through analyzing the statistical relationships between the F scale and the Dogmatism scale (constructed by Rokeach); the other is through comparing the responses of members of various political parties. Two statistical studies have demonstrated that the F scale and the Dogmatism scale are not completely overlapping in their measurements. Kerlinger and Rokeach (1966) factor analyzed the items from the F scale and the Dogmatism scale and found a common core of authoritarianism in both scales. But a further analysis, seeking other factors, found that the two scales were factorially discriminable, with dogmatism representing a general authoritarianism free of any particular ideological content. The purpose of another study (by E. N. Barker, 1963) was to see whether levels of dogmatism were related to a person's degree of commitment to a particular position on the political spectrum. Although dogmatism was unrelated to any particular political ideology, it was related—as expected—to intensity of commitment to a particular position.

If dogmatism indicates general authoritarianism, we would expect members of both the Communist and Fascist political parties to be highly dogmatic. Rokeach found groups of English college students who identified themselves as members of the Conservative, Liberal, Labour, or Communist party. In 1954, these students were administered the Dogmatism scale, the F scale, and the Ethnocentrism scale. Mean scores are reported in Table 18-2. Note that of all groups the Communists scored lowest on the F scale and on the Ethnocentrism scale, indicating their lack of right-wing authoritarianism and prejudice.[1] (Communist students were significantly lower on right-wing authoritarianism and prejudice than three of the other four groups.) In contrast, the Communists scored highest on dogma-

---

[1] In 1953 Coulter gave the F scale to 53 members of an English Fascist group and found their scores to be among the highest ever recorded (reported in Christie, 1956; R. Brown, 1965).

Table 18-2
Comparisons of various political groups among English university students

Group	N	Dogmatism		F Scale		Ethnocentrism Scale	
		Mean	Standard Deviation	Mean	Standard Deviation	Mean	Standard Deviation
Conservatives	54	258.8	49.7	115.5	25.0	29.9	9.0
Liberals	22	242.9	29.2	98.4	14.0	24.8	7.9
Labourites (pro-Attlee)	27	252.7	36.6	101.8	21.4	22.7	9.3
Labourites (pro-Bevan)	19	255.2	37.9	90.4	24.3	23.5	9.4
Communists	13	261.6	32.6	82.9	20.3	16.5	4.2

Adapted from *The Open and Closed Mind*, by M. Rokeach. Copyright © 1960 by Basic Books, Inc., Publishers. Used by permission.

tism—although the only difference between groups that approaches statistical significance was the difference between Communists and Liberals.

At first these results may sound conflicting. Can a group be unprejudiced, unauthoritarian, but highly dogmatic? Perhaps the Communists' tolerance of minority groups reflects a rigid adherence to the content of communist ideology. (Notice the extremely low standard deviation of the Communists on Ethnocentrism.) Yet as indicated by the Dogmatism scale, English Communists formed the group that was most intolerant of those who disagreed with communist views. They represent an exaggeration of what Triandis and Davis referred to in Chapter 10 as belief-prejudiced persons—those who are more concerned with the beliefs than with the race of stimulus persons. Beyond this, communist ideology is authoritarian in that (1) strong pressures are exerted on its members to maintain discipline, (2) its leadership derives from an elitist group rather than from democratic procedures, and (3) it stifles opposition by repressive measures. It is not surprising that Communists scored high on a measure of dogmatism.

As a measure of general authoritarianism uncontaminated by political ideology, the Dogmatism scale appears more appropriate than the F scale (Vacchiano, Strauss, & Hochman, 1969). However, the Dogmatism scale is quite possibly not so free of ideological content as Rokeach had hoped.

In some ways the Dogmatism scale suffers from the same limitations as the F scale. For example, all 40 items are scored in such a way that agreement with the item is indicative of dogmatism. The presence of an acquiescent response set must again be considered as a possible explanation of the results (Peabody, 1961, 1966). However, in one thorough review (Vacchiano et al., 1969), so many substantive differences between persons scoring high and low on the scale were found that the reviewers came to the conclusion that "more than a response bias is operative and that the [Dogmatism scale] is a generally reliable and valid instrument" (1969, p. 269).

Researchers have related dogmatism to many of the same variables that have been linked with authoritarianism. The findings of a sampling of these studies on dogmatism are outlined below.

1. Compared with their less dogmatic counterparts, highly dogmatic subjects are more dependent on authority figures in a conformity-inducing task (Vidulich & Kaiman, 1961).

2. Highly dogmatic persons are more likely to accept the official police explanation of the causes of a riot than are less dogmatic subjects (J. McCarthy & Johnson, 1962) and are more responsive to group pressures to become more prejudiced (Kirtley, 1968).

3. Less dogmatic subjects perceive authority figures in a more realistic way, reporting both their negative and their positive characteristics (Kemp, 1963).

4. In an unstructured classroom situation, highly dogmatic students are more concerned with rules and procedures regarding leadership selection and group structure. Intellectual lethargy and an unwillingness to relate to other students, the instructor, or the subject matter are characteristic of classrooms composed of highly dogmatic students (Zagona & Zurcher, 1964, 1965).

5. In two studies, students with low Dogmatism scores were found to be more critical of United States' foreign policies during the time of the country's involvement in the Vietnam War (Guller & Bailes, 1968; Karabenick & Wilson, 1969).

6. Less dogmatic persons are more accurate in their perceptions of the degree of dogmatism in a stimulus person than are highly dogmatic persons (Burke, 1966; Jacoby, 1971).

The fact that dogmatism is seen as a relatively closed cognitive organization of beliefs and disbeliefs leads one to expect that highly dogmatic students are less able to learn or process new information or to utilize new information presented to them (Brightman & Urban, 1974). Rokeach and Vidulich (1960) found that dogmatic subjects were less successful at solving a problem that required adopting novel learning sets. Numerous other studies have also generally confirmed such an expectation (Long & Ziller, 1965). For example, among introductory sociology students, those high in dogmatism entered the class with less information, learned less as a result of classroom exposure, and retained what they learned to a significantly lesser degree than did the less dogmatic students (H. J. Ehrlich, 1961a). Even five years later, the differences in regard to retention of learned material held up between groups differing in dogmatism (H. J. Ehrlich, 1961b). A general, if tentative, conclusion would be that the Dogmatism scale is able to distinguish between people in respect to how well they can learn new beliefs and change old beliefs (H. J. Ehrlich & Lee, 1969).

II. Destructive obedience— A behavioral analogue of authoritarianism?

A. Obedience in the real world

We may view the authoritarian personality as an extension of characteristics present in most of us. Within the realm of behavior the phenomenon of *destructive obedience* may be analogous to the authoritarian personality.[2] All of us feel some degree of pressure to obey certain symbols of authority, such as parents, college deans, and traffic lights. In order to exist in an environment where the rights and needs of others are to be respected, laws and rules are established with the expectation that they will be obeyed.

The question is whether obedience can assume so powerful a position within a person's domain of behavior that it causes the person to perform socially unacceptable acts. Can destructive obedience occur? The cases of Adolf Eichmann, Lieutenant Calley, and some of the employees of the Committee to Re-Elect the President (see Figure 18-4) are relevant. When he was tried for killing 100 Vietnamese villagers, Lieutenant Calley stated that he was simply following orders. Adolf Eichmann, in charge of extermi-

---

[2]In fact, one of the items measuring authoritarianism on the California F scale is: "Obedience and respect for authority are the most important virtues children should learn."

nating 6 million Jews in Nazi Germany, also did what he was told. At his trial for war crimes, Eichmann denied any moral responsibility, since —he said—he was simply doing his job. Likewise, overzealous supporters of Richard Nixon

Figure 18-4
Obedience to the authority of the federal government. At the U. S. Senate hearings during the summer of 1973, James W. McCord, a veteran of distinguished service in the government and a former FBI agent, testified that his participation in the break-in at the Democratic party headquarters was instigated primarily by his belief that the operation had been sanctioned by the then Attorney General John Mitchell and indirectly by President Nixon. Other witnesses, many of whom had a background in professional law enforcement, also testified that, while they knew their deeds were illegal, they did them out of loyalty to their superiors or to President Nixon (Cohen, 1973). (Photo by George Tames/New York Times Pictures.)

did not question their superiors when told to engage in clearly illegal campaign activities. Did Calley or Eichmann or Jeb Magruder not realize that following the expectations of a job might violate their moral responsibilities as decent human beings? When obeying the demands of others requires the violation of one's moral responsibilities, we refer to the response as *destructive obedience.*

Real-life conflicts between obedience and morality are not confined to Nazi Germany of 30 years ago, Vietnamese villages thousands of miles from us, and high-level political campaigns. A salesperson may have to choose between obeying instructions to misrepresent a dangerous product and risking loss of the job. A plant manager may be told that he has to fire 10% of his best workers or the plant will go bankrupt. A student may have to choose between echoing the instructor's viewpoint on an essay question and possibly flunking the exam.

B. Milgram's laboratory studies of destructive obedience

Although the Eichmann, Calley, and Watergate examples are real, they may be unusual cases. Let us consider other specific conflicts. Stanley Milgram, a social psychologist, tried to determine how many persons would continue to obey the commands of an authority figure, even when they believed (incorrectly) that they were endangering the life of another person. Milgram's procedure (1963) required the subject to give increasingly powerful electric shocks to another person whenever the latter erred on a learning task. The original subjects were 40 males who responded to newspaper advertisements and a direct-mail solicitation. Although such a self-selected sample of volunteers clearly was not random, it was heterogeneous in regard to age (20 to 50) and occupation (postal clerks, secondary-school teachers, salesmen, engineers, laborers, and others). Subjects were paid $4.50 for their participation in the project at Yale University.

When each subject arrived for the experiment, he was introduced to the experimenter and another subject (actually an accomplice of the experimenter). The subjects were told that the purpose of the experiment was to determine the effects of punishment on learning. The introduction continued as follows:

> So, in this study we are bringing together a number of adults of different occupations and ages. And we're asking some of them to be teachers and some of them to be learners.
>
> We want to find out just what effect different people have on each other as teachers and learners, and also what effect *punishment* will have on learning in this situation.
>
> Therefore, I'm going to ask one of you to be the teacher here tonight and the other one to be the learner [Milgram, 1963, p. 373].

Subjects drew lots to determine which would be the teacher and which would be the learner, but the drawing was rigged so that the true subject was always the teacher and the accomplice was always the learner. After the drawing, both subjects were taken to an adjacent room, where the learner was strapped to a chair. The purpose of this procedure was explained as to restrict the learner and keep him from escaping. An electrode was then attached to the learner's wrist, and the teacher and the experimenter returned to the original room.

There the subject was instructed in his task. The lesson to be administered by the subject was a paired-associate learning task, in which the subject was to read a series of word pairs to the learner and then read the first word of the pair along with four terms. The learner's job was to indicate which of the four terms was the correct associate; he did this by pressing a switch, which lit a light in the teacher's room.

The response lights were in an answer box located on top of the shock generator in the teacher's room. The instrument panel of the shock generator consisted of 30 switches, each clearly labeled with a designation of its voltage. These switches increased by 15-volt increments from 15 to 450 volts. To clarify the degree of shock, groups of four switches were consecutively labeled Slight Shock, Moderate Shock, Strong Shock, Very Strong Shock, Intense Shock, Extreme-Intensity Shock, Danger—Severe Shock, and, the last, only XXX. In actuality this equipment was a dummy shock generator and the confederate never received an actual shock, but its appearance was quite convincing. Moreover, the seeming authenticity of the shock was communicated to the teacher by giving him a sample shock of 45 volts.

The teacher was told to administer a shock to the learner each time that he gave a wrong response. (The learner, being an accomplice, had been instructed to err often, but of course the true subject did not know this.) After each wrong answer, the subject was instructed to move one level higher on the shock generator. The teacher-subject also had to announce the voltage level before administering a shock—a device that served to remind him of the level of shock he was giving another person. After the learner had committed enough errors so that the shock level was supposedly at 300 volts, according to prearranged plans, he began to pound on the wall between the two experimental rooms. From that point on, he no longer answered.

The usual response of a subject at this point was to turn to the experimenter for guidance. In a stoic and rather stern way, the experimenter replied that no answer was to be treated as a wrong answer, and the subject was to be shocked according to the usual schedule. The subject then was to wait five to ten seconds and, assuming the learner had made no response, increase the shock level again. After the administration of the 315-volt shock, the teacher heard the learner pound on the walls again, but no answer materialized. From that point on, no sound or answer emanated from the learner's room.

Milgram's basic experimental question was simply how many subjects would continue administering shocks to the end of the shock series. Table 18-3 presents the results. Of the 40 subjects, 26 (65%) continued to the end of the shock series. No subject stopped prior to administering 300 volts—the point at which the learner began kicking the wall. Five refused to obey at that point; at some point, 14 of the 40 subjects defied the experimenter. Milgram concludes that obedience to commands is a strong force in our society, since 65% of his subjects obeyed the experimenter's instructions even though they knew that they were hurting a powerless person.

Milgram (1964a; 1965; 1974) then extended his program of research to study some of the situational factors that may cause a subject to obey or to refuse to obey when the experimenter (the authority figure) tells the subject to hurt another person. After demonstrating that the majority of subjects would continue to shock another person to the limit of the apparatus, Milgram tested whether the closeness of the victim's presence to the subject had any effect on the subject's behavior. Milgram used the following four conditions.

1. In the *remote-feedback condition*, the victim was in another room and could not be heard or seen by the subject, with the exception that, when the 300-volt level was reached, the victim pounded on the wall. After 300 volts the victim no longer answered or made any noise.

2. The *voice-feedback condition* was identical to the first condition except that the victim made vocal protests that could be heard through the walls and through the slightly open doorway between rooms.

3. In the *proximity condition*, the victim was placed in the same room as the subject, about 1½ feet away. Thus, both visual and aural clues to the victim's pain were available to the subject.

4. The *touch-proximity condition* was identical to the proximity condition, except that, beyond the 150-volt level, the victim refused to put his hand on the shockplate. On every subsequent trial the experimenter ordered the subject to force the victim's hand onto the shockplate.

A different set of 40 adult males participated in each of the four conditions. The percentages of subjects who obeyed the experimenter were: remote-feedback, 66%; voice-feedback, 62.5%; proximity, 40%; and touch-proximity, 30%. Thus, as one might expect, when the victim was closer, more subjects refused to obey.

Table 18-3

Distribution of breakoff points in Milgram's study of obedience

Verbal Designation and Voltage Indication	Number of Subjects for Whom This Was Maximum Shock
Slight shock	
15	0
30	0
45	0
60	0
Moderate shock	
75	0
90	0
105	0
120	0
Strong shock	
135	0
150	0
165	0
180	0
Very strong shock	
195	0
210	0
225	0
240	0
Intense shock	
255	0
270	0
285	0
300	5
Extreme-intensity shock	
315	4
330	2
345	1
360	1
Danger—severe shock	
375	1
390	0
405	0
420	0
XXX	
435	0
450	26

From "Behavioral Study of Obedience," by S. Milgram, *Journal of Abnormal and Social Psychology*, 1963, *67*, 376. Copyright 1963 by the American Psychological Association. Reprinted by permission.

The relationship of the subject to the experimenter also determines the amount of obedience (Milgram, 1965; Rada & Rogers, 1973). In one condition, the experimenter sat only a few feet away from the subject. In a second condition, the experimenter was present at the beginning to give initial instructions and then left the room, using the telephone for further instructions. In a third condition, the experimenter was never present, the instructions being given by a tape recording. Obedience was almost three times more frequent when the experimenter remained physically present. Moreover, when the experimenter was absent, several subjects administered shocks of a lower voltage than was required. As Milgram indicates, this kind of response clearly violated the avowed purpose of the experiment, but perhaps it was easier for the subject to handle conflict this way than to defy authority openly.

As Rada and Rogers (1973) note, the situation in which the authority figure is absent is probably more typical of everyday living. It is easier to defy authority when authority is not physically present. But Rada and Rogers found that when the authority figure had previously issued a strong command to obey, the subjects tended to obey whether the authority figure was present or not.

C. Criticisms of Milgram's study of obedience

As provocative as these findings are, Milgram's program of research has not gone without criticism. Perhaps the strongest of the critics is Baumrind (1964), who believes the studies were not only unethical but lacking in generalizability to real-world obedience situations.[3] These two lines of criticism will be examined in turn.

Criticisms of the ethics of the experiment. Milgram's study has been called unethical on several grounds. One claim is that the subjects' rights

were not protected. No health examinations were given to the subjects prior to the experiment to determine whether some psychological maladjustment or physical problem might exclude certain subjects. No prior permission was obtained from the subjects allowing the experimenters to place them in distressful conflict situations.

A second claim is that there could have been long-term effects on the subjects from having participated in the study. Among these effects is the subjects' loss of trust in future experimenters, the university, or science in general. Having been deceived in a study in which their emotions were displayed so openly, subjects could have become strongly skeptical about psychological researchers. Another type of long-term effect might have been on the subjects' self-concepts. Prior to the experiment, most subjects probably saw themselves as persons who would not deliberately inflict pain on another person unless the circumstances were extreme. As a result of the experiment, they would have discovered otherwise. Milgram apparently believes that such self-education is beneficial, regardless of its consequences. Some social psychologists—following D. J. Bem's (1970) self-perception theory—would disagree; they would say that when people know they have acted heinously in one situation, the bonds against their doing the same thing in the future would be loosened.

A third criticism regarding the ethicality of the experiment centers on Milgram's reaction to the anguish and tension shown by some subjects as they methodically increased the shock levels trial by trial. Milgram reports with some awe, if not relish, the extreme degrees of tension experienced by some subjects. Consider his quotation from one observer:

> I observed a mature and initially poised businessman enter the laboratory smiling and confident. Within 20 minutes he was reduced to a twitching, stuttering wreck, who was rapidly approaching a point of nervous collapse. He constantly pulled on his earlobe, and twisted his hands. At one point he pushed his fist into his forehead and muttered: "Oh, God, let's stop it." And yet he continued to respond to every

---

[3]Baumrind advocates that only research of unquestioned relevance to real-world issues justifies harm to subjects. Yet, who is to determine what is relevant?

word of the experimenters, and obeyed to the end [1963, p. 377].

Milgram tells us that other subjects were observed to "sweat, stutter, tremble, groan, bite their lips, and dig their fingernails into their flesh. Full-blown, uncontrollable seizures were observed for three subjects" (1963, p. 375). One subject had such a violently convulsive seizure that it was necessary to terminate his participation. Critics have asked why the whole experiment was not terminated in the face of all these tensions. Milgram apparently believed that debriefing at the end of the experiment was sufficient to eradicate these tensions. In describing the debriefing procedure, Milgram stated: "After the interview, procedures were undertaken to assure that the subject would leave the laboratory in a state of well-being. A friendly reconciliation was arranged between the subject and the victim, and an effort was made to reduce any tensions that arose as a result of the experiment" (1963, p. 374). It is hard to believe, however, that such extreme examples of tension could be erased by any such momentary debriefing procedure. Milgram's critics are not convinced by his reports (1964b, 1968, 1974) that interviews by psychiatrists and follow-up questionnaires completed by the subjects indicated no long-term deleterious effects.

Criticisms of the lack of generalizability. Baumrind and others have also questioned whether the extreme degrees of obedience found in Milgram's subjects may be generalized to the real world. The specific criticisms are as follows.

1. The nonrandom, nonrepresentative nature of the subjects is one difficulty. The representativeness of men who would respond to a newspaper ad to participate in a laboratory experiment can certainly be doubted. Some of these men may indeed have been crying for help or otherwise showing concern about themselves. We cannot say, however, whether they were more obedient than a truly representative sample of adult males would have been.

2. Trust in the authority figure and obedience to him may be demand characteristics that are especially salient for subjects in experiments (Orne & Holland, 1968). In other words, subjects who will do as they are told in an experiment might disobey another authority figure, such as the physician who tells them to exercise daily, or the employer who tells them to fire a popular coworker. Along with this criticism is the claim that the prestige of Yale University contributed to the high obedience rate; subjects assumed that anything carried out at Yale must be scientifically and socially acceptable—hence, they were more inclined to obey. The available evidence, as scant as it is, contradicts this last claim. Milgram repeated the experiment in a nonuniversity setting to determine whether the Yale setting contributed to extreme degrees of obedience. Men recruited for the experiment reported to a rather rundown office building in a deteriorating area of Bridgeport, Connecticut. Placed in the same task as that of the original Yale study, almost 50% of the men obeyed the experimenter to the end of the shock series. While the prestige of Yale apparently accounted for some obedience, the phenomenon still occurred in a blatantly nonuniversity setting. Perhaps, as Etzioni (1968) concludes, humans are latently Eichmannistic, at least when faced with the dilemma Milgram gave them.

3. The role of "prods" by the experimenter may have contributed significantly to the high rate of obedience. In the Milgram task, if a subject was unwilling to continue, four prods were used to urge him to continue: Prod 1, "Please continue," or "Please go on"; Prod 2, "The experiment requires that you continue"; Prod 3, "It is absolutely essential that you continue"; and Prod 4, "You have no other choice, you *must* go on." These prods were always used in sequence. If Prod 1 had not brought the subject into line, Prod 2 was introduced, and so on. The experiment was terminated only when Prod 4 had failed to keep the subject at his task. We do not know what the rejection rate would have been if the prods had not been used, but certainly more subjects would have terminated earlier. The fact that the experimenter responded to the subject's concern in such a firm and persistent

manner may have convinced some subjects to continue their participation.

Certainly there are problems in making a blanket generalization of Milgram's findings to real-world cases of obedience and destructive obedience. Several replications (Rada & Rogers, 1973; Kilham & Mann, 1974) have reported lower rates of obedience. But in real-world situations where prods or similar devices are used to keep people at tasks that are personally abhorrent, Milgram's findings probably are applicable. Perhaps the most provocative finding in Milgram's work is the demonstration that obedience is a much more pervasive phenomenon than had been thought. Neither a group of undergraduates nor a group of psychologists and psychiatrists, when told of the procedures, predicted that subjects would continue to obey when the high voltage levels were reached. Assumptions about human nature were more favorable than the outcomes.

D. Relationship of obedience to authoritarianism and other psychological characteristics

Milgram's approach to obedience was primarily oriented toward the effects of situational variations. But the fact that some subjects obeyed while others did not has led to a search for characteristics of individuals that could be related to the differences. Again, a combination of situational and intrapersonal factors affected social behavior.

Elms and Milgram (1966) administered various personality scales to participants in an obedience study. The men who obeyed had significantly higher scores on the California F scale than did those men who defied the authority figure. Elms and Milgram reported that "significant attitudinal differences [between these two groups] were displayed toward [one's] own father, the experimenter, the sponsoring university, willingness to shoot at men in wartime, and other concepts, in patterns somewhat similar to 'authoritarian personalities' " (1966, p. 282). Sim-

ilarly, Haas (1966) has demonstrated that more hostile subjects are more likely to obey. A behavioral response such as obedience is partly influenced by the presence of components of the authoritarian syndrome within the person. The decision to obey or disobey is also related to the subject's level of moral development, as measured by responses to Kohlberg's stories (described in Chapter 8). Subjects who refuse to continue their participation in Milgram's experiment generally have more mature moral-judgment scores than subjects who obey.

III. Authoritarianism in our society

A. Freud and Marcuse — Two views on the repressive nature of society

Sigmund Freud believed that culture demands repression and that society must act in an authoritarian way. His view, expressed in *Civilization and Its Discontents* (1930), was that culture serves two functions: to protect people from the dangers of the natural world and to regulate contacts between human beings so that they do not destroy one another (C. S. Hall & Lindzey, 1968). Freud scorned any suggestion that culture or civilization serves to free people. To Freud, civilization deprives us of freedom because it imposes regulations, standards, and prohibitions on each individual. Although Freud acknowledged the benefits of a complex society, he nevertheless believed that it generates restrictions that eventually lead to hostilities and frustrations.

Authoritarianism is a characteristic both of individual persons and of whole societies. That is, civilizations can differ in the degrees to which they reflect repression of differing viewpoints, exaltation of leaders, and denial of human values.

Herbert Marcuse has responded on several occasions to Freud's conclusions about the repressive nature of civilization; Marcuse has ranged from optimism to pessimism and back to optimism again. In *Eros and Civilization* (1955/1962) Marcuse rejected Freud's conclusion. He agreed that some degree of repression is necessary for the successful operation of a society, but he also stated that society has *surplus repression* arising from various dominating institutions. Surplus repression is what a particular group or individual imposes on others in order to enhance or maintain a privileged position. Attempts by governmental officials to curtail the flow of information through the mass media might exemplify surplus repression. Marcuse proposed a rechanneling of these repressions into desirable activities. He wrote "To the degree to which the struggle for existence becomes cooperation for the free development and fulfillment of individual needs, repressive reason gives way to a new rationality of gratification in which reason and happiness converge" (Marcuse, 1955/1962, p. 205).

Marcuse also claimed that a nonrepressive society was possible only under conditions of abundance. The new rationality of gratification and a play ethic could not emerge under conditions of scarcity; the sensuous element would give way to discipline and work (Marks, 1970, p. 59). However, given a state of freedom from want and from stuporous work, we could develop a new life-style, a gentleness, and an eroticism far different from our present perversions. We must question, however, whether certain governments would not strive to perpetuate a work ethic. Would not a conservative government be frightened by the possibility of a civilization in which the problems of productivity had been mastered, a work ethic had been replaced by a play ethic, and the performance orientation had been replaced by a display orientation?

Marcuse's earlier optimism about the future of complex society was dramatically rejected in his later book *One-Dimensional Man* (1964), which appeared nine years after *Eros and Civilization* was first published. (Marcuse's recent beliefs have been summarized by Kateb, 1970, and reprinted in Table 18-4). *One-Dimensional Man* emphasized the irrationality of advanced industrial

Table 18-4
Marcuse's theses regarding the nature of technological society and our role in it

1. The advanced industrial society, or the affluent society in the West, with the United States farthest along, is preponderantly evil—both for the harm it does and for the good it prevents, internally and externally.
2. On balance, and internally, the Soviet Union is worse in actuality, better in potentiality, but with no guarantee that it will in fact become better. In the early 1970s there were still "progressive and liberal forces" active in the United States. But this country is in the midst of a counterrevolution that is moving toward fascism.
3. The evil of each system is not correctable peacefully by those in control or by their likely heirs.
4. In the abstract, revolution may therefore be justifiable.
5. We may be witnessing the emergence of certain forces that could perhaps bring about qualitative, genuinely revolutionary changes in the West, while developments in the Soviet bloc are, if anything, more problematic.

Adapted from Kateb, 1970, pp. 48–49, and from Keen & Raser, 1971.

civilization. Marcuse had come to doubt that a highly complex, technological society is capable of any qualitative change in the foreseeable future (Marks, 1970). Although industrial society has been quite successful in developing its technological resources, it becomes repressive when the success of its technological development opens up new "dimensions of social well-being." Industrial society is a juggernaut that crushes individuality, liberty, and social equality. Such a society pulverizes efforts to discover a new consciousness (Reich, 1970), a new set of values, and a life-style that emphasizes human freedom, authenticity, and genuine emotion. Technological society cannot tolerate the possibility of these developments; it dominates people under the guise of offering them material affluence and apparent freedom. The individual becomes a "willing subject of the technological domination; he is bought out by his material gains. On all sides there is promise of easier and better living, of more gadgetry, more alienation" (Marks, 1970, p. 68). Rather than finding themselves in their own being, "people recognize themselves in their commodities; they find their souls in their automobile, hi-fi set, split-level home, kitchen equipment" (Marcuse, 1964, p. 9). Hence there develops a "progressive moronization of humanity" and one-dimensional men—like the robot types in Aldous Huxley's *Brave New World*—are content to do their assigned tasks and never realize how unhappy and unfulfilled they really are.

In *One-Dimensional Man*, Marcuse advocated revolution as a necessary response to technological domination, but he saw little chance for a change.[4] The mass media and the political and economic systems perpetuate a one-dimensional view of man. The few individuals who refuse to be absorbed by the organization are disparaged as nonconformists or neurotics. Some of them are coopted by the system. Even activities that might be interpreted as protests—the use of drugs, encounter groups, and Zen—are largely ceremonial, in Marcuse's opinion.[5] They may even sap the strength of a revolutionary theorist.

An Essay on Liberation (Marcuse, 1969) is described by John Raser (1971) as Marcuse's most hopeful statement. In this work and his more recent *Counterrevolution and Revolt* (1972) Marcuse sees militant young people as perhaps the beginning of a new sensibility in the United States that will lead to desired changes in fun-

damental values and the politicoeconomic structure of our society. But in none of his books does Marcuse offer facts to justify his conclusions. A social-psychological orientation such as ours would urge the provision of some documentation.

B. A more optimistic view of the future of society

Other social analysts, including some liberals and radicals, do not share Marcuse's modified pessimism. Irving Howe (1969) feels that actual society in the United States is more complex than Marcuse allows; Howe believes that human beings possess far more independence and autonomy than the "one-dimensional" label suggests. Charles Reich, author of *The Greening of America* (1970), holds that youth around the world are leading a nonviolent revolution that will bring about a new life-style and a new consciousness. Consciousness III, as Reich calls it, believes that "the individual self is the only true reality" (p. 225). A sense of community and the importance of personal relationships are emphasized.[6] People become responsible for their acts. In short, the developments that Marcuse sees as ceremonial, Reich views as antecedents to a new consciousness in the United States. Reich's *The Greening of America* was an instant success when it was published in 1970; many people saw it as a blueprint for the future. But as North America and Western Europe faced massive inflation, rising unemployment and scarcity of food and

---

[4]Admired by many followers of the New Left because of his neo-Marxist views, Marcuse is not held in favor by the American Maoists, partly because he worked for a U. S.–government propaganda agency during World War II.

[5]Marcuse's is not the only voice bewailing the usurpation of "humanness" in technological society. His work is selected for review here because his view is an extreme one and because students in rebellion all over the world claim him as a prophet of the new life (Keen & Raser, 1971).

[6]In somewhat the same vein as Charles Reich's delimitation of Consciousness III, Marcuse describes the new revolutionary person as follows: "It would be a psyche, a mind, an instinctual structure that could no longer tolerate aggression, domination, exploitation, ugliness, hypocrisy, or dehumanizing, routine performance. Positively you can see it in the growth of the esthetic and the erotic components in the instinctual and mental structure. I see it manifested today in the protest against the commercial violation of nature, against plastic beauty and real ugliness, against pseudovirility and brutal heroism" (H. Marcuse, quoted in Keen & Raser, 1971, p. 62).

fuel in the mid-1970s, the achievement of Consciousness III seemed to be forgotten.

IV. Authoritarianism in the future

Certain developments lead us to believe that average F-scale scores will decrease in the future. Increased levels of education and sophistication should reduce the tendency to agree with the clichés and emotional tone of F-scale statements. Even though lower scores do not necessarily indicate a decreased authoritarianism in the individual, increased educational opportunities should help decrease authoritarianism per se. Social critic Eric Hoffer believes that in the future all technologically advanced societies will have their citizens "spend a good part of their lives in some form of education or reeducation, and everyone will therefore become, in a sense, an intellectual" (quoted by Tomkins, 1967, p. 34). And there are fewer authoritarians within the intellectual community. Nonetheless, societal pressures can increase personal authoritarianism. An increase in political-extremist groups, on both left and right, leads the average citizen to move in a direction that is more supportive of authoritarian actions.

For example, Sales (1972) has found that in periods of economic hard times, such as the Great Depression of the 1930s, more people join authoritarian organizations, such as those churches that stress the punitiveness of God, demand absolute obedience to the leadership of the church or the Divine, condemn heretics, and manifest other qualities of an authoritarian syndrome. From 1930 through 1939, the number of converts added to relatively nonauthoritarian denominations was less, in contrast to the rates for a preceding period of economic prosperity (1920–1929). Such findings, which were replicated on a smaller base in Seattle during a period of increased unemployment in its aerospace industry in 1969–1970, will probably characterize the last few years of the 1970s, in light of the rising unemployment rate, increased inflation, and the scarcity of necessary products.

Sales, in a later article (1973), even questions whether a democratic society can flourish except in times of prosperity. Regardless, a democratic society always faces the need to protect itself from antisocial forces while maintaining protection of personal privacy and freedom (Lingle, 1974). At times the balance swings too far in one direction. In the early 1970s in the United States surveillance by both the government and private organizations heightened (Cowan, Egleson, & Hentoff, 1974). The FBI and police at times hired overzealous *agents provocateurs* to infiltrate organizations and entrap their victims. Westin (1967) reports a survey showing that 24.6% of the businesses surveyed used surveillance techniques to observe their employees without their knowledge.

A proposal first made in 1970 by Arnold Hutschnecker, a New York psychiatrist, is an omen for the decade. Hutschnecker suggested a mass testing of the mental and personality characteristics of all United States children between the ages of 6 and 8 in order to identify potential juvenile delinquents and criminals. This proposal would have instituted "corrective treatment" right away for all children who showed "delinquent tendencies"; after-school "counseling" would have been required of all children, and older, more "difficult" youths would have been placed in special camps (*New York Times,* April 19, 1970, p. 13). Since there is no evidence that personality tests would be accurate enough to identify potentially delinquent individuals—and perhaps for other reasons—the proposal was rejected by the U. S. Department of Health, Education, and Welfare. But the fact that the suggestion was seriously advanced (and drew some significant support) reminds us that George Orwell's *1984* may be even closer than its date indicates.

There are already massive data banks, kept by private corporations, that contain a great deal of confidential information. Credit bureaus, originally established to assess applicants for credit, maintain files on more than 110 million United States citizens and a proportionate number in Canada. Information swapping by various credit information systems across the two countries is a common occurrence. What is to prevent either government from obtaining these files? Alan F. Westin, who has studied the invasions of our privacy, foresees a vast credit bureau of the future that contains four "master files" on every United States resident. "Most important of all," he states, "these four master files on education, employment, finances and citizenship can be put together in one unified printout whenever a government agency with subpoena power chooses to do so" (quoted in *AFL-CIO American Federationist*, April 1971, p. 8).

In the law-enforcement area there appear to be strong counterreactions to the 1960s U. S. Supreme Court decisions that had liberalized the rights of accused criminals.[7] In contrast to trends in the preceding years, responses to Gallup-type polls in the period of 1967–1972 were more in favor of capital punishment for criminals (Erskine, 1970; Sales, 1973). Further indications that the 1970s are becoming a more repressive period were the frequent attacks by then U. S. Vice President Agnew and others on the mass media during the early 1970s, even though such threatening attacks were temporarily stilled because of the beneficial role the mass media played in exposing governmental lawbreaking.

---

[7]First indications of a shift in the Supreme Court to a more conservative position in regard to rights of the accused came on February 24, 1971, with the ruling in *Harris v. New York State*. The defendant was arrested for selling heroin and made certain statements to the police that were inadmissible in court under the Miranda Doctrine. The U. S. Supreme Court ruled that these statements could not be admitted into evidence by the prosecution, but that if the defendant took the stand in his own behalf these statements could be used to attack his credibility as a witness. This is a dangerous precedent. It discourages the witness from taking the stand in his own behalf (a fact that could well influence the jury) and circumvents the Miranda Doctrine (J. Geary, personal communication, January 5, 1975).

All is not pessimistic, however. There are active efforts to reduce the authoritarian nature of our society. A recent U. S. law permits individuals to learn what is kept in their credit files and records. A similar law has been enacted in Canada. Censorship and restrictions on the availability of erotic material are being reduced; new life-styles are tolerated if they do not violate the rights of others. More individuals are protesting invasions of privacy; institutions such as the American Civil Liberties Union (whose goal is the protection of every citizen's rights) are gaining support. (See Chapter 19 for more detail.)

Police departments in many United States cities are also undergoing changes. In some police departments, the traditional policeman's uniform has been discarded and replaced by blue blazers and contrasting slacks. Police have been encouraged to develop a new role in their dealings with citizens. Moreover, they are receiving training in human relations and community relations. "Ride alongs," in which parents and children accompany police on night patrol, have increased communication between the police and the community. Although the general atmosphere of life in the United States in the mid-1970s has rejected the governmental authoritarianism and repression of the Nixon administration, the future is uncertain.

V. Summary

Authoritarianism is both personal and societal; tendencies toward authoritarianism differ among individuals as well as among various societies and governments.

The program of research on authoritarianism at the University of California at Berkeley began with a concern about anti-Semitism, moved to a study of ethnocentrism and politico-economic conservatism, and culminated in the measurement of authoritarianism, or an antidemocratic ideology.

Ethnocentrism is a belief that one's own group is superior to all other groups. Other racial and ethnic groups, foreigners, and all deviant groups are rejected.

Authoritarianism was conceptualized as a basic personality style—a syndrome of organized beliefs and symptoms.

The California researchers posited nine components of authoritarianism: conventionalism, authoritarian aggression, authoritarian submission, power and toughness, anti-intraception, superstition and stereotypy, destructiveness and cynicism, projectivity, and overconcern with sex.

In conceptualizing the authoritarian personality, the California researchers used psychoanalytic theory to explain how authoritarianism developed in a person. The highly authoritarian and ethnocentric person was seen as possessing a weak ego, a rigid and externalized superego, and a strong, primitive id.

The California F scale was designed to measure authoritarianism. It has been criticized because, in each of its items, agreement with the statement is scored as an indication of authoritarianism. This characteristic results in high scores for respondents with an acquiescent response set, the tendency to agree with a statement regardless of the statement's content.

There is a great deal of evidence that degree of authoritarianism, as measured by the F scale, is related to a variety of psychological constructs. For example, highly authoritarian subjects are more prejudiced, less sensitive to the feelings of others, less likely to volunteer for psychological experiments, and more likely to support conservative political candidates.

Methodological flaws in the authoritarian-personality study lead us to conclude that it has not yet been proven that authoritarianism is an ideology that generally includes preju-dice, rigidity, politicoeconomic conservatism, and other attributes.

Dogmatism is a concept somewhat related to authoritarianism. Dogmatism is defined as a relatively closed cluster of beliefs organized around a set of attitudes toward absolute authority.

Milgram's program of studies on obedience indicates that (1) the majority of subjects obey the instructions of the experimenter even when it means inflicting great pain on a fellow subject, and (2) the extent of obedience is much greater than anticipated.

Variations in Milgram's basic procedure indicate that (1) when the victim is closer to the subject administering the electric shocks, the subject demonstrates less obedience, and (2) when the experimenter is closer to the subject administering the shocks, the subject shows a greater degree of obedience.

Among the criticisms of Milgram's study on obedience are those questioning its ethicality. Specifically, critics are concerned about the possible long-term effects on the subjects, the rights of consent of the subjects, and the researcher's wisdom in continuing the study despite tensions shown by subjects.

The findings regarding the pervasiveness of obedience in Milgram's studies have also been questioned. Some critics do not believe that the findings can be generalized to real-life situations because of (1) the nonrepresentative nature of the subjects, (2) the use of prods to keep the subjects at the task, and (3) the essential nature of trust in an experiment.

Finally, sociological theorists have proposed that advanced industrialized civilizations necessarily become repressive and authoritarian. The current causes for increased repression and some less-discouraging trends in our society are described.

I. Definitions of conformity and related phenomena
   A. Conformity
   B. Compliance versus private acceptance: Two types of conformity
   C. Uniformity
   D. Conventionality
   E. Independence
   F. Anticonformity or counterconformity

II. Early procedures and findings in the study of conformity (compliance)
   A. The Asch situation: Conformity (compliance) in the laboratory
   B. Limitations of the Asch procedure
   C. Refinements in the conceptualization of conformity

III. The extent of conformity
   A. The autokinetic-effect situation
   B. Situational influences on extent of conformity in Asch's studies
   C. Crutchfield's procedure: Conformity across content areas

IV. Is there a conforming personality?

V. Is conformity increasing in our society?

VI. Unresolved issues in the study of conformity and nonconformity

VII. Other effects of social influence: Group risk taking and polarization
   A. Group risk taking: Is it the best label?
   B. Is willingness to take a greater risk a group phenomenon or a pseudoeffect?
   C. Another shift: From direction to extremity
   D. Summary on group risk taking and group polarization

VIII. Hypnosis: Something more than simply social influence?

IX. Summary

Conformity and social influence

19

Every new opinion, at its starting, is precisely in the minority of one.

Thomas Carlyle

As for conforming outwardly, and living your own life inwardly, I do not think much of that.

Henry David Thoreau

Consider these events:

Jack and Sally Klein bought a house in the huge Westlake subdivision near San Francisco. They went right to work on the lawn and soon had the most beautiful one in the neighborhood. But their grass became infected with a fungus that resisted all efforts at treatment. After two years of fighting it, the Kleins dug up the sick grass and planted ivy. They also grew hedges on their property line and put in a rock garden and a birdbath—all in disregard of the bylaws of the Westlake Subdivision Improvement Association. Homeowners all over the subdivision rose in anger against the Kleins, and vandals attacked the ivy with gasoline. The Improvement Association brought suit to force the Kleins to conform.

Dr. Jeremiah Stamler, a respected heart specialist in Chicago, was subpoenaed to appear before the U. S. House Committee on Un-American Activities (commonly called HUAC) to testify regarding an alleged resurgence of Communist activities in Chicago. The committee never revealed why it wanted testimony from Dr. Stamler, but it did release the names of subpoenaed witnesses, leading to local news-

paper headlines such as "City Doctor Gets Red Quiz Subpoena" and "Heart Expert Subpoenaed in Red Quiz." Such invasions of privacy of innocent people were not uncommon in the years that HUAC was in existence (Goodman, 1968). What was uncommon was Dr. Stamler's response. Along with Mrs. Yolanda F. Hall, a nutritionist who had also been called to testify, he not only refused to but also brought suit challenging the committee's constitutionality. After nine years in court, at legal costs of $300,000, Dr. Stamler and Mrs. Hall won their case.

For a full six months after she began wearing her hair in a natural, or Afro, style, everything went smoothly for Deborah Ruth Renwick, a Black stewardess with United Air Lines. But then a supervisor complained, and Ms. Renwick was asked to cut her hair by about an inch. She refused to, and was fired—for failing to maintain the airline's standards of good grooming *(Newsweek,* October 6, 1969).

Members of the Amish religious sect in Wisconsin, Pennsylvania, and Iowa refused to send their children to the local public high schools, because of their religious beliefs. Their religious doctrine holds that higher education of any kind is a deterrent to salvation (Erickson, 1966). After a number of years of litigation the U. S. Supreme Court decided in 1972 that members of the Amish religious group are not subject to state compulsory-education laws (*Newsweek*, May 29, 1972).

All these true events reflect the pervasiveness of conformity pressures in our everyday lives. One of the purposes of this chapter is to explore types of conformity, the extent of conformity in our society, and the ways in which others cause us to accept beliefs or adopt behaviors that we had not held earlier. The chapter also considers social influence in a broader context, for the influence process is at the core of social psychology (Moscovici, 1974) and can have a variety of results. Pressures from a supervisor can make workers obedient even to the extent of administering extremely dangerous electric shocks to other persons, as Chapter 18 showed. A person who is unsure of the appropriate *emotional* response to a novel situation will imitate the behavior of another person in the same situation. Social influence can be particularly effective under cases of deindividuation in group members (see Chapter 17). Rather than reexamining these phenomena, the final sections of this chapter deal with two other manifestations of social influence —hypnosis and risk taking in groups.

I. Definitions of conformity and related phenomena

Margaret Williams vigorously brushes her teeth after every meal. Is she demonstrating conformity because she does what her dentist tells her to do? Eddie Stephens, a 12-year-old, rejects every sugggestion that his parents lay before him. If his mother tells him that his green shirt would look nice for the dance, he wears the purple and orange one. Does such a choice simply ignore pressures toward conformity, or is it a

motivated, deliberately anticonforming behavior on Eddie's part? Or does the action represent Eddie's healthy search for identity and independence? Commander Lloyd Bucher of the U. S. Navy ship *Pueblo* signed a statement of guilt in order to save his crew from punishments and torture by the North Koreans. Did his behavior reflect conformity?

These vignettes reflect the possibility of confusion when we consider terms such as *conformity, uniformity, conventionality, anticonformity,* and others. When used by social psychologists, each of these terms has a separate meaning. We shall define them in the following paragraphs.

A. Conformity

One reason *conformity* is a confusing term is that social psychologists use it as a label for different phenomena. C. A. Kiesler (1969) identifies three uses of the term *conformity:* (1) going along with the group, or behaving in a way consistent with that of the majority; (2) a change in attitudes or beliefs as a result of group pressure; and (3) a basic personality trait. All these usages will be discussed in this chapter.

Because of these varied meanings, we believe it is best to think of conformity as a generic term, defined as *yielding to group pressures.* But, we should ask, what is yielded? C. A. Kiesler and Kiesler have defined conformity as "a change in *behavior or belief* toward a group as a result of real or imagined group pressure" (1969, p. 2; italics added). Note that the word *change* in this definition of conformity implies that the resulting response is different from the person's earlier private opinion, preference, or perception. For example, if a student does not want to join in a protest against the dormitory head resident but does so because everybody in his dormitory is doing it, the student clearly shows conformity. But what if he privately lacks any opinion—favorable or unfavorable—about the head resident but joins in the protest because his roommates ask him to? Does his action then reflect conform-

Figure 19-1

Conformity pressures at Disneyland. A happy crowd of teenagers prepares to
enter the gates and spend a day at Disneyland. It is a hot summer day, and
people are dressed comfortably for the occasion. But a Disneyland gate guard
stops one girl and says "Excuse me, Miss, but do you have a sweater or jacket?"
The girl, already sweating in her halter top, asks "What for?" "Miss," replies
the guard, "Disneyland is just family fun, and, frankly, we can't let you in with
a halter top that looks like that." Of the 20 million people who visit Walt
Disney World or Disneyland annually, 10,000 get turned away at the gate
because of their dress or appearance. For example, *no* controversial or political
messages on jackets, buttons, or T-shirts are allowed; these include "Don't
blame me—I voted for McGovern" and "Make Love, Not War." (Source: E. Black,
"Brave, New Tomorrowland," *New Times*, Vol. 3, No. 12, Dec. 13, 1974, p. 51;
photo courtesy of Disneyland.)

ity? It does, because his action is still a change in behavior resulting from pressure by others.

B. Compliance versus private acceptance: Two types of conformity

Changes in actions *or* in private attitudes can reflect conformity, but these two types of change reflect different phenomena. If a student is asked to join a protest, his response will reflect one of the following four possible combinations (V. L. Allen, 1965):

1. His behavior conforms (he joins in the protest), and his private attitude is in support of the protest.

2. His behavior conforms (he joins in the protest), but his private attitude is contradictory. (Privately he feels it is improper to protest, but he does so to please a friend or to gain favor.)

3. His behavior is nonconforming (he refuses to join in the protest), and his private attitude is resistant to the protest.

4. His behavior is nonconforming (he refuses to join in the protest), even though his private attitude is in support of the protest. (Perhaps he is afraid that his parents or the college authorities will hear about it and that they will reprimand him.)

Festinger (1953a) and, more recently, C. A. Kiesler and Kiesler (1969) distinguish between these two types of changes by labeling conforming behavior *compliance* and conforming private attitudes *private acceptance*. While this is a very useful distinction, it has had little impact on the research literature. The early studies on conformity—now considered "classics"—usually dealt only with conforming *behavior*; thus, in our subsequent descriptions of the studies by Sherif, Asch, and others, we shall keep in mind this limitation by labeling such projects as *studies of conformity (compliance)*. Private acceptance of pressures to conform reflects an internalization of the action (Kelman, 1958) and may be equated with the phenomena of *attitude change* (see Chapter 11).

C. Uniformity

Uniformity does not reflect the same process as conformity. As Krech, Crutchfield, and Ballachey (1962, p. 505) indicate, there may be general agreement in a society over facts or beliefs without its being the result of social pressures.[1] Most people would agree that children should be given a nutritious and balanced diet. The near uniformity of this response is not a function of majority pressures; similarity in response occurs for reasons other than group influence.

D. Conventionality

Conventionality may be defined as acting in what is a customary or usual fashion, or as adherence to the standard practices of society. Saying good-bye at the end of a telephone conversation is, in our society, a conventional response; it does not reflect conformity as we have defined it. Yet we acknowledge, as do Krech et al. (1962), that highly conforming individuals are more likely to adopt and maintain conventional values. (You may recall that conventionalism was one of the nine components of the authoritarian personality described in Chapter 18). But even if people are highly conventional in matters of dress, spoken speech, or even basic values, their behavior will not necessarily conform to group pressures.

E. Independence

If conformity is yielding to group pressures, what is the opposite of conformity? We may think of two different types of opposing, nonconforming responses. One is *independence*, defined

---

[1]Probably there is no belief that is held with complete uniformity by all adults in a society. For example, a survey by the Knight newspapers in early 1970 indicated that a significant minority of United States adults did not believe that two men walked on the moon on July 20, 1969. A total of 1721 persons were surveyed in cities and several rural areas. Percentages of persons who doubted that the moon walk had actually occurred ranged from 8% in one community to 54% in another.

as the maintenance and expression (through behavior) of one's private beliefs in the face of group pressures to do something to the contrary. If a student believed that the dormitory head resident was doing a good job and hence refused to join in a protest even though all his friends were doing so, his reaction would be characterized as *independence.* The essential ingredient of an independent response is the *prior establishment* of a private opinion that is expressed unremittingly, even though it contradicts majority opinion or group pressure.

F. Anticonformity or counterconformity

What about the person who rejects group pressures to conform simply because he or she is rebellious? Regardless of the content of the issue advocated by others, the person rejects the influence attempt. The term **anticonformity,** or **counterconformity,** is used to label a response that is opposed to the majority response out of a desire to be negative or different. As in the case of independence, the important determinant is the individual's motivation for his or her chosen response; if a particular response is made only in order to be rebellious or to be contrary to what others advocate, the response is labeled as anticonforming. If Eddie selects an outrageous purple and orange shirt *only* because his parents insist that he wear "the lovely green one," he is manifesting not independence, but anticonformity. When anticonformity occurs, the group's position serves as a negative reference point.

Thus the actions of two persons who behave in the same manner may reflect different motivations and hence may be labeled as different processes (R. J. Smith, 1967). For example, in studying the reasons why some United States soldiers who were prisoners of war did not collaborate with their Communist Chinese captors during the Korean War, psychologists identified two types of resisters. (A resister was a United States soldier who did not succumb to the Chinese appeals to collaborate.) Some resisted be-

cause they knew that admitting guilt for the war, broadcasting peace appeals, and the like were wrong actions; these men were labeled as independent resisters. Another type had a long history of unwillingness to accept any kind of authority; they did not conform to commands from officers in the U. S. Army *or* orders from the Chinese (Schein, 1957; Kinkead, 1959). These men could justifiably be classified as showing anticonformity or counterconformity.

II. Early procedures and findings in the study of conformity (compliance)

A. The Asch situation: Conformity (compliance) in the laboratory

Suppose that a male college student who has volunteered to participate in a research project finds that he is a subject in a visual perception experiment. Along with six other subjects (in actuality, confederates), he is seated at a circular table. The group is shown a board with a vertical line drawn on it. With this line still in view, all the group members look at another board, which has three vertical lines of differing lengths. One of these lines is actually identical in length to the line of the first board; the other two lines are different enough so that in controlled tests (done individually, not in groups) more than 95% of subjects make correct judgments about the length of the lines. The subjects are instructed to state their choices out loud and one at a time. The actual subject always responds next to last. On the first trial and again on the second trial, everyone gives the same response—namely, the response that the real subject has judged to be the correct one. The volunteer may begin to think that this task is easy. The same outcome occurs on several more trials; then, on a subsequent trial—where the choice appears as clear-cut as those before—the first subject-confederate gives a response that the actual subject perceives to be clearly incorrect. All the other subject-confederates follow suit, giving the wrong response (all the confederates are trained in advance to give the same incorrect response on certain critical trials). When it comes time for the actual subject to respond, all the other preceding respondents at the table have given an answer that he believes is wrong. What does he do? Does he stick by his convictions, remain independent, and give the correct response? Does he comply with the group, giving an answer he knows is wrong? Or does he convince himself that he must be wrong and that the group's answer is correct?

This was the procedure used in an early set of studies on conformity (compliance) by social psychologist Solomon Asch (1951, 1956, 1958). Since this set of studies is regarded as a classic in social psychology, we are obligated to report the findings. Our attention, however, will be focused on the conceptual and procedural limitations of these studies as tests of conformity.[2]

How does the volunteer in the Asch conformity situation respond? We cannot make one statement that applies to all subjects. In the original Asch studies, a significant minority (about 33%) never conformed, but a very small percentage (8%) conformed to the group pressure on almost all the critical trials. Overall, 32% of the subjects conformed on critical trials, and 68% remained independent. The usefulness of this summary is very limited, however, because of wide individual differences. We will have more to say about these individual differences later.

B. Limitations of the Asch procedure

Conformity, as used by Asch, refers to behavior that is consistent with the behavior of others in a group and is contradictory to the subject's private opinion or preferences. Thus, ac-

cording to Asch's procedures, on each critical trial the subject's response must either conform (that is, yield to the majority) or be independent. The conformity score for each subject is the number of times he or she conforms on critical trials.

Asch's operational definition has two important limitations. First, as he used the term, *conformity* refers to public compliance and has nothing to say about private acceptance. Some of Asch's conformists may have changed their private opinions; others may have been expedient conformers in the sense that they conformed in order to gain acceptance by the group. Asch's operational definition does not distinguish between these two types of response. Interviews with subjects afterward led Asch to conclude that only a few of them internalized the group's answer. Most subjects came to doubt their perceptions, however, in the face of the consensus.

A second limitation of Asch's procedure is that it makes the occurrence of anticonformity or counterconformity very difficult. In everyday life, as indicated previously, we interpret some actions as primarily the result of a need to be different; on the critical trials in the Asch situation, there is no way for a person to show anticonformity. (On the noncritical trials, the subject could show anticonformity by giving an incorrect judgment when the group gave a correct judgment.)

A problem with Asch's procedure as a predictor of real-life conformity relates to the subject's involvement in the task. Just how important is this task to the average subject? On the one hand, we might assume that a subject becomes very ego-involved in the task when he finds that others disagree with him. He may strain to do well and may feel great conflict. On the other hand, a subject may think "What the hell! It's only a silly psychology experiment. Why sweat it? I may as well answer the way everyone else does." The latter reaction could cause a rate of conformity (compliance) that would differ from the rate of conformity in real-life situations in which the degree of ego involvement is greater. In a similar fashion, the subject in the experiment

---

[2]After the 25-year interim that has passed since the time of these pioneering studies, it is easy to be critical. The Asch studies were, indeed, a groundbreaking contribution to the study of conformity and social influence. Unfortunately, research methodology has not developed as fast as new conceptualizations of conformity.

may see the demand characteristics as dictating a conforming response on his part. This is speculation; as yet, we do not know the facts. Would the subject who yields in the Asch experiment yield in the same way to pressures from friends who wish to involve him in their all-night poker game? The two situations differ in many ways—the risks of conforming, the degree of clarity in identifying the correct response, the nature of the social pressure, and so on. Rates of yielding in real-life situations may differ greatly from those found on Asch's task.

Undoubtedly, conformity does occur in the laboratory even at the price of great tension and conflict, as Milgram's study on obedience, reported in Chapter 18, indicated. But in both the Milgram and Asch experiments some of the subjects may have been manifesting an "as if" reaction—that is, they may have been behaving *as if* the conditions were valid, while still being highly suspicious of the reality of the conditions. For these and other reasons, it is hazardous to assume that the extent of conformity found in the Asch tasks would occur in real-life situations.

C. Refinements in the conceptualization of conformity

Because of concerns like those described in the preceding section, several social psychologists have emphasized that conformity is not a simple, unitary process. Conformity in situations in which investment is low (as in the Asch situation) is a different process from conforming in situations in which the investment is high (as when someone's friends decide to steal a car and try to persuade him or her to participate). Similarly, there is a difference in a practical sense as well as in a conceptual sense between a situation in which the advocated position agrees with local norms and one in which it conflicts with them. When a person is pressured to adopt a new position that varies from the position defined by social custom but refuses, is the person conforming or not? For example, in the mid-1970s some White parents living in Boston refused to register their children when previously all-White schools were desegregated. These parents were labeled nonconformists, but they were clearly conforming to popular local traditions. Analysts of the conformity process, such as Jahoda (1959), R. H. Willis (1963, 1965), and C. A. Kiesler and Kiesler (1969), tell us that conformity is not an either-or process; a single act can be in compliance with laws and at variance with pressures from the group, or vice versa. We must know the total context in which behavior occurs before we can decide whether it is conforming.

Another complexity derives from the fact that a person can change his or her public position—to avoid torture, to get elected, to persuade a close friend—while maintaining his or her original private opinion. In such cases, has the person conformed? Galileo was forced by the Roman Catholic Church to recant publicly his heretical position that the earth revolved around the sun. He finally did so—yet murmured "It still moves." Galileo complied publicly but did not privately accept the Church's position.

We have already indicated that several social psychologists have refined the distinctions between conformity processes outlined in the preceding sections. We discuss two such distinctions here.

Kelman's distinctions between internal processes. Herbert Kelman (1958, 1961) has offered a model of conformity that makes a distinction between different consequences for the recipient of pressures to conform. He describes three different processes, called *compliance, identification,* and *internalization.* Kelman proposes that when a person agrees with the majority in order to receive a reward or to avoid a punishment for nonconformity, his or her reaction reflects *compliance.* The response is made only as an instrumental act to achieve some other goal. Prisoners of war who signed statements of guilt in order to receive food or their mail exemplify *compliance.*

In contrast, a conforming response made in order to maintain an important relationship with others is called *identification.* If the subject in an Asch situation strongly identified with the others and used them as models, he or she would continue to conform as long as the relationship with the others was important.

The third process, *internalization*, reflects an acceptance of the others' influence attempt because it is congruent with the subject's value system. In this case, the private acceptance of the material is less dependent on the continued presence of the others.

But further distinctions in response still need to be made.

Jahoda's model: Three aspects of conformity. To represent the complexities adequately, Marie Jahoda (1959) proposed eight possible types of action, each a different combination of three conditions. These are represented in Figure 19-2. Notice that adoption or rejection of the advocated position is represented on the second line and that the consistency between the subject's public position and his or her final private position is shown on the third line. The eight possible results are labeled on the last line. Let us take a concrete example and see how each action might be represented. Suppose a male college student is approached by a friend and asked to sign a petition in favor of equal pay for women. If we assume that the student has a great deal of initial investment in the issue (that is, has strong feelings about it), processes *a* through *d* apply. Though Jahoda is not explicit here, we assume

that in most cases the student's initial private desire is to reject the request.

Process *a* is called by Jahoda *independent dissent*. Here the person has strong feelings about the issue, does not adopt the advocated position (refuses to sign the petition), and maintains a private opinion that coincides with his public action. We would infer that this person has strong feelings against the feminist movement before he is approached; we know that he refuses to sign and is—in Jahoda's words—at ease with himself about the public position he has taken.

Process *b* refers to a case in which a person is also involved in the issue, also refuses to sign the petition, but experiences a shift in his private opinion. That is, his initial antifeminist position causes him to refuse to sign the petition, but somehow he is now privately convinced that the petition is a good thing. Jahoda calls this *undermined independence*, which indicates that the influence process has undermined the student's private position. If we can assume that subjects in the Asch study were involved in their task, the nonyielders who continued to report their true answers but developed doubts about their eyesight would represent process *b*[3]

[3]Many arguments between husbands and wives may represent process *b*. Both parties are involved; one refuses to go along with the request of the other, even though he or she has privately become convinced that the other's position is right.

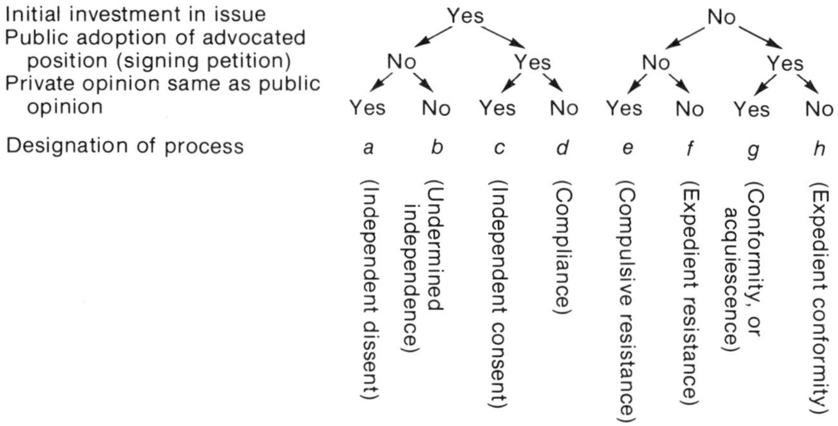

Figure 19-2
Types of conformity and independence (modified from Jahoda, 1959).

Initial investment in issue							Yes				No			
Public adoption of advocated position (signing petition)		No			Yes		No			Yes	
Private opinion same as public opinion	Yes	No	Yes	No	Yes	No	Yes	No
Designation of process	*a*	*b*	*c*	*d*	*e*	*f*	*g*	*h*
	(Independent dissent)	(Undermined independence)	(Independent consent)	(Compliance)	(Compulsive resistance)	(Expedient resistance)	(Conformity, or acquiescence)	(Expedient conformity)

Processes c and d represent persons who are initially against women's liberation, and are very involved in the issue, but whose public position is influenced by the request. They sign the petition ("Yes" on line 2 of Figure 19-2). Process c reflects what happens to the person who not only publicly advocates the position of the petition but also privately comes to accept this viewpoint. Jahoda calls this *independent consent*. This subject's position is now free of conflict, since both his public and private positions are consistent. Perhaps this student restructured or clarified the manner in which he viewed the issue—almost a necessity in light of his initial involvement in the topic and his changed position.

Process d reflects public adoption of the advocated position combined with a failure to adopt a consistent private opinion. An example of process d would occur when the college student signs the petition despite his continued strong feelings against women's liberation. Galileo's action is a prime example of this process, which Jahoda calls *compliance*; such an example indicates that severe threats upon the person may cause the apparently inconsistent behavior and beliefs of process d. Certain members of Congress or Parliament—particularly those in the same political party as the President or Prime Minister—may vote for a bill or a court nominee even though their privately held negative feelings have not been changed by pressures from the political leader.

The remaining four processes in Figure 19-2 reflect cases in which the student's initial involvement in the issue is minimal. In this case, the student may never have thought about feminism before and may not care about it presently. In process e, the student refuses to sign the petition and does not feel any conflict between what he has done and what he believes. Jahoda labels this *compulsive resistance* and describes it as an unreasonable position. She expects this type of behavior only "in those who lack the essential ability to respond to external pressure, or in those who reject a stand just because it is demanded by others" (1959, p. 114). There is a tone of anticonformity, then, to this response.

Process f, called *expedient resistance*, represents the action taken by a person who has no initial investment in the issue, who refuses to sign the petition, but who feels in his heart that the goal of the petition is appropriate. As Jahoda indicates, this reaction does not appear to be psychologically plausible; however, other factors, such as a momentary dislike for the friend, might cause this response.

If a person is asked by a friend to sign a petition favoring an issue about which he has no strong feelings, he may do so as a favor to the friend, or because he trusts his friend's judgment. He may even privately adopt the position. This response (process g) Jahoda labels *conformity*; she evaluates it as a very reasonable type of behavior in cases in which the person has little investment in the issue. Note that Jahoda reserves the term *conformity* for cases in which the subject has little investment in the issue. We prefer to use *conformity* as a generic term that also applies in high-investment situations, and therefore we would rather refer to process g as *acquiescence*.

The remaining possibility, process h, describes the result when an initially uninvolved person signs the petition even though the recruitment has not influenced his private opinion. This *expedient conformity* may reflect a responsiveness to social pressures; this person may think "I'll sign it to please my friend, even though I don't agree with it; after all, it's no big deal to me." United States prisoners of war who did not feel much concern about national issues and hence made peace broadcasts for the North Koreans and Communist Chinese reflected expedient conformity. Opportunistic prisoners of war found that such collaboration brought them special treatment—their mail from home was delivered more quickly, and their work details were easier. Thus, it was expedient to conform.

The refinements proposed by Kelman, by Jahoda, and by Stricker et al. (in Figure 19-3) are not only helpful but should serve as organizing principles for future research. So far these refinements have had little effect upon empirical studies. When we face the question of the extent of conformity in the next section, we must unfortunately rely in most cases upon inadequate operational definitions of conformity.

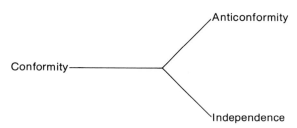

Figure 19-3
One model of the relationship of responses to group pressure. In more traditional measures of conformity an arrow-shaped model such as this one may be most accurate. Stricker, Messick, and Jackson (1970) tested the extent of conformity, anticonformity, and independence in four different tasks. The relationships found in their study suggest that conformity responses have strong negative relationships with both independence responses and anticonformity responses; however, anticonformity and independence are not related. Thus the drawing represents each of these as an opposite pole of conformity. (From "Conformity, Anticonformity, and Independence: Their Dimensionality and Generality," by L. J. Stricker, S. Messick, and D. N. Jackson, *Journal of Personality and Social Psychology*, 1970, *16*, 494–507. Copyright 1970 by the American Psychological Association. Reprinted by permission.)

III. The extent of conformity

A. The autokinetic-effect situation

The empirical study of conformity was highly influenced by the pioneering work of Muzafer Sherif (1935) on the **autokinetic effect.** If you look at a stationary light in an otherwise completely dark room, the light will appear to move. Perhaps it will move to the left, perhaps to the right, perhaps up or down—but it will appear to move in some direction, because your eyes have no other reference point (J. Levy, 1972). Sherif capitalized on this autokinetic phenome-

non to study the effects of another person's response on one's own response. He found that a subject's reports of movement were highly influenced by the estimates of other participants. Even the responses of only one other person influenced the subject's response.[4] It is not surprising that the subject's estimates were modified by the responses of others; after all, there was no other source of information, and the light was not really moving anyway. Yet despite these and other manifestations of artificiality in the situation, the study using the autokinetic effect stimulated more advanced studies of conformity. The influence of the procedure on Asch's work is evident, even though Sherif used an ambiguous stimulus and Asch's stimulus was almost devoid of ambiguity.

B. Situational influences on extent of conformity in Asch's studies

Asch's usual procedure employed six confederates who gave false answers on certain trials in a line-judging task. With these influences operating, 32% of the true subjects' responses were conforming, and 68% were independent. These averages include responses of all true subjects on all the critical trials. (There were 50 true subjects, and 12 critical trials interspersed with a large number of trials in which all confederates gave the correct answer.)

But averages are deceiving; in the Asch study the distribution of conforming responses is more important because of the great degree of individual differences. Table 19–1 presents the distribution of conforming responses. Notice that

[4]Apparently, the response in Sherif's experiment reflects both public compliance and private acceptance. The effect lasts a long time (M. Sherif, 1935; Bovard, 1948), and subjects report that they were unaware that the responses of others influenced them (Hood & Sherif, 1962). On the other hand, if subjects are told at the beginning of the experiment that the light is actually stationary and that its "movement" is an illusion, subjects' estimates are not influenced by the estimates of others (C. N. Alexander, Zucker, & Brody, 1970).

13 of the 50 subjects never yielded to the majority on any of the 12 critical trials. One subject yielded on 11 of the 12 trials, and 3 subjects yielded on 10 of the 12 trials. Although the mean number of conforming responses is 3.84 (out of a possible 12), the modal number is 0. With a distribution as J-shaped as this one, it is rather meaningless to say that the mean adequately represents the entire group.

Table 19-1
Distribution of conforming responses in the original Asch study

Number of Conforming Responses	Number of True Subjects Who Gave This Number of Conforming Responses
0	13
1	4
2	5
3	6
4	3
5	4
6	1
7	2
8	5
9	3
10	3
11	1
12	0
Total	50 subjects
Mean 3.84	

Modified from Asch (1958, p. 177).

Asch continued his work using this basic procedure to assess the extent to which various situational factors affect a conforming response. The relevant findings of more recent studies that have varied other situational factors are summarized here.[5]

[5]The reader is referred to Nord (1969), C. A. Kiesler (1969, pp. 255–272), and V. L. Allen (1965, pp. 157–164) for more detailed treatments of these and other situational effects on the extent of conformity.

What is the effect of group size? One might expect that the larger the number of subjects who form a unanimous majority, the more often the true subject would conform. This is true, but only to a degree. Asch (1956, 1958) and others (L. A. Rosenberg, 1961; S. C. Goldberg, 1954) studied the extent of yielding to unanimous majorities of 2, 3, 4, 6, 7, 8, and 10 to 15 persons. Also, the limiting case was studied in which the true subject participated with only one confederate. More conformity resulted from participation with two confederates giving false answers than with one (see Table 19-2). Groups of three or four confederates had the greatest influence in inducing conformity responses; groups of eight or more persons were somewhat less effective, indicating the possible emergence of a **ceiling effect** (Stang, 1976). In the real world, however, further increases in group size may increase conformity; Krech et al. (1962) see threats of reprisal as one reason why conformity may increase with increases in size of real-life groups.

What is the effect of a nonunanimous majority? In the studies described thus far, all the confederates were instructed to respond falsely on predetermined trials. But it is unclear whether conformity results from the sheer number of others or from the *unanimity* of their response (Moscovici, 1974; Allen & Levine, 1968). What if one of the eight confederates (the one seated fourth in the row) were to give the correct response on every trial? This results in much less conformity on the part of the true subject. In such experiments, 5.5% of the responses were conforming, compared with 32% in the original experiment. When two *true subjects* participated along with the eight confederates, a conforming response occurred 10% of the time.

The presence of one other kindred soul within a relatively large group (eight to ten persons) is a greater deterrent to conformity than being in a smaller group (four persons) where everyone else disagrees with you. Even if the kindred soul is not present but the subject knows that someone else *has* responded as he desires

Table 19-2
Extent of conformity in true subjects with unanimous majorities of different sizes

Size of majority	1	2	3	4	8	10–15
N of true subjects	10	15	10	10	50	12
Mean no. of conforming responses	0.33	1.53	4.0	4.20	3.84	3.75
Range in no. of conforming responses per subject	0–1	0–5	1–12	0–11	0–11	0–10

From Asch (1958, p. 181).

to, he is somewhat less conforming (Wilder & Allen, 1973). Clearly, such findings have implications for attempts to persuade. "Divide and conquer" has validity in the sense that, when a person is removed from all others who give human support, he or she is much more likely to succumb to the pressures of the majority, even if the unanimous majority has few members (D. Graham, 1962; Moscovici & Faucheux, 1972).

What is the effect when an initial supporter defects to the majority? In one condition Asch arranged for one of the confederates (seated in the fourth position) to give the correct response on the first half of the critical trials but then switch to the false response of the majority on the remaining trials. The experience of having and then losing a supporter restored the majority effect to almost full force; in such cases the true subject conformed an average of 28.5% of the time after his supporter defected.

Further research has indicated that the status and competence of the group members influence the extent of conformity expressed by the true subject (Endler & Hartley, 1973; Wiesenthal, Endler, Coward, & Edwards, 1974). One would expect a high school student to conform more to the majority's judgments when the other participants are introduced as college seniors than when they are introduced as other high school students. Crutchfield (cited in Krech et al., 1962) used a conformity procedure similar to Asch's and found that subjects who were members of an ethnic or racial minority con-

formed highly when participating in groups of which they were the only minority-group member.

How does compliance with a small request affect later compliance with a larger request? The foot-in-the-door technique is an age-old device that is certainly not limited to door-to-door salesmen. The basic premise is that if you can get a person to do a small thing for you, he or she is more likely to agree to another request later—a request that may ordinarily have been rejected. Consider the following example. J. L. Freedman and Fraser (1966) arranged an experiment whereby a fictitious California consumer's group contacted housewives by phone. The housewives were told that a survey of household products was being conducted. The survey would involve five or six staff members entering the home some morning for about two hours to enumerate and classify all of the household products. These men would need to have full freedom in the house to go through cupboards and storage places. All the information would then be used in writing reports for a public-service publication called *The Guide*. Of the housewives with whom there had been no earlier contact, 22% complied with this request. In contrast, another group of housewives was called earlier and asked to answer a brief telephone survey conducted by the same consumer organization; on this first contact, eight questions were asked about brands of soaps used in the home. Of the housewives who had been exposed to this foot-in-the-door gambit, a much larger number—53%—agreed to allow the consumer group to enter their home.

These and similar findings (Pliner, Hart, Kohl, & Saari, 1974) would seem to support the notion of "if they give you an inch, you can take a mile." But it should be noted that Freedman and Fraser's findings may be limited to situations in which the respondent has a low degree of initial commitment—Jahoda's conditions *e, f, g,* and *h* in Figure 19-2. Fish and Kaplan (1974), in replicating the above study with another type of request, found that respondents who had high degrees of initial commitment would comply with a smaller request but reject the larger one, saying in effect "I have done my share."

C. Crutchfield's procedure:
Conformity across
content areas

Every beginning project can do only so much, and as beginning studies Asch's experiments had unavoidable limitations. We would like to know, for example, whether the conforming effect occurs to the same degree with other types of tasks than line judging, and whether it occurs in other types of subjects than the ubiquitous college sophomore. A study by Crutchfield (1955) gives us additional information. However, Crutchfield's procedure requires some detailed description.

Crutchfield's subjects were businessmen or military officers in management positions who were participating in a three-day assessment program at the Institute of Personality Assessment and Research at the University of California at Berkeley. On the final day of activities, the men were placed in groups of five and were put in front of an apparatus consisting of five adjacent electrical panels. Each panel formed three sides of a cubicle, which prevented the subject from seeing the panels of his four fellow subjects. The subjects were to respond to a series of questions projected on the wall in front of each man. Each question was multiple-choice, and the subject was to indicate his response by flipping a switch

on his panel. Moreover, he was to respond in order, as indicated by one of five lights lettered A, B, C, D, and E on his panel. If he were A, he responded first; B responded second, and so on. Each subject found that he responded first for a while, then third, then fourth, then second, and finally last.

Another important set of lights was on each man's panel. These lights informed the subject of the other subjects' answers before he himself responded (unless it was his turn to answer first). In other words, each subject had feedback about the answers of the other four men, in turn. Crutchfield described what happened when a subject answered last:

> Eventually the man finds himself for the first time in position E, where he is to respond last. The next slide shows a standard line and five comparison lines, of which he is to pick the one equal in length to the standard. Among the previous slides he has already encountered this kind of perceptual judgment and has found it easy. On looking at this slide it is immediately clear to him that line number 4 is the correct one. But as he waits his turn to respond, he sees light number 5 in row A go on, indicating that the person has judged line number 5 to be correct. And in fairly quick succession light 5 goes on also in rows B, C, and D.
>
> At this point the man is faced with an obvious conflict between his own clear perception and a unanimous contradictory consensus of the other four men. What does he do? Does he rely on the evidence of his own senses and respond independently? Or does he defer to the judgment of the group, complying with their perception rather than his own? [1955, p. 192].

The experimental procedure, to this point, has been described as the participating subjects viewed it. But each subject had been deceived. The apparatus was not wired as he thought, and there was no connection among the five panels. Instead, each panel was wired to the experimenter's panel, and it was he who sent all the information to all subjects. Moreover, each subject at any one time received the same information sent to the other four subjects, so that on any given trial, all five men were responding first, or, later, all were responding last *at the same time.*

Thus, Crutchfield's equipment permits a test of compliance, as it assesses public behavior in response to information about others' responses. But from the subject's responses, we can say nothing about private acceptance. Nonetheless, Crutchfield's procedure is more efficient than Asch's because it does not require the use of confederates and because it permits the testing of five subjects at one time. However, the subjects are not visible to each other. No subject sees or hears the actual responses of others—he sees only the lights representing these—and the fact that his actions are not identified to the others may limit the effect of group pressure in this situation. We may question whether this private form of responding affects conformity. Deutsch and Gerard (1955) used the Asch task to evaluate the effect of physical presence and visual communication on degree of conformity. Some subjects judged length of lines while in the presence of three confederates. Other subjects were separated by partitions and responded anonymously by pressing a button. Deutsch and Gerard found less conformity in the latter condition, perhaps indicating that the need to be accepted by others is one reason for conformity effects. These procedural effects are extensive enough to allow us to question how appropriate it is to compare percentages of conformity in the Crutchfield and Asch tasks (L. Levy, 1960).

Crutchfield's study had the advantage of presenting the subject with a wider variety of judgments than those presented in the Asch study. For example, on the first of 21 critical slides including a standard line and five comparison lines, 15 of 50 men, or 30%, conformed to the false consensus. On a question asking for the simple completion of a number series (like those found on mental tests), 30% of the men conformed to the false majority. (See Figure 19-4 for another example.)

Conformity was found by Crutchfield on items dealing with opinions and attitudes. For example, almost all the subjects in a control testing (done individually, without feedback about others' "responses") agreed with the statement "I believe we are made better by the trials and hardships of life." Yet among the men subjected to false feedback about the majority, 31% disagreed with the statement. Conformity was found even on a highly personal attitude such as expressed in the statement "I doubt whether I would make a good leader." No participant in the control group agreed with the statement, but when they were told that the other four men had agreed, 37% of the group participants agreed.

Only 2 of the 21 critical items did not produce a significant conforming response. Both these items required extremely personal and subjective judgments; they asked the subject which of two line drawings he *preferred.* Only one man out of 50 expressed agreement with the false group consensus.

As in the Asch study, a total conformity score was determined by counting the number of times each subject conformed on the 21 critical items. Of the 50 subjects, 1 conformed on 17 of 21 items. At the other extreme, several men conformed on only 1 or 2 items. The rest of the men were distributed between these extremes; the mean was approximately 8 items, or about 38%. However, as before, the mean "conformity score" diminishes in importance when placed in the context of extensive individual differences.

IV. Is there a conforming personality?

We have indicated the significant ways that situational factors may influence the extent of conformity manifested by a subject in a situation in which everyone else's response differs from his or her own. We have seen that the content of the material may determine whether the response is a conforming one or not. But in every study there were large individual differences. May we then conclude that some people are, by their nature, more conforming than others? Is conforming behavior a personality characteristic?

Opinions of social psychologists vary on this issue. This section reviews the findings and interpretations relevant to these questions.

Since subjects in Crutchfield's study were participating in a thorough assessment procedure, it was feasible to compare the conformers and the independent subjects on a number of measures in order to see which characteristics, if any, distinguished the two groups. Crutchfield found that the two groups differed in many respects; in contrast to the highly conformist subjects, the independent subjects showed "more intellectual effectiveness, ego strength, leadership ability, and maturity of social relations, together with a conspicuous absence of inferiority feelings, rigid and excessive self-control, and authoritarian atti-

tudes" (1955, p. 194). For example, the degree of conformity correlated −.63 with a staff rating of subjects' intellectual competence, −.33 with Barron's ego-strength scale, and +.39 with authoritarianism (as measured by the California F scale).

Other studies using modifications of the Crutchfield procedure have found conforming subjects to have a stronger need for affiliation (McGhee & Teevan, 1967), stronger tendencies to blame themselves (Costanzo, 1970), and lessened degrees of self-esteem (Stang, 1972).

Conformers and independent subjects also tended to differ in the personality statements that they accepted as applicable to themselves. Independent subjects more frequently indicated that

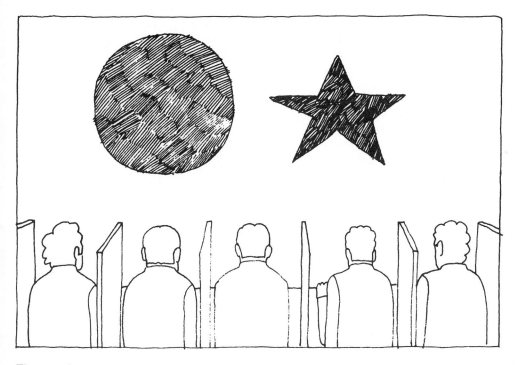

Figure 19-4

The Crutchfield conformity procedure and results. Five subjects sit in adjacent booths and respond to questions presented on a screen in front of them. In this example, the circle is about one-third larger than the star. But when each subject is led to believe that the other subjects have chosen the star as being larger, 46% of the subjects go along with the others and choose the star.

each of the following statements was true about themselves: "Sometimes I rather enjoy going against the rules and doing things I'm not supposed to." "I like to fool around with new ideas, even if they turn out later to be a total waste of time." "A person needs to 'show off' a little now and then." "It is unusual for me to express strong approval or disapproval of the actions of others." "I am often so annoyed when someone tries to get ahead of me in a line of people that I speak to him about it." "Compared to your own self-respect, the respect of others means very little." Such a pattern indicates that independent subjects feel freed from the compulsive limits of rules and are more adventurous and even exhibitionistic than conformers. They possess self-confidence and internal determinants of right and wrong. We would expect them to possess more principled levels of moral judgment than the conformists (see Chapter 8).

Conversely, conformists more often indicated that the following items applied to them: "I am in favor of very strict enforcement of all laws, no matter what the consequences." "It is all right to get around the law if you don't actually break it." "Most people are honest chiefly through fear of being caught." "I don't like to work on a problem unless there is a possibility of coming out with a clear-cut and unambiguous answer." "Once I have made up my mind I seldom change it." "I always follow the rule: business before pleasure." "The trouble with many people is that they don't take things seriously enough." "I am afraid when I look down from a high place." "I am often bothered by useless thoughts which keep running through my head." "I commonly wonder what hidden reason another person may have for doing something nice to me." "People pretend to care more about one another than they really do." "Sometimes I am sure that other people can tell what I am thinking." Thus conformists are oriented toward laws as determining what is right; at the same time there is an underlying cynicism in their views of others.

Conformists, in reporting attitudes concerning parents and children, describe their parents in highly idealized and uncritical terms, suggestive of the orientation of the highly authoritarian personality. Extremely conformist subjects prefer more restrictive child-rearing practices for their children, while independent subjects are more permissive (Block, 1955).

Apparently the independent subjects represent everything psychologists would define as characteristic of an effectively functioning person, while the conformists possess qualities—both cognitive and temperamental—that inhibit effective functioning. There are only two pieces of evidence in Crutchfield's findings that fail to fit. First, the highly conformist subjects almost always report coming from stable homes, while the independent subjects much more frequently report broken homes and unstable home environments. (Crutchfield does not report just how frequently, and we can make little of this.) Second, on measures of psychological maladjustment, conformists do not appear to be any more neurotic than independent subjects. Neither Crutchfield's conformists nor those in an Asch-type study by Barron (1953) differed significantly from independent subjects on any of the neuroticism scales of the Minnesota Multiphasic Personality Inventory. Nor did Barocas and Gorlow (1967) discover any personality characteristics that consistently differentiated between independent and conformist subjects *across several samples.*

Despite these imperfections, the picture of the extreme conformists has been painted with heavy strokes. Crutchfield described them as "having less ego strength, less ability to tolerate own impulses and to tolerate ambiguity, less ability to accept responsibility, less self-insight, less spontaneity and productive originality, and as having more prejudiced and authoritarian attitudes, more idealization of parents, and greater emphasis on external and socially approved values" (1955, p. 196). Such a strong consistency of relationships tempts one to conclude that there exists a conforming personality or a psychological trait of conformity. But the presence of a trait implies a consistency of behavior. In other words, a subject who yielded in the Asch or the Crutchfield procedure would also defer to the opinion of the majority if he were a jury member, or would submit to his captors if he were a prisoner of war. However, studies on the generality of conformity behavior indicate a modest amount of consistency (reviewed by McGuire, 1968b). Rosner (1957), for example, placed student nurses in a conformity task in which some peers were confederates on one occasion and other peers were confederates on another occasion. The degree of conformity of specific nurses was similar across occasions. In another study, subjects who conformed in regard to perceptual judgments in the Crutchfield procedure were more likely to report acceptance of peer-group norms and acceptance of authority pressures (Back & Davis, 1965). Abelson and Lesser (1959) found that children who conformed to teachers' judgments responded similarly to their mothers' judgments. Stricker et al. (1970) reported correlation coefficients of +.09 to +.60 between conformity and scores on four different tasks. However, as McGuire (1968b) points out, in these and other studies, the degree of variance accounted for is seldom as high as 50%. Thus, we conclude that there are some people whose tendency is to conform regardless of behavioral setting. Likewise, some persons are characteristically independent, and others lean toward anticonformity. But we must be careful not to put too much weight on these conclusions. Not all people show consistent response patterns. Also, labeling a person as generally a conformist on the basis of his or her behavior in one setting is highly speculative, since it ignores the powerful role of the situation in influencing behavior.

Thirty years ago most psychologists saw personality traits as the central determinants of much of our social behavior. Whether the behavior was crossing a street against the light, resisting the temptation to steal money from an open wallet, or demanding a raise from one's boss, it was assumed at that time that personality traits had a predominant influence. But more recent reviews, such as those by W. Mischel (1968, 1969), question whether (1) there is much consistency in traits over time and (2) these traits really do relate very much to behavior. Although some

traits may remain consistent over time (Bloom, 1964), the overall results are certainly disappointing to those who seek to find a simple, consistent, straightforward relationship between personality and behavior. Correlations of only +.30 to +.40 are typical.

Both Mischel's analysis and provocative reviews by Marlowe and Gergen (1968, 1970) encourage the development of more sophisticated theories of personality, ones that "recognize that behavior tends to change with alterations in the situation in which it occurs" (W. Mischel, 1968, p. 38). One of the reasons why such theories have been so slow to develop is the lack of a classification system for the variety of situations in which certain types of personality may be manifested (D. J. Bem, 1972).

Studies that correlate a single personality characteristic (such as degree of extroversion or anxiety) with social behavior have produced meager results (reviewed by Marlowe and Gergen, 1968, 1970). Among the errors of such a simplified approach is the assumption that personality traits operate independently of one another. More recently, research concern has shifted to the ways that one personality characteristic may influence or *moderate* the effect of another on social behavior. For example, it may appear that there is very little relationship between authoritarianism and conformity. But we may find that when the authoritarian person is in the presence of a high-status model, he or she conforms more than is normal, and that if the person is with a low-status model, he or she conforms much less than usual. The use of certain characteristics as moderator variables is now being developed (Kogan & Wallach, 1964). Similarly, an attitude or trait may have clear-cut effects on social behavior but only within the limits prescribed by the nature of the task or situation (as Christie and Geis, 1970, found with Machiavellianism).

When looking at personality factors versus situational factors in relationship to social behavior, some social psychologists conclude that their *interactions* are of greatest importance (for example, Endler, 1973; Endler & Hunt, 1968). In one study on the effect of the two types of influences, J. McV. Hunt (1965) found that most of the variance in the relationship was accounted for by interactions between personality and situational variables. Hunt wrote "Thus, it is neither the individual differences among subjects, *per se*, nor the variations among situations, *per se*, that produce the variations in behavior. It is, rather, the interactions among these..." (1965, p. 83). A study by Rule and Sandilands (1969) exemplifies this point; these investigators found that highly test-anxious subjects conformed more on a task that required a high commitment than on one with low commitment. Subjects low in test anxiety conformed more on the task that required little commitment. Higher-order analyses of relationships between personality and situational factors appear much more fruitful than simplified statements about a conforming personality—even though such statements may include a grain of truth.

V. Is conformity increasing in our society?

There are strong pressures toward uniformity in any organized society. To a degree, this is necessary and functional. Uniformity leads to predictability, and predictability is important in human interactions, as we have indicated at several places throughout this book. But pressures toward uniformity and conventionality can become too strong, and a complex society can often confuse what is conventional with what is commendable. A survey conducted by pollster Louis Harris in 1965 indicated just how pervasive are the conformity pressures in contemporary life. A cross-section of United States adults was asked whether they felt that certain actions were "more helpful" or "more harmful" to "American" life. Despite our lip service to the ideal that the United States is the home of rugged individualists, there are stronger forces in the opposite direction. For example, 69% of United States adults believed that anti–Vietnam War pickets were

more harmful than helpful. Only 5% said such pickets were more helpful. Of those surveyed, 58% felt that college professors active in unpopular causes were more harmful; only 6% felt these professors were more helpful. Even though the Constitution requires that any person accused of a crime be given adequate legal counsel, 34% of those surveyed considered the "lawyer who defends notorious criminals" as being more harmful to life in the United States. Alas, even women who wear bikini swimsuits do not escape conformity pressures; they were considered deleterious to U. S. life by more than 33% of the adults in the United States. These figures should be taken as evidence for the existence not of conformity, but of strong pressures to conform.

What difference do these pressures to conform make in everyday life? One is that many of us treat different-looking people differently. Table 19-3 reflects what happened when conventionally dressed or hippie-looking college students approached 1200 people in a supermarket and made the trivial request "Excuse me, do you have two nickels for a dime?" In this study, Raymond and Unger (1972) found that White subjects helped more Whites than Blacks and helped conventionally dressed requesters more than hippies. Black subjects also cooperated with hippies somewhat less than with conventionally dressed requesters. Persons over 30 were less helpful to the hippies than were younger adults.

The subjects in Raymond and Unger's study probably responded to the conventionally dressed White more often because they assumed his values were like their own, reflecting the power of belief similarity (Rokeach & Mezei, 1966) discussed in Chapters 5 and 10. Many of the subjects may have associated a difference in appearance and style with differences in health and sanitation habits, sexual behavior, and use of drugs (M. E. Brown, 1969; Sarbin, 1969). At any rate, the results of several studies on the effect of hippie-style dress on responses to help are generally consistent (Darley & Cooper, 1972; Samuel, 1972; Suedfeld, Bochner, & Matas, 1971), indicating that students are ineffective or

Table 19-3

Percentage of subjects in Raymond and Unger's study cooperating in each of
four experimental conditions

Requester's Appearance	Experiment I (N = 581) White Subjects	Experiment II (N = 207) Black Subjects	Experiment III (N = 480) Under Age 30	Experiment III (N = 480) Over Age 30
Conventional dress				
White	82	80	95	91
Black	72	70	82	75
Deviant dress ("hippie")				
White	60	60	88	66
Black	54	81	85	55

Note: In all cases, requester approached subject in supermarket and asked "Excuse me, do you have two nickels for a dime?" or "Excuse me, do you have a dime for two nickels?" The requesters were two male students at Hofstra University, aged 20 and 22, one Black and the other White. "Conventional dress" meant business suit and tie, short and neatly combed hair, and black-rimmed prescription glasses. Deviant, or "hippie," appearance, for the White requester, meant an embroidered outershirt, bell-bottom pants, beads and sandals, a shoulder-length wig of unruly, uncombed hair, a headband, and dark sunglasses with metal frames. For the Black requester, deviant appearance meant a colorful dashiki over bell-bottom pants, sneakers, a medallion around his neck, one earring, an Afro wig, and dark sunglasses with metal frames.

Adapted from "The Apparel Oft Proclaims the Man: Cooperation with Deviant and Conventional Youths," by B. J. Raymond and R. K. Unger, *Journal of Social Psychology,* 1972, *87,* 75–82. Copyright 1972 by the American Psychological Association. Used by permission.

actually detrimental as political campaigners unless they alter their appearance in the direction of conventionality (Glassner & Stires, 1973).

In Canada, too, nonconformity, as exemplified by the hippie style, is treated with rejection. In fact, an unpublished survey conducted in 1970 by Denis Szabo, a University of Montreal criminologist, found that Quebec policemen expressed more hostility toward hippies than toward criminals. In the St. Lawrence River community of Rimouski, 54% of the policemen reported feelings of hostility toward hippies, while only 28% expressed such feelings toward criminals. Montreal police were somewhat more tolerant; 23.3% described their feelings toward hippies as hostile, compared with 22.9% who expressed such feelings about criminals. Only 8% of the Montreal policemen described their feelings toward hippies as friendly.

Social critics such as David Riesman (1950) and William H. Whyte, Jr. (1956), believe that from the 1920s to the 1950s, the degree of conformity in U. S. society increased. In *The Organization Man,* Whyte argued that the complexities of modern society had increased the need to rely on others. A social ethic that emphasized "getting along with others" as a norm or standard was replacing a Protestant ethic that valued hard work. Whyte wrote:

By Social Ethic I mean that contemporary body of thought which makes morally legitimate the pressures of society against the individual. Its major propositions are three: a belief in the group as a source of creativity; a belief in "belongingness" as the ultimate need of the individual; and a belief in the application of science to achieve the belongingness . . . Man exists as a unit of society. Of himself, he is isolated, meaningless; only as he collaborates with others does he become worthwhile, for by sublimating himself in the group, he helps produce a whole that is greater than the sum of its parts [1956, pp. 7–8].

Whyte saw people as motivated primarily by social considerations. They were not oriented toward achieving as much as toward being accepted. Rewards accrued not from hard work but from the ability to work with and through other people.

David Riesman's (1950) view of the prevalence of the other-directed person in our society reflects a similar conceptualization. To Riesman, United States citizens several generations ago were more "inner-directed," meaning that they determined their own values and goals. "Other-directed" individuals must seek definition of right and wrong from their peers; they have no internalized values. Riesman believed the incidence of other-directedness in our society had increased.

Figure 19-5
The case of Mark Painter

The Mark Painter case is a specific example of how nonconformity to middle-class values is punished in the United States. Mark was seven years old in 1966 when the Iowa Supreme Court awarded custody of him to his "conventional" grandparents rather than his "bohemian" father. Four years before, Mark's mother and sister had been killed in a car wreck; upset and distraught, his father, Harold Painter, had sent Mark to live temporarily with his maternal grandparents on a farm near Ames, Iowa. Mr. Painter married again; his new wife was an honors graduate of

the University of California (Berkeley), an artist, and a former Red Cross worker in Japan and Korea. After renovating a ramshackle Victorian house near San Francisco, the Painters felt it was time to bring Mark home. But the grandparents had become fond of Mark; they refused to let the boy go. The Painters filed a suit in the county district court, but their writ of habeas corpus was rejected by both the district court and the Iowa Supreme Court.

The latter court's decision noted that Mark's grandfather was "highly respected" and "has served on the schoolboard and regularly teaches a Sunday-school class at the Gilbert Congregational Church." In contrast, Painter had held seven jobs in ten years and was "either an agnostic or an atheist and has no concern for formal religious training. He has read a lot of Zen Buddhism." Life with the Painters, according to the court, would be "unstable, unconventional, arty, bohemian, and probably intellectually stimulating." By comparison, the court saw the grandparents' home as offering Mark "a stable, dependable, conventional, middle-class Middle West background and an opportunity for a college education and profession." The court concluded that "security and stability in the home are more important than intellectual stimulation" (*Time*, Feb. 26, 1966).

Two years later, in 1968, Mark was allowed to live with his father and his stepmother. But the decision did not result from an overturning of the court's action; rather, Mark's grandmother consented to let Mark live where he wanted to live. (In fact, the United States Supreme Court had refused to hear arguments in the case.) Despite the happy ending of this case, the courts still have the power to disrupt family life (*Christian Century*, 1968).

The trends identified by Riesman and Whyte were largely the products of the inevitably increasing complexity of an overpopulated industrialized society, which still exists today. Beyond these forces, there can be political reasons to increase conformity, and governments in power have chosen to use methods at their disposal to restrict the expression of dissenting opinions. Actions by the executive branch of the United States government under the Nixon administration reflected extreme efforts to achieve uniformity, or at least to control dissent. The attempt to use the Internal Revenue Service to threaten tax reviews, the "bugging" of the Democratic party national headquarters, the break-in of the office of Daniel Ellsberg's psychiatrist—all these reflect increased efforts at repression of dissenting opinions. Likewise, requests for parade permits for protest groups have been denied by both the federal and local governments. Preventive detention of "potential criminals" is now the law in Washington, D. C.

But we sometimes forget that such attempts to force conformity by the government have also been made at numerous other times in United States history. Even though the United States was founded by minority dissenters, within 20 years of its founding (1798), its Congress passed the Alien and Sedition Acts, empowering the government to prosecute newspaper editors who were critical of the United States' undeclared naval war against France. Sixty-five years later, President Lincoln suspended the right of habeas corpus for those arrested as being disloyal during the Civil War—and he did not even consult Congress before doing so. Furthermore, 20-year terms for war dissent were prescribed by the Sedition Act of 1918.

Nonetheless, freedom to criticize, protest, and deviate has grown. Organizations such as the American Civil Liberties Union (ACLU), whose goal is the protection of individual rights, have increased budgets and membership. The repressive quality of the Nixon administration has been exposed for all to see. Many state legislatures have adopted "sunshine laws," requiring all legislative committee meetings to be open to the public or the mass media.

Doubtless, tolerance for dissent has not increased in a straightforward manner throughout the years. Periods of wartime create strong pressures against dissent. During periods of peace-

time and general prosperity, more dissent can be tolerated. Governmental policies can deliberately encourage dissent or suppress it. In today's self-conscious society, we ask more of ourselves, and because of this heightened expectation we may often be discouraged by restrictions against dissent. Yet freedom to dissent or not conform does continue to exist and grow.

VI. Unresolved issues in the study of conformity and nonconformity

We have seen that its very nature as a pervasive social phenomenon has made conformity a difficult concept to define and measure. Its relevance has encouraged value judgments that fail to facilitate the resolution of problems. The purpose of this section is to review these unresolved problems as a summary of the scientific study of conformity. A decade ago Hollander and Willis (1967) listed the following issues as among the unresolved concerns in the study of conformity and nonconformity; today they largely remain problems to be solved.

1. Research and thinking have emphasized conformity to a much greater degree than nonconformity. Similarly, it had been assumed that one dimension can describe all types of conforming and nonconforming behavior. We have described a number of studies, generated by the work of Sherif, Asch, and Crutchfield, that focused on yielding, or conformity to group pressures. Such paradigms do not provide for a separation between independence and anticonformity, which are clearly two different phenomena. More recent conceptualizations, particularly those of R. H. Willis (1965) and of Stricker, Messick, and Jackson (1970), have put greater emphasis on dimensions or types of nonconformity.

2. There has been a failure to distinguish between descriptions of overt behavior and explanations of underlying processes. Did Galileo conform when he publicly recanted while main-

taining his private opinion? Since *conformity* is a generic term, we must conclude that he did. But current thinking prefers to call Galileo's act compliance, which is a type of conformity. Likewise, we now describe 32% of the Asch responses as compliance, meaning the adoption of a new public position while the private opinion remains unchanged. The Asch and Crutchfield procedures do not permit a determination of the extent of change in private acceptance or private opinion.

3. Often it is assumed that conformity is bad and nonconformity is good. Hollander and Willis, in evaluating the viewpoint of social critics such as Riesman and Whyte, conclude:

> The most characteristic tack in such critiques is to describe conventional behavior in modern American society, label it conformity, invoke the "self-evident" premise that conformity is oppositional to individuality or independence, and therefore conclude that modern society and its component institutions hamper constructive initiative and are accordingly bad [1967, p. 71].

Hollander and Willis are reluctant to accept the judgment that conformity is necessarily bad. They feel that conformity often functions to meet a person's goals, whether social (such as need for acceptance) or nonsocial (such as need for food). Such needs are basic to all of us. Beyond this, we all rely on other people as sources of information; other people inevitably influence us. Barry Collins concludes:

> It would be a mistake to oversimplify the question and ask whether conformity is good or bad. A person who refused to accept anyone's word of advice on any topic whatsoever . . . would probably make just as big a botch of his life . . . as a person who always conformed and never formed a judgment on the basis of his own individual sources of information [1970, p. 21].

4. It is often assumed that conformity to group norms is defined in the same terms and serves the same functions for all group members. Research in reciprocity and social exchange (J. Adams, 1965; Gouldner, 1960) indicates that a conforming response may serve for some persons as a deserved reward. To others, it may be a payment in advance for expected rewards (Hollander & Willis, 1967, p. 72).

In similar ways, conformity may be used by low-status group members to ingratiate themselves with the group leader (E. E. Jones, 1965). Such behavior is reminiscent of Jahoda's *expedient conformity*; it serves to meet other goals of these group members. But conformity in a high-status group member or leader may serve another function. For a long time, disagreement has raged over the relative degree of conformity shown by leaders. Are group leaders more conforming to the group norms than followers? Clarification of the matter comes through Hollander's (1958, 1964) **idiosyncrasy-credit model.** In initial stages of group development, the leader may conform strongly to group norms, accumulating credits in the form of positive impressions by the other group members. This accumulation of credit then permits the leader to spend part of it later in the form of greater nonconformity and deviation from group norms. Thus, for different group members, and at different times, conformity can serve different functions. To some degree it may be considered person specific and related to the level of status in the group.

VII. Other effects of social influence: Group risk taking and polarization

A. Group risk taking: Is it the best label?

An individual decision to conform to others is one way a person can respond to pressures from other group members. But groups make decisions as groups, too, and often the nature of these decisions is not what would have been made by the group's separate members. For example, it has frequently been asserted that a group exerts a cautionary, conservative influence on its individual members, so that problem solutions reached by group decision are likely to be less creative or satisfactory than solutions developed by individuals. (Someone has described a camel as "a horse designed by a committee"; also, there's a poster that reads "God so loved the world that He didn't send a committee.") According to this line of thought, the widespread use of the committee as the decision-making unit in business, the military, and education would always and inexorably limit the degree of boldness and risk taking in these institutions. Fortunately a body of research findings has accumulated over the last two decades from which we can answer the question of whether group decisions take fewer risks. Actually, there are two answers. The first, it develops, is not a complete answer, because it responded to the question "Do groups make more conservative decisions than would their individual members?" This was the wrong question; a better one is "Do groups tend to make *more extreme* decisions in the direction that their individual members are leaning?" Before answering the second question, we need to examine the methodology used in answering both questions.

Following early work on group decision making by Ziller (1957), initial studies by Stoner (1961) and Wallach, Kogan, and Bem (1962) set out to evaluate experimentally the effect of the group's influence on the willingness of individual members to take risks. The experiment by Wallach, Kogan, and Bem involved 14 all-male and 14 all-female groups of college students, with 6 subjects in each group. At the beginning of the experiment, each subject completed a questionnaire containing descriptions of 12 hypothetical choice-dilemma situations. A specimen item from this questionnaire is reprinted in Figure 19-6. Note that the definition of a risky choice is rather specific in this figure (Mackenzie &

Bernhardt, 1968). The subject was not asked whether he or she would recommend a risky or a conservative decision, but rather was asked what the odds must be for success before ad-

---

Figure 19-6
A choice-dilemma questionnaire item

Mr. A., an electrical engineer who is married and has one child, has been working for a large electronics corporation since graduating from college five years ago. He is assured of a life-time job with a modest, though adequate, salary and liberal pension benefits upon retirement. On the other hand, it is very unlikely that his salary will increase much before he retires. While attending a convention, Mr. A. is offered a job with a small, newly founded company which has a highly uncertain future. The new job would pay more to start and would offer the possibility of a share in the ownership if the company survived the competition of the larger firms.

Imagine that you are advising Mr. A. Listed below are several probabilities or odds of the new company proving financially sound. *Please check the lowest probability that you would consider acceptable to make it worthwhile for Mr. A. to take the new job.*

_____The chances are 1 in 10 that the company will prove financially sound.

_____The chances are 3 in 10 that the company will prove financially sound.

_____The chances are 5 in 10 that the company will prove financially sound.

_____The chances are 7 in 10 that the company will prove financially sound.

_____The chances are 9 in 10 that the company will prove financially sound.

_____Place a check here if you think Mr. A. should *not* take the new job no matter what the probabilities.

From *Risk-Taking: A Study in Cognition and Personality*, by N. Kogan and M. A. Wallach. Copyright 1964 by Holt, Rinehart and Winston. Reprinted by permission.

vocating a riskier but potentially more beneficial action.[6]

After each of the six members in a group had answered the choice-dilemma questionnaire, they were asked to move together in a discussion group. They were each given another copy of the questionnaire and, under careful instructions, were now asked to discuss each hypothetical choice and to arrive at a unanimous group decision. After this discussion was finished, the experimenter asked the group members to separate for some further individual work and to take their questionnaires with them. Each subject was to go back over the 12 items on the questionnaire and indicate his or her own present decision. Then each subject was asked to rank everyone in the group, including himself or herself, on how much each individual had influenced the final group decision. Two to six weeks later, a representative sample of the subjects came back to take the questionnaire again, on an individual basis.

The control groups were formed in the same way as the experimental groups. Members of the control groups were given an individual questionnaire session and a second individual decision session in which they were asked to reconsider their earlier responses to the questionnaire. They did not participate in any group discussion of the proper degree of risk to take.

The results indicated that after the group decision there was increased willingness to take

risks on 10 of the 12 situations. This was the case in both male and female groups. On 9 of the 10 changes, the shift was so great that there was little likelihood that it occurred by coincidence. When the same kind of analysis was made for the control groups on two separate responses to the questionnaire, no significant differences were found between the first and second sessions in the degree of willingness to take risk. Wallach, Kogan, and Bem therefore concluded that the group decision leads to taking greater risks.

When a random sample of the original subjects was brought back after two to six weeks, it was found that the results of the group discussion persisted over this length of time. The risk-taking propensities of these people at this final session were still significantly greater than those they had displayed before the group discussion.

B. Is willingness to take a greater risk a group phenomenon or a pseudoeffect?

Researchers became quite fascinated over the apparent conclusion that groups make riskier decisions than individuals, for several reasons. It was a "nonobvious" finding, one that went against conventional wisdom (Cartwright, 1971). Making such discoveries in their laboratories seems always to encourage social psychologists that what they are doing is meaningful in the sense that they are making discoveries beyond those that "everybody knows." The apparent shift toward risk in groups also has great implications for any society like ours where momentous decisions of war policy are made by committees. So the researchers pursued the question of *why* a riskier decision emerged from group deliberations. We now know that a better choice would have been to focus on the *extremity* characteristic of the group rather than its "risky" *direction*, but after several studies (Kogan & Wallach, 1967a; 1967b; 1967c) replicated the findings, researchers advanced several possible explanations; these are presented in the following paragraphs.

---

[6]According to a comprehensive review of research to that time by Dion, Baron, and Miller (1970), the choice-dilemma task is the instrument used to measure risky shifts in about 80% of the group risk-taking studies. Another type of group risk-taking task requiring subjects to choose the level of difficulty they want to answer on mental-aptitude items accounts for about 14% of the studies, and stimulus-judging tasks account for the remaining 6%. More recently, social psychologists at the University of Nevada at Reno (Blascovich, Veach, & Ginsburg, 1973; Blascovich & Ginsburg, 1974) have used a blackjack game as the group task. The social-psychological laboratory there includes a gambling casino with several slot machines and an authentically furnished blackjack table.

The familiarization hypothesis. The role of group decision in the willingness to take risk was questioned when it was discovered that in two studies *greater familiarization* with the situations led to the risky shift in the absence of any group participation (Bateson, 1966; Flanders & Thistlethwaite, 1967). (Familiarization was accomplished by having the subjects read over the material alone or write arguments for their choices.) According to this notion, the shift toward greater risk taking is a *pseudoeffect*—an artifact of increased familiarity with the test items. Other studies failed to confirm this finding, however (P. R. Bell & Jamieson, 1970; Fraser, 1971; Stokes, 1971; Teger, Pruitt, St. Jean, & Haaland, 1970; Dion & Miller, 1971; St. Jean, 1970), and it still remains unlikely that a risky shift can be consistently produced with isolated individuals (Dion, Baron, & Miller, 1970). Apparently, the actual experiencing of group interaction is needed to account for the full risky-shift phenomenon.

Diffusion of responsibility as a hypothesis. If the risky shift is truly a group phenomenon—if it does not occur in isolated individuals—it may result from a *diffusion of responsibility,* which develops emotional bonds and reduces fear of failure, enabling persons to make riskier decisions. The group may free the individual from full responsibility, somewhat as happened in Darley and Latané's call-for-help studies described in Chapter 9. Kogan and Wallach, for example, argue that the "failure of a risky course is easier to bear when others are implicated in a decision..." (1967b, p. 51). It is unclear whether this proposed relaxation derives from the emotional relationship that is established in the group, the anonymity that a group (particularly a large group) provides the individual, or other factors. In fact, whether a sharing of responsibility leads to the increased risk taking remains an unsettled question (Dion et al., 1970). For example, presentation of relevant arguments can produce a risky shift in individual decisions, even without development of group cohesion or emotional bonds

(Pruitt & Teger, 1969; R. D. Clark & Willems, 1970). But this explanation would explain only a risky shift, not a shift toward caution (Pruitt, 1971a; 1971b). Since there *is* a shift toward caution on 2 of Kogan and Wallach's 12 choice-dilemma situations as well as on other tasks (Zajonc, Wolosin, Wolosin, & Sherman, 1968, 1969; D. L. Johnson & Andrews, 1971), diffusion of responsibility is inadequate as a general explanation of group-induced changes. As we shall see, the general explanation is what is needed, rather than one that covers only risky shifts.

The persuasion hypothesis (or leadership hypothesis). Perhaps groups make riskier decisions because the group members whose initial decisions were riskier exert more influence in the group discussion (Marquis, 1962). This explanation emphasizes *persuasion,* or the notion that group leaders and frequent speakers in the discussion are more willing to take risks and hence influence other group members in that direction. Evidence for such a phenomenon is usually indirect and often contradictory. Several studies (Flanders & Thistlethwaite, 1967; Wallach, Kogan, & Bem, 1962; Wallach, Kogan, & Burt, 1968) find significant positive relationships between participants' initial risk-taking levels and ratings by others (made after the session) of the participants' apparent influence. This would argue for the accuracy of the persuasion hypothesis.

But the relationship may exist only in the eye of the beholder. Kelley and Thibaut suggest "The correlations between initial riskiness and influence may simply reflect what has happened: Subjects observe the shift to occur and infer from it that the initially risky person must have been more influential" (1968, p. 81). Bolstering this interpretation, Wallach, Kogan, and Burt (1968) found that subjects were aware that a shift toward greater risk was occurring but were not accurate in estimating the extent of shift. Also, more direct tests of the leadership hypothesis fail to confirm an expectation that leadership per se leads to the shift (Vidmar, 1970; G. C. Hoyt &

Stoner, 1968). We may also utilize the earlier finding that personality factors play a definite but minor role in conformity and persuasibility. Although it is plausible that initial risk takers assume a vigorous role in groups, there is no direct evidence that this behavior accounts for the risky shift.

Risk as a cultural value. The typical subject, in making his or her individual judgments on the choice-dilemma tasks, expects others to make choices that are no riskier than his or her own (Hinds, 1962). On the basis of this finding, it has been hypothesized that risk represents more of a *cultural value* than does conservatism (R. Brown, 1965; Teger & Pruitt, 1967; R. D. Clark, Crockett, & Archer, 1971). According to this explanation, those group members whose initial risk-taking scores were below the group average came to realize, through the discussion, that their positions were not as risky as others'. Thus, they became willing to recommend greater risk taking after the group discussion. Harold Miller (1970) found that subjects at both extremes on the initial measure had the greatest interest in the task, but that there were many more subjects at the extremely risky end, which gives some confirmation of the hypothesis of risk as a cultural value.

Along with this cultural-value explanation, it may be that the proximal cause of change is the relevant arguments that occur during discussion (Madaras & Bem, 1968). The opportunity for *information exchange* has also been proposed as playing a participatory role (Pruitt & Teger, 1969; R. D. Clark & Willems, 1969; Willems & Clark, 1969; Myers & Bishop, 1971). For example, R. Brown (1965) predicted that if members simply report their previous choices in the group, no further discussion may be necessary to produce the shift. The information exchange, Brown argued, may show the dubious subject that others are more risk taking and that support exists for a shift toward risk. To test this suggestion, St. Jean (1970) varied the amount of information available in discussion groups. Some subjects participated in the usual type of discussions, and some subjects had available only the information about the risk levels advocated by others. A third group had all information except the specific risk levels of others. St. Jean found that merely exchanging information about risk levels did not shift risk levels; rather, relevant arguments by the others appeared to be the essential causes of the risky shift.

Many of the early studies suffered from theoretical chauvinism, or an expectation that only one explanation can account for an observed effect (Dion et al., 1970). Numerous reasons can plausibly serve as explanations, and each can benefit by the same empirical documentation. Several of the proposed explanations presented in this section may work hand in hand (Pruitt, 1971a). As Dion et al. stated; "It may be the case that those whose initial decisions are riskier do in fact exert more influence in the group setting, but, further, that this greater influence is restricted to situations in which the value of risk is salient" (1970, p. 364).

It appears that three conditions must be present for the shift toward risk to occur in a group; these are group discussion, "a certain divergence between the individual positions, and a certain normative quality in the material on which the discussion is based" (Moscovici & Doise, 1974, pp. 271–272).

C. Another shift: From direction to extremity

Most recently the apparent shift toward risk by groups is being reevaluated as a "group-induced shift" or a "choice shift" (Pruitt, 1971a; Schroeder, 1973). Moreover, it is now being explained as a special case of a more general phenomenon, labeled *group polarization.* A consistent finding is that group members' responses following discussion are, on the average, *more extreme* in the same direction as the average of those individuals' pregroup preferences (Doise, 1969;

Fraser, Gouge, & Billig, 1971; Myers, 1974; Moscovici & Doise, 1974). That is, talking in a group enhances the response tendencies initially favored by participants. (Pruitt, 1971b, calls this explanation a "value theory," because it explains the energy behind the shift in terms of human values.)

If group polarization is the explanation for what has been called the "risky shift," we should be able to demonstrate a *shift toward caution* in groups on materials for which the individual responses were already in the direction of caution. That is what Fraser (1971) has done. He used four situations in which the individual responses were initially risky and four in which the initial responses were initially cautious. He found, using the Kogan and Wallach procedure described earlier, that polarization occurred on each item; after discussion, the group's response to risky items was more risky, but to cautious items it was more cautious. Other studies have shown that the polarization hypothesis explains group effects on a variety of tasks (McCauley, 1972; Moscovici & Zavalloni, 1969; Gouge & Fraser, 1972). For example, group discussion led highly racist high school students to become more racist, while groups composed of only unprejudiced members shifted in the opposite direction (Myers & Bishop, 1970).

D. Summary on group risk taking and group polarization

At present it appears that, in a variety of problem situations, increased exposure to the situation leads to a *more extreme* decision; in many situations, this is a riskier decision. In *those situations*, the assumption that putting a major decision in the hands of a group, rather than in the hands of one individual, will ensure a safer, more conservative decision seems unwarranted. But in other situations, the group's effect may be more conservative *if* the group members' responses were originally in a cautionary direction. The

person's initial values, along with the importance of the situation (R. S. Baron, Roper, & Baron, 1974), contribute to determining whether a "risky shift" will occur.

VIII. Hypnosis: Something more than simply social influence?

Traditionally, hypnosis has been viewed by most people as a trance state during which the hypnotist possesses an almost magical control over the hypnotized subject. We have all probably witnessed or read about cases in which hypnotized subjects were encouraged to recall things or do things that they normally were not able to do. What is the nature of this hypnotized state, and what causes its apparently paranormal abilities? May the state of being hypnotized simply be a case of extreme social influence?

The sleepwalker has traditionally served as a kind of model for conceptualizing the characteristics of the person who is deeply hypnotized (Barber, 1973). But more research has been conducted on hypnotism in the last 15 years than during the previous 200 years. This recent work has suggested that many of the traditional conceptions of hypnosis are myths (T. X. Barber, 1973). In fact, hypnosis may be viewed as *a state of extreme suggestibility;* the deeply hypnotized person is simply extremely suggestible and, according to some conceptions (Sarbin & Coe, 1972), adopts a subservient, compliant, helpful *role* and comes to behave according to that role.

Such conceptions may be hard for us to accept because of our awareness of the kinds of things that hypnotized persons can do and tolerate, including participating in childbirth or having dental work done without pain, showing age regression (that is, reinstating behaviors that were actually present during childhood), developing amnesia on instructions from the hypnotist, or carrying out illegal or immoral acts. The point is that if people are given a strong suggestion to do these things, *without being hypnotized*, they will often do so. It was only relatively recently that researchers used control groups that were tested for responses to suggestions of age-regression, hallucination, or pain reduction without undergoing a hypnotic-induction procedure. T. X. Barber (1973), in reviewing these studies, reports that:

1. Suggestions that pain will not be felt are effective in reducing verbally reported pain in most control subjects (Barber & Calverley, 1969; Spanos, Barber, & Lang, 1969).

2. In the case of about 10% of control subjects, suggestions to regress to an earlier time of life elicit testimony that they "thoroughly" believed they had returned to this earlier time (Barber & Calverley, 1966).

3. Suggestions to see an object that is not present or hear a musical sound that is not being played elicit an "auditory hallucination" in from 33% to 50% of control subjects, about the same rate as for hypnotized subjects (Barber & Calverley, 1964; Bowers, 1967; Spanos & Barber, 1968).

4. Suggestions that are intended to inhibit allergic responses do produce a significant inhibition of those responses in most allergic persons assigned to a high-suggestion control group (Ikemi & Nakagawa, 1962).

We have already seen in the Milgram obedience studies described in Chapter 18 the degree to which "normal" adults will carry out harmful acts when given direct suggestions to do so.

Thus Barber advocates a position that putting a person into a trance—the essence of hypnosis—is not necessary in order to achieve the outcomes most of us attribute to hypnosis. Whether the induction of hypnosis does contribute something extra is now a matter of great controversy (Hilgard, 1973; Orne, 1959; R. F. Q. Johnson, 1972; Sheehan, 1973). Ernest Hilgard, a critic of Barber's position, acknowledges that inducing hypnosis does not produce effects that are much beyond those that occur with control

groups given a role-playing orientation. But he notes that the fact that trance induction does produce some special effects indicates the essential nature of the hypnotic trance. Controversy continues, but it does appear that a major part of what we attribute to the hypnotic trance is a result of heightened responsiveness to the influence attempt by another person.

IX. Summary

Conformity is defined as a yielding to group pressures. It may refer to a behavior or action (called compliance) or a change in attitude or belief (called private acceptance). *Uniformity* is not the same phenomenon as conformity. In contrast to conformity, *conventionality* is defined as acting in what is the customary or usual fashion, or adhering to the standard practices of society.

Two possible opposites to conformity are *independence* and *anticonformity*. Independence is the maintenance and expression of one's private beliefs in the face of group pressures to do something to the contrary. *Anticonformity* refers to actions or beliefs that develop in opposition to majority opinion.

In the Asch studies about one-third of the responses were conforming and two-thirds were independent, but the range in reactions between subjects was so great that an average is rather meaningless.

Apparently, conforming acts may reflect different processes, according to whether (1) the person is involved or not involved in the issue, and (2) his or her public action is or is not consistent with his or her private attitude.

Situational factors may influence the extent of conformity. Groups of three to four people have greater influence on a lone subject than do two people. Nonunanimous majorities have less effect than unanimous ones.

Personality factors also have an influence —at least in laboratory studies of conformity. Subjects who yield to group pressure are more likely to possess intolerance of ambiguity, rigid authoritarian and moralistic attitudes, conventional values, and negative assumptions about human nature.

Although theorists have speculated that pressures toward conformity are increasing in our society, such claims are hard to document.

A judgment that conformity is always bad and independence or nonconformity is always good fails to reflect an understanding of the numerous social needs that conformity serves in contemporary life.

Numerous studies indicate that, within the limits of the procedures used, groups make riskier decisions than do separate individuals. Among the various explanations proposed for this consistent finding, the most plausible are ones that recognize a polarization of responses resulting from group interaction.

Hypnosis may be considered to be a reflection of social influence. Many of the behavior outcomes earlier attributed to some magical power of hypnosis may be interpreted as responses to heightened states of suggestibility.

I. Early approaches to leadership—The search for distinguishing traits
   A. The result: Few characteristics that differentiate consistently
   B. Why is the relationship no stronger?
   C. The "great man" theory of leadership

II. Leadership as an influence on group functioning
   A. Leadership versus the designated leader
   B. Actual dimensions of the leader's behavior
   C. The relationship between the leader's functions and the leader's success

III. Fiedler's contingency theory of leadership

IV. Leadership, organizational effectiveness, and assumptions about human nature
   A. The rational-economic conception
   B. The conception of social man
   C. The self-actualizing conception of the worker
   D. The conception of the complex worker

V. Summary

636

The social psychology of leadership and organizational effectiveness

20

I must follow the people. Am I not their leader?
Benjamin Disraeli

What most frequently distinguishes the leader from his coworkers is that he knows more about the group task or that he can do it better.
Fred E. Fiedler

The study of leadership is a fitting topic for the final chapter of a social-psychology textbook. The nature of leadership has been a topic of interest ever since social psychology began, 75 years ago. To understand leadership fully we must draw on the research of sociologists, psychologists, and anthropologists. Our comprehension will be heightened by the autobiographies of leaders and their interpretations of leadership, and by theories offered by political scientists and historians. We shall see that conceptions of leadership are strongly related to assumptions about human nature and specifically to the motivations of workers.

The study of leadership has moved from searching for simplicity to recognizing complexity. In early attempts to study leadership objectively, researchers attempted to find characteristics that all leaders possessed and that no followers did. Implicit in this approach was an assumption that certain traits within a person lead that person to assume a leadership role on every occasion, whether it is the election of a captain of the church bowling team, the promotion of a company vice-president, or the selection of a jury foreperson. But such a simplified approach was doomed to failure because it did not recognize the numerous functions of leaders, the nature of the group task, the relative amount of power held by the leader, and other very important factors.

As research progressed, more complex interactions between the leader's personality and aspects of the situation have been studied, in an effort to make a more accurate statement about which people are successful leaders. The concept of leadership has been refined, and its functions have been analyzed. The most complex viewpoint—and the most promising—is the *contingency theory of leadership*, developed by Fred Fiedler; it will be described in detail later in this chapter.

I. Early approaches to leadership—The search for distinguishing traits

A. The result: Few characteristics that differentiate consistently

What makes one person a successful leader, while another person fails in the same position? The answer would be a simple one if we could identify basic personality characteristics that make people more or less likely to become leaders. It was in this direction that the scientific study of leadership began; in the first three decades of this century leaders and nonleaders were compared on a variety of personality and intelligence measures in order to isolate differences. Bird (1940) summarized the findings of many early studies. In these studies, leadership was usually defined in terms of activities at school, but there was great variation in the settings; they included student councils, Girl Scout and Boy Scout troops, speech and drama groups, and athletic teams.

In the 20 or so studies reviewed by Bird, 79 different traits were identified that distinguished leaders from nonleaders. Bird was surprised that little consistency was found from one study to another. Of the 79 traits, 51 made a difference in only one study. While this lack of consistency was partly the result of using different, but almost synonymous, terms in different studies ("more reliable" versus "more accurate in work"), the general result was a disappointment for those who assumed that leaders were somehow "special" in regard to many traits. Only four characteristics—intelligence, initiative, sense of humor, and extroversion—were identified often enough for Bird to consider them "general traits of leadership" (1940, p. 380).

We believe that Bird's conclusion was neither the result of the poor quality of early measuring instruments nor the outgrowth of hazy definitions of leadership. Later reviews of the characteristics of leaders (Stogdill, 1948; R. D. Mann, 1959; Bass, 1960; J. H. Davis, 1969) arrived at the same conclusion: *there is no consistent pattern of traits that characterizes leaders* (Gibb, 1969, p. 227). Stogdill's review concluded that successful leaders generally differ from followers in possessing higher degrees of persistence, self-confidence, sociability, and dependability. However, as Bass (1960) indicates, these factors are manifested in the leader's increased motivation to develop relationships with other group members and influence them.

Throughout the life span of this research effort, intelligence has remained the one characteristic most consistently related to leadership: in most cases, successful leaders are superior to nonleaders in intelligence. But even here two qualifications must be mentioned. First, the relationship is not as high as one might expect (J. P. Campbell, Dunnette, Lawler, & Weick, 1970; Csoka, 1972). For example, Mann's review concludes "Considering independent studies as the unit of research, the positive association between intelligence and leadership is found to be highly significant. . . . However, the magnitude of the relationship is less impressive; no correlation reported exceeds .50 and the median *r* [correlation coefficient] is roughly .25" (1959, p. 248). In some situations the relationship between leadership and intelligence is negligible or even inverse (Lonetto & Williams, 1974). Such outcomes lead to a second qualification: apparently, if too much discrepancy exists between a potential leader's level of intelligence and the intelligence of other group members, his or her success in initiating and maintaining leadership is hampered. Leaders can be too bright for their followers. According to Gibb, "the evidence suggests that every increment of intelligence means wiser government, but that the crowd prefers to be ill-governed by people it can understand" (1969, p. 218).

B. Why is the relationship no stronger?

We should wonder why there is not a greater relationship between personality traits and leadership. After all, even despite the exposés of immoral leadership in the Watergate coverup, both philosophers and window-washers expect their leaders to be a cut above the average. Plato 2500 years ago wrote that those who lead the citizenry must prove themselves to be courageous, just, enlightened, and wise; and even today most people describe leadership in terms of personal qualities or virtues that are held desirable in that society (Gibb, 1969). There are four possible causes for this limited degree of relationship, according to Gibb (1969, pp. 227–228); each is correct to some extent.

1. The description and measurement of

personality may still be inadequate; the really important aspects of personality may not have been investigated yet (Cartwright & Zander, 1968).

2. Situational factors may override personality factors in determining leadership, just as they do in determining cooperation and competition (Chapter 9) or conformity (Chapter 19).

3. In a complex society such as ours, leadership is composed of a mixture of functions. In certain groups and on certain tasks, some functions may take precedence over others. The leader of a rescue squad may need to possess knowledge of the geographical area or certain lifesaving skills. Since different functions may be accentuated in different groups, and since a particular type of personality may be appropriate for one function and not another, it is unrealistic to expect personality to relate consistently to leadership across functions. For example, Clifford and Cohn (1964) found that children selected as swimming-team captains or picnic hosts and hostesses were those who were perceived as specifically qualified for those tasks. This explanation does not find fault with personality measures; rather, it concludes that leadership is too vague or complex a criterion to allow for a highly consistent relationship. This type of criticism has led to refinements in the definition of leadership that are described later in this chapter.

4. The groups studied have been quite different in composition from each other. Many studies have used students; many have not. Perhaps more homogeneous sets of groups would provide a greater relationship. Clarification of this point can be achieved by studying the personalities of governmental and political leaders. The study of political leaders also permits exploration of what has been called, in sexist terms, the "great man" theory of leadership.

C. The "great man" theory of leadership

The "great man" theory of leadership, in its boldest form, proposes that major events in national and international affairs are influenced by the people who hold positions of leadership "and that all factors in history, save great men, are inconsequential" (Hook, 1955, p. 14). A sudden act by a great leader could, according to this theory, change the fate of a nation.[1] Thus, Germany became overtly nationalistic and belligerent in the 1930's solely because Adolf Hitler was in power; had there been no Hitler, says the theory, there would have been no World War II. The extreme form of the theory would go on to propose that, had a "great man" been in power in Great Britain or the United States at that time, World War II could have been averted even despite Hitler's belligerence. Implicit in the "great man" theory is the assumption that leaders possess **charisma,** a set of personality characteristics that facilitate the accomplishment of their goals, even in the face of great obstacles.

Another variant of the "great man" theory suggests that people who possess *some* of the qualities necessary for successful leadership will possess *all* such necessary qualities. This is an extremely naïve idea, in that it assumes that all desirable qualities (interpersonal sensitivity, intelligence, high energy level, ability to delegate, and so on) are present in the same persons. This notion of the status ordering of people in regard to leadership has been rejected by empirical studies (Bales, 1958; Collins, 1970). For example, the most valuable group member in terms of initiating solutions to the group's tasks is seldom the best-liked group member (Bales, 1970; Borgatta & Bales, 1956; M. E. Shaw & Gilchrist, 1956; Stang, 1973).

An opposing viewpoint: The Zeitgeist *and social determinism.* A strong rebuttal to the "great man" theory is found in approaches that place emphasis on social forces, social movements, and changing social values as determinants of historic

---

[1] Perhaps the greatest exponent of the "great man" theory was the historian Thomas Carlyle, who believed that genius would exert its influence wherever it was found. William James proposed that the mutations, or drastic changes, in society were due to great men, who initiated movement and hindered others from moving society in another direction.

Figure 20-1

Does each President of the United States possess a certain personality style?
James D. Barber, a political scientist, proposes that a President's personality is
an important shaper of his presidential behavior. This style may be either active
or passive and either positive or negative, so that there are four possible types:
(1) *Active-positive.* This person has the ability to adapt to the task, enjoys the
activities, and has high self-esteem. (2) *Active-negative.* This person shows a lot
of effort but feels relatively little satisfaction. He or she sees life as a hard
struggle to achieve and hold power and is hampered by a perfectionist superego.
(3) *Passive-positive.* This is a receptive, compliant, other-directed person whose
life is a search for affection as a reward for being agreeable. He or she has
superficial optimism but lacks self-esteem. (4) *Passive-negative.* This person does
little and enjoys it less but is in politics out of a sense of duty. He or she is
oriented toward doing dutiful service but tends to withdraw from decision
making. Barber has placed each President in one of these four categories.
Perhaps you can guess how each of those pictured was classified. (Source: J.
D. Barber, *The Presidential Character.* Englewood Cliffs, N. J.: Prentice-Hall, 1972;
photos courtesy of the Library of Congress.)

events. According to the *Zeitgeist* theory of history, leaders are like actors who play out the roles designed for them by broad social forces. *Zeitgeist* means "the spirit of the times" or "the temper of the times"; this theory sees the leader's temperament, motives, and ability as having little real influence in the face of social movements. As Victor Hugo wrote, "There is nothing in this world so powerful as an idea whose time has come"—a statement reflecting the perspective of the *Zeitgeist*, or social determinism. This perspective has been adopted by the majority of 20th-century historians (Hook, 1955). In seeking a determination of whether the "great man" or the *Zeitgeist* theory is more nearly correct, let us first discuss the historical evidence and then report empirical studies.

A study of the history of scientific discovery gives little credence to a hypothesis of "great men" in science. Although we give recognition to a Freud, a Darwin, or a Copernicus, we also acknowledge the fact that the discoveries made by each of them had a clear line of historical development. If Freud had not existed, someone else would soon have advanced similar theories about the role of the unconscious in our behavior. Darwin's theory of evolution was developed independently at the same time by Alfred Wallace. Newton and Leibnitz each created a differential calculus. Even scientific breakthroughs and new paradigms (Kuhn, 1970) rest on previous work in science.

In other areas of thought, the progression is less clear. If one considers great works of art, one concludes along with Hook that "Beethoven's sonatas and symphonies without Beethoven are inconceivable" (1955, p. 35). Yet surely the *Zeitgeist* strongly influenced the style of music in which Beethoven's unique genius found expression.

If we turn to the topic of political leaders, we find a vast amount of material that needs interpretation. Could the "great man" theory of leadership be tested by relating the personal qualities of ruling monarchs to the extent of growth or decline in their countries during their time?

Frederick Adams Wood (1913), an early-20th-century American historian, tried to do so. He made a detailed study of 386 rulers in 14 countries in Western Europe who lived between A.D. 1000 and the time of the French Revolution. All the rulers that he studied had absolute power over their kingdoms. Each was classified as strong, weak, or mediocre, on the basis of knowledge about his intellectual and personal characteristics.[2] The condition of each country was also classified as to whether it exhibited a state of prosperity, a state of decline, or no clear indication of either. (This classification was based on the country's economic and political status, not on its artistic, educational, or scientific development.)

Wood found a high relationship between the strength of the monarch and the condition of the country—a correlation coefficient between $+.60$ and $+.70$. He states his results as follows: "Strong, mediocre, and weak monarchs are associated with strong, mediocre, and weak periods respectively in about 70 percent of the cases" (1913, p. 246). The 70% appears to be a misinterpretation by Wood of the meaning of a correlation value; actually, less than 50% of the difference between the conditions in different countries is accounted for by the relative strength of their monarchs. And, as with any correlation, we cannot infer cause and effect, as Wood would like to. Wood clearly favors the interpretation that strong leaders cause their countries to flourish. However, it is equally possible that a state of prosperity in a country permits bright or brilliant rulers to emerge. Then again, both the ruler's success and the quality of conditions could be products of a third set of factors. In addition to these difficulties, there are problems in establishing independent and objective measures of the quality of a monarch and his or her country's development. It is exceedingly difficult

[2]Wood's goal was to classify the characteristics of the ruler, not the strength or weakness of the nation at that time. However, it is likely that this second issue became a contaminating factor in classifying the first.

to evaluate the personality characteristics of a monarch without considering the outcome of his or her reign. King Charles I of England is a case in point. It is not enough that King Charles lost his crown and his head; the final indignity is that Wood calls him two-faced and obstinate. As Hook states, other observers might describe Charles as "shrewd and principled." Although we admire Wood's exhaustive approach to the study of "great men," we must conclude that his data do not permit an answer to his question.

Another reason why we have little confidence in Wood's conclusions comes from Spiller's (1929) analysis of the biographies of great men. Spiller, a sociologist, comes to the opposite conclusion: that the personal characteristics and abilities of great men have little relation to the degree of their influence upon society. Spiller writes "If a sweeping survey of the field of human progress were made perhaps ninety-five percent of the advance would be found unconnected with the great men" (1929, p. 218).

How may the conflicting approaches of the "great man" theory and the *Zeitgeist* hypothesis be resolved? We have emphasized throughout this book that no one theory is always correct and that conflicting theories can each make a contribution to the understanding of complex social phenomena. Hook believes the "great man" plays a unique and decisive role "only where the historical situation permits of major *alternative* paths of development" (1955, p. 109). Even if Christopher Columbus had not set sail in 1492, a fellow explorer would have "discovered" the New World soon thereafter. The forces at work gave no alternative. Only when choices exist does the great man or woman influence history. On Elba, Napoleon still had alternatives—to remain or to escape and return to power. On St. Helena, he had none.

How different would have been the United States' involvement in Southeast Asia had President Kennedy lived through a second term in office? It is a much debated, but unanswered, question. Even Kennedy—who adopted a strong activist philosophy of the presidency—complained about how his decisions got lost in the

State Department. This would imply that the actual number of alternatives available to the President were less than might at first appear.[3] Although Presidents and Prime Ministers influence national thought and action, the *Zeitgeist* is a force that permits these particular individuals to be elected in the first place.

What may arise out of a clash between a particular leader and his times is a new set of values; one effect of the nonviolent protest for Black rights led by Martin Luther King, Jr., was the consciousness among many Whites that certain citizens in the United States were being unfairly treated. This effect cannot be attributed to the man alone or to his times; it resulted from a creative interaction between the two (Elkind, 1971).

The "great man" theory in the laboratory. A quite different approach to the "great man" theory of leadership is to bring the phenomenon into the laboratory and use manipulations and experimental controls to determine how the behavior of the single person in the top position affects organizational performance. Borgatta, Couch, and Bales (1954) used three-man groups of military recruits in an attempt to test the theory under controlled conditions. Each man participated in four sessions of 24 minutes each, with two new participants in each session. "Great

---

[3]It should be noted that George Reedy, former press secretary and special assistant to President Lyndon Johnson, holds a dissenting view: "Presidents glory in telling people that they are prisoners of a system and of circumstances beyond their control. This is probably the subconscious device by which the chief executive prepares his alibi for history. It is true that they must deal with forces and circumstances which they did not create and cannot ignore. But how they deal with them is up to the presidents themselves. A president, in a peculiar sense that does not apply to other people, is the master of his own fate and the captain of his soul" (1970, p. 31). But Reedy's own examples defy his statement: "If Congress is balky, this is a political problem and a president is supposedly a political expert. . . . If foreign relations are contentious and unruly, this is merely one of the conditions under which he operates and not a 'reason' for failure" (p. 31). The assumption that the President is somehow superhuman in the task of mastering his own fate strikes us as an extremely simplified view of leadership.

men" were selected on the basis of their perform-ance in the first session; the top 11 of 123 men were so classified. These men were followed through the subsequent sessions so that their productivity could be assessed. (Productivity was measured by the number of acts initiated per time unit, the leadership ratings given each man by his coparticipants, and the popularity ratings each man received.) "Great men" selected on the basis of the first session continued to have an influence that led to relatively superior perform-ance in their subsequent groups. Of the 11 top men, 8 were in the top 11 productivity ranks in the second and third sessions (among 123 sub-jects). Seven of the 11 were still in the top rank in the fourth session. Groups in the second, third, and fourth sessions with "great men" as partici-pants demonstrated smoother functioning, with fewer cases of anxiety or withdrawal from partic-ipation. This result implies that groups with a "great man" as a participant were also more sat-isfied with their performances.

As impressive as these findings are, we are still a long way from verifying a "great man" theory of leadership in practice. The study by Borgatta et al. (1954) does indicate some consis-tency in group performance across groups with different leaders. But it does not show the degree to which a charismatic leader can manipulate the content of eventful decisions.

II. Leadership as an influence on group functioning

A. Leadership versus the designated leader

The relative futility of the quest for distin-guishing traits of leaders had several ramifica-tions. One was a rethinking of the difference between a designated leader and a person who exercised leadership (Stogdill, 1974). During the 1940s and 1950s, study concentrated on the *func-tions* of leaders; influential work was done by R. F. Bales at Harvard University and by John Hemp-hill, Ralph Stogdill, Carroll Shartle, and others at the Personnel Research Board of Ohio State University. The result of these efforts was a new focus on *influence* as the salient aspect of leader-ship (Hammer, 1974). For example, Stogdill de-fined leadership as "the process (act) of influenc-ing the activities of an organized group in its efforts toward goal setting and goal achieve-ment" (1950, p. 3).

According to such a definition, almost every member of every group has some leader-ship function. Certainly all members of a football team have some such function—even the water boy, if his refreshment really renews energy, ef-fort, and efficiency. Of course, some group members exert much more influence toward goal attainment than do others, as Stogdill recognized. Members of a group, team, or organization can often be rank ordered in regard to the amount of influence they exert on each aspect of the group's task. In the case of a football team, the coaching staff and the quarterback may exert the most influence when it comes to selecting plays that are successful in moving the team toward the goal line. However, insofar as inspiration and motivation are concerned, some other player may be more important. Such a phenomenon demon-strates the place of *emergent leadership* (R. T. Stein, 1975; R. T. Stein, Geis, & Damarin, 1973), or the assumption of leadership functions by persons who are not designated leaders.

An emphasis on goal-oriented functions of leaders is a far cry from the earlier search for personality characteristics that were unique to leaders. In studying the functions of leadership, the initial research efforts asked what kinds of things leaders actually do. For example, the Unit-ed States Army adopted 11 "principles of leader-ship" (Carter, 1952), which Gibb (1969, p. 228) has converted into 7 possible behaviors: (1) per-forming professional and technical specialities, (2) knowing subordinates and showing consider-ation for them, (3) keeping channels of commun-ication open, (4) accepting personal responsi-bility and setting an example, (5) initiating and directing action, (6) training people as a team, and (7) making decisions. Similar in purpose was the survey by Hemphill, Halpin, and their associates in the Ohio State Leadership Studies (Hemphill & Coons, 1950) that proposed 9 basic dimensions of the leader's behavior; these are listed in Table 20-1.

Table 20-1
Nine proposed dimensions of leader behavior

1. *Initiation.* Described by the frequency with which a leader originates, facilitates, or resists new ideas and new practices

2. *Membership.* Described by the frequency with which a leader mixes with the group, stresses informal interaction between himself and members, or interchanges personal services with members

3. *Representation.* Described by the frequency with which the leader defends his group against attack, advances the interests of his group, and acts in behalf of his group

4. *Integration.* Described by the frequency with which a leader subordinates individual behavior, encourages pleasant group atmosphere, reduces conflict between members, or promotes individual adjustment to the group

5. *Organization.* Described by the frequency with which the leader defines or structures his own work, the work of other members, or the relationships among members in the performance of their work

6. *Domination.* Described by the frequency with which the leader restricts individuals or the group in action, decision making, or expression of opinion

7. *Communication.* Described by the frequency with which a leader provides information to members, seeks information from them, facilitates exchange of information, or shows awareness of affairs pertaining to the group

8. *Recognition.* Described by the frequency with which a leader engages in behavior that expresses approval or disapproval of group members

9. *Production.* Described by the frequency with which a leader sets levels of effort or achievement or prods members for greater effort or achievement.

Adapted from Hemphill (1950, pp. 5–6); reprinted with permission of the author.

B. Actual dimensions of the leader's behavior

So much for analysis; what does a leader actually do? Halpin and Winer (1952) set out to identify empirically the dimensions of a leader's behavior. After constructing questionnaire items and administering them to varying sets of group members, the Ohio State researchers did a factor analysis of the responses (Stogdill, 1963). Four factors of leadership, or clusters of behaviors, emerged; of concern to us here are the two major ones, labeled *consideration* and *initiating structure.* (The other two factors were production emphasis, accounting for only about 10% of the variability, and sensitivity, or social awareness, accounting for only about 7% of the variability.)

Consideration. Halpin and Winer called the first dimension of leadership behavior **consideration.** This dimension reflects the extent to which the leader shows behavior that is "indicative of friendship, mutual trust, respect, and warmth" in relationships between himself and the other group members (Halpin, 1966, p. 86). Genuine consideration by the leader reflects an awareness of the needs of each member of the group (Fleishman & Peters, 1962). Leaders high in this behavioral characteristic encourage their co-workers to communicate with them and to share their feelings (Korman, 1966). In Halpin and Winer's study, consideration accounted for almost half of the variability in behavior between different leaders.

Initiating structure. A second dimension was called **initiating structure,** which was defined as "the leader's behavior in delineating the relationship between himself and members of the work group, and in endeavoring to establish well-defined patterns of organization, channels of communication, and methods of procedure" (Halpin, 1966, p. 86). Thus, *initiating structure* refers to the leader's task of getting the group moving toward its designated goal. (A part of initiating structure may be identifying and agreeing upon the goal.) Initiating structure accounted for about one-third of the variability in behavior among leaders.

We believe it is important to emphasize here that other analyses of the leader's behavior have produced similar divisions into two primary dimensions. Bales (1953) has concluded that leadership may be differentiated into two functions: *task orientation* (or thrust to achieve the group's goals) and a *socioemotional orientation*, in which the leader wishes to keep high the group members' morale and cohesiveness. Because there have been independent confirmations of these results by Bales (1958) and others (Fleishman, Harris, & Burtt, 1955), we conclude that *initiating structure* and *consideration* (or similar factors) are two major dimensions of leadership behavior and not simply mutually exclusive leadership patterns (Gibb, 1969).

A leader's place on each of these dimensions can be assessed by asking the group's members to rate the leader on a set of descriptive statements, reprinted in Table 20-2. These statements form the Leader Behavior Description Questionnaire (abbreviated LBDQ), devised by the Personnel Research Board at Ohio State University (Halpin, 1966; Stogdill, 1963, 1969; Schriesheim & Kerr, 1974). Each group member indicates the frequency with which his or her leader engages in each form of behavior by checking one of five adverbs: *always, often, occasionally, seldom,* or *never.*

Table 20-2
The Leader Behavior Description Questionnaire*

Initiating Structure

1. He makes his attitudes clear to the staff.
2. He tries out his new ideas with the staff.
3. He rules with an iron hand.[a]
4. He criticizes poor work.
5. He speaks in a manner not to be questioned.
6. He assigns staff members to particular tasks.

7. He works without a plan.[a]
8. He maintains definite standards of performance.
9. He emphasizes the meeting of deadlines.
10. He encourages the use of uniform procedures.
11. He makes sure that his part in the organization is understood by all members.
12. He asks that staff members follow standard rules and regulations.
13. He lets staff members know what is expected of them.
14. He sees to it that staff members are working up to capacity.
15. He sees to it that the work of staff members is coordinated.

Consideration

1. He does personal favors for staff members.
2. He does little things to make it pleasant to be a member of the staff.
3. He is easy to understand.
4. He finds time to listen to staff members.
5. He keeps to himself.[a]
6. He looks out for the personal welfare of individual staff members.
7. He refuses to explain his actions.[a]
8. He acts without consulting the staff.[a]
9. He is slow to accept new ideas.[a]
10. He treats all staff members as his equals.
11. He is willing to make changes.
12. He is friendly and approachable.
13. He makes staff members feel at ease when talking with them.
14. He puts suggestions made by the staff into operation.
15. He gets staff approval on important matters before going ahead.

*This questionnaire, developed 20 years ago, fails to recognize that leaders may be either "he" or "she."

[a]Scored negatively. (Reprinted with permission of The Macmillan Company from *Theory and Research in Administration*, by A. W. Halpin. © Copyright by Andrew W. Halpin, 1966.)

Is it likely that a leader will be skilled in both initiating structure and showing consideration for others? Often the same person cannot fulfill both these functions successfully. The achievement-oriented leader must often be critical of the ideas or actions of other members; such a leader must constantly turn the members' attention back toward the goal when they have digressed into some diversionary activity. The task-oriented leader must make unpleasant decisions, often when unanimity is lacking. Often the leader reports how difficult it is to be task-oriented and considerate at the same time. Hence another member of the organization may become the group-maintenance expert, concerned with arbitrating task-oriented disputes, relieving tension, and giving every person a pat on the back or a chance to be heard. Traditionally many families have developed an unstated understanding that the father is the task specialist and the mother is the socioemotional specialist, although contemporary changes in family structure are altering this pattern.

In an organized group—whether it is a professional basketball team, the teaching staff at an elementary school, or a fire-fighting crew for an oil company—an evaluation can be made of how successful the leader is in initiating structure and showing consideration. Research indicates that the correlation between skill in these two functions is quite low (Greenwood & McNamara, 1969); sales managers who keep their sales staff task oriented are likely not to be particularly considerate or sensitive to them. However, sometimes a given behavior may facilitate the achievement of both functions; a leader who helps a group solve a difficult problem may, by that action, develop solidarity and better morale (Cartwright & Zander, 1968). There may be a few leaders who are skilled at both functions, but such persons are rare. You may wish to consider, for example, how many Presidents of the United States or Prime Ministers of Canada were successful both in "getting the country moving again" and in "bringing people together."

C. The relationship between the leader's functions and the leader's success

We have described how the leader's performance in two functions can be assessed by the ratings given him by his coworkers. But what difference do such ratings make? Can we show that leaders who receive more positive ratings have more successful groups? Studies on two diverse types of groups—departmental faculties at a liberal arts college and crews of Air Force bombing planes—provide answers for these questions.

During the Korean War, LBDQ scores were obtained from the flight crews of 52 B-29 commanders; 33 of these commanders were later rated by their supervisors in regard to their combat performance in the war (Halpin, 1954). Negative correlations were found between the supervisors' ratings and the commanders' consideration scores; in other words, pilots who were rated as successful by their superiors were judged by their crews' ratings as being *low* in consideration. The correlations between the supervisors' ratings and the pilots' initiating-structure scores were positive; that is, good pilots were seen by their crews as more task oriented and better at achieving goals. Each crew also completed a Crew Satisfaction Index. The correlations between the Crew Satisfaction Index and consideration scores were high and positive, indicating that pilots who were considerate had more satisfied crews. Notice the discrepancy; pilots high on consideration were rated as less successful by superiors but maintained crews who were more satisfied. Thus is encapsulated a basic conflict in role expectations faced by many leaders—to achieve or to care for others?

In a similar study, also conducted during the Korean War (Halpin, 1953), 87 B-29 aircraft commanders were rated on overall effectiveness by their superiors, while their crews completed the LBDQ. The commanders were then classified as to whether they were above or below the means on both dimensions of leadership. Table 20-3 indicates that of the 9 commanders who were in the upper 10% in overall effectiveness, 8 were above the mean on both consideration and initiating structure. Of the 10 commanders who were in the bottom 12% in overall effectiveness, 6 were below the mean on both dimensions of leader behavior. The successful leader, as rated by his superiors, facilitates both group achievement and group maintenance.

In an entirely different setting, Hemphill (1955) asked faculty members at a liberal arts college to name the five departments in the college that had the reputation of being the best led or administered and the five departments that were least well administered. Faculty members in each department then rated their department chairman on the LBDQ. The average LBDQ scores for chairmen were tabulated, and the results are shown in Table 20-4. Eight of the nine chairmen of well-administered departments had scores above the median on both LBDQ meas-

Table 20-3
Bomber pilots' effectiveness and ratings by their crews (Halpin, 1953)

	Below mean on both consideration and initiating structure	Above mean on both consideration and initiating structure
Upper 10% on overall effectiveness	1	8
Lower 12% on overall effectiveness	6	4

Figures indicate the number of commanders in high and low groups on ratings of overall effectiveness scoring above and below the mean on both leader-behavior dimensions.

Table 20-4
The relationship between the reputation achieved by college departments and the consideration and initiating-structure scores of department chairmen taken conjunctively ($N = 18$)

	Number of Chairmen	
Chairman's Leadership	*With Dept. below Median in Reputation*	*With Dept. above Median in Reputation*
Score of 41 or higher on consideration and a score of 36 or more on initiating structure	1	8
Score of less than 41 on consideration or less than 36 on initiating structure	8	1

From "Leadership Behavior Associated with the Administrative Reputation of College Departments," by J. K. Hemphill, *Journal of Educational Psychology*, 1955, 46(7), 396. Copyright 1955. Reprinted by permission of Abrahams Magazine Service.

ures, whereas only one of nine poorly administered departments had a chairman who was rated favorably by his staff. The department's administrative reputation is quite consistent with the ratings that its staff gives its chairman. Of course, part of the department's reputation stems directly from the gossip and faculty-room grumblings or enthusiasms of its staff members; thus, "departmental administrative reputation" is a criterion not completely free of contamination. Even though these studies were only partially successful in achieving a completely pure criterion of leadership quality, they support the conclusion that effective leadership behavior is associated with accomplishing both initiating structure and consideration for coworkers (Kerr, Schriesheim, Murphy, & Stogdill, 1974).

III. Fiedler's contingency theory of leadership

In our review of studies on leadership, we have seen how the search for basic personality traits in the 1930s and 1940s produced little in the way of tangible results. The 1950s saw a shift toward analyzing the functions or dimensions of a leader's behavior, along with documenting the relationships between the leader's effectiveness and the ratings he or she received from supervisors, coworkers, and subordinates. But a functional analysis was not enough. Not until the 1960s—and the work of Fred E. Fiedler—were the trait approach and the functional analysis put together meaningfully.

Fiedler (1967) defines the leader as the individual in the group who is given the task of directing and coordinating task-relevant activities, or who—in the absence of a designated leader—carries the primary responsibility for performing these functions in a group. Fiedler's theory is called a *contingency theory of leadership* because it relates the effectiveness of the leader to aspects of the situation in which the group operates. Specifically, the theory predicts that the

leader's contribution to group effectiveness is dependent on both the characteristics of the leader and the favorableness of the situation for the leader (Graen, Alvares, Orris, & Martella, 1970). To Fiedler, there is no one successful type of leader; task-oriented leaders may be effective under some circumstances but not under others. A permissive leader who is oriented toward human relations and who has been successful with one group may not be successful in another group whose situation differs.

One virtue of Fiedler's theory is that it reconciles previous findings, which were contradictory in regard to what makes a good leader. It is an inductive theory, developed on the basis of a 20-year research program that has studied more than 800 groups. The theory is now used to predict the outcome of later studies. To Fiedler, the basic dimension is *leadership style*, which is defined as "the underlying need-structure of the individual that motivates his behavior in various leadership situations" (Graen et al., 1970, p. 286). Leadership style is assessed by the extent of the leader's esteem for his or her "least-preferred coworker," or the LPC measure.[4] Each leader is asked to think of all the people with whom he or she has ever worked and then to select the one with whom it has been most difficult to cooperate. This person represents the "least-preferred coworker," or LPC.[5] The leader is then given a set of bipolar rating scales and

---

[4]Fiedler makes a distinction between leadership style and a particular leader's style. The latter refers to "the specific acts in which a leader engages while directing or coordinating the work of his group." Actions or behavior may change to fit the situation, but leadership style remains relatively constant. Because of this operational definition of leadership style, its essence remains rather vague to many readers.

[5]The LPC need not be someone with whom the leader is currently working. As a matter of fact, most subjects describe someone with whom they previously worked (J. G. Hunt, 1967). In some of his research, Fiedler has used the ASO scale (Assumed Similarity of Opposites) to measure similarity between the ratings a leader gives to his or her best- and least-liked coworkers. ASO scores and LPC scores correlate highly with each other (from +.70 to +.93).

is asked to rate this least-preferred coworker on each of these dimensions. The number used is usually between 16 and 24; Table 20-5 gives a set of rating scales from a study by one of Fiedler's coworkers (J. G. Hunt, 1967, p. 291). In this case, the LPC score is the sum of the ratings circled on the 21 dimensions. Notice that for each dimension the favorable end is given a value of 8, the unfavorable end a value of 1.

The LPC score may be thought of as an indication of a leader's emotional reaction to people with whom the leader could not work well (Fiedler, 1969). When we sum the ratings given by different leaders to their designated LPC, we find that some of these leaders give their LPC extremely unfavorable ratings, which usually average around 2 (Fiedler, 1971). Fiedler first hy-

pothesized that these leaders, called *Low-LPC leaders*, were task-oriented administrators, who gain satisfaction and self-esteem from the group's completion of its tasks, even if the leader himself must suffer poor interpersonal relationships for them to be completed. Low-LPC leaders tend to be punitive toward others, though not necessarily more distant. In contrast, there are other leaders who give even their designated least-preferred coworkers relatively favorable ratings; Fiedler called these persons *High-LPC leaders* and considered them to be more concerned about interpersonal relations. To High-LPC leaders, satisfaction comes from happy group relationships; they are more relaxed, compliant, and nondirective. Thus High-LPC and Low-LPC leaders seek to satisfy different basic

Table 20-5
Bipolar ratings used in rating least-preferred coworker

Pleasant	8	7	6	5	4	3	2	1	Unpleasant
Friendly	8	7	6	5	4	3	2	1	Unfriendly
Bad	1	2	3	4	5	6	7	8	Good
Distant	1	2	3	4	5	6	7	8	Close
Supportive	8	7	6	5	4	3	2	1	Hostile
Contented	8	7	6	5	4	3	2	1	Discontented
Stubborn	1	2	3	4	5	6	7	8	Not stubborn
Not enterprising	1	2	3	4	5	6	7	8	Enterprising
Tense	1	2	3	4	5	6	7	8	Relaxed
Not studious	1	2	3	4	5	6	7	8	Studious
Unsympathetic	1	2	3	4	5	6	7	8	Sympathetic
Impatient	1	2	3	4	5	6	7	8	Patient
Happy	8	7	6	5	4	3	2	1	Depressed
Unenthusiastic	1	2	3	4	5	6	7	8	Enthusiastic
Not confident	1	2	3	4	5	6	7	8	Confident
Disagreeable	1	2	3	4	5	6	7	8	Agreeable
Unproductive	1	2	3	4	5	6	7	8	Productive
Unadventurous	1	2	3	4	5	6	7	8	Adventurous
Sociable	8	7	6	5	4	3	2	1	Unsociable
Satisfied	8	7	6	5	4	3	2	1	Dissatisfied
Unambitious	1	2	3	4	5	6	7	8	Ambitious

Adapted from "Fiedler's Leadership Contingency Model: An Empirical Test in Three Organizations," by J. G. Hunt, *Organizational Behavior and Human Performance*, 1967, 2, 291. Copyright 1967 by Academic Press, Inc. Reprinted by permission.

needs in the group. Leadership style, an underlying motivation, is seen as one central determinant of the leader's success. More recently, Fiedler (1971, 1972) has been less willing to equate Low-LPC leaders with task orientation and High-LPC leaders with a relationship orientation. High-LPC leaders also seem to be higher in cognitive complexity.[6]

There is evidence that the LPC measure is valid and reliable (Shima, 1968). In a laboratory task, High-LPC leaders acted in a more socioemotionally facilitative manner; Low-LPC leaders were more task oriented (Gruenfeld, Rance, & Weissenberg, 1969). The split-half reliability for a 20-item LPC scale is about +.90 (Fiedler, 1967). Test-retest correlations are not as high. A total of 54 experienced leaders completed the LPC form and repeated it eight weeks later; the reliability coefficient was +.57. For 32 inexperienced leaders under the same conditions the reliability coefficient was +.47. However, these groups were composed of military recruits undergoing eight weeks of basic training. Using mature U. S. Air Force officers in a reliability study with an eight-week time interval, Fiedler (1967) found a test-retest reliability coefficient of +.68.

The reason that a contingency theory is important is that it assumes an *interaction* between the situation and characteristics of the leader (Yukl, 1971); both of these, according to Fiedler, play a role in determining the nature of the leader's influence and the extent of the leader's effectiveness. Fiedler proposed that the following three situational and relationship components were important.

1. The leader's personal relations with members of his or her organization is one component. Relationships can range from very good to very poor; they are partially determined, of course, by the leader's personality. Fiedler finds that the leader-group relationship is the single most important factor determining the leader's influence in a small group (Fiedler, 1964, p. 159).[7] To some extent, leaders with good relationships can overcome the limitation of being weak in the second component, "position power."

2. The leader's "legitimate power" or "position power" is a second important component in a leader's effectiveness. How much power and authority is provided the leader by the position held? Does the leader have the authority to hire and fire? Can he or she reward persons by giving raises in pay or status? Or is he or she limited in means of regulating the behavior of other members? Does the organization back up his or her authority? For example, the person in charge of a group of volunteer workers in a political campaign would ordinarily have little position power over the volunteers. A football coach, an owner of a small business, and a police chief carry high degrees of power. Leaders with high position power carry some kind of separate rank or status and have "clout," whereas leaders low in position power cannot punish or reward their members by altering their rank or status. In fact, low-position-power leaders may be deposed by the group members. Position power, measured by a checklist of behaviors, is considered the least important of the three components of a leader's effectiveness, because group success can often result from a structured task or a popular leader even if the leader lacks authority and power.

3. The amount of structure in the task that the group has been assigned to perform is a third

[6]We may still expect that Low-LPC leaders will emphasize initiating structure and productivity, whereas High-LPC leaders emphasize consideration and sensitivity. Likewise, Low-LPC leaders would use coercion and High-LPC leaders would use persuasion in influencing others (McGinnies, 1970).

[7]The leader's relationship with the group has been measured in two ways: (1) by determining to what extent the leader sees himself or herself as the group's most-preferred member, and (2) by a "group atmosphere" scale on which the leader defines the climate of the group. Again, the relationship of conceptual definition to measurement is ambiguous. The group's atmosphere and the leader's perception of the group's liking for him may not be highly related. The use of the leader as the sole definer of group atmosphere also has limitations (E. P. Hollander, 1972).

component. How well does the leader know how to proceed? Some tasks possess a great deal of *goal clarity;* the requirements of the task are clearly known or programmed. Other tasks, such as those of ad hoc committees, policymaking groups, and creative groups, often lack goal clarity and structure—no one knows what the group purposes are or how the group should proceed. A second element of task structure is its degree of *solution specificity* (M. E. Shaw, 1963); that is, whether there is more than one correct solution for the group's task. A third aspect is the degree of *decision verifiability;* once a decision has been made, how clearly does the group know that it is a correct one? All these aspects of task structure play a role in determining the effectiveness of different types of leaders.[8] However, task structure clearly interacts with position power. If the task is clearly structured, the leader needs less position power to get the job done, because everybody's role has already been specified.

For purposes of simplification and analysis, Fiedler considered each of these three situational and relationship components as a dichotomy. Leader-member relationships are either good or poor; position power is either strong or weak; and task structure is either clear or unclear. As there are two categories in each of three aspects, we may conceive of a system of eight classifications (2 x 2 x 2), which would encompass all possible combinations of these aspects. Fiedler has set up such a system, to see what leadership style works best in each combination; it is shown in Table 20-6. Fiedler has added a ninth category (category VIII-A) to cover instances in which the leader-member relationships are extremely poor.

In seeking an understanding of the determinants of effectiveness, Fiedler hypothesized that the degree to which the conditions are favorable or unfavorable to the leader is another important characteristic. Favorable conditions emerge from situations that permit the leader to exert a great deal of influence on his group. For

example, good leader-member relations, strong position power, and clear task structure are considered favorable for the leader. The nine classifications in Table 20-6 are listed in order of their favorability for the leader. Class I, for example, is most favorable. Class VIII-A is quite unfavorable, because the personal relations are poor, task structure is unclear, and position power is weak. Fiedler concludes that Low-LPC leaders (task-oriented, controlling types) are most effective under group conditions that are either *very favorable* (classes I, II, III) or *very unfavorable to the leader* (classes VII, VIII, and VIII-A). In other words, the Low-LPC leader is most effective in cases in which he or she has either a great deal of influence and power or no influence and power. However, High-LPC leaders (permissive, relationship-oriented types) are most effective under conditions that are *moderately favorable or unfavorable* and in which *the leader's influence and power are mixed or moderate* (classes IV, V, VI). Let us look at these situations in greater detail.

Categories II and VI in Table 20-6 represent clear task structure (formal task groups) with weak position power (basketball teams, surveying groups, laboratory groups). Groups in category II have good leader-member relationships, whereas in category VI these relationships are poor. When these two categories were compared, it was found that task-oriented leaders with low LPC scores were more effective when relationships were good (category II), whereas High-LPC leaders (relationship-oriented) were more effective when relationships were poor (category VI). High school basketball teams with good relationships between the captain and the other team members win more games if the captain is a task-oriented leader (Fiedler, 1964).

Categories I and V represent clear task structure with strong position power (bomber crews, open-hearth crews, infantry squads, service-station crews). Again, groups with good leader-member relationships (category I) performed better under task-oriented Low-LPC leaders. Groups with relatively poor leader-member relationships (category V) performed

---

[8]Fiedler has used scales developed by M. E. Shaw (1963) to measure degree of structure.

Table 20-6
Classification of group-task situations on the basis of three factors

	Leader's Personal Relations with Members	Task Structure	Position Power	Number of Studies	Median Correlation
I	Good	Clear, or structured	Strong	8	−.52
II	Good	Clear	Weak	3	−.58
III	Good	Unclear, or unstructured	Strong	12	−.33
IV	Good	Unclear	Weak	10	+.47
V	Moderately poor	Clear	Strong	6	+.42
VI	Moderately poor	Clear	Weak	0	Not avail.
VII	Moderately poor	Unclear	Strong	12	+.05
VIII	Moderately poor	Unclear	Weak	12	−.43
VIII-A	Very poor	Clear	Strong	1	−.67

Note: A positive correlation means that a High-LPC leader (relationship-oriented leader) is more effective in that situation, whereas a negative correlation means that a Low-LPC (task-oriented) leader is more effective. (From *A Theory of Leadership Effectiveness*, by F. E. Fiedler. Copyright 1967 by McGraw-Hill Book Company. Reprinted by permission.)

better under relationship-oriented, High-LPC leaders.

Subsequent analyses showed that in groups with extremely poor leader-member relationships (those in which the group members rejected the leader), Low-LPC leaders were more effective than High-LPC leaders. These findings led Fiedler to compose the additional category VIII-A for groups with clear task structure, strong position power, and *very* poor leader-member relations (Fiedler, 1967, p. 84). Perhaps in these groups the leader and group members are so much at odds that the concern and liking of the High-LPC leader is ineffective; the group members may hate their leader but be more responsive to him if he is task oriented. It is also possible that in a situation that is so unfavorable for them, Low-LPC leaders intensify the task-controlling nature of their behavior (Billings, 1974).

These findings are additionally important because they lead to the conclusion that Low-

LPC, controlling leaders are more effective in groups that are either very favorable (category I) or very unfavorable (category VIII-A) for the leader. Some confirmation for this conclusion is found in Chemers' (1972; Chemers & Skrzypek, 1972) laboratory task groups and in Hill's (1969) investigation of supervision in two organizations. The evidence from Hill's study reveals that this relationship is very tenuous, as Graen et al. point out (1970, p. 291), but Chemers' findings give considerable support to the validity of the contingency model.

Categories IV and VIII in Table 20-6 represent groups with unclear task structure and weak position power (faculty ad hoc committees, Sunday school curriculum committees, weekend encounter groups). According to Fiedler, such groups are often concerned with creative problems and goals. Their task is not clearly defined, and the leader has little authority. Fiedler concludes "The relationship-oriented leaders (High LPC) performed best in groups which were relatively pleasant or relaxed (category IV). Task-oriented leaders (Low LPC) performed best in groups which were relatively tense and unpleasant and in which the leader felt less well-accepted (category VIII)" (1967, p. 120). Notice that the direction of the difference in effectiveness between High-LPC and Low-LPC leaders is opposite to that in categories II and VI and in categories I and V.

Categories III and VII represent groups with unclear task structure and powerful leaders (ROTC groups with creativity tasks). Results are quite obscure here; there was some tendency for "groups directed by task-oriented leaders who experienced a relatively pleasant group atmosphere [to perform] better on all tasks except one" (Fiedler, 1967, p. 129).

The most basic conclusion of Fiedler's massive program of research is that *there is no such thing as a good leader for all situations.* "A leader who is effective in one situation may or may not be in another" (Fiedler, 1969, p. 42). The organization, the tasks, and the power of the leader, the leader's popularity, and his or her relationship with coworkers all play a role. If a leader is not currently successful in meeting the goals of the group, it may be possible to introduce changes in the situation in order to facilitate success. The leader's position power may be changed, or greater structure may be introduced into the tasks given the group. Laboratory training in sensitivity groups may help leaders learn which skills they have and which they do not. They can learn to avoid situations where they are weakest and to find tasks and groups that fit their leadership styles. Fiedler believes that it is more fruitful to try to change the leader's work environment than to try to change his or her personality or leadership style (Fiedler, 1969, p. 43; also Fiedler, 1973). However, other social scientists report that the application of positive reinforcement, dissonance, reactance, and other psychological principles can modify unsuccessful communication habits in a supervisor (Varela, 1969).

Although Fiedler's approach should be commended as being the most comprehensive

attack on leadership effectiveness yet developed, undoubtedly it will require refinement as more data are accumulated. Even now, there are failures to verify the model when the criteria for leadership success are extended beyond productivity measures to supervisors' ratings, a second type of criterion (J. F. Duffy, 1970; J. F. Duffy, Kavanagh, MacKinney, Wolins, & Lyons, 1970). Another limitation to Fiedler's approach is the ambiguity of the LPC measure (Strickland, 1967). What does the LPC measure? What is the difference between leaders with high and low LPC scores? Initially, the LPC score seemed to reflect the degree of a leader's tolerance for inept coworkers. But Fishbein, Landy, and Hatch (1969) have concluded that the major function of the LPC measure is that it identifies people who have different types of least preferred coworkers. This point should be clarified through future research.

One other difficulty with Fiedler's theory is the choice of a criterion for a successful test of the theory. Ordinarily, we would expect that a statistically significant correlation in the expected direction between LPC and group performance scores would be used to demonstrate the accuracy of the theory. Most of the correlations in Fiedler's studies and in the studies of his coworkers are nonsignificant. Fiedler chooses to verify the theory by showing that the general majority of observed correlations are in the direction predicted by the theory. For example, in discussing the results of one study, he reports "While only one of the 16 [sic] correlations was significant, only one of the eight correlations, namely, .03, was not in the hypothesized direction" (1967, p. 119). Similar statements may be found in Fiedler's (1971) review of more recent validations. Reliance on such a weak criterion does not establish confidence in the accuracy of the theory (Graen et al., 1970; Butterfield, 1968).

Thus the contingency model of leadership is not the final answer. Previous approaches have tended to treat the leader and the situation as separate; "the reality of the leader as part of the situation for the followers, and also as one who defines it for the followers, was largely disregarded" (E. P. Hollander, 1972, p. 2). Fiedler's more recent writings (for example, Fiedler, 1972) suggest more concern about how situational aspects actually *moderate* the relationship between the leader's style and task behaviors (Billings, 1974). Yet there still is little study of the *process* of leadership; as E. P. Hollander (1972) notes, the major challenge for many leaders is the maintenance of their position in the face of challenges from above or below. Some leaders attempt to instill trust, others loyalty, others a sense of equity (E. P. Hollander & Julian, 1970).

To study leadership, we also need to study "followership." As Fillmore Sanford presciently noted more than 25 years ago, "Not only is it the follower who accepts or rejects leadership, but it is the follower who *perceives* both the leader and the situation and who reacts in terms of what he perceives" (1950, p. 4).

To reflect this need to study leaders and followers in relation to each other, the following sections of this chapter describe the effects of leader's assumptions about followers and the implications of these assumptions for group performance.

IV. Leadership, organizational effectiveness, and assumptions about human nature

Two types of leaders have been identified in this chapter—the task-oriented, controlling type and the group-oriented, egalitarian type. Each type of leader reflects different assumptions about human nature—assumptions that have great impact on the ways that leaders deal with their superiors and their subordinates. This section reviews changing conceptions of human nature held by leaders; we shall see an increasing sophistication and complexity arising from an accumulation of research and thought (Cyert & MacCrimmon, 1968).

Any member of any group possesses a variety of skills and resources. If the group is the Los Angeles Rams, a particular member may be valued because of his quickness, strength, or endurance. But each member possesses skills other than his physical ones. He has social skills, which may facilitate team harmony, and cognitive skills, which may aid in the development of a game plan. The coach's assumptions about the skills of each player may emphasize only the physical ones. (One of the central themes in recent exposés written by football players, such as *Out of Their League* by Meggyesy, 1971, and *Meat on the Hoof*, by G. Shaw, 1972, is that football coaches are oriented toward players as objects, not as fully developed beings.)

Edgar Schein (1971), in a stimulating text called *Organizational Psychology*, introduces four different assumptions about the nature of the worker that may be held by leaders. These four assumptions, described in detail below, refer to the *rational-economic man*, the *social man*, the *self-actualizing man*, and the *complex man*. If we ask a used-car lot's sales manager, a homecoming-committee chairperson, or a basketball coach about the best way to get the highest quality of production from his or her coworkers, the answer will probably reflect one of these four assumptions.

A. The rational-economic conception

In the first quarter of this century the most influential voice in managerial psychology was that of Frederick Taylor (1911), who advocated what was called a scientific-management approach. In Taylor's view, the worker's only motivation was to make money, and hence Taylor's answer to the problem of motivating workers was a piecework system of pay (Tannenbaum, 1966).

If people are motivated by money—as assumed by the rational-economic theory—the leader's task is one of manipulating and motivating workers to perform their best within the limits of what they can be paid. The theory holds that workers' feelings are irrational and must be prevented from obstructing the expression of the worker's rational self-interest (Schein, 1971).

This narrow conception resembles what Douglas McGregor (1960, 1966, 1967) called Theory X, or management's traditional conception of the worker. (McGregor included some additional assumptions under Theory X that are compatible with the rational-economic theory—namely that human nature is inherently passive, lazy, and gullible, and that people are incapable of self-discipline and self-control). Altogether, the rational-economic theory says there is little to workers' motivations beyond their desire to obtain the largest possible paycheck at the end of the week.

The assembly line is an outgrowth of the rational-economic conception. The production of a light switch, a radio, or an automobile is broken down into thousands of specific tasks. A worker may have to make only one response—perhaps he may tighten one screw in every light switch that passes in front of him on the never-ending assembly line. (See Figure 20-2.) His pay can be related to the number of switches he processes. The goal of management is to produce as many finished products as possible; according to this conception, whether the worker is satisfied or bored is quite unimportant. "The fact that the employee's emotional needs were not fulfilled on the job was of little consequence because he often did not expect them to be fulfilled" (Schein, 1971, p. 52).

There is no denying that better pay and merit bonuses are important motivators for workers. To that degree, the rational-economic theory has some applicability. But the theory does not suffice; it fails to recognize other needs of workers that contribute to satisfaction and productivity or, when unfulfilled, to employee turnover and malingering.

B. The conception of social man

Between 1927 and 1932 a series of studies used employees of the Western Electric Company's Hawthorne works in Chicago (Roethlis-

berger & Dickson, 1939).[9] A group of female workers assembling relay switches for telephones was moved to a special room, and a number of innovations were introduced to study their effects on these workers' productivity. The researchers expected some of these innovations to lower productivity—the lighting was dimmed; the working day was shortened by an hour; and coffee breaks were added, thus reducing time on the job. Finally, a longer work day was instituted without any rest periods or coffee breaks. To the surprise of the researchers, *every* innovation had the effect of *increasing* productivity. Output became higher than ever before. The researchers concluded that the workers' productivity had increased because the workers felt that management was interested in them. Previous feelings of alienation and loss of identity in the workers were replaced with a feeling that they were special. The *Hawthorne effect* subsequently became a term used to label this phenomenon of working harder and producing more because of a feeling of participating in something new and special.

One of the Hawthorne researchers, Elton Mayo (1945), developed a set of assumptions about the worker that reflect a model emphasizing *social man*. These assumptions included the following:

1. Workers are basically motivated by social needs and determine their basic sense of identity through relationships with others.

2. As a result of the industrial revolution and the segmenting of tasks into specific activities, meaning has gone out of work itself for many workers, who—now alienated—seek its meaning in the social relationships available on the job (Creedman & Creedman, 1972).

3. Working people are more responsive to the social forces of their peer group than to the incentives and controls of management. The

[9]A thorough review and critique of the extensive Hawthorne studies is found in H. A. Landsberger, *Hawthorne Revisited* (Ithaca, N. Y.: Cornell University, 1958). Other critiques and reinterpretations include those by Carey (1967) and Parsons (1974).

Figure 20-2
Life on the assembly line. The single source of cohesiveness uniting auto
workers on the assembly line is the never-ending monotony of it all. Partially
assembled cars pass by at the rate of 50 to 65 an hour, and workers have less
than a minute each to do their specific tasks—for example, to pound out a dent
in a fender or reweld an improperly joined seam. At the Dodge plant in
Hamtramck, Michigan, the assembly line begins promptly at 6 A.M. There is
a 30-minute lunch break at 10 A.M.—not enough time for some workers to get
a hot lunch at the cafeteria. Some workers munch a sandwich from a bag, often
while waiting in the long line to use the toilet. The only other breaks are an
11-minute one in the morning and a 12-minute one in the afternoon. This work
shift ends at 2:30 P.M. To quote Henry Belcher, a welder, "Everything is
regulated. No time to stop and think about what you are doing; your life is
geared to the assembly line. I have lost my freedom" (*Time*, Sept. 28, 1970, p.
70). (Photo courtesy of Ford Motor Company.)

working group can often determine and control what constitutes a normal rate of production, despite management's frenzied efforts to increase output. In another work group in the Hawthorne plant, one new worker was at first a "rate buster"—she turned out almost twice as many products a day as the others. But soon the other women had convinced her of what was an appropriate or justified rate.

4. Working man is responsive to management to the extent that a supervisor can meet a subordinate's social needs and needs for acceptance. (Adapted from Schein, 1965, p. 51.)

Thus, according to the assumptions of *social man*, the tasks of a shop foreperson or department chairperson require that some attention be given to the needs of his or her subordinates. Even with feelings of alienation, workers may perform tolerably or adequately, but productivity (as well as worker morale and satisfaction) can be increased by a leader's or manager's recognition of the workers' needs.

Despite the fact that Mayo's model of the worker as a social being was an improvement over the rational-economic conception of man, it was justifiably criticized by liberal sociologists such as C. Wright Mills (1948) as being promanagement and seeing the worker as only a means to ends defined by the company ownership. Yet a variety of studies in the 1940s and 1950s demonstrated the potency of the conception of *social man*. Many of these studies were stimulated by the thinking of Kurt Lewin, the father of group dynamics, who sensitized industry to the powerful effect of participatory decision making on job efficiency.

A prototype of a Lewinian study was conducted in a pajama plant in rural Virginia. One of the officers of the company, psychologist Alfred Marrow, invited Lewin to meet with the plant staff to discuss a basic problem: the inexperienced workers hired by the new company were not reaching the level of skill that was expected of them by management. The company officials felt that they had tried everything. The workers were being paid more than they had been receiving on their previous jobs. The man-

agement had tried a multitude of reward systems, and all had failed.

Lewin made a number of interpretations. One was that the inability of the workers to meet management's standard might derive from their belief that the company's standard was impossible to attain. Lewin advocated the importing of some experienced workers from other communities to work alongside the local workers. Although this was an unpopular suggestion—because the town officials strongly opposed giving jobs to outsiders—the unnerved plant officials tried it. The skilled, experienced operators who were imported adapted to management's standards. When the local, unskilled workers saw the performance of the experienced outsiders, they vowed that they could also reach the desired level, and their production rate gradually began to increase.

Later studies at this same plant (French & Coch, 1948) dealt with resistance by production workers to changes in working methods. This resistance was manifested by higher rates of turnover, lowered levels of production, and verbal hostility toward the plant and their coworkers. French, one of Lewin's associates, and Coch, the personnel manager, decided to try three methods of instituting changes in job duties, each involving a different amount of participation by the workers in planning the details of new job activities. The first group of workers was simply told about the planned changes in their jobs and what was now expected of them; they did not participate in the decision. The second group appointed representatives from among themselves to meet with management to consider problems involved in changing working methods. The third group procedure involved every worker in the unit, not just representatives. All members of the third group met with management, participated actively in discussions, shared many suggestions, and helped plan the most efficient methods for mastering the new jobs.

Marrow reports the differences between groups in job adaptation. These findings support the conception of *social man*.

The differences in outcome of the three procedures were clear-cut and dramatic. Average production in the non-participating group dropped 20 percent immediately and did not regain the pre-change level. Nine percent of the group quit. Morale fell sharply, as evidenced by marked hostility toward the supervisor, by slowdowns, by complaints to the union, and by other instances of aggressive behavior.

The group which participated through representatives required two weeks to recover its pre-change output. Their attitude was cooperative, and none of the members of the group quit their jobs.

The consequences in the total-participation group were in sharp contrast to those in the non-participating group. It regained the pre-change output after only two days and then climbed steadily until it reached a level about 14 percent above the earlier average. No one quit; all members of the group worked well with their supervisors, and there were no signs of aggression [1969, pp. 150–151].

A more recent study (Zander & Armstrong, 1972) reported that when work groups in a slipper factory were asked to set their own daily production goals, they tended to aim for high goals—even higher than the standard set by the manager.

Lewinian methods and conceptions of social man may lead to better employee-leader relations, as well as heightened productivity. Such effects are not limited to the industrial plant. More democratic procedures in the selection of college presidents and boards of trustees may improve faculty and student morale and productivity. Lewin, Lippitt, and White's (1939) classic study of the social climate of boys' task groups has shown the wide applicability of the conception of social man. Small groups of 11-year-old boys met after school for several weeks in order to make masks and carry out similar activities. The adult leader of the groups acted in either an authoritarian, a democratic, or a laissez-faire manner. The authoritarian leader usually started by giving an order, frequently criticized the work, and often disrupted activity by suddenly making the children begin a new project. This type of leader gave the boys no indication of long-range goals and frequently remained aloof. The democratic leader worked together with the group to develop goals and the means for attaining them. All decisions were made by the entire group. The laissez-faire leader was noncommittal and passive throughout the boys' activity periods. This type of leader gave out information only on request and did not enter into the spirit of the task. As in the pajama factory, these experimental variations produced changes in both productivity and satisfaction. Authoritarian leadership resulted in more restlessness, discontent, aggression, fighting, damage to play materials, and apathy. Apathy dominated in groups with laissez-faire leaders, also. All but 1 of 20 boys in the groups preferred the democratic leadership. (Preferences were not a result of the specific person who served as leader, since three different men served as leaders in all three social climates.)

Results regarding productivity were not as clear-cut. The largest number of masks was produced by the authoritarian groups, but democratic groups were better able to put forth a sustained effort when the leader was absent. Laissez-faire leadership led to low rates of productivity.

Productivity as used in this study referred to the number of masks made during the brief time of the group sessions. But we need to distinguish between performance in the short run and in the long run. The more simple, concrete, and terminal the task of the group, the more effective is authoritarian leadership (Adams, 1954; reviewed in Anderson, 1959). In a complex or creative task or in one requiring cooperation among members, democratic leadership may be more effective. (The distinction here touches upon structured and unstructured situations, in which, according to Fiedler, High-LPC and Low-LPC leaders have different degrees of effectiveness.)

If we assume that democratic leadership instills in group members a greater desire to succeed, even without continuous supervision, we may conclude that democratic leadership has better long-term effects. This assumption is clearly behind the advocacy of a student-centered approach to learning. To Carl Rogers

(1969), a teacher-centered approach to the classroom has no long-range benefits in the development of the student as an authentic person. To be of real value to the learner, the quest for learning must come from inside; authoritarian threats are of short-term value only.

C. The self-actualizing conception of the worker

The social view of human nature is more mature and humane than the rational-economic view, but it is still not a satisfactory view to some social psychologists and social philosophers. To Abraham Maslow (1954), for example, people at their best are *self-actualizing* and make maximum use of all their resources. To Maslow, to Argyris (1964), and to McGregor (1960, 1966, 1967)—all social psychologists concerned with leadership in industry—most jobs in contemporary factories, offices, and shops do not permit workers to use their capacities fully. These jobs do not facilitate workers' understanding of the relationship between what they are doing and the total purpose of the employing organization (Schein, 1971).

The leader who adopts the view of people as self-actualizing feels concern about his or her employees but is more interested in making their work meaningful and satisfying than in fulfilling their social needs. Workers will be given as much responsibility as they can handle; as they achieve certain degrees of skill and responsibility, they are encouraged to move upward. According to the self-actualizing conception, people are intrinsically motivated—they have deeply personal, internalized reasons for doing a good job. They take pride in their work because it is *their* work (D. A. Wood, 1974). (Prior conceptions saw the worker as extrinsically motivated; reasons for working were artificially related to the job.) If we ask people why they feel good about their jobs, as Herzberg, Mausner, and Snyderman (1959) have done, their reasons are often centered around their accomplishments and their feeling of increasing job competence. We interpret these interview responses as indications that

self-actualization is a part of the nature of the worker.[10]

It may be true that a self-actualization conception of human nature is more idealistic than realistic. Some workers may not care whether their job provides any challenge or autonomy (B. Schneider & Bartlett, 1970; Meir & Barak, 1974). Self-actualization may not be applicable to many unskilled jobs or temporary activities (Larson & Spreitzer, 1973). Perhaps for these positions the goal should be to provide the worker with enough money so that he or she can find meaning and challenge off the job (Schein, 1971, p. 60). But, as Argyris (1964) and others have indicated, there is a great risk that rejecting self-actualization as a goal can lead to a waste of human resources, which are our most precious commodity.

D. The conception of the complex worker

Each of the previous sets of assumptions about the nature of the worker is oversimplified and overgeneralized. Each may have some accuracy; each may be applicable to some individuals or partially applicable to many individuals. Schein postulates that man is not only "more complex within himself, being possessed of many needs and potentials, but he is also likely to differ from his neighbor in the patterns of his own complexity" (1965, p. 60). Thus, a model of man as a *complex being* is necessary to complete our picture of the nature of the worker (Lawler, 1972). Since the ramifications of a complex view of the nature of the worker are complex in and of themselves, we quote Schein's description at length.

a. Man is not only complex, but also highly variable; he has many motives which are arranged in some sort of hierarchy of importance

[10]Factors that made people feel bad about their job—such as poor pay, bad working conditions, and inadequate job security—are unrelated to self-actualization (Herzberg et al., 1959).

to him, but this hierarchy is subject to change from time to time and situation to situation; furthermore, motives interact and combine into complex motive patterns (for example, since money can facilitate self-actualization, for some people economic strivings are equivalent to self-actualization).

b. Man is capable of learning new motives through his organizational experiences, hence ultimately his pattern of motivation and the psychological contract which he establishes with the organization is the result of a complex interaction between initial needs and organizational experiences.

c. Man's motives in different organizations or different subparts of the same organization may be different; the person who is alienated in the formal organization may find fulfillment of his social and self-actualization needs in the union or in the informal organization; if the job itself is complex, such as that of a manager, some parts of the job may engage some motives while other parts engage other motives.

d. Man can become productively involved with organizations on the basis of many different kinds of motives; his ultimate satisfaction and the ultimate effectiveness of the organization depend only in part on the nature of his motivation. The nature of the task to be performed, the abilities and experience of the person on the job, and the nature of the other people in the organization all interact to produce a certain pattern of work and feelings. For example, a highly skilled but poorly motivated worker may be as effective *and satisfied* as a very unskilled but highly motivated worker.

e. Man can respond to many different kinds of managerial strategies, depending on his own motives and abilities and the nature of the task; in other words, there is no one correct managerial strategy that will work for all men at all times [1971, p. 62].[11]

The leader who holds a belief in the complexity of human nature must be sensitive to individual differences in the needs, fears, and

[11]From *Organizational Psychology,* by E. H. Schein. © 1965. Reprinted by permission of Prentice-Hall, Inc., Englewood Cliffs, N. J.

abilities of workers. He or she must be able to appreciate these differences and adapt to each. Unlimited or unqualified application of any one of the previous conceptions by a leader will be wrong in many cases. (See Figure 20-3.)

There are many examples of the usefulness of a conception of *complex man* in the study of leaders and organizations. In effect, the failure of any intervention to bring about identical results in every subject is an indication of the human complexity involved. When 19 out of 20 11-year-olds prefer democratic leadership, we must not overlook the single deviant and the interindividual variability his response represents. (Very few interventions produce the almost unanimous response that was obtained in the authoritarian-democratic leadership studies!) This represents one level of complexity resulting from individual differences. But there are complexities within each individual—variability in needs across time or duties. Another example of individual differences in response comes from a study of a large trucking company (Vroom, 1960; Vroom & Mann, 1960). This study found that workers with different kinds of jobs and different personalities preferred different leadership styles. Men with relatively independent, solitary jobs (such as truck drivers and dispatchers) preferred a more task-oriented, authoritarian supervisor. But men whose work was interdependent preferred employee-oriented supervision. Successful attempts to change the leadership preferences of workers further document the conclusion that it is desirable for every successful manager, chairperson, or group leader to possess a complex view of human nature (Hulin & Blood, 1968).

V. Summary

In the early search for characteristics that distinguished leaders from nonleaders, little consistency in results from one study to another was found. However, some traits did appear in sever-

Figure 20-3
What makes a successful supervisor of others? In a review of studies on worker motivation, Katz and Kahn (1966) list several qualities that successful supervisors have to a greater degree than do supervisors of less productive groups: (1) *More differentiation.* The successful supervisor spends more time on special problems and on planning; he or she does not simply "pitch in" and do the same activities as the other workers. (2) *Less close supervision.* Successful supervisors give their workers more autonomy. While they do not abdicate responsibility for supervision, they do not "look over the shoulder" of their workers as closely as do less successful managers. (3) *Greater employee orientation.* Successful supervisors are oriented toward employees more than toward the hiring institution. They are concerned with maintenance of relationships as well as production. (Photo © Larry Keenan, 1976, NEST, S.F.)

al studies; leaders were higher in intelligence, persistence, initiative, sense of humor, extraversion, sociability, self-confidence, and dependability.

Leadership has been conceptualized as actions on the part of a group member that influence the group in its movement toward goal setting and goal achievement. In this conception, each member of the group may play a role in the group's leadership.

Designated leaders of groups have two major leadership functions: *initiating structure* and *consideration.* Initiating structure refers to the leader's behavior in identifying the group's goal and moving the group toward its goal. *Consideration* refers to the leader's concern with relationships between himself or herself and other group members. Leaders high in consideration reflect their awareness of the needs of each group member.

Designating leadership functions as either task oriented or group-maintenance oriented parallels the division into initiating structure and consideration. While a task orientation and a group-maintenance orientation are not mutually exclusive, many groups develop different leaders for the two functions.

Fiedler's contingency theory of leadership emphasizes that there is no one successful type of leader; rather, aspects of the leader's power, the task structure, and the leader's personal relations with members of his or her group interact to determine what kind of leader will be most successful.

Leaders of organizations and groups operate according to assumptions about human nature. Four different types of models may be distinguished: rational-economic man, social man, self-actualizing man, and complex man.

The model of *rational-economic man* sees the worker as motivated by money and self-interest. Hence, the leader's task is seen as one of motivating workers to turn out the most they can within the limits of what they can be paid.

The model of *social man* sees workers as basically motivated by social needs; relationships with others are primary. The task of the manager is to recognize these social needs and facilitate their fulfillment in order to increase production.

The model of *self-actualizing man* views workers as striving to use their capacities fully. The leader employing this model seeks to make other employees' work meaningful and satisfying. The worker is given the most challenging jobs that he or she can handle and is encouraged to develop new skills and goals.

The model of *complex man* reflects beliefs that different workers have different needs and capabilities. The leader who believes in the complexity of human nature must be sensitive to individual differences in the needs, fears, and abilities of workers.

Glossary

acquiescent response set. A tendency to agree with an attitude statement regardless of the nature of its content.

action research. Research whose goal is the understanding or solution of social problems.

adaptation. A cognitive process through which a person becomes relatively unaware of an aversive condition or reassesses it as relatively harmless.

adaptation-level theory. A theory of content effects, which suggests that the individual's background acts to set a standard against which events or objects are perceived.

affiliation. A basic social need: being with other people.

aggression. A type of behavior in which the goal is to harm or injure another person.

aggressiveness. Behavior that reflects impulsiveness, activity without thought, and forcefulness.

altruism. A special form of helping behavior that is voluntary, costly, and motivated by something other than the anticipation of reward.

anal stage. The Freudian developmental stage that is characteristic of the 2- to 3-year-old child and centered on toilet training and elimination of waste.

androgyny. The state of possessing both masculine and feminine traits; generally refers to psychological rather than physical characteristics.

anomie. A feeling of personal worthlessness, futility, and alienation.

anticonformity. Behavior that is directly antithetical to the normative group expectations.

anti-intraception. Opposition to the subjective, the imaginative, the tender-minded. A characteristic of the authoritarian-personality syndrome.

anti-Semitism. A generalized negative attitude toward Jews.

anxiety. A generalized, diffuse apprehension about the future.

archival research. Analysis of existing documents or records, especially those contained in public archives.

area sampling. A form of probability sampling in which geographic area serves as a basis of selection of a stratified random sample. For instance, a few counties, and within each county a few precincts, and within each precinct a few dwellings, may be randomly chosen for a sample.

arousal. A state of heightened emotion.

artifact. A research finding that does not reflect the true state of affairs in an area but, instead, reflects the results of an arbitrary methodological approach.

Asch situation. An experimental situation in which a subject is led to believe that his or her perceptions are different from those of all the other subjects. Used to test the extent of conformity to group opinion.

assumed similarity. Correspondence between one's judgments or ratings of another person and one's own characteristics. A response set in person-perception tasks. Sometimes called *projection*, because it represents an attribution of one's characteristics to another person.

assumption about human nature. Belief that people in general possess certain common characteristics.

attitude. A positive or negative affective reaction of a relatively enduring nature to an object or proposition.

attribution theory. A theory, stemming from the work of Fritz Heider and from Gestalt theory, concerning the way in which people assign characteristics or intentions to other persons or to objects.

authoritarian aggression. A tendency to be on the lookout for and to condemn, reject, and punish people who violate conventional values. A characteristic of the authoritarian-personality syndrome.

authoritarianism. A basic personality style that includes a set of organized beliefs, values, and pref-

663

erences, including submission to authority, identification with authority, denial of feelings, cynicism, and others.

authoritarian submission. A submissive, uncritical
attitude toward the idealized moral authorities of
the in-group. A characteristic of the authoritarian-personality syndrome.

autokinetic effect. The tendency for a stationary
light, when viewed in an otherwise completely darkened room, to appear to be moving.

autonomous stage of morality. A later stage of moral
development in which rules are seen as modifiable
in order to fit the needs of a given situation.

balance theory. An attitude theory, which hypothesizes that people prefer to hold consistent or compatible beliefs and avoid inconsistent or incompatible ones.

base rate. The rate of response in the general population, or frequency of occurrence of an action or
attitude in the general population.

behavior settings. A term used in Barker's ecological
psychology to refer to every location-activity combination. Thus the term "behavior settings" refers
not only to physical localities (a gymnasium, a
street corner, a drugstore) but also to the activities
that take place within them.

bystander effect. The finding that a person is less
likely to provide help when in the presence of
other witnesses than when alone.

ceiling effect. An artificial limit on the highest possible score, due to some characteristic of the
measure.

central trait. A personal characteristic that strongly
influences a perceiver's impressions of the person
possessing it. Asch showed that the *warm-cold* personality dimension was such a central trait.

charisma. A particular appeal or personal magnetism
attributed to certain persons.

chauvinist. One who displays excessive pride and de-
votion to his or her own group. For example, a
male chauvinist is one who believes that men are
better than women in nearly all respects.

closed-ended question. One that presents two or
more response alternatives for the respondent to
choose between.

coefficient of correlation. A measure of the degree
of relationship between two variables or scores
obtained from the same set of individuals. Correlation coefficients range from $+1.00$ through 0.00
to -1.00.

cofigurative culture. A culture in which both children
and adults learn from their peers.

cognition. A mental event in which perceptions,
memories, beliefs, or thoughts are processed.

cognitive. Referring to thought or mental, rather than
emotional, orientation.

cognitive complexity. The use of many dimensions
in interpreting other people's behavior.

cognitive dissonance. A state in which a person holds
two beliefs or cognitions that are inconsistent with
each other.

cohesiveness. The attractiveness that a group has for
its members and that the members have for one
another; the force that holds a group together.

communication networks. Representations of the
acceptable paths of communication between persons in a group or organization.

compensatory reaction. A response that may occur
when another person exhibits too much or too little
verbal or nonverbal intimacy. It involves an adjustment in one or more signals of immediacy (for
example, eye contact, smiling, or proximity). Predicted in a theory by Argyle and Dean (1965).

competition. Striving to excel in order to obtain an
exclusive goal.

competitive motive. A condition that leads an individual to seek personal success and the failure of
other participants in a situation.

competitive reward structure. A reward structure
such that not all people striving for a reward can
attain it and such that movement toward the goal
by one decreases the chances that others will attain
it.

conceptual systems. The outcome of an individual's
efforts to organize his or her beliefs, knowledge,
and values.

confederates. Assistants of the experimenter who
take part in an experiment, acting as subjects and
acting or speaking in preplanned ways.

conformity. As defined by Kiesler and Kiesler, a
change in behavior or belief toward a group consensus as a result of real or imagined group pressure. As defined in this text, a yielding to group
pressures.

consideration. A dimension of leadership; the leader's concern with relationships between himself
and other group members and the maintenance
of group morale and cohesiveness.

construct. A concept, defined in terms of observable
events, used by a theory to account for regularities
or relationships in data.

content analysis. A method for the objective, systematic, and usually quantitative description of various

characteristics of the content of verbal communication.

conventionalism. Rigid adherence to conventional middle-class values. A characteristic of the authoritarian-personality syndrome.

cooperation. Working together for mutual benefit. A prosocial behavior.

cooperative motive. A condition that leads an individual to seek the outcome most beneficial to all participants in a situation.

cooperative reward structure. A reward structure such that all those who strive must achieve the reward in order for it to be attained by any one participant. Each person's efforts advance the group's chances.

coping behavior. Response to a stress-producing situation designed to reduce the stress conditions.

correlational method. A nonmanipulative, nonexperimental method of science that studies the relationships among the naturally occurring characteristics of individuals or events.

counterconformity. Anticonformity. Acting in a manner opposite to that advocated by others.

cross-cultural. Pertaining to a study or method that compares responses of people from different societies to the same stimulus.

cross-sectional studies. Studies that compare subjects of different ages at the same point in time.

crowding. A psychological state of stress that sometimes accompanies high population density. (A similar term, *crowded*, refers to situations in which population density is relatively high.)

culture free. Free from biases that invalidly deflate the scores of subjects from certain cultures, ethnic groups, or social classes.

death instinct. A concept developed by Freud, which holds that all human beings have a compulsion "to return to [an] inorganic state."

deduction. The process of logical reasoning from premises to conclusions. Used in deriving predictions from a theory.

defensible space. Refers to multiple-family dwellings and describes space with well-defined boundaries and ample opportunities by residents to maintain surveillance over visitors (Newman, 1972).

deindividuation. A state of relative anonymity, in which a group member does not feel singled out or identifiable.

demand characteristics. The perceptual cues, both explicit and implicit, that communicate what behavior is expected in a situation.

demographic. Relating to characteristics by which a population can be classified into separate statistical subgroups (for example, age or sex).

dependent variable. A variable whose changes are considered to be consequences or effects of changes in other (independent) variables. (*the reaction.*)

destructiveness and cynicism. Generalized hostility; vilification of the human. A characteristic of the authoritarian-personality syndrome.

determinism. A basic assumption of science, which states that nature is orderly and lawful and that all events are caused. In line with this assumption, all behavior is believed to be the result of natural causes and therefore potentially predictable.

developmental quotient (DQ). A measure of the rate of mental development in infants.

differential accuracy. The ability to judge correctly the differences between individuals on any given trait (or difference between an individual and the group mean, or norm).

diffusion of responsibility. A hypothesized cause of the *bystander effect*, whereby an individual is less likely to accept personal responsibility for helping when in the presence of other witnesses than when alone.

discrimination. Any action that reflects the acceptance of one person or rejection of another solely on the basis of that person's membership in a particular group.

dogmatism. A closed-minded, rigid style combined with beliefs that are authoritarian in content.

dominance hierarchy. In a group, the ranking of the members in terms of influence or power. The most powerful or dominant member is highest in the hierarchy.

donation. A helping behavior in which goods or services are provided to a person or organization in need.

double-barreled item. A questionnaire item that actually asks two different questions at once. Such items should be avoided because they are ambiguous.

dyad. A two-person group.

ecological perspective. A viewpoint that encourages social scientists to study the behavior of the organism in the environment in which it occurs.

ecological psychology. A viewpoint in social psychology that encourages us to study the behavior of the organism in the environment in which it occurs.

ecology. The study of relationships between organism and environment, where both are viewed as part of an ongoing, dynamic system.

ego. According to Freud, that part of the personality that is oriented toward acting reasonably and realistically; the "executive" part of personality.

ego ideal. The person's perception of the kind of person he or she would like to be.

Electra complex. According to psychoanalytic theory, the young girl's feeling of attraction toward her father and hence envy of her mother for occupying the place, vis-à-vis her father, that the girl would like to occupy.

empathy. Ability to understand the feelings of another; role-taking ability.

empirical approach. An active, planned collection of factual information. Contrasted with a rational (or armchair) approach.

empirical-rational strategy. A strategy of planned change, which holds that publishing the facts that support change is sufficient to initiate that change.

environmental psychology. A recently developed, multidisciplinary field concerned with the interplay of individual behavior, social milieu, and physical setting. Researchers in the field include architects, anthropologists, planners, psychologists, and other professionals.

equity theory. A minitheory that specifies how people assign rewards to contributions; each person's rewards should be equitable in light of his or her costs.

ethnic group. A group sharing a common culture, customs, and language.

ethnocentrism. A rejection of foreigners, aliens, and all out-groups, abetted by a belief that one's own group is best in all respects.

ethology. The study of the behavior of animals in their natural settings.

evaluation apprehension. A concern on the part of a subject in a study that he or she is performing correctly and will be positively evaluated by the researcher.

experimental method. A method of science that involves manipulation of one or more independent variables, control of related variables, and observation of one or more dependent variables.

experimental realism. Arrangement of the events of an experiment so that they will seem convincing and have the maximum possible impact on the subjects. This is sometimes accomplished through the use of deception.

experimenter effects. Changes or distortions in the results of an experiment produced by the experimenter's characteristics or behavior.

expiatory punishment. According to Piaget, the belief held by younger children that wrongdoers should suffer a punishment that is painful in proportion to the seriousness of the offense but not necessarily adapted to the nature of the offense (see *reciprocity*).

external validity. The generalizability of a research finding (for example, to other populations, settings, treatment arrangements, and measurement arrangements).

fact. An observation that has been made (or could be made) repeatedly and consistently by different observers.

factorial design. A design in which each level of one independent variable is combined with each level of another independent variable (or several others).

favor. A form of helping behavior that requires little self-sacrifice in time and effort.

field experiment. An experiment done in a natural, real-life situation, often without the awareness of subjects.

field study. Social research done in a natural setting, usually over a long period of time and usually with observational methods, though other methods of data collection may also be used.

field theory. A basic point of view in social psychology, first developed by Kurt Lewin, which proposes that one's social behavior is a function not only of one's own attitudes, personality, and other intrapersonal factors, but also of one's environment, or "field."

"foot-in-the-door" effect. The case in which previous compliance with a small request makes it more likely that the person will comply with a larger (and less desirable) request.

frustration. The blocking of, or interference with, ongoing motivated behavior.

functional distance. The extent to which the physical proximity of two persons' residences, along with the physical layout of the residences, affects their opportunities to interact. Close functional proximity implies frequent opportunity to interact (Festinger, Schachter, & Back, 1950).

funnel sequence. Arrangement of questions in an interview with broad, open-ended questions first, then somewhat narrower ones, and finally very narrow and specific questions.

future shock. Alvin Toffler's term for the disorientation that results from the superimposition of a new culture on an old one; a product of a greatly accelerated rate of change in society.

gender identity. One's self-awareness of being male or female.

generative mechanism. The process by which a phenomenon is produced.

genital stage. The Freudian developmental stage from age 14 up, centered on the development of mature sexuality and love for others.

genotype. An underlying characteristic; often a causal factor.

Gestalt (German). Form or pattern.

halo effect. A rating error in which the rater lets his or her general, overall impression of another influence the rating he or she gives the other person on some specific characteristic.

haphazard sampling. Sampling without any systematic method and, therefore, unrepresentative.

helping behavior. Prosocial behavior that benefits another person rather than oneself.

hereditarian. An individual who believes that variations in behavior are the result of biological differences between individuals that are determined genetically. The hereditarian point of view can be contrasted with that of the advocates of socialization, who argue that learning and experience are the major determinants of behavior.

heritability. The degree to which individual differences in a particular trait can be attributed to genetic factors.

hermaphrodite. A person who possesses a combination of male and female bodily organs and hormonal patterns, so that the person's sex cannot be clearly defined as entirely female or entirely male.

heteronomous stage. An early stage of moral development, in which the child accepts rules as given from authority.

homeostatic model. A model of motivation that assumes that an organism seeks an optimal amount or degree of stimulation and that large discrepancies from the optimum result in tension and a motive to achieve a level of stimulation closer to the optimum.

hypothesis. A tentative explanation of a relationship between variables, or a supposition that a relationship may exist. A hypothesis generates some scientific method (such as an experiment) that seeks to confirm or disprove the hypothesis.

id. According to Freud, a set of drives that is the repository of our basic unsocialized impulses, including sex and aggression.

ideology. A set of beliefs on various topics that "hang together."

idiosyncrasy-credit model. Hollander's model, according to which a leader has the opportunity to deviate more from group norms because he or she has developed "credits" through past efforts in the organization.

immanent justice. According to Piaget, the belief held by younger children that misdeeds will lead naturally to negative consequences, that punishments emanate automatically from things themselves.

immediacy behavior. A behavior that signals intimacy or psychological closeness, such as making eye contact, adopting close physical proximity, touching, leaning forward, or facing directly.

implicit personality theories. Assumptions that two or more traits are related to each other, so that if a person possesses one of them, he or she will possess the other also.

impression management. The process of attempting to control the images that others form of us.

independent variable. A variable that is manipulated in an experiment; a variable whose changes are considered to be the cause of changes in another (dependent) variable.

individualistic motive. A condition that leads an individual to optimize personal rewards, without regard to how other participants in the situation fare.

individualistic reward structure. A reward structure in which goal attainment by one participant has no effect on the probability of goal attainment by others.

induction. The process of making inferences from some specific observations to a more general rule. Used in constructing a theory on the basis of observed facts.

informed consent. An important ethical principle in research with human subjects, requiring that subjects be given a choice about their participation in research and that they be told beforehand about all the relevant conditions of the research that might make them wish to withdraw.

ingratiation. A tactic used for impression management, in which the person tries to make others like him or her.

initiating structure. A dimension of leadership; the leader's behavior in identifying the group's goal and moving the group toward its goal.

inside density. Density within a dwelling or residence —for example, the number of persons per room.

instinct. An unlearned behavior pattern that appears in full form in all members of the species whenever there is an adequate stimulus.

interaction. A joint effect of two or more variables such that the effect of one variable is different for various levels of the other variable.

interaction territory. An area around two or more

people as they talk, into which passersby are not welcome. Analogous to a group personal space.

internal validity. The conclusiveness with which the effects of the independent variables are established in a scientific investigation, as opposed to the possibility that some confounding variable(s) may have caused the observed results.

interpersonal trust. A person's generalized expectancy that promises of other individuals or groups, with regard to the future, can be relied upon.

intervention in an emergency. A helping behavior that is potentially costly and performed under stress, with little possibility of reward.

intrusion. A violation of interpersonal-distance norms (or some other sign of excessive immediacy) that occurs as two people talk.

invariant. Consistent; following a set sequence without modification.

"just-world" phenomenon. The belief that persons get what they deserve in life.

laboratory experiment. An experiment in which a great degree of precision and control over the variables is achieved, so that factors that normally go together can be separated and the operation of each factor can be seen independent of other factors.

latency period. Freudian developmental stage characteristic of the 6- to 14-year-old child; a period of relative quiescence.

libido. In psychoanalytic theory, psychic energy that is expended in the satisfying of different needs.

life space. In field theory, the person plus his or her environment, all of which is viewed as one set of interdependent factors.

Likert-type scale. A type of attitude scale that poses statements and asks the respondent to indicate how much he or she agrees or disagrees with each statement.

longitudinal studies. Studies that compare responses of the same group of subjects at two points in time.

LPC. Least preferred coworker.

Machiavellianism. A belief that people can be manipulated through such means as flattery, threats, and deceit, in combination with a zest for carrying out such manipulations.

marker. A device used to signal occupancy or possession of a territory.

measure. To quantify a variable, using a continuous numerical scale.

modeling. The tendency for a person to reproduce the actions, attitudes, and emotional responses exhibited by a real-life or symbolic model. Also called "observational learning."

moderator variable. A variable that links two other variables or affects the influence of one on the other.

moral independence. According to Piaget, the second stage in moral development, in which the child comes to believe in the modification of rules to fit the needs of the situation.

moral judgment. As studied by Piaget, Kohlberg, and others, a subject's beliefs regarding good and bad behavior in certain situations.

moral realism. According to Piaget, a belief held by younger children that good behavior is obedient behavior and that acts should be judged in terms of the consequences, not on the basis of the motives behind the acts.

motive to avoid success. A hypothesized personality trait. People who score high on this trait are believed to avoid success out of fear of negative consequences.

natural experiment. An experiment in which the change in the independent variable occurs without the intervention of the investigator.

naturalistic observation. Unselective observation and recording of typical behavior in natural settings; a favorite method of anthropologists.

neo-Freudians. Followers of Freud who depart in various ways from some of Freud's doctrines.

nonmanipulative method. The so-called correlational method of science.

nonreactive measure. A type of measurement that does not change the phenomenon being measured.

normative-reeducative strategy. A strategy of planned change, which assumes that before trying to change a person or group, the cultural or normative factors (such as the past history of the person or group) must be taken into account.

norms. Socially defined and enforced standards concerning the way an individual should interpret the world and/or behave in it.

objectivity. Openness to observation by many observers; hence, a display of consensual agreement, a factual nature.

obscenity. That which is considered to be offensive to the mass populace, and hence which should be proscribed. Recent definitions have limited *obscenity* to offensive sexual materials.

observational method. A scientific method involving planned, systematic watching, guided by certain rules and conditions designed to improve accuracy.

Oedipus conflict. The attraction of the child toward the parent of the other sex, accompanied by envy and hostility toward the parent of the same sex.

A part of the phallic stage of personality development, according to Freud.

office landscaping *(Burolandschaft)*. A German innovation in office design in which office workers are separated not by walls, but by office furniture, plants, bookcases, and other movable articles.

open-ended question. One that the respondent answers in his own words.

operational definition. Definition of a concept by specifying the procedures or operations by which it is measured.

oral stage. The first stage in personality development, according to Freud. In this stage the child is concerned with satisfying the oral needs to suck and bite.

outside density. Density within neighborhoods, outside of dwellings.

paradigm. A broad method by which science progresses. A paradigm includes laws and theories; it poses problems for science to solve.

parametric study. An experiment in which three or more values of the independent variable are used.

participant observation. An observation method in which the observer becomes a member of a group being observed and participates in its activities but tries not to influence the activities himself.

perception. A person's immediate experience of other persons or objects, gained through the sense organs, but somewhat modified by the perceiver's personal characteristics and by social influences.

personal space. An area around a person's body inside which other people are not welcome; the zone of interpersonal distance "too close for comfort."

personal-space invasion. A violation of interpersonal-distance norms in which another person approaches to an uncomfortably close distance in uncrowded conditions, without attempting to initiate conversation. It usually results in signs of discomfort and eventual flight.

phallic stage. A stage of personality development, according to Freud. In this stage the child's concern is directed toward his or her sex organs.

phenomenological approach. A point of view in social psychology stating that the environment, *as the person perceives it*, is an important influence on behavior.

phenotype. A surface or observable characteristic; often a resultant rather than a causal factor.

philosophies of human nature. Expectations that people possess certain qualities and will behave in certain ways.

placebo. A substance that has no effects on an organism when ingested. Used for a control condition in studies on drug effects.

population. All the people having certain characteristics in common. An example would be all the registered voters in Canada. Also, the total group from which a sample is selected for study.

population density. The number of persons (or other animals) per unit of space, for example the number of persons per acre.

pornography. Written, oral, or visual materials that are considered to be sexually stimulating.

postfigurative culture. A culture in which children learn primarily from their elders.

power and toughness. Preoccupation with the dominance-submission, strong-weak, leader-follower dimension; identification with power figures; a characteristic of the authoritarian personality syndrome.

power-coercive strategy. A strategy that uses either violent or nonviolent pressures (lobbying, petitions, strikes, riots, and so on) to bring about social change.

prefigurative culture. A culture in which adults learn from their children.

prejudice. An unjustified evaluative reaction to a member of a racial, ethnic, or other group, which results solely from the object's membership in that group.

primacy effect. The tendency for the first information received to have the predominant effect on one's judgments or opinions about persons, objects, or issues.

primary environment. A place where a person spends a relatively large amount of time, relates to others on a personal basis, and performs a wide range of personally important activities. In such settings, the experience of crowding may be relatively difficult to resolve (Stokols, 1974).

primary territory. An area that an individual or group owns and controls on a relatively permanent basis. Such areas are central to the everyday lives of the occupants (Altman, 1975).

privacy. The selective control over access by others to oneself or one's group. Includes control over inputs from others and transmission of information to others (Altman, 1975).

probability sampling. Sampling done in such a way that every member of the population has a known probability (usually an equal probability) of being included.

probe. An optional follow-up question designed to obtain a complete answer in an interview.

projection. A defense mechanism in which a person seeks to alleviate conflict by seeing in others the motives or attributes about which he or she is anxious. (See also *assumed similarity*.)

projectivity. The disposition to believe that wild and dangerous things go on in the world; the projection outward of unconscious emotional responses. A characteristic of the authoritarian-personality syndrome.

prosocial behavior. Behavior that has positive social consequences, that improves the physical or psychological well-being of another person or persons.

proxemics. The study of interpersonal proximity and spatial behavior; it includes the study of crowding and territoriality.

psychoanalytic theory. A theory of personality first developed by Sigmund Freud, which has implications for social behavior.

psychological reactance. (See *reactance*.)

public territory. A space in a public place that is temporarily used by an individual or group (for example, a bench, cafeteria table, or bus seat).

quasi-experimental research. Social research in which the investigator does not have full experimental control over the independent variable, but does have extensive control over how, when, and for whom the dependent variable is measured.

quota sampling. Sampling done by assigning each interviewer a quota of respondents who are in specified categories of a classification system (usually using several dimensions such as urban-rural, sex, age, and so on). The total sample has the same proportion of people in each category as does the population, but it still is not completely representative because of probable bias in the interviewers' choices of respondents.

race. A population that is geographically contiguous and whose members breed together.

randomization. Assignment of conditions (for instance, assignment of subjects to treatment conditions) in a completely random manner—that is, a manner determined entirely by chance.

random sampling. A form of probability sampling that involves a completely random selection from a list that enumerates the whole population.

rational approach. Reaching conclusions by reasoning or speculating about wants rather than actively collecting data. Contrasted with the empirical approach.

reactance. A theory stating that if the opportunity to choose an object or activity is severely limited, its desirability is increased.

reaction to transgression. Emotional reaction to actions that violate some norm or moral code.

reactive measure. A measurement of a variable whose characteristics may be changed by the very act of measuring it.

real similarity. Correspondence between a perceiver's own personal characteristics and those of a person whom he or she is judging or describing (the criterion data).

recency effect. The tendency for the most recent information received to be predominant on one's judgment or opinion about persons, objects, or issues.

reciprocity. According to Piaget, a belief held by older children that punishment should be logically related to the offense so that the rule breaker will understand the implications of his or her misconduct. (See *expiatory punishment*.)

reciprocity norm. A norm or standard of behavior that says that people should help those who have helped them and refrain from injuring those who have helped them.

reinforcement. A consequence of a response that increases the probability that the response will be made again under the same stimulus conditions.

reinforcement theory. A theory that emphasizes that behavior is determined by the rewards or punishments given in response to it.

relative deprivation. One's perceived state in relation to the perceived state of others or in relation to unfulfilled expectations.

reliability. Consistency of measurement. Stability of scores over time, equivalence of scores on two forms of a test, and similarity of two raters' scoring of the same behavior are examples of three different kinds of reliability.

representativeness. Similarity of a sample to the population from which it is drawn—an essential characteristic of scientific sampling.

resistance to temptation. Suppression of a behavior that would have a high incidence if it were not for the influence of a prohibition or norm.

response. An alteration in a person's behavior that results from an external or internal stimulus.

response sets. Systematic ways of answering questions that are not directly related to the content of the question but related to the form or the social characteristics of the alternative answers. Common types of response sets are social desirability and acquiescence.

role. The socially defined pattern of behaviors that is expected of an individual who is assigned a certain social function, such as mother-in-law, clergyman, or baseball umpire.

sampling. Selecting a portion of a population— generally a relatively small proportion—for study.

sampling error. The inevitable margin of error in estimating the characteristics of a population from data on the characteristics of a sample.

scapegoating. The displacement of hostility upon less powerful groups when the source of frustration is not available for attack or not attackable for other reasons.

secondary deviance. A term used to refer to the proposition that so called "deviants" in society may be maladjusted as a result of the way society treats people in their condition, rather than as a result of the condition itself.

secondary environment. A place where a person spends little time, relates to others on an impersonal basis, and performs relatively unimportant activities (Stokols, 1974).

secondary territory. A physical area often claimed by a person or group, even though it is recognized that others may occupy that area at times.

self-fulfilling prophecy. A belief that certain events are true that leads them to become true in reality.

sensitivity training. A method by which normal persons gain feedback about their interpersonal skills and their effectiveness in groups.

set. Readiness to respond in a certain way to some stimulus situation; some types are response sets, perceptual sets, and verbal-response sets.

sex-role socialization. The process by which an individual learns the roles that society has defined as appropriate for men and for women and adopts those behaviors that are consistent with his/her own gender.

sex-typed. Referring to actions that are consistent with the society's norms regarding male and female behavior.

significance (statistical). The statistical probability *(p)* that a given numerical finding could have occurred by chance alone; the lower the probability of chance occurrence, the greater the significance of the finding.

simulation. A research method that attempts to imitate some crucial aspects of a real-world situation in order to gain more understanding of the underlying mechanisms that operate in that situation.

situated identities, theory of. A theory proposing that for each social situation, there is a certain pattern of behavior that conveys an identity that is appropriate for that setting.

social class. A grouping of persons who share common values, interests, income level, and educational level.

social-comparison theory. A theory, developed by Festinger, that proposes that we use other people as sources for comparison, so that we can evaluate our own attitudes and abilities.

social density. The number of persons in an area, which determines the amount of space per person and the potential number of interaction partners.

social-desirability bias. A response set to answer questions about oneself in the socially approved manner.

social distance. A person's acceptable degree of closeness (physically, socially, or psychologically) in regard to members of an ethnic, racial, or religious group.

social facilitation. The state in which the presence of others improves the quality or rate of an individual's performance.

social indicator. A statistic of direct normative interest, which facilitates concise, comprehensive, and balanced judgments about the condition of major aspects of a society.

social influence. An hypothesized cause of the *bystander effect*; a process by which a person in a group is less likely than a person who is alone to interpret an event as a situation calling for helping behavior.

socialization. A growing-up process in which children learn the norms of their society and acquire their own distinctive values, beliefs, and personality characteristics.

social-learning theory. A theory that proposes that social behavior develops as a result of observing others and of being rewarded for certain acts.

social movement. A form of collective behavior organized for the purpose of bringing about social change.

social psychology. The field of study concerned with the effects of other people on an individual's attitudes and behavior.

social-responsibility norm. A norm or standard of behavior that dictates that people should help persons who are dependent or in need of help.

sociofugal space. An arrangement of space that keeps people apart.

sociopetal space. An arrangement of space that brings people together.

spatial density. In research on crowding, the effect

of variations in the size of a room with a constant-sized group.

specimen record. A relatively complete, nonselective, sequential, narrative description of an individual's behavior, usually over a period of several hours.

statistical test. A mathematical procedure for determining the significance of a numerical finding—that is, the likelihood that it is a dependable finding that would occur regularly if repeated observations were made under the same conditions. The significance of the finding is stated in terms of a *p* value.

stereotype. A relatively rigid and oversimplified conception of a group of people, in which all individuals in the group are labeled with the so-called group characteristics.

stereotype accuracy. The ability to judge correctly the group mean, or norm, on any given trait; knowledge of "the generalized other."

stimulus. Any event, internal or external to the person, that brings about an alteration in the person's behavior.

stimulus generalization. The process in which, after a person learns to make a certain response to a certain stimulus, other similar but previously ineffective stimuli will also elicit that response.

stratified random sampling. A form of probability sampling that involves dividing the population into several categories (strata) on one or more dimensions (for example, region of the country, rural or urban residence) and then selecting respondents *randomly* from each category. This is a representative sample because the selection of respondents is random (in contrast to a quota sample, in which it is not).

stress. A psychological and physiological state that results from conditions perceived as threatening.

superego. According to Freud, the part of personality oriented toward doing what is morally proper; the conscience. The superego includes one's ego ideal, or ideal self-image.

superordinate goal. A goal that is an important one for several people and that cannot be achieved by any of the people working alone but only by their working together.

superstition and stereotypy. A component of authoritarianism, reflecting rigid thinking and a shift in responsibility from within one onto outside forces beyond one's control, especially to mystical determinants.

survey method. Asking questions systematically of a group of people.

systematically biased sampling. Sampling that misrepresents the characteristics of the population in some consistent way. For example, a sample drawn from lists of college alumni would not correctly represent the total population of adults in regard to educational level.

systematic sampling. A form of probability sampling that involves choosing in a systematic but unbiased manner from a list that enumerates the whole population (for example, choosing every tenth name from an alphabetical list).

territorial dominance. The phenomenon in which an individual dominates interactions with others when the interactions occur in the individual's own territory.

territoriality. Our tendency to control the use of physical areas and maintain them as our own.

territory. For many nonhuman species, a specific geographic region that an animal marks with scents or calls, uses as a nesting place, and defends against intrusion by other animals of the same species. For humans, an area whose occupant(s) perceive it as under their own control.

theory. A system of ideas containing some abstract concepts, some rules about the interconnections of these concepts, and some ways of linking these concepts to observed facts.

time samples. Observations made during a series of short periods of time, usually spread over many days or weeks.

transsexualism. A gender identity opposite to one's biological structure and hormonal balance. A person with male sex organs whose gender identity is female, or vice versa, is a transsexual.

unconscious. According to Freud, that part of the human psyche that is below the level of awareness.

understaffed setting. A behavior setting occupied by fewer people than are required to fill all the roles (also called *undermanned*).

unobtrusive measure. A measurement that can be made without the knowledge of the person being studied. An unobtrusive measure is also nonreactive.

validity. Accuracy or correctness of measurement (for example, the degree to which a test actually measures what it was intended to measure).

verification. The process of collecting facts to support or refute theoretical predictions.

References

Note: Those references that are especially recommended to students for supplementary reading are marked with an asterisk.

Abelson, R. P. Computers, polls, and public opinion—some puzzles and paradoxes. *Trans-Action,* 1968, *5,* 20–27.

Abelson, R. P., Aronson, E., McGuire, W. J., Newcomb, T. M., Rosenberg, M. J., & Tannenbaum, P. H. (Eds.). *Theories of cognitive consistency: A sourcebook.* Chicago: Rand-McNally, 1968.

Abelson, R. P., & Lesser, G. S. The measurement of persuasibility in children. In I. L. Janis and C. I. Hovland (Eds.), *Personality and persuasibility.* New Haven: Yale University Press, 1959. Pp. 141–166.

Abrahams, W. E. *The mind of Africa.* Chicago: University of Chicago Press, 1962.

Abramowitz, S. I., Abramowitz, C. V., Jackson, C., & Gomes, B. The politics of clinical judgment: What nonliberal examiners infer about women who don't stifle themselves. *Journal of Consulting and Clinical Psychology,* 1973, *41,* 385–391.

*Adair, J. G. *The human subject: The social psychology of the psychological experiment.* Boston: Little Brown, 1973.

Adams, D. K., Harvey, O. J., & Heslin, R. E. Variation in flexibility and creativity as a function of hypnotically induced past histories. In O. J. Harvey (Ed.), *Experience, structure, and adaptability.* New York: Springer, 1966. Pp. 217–234.

Adams, J. Inequity in social exchange. In L. Berkowitz (Ed.), *Advances in experimental social psychology* (Vol. 2). New York: Academic Press, 1965. Pp. 267–299.

Adams, S. Social climate and productivity in small groups. *American Sociological Review,* 1954, *19,* 421–425.

Adelson, J. What generation gap? *New York Times Magazine,* January 18, 1970, pp. 1–11ff.

Aderman, D. Elation, depression, and helping behavior. *Journal of Personality and Social Psychology,* 1972, *24,* 91–101.

Aderman, D., & Berkowitz, L. Observational set, empathy, and helping. *Journal of Personality and Social Psychology,* 1970, *14,* 141–148.

Aderman, D., Brehm, S. S., & Katz, L. B. Empathic observation of an innocent victim: The just world revisited. *Journal of Personality and Social Psychology,* 1974, *29,* 342–347.

*Adorno, T., Frenkel-Brunswik, E., Levinson, D., & Sanford, N. *The authoritarian personality.* New York: Harper, 1950.

AFL-CIO American Federationist. The credit intelligence web. April 1971, pp. 7–14.

Aiello, J. R. A test of equilibrium theory: Visual interaction in relation to orientation, distance and sex of interactants. *Psychonomic Science,* 1972, *27,* 335–336.

Aiello, J. R., & Aiello, T. The development of personal space: Proxemic behavior of children 6 through 16. *Human Ecology,* 1974, *2*(3), 177–189.

Aiello, J. R., & Cooper, R. E. Use of personal space as a function of social affect. *Proceedings, 80th Annual Convention, American Psychological Association,* 1972, *7,* 207–208.

Aiello, J. R., Epstein, Y. M., & Karlin, R. A. Effects of crowding on electrodermal activity. *Sociological Symposium,* 1975, *14,* 43–57. (a)

Aiello, J. R., Epstein, Y. M., & Karlin, R. A. *Field experimental research on human crowding.* Paper presented at the meeting of the Eastern Psychological Association, New York City, April 1975. (b)

Ainsworth, M. D. S. *Infancy in Uganda.* Baltimore: Johns Hopkins University Press, 1967.

Ajzen, I., & Fishbein, M. The prediction of behavioral intentions in a choice situation. *Journal of Experimental Social Psychology,* 1969, *5,* 400–416.

Ajzen, I., & Fishbein, M. The prediction of behavior from attitudinal and normative behaviors. *Journal of Experimental Social Psychology,* 1970, *6,* 466–487.

Ajzen, I., & Fishbein, M. Attitudes and normative beliefs as factors influencing behavioral intentions. *Journal of Personality and Social Psychology,* 1972, *21,* 1–9.

Alexander, C. N., & Knight, G. W. Situated identities and social psychological experimentation. *Sociometry,* 1971, *34,* 65–82.

Alexander, C. N., & Sagatun, I. An attributional analysis of experimental norms. *Sociometry,* 1973, *36,* 127–142.

Alexander, C. N., Jr., Zucker, L. G., & Brody, C. L. Experimental expectations and autokinetic experiences: Consistency theories and judgmental convergence. *Sociometry,* 1970, *33,* 108–122.

Alexander, H. B. A comparison of the ranks of the American states in Army Alpha and in socioeconomic status. *School and Society,* 1922, *16,* 388–392.

673

Alfert, E. Comment on promotion of prejudice. *Journal of Social Issues*, 1969, *25*(4), 206–212. (a)

Alfert, E. Response to Jensen's rejoinder. *Journal of Social Issues*, 1969, *25*(4), 217–219. (b)

Alger, I., & Rusk, H. The rejection of help by some disabled people. *Archives of Physical Medicine Rehabilitation*, 1955, *36*, 279–281.

Alinsky, S. *Rules for radicals*. New York: Random House, 1971.

Allen, G., & Pettigrew, K. D. Heritability of IQ by social class: Evidence inconclusive. *Science*, 1973, *182*, 1042–1044.

Allen, V. L. Situational factors in conformity. In L. Berkowitz (Ed.), *Advances in experimental social psychology* (Vol. 2). New York: Academic Press, 1965. Pp. 133–170.

*Allen, V. L. (Issue Ed.) Ghetto riots. *Journal of Social Issues*, 1970, *26*(1). (a)

Allen, V. L. Toward understanding riots: Some perspectives. *Journal of Social Issues*, 1970, *26*(1), 1–19. (b)

Allen, V. L., & Levine, J. M. Social support, dissent, and conformity. *Sociometry*, 1968, *31*, 138–149.

Allinsmith, W. Moral standards: II. The learning of moral standards. In D. R. Miller & G. E. Swanson (Eds.), *Inner conflict and defense*. New York: Holt, 1960. Pp. 141–176.

Allport, F. H. *Social psychology*. Cambridge, Mass.: Riverside Press, 1924.

Allport, G. W. Attitudes. In C. Murchison (Ed.), *Handbook of social psychology*. Worcester, Mass.: Clark University Press, 1935. Pp. 789–844.

Allport, G. W. Prejudice, a problem in psychological and social causation. *Journal of Social Issues*, Supplement Series, No. 4, 1950.

*Allport, G. W. *The nature of prejudice*. Garden City, N.Y.: Doubleday Anchor, 1958. (Originally published, 1954.)

Allport, G. W. What units shall we employ? In G. Lindzey (Ed.), *Assessment of human motives*. New York: Rinehart, 1958. Pp. 239–260.

Allport, G. W. *Pattern and growth in personality*. New York: Holt, Rinehart & Winston, 1961.

Allport, G. W. The general and the unique in psychological science. *Journal of Personality*, 1962, *30*, 405–422.

Allport, G. W. Traits revisited. *American Psychologist*, 1966, *21*, 1–10.

Allport, G. W. The historical background of modern social psychology. In G. Lindzey & E. Aronson (Eds.), *Handbook of social psychology* (Vol. 1) (2nd ed.). Reading, Mass.: Addison-Wesley, 1968. Pp. 1–80.

Allport, G. W., & Kramer, B. M. Some roots of prejudice. *Journal of Psychology*, 1946, *22*, 9–39.

Almedingen, E. M. *The Empress Alexandra: 1872–1918*. London: Hutchison, 1961.

Almquist, E. M., & Angrist, S. S. Role model influences on college women's career aspirations. *Merrill-Palmer Quarterly*, 1971, *17*, 263–279.

Alper, T. G. Achievement motivation in college women: A now-you-see-it-now-you-don't phenomenon. *American Psychologist*, 1974, *29*, 194–203.

Alper, T. G., & Boring, E. G. Intelligence-test scores of north-ern and southern White and Negro recruits in 1918. *Journal of Abnormal and Social Psychology*, 1944, *39*, 471–474.

Altemeyer, R. A. *Balancing the F scale*. Paper presented at the meeting of the American Psychological Association, Washington, D.C., September 1969.

Altemeyer, R. A., & Jones, K. Sexual identity, physical attractiveness, and seating position as determinants of influence in discussion groups. *Canadian Journal of Behavioural Science*, 1974, *6*, 357–375.

*Altman, I. *The environment and social behavior: Privacy, personal space, territory, and crowding*. Monterey, Calif.: Brooks/Cole, 1975.

Altman, I., Nelson, P. A., & Lett, E. E. The ecology of home environments. *Catalog of Selected Documents in Psychology*. Washington, D.C.: American Psychological Association, Spring 1972.

*Altman, I., & Taylor, D. A. *Social penetration: The development of interpersonal relations*. New York: Holt, 1973.

Altman, I., Taylor, D., & Wheeler, L. Ecological aspects of group behavior in isolation. *Journal of Applied Social Psychology*, 1971, *1*, 76–100.

Altus, W. D. Birth order and its sequelae. *Science*, 1966, *151*, 44–49.

American Psychological Association. *Ethical standards of psychologists*. Washington, D.C.: American Psychological Association, 1953.

American Psychological Association. Special Issue: Testing and public policy. *American Psychologist*, 1965, *20*, 855–1005.

American Psychological Association. *Casebook on ethical standards of psychologists*. Washington, D.C.: American Psychological Association, 1967.

American Psychological Association. *Ethical principles in the conduct of research with human participants*. Washington, D.C.: American Psychological Association, 1973.

Amir, Y. Contact hypothesis in ethnic relations. *Psychological Bulletin*, 1969, *71*, 319–342.

Amoroso, D. M., & Brown, M. *Some problems in studying the effects of erotic materials*. Research Report No. 28. Waterloo, Ontario, Canada: Department of Psychology, University of Waterloo, September 1971.

Amoroso, D. M., Brown, M., Pruesse, M., Ware, E. E., & Pilkey, D. W. An investigation of behavioral, psychological, and physiological reactions to pornographic stimuli. *Technical Reports of the Commission on Obscenity and Pornography* (Vol. 8). Washington, D. C.: U. S. Government Printing Office, 1971.

Amsel, A. The role of frustrative nonreward in noncontinuous reward situations. *Psychological Bulletin*, 1958, *55*, 102–119.

Amsel, A. Frustrative nonreward in partial reinforcement and discrimination learning: Some recent history and a theoretical extension. *Psychological Review*, 1962, *69*, 306–328.

Anastasi, A. *Differential psychology* (3rd ed.). New York: Macmillan, 1958.

Anastasi, A., & D'Angelo, R. Y. A comparison of Negro and

White preschool children in language development and Goodenough Draw-A-Man I.Q. *Journal of Genetic Psychology*, 1952, *81*, 147–165.

Anchor, K. N., & Cross, H. J. Maladaptive aggression, moral perspective, and the socialization process. *Journal of Personality and Social Psychology*, 1974, *30*, 163–168.

Anderson, J. P., & Perlman, D. Effects of an adult's preaching and responsibility for hypocritical behavior on children's altruism. *Proceedings of the 81st Annual Convention, American Psychological Association*, 1973, *8*, 291–292.

Anderson, N. H. Application of an additive model to impression formation. *Science*, 1962, *138*, 817–818.

Anderson, N. H. Averaging versus adding as a stimulus-combination rule in impression formation. *Journal of Experimental Psychology*, 1965, *70*, 394–400.

Anderson, N. H. Likableness ratings of 555 personality-trait words. *Journal of Personality and Social Psychology*, 1968, *9*, 272–279. (a)

Anderson, N. H. A simple model of information integration. In R. P. Abelson, E. Aronson, W. J. McGuire, T. M. Newcomb, M. J. Rosenberg, & P. H. Tannenbaum (Eds.), *Theories of cognitive consistency: A sourcebook*. Chicago: Rand-McNally, 1968. Pp. 731–743. (b)

Anderson, N. H. Cognitive algebra: Integration theory applied to social attribution. In L. Berkowitz (Ed.), *Advances in experimental social psychology* (Vol. 7). New York: Academic Press, 1974. Pp. 1–101.

Anderson, N. H., & Alexander, G. R. Choice test of the averaging hypothesis for information integration. *Cognitive Psychology*, 1971, *2*, 313–324.

Anderson, N. H., Lindner, R., & Lopes, L. L. Integration theory applied to judgments of group attractiveness. *Journal of Personality and Social Psychology*, 1973, *26*, 400–408.

Anderson, R. C. Learning in discussions: A résumé of the authoritarian-democratic studies. *Harvard Educational Review*, 1959, *29*, 201–215.

Andreoli, V. A., Worchel, S., & Folger, R. Implied threat to behavioral freedom. *Journal of Personality and Social Psychology*, 1974, *30*, 765–771.

Andrews, I. R., & Johnson, D. L. Small-group polarization of judgments. *Psychonomic Science*, 1971, *24*, 191–192.

Appley, M. H. (Ed.). *Adaptation-level theory: A symposium*. New York: Academic Press, 1971.

Arbuthnot, J. Modification of moral judgment through role playing. *Developmental Psychology*, 1975, *11*, 319–324.

Arbuthnot, J., & Andrasik, F. *Situational influences on moral judgment*. Paper presented at the meeting of the American Psychological Association, Montreal, August 1973.

Ardrey, R. *African genesis*. New York: Delta Books, 1961.

Ardrey, R. *The territorial imperative*. New York: Atheneum, 1966.

Ardrey, R. *The social contract*. New York: Atheneum, 1970.

Argyle, M., & Dean, J. Eye-contact, distance, and affiliation. *Sociometry*, 1965, *28*, 289–304.

Argyle, M., & Ingham, R. Gaze, mutual gaze, and proximity. *Semiotica*, 1972, *6*(2), 32–50.

Argyris, C. *Integrating the individual and the organization*. New York: Wiley, 1964.

Argyris, C. Dangers in applying results from experimental social psychology. *American Psychologist*, 1975, *30*, 469–485.

Aronfreed, J. The nature, variety, and social patterning of moral responses to transgression. *Journal of Abnormal and Social Psychology*, 1961, *63*, 223–241.

Aronfreed, J. *Conduct and conscience: The socialization of internalized control over behavior*. New York: Academic Press, 1968.

Aronfreed, J., & Paskal, V. *Altruism, empathy, and the conditioning of positive affect*. Unpublished manuscript, University of Pennsylvania, 1965.

Aronson, E. The effect of effort on the attractiveness of rewarded and unrewarded stimuli. *Journal of Abnormal and Social Psychology*, 1961, *63*, 375–380.

*Aronson, E. Some antecedents of interpersonal attraction. In W. J. Arnold & D. Levine (Eds.), *Nebraska symposium on motivation, 1969*. Lincoln, Nebr.: University of Nebraska Press, 1970. Pp. 143–173.

*Aronson, E. *The social animal*. San Francisco: Freeman, 1972.

Aronson, E., Blaney, N., Sikes, J., Stephan, C., & Snapp, M. Busing and racial tension: The jigsaw route to learning and liking. *Psychology Today*, 1975, *8*(9), 43–50.

Aronson, E., Blaney, N., & Stephan, C. *Cooperation in the classroom: The jigsaw puzzle model*. Paper presented at the meeting of the American Psychological Association, Chicago, September 1975.

Aronson, E., & Carlsmith, J. M. Experimentation in social psychology. In G. Lindzey & E. Aronson (Eds.), *Handbook of social psychology* (Vol. 2) (2nd ed.). Reading, Mass.: Addison-Wesley, 1968. Pp. 1–79.

Aronson, E., & Cope, V. My enemy's enemy is my friend. *Journal of Personality and Social Psychology*, 1968, *8*, 8–12.

Aronson, E., & Golden, B. W. The effect of relevant and irrelevant aspects of communicator credibility on attitude change. *Journal of Personality*, 1962, *30*, 135–146.

Aronson, E., & Mills, J. The effect of severity of initiation on liking for a group. *Journal of Abnormal and Social Psychology*, 1959, *59*, 177–181.

Aronson, E., Willerman, B., & Floyd, J. The effect of a pratfall on increasing interpersonal attractiveness. *Psychonomic Science*, 1966, *4*, 157–158.

Asch, S. E. Forming impressions of personality. *Journal of Abnormal and Social Psychology*, 1946, *41*, 258–290.

Asch, S. E. Effects of group pressure upon the modification and distortion of judgments. In H. Guetzkow (Ed.), *Groups, leadership, and men*. Pittsburgh: Carnegie Press, 1951. Pp. 177–190.

*Asch, S. E. *Social psychology*, Englewood Cliffs, N.J.: Prentice-Hall, 1952.

Asch, S. E. Studies of independence and conformity: A minority of one against a unanimous majority. *Psychological Monographs*, 1956, *70*(9, Whole No. 416).

Asch, S. E. Effects of group pressure upon modification and distortion of judgments. In E. E. Maccoby, T. M. Newcomb, & E. L. Hartley (Eds.), *Readings in social psychology* (3rd ed.). New York: Holt, 1958. Pp. 174–183.

Asher, E. J. The inadequacy of current intelligence tests for testing Kentucky mountain children. *Journal of Genetic Psychology*, 1935, *46*, 480–486.

Ashmore, R. D. Prejudice: Causes and cures. In B. E. Collins, *Social psychology*. Reading, Mass.: Addison-Wesley, 1970. Pp. 243–339.

*Ashmore, R. D., & McConahay, J. B. *Psychology and America's urban dilemmas*. New York: McGraw-Hill, 1975.

Ashmore, R. D., Ramchandra, V., & Jones, R. A. *Censorship as an attitude change induction*. Paper presented at the meeting of the Eastern Psychological Association, New York City, April 1971.

Astin, H. S. *The woman doctorate in America*. New York: Russell Sage Foundation, 1969.

Athanasiou, R. A review of public attitudes on sexual issues. In J. Zubin & J. Money (Eds.), *Critical issues in contemporary sexual behavior*. Baltimore: Johns Hopkins University Press, 1973. Pp. 361–390.

Athanasiou, R., & Sarkin, R. Premarital sexual behavior and postmarital adjustment. *Archives of Sexual Behavior*, 1974, *3*(3), 207–225.

Athanasiou, R., Shaver, P., & Tavris, C. Sex. *Psychology Today*, 1970, *4*(3), 39–52.

Athanasiou, R., & Yoshioka, G. A. The spatial character of friendship formation. *Environment and Behavior*, 1973, *5*, 43–65.

Atkins, A., Deaux, K., & Bieri, J. Latitude of acceptance and attitude change: Empirical evidence for a reformulation. *Journal of Personality and Social Psychology*, 1967, *6*, 47–54.

Atyas, J., & Wrightsman, L. S. A time for taking stock. In L. S. Wrightsman, *Assumptions about human nature: A social-psychological analysis*. Monterey, Calif.: Brooks/Cole, 1974. Pp. 210–223.

Austin, W. T., & Bates, F. L. Ethological indicators of dominance and territory in a human captive population. *Social Forces*, 1974, *52*, 447–455.

Averill, J. R. Personal control over aversive stimuli and its relation to stress. *Psychological Bulletin*, 1973, *80*, 286–303.

Ax, A. F. The physiological differentiation of emotional states. *Psychosomatic Medicine*, 1953, *15*, 433–442.

Azrin, N. H., Hutchinson, R. R., & Hake, D. F. Attack, avoidance, and escape reactions to aversive shock. *Journal of Experimental Analysis of Behavior*, 1966, *9*, 191–204.

Bachtold, L. M., & Werner, E. E. Personality profiles of gifted women: Psychologists. *American Psychologist*, 1970, *25*, 234–243.

Back, K. W. Influence through social communication. *Journal of Abnormal and Social Psychology*, 1951, *46*, 9–23.

*Back, K. W. *Beyond words: The story of sensitivity training and the encounter movement*. New York: Russell Sage Foundation, 1972.

Back, K. W., & Davis, K. E. Some personal and situational factors relevant to the consistency and prediction of con-

forming behavior. *Sociometry*, 1965, *28*, 227–240.

Backman, C. W., & Secord, P. F. The effect of perceived liking on interpersonal attraction. *Human Relations*, 1959, *12*, 379–384.

Baer, D. M., & Wright, J. C. Developmental psychology. In M. R. Rosenzweig & L. W. Porter (Eds.), *Annual review of psychology* (Vol. 25). Palo Alto, Calif.: Annual Reviews, 1974, Pp. 1–82.

Bailey, K., Hartnett, J., & Gibson, S. Implied threat and the territorial factor in personal space. *Psychological Reports*, 1972, *30*, 263–270.

Baker, N. J., & Wrightsman, L. S. The *Zeitgeist* and philosophies of human nature, or where have all the idealistic imperturbable freshmen gone? In L. S. Wrightsman, *Assumptions about human nature: A social-psychological approach*. Monterey, Calif.: Brooks/Cole, 1974. Pp. 166–180.

Baker, R. K., & Ball, S. J. (Eds.). *Mass media and violence* (Vol. 9). National Commission on the Causes and Prevention of Violence Staff Study Series. Washington, D.C.: U.S. Government Printing Office, 1969.

Baldwin, A. L. A cognitive theory of socialization. In D. A. Goslin (Ed.), *Handbook of socialization theory and research*. Chicago: Rand-McNally, 1969. Pp. 325–345.

Bales, R. F. The equilibrium problem in small groups. In T. Parsons, R. F. Bales, & E. A. Shils (Eds.), *Working papers in the theory of action*. Glencoe, Ill.: Free Press, 1953. Pp. 111–161.

Bales, R. F. Task roles and social roles in problem-solving groups. In E. E. Maccoby, T. M. Newcomb, & E. L. Hartley (Eds.), *Readings in social psychology* (3rd ed.). New York: Holt, Rinehart, & Winston, 1958. Pp. 396–413.

Bales, R. F. *Personality and interpersonal behavior*. New York: Holt, Rinehart, & Winston, 1970.

Bandler, R. J., Madaras, G. R., & Bem, D. J. Self-observation as a source of pain perception. *Journal of Personality and Social Psychology*, 1968, *9*, 205–209.

Bandura, A. Influence of model's reinforcement contingencies on the acquisition of imitative responses. *Journal of Personality and Social Psychology*, 1965, *1*, 589–595. (a)

Bandura, A. Vicarious processes: A case of no-trial learning. In L. Berkowitz (Ed.), *Advances in experimental social psychology* (Vol. 2). New York: Academic Press, 1965. Pp. 1–55. (b)

Bandura, A. Theoretical approaches to socialization. In D. A. Goslin (Ed.), *Handbook of socialization theory and research*. Chicago: Rand-McNally, 1969. Pp. 213–262.

Bandura, A. (Ed.) *Psychological modeling: Conflicting theories*. Chicago: Aldine-Atherton, 1971.

*Bandura, A. *Aggression: A social learning analysis*. Englewood Cliffs, N.J.: Prentice-Hall, 1973.

*Bandura, A. Behavior theory and the models of man. *American Psychologist*, 1974, *29*, 859–869.

Bandura, A., & McDonald, F. J. Influence of social reinforcement and the behavior of models in shaping children's moral judgments. *Journal of Abnormal and Social Psychology*, 1963, *57*, 274–281.

Bandura, A., & Mischel, W. Modification of self-imposed delay of reward through exposure to live and symbolic models. *Journal of Personality and Social Psychology*, 1965, *2*, 698–705.

Bandura, A., Ross, D., & Ross, S. Transmission of aggression through imitation of aggressive models. *Journal of Abnormal and Social Psychology*, 1961, *63*, 575–582.

Bandura, A., Ross, D., & Ross, S. Imitation of film-mediated aggressive models. *Journal of Abnormal and Social Psychology*, 1963, *66*, 3–11.

Bandura, A., & Walters, R. *Social learning and personality development*. New York: Holt, Rinehart, & Winston, 1963.

Banfield, E. C. *The unheavenly city*. Boston: Little-Brown, 1970.

Bannister, D. (Ed.). *Perspectives on personal construct theory*. New York: Academic Press, 1970.

Barach, J. A. Self-confidence, risk-handling, and mass communications. In P. R. McDonald (Ed.), *Marketing involvement in society and the economy*. Fall Conference Proceedings of the American Marketing Association, Series #30, 1969. Pp. 323–329.

Barach, J. A. *A resolution for conflicting theories and data concerning generalized self-confidence and persuasibility*. Paper presented at the meeting of the American Psychological Association, New Orleans, September 1974.

Barash, D. P. Human ethology: Personal space reiterated. *Environment and Behavior*, 1973, *5*, 67–73.

Barber, J. D. *The presidential character*. Englewood Cliffs, N. J.: Prentice-Hall, 1972.

Barber, T. X. Experimental hypnosis. In B. B. Wolman (Ed.), *Handbook of general psychology*. Englewood Cliffs, N. J.: Prentice-Hall, 1973. Pp. 942–963.

Barber, T. X., & Calverley, D. S. An experimental study of "hypnotic" (auditory and visual) hallucinations. *Journal of Abnormal and Social Psychology*, 1964, *63*, 13–20.

Barber, T. X., & Calverley, D. S. Effects on recall of hypnotic induction, motivational suggestions, and suggested regression: A methodological and experimental analysis. *Journal of Abnormal Psychology*, 1966, *71*, 169–180.

Barber, T. X., & Calverley, D. S. Effects of hypnotic induction, suggestions of anesthesia, and distraction on subjective and physiological responses to pain. Paper presented at the meeting of the Eastern Psychological Association, Philadelphia, April 1969.

Barber, T. X., & Silver, M. J. Fact, fiction, and the experimenter-bias effect. *Psychological Bulletin Monograph Supplement*, 1968, *70*(6, Pt. 2), 1–29. (a)

Barber, T. X., & Silver, M. J. Pitfalls in data analysis and interpretation: A reply to Rosenthal. *Psychological Bulletin Monograph Supplement*, 1968, *70*(6, Pt. 2), 48–62. (b)

Barch, A. M., Trumbo, D., & Nangle, J. Social setting and conformity to a legal requirement. *Journal of Abnormal and Social Psychology*, 1957, *55*, 396–398.

Barclay, A. M. Urinary acid phosphate secretion in sexually aroused males. *Journal of Experimental Research in Personality*, 1970, *4*, 233–238.

Bard, M. Alternatives to traditional law enforcement. In F. Korten, S. W. Cook., & J. I. Lacey (Eds.), *Psychology and the problems of society*. Washington, D.C.: American Psychological Association, 1970. Pp. 128–132.

Bardwick, J. M. *Psychology of women*. New York: Harper & Row, 1971.

Barefoot, J. C., Hoople, H., & McClay, D. Avoidance of an act which would violate personal space. *Psychonomic Science*, 1972, *28*, 205–206.

Barker, E. N. Authoritarianism of the political right, center, and left. *Journal of Social Issues*, 1963, *19*(2), 63–74.

Barker, R. G. Ecology and motivation. In M. R. Jones (Ed.), *Nebraska symposium on motivation, 1960*. Lincoln: University of Nebraska Press, 1960. Pp. 1–49.

Barker, R. G. (Ed.) *The stream of behavior*. New York: Appleton-Century-Crofts, 1963.

Barker, R. G. Explorations in ecological psychology. *American Psychologist*, 1965, *20*, 1–14.

*Barker, R. G. *Ecological psychology: Concepts and methods for studying the environment of human behavior*. Stanford, Calif.: Stanford University Press, 1968.

Barker, R. G., Dembo, T., & Lewin, K. Frustration and regression: A study of young children. *University of Iowa Studies in Child Welfare*, 1941, *18*, No. 1.

Barker, R. G., & Schoggen, P. *Qualities of community life*. San Francisco: Jossey-Bass, 1973.

Barnett, S. A. On the hazards of analogies. In M. F. A. Montagu (Ed.), *Man and aggression* (2nd ed.). New York: Oxford University Press, 1973. Pp. 75–83.

Barocas, R., & Gorlow, L. Self-report personality measurement and conformity behavior. *Journal of Social Psychology*, 1967, *71*, 227–234.

Barocas, R., & Karoly, P. Effects of physical appearance on social responsiveness. *Psychological Reports*, 1972, *31*, 495–500.

Barocas, R., & Vance, F. L. *Physical appearance and personal adjustment counseling*. Paper presented at the meeting of the Eastern Psychological Association, Boston, April 1972.

Baron, R. A. Aggression as a function of ambient temperature and prior anger arousal. *Journal of Personality and Social Psychology*, 1972, *21*, 183–189.

Baron, R. A. *Threatened retaliation as an inhibitor of human aggression: Mediating effects of the instrumental value of aggression*. Paper presented at the meeting of the Midwestern Psychological Association, Chicago, May 1973.

Baron, R. A. Aggression as a function of victim's pain cues, level of prior anger arousal, and exposure to an aggressive model. *Journal of Personality and Social Psychology*, 1974, *29*, 117–124.

Baron, R. A., & Bell, P. A. Aggression and heat: Mediating effects of prior provocation and exposure to an aggressive model. *Journal of Personality and Social Psychology*, 1975, *31*, 825–832.

Baron, R. A., Byrne, D., & Griffitt, W. *Social psychology: Understanding human interaction*. Boston: Allyn & Bacon, 1974.

Baron, R. A., & Kepner, C. R. Model's behavior and attraction toward the model as determinants of adult aggressive behavior. *Journal of Personality and Social Psychology*, 1970, *14*, 335–344.

Baron, R. A., & Lawton, S. F. Environmental influences on aggression: The facilitation of modeling effects by high ambient temperatures. *Psychonomic Science*, 1972, *26*, 80–83.

Baron, R. S., Baron, P. H., & Miller, N. The relation between distraction and persuasion. *Psychological Bulletin*, 1973, *80*, 310–323.

Baron, R. S., Roper, G., & Baron, P.H. Group discussion and the stingy shift. *Journal of Personality and Social Psychology*, 1974, *30*, 538–545.

Barron, F. Some personality correlates of independence of judgment. *Journal of Personality*, 1953, *21*, 287–297.

Barron, F. Review of the Edwards Personal Preference Schedule. In O. K. Buros (Ed.), *The fifth mental measurements yearbook*. Highland Park, N. J.: Gryphon Press, 1959. Pp. 114–117.

Barry, H., III, Bacon, M. K., & Child, I. L. A cross-cultural survey of some sex differences in socialization. *Journal of Abnormal and Social Psychology*, 1957, *55*, 327–332.

Baruch, G. K. Maternal influences upon college women's attitudes toward women and work. *Developmental Psychology*, 1972, *6*, 32–37.

Bass, B. M. Authoritarianism or acquiescence? *Journal of Abnormal and Social Psychology*, 1955, *51*, 616–623.

Bass, B. M. *Leadership, psychology, and organizational behavior*. New York: Harper & Row, 1960.

Bateson, N. Familiarization, group discussion, and risk taking. *Journal of Experimental Social Psychology*, 1966, *2*, 119–129.

Bauer, R. A. (Ed.) *Social indicators*. Cambridge, Mass.: M.I.T. Press, 1966.

Bauer, R. A. Self-confidence and persuasibility: One more time. *Journal of Marketing Research*, 1970, *7*, 256–258.

Baum, A., & Davis, G. E. *Spatial and social aspects of crowding perception*. Unpublished manuscript, Department of Psychology, State University of New York at Stony Brook, 1974.

Baum, A., & Greenberg, C. I. The behavioral and perceptual effects of anticipated crowding. *Journal of Personality and Social Psychology*, 1975, *32*, 671–679.

Baum, A., Harpin, R. E., & Valins, S. *The role of group phenomena in the experience of crowding*. Unpublished manuscript, Department of Psychology, Trinity College, 1975.

Baum, A., Riess, M., & O'Hara, J. Architectural variants of reaction to spatial invasion. *Environment and Behavior*, 1974, *6*, 91–100.

Baum, A., & Valins, S. Residential environments, group size, and crowding. *Proceedings, 81st Annual Convention, American Psychological Association*, 1973, *8*, 211–212.

Baumrin, B. H. The immorality of irrelevance: The social role of science. In F. F. Korten, S. W. Cook, & J. I. Lacey (Eds.), *Psychology and the problems of society*. Washington, D. C.: American Psychological Association, 1970. Pp. 73–83.

Baumrind, D. Some thoughts on the ethics of research: After reading Milgram's "Behavioral study of obedience." *American Psychologist*, 1964, *19*, 421–423.

Baxter, G. W., Jr. *Changes in PHN after one year and two years in college*. Unpublished master's thesis, Department of Psychology, George Peabody College for Teachers, 1968.

Baxter, J. C., & Deanovich, B. F. Anxiety arousing effects of inappropriate crowding. *Journal of Personality and Social Psychology*, 1970, *35*, 174–178.

Beach, F. A. (Ed.) *Sex and behavior*. New York: Wiley, 1965.

Beardslee, D. C., & Fogelson, R. Sex differences in sexual imagery aroused by musical stimulation. In J. W. Atkinson (Ed.), *Motives in fantasy, action, and society*. Princeton, N. J.: Van Nostrand, 1958. Pp. 132–142.

Becker, F. D. Study of spatial markers. *Journal of Personality and Social Psychology*, 1973, *26*, 439–445.

Becker, F. D., & Mayo, C. Delineating personal distance and territoriality. *Environment and Behavior*, 1971, *3*, 375–381.

Becker, G. Affiliate perception and the arousal of the participation-affiliation motive. *Perceptual and Motor Skills*, 1967, *24*, 991–997.

Beez, W. V. Influence of biased psychological reports on teacher behavior and pupil performance. *Proceedings, 76th Annual Convention, American Psychological Association*, 1968, *3*, 605–606.

Beilin, L. A. *Program design and curriculum development for police training*. Paper presented at the meeting of the American Psychological Association, New Orleans, September 1974.

Bell, P. R., & Jamieson, B. D. Publicity of initial decisions and the risky shift phenomenon. *Journal of Experimental Social Psychology*, 1970, *6*, 329–345.

Bell, R. *Self-concept and aspirations of working-class mothers*. Paper presented at the meeting of the American Psychological Association, New York, September 1964.

Bell, R. R., & Chaskes, J. B. Premarital sexual experience among coeds, 1958 and 1968. *Journal of Marriage and the Family*, 1970, *32*, 81–84.

Bellow, S. A talk with the Yellow Kid. *The Reporter*, September 6, 1956, pp. 41–44.

Bem, D. J. An experimental analysis of self-persuasion. *Journal of Experimental Social Psychology*, 1965, *1*, 199–218.

Bem, D. J. Self-perception: An alternative interpretation of cognitive dissonance phenomena. *Psychological Review*, 1967, *74*, 183–200.

*Bem, D. J. *Beliefs, attitudes, and human affairs*. Monterey, Calif.: Brooks/Cole, 1970.

Bem, D. J. Constructing cross-situational consistencies in behavior: Some thoughts on Alker's critique of Mischel. *Journal of Personality*, 1972, *40*, 17–26. (a)

Bem, D. J. Self-perception theory. In L. Berkowitz (Ed.), *Advances in experimental social psychology*. Vol. 6. New York: Academic Press, 1972. Pp. 1–62. (b)

Bem, D. J., & McConnell, H. K. Testing the self-perception explanation of dissonance phenomena: On the salience of premanipulation attitudes. *Journal of Personality and Social Psychology*, 1970, *14*, 23–31.

Bem, S. L. Sex role adaptability: One consequence of psychological androgyny. *Journal of Personality and Social Psychology*, 1975, *31*, 634–643.

Bem, S. L., & Bem, D. J. Case study of a nonconscious ideology: Training the woman to know her place. In D. J. Bem, *Beliefs, attitudes, and human affairs.* Monterey, Calif.: Brooks/Cole, 1970. Pp. 89–99.

Bender, P. Definition of "obscene" under existing law. *Technical Reports of the Commission on Obscenity and Pornography* (Vol. 2). Washington, D. C.: U. S. Government Printing Office, 1971.

Bengston, V. L. Inter-age differences in perception and the generation gap. *The Gerontologist*, 1971, *11*, 85–90.

Bengston, V. L., Furlong, M. J., & Laufer, R. S. Time, aging, and the continuity of social structure: Themes and issues in generational analysis. *Journal of Social Issues*, 1974, *30*(2), 1–30.

*Bengston, V. L., & Laufer, R. S. (Issue Eds.). Youth, generations, and social change. *Journal of Social Issues*, 1974, *30*(2 & 3).

Benjamin, H. (Ed.) *The transsexual phenomenon.* New York: Julian Press, 1966.

Benjamin, H., & Masters, R. E. L. (Eds.). *Prostitutes and morality.* New York: Julian Press, 1964.

Bennis, W. G., Benne, K. D., & Chin, R. *The planning of change.* New York: Holt, Rinehart & Winston, 1968.

Bereiter, C., & Engelmann, S. *Teaching disadvantaged children in the preschool.* Englewood Cliffs, N. J.: Prentice-Hall, 1966.

Berelson, B. Content analysis. In G. Lindzey (Ed.), *Handbook of social psychology* (Vol. 1). Cambridge, Mass.: Addison-Wesley, 1954. Pp. 488–522.

Bergamini, J. *The tragic dynasty: A history of the Romanovs.* New York: Putnam's, 1969.

Berger, S. M. Conditioning through vicarious instigation. *Psychological Review*, 1962, *69*, 450–466.

Berger, S. M., & Lambert, W. W. Stimulus-response theory in contemporary social psychology. In G. Lindzey & E. Aronson (Eds.), *Handbook of social psychology* (Vol. 1) (2nd ed.). Reading, Mass.: Addison-Wesley, 1968. Pp. 81–178.

Bergman, B. A. *The effects of group size, personal space, and success-failure on physiological arousal, test performance, and questionnaire response.* Unpublished doctoral dissertation, Department of Psychology, Temple University, Philadelphia, Pa., 1971.

Berkowitz, L. Group standards, cohesiveness and productivity. *Human Relations*, 1954, *7*, 505–519.

Berkowitz, L. Aggressive cues in aggressive behavior and hostility catharsis. *Psychological Review*, 1964, *71*, 104–122.

Berkowitz, L. Some aspects of observed aggression. *Journal of Personality and Social Psychology*, 1965, *2*, 359–369. (a)

Berkowitz, L. The concept of aggressive drive: Some additional considerations. In L. Berkowitz (Ed.), *Advances in experimental social psychology* (Vol. 2). New York: Academic Press, 1965. Pp. 301–329. (b)

Berkowitz, L. The frustration-aggression hypothesis revisited.

In L. Berkowitz (Ed.), *Roots of aggression: A re-examination of the frustration-aggression hypothesis.* New York: Atherton, 1969. Pp. 1–20. (a)

*Berkowitz, L. (Ed.). *Roots of aggression: A re-examination of the frustration-aggression hypothesis.* New York: Atherton, 1969. (b)

Berkowitz, L. Social norms, feelings, and other factors affecting helping and altruism. In L. Berkowitz (Ed.), *Advances in experimental social psychology* (Vol. 6). New York: Academic Press, 1972. Pp. 63–108.

Berkowitz, L. Some determinants of impulsive aggression: Role of mediated associations with reinforcements for aggression. *Psychological Review*, 1974, *81*, 165–176.

Berkowitz, L., & Alioto, J. T. The meaning of an observed event as a determinant of its aggressive consequences. *Journal of Personality and Social Psychology*, 1973, *28*, 206–217.

Berkowitz, L., & Daniels, L. R. Responsibility and dependency. *Journal of Abnormal and Social Psychology*, 1963, *66*, 664–669.

Berkowitz, L., & Geen, R. G. Film violence and cue properties of available targets. *Journal of Personality and Social Psychology*, 1966, *3*, 525–530.

Berkowitz, L., & Geen, R. G. Stimulus qualities of the target of aggression: A further study. *Journal of Personality and Social Psychology*, 1967, *5*, 364–368.

Berkowitz, L., & Knurek, D. A. Label-mediated hostility generalization. *Journal of Personality and Social Psychology*, 1969, *13*, 200–206.

Berkowitz, L., & LePage, A. Weapons as aggression-eliciting stimuli. *Journal of Personality and Social Psychology*, 1967, *7*, 202–207.

Berkowitz, N. H., & Wolkon, G. H. A forced choice form of the F scale—free of acquiescent response set. *Sociometry*, 1964, *27*, 54–65.

Berscheid, E., & Walster, E. When does a harm-doer compensate a victim? *Journal of Personality and Social Psychology*, 1967, *6*, 435–441.

*Berscheid, E., & Walster, E. H. *Interpersonal attraction.* Reading, Mass.: Addison-Wesley, 1969.

Bickman, L. Social influence and diffusion of responsibility in an emergency. *Journal of Experimental Social Psychology*, 1972, *8*, 438–445.

Bickman, L., & Henchy, T. (Eds.). *Beyond the laboratory: Field research in social psychology.* New York: McGraw-Hill, 1972.

Bickman, L., & Kamzan, M. The effect of race and need on helping behavior. *Journal of Social Psychology*, 1973, *89*, 73–77.

Bickman, L., Teger, A., Gabriele, T., McLaughlin, C., Berger, M., & Sunday, E. Dormitory density and helping behavior. *Environment and Behavior*, 1974, *5*, 465–490.

Biddle, B. J., & Thomas, E. J. (Eds.). *Role theory: Concepts and research.* New York: Wiley, 1966.

Biddle, W. W., & Biddle, L. *The community development process.* New York: Holt, Rinehart & Winston, 1965.

Bieber, I., Dain, H. J., Dince, P. R., Drellich, M. G., Girand,

H. G., Gundlach, R. H., Kremer, M. W., Rifkin, A. H., Wilbur, C. B., & Bieber, T. B. *Homosexuality: A psychoanalytic study.* New York: Basic Books, 1962.

Bienen, H. *Violence and social change: A review of current literature.* Chicago: University of Chicago Press, 1968.

Bieri, J., Atkins, A., Briar, S., Leaman, R. L., Miller, H., & Tripodi, T. *Clinical and social judgment.* New York: Wiley, 1966.

Billings, R. S. *Fiedler's contingency theory of leadership revisited: An analysis of group process.* Paper presented at the meeting of the American Psychological Association, New Orleans, August 1974.

Bird, C. *Social psychology.* New York: Appleton-Century-Crofts, 1940.

Bishop, G. F. Resolution and tolerance of cognitive inconsistency in a field situation: Change in attitude and beliefs following the Watergate affair. *Psychological Reports,* 1975, *36,* 747–753.

Black, E. Brave, new Tomorrowland. *New Times,* 1974, *3*(12), 51.

Blake, R. R., Rhead, C. C., Wedge, B., & Mouton, J. S. Housing architecture and social interaction. *Sociometry,* 1956, *19,* 133–139.

Blalock, H. M., Jr. *Toward a theory of minority-group relations.* New York: Wiley, 1957.

Blanchard, F. A., Weigel, R. H., & Cook, S. W. *The effect of relative competence of group members upon interpersonal attraction in cooperating interracial groups.* Unpublished manuscript, Institute of Behavioral Science, University of Colorado, 1974.

Blascovich, J., & Ginsburg, G. P. Emergent norms and choice shifts involving risk. *Sociometry,* 1974, *37,* 205–218.

Blascovich, J., Veach, T. L., & Ginsburg, G. P. Blackjack and the risky shift. *Sociometry,* 1973, *36,* 42–55.

Blatt, M. M., & Kohlberg, L. *The effects of classroom moral discussions upon children's level of moral judgment.* Unpublished manuscript, University of Chicago, 1969.

Blau, P. Cooperation and competition in a bureaucracy. *American Journal of Sociology,* 1954, *59,* 530–535.

Blauner, R. Internal colonialism and ghetto revolt. *Social Problems,* 1969, *16,* 393–408.

Bleda, P. R., & Castore, C. H. Social comparison, attraction, and choice of a comparison other. *Memory and Cognition,* 1973, *1,* 420–424.

Block, J. The assessment of communication role variations as a function of interactional context. *Journal of Personality,* 1952, *21,* 272–286.

Block, J. Personality characteristics associated with father's attitudes toward child rearing. *Child Development,* 1955, *26,* 41–48.

Block, J. *The challenge of response sets: Unconfounding meaning, acquiescence, and social desirability in the MMPI.* New York: Appleton-Century-Crofts, 1965.

Block, J., Haan, N., & Smith, M. B. Activism and apathy in contemporary adolescents. In J. F. Adams (Ed.), *Understanding adolescents: Current developments in adolescent psycholo-*gy. Boston: Allyn & Bacon, 1968. Pp. 198–231.

Bloom, B. S. *Stability and change in human characteristics.* New York: Wiley, 1964.

Bloom, B. S., Davis, A., & Hess, R. D. *Compensatory education for cultural deprivation.* New York: Holt, 1965.

Bloom, L. M., & Clark, R. D., III. The cost-reward model of helping behavior: A nonconfirmation. *Journal of Applied Social Psychology,* in press.

Blumenthal, M. D., Kahn, R. L., Andrews, F. M., & Head, K. B. *Justifying violence: Attitudes of American men.* Ann Arbor, Mich.: Institute for Social Research, 1972.

Blumer, D. Transsexualism, sexual dysfunction and temporal lobe disorder. In R. Green and J. Money (Eds.), *Transsexualism and sex reassignment.* Baltimore: Johns Hopkins Press, 1969. Pp. 213–219.

Bochner, S., & Insko, C. Communicator discrepancy, source credibility, and influence. *Journal of Personality and Social Psychology,* 1966, *4,* 614–621.

Boehm, V. R. *Changing career patterns for women in the Bell System.* Paper presented at the meeting of the American Psychological Association, New Orleans, August 1974.

Boeth, R. The great IQ controversy. *Newsweek,* December 17, 1973 issue, pp. 109–111.

*Boguslaw, R. *The new utopians: A study of system design and social change.* Englewood Cliffs, N.J.: Prentice-Hall, 1965.

Booth, A., & Welch, S. *The effects of crowding: A cross-national study.* Unpublished manuscript, Ministry of State for Urban Affairs, Ottawa, Canada, 1973.

Booth, A., & Welch, S. *Crowding and urban crime rates.* Paper presented at the meeting of the Midwest Sociological Association, Omaha, Nebraska, 1974.

Borgatta, E. F., & Bales, R. F. Sociometric status patterns and characteristics of interaction. *Journal of Abnormal and Social Psychology,* 1956, *43,* 289–297.

Borgatta, E. F., Couch, A. S., & Bales, R. F. Some findings relevant to the Great Man theory of leadership. *American Sociological Review,* 1954, *19,* 755–759.

Borrow, G. *Lavengro: The scholar, the gypsy, the priest.* London: T. N. Foulis, 1914.

Bose, C. E. *Jobs and gender: Sex and occupational prestige.* Baltimore, Md.: Center for Metropolitan Planning and Research, Johns Hopkins University, August 1973.

*Bosworth, A. R. *America's concentration camps.* New York: Bantam Books, 1968.

Bouchard, T. J., Jr. Personality, problem-solving procedure, and performance in small groups. *Journal of Applied Psychology,* 1969, *53,* 1–29.

Bouchard, T. J., Jr. Training, motivation, and personality as determinants of the effectiveness of brainstorming groups and individuals. *Journal of Applied Psychology,* 1972, *56,* 324–331.

Bouchard, T. J., Jr., Barsaloux, J., & Drauden, G. Brainstorming procedure, group size, and sex as determinants of the problem-solving effectiveness of groups and individuals. *Journal of Applied Psychology,* 1974, *59,* 135–138.

Bourlière, F. *The natural history of mammals.* New York: Knopf,

1956. (Originally published, 1954).

Bovard, E. W., Jr. Social norms and the individual. *Journal of Abnormal and Social Psychology*, 1948, *43*, 62–69.

Bowers, K. S. The effect of demands for honesty on reports of visual and auditory hallucinations. *International Journal of Clinical and Experimental Hypnosis*, 1967, *15*, 31–36.

Boyd, W. C. *Genetics and the races of man*. Boston: Little, Brown, 1950.

Braginsky, D. Machiavellianism and manipulative interpersonal behavior in children. *Journal of Experimental Social Psychology*, 1970, *6*, 77–99.

Brainerd, C. J. *Structures-of-the-whole: Is there any glue to hold the concrete-operational "stage" together?* Paper presented at the meeting of the Canadian Psychological Association, Windsor, Ontario, June 1974.

Bramel, D. Interpersonal attraction, hostility, and perception. In J. Mills (Ed.), *Experimental social psychology*. New York: Macmillan, 1969. Pp. 1–120.

Bramson, L., & Goethals, G. W. (Eds.). *War* (Rev. ed.). New York: Basic Books, 1968.

Brecher, R., & Brecher, E. (Eds.). *An analysis of human sexual response*. New York: Signet, 1966.

Brehm, J. W. *A theory of psychological reactance*. New York: Academic Press, 1966.

*Brehm, J. W. *Responses to loss of freedom: A theory of psychological reactance*. Morristown, N.J.: General Learning Press, 1972.

Brehm, J. W., & Cohen, A. R. *Explorations in cognitive dissonance*. New York: Wiley, 1962.

Brehm, J. W., & Cole, A. H. Effect of a favor which reduces freedom. *Journal of Personality and Social Psychology*, 1966, *3*, 420–426.

Brehm, J. W., Gatz, M., Goethals, G., McCrimmon, J., & Ward, L. *Psychological arousal and interpersonal attraction*. Unpublished manuscript, Duke University, 1970.

Breland, H. M. Birth order effects: A reply to Schooler. *Psychological Bulletin*, 1973, *80*, 210–212.

Brewer, M. B. Averaging versus summation in composite ratings of complex social stimuli. *Journal of Personality and Social Psychology*, 1968, *8*, 20–26.

Briand, P. L., Jr. (Ed.). *Hearings on mass media and violence* (Vol. 9-A). National Commission on the Causes and Prevention of Violence Staff Study Series. Washington, D.C.: U.S. Government Printing Office, 1969.

Brickman, P., & Bryan, J. H. Moral judgment of theft, charity, and third-party transfers that increase or decrease equality. *Journal of Personality and Social Psychology*, 1975, *31*, 156–161.

Brigham, J. C. Ethnic stereotypes. *Psychological Bulletin*, 1971, *76*, 15–38. (a)

Brigham, J. C. *Instructional set, attribution of traits to Blacks and racial attitude*. Paper presented at the meeting of the Southeastern Psychological Association, Miami Beach, April 1971. (b)

Brigham, J. C., & Severy, L. *Personality and attitude predictors of voting behavior*. Unpublished manuscript, Department of Psychology, Florida State University, 1973.

Brightman, H. J., & Urban, T. F. The influence of the dogmatic personality upon information processing: A comparison with a Bayesian information processor. *Organizational Behavior and Human Performance*, 1974, *11*, 266–276.

Brislin, R. W., & Lewis, S. A. Dating and physical attractiveness: Replication. *Psychological Reports*, 1968, *22*, 976.

Bristow, A. T. Furor over Shockley grows. *Race Relations Reporter*, December 3, 1973, 4(23), 1–3.

Brock, T. C., & Becker, L. A. Ineffectiveness of "overheard" counterpropaganda. *Journal of Personality and Social Psychology*, 1965, *2*, 654–660.

Brodsky, S. L. After the courtship: Psychologists and policemen work together. Paper presented at the meeting of the American Psychological Association, New Orleans, September 1974.

Brody, R. A. Some systemic effects of the spread of nuclear weapons technology: A study through simulation of a multi-nuclear future. *Journal of Conflict Resolution*, 1963, *7*, 663–753.

Bromley, D. D., & Britten, F. H. *Youth and sex: A study of 1300 college students*. New York: Harper, 1938.

Bronfenbrenner, U. *Two worlds of childhood: U.S. and U.S.S.R.* New York: Russell Sage Foundation, 1970.

Bronfenbrenner, U., & Devereux, E. G., Jr. *Adults and peers as sources of conformity and autonomy*. Paper presented at the Conference on Socialization for Competence, Puerto Rico, April 1965.

Brookes, M. J., & Kaplan, A. The office environment: Space planning and affective behavior. *Human Factors*, 1972, *14*(5), 373–391.

Broverman, D. M., Klaiber, E. L., Kobayashi, Y., & Vogel, W. Roles of activation and inhibition in sex differences in cognitive abilities. *Psychological Review*, 1968, *75*, 23–50.

Broverman, I. K., Broverman, D. M., Clarkson, F. E., Rosenkrantz, P. S., & Vogel, S. R. Sex-role stereotypes and clinical judgments of mental health. *Journal of Consulting and Clinical Psychology*, 1970, *34*, 1–7.

Broverman, I. K., Vogel, S. R., Broverman, D. M., Clarkson, F. E., & Rosenkrantz, P. S. Sex-role stereotypes: A current appraisal. *Journal of Social Issues*, 1972, *28*(2), 59–78.

Brown, B. R. The effects of need to maintain face on interpersonal bargaining. *Journal of Experimental Social Psychology*, 1968, *4*, 107–122.

Brown, B. R. Face-saving following experimentally induced embarrassment. *Journal of Experimental Social Psychology*, 1970, *6*, 255–271.

Brown, B. R., & Garland, H. The effects of incompetency, audience acquaintanceship, and anticipated evaluative feedback on face-saving behavior. *Journal of Experimental Social Psychology*, 1971, *7*, 490–502.

Brown, D. G., & Lynn, D. B. Human sexual development: An outline of components and concepts. In D. L. Taylor (Ed.), *Human sexual development: Perspectives in sex education*. Philadelphia: F. A. Davis, 1970. Pp. 73–87.

*Brown, J. A. C. *Techniques of persuasion: From propaganda to brainwashing*. Baltimore: Penguin, 1963.

Brown, J. S., & Farber, I. E. Emotions conceptualized as intervening variables—with suggestions toward a theory of frustration. *Psychological Bulletin*, 1951, *48*, 465–495.

Brown, M. E. The condemnation and persecution of hippies. *Trans-Action*, September 1969, pp. 33–34ff.

Brown, N. W., & Renz, P. Altering the reality self-concept of seventh grade culturally deprived girls in the inner city. *Adolescence*, 1973, *8*, 463–474.

Brown, P., & Elliott, R. Control of aggression in a nursery-school class. *Journal of Experimental Child Psychology*, 1965, *2*, 103–107.

Brown, R. *Social psychology*. New York: Free Press, 1965.

Brown, R., & Herrnstein, R. J. *Psychology*. Boston, Mass.: Little, Brown, 1975.

Brown, R. M. Historical patterns of violence in America. In H. D. Graham & T. R. Gurr (Eds.), *Violence in America*. New York: New American Library, 1969. Pp. 43–80.

Bruce, M. Factors affecting intelligence test performance of Whites and Negroes in the rural South. *Archives of Psychology*, 1940, No. 252.

Bruner, J. S., & Tagiuri, R. The perception of people. In G. Lindzey (Ed.), *Handbook of social psychology* (Vol. 2). Reading, Mass.: Addison-Wesley, 1954. Pp. 634–654.

Bruning, J. L., & Husa, F. T. Given names and stereotyping. *Developmental Psychology*, 1972, *7*, 91.

Bruvold, W. H. *Are beliefs and behavior consistent with attitudes? A preliminary restatement and some evidence from a survey research project*. Paper presented at the meeting of the Western Psychological Association, Los Angeles, April 1970.

Bryan, J. H. Why children help: A review. *Journal of Social Issues*, 1972, *28*(3), 87–104.

Bryan, J. H., & Davenport, M. *Donations to the needy: Correlates of financial contributions to the destitute* (Research Bulletin No. 68-1). Princeton, N. J.: Educational Testing Service, 1968.

Bryan, J. H., & London, P. Altruistic behavior by children. *Psychological Bulletin*, 1970, *73*, 200–211.

Bryan, J. H., & Schwartz, T. Effects of film material upon children's behavior. *Psychological Bulletin*, 1971, *75*, 50–59.

Bryan, J. H., & Test, M. A. Models and helping: Naturalistic studies in aiding behavior. *Journal of Personality and Social Psychology*, 1967, *6*, 400–407.

Bryan, J. H., & Walbek, N. The impact of words and deeds concerning altruism upon children. *Child Development*, 1970, *41*, 747–757. (a)

Bryan, J. H., & Walbek, N. Preaching and practicing self sacrifice: Children's actions and reactions. *Child Development*, 1970, *41*, 329–353. (b)

Buchanan, W., & Cantril, H. *How nations see each other*. Urbana, Ill.: University of Illinois Press, 1953.

Buck, R. W., & Parke, R. D. Behavioral and physiological response to the presence of a friendly or neutral person in two types of stressful situations. *Journal of Personality and Social Psychology*, 1972, *24*, 143–153.

Buckhout, R., Alper, A., Chern, S., Silverberg, G., & Slomovits, M. Determinants of eyewitness performance on a lineup. *Bulletin of the Psychonomic Society*, 1974, *4*, 191–192.

Buckhout, R., Figueroa, D., & Hoff, E. *Eyewitness identification: Effects of suggestion and bias in identifications from photographs* (Report No. CR-11). Center for Responsive Psychology, Brooklyn College, Brooklyn, N. Y., May 1, 1974.

Buechner, H. K. Territorial behavior in the Uganda kob. *Science*, 1961, *133*, 698–699.

Buechner, H. K. Territoriality as a behavioral adaptation to environment in the Uganda kob. *Proceedings of the XVI International Congress of Zoology*, 1963, *3*, 59–62.

Bureau of the Census, U. S. Department of Commerce. U. S. population, 1790–2000. Cited in F. Pullara, Trends in U. S. population. *A.F.L. Federationist*, June 1970, p. 10.

Burgess, T. D. G., & Sales, S. M. Attitudinal effects of mere exposure: A re-evaluation. *Journal of Experimental Social Psychology*, 1971, *7*, 461–472.

Burk, B. A., Zdep, S. M., & Kushner, H. Affiliation patterns among American girls. *Adolescence*, 1973, *8*, 541–546.

Burke, W. W. Social perception as a function of dogmatism. *Perceptual and Motor Skills*, 1966, *23*, 863–868.

Burma, J. H. The measurement of Negro "passing." *American Journal of Sociology*, 1946, *52*, 18–22.

Burney, C. *Solitary confinement* (2nd ed.). London: Colin MacMillan, 1961.

Burt, C. The evidence for the concept of intelligence. *British Journal of Educational Psychology*, 1955, *25*, 158–177.

Burt, C. The inheritance of mental ability. *American Psychologist*, 1958, *13*, 1–15.

Burton, R. V. Generality of honesty reconsidered. *Psychological Review*, 1963, *70*, 481–499.

Burtt, H. E. Sex differences in the effect of discussion. *Journal of Experimental Psychology*, 1920, *3*, 390–395.

Buss, A. *The psychology of aggression*. New York: Wiley, 1961.

Buss, A. Physical aggression in relation to different frustrations. *Journal of Abnormal and Social Psychology*, 1963, *67*, 1–7.

Buss, A. H. Instrumentality of aggression, feedback, and frustration as determinants of physical aggression. *Journal of Personality and Social Psychology*, 1966, *3*, 153–162.

Buss, A. H., Booker, A., & Buss, E. Firing a weapon and aggression. *Journal of Personality and Social Psychology*, 1972, *22*, 296–302.

Butterfield, D. A. *An integrative approach to the study of leadership effectiveness in organizations*. Unpublished doctoral dissertation, University of Michigan, 1968.

Buxhoeveden, S. *The life and tragedy of Alexandra Feodorovna, Empress of Russia: A biography*. New York and London: Longmans-Greene, 1930.

Byrd, R. E. *Alone*. New York: Putnams, 1938.

Byrne, D. Attitudes and attraction. In L. Berkowitz (Ed.), *Advances in experimental social psychology* (Vol. 4). New York: Academic Press, 1969. Pp. 36–86.

*Byrne, D. *The attraction paradigm*. New York: Academic Press, 1971.

Byrne, D., Ervin, C., & Lamberth, J. Continuity between the

experimental study of attraction and real-life computer dating. *Journal of Personality and Social Psychology*, 1970, *16*, 157–165.

Byrne, D., & Rhamey, R. Magnitude of positive and negative reinforcements as a determinant of attraction. *Journal of Personality and Social Psychology*, 1965, *2*, 884–889.

Byrne, D., & Wong, T. J. Racial prejudice, interpersonal attraction, and assumed dissimilarity of attitudes. *Journal of Abnormal and Social Psychology*, 1962, *65*, 246–253.

Calder, B. J., Ross, M., & Insko, C. A. Attitude change and attitude attribution: Effects of incentive, choice, and consequences. *Journal of Personality and Social Psychology*, 1973, *25*, 84–99.

*Calder, N. *Technopolis: Social control of the uses of science.* New York: Simon & Schuster, 1970.

Calhoun, J. B. Population density and social pathology. *Scientific American*, 1962, *206*(2), 139–148.

Calvin, A. Social reinforcement. *Journal of Social Psychology*, 1962, *56*, 15–19.

Cameron, N. A. Role concepts in behavior pathology. *American Journal of Sociology*, 1950, *55*, 464–467.

Campbell, A. Personal communication, 1967.

Campbell, A., Gurin, G., & Miller, W. E. *The voter decides.* New York: Harper & Row, 1954.

Campbell, D. T. *The generality of a social attitude.* Unpublished doctoral dissertation, University of California, 1947.

Campbell, D. T. Social attitudes and other acquired behavioral dispositions. In S. Koch (Ed.), *Psychology: A study of a science* (Vol. 6). New York: McGraw-Hill, 1963. Pp. 94–172.

Campbell, D. T. Ethnocentric and other altruistic motives. In D. Levine (Ed.), *Nebraska symposium on motivation, 1965.* (Vol. 13). Lincoln: University of Nebraska Press, 1965. Pp. 283–311.

Campbell, D. T. Reforms as experiments. *American Psychologist*, 1969, *24*, 409–429.

Campbell, D. T. On the genetics of altruism and the counterhedonic components in human culture. *Journal of Social Issues*, 1972, *28*(3), 21–37.

Campbell, D. T. On the genetics of altruism and the counterhedonic components in human culture. In L. Wispé (Ed.), *Psychology of sympathy and altruism.* Cambridge, Mass.: Harvard University Press, 1977.

Campbell, D. T., & Erlebacher, A. How regression artifacts in quasi-experimental evaluations can mistakenly make compensatory education look harmful. In J. Hellmuth (Ed.), *Disadvantaged child (Vol. 3). Compensatory education: A national debate.* New York: Brunner/Mazel, 1970. Pp. 185–210.

Campbell, D. T., & Fiske, D. W. Convergent and discriminant validation by the multitrait multimethod matrix. *Psychological Bulletin*, 1959, *56*, 81–105.

Campbell, D. T., Kruskal, W. H., & Wallace, W. P. Seating aggregation as an index of attitude. *Sociometry*, 1966, *29*, 1–15.

Campbell, D. T., & McCandless, B. R. Ethnocentrism, xeno-

phobia, and personality. *Human Relations*, 1951, *4*, 185–192.

Campbell, D. T., Siegman, C., & Rees, M. B. Direction-of-wording effects in the relationships between scales. *Psychological Bulletin*, 1967, *68*, 293–303.

*Campbell, D. T., & Stanley, J. C. *Experimental and quasi-experimental designs for research.* Chicago: Rand-McNally, 1966.

Campbell, J. P., Dunnette, M. D., Lawler, E. E., & Weick, K. E. *Managerial behavior, performance, and effectiveness.* New York: McGraw-Hill, 1970.

Candee, D., & Kohlberg, L. *Watergate as a moral issue.* Paper presented at the meeting of the American Psychological Association, New Orleans, September 1974.

Cannavale, F. J., Scarr, H. A., & Pepitone, A. Deindividuation in the small group: Further evidence. *Journal of Personality and Social Psychology*, 1970, *16*, 141–147.

Cannell, C. F., & Kahn, R. L. Interviewing. In G. Lindzey and E. Aronson (Eds.), *Handbook of social psychology* (Vol. 2) (2nd ed.). Reading, Mass.: Addison-Wesley, 1968. Pp. 526–595.

Canter, D., & Canter, S. Close together in Tokyo. *Design and Environment*, 1971, *2*(2), 60–63.

Cantor, G. N. Sex and race effects in the conformity behavior of upper-elementary-school-aged children. *Iowa Testing Programs Occasional Papers*, No. 16, July 1975.

Caplan, N. The new ghetto man: A review of recent empirical studies. *Journal of Social Issues*, 1970, *26*(1), 59–73.

Caplan, N., & Nelson, S. D. Who's to blame? *Psychology Today*, 1974, *8*(6), 99–104.

Caplan, N. S., & Paige, J. M. A study of ghetto rioters. *Scientific American*, 1968, *219*(2), 15–21.

Carey, A. The Hawthorne studies: A radical criticism. *American Sociological Review*, 1967, *32*, 403–416.

Carlsmith, J. M., Collins, B. E., & Helmreich, R. L. Studies in forced compliance: I. The effect of pressure for compliance on attitude change produced by face-to-face role playing and anonymous essay writing. *Journal of Personality and Social Psychology*, 1966, *4*, 1–13.

Carlsmith, J. M., & Gross, A. E. Some effects of guilt on compliance. *Journal of Personality and Social Psychology*, 1969, *11*, 232–239.

Carlson, H., Thayer, R. E., & Germann, A. C. Social attitudes and personality differences among members of two kinds of police departments (innovative vs. traditional) and students. *Journal of Criminal Law, Criminology and Police Science*, 1971, *62*, 564–567.

Carlson, R. Personality. In M. R. Rosenzweig & L. W. Porter (Eds.), *Annual review of psychology* (Vol. 26). Palo Alto, Calif.: Annual Reviews, 1975. Pp. 393–414.

Carlsson, G. Social class, intelligence, and the verbal factor. *Acta Psychologia*, 1955, *11*, 269–278.

Carmichael, S., & Hamilton, C. V. *Black power: The politics of liberation in America.* New York: Random House, 1967.

Carnegie, D. *How to win friends and influence people.* New York: Simon & Schuster, 1936.

Carpenter, C. R. A field study of the behavior and social relations of howling monkeys. *Comparative Psychology Monographs*, 1934, *10*(2), Whole No. 48.

Carpenter, C. R. Territoriality: A review of concepts and problems. In A. Roe & G. Simpson (Eds.), *Behavior and evolution.* New Haven, Conn.: Yale University Press, 1958. Pp. 224–250.

Carroll, J. S. *A multimethod individual differences study of implicit personality theory.* Paper presented at the meeting of the American Psychological Association, New Orleans, September 1974.

Carstairs, G. M. Overcrowding and human aggression. In H. D. Graham & T. R. Gurr (Eds.), *Violence in America.* New York: New American Library, 1969. Pp. 730–742.

Carter, J. H. Military leadership. *Military Review*, 1952, *32*, 14–18.

Carthy, J. H., & Ebling, F. J. (Eds.). *The natural history of aggression.* New York: Academic Press, 1964.

Cartwright, D. Risk taking by individuals and groups: An assessment of research employing choice dilemmas. *Journal of Personality and Social Psychology*, 1971, *20*, 361–378.

Cartwright, D., & Zander, A. Leadership and performance of group functions: Introduction. In D. Cartwright & A. Zander (Eds.), *Group dynamics* (3rd ed.). New York: Harper & Row, 1968. Pp. 301–317.

Castore, C. H., & DeNinno, J. *Role of relevance in the selection of comparison others.* Paper presented at the meeting of the American Psychological Association, Honolulu, August 1972.

Cattell, R. B., Kawash, G. F., & DeYoung, G. E. Validation of objective measures of ergic tension: Response of the sex erg to visual stimulation. *Journal of Experimental Research in Personality*, 1972, *6*, 76–83.

Cattell, R. B., & Marony, J. H. The use of the 16 PF in distinguishing homosexuals, normals, and general criminals. *Journal of Consulting Psychology*, 1962, *26*, 531–540.

Cavalli-Sforza, L. L. The genetics of human populations. *Scientific American*, 1974, *231*(3), 80–89.

Cavan, S. Interaction in home territories. *Berkeley Journal of Sociology*, 1963, *8*, 17–32.

Chance, N. A. Acculturation, self-identification, and adjustment. *American Anthropologist*, 1965, *67*, 372–393.

Chandler, M. *Accurate and accidental empathy.* Paper presented at the meeting of the American Psychological Association, New Orleans, September 1974.

Chapanis, N. P., & Chapanis, A. C. Cognitive dissonance: Five years later. *Psychological Bulletin*, 1964, *61*, 1–22.

Chemers, M. M. *Current status and future potential of the contingency model.* Paper presented at the meeting of the American Psychological Association, Honolulu, September 1972.

Chemers, M. M., & Skrzypek, G. J. Experimental test of the contingency model of leadership effectiveness. *Journal of Personality and Social Psychology*, 1972, *24*, 172–177.

Cherry, F., & Deaux, K. *Fear of success vs. fear of gender-inconsistent behavior: A sex similarity.* Paper presented at the meet-

ing of the Midwestern Psychological Association, Chicago, May 1975.

Chesler, M., & Schmuck, R. Social psychological characteristics of superpatriots. In R. A. Schoenberger (Ed.), *The American right wing.* New York: Holt, 1969. Pp. 164–192.

Chesler, P. *Women and madness.* Garden City, N. Y.: Doubleday, 1972.

Cheyne, J. A., & Efran, M. G. The effect of spatial and interpersonal variables on the invasion of group controlled territories. *Sociometry*, 1972, *35*, 477–489.

Cheyne, J. A., & Walters, R. H. Intensity of punishment, timing of punishment and cognitive structure as determinants of response inhibition. *Journal of Experimental Child Psychology*, 1969, *7*, 231–244.

Cheyne, J. A., & Walters, R. H. Punishment and prohibition: Some origins of self control. In T. M. Newcomb (Ed.), *New directions in psychology* (Vol. 4). New York: Holt, Rinehart & Winston, 1970.

Child, I. *Italian or American? The second generation in conflict.* New Haven: Yale University Press, 1943.

Child, I. L., Potter, E. H., & Levine, E. M. Children's textbooks and personality development: An exploration in the social psychology of education. *Psychological Monographs*, 1946, *60*, (3, Whole No. 279).

Christensen, H. T. Sex, science, and values. In SEICUS (Ed.), *Sexuality and man.* New York: Scribners, 1970.

Christensen, H. T., & Gregg, C. F. Changing sex norms in America and Scandinavia. *Journal of Marriage and the Family*, 1970, *32*, 616–627.

Christian Century. Painter case has happy ending. September 18, 1968, pp. 1162–1163.

Christian, J. J., Flyger, V., & Davis, D. E. Factors in the mass mortality of a herd of Sika deer, Cervus Nippon. *Chesapeake Science*, 1960, *1*, 79–95.

Christie, R. Eysenck's treatment of the personality of Communists. *Psychological Bulletin*, 1956, *53*, 411–430.

Christie, R., & Cook, P. A guide to the published literature relating to the authoritarian personality through 1956. *Journal of Psychology*, 1958, *45*, 171–199.

*Christie, R., & Geis, F. L. (Eds.). *Studies in Machiavellianism.* New York: Academic Press, 1970.

Christie, R., Havel, J., & Seidenberg, B. Is the F scale irreversible? *Journal of Abnormal and Social Psychology*, 1958, *56*, 143–159.

Christie, R., & Jahoda, M. (Eds.). *Studies in the scope and method of "The Authoritarian Personality."* New York: Free Press, 1954.

Chun, K., & Campbell, J. B. Dimensionality of the Rotter Interpersonal Trust Scale. *Psychological Reports*, 1974, *35*, 1059–1070.

Cialdini, R. B. *A test of two techniques for inducing verbal, behavioral, and further compliance with a request to give blood.* Unpublished manuscript, Department of Psychology, Arizona State University, 1975.

Cialdini, R. B., Darby, B. L., & Vincent, J. E. Transgression and altruism: A case for hedonism. *Journal of Experimental Social Psychology*, 1973, 9, 502–516.

Cialdini, R. B., Vincent, J. E., Lewis, S. K., Catalan, J., Wheeler, D., & Darby, B. L. A reciprocal concessions procedure for inducing compliance: The door-in-the-face technique. *Journal of Personality and Social Psychology*, 1975, 21, 206–215.

Clark, D. H., Lesser, G. S., & Fifer, G. *Mental abilities of young children from different cultural and social class backgrounds.* Paper presented at the meeting of the American Psychological Association, Los Angeles, September 1964.

Clark, K. B. *Dark ghetto.* New York: Harper & Row, 1965.

Clark, K. B., & Clark, M. P. Racial identification and preference in Negro children. In T. M. Newcomb & E. L. Hartley (Eds.), *Readings in social psychology.* New York: Holt, 1947. Pp. 169–178.

Clark, K. B., & Clark, M. P. Emotional factors in racial identification and preference in Negro children. *Journal of Negro Education*, 1950, 19, 341–350.

Clark, R. D., III, Crockett, W. H., & Archer, R. L. Risk-as-value hypothesis: The relationship between perception of self, others, and the risky shift. *Journal of Personality and Social Psychology*, 1971, 20, 425–429.

Clark, R. D., III, & Willems, E. P. Risk preferences as related to judged consequences of failure. *Psychological Reports*, 1969, 25, 827–830.

Clark, R. D., III, & Willems, E. P. The risky shift phenomenon: The diffusion-of-responsibility hypothesis or the risk-as-value hypothesis. Paper presented at the meeting of the Southwestern Psychological Association, St. Louis, April 1970.

Clark, R. D., III, & Willems, E. P. Two interpretations of Brown's hypothesis for the risky shift. *Psychological Bulletin*, 1972, 78, 62–63.

Clark, R. D., III, & Word, L. E. Why don't bystanders help? Because of ambiguity? *Journal of Personality and Social Psychology*, 1972, 24, 392–400.

Clark, R. D., III, & Word, L. E. Where is the apathetic bystander? Situational characteristics of the emergency. *Journal of Personality and Social Psychology*, 1974, 29, 279–287.

Claxton, R. N. Changes in the philosophies of human nature of a disadvantaged group as a function of occupation and attitudinal training. Unpublished master's thesis, Department of Psychology, George Peabody College for Teachers, 1971.

Clifford, C., & Cohn, T. S. The relationship between leadership and personality attributes perceived by followers. *Journal of Social Psychology*, 1964, 64, 57–64.

Cline, V. B. Interpersonal perception. In B. A. Maher (Ed.), *Progress in experimental personality research* (Vol. 1). New York: Academic Press, 1964. Pp. 221–284.

Cline, V. B., Croft, R. G., & Courrier, S. Desensitization of children to television violence. *Journal of Personality and Social Psychology*, 1973, 27, 360–365.

Cline, V. B., & Richards, J. M., Jr. Accuracy of interpersonal perception—a general trait? *Journal of Abnormal and Social Psychology*, 1960, 60, 1–7.

Cobb, W. M. The physical constitution of the American Negro. *Journal of Negro Education*, 1934, 3, 340–388.

Cobb, W. M. Race and runners. *Journal of Health and Physical Education*, 1936, 7, 3–7; 52–56.

*Cohen, A. R. *Attitude change and social influence.* New York: Basic Books, 1964.

Cohen, D., Whitmyre, J. W., & Funk, W. H. Effect of group cohesiveness and training upon creative thinking. *Journal of Applied Psychology*, 1960, 44, 319–322.

Cohen, J. L., Sladen, B., & Bennett, B. The effects of situational variables on judgments of crowding. *Sociometry*, 1975, 38, 273–281.

Cohen, R. J. Loyalty or legality in obedience: Note on the Watergate proceedings. *Psychological Reports*, 1973, 33, 964.

Coleman, A. D. Territoriality in man: A comparison of behavior in home and hospital. *American Journal of Orthopsychiatry*, 1968, 38, 464–468.

Coleman, J., Campbell, E., Hobson, C., McPartland, J., Mood, A., Weinfield, F., & York, R. *Equality of educational opportunity.* Washington, D. C.: U. S. Government Printing Office, 1966.

Coles, R. Praise and imitation. *Saturday Review*, January 16, 1971, pp. 51, 55.

Collins, B. E. Attribution theory analysis of forced compliance. *Proceedings, 77th Annual Convention, American Psychological Association*, 1969, 4, 309–310.

Collins, B. E. *Social psychology.* Reading, Mass.: Addison-Wesley, 1970.

Collins, B. E. Four components of the Rotter Internal-External scale: Belief in a difficult world, a just world, a predictable world, and a politically responsive world. *Journal of Personality and Social Psychology*, 1974, 29, 381–391.

Collins, B. E., & Hoyt, M. F. Personal responsibility-for-consequences: An integration and extension of the forced compliance literature. *Journal of Experimental Social Psychology*, 1972, 8, 558–593.

Conroy, J., & Sundstrom, E. *Effects of disagreement on territorial dominance in a dyadic conversation.* Paper presented at the meeting of the Southeastern Psychological Association, Atlanta, March 1975.

Constantinople, A. Masculinity-femininity: An exception to a famous dictum? *Psychological Bulletin*, 1973, 80, 389–407.

Cook, M. Experiments on orientation and proxemics. *Human Relations*, 1970, 23, 61–76.

Cook, S. W. Desegregation: A psychological analysis. *American Psychologist*, 1957, 12, 1–13.

Cook, S. W. *An experimental analysis of attitude change in a natural social setting.* Small grant proposal submitted to U. S. Commission of Education, July 1964.

*Cook, S. W. Motives in a conceptual analysis of attitude-related behavior. In W. J. Arnold & D. Levine (Eds.), *Nebraska symposium on motivation, 1969.* Lincoln: University of Nebraska Press, 1970. Pp. 179–231.

Cook, S. W. *The effect of unintended racial contact upon racial interaction and attitude change* (Final report, Project No. 5-1320, Contract No. OEC-4-7-051320-0273). Washington, D. C.: U. S. Office of Education, Bureau of Research, August 1971.

Cook, S. W., & Selltiz, C. A. Multiple-indicator approach to attitude measurement. *Psychological Bulletin*, 1964, *62*, 36–55.

Cook, S. W., & Wrightsman, L. S. *The factorial structure of "positive attitudes toward people."* Symposium paper presented at the meeting of the Southeastern Psychological Association, Atlanta, April 1967.

Cooley, C. H. *Human nature and the social order* (Rev. ed.). New York: Scribner's, 1922. (Originally published, 1902.)

Cooper, J., & Jones, E. E. Opinion divergence as a strategy to avoid being miscast. *Journal of Personality and Social Psychology*, 1969, *13*, 23–40.

Cory, D. W. Homosexuality. In A. Ellis & A. Abarbanel (Eds.), *The encyclopedia of sexual behavior* (Rev. ed.). New York: Jason Aronson, 1973. Pp. 485–493.

Costanzo, P. R. Conformity development as a function of self-blame. *Journal of Personality and Social Psychology*, 1970, *14*, 366–374.

Cottrell, N. Social facilitation. In C. McClintock (Ed.), *Experimental social psychology*. New York: Holt, Rinehart & Winston, 1972. Pp. 185–236.

Cottrell, N., Wack, D., Sekerak, G., & Rittle, R. Social facilitation of dominant responses by the presence of an audience and the mere presence of others. *Journal of Personality and Social Psychology*, 1968, *9*, 245–250.

Couch, A., & Keniston, K. Yeasayers and naysayers: Agreeing response set as a personality variable. *Journal of Abnormal and Social Psychology*, 1960, *60*, 151–174.

Cowan, P., Egleson, N., & Hentoff, N. *State secrets*. New York: Holt, Rinehart & Winston, 1974.

Cowan, P. A., Langer, J., Heavenrich, J., & Nathanson, M. Social learning and Piaget's cognitive theory of moral development. *Journal of Personality and Social Psychology*, 1969, *11*, 261–274.

Cox, D. F., & Bauer, R. A. Self-confidence and persuasibility in women. *Public Opinion Quarterly*, 1964, *28*, 453–466.

Cox, O. C. *Caste, class, and race*. New York: Doubleday, 1948.

Cozby, P. C. Self-disclosure, reciprocity, and liking. *Sociometry*, 1972, *35*, 151–160.

Cozby, P. C. Effects of density, activity, and personality on environmental preferences. *Journal of Experimental Research in Personality*, 1973, *7*, 45–60. (a)

*Cozby, P. C. Self-disclosure: A literature review. *Psychological Bulletin*, 1973, *79*, 73–91. (b)

Cozby, P. C. Student reactions to Agnew's resignation: Inconsistency reduction in another natural-occurring event. *Sociometry*, 1974, *37*, 450–457.

Craig, K. D., & Neidermayer, H. Autonomic correlates of pain thresholds influenced by social modeling. *Journal of Personality and Social Psychology*, 1974, *29*, 246–252.

Craik, K. H. Environmental psychology. In P. H. Mussen &

M. R. Rosenzweig (Eds.), *Annual review of psychology* (Vol. 24). Palo Alto, Calif.: Annual Reviews, Inc., 1973. Pp. 403–422.

Crandall, R. Social facilitation: Theories and research. In A. Harrison (Ed.), *Explorations in psychology*. Monterey, Calif.: Brooks/Cole, 1974. Pp. 94–106.

Crane, V., & Ballif, B. L. Effects of adults' modeling and rule structure on responses to moral situations of children in fifth-grade classrooms. *Journal of Experimental Education*, 1973, *41*, 49–52.

Crano, W. D. *Order effects in recall of counterattitudinal information*. Paper presented at the meeting of the Midwestern Psychological Association, Chicago, May 1973.

Creedman, N., & Creedman, M. Angst, the curse of the working class. *Human Behavior*, 1972, *1*(6), 8–14.

Crombag, H. F. Cooperation and competition in means-interdependent triads: A replication. *Journal of Personality and Social Psychology*, 1966, *4*, 692–695.

Cronbach, L. J. Processes affecting scores on "understanding others" and "assumed similarity." *Psychological Bulletin*, 1955, *52*, 177–193.

Cronbach, L. J. The two disciplines of scientific psychology. *American Psychologist*, 1957, *12*, 671–684.

Cronbach, L. J. Proposals leading to analytic treatment of social perception scores. In R. Tagiuri & L. Petrullo (Eds.), *Person perception and interpersonal behavior*. Stanford, Calif.: Stanford University Press, 1958. Pp. 353–379.

*Cronbach, L. J. Five decades of public controversy over mental testing. *American Psychologist*, 1975, *30*, 1–14.

Crook, J. H. The nature and function of territorial aggression. In M. F. A. Montagu (Ed.), *Man and aggression* (2nd ed.). New York: Oxford University Press, 1973. Pp. 183–220.

Cross, H. J., & Pruyn, E. L. Adjustment and the counter culture. In J. F. Adams (Ed.), *Psychology of adjustment*. New York: Holbrook Press, 1972.

Cross, K. Is there a generation gap? *Journal of the National Association of Women Deans and Counselors*, 1968, *31*, 53–56.

Crow, W. J. The effect of training upon accuracy and variability in interpersonal perception. *Journal of Abnormal and Social Psychology*, 1957, *55*, 355–359.

Crow, W. J., & Hammond, K. R. The generality of accuracy and response sets in interpersonal perception. *Journal of Abnormal and Social Psychology*, 1957, *54*, 384–390.

*Crowne, D. P., & Marlowe, D. *The approval motive*. New York: Wiley, 1964.

Crutchfield, R. S. Conformity and character. *American Psychologist*, 1955, *10*, 191–198.

Csoka, L. S. *Intelligence: A critical variable for leadership experience* (Technical Report 72-34). Seattle: University of Washington, May 1972.

Curry, T. J., & Emerson, R. M. Balance theory: A theory of interpersonal attraction? *Sociometry*, 1970, *33*, 216–238.

Cyert, R. M., & MacCrimmon, K. R. Organizations. In G. Lindzey & E. Aronson (Eds.), *Handbook of social psychology* (Vol. 1) (2nd ed.). Reading, Mass.: Addison-Wesley, 1968. Pp. 568–611.

Dabbs, J. M. Sex, setting, and reactions to crowding on sidewalks. *Proceedings, 80th Annual Convention, American Psychological Association*, 1972, 7, 205–206.

Dabbs, J. M., Fuller, J. P., & Carr, T. S. Personal space when "cornered": College students and prison inmates. *Proceedings, 81st Annual Convention, American Psychological Association*, 1973, 8, 213–214.

Dabbs, J. M., & Janis I. L. Why does eating while reading facilitate opinion change?—An experimental inquiry. *Journal of Experimental Social Psychology*, 1965, 1, 133–144.

Daly, J. D. *Factors affecting the measurement of self-esteem and achievement of inner-city Afro-American college students.* Paper presented at the meeting of the American Psychological Association, New Orleans, September 1974.

Dan, A. J., & Beekman, S. Male versus female representation in psychological research. *American Psychologist*, 1972, 27, 1078.

D'Andrade, R. Sex differences and cultural institutions. In E. Maccoby (Ed.), *The development of sex differences.* Stanford, Calif.: Stanford University Press, 1966. Pp. 173–204.

Daniels, J. *Ordeal of ambition: Jefferson, Hamilton, Burr.* Garden City, N.Y.: Doubleday, 1970.

Daniels, L. R., & Berkowitz, L. Liking and response to dependency relationships. *Human Relations*, 1963, 16, 141–148.

Danish, S. A. *A training program in helping skills: An examination of what, how and if it works.* Paper presented at the meeting of the American Psychological Association, New Orleans, August 1974.

Danish, S. J., & Hauer, A. L. *Helping skills: A basic training program.* New York: Behavioral Publications, 1973.

Dank, B. M. Coming out in the gay world. *Psychiatry*, 1971, 34, 180–197.

Darley, J. M., & Batson, C. D. "From Jerusalem to Jericho": A study of situational and dispositional variables in helping behavior. *Journal of Personality and Social Psychology*, 1973, 27, 100–108.

Darley, J. M., & Cooper, J. The "clean for Gene" phenomenon: The effect of students' appearance on political campaigning. *Journal of Applied Social Psychology*, 1972, 2, 24–33.

Darley, J. M., & Latané, B. Bystander intervention in emergencies: Diffusion of responsibility. *Journal of Personality and Social Psychology*, 1968, 8, 377–383. (a)

Darley, J. M., & Latané, B. When will people help in a crisis? *Psychology Today*, 1968, 2(7), 54–57; 70–71. (b)

Darley, J. M., Teger, A. I., & Lewis, L. D. Do groups always inhibit individuals' responses to potential emergencies? *Journal of Personality and Social Psychology*, 1973, 26, 395–399.

Darley, S. A., & Cooper, J. Cognitive consequences of forced noncompliance. *Journal of Personality and Social Psychology*, 1972, 24, 321–326.

Darsie, M. L. Mental capacity of American-born Japanese children. *Comparative Psychology Monographs*, 1926, 15 (No. 3).

Dasen, P. R. Preliminary study of sensori-motor development in Baoulé children. *Early Child Development and Care*, 1973, 2, 345–354.

Dasen, P. R. Le développement psychologique du jeune enfant Africain. *Archives de Psychologie*, 1974, 16, 341–386.

Davé, R. H. *The identification and measurement of environmental process variables that are related to educational achievement.* Unpublished doctoral dissertation, University of Chicago, 1963.

Davenport, R. K. Implications of military selection and classification in relation to universal military training. *Journal of Negro Education*, 1946, 15, 585–594.

Davie, M. R. *Negroes in American society.* New York: McGraw-Hill, 1949.

Davies, J. C. Toward a theory of revolution. *American Sociological Review*, 1962, 27, 5–19.

Davies, J. C. The J-curve of rising and declining satisfactions as a cause of great revolutions and a contained rebellion. In H. D. Graham & T. R. Gurr (Eds.), *Violence in America.* New York: New American Library, 1969. Pp. 671–709.

Davis, A. J. Sexual assaults in the Philadelphia prison system and sheriff's vans. *Trans-Action*, 1968, 6, 8–16.

Davis, F. B., Lesser, G. S., & French, E. G. Identification and classroom behavior of gifted elementary school children. *Cooperative Research Monographs*, 1960 (No. 2).

*Davis, J. H. *Group performance.* Reading, Mass.: Addison-Wesley, 1969.

Davis, J. H., Kerr, N. L., Atkin, R. S., Holt, R., & Meek, D. The decision processes of 6- and 12-person mock juries assigned unanimous and two-thirds majority rules. *Journal of Personality and Social Psychology*, 1975, 32, 1–14.

Davis, J. H., & Restle, F. The analysis of problems and prediction of group problem solving. *Journal of Abnormal and Social Psychology*, 1963, 66, 103–116.

Davis, K. E., & Braucht, G. N. Exposure to pornography, character, and sexual deviance: A retrospective survey. *Journal of Social Issues*, 1973, 29(3), 183–196.

Davitz, J. R. The effects of previous training on postfrustration behavior. *Journal of Abnormal and Social Psychology*, 1952, 47, 309–315.

Dawes, R. M. IQ: Methodological and other issues (letter to the editor). *Science*, 1972, 178, 229–230.

Dawes, R. M. *Formal models of dilemmas in social decision-making.* Paper presented at the Human Judgment and Decision Processes Symposium, Northern Illinois University, October 1974.

Day, C. B. *A study of some Negro-White families in the United States.* Cambridge, Mass.: Harvard African Studies, 1932.

Day, H. R., & White, C. *International prejudice as a factor in domestic versus foreign car ownership and preferences.* Paper presented at the 20th International Congress of Psychology, Tokyo, Japan, August 1973.

*Deaux, K. *The behavior of women and men.* Monterey, Calif.: Brooks/Cole, 1976.

Deaux, K., & Emswiller, T. Explanations of successful performance on sex-linked tasks: What is skill for the male is luck for the female. *Journal of Personality and Social Psychology*, 1974, 29, 80–85.

Deaux, K., & Farris, E. *Attributing causes for one's performance:*

The effects of sex norms and outcome. Unpublished manuscript, Purdue University, 1974.

Deaux, K., White, L., & Farris, E. Skill versus luck: Field and laboratory studies of male and female preferences. *Journal of Personality and Social Psychology,* 1975, *32,* 629–636.

deCharms, R. C. *Personal causation: The internal affective determinants of behavior.* New York: Academic Press, 1968.

deFleur, M. L., & Westie, F. R. Verbal attitudes and overt acts: An experiment on the salience of attitudes. *American Sociological Review,* 1958, *23,* 667–673.

DeLamater, J. A definition of "group." *Small Group Behavior,* 1974, *5*(1), 30–44.

*Demerath, N. J., III, Larsen, O., & Schuessler, K. F. (Eds.). *Social policy and sociology.* New York: Academic Press, 1975.

Deniels, A. K. The captive professional: Bureaucratic limitations in the practice of military psychiatry. *Journal of Health and Social Welfare,* 1969, *10*(4), 255–265.

Desor, J. A. Toward a psychological theory of crowding. *Journal of Personality and Social Psychology,* 1972, *21,* 79–83.

Deur, J. D., & Parke, R. D. Effects of inconsistent punishment on aggression in children. *Developmental Psychology,* 1970, *2,* 403–411.

Deutsch, M. An experimental study of the effects of cooperation and competition upon group process. *Human Relations,* 1949, *2,* 196–231. (a)

Deutsch, M. A theory of cooperation and competition. *Human Relations,* 1949, *2,* 129–152. (b)

Deutsch, M. Field theory in social psychology. In G. Lindzey & E. Aronson (Eds.), *Handbook of social psychology* (Vol. 1) (2nd ed.). Reading, Mass.: Addison-Wesley, 1968. Pp. 412–487.

*Deutsch, M. *The resolution of conflict: Constructive and destructive processes.* New Haven, Conn.: Yale University Press, 1973.

Deutsch, M., & Collins, M. *Interracial housing: A psychological evaluation of a social experiment.* Minneapolis, Minn.: University of Minnesota Press, 1951.

Deutsch, M., & Gerard, H. A study of normative and informational social influences on individual judgment. *Journal of Abnormal and Social Psychology,* 1955, *51,* 629–636.

*Deutsch, M., & Krauss, R. M. *Theories in social psychology.* New York: Basic Books, 1965.

DeVries, D. L., & Slavin, R. E. *Effects of team competition on race relations in the classroom: Further supportive evidence.* Paper presented at the meeting of the American Psychological Association, Chicago, September 1975.

Dewey, J. *Freedom and culture.* New York: Putnam, 1939.

Diamond, M. J., & Lobitz, W. C. When familiarity breeds respect: The effects of the experimental depolarization program on police and student attitudes toward each other. *Journal of Social Issues,* 1973, *29*(4), 95–109.

Dienstbier, R. A., & Munter, P.O. Cheating as a function of the labeling of natural arousal. *Journal of Personality and Social Psychology,* 1971, *17,* 208–213.

Dillehay, R. C. On the irrelevance of the classical negative evidence concerning the effect of attitudes on behavior.

American Psychologist, 1973, *28,* 887–891.

Dimond, R. E., & Hellkamp, D. T. Race, sex, ordinal position of birth, and self-disclosure in high school students. *Psychological Reports,* 1969, *25,* 235–238.

Dimond, R. E., & Munz, D. C. Ordinal position of birth and self-disclosure in high school students. *Psychological Reports,* 1967, *21,* 827–833.

Dinges, N. G., & Oetting, E. R. Interaction distance anxiety in the counseling dyad. *Journal of Counseling Psychology,* 1972, *19*(2), 146–149.

Dion, K. Physical attractiveness and evaluation of children's transgressions. *Journal of Personality and Social Psychology,* 1972, *24,* 207–213.

Dion, K. K., Berscheid, E., & Walster, E. What is beautiful is good. *Journal of Personality and Social Psychology,* 1972, *24,* 285–290.

Dion, K. L., Baron, R. S., & Miller, N. Why do groups make riskier decisions than individuals? In L. Berkowitz (Ed.), *Advances in experimental social psychology* (Vol. 5). New York: Academic Press, 1970. Pp. 305–377.

Dion, K.L., & Miller, N. An analysis of the familiarization explanation of the risky-shift. *Journal of Experimental Social Psychology,* 1971, *7,* 524–533.

Dipboye, R. L., Fromkin, H. L., & Wiback, K. Relative importance of applicant sex, attractiveness, and scholastic standing in evaluation of job applicant résumés. *Journal of Applied Psychology,* 1975, *60,* 39–45.

Dittes, J. E., & Capra, P. C. *Affiliation: Comparability or compatibility?* Paper presented at the meeting of the American Psychological Association, St. Louis, August 1962.

Dmitruk, V. M. Intangible motivation and resistance to temptation. *Journal of Genetic Psychology,* 1973, *123,* 47–53.

Doise, W. Intergroup relations and polarization of individual and collective judgments. *Journal of Personality and Social Psychology,* 1969, *12,* 136–143.

Dollard, J., Doob, L. W., Miller, N. E., Mowrer, O. H., & Sears, R. R. *Frustration and aggression.* New Haven, Conn.: Yale University Press, 1939.

*Doniger, S. (Ed.). *The nature of man.* New York: Harper, 1962.

Donley, R. E., & Winter, D. G. Measuring the motives of public officials at a distance: An exploratory study of American presidents. *Behavioral Science,* 1970, *15,* 227–236.

Donnerstein, E., Donnerstein, M., Simon, S., & Ditrichs, R. Variables in interracial aggression: Anonymity, expected retaliation, and a riot. *Journal of Personality and Social Psychology,* 1972, *22,* 236–245.

Dooley, B. Crowding stress: The effects of social density on men with close or far personal space. Unpublished doctoral dissertation, University of California at Los Angeles, 1974.

Dorris, J. W. Reactions to unconditional cooperation: A field study emphasizing variables neglected in laboratory research. *Journal of Personality and Social Psychology,* 1972, *22,* 387–397.

Douvan, E. A., & Adelson, J. *The adolescent experience.* New York: Wiley, 1966.

Downs, R. M., & Stea, D. (Eds.). *Image and environment: Cognitive mapping and spatial behavior.* Chicago: Aldine, 1973.

Doyle, C. *Psychology, science, and the Western democratic tradition.* Unpublished doctoral dissertation, University of Michigan, 1965.

Doyle, C. *An empirical study of the attitudes of psychologists and other scientists and humanists toward science, freedom, and related issues.* Paper presented at the meeting of the American Psychological Association, New York, September 1966.

Drake, D. Crossing the sex barrier. *Saturday Review/World,* April 20, 1974, pp. 48–49ff.

Draper, P. Crowding among hunter-gatherers: The !Kung bushmen. *Science,* 1973, *182,* 301–303.

Draper, P. !Kung women: Contrasts in sex egalitarianism in the foraging and sedentary contexts. In R. Reiter (Ed.), *Toward an anthropology of women.* New York: Monthly Review Press, in press.

Dreger, R. M., & Miller, K. S. Comparative psychological studies of Negroes and Whites in the United States. *Psychological Bulletin,* 1960, *57,* 361–402.

Dreger, R. M., & Miller, K. S. Comparative psychological studies of Negroes and Whites in the United States: 1959–1965. *Psychological Bulletin Monograph Supplement,* 1968, *70* (No. 3, Part 2).

Driscoll, J. M., Meyer, R. G., & Schanie, C. F. Training police in family crisis intervention. *Journal of Applied Behavioral Science,* 1973, *9,* 62–81.

Driscoll, J. P. Transsexuals. *Trans-Action,* 1971, *8,* 28–37ff.

Driscoll, R., Davis, K. E., & Lipetz, M. E. Parental influence and romantic love: The Romeo and Juliet effect. *Journal of Personality and Social Psychology,* 1972, *24,* 1–10.

Driver, M. J., Streufert, S., & Nataupsky, M. Effects of immediate and remote incongruity experience on response to dissonant information. *Proceedings, 77th Annual Convention, American Psychological Association,* 1969, *4,* 323–324.

DuBois, P. H. A test standardized on Pueblo Indian children. *Psychological Bulletin,* 1939, *36,* 523.

Du Bois, W. E. B. *The world and Africa: An inquiry into the part which Africa has played in world history.* New York: Viking Press, 1947.

Dubos, R. *Man adapting.* New Haven, Conn.: Yale University Press, 1965.

Duffy, J. Masturbation and clitoridectomy. *Journal of the American Medical Association,* 1963, *19,* 246–248.

Duffy, J. Masturbation and clitoris amputation. *Sexology,* May 1964, pp. 668–671.

Duffy, J. F. *A field extension of Fiedler's contingency model.* Unpublished master's thesis, Department of Psychology, Iowa State University of Science and Technology, 1970.

Duffy, J. F., Kavanagh, M. J., MacKinney, A. C., Wolins, L., & Lyons, T. F. *A field extension of Fiedler's contingency model.* Paper presented at the meeting of the Midwestern Psychological Association, Cincinnati, April 1970.

Dunn, L. C., & Dobzhansky, T. *Heredity, race, and society* (Rev. ed.). New York: New American Library, 1952.

Dunn, R. E., & Goldman, M. Competition and noncompetition in relation to satisfaction and feelings toward group and nongroup members. *Journal of Social Psychology,* 1966, *68,* 299–311.

Dunnette, M. D. *Forms of interpersonal accommodation: Processes, problems, and research avenues.* Paper presented at the meeting of the American Psychological Association, New York, September 1968.

Dunnette, M. D., Campbell, J., & Jaastad, K. The effect of group participation on brainstorming effectiveness for two industrial samples. *Journal of Applied Psychology,* 1963, *47,* 30–37.

Durkheim, E. Représentations individuelles et représentations collectives. *Revue de Métaphysique,* 1898, *6,* 274–302. (In D. F. Pocock (trans.), *Sociology and philosophy.* New York: Free Press, 1953.)

Dutton, D. G., & Aron, A. P. Some evidence for heightened sexual attraction under conditions of high anxiety. *Journal of Personality and Social Psychology,* 1974, *30,* 510–517.

Dutton, D. G., & Lake, R. A. Threat of own prejudice and reverse discrimination in interracial situations. *Journal of Personality and Social Psychology,* 1973, *28,* 94–100.

Dutton, D. G., & Lennox, V. L. Effect of prior "token" compliance on subsequent interracial behavior. *Journal of Personality and Social Psychology,* 1974, *29,* 65–71.

*Duval, S., & Wicklund, R. A. *A theory of objective self-awareness.* New York: Academic Press, 1972.

Eagleson, O. W., & Clifford, A. D. A comparative study of the names of White and Negro women college students. *Journal of Social Psychology,* 1945, *21,* 57–64.

Eagly, A., & Telaak, K. Width of the latitude of acceptance as a determinant of attitude change. *Journal of Personality and Social Psychology,* 1972, *23,* 388–397.

Eaton, J. W., & Weil, R. J. *Culture and mental disorders.* New York: Free Press, 1955.

Edney, J. Property, possession, and performance: A field study in human territoriality. *Journal of Applied Social Psychology,* 1972, *2,* 275–282.

Edney, J. J. Human territoriality. *Psychological Bulletin,* 1974, *81,* 959–975.

Edney, J. J. Territoriality and control: A field experiment. *Journal of Personality and Social Psychology,* 1975, *31,* 1108–1115.

Edney, J. J. Human territories: Comment on functional properties. *Environment and Behavior,* 1976, *8*(1), 31–47.

Edney, J. J., & Jordan-Edney, N. L. Territorial spacing on a beach. *Sociometry,* 1974, *37,* 92–104.

Edwards, A. L. *Manual for the Edwards Personal Preference Schedule.* New York: Psychological Corporation, 1953.

Edwards, D. J. A. Approaching the unfamiliar: A study of human interaction distances. *Journal of Behavioral Sciences,* 1972, *1*(4), 249–250.

Edwards, K. J. *Expectancy theory and cooperation-competition in the classroom.* Paper presented at the meeting of the American Psychological Association, New Orleans, August 1974.

Edwards, T. *The new dictionary of thoughts.* Garden City, N. Y.: Doubleday, 1972.

Efran, M. G., & Cheyne, J. A. The study of movement and affect in territorial behavior. *Man-Environment Systems,* 1972, *2,* 348–350.

Efran, M. G., & Cheyne, J. A. Shared space: The cooperative control of spacial areas by two interacting individuals. *Canadian Journal of Behavioural Science,* 1973, *5,* 201–210.

Efran, M. G., & Cheyne, J. A. Affective concommitants of the invasion of shared space: Behavioral, physiological and verbal indicators. *Journal of Personality and Social Psychology,* 1974, *29,* 219–226.

Ehlert, J., Ehlert, N., & Merrens, M. The influence of ideological affiliation on helping behavior. *Journal of Social Psychology,* 1973, *89,* 315–316.

Ehrlich, D., Guttman, I., Schönbach, P., & Mills, J. Postdecision exposure to relevant information. *Journal of Abnormal and Social Psychology,* 1957, *54,* 98–102.

Ehrlich, H. J. Dogmatism and learning. *Journal of Abnormal and Social Psychology,* 1961, *62,* 148–149. (a)

Ehrlich, H. J. Dogmatism and learning: A five year follow-up. *Psychological Reports,* 1961, *9,* 283–286. (b)

*Ehrlich, H. J. *The social psychology of prejudice: A systematic theoretical review and propositional inventory of the American social psychological study of prejudice.* New York: Wiley, 1973.

Ehrlich, H. J., & Graeven, D. B. Reciprocal self-disclosure in a dyad. *Journal of Experimental Social Psychology,* 1971, *7,* 389–400.

Ehrlich, H. J., & Lee, D. Dogmatism, learning, and resistance to change: A review and a new paradigm. *Psychological Bulletin,* 1969, *71,* 249–260.

Ehrlich, P. R., & Holdren, J. P. The "lost genius" debate. *Saturday Review,* May 1, 1971, p. 61.

Ehrmann, W. *Premarital dating behavior.* New York: Holt, Rinehart & Winston, 1959.

Eibl-Eibesfeldt, I. [*Ethology: The biology of behavior*] (E. Klinghammer, trans.) New York: Holt, Rinehart & Winston, 1970.

Eichenwald, H. F., & Fry, P. C. Nutrition and learning. *Science,* 1969, *163,* 644–648.

Eisenberg, L. The *human* nature of human nature. *Science,* 1972, *176,* 123–128.

Eiser, J. R., & Stroebe, W. *Categorization and social judgement.* London: Academic Press, 1972.

Ekman, P. *A comparison of verbal and nonverbal behavior as reinforcing stimuli of opinion responses.* Unpublished doctoral dissertation, Adelphi College, 1958.

Ekman, P., & Friesen, W. V. Nonverbal leakage and clues to deception. *Psychiatry,* 1969, *32,* 88–106.

Ekman, P., & Friesen, W. V. Detecting deception from the body or face. *Journal of Personality and Social Psychology,* 1974, *29,* 288–298.

Elkind, D. Praise and imitation. *Saturday Review,* January 16, 1971, 51ff.

Elkind, D. Erik Erikson's eight ages of man. *Command and Management Course 1 Phase 1 Management Fundamental Lesson #2: Individual Behavior,* 1974.

Ellis, A. *The art and science of love.* New York: Lyle Stuart, 1960.

Ellis, A. The right to be wrong. *Journal of Sex Research,* 1968, *4,* 96–107.

Ellis, L. J., & Bentler, P. M. Traditional sex-determined role standards and sex stereotypes. *Journal of Personality and Social Psychology,* 1973, *25,* 28–34.

Ellsworth, P. C., & Carlsmith, J. M. Effect of eye contact and verbal consent on affective response to a dyadic interaction. *Journal of Personality and Social Psychology,* 1968, *10,* 15–20.

Ellsworth, P. C., & Ross, L. D. *Eye contact and intimacy.* Unpublished manuscript, Stanford University, 1972.

Elms, A. C. Right wingers in Dallas. *Psychology Today,* 1970, *3*(9), 27–31ff.

Elms, A. C. Horoscopes and Ardrey. *Psychology Today,* 1972, *6*(5), 36–44ff. (a)

Elms, A. C. *Social psychology and social relevance.* Boston: Little, Brown, 1972. (b)

Elms, A. C. The crisis of confidence in social psychology. *American Psychologist,* 1975, *30,* 967–976.

Elms, A., & Milgram, S. Personality characteristics associated with obedience and defiance toward authoritative command. *Journal of Experimental Research in Personality,* 1966, *1,* 282–289.

Emiley, S. F. The effects of crowding and interpersonal attraction on affective responses, task performance, and verbal behavior. *Journal of Social Psychology,* 1975, *97,* 267–278.

Emswiller, T., Deaux, K., & Willits, J. E. Similarity, sex, and requests for small favors. *Journal of Applied Social Psychology,* 1971, *1,* 284–291.

Endler, N. S. The person versus the situation—A pseudo-issue? A reply to Alker. *Journal of Personality,* 1973, *41,* 287–303.

Endler, N. S., & Hartley, S. Relative competence, reinforcement and conformity. *European Journal of Social Psychology,* 1973, *3,* 63–72.

Endler, N. S., & Hunt, J. McV. Inventories of hostility and comparisons of the proportions of variance from persons, responses, and situations for hostility and anxiousness. *Journal of Personality and Social Psychology,* 1968, *9,* 309–315.

Eoyang, C. K. Effects of group size and privacy in residential crowding. *Journal of Personality and Social Psychology,* 1974, *30,* 389–392.

Epley, S. W. Reduction of the behavioral effects of aversive stimulation by the presence of companions. *Psychological Bulletin,* 1974, *81,* 271–283.

Epley, S. W. The presence of others may reduce anxiety—the evidence is not conclusive. *Psychological Bulletin,* 1975, *82,* 886.

Epps, E. G. Correlates of academic achievement among Northern and Southern urban Negro students. *Journal of Social Issues,* 1969, *25*(3), 55–70.

Epstein, R., & Komorita, S. S. The development of a scale of parental punitiveness toward aggression. *Child Development,* 1965, *19,* 129–142. (a)

Epstein, R., & Komorita, S. S. Parental discipline, stimulus characteristics of outgroups, and social distance in children. *Journal of Personality and Social Psychology*, 1965, *2*, 416–420. (b)

Epstein, R., & Komorita, S. S. Prejudice among Negro children as related to parental ethnocentrism and punitiveness. *Journal of Personality and Social Psychology*, 1966, *4*, 643–647.

Epstein, Y., & Aiello, J. R. Effects of crowding on electrodermal activity. Paper presented at the meeting of the American Psychological Association, New Orleans, August 1974.

Epstein, Y., & Karlin, R. A. Effects of acute experimental crowding. *Journal of Applied Social Psychology*, 1975, *5*, 34–53.

Erickson, D. A. The plain people vs. the common schools. *Saturday Review*, November 19, 1966, pp. 85–87ff.

Erickson, V. Psychological growth for women: A cognitive developmental curriculum intervention. *Counseling and Values*, 1974, *18*(2), 102–116.

*Erikson, E. H. *Childhood and society* (2nd ed.). New York: Norton, 1963. (a)

Erikson, E. H. (Ed.). *Youth: Change and challenge*. New York: Basic Books, 1963. (b)

Erikson, E. H. Inner and outer space: Reflections on womanhood. *Daedalus*, 1964, *93*, 582–606. (a)

Erikson, E. H. *Insight and responsibility*. New York: Norton, 1964. (b)

Erikson, E. H. *Identity: Youth and crisis*. New York: Norton, 1968.

Erlenmeyer-Kimling, L., & Stern, S. E. Heritability of IQ by social class: Evidence inconclusive. *Science*, 1973, *182*, 1044–1045.

Erlich, J., & Riesman, D. Age and authority in the interview. *Public Opinion Quarterly*, 1961, *25*, 39–56.

Eron, L. D. Relationship of TV viewing habits and aggressive behavior in children. *Journal of Abnormal and Social Psychology*, 1963, *67*, 193–196.

Eron, L. D., Huesman, L. R., Lefkowitz, M. M., & Walder, L. O. Does television violence cause aggression? *American Psychologist*, 1972, *27*, 253–263.

Erskine, H. The polls: Capital punishment. *Public Opinion Quarterly*, 1970, *34*, 290–307.

Esman, A. Toward an understanding of racism. *Psychiatry and Social Science Review*, 1970, *4*, 7–9.

Esser, A. H. Cottage fourteen: Dominance and territoriality in a group of institutionalized boys. *Small Group Behavior*, 1973, *4*, 131–146.

Esser, A. H., Chamberlain, A. S., Chapple, E., & Kline, N. S. Territoriality of patients on a research ward. In J. Wortis (Ed.), *Recent advances in biological psychiatry*. New York: Plenum Press, 1964. Pp. 37–44.

Etzioni, A. A model of significant research. *International Journal of Psychiatry*, 1968, *6*, 279–280.

Evans, G., & Howard, R. B. Personal space. *Psychological Bulletin*, 1973, *80*, 334–344.

Evans, J. F. Motivational effects of being promised an opportunity to engage in social comparison. *Psychological Reports*, 1974, *34*, 175–181.

Evans, J. F. *The stressfulness of impending social comparison*. Paper presented at the Conference on "Dimensions in anxiety and stress," Olso, Norway, June 29–July 3, 1975.

Evans, R. B. Childhood parental relationships of homosexual men. *Journal of Consulting and Clinical Psychology*, 1969, *33*, 129–135.

*Evans, R. I. *Dialogue with Erik Erikson*. New York: Dutton, 1969.

*Fairfield, D. (Ed.). Communes, U. S. A. *The Modern Utopian*, 1971, *5*, Nos. 1, 2, and 3 combined.

Fairweather, G. W. *Social change: The challenge to survival*. Morristown, N. J.: General Learning Press, 1972.

*Fancher, R. E. *Psychoanalytic psychology: The development of Freud's thought*. New York: Norton, 1973.

*Fanon, F. *The wretched of the earth*. New York: Grove Press, 1965.

Farina, A., Allen, J. G., & Saul, B. B. B. The role of the stigmatized in affecting social relationships. *Journal of Personality*, 1968, *36*, 169–182.

Farina, A., Gliha, D., Boudreau, L. A., Allen, J. G., & Sherman, M. Mental illness and the impact of believing others know about it. *Journal of Abnormal Psychology*, 1971, 77, 1–5.

Farley, R., & Hermalin, A. The 1960s: A decade of progress for Blacks? *Demography*, 1972, *9*(3), 353–370.

Fast, J. *Body language*. New York: Evans, 1970.

Fawl, C. L. Disturbances experienced by children in their natural habitats. In R. G. Barker (Ed.), *The stream of behavior*. New York: Appleton-Century-Crofts, 1963. Pp. 99–126.

Feather, N. T. Cognitive dissonance, sensitivity, and evaluation. *Journal of Abnormal and Social Psychology*, 1963, *66*, 157–163.

Feather, N. T. Attribution of responsibility and valence of success and failure in relation to initial confidence and task performance. *Journal of Personality and Social Psychology*, 1969, *13*, 129–144.

Feather, N. T. Positive and negative reactions to male and female success and failure in relation to the perceived status and sex-typed appropriateness of occupations. *Journal of Personality and Social Psychology*, 1975, *31*, 536–549.

Feather, N. T., & Simon, J. G. Reactions to male and female success and failure in sex-linked occupations: Impressions of personality, causal attributions, and perceived likelihood of different consequences. *Journal of Personality and Social Psychology*, 1975, *31*, 20–31.

Feldman, R. E. Response to compatriot and foreigner who seek assistance. *Journal of Personality and Social Psychology*, 1968, *10*, 202–214.

Feldman, S. (Ed.). *Cognitive consistency: Motivational antecedents and behavioral consequents*. New York: Academic Press, 1966.

Feldman-Summers, S., & Kiesler, S. B. Those who are number two try harder: The effect of sex on attribution of causality. *Journal of Personality and Social Psychology*, 1974, *30*, 846–855.

Felipe, N. J., & Sommer, R. Invasions of personal space. *Social Problems*, 1966, *14*, 206–214.

Felknor, C., & Harvey, O. J. *Cognitive determinants of concept formation and attainment* (Technical Report No. 10). Contract with Office of Naval Research (Nonr 1147), University of Colorado, 1968.

Fendrich, J. M. A study of the association among verbal attitudes, commitment, and overt behavior in different experimental situations. *Social Forces*, 1967, 45, 347–355.

Fenichel, O. *The psychoanalytic theory of neurosis.* New York: Norton, 1945.

Ferguson, G. O., Jr. The intelligence of Negroes at Camp Lee, Virginia. *School and Society*, 1919, 9, 721–726.

Ferkiss, V. C. *Technological man: The myth and the reality.* New York: Braziller, 1969.

Feshbach, S. *Film violence and its effects on children: Some comments on the implications of research for public policy.* Paper presented at the meeting of the American Psychological Association, Washington, D.C., September 1969.

Feshbach, S., & Singer, R. D. The effects of personal and shared threats upon social prejudice. *Journal of Abnormal and Social Psychology*, 1957, 54, 411–416.

Feshbach, S., & Singer, R. D. *Television and aggression.* San Francisco: Jossey-Bass, 1970.

Festinger, L. Informal social communication. *Psychological Review*, 1950, 57, 271–282.

Festinger, L. An analysis of compliant behavior. In M. Sherif & M. O. Wilson (Eds.), *Group relations at the crossroads.* New York: Harper & Row, 1953. Pp. 232–256. (a)

Festinger, L. Laboratory experiments. In L. Festinger & D. Katz (Eds.), *Research methods in the behavioral sciences.* New York: Dryden, 1953. Pp. 136–172. (b)

Festinger, L. A theory of social comparison processes. *Human Relations*, 1954, 7, 117–140.

Festinger, L. *A theory of cognitive dissonance.* Stanford, Calif.: Stanford University Press, 1957.

Festinger, L., & Carlsmith, J. M. Cognitive consequences of forced compliance. *Journal of Abnormal and Social Psychology*, 1959, 58, 203–210.

Festinger, L., Gerard, H., Hymovitch, B., Kelley, H. H., & Raven, B. The influence process in the presence of extreme deviates. *Human Relations*, 1952, 5, 327–346.

Festinger, L., Pepitone, A., & Newcomb, T. Some consequences of deindividuation in a group. *Journal of Abnormal and Social Psychology*, 1952, 47, 382–389.

*Festinger, L., Riecken, H., & Schachter, S. *When prophecy fails.* Minneapolis, Minn.: University of Minnesota Press, 1956.

Festinger, L., Schachter, S., & Back, K. *Social pressures in informal groups: A study of human factors in housing.* New York: Harper, 1950.

Fidell, L. S. Empirical verification of sex discrimination in hiring practices in psychology. *American Psychologist*, 1970, 25, 1094–1098.

Fiedler, F. E. A contingency model of leadership effectiveness. In L. Berkowitz (Ed.), *Advances in experimental social psychology* (Vol. 1). New York: Academic Press, 1964. Pp. 149–190.

*Fiedler, F. E. *A theory of leadership effectiveness.* New York: McGraw-Hill, 1967.

Fiedler, F. E. Style or circumstance: The leadership enigma. *Psychology Today*, 1969, 2(10), 38–43.

Fiedler, F. E. Validation and extension of the contingency model of leadership effectiveness: A review of empirical findings. *Psychological Bulletin*, 1971, 76, 128–148.

Fiedler, F. E. Personality, motivational systems, and behavior of High and Low LPC persons. *Human Relations*, 1972, 25, 391–412.

Fiedler, F. E. The trouble with leadership training is that it doesn't train leaders. *Psychology Today*, 1973, 6(9), 23–30ff.

Fink, H. C. *Attitudes toward the Calley–My Lai case, authoritarianism, and political beliefs.* Paper presented at the meeting of the Eastern Psychological Association, Washington, D.C., May 1973.

Firestone, I. J., Kaplan, K. J., & Russell, J. C. Anxiety, fear, and affiliation with similar-state versus dissimilar-state others: Misery sometimes loves nonmiserable company. *Journal of Personality and Social Psychology*, 1973, 26, 409–414.

Fischer, W. F. Sharing in preschool children as a function of amount and type of reinforcement. *Genetic Psychology Monographs*, 1963, 68, 215–245.

Fish, B., & Kaplan, K. J. Does a "foot-in-the-door" get you in or out? *Psychological Reports*, 1974, 34, 35–42.

Fishbein, M. The relationships between beliefs, attitudes, and behavior. In S. Feldman (Ed.), *Cognitive consistency.* New York: Academic Press, 1966.

Fishbein, M., & Ajzen, I. *Belief, attitude, intention and behavior.* Reading, Mass.: Addison-Wesley, 1975.

Fishbein, M., & Hunter, R. Summation versus balance in attitude organization and change. *Journal of Abnormal and Social Psychology*, 1964, 69, 505–510.

Fishbein, M., Landy, E., & Hatch, G. Some determinants of an individual's esteem for his least preferred coworker: An attitudinal analysis. *Human Relations*, 1969, 22, 173–188.

Fisher, J. D. Situation-specific variables as determinants of perceived environmental aesthetic quality and perceived crowdedness. *Journal of Research in Personality*, 1974, 8, 177–188.

Fisher, J. D., & Byrne, D. Too close for comfort: Sex differences in response to invasions of personal space. *Journal of Personality and Social Psychology*, 1975, 32, 15–21.

Fisher, J. D., & Nadler, A. The effect of similarity between donor and recipient on recipient's reactions to aid. *Journal of Applied Social Psychology*, 1974, 4, 230–243.

Fisher, J. E., O'Neal, E. C., & McDonald, P. J. *Female competitiveness as a function of prior performance outcome, competitor's evaluation, and sex of competitor.* Paper presented at the meeting of the Midwestern Psychological Association, Chicago, May 1974.

Fishkin, J., Keniston, K., & MacKinnon, C. Moral reasoning and political ideology. *Journal of Personality and Social Psychology*, 1973, 27, 109–119.

Flacks, R. The liberated generation: An exploration of the roots of student protest. *Journal of Social Issues*, 1967, 23(3), 52–75.

Flanders, J. P., & Thistlethwaite, D. L. Effects of familiarization and group discussion upon risk-taking. *Journal of Experimental Social Psychology*, 1967, 5, 91–98.

Flaschman, S., & Weinrub, A. Heritability: A scientific snow job. *Science for the People*, March 1974, pp. 21–22.

Flavell, J. H. The development of inferences about others. In T. Mischel (Ed.), *Understanding other persons*. London: Blackwell, 1973. Pp. 66–116.

Fleishman, E. A., Harris, E. F., & Burtt, H. E. *Leadership and supervision in industry*. Columbus: Ohio State University Press, 1955.

Fleishman, E. A., & Peters, D. R. Interpersonal values, leadership attitudes and managerial success. *Personnel Psychology*, 1962, *15*, 127–143.

Flerx, V. C., & Rogers, R. W. *Sex-role stereotypes: Developmental aspects and early intervention*. Unpublished manuscript, Department of Psychology, University of South Carolina, 1975.

Flynn, J. P., Edwards, S. B., & Bandler, R. J. Changes in sensory and motor systems during centrally elicited attack. *Behavioral Science*, 1971, *16*, 1–20.

Flynn, J. T., & Peterson, M. The use of regression analysis in police patrolman selection. *Journal of Criminal Law, Criminology, and Police Science*, 1972, *63*, 564–569.

Fontana, A., & Noel, B. Moral reasoning in the university. *Journal of Personality and Social Psychology*, 1973, *27*, 419–429.

*Ford, C. S., & Beach, F. A. *Patterns of sexual behavior*. New York: Harper & Row, 1970 (Originally published, 1951.)

Form, W. H., & Nosow, S. *Community in disaster*. New York: Harper, 1958.

Forrester, B. J., & Klaus, R. A. The effect of race of the examiner on intelligence test scores of Negro kindergarten children. *Peabody Papers in Human Development*, 1964, *2*(7), 1–7.

Fortune, R. F. Arapesh warfare. *American Anthropologist*, 1939, *41*, 28.

Foulds, G. A., & Raven, J. C. Intellectual ability and occupational grade. *Occupational Psychology, London*, 1948, *22*, 197–203.

Fraczek, A., & Macaulay, J. R. Some personality factors in reaction to aggressive stimuli. *Journal of Personality*, 1971, *39*, 163–177.

Fraser, C. Group risk-taking and group polarization. *European Journal of Social Psychology*, 1971, *1*, 493–510.

Fraser, C., Gouge, C., & Billig, M. Risky shifts, cautious shifts, and group polarization. *European Journal of Social Psychology*, 1971, *1*, 7–30.

Freedman, J. L. How important is cognitive consistency? In R. P. Abelson, E. Aronson, W. J. McGuire, T. M. Newcomb, M. J. Rosenberg & P. H. Tannenbaum (Eds.), *Theories of cognitive consistency: A sourcebook*. Chicago: Rand-McNally, 1968. Pp. 497–503.

Freedman, J. L. The effects of population density on humans. In J. T. Fawcett (Ed.), *Psychological perspectives on population*. New York: Basic Books, 1972. Pp. 209–238.

Freedman, J. L. *Crowding and behavior*. San Francisco: Freeman, 1975.

Freedman, J. L., & Fraser, S. C. Compliance without pressure: The foot-in-the-door technique. *Journal of Personality and Social Psychology*, 1966, *4*, 195–202.

Freedman, J. L., Klevansky, S., & Ehrlich, P. R. The effect of crowding on human task performance. *Journal of Applied Social Psychology*, 1971, *1*, 7–25.

Freedman, J. L., Levy, A. S., Buchanan, R. W., & Price, J. Crowding and human aggressiveness. *Journal of Experimental Social Psychology*, 1972, *8*, 528–548.

Freedman, J., & Sears, D. O. Selective exposure. In L. Berkowitz (Ed.), *Advances in experimental social psychology* (Vol. 2). New York: Academic Press, 1965. Pp. 57–97.

Freedman, M. Homosexuals may be healthier than straights. *Psychology Today*, 1975, *8*(10), 28–32.

Freeman, H. A., & Freeman, R. S. Senior college women: Their sexual standards and activity. *Journal of the National Association of Women Deans and Counselors*, 1966, *29*(3), 136–143.

French, J. R. P., Jr. & Coch, L. Overcoming resistance to change. *Human Relations*, 1948, *1*, 512–532.

Freud, E. L. (Ed.) *Letters to Sigmund Freud*. New York: Basic Books, 1960.

Freud, S. *Totem and taboo*. London: Hogarth Press, 1913.

Freud, S. Some psychological consequences of the anatomical distinction between the sexes. *International Journal of Psychoanalysis*, 1927, *8*, 133–142.

Freud, S. *Civilization and its discontents*. London: Hogarth Press, 1930.

Freud, S. Female sexuality. *International Journal of Psychoanalysis*, 1932, *13*, 281–297.

Freud, S. The psychology of women. *New introductory lectures on psychoanalysis*. New York: Norton, 1933.

Freud, S. *Moses and monotheism*. London: Hogarth Press. 1939.

Freud, S. Fragment of an analysis of a case of hysteria. In *Collected Papers* (Vol. 3). New York: Basic Books, 1959. (Originally published, 1905.)

Freud, S. Introductory lectures on psychoanalysis. In J. Strachey (Ed.), *The standard edition of the complete psychological works* (Vols. 15 & 16). London: Hogarth Press, 1963. (First German edition, 1917.)

Freud, S., & Bullitt, W. C. *Thomas Woodrow Wilson*. Boston: Houghton-Mifflin, 1967.

Freund, K., Sedlacek, F., & Knob, K. A simple transducer for mechanical plethysmography of the male genital. *Journal of the Experimental Analysis of Behavior*, 1965, *8*, 169–170.

Frey, D., & Irle, M. Some conditions to produce a dissonance and an incentive effect in a "forced compliance" situation. *European Journal of Social Psychology*, 1972, *2*, 45–54.

Fried, M. H. The need to end the pseudoscientific investigation. In M. Mead, T. Dobzhansky, E. Tobach, & R. E. Light (Eds.), *Science and the concept of race*. New York: Columbia University Press, 1968. Pp. 122–131.

Fried, S., Gumpper, D. C., & Allen, J. C. Ten years of social psychology: Is there a growing commitment to field research? *American Psychologist*, 1973, *28*, 155–156.

Friedenberg, E. Z. Current patterns of generational conflict. *Journal of Social Issues*, 1969, *25*(2), 21–38.

Frieze, I. H. *Changing self-images and sex-role stereotypes in college women*. Paper presented at the meeting of the American Psychological Association, New Orleans, August 1974.

Frieze, I. H., Hanusa, B. H., Fisher, J., & McHugh, M. C. Sex differences in achievement behavior: An attributional analysis. *Journal of Social Issues*, in press.

Frodi, A. The effects of exposure to aggression-eliciting and aggression-inhibiting stimuli on subsequent aggression. *Göteborg Psychological Reports*, 1973, 3, No. 8.

Fromkin, H. L. *The psychology of uniqueness: Avoidance of similarity and seeking of differentness.* Paper No. 438, Institute for Research in the Behavioral, Economic, and Management Sciences, Krannert Graduate School of Industrial Administration, Purdue University, December 1973.

Fromkin, H. L., Brandt, J., King, D. C., Sherwood, J. J., & Fisher, J. *An evaluation of human relations training for police.* Paper No. 469, Institute for Research in the Behavioral, Economic, and Management Sciences, Krannert Graduate School of Industrial Administration, Purdue University, August 1974.

Fromkin, H. L., & Brock, T. C. Erotic materials: A commodity theory analysis of the enhanced desirability that may accompany their unavailability. *Journal of Applied Social Psychology*, 1973, 3, 219–231.

Fromkin, H. L., Klimoski, R. J., & Flanagan, M. F. Race and task competency as determinants of newcomer acceptance in work groups. *Organizational Behavior and Human Performance*, 1972, 7, 25–42.

Fromm, E. *Man for himself.* New York: Rinehart, 1955.

Fromme, A. *Sex and marriage.* New York: Barnes & Noble, 1955.

Fryer, D. Occupational intelligence standards. *School and Society*, 1922, 16, 273–277.

Fugita, S. S. Effects of anxiety and approval on visual interaction. *Journal of Personality and Social Psychology*, 1974, 29, 586–592.

*Fuller, E. *Man in modern fiction.* New York: Random House Vintage Books, 1958.

Gaebelein, J. W. Instigative aggression in females. *Psychological Reports*, 1973, 33, 619–622. (a)

Gaebelein, J. W. Third party instigation of aggression: An experimental approach. *Journal of Personality and Social Psychology*, 1973, 27, 389–395. (b)

Gaebelein, J. W., & Hay, W. M. Third party instigation of aggression as a function of attack and vulnerability. *Journal of Research in Personality*, 1974, 7, 324–333.

Gaebelein, J. W., & Taylor, S. P. The effects of competition and attack on physical aggression. *Psychonomic Science*, 1971, 24, 65–67.

Gaertner, S. L. Helping behavior and racial discrimination among liberals and conservatives. *Journal of Personality and Social Psychology*, 1973, 25, 335–341.

Gaertner, S. L. *Racial attitudes of liberals.* Paper presented at the meeting of the American Psychological Association, New Orleans, September 1974.

Gaertner, S., & Bickman, L. Effects of race on the elicitation of helping behavior: The wrong number technique. *Journal of Personality and Social Psychology*, 1971, 20, 218–222.

Gage, N. L. Judging interests from expressive behavior. *Psychological Monographs*, 1952, 66 (18, Whole No. 350).

*Gage, N. L., & Cronbach, L. J. Conceptual and methodological problems in interpersonal perception. *Psychological Review*, 1955, 62, 411–422.

Gage, N. L., Leavitt, G. S., & Stone, G. C. The psychological meaning of acquiescence set for authoritarianism. *Journal of Abnormal and Social Psychology*, 1957, 55, 98–103.

*Gagnon, J. H., & Simon, W. *Sexual conduct: The social sources of human sexuality.* Chicago: Aldine, 1973.

Galizio, M., & Hendrick, C. Effect of musical accompaniment on attitude: The guitar as a prop for persuasion. *Journal of Applied Social Psychology*, 1972, 2, 350–359.

Galle, O. R., Gove, W. R., & McPherson, J. M. Population density and pathology: What are the relations for man? *Science*, 1972, 176, 23–30.

Gallup, G. H. *The Gallup poll: Public opinion 1935–1971.* New York: Random House, 1972.

Galton, F. *Hereditary genius: An inquiry into its laws.* New York: Horizon Press, 1952. (Originally published, 1870.)

Gamson, W. A. Violence and political power: The meek don't make it. *Psychology Today*, 1974, 8(2), 35–41.

Gamson, W. A. *The strategy of social protest.* Homewood, Ill.: Dorsey, 1975.

Gans, H. J. Planning and social life: Friendship and neighbor relations in suburban communities. In H. Proshansky, W. Ittelson, & L. Rivlin (Eds.), *Environmental psychology.* New York: Holt, Rinehart & Winston, 1970. Pp. 501–509.

Garai, J. E., & Scheinfeld, A. Sex differences in mental and behavioral traits. *Genetic Psychology Monographs*, 1968, 77, 169–299.

*Gardner, J. *Grendel.* New York: Knopf, 1971.

Garrett, H. E. A note on the intelligence scores of Negroes and Whites in 1918. *Journal of Abnormal and Social Psychology*, 1945, 40, 344–346.

Garrett, H. E. Klineberg's chapter on race and psychology: A review. *Mankind Quarterly*, 1960, 1, 15–22.

Garrett, H. E. The SPSSI and racial differences ("Comment" section). *American Psychologist*, 1962, 17, 260–263.

Garrett, H. E. McGraw's need for denial ("Comment" section). *American Psychologist*, 1964, 19, 815.

Garrett, H. E. *A critical review of Thomas Pettigrew's A profile of the Negro American.* Charlottesville, Va.: Author, 1965.

Garrett, H. E. Reply to Psychology Class 338 (Honors Section). *American Psychologist*, 1969, 24, 390–391.

Garrett, J. B., & Wallace, B. Cognitive consistency, repression-sensitization, and level of moral judgment: Reactions of college students to the Watergate scandal. *Journal of Social Psychology*, 1976, 98, 3–8.

Garth, T. R., Schuelke, N., & Abell, W. The intelligence of mixed-blood Indians. *Journal of Applied Psychology*, 1927, 11, 268–275.

*Gartner, A., Greer, C., & Riessman, F. (Eds.) *The new assault on equality: IQ and social stratification.* New York: Harper & Row, 1974.

Garwood, S. G., & McDavid, J. W. *Ethnic factors in stereotypes of given names.* Paper presented at the meeting of the American Psychological Association, New Orleans, September 1974.

Gay, J. & Cole, M. *The new mathematics and an old culture.* New York: Holt, 1967.

Geber, M. Développement psychomoteur de l'enfant africain. *Courrier* (Paris: UNESCO), 1956, *6*, 17–29.

Geber, M., & Dean, R. F. A. Development rates of African children in Uganda. *Lancet*, 1957, *272* (6981), 1216–1219. (a)

Geber, M., & Dean, R. F. A. Gesell tests on African children. *Pediatrics*, 1957, *6*, 1056–1065. (b)

Gecas, V. Parental behavior and dimensions of adolescent self-evaluation. *Sociometry*, 1971, *34*, 466–482.

Geen, R. G. *Aggression.* Morristown, N.J.: General Learning Press, 1972. (Module No. 4039 V00)

Geen, R. G. *Interpretations of observed violence and their influence on human aggression.* Paper presented at the meeting of the Midwestern Psychological Association, Chicago, May 1973.

Geen, R. G., & Berkowitz, L. Name-mediated aggressive cue properties. *Journal of Personality*, 1966, *34*, 456–465.

Geen, R. G., & Berkowitz, L. Some conditions facilitating the occurrence of aggression after the observation of violence. *Journal of Personality*, 1967, *35*, 666–676.

Geen, R. G., & O'Neal, E. C. Activation of cue-elicited aggression by general arousal. *Journal of Personality and Social Psychology*, 1969, *11*, 289–292.

Geen, R. G., Rakosky, J. J., & O'Neal, E. C. Methodological study of measurement of aggression. *Psychological Reports*, 1968, *23*, 59–62.

Geen, R. G., & Stonner, D. Context effects in observed violence. *Journal of Personality and Social Psychology*, 1973, *25*, 145–150.

Geer, J. H. *Cognitive factors in sexual arousal—toward an amalgam of research strategies.* Paper presented at the meeting of the American Psychological Association, New Orleans, August 1974.

Geer, J. H., & Jarmecky, L. The effect of being responsible for reducing another's pain on subject's response and arousal. *Journal of Personality and Social Psychology*, 1973, *26*, 232–237.

Geis, F., Christie, R., & Nelson, C. In search of the Machiavel. In R. Christie & F. L. Geis (Eds.), *Studies in Machiavellianism.* New York: Academic Press, 1970. Pp. 76–95.

Geis, F. L., & Levy, M. The eye of the beholder. In R. Christie & F. L. Geis (Eds.), *Studies in Machiavellianism.* New York: Academic Press, 1970. Pp. 210–235.

Gelfand, D. M., Hartmann, D. P., Walder, P., & Page, B. Who reports shoplifters? A field-experimental study. *Journal of Personality and Social Psychology*, 1973, *25*, 276–285.

Gentry, W. D. Effects of frustration, attack, and prior aggressive training on overt aggression and vascular processes. *Journal of Personality and Social Psychology*, 1970, *16*, 718–725.

Gentry, W. D. *Aggression in fairy tales: A study of three cultures.*

Paper presented at the meeting of the Southeastern Psychological Association, Hollywood, Fla., April 1974.

Gerard, H. B., & Mathewson, G. D. The effects of severity of initiation on liking for a group: A replication. *Journal of Experimental Social Psychology*, 1966, *2*, 278–287.

Gerard, H. B., & Rabbie, J. M. Fear and social comparison. *Journal of Abnormal and Social Psychology*, 1961, *62*, 586–592.

Gergen, K. J. Personal consistency and the presentation of self. In C. Gordon & K. J. Gergen (Eds.), *The self in social interaction.* New York: Wiley, 1968. Pp. 299–308.

*Gergen, K. J. *The psychology of behavior exchange.* Reading, Mass.: Addison-Wesley, 1969.

Gergen, K. J. Social psychology as history. *Journal of Personality and Social Psychology*, 1973, *26*, 309–320. (a)

Gergen, K. J. The codification of research ethics: Views of a doubting Thomas. *American Psychologist*, 1973, *28*, 907–912. (b)

Gergen, K. J. *Experimental paradigm: Death and transfiguration.* Paper presented at the meeting of the American Psychological Association, Chicago, September 1975.

Gergen, K. J., Gergen, M. M., & Meter, K. Individual orientations to prosocial behavior. *Journal of Social Issues*, 1972, *28*(3), 105–130.

Gergen, K. J., Gergen, M. M., & Meter, K. Individual orientations to prosocial behavior. In L. Wispé (Ed.), *The psychology of sympathy and altruism.* Cambridge, Mass.: Harvard University Press, 1977.

*Gergen, K. J., & Marlowe, D. (Eds.). *Personality and social behavior.* Reading, Mass.: Addison-Wesley, 1970.

Gergen, K. J., & Taylor, M. G. Social expectancy and self-presentation in a status hierarchy. *Journal of Experimental Social Psychology*, 1969, *5*, 79–92.

Gergen, K. J., & Wishnov, B. Others' self-evaluations and interaction anticipation as determinants of self-presentation. *Journal of Personality and Social Psychology*, 1965, *2*, 348–358.

Geschwender, J. A. Social structure and the Negro revolt: An examination of some hypotheses. *Social Forces*, 1964, *43*, 248–256.

Gesell, A., Ilg, F. L., & Ames, L. B. *Youth: The years from ten to sixteen.* New York: Harper & Row, 1956.

Getzels, J. W., & Walsh, J. J. The method of paired direct and projective questionnaires in the study of attitude structure and socialization. *Psychological Monographs*, 1958, *72*(1, Whole No. 254).

Gibb, C. A. Leadership. In G. Lindzey & E. Aronson (Eds.), *Handbook of social psychology* (Vol. 4) (2nd ed.). Reading, Mass.: Addison-Wesley, 1969. Pp. 205–282.

Ginsburg, B. E., & Laughlin, W. S. The distribution of genetic differences in behavioral potential in the human species. In M. Mead, T. Dobzhansky, E. Tobach, & R. E. Light (Eds.), *Science and the concept of race.* New York: Columbia University Press, 1968. Pp. 26–36.

Glass, B. The genetic basis of human races. In M. Mead, T. Dobzhansky, E. Tobach, & R. E. Light (Eds.), *Science and the concept of race.* New York: Columbia University Press, 1968. Pp. 88–93.

Glass, B., & Li, C. C. The dynamics of racial intermixture: An analysis based on the American Negro. *American Journal of Human Genetics,* 1953, *5,* 1–20.

Glass, D. C., & Singer, J. E. *Urban stress.* New York: Academic Press, 1972.

Glass, D. C., & Singer, J. E. Experimental studies of uncontrollable and unpredictable noise. *Representative Research in Social Psychology,* 1973, *4,* 165–183.

Glassner, W. J., & Stires, L. K. *The effect of appearance on the acceptance of a political leaflet.* Paper presented at the meeting of the Eastern Psychological Association, Washington, D.C., May 1973.

Goethals, G. R., & Cooper, J. Role of intention and post-behavioral consequence in the arousal of cognitive dissonance. *Journal of Personality and Social Psychology,* 1972, *23,* 298–301.

Goffman, E. On face-work: An analysis of ritual elements in social interaction. *Psychiatry,* 1955, *18,* 213–231.

*Goffman, E. *The presentation of self in everyday life.* Garden City, N.Y.: Doubleday Anchor, 1959.

Goffman, E. *Asylums.* Garden City, N.Y.: Doubleday Anchor, 1961.

Goffman, E. *Behavior in public places: Notes on the social organization of gatherings.* Glencoe, Ill.: Free Press, 1963. (a)

*Goffman, E. *Stigma: Notes on the management of spoiled identity.* Englewood Cliffs, N. J.: Prentice-Hall, 1963. (b)

Goffman, E. *Interaction ritual: Essays on face-to-face behavior.* Garden City, N. Y.: Doubleday, 1967.

Goffman, E. *Relations in public.* New York: Basic Books, 1971.

Goldberg, G. N., Kiesler, C. A., & Collins, B. E. Visual behavior and face-to-face distance during interaction. *Sociometry,* 1969, *32,* 43–53.

Goldberg, P. Are women prejudiced against women? *Trans-Action,* 1968, *5,* 28–30.

Goldberg, S. C. Three situational determinants of conformity to social norms. *Journal of Abnormal and Social Psychology,* 1954, *49,* 325–329.

Golden, J. Roundtable: Marital discord and sex. *Medical Aspects of Human Sexuality,* 1971, *1,* 160–190.

Goldsmith, N. F. Women in science: Symposium and job mart. *Science,* 1970, *168,* 1124–1127.

Goldstein, J. H., & Arms, R. L. Effects of observing athletic contests on hostility. *Sociometry,* 1971, *34,* 83–90.

Goldstein, M. J. Exposure to erotic stimuli and sexual deviance. *Journal of Social Issues,* 1973, *29*(3), 197–219.

Goldstein, M. J., & Wilson, W. C. Introduction. *Journal of Social Issues,* 1973, *29*(3), 1–5.

Gomes, B., & Abramowitz, S. I. Sex-related therapist and patient effects on clinical judgment. *Sex Roles: A Journal of Research,* 1976, *2,* 1–14.

Goode, W. The theoretical importance of love. *American Sociological Review,* 1959, *24,* 38–47.

Goodman, W. *The committee: The extraordinary career of the House Committee on Un-American Activities.* New York: Farrar,

Straus, & Giroux, 1968.

Goodwin, L. *Do the poor want to work? A social-psychological study of work orientations.* Washington, D. C.: The Brookings Institution, 1972.

Goranson, R. E., & Berkowitz, L. Reciprocity and responsibility reactions to prior help. *Journal of Personality and Social Psychology,* 1966, *3,* 227–232.

Goranson, R., & King, D. Rioting and daily temperature: Analysis of the U. S. riots in 1967. (Unpublished manuscript, York University, 1970, cited in Baron, R., Byrne, D., & Griffitt, W., *Social psychology: Understanding human interaction.* Boston: Allyn & Bacon, 1974.)

Gordon, K. Group judgments in the field of lifted weights. *Journal of Experimental Psychology,* 1924, *7,* 389–400.

Gordon, S. Untitled "letter to the editor." *Ms.,* 1973, *2*(1), 4. (July 1973 issue.)

Gorer, G. Man has no "killer" instinct. In M. F. A. Montagu (Ed.), *Man and aggression.* New York: Oxford University Press, 1968. Pp. 27–36.

*Gossett, T. F. *Race: The history of an idea in America.* Dallas: Southern Methodist University Press, 1963.

Gouge, C., & Fraser, C. A further demonstration of group polarization. *European Journal of Psychology,* 1972, *2,* 95–97.

Gough, H. G. *California Psychological Inventory manual.* Palo Alto: Calif.: Consulting Psychologists Press, 1957.

Gouldner, A. W. The norm of reciprocity: A preliminary statement. *American Sociological Review,* 1960, *25,* 161–178.

Graen, G., Alvares, K., Orris, J. B., & Martella, J. A. Contingency model of leadership effectiveness: Antecedent and evidential results. *Psychological Bulletin,* 1970, *74,* 284–296.

Graham, D. Experimental studies of social influence in simple judgment situations. *Journal of Social Psychology,* 1962, *56,* 245–269.

*Graham, H. D., & Gurr, T. R. (Eds.). *Violence in America: Historical and comparative perspectives.* New York: New American Library, 1969.

Graham, W. K., & Dillon, P. C. Creative supergroups: Group performance as a function of individual performance on brainstorming tasks. *Journal of Social Psychology,* 1974, *93,* 101–105.

Granberg, D. Authoritarianism and the assumption of similarity to self. *Journal of Experimental Research in Personality,* 1972, *6,* 1–4.

Granberg, D., & Steele, L. Procedural considerations in measuring latitudes of acceptance, rejection, and noncommitment. *Social Forces,* 1974, *52,* 538–542.

Gray, D. B., & Revelle, W. A cluster analytic critique of the Multifactor Racial Attitude Inventory. *Psychological Record,* 1972, *22,* 103–112.

Gray, S. W. The performance of the culturally deprived child: Contributing variables. *Proceedings of Section II, Annual Professional Institute of the Division of School Psychologists, American Psychological Association,* 1962. Pp. 30–36. (Mimeographed)

Gray, S. W. *Selected longitudinal studies of compensatory education—a look from the inside.* Paper presented at the meeting of the American Psychological Association, Washington, D. C., September 1969.

Gray, S. W. & Klaus, R. A. An experimental preschool program for culturally deprived children. *Child Development*, 1965, *36*, 887–898.

Gray, S. W., & Klaus, R. A. The Early Training Project: A seventh year report. *Child Development*, 1970, *41*, 909–924.

Greaves, G. Conceptual system functioning and selective recall of information. *Journal of Personality and Social Psychology*, 1972, *21*, 327–332.

Green, D. Dissonance and self-perception analyses of "forced compliance": When two theories make competing predictions. *Journal of Personality and Social Psychology*, 1974, *29*, 819–828.

Green, J. A. Attitudinal and situational determinants of intended behavior toward Negroes. (Doctoral dissertation, University of Colorado.) Ann Arbor, Mich.: University Microfilms, 1968. No. 68-2644.

Green, R., & Money, J. (Eds.). *Transsexualism and sex reassignment*. Baltimore, Md.: Johns Hopkins Press, 1969.

Green, R. F. *On the correlation between I.Q. and amount of "White" blood*. Paper presented at the meeting of the American Psychological Association, Honolulu, August 1972.

Green, R. L. *The effects of nonschooling on measured intelligence among elementary school-age children*. Paper presented at the meeting of the American Psychological Association, Chicago, September 1965.

Greenberg, B. S., & Parker, E. G. (Eds.). *The Kennedy assassination and the American public: Social communication in crisis*. Stanford, Calif.: Stanford University Press, 1965.

Greenberg, M. S., & Frisch, D. M. Effect of intentionality on willingness to reciprocate a favor. *Journal of Experimental Social Psychology*, 1972, *8*, 99–111.

Greenberg, M. S., & Shapiro, S. P. Indebtedness: An adverse aspect of asking for and receiving help. *Sociometry*, 1971, *34*, 290–301.

Greenfield, S. M. *Love: Some reflections by a social anthropologist*. Paper presented at the meeting of the American Psychological Association, Miami Beach, September 1970.

Greenwald, A. G. On the inconclusiveness of "crucial" cognitive tests of dissonance versus self-perception theories. *Journal of Experimental Social Psychology*, 1975, *11*, 490–499.

Greenwood, J. M., & McNamara, W. J. Leadership styles of structure and consideration and managerial effectiveness. *Personnel Psychology*, 1969, *22*, 141–152.

Gregor, G. L., Smith, R. F., Simons, L. S., & Parker, H. B. Behavioral consequences of crowding in the deermouse. *Journal of Comparative and Physiological Psychology*, 1970, *79*, 488–493.

Griffitt, W. Environmental effects on interpersonal behavior: Ambient effective temperature and attraction. *Journal of Personality and Social Psychology*, 1970, *15*, 240–244.

Griffitt, W. Attitude similarity and attraction. In T. L. Huston (Ed.), *Foundations of interpersonal attraction*. New York: Academic Press, 1974. Pp. 285–308.

Griffitt, W., & Veitch, R. Influences of population density on interpersonal affective behavior. *Journal of Personality and Social Psychology*, 1971, *17*, 92–98.

Griffitt, W., & Veitch, R. Preacquaintance attitude similarity and attraction revisited: Ten days in a fall-out shelter. *Sociometry*, 1974, *37*, 163–173.

Gross, A. E. *Sex and helping: Intrinsic glow and extrinsic show*. Paper presented at the meeting of the American Psychological Association, Honolulu, September 1972.

Gross, A. E., & Latané, J. G. Receiving help, reciprocation, and interpersonal attraction. *Journal of Applied Social Psychology*, 1974, *4*, 210–223.

Gross, A. E., Piliavin, I. M., Wallston, B. S., & Broll, L. *When humanitarianism is not humane: Helping—the recipient's view*. Paper presented at the meeting of the American Psychological Association, Honolulu, September 1972.

Gross, A. E., Wallston, B. S., & Piliavin, I. M. Beneficiary attractiveness and cost as determinants of responses to routine requests for help. *Sociometry*, 1975, *38*, 131–140.

Gross, A. E., Wallston, B. S., & Piliavin, I. M. The help recipient: A social psychological perspective. In D. H. Smith & J. Macauley (Eds.), *Voluntary action 1975: Individual voluntary action, altruism and leisure activity*. Lexington, Mass.: Heath, in press.

Grossack, M. M., & Gardner, H. *Man and men: Social psychology as a social science*. Scranton, Pa.: International Textbook, 1970.

Groves, W. E., Rossi, P. H., & Grafstein, D. *Study of life styles and campus communities: A preliminary report to students who participated*. Baltimore, Md.: Department of Social Relations, Johns Hopkins University, 1970.

Gruen, W. *The composition and some correlates of the American core culture*. Canandaigua, N. Y.: Veterans Administration Hospital, 1964. (Mimeographed)

Gruenfeld, L. W., Rance, D. E., & Weissenberg, P. The behavior of task-oriented (low LPC) and socially-oriented (high LPC) leaders under several conditions of social support. *Journal of Social Psychology*, 1969, *79*, 99–107.

Grusec, J. E., & Skubiski, S. L. Model nurturance, demand characteristics of the modeling experiment, and altruism. *Journal of Personality and Social Psychology*, 1970, *14*, 352–359.

Guetzkow, H., Alger, C., Brody, R., Noel, R., & Snyder, R. *Simulation in international relations: Developments for research and teaching*. Englewood Cliffs, N. J.: Prentice-Hall, 1963.

Gullahorn, J. T. Distance and friendship as factors in the gross interaction matrix. *Sociometry*, 1952, *15*, 123–134.

Guller, I. B., & Bailes, D. W. *Dogmatism and attitudes toward the Viet Nam war*. Paper presented at the meeting of the Eastern Psychological Association, Washington, D. C., April 1968.

Gump, P. V., Schoggen, P., & Redl, F. The camp milieu and its immediate effects. *Journal of Social Issues*, 1957, *13*(1), 40–46.

Gurin, P., Gurin, G., Lao, R. C., & Beattie, M. Internal-external control in the motivational dynamics of Negro youth. *Journal of Social Issues*, 1969, *25*(3), 29–53.

Gurnee, H. A comparison of collective and individual judgments of facts. *Journal of Experimental Psychology*, 1937, *21*, 106–112.

Gurr, T. R. *Why men rebel.* Princeton, N. J.: Princeton University Press, 1970.

Gusfield, J. The study of social movements. In *International encyclopedia of the social sciences* (Vol. 14). New York: Macmillan, 1968. Pp. 445–452.

Gutkin, D. C. The effect of systematic story changes on intentionality in children's moral judgments. *Child Development*, 1972, *43*, 187–195.

Gutkin, D. C. An analysis of the concept of moral intentionality. *Human Development*, 1973, *16*, 371–381.

Haan, N., Smith, M. B., & Block, J. Moral reasoning of young adults: Political-social behavior, family background, and personality correlates. *Journal of Personality and Social Psychology*, 1968, *10*, 183–201.

Haan, N., Stroud, J., & Holstein, C. Moral and ego stages in relationship to ego processes: A study of "hippies." *Journal of Personality*, 1973, *4*, 596–612.

Haas, K. Obedience: Submission to destructive orders as related to hostility. *Psychological Reports*, 1966, *19*, 32–34.

Haase, R. S. The relationship of sex and instructional set to the regulation of interpersonal interaction distance in a counseling analogue. *Journal of Counseling Psychology*, 1970, *17*, 233–236.

Hackman, J. R., & Vidmar, N. Effects of size and task type on group performance and member reactions. In L. Marlowe (Ed.), *Basic topics in social psychology*. Boston: Holbrook Press, 1972. Pp. 244–258.

Hagen, E. E. *On the theory of social change.* Homewood, Ill.: Dorsey, 1962.

Haggstrom, W. C. The power of the poor. In F. Reissman, J. Cohen, & A. Pearl (Eds.), *Mental health of the poor.* New York: Free Press, 1964.

Hain, J. D., & Linton, P. H. Physiological response to visual sexual stimuli. *Journal of Sex Research*, 1969, *5*, 292–302.

Haines, D. B., & McKeachie, W. J. Cooperative versus competitive discussion methods in teaching introductory psychology. *Journal of Educational Psychology*, 1967, *58*, 386–390.

Hall, C. S., & Lindzey, G. The relevance of Freudian psychology and related viewpoints for the social sciences. In G. Lindzey & E. Aronson (Eds.), *Handbook of social psychology* (Vol. 1) (2nd ed.). Reading, Mass.: Addison-Wesley, 1968. Pp. 245–319.

Hall, C. S., & Lindzey, G. *Theories of personality* (2nd ed.). New York: Wiley, 1970.

Hall, E. T. *The silent language.* Garden City, N. Y.: Doubleday, 1959.

Hall, E. T. A system for the notation of proxemic behavior. *American Anthropologist*, 1963, *65*, 1003–1026.

*Hall, E. T. *The hidden dimension.* Garden City, N. Y.: Doubleday, 1966.

Hall, K. R. L. Aggression in monkey and ape societies. In J. D. Carthy & F. J. Ebling (Eds.), *The natural history of aggression.* New York: Academic Press, 1964. Pp. 51–64.

Halpin, A. W. Studies in aircrew composition: III. In *The combat leader behavior of B-29 aircraft commanders.* Washington, D. C.: Human Factors Operations Research Laboratory, Bolling Air Force Base, September 1953.

Halpin, A. W. The leadership behavior and combat performances of airplane commanders. *Journal of Abnormal and Social Psychology*, 1954, *49*, 19–22.

*Halpin, A. W. *Theory and research in administration.* New York: Macmillan, 1966.

Halpin, A. W., & Winer, B. J. *The leadership behavior of the airplane commander.* Research Foundation, Columbus: Ohio State University, 1952. (Mimeographed)

Hamilton, D. L., & Huffman, L. J. Generality of impression-formation processes for evaluative and nonevaluative judgments. *Journal of Personality and Social Psychology*, 1971, *20*, 200–207.

Hammer, T. H. *Leadership as a multi-faceted concept: Integrating leadership, motivation and power.* Paper presented at the meeting of the American Psychological Association, New Orleans, August 1974.

Haney, C., Banks, C., & Zimbardo, P. Interpersonal dynamics in a simulated prison. *International Journal of Criminology and Penology*, 1973, *1*, 69–97.

Hanratty, M. A., O'Neal, E., & Sulzer, J. L. Effect of frustration upon imitation of aggression. *Journal of Personality and Social Psychology*, 1972, *21*, 30–34.

Harari, H., & McDavid, J. W. Name stereotypes and teachers' expectations. *Journal of Educational Psychology*, 1973, *65*, 222–225.

Harding, J., Kutner, B., Proshansky, H., & Chein, I. Prejudice and ethnic relations. In G. Lindzey (Ed.), *Handbook of social psychology* (Vol. 5) (2nd ed.). Reading, Mass.: Addison-Wesley, 1969. Pp. 1–76.

*Hardwick, E. *Women and literature.* New York: Random House, 1974.

Harlow, H. F. The nature of love. *American Psychologist*, 1958, *13*, 673–685.

Harré, R., & Secord, P. F. *The explanation of social behavior.* Oxford, England: Blackwell, 1972.

Harrell, J. V., & Caldwell, M. D. *The effects of polling information on candidate selection behavior.* Paper presented at the meeting of the Southeastern Psychological Association, Atlanta, March 1975.

Harrell, R. F., Woodyard, E. R., & Gates, A. I. Influence of vitamin supplementation of diets of pregnant and lactating women on intelligence of their offspring. *Metabolism*, 1956, *5*, 555–562.

Harrell, T. W., & Harrell, M. S. Army general classification test scores for civilian populations. *Educational and Psychological Measurement*, 1945, *5*, 229–239.

Harris, A. S. The second sex in academe. *American Association of University Professors Bulletin*, 1970, *56*, 283–295.

Harris Survey. Nonconformity is eyed askance. Honolulu *Advertiser*, September 27, 1965, p. 17.

Harrison, A. A. Exposure and popularity. *Journal of Personality*, 1969, *37*, 359–377.

*Harrison, R. P. *Beyond words: An introduction to nonverbal com-

munication. Englewood Cliffs, N. J.: Prentice-Hall, 1974.

Hart, H. *Selective migration as a factor in child welfare in the United States, with special reference to Iowa.* Iowa City: University of Iowa Studies in Child Welfare, I, 1921.

Hartley, E. L. *Problems in prejudice*. New York: King's Crown Press, 1946.

Hartman, A. A., Nicolay, R. C., & Hurley, J. Unique personal names as a social adjustment factor. *Journal of Social Psychology*, 1968, 75, 107–110.

Hartmann, D. P. *Comments on the choice of a dependent variable in laboratory investigations of human aggression.* Paper presented at the meeting of the American Psychological Association, Miami Beach, September 1970.

Hartmann, H., Kris, E., & Loewenstein, R. M. Notes on a theory of aggression. *Psychoanalytic Study of the Child*, 1949, 3–4, 9–36.

Hartshorne, H., & May, M. A. *Studies in the nature of character* (Vol. 1). *Studies in deceit*. New York: Macmillan, 1928.

Harvey, J. H., Arkin, R. M., Gleason, J. M., & Johnston, S. Effect of expected and observed outcome of an action on the differential causal attributions of actor and observer. *Journal of Personality*, 1974, 42, 62–77.

Harvey, J., & Hays, D. G. Effect of dogmatism and authority of the source of communication upon persuasion. *Psychological Reports*, 1972, 30, 119–122.

Harvey, J., & Mills, J. Effect of a difficult opportunity to revoke a counterattitudinal action upon attitude change. *Journal of Personality and Social Psychology*, 1971, 18, 201–209.

Harvey, O. J. System structure, flexibility and creativity. In O. J. Harvey (Ed.), *Experience, structure, and adaptability*. New York: Springer, 1966.

Harvey, O. J. *Belief systems and education: Some implications for change.* Unpublished manuscript, Department of Psychology, University of Colorado, 1969.

*Harvey, O. J., Hunt, D. E., & Schroder, H. M. *Conceptual systems and personality organization*. New York: Wiley, 1961.

Harvey, O. J., & Ware, R. Personality differences in dissonance reduction. *Journal of Personality and Social Psychology*, 1967, 7, 227–230.

Hastorf, A. H., Schneider, D. J., & Polefka, J. *Person perception*. Reading, Mass.: Addison-Wesley, 1970.

Hathaway, S. R., & McKinley, J. C. *Minnesota Multiphasic Personality Inventory manual* (Rev. ed.). New York: Psychological Corporation, 1951.

Haywood, H. C. Experiential factors in intellectual development: The concept of dynamic intelligence. In J. Zubin (Ed.), *Psychopathology of mental development*. New York: Grune & Stratton, 1967. Pp. 69–104.

Hebb, D. O. *The organization of behavior*. New York: Wiley, 1949.

Hebb, D. O. Drives and the C.N.S. (conceptual nervous system). *Psychological Review*, 1955, 62, 243–254.

Hebb, D. O. What psychology is about. *American Psychologist*, 1974, 29, 71–79.

Heber, R., & Garber, H. *An experiment in the prevention of cultural-familial retardation.* Paper presented at the Second Con-gress of the International Association for the Scientific Study on Mental Deficiency, Warsaw, Poland, September 1970.

Hedblom, J. H. Dimensions of lesbian sexual experience. *Archives of Sexual Behavior*, 1973, 2(4), 329–341.

Heider, F. Social perception and phenomenal causality. *Psychological Review*, 1944, 51, 358–374.

Heider, F. Attitudes and cognitive organization. *Journal of Psychology*, 1946, 21, 107–112.

Heider, F. *The psychology of interpersonal relations*. New York: Wiley, 1958.

Heilbroner, R. L. *An inquiry into the human prospect*. New York: Norton, 1974.

*Heilbroner, R., Mintz, M., McCarthy, C., Ungar, S. J., Vandivier, K., Friedman, S., & Boyd, J. *In the name of profit: Profiles in corporate responsibility.* Garden City, N. Y.: Doubleday, 1972.

*Heilbrun, C. G. *Toward a recognition of androgyny*. New York: Knopf, 1973.

Heiman, J. R. *Facilitating erotic arousal: Toward sex-positive sex research.* Paper presented at the meeting of the American Psychological Association, New Orleans, August 1974.

Heiman, J. R. The physiology of erotica: Women's sexual arousal. *Psychology Today*, 1975, 8(11), 90–94.

Helmreich, R., Aronson, E., & LeFan, J. To err is humanizing—sometimes: Effects of self-esteem, competence, and a pratfall on interpersonal attraction. *Journal of Personality and Social Psychology*, 1970, 16, 259–264.

Helmreich, R., Bakeman, R., & Scherwitz, L. The study of small groups. In P. H. Mussen & M. R. Rosenzweig (Eds.), *Annual review of psychology* (Vol. 24). Palo Alto, Calif.: Annual Reviews, Inc., 1973. Pp. 337–354.

Helmreich, R. L., & Collins, B. E. Situational determinants of affiliative preference under stress. *Journal of Personality and Social Psychology*, 1967, 6, 79–85.

Helmreich, R. L., & Collins, B. E. Studies in forced compliance: Commitment and magnitude of inducement to comply as determinants of opinion change. *Journal of Personality and Social Psychology*, 1968, 10, 75–81.

Helson, H. Adaptation-level theory. In S. Koch (Ed.), *Psychology: A study of a science* (Vol. 1). *Sensory, perceptual, and physiological formulations*. New York: McGraw-Hill, 1959, Pp. 565–621.

Helson, H. *Adaptation-level theory: An experimental and systematic approach to behavior*. New York: Harper & Row, 1964.

Hemphill, J. K. Leadership behavior associated with the administrative reputation of college departments. *Journal of Educational Psychology*, 1955, 46, 385–401.

Hemphill, J. K., & Coons, A. E. *Leader behavior description*. Personnel Research Board, Ohio State University, 1950.

Hendrick, C. Averaging versus summation in impression formation. *Perceptual and Motor Skills*, 1968, 27, 443–446.

Hendrick, C. *Race versus belief as determinants of attraction.* Paper presented at the meeting of the American Psychological Association, New Orleans, September 1974. (a)

Hendrick, C. *Social psychology and history: An analysis of the defense of traditional science.* Unpublished paper, Kent State University, September 15, 1974. (b)

Hendrick, C., Bixenstine, V. E., & Hawkins, G. Race versus belief similarity as determinants of attraction: A search for a fair test. *Journal of Personality and Social Psychology,* 1971, *17,* 250–258.

Hendrick, C., & Jones, R. A. *The nature of theory and research in social psychology.* New York: Academic, 1972.

Hendrick, C., Stikes, C. S., Murray, E. J., & Puthoff, C. Race versus belief as determinants of attraction in a group interaction context. *Memory and Cognition,* 1973, *1,* 41–46.

Herold, P. L. *Patterns of political preference and attribution related to authoritarianism.* Paper presented at the meeting of the Western Psychological Association, Los Angeles, April 1970.

Herrnstein, R. I. Q. *Atlantic Monthly,* September 1971, *228*(8), 43–64.

Herrnstein, R. *IQ in the meritocracy.* Boston: Atlantic Monthly Press and Little, Brown, 1973.

Herzberg, F. *Work and the nature of man.* Cleveland: World, 1966.

Herzberg, F., Mausner, B., & Snyderman, B. *The motivation to work.* New York: Wiley, 1959.

Herzog, E. Some assumptions about the poor. *Monthly Labor Review,* 1970, *93*(2), 42–49.

Heshka, S., & Nelson, Y. Interpersonal speaking distance as a function of age, sex and relationship. *Sociometry,* 1972, *35,* 491–498.

Heslin, R. Predicting group task effectiveness from member characteristics. *Psychological Bulletin,* 1964, *62,* 248–256.

Hess, E. H. Ethology. In R. Brown, E. Galanter, E. H. Hess, & G. Mandler, *New directions in psychology.* New York: Holt, 1962. Pp. 157–266.

Hess, R. D. Educability and rehabilitation: The future of the welfare class. *Journal of Marriage and the Family,* 1964, *26,* 422–429.

Hess, R. D., & Shipman, V. Early experience and the socialization of cognitive modes in children. *Child Development,* 1965, *36,* 869–886.

Hetherington, M. E., & McIntyre, C. W. Developmental psychology. In M. R. Rosenzweig & L. W. Porter (Eds.), *Annual review of psychology* (Vol. 26). Palo Alto, Calif.: Annual Reviews, Inc., 1975. Pp. 97–136.

Heussenstamm, F. K. Bumper stickers and the cops. *Trans-Action,* 1971, *8,* 32–33.

Heuyer, G., et al. Le niveau intellectuel des enfants, d'age scolaire. *Institut nationale d'etudes demographiques: Travaux et documents.* Cashier/3, 1950. (Reported in A. Anastasi, *Differential psychology.* New York: Macmillan, 1958.)

Hicks, R. A., & Pellegrini, R. J. The meaningfulness of Negro-White differences in intelligence test performance. *Psychological record,* 1966, *16,* 43–46.

Higbee, K. L. *Experimentation in social-personality research.* Paper presented at meeting of the Psychonomic Society, Denver, November 1975.

Higbee, K. L., & Wells, M. G. Some research trends in social psychology during the 1960's. *American Psychologist,* 1972, *27,* 963–966.

Higgins, J. Authoritarianism and candidate preference. *Psychological Reports,* 1965, *16,* 603–604.

Hildum, D., & Brown, R. Verbal reinforcement and interview bias. *Journal of Abnormal and Social Psychology,* 1956, *53,* 108–111.

Hilgard, E. R. The domain of hypnosis: With some comments on alternative paradigms. *American Psychologist,* 1973, *28,* 972–982.

Hilgard, E. R., & Payne, S. L. Those not at home: Riddle for pollsters. *Public Opinion Quarterly,* 1944, *8,* 245–261.

Hill, W. A situational approach to leadership effectiveness. *Journal of Applied Psychology,* 1969, *53,* 513–517.

Hills, L. R. The cruel rules of social life. *Newsweek,* 1973, *81*(14), 15. (October 1, 1973 issue.)

Hiltner, S. The dialogue on man's nature. In S. Doniger (Ed.), *The nature of man.* New York: Harper, 1962. Pp. 237–261.

Hilton, I. Differences in the behavior of mothers toward first- and later-born children. *Journal of Personality and Social Psychology,* 1967, *7,* 282–290.

Himmelweit, H. Frustration and aggression: A review of recent experimental work. In T. H. Pear (Ed.), *Psychological factors of peace and war.* London: Hutchison, 1950. Pp. 161–191.

Hinds, W. C. *Individual and group decisions in gambling situations.* Unpublished master's thesis, School of Industrial Management, M.I.T., 1962.

Hirota, K. Group problem solving and communication. *Japanese Journal of Psychology,* 1953, *24,* 176–177.

Hochreich, D. J., & Rotter, J. B. Have college students become less trusting? *Journal of Personality and Social Psychology,* 1970, *15,* 211–214.

Hodge, R. W., Siegel, P. M., & Rossi, P. H. Occupational prestige in the United States, 1925–1963. *American Journal of Sociology,* 1964, *70,* 286–302.

Hodgkinson, H. *Education, interaction, and social change.* Englewood Cliffs, N. J.: Prentice-Hall, 1967.

Hoenig, J., & Kenna, J. C. The nosological position of transsexualism. *Archives of Sexual Behavior,* 1974, *3,* 273–287.

Hoffer, E. *The true believer.* New York: Harper, 1951.

Hoffer, E. *The ordeal of change.* New York: Harper Colophon, 1964.

Hoffman, L. W. Early childhood experiences and women's achievement motives. *Journal of Social Issues,* 1972, *28*(2), 129–155.

Hoffman, L. W. Fear of success in males and females: 1965 and 1971. *Journal of Consulting and Clinical Psychology,* 1974, *42,* 353–358.

*Hoffman, M. *The gay world.* New York: Basic Books, 1968.

Hoffman, M. L., & Saltzstein, H. D. Parent discipline and the child's moral development. *Journal of Personality and Social Psychology,* 1967, *5,* 45–57.

Hogan, R. Moral conduct and moral character: A psychological perspective. *Psychological Bulletin*, 1973, *79*, 217–232.

Hollander, E. P. Conformity, status, and idiosyncrasy credit. *Psychological Review*, 1958, *65*, 117–127.

Hollander, E. P. *Leaders, groups, and influence.* New York: Oxford University Press, 1964.

Hollander, E. P. *Principles and methods of social psychology* (2nd ed.). New York: Oxford University Press, 1971.

Hollander, E. P. *Some future potentials in leadership research.* Paper presented at the meeting of the American Psychological Association, Honolulu, September 1972.

Hollander, E. P., & Julian, J. W. Studies in leader legitimacy, influence, and innovation. In L. Berkowitz (Ed.), *Advances in experimental social psychology* (Vol. 5). New York: Academic Press, 1970. Pp. 33–69.

Hollander, E. P., & Willis, R. H. Some current issues in the psychology of conformity and nonconformity. *Psychological Bulletin*, 1967, *68*, 62–76.

Hollingshead, A. B. & Redlich, F.C. *Social class and mental illness.* New York: Wiley, 1958.

Holmes, D. S., & Bennett, D. H. Experiments to answer questions raised by the use of deception in psychological research: I. Role playing as an alternative to deception; II. Effectiveness of debriefing after a deception; III. Effect of informed consent on deception. *Journal of Personality and Social Psychology*, 1974, *29*, 358–367.

Holmes, D. S., & Jorgensen, B. W. Do personality and social psychologists study men more than women? *Representative Research in Social Psychology*, 1971, *2*, 71–76.

Holstein, C. E. *The relation of children's moral judgment level to that of their parents and to communication patterns in the family.* Unpublished doctoral dissertation, University of California, Berkeley, 1969. (Reprinted in R. C. Smart & M. S. Smart [Eds.], *Readings in child development and relationships.* New York: Macmillan, 1972.)

Holsti, O. R. Content analysis. In G. Lindzey and E. Aronson (Eds.), *The handbook of social psychology* (Vol. 2) (2nd ed.). Reading, Mass.: Addison-Wesley, 1968. Pp. 596–692.

Homans, G. C. Social behavior and exchange. *American Journal of Sociology*, 1958, *63*, 597–606.

Homans, G. C. *Social behavior: Its elementary forms.* New York: Harcourt, Brace & World, 1961.

Homans, G. C. The relevance of psychology to the explanation of social phenomena. In R. Borger & F. Cioffi (Eds.), *Explanation in the behavioural sciences.* Cambridge: Cambridge University Press, 1970. Pp. 313–328.

Honigmann, J. J. *Culture and personality.* New York: Harper, 1954.

Hood, W. R., & Sherif, M. Verbal report and judgment of an unstructured stimulus. *Journal of Psychology*, 1962, *54*, 121–130.

Hook, S. *The hero in history.* Boston: Beacon Press, 1955.

Hooker, E. The adjustment of the male overt homosexual. *Journal of Projective Techniques*, 1957, *21*, 18–31.

Hooker, E. Parental relations and male homosexuality in patient and nonpatient samples. *Journal of Consulting and Clini-*

cal Psychology, 1969, *33*, 140–142.

Hoppe, R. A., Greene, M. S., & Kenny, J. W. Territorial markers: Additional findings. *Journal of Social Psychology*, 1972, *88*, 305–306.

Horner, M. S. Femininity and successful achievement: A basic inconsistency. In J. Bardwick, E. Douvan, M. S. Horner, & D. Gutmann, *Feminine personality and conflict.* Monterey, Calif.: Brooks/Cole, 1970. Pp. 45–74.

Horner, M. S. Toward an understanding of achievement-related conflicts in women. *Journal of Social Issues*, 1972, *28*(2), 157–176.

Horney, K. On the genesis of the castration complex in women. *International Journal of Psychoanalysis*, 1924, *5*, 50–56.

Horney, K. The flight from womanhood. *International Journal of Psychoanalysis*, 1926, *7*, 324–339.

Horney, K. *The neurotic personality of our time.* New York: Norton, 1937.

Horney, K. *New ways in psychoanalysis.* New York: Norton, 1939.

Hornstein, H. A., Fisch, E., & Holmes, M. Influence of a model's feeling about his behavior and his relevance as a comparison other on observers' helping behavior. *Journal of Personality and Social Psychology*, 1968, *10*, 222–226.

Horowitz, M. J., Duff, D. F., & Stratton, L. Personal space and the body buffer zone. *Archives of General Psychiatry*, 1964, *11*, 651–666.

Horton, C. P., & Crump, E. P. Growth and development: XI. Descriptive analysis of the background of 76 Negro children whose scores are above or below average on the Merrill-Palmer scale of mental tests of three years of age. *Journal of Genetic Psychology*, 1962, *100*, 255–269.

Hostetler, J. A. *Hutterite society.* Baltimore, Md.: Johns Hopkins University Press, 1974.

*Houriet, R. *Getting back together.* New York: Coward, McCann, & Geoghagan, 1971.

Houston, J. W., & Houston, J. D. *Farewell to Manzanar.* Boston: Houghton-Mifflin, 1973.

Hovland, C., Harvey, O. J., & Sherif, M. Assimilation and contrast effects in reactions to communication and attitude change. *Journal of Abnormal and Social Psychology*, 1957, *55*, 244–252.

Hovland, C., Janis, I., & Kelley, H. H. *Communication and persuasion.* New Haven, Conn.: Yale University Press, 1953.

Hovland, C., & Mandell, W. An experimental comparison of conclusion drawing by the communicator and by the audience. *Journal of Abnormal and Social Psychology*, 1952, *47*, 581–588.

Hovland, C. I., & Weiss, W. The influence of source credibility on communication effectiveness. *Public Opinion Quarterly*, 1951, *15*, 635–650.

Howard, E. *Territory and bird life.* London: John Murray, 1920.

Howard, J. L., Liptzin, M. B., & Reifler, C. B. Is pornography a problem? *Journal of Social Issues*, 1973, *29*(3), 133–145.

Howard, J. L., Reifler, C. B., & Liptzin, M. B. Effects of exposure to pornography. In *Technical report of the Commission on Obscenity and Pornography* (Vol. 8). Washington, D. C.: U. S. Government Printing Office, 1971. Pp. 97–132.

Howard, P. Office landscaping revisited. *Design and Environment*, 1972, Fall, 40–47.

Howe, I. Herbert Marcuse or Milovan Djilas? The inescapable choice for the next decade. *Harpers*, 1969, *239*, 84–92.

Hoyt, G. C., & Stoner, J. A. F. Leadership and group decisions involving risk. *Journal of Experimental Social Psychology*, 1968, *4*, 275–285.

Hoyt, J. L. Effect of media violence "justification" on aggression. *Journal of Broadcasting*, 1970, *16*, 455–464.

Hoyt, M. F., & Raven, B. H. Birth order and the 1971 Los Angeles earthquake. *Journal of Personality and Social Psychology*, 1973, *28*, 123–128.

Hoyt, M. F., Henley, M. D., & Collins, B. E. Studies in forced compliance: Confluence of choice and consequence on attitude change. *Journal of Personality and Social Psychology*, 1972, *23*, 205–210.

Hulin, C., & Blood, M. Job enlargement, individual differences, and worker responses. *Psychological Bulletin*, 1968, *69*, 41–55.

Humphreys, L. New styles in homosexual manliness. *Trans-Action*, 1971, *8*, 38–46ff.

Humphreys, L. *Tearoom trade: Impersonal sex in public places* (2nd ed.). Chicago: Aldine, 1975.

Hundert, A. J., & Greenfield, N. Physical space and organizational behavior: A study of an office landscape. *Proceedings, 77th Annual Convention, American Psychological Association*, 1969, *4*, 601–602.

Hunt, J. G. Fiedler's leadership contingency model: An empirical test in three organizations. *Organizational Behavior and Human Performance*, 1967, *2*, 290–308.

Hunt, J. McV. *Intelligence and experience*. New York: Ronald, 1961.

Hunt, J. McV. The intellectual performance of the culturally deprived child. *Proceedings of Section II, Annual Professional Institute of the Division of School Psychologists, American Psychological Association*, 1962, Pp. 25–27. (Mimeographed)

Hunt, J. McV. Traditional personality theory in the light of recent evidence. *American Scientist*, 1965, *53*, 60–96.

Hunt, J. McV., Cole, M. W., & Reis, E. E. S. Situational cues distinguishing anger, fear, and sorrow. *American Journal of Psychology*, 1958, *71*, 136–151.

*Hunt, M. *Sexual behavior in the 1970s*. Chicago: Playboy Press, 1974.

Husband, R. W. Cooperative versus solitary problem solution. *Journal of Social Psychology*, 1940, *11*, 405–409.

*Huston, T. L. (Ed.). *Foundations of interpersonal attraction*. New York: Academic Press, 1974. (a)

Huston, T. L. *The good Samaritan reconsidered*. Paper presented at the meeting of the American Psychological Association, New Orleans, September 1974. (b)

Huston, T. L., & Korte, C. The responsive bystander: Why he helps. In T. Lickona (Ed.), *Morality: A handbook of moral development and behavior*. New York: Holt, Rinehart & Win-

ston, 1976. Pp. 269–283.

Hutt, C., & Vaizey, M. J. Differential effects of group density on social behavior. *Nature*, 1966, *209*, 1371–1372.

Huxley, A. *Brave new world*. Garden City, N. Y.: Garden City Publishing Co., 1933.

Hyman, H. H. Do they tell the truth? *Public Opinion Quarterly*, 1944, *8*, 557–559.

Hyman, H. H. & Sheatsley, P. B. "The authoritarian personality"—A methodological critique. In R. Christie and M. Jahoda (Eds.), *Studies in the scope and method of "The Authoritarian Personality."* New York: Free Press, 1954. Pp. 50–122.

*Ibsen, H. A doll's house. In *Eleven Plays of Henrik Ibsen*. New York: Modern Library, 1949. Pp. 1–52. (Originally published, 1879.)

Ickes, W. J. *Social facilitation and self-evaluation: An objective self-awareness analysis*. Paper presented at the meeting of the American Psychological Association, New Orleans, September 1974.

Ikemi, Y., & Nakagawa, S. A psychosomatic study of contagious dermatitis. *Kyushu Journal of Medical Science*, 1962, *13*, 335–350.

Insko, C. Primacy versus recency in persuasion as a function of timing of arguments and measures. *Journal of Abnormal and Social Psychology*, 1964, *69*, 381–391.

Insko, C. A. Verbal reinforcement of attitude. *Journal of Personality and Social Psychology*, 1965, *2*, 621–623.

*Insko, C. A. *Theories of attitude change*. New York: Appleton-Century-Crofts, 1967.

Insko, C. A., & Robinson, J. E. Belief similarity vs. race as determinants of reactions to Negroes by Southern White adolescents: A further test of Rokeach's theory. *Journal of Personality and Social Psychology*, 1967, *7*, 216–221.

Insko, C. A., & Schopler, J. Triadic consistency: A statement of affective-cognitive-conative consistency. *Psychological Review*, 1967, *74*, 361–376.

Insko, C. A., Songer, E., & McGarvey, W. Balance, positivity, and agreement in the Jordan paradigm: A defense of balance theory. *Journal of Experimental Social Psychology*, 1974, *10*, 53–83.

Isaacs, S. *Intellectual growth in young children*. New York: Schocken, 1966.

Isen, A. M. Success, failure, attention and reactions to others: The warm glow of success. *Journal of Personality and Social Psychology*, 1970, *15*, 294–301.

Isen, A. M., Horn, N., & Rosenhan, D. L. Effects of success and failure on children's generosity. *Journal of Personality and Social Psychology*, 1973, *27*, 239–247.

Isen, A. M., & Levin, P. F. Effect of feeling good on helping: Cookies and kindness. *Journal of Personality and Social Psychology*, 1972, *21*, 384–388.

Israel, J., & Tajfel, H. *The context of social psychology: A critical assessment*. New York: Academic Press, 1972.

Ittelson, W. (Ed.). *Environment and cognition*. New York: Seminar Press, 1973.

Ittelson, W., Proshansky, H., & Rivlin, L. A study of bedroom use on two psychiatric wards. *Hospital and Community Psy-*

chiatry, 1972, *21*(6), 177–180.

*Ittelson, W., Proshansky, H., Rivlin, L., & Winkel, G. *An introduction to environmental psychology.* New York: Holt, Rinehart & Winston, 1974.

Iverson, M. A. Personality impressions of punitive stimulus persons of differential status. *Journal of Abnormal and Social Psychology*, 1964, *68*, 617–626.

Ivey, M. E., & Bardwick, J. M. Patterns of affective fluctuation in the menstrual cycle. *Psychosomatic Medicine*, 1968, *30*, 336–345.

Izzett, R. Authoritarianism and attitudes toward the Vietnam War as reflected in behavioral and self-report measures. *Journal of Personality and Social Psychology*, 1971, *17*, 145–148.

Jackson, D. N., & Messick, S. Acquiescence: The nonvanishing variance component. *American Psychologist*, 1965, *20*, 498. (Abstract)

Jacobs, R. C., & Campbell, D. T. The perpetuation of an arbitrary tradition through several generations of a laboratory micro-culture. *Journal of Abnormal and Social Psychology*, 1961, *62*, 649–658.

Jacoby, J. Interpersonal perceptual accuracy as a function of dogmatism. *Journal of Experimental Social Psychology*, 1971, *7*, 221–236.

Jahoda, M. Conformity and independence—a psychological analysis. *Human Relations*, 1959, *12*, 99–120.

*Janeway, E. *Between myth and morning: Women awakening.* New York: Morrow, 1974.

Janis, I. L. Groupthink. *Psychology Today*, 1971, *5*(6), 43–46ff.

Janis, I. L. *Victims of groupthink: A psychological study of foreign-policy decisions and fiascoes.* Boston: Houghton Mifflin, 1972.

Janis, I. L., & Field, P. B. Sex differences and personality factors related to persuasibility. In I. L. Janis, C. I. Hovland, P. B. Field, H. Linton, E. Graham, A. R. Cohen, D. Rife, R. P. Abelson, G. S. Lesser, & B. T. King (Eds.), *Personality and persuasibility.* New Haven, Conn.: Yale University Press, 1959. Pp. 55–68.

Janis, I. L., Kaye, D., & Kirschner, P. Facilitating effects of "eating-while-reading" on responsiveness to persuasive communications. *Journal of Personality and Social Psychology*, 1965, *1*, 181–186.

Jellison, J. M. *Behavior change as a function of communicator credibility and receptivity to a communication.* Paper presented at the meeting of the Midwestern Psychological Association, Chicago, May 1970.

Jellison, J. M., Jackson-White, R., & Bruder, R. A. *Fear of success? A situational approach.* Paper presented at the meeting of the Western Psychological Association, San Francisco, April 1974.

Jenkins, J. J. Remember that old theory of memory? Well, forget it! *American Psychologist*, 1974, *29*, 785–795.

Jenness, A. The role of discussion in changing opinion regarding a matter of fact. *Journal of Abnormal and Social Psychology*, 1932, *27*, 279–296.

Jensen, A. R. *Patterns of mental ability and socioeconomic status.* Paper presented at the meeting of the National Academy of Sciences, Washington, D. C., April 1968. (a)

Jensen, A. R. *Uses of twin and sibling data.* Paper presented at the meeting of the American Psychological Association, San Francisco, August 1968. (b)

Jensen, A. R. Counter response. *Journal of Social Issues*, 1969, *25*(4), 219–222. (a)

Jensen, A. R. How much can we boost IQ and scholastic achievement? *Harvard Educational Review*, 1969, *39*, 1–123. (b)

Jensen, A. R. Input: Arthur Jensen replies. *Psychology Today*, 1969, *3*(5), 4–6. (c)

Jensen, A. R. Reducing the heredity-environment uncertainty: A reply. *Harvard Educational Review*, 1969, *39*, 449–483. (d)

Jensen, A. R. Rejoinder. *Journal of Social Issues*, 1969, *25*(4), 212–217. (e)

Jensen, A. R. The differences are real. *Psychology Today*, 1973, *7*(7), 80–86.

Jensen, A. R. Kinship correlations reported by Sir Cyril Burt. *Behavior Genetics*, 1974, *4*(1), 1–28.

Jensen, B. T., & Terebinski, S. J. The railroad game: A tool for research in social sciences. *Journal of Social Psychology*, 1963, *60*, 85–87.

Jensen, D. L. (Ed.). *Machiavelli: Cynic, patriot, or political scientist.* Lexington, Mass.: Heath, 1960.

Jensen, L. C., & Hughston, K. The relationship between type of sanction, story content, and children's judgments which are independent of sanction. *Journal of Genetic Psychology*, 1973, *122*, 49–54.

Joesting, J. Women in academe. *American Psychologist*, 1974, *29*, 520–523.

Johnson, D. L., & Andrews, I. R. Risky-shift phenomenon tested with consumer products as stimuli. *Journal of Personality and Social Psychology*, 1971, *20*, 382–385.

Johnson, R. F. Q. Trance logic revisited: A reply to Hilgard's critique. *Journal of Abnormal Psychology*, 1972, *79*, 212–220.

*Jones, E. E. *Ingratiation.* New York: Appleton-Century-Crofts, 1964.

Jones, E. E. Conformity as a tactic of ingratiation. *Science*, 1965, *149*, 144–150.

Jones, E. E., & Davis, K. E. From acts to dispositions: The attribution process in person perception. In L. Berkowitz (Ed.), *Advances in experimental social psychology* (Vol. 2). New York: Academic Press, 1965. Pp. 219–266.

Jones, E. E., Davis, K. E., & Gergen, K. J. Role playing variations and their informational value for person perception. *Journal of Abnormal and Social Psychology*, 1961, *63*, 302–310.

Jones, E. E., Gergen, K. J., & Davis, K. Some reactions to being approved or disapproved as a person. *Psychological Monographs*, 1962, *76* (Whole No. 521).

Jones, E. E., Gergen, K. J., Gumpert, P., & Thibaut, J. Some conditions affecting the use of ingratiation to influence performance evaluation. *Journal of Personality and Social Psychology*, 1965, *1*, 613–625.

Jones, E. E., Gergen, K. J., & Jones, R. G. Tactics of ingratiation among leaders and subordinates in a status hierarchy. *Psychological Monographs*, 1963, *77* (Whole No. 566).

Jones, E. E., & Harris, V. A. The attribution of attitudes. *Journal of Experimental Social Psychology*, 1967, *3*, 1–24.

Jones, E. E., & Nisbett, R. E. *The actor and the observer: Divergent perceptions of the causes of behavior.* Morristown, N. J.: General Learning Press, 1971.

Jones, J. M. *Prejudice and racism.* Reading, Mass.: Addison-Wesley, 1972.

Jones, R. Beyond behaviorism. *Contemporary Psychology*, 1970, *15*, 741–742.

Jordan, W. D. *White over Black: American attitudes toward the Negro, 1550–1812.* Baltimore, Md.: Penguin, 1969.

Jorgensen, B. W. *Group size: Its effect on group performance and on individual acquisition of knowledge.* Paper presented at the meeting of the Eastern Psychological Association, Washington, D. C., May 1973.

Jorgensen, C. *Christine Jorgensen: A personal autobiography.* New York: Paul G. Erikson, 1967.

Jorgensen, C. Personal communication on draft of Chapter 15. June 16, 1975.

Jourard, S. M. Healthy personality and self-disclosure. *Mental Hygiene.* 1959, *43*, 499–507.

Jourard, S. M. *The transparent self.* Princeton, N. J.: Van Nostrand, 1964.

Jourard, S. M., & Landsman, M. J. Cognition, cathexis, and the "dyadic effect" in men's self-disclosing behavior. *Merrill-Palmer Quarterly*, 1960, *6*, 178–186.

Jourard, S. M., & Lasakow, P. Some factors in self-disclosure. *Journal of Abnormal and Social Psychology*, 1958, *56*, 91–98.

Jovanovic, U. J. The recording of physiological evidence of genital arousal in human males and females. *Archives of Sexual Behavior*, 1971, *1*, 309–320.

Kaats, G. R. *Belief systems and person perception: Analyses in a service academy environment.* Unpublished doctoral dissertation, Department of Psychology, University of Colorado, 1969.

Kaats, G. R., & Davis, K. E. The dynamics of sexual behavior of college students. *Journal of Marriage and the Family*, 1970, *32*, 390–399.

Kaats, G. R., & Davis, K. E. The social psychology of sexual behavior. In L. S. Wrightsman, *Social psychology in the seventies.* Monterey, Calif.: Brooks/Cole, 1972. Pp. 549–580.

Kafrissen, S. R., Heffron, E. F., & Zusman, J. Mental health problems in environmental disasters. In H. L. P. Resnik, H. L. Ruben, & D. D. Ruben (Eds.), *Emergency psychiatric care: The management of mental health crises.* Bowie, Md.: Charles Press, 1975. Pp. 159–170.

*Kamin, L. J. *The science and politics of I.Q.* Potomac, Md.: Erlbaum Associates, 1974.

Kalven, H., Jr., & Zeisel, H. *The American jury.* Boston: Little, Brown, 1966.

*Kanter, R. M. *Commitment and community: Communes and utopias in social perspective.* Cambridge, Mass.: Harvard University Press, 1972.

Kanter, R. M., Jaffe, D., & Weisberg, D. K. *Coupling, parenting, and the presence of others: Intimate relationships in communal households.* Paper presented at the meeting of the American

Psychological Association, New Orleans, September 1974.

Kaplan, B. J. Malnutrition and mental deficiency. *Psychological Bulletin*, 1972, *78*, 321–334.

Kaplan, J. A legal look at prosocial behavior: What can happen for failing to help or trying to help someone. *Journal of Social Issues*, 1972, *28*(3), 219–226.

Kaplan, J. A. A legal look at prosocial behavior: What can happen for failing to help or trying to help someone. In L. Wispé (Ed.), *The psychology of sympathy and altruism.* Cambridge, Mass.: Harvard University Press, 1977.

Kaplan, M. F. Interpersonal attraction as a function of relatedness of similar and dissimilar attitudes. *Journal of Experimental Research in Personality*, 1972, *6*, 17–21.

Karabenick, S. A., Lerner, R. M., & Beecher, M. D. Relation of political affiliation to helping behavior on election day, November 7, 1972. *Journal of Social Psychology*, 1973, *91*, 223–227.

Karabenick, S. A., & Wilson, W. Dogmatism among war hawks and peace doves. *Psychological Reports*, 1969, *25*, 419–422.

Kardiner, A., & Ovesey, L. *The mark of oppression.* New York: Norton, 1951.

Karlins, M., & Abelson, H. I. *How opinions and attitudes are changed* (2nd ed.). New York: Springer, 1970.

Karlins, M., Coffman, T. L., & Walters, G. On the fading of social stereotypes: Studies in three generations of college students. *Journal of Personality and Social Psychology*, 1969, *13*, 1–16.

Karnes, M. B. *Research and development program on disadvantaged children.* Final Report, Vol. 1, May 1969. University of Illinois, Contract No. DE-6-10-325, U. S. Office of Education.

Karon, B. P. *The Negro personality.* New York: Springer, 1958.

*Katchadourian, H. A., & Lunde, D. T. *Fundamentals of human sexuality* (2nd ed.). New York: Holt, Rinehart & Winston, 1975.

Kateb, G. The political thought of Herbert Marcuse. *Commentary*, 1970, *49*(1), 48–63.

Katz, D. The functional approach to the study of attitudes. *Public Opinion Quarterly*, 1960, *24*, 163–204.

Katz, D. Consistency for what? The functional approach. In R. P. Abelson, E. Aronson, W. J. McGuire, T. M. Newcomb, M. J. Rosenberg, & P. H. Tannenbaum (Eds.), *Theories of cognitive consistency: A sourcebook.* Chicago: Rand-McNally, 1968. Pp. 179–191.

Katz, D., & Kahn, R. L. *The social psychology of organizations.* New York: Wiley, 1966.

Katz, D., Sarnoff, I., & McClintock, C. G. Ego-defense and attitude change. *Human Relations*, 1956, *9*, 27–45.

Katz, D., & Stotland, E. A preliminary statement to a theory of attitude structure and change. In S. Koch (Ed.), *Psychology: A study of a science* (Vol. 3). New York: McGraw-Hill, 1959. Pp. 423–475.

Katz, I. Review of evidence relating to effects of desegregation on the intellectual performance of Negroes. *American Psychologist*, 1964, *19*, 381–399.

Katz, I. Some motivational determinants of racial differences in intellectual achievement. *International Journal of Psychology*, 1967, *2*, 1–12.

Katz, I. A critique of personality approaches to Negro performance with research suggestions. *Journal of Social Issues*, 1969, *25*(3), 13–28.

Katz, I., & Benjamin, L. Effects of White authoritarianism in biracial groups. *Journal of Abnormal and Social Psychology*, 1960, *61*, 448–456.

Katz, I., & Cohen, M. The effects of training Negroes upon cooperative problem solving in biracial teams. *Journal of Abnormal and Social Psychology*, 1962, *64*, 319–325.

Katz, I., Epps, E. G., & Axelson, L. J. Effect upon Negro digit-symbol performance of anticipated comparison with Whites and with other Negroes. *Journal of Abnormal and Social Psychology*, 1964, *69*, 77–83.

Katz, I., & Greenbaum, C. Effects of anxiety, threat, and racial environment on task performance of Negro college students. *Journal of Abnormal and Social Psychology*, 1963, *66*, 562–567.

Katz, I., Henchy, J., & Allen, H. Effects of race of tester, approval-disapproval, and need on Negro children's learning. *Journal of Personality and Social Psychology*, 1968, *8*, 38–42.

Katz, J. *No time for students.* San Francisco: Jossey-Bass, 1968.

Kauffman, D. R., & Steiner, I. D. Conformity as an ingratiation technique. *Journal of Experimental Social Psychology*, 1968, *4*, 400–414.

Kaufmann, H. *Social psychology; The study of human interaction.* New York: Holt, Rinehart & Winston, 1973.

Keasey, C. B. Experimentally induced changes in moral opinions and reasoning. *Journal of Personality and Social Psychology*, 1973, *26*, 30–38.

Keen, S., & Raser, J. A conversation with Herbert Marcuse. *Psychology Today*, 1971, *4*(9), 35–40ff.

Keiffer, M. G., & Cullen, D. M. *Discrimination experienced by academic female psychologists.* Paper presented at the meeting of the American Psychological Association, Washington, D. C., September 1969.

Kelley, H. H. The warm-cold variable in first impressions of persons. *Journal of Personality*, 1950, *18*, 431–439.

Kelley, H. H. Attribution theory in social psychology. In D. Levine (Ed.), *Nebraska symposium on motivation, 1967* (Vol. 15). Lincoln: University of Nebraska Press, 1967. Pp. 192–238.

Kelley, H. H. *Attribution in social interaction.* Morristown, N. J.: General Learning Press, 1971.

Kelley, H. H. *Causal schemata and the attribution process.* Morristown, N. J.: General Learning Press, 1972.

Kelley, H. H. The processes of causal attribution. *American Psychologist*, 1973, *28*, 107–128.

Kelley, H. H., Shure, G. H., Deutsch, M., Faucheux, C., Lanzetta, J. T., Moscovici, S., Nuttin, J. M., Jr., Rabbie, J. M., & Thibaut, J. W. A comparative experimental study of negotiation behavior. *Journal of Personality and Social Psychology*, 1970, *16*, 411–438.

Kelley, H. H., & Thibaut, J. W. Group problem solving. In G. Lindzey & E. Aronson (Eds.), *Handbook of social psychology* (Vol. 4) (2nd ed.). Reading, Mass.: Addison-Wesley, 1968. Pp. 1–104.

Kelly, G. A. *The psychology of personal constructs* (2 vols.). New York: Norton, 1955.

Kelly, G. A. *A theory of personality: The psychology of personal constructs.* New York: Norton, 1963.

Kelly, G. F. Bisexuality and the youth culture. *Homosexual Counseling Journal*, 1974, *1*(2), 16–25.

Kelman, H. C. Compliance, identification, and internalization: Three processes of attitude change. *Journal of Conflict Resolution*, 1958, *2*, 51–60.

Kelman, H. C. Processes of opinion change. *Public Opinion Quarterly*, 1961, *25*, 57–78.

Kelman, H. C. Human use of human subjects: The problem of deception in social psychological experiments. *Psychological Bulletin*, 1967, *67*, 1–11.

Kelman, H. C. Violence without moral restraint: Reflections on the dehumanization of victims and victimizers. *Journal of Social Issues*, 1973, *29*(4), 25–61.

Kelman, H. C. Attitudes are alive and well and gainfully employed in the sphere of action. *American Psychologist*, 1974, *29*, 310–335.

Kelman, H. C., & Lawrence, L. H. Assignment of responsibility in the case of Lt. Calley: Preliminary report on a national survey. *Journal of Social Issues*, 1972, *28*(1), 177–212. (a)

Kelman, H. C., & Lawrence, L. H. American response to the trial of Lt. William L. Calley. *Psychology Today*, 1972, *6*(1), 41–45. (b)

*Kemeny, J. G. *A philosopher looks at science.* Princeton, N. J.: Van Nostrand, 1959.

Kemp, C. G. Perception of authority in relation to open and closed belief systems. *Science Education*, 1963, *47*, 482–484.

Keniston, K. *The uncommitted: Alienated youth in American society.* New York: Harcourt, Brace & World, 1965.

Keniston, K. The sources of student dissent. *Journal of Social Issues*, 1967, *23*(3), 108–137.

*Keniston, K. *Young radicals: Notes on committed youth.* New York: Harcourt, Brace & World, 1968.

Keniston, K. Counter culture: Cop-out, or wave of the future? *Life*, 1969, *67*(19), 8–9. (November 7, 1969 issue.)

Keniston, K. Youth: A "new" stage of life. *American Scholar*, Autumn 1970, *39*, 632–654.

Kerckhoff, A. C. The social context of interpersonal attraction. In T. L. Huston (Ed.), *Foundations of interpersonal attraction.* New York: Academic Press, 1974. Pp. 61–78.

Kerckhoff, A. C., & Davis, K. E. Value consensus and need complementarity in mate selection. *American Sociological Review*, 1962, *27*, 295–303.

Kerlinger, F. N., & Rokeach, M. The factorial structure of the F and D scales. *Journal of Personality and Social Psychology*, 1966, *4*, 391–399.

Kerner, O., Lindsay, J., Harris, F. R., Brooke, E. W., Corman, J. C., McCulloch, W. M., Abel, I. W., Thornton, C. B.,

Wilkins, R., Peden, K. W., Jenkins, H., et al. *Report of the National Advisory Commission on Civil Disorders.* New York: Bantam Books, 1968.

Kerr, S., Schriesheim, C. A., Murphy, C. J., & Stogdill, R. M. Toward a contingency theory of leadership based upon the consideration and initiating structure literature. *Organizational Behavior and Human Performance,* 1974, *12,* 62-82.

Kibler, B. K., & Harari, H. *Stereotypes of given names: Case studies and anecdotal evidence.* Paper presented at the meeting of the American Psychological Association, New Orleans, September 1974.

Kiesler, C. A. Group pressure and conformity. In J. Mills (Ed.), *Experimental social psychology.* New York: Macmillan, 1969. Pp. 233-306.

Kiesler, C. A. *The psychology of commitment: Experiments linking behavior to belief.* New York: Academic Press, 1971.

*Kiesler, C. A., Collins, B. E., & Miller, N. *Attitude change: A critical analysis of theoretical approaches.* New York: Wiley, 1969.

*Kiesler, C. A., & Kiesler, S. B. *Conformity.* Reading, Mass.: Addison-Wesley, 1969.

Kiesler, C. A., & Munson, P. A. Attitudes and opinions. In M. R. Rosenzweig & L. W. Porter (Eds.), *Annual review of psychology* (Vol. 26). Palo Alto, Calif.: Annual Reviews, Inc., 1975. Pp. 415-456.

Kiesler, S. B. The effect of perceived role requirements on reactions to favor doing. *Journal of Experimental Social Psychology,* 1966, *2,* 298-310.

Kilham, P., & Klopfer, P. H. The construct race and the innate differential. In M. Mead, T. Dobzhansky, E. Tobach, & R. E. Light (Eds.), *Science and the concept of race.* New York: Columbia University Press, 1968. Pp. 26-36.

Kilham, W., & Mann, L. Level of destructive obedience as a function of transmitter and executant roles in the Milgram obedience paradigm. *Journal of Personality and Social Psychology,* 1974, *29,* 696-702.

Kimble, G. A. *Hilgard and Marquis's conditioning and learning.* New York: Appleton-Century-Crofts, 1961.

Kimbrell, D. L., & Blake, R. R. Motivational factors in a violation of prohibition. *Journal of Abnormal and Social Psychology,* 1958, *56,* 132-133.

Kimmel, E. Status of women in the psychological community in the Southeast: A case study. *American Psychologist,* 1974, *29,* 519-520.

Kinkade, K. *A Walden II experiment: The first five years of Twin Oaks community.* New York: Morrow, 1973.

Kinkead, E. *In every war but one.* New York: Norton, 1959.

Kinsey, A. C., Pomeroy, W. B., & Martin, C. E. *Sexual behavior in the human male.* Philadelphia: Saunders, 1948.

Kinsey, A. C., Pomeroy, W. B., Martin, C. E., & Gebhard, P. H. *Sexual behavior in the human female.* Philadelphia: Saunders, 1953.

Kipnis, D. M. Interaction between members of bomber crews as a determinant of sociometric choice. *Human Relations,* 1957, *10,* 263-270.

Kirkendall, L. A., & Libby, R. W. Interpersonal relationships:

Crux of the sexual renaissance. *Journal of Social Issues,* 1966, *22*(2), 45-59.

*Kirscht, J. P., & Dillehay, R. C. *Dimensions of authoritarianism: A review of research and theory.* Lexington, Ky.: University of Kentucky Press, 1967.

Kirtley, D. Conformity and prejudice in authoritarians of opposing political ideologies. *Journal of Psychology,* 1968, *70,* 199-204.

Klaus, R. A., & Gray, S. W. Murfreesboro preschool program for culturally deprived children. *Childhood Education,* 1965, *42,* 92-95.

Klaus, R. A., & Gray, S. W. The early training project for disadvantaged children: A report after five years. *Monographs of the Society for Research in Child Development,* 1968, *33*(4, Whole No. 120).

Kleck, R. E., Buck, P. L., Goller, W. C., London, R. S., Pfeiffer, J. R., & Vukcevic, D. P. Effect of stigmatizing conditions on the use of personal space. *Psychological Reports,* 1968, *23,* 111-118.

Kleeman, J. L. *The Kendall College human potential seminar model and philosophies of human nature.* Unpublished doctoral dissertation, College of Education, University of Illinois at Champaign-Urbana, 1972.

Kleiber, D., Veldman, D. J., & Menaker, S. L. The multidimensionality of locus of control. Paper presented at the meeting of the Eastern Psychological Association, Washington, D. C., May 1973.

Kleinke, C. L. Effects of false feedback about response lengths on subjects' perception of an interview. *Journal of Social Psychology,* 1975, *95,* 99-104. (a)

Kleinke, C. L. *First impressions.* Englewood Cliffs, N. J.: Prentice-Hall, 1975. (b)

Kline, P. *Fact and fantasy in Freudian theory.* London: Methuen, 1972.

Klineberg, O. *Negro intelligence and selective migration.* New York: Columbia University Press, 1935.

Klineberg, O. (Ed.) *Characteristics of the American Negro.* New York: Harper, 1944.

Klineberg, O. Black and White in international perspective. *American Psychologist,* 1971, *26,* 119-128.

Kluckhohn, C. Have there been discernible shifts in American values during the past generation? In E. Morison (Ed.), *The American style.* New York: Harper, 1958. Pp. 145-217.

Knapp, M. L. *Nonverbal communication in human interaction.* New York: Holt, 1972.

Knight, H. C. *A comparison of the reliability of group and individual judgments.* Unpublished master's thesis, Columbia University, 1921. (Cited in Shaw, 1971.)

Knowles, E. S. Boundaries around social space: Dyadic responses to an invader. *Environment and Behavior,* 1972, *4,* 437-445.

Knowles, E. S. Boundaries around group interaction: The effect of group size and member status on boundary permeability. *Journal of Personality and Social Psychology,* 1973, *26,* 327-331.

Knox, R. E., & Inkster, J. A. Postdecision dissonance at post time. *Journal of Personality and Social Psychology*, 1968, *8*, 319–323.

Koenig, K. *The relationship of political attitudes, interest and activity to nonauthoritarianism.* Paper presented at the meeting of the American Psychological Association, Los Angeles, September 1964.

Koffka, W. *Principles of Gestalt psychology.* New York: Harcourt Brace, 1935.

Kogan, N., & Wallach, M. A. *Risk-taking: A study in cognition and personality.* New York: Holt, 1964.

Kogan, N., & Wallach, M. A. Effects of physical separation of group members upon group risk taking. *Human Relations*, 1967, *20*, 41–48. (a)

Kogan, N., & Wallach, M. A. Group risk taking as a function of members' anxiety and defensiveness labels. *Journal of Personality*, 1967, *35*, 50–63. (b)

Kogan, N., & Wallach, M. A. The risky-shift phenomenon in small decision-making groups: A test of the information-exchange hypothesis. *Journal of Experimental Social Psychology*, 1967, *3*, 75–85. (c)

Kohlberg, L. *The development of modes of moral thinking and choice in the years ten to sixteen.* Unpublished doctoral dissertation, University of Chicago, 1958.

Kohlberg, L. Moral development and identification. In H. Stevenson (Ed.), *Child psychology* (62nd Yearbook of the National Society for the Study of Education). Chicago: University of Chicago Press, 1963.

*Kohlberg, L. Development of moral character and moral ideology. In M. L. Hoffman & L. W. Hoffman (Eds.), *Review of child development research* (Vol. 1). New York: Russell Sage Foundation, 1964. Pp. 383–431.

Kohlberg, L. The child as a moral philosopher. *Psychology Today*, 1968, *2*(4), 24–30.

Kohlberg, L. The cognitive-developmental approach to socialization. In D. A. Goslin (Ed.), *Handbook of socialization theory and research.* Chicago: Rand-McNally, 1969. Pp. 347–480.

Kohlberg, L. Moral development and the education of adolescents. In R. Purnell (Ed.), *Adolescents and the American high school.* New York: Holt, Rinehart & Winston, 1970. Pp. 144–163.

Kohlberg, L. *Moral education in schools and prisons.* Colloquium address, George Peabody College for Teachers, March 4, 1971.

Kohlberg, L. Stages and aging in moral development: Some speculations. *Gerontologist*, 1973, *13*, 497–502.

Köhler, W. Psychological remarks on some questions of anthropology. In M. Henle (Ed.), *Documents of Gestalt psychology.* Berkeley, Calif.: University of California Press, 1961. Pp. 203–221.

Komarovsky, M. Functional analysis of sex roles. *American Sociological Review*, 1959, *15*, 508–516.

Komorita, S. S. Attitude content, intensity, and the neutral point on a Likert scale. *Journal of Social Psychology*, 1963, *61*, 327–334.

Konečni, V. J. Some effects of guilt on compliance: A field

replication. *Journal of Personality and Social Psychology*, 1972, *23*, 30–32.

Koning, H. Did the Pentagon Papers make any difference? *Saturday Review*, 1972, *55*(24), 13–15. (June 10, 1972 issue.)

Korman, A. K. "Consideration," "initiating structure," and organizational criteria—A review. *Personnel Psychology*, 1966, *19*, 349–361.

Korner, A. F. Early stimulation and maternal care as related to infant capabilities and individual differences. *Early Child Development and Care*, 1973, *2*, 307–327.

Korte, C. *Group effects on help giving in an emergency.* Paper presented at the meeting of the American Psychological Association, Washington, D. C., September 1969.

Korte, C. Effects of individual responsibility and group communication on help-giving in an emergency. *Human Relations*, 1971, *24*, 149–159.

*Korten, F. F., Cook, S. W., & Lacey, J. I. (Eds.) *Psychology and the problems of society.* Washington, D. C.: American Psychological Association, 1970.

Kovel, J. *White racism: A psychohistory.* New York: Pantheon, 1970.

Kramer, R. *Moral development in young adulthood.* Unpublished doctoral dissertation. University of Chicago, 1968.

Krasner, L. The behavior scientist and social responsibility: No place to hide. *Journal of Social Issues*, 1965, *21*(2), 9–30.

Kraut, R. E. Effects of social labeling on giving to charity. *Journal of Experimental Social Psychology*, 1973, *9*, 551–562.

Krebs, D. L. Altruism—an examination of the concept and a review of the literature. *Psychological Bulletin*, 1970, *73*, 258–302.

Krebs, R. *Some relations between moral judgment, attention, and resistance to temptation.* Unpublished doctoral dissertation, University of Chicago, 1967.

Krech, D., Crutchfield, R., & Ballachey, E. *Individual in society.* New York: McGraw-Hill, 1962.

Kronhausen, E., & Kronhausen, P. *Pornography and the law* (Rev. ed.). New York: Ballantine, 1964.

Krug, R. E. An analysis of the F scale: I. Item factor analysis. *Journal of Social Psychology*, 1961, *53*, 285–291.

Krupat, E. Context as a determinant of perceived threat: The role of prior experience. *Journal of Personality and Social Psychology*, 1974, *29*, 731–736.

Krupat, E., & Epstein, Y. "I'm too busy": The effects of overload and diffusion of responsibility on working and helping. *Proceedings, 81st Annual Convention, American Psychological Association*, 1973, *8*, 293–294.

Kuhn, D. Z., Madsen, C. H., Jr., & Becker, W. C. Effects of exposure to an aggressive model and frustration on children's aggressive behavior. *Child Development*, 1967, *38*, 739–746.

Kuhn, T. S. *The structure of scientific revolutions* (2nd edition). Chicago: University of Chicago Press, 1970.

Kurtines, W., & Greif, E. B. The development of moral thought: Review and evaluation of Kohlberg's approach. *Psychological Bulletin*, 1974, *81*, 453–470.

Kutchinsky, B. The effect of easy availability of pornography on the incidence of sex crimes: The Danish experience. *Journal of Social Issues,* 1973, *29*(3), 163–181.

Kutner, B., Wilkins, C., & Yarrow, P. R. Verbal attitudes and overt behavior involving racial prejudice. *Journal of Abnormal and Social Psychology,* 1952, *47,* 649–652.

Lagarspertz, K. Genetics and the social causes of aggressive behavior in mice. *Scandinavian Journal of Psychology,* 1961, *2,* 167–173.

Lambert, W. E., Libman, E., & Poser, E. G. The effect of increased salience of a membership group on pain tolerance. *Journal of Personality,* 1960, *28,* 350–357.

Lamm, H., Trommsdorff, G., & Rost-Schaude, E. Group-induced extremization: Review of evidence and a minority-change explanation. *Psychological Reports,* 1973, *33,* 471–484.

Lana, R. Controversy of the topic and order of presentation in persuasive communications. *Psychological Reports,* 1963, *12,* 163–170. (a)

Lana, R. Interest, media, and order effects in persuasive communications. *Journal of Psychology,* 1963, *56,* 9–13. (b)

Lana, R. The influence of the pretest on order effects in persuasive communications. *Journal of Abnormal and Social Psychology,* 1964, *69,* 337–341. (a)

Lana, R. Three theoretical interpretations of order effects in persuasive communications. *Psychological Bulletin,* 1964, *61,* 314–320. (b)

Landsberger, H. A. *Hawthorne revisited.* Ithaca, N. Y.: Cornell University, 1958.

Lang, J., Burnette, C., Moleski, W., & Vachon, D. (Eds.) *Designing for human behavior. Architecture and the behavioral sciences.* Stroudsburg, Pa.: Dowden, Hutchinson, & Ross, 1974.

Langman, B., & Cockburn, A. Sirhan's gun. *Harper's,* January 1975, *250*(No. 1496), 16–27.

Lantz, H. R. Population density and psychiatric diagnosis. *Sociology and Social Research,* 1953, *37,* 322–326.

LaPiere, R. T. Attitudes and actions. *Social Forces,* 1934, *13,* 230–237.

Larson, D. L., & Spreitzer, E. A. Education, occupation, and age as correlates of work orientation. *Psychological Reports,* 1973, *33,* 879–884.

Latané, B. (Ed.) Studies in social comparison. *Journal of Experimental Social Psychology, Supplement,* 1966, No. 1.

Latané, B. Field studies of altruistic compliance. *Representative Research in Social Psychology,* 1970, *1,* 49–61.

Latané, B., & Darley, J. M. Group inhibition of bystander intervention in emergencies. *Journal of Personality and Social Psychology,* 1968, *10,* 215–221.

*Latané, B., & Darley, J. *The unresponsive bystander: Why doesn't he help?* New York: Appleton-Century-Crofts, 1970.

Latané, B., & Rodin, J. A lady in distress: Inhibiting effects of friends and strangers on bystander intervention. *Journal of Experimental Social Psychology,* 1969, *5,* 189–202.

LaVoie, J. C. Punishment and adolescent self-control. *Developmental Psychology,* 1973, *8,* 16–24.

LaVoie, J. C. Aversive, cognitive, and parental determinants

of punishment generalization in adolescent males. *Journal of Genetic Psychology,* 1974, *124,* 29–39. (a)

LaVoie, J. C. Cognitive determinants of resistance to deviation in seven-, nine-, and eleven-year-old children of low and high maturity of moral judgment. *Developmental Psychology,* 1974, *10,* 393–403. (b)

LaVoie, J. C., & Adams, G. R. *Pygmalion in the classroom: An experimental investigation of the characteristics of children on teacher expectancy.* Paper presented at the meeting of the Midwestern Psychological Association, Chicago, May 1973.

Lawler, E. E. *Individualizing organizations.* Paper presented at the meeting of the Midwestern Psychological Association, Chicago, May 1972.

Lawrence, J. *A history of Russia.* New York: Farrar, Straus, & Cudahy, 1960.

Lawson, E. D. Semantic differential analysis of men's first names. *Journal of Psychology,* 1971, *78,* 229–240.

Lay, C. H., Burron, B. F., & Jackson, D. N. Base rates and informational value in impression formation. *Journal of Personality and Social Psychology,* 1973, *28,* 390–395.

Layzer, D. Heritability analyses of IQ scores: Science or numerology? *Science,* 1974, *183,* 1259–1266.

Lazarus, R. S. *Psychological stress and the coping process.* New York: McGraw-Hill, 1966.

Leach, C. The importance of instructions in assessing sequential effects in impression formation. *British Journal of Social and Clinical Psychology,* 1974, *13,* 151–156.

Lear, J. Do we need new rules for experiments on people? *Saturday Review,* 1966, *49*(6), 61–70. (February 5, 1966 issue.)

Leavitt, H. J. Some effects of certain communication patterns on group performance. *Journal of Abnormal and Social Psychology,* 1951, *46,* 38–50.

LeBon, G. *The crowd.* London: Ernest Benn, 1896.

Lee, E. S. Negro intelligence and selective migration: A Philadelphia test of the Klineberg hypothesis. *American Sociological Review,* 1951, *16,* 227–233.

Lehmann, S. Community and psychology and community psychology. *American Psychologist,* 1971, *26,* 554–560.

Lehrer, L. *Sex differences in moral behavior and attitudes.* Unpublished doctoral dissertation, University of Chicago, 1967.

*Lehrman, N. *Masters and Johnson explained.* Chicago: Playboy Press, 1970.

Leipold, W. D. *Psychological distance in a dyadic interview as a function of introversion-extroversion, anxiety, social desirability, and stress.* Unpublished doctoral dissertation, University of North Dakota, 1963.

Lemert, E. M. *Social pathology: A systematic approach to the theory of sociopathic behavior.* New York: McGraw-Hill, 1951.

Lerner, E. *Constraint areas and the moral judgment of children.* Menasha, Wisc.: Banta, 1937.

Lerner, M. J. Evaluation of performance as a function of performer's reward and attractiveness. *Journal of Personality and Social Psychology,* 1965, *3,* 355–360.

Lerner, M. J. *The unjust consequences of the need to believe in a just world*. Paper presented at the meeting of the American Psychological Association, New York, September 1966.

Lerner, M. J. The desire for justice and reactions to victims. In J. Macaulay & L. Berkowitz (Eds.), *Altruism and helping behavior: Social psychological studies of some antecedents and consequences*. New York: Academic Press, 1970. Pp. 205–229.

Lerner, M. J. Social psychology of justice and interpersonal attraction. In T. L. Huston (Ed.), *Foundations of interpersonal attraction*. New York: Academic Press, 1974. Pp. 331–351.

Lerner, M. J., & Becker, S. W. Interpersonal choice as a function of ascribed similarity and definition of the situation. *Human Relations*, 1962, *15*, 27–34.

Lerner, M. J., & Matthews, G. Reactions to suffering of others under conditions of indirect responsibility. *Journal of Personality and Social Psychology*, 1967, *5*, 319–325.

Lerner, M. J., & Simmons, C. H. Observer's reactions to the "innocent victim": Compassion or rejection? *Journal of Personality and Social Psychology*, 1966, *4*, 203–210.

Lesser, G. S., Fifer, G., & Clark, D. H. Mental abilities of children from different social class and cultural groups. *Monographs of the Society for Research in Child Development*, 1965, *30*(4), 1–115.

Levenson, H., Gray, M. J., & Ingram, A. *Research methods in personality/social: Five years after Carlson's survey*. Paper presented at the meeting of the American Psychological Association, Chicago, August 1975.

Lever, J., & Goodman, L. W. Toys, play, and sex role socialization of children. Paper presented at meetings of the Society for the Study of Social Problems, 1972.

Levin, F. M., & Gergen, K. J. Revealingness, ingratiation, and the disclosure of self. *Proceedings of the 77th Annual Convention, American Psychological Association*, 1969, *4*(Pt. 1), 447–448.

Levin, H. Psychologist to the powerless. In F. F. Korten, S. W. Cook, & J. I. Lacey (Eds.), *Psychology and the problems of society*. Washington, D. C.: American Psychological Association, 1970. Pp. 121–127.

Levine, F. J., & Tapp, J. L. The psychology of criminal investigation. *University of Pennsylvania Law Review*, 1973, *121*(5), 1079–1131.

Levine, S. The effects of differential infantile stimulation on emotionality at weaning. *Canadian Journal of Psychology*, 1959, *13*, 243–247.

Levinger, G. Little sand box and big quarry: Comment on Byrne's paradigmatic spade for research on interpersonal attraction. *Representative Research in Social Psychology*, 1972, *3*, 3–19.

Levinger, G. A three-level approach to attraction: Toward an understanding of pair relatedness. In T. L. Huston (Ed.), *Foundations of interpersonal attraction*. New York: Academic Press, 1974. Pp. 99–120.

Levinger, G., & Senn, D. J. Disclosure of feelings in marriage. *Merrill-Palmer Quarterly*, 1967, *13*, 237–249.

Levinger, G., Senn, D. J., & Jorgensen, B. W. Progress toward permanence in courtship: A test of the Kerckhoff-Davis

hypotheses. *Sociometry*, 1970, *33*, 427–443.

Levinson, D. J., & Huffman, P. E. Traditional family ideology and its relation to personality. *Journal of Personality*, 1955, *23*, 251–273.

Levy, J. Autokinetic illusion: A systematic review of theories, measures, and independent variables. *Psychological Bulletin*, 1972, *78*, 457–474.

Levy, L. Studies in conformity behavior: A methodological note. *Journal of Psychology*, 1960, *50*, 39–41.

Levy, S. G. A 150-year study of political violence in the United States. In H. D. Graham & T. R. Gurr (Eds.), *Violence in America*. New York: New American Library, 1969. Pp. 81–92.

Lewin, A. Y., & Duchan, L. Women in academia. *Science*, 1971, *173*, 892–895.

Lewin, K. *A dynamic theory of personality*. New York: McGraw-Hill, 1935.

Lewin, K. The conceptual representation and measurement of psychological forces. *Contributions to Psychological Theory*, Vol. I, No. 4. Durham, N. C.: Duke University Press, 1938.

Lewin, K. *Resolving social conflicts*. New York: Harper, 1948. (a)

Lewin, K. Some social-psychological differences between the United States and Germany. In K. Lewin (Ed.), *Resolving social conflicts: Selected papers on group dynamics, 1935–1946*. New York: Harper, 1948. (b)

Lewin, K. *Field theory in social science*. New York: Harper, 1951.

Lewin, K. Behavior and development as a function of the total situation. In L. Carmichael (Ed.), *Manual of child psychology* (2nd ed.). New York: Wiley, 1954.

Lewin, K., Lippitt, R., & White, R. K. Patterns of aggressive behavior in experimentally created "social climates." *Journal of Social Psychology*, 1939, *10*, 271–299.

Lewis, E. C. *Developing woman's potential*. Ames, Ia.: Iowa State University Press, 1968.

Lewis, O. Privacy and crowding in poverty. In H. Proshansky, W. Ittelson, & L. Rivlin (Eds.), *Environmental psychology: Man and his physical setting*. New York: Holt, Rinehart & Winston, 1970. Pp. 267–269.

Lewis, R. A. Social reaction and the formation of dyads: An interactionist approach to mate selection. *Sociometry*, 1973, *36*, 409–418.

Leyens, J.-P. The role of a positive model, a frustrating situation and aggressive context on imitation. *European Journal of Social Psychology*, 1972, *2*, 5–17.

Leyens, J. P., Camino, L., Parke, R. D., & Berkowitz, L. Effects of movie violence on aggression in a field setting as a function of group dominance and cohesion. *Journal of Personality and Social Psychology*, 1975, *32*, 346–360.

Leyhausen, P. The communal organization of solitary mammals. *Symposium of the Zoological Society of London*, 1965, *14*, 249–263.

*Lickona, T. (Ed.) *Morality: Theory, research, and social issues*. New York: Holt, Rinehart & Winston, 1976.

Lieberman, M. A., Yalom, I. D., & Miles, M. B. *Encounter groups: First facts*. New York: Basic Books, 1973. (a)

Lieberman, M. A., Yalom, I. D., & Miles, M. B. Encounter: The leader makes a difference. *Psychology Today*, 1973, *6*(10), 69–76. (b)

*Liebert, R. M., Neale, J. M., & Davidson, E. S. *The early window: Effects of television on children and youth.* Elmsford, N.Y.: Pergamon, 1973.

Liebhart, E. H. Empathy and emergency helping: The effects of personality, self-concern, and acquaintance. *Journal of Experimental Social Psychology*, 1972, *8*, 404–411.

Lief, H. I. Teaching doctors about sex. In R. Brecher & E. Brecher (Eds.), *An analysis of the human sexual response.* Boston: Little, Brown, 1966.

Lifton, R. J. *Home from the war: Vietnam veterans neither victims nor executioners.* New York: Simon & Schuster, 1973.

Lindgren, H. C. Political conservatism and its social environment: An appraisal of the American presidential election of 1972. *Psychological Reports*, 1974, *34*, 55–62.

*Lindzey, G., & Aronson, E. (Eds.) *Handbook of social psychology* (Vols. 1–5) (2nd ed.). Reading, Mass.: Addison-Wesley, 1968, 1969.

Lingle, J. H. *Catch-as-catch-can: When surveillance turns to entrapment.* Paper presented at the meeting of the American Psychological Association, New Orleans, August 1974.

Linn, L. S. Verbal attitudes and overt behavior: A study of racial discrimination. *Social Forces*, 1965, *44*, 353–364.

Lippitt, G. L. Organizations for the future: Implications for management. *Optimum*, 1974, *5*(1), 36–53.

Lippitt, R. *Training in community relations.* New York: Harper, 1949.

Lippitt, R., Watson, J., & Westley, B. *The dynamics of planned change.* New York: Harcourt, Brace & World, 1958.

Little, K. B. Personal space. *Journal of Experimental Social Psychology*, 1965, *1*, 237–247.

Livesay, T. M. Racial comparisons in test-intelligence. *American Journal of Psychology*, 1942, *55*, 90–95.

Livesay, T. M. Relation of economic status to "intelligence" and to the racial deprivation of high school seniors in Hawaii. *American Journal of Psychology*, 1944, *57*, 77–82.

Loftus, E. F. Reconstructing memory: The incredible eyewitness. *Psychology Today*, 1974, *8*(7), 116–119.

Loftus, E. F., & Palmer, J. C. Reconstruction of automobile destruction: An example of the interaction between language and memory. *Journal of Verbal Learning and Verbal Behavior*, 1974, *11*, 585–589.

Logan, R. W. *The Negro in the United States.* Princeton, N.J.: Van Nostrand, 1957.

Loiselle, R. H., & Mollenauer, S. Galvanic skin response to sexual stimuli in a female population. *Journal of General Psychology*, 1965, *73*, 273–278.

London, P. The rescuers: Motivational hypotheses about Christians who saved Jews from the Nazis. In J. Macaulay & L. Berkowitz (Eds.), *Altruism and helping behavior: Social psychological studies of some antecedents and consequences.* New York: Academic Press, 1970. Pp. 241–250.

Lonetto, R., & Williams, D. Personality, behavioural and output variables in a small group task situation: An examina-

tion of consensual leader and non-leader differences. *Canadian Journal of Behavioural Science*, 1974, *6*(1), 59–74.

Long, B. H., & Ziller, R. C. Dogmatism and predecisional information search. *Journal of Applied Psychology*, 1965, *49*, 376–378.

Loo, C. M. The effects of spatial density on the social behavior of children. *Journal of Applied Social Psychology*, 1972, *4*, 372–381.

Lorenz, K. *King Solomon's ring.* New York: Crowell, 1952.

*Lorenz, K. *On aggression.* New York: Harcourt, Brace & World, 1966.

Lorenz, K. [*Studies in animal and human behavior*] (Vol. 1),(R. Martin, trans.) Cambridge, Mass.: Harvard University Press, 1970.

Lorge, I., Fox, D., Davitz, J., & Brenner, M. A survey of studies contrasting the quality of group performance and individual performance, 1920–1957. *Psychological Bulletin*, 1958, *55*, 337–372.

Lott, A. J., & Lott, B. E. Group cohesiveness, communication level, and conformity. *Journal of Abnormal and Social Psychology*, 1961, *62*, 408–412.

Lottier, S. Distribution of criminal offenses in metropolitan regions. *Journal of Criminal Law and Criminology*, 1938, *29*, 39–45.

Love, R. E. *The political heckler—Friend or foe?* Paper presented at the meeting of the Eastern Psychological Association, Washington, D.C., May 1973.

Lubell, S. That "generation gap." *Public Interest*, 1968, *13*, 52–60.

Lucas, O., Finkelman, A., & Tocantino, L. M. Management of tooth extractions in hemophiliacs by the combined use of hypnotic suggestion, protective splints, and packing sockets. *Journal of Oral Surgery Anesthesia and Hospital Dental Service*, 1962, *20*, 489–500.

Luce, R. D., & Raiffa, H. *Games and decisions.* New York: Wiley, 1957.

Luchins, A. S. Experimental attempts to minimize the impact of first impressions. In C. I. Hovland (Ed.), *The order of presentation in persuasion.* New Haven: Yale University Press, 1957. Pp. 62–75. (a)

Luchins, A. S. Primacy-recency in impression formation. In C. I. Hovland (Ed.), *The order of presentation in persuasion.* New Haven: Yale University Press, 1957. Pp. 33–61. (b)

Luchins, A. S. Definitiveness of impression and primacy-recency in communications. *Journal of Social Psychology*, 1958, *48*, 275–290.

Luckey, E., & Nass, G. D. A comparison of sexual attitudes and behavior in an international sample. *Journal of Marriage and the Family*, 1969, *31*, 364–379.

Luft, J. On nonverbal interaction. *Journal of Psychology*, 1966, *63*, 261–268.

Lund, F. The psychology of belief. IV. The law of primacy in persuasion. *Journal of Abnormal and Social Psychology*, 1925, *20*, 183–191.

Lyman, S. M., & Scott, M. B. Territoriality: A neglected sociological dimension. *Social Problems*, 1967, *15*, 236–249.

*Maccoby, E. E., & Jacklin, C. N. *The psychology of sex differences.* Stanford, Calif.: Stanford University Press, 1974. (a)

Maccoby, E. E., & Jacklin, C. N. What we know and don't know about sex differences. *Psychology Today,* 1974, *8*(7), 109–112. (b)

Macaulay, J. R. A shill for charity. In J. Macaulay & L. Berkowitz (Eds.), *Altruism and helping behavior: Social psychological studies of some antecedents and consequences.* New York: Academic Press, 1970. Pp. 43–59.

MacDonald, A. P., Jr. Anxiety, affiliation, and social isolation. *Developmental Psychology,* 1970, *3,* 242–254.

MacDonald, A. P., Jr., & Majumder, R. K. On the resolution and tolerance of cognitive inconsistency in another naturally occurring event: Attitudes and beliefs following the Senator Eagleton incident. *Journal of Applied Social Psychology,* 1973, *3,* 132–143.

MacDougald, D., Jr. Aphrodisiacs and anaphrodisiacs. In A. Ellis & A. Abarbanel (Eds.), *The encyclopedia of sexual behavior.* New York: Jason Aronson, 1973. Pp. 145–153.

Machiavelli, N. *The prince.* New York: Modern Library, 1940.

Mack, R. *Transforming America: Patterns of social change.* New York: Random House, 1967.

Mackenzie, K. D., & Bernhardt, I. *The effect of status upon group risk taking.* Unpublished manuscript, Wharton School of Finance and Commerce, University of Pennsylvania, 1968.

MacNeil, M. K. *Persistence and change of norms established under differing arbitrary conditions.* Unpublished master's thesis, University of Oklahoma, 1965. (Cited by Montgomery, Hinkle, & Enzie, 1975.)

MacRae, D., Jr. A test of Piaget's theories of moral development. *Journal of Abnormal and Social Psychology,* 1954, *49,* 14–18.

Madaras, G. R., & Bem, D. J. Risk and conservatism in group decision-making. *Journal of Experimental Social Psychology,* 1968, *4,* 350–365.

Madsen, M. C. Cooperative and competitive motivation of children in three Mexican subcultures. *Psychological Reports,* 1967, *20,* 1307–1320.

Madsen, M. C. Developmental and cross-cultural differences in the cooperative and competitive behavior of young children. *Journal of Cross-Cultural Psychology,* 1971, *2,* 365–371.

Madsen, M. C., & Shapira, A. Cooperative and competitive behavior of urban Afro-American, Anglo-American, Mexican-American, and Mexican village children. *Developmental Psychology,* 1970, *3,* 16–20.

Magruder, J. S. *An American life: One man's road to Watergate.* New York: Atheneum, 1974.

Mahoney, E. R. Compensatory reactions to spatial immediacy. *Sociometry,* 1974, *37,* 423–431.

Maitland, K. A., & Goldman, J. R. Moral judgment as a function of peer-group interaction. *Journal of Personality and Social Psychology,* 1974, *30,* 699–704.

Malcolm X, with the assistance of A. Haley. *The autobiography of Malcolm X.* New York: Grove Press, 1964.

Mallick, S. K., & McCandless, B. R. A study of catharsis of aggression. *Journal of Personality and Social Psychology,* 1966, *4,* 591–596.

Mander, A., & Gaebelein, J. W. *The antagonistic effects of veto power and noncooperation on third party instigated aggression.* Paper presented at the meeting of the Southeastern Psychological Association, Atlanta, March 1975.

Mann, J. H. The differential nature of prejudice reduction. *Journal of Social Psychology,* 1960, *52,* 339–343.

Mann, J., Berkowitz, L., Sidman, J., Starr, S., & West, S. Satiation of the transient stimulating effect of erotic films. *Journal of Personality and Social Psychology,* 1974, *30,* 729–735.

Mann, J., Sidman, J., & Starr, S. Effects of erotic films on sexual behavior of married couples. In *Technical report of the Commission on Obscenity and Pornography* (Vol. 8). Washington, D. C.: U. S. Government Printing Office, 1971. Pp. 170–254.

Mann, J., Sidman, J., & Starr, S. Evaluating social consequences of erotic films: An experimental approach. *Journal of Social Issues,* 1973, *29*(3), 113–131.

Mann, R. D. A review of the relationship between personality and performance in small groups. *Psychological Bulletin,* 1959, *56,* 241–270.

Marcus, S. *The other Victorians.* New York: Basic Books, 1966.

Marcuse, H. *Eros and civilization: A philosophical inquiry into Freud.* New York: Vintage, 1962. (Originally published, 1955.)

Marcuse, H. *One-dimensional man: Studies in the ideology of advanced industrial society.* Boston: Beacon Press, 1964.

Marcuse, H. *An essay on liberation.* Boston: Beacon Press, 1969.

Marcuse, H. *Counterrevolution and revolt.* Boston: Beacon Press, 1972.

Markley, O. W. Latitude of rejection: An artifact of own position. *Psychological Bulletin,* 1971, *75,* 357–359.

Markley, O. W. Rejoinder to Sherif. *Psychological Bulletin,* 1972, *78,* 479.

*Marks, R. W. *The meaning of Marcuse.* New York: Ballantine, 1970.

Marlatt, G. A., & Kaplan, B. E. Self-initiated attempts to change behavior: A study of New Year's resolutions. *Psychological Reports,* 1972, *30,* 123–131.

Marlowe, D., & Gergen, K. J. Personality and social interaction. In G. Lindzey & E. Aronson (Eds.), *Handbook of social psychology* (Vol. 3) (2nd ed.). Reading, Mass.: Addison-Wesley, 1968. Pp. 590–665.

Marlowe, D., & Gergen, K. J. Personality and social behavior. In K. J. Gergen & D. Marlowe (Eds.), *Personality and social behavior.* Reading, Mass.: Addison-Wesley, 1970. Pp. 1–75.

Marquis, D. G. Individual responsibility and group decisions involving risk. *Industrial Management Review,* 1962, *3,* 8–23.

Marriott, C. Psycho-social patterns of dying. Paper presented at the meeting of the American Psychological Association, New Orleans, August 1974.

Marriott, C., & Harshbarger, D. The hollow holiday: Christmas, a time of death in Appalachia. *Omega,* 1973, *4,* 259–266.

Marrow, A. J. *The practical theorist: The life and work of Kurt Lewin.* New York: Basic Books, 1969.

Marsden, H. M. Crowding and animal behavior. In J. F. Wohlwill & D. H. Carson (Eds.), *Environment and the social sciences: Perspective and applications.* Washington, D. C.: American Psychological Association, 1972. Pp. 5–14.

Marsella, A. J., Escudero, M., & Gordon, P. The effects of dwelling density on mental disorders in Filipino men. *Journal of Health and Social Behavior,* 1970, *11,* 288–294.

Marshall, J. E., & Heslin, R. Boys and girls together: Sexual composition and the effect of density and group size on cohesiveness. *Journal of Personality and Social Psychology,* 1975, *31,* 952–961.

Marston, W. M. Studies in testimony. *Journal of Criminal Law and Criminology,* 1924, *15,* 5–31.

Martin, J., & Westie, F. The tolerant personality. *American Sociological Review,* 1959, 24, 521–528.

Martindale, D. A. Territorial dominance behavior in dyadic verbal interactions. *Proceedings, 79th Annual Convention, American Psychological Association,* 1971, *6,* 305–306.

Marx, G. T. Civil disorder and agents of social control. *Journal of Social Issues,* 1970, *26*(1), 19–57.

Masangkay, Z. S., McCluskey, K. A., McIntyre, C. W., Sims-Knight, J., Vaughn, B. E., & Flavell, J. H. The early development of inferences about the visual precepts of others. *Child Development,* 1973, *45,* 357–366.

Maslow, A. H. *Motivation and personality.* New York: Harper & Row, 1954.

Maslow, A. H., & Mintz, N. L. Effects of esthetic surroundings: I. Initial effects of three esthetic conditions upon perceiving "energy" and "well-being" in faces. *Journal of Psychology,* 1956, *41,* 247–254.

*Massie, R. K. *Nicholas and Alexandra.* New York: Atheneum, 1967.

Masters, W. H., & Johnson, V. E. *Human sexual response.* Boston: Little, Brown, 1966.

Masters, W. H., & Johnson, V. E. *Human sexual inadequacy.* Boston: Little, Brown, 1970.

Matlin, M. W. Response competition as a mediating factor in the frequency-affect relationship. *Journal of Personality and Social Psychology,* 1970, *16,* 536–552.

Mattson, A., & Gross, S. *Adaptational and defensive behavior in young hemophiliacs and their parents.* Paper presented at the meeting of the American Psychiatric Association, New York, May 1965. (Cited in Massie, 1967.) (a)

Mattson, A., & Gross, S. *Social and behavioral studies on hemophilic children and their families.* Paper presented at the meeting of the American Psychiatric Association, New York, May 1965. (Cited in Massie, 1967.) (b)

Maykovich, M. K. Reciprocity in racial stereotypes: White, Black, and Yellow. *American Journal of Sociology,* 1972, *77,* 876–897.

Mayo, C. W., & Crockett, W. H. Cognitive complexity and primacy-recency effects in impression formation. *Journal of Abnormal and Social Psychology,* 1964, *68,* 335–338.

Mayo, E. *The social problems of an industrial civilization.* Boston:

Harvard Graduate School of Business, 1945.

Mbiti, J. S. *African religions and philosophy.* New York: Anchor, 1970.

McArthur, L. A. The how and what of why: Some determinants and consequences of causal attribution. *Journal of Personality and Social Psychology,* 1972, *22,* 171–193.

McArthur, L. Z., & Resko, B. G. The portrayal of men and women in American television commercials. *Journal of Social Psychology,* in press.

McBride, G., King, M. G., & James, J. W. Social proximity effects on galvanic skin responses in adult humans. *Journal of Psychology,* 1965, *61,* 153–157.

McCall, G. J. A symbolic interactionist approach to attraction. In T . L. Huston (Ed.), *Foundations of interpersonal attraction.* New York: Academic Press, 1974. Pp. 217–231.

McCarrey, M., Peterson, L., Edwards, S., & VonKulmiz, P. Landscape office attitudes: Reflections of perceived degree of control over transactions with the environment. *Journal of Applied Psychology,* 1974, *50,* 401–403.

McCarthy, J., & Johnson, R. C. Interpretation of the "city hall riots" as a function of general dogmatism. *Psychological Reports,* 1962, *11,* 243–245.

McCary, J. L. Myths about sex. *Sexual Behavior,* 1971, *1*(1), 22–31.

McCary, J. L. *Human sexuality: Physiological, psychological, and sociological factors* (2nd ed.). New York: Van Nostrand, 1973.

McCary, J. L. Teaching the topic of human sexuality. *Teaching of Psychology,* 1975, *2*(1), 16–21.

McCauley, C. R. Extremity shifts, risky shifts and attitude shifts after group discussion. *European Journal of Social Psychology,* 1972, *2,* 417–436.

McClearn, G. E., & Meredith, H. W. Behavioral genetics. In P. R. Farnsworth, O. McNemar, & Q. McNemar (Eds.), *Annual review of psychology* (Vol. 17). Palo Alto, Calif.: Annual Reviews, 1966. Pp. 515–550.

McClintock, C. G. Personality syndromes and attitude change. *Journal of Personality,* 1958, *26,* 479–493.

McCord, W., & Howard, J. Negro opinions in three riot cities. *American Behavioral Scientist,* 1968, *11,* 24–27.

McCord, W., McCord, J., & Howard, A. Familial correlates of aggression in nondelinquent male children. *Journal of Abnormal and Social Psychology,* 1961, *62,* 79–93.

McCorkle, L. W., & Korn, R. R. Resocialization within walls. *Annals of the American Academy of Political and Social Science,* 1954, *293,* 88–98.

McDavid, J. W., & Harari, H. Stereotyping of names and popularity in grade-school children. *Child Development,* 1966, *37,* 453–459.

McDavid, J. W., & Harari, H. *Psychology and social behavior.* New York: Harper & Row, 1974.

McDougall, W. *An introduction to social psychology.* London: Methuen, 1908.

McDowell, K. V. Violations of personal space. *Canadian Journal of Behavioural Science,* 1972, *4,* 210–217.

McGarry, J., & Hendrick, C. *Communicator credibility and persuasion: A reappraisal.* Unpublished manuscript, Kent State

University, 1975.

McGee, R. *Social disorganization in America.* San Francisco: Chandler, 1962.

McGhee, P. E., & Teevan, R. C. Conformity behavior and need for affiliation. *Journal of Social Psychology,* 1967, *72,* 117–121.

McGinnies, E. Studies in persuasion: III. Reactions of Japanese students to one-sided and two-sided communications. *Journal of Social Psychology,* 1966, *70,* 87–93.

McGinnies, E. *Social behavior: A functional analysis.* Boston: Houghton-Mifflin, 1970.

McGinnies, E., & Ward, C. D. Persuasibility as a function of source credibility and locus of control: Five cross cultural experiments. *Journal of Personality,* 1974, *42,* 360–371.

McGinniss, J. *The selling of the President, 1968.* New York: Pocket Books, 1970.

McGrath, J. E., & Altman, I. *Small group research.* New York: Holt, Rinehart & Winston, 1966.

*McGregor, D. *The human side of enterprise.* New York: McGraw-Hill, 1960.

McGregor, D. *Leadership and motivation* (W. G. Bennis & E. H. Schein, Eds.). Cambridge, Mass.: M.I.T. Press, 1966.

McGregor, D. *The professional manager* (C. McGregor and W. G. Bennis, Eds.). New York: McGraw-Hill, 1967.

McGrew, P. L. Social and spatial density effects on spacing behavior in preschool children. *Journal of Child Psychology and Psychiatry,* 1970, *11,* 197–205.

McGuire, W. J. Attitudes and opinions. In P. R. Farnsworth, O. McNemar, & Q. McNemar (Eds.), *Annual review of psychology* (Vol. 17). Palo Alto, Calif.: Annual Reviews, 1966. Pp. 475–514.

McGuire, W. J. Some impending reorientations in social psychology: Some thoughts provoked by Kenneth Ring. *Journal of Experimental Social Psychology,* 1967, *3,* 124–139. (a)

McGuire, W. J. *Theory-oriented research in natural settings: The best of both worlds for social psychology.* Symposium paper presented at Pennsylvania State University, May 1967. (b)

McGuire, W. J. Personality and attitude change: A theoretical housing. In A. G. Greenwald, T. C. Brock, & T. M. Ostrom (Eds.), *Psychological foundations of attitudes.* New York: Academic Press, 1968. Pp. 171–196. (a)

McGuire, W. J. Personality and susceptibility to social influence. In E. F. Borgatta & W. W. Lambert (Eds.), *Handbook of personality theory and research.* Chicago: Rand-McNally, 1968. Pp. 1130–1187. (b)

McGuire, W. J. The nature of attitudes and attitude change. In G. Lindzey & E. Aronson (Eds.), *Handbook of social psychology* (Vol. 3) (2nd ed.). Reading, Mass.: Addison-Wesley, 1969. Pp. 136–314.

McGuire, W. J. Attitude change: The information-processing paradigm. In C. G. McClintock (Ed.), *Experimental social psychology.* New York: Holt, Rinehart & Winston, 1972. Pp. 108–141.

McGuire, W. J. The yin and yang of progress in social psychology: Seven koan. *Journal of Personality and Social Psychology,* 1973, *26,* 446–456.

McIntyre, C. W., Vaughn, B. E., & Flavell, J. H. Early developmental changes in the ability to infer the visual percepts of others. *Proceedings of the 81st Annual Convention, American Psychological Association,* 1973, *8,* 99–100.

McKinley, J. C., Hathaway, S. R., & Meehl, P. E. The MMPI: VI. The K scale. *Journal of Consulting Psychology,* 1948, *12,* 20–31.

McKinney, T. T. *All White America.* Boston: Meador, 1937.

McKusick, V. A. The royal hemophilia. *Scientific American,* 1965, *213*(2), 88–95.

McLuhan, M. *Understanding media: The extensions of man.* New York: McGraw-Hill, 1964.

McMahon, I. D. *Sex differences in causal attributions following success and failure.* Paper presented at the meeting of the Eastern Psychological Association, New York City, April 1971.

McManis, D. L. Effects of peer-models vs. adult-models and social reinforcement on intentionality of children's moral judgments. *Journal of Psychology,* 1974, *87,* 159–170.

McMillen, D. L. Transgression, self-image, and compliant behavior. *Journal of Personality and Social Psychology,* 1971, *20,* 176–179.

McNeel, S. P., & Messick, D. M. A Bayesian analysis of subjective probabilities of interpersonal relationships. *Acta Psychologica,* 1970, *34,* 311–321.

McNemar, Q. *The revision of the Stanford-Binet scale: An analysis of the standardization data.* Boston: Houghton Mifflin, 1942.

Mead, G. H. *Mind, self and society.* (C. W. Morris, Ed.) Chicago: University of Chicago Press, 1934.

Mead, M. *Sex and temperament in three primitive societies.* New York: Morrow, 1935.

*Mead, M. *Culture and commitment: A study of the generation gap.* Garden City, N. Y.: Doubleday, 1970.

*Mead, M., Dobzhansky, T., Tobach, E., & Light, R. E. (Eds.). *Science and the concept of race.* New York: Columbia University Press, 1968.

Megargee, E. I., & Hokanson, J. E. (Eds.). *The dynamics of aggression.* New York: Harper & Row, 1970.

Meggyesy, D. *Out of their league.* New York: Paperback Library, 1971.

Mehrabian, A. Inference of attitudes from the posture, orientation, and distance of a communicator. *Journal of Consulting and Clinical Psychology,* 1968, *32,* 296–308. (a)

Mehrabian, A. Relationship of attitude to seated posture, orientation, and distance. *Journal of Personality and Social Psychology,* 1968, *10,* 26–30. (b)

Mehrabian, A. *Nonverbal communication.* Chicago, Ill.: Aldine-Atherton, 1972.

Mehrabian, A., & Diamond, S. Effects of furniture arrangement, props, and personality on social interaction. *Journal of Personality and Social Psychology,* 1971, *20,* 18–30. (a)

Mehrabian, A., & Diamond, S. Seating arrangement and conversation. *Sociometry,* 1971, *34,* 281–289. (b)

Meier, G. W. Infantile handling and development in Siamese kittens. *Journal of Comparative and Physiological Psychology,* 1961, *54,* 284–286.

Meir, E. I., & Barak, A. Pervasiveness of the relationship between intrinsic-extrinsic needs and persistence at work. *Journal of Applied Psychology*, 1974, *59*, 103–104.

Meisels, M., & Canter, F. Personal space and personality characteristics: A nonconfirmation. *Psychological Reports*, 1970, *27*, 287–290.

*Melville, K. *Communes in the counter culture: Origins, theories, styles of life.* New York: William Morrow, 1972.

Menne, J. M. C., & Sinnett, E. R. Proximity and social interaction in residence halls. *Journal of College Student Personnel*, 1971, *12*, 26–31.

Merbaum, A. D. *Need for achievement in Negro children.* Unpublished master's thesis, Department of Psychology, University of North Carolina, 1960.

Mercer, J. IQ: The lethal label. *Psychology Today*, 1972, *6*(4), 44–47ff.

Merrens, M. R. Nonemergency helping behavior in various sized communities. *Journal of Social Psychology*, 1973, *90*, 327–329.

Merton, R. K. The social psychology of housing. In W. Dennis (Ed.), *Current trends in social psychology.* Pittsburgh: University of Pittsburgh Press, 1947. Pp. 163–217.

Merton, R. K. *Social theory and social structure* (Rev. ed.). New York: Free Press, 1968.

Mesthene, E. G. The role of technology in society. In A. H. Teich (Ed.), *Technology and man's future.* New York: St. Martin's Press, 1972. Pp. 127–151.

Mettee, D. R., & Wilkins, P. C. When similarity "hurts": Effects of perceived ability and a humorous blunder on interpersonal attractiveness. *Journal of Personality and Social Psychology*, 1972, *22*, 246–258.

Meyer, T. P. Effects of viewing justified and unjustified real film violence on aggressive behavior. *Journal of Personality and Social Psychology*, 1972, *23*, 21–29.

Michael, S. T. Authoritarianism, anomie, and the disordered mind. *Acta Psychiatrica Scandinavica*, 1967, *43*, 286–299.

Michelini, R. L., Wilson, J. P., & Messé, L. A. *The influence of psychological needs on helping behavior.* Paper presented at the meeting of the Midwestern Psychological Association, Chicago, May 1973.

Michelson, W. *Man and his urban environment: A sociological approach.* Reading, Mass.: Addison-Wesley, 1970.

Midlarsky, E., & Bryan, J. H. Affect expressions and children's imitative altruism. *Journal of Experimental Research in Personality*, 1972, *6*, 195–203.

Milgram, S. Behavioral study of obedience. *Journal of Abnormal and Social Psychology*, 1963, *67*, 371–378.

Milgram, S. Group pressure and action against a person. *Journal of Abnormal and Social Psychology*, 1964, *69*, 137–143. (a)

Milgram, S. Issues in the study of obedience: A reply to Baumrind. *American Psychologist*, 1964, *19*, 848–852. (b)

Milgram, S. Some conditions of obedience and disobedience to authority. *Human Relations*, 1965, *18*, 57–76.

Milgram, S. Reply to the critics. *International Journal of Psychiatry*, 1968, *6*, 294–295.

Milgram, S. The experience of living in cities. *Science*, 1970, *167*, 1461–1468.

*Milgram, S. *Obedience to authority.* New York: Harper & Row, 1974.

Milgram, S., Bickman, L., & Berkowitz, L. Note on the drawing power of crowds of different size. *Journal of Personality and Social Psychology*, 1969, *13*, 79–82.

Milgram, S., & Toch, H. Collective behavior: Crowds and social movements. In G. Lindzey & E. Aronson (Eds.), *Handbook of social psychology* (Vol. 4) (2nd ed.). Reading, Mass.: Addison-Wesley, 1969. Pp. 507–610.

Miller, A. G., & Thomas, R. Cooperation and competition among Blackfoot Indian and urban Canadian children. *Child Development*, 1972, *43*, 1104–1110.

Miller, G. A. Psychology as a means of promoting human welfare. *American Psychologist*, 1969, *24*, 1063–1075. Reprinted in F. F. Korten, S. W. Cook, & J. I. Lacey (Eds.), *Psychology and the problems of society.* Washington, D. C.: American Psychological Association, 1970. Pp. 5–21.

Miller, H. Is the risky shift a result of a rational group decision? *Proceedings, 78th Annual Convention, American Psychological Association*, 1970, *5*, 333–334.

Miller, K. S., & Dreger, R. M. (Eds.). *Comparative studies of Blacks and Whites in the United States: Psychological, social, physiological.* New York: Seminar Press, 1973.

Miller, L. K., & Hamblin, R. L. Interdependence, differential rewarding, and productivity. *American Sociological Review*, 1963, *28*, 768–778.

Miller, N. E. The frustration-aggression hypothesis. *Psychological Review*, 1941, *48*, 337–342.

Miller, N. E. Some implications of modern behavior theory for personality change and psychotherapy. In P. Worchel & D. Byrne (Eds.), *Personality change.* New York: Wiley, 1964. Pp. 149–175.

Miller, N. E., & Dollard, J. *Social learning and imitation.* New Haven: Yale University Press, 1941.

Miller, Norman. Involvement and dogmatism as inhibitors of attitude change. *Journal of Experimental Social Psychology*, 1965, *1*, 121–132.

Miller, Norman, & Zimbardo, P. G. Motives for fear-induced affiliation: Emotional comparison or interpersonal similarity? *Journal of Personality*, 1966, *34*, 481–503.

Mills, C. W. The contributions of sociology to studies of industrial relations. *Proceedings of the First Annual Meeting, Industrial Relations Research Association*, 1948, *1*, 199–222.

Mills, J. Opinion change as a function of the communicator's desire to influence and liking for the audience. *Journal of Experimental Social Psychology*, 1966, *2*, 152–159.

Mills, J., & Aronson, E. Opinion change as a function of communicator's attractiveness and desire to influence. *Journal of Personality and Social Psychology*, 1965, *1*, 173–177.

Milton, G. A. *Five studies of the relation between sex role identification and achievement in problem-solving* (Technical Report No. 3). New Haven, Conn.: Yale University, 1958.

Milton, G. A. Sex differences in problem solving as a function of role appropriateness of the problem content. *Psychological Reports*, 1959, 5, 705–708.

Milton, O. Presidential choice and performance on a scale of authoritarianism. *American Psychologist*, 1952, 7, 597–598.

Mintz, N. L. Effects of esthetic surroundings: II. Prolonged and repeated experience in a "beautiful" and an "ugly" room. *Journal of Psychology*, 1956, 41, 459–466.

Mischel, H. Sex bias in the evaluation of professional achievements. *Journal of Educational Psychology*, 1974, 66, 157–166.

Mischel, W. A social learning view of sex differences in behavior. In E. E. Maccoby (Ed.), *The development of sex differences*. Stanford, Calif.: Stanford University Press, 1966. Pp. 56–81.

Mischel, W. *Personality and assessment*. New York: Wiley, 1968.

Mischel, W. Continuity and change in personality. *American Psychologist*, 1969, 24, 1012–1018.

Mischel, W. *The construction of personality: Some facts and fantasies about cognition and social behavior*. Paper presented at the meeting of the American Psychological Association, Washington, D. C., September 1971.

Mitchell, R. E. Some social implications of high density housing. *American Sociological Review*, 1971, 36, 18–29.

Mitnick, L., & McGinnies, E. Influencing ethnocentrism in small discussion groups through a film communication. *Journal of Abnormal and Social Psychology*, 1958, 56, 82–90.

Modigliani, A. Embarrassment and embarrassability. *Sociometry*, 1968, 31, 313–326.

Monahan, L., Kuhn, D., & Shaver, P. Intrapsychic versus cultural explanations of the "fear of success" motive. *Journal of Personality and Social Psychology*, 1974, 29, 60–64.

*Money, J., & Athanasiou, R. Pornography: Review and bibliographic annotations. *American Journal of Obstetrics and Gynecology*, 1973, 115(1), 130–146.

Money, J., & Brennan, J. G. Sexual dimorphism in the psychology of female transsexuals. In R. Green & J. Money (Eds.), *Transsexualism and sex reassignment*. Baltimore: Johns Hopkins Press, 1969.

Money, J., & Ehrhardt, A. A. *Man and woman; boy and girl*. Baltimore: Johns Hopkins Press, 1972.

Money, J., & Primrose, C. Sexual dimorphism and dissociation in the psychology of male transsexuals. In R. Green & J. Money (Eds.), *Transsexualism and sex reassignment*. Baltimore: Johns Hopkins Press, 1969.

Montagu, M. F. A. *Man: His first million years*. Cleveland: World, 1957.

Montagu, M. F. A. *Man's most dangerous myth: The fallacy of race* (4th ed.). Cleveland: World, 1964.

*Montagu, M. F. A. *Man and aggression* (2nd ed.). New York: Oxford University Press, 1973. (a)

Montagu, M. F. A. The new litany of "innate depravity," or "Original Sin" revisited. In M. F. A. Montagu (Ed.), *Man and aggression* (2nd ed.). New York: Oxford University Press, 1973. Pp. 3–18. (b)

Montgomery, R. L., Hinkle, S. W., & Enzie, R. F. Arbitrary norms and social change in high and low authoritarian

societies. *Journal of Personality and Social Psychology*, 1976, 33(6), 698–708.

Moore, B. S., Underwood, B., & Rosenhan, D. Affect and self-gratification. *Developmental Psychology*, 1973, 8, 209–214.

Moore, W. *Social change*. Englewood Cliffs, N. J.: Prentice-Hall, 1963.

Moore, W. *Order and change: Essays in comparative sociology*. New York: Wiley, 1967.

Moore, W. Social change. In *International Encyclopedia of the Social Sciences*. Vol. 14. New York: Macmillan, 1968.

Moorehead, A. *The Russian revolution*. New York: Harper, 1958.

*Moos, R., & Insel, P. (Eds.) *Issues in social ecology: Human milieus*. Palo Alto, Calif.: National Press Books, 1974.

Morgan, L. B. Counseling for future shock. *Personnel and Guidance Journal*, 1974, 52, 283–287.

Moriarty, T. Crime, commitment and the responsive bystander: Two field experiments. *Journal of Personality and Social Psychology*, 1975, 31, 370–376.

Morin, S. F. *On being a gay professional or professionally gay*. Paper presented at the meeting of the American Psychological Association, New Orleans, August 1974.

Morin, S. F., & Miller, J. S. Coming out. In E. Rosenberg (Ed.), *Survival manual for alternative health care agencies*. Madison, Wisc.: STASH Press, 1975.

Morris, D. *The naked ape*. London: Jonathan Cape, 1967.

Morris, D. *The human zoo*. New York: McGraw-Hill, 1969.

*Morris, J. *Conundrum*. New York: Harcourt, Brace, Jovanovich, 1974.

Morton, J. R. C., Denenberg, V. H., & Zarrow, M. X. Modification of sexual development through stimulation in infancy. *Journal of Endocrinology*, 1963, 72, 439–442.

Moscovici, S. Society and theory in social psychology. In J. Israel & H. Tajfel (Eds.), *The context of social psychology: A critical assessment*. New York: Academic Press, 1972.

Moscovici, S. Social influence I: Conformity and social control. In C. Nemeth (Ed.), *Social psychology: Classic and contemporary integrations*. Chicago: Aldine, 1974. Pp. 179–216.

Moscovici, S., & Doise, W. Decision making in groups. In C. Nemeth (Ed.), *Social psychology: Classic and contemporary integrations*. Chicago: Rand McNally, 1974. Pp. 250–287.

Moscovici, S., & Faucheux, C. Social influence, conformity bias, and the study of active minorities. In L. Berkowitz (Ed.), *Advances in experimental social psychology* (Vol. 6). New York: Academic Press, 1972. Pp. 149–202.

Moscovici, S., & Zavalloni, M. The group as a polarizer of attitudes. *Journal of Personality and Social Psychology*, 1969, 12, 125–135.

Moscovici, S., Zavalloni, M., & Louis-Guérin, C. Studies on polarization of judgments: I. Group effects on person perception. *European Journal of Social Psychology*, 1972, 2, 87–91.

Mosher, D. L. Sex differences, sex experience, sex guilt, and explicitly sexual films. *Journal of Social Issues*, 1973, 29(3), 95–112.

Moss, H. A. Sex, age, and state as determinants of mother-infant interaction. *Merrill-Palmer Quarterly,* 1967, *13,* 19–36.

Moss, M. K., & Andrasik, F. Belief similarity and interracial attraction. *Journal of Personality,* 1973, *41,* 192–205.

Moss, M. K., & Page, R. A. Reinforcement and helping behavior. *Journal of Applied Social Psychology,* 1972, *2,* 360–371.

Mosteller, F., Hyman, H., McCarthy, P. J., Marks, E. S., & Truman, D. B. The pre-election polls of 1948: Report to the committee on analysis of pre-election polls and forecasts. *Social Science Research Council Bulletin,* 1949, No. 60, 1–396.

Mosteller, F., & Wallace, D. L. *Inference and disputed authorship: The Federalist.* Reading, Mass.: Addison-Wesley, 1964.

Mostert, N. *Supership.* New York: Knopf, 1974.

Mouchanow, M. *My empress: Twenty-three years of intimate life with the empress of all the Russias from her marriage to the day of her exile.* New York: John Lane, 1918.

Moyer, K. E. *The physiology of hostility.* Chicago: Markham, 1971.

Moyer, K. E. A physiological model of aggression: Does it have different implications? (Report No. 72–3). Pittsburgh, Pa.: Carnegie-Mellon University, 1972.

Mulvihill, D. J., & Tumin, M. M. *Crimes of violence. Staff report to the National Commission on the Causes and Prevention of Violence* (Vol. 11). Washington, D. C.: United States Government Printing Office, 1969.

Murphy, R. J., & Watson, J. M. The structure of discontent. In N. E. Cohen (Ed.), *The Los Angeles riots: A socio-psychological study.* New York: Praeger, 1970.

*Murstein, B. I. (Ed.) *Theories of attraction and love.* New York: Springer, 1971.

Murstein, B. I. Physical attractiveness and marital choice. *Journal of Personality and Social Psychology,* 1972, *22,* 8–12.

Mussen, P. Differences between the TAT responses of Negro and White boys. *Journal of Consulting Psychology,* 1953, *17,* 373–376.

Myers, D. G. The polarizing effects of group discussion. Unpublished manuscript, Hope College, 1974.

Myers, D. G., & Bishop, G. D. Discussion effects on racial attitudes. *Science,* 1970, *169,* 778–789.

Myers, D. G., & Bishop, G. D. Enhancement of dominant attitudes in group discussion. *Journal of Personality and Social Psychology,* 1971, *20,* 386–391.

Naeye, R. L., Diener, M. M., & Dellinger, W. S. Urban poverty: Effects on prenatal nutrition. *Science,* 1969, *166,* 1026.

National Center for Educational Statistics. *Salaries and tenure of full-time instructional faculty, 1974–1975.* Washington, D. C.: U. S. Department of Health, Education, and Welfare, 1975.

National Commission on the Causes and Prevention of Violence. *To establish justice, to insure domestic tranquility.* New York: Award Books, 1969.

National Science Foundation. *Knowledge into action: Improving the nation's use of the social sciences.* Washington, D. C.: U. S. Government Printing Office, 1969.

Neary, J. A scientist's variation on a disturbing racial theme.

Life, 1970, *68*(24), 58B-65. (June 12, 1970 issue.)

Neff, F. W. *Problems of the psychologist in designing and implementing instruction for a police organization.* Paper presented at the meeting of the American Psychological Association, New Orleans, September 1974.

Neff, W. *Work and human behavior.* New York: Atherton Press, 1968.

Neiman, L. J., & Hughes, J. W. The problem of the concept of role—a resurvey of the literature. *Social Forces,* 1951, *30,* 141–149.

Nelson, E. A., Grinder, R. E., & Mutterer, M. L. Sources of variance in behavioral measures of honesty in temptation situation: Methodological analyses. *Developmental Psychology,* 1969, *1,* 265–279.

Nemecek, J., & Grandjean, E. Results of an ergonomic investigation of large-scale offices. *Human Factors,* 1973, *15*(2) 111–124.

Nemeth, C. A critical analysis of research utilizing the Prisoner's Dilemma paradigm for the study of bargaining. In L. Berkowitz (Ed.), *Advances in experimental social psychology* (Vol. 6). New York: Academic Press, 1972.

*Nemeth, C. (Ed.) *Social psychology: Classic and contemporary integrations.* Chicago: Rand McNally, 1974.

Neufeld, E., Langmeyer, D., & Seeman, W. Some sex-role stereotypes and personal preferences, 1950 and 1970. *Journal of Personality Assessment,* 1974, *38,* 247–254.

Neulinger, J. *Perceptions of the optimally integrated person: A redefinition of mental health.* Paper presented at the meeting of the American Psychological Association, San Francisco, September 1968.

Newbrough, J. R. *Adolescent participation in civil disturbances* (Final Report). Center for Community Studies, George Peabody College for Teachers, November 1968.

Newbrough, J. R. Community psychology: A new holism. *American Journal of Community Psychology,* 1973, *1,* 201–211.

Newcomb, T. M. *The acquaintance process.* New York: Holt, Rinehart & Winston, 1961.

Newcomb, T. M., Turner, R. H., & Converse, P. E. *Social psychology.* New York: Holt, 1965.

*Newman, O. *Defensible space.* New York: Macmillan, 1973.

Newsweek. Taking the Chitling Test. 1968, *72*(3), 51–52. (July 15, 1968 issue.)

Newsweek. A question of style. 1969, *14*(14), 104. (October 6, 1969 issue.)

Newsweek. Why the pollsters failed. 1970, *76*(1), 58. (July 6, 1970 issue.)

Newsweek. M*A*S*H*E*D. 1971, *77*(8), 45–46. (February 22, 1971 issue.)

Newsweek. Victory for the Amish. 1972, *79*(22), 89. (May 29, 1972 issue.)

Newsweek. The guilty victim. 1974, *83*(24), 66. (June 17, 1974 issue.)

Newsweek. La Presidente. 1974, *84*(11), 41. (September 9, 1974 issue.)

Newtson, D., & Czerlinsky, T. Adjustment of attitude communications for contrasts by extreme audiences. *Journal of Personality and Social Psychology*, 1974, *30*, 829–837.

New York Times. Few cheers for "bad seed" tests for the young. April 19, 1970, p. E-13.

Nisbett, R. E., Caputo, C., Legant, P., & Maracek, J. Behavior as seen by the actor and as seen by the observer. *Journal of Personality and Social Psychology*, 1973, *27*, 154–164.

Nisbett, R. E., & Schachter, S. Cognitive manipulation of pain. *Journal of Experimental Social Psychology*, 1966, *2*, 227–236.

Nisbett, R. E., & Temoshok, L. Is there an "external" cognitive style? *Journal of Personality and Social Psychology*, 1976, *33*, 36–47.

Nobles, W. W. Psychological research and Black self-concept: A critical review. *Journal of Social Issues*, 1973, *29*(1), 11–31.

Nord, W. R. Social exchange theory: An integrative approach to social conformity. *Psychological Bulletin*, 1969, *71*, 174–208.

Novak, D., & Lerner, M. J. Rejection as a consequence of perceived similarity. *Journal of Personality and Social Psychology*, 1968, *9*, 147–152.

Nutt, R. L., & Sedlacek, W. E. Freshman sexual attitudes and behavior. *Journal of College Student Personnel*, 1974, *15*, 346–351.

Oakes, W. F. External validity and the use of real people as subjects. *American Psychologist*, 1972, *27*, 959–962.

Oberschall, A. *Social conflict and social movements.* Englewood Cliffs, N.J.: Prentice-Hall, 1973.

O'Connor, J. *Developmental changes in abstractness and moral reasoning.* Unpublished doctoral dissertation, Department of Psychology, George Peabody College for Teachers, 1971.

O'Leary, V. E. Some attitudinal barriers to occupational aspirations in women. *Psychological Bulletin*, 1974, *81*, 809–826.

Oliver, L. Women in aprons: The female stereotype in children's readers. *Elementary School Journal*, 1974, *74*, 253–259.

O'Neal, E. *Arousal and impulsive aggression.* Paper presented at the meeting of the Midwestern Psychological Association, Chicago, May 1973.

Orlofsky, J. L., Marcia, J. E., & Lesser, I. M. Ego identity status and the intimacy versus isolation crisis of young adulthood. *Journal of Personality and Social Psychology*, 1973, *27*, 211–219.

Orne, M. T. The nature of hypnosis: Artifact and essence. *Journal of Abnormal and Social Psychology*, 1959, *58*, 277–299.

Orne, M. T. Demand characteristics and the concept of quasi-controls. In R. Rosenthal & R. L. Rosnow (Eds.), *Artifact in behavioral research.* New York: Academic Press, 1969. Pp. 143–179.

Orne, M. T., & Holland, C. C. On the ecological validity of laboratory deceptions. *International Journal of Psychiatry*, 1968, *6*, 282–293.

Orpen, C., & Van der Schyff, L. Prejudice and personality in White South Africa: A "differential learning" alternative to the authoritarian personality. *Journal of Social Psychology*, 1972, *87*, 313–314.

Orwell, G. *1984.* New York: Harcourt-Brace, 1949.

Osborn, A. F. *Applied imagination.* New York: Scribner, 1957.

Osgood, C. E., & Tannenbaum, P. H. The principle of congruity in the prediction of attitude change. *Psychological Review*, 1955, *62*, 42–55.

Osmond, H. Function as the basis of psychiatric ward design. *Mental Hospitals*, 1957, *8*, 23–30.

Osterhouse, R. A., & Brock, T. C. Distraction increases yielding to propaganda by inhibiting counterarguing. *Journal of Personality and Social Psychology*, 1970, *15*, 344–358.

Packard, V. *The sexual wilderness.* New York: McKay, 1968.

Page, E. B. Miracle in Milwaukee: Raising the IQ. *Educational Researcher*, 1972, *1*(10), 8–10; 15–16.

Page, M. M. Social psychology of a classical conditioning of attitudes experiment. *Journal of Personality and Social Psychology*, 1969, *11*, 177–186.

Page, M. M. Postexperimental assessment of awareness in attitude conditioning. *Educational and Psychological Measurement*, 1971, *31*, 891–906.

Page, M. M. Demand characteristics and the classical conditioning of attitudes experiment. *Journal of Personality and Social Psychology*, 1974, *30*, 468–476.

Page, M., & Scheidt, R. The elusive weapons effect: Demand awareness, evaluation and slightly sophisticated subjects. *Journal of Personality and Social Psychology*, 1971, *20*, 304–318.

Paige, J. M. Changing patterns of anti-White attitudes among Blacks. *Journal of Social Issues*, 1970, *26*(4), 69–86.

Panel on Privacy and Behavioral Research. Preliminary summary of report. *Science*, 1967, *155*, 535–538.

Panos, R. J. *Correlates of birth order: Effect or artifact?* Paper presented at the meeting of the American Educational Research Association, Chicago, February 1968.

Parke, R. D. Effectiveness of punishment as an interaction of intensity, timing, agent nurturance, and cognitive structuring. *Child Development*, 1969, *40*, 213–235.

Parke, R. D., Berkowitz, L., Leyens, J-P., & Sebastian, R. The effects of repeated exposure to movie violence on aggressive behavior in juvenile delinquent boys: Field experimental studies. In L. Berkowitz (Ed.), *Advances in experimental social psychology* (Vol. 9). New York: Academic Press, in press.

Parlee, M. B. Comments on D. M. Broverman, E. L. Klaiber, Y. Kobayashi, and W. Vogel: Roles of activation and inhibition in sex differences in cognitive abilities. *Psychological Review*, 1972, *79*, 180–184.

Parlee, M. B. The premenstrual syndrome. *Psychological Bulletin*, 1973, *80*, 454–465.

Parnes, S. J., & Meadow, A. Effects of "brainstorming" instructions on creative problem solving by trained and untrained subjects. *Journal of Educational Psychology*, 1959, *50*, 171–176.

Parry, H. J., & Crossley, H. M. Validity of responses to survey questions. *Public Opinion Quarterly*, 1950, *14*, 61–80.

Parsons, H. M. What happened at Hawthorne? *Science*, 1974, *183*, 922–932.

Pasamanick, B. A., & Knobloch, H. Early language behavior

in Negro children and the testing of intelligence. *Journal of Abnormal and Social Psychology*, 1955, *50*, 401–402.

Pasamanick, B. A., & Knobloch, H. Brain damage and reproductive casualty. *American Journal of Orthopsychiatry*, 1960, *30*, 298–305.

Patterson, M. L. Compensation in nonverbal immediacy behaviors: A review. *Sociometry*, 1973, *36*, 237–252. (a)

Patterson, M. L. Stability of nonverbal immediacy behaviors. *Journal of Experimental Social Psychology*, 1973, *9*, 97–109. (b)

Patterson, M. L., & Holmes, D. S. Social interaction correlates of the MPI introversion-extroversion scale. *American Psychologist*, 1966, *21*, 724–725. (Abstract)

Patterson, M. L., Mullens, S., & Romano, J. Compensatory reactions to spatial intrusion. *Sociometry*, 1971, *34*, 114–121.

Patterson, M. L., & Sechrest, L. B. Interpersonal distance and impression formation. *Journal of Personality*, 1970, *38*, 161–166.

Paulus, P., Cox, V., McCain, G., & Chandler, J. Some effects of crowding in a prison environment. *Journal of Applied Social Psychology*, 1975, *5*, 86–91.

Peabody, D. Attitude content and agreement set in scales of authoritarianism, dogmatism, anti-Semitism, and economic conservatism. *Journal of Abnormal and Social Psychology*, 1961, *63*, 1–11.

Peabody, D. Authoritarianism scales and response bias. *Psychological Bulletin*, 1966, *65*, 11–23.

Peck, R. F., & Havighurst, R. J. *The psychology of character development.* New York: Wiley, 1960.

Pederson, D. M., & Higbee, K. L. Personality correlates of self-disclosure. *Journal of Social Psychology*, 1969, *78*, 81–89.

Penman, K. A., Hastad, D. N., & Cords, W. L. Success of the authoritarian coach. *Journal of Social Psychology*, 1974, *92*, 155–156.

Pepitone, A. Some conceptual and empirical problems of consistency theories. In S. Feldman (Ed.), *Cognitive consistency.* New York: Academic Press, 1966. Pp. 257–297.

Perlman, D. The sexual standards of Canadian university students. In D. Koulack & D. Perlman (Eds.), *Readings in social psychology: Focus on Canada.* Toronto: Wiley, 1973. Pp. 139–160.

Perlman, D. Self-esteem and sexual permissiveness. *Journal of Marriage and the Family*, 1974, *34*, 470–473.

Perlman, D., & Oskamp, S. The effects of picture content and exposure frequency on evaluations of Negroes and Whites. *Journal of Experimental Social Psychology*, 1971, *7*, 503–514.

Person, E., & Ovesey, L. The transsexual syndrome in males: I. Primary transsexualism. *American Journal of Psychotherapy*, 1974, *28*, 4–20.

Peterson, J., & Lanier, L. H. Studies in the comparative abilities of Whites and Negroes. *Mental Measurement Monographs*, 1929, No. 5.

Peterson, J. H. *A disguised structured instrument for the assessment of attitudes toward the poor.* Unpublished doctoral dissertation, University of Oklahoma, 1967.

Peterson, M. Guidelines for psychologists in police consultation. Paper presented at the meeting of the American Psychological Association, New Orleans, September 1974.

Peterson, P. D., & Koulack, D. Attitude change as a function of latitudes of acceptance and rejection. *Journal of Personality and Social Psychology*, 1969, *11*, 309–311.

Petronko, M. R., & Perin, C. T. A consideration of cognitive complexity and primacy-recency effects in impression formation. *Journal of Personality and Social Psychology*, 1970, *15*, 151–157.

Pettigrew, T. F. Regional differences in anti-Negro prejudice. *Journal of Abnormal and Social Psychology*, 1959, *59*, 28–36.

Pettigrew, T. F. Social psychology and desegregation research. *American Psychologist*, 1961, *16*, 105–112.

*Pettigrew, T. F. *A profile of the Negro American.* Princeton, N. J.: Van Nostrand, 1964.

Phares, E. J. *Locus of control in personality.* Morristown, N. J.: General Learning Press, 1976.

Pheterson, G. I., Kiesler, S. B., & Goldberg, P. A. Evaluation of the performance of women as a function of their sex, achievement and personal history. *Journal of Personality and Social Psychology*, 1971, *19*, 114–118.

Phillips, D. P. *Dying as a form of social behavior.* (Doctoral dissertation, Princeton University). Ann Arbor, Mich.: University Microfilms, 1970. No. 70–19, 799.

Phillips, D. P. Deathday and birthday: An unexpected connection. In J. M. Tanur (Ed.), *Statistics: A guide to the unknown.* San Francisco: Holden-Day, 1972.

Piaget, J. *The language and thought of the child.* New York: Harcourt-Brace, 1926.

Piaget, J. The general problems of the psychobiological development of the child. In J. M. Tanner & B. Inhelder (Eds.), *Discussions of child development: Proceedings of the World Health Organization study group on the psychobiological development of the child* (Vol. 4). New York: International Universities Press, 1960. Pp. 3–27.

*Piaget, J. *The moral judgment of the child.* New York: Free Press, 1965. (Originally published, 1932.)

Piaget, J. The theory of stages in cognitive development. In D. R. Green, M. P. Ford, & G. B. Flamer (Eds.), *Measurement and Piaget.* New York: McGraw-Hill, 1971. Pp. 1–11.

Piliavin, I. M., Piliavin, J. A., & Rodin, J. Costs, diffusion, and the stigmatized victim. *Journal of Personality and Social Psychology*, 1975, *32*, 429–438.

Piliavin, I. M., Rodin, J., & Piliavin, J. A. Good Samaritanism: An underground phenomenon? *Journal of Personality and Social Psychology*, 1969, *13*, 289–299.

Piliavin, J. A., & Piliavin, I. M. Effect of blood on reactions to a victim. *Journal of Personality and Social Psychology*, 1972, *23*, 353–361.

Piliavin, J. A., & Piliavin, I. M. *The Good Samaritan: Why does he help?* Unpublished manuscript, University of Wisconsin, 1973.

Pintner, R. *Intelligence testing.* New York: Holt, 1931.

Pizer, S. A., & Travers, J. R. *Psychology and social change.* New York: McGraw-Hill, 1975.

Pleck, J. H., & Sawyer, J. (Eds.) *Men and masculinity.* Englewood Cliffs, N.J.: Prentice-Hall, 1974.

Pliner, P., Hart, H., Kohl, J., & Saari, D. Compliance without pressure: Some further data on the foot-in-the door technique. *Journal of Experimental Social Psychology,* 1974, *10,* 17–22.

Plog, S. C. The disclosure of self in the United States and Germany. *Journal of Social Psychology,* 1965, *65,* 193–203.

Polanyi, M. *Knowing and being.* Chicago: University of Chicago Press, 1969.

Poley, W. Dimensionality in the measurement of authoritarian and political attitudes. *Canadian Journal of Behavioural Science,* 1974, *6,* 83–94.

Pollock, H. M., & Furbush, A. M. Mental disease in 12 states, 1919. *Mental Hygiene,* 1921, *5,* 353–389.

Pomazal, R. J., & Clore, G. L. Helping on the highway: The effects of dependency and sex. *Journal of Applied Social Psychology,* 1973, *3,* 150–164.

*Pomeroy, W. B. *Dr. Kinsey and the Institute for Sex Research.* New York: Harper & Row, 1972.

Poor, D. *The social psychology of questionnaires.* Unpublished bachelor's thesis, Harvard University, 1967. (Cited in R. Rosenthal & R. L. Rosnow (Eds.), *Artifact in behavioral research.* New York: Academic Press, 1969.)

Poppen, P. J. *Sex differences in moral judgment.* Paper presented at the meeting of the American Psychological Association, New Orleans, September 1974.

Popper, K. R. *Objective knowledge: An evolutionary approach.* Oxford: Clarendon, 1972.

Porter, E., Argyle, M., & Salter, V. What is signalled by proximity? *Perceptual and Motor Skills,* 1970, *30,* 39–42.

Porter, J. A. *The vertical mosaic.* Toronto: University of Toronto Press, 1965.

*Porter, L. W., Lawler, E. E., III, & Hackman, J. R. *Behavior in organizations.* New York: McGraw-Hill, 1975.

Potter, D. A. Personalism and interpersonal attraction. *Journal of Personality and Social Psychology,* 1973, *28,* 192–198.

Prentice, N. M. The influence of live and symbolic modeling on promoting moral judgment of adolescent delinquents. *Journal of Abnormal Psychology,* 1972, *80,* 157–161.

Preston, M. Note on the reliability and validity of group judgment. *Journal of Experimental Psychology,* 1938, *22,* 462–471.

Price, C. R. Between cultures: The current crisis of transition. In W. Schmidt (Ed.), *Organizational frontiers and human values.* Belmont, Calif.: Wadsworth, 1970. Pp. 27–44.

Price, G. H., & Dabbs, J. M., Jr. *Sex, setting, and personal space: Changes as children grow older.* Paper presented at the meeting of the American Psychological Association, New Orleans, August 1974.

Price, J. L. *The effects of crowding on the social behavior of children.* Unpublished doctoral dissertation, Columbia University, 1971. (University Microfilms, 1972, No. 72-19, 151).

Price, K. O., Harburg, E., & Newcomb, T. M. Psychological balance in situations of negative interpersonal attitudes. *Journal of Personality and Social Psychology,* 1966, *3,* 265–270.

Prince, V., & Butler, P. M. Survey of 504 cases of transvestism. *Psychological Reports,* 1972, *31,* 903–917.

Prociuk, T. J., & Lussier, R. I. Internal-external locus of control: An analysis and bibliography of two years' research (1973-1974). *Psychological Reports,* in press.

*Proshansky, H., Ittelson, W., & Rivlin, L. (Eds.). *Environmental psychology: Man and his physical setting.* New York: Holt, Rinehart & Winston, 1970. (a)

Proshansky, H., Ittelson, W., & Rivlin, L. Freedom of choice and behavior in a physical setting. In H. Proshansky, W. Ittelson, and L. Rivlin (Eds.), *Environmental psychology: Man and his physical setting.* New York: Holt, Rinehart & Winston, 1970. Pp. 173–183. (b)

Proshansky, H., & Newton, P. The nature and meaning of Negro self-identity. In M. Deutsch, I. Katz, & A. R. Jensen (Eds.), *Social class, race, and psychological development.* New York: Holt, Rinehart & Winston, 1968. Pp. 178–218.

Prothro, E. T. Ethnocentrism and anti-Negro attitudes in the deep South. *Journal of Abnormal and Social Psychology,* 1952, *47,* 105–108.

Pruitt, D. G. Reward structure and cooperation: The decomposed Prisoner's Dilemma game. *Journal of Personality and Social Psychology,* 1967, *7,* 21–27.

Pruitt, D. G. Reciprocity and credit building in a laboratory dyad. *Journal of Personality and Social Psychology,* 1968, *8,* 143–147.

Pruitt, D. G. Choice shifts in group discussion: An introductory review. *Journal of Personality and Social Psychology,* 1971, *20,* 339–360. (a)

Pruitt, D. G. Conclusions: Toward an understanding of choice shifts in group discussion. *Journal of Personality and Social Psychology,* 1971, *20,* 495–510. (b)

Pruitt, D. G., & Teger, A. I. The risky shift in group betting. *Journal of Experimental Social Psychology,* 1969, *5,* 115–126.

Rabbie, J. M. Differential preference for companionship under threat. *Journal of Abnormal and Social Psychology,* 1963, *67,* 643–648.

Rabbie, J. M. *Effects of expected intergroup competition and cooperation.* Paper presented at the meeting of the American Psychological Association, New Orleans, August 1974.

Rabbie, J. M., & Wilkens, G. Intergroup competition and its effect on intragroup and intergroup relations. *European Journal of Social Psychology,* 1971, *1,* 215–234.

Rada, J. B., & Rogers, R. W. *Obedience to authority: Presence of authority and command strength.* Paper presented at the meeting of the Southeastern Psychological Association, New Orleans, April 1973.

Radloff, R. Opinion evaluation and affiliation. *Journal of Abnormal and Social Psychology,* 1961, *62,* 578–585.

Ralls, K. Mammalian scent marking. *Science,* 1971, *171,* 443–450.

Rand, A. *The fountainhead.* Indianapolis: Bobbs-Merrill, 1943.

Ransford, H. E. Isolation, powerlessness, and violence: A study of attitudes and participation in the Watts riot. *American Journal of Sociology*, 1968, *73*, 581–591.

Rapoport, A., & Chammah, A. *Prisoner's dilemma.* Ann Arbor: University of Michigan Press, 1965.

Raser, J. "Mar-coo-za, Mar-coo-za." *Psychology Today*, 1971, *4*(9), 38–39ff.

Ratcliffe, J. M. (Ed.) *The Good Samaritan and the law.* Garden City, N.Y.: Doubleday Anchor, 1966.

*Rather, D., & Gates, G. P. *The palace guard.* New York: Harper & Row, 1974.

Raven, B. H., & Eachus, H. T. Cooperation and competition in means-interdependent triads. *Journal of Abnormal and Social Psychology*, 1963, *67*, 307–316.

Rawlings, E. I. Reactive guilt and anticipatory guilt in altruistic behavior. In J. Macaulay & L. Berkowitz (Eds.), *Altruism and helping behavior: Social psychological studies of some antecedents and consequences.* New York: Academic Press, 1970. Pp. 163–177.

Raymond, B. J., & Unger, R. K. "The apparel oft proclaims the man": Cooperation with deviant and conventional youths. *Journal of Social Psychology*, 1972, *87*, 75–82.

Rechy, J. *City of night.* New York: Grove Press, 1963.

Reed, T. E. Caucasian genes in American Negroes. *Science*, 1969, *165*, 762–768.

Reedy, G. *The twilight of the presidency.* New York and Cleveland: World, 1970.

Regan, D. T. Effects of a favor and liking on compliance. *Journal of Experimental Social Psychology*, 1971, *7*, 627–639.

Reich, C. A. *The greening of America.* New York: Random House, 1970.

Reichart, S. A greater space in which to breathe: What art and drama tell us about alienation. *Journal of Social Issues*, 1969, *25*(2), 137–146.

Reiss, I. *Premarital sexual standards in America.* New York: Free Press, 1960.

Reiss, I. *The social context of premarital sexual permissiveness.* New York: Holt, Rinehart & Winston, 1967.

Rest, J. R. *Developmental hierarchies of comprehension and preference in moral thinking.* Paper presented at the meeting of the Society for Research in Child Development, Santa Monica, March 1969.

Rest, J. R. The hierarchical nature of moral judgment: A study of patterns of comprehension and preference of moral stages. *Journal of Personality*, 1973, *41*, 86–109.

Rest, J., Turiel, E., & Kohlberg, L. Level of moral development as a determinant of preference and comprehension of moral judgments made by others. *Journal of Personality*, 1969, *37*, 225–252.

Rettig, S., & Rawson, H. E. The risk hypothesis in predictive judgments of unethical behavior. *Journal of Abnormal and Social Psychology*, 1963, *66*, 243–248.

Reuben, D. *Everything you always wanted to know about sex but were afraid to ask.* New York: David McKay, 1969.

Rhine, R., & Severance, L. Ego-involvement, discrepancy, source credibility, and attitude change. *Journal of Personal-ity and Social Psychology*, 1970, *16*, 175–190.

Richardson, S. A. *A study of selected personality characteristics of social science field workers.* Unpublished doctoral dissertation, Cornell University, 1954.

Rider, R. V., Taback, M., & Knobloch, H. Associations between premature birth and socio-economic status. *American Journal of Public Health*, 1955, *45*, 1022–1028.

*Riesman, D. (in association with N. Glazer & R. Denney). *The lonely crowd: A study of the changing American character.* New Haven: Yale University Press, 1950.

Ring, K. Experimental social psychology: Some sober questions about frivolous values. *Journal of Experimental Social Psychology*, 1967, *3*, 113–123.

Ring, K. *Let's get started: An appeal to what's left in psychology.* Unpublished manuscript, Department of Psychology, University of Connecticut, 1971.

Ring, K., Lipinski, C. E., & Braginsky, D. The relationship of birth order to self-evaluation, anxiety reduction, and susceptibility to emotional contagion. *Psychological Monographs*, 1965, *79*(10, Whole No. 603).

Ritchie, E., & Phares, E. J. Attitude change as a function of internal-external control and communicator status. *Journal of Personality*, 1969, *37*, 429–443.

Roberts, P. F. The dynamics of racial intermixture in the American Negro: Some anthropological considerations. *American Journal of Human Genetics*, 1955, *7*, 361–367.

Roberts, R. E. *The new communes: Coming together in America.* Englewood Cliffs, N. J.: Prentice-Hall, 1971.

Robinson, D., & Rohde, S. Two experiments with an anti-Semitism poll. *Journal of Abnormal and Social Psychology*, 1946, *41*, 136–144.

Robinson, D. L., & O'Conner, J. *The impact of teaching race relations on cadet instructors.* Paper presented at the meeting of the American Psychological Association, New Orleans, September 1974.

Robinson, I. E., King, K., Dudley, C. J., & Cline, F. J. Change in sexual behavior and attitude of college students. *Family Life Coordinator*, 1968, *17*, 119–123.

Rodin, J. *Menstruation, reattributions and competence.* Unpublished manuscript, Department of Psychology, Yale University, 1974.

Roethlisberger, F. J., & Dickson, W. J. *Management and the worker.* Cambridge, Mass.: Harvard University Press, 1939.

Rogers, C. R. A note on the "nature of man." *Journal of Counseling Psychology*, 1957, *4*, 199–203.

*Rogers, C. R. *Freedom to learn.* Columbus, Ohio: Charles E. Merrill, 1969.

*Rogers, C. R. *Becoming partners: Marriage and its alternatives.* New York: Dell, 1974.

*Rogers, C. R., & Skinner, B. F. Some issues concerning the control of human behavior. *Science*, 1956, *124*, 1057–1066.

Rogers, E. M. *Diffusion of innovations.* New York: Free Press, 1962.

Rogers, E. M., & Havens, E. Prestige rating and mate selection on a college campus. *Journal of Marriage and Family Living*, 1960, *22*, 55–59.

Rohe, W., & Patterson, A. H. *The effects of varied levels of resources and density on behavior in a day care center.* Paper presented at the annual conference of the Environmental Design Research Association, Milwaukee, Wisc., 1974.

Rohrer, J. H. The test intelligence of Osage Indians. *Journal of Social Psychology,* 1942, *16,* 99–105.

*Rokeach, M. *The open and closed mind.* New York: Basic Books, 1960.

Rokeach, M. *Beliefs, attitudes, and values.* San Francisco: Jossey-Bass, 1968.

Rokeach, M. Faith, hope, bigotry. *Psychology Today,* 1970, *3*(11), 33–37ff.

*Rokeach, M. *The nature of human values.* New York: Free Press, 1973.

Rokeach, M., Homant, R., & Penner, L. A value analysis of the disputed Federalist Papers. *Journal of Personality and Social Psychology,* 1970, *16,* 245–250.

Rokeach, M., & Mezei, L. Race and shared belief as factors in social choice. *Science,* 1966, *151,* 167–172.

Rokeach, M., Smith, P. W., & Evans, R. I. Two kinds of prejudice or one? In M. Rokeach, *The open and closed mind.* New York: Basic Books, 1960. Pp. 196–214.

Rokeach, M., & Vidulich, R. N. The formation of new belief systems. In M. Rokeach, *The open and closed mind.* New York: Basic Books, 1960. Pp. 196–214.

Rollin, B. Everything Dr. Reuben doesn't know about sex. *Playboy,* 1972, *19*(11), 123–126ff. (November 1972 issue.)

Rorer, L. G. The great response style myth. *Psychological Bulletin,* 1965, *63,* 129–156.

Rorer, L. G., & Goldberg, L. R. Acquiescence in the MMPI? *Educational and Psychological Measurement,* 1965, *25,* 801–817.

*Rosaldo, M. Z., & Lamphere, L. (Eds.). *Women, culture and society.* Stanford, Calif.: Stanford University Press, 1974.

Rose, A. M. Anti-Semitism's root in city-hatred. *Commentary,* 1948, *6,* 374–378.

Rosen, B. C., & D'Andrade, R. The psychosocial origins of achievement motivation. *Sociometry,* 1959, *22,* 188–218.

Rosen, B., & Jerdee, T. H. Effects of applicant's sex and difficulty of job on evaluations of candidates for managerial positions. *Journal of Applied Psychology,* 1974, *59,* 511–512. (a)

Rosen, B., & Jerdee, T. H. Influence of sex role stereotypes on personal decisions. *Journal of Applied Psychology,* 1974, *59,* 9–14. (b)

Rosen, B., & Jerdee, T. H. Sex stereotyping in the executive suite. *Harvard Business Review,* 1974, *52,* 45-58. (c)

Rosen, E. Differences between volunteers and non-volunteers for psychological studies. *Journal of Applied Psychology,* 1951, *35,* 185–193.

Rosen, S. Post-decision affinity for incompatible information. *Journal of Abnormal and Social Psychology,* 1961, *63,* 188–190.

Rosenbaum, R. Tales of the heartbreak biz. *Esquire,* 1974, *82*(1), 67–73; 155–158.

Rosenberg, L. A. Group size, prior experience, and conformity. *Journal of Abnormal and Social Psychology,* 1961, *63,* 436–437.

Rosenberg, M. J. When dissonance fails: On eliminating evaluation apprehension from attitude measurement. *Journal of Personality and Social Psychology,* 1965, *1,* 28–42.

Rosenberg, S., Nelson, C., & Vivekananthan, P. S. A multidimensional approach to the structure of personality impressions. *Journal of Personality and Social Psychology,* 1968, *9,* 283–294.

Rosenblatt, P. C. Origins and effects of group ethnocentrism and nationalism. *Journal of Conflict Resolution,* 1964, *8,* 131–146.

Rosenblatt, P. C., & Stevenson, L. G. *Territoriality and privacy in married and unmarried cohabiting couples.* Unpublished manuscript, Department of Psychology, University of Minnesota, 1973.

Rosenfeld, H. M. Effect of an approval-seeking induction on interpersonal proximity. *Psychological Reports,* 1965, *17,* 120–122.

Rosenfeld, H. M. Approval-seeking and approval-inducing functions of verbal and nonverbal responses in the dyad. *Journal of Personality and Social Psychology,* 1966, *4,* 597–605.

Rosenhan, D. Effects of social class and race on responsiveness to approval and disapproval. *Journal of Personality and Social Psychology,* 1966, *4,* 253–259.

Rosenhan, D. The natural socialization of altruistic autonomy. In J. Macaulay & L. Berkowitz (Eds.), *Altruism and helping behavior: Social psychological studies of some antecedents and consequences.* New York: Academic Press, 1970. Pp. 251–268.

Rosenkoetter, L. I. Resistance to temptation: Inhibitory and disinhibitory effects of models. *Developmental Psychology,* 1973, *8,* 80–84.

Rosenkrantz, P. S., & Crockett, W. H. Some factors influencing the assimilation of disparate information in impression formation. *Journal of Personality and Social Psychology,* 1965, *2,* 397–402.

Rosenkrantz, P. S., Vogel, S. R., Bee, H., Broverman, I. K., & Broverman, D. M. Sex-role stereotypes and self-concepts in college students. *Journal of Consulting and Clinical Psychology,* 1968, *32,* 287–295.

*Rosenthal, A. M. *Thirty-eight witnesses.* New York: McGraw-Hill, 1964.

Rosenthal, R. The effect of the experimenter on the results of psychological research. In B. A. Maher (Ed.), *Progress in experimental personality research* (Vol. 1). New York: Academic Press, 1964. Pp. 79–114.

Rosenthal, R. *Experimenter effects in behavioral research.* New York: Appleton-Century-Crofts, 1966.

Rosenthal, R. Interpersonal expectations: Effects of the experimenter's hypothesis. In R. Rosenthal & R. L. Rosnow (Eds.), *Artifact in behavioral research.* New York: Academic Press, 1969, Pp. 181–277.

Rosenthal, R., & Fode, K. L. The effect of experimenter bias on the performance of the albino rat. *Behavioral Science,* 1963, *8,* 183–189.

Rosenthal, R., & Jacobson, L. *Pygmalion in the classroom: Teacher expectation and pupils' intellectual development.* New York: Holt, Rinehart & Winston, 1968.

Rosenthal, R., & Rosnow, R. L. The volunteer subject. In R. Rosenthal & R. L. Rosnow (Eds.), *Artifact in behavioral research.* New York: Academic Press, 1969. Pp. 59–118.

Rosenthal, R., & Rosnow, R. L. *The volunteer subject.* New York: John Wiley, 1975.

Rosner, S. Consistency in response to group pressures. *Journal of Abnormal and Social Psychology,* 1957, *55,* 145–146.

Rosnow, R. L. Whatever happened to the "Law of Primacy"? *Journal of Communication,* 1966, *16,* 10–31.

Rosnow, R. L. One-sided versus two-sided communication under indirect awareness of persuasive intent. *Public Opinion Quarterly,* 1968, *32,* 95–101.

Rosnow, R. L. When he lends a helping hand, bite it. *Psychology Today,* 1970, 4(1), 26–30.

Rosnow, R. L., & Arms, R. L. Adding versus averaging as a stimulus-combination rule in forming impressions of groups. *Journal of Personality and Social Psychology,* 1968, *10,* 363–369.

Rosnow, R., & Robinson, E. (Eds.). *Experiments in persuasion.* New York: Academic Press, 1967.

Rosow, I. The social effects of the physical environment. *Journal of the American Institute of Planners,* 1961, *27,* 127–133.

Ross, A. S. Effect of increased responsibility on bystander intervention: The presence of children. *Journal of Personality and Social Psychology,* 1971, *19,* 306–310.

Ross, H. L., Campbell, D. T., & Glass, G. V. Determining the social effects of a legal reform: The British "Breathalyser" crackdown of 1967. *American Behavioral Scientist,* 1970, *13,* 493–509.

Ross, L., Rodin, J., & Zimbardo, P. G. Toward an attribution therapy: The reduction of fear through induced cognitive-emotional misattribution. *Journal of Personality and Social Psychology,* 1969, *12,* 279–288.

Ross, M., Layton, B., Erickson, B., & Schopler, J. Affect, facial regard, and reactions to crowding. *Journal of Personality and Social Psychology,* 1973, *28,* 69–76.

Ross, M., & Shulman, R. F. Increasing the salience of initial attitudes: Dissonance versus self-perception theory. *Journal of Personality and Social Psychology,* 1973, *28,* 138–144.

*Rossi, A. S. (Ed.). *The feminist papers: From Addams to de Beauvoir.* New York: Bantam Books, 1973.

Roszak, T. *The making of a counter culture.* Garden City, N. Y.: Doubleday, 1969.

Rothbart, M. K. Birth order and mother-child interaction in an achievement situation. *Journal of Personality and Social Psychology,* 1971, *17,* 113–120.

Rothbart, M. K., & Maccoby, E. E. Parents' differential reactions to sons and daughters. *Journal of Personality and Social Psychology,* 1966, *4,* 237–243.

Rotter, J. B. *Social learning and clinical psychology.* Englewood Cliffs, N. J.: Prentice-Hall, 1954.

Rotter, J. B. Generalized expectancies for internal versus external control of reinforcement. *Psychological Monographs,* 1966, *80*(1, Whole No. 609).

Rotter, J. B. A new scale for the measurement of interpersonal trust. *Journal of Personality,* 1967, *35,* 651–665.

Rotter, J. B. Generalized expectancies for interpersonal trust. *American Psychologist,* 1971, *26,* 443–452.

Rotter, J. B. Some problems and misconceptions related to the construct of internal versus external control of reinforcement. *Journal of Consulting and Clinical Psychology,* 1975, *43,* 56–67.

Rotter, J. B., Chance, J., & Phares, E. J. (Eds.). *Applications of a social learning theory of personality.* New York: Holt, Rinehart & Winston, 1972.

Rozelle, R. M., Evans, R. I., Lasater, T. M., Dembroski, T. M., & Allen, B. P. Need for approval as related to the effects of persuasive communications on actual, reported and intended behavior change—A viable predictor? *Psychological Reports,* 1973, *33,* 719–725.

Rubin, I. Common sex myths. *Sexology,* 1966, *32,* 512–514.

Rubin, Z. Measurement of romantic love. *Journal of Personality and Social Psychology,* 1970, *16,* 265–273.

*Rubin, Z. *Liking and loving: An invitation to social psychology.* New York: Holt, Rinehart & Winston, 1973.

Rudé, G. *The crowd in history, 1730–1848.* New York: Wiley, 1964.

Ruesch, J., & Kees, W. Function and meaning in the physical environment. In H. Proshansky, W. Ittelson, & L. Rivlin (Eds.), *Environmental psychology.* New York: Holt, Rinehart & Winston, 1970. Pp. 141–153.

Rule, B. G., & Hewitt, L. S. Effects of thwarting on cardiac response and physical aggression. *Journal of Personality and Social Psychology,* 1971, *19,* 181–187.

Rule, B. G., & Percival, E. The effects of frustration and attack on physical aggression. *Journal of Experimental Research in Personality,* 1971, *5,* 111–118.

Rule, B. G., & Sandilands, M. L. Test anxiety, confidence, commitment, and conformity. *Journal of Personality,* 1969, *37,* 460–467.

Russo, N. F. Eye contact, interpersonal distance, and the equilibrium theory. *Journal of Personality and Social Psychology,* 1975, *31,* 497–502.

*Ryan, W. *Blaming the victim.* New York: Pantheon, 1971.

Rychlak, J. F. *Introduction to personality and psychotherapy: A theory-construction approach.* Boston: Houghton Mifflin, 1973.

Saegert, S., Swap, W., & Zajonc, R. B. Exposure, context, and interpersonal attraction. *Journal of Personality and Social Psychology,* 1973, *25,* 234–242.

Sagarin, E. *Deviants and deviance: An introduction to the study of disvalued people and behavior.* New York: Praeger, 1975.

*Sahakian, W. S. *Systematic social psychology.* New York: Intext, 1974.

Sahlein, W. J. *A neighborhood solution to the social services dilemma.* Lexington, Mass.: D. C. Heath, 1973.

St. Jean, R. Reformulation of the value hypothesis in group risk taking. *Proceedings, 78th Annual Convention, American Psychological Association,* 1970, *5,* 339–340.

Saks, M. J., & Ostrom, T. M. Jury size and consensus requirements: The laws of probability versus the laws of the land. *Journal of Contemporary Law,* 1975, *1,* 163–173.

Sales, S. M. Economic threat as a determinant of conversion rates in authoritarian and nonauthoritarian churches. *Jour-*

nal of Personality and Social Psychology, 1972, 23, 420–428.

Sales, S. M. Threat as a factor in authoritarianism: An analysis of archival data. Journal of Personality and Social Psychology, 1973, 28, 44–57.

Salinger, J. D. The catcher in the rye. New York: Little, Brown, 1951.

Sampson, E. E. The study of ordinal position: Antecedents and outcomes. In B. Maher (Ed.), Progress in experimental personality research (Vol. 2). New York: Academic Press, 1965. Pp. 175–228.

Samuel, W. Response to Bill of Rights paraphrases as influenced by the hip or straight attire of the opinion solicitor. Journal of Applied Social Psychology, 1972, 2, 47–62.

Sandiford, P., & Kerr, R. Intelligence of Chinese and Japanese children. Journal of Educational Psychology, 1926, 17, 361–367.

Sanford, F. H. Authoritarianism and leadership. Philadelphia: Institute for Research in Human Relations, 1950.

Sanford, N. The approach of the authoritarian personality. In J. L. McCary (Ed.), Psychology of personality. New York: Grove Press, 1956. Pp. 253–319.

Sanford, N. Whatever happened to action research? Journal of Social Issues, 1970, 26(4), 3–23.

Sarbin, T. R. On the distinction between social roles and social types, with special reference to the hippie. American Journal of Psychiatry, 1969, 125, 1024–1031.

Sarbin, T. R., & Allen, V. L. Role theory. In G. Lindzey and E. Aronson (Eds.), Handbook of social psychology (Vol. 1) (2nd ed.). Reading, Mass.: Addison-Wesley, 1968. Pp. 488–567.

Sarbin, T. R., & Coe, W. C. Hypnosis: A social psychological analysis of influence communication. New York: Holt, Rinehart & Winston, 1972.

Sarnoff, I. R., & Zimbardo, P. G. Anxiety, fear, and social affiliation. Journal of Abnormal and Social Psychology, 1961, 62, 356–363.

Satow, K. L. The role of social approval in altruistic behavior. Paper presented at the meeting of the Eastern Psychological Association, Washington, D. C., April 1973.

Saxe, L., Greenberg, M. S., & Bar-Tal, D. Perceived relatedness of trait-dispositions to ability and effort. Perceptual and Motor Skills, 1974, 38, 39–42.

Scarr-Salapatek, S. Race, social class, and IQ. Science, 1971, 174, 1285–1295. (a)

Scarr-Salapatek, S. Unknowns in the IQ equation. Science, 1971, 174, 1223–1228. (b)

Schachter, S. Deviation, rejection, and communication. Journal of Abnormal and Social Psychology, 1951, 46, 190–207.

Schachter, S. The psychology of affiliation. Stanford, Calif.: Stanford University Press, 1959.

Schachter, S. The interaction of cognitive and physiological determinants of emotional state. In L. Berkowitz (Ed.), Advances in experimental social psychology (Vol. 1). New York: Academic Press, 1964. Pp. 49–80.

Schachter, S. Cognitive effects on bodily functioning: Studies of obesity and eating. In D. C. Glass (Ed.), Neurophysiology and emotion. New York: Rockefeller University Press and Russell Sage Foundation, 1967. Pp. 117–144.

Schachter, S. Eat, eat. Psychology Today, 1971, 4(11), 44–47ff. (a)

Schachter, S. Emotion, obesity, and crime. New York: Academic Press, 1971. (b)

Schachter, S., Ellertson, N., McBride, D., & Gregory, D. An experimental study of cohesiveness and productivity. Human Relations, 1951, 4, 229–238.

*Schachter, S., & Rodin, J. Obese humans and rats. Potomac, Md.: Lawrence Erlbaum Associates, 1974.

Schachter, S., & Singer, J. Cognitive, social, and physiological determinants of emotional state. Psychological Review, 1962, 69, 379–399.

Schachter, S., & Wheeler, L. Epinephrine, chlorpromazine, and amusement. Journal of Abnormal and Social Psychology, 1962, 65, 121–128.

Schaller, G. B. The Serengeti lion: A study of predator-prey relations. Chicago: University of Chicago Press, 1972.

Schaps, E. Cost, dependency, and helping. Journal of Personality and Social Psychology, 1972, 21, 74–78.

Schein, E. H. The Chinese indoctrination program for prisoners of war. Psychiatry, 1956, 19, 149–172.

Schein, E. H. Reaction patterns to severe chronic stress in American army prisoners of war of the Chinese. Journal of Social Issues, 1957, 13(3), 21–30.

*Schein, E. H. Organizational psychology (2nd ed.). Englewood Cliffs, N. J.: Prentice-Hall, 1971.

Schein, V. E. The relationship between sex role stereotypes and requisite management characteristics. Journal of Applied Psychology, 1973, 57, 95–100.

Schellenberg, J. A. An introduction to social psychology (2nd ed.). New York: Random House, 1974. (1st ed., 1970.)

Scherer, S. E. Proxemic behavior of primary school children as a function of their socioeconomic class and subculture. Journal of Personality and Social Psychology. 1974, 29, 800–805.

Schleifer, M., & Douglas, V. Effects of training on the moral judgment of young children. Journal of Personality and Social Psychology, 1973, 28, 62–68.

Schlenker, B. R. Liking for a group following an initiation: Impression management or dissonance reduction? Paper presented at the meeting of the Southeastern Psychological Association, New Orleans, March 1973.

Schlenker, B. R. Social psychology and science. Journal of Personality and Social Psychology, 1974, 29, 1–15.

Schmideberg, M. Some observations on individual reactions to air raids. International Journal of Psychoanalysis, 1942, 23, 146–176.

Schmidt, G., & Sigusch, V. Sex differences in responses to psychosexual stimulation by film and slides. Journal of Sex Research, 1970, 6, 268–283.

Schmidt, G., Sigusch, V., & Meyberg, V. Psychosexual stimulation in men: Emotional reactions, changes of sex behavior, and measures of conservative attitudes. Journal of Sex Research, 1969, 5, 199–217.

Schmitt, R. C. Implications of density in Hong Kong. American Institute of Planners Journal, 1963, 29, 210–217.

Schmitt, R. C. Density, health and social disorganization.

American Institute of Planners Journal, 1966, *32*, 38–40.

Schneider, B., & Bartlett, C. J. Individual differences and organizational climate, II: Measurement of organizational climate by the multitrait-multirater matrix. *Personnel Psychology*, 1970, *23*, 493–512.

Schneider, D. J. Tactical self-presentation after success and failure. *Journal of Personality and Social Psychology*, 1969, *13*, 262–268.

Schneider, D. J. Implicit personality theory: A review. *Psychological Bulletin*, 1973, *79*, 294–309.

Schneider, F. W. When will a stranger lend a helping hand? *Journal of Social Psychology*, 1973, *90*, 335–336.

*Schoenberger, R. A. (Ed.). *The American right wing*. New York: Holt, 1969.

Schoenfeld, W. N. Notes on a bit of psychological nonsense: "Race differences in intelligence." *Psychological Record*, 1974, *24*, 17–32.

Schofield, M. *Sexual behavior of young people*. Boston: Little-Brown, 1965.

Schooler, C. Birth order effects: Not here, not now! *Psychological Bulletin*, 1972, *78*, 161–175.

Schooler, C. Birth order effects: A reply to Breeland. *Psychological Bulletin*, 1973, *80*, 213–214.

Schopler, J., & Walton, M. *The effects of structure, expected enjoyment, and participants' internality-externality upon feelings of being crowded*. Unpublished manuscript, Department of Psychology, University of North Carolina at Chapel Hill, 1974.

Schriesheim, C., & Kerr, S. Psychometric properties of the Ohio State leadership scales. *Psychological Bulletin*, 1974, *81*, 756–765.

Schroeder, H. E. The risky shift as a general choice shift. *Journal of Personality and Social Psychology*, 1973, *27*, 297–300.

Schuman, H., & Harding, J. Sympathetic identification with the underdog. *Public Opinion Quarterly*, 1963, *37*, 230–241.

Schuman, H., & Hatchett, S. *Black racial attitudes: Trends and complexities*. Ann Arbor, Mich.: Institute for Social Research, University of Michigan, 1974.

Schur, E. M. *Labeling deviant behavior: Its sociological implications*. New York: Harper & Row, 1971.

Schur, E. M. *The concept of secondary deviation: Its theoretical significance and empirical elusiveness*. Paper presented at the University of Massachusetts, Amherst, April 19, 1974.

Schwartz, M., & Schwartz, J. Evidence against a genetical component to performance on IQ tests. *Nature*, 1974, *248*(No. 5443), 84–85.

Schwartz, S. H. Normative explanations of helping behavior: A critique, proposal, and empirical test. *Journal of Experimental Social Psychology*, 1973, *9*, 349–364.

Schwartz, S. H., & Clausen, G. T. Responsibility, norms, and helping in an emergency. *Journal of Personality and Social Psychology*, 1970, *16*, 299–310.

Schwartz, S. H., Feldman, K. A., Brown, M. E., & Heingartner, A. Some personality correlates of conduct in two situations of moral conflict. *Journal of Personality*, 1969, *37*, 41–57.

Schweitzer, D., & Ginsburg, G. P. Factors in communication credibility. In C. W. Backman & P. F. Secord (Eds.), *Problems in social psychology*. New York: McGraw-Hill, 1966. Pp. 94–102.

Scodel, A., & Mussen, P. Social perceptions of authoritarians and nonauthoritarians. *Journal of Abnormal and Social Psychology*, 1953, *48*, 181–184.

Scott, J. P. *Aggression*. Chicago: University of Chicago Press, 1958.

Scott, J. P. The social psychology of infra-human animals. In G. Lindzey & E. Aronson (Eds.), *Handbook of social psychology* (Vol. 4) (2nd ed.). Reading, Mass.: Addison-Wesley, 1969. Pp. 611–642.

Scott, W. A. Attitude measurement. In G. Lindzey & E. Aronson (Eds.), *Handbook of social psychology* (Vol. 2) (2nd ed.). Reading, Mass.: Addison-Wesley, 1968. Pp. 204–273.

Scottish Council for Research in Education. *Social implications of the 1947 Scottish mental survey*. London: University of London Press, 1953.

Sears, D. O., & Abeles, R. P. Attitudes and opinions. In P. H. Mussen & M. R. Rosenzweig (Eds.), *Annual review of psychology* (Vol. 20). Palo Alto, Calif.: Annual Reviews, 1969. Pp. 253–288.

Sears, R., Maccoby, E., & Levin, H. *Patterns of child rearing*. Evanston, Ill.: Row, Peterson, 1957.

Seashore, H., Wesman, A., & Doppelt, J. The standardization of the Wechsler Intelligence Scale for Children. *Journal of Consulting Psychology*, 1950, *14*, 99–110.

Seaver, W. B. Effects of naturally induced teacher expectancies. *Journal of Personality and Social Psychology*, 1973, *28*, 333–342.

Secord, P. *Social psychology in search of a paradigm*. Paper presented at the meeting of the American Psychological Association, Chicago, September 1975.

Seidel, H. E., Jr., Barkley, M. J., & Stith, D. Evaluation of a program for Project Head Start. *Journal of Genetic Psychology*, 1967, *110*, 185–197.

Selltiz, C., Jahoda, M., Deutsch, M., & Cook, S. W. *Research methods in social relations* (Rev. ed.). New York: Holt, 1959.

Selltiz, C., Wrightsman, L. S., & Cook, S. W. *Research methods in social relations* (3rd ed.). New York: Holt, Rinehart & Winston, 1976.

Sensenig, J., & Brehm, J. W. Attitude change from an implied threat to attitudinal freedom. *Journal of Personality and Social Psychology*, 1968, *8*, 324–330.

Severy, L. J. Comment on: "Positive forms of social behavior: An overview." *Journal of Social Issues*, 1974, *30*(3), 189–194.

Severy, L. J., & Ashton, N. L. *Measuring differing prosocial tendencies*. Paper presented at the meeting of the Southeastern Psychological Association, New Orleans, April 1973.

Severy, L. J., & Brigham, J. C. *Personality, prejudice and voting behavior under conditions of high involvement*. Paper presented at the meeting of the Rocky Mountain Psychological Association, Denver, May 1971.

Seyfried, B. A., & Hendrick, C. When do opposites attract? When they are opposite in sex and sex-role attitudes. *Journal of Personality and Social Psychology*, 1973, *25*, 15–20.

Shafer, E., & Burke, H. Preferences for outdoor recreation facilities in four state parks. *Journal of Forestry,* 1965, *63,* 512–518.

Shaffer, D. R. *Some effects of initial attitude importance on attitude change.* Paper presented at the meeting of the Southeastern Psychological Association, Atlanta, April 1975. (Also in *Journal of Social Psychology,* 1975, *97,* 279–288.)

Shaffer, D. R. Social psychology from a social-developmental perspective. In C. Hendrick (Ed.), *Perspectives on social psychology.* Potomac, Md.: Lawrence Erlbaum Associates, in press.

Shantz, C. U. *Empathy in relation to social cognitive development.* Paper presented at the meeting of the American Psychological Association, New Orleans, September 1974.

Shapira, A., & Madsen, M. C. Cooperative and competitive behavior of kibbutz and urban children in Israel. *Child Development,* 1969, *40,* 609–617.

*Sharp, G. *Exploring nonviolent alternatives.* Boston: Porter Sargent, 1970.

Sharp, G. *The politics of nonviolent action.* Philadelphia, Pa.: Pilgrim Press, 1971.

*Shaver, K. G. *An introduction to attribution processes.* Cambridge, Mass.: Winthrop, 1975.

Shaver, P. European perspectives on the crisis in social psychology. *Contemporary Psychology,* 1974, *19,* 356–358.

Shaw, C., & McKay, H. D. *Juvenile delinquency and urban areas.* Chicago: University of Chicago Press, 1942.

Shaw, E. A. Differential impact of negative stereotyping in employee selection. *Personnel Psychology,* 1972, *25,* 333–338.

Shaw, G. *Meat on the hoof: The hidden world of Texas football.* New York: St. Martin's, 1972.

Shaw, J. I., & Skolnick, P. An investigation of relative preference for consistency motivation. *European Journal of Social Psychology,* 1973, *3,* 271–280.

Shaw, M. E. A comparison of individuals and small groups in the rational solution of complex problems. *American Journal of Psychology,* 1932, *44,* 491–504.

Shaw, M. E. Some effects of unequal distribution of information upon group performance in various communication nets. *Journal of Abnormal and Social Psychology,* 1954, *49,* 547–553.

Shaw, M. E. *Scaling group tasks: A method for dimensional analysis.* Unpublished manuscript, Department of Psychology, University of Florida, 1963. (Mimeographed)

Shaw, M. E. Communication networks. In L. Berkowitz (Ed.), *Advances in experimental social psychology* (Vol. 1). New York: Academic Press, 1964. Pp. 111–147.

*Shaw, M. E. *Group dynamics: The psychology of small group behavior* (2nd ed.). New York: McGraw-Hill, 1976.

*Shaw, M. E., & Costanzo, P. R. *Theories in social psychology.* New York: McGraw-Hill, 1970.

Shaw, M. E., & Gilchrist, J. C. Intragroup communication and leader choice. *Journal of Social Psychology,* 1956, *43,* 133–138.

Shaw, M. E., & Rothschild, G. H. Some effects of prolonged experience in communication nets. *Journal of Applied Psychology,* 1956, *40,* 281–286.

Sheehan, P. W. Escape from the ambiguous: Artifact and methodologies of hypnosis. *American Psychologist,* 1973, *28,* 983–993.

Sheldon, E. B., & Freeman, H. E. *Notes on social indicators: Promises and potential.* New York: American Elsevier, 1970.

Sherif, C. W. Comment on interpretation of latitude of rejection as an "artifact." *Psychological Bulletin,* 1972, *78,* 476–478.

Sherif, C. W., Kelly, M., Rodgers, H. L., Jr., Sarup, G., & Tittler, B. I. Personal involvement, social judgment, and action. *Journal of Personality and Social Psychology,* 1973, *27,* 311–328.

Sherif, C. W., Sherif, M., & Nebergall, R. E. *Attitude and attitude change: The social judgment approach.* Philadelphia: Saunders, 1965.

Sherif, M. A study of some social factors in perception. *Archives of Psychology,* 1935, *27,* No. 187, 1–60.

Sherif, M. *In common predicament: Social psychology of intergroup conflict and cooperation.* Boston: Houghton-Mifflin, 1966.

Sherif, M. On the relevance of social psychology. *American Psychologist,* 1970, *25,* 144–156.

Sherif, M., Harvey, O. J., White, B. J., Hood, W. E., & Sherif, C. W. *Intergroup conflict and cooperation: The Robber's Cave experiment.* Norman, Okla.: University of Oklahoma Book Exchange, 1961.

Sherif, M., & Hovland, C. *Social judgment.* New Haven, Conn.: Yale University Press, 1961.

Sherif, M., Taub, D., & Hovland, C. I. Assimilation and contrast effects of anchoring stimuli on judgments. *Journal of Experimental Psychology,* 1958, *55,* 150–155.

Sherman, J. A. *On the psychology of women.* Springfield, Ill.: Charles C Thomas, 1971.

Sherrod, D. R. Crowding, perceived control, and behavioral after effects. *Journal of Applied Social Psychology,* 1974, *4,* 171–186.

Sherrod, D. R., & Downs, R. Environmental determinants of altruism: The effects of stimulus overload and perceived control on helping. *Journal of Experimental Social Psychology,* in press.

Sherwood, J. J. Authoritarianism, moral realism, and President Kennedy's death. *British Journal of Social and Clinical Psychology,* 1966, *5,* 264–269.

Sherwood, J. J., Barron, J. W., & Fitch, H. G. Cognitive dissonance: Theory and research. In R. V. Wagner & J. J. Sherwood (Eds.), *The study of attitude change.* Monterey, Calif.: Brooks/Cole, 1969. Pp. 56–86.

Sheth, J. N. *A field study of attitude structure and attitude-behavior relationship* (Faculty Working Paper No. 116). College of Commerce and Business Administration, University of Illinois at Urbana-Champaign, July 1973.

Shields, S. A. *The psychology of women: An historical perspective.* Paper presented at the meeting of the American Psychological Association, New Orleans, September 1974.

Shils, E. Authoritarianism: "Right" and "Left." In R. Christie & M. Jahoda (Eds.), *Studies in the scope and method of "The Authoritarian Personality."* New York: Free Press, 1954. Pp. 24–49.

Shima, H. The relationship between the leader's modes of

interpersonal cognition and the performance of the group. *Japanese Psychological Research*, 1968, *10*, 13–30.

Shipman, V. C., & Hess, R. D. *Children's conceptual styles as a function of social status and maternal conceptual styles.* Paper presented at the meeting of the American Psychological Association, Chicago, September 1965.

Shoffeitt, P. G. *The moral development of children as a function of parental moral judgments and child-rearing practices.* Unpublished doctoral dissertation, Department of Psychology, George Peabody College for Teachers, 1971.

Shotz, M., & Gelman, R. The development of communications skills: Modifications in the speech of young children as a function of the listener. *Monographs for the Society for Research in Child Development*, 1973, *38*(5, Serial No. 152).

Shuey, A. M. *The testing of Negro intelligence.* New York: Social Science Press, 1966.

Siegel, A. E. The influence of violence in the mass media upon children's role expectations. *Child Development*, 1958, *29*, 35–56.

Siegel, A. E. Mass media and violence: Effects on children. *Stanford M.D.*, 1969, *8*(2), 11–14.

Siegelman, M. Adjustment of male homosexuals and heterosexuals. *Archives of Sexual Behavior*, 1972, *2*(1), 9–25.

Sigall, H., & Landy, D. Radiating beauty: The effects of having a physically attractive partner on person perception. *Journal of Personality and Social Psychology*, 1973, *28*, 218–224.

Silverman, I. On the resolution and tolerance of cognitive consistency in a natural-occurring event: Attitudes and beliefs following the Senator Edward M. Kennedy incident. *Journal of Personality and Social Psychology*, 1971, *17*, 171–178.

Simon, L. M., & Leavitt, E. A. The relation between Wechsler-Bellevue IQ scores and occupational area. *Occupations*, 1950, *29*, 23–25.

Simons, H. W. Authoritarianism and social perceptiveness. *Journal of Social Psychology*, 1966, *68*, 291–297.

Simpson, E. Moral development research: A case study of scientific cultural bias. *Human Development*, 1974, *17*(2), 81–106.

Simpson, G. E., & Yinger, J. M. *Racial and cultural minorities: An analysis of prejudice and discrimination* (4th ed.). New York: Harper & Row, 1972.

Singer, D. G., & Singer, J. L. *Family television viewing habits and the spontaneous play of preschool children.* Paper presented at the meeting of the American Psychological Association, New Orleans, September 1974.

Singer, J. E. The use of manipulative strategies: Machiavellianism and attractiveness. *Sociometry*, 1964, *27*, 128–140.

Singer, J. E., Brush, C. A., & Lublin, S. C. Some aspects of deindividuation: Identification and conformity. *Journal of Experimental Social Psychology*, 1965, *1*, 356–378.

Singer, J. E., & Shockley, V. L. Ability and evaluation. *Journal of Personality and Social Psychology*, 1965, *1*, 95–100.

*Siroka, R. W., Siroka, E. K., & Schloss, G. A. (Eds.). *Sensitivity training and group encounter: An introduction.* New York:

Grosset & Dunlap, 1971.

Sistrunk, F., & McDavid, J. W. Sex variables in conforming behavior. *Journal of Personality and Social Psychology*, 1971, *17*, 200–207.

Sizer, M. F., & Sizer, T. R. *Moral education.* Cambridge, Mass.: Harvard University Press, 1970.

Skinner, B. F. *Walden two.* New York: Macmillan, 1948.

Skinner, B. F. *Science and human behavior.* New York: Macmillan, 1953.

*Skinner, B. F. *Beyond freedom and dignity.* New York: Knopf, 1971.

*Slater, P. *The pursuit of loneliness.* Boston: Beacon Press, 1970.

Slater, P. E. Contrasting correlates of group size. *Sociometry*, 1958, *25*, 129–139.

Sloan, L. R., & Brock, T. C. *The persuasiveness of disrupted speeches.* Paper presented at the meeting of the Eastern Psychological Association, Washington, D. C., May 1973.

Sloan, L. R., Love, R. E., & Ostrom, T. M. Political heckling: Who really loses? *Journal of Personality and Social Psychology*, 1974, *30*, 518–525.

Slosnerick, M. *Social interaction by preschool children in conditions of crowding.* Paper presented at the meeting of the Midwestern Psychological Association, Chicago, May 1974.

Small, L. *Effects of discrimination training on stage of moral judgment.* Paper presented at the meeting of the American Psychological Association, New Orleans, September 1974.

*Smelser, N. *Essays in sociological explanation.* Englewood Cliffs, N. J.: Prentice-Hall, 1968.

Smigel, E. O., & Seiden, R. The decline and fall of the double standard. *Annals of the American Academy of Political and Social Sciences*, 1968, *376*, 1–14.

Smith, C. R., Williams, L., & Willis, R. H. Race, sex, and beliefs as determinants of friendship acceptance. *Journal of Personality and Social Psychology*, 1967, *5*, 127–137.

Smith, E. E. The effects of clear and unclear role expectations on group productivity and defensiveness. *Journal of Abnormal and Social Psychology*, 1957, *55*, 213–217.

Smith, H., & Rosen, E. Some psychological correlates of world mindedness and authoritarianism. *Journal of Personality*, 1958, *26*, 170–183.

Smith, H. L., & Hyman, H. The biasing effect of interviewer expectations on survey results. *Public Opinion Quarterly*, 1950, *14*, 491–506.

*Smith, M. B. Is experimental social psychology advancing? *Journal of Experimental Social Psychology*, 1972, *8*, 86–96.

*Smith, M. B., Bruner, J. S., & White, R. W. *Opinions and personality.* New York: Wiley, 1956.

Smith, P. W., & Brigham, J. C. The functional approach to attitude change: An attempt at operationalization. *Representative Research in Social Psychology*, 1972, *3*, 73–80.

Smith, R. E., Smythe, L., & Lien, D. Inhibition of helping behavior by a similar or dissimilar nonreactive fellow bystander. *Journal of Personality and Social Psychology*, 1972, *23*, 414–419.

Smith, R. G. Source credibility context effects. *Speech Monographs*, 1973, *40*, 303–309.

Smith, R. J. Explorations in nonconformity. *Journal of Social Psychology*, 1967, *71*, 133–150.

Smith, S. Language and nonverbal test performance of racial groups in Honolulu before and after a 14-year interval. *Journal of General Psychology*, 1942, *26*, 51–93.

Smith, S., & Haythorn, W. W. Effects of compatibility, crowding, group size, and leadership seniority on stress, anxiety, hostility, and annoyance in isolated groups. *Journal of Personality and Social Psychology*, 1972, *22*, 67–79.

Snow, R. E. Review of R. Rosenthal and L. Jacobson, *Pygmalion in the classroom*. *Contemporary Psychology*, 1969, *14*, 197–199.

*Snyder, M. The self-monitoring of expressive behavior. *Journal of Personality and Social Psychology*, 1974, *30*, 526–537.

Snyder, M., & Cunningham, M. R. To comply or not to comply: Testing the self-perception explanation of the "foot-in-the-door" phenomenon. *Journal of Personality and Social Psychology*, 1975, *31*, 64–67.

Snyder, M., & Ebbesen, E. B. Dissonance awareness: A test of dissonance theory versus self-perception theory. *Journal of Experimental Social Psychology*, 1972, *8*, 502–517.

Snyder, M., Grether, J., & Keller, K. Staring and compliance: A field experiment on hitch-hiking. *Journal of Applied Social Psychology*, 1974, *4*, 165–170.

Snyder, M., & Monson, T. C. Persons, situations, and the control of social behavior. *Journal of Personality and Social Psychology*, 1975, *32*, 637–644.

Snyder, M., & Rothbart, M. Communicator attractiveness and opinion change. *Canadian Journal of Behavioural Science*, 1971, *3*, 377–387.

Society for the Psychological Study of Social Issues Council. Statement on race and intelligence. *Journal of Social Issues*, 1969, *25*(3), 1–3.

Sommer, R. Studies in personal space. *Sociometry*, 1959, *22*, 247–260.

Sommer, R. The distance for comfortable conversation: A further study. *Sociometry*, 1962, *25*, 111–116.

Sommer, R. Further studies of small group ecology. *Sociometry*, 1965, *28*, 337–348.

Sommer, R. The ecology of privacy. *Library Quarterly*, 1966, *36*, 234–248.

Sommer, R. Classroom ecology. *Journal of Applied Behavioral Science*, 1967, *3*, 489–503.

*Sommer, R. *Personal space: The behavioral basis of design*. Englewood Cliffs, N. J.: Prentice-Hall, 1969.

Sommer, R. *Tight spaces*. Englewood Cliffs, N. J.: Prentice-Hall, 1974.

Sommer, R., & Becker, F. D. Territorial defense and the good neighbor. *Journal of Personality and Social Psychology*, 1969, *11*, 85–92.

Sommer, R., & Ross, H. Social interaction on a geriatrics ward. *International Journal of Social Psychiatry*, 1958, *4*, 128–133.

Sorrentino, R. M., & Boutilier, R. G. Evaluation of a victim as a function of fate similarity/dissimilarity. *Journal of Experimental Social Psychology*, 1974, *10*, 84–93.

Southam, A. L., & Gonzaga, G. P. Systemic changes during the menstrual cycle. *American Journal of Obstetrics and Gynecology*, 1965, *91*, 142–157.

Southwick, C. H. The population dynamics of confined house mice supplied with unlimited food. *Ecology*, 1955, *36*, 212–225.

Spanos, N. P., & Barber, T. X. "Hypnotic" experiences as inferred from subjective reports: Auditory and visual hallucinations. *Journal of Experimental Research in Personality*, 1968, *3*, 136–150.

Spanos, N. P., Barber, T. X., & Lang, G. *Effects of hypnotic induction, suggestions of analgesia, and demands for honesty on subjective reports of pain*. Department of Sociology, Boston University, 1969. (Mimeographed)

Spence, J. T. The Thematic Apperception Test and attitudes toward achievement in women: A new look at the motive to avoid success and a new method of measurement. *Journal of Counseling and Clinical Psychology*, 1974, *42*, 427–437.

Spence, J. T., & Helmreich, R. Who likes competent women? Competence, sex-role congruence of interests, and subjects' attitudes toward women as determinants of interpersonal attraction. *Journal of Applied Social Psychology*, 1972, *3*, 197–213.

Spence, J. T., Helmreich, R., & Stapp, J. Ratings of self and peers on sex-role attributes and their relation to self-esteem and conceptions of masculinity and femininity. *Journal of Personality and Social Psychology*, 1975, *32*, 29–39.

Spiller, G. The dynamics of greatness. *Sociological Review*, 1929, *21*, 218–232.

Stack, L. C. Trust everybody but cut the cards. In H. London & J. Exner (Eds.), *Dimensions of personality*. New York: Wiley, in press.

Stang, D. J. Conformity, ability, and self-esteem. *Representative Research in Social Psychology*, 1972, *3*, 97–103.

Stang, D. J. Effect of interaction rate on ratings of leadership and liking. *Journal of Personality and Social Psychology*, 1973, *27*, 405–408.

Stang, D. J. Methodological factors in mere exposure research. *Psychological Bulletin*, 1974, *12*, 1014–1025.

Stang, D. J. Group size effects on conformity. *Journal of Social Psychology*, 1976, *98*, 175–181.

Starr, J. M. The peace and love generation: Changing attitudes toward sex and violence among college youth. *Journal of Social Issues*, 1974, *30*(2), 73–106.

Staub, E. A child in distress: The influence of age and number of witnesses on children's attempts to help. *Journal of Personality and Social Psychology*, 1970, *14*, 130–140.

Staub, E. Helping a person in distress: The influence of implicit and explicit "rules" of conduct on children and adults. *Journal of Personality and Social Psychology*, 1971, *17*, 137–144.

Staub, E. Helping a distressed person: Social, personality, and stimulus determinants. In L. Berkowitz (Ed.), *Advances in experimental social psychology* (Vol. 7). New York: Academic Press, 1974. Pp. 293–341.

Stein, A. H. A view through the electronic window. *Contemporary Psychology*, 1974, *19*, 438–439.

Stein, A. H., & Bailey, M. M. The socialization of achievement orientation in females. *Psychological Bulletin*, 1973, *80*, 345–366.

Stein, A. H., & Friedrich, L. K. (with F. Vondracek). Television content and young children's behavior. In J. P. Murray, E. A. Rubinstein, & G. A. Comstock (Eds.), *Television and social behavior* (A Technical Report to the Surgeon General's Scientific Advisory Committee on Television and Social Behavior). Rockville, Md.: National Institutes of Health, 1971.

Stein, D. D. The influence of belief systems on interpersonal preference: A validation study of Rokeach's theory of prejudice. *Psychological Monographs*, 1966, *80*(8, Whole No. 616), 1–29.

Stein, D. D., Hardyck, J. A., & Smith, M. B. Race and belief: An open and shut case. *Journal of Personality and Social Psychology*, 1965, *1*, 281–289.

Stein, R. T. Identifying emergent leaders from verbal and nonverbal communications. *Journal of Personality and Social Psychology*, 1975, *32*, 125–135.

Stein, R. T., Geis, F. L., & Damarin, F. The perception of emergent leadership hierarchies in task groups. *Journal of Personality and Social Psychology*, 1973, *28*, 77–87.

Steiner, I. D. *Group process and productivity*. New York: Academic Press, 1972.

Steiner, I. D. Whatever happened to the group in social psychology? *Journal of Experimental Social Psychology*, 1974, *10*, 94–108.

Steiner, I. D., & Dodge, J. S. Interpersonal perception and role structure as determinants of group and individual efficiency. *Human Relations*, 1956, *9*, 467–480.

Steiner, I. D., & Johnson, H. Authoritarianism and "tolerance of trait inconsistency." *Journal of Abnormal and Social Psychology*, 1963, *67*, 388–391.

Steinzor, B. The spatial factor in face to face discussion groups. *Journal of Abnormal and Social Psychology*, 1950, *45*, 522–555.

Stephan, C. Attributions of intention and perception of attitude as a function of liking and similarity. *Sociometry*, 1973, *36*, 463–475.

Stephenson, G. M., & Rutter, D. R. Eye-contact, distance and affiliation: A re-evaluation. *British Journal of Psychology*, 1970, *61*, 385–393.

Stewart, L. H., Dole, A. A., & Harris, Y. Y. Cultural differences in abilities during high school. *American Journal of Educational Research*, 1967, *4*, 19–29.

Stewart, N. AGCT scores of army personnel grouped by occupations. *Occupations*, 1947, *26*, 5–41.

Stinchcombe, A. L., McDill, M., & Walker, D. Is there a racial tipping point in changing schools? *Journal of Social Issues*, 1969, *25*(1), 127–136.

Stires, L. K., & Jones, E. E. Modesty versus self-enhancement as alternative forms of ingratiation. *Journal of Experimental Social Psychology*, 1969, *5*, 172–188.

Stodolsky, S. S., & Lesser, G. Learning patterns in the disadvantaged. *Harvard Educational Review*, 1967, *37*, 546–593.

Stogdill, R. M. Personal factors associated with leadership. *Journal of Psychology*, 1948, *23*, 36–71.

Stogdill, R. M. Leadership, membership, and organization. *Psychological Bulletin*, 1950, 47, 1–14.

Stogdill, R. M. *Manual for the Leader Behavior Description Questionnaire—Form XII*. Bureau of Business Research, Ohio State University, 1963.

Stogdill, R. M. Validity of leader behavior descriptions. *Personnel Psychology*, 1969, *22*, 153–158.

*Stogdill, R. M. *Handbook of leadership: A survey of theory and research*. New York: Free Press, 1974.

Stokes, J. P. Effects of familiarization and knowledge of others' odds choices on shifts to risk and caution. *Journal of Personality and Social Psychology*, 1971, *20*, 402–412.

Stokols, D. A social-psychological model of human crowding phenomena. *Journal of the American Institute of Planners*, 1972, *38*, 72–83. (a)

Stokols, D. On the distinction between density and crowding: Some implications for future research. *Psychological Review*, 1972, *79*, 275–277. (b)

Stokols, D. The experience of crowding in primary and secondary environments. *Environment and Behavior*, 1976, *8*(1), 49–86.

Stokols, D., Rall, M., Pinner, B., & Schopler, J. Physical, social, and personal determinants of the perception of crowding. *Environment and Behavior*, 1973, *5*, 87–115.

Stokols, D., & Resnick, S. *An experimental assessment of neutral and personal crowding experiences*. Paper presented at the meeting of the Southeastern Psychological Association, Atlanta, March 1975. (a)

Stokols, D., & Resnick, S. M. *The generalization of residential crowding experiences to nonresidential settings*. Paper presented at the meeting of the Environmental Design Research Association, Lawrence, Kansas, April 1975. (b)

Stokols, D., Smith, T. E., & Prostor, J. J. Partitioning and perceived crowding in a public space. *American Behavioral Scientist*, 1975, *18*, in press.

Stoller, R. J. A contribution to the study of gender identity. *International Journal of Psychoanalysis*, 1964, *45*, 220–226.

*Stone, W. F. *The psychology of politics*. New York: Free Press, 1974.

Stoner, J. A. F. *A comparison of individual and group decisions involving risk*. Unpublished master's thesis, School of Industrial Management, M.I.T., 1961.

Storms, M. D., & Nisbett, R. E. Insomnia and the attribution process. *Journal of Personality and Social Psychology*, 1970, *16*, 319–328.

Stotland, E., & Dunn, R. E. Identification, "oppositeness," authoritarianism, self-esteem, and birth order. *Psychological Monographs*, 1962, *76*, No. 528.

Stotland, E., & Hillmer, M. L., Jr. Identification, authoritarian defensiveness, and self-esteem. *Journal of Abnormal and Social Psychology*, 1962, *64*, 334–342.

Stotland, E., Katz, D., & Patchen, M. The reduction of prejudice through the arousal of self-insight. *Journal of Personal-*

ity, 1959, 27, 507–531.

Stricker, L. J., Messick, S., & Jackson, D. N. Conformity, anticonformity, and independence: Their dimensionality and generality. *Journal of Personality and Social Psychology*, 1970, 16, 494–507.

Strickland, L. H. Need for approval and the components of the ASO score. *Perceptual and Motor Skills*, 1967, 24, 875–878.

Stuckert, R. P. Race mixture: The African ancestry of White Americans. In P. B. Hammond (Ed.), *Physical anthropology and archeology, selected readings*. New York: Macmillan, 1964. Pp. 192–197.

Strodtbeck, F., & Hook, H. The social dimensions of a 12-man jury table. *Sociometry*, 1961, 24, 397–415.

Stroebe, W., & Fraser, C. Riskiness and confidence in Choice Dilemma decisions. *European Journal of Social Psychology*, 1971, 1, 519–526.

Stroop, J. R. Is the judgment of the group better than that of the average member of the group? *Journal of Experimental Psychology*, 1932, 15, 550–562.

*Student Committee on Human Sexuality, Yale University. *The student guide to sex on campus*. New York: New American Library, 1971.

Sue, S., Sue, D. W., & Sue, D. W. Asian Americans as a minority group. *American Psychologist*, 1975, 30, 906–910.

Suedfeld, P. Social isolation: A case for interdisciplinary research. *Canadian Psychologist*, 1974, 15, 1–15.

Suedfeld, P., Bochner, S., & Matas, C. Petitioner's attire and petition signing by peace demonstrators: A field experiment. *Journal of Applied Social Psychology*, 1971, 1, 278–283.

Suedfeld, P., Bochner, S., & Wnek, D. Helper-sufferer similarity and a specific request for help: Bystander intervention during a peace demonstration. *Journal of Applied Social Psychology*, 1972, 2, 17–23.

Sullivan, H. S. *The interpersonal theory of psychiatry*. New York: Norton, 1953.

Sundstrom, E. An experimental study of crowding: Effects of room-size, intrusion, and goal-blocking on nonverbal behaviors, self-disclosure, and self-reported stress. *Journal of Personality and Social Psychology*, 1975, 32, 645–654. (a)

Sundstrom, E. Toward an interpersonal model of crowding. *Sociological Symposium*, 1975, 14, 129–144. (b)

Sundstrom, E., & Altman, I. *Relationships between dominance and territorial behavior: A field study in a youth rehabilitation setting*. (Technical Report). Department of Psychology, University of Utah, 1972.

Sundstrom, E., & Altman, I. Field study of territorial behavior and dominance. *Journal of Personality and Social Psychology*, 1974, 30, 115–124.

Sundstrom, E., & Altman, I. Personal space and interpersonal relationships: Research review and theoretical model. *Human Ecology*, 1976, 4(1), 47–67.

Swingle, P. (Ed.). *The structure of conflict*. New York: Academic Press, 1970.

Szabo, D. Personal communication, August 1, 1970.

Taft, R. The ability to judge people. *Psychological Bulletin*, 1955, 52, 1–23.

*Tagiuri, R. Person perception. In G. Lindzey & E. Aronson (Eds.), *Handbook of social psychology* (Vol. 3) (2nd ed.). Reading, Mass.: Addison-Wesley, 1969. Pp. 395–449.

*Tajfel, H. Social and cultural factors in perception. In G. Lindzey & E. Aronson (Eds.), *Handbook of social psychology* (Vol. 3) (2nd ed.). Reading, Mass.: Addison-Wesley, 1969. Pp. 315–394.

*Tannenbaum, A. S. *Social psychology of the work organization*. Belmont, Calif.: Wadsworth, 1966.

Tanner, K. L., & Catron, D. W. *The effects of examiner-subject variables (length of acquaintance and race of E) on WPPSI scores of preschool Negro boys*. Paper presented at the meeting of the Southeastern Psychological Association, Miami Beach, April 1971.

Tanser, H. A. *The settlement of Negroes in Kent County, Ontario, and the study of the mental capacity of their descendants*. Chatham, Ont.: Shepard, 1939.

Tanter, R., & Midlarsky, M. A theory of revolution. *Journal of Conflict Resolution*, 1967, 11, 264–280.

Taylor, D. A., & Altman, I. Self-disclosure as a function of reward-cost outcomes. *Sociometry*, 1975, 38, 18–31.

Taylor, D. A., Altman, I., & Sorrentino, R. Interpersonal exchange as a function of rewards and costs and situational factors: Expectancy confirmation-disconfirmation. *Journal of Experimental Social Psychology*, 1969, 5, 324–339.

Taylor, D. W., Berry, P. C., & Block, C. H. Does group participation when using brainstorming facilitate or inhibit creative thinking? *Administrative Science Quarterly*, 1958, 3, 23–47.

Taylor, D. W., & Faust, W. L. Twenty questions: Efficiency of problem solving as a function of the size of the group. *Journal of Experimental Psychology*, 1952, 44, 360–363.

Taylor, F. W. *Scientific management*. New York: Harper, 1911.

Taylor, J. B., Zurcher, L. A., & Key, W. H. *Tornado: A community responds to disaster*. Seattle: University of Washington Press, 1970.

Taylor, S. E., & Mettee, D. R. When similarity breeds contempt. *Journal of Personality and Social Psychology*, 1971, 20, 75–81.

Taylor, S. P., & Pisano, R. Physical aggression as a function of frustration and physical attack. *Journal of Social Psychology*, 1971, 84, 261–267.

Taynor, J., & Deaux, K. When women are more deserving than men: Equity, attribution, and perceived sex differences. *Journal of Personality and Social Psychology*, 1973, 28, 360–367.

Taynor, J., & Deaux, K. Equity and perceived sex differences: Role behavior as defined by the task, the mode, and the actor. *Journal of Personality and Social Psychology*, 1975, 32, 381–390.

Tedeschi, J. T., Schlenker, B. R., & Bonoma, T. V. Cognitive dissonance: Private ratiocination or public spectacle? *American Psychologist*, 1971, 26, 685–695.

Teger, A. I. Defining the socially responsible response. Paper presented at the meeting of the American Psychological Association, Miami Beach, September 1970.

Teger, A. I., & Pruitt, D. G. Components of group risk taking. *Journal of Experimental Social Psychology*, 1967, *3*, 189–205.

Teger, A. I., Pruitt, D. G., St. Jean, R., & Haaland, G. A re-examination of the familiarization hypothesis in group risk taking. *Journal of Experimental Social Psychology*, 1970, *6*, 346–350.

Teich, A. H. (Ed.). *Technology and man's future*. New York: St. Martin's Press, 1972.

Teichman, Y. Emotional arousal and affiliation. *Journal of Experimental Social Psychology*, 1973, *9*, 591–605.

Tennis, G. H., & Dabbs, J. M., Jr. Sex, setting and personal space: First grade through college. *Sociometry*, 1975, *38*, 385–394.

Terborg, J. R., & Ilgen, D. R. A theoretical approach to sex discrimination in traditionally masculine occupations. *Organizational Behavior and Human Performance*, 1975, *13*, 352–376.

Terman, L. M., & Merrill, M. A. *Measuring intelligence*. Boston: Houghton-Mifflin, 1937.

*TeSelle, S. (Ed.). *The family, communes, and utopian societies*. New York: Harper & Row, 1972.

Tesser, A., Gatewood, R., & Driver, M. Some determinants of gratitude. *Journal of Personality and Social Psychology*, 1968, *9*, 233-236.

Thayer, G. *The war business: The international trade in armaments*. New York: Simon & Schuster, 1969.

Theman, V., & Witty, P. A. Case studies and genetic records of two gifted Negroes. *Journal of Psychology*, 1943, *15*, 165–181.

Thibaut, J. W., & Kelley, H. H. *The social psychology of groups*. New York: Wiley, 1959.

Thomas, L. E. Generational discontinuity in beliefs: An exploration of the generation gap. *Journal of Social Issues*, 1974, *30*(3), 1–22.

Thompson, R. J., Jr., & Kolstoe, R. H. Physical aggression as a function of strength of frustration and instrumentality of aggression. *Journal of Research in Personality*, 1974, *7*, 314–323.

Thorngate, W. *Possible limits on a science of man* (Report 73-3). Social Psychology Labs, University of Alberta, Canada, 1973.

*Tiger, L. *Men in groups*. New York: Random House, 1969.

Tilker, H. Socially responsible behavior as a function of observer responsibility and victim feedback. *Journal of Personality and Social Psychology*, 1970, *14*, 95–100.

Tilly, C. Collective violence in European perspective. In H. D. Graham & T. R. Gurr (Eds.), *Violence in America*. New York: New American Library, 1969. Pp. 4–42.

Time. Choosing parents in Iowa. 1966, *87*(8), 45. (February 25, 1966, issue.)

Time. A gun-toting nation. 1966, *88*(7), 15. (August 12, 1966, issue.)

Time. Moynihan's memo fever. 1970, *95*(12), 15–16. (March 23, 1970, issue.)

Time. The grueling life on the line. 1970, *96*(13), 70–71. (September 28, 1970, issue.)

Time. The new American Samaritans. 1971, *98*(26), 12–14; 19–20. (December 27, 1971, issue.)

Time. Cutthroat pre-meds. 1974, *103*(21), 62. (May 20, 1974, issue.)

Tinbergen, N. *The study of instinct*. Oxford: Clarendon Press, 1951.

Tinbergen, N. The curious behavior of the stickleback. *Scientific American*, 1952, *187*(6), 22–26.

Tinbergen, N. On war and peace in animals and man. *Science*, 1968, *196*, 1411–1418.

Tipton, R. M., & Jenkins, L. Altruism as a function of response cost to the benefactor. *Journal of Psychology*, 1974, *86*, 209–216.

Tittler, B. I. *The relationship between attitude change and ego involvements and its relevance to sex differences in attitude change*. Unpublished master's thesis, Pennsylvania State University, 1967.

Titus, H. E., & Hollander, E. P. The California F scale in psychological research. *Psychological Bulletin*, 1957, *54*, 47–64.

Toch, H. *The social psychology of social movements*. Indianapolis: Bobbs-Merrill, 1965.

Toder, N. L., & Marcia, J. E. Ego identity status and response to conformity pressure in college women. *Journal of Personality and Social Psychology*, 1973, *26*, 287–294.

*Toffler, A. *Future shock*. New York: Random House, 1970.

Tognoli, J. Response matching in interpersonal information exchange. *British Journal of Social and Clinical Psychology*, 1969, *8*, 116–123.

Tomkins, C. The creative situation. *New Yorker*, January 7, 1967, *42*(1), 34–36ff.

Tomlinson, T. M. The development of a riot ideology among urban Negroes. *American Behavioral Scientist*, 1968, *11*(4), 27–31.

Touhey, J. C. Individual differences in attitude change following two acts of forced compliance. *Journal of Personality and Social Psychology*, 1973, *27*, 96–99.

Touhey, J. C. Effects of additional women professionals on ratings of occupational prestige and desirability. *Journal of Personality and Social Psychology*, 1974, *29*, 86–89. (a)

Touhey, J. C. Effects of additional men on prestige and desirability of occupations typically performed by women. *Journal of Applied Social Psychology*, 1974, *4*, 330–335. (b)

Toynbee, A. J. *A study of history* (Vol. 1). New York: Oxford University Press, 1948.

Tresemer, D. Fear of success: Popular but unproven. *Psychology Today*, 1974, *7*(10), 82–85.

Triandis, H. C. A note on Rokeach's theory of prejudice. *Journal of Abnormal and Social Psychology*, 1961, *62*, 184–186.

Triandis, H. C. *Attitude and attitude change*. New York: Wiley, 1971.

Triandis, H. C. Social psychology and cultural analysis. *Journal for the Theory of Social Behaviour*, 1975, *5*, 81–106.

Triandis, H. C. *Interpersonal behavior*. Monterey, Calif.: Brooks/Cole, 1976.

Triandis, H. C., & Davis, E. Race and belief as determinants of behavioral intentions. *Journal of Personality and Social Psychology*, 1965, *2*, 715–725.

Triandis, H. C., & Vassiliou, V. Frequency of contact and stereotyping. *Journal of Personality and Social Psychology*, 1967, *7*, 316–328.

Trimble, J. E. *The consonance of agreement of stereotypic descriptions of the American Indian*. Unpublished manuscript, Oklahoma City University, 1968.

Trimble, J. E. *An index of the social indicators of the American Indian in Oklahoma*. Oklahoma City, Okla.: Oklahoma Indian Affairs Commission Publication, 1972.

Trimble J. E. *A reexamination of the stereotypic agreement patterns of American Indians and non-Indians*. Unpublished manuscript, Oklahoma City University, 1974. (a)

Trimble, J. E. *Say goodbye to the Hollywood Indian: Results of a nationwide survey of the self-image of the American Indian*. Paper presented at the meeting of the American Psychological Association, New Orleans, August 1974. (b)

Triplett, N. The dynamogenic factors in pacemaking and competition. *American Journal of Psychology*, 1897, *9*, 507–533.

Truax, C. B., & Carkhuff, R. R. Client and therapist transparency in the psychotherapeutic encounter. *Journal of Counseling Psychology*, 1965, *12*, 3–9.

Tucker, J., & Friedman, S. T. Population density and group size. *American Journal of Sociology*, 1972, *77*, 742–749.

Tulkin, S. Race, class, family, and school achievement. *Journal of Personality and Social Psychology*, 1968, *9*, 31–37.

Turiel, E., & Rothman, G. R. The influence of reasoning on behavioral choices at different stages of moral development. *Child Development*, 1972, *43*, 741–756.

Turkle, B. *Thy friend, Obadiah*. New York: Viking Press, 1969.

Turner, C. W., & Simons, L. S. Effects of subject sophistication and evaluation apprehension on aggressive responses to weapons. *Journal of Personality and Social Psychology*, 1974, *30*, 341–348.

Tyler, L. E. *The psychology of human differences* (3rd ed.). New York: Appleton-Century-Crofts, 1965.

UNESCO. Biological aspects of race. *UNESCO Courier*, April 1, 1965, pp. 8–11.

Unger, R. K., & Siiter, R. *Sex-role stereotypes: The weight of a "grain of truth."* Paper presented at the meeting of the Eastern Psychological Association, Philadelphia, April 1974.

U. S. Commission on Civil Rights. *Racism in America and how to combat it*. U. S. Government Printing Office, 1969.

U. S. Department of Health, Education, and Welfare. *Toward a social report*. Washington, D. C.: U. S. Government Printing Office, 1969.

U. S. Department of Labor. *The Negro family: The case for national action*. Washington, D. C.: Office of Policy Planning and Research, U. S. Department of Labor, 1965.

Vacc, N. A., & Vacc, N. E. An adaptation for children of the Modified Role Repertory Test—A measure of cognitive complexity. *Psychological Reports*, 1973, *33*, 771–776.

Vacchiano, R. B., Strauss, P. S., & Hochman, L. The open and closed mind: A review of dogmatism. *Psychological Bulletin*, 1969, *71*, 261–273.

Valins, S. Cognitive effects of false heart-rate feedback. *Journal of Personality and Social Psychology*, 1966, *4*, 400–408.

Valins, S. Emotionality and autonomic reactivity. *Journal of Experimental Research in Personality*, 1967, *2*, 41–48. (a)

Valins, S. Emotionality and information concerning internal reactions. *Journal of Personality and Social Psychology*, 1967, *6*, 458–463. (b)

Valins, S. The perception and labeling of bodily changes as determinants of emotional behavior. In P. Black (Ed.), *Physiological correlates of emotion*. New York: Academic Press, 1970. Pp. 229–243.

Valins, S., & Baum, A. Residential group size, social interaction, and crowding. *Environment and Behavior*, 1974, *5*, 421–439.

Varela, J. A. Aplicación de hallazgos provenientes de las ciencias sociales. *Revista Interamericana de Psicologia*, 1969, *3*, 45–52.

Vernadsky, G. *A history of Russia*. Philadelphia: Blakiston, 1944.

Vidmar, N. Group composition and the risky shift. *Journal of Experimental Social Psychology*, 1970, *6*, 153–166.

Vidulich, R. N., & Kaiman, I. P. The effects of information source status and dogmatism upon conformity behavior. *Journal of Abnormal and Social Psychology*, 1961, *63*, 639–642.

Vockell, E. L., Felker, D. W., & Miley, C. H. Birth order literature 1967–1971: Bibliography and index. *Journal of Individual Psychology*, 1973, *29*, 39–53.

Vollmer, H. M. Basic rules for applying social science to urban and social problems. *Urban and Social Change Review*, 1970, *3*(2), 32–33.

Vonhoff, H. *People who care: An illustrated history of human compassion*. Philadelphia: Fortress Press, 1971.

Vontress, C. E. *Self-hatred in Americans of African descent*. Paper presented at the meeting of the American Psychological Association, New Orleans, August 1974.

Vraa, C. W. Emotional climate as a function of group composition. *Small Group Behavior*, 1974, *5*, 105–120.

Vroom, V. H. *Some personality determinants of the effects of participation*. Englewood Cliffs, N. J.: Prentice-Hall, 1960.

Vroom, V. H., & Mann, F. C. Leader authoritarianism and employee attitudes. *Personnel Psychology*, 1960, *13*, 125–140.

*Wagner, R. V., & Sherwood, J. J. (Eds.). *The study of attitude change*. Monterey, Calif.: Brooks/Cole, 1969.

Wainwright, L. The dying girl that no one helped. *Life*, 1964, *56*(16), 21. (April 10, 1964 issue.)

Walker, E. L. *Psychology as a natural and social science*. Monterey, Calif.: Brooks/Cole, 1970.

Walker, N. *Crime and punishment in Britain*. Edinburgh: Edinburgh University Press, 1965.

Wall, P. M. *Eye-witness identification in criminal cases*. Springfield, Ill.: Charles C Thomas, 1971.

Waller, W. The rating and dating complex. *American Sociological Review*, 1937, *2*, 727–737.

Wallach, M. A., Kogan, N., & Bem, D. J. Group influence on individual risk taking. *Journal of Abnormal and Social Psychology*, 1962, *65*, 75–86.

Wallach, M. A., Kogan, N., & Burt, R. Are risk takers more persuasive than conservatives in group decisions? *Journal of Experimental Social Psychology*, 1968, *4*, 76–89.

Walster, E. The effect of self-esteem on romantic liking. *Journal of Experimental Social Psychology*, 1965, *1*, 184–197.

Walster, E. Passionate love. In B. Murstein (Ed.), *Theories of attraction and love*. New York: Springer, 1971. Pp. 85–99.

Walster, E., Aronson, E., & Abrahams, D. On increasing the persuasiveness of a low prestige communicator. *Journal of Experimental Social Psychology*, 1966, *2*, 325–342.

Walster, E., Aronson, V., Abrahams, D., & Rottmann, L. Importance of physical attractiveness in dating behavior. *Journal of Personality and Social Psychology*, 1966, *4*, 508–516.

Walster, E., & Berscheid, E. Adrenaline makes the heart grow fonder. *Psychology Today*, 1971, *5*(1), 46–50ff.

Walster, E., Berscheid, E., & Walster, G. W. The exploited: Justice or justification? In J. Macaulay & L. Berkowitz (Eds.), *Altruism and helping behavior: Social psychological studies of some antecedents and consequences*. New York: Academic Press, 1970. Pp. 179–204.

Walster, E., & Piliavin, J. A. Equity and the innocent bystander. *Journal of Social Issues*, 1972, *28*(3), 165–189.

Walster, E., Piliavin, J. A., & Walster, G. W. The hard-to-get woman. *Psychology Today*, 1973, *7*(4), 80–83.

Walster, E., Walster, G. W., Piliavin, J., & Schmidt, L. "Playing hard to get": Understanding an elusive phenomenon. *Journal of Personality and Social Psychology*, 1973, *26*, 113–121.

Walters, C. E. Comparative development of Negro and White infants. *Journal of Genetic Psychology*, 1967, *110*, 235–251.

Walters, R. H. Implications of laboratory studies of aggression for the control and regulation of violence. *Annals*, 1965, *364*, 60–72.

Walters, R. H., Llewellyn-Thomas, E., & Acker, C. W. Enhancement of punitive behavior by audio-visual displays. *Science*, 1962, *135*, 872–873.

Walters, R. H., & Parke, R. D. Social motivation, dependency, and susceptibility to social influence. In L. Berkowitz (Ed.), *Advances in experimental social psychology* (Vol. 1). New York: Academic Press, 1964. Pp. 231–276.

Walters, R., & Willows, D. Imitation behavior of disturbed children following exposure to aggressive and nonaggressive models. *Child Development*, 1968, *39*, 79–91.

Wandersman, A., Schaffner, P., & Stang, D. J. *An extension of the attitudinal effects of exposure to voting behavior*. Unpublished manuscript, Cornell University, 1974.

Ware, R., & Harvey, O. J. A cognitive determinant of impression formation. *Journal of Personality and Social Psychology*, 1967, *5*, 38–44.

Warner, W. L., Meeker, M., & Eells, K. W. *Social class in America*. Chicago: Science Research Associates, 1949.

Warr, P. B., & Knapper, C. *The perception of people and events*. New York: Wiley, 1968.

Warren, N. African infant precocity. *Psychological Bulletin*, 1972, *78*, 353–367.

Warren, J. R. Birth order and social behavior. *Psychological Bulletin*, 1966, *65*, 38–49.

Warriner, C. H. Groups are real: A reaffirmation. *American Sociological Review*, 1956, *21*, 549–554.

Warwick, D. P. Social scientists ought to stop lying. *Psychology Today*, 1975, *8*(9), 38–40ff.

Washburn, S. L. The study of race. In M. F. A. Montagu (Ed.), *The concept of race*. New York: Free Press, 1964. Pp. 242–260.

Waters, H. F., & Malamud, P. "Drop that gun, Captain Video." *Newsweek*, 1975, *85*(10), 81–82. (March 10, 1975 issue.)

Watson, G. *Action for unity*. New York: Harper, 1947.

Watson, G. B. Do groups think more effectively than individuals? *Journal of Abnormal and Social Psychology*, 1928, *23*, 328–336.

Watson, J. B. *Behaviorism*. New York: Norton, 1930.

Watson, J. D. *The double helix: A personal account of the discovery of the structure of DNA*. New York: Atheneum, 1968.

Watts, R. E. Influence of population density on crime. *Journal of American Statistical Association*, 1931, *26*, 11–21.

Watts, W., Lynch, S., & Whittaker, D. Alienation and activism in today's college age youth: Socialization patterns and current family relationships. *Journal of Counseling Psychology*, 1969, *16*, 1–7.

*Webb, E. J., Campbell, D. T., Schwartz, R. D., & Sechrest, L. *Unobtrusive measures: Nonreactive research in the social sciences*. Chicago: Rand-McNally, 1966.

Weber, M. *The Protestant ethic and the spirit of capitalism*. New York: Scribner's, 1930.

Weber, S. J., & Cook, T. D. Subject effects in laboratory research: An examination of subject roles, demand characteristics, and valid inference. *Psychological Bulletin*, 1972, *77*, 273–295.

Webster, S. W. The influence of interracial contact on social acceptance in a newly integrated school. *Journal of Educational Psychology*, 1961, *52*, 292–296.

Wegner, M. A., Averill, J. R., & Smith, D. B. Autonomic activity during sexual arousal. *Psychophysiology*, 1968, *4*, 468–478.

Weigel, R. H., Wiser, P. L., & Cook, S. W. The impact of cooperative learning experiences on cross-ethnic relations and attitudes. *Journal of Social Issues*, 1975, *31*(1), 219–244.

Weick, K. E. Systematic observational methods. In G. Lindzey & E. Aronson (Eds.), *The handbook of social psychology* (Vol. 2) (2nd ed.). Reading, Mass.: Addison-Wesley, 1968. Pp. 357–451.

Weinberg, G. *Society and the healthy homosexual*. New York: St. Martin's Press, 1972.

Weinberg, M. S., & Williams, C. J. *Male homosexuals: Their problems and their adaptations.* New York: Oxford University Press, 1974.

Weiss, R. F., Buchanan, W., Altstatt, L., & Lombardo, J. P. Altruism is rewarding. *Science,* 1971, *171,* 1262-1263.

Weiss, W. Effects of the mass media of communication. In G. Lindzey & E. Aronson (Eds.), *The handbook of social psychology* (Vol. 5) (2nd ed.). Reading, Mass.: Addison-Wesley, 1969. Pp. 77-195.

Weissberg, N. C. On de Fleur and Westie's "Attitudes as a scientific concept." *Social Forces,* 1965, *43,* 422-425.

Weitz, S. Attitude, voice, and behavior: A repressed affect model of interracial interaction. *Journal of Personality and Social Psychology,* 1972, *24,* 14-21.

*Weitz, S. (Ed.). *Nonverbal communication.* New York: Oxford University Press, 1974.

Weitzman, L. J., Eifler, D., Hokada, E., & Ross, C. Sex-role socialization in picture books for preschool children. *American Journal of Sociology,* 1972, *77,* 1125-1149.

Weizmann, F. Correlational statistics and the nature-nurture problem. *Science,* 1971, *171,* 589.

Wells, W. D. *Television and aggression: Replication of an experimental field study.* Unpublished manuscript, University of Chicago, 1973.

Werner, E. E. Infants around the world: Cross-cultural studies of psychomotor development, birth to two years. *Journal of Cross-Cultural Psychology,* 1972, *3*(2), 111-134.

West, S. G., Gunn, S. P., & Chernicky, P. Ubiquitous Watergate: An attributional analysis. *Journal of Personality and Social Psychology,* 1975, *32,* 55-65.

Westhues, K. *On marginality and its solutions in contemporary society.* Lecture presented at St. Francis Xavier University, Antigonish, Nova Scotia, February 1972.

Westie, F. R. A technique for the measurement of race attitudes. *American Sociological Review,* 1953, *18,* 73-78.

Westin, A. F. *Privacy and freedom.* New York: Atheneum, 1967.

Wheeler, L., & Smith, S. Censure of the model in the contagion of aggression. *Journal of Personality and Social Psychology,* 1967, *6,* 93-98.

Wheeler, L. R. A comparative study of the intelligence of East Tennessee mountain children. *Journal of Educational Psychology,* 1942, *33,* 321-334.

White, G. M. Immediate and deferred effects of model observation and guided and unguided rehearsal on donating and stealing. *Journal of Personality and Social Psychology,* 1972, *21,* 139-148.

Whiting, B., & Edwards, C. P. A cross-cultural analysis of sex differences in the behavior of children aged three through 11. *Journal of Social Psychology,* 1973, *91,* 171-188.

*Whyte, W. H., Jr. *The organization man.* New York: Simon & Schuster, 1956.

Wicker, A. W. Undermanning, performances, and students' subjective experiences in behavior settings of large and small schools. *Journal of Personality and Social Psychology,* 1968, *10,* 255-261.

Wicker, A. W. Attitudes versus actions: The relationship of verbal and overt behavioral responses to attitude objects. *Journal of Social Issues,* 1969, *25*(4), 41-78. (a)

Wicker, A. W. Size of church membership and members' support of church behavior settings. *Journal of Personality and Social Psychology,* 1969, *13,* 278-288. (b)

Wicker, A. W. An examination of the "other variables" explanation of attitude-behavior inconsistency. *Journal of Personality and Social Psychology,* 1971, *19,* 18-30.

Wicker, A. W. Undermanning theory and research: Implications for the study of psychological and behavioral effects of excess populations. *Representative Research in Social Psychology,* 1973, *4,* 185-206.

Wicker, A. W., & Kirmeyer, S. *From church to laboratory to national park: A program of research on excess and insufficient populations in behavior settings.* Unpublished manuscript, Claremont Graduate School, 1975.

Wiesenthal, D. L., Endler, N. S., Coward, T. R., & Edwards, J. *Reversibility of relative competence as a determinant of conformity across different perceptual tasks.* Paper presented at the meeting of the Eastern Psychological Association, Philadelphia, May 1974.

Wilder, D. A., & Allen, V. L. *The effect of absent social support on conformity.* Paper presented at the meeting of the Midwestern Psychological Association, Chicago, May 1973.

Wilder, J. Values and the psychology of the superego. *American Journal of Psychotherapy,* 1973, *27,* 187-203.

Willems, E. P., & Clark, R. D., III. Dependence of the risky shift on instructions: A replication. *Psychological Reports,* 1969, *25,* 811-814.

Willerman, L. IQ: Methodological and other issues (letter to the editor). *Science,* 1972, *178,* 230.

Williams, R. M., Jr. *The reduction of intergroup tensions.* New York: Social Science Research Council, 1947.

*Willie, C. V., Kramer, B. M., & Brown, B. S. (Eds.). *Racism and mental health.* Pittsburgh, Pa.: University of Pittsburgh Press, 1973.

Willis, F. N. Initial speaking distance as a function of the speakers' relationship. *Psychonomic Science,* 1966, *5,* 221-222.

Willis, R. H. Two dimensions of conformity—nonconformity. *Sociometry,* 1963, *26,* 499-513.

Willis, R.H. Conformity, independence, and anti-conformity. *Human Relations,* 1965, *18,* 373-388.

Willis, R. H., & Burgess, T. D. G., II. Cognitive and affective balance in sociometric dyads. *Journal of Personality and Social Psychology,* 1974, *29,* 145-152.

Wilner, D. M., Walkley, R., & Cook, S. W. *Human relations in interracial housing: A study of the contact hypothesis.* Minneapolis, Minn.: University of Minnesota Press, 1955.

Wilson, E. O. The natural history of lions. *Science,* 1973, *179,* 466-467.

Wilson, G. D., & Nias, D. K. B. Measurement of social attitudes: A new approach. *Perceptual and Motor Skills,* 1972, *35,* 827-834.

Wilson, W., & Miller, H. Repetition, order of presentation, timing of arguments and measures as determinants of opinion change. *Journal of Personality and Social Psychology*, 1968, 9, 184–188.

Wilson, W. C. Pornography: The emergence of a social issue and the beginning of psychological study. *Journal of Social Issues*, 1973, 29(3), 7–17.

Winch, R. F. *The modern family.* New York: Holt, 1952.

Winch, R. F., Ktsanes, T., & Ktsanes, V. The theory of complementary needs in mate selection: An analytic and descriptive study. *American Sociological Review*, 1954, 19, 241–249.

Winsborough, H. The social consequences of high population density. *Law and Contemporary Problems*, 1965, 30, 120–126.

Winsome, R. Connotative meanings of first names. *Parade Magazine*, October 20, 1973 (cited in Kibler & Harari, 1974).

Wishner, J. Reanalysis of "impressions of personality." *Psychological Review*, 1960, 67, 96–112.

Wispé, L. G. Positive forms of social behavior: An overview. *Journal of Social Issues*, 1972, 28(3), 1–19.

Wispé, L. A quantitative study of positive and negative studies of social behavior. In L. Wispé (Ed.), *The psychology of sympathy and altruism.* Cambridge, Mass.: Harvard University Press, 1977.

Wispé, L. G. & Freshley, H. B. Race, sex and sympathetic helping behavior: The broken bag caper. *Journal of Personality and Social Psychology*, 1971, 17, 59–65.

Witcover, J. *The resurrection of Richard Nixon.* New York: Putnam, 1970.

Witty, P. A., & Jenkins, M. D. The case of "B," a gifted Negro girl. *Journal of Social Psychology*, 1935, 6, 117–124.

Wodarski, J. S., Hamblin, R. L., Buckholdt, D. R., & Ferritor, D. E. Individual consequences versus different shared consequences contingent on the performance of low-achieving group members. *Journal of Applied Social Psychology*, 1973, 3, 276–290.

Wohlwill, J. Amount of stimulus exploration and preference as differential functions of stimulus complexity. *Perception and Psychophysics*, 1968, 4, 307–312.

Wohlwill, J. The emerging discipline of environmental psychology. *American Psychologist*, 1970, 25, 303–312.

Wohlwill, J. Behavioral response and adaptation to environmental stimulation. In A. Damon (Ed.), *Physiological anthropology.* Cambridge, Mass.: Harvard University Press, 1971.

Wohlwill, J. Human adaptation to levels of environmental stimulation. *Human Ecology*, 1974, 2(2), 127–147.

*Wohlwill, J., & Carson, D. (Eds.). *Environment and the social sciences: Perspectives and applications.* Washington, D.C.: American Psychological Association, 1972.

Wolf, R. M. *The identification and measurement of environmental process variables related to intelligence.* Unpublished doctoral dissertation, University of Chicago, 1963.

Wolfe, B. *Three who made a revolution* (2 vols.). New York: Time Reading Program, 1964.

Wolfgang, M. Crime: Homicide. In D. L. Sells (Ed.), *International encyclopedia of the social sciences* (Vol. 3). New York: Macmillan, 1968.

Women on Words and Images. *Dick and Jane as victims: Sex stereotyping in children's readers.* Princeton, N.J.: Women on Words and Images, 1972.

Wood, D. A. Effect of worker orientation differences on job attitude correlates. *Journal of Applied Psychology*, 1974, 59, 54–60.

Wood, F. A. *The influence of monarchs.* New York: Macmillan, 1913.

Wood, R. Popular sex superstitions. *Sexology*, 1963, 29, 752–754.

Woodmansee, J., & Cook, S. W. Dimensions of verbal racial attitudes. *Journal of Personality and Social Psychology*, 1967, 7, 240–250.

Worchel, S. The effect of films on the importance of behavioral freedom. *Journal of Personality*, 1972, 40, 417–435.

Worchel, S., & Arnold, S. E. The effects of censorship and attractiveness of the censor on attitude change. *Journal of Experimental Social Psychology*, in press.

Worchel, S., & Brehm, J. W. Direct and implied social restoration of freedom. *Journal of Personality and Social Psychology*, 1971, 18, 294–304.

Worchel, S., & Teddlie, C. Factors affecting the experience of crowding: A two-factor theory. Unpublished paper, University of Virginia, 1976.

Worthington, M. Personal space as a function of the stigma effects. *Environment and Behavior*, 1974, 6, 289–297.

Worthy, M. *Eye-darkness, race and self-paced athletic performance.* Paper presented at the meeting of the Southeastern Psychological Association, Miami Beach, April 1971.

Worthy, M. *Eye color and hitting vs. pitching success in major league baseball: 1973 season.* Paper presented at the meeting of the Midwestern Psychological Association, Chicago, May 1974. (a)

Worthy, M. *Eye-color, sex, and race.* Anderson, S. C.: Droke House/Hallux, 1974. (b)

Worthy, M., & Markle, A. Racial differences in self-paced versus reactive sports activities. *Journal of Personality and Social Psychology*, 1970, 16, 439–443.

Wrench, D. F. *Psychology: A social approach.* New York: McGraw-Hill, 1969.

Wright, B. A. Altruism in children and perceived conduct of others. *Journal of Abnormal and Social Psychology*, 1942, 37, 218–233.

Wright, P. H., & Crawford, A. C. Agreement and friendship: A close look and some second thoughts. *Representative Research in Social Psychology*, 1971, 2, 52–69.

Wrightsman, L. S. The effects of purported validity of a test on motivation and achievement. *Journal of Educational Research*, 1960, 54, 153–156. (a)

Wrightsman, L. S. Effects of waiting with others on changes in level of felt anxiety. *Journal of Abnormal and Social Psychology*, 1960, 61, 216–222. (b)

Wrightsman, L. S. Dimensionalization of attitudes toward the Negro. *Psychological Reports*, 1962, 11, 439–448. (a)

Wrightsman, L. S. The effects of anxiety, achievement motivation, and task importance upon performance on an intelligence test. *Journal of Educational Psychology*, 1962, 53, 150–156. (b)

Wrightsman, L. S. Measurement of philosophies of human nature. *Psychological Reports*, 1964, *14*, 743–751. (a)

Wrightsman, L. S. Some subtle factors affecting students' evaluations of teachers. *S.P.A.T.E. Journal*, 1964, *3*, 42–51. (b)

Wrightsman, L. S. *Attitudinal and personality correlates of presidential voting preferences.* Paper presented at the meeting of the American Psychological Association, Chicago, September 1965.

Wrightsman, L. S. Wallace supporters and adherence to "law and order." *Journal of Personality and Social Psychology*, 1969, *13*, 17–22.

*Wrightsman, L. S. *Assumptions about human nature: A social-psychological approach.* Monterey, Calif.: Brooks/Cole, 1974.

Wrightsman, L. S. The presence of others does make a difference—sometimes. *Psychological Bulletin*, 1975, *82*, 884–885.

Wrightsman, L. S., & Baker, N. J. Where have all the idealistic imperturbable freshmen gone? *Proceedings of the 77th Annual Convention, American Psychological Association*, 1969, *4*, 299–300.

Wrightsman, L. S., Baxter, G. W., Jr., & Jackson, V. W. *Effects of school desegregation upon attitudes toward Negroes held by Southern junior high school students.* Final report, CEMREL research contract, 1967. (Mimeographed)

Wrightsman, L. S., & Cook, S. W. *Factor analysis and attitude change.* Paper presented at the meeting of the Southeastern Psychological Association, Atlanta, April 1965.

Wrightsman, L. S., & Noble, F. C. Reactions to the President's assassination and changes in philosophies of human nature. *Psychological Reports*, 1965, *16*, 159–162.

Wrightsman, L. S., O'Connor, J., & Baker, N. J. (Eds.). *Cooperation and competition: Readings on mixed-motive games.* Monterey, Calif.: Brooks/Cole, 1972.

Wrightsman, L. S., & Sanford, F. H. *Psychology: A scientific study of human behavior* (4th ed.). Monterey, Calif.: Brooks/Cole, 1975.

Wrightsman, L. S., & Satterfield, C. H. *Additional norms and standardization of the Philosophies of Human Nature scale—1967 Revision.* George Peabody College for Teachers, 1967. (Mimeographed)

Wynne-Edwards, V. *Animal dispersion in relation to social behavior.* New York: Hafner, 1962.

Yakimovich, D., & Saltz, E. Helping behavior: The cry for help. *Psychonomic Science*, 1971, *23*, 427–428.

Yancey, W. L. Architecture and social interaction: The case of a large-scale public housing project. *Environment and Behavior*, 1971, *3*, 3–21.

Yankelovich, D. *The new morality: A profile of American youth in the 70's.* New York: McGraw-Hill, 1974.

Yerkes, R. M. Psychological examining in the United States Army. *Memoirs of the National Academy of Science* (Vol. 15). Washington, D. C.: U. S. Government Printing Office, 1921.

Young, J. *The effects of laboratory training on self-concept, philosophies of human nature, and perceptions of group behavior.* Unpublished doctoral dissertation, Department of Special Education, George Peabody College for Teachers, 1970.

Yussoupoff (Yussoupov), F. *Rasputin: His malignant influence and his assassination.* New York: Cape, 1927.

Yukl, G. Toward a behavioral theory of leadership. *Organizational Behavior and Human Performance*, 1971, *6*, 414–440.

*Zablocki, B. *The joyful community.* Baltimore, Md.: Penguin, 1971.

Zacker, J. Authoritarian avoidance of ambiguity. *Psychological Reports*, 1973, *33*, 901–902.

Zagona, S. V., & Zurcher, L. A. Participation, interaction, and role behavior in groups selected from the extremes of the open-closed cognitive continuum. *Journal of Psychology*, 1964, *58*, 255–264.

Zagona, S. V., & Zurcher, L. A. The relationship of verbal ability and other cognitive variables to the open-closed cognitive dimension. *Journal of Psychology*, 1965, *60*, 213–219.

Zajonc, R. B. The concepts of balance, congruity, and dissonance. *Public Opinion Quarterly*, 1960, *24*, 280–296.

Zajonc, R. B. Social facilitation. *Science*, 1965, *149*, 269–274.

Zajonc, R. B. Attitudinal effects of mere exposure. *Journal of Personality and Social Psychology Monograph Supplement*, 1968, *9*(2, Part 2), 2–27. (a)

Zajonc, R. B. Cognitive theories in social psychology. In G. Lindzey & E. Aronson (Eds.), *Handbook of social psychology* (Vol. 1) (2nd ed.). Reading, Mass.: Addison-Wesley, 1968. Pp. 320–411.(b)

Zajonc, R. B., & Sales, S. Social facilitation of dominant and subordinate responses. *Journal of Experimental Social Psychology*, 1966, *2*, 160–168.

Zajonc, R. B., Wolosin, R. J., Wolosin, M. A., & Sherman, S. J. Individual and group risk taking in a two-choice situation. *Journal of Experimental Social Psychology*, 1968, *4*, 89–107.

Zajonc, R. B., Wolosin, R. J., Wolosin, M. A., & Sherman, S. J. Group risk-taking in a two-choice situation: Replication, extension, and a model. *Journal of Experimental Social Psychology*, 1969, *5*, 127–140.

Zander, A., & Armstrong, W. Working for group pride in a slipper factory. *Journal of Applied Social Psychology*, 1972, *2*, 293–307.

Zanna, M. P., & Pack, S. J. On the self-fulfilling nature of apparent sex differences in behavior. *Journal of Experimental Social Psychology*, 1975, *11*, 583–591.

Ziller, R. C. Four techniques of group decision making under uncertainty. *Journal of Applied Psychology*, 1957, *41*, 384–388.

Zillman, D. Excitation transfer in communication-mediated aggressive behavior. *Journal of Experimental Social Psychology*, 1971, *7*, 419–434.

Zillman, D., Katcher, A., & Milavsky, B. Excitation transfer from physical exercise to subsequent aggressive behavior. *Journal of Experimental Social Psychology*, 1972, *8*, 247–259.

Zimbardo, P. G. *The cognitive control of motivation: The consequences of choice and dissonance.* Glenview, Ill.: Scott, Foresman, 1969.

Zimbardo, P. G. The human choice: Individuation, reason, and order versus deindividuation, impulse, and chaos. In W. J. Arnold & D. Levine (Eds.), *Nebraska symposium on motivation, 1969.* Lincoln: University of Nebraska Press, 1970. Pp. 237–307. (a)

Zimbardo, P. G. *Symposium on social and developmental issues in moral research.* Paper presented at the meeting of the Western Psychological Association, Los Angeles, April 1970. (b)

Zimbardo, P. G., & Ebbesen, E. B. *Influencing attitudes and changing behavior.* Reading, Mass.: Addison-Wesley, 1969.

Zimbardo, P. G., & Formica, R. Emotional comparison and self-esteem as determinants of affiliation. *Journal of Personality,* 1963, *31,* 141–162.

Zimmerman, E., & Parlee, M. B. Behavioral changes associated with the menstrual cycle: An experimental investigation. *Journal of Applied Social Psychology,* 1973, *3,* 335–344.

Zlutnick, S., & Altman, I. Crowding and human behavior. In J. Wohlwill & D. Carson (Eds.), *Environment and the social sciences.* Washington, D.C.: American Psychological Association, 1972. Pp. 44–60.

Zuckerman, M. Does the penis lie? Paper presented at the meeting of the American Psychological Association, Washington, D.C., September 1971. (a)

Zuckerman, M. Physiological measures of sexual arousal in the human. *Psychological Bulletin,* 1971, *75,* 297–329. (b)

Zurcher, L. A., Jr. The "friendly" poker game: A study of an ephemeral role. *Social Forces,* 1970, *49,* 173–186.

Author Index

Abeles, R. P., 340, 386
Abell, W., 482
Abelson, H. I., 393, 394
Abelson, R. P., 352, 360, 623
Abrahams, D., 164, 393
Abrahams, W. E., 495
Abramowitz, C. V., 328, 464
Abramowitz, S. I., 328, 464
Acker, C. W., 231
Adams, D. K., 89
Adams, G. R., 69
Adams, J., 298, 628
Adams, S., 658
Adelson, J., 436, 438
Aderman, D., 85, 86, 292, 297
Adorno, T., 15, 319, 583
Aiello, J. R., 515, 516, 518, 541, 545, 546
Aiello, T., 516
Ainsworth, M. D. S., 484, 485
Ajzen, I., 347
Alexander, C. N., Jr., 118, 616
Alexander, G. R., 97
Alexander, H. B., 491
Alfert, E., 485, 489
Alger, C., 56
Alger, I., 309
Alinsky, S., 425, 426
Alioto, J. T., 224
Allen, B. P., 392
Allen, G., 487
Allen, H., 494
Allen, J. C., 73
Allen, J. G., 127, 128
Allen, V. L., 18, 19, 235, 610, 617, 618
Allinsmith, W., 254
Allport, G. W., 3, 6, 86, 87, 252, 315,
    324, 332, 335
Almedingen, E. M., 15
Almquist, E. M., 454
Alper, A., 111
Alper, T. G., 460, 480
Altemeyer, R. A., 520, 591
Altman, I., 138, 139, 513, 515, 516, 517,
    520, 522, 523, 524, 528, 529, 537,
    538, 539, 540, 545, 547, 552
Altstatt, L., 280, 291
Altus, W. D., 154

Alvares, K., 648
Ames, L. B., 264
Amir, Y., 395
Amoroso, D. M., 206
Amsel, A., 219
Anastasi, A., 482, 496, 499, 505
Anchor, K. N., 265
Anderson, J. P., 293
Anderson, N. H., 97, 98
Anderson, R. C., 658
Andrasik, F., 161, 269
Andreoli, V. A., 367
Andrews, F. M., 35, 213
Andrews, I. R., 563, 631
Angrist, S. S., 454
Appley, N. H., 357
Arbuthnot, J., 269
Archer, R. L., 632
Ardrey, R., 217, 218, 522
Argyle, M., 138, 513, 516, 518, 519
Argyris, C., 94, 659
Arkin, R. M., 100
Arms, R. L., 97, 230
Armstrong, W., 658
Arnold, S. E., 367
Aron, A. P., 173
Aronfreed, J., 245, 254, 271, 272, 280
Aronson, E., 72, 163, 164, 165, 167, 168,
    352, 370, 393, 394, 396, 397
Aronson, V., 164
Asch, S. E., 22, 24, 96, 97, 612, 617, 618
Asher, E. J., 500
Ashmore, R. D., 332, 335, 341, 367
Ashton, N. L., 301
Astin, H. S., 327
Athanasiou, R., 167, 199, 201, 207, 532
Atkin, R. S., 565
Atkins, A., 87, 359, 362
Atyas, J., 572
Austin, W. T., 528
Averill, J. R., 205, 536, 537
Ax, A. F., 157
Axelson, L. J., 494
Azrin, N. H., 220

Bachtold, L. M., 327
Back, K. W., 167, 531, 569, 623

Backman, C. W., 165
Bacon, M. K., 450, 451
Baer, D. M., 264
Bailes, D. W., 594
Bailey, K., 516
Bailey, M. M., 459
Bakeman, R., 552
Baker, N. J., 81, 284, 411
Baker, R. K., 233
Baldwin, A. L., 244
Bales, R. F., 639, 642, 645
Ball, S. J., 233
Ballachey, E., 6, 317, 496, 610
Ballif, B. L., 245
Bandler, R. J., 217, 348
Bandura, A., 20, 219, 226, 227, 228, 231,
    239, 245, 270, 272, 273, 274
Banfield, E. C., 337
Banks, C., 54, 55
Bannister, D., 86, 87
Barach, J. A., 391
Barak, A., 659
Barash, D. P., 518
Barber, J. D., 640
Barber, T. X., 69, 633, 634
Barch, A. M., 51
Barclay, A. M., 205
Bard, M., 423, 424
Bardwick, J. M, 449, 454, 460
Barefoot, J. C., 518
Barker, E. N., 592
Barker, R. G., 18, 27, 28, 48, 417, 525,
    546
Barkley, M. J., 503
Barnett, S. A., 218, 229
Barocas, R., 164, 622
Baron, P. H., 391, 633
Baron, R. A., 207, 230, 239, 535
Baron, R. S., 391, 630, 631, 633
Barron, F., 62, 622
Barron, J. W., 366
Barry, H., 450, 451
Barsaloux, J., 562
Bar-Tal, D., 100
Bartlett, C. J., 659
Baruch, G. K., 454
Bass, B. M., 63, 591, 638

Bates, F. L., 528
Bateson, N., 631
Batson, C. D., 297
Bauer, R. A., 391, 429
Baum, A., 518, 542, 543, 544
Baumrin, B. H., 412
Baumrind, D., 598
Baxter, G. W., Jr., 91, 339
Baxter, J. C., 518
Beach, F. A., 448
Beardslee, D. C., 207
Beattie, M., 83, 325, 495
Becker, F. D., 217, 526, 527
Becker, G., 153
Becker, L. A., 393
Becker, S. W., 84
Becker, W. C., 227
Bee, H., 463
Beecher, M. D., 304
Beekman, S., 459
Beez, W. V., 69
Beilin, L. A., 423
Bell, P. A., 535
Bell, P. R., 631
Bell, R., 504
Bell, R. R., 202
Bellow, S., 134
Bem, D. J., 102, 104, 160, 161, 318, 347,
    348, 360, 372, 379, 380, 465, 598,
    623, 629, 631, 632
Bem, S. L., 462, 465
Bender, P., 204
Bengston, V. L., 438
Benjamin, H., 181, 196
Benjamin, L., 494
Benne, K. D., 418
Bennett, B., 542
Bennett, D. H., 72
Bennis, W. G., 418
Bentler, P. M., 463
Bereiter, C., 503
Berelson, B., 57
Bergamini, J., 10
Berger, M., 545
Berger, S. M., 20, 272
Bergman, B. A., 543
Berkowitz, L., 53, 205, 215, 217, 219,
    221, 222, 223, 224, 225, 229, 231,
    233, 292, 296, 297, 302, 303, 305,
    306, 568
Berkowitz, N. H., 591
Bernhardt, I., 629
Berry, P. C., 563
Berscheid, E., 164, 169, 172, 173, 298,
    299
Bickman, L., 53, 72, 73, 295, 303, 304,
    545
Biddle, B. J., 16
Biddle, L., 420
Biddle, W. W., 420
Bieber, I., 188
Bieber, T. B., 188
Bienen, H., 424

Bieri, J., 87, 359, 362
Billig, M., 633
Billings, R. S., 652, 654
Bird, C., 638
Bishop, G. D., 563, 564, 632, 633
Bishop, G. F., 375, 377
Bixenstine, V., E., 341
Black, E., 609
Blake, R. R., 272, 532
Blalock, H. M., 327
Blanchard, F. A., 397
Blaney, N., 396, 397
Blascovich, J., 630
Blatt, M. M., 269
Blau, P., 285, 286
Blauner, R., 333
Bleda, P. R., 150
Block, C. H., 563
Block, J., 63, 265, 266, 435, 622
Blood, M., 660
Bloom, B. S., 502, 506, 623
Bloom, L. M., 307
Blumenthal, M. D., 35, 213
Blumer, D., 182
Bochner, S., 290, 360, 361, 393, 624
Boehm, V. R., 470
Boeth, R., 490
Boguslaw, R., 434, 441, 443
Bonoma, T. V., 372
Booker, A., 225
Booth, A., 539, 540, 541, 546, 547
Borgatta, E. F., 639, 642, 643
Boring, E. G., 480
Borrow, G., 141
Bose, C. E., 470
Bosworth, A. R., 331
Bouchard, T. J., Jr., 562, 563
Boudreau, L. A., 127
Bourlière, F., 218
Boutilier, R. G., 84, 85
Bovard, E. W., Jr., 616
Bowers, K. S., 634
Braginsky, D., 135, 155
Brainerd, C. J., 255
Bramel, D., 163, 285
Bramson, L., 237
Brandt, J., 424
Braucht, G. N., 207
Brehm, J. W., 172, 173, 305, 367, 378
Brehm, S. S., 85, 86
Breland, H. M., 154
Brennan, J. G., 182
Brenner, M., 560
Brewer, M. B., 97
Briand, P. L., Jr., 233
Briar, S., 87
Brickman, P., 259
Brigham, J. C., 89, 331, 337, 342, 385
Brightman, H. J., 594
Brislin, R. W., 165
Bristow, A. T., 490
Britten, F. H., 202
Brock, T. C., 367, 391, 393

Brodsky, S., 424
Brody, C. L., 616
Brody, R. A., 56
Broll, L., 309
Bromley, D. D., 202
Bronfenbrenner, U., 264, 269, 308
Brooks, M. J., 532
Broverman, D. M., 328, 449, 463, 464
Broverman, I. K., 328, 463, 464
Brown, B. R., 118
Brown, D. G., 182
Brown, J. S., 219
Brown, M., 206
Brown, M. E., 265, 624
Brown, N. W., 495
Brown, P., 239
Brown, R., 63, 127, 258, 259, 260, 269,
    356, 592, 632
Brown, R. M., 234
Bruce, M., 483
Bruder, R. A., 461
Bruner, J. S., 96, 382, 383
Bruning, J. L., 325
Brush, C. A., 554
Bruvold, W. H., 316
Bryan, J. H., 229, 232, 239, 259, 292,
    293, 303, 305
Buchanan, W., 280, 291, 335
Buck, P. L., 516
Buck, R. W., 156
Buckholdt, D. R., 285
Buckhout, R., 111, 112
Buechner, H. K., 217
Bullitt, W. C., 83
Burgess, T. D. G., 168, 365
Burk, B. A., 149
Burke, H., 537
Burke, W. W., 594
Burnette, C., 511
Burney, C., 149
Burron, B. F., 103
Burt, C., 485, 486
Burt, R., 631
Burton, R. V. 252
Burtt, H. E., 560, 645
Buss, A. H., 215, 220, 225
Buss, E., 225
Butler, P. M., 182
Butterfield, D. A., 653
Buxhoeveden, S., 14, 15, 18
Byrd, R. E., 149
Byrne, D., 161, 167, 207, 341, 515, 518

Calder, B. J., 372
Caldwell, M. D., 64
Calhoun, J. B., 237, 538
Calverly, D. S., 634
Calvin, A. 356
Cameron, N. A., 18
Camino, L., 233
Campbell, A., 62, 64
Campbell, D. T., 35, 50, 51, 52, 63, 69,
    73, 280, 318, 319, 343, 428, 430,

Campbell, D. T. (continued)
588, 591
Campbell, E., 491
Campbell, J. B., 81
Campbell, J. P., 563, 638
Candee, D., 263
Cannavale, F. J., 553, 554
Cannell, C. F., 61, 64
Canter, D., 541
Canter, F., 516
Cantor, G. N., 495, 541
Cantril, H., 335
Caplan, N. S., 29, 235
Capra, P. C., 153
Caputo, C., 100
Carey, A., 655
Carkhuff, R. R., 138
Carlsmith, J. M., 72, 133, 297, 370, 372, 373, 379
Carlson, H., 424
Carlson, R., 254, 274
Carlsson, G., 499
Carmichael, S., 323
Carnegie, D., 128
Carpenter, C. R., 522
Carr, T. S., 516
Carroll, J. S., 96
Carstairs, G. M., 237
Carter, J. H., 643
Cartwright, D., 630, 639, 646
Castore, C. H., 150
Catalan, J., 122
Catron, D. W., 495
Cattell, R. B., 188, 206
Cavalli-Sforza, L. L., 476
Cavan, C. 523
Chamberlain, A. S., 528
Chammah, A., 284
Chance, J., 83
Chance, N. A., 325
Chandler, J., 544
Chandler, M., 104
Chapanis, A. C., 370
Chapanis, N. P., 370
Chapple, E., 528
Chaskes, J. B., 202
Chein, I., 319
Chemers, M. M., 652
Chern, S., 111
Chernicky, P., 101, 102, 103, 263
Cherry, F., 460
Chesler, M., 586
Chesler, P., 328
Cheyne, J. A., 272, 523
Child, I. L., 438, 450, 451, 453
Chin, R., 418
Christensen, H. T., 201, 202, 203
Christian, J. J., 539
Christie, R., 63, 134, 135, 136, 347, 587, 589, 592, 623
Chun, K., 81
Cialdini, R. B., 122, 298, 309
Clark, D. H., 480, 504, 505

Clark, K. B., 333, 427
Clark, M. P., 427
Clark, R. D. III, 295, 307, 631, 632
Clarkson, F. E., 328, 463, 464
Clausen, G. T., 294, 296, 301
Claxton, R. N., 91
Clifford, A. D., 324
Clifford, C., 639
Cline, F. J., 202
Cline, V. B., 105, 110, 233
Clore, G. L., 303
Cobb, W. M., 487
Coch, L., 657
Cockburn, A., 111
Coe, W. C., 633
Coffman, T. L., 331
Cohen, A. R., 342, 378
Cohen, D., 563
Cohen, J. L., 542
Cohen, M., 494
Cohen, R. J., 595
Cohn, T. S., 639
Cole, A. H., 305
Cole, M., 493
Cole, M. W., 157
Coleman, A. D., 529
Coleman, J., 491, 498
Collins, B. E., 83, 153, 342, 354, 372, 379, 382, 383, 518, 628, 639
Collins, M., 396
Conroy, J., 529
Constantinople, A., 462
Converse, P. E., 317
Cook, M., 516, 520
Cook, P., 587, 589
Cook, S. W., 44, 318, 319, 346, 395, 396, 397, 404, 405, 406, 407
Cook, T. D., 67
Cooley, C. H., 18, 117
Coons, A. E., 644
Cooper, J., 119, 373, 379, 624
Cooper, R. E., 515
Cope, V., 167
Cords, W. L., 590
Cory, D. W., 186
Costanzo, P. R., 16, 19, 621
Cottrell, N., 559
Couch, A. S., 63, 642
Courrier, S., 233
Cowan, P., 603
Cowan, P. A., 272, 273
Coward, T. R., 618
Cox, D. F., 391
Cox, O. C., 333
Cox, V., 544
Cozby, P. C., 138, 139, 375, 542
Craig, K. D., 159
Craik, K. H., 511
Crandall, R., 559
Crane, V., 245
Crano, W. D., 394
Crawford, A. C., 161
Creedman, M., 655

Creedman, N., 655
Crockett, W. H., 87, 99, 632
Croft, R. G., 233
Crombag, H. F., 286
Cronbach, L. J., 43, 95, 107, 108, 109, 110
Crook, J. H., 216, 217, 218
Cross, H. J., 265, 573
Cross, K., 438
Crossley, H. M., 62
Crow, W. J., 109, 110
Crowne, D. P., 128, 392
Crump, E. P., 499
Crutchfield, R. S., 6, 317, 496, 610, 618, 619, 621, 622
Csoka, L. S., 638
Cullen, D. M., 327
Cunningham, M. R., 121, 122
Curry, T. J., 167
Cyert, R. M., 654
Czerlinsky, T., 119

Dabbs, J. M., 391, 516, 517
Dain, H. J., 188
Daly, J. D., 495
Damarin, F., 643
Dan, A. J., 459
D'Andrade, R., 448, 494
D'Angelo, R. Y., 482
Daniels, J., 4
Daniels, L. R., 302, 303
Danish, S. A., 309
Dank, B. M., 186
Darby, B. L., 122, 298
Darley, J. M., 36, 38, 39, 42, 43, 44, 56, 57, 81, 288, 289, 290, 293, 294, 295, 297, 300, 303, 306, 310, 379
Darley, S. A., 624
Darsie, M. L., 496
Dasen, P. R., 482
Davé, R. H., 507
Davenport, M., 303
Davies, J. C., 235, 236
Davis, A., 502
Davis, A. J., 185
Davis, D. E., 539
Davis, E., 338, 340
Davis, F. B., 504
Davis, G. E., 542
Davis, J. H., 560, 565, 566, 568, 638
Davis, K. E., 18, 22, 102, 120, 125, 130, 131, 162, 172, 177, 178, 192, 196, 199, 200, 201, 202, 203, 204, 207, 623
Davitz, J. R., 239, 560
Dawes, R. M., 284, 487
Day, C. B., 478
Day, H. R., 583
Dean, J., 138, 513, 518, 519
Dean, R. F. A., 483
Deanovich, B. F., 518
Deaux, K., 304, 359, 362, 447, 460, 465, 466, 467

deCharms, R. C., 348
deFleur, M. L., 344
DeLamater, J., 551, 552
Dellinger, W. S., 501
Dembo, T., 417
Dembroski, T. M., 392
Denenberg, V. H., 502
Deniels, A. K., 309
DeNinno, J., 150
Desor, J. A., 542
Deur, J. D., 239
Deutsch, M., 26, 27, 31, 38, 283, 396, 620
Devereux, E. G., Jr., 269
DeVries, D. L., 396
DeYoung, G. E., 206
Diamond, M. J., 424
Diamond, S., 516, 533
Dickson, W. J., 655
Diener, M. M., 501
Dienstbier, R. A., 159
Dillehay, R. C., 343, 587, 589
Dillon, P. C., 563
Dimond, R. E., 138
Dince, P. R., 188
Dinges, N. G., 519
Dion, K. K., 164,
Dion, K. L., 630, 631, 632
Dipboye, R. I., 469
Ditrichs, R., 239
Dittes, J. E., 153
Dmitruk, V. M., 271
Dobzhansky, T., 476
Dodge, J. S., 18
Doise, W., 632, 633
Dole, A. A., 496
Dollard, J., 19, 218, 219
Donley, R. E., 35, 36, 45
Donnerstein, E., 239
Donnerstein, M., 239
Doob, L. W., 218
Dooley, B., 542
Doppelt, J., 499
Dorris, J. W., 57
Douglas, V., 273
Douvan, E. A., 438, 460
Downs, R., 310
Downs, R. M., 511
Doyle, C., 83
Drake, D., 183
Draper, P., 238, 451, 537
Drauden, G., 562
Dreger, R. M., 479
Drellich, M. G., 188
Driscoll, J. M., 423
Driscoll, J. P., 182
Driscoll, R., 172
Driver, M., 306
Driver, M. J., 370
DuBois, P. H., 492
Du Bois, W. E. B., 483
Dubos, R., 536
Duchan, L., 469

Dudley, C. J., 202
Duff, D. F., 516
Duffy, J., 194
Duffy, J. F., 653
Dunn, L. C., 476
Dunn, R. E., 163, 286
Dunnette, M. D., 112, 563, 638
Durkheim, E., 553
Dutton, D. G., 122, 125, 173
Eachus, H. T., 285, 286
Eagleson, O. W., 324
Eagly, A., 359, 362, 363
Eaton, J. W., 228
Ebbesen, E. B., 352, 380, 381
Edney, J. J., 523, 524, 525, 526, 529
Edwards, A. L., 62
Edwards, C. P., 448, 451, 452
Edwards, D. G. A., 515, 516
Edwards, J., 618
Edwards, K. J., 283
Edwards, S., 532
Edwards, S. B., 217
Edwards, T., 130
Eells, K. W., 504
Efran, M. G., 523
Egleson, N., 603
Ehlert, J., 300
Ehlert, N., 300
Ehrhardt, A. A., 181, 183, 449
Ehrlich, J., 370
Ehrlich, H. J., 138, 139, 594
Ehrlich, P. R., 500, 542
Ehrmann, W., 202
Eibl-Eibesfeldt, I., 216
Eichenwald, H. F., 491, 501, 502
Eifler, D., 46, 453
Eisenberg, L., 229
Eiser, J. R., 357
Ekman, P., 141, 356
Elkind, D., 251, 642
Elkins, D., 142
Ellertson, N., 568
Elliott, R., 239
Ellis, A., 188, 195
Ellis, L. J., 463
Ellsworth, P. C., 133, 139
Elms, A. C., 31, 219, 586, 600
Emerson, R. M., 167
Emily, S. F., 542
Emswiller, T., 304, 466
Endler, N. S., 618, 623
Engelmann, S., 503
Enzie, R. I., 429
Eoyang, C. K., 544
Epley, S. W., 156
Epps, E. G., 494, 499
Epstein, R., 335
Epstein, Y. M., 541, 542, 545
Erickson, B., 541
Erickson, D. A., 608
Erickson, V., 268
Erikson, E. H., 248, 250, 287, 456
Erlebacher, A., 69
Erlenmeyer-Kimling, L., 487

Erlich, J., 64
Eron, L. D., 231
Erskine, H., 604
Ervin, C., 515
Escudero, M., 539
Esman, A., 334
Esser, A. H., 528
Etzioni, A., 599
Evans, G., 513
Evans, J. F., 150
Evans, R. B., 188, 190
Evans, R. I., 248, 249, 338, 392

Fairweather, G. W., 422, 424
Farber, J. E., 219
Farina, A., 127, 128
Farley, R., 483
Farris, E., 467
Fast, J., 141
Faucheux, C., 31, 618
Faust, W. L., 560
Fawl, C. L., 417
Feather, N. T., 370, 460, 466, 467
Feldman, K., 265
Feldman, R. E., 93, 94, 304
Feldman, S., 352
Feldman-Summers, S., 466
Felipe, N. J., 517
Felker, D. W., 154
Felknor, C., 88
Fendrich, J. M., 344
Fenichel, O., 246
Ferguson, G. O., Jr., 482
Ferkiss, V. C., 433
Ferritor, D. E., 285
Feshbach, S., 233, 234, 335, 416
Festinger, L., 25, 29, 73, 150, 167, 347, 366, 370, 373, 379, 380, 531, 553, 563, 569, 610
Fidell, L. S., 327, 468
Fiedler, F. E., 648, 649, 650, 651, 652, 653, 654
Field, P. B., 31, 391, 458
Fifer, G., 480, 504, 505
Figueroa, D., 112
Fink, H. C., 589
Finkelman, A., 9
Firestone, I. G., 153
Fisch, E., 292
Fischer, W. F., 291
Fish, B., 619
Fishbein, M., 97, 345, 347, 653
Fisher, J., 467
Fisher, J. D., 309, 424, 518
Fisher, J. E., 461
Fishkin, J., 261, 268
Fiske, D. W., 318
Fitch, H. G., 366
Flacks, R., 435
Flanagan, M. F., 341
Flanders, J. P., 631
Flaschman, S., 487
Flavell, J. H., 264

Fleishman, E. A., 644, 645
Flerx, V. C., 453
Floyd, J., 163, 164
Flyger, V., 539
Flynn, J. P., 217
Flynn, J. T., 423
Fode, K. L., 68
Fogelson, R., 207
Folger, R., 367
Fontana, A., 268
Form, W. H., 303
Formica, R., 153
Forrester, B. J., 494
Fortune, R. F., 228
Foulds, G. A., 499
Fox, D., 560
Fraczek, A., 225
Fraser, C., 563, 564, 631, 633
Fraser, S. C., 121, 122, 309, 618
Freedman, J. L., 121, 122, 309, 370, 378,
    538, 539, 542, 618
Freedman, M., 185, 188
Freeman, H. A., 199
Freeman, H. E., 429
Freeman, R. S., 199
French, E. G., 504
French, J. R. P., Jr., 657
Frenkel-Brunswik, E., 15, 319
Freshley, H. B., 304
Freud, E. L., 79
Freud, S., 13, 83, 140, 141, 215, 245, 456,
    600
Freund, K., 205
Frey, D., 372
Fried, M. H., 478
Fried, S., 73
Friedenberg, E. Z., 438
Friedman, S. T., 544
Friedrich, L. K., 452
Friesen, W. V., 141
Frieze, I. H., 463, 467
Fri_ch, D. M., 306
Frodi, A., 225
Fromkin, H. L., 86, 341, 367, 424, 469
Fromm, E., 253
Fry, P. C., 491, 501, 502
Fryer, D., 499
Fugita, S. S., 126
Fuller, J. P., 516
Funk, W. H., 563
Furbush, A. M., 539
Furlong, M. J., 438

Gabriele, T., 545
Gaebelein, J. W., 220, 221
Gaertner, S. L., 304, 345, 346
Gage, N. L., 63, 107, 109
Gagnon, J. H., 177, 191
Galizio, M., 391
Galle, O. R., 539
Gallup, G. H., 60
Galton, F., 499
Gamson, W. A., 422

Gans, H. J., 531
Garai, J. E., 458
Garber, H., 503
Gardner, H., 237, 441, 442
Garland, H., 118
Garrett, H. E., 479, 480
Garrrett, J. B., 376
Garth, T. R., 482
Garwood, S. G., 325
Gates, A. I., 501
Gates, G. P., 566
Gatewood, R., 306
Gatz, M., 173
Gay, J., 493
Geary, J., 604
Geber, M., 482, 489
Gebhard, P. H., 184
Gecas, V., 169
Geen, R. G., 217, 223, 224, 229, 230,
    231, 536
Geer, J. H., 205, 295
Geis, F. L., 134, 135, 136, 347, 623, 642
Gelfand, D. M., 300
Gelman, R., 264
Gentry, W. D., 220, 230
Gerard, H. B., 153, 169, 569, 620
Gergen, K. J., 18, 31, 32, 72, 118, 119,
    120, 125, 130, 131, 132, 138, 285,
    301, 623
Gergen, M. M., 301
Germann, A. C., 424
Geschwender, J. A., 236
Gesell, A., 264
Getzels, J. W., 404
Gibaud-Wallston, J., 572
Gibb, C. A., 638, 643, 645
Gibson, S., 516
Gilchrist, J. C., 639
Ginsburg, B. E., 476, 477
Ginsburg, G. P., 393, 630
Girand, H. G., 188
Glass, B., 476, 478
Glass, D. C., 531, 536, 542
Glass, G. V., 50
Glassner, W. J., 625
Gleason, J. M., 100
Gliha, D., 127
Goethals, G. R., 173, 373
Goethals, G. W., 237
Goffman, E., 18, 117, 127, 523, 527
Goldberg, G. N., 518
Goldberg, L. R., 63
Goldberg, P. A., 465
Goldberg, S. C., 617
Golden, B. W., 394
Golden, J., 195, 196
Goldman, J. R., 269
Goldman, M., 286
Goldsmith, N. F., 327
Goldstein, M. J., 204, 207, 230
Goller, W. C., 516
Gomes, B., 328, 464
Gonzaga, G. P., 449

Goode, W., 170
Goodman, L. W., 453
Goodman, W., 607
Goodwin, L., 333
Goranson, R. E., 306, 535
Gordon, K., 560
Gordon, P., 539
Gordon, S., 466
Gorer, G., 228
Gorlow, L., 622
Gossett, T. F., 475
Gouge, C., 563, 633
Gough, H. G., 62
Gouldner, A. W., 305, 628
Gove, W. R., 539
Graen, G., 648, 652, 653
Graeven, D. B., 138, 139
Grafstein, D., 202
Graham, D., 618
Graham, H. D., 236
Graham, W. K., 563
Granberg, D., 358, 588
Grandjean, E., 532
Gray, D. B., 319
Gray, M. J., 31
Gray, S. W., 491, 492, 500, 502, 503
Greaves, G., 88
Green, D., 380
Green, J. A., 343
Green, R., 181, 183
Green, R. F., 482, 483
Green, R. L., 500
Greenbaum, C., 494
Greenberg, B. S., 51
Greenberg, C. I., 543
Greenberg, M. S., 100, 306, 309
Greene, M. S., 527
Greenfield, N., 532
Greenfield, S. M., 170
Greenwald, A. G., 381, 382
Greenwood, J. M., 646
Gregg, C. F., 202, 203
Gregor, G. L., 538
Gregory, D., 568
Greif, E. B., 270
Grether, J., 137
Griffitt, W., 161, 207, 535, 541
Grinder, R. E., 252
Gross, A. E., 297, 300, 303, 304, 306, 309
Gross, S., 9
Grossack, M. M., 237, 441, 442
Groves, W. E., 202
Gruen, W., 504
Gruenfeld, L. W., 650
Grusec, J. E., 293
Guetzkow, H., 56
Gullahorn, J. T., 532
Guller, I. B., 594
Gump, P. V., 28
Gumpert, P., 132
Gumpper, D. C., 73
Gundlach, R. H., 188
Gunn, S. P. 101, 102, 103, 263

Gurin, G., 64, 83, 325, 495
Gurin, P., 83, 325, 495
Gurnee, H., 560
Gurr, T. R., 211, 236
Gusfield, J., 431
Gutkin, D. C., 256, 264
Gutmann, D., 460
Guttman, I., 370

Haaland, G., 631
Haan, N., 246, 265, 266, 435
Hass, K., 600
Haase, R. S., 519
Hackman, J. R., 564
Hagen, E. E., 429
Haggstrom, W. C., 309
Hain, J. D., 205
Haines, D. B., 285
Hake, D. F., 220
Hall, C. S., 6, 7, 12, 13, 215, 237, 600
Hall, E. T., 511, 513, 514, 515, 516, 518
Hall, K. R. L., 218
Halpin, A. W., 644, 645, 646, 647
Hamblin, R. L., 285, 286
Hamilton, C. V., 323
Hamilton, D. L., 103
Hammer, T. H., 643
Hammond, K. R., 110
Haney, C., 54, 55
Hanratty, M. A., 220
Hanusa, B. H., 467
Harari, H., 20, 324, 325
Harburg, E., 378
Harding, J., 319, 320
Hardyck, J. A., 161, 338
Harlow, H. F., 174, 175
Harpin, R. E., 544
Harré, R., 31, 44
Harrell, J. V., 64
Harrell, M. S., 499, 507
Harrell, R. F., 501
Harrell, T. W., 499, 507
Harris, A. S., 327
Harris, E. F., 645
Harris, V. A., 103
Harris, Y. Y., 496
Harrison, A. A., 168
Harrison, R. P., 140
Harshbarger, D., 5
Hart, H., 309, 478, 619
Hartley, E. L., 367
Hartley, S., 618
Hartman, A. A., 325
Hartmann, D. P., 223, 300
Hartmann, H., 216
Hartnett, J., 516
Hartshorne, H., 252
Harvey, J. H., 100, 379, 393
Harvey, O. J., 86, 88, 89, 239, 253, 357
Hastad, D. N., 590
Hastorf, A. H., 104
Hatch, G., 653
Hatchett, S., 64

Hathaway, S. R., 62
Hauer, A. L., 309
Havel, J., 63
Havens, E., 165
Havighurst, R. J., 12, 252, 253
Hawkins, G., 341
Hay, W. M., 221
Hays, D. G., 393
Haythorne, W. W., 544
Haywood, H. C., 501
Head, K. B., 35, 213
Heavenrick, J., 272
Hebb, D. O., 31, 149, 502
Heber, R., 503
Hedblom, J. H., 186
Heffron, E. F., 420
Heider, F., 25, 100, 165, 170, 364
Heilbroner, R. L., 92
Heiman, J. R., 205
Heingartner, A., 265
Hellkamp, D. T., 138
Helmreich, R. L., 153, 163, 164, 165, 372, 379, 462, 552
Helson, H., 357, 513, 544
Hemphill, J. K., 644, 646
Henchy, J., 494
Henchy, T., 72, 73
Hendrick, C., 6, 32, 97, 162, 341, 391, 393
Henley, M. D., 372
Hentoff, N., 603
Hermalin, A., 483
Herold, P. L., 588
Herrnstein, R. J., 269, 500
Herzberg, F., 659
Herzog, E., 334
Heshka, S., 515
Heslin, R., 542, 563
Heslin, R. E., 89
Hess, E. H., 216
Hess, R. D., 502, 503
Hetherington, M. E., 264, 273
Heussenstamm, F. K., 49
Heuyer, G., 499
Hewitt, L. S., 220
Hicks, R. A., 489
Higbee, K. L., 138, 415
Higgins, J., 589
Hildum, D., 63, 356
Hilgard, E. R., 64, 634
Hill, W. A., 652
Hillmer, M. L., 163
Hills, L. R., 366
Hiltner, S., 86
Hilton, J., 154
Himmelweit, H., 229
Hinds, W. C., 632
Hinkle, S. W., 429
Hirota, K., 566
Hobson, C., 491
Hochman, L., 593
Hochreich, D. J., 81
Hodge, R. W., 496, 498

Hodgkinson, H., 433, 434
Hoenig, J., 182
Hoff, E., 112
Hoffer, E., 13
Hoffman, L. W., 459
Hoffman, M., 185, 189
Hoffman, M. L., 254
Hogan, R., 274
Hokada, E., 46, 453
Hokanson, J. E., 229, 238
Holdren, J. P., 500
Holland, C. C., 599
Hollander, E. P., 22, 587, 589, 627, 628, 650, 653, 654
Hollingshead, A. B., 539
Holmes, D. S., 72, 459, 516
Holmes, M., 292
Holstein, C. E., 246, 254, 268
Holsti, O. R., 57
Holt, R., 565
Homans, G. C., 19, 20, 132
Homant, R., 40
Honigmann, J. J., 228
Hood, W. E., 239
Hood, W. R., 616
Hook, H., 520
Hook, S., 639, 641, 642
Hooker, E., 188, 189
Hoople, H., 518
Hoppe, R. A., 527
Horn, N., 297
Horner, M. S., 459, 460
Horney, K., 13, 456
Hornstein, H. A., 292
Horowitz, M. J., 516
Horton, C. P., 499
Hostetler, J. A., 574
Houston, J. D., 330
Houston, J. W., 330
Hovland, C. I., 354, 357, 359, 393, 394
Howard, A., 228
Howard, E., 522
Howard, J., 235
Howard, J. L., 205
Howard, P., 532
Howard, R. B., 513
Howe, I., 602
Hoyt, G. C., 631
Hoyt, J. L., 224
Hoyt, M. F., 155, 372
Huesman, L. R., 231
Huffman, L. J., 103
Huffman, P. E., 588
Hughes, J. W., 16
Hughston, K., 274
Hulin, C., 660
Humphreys, L., 185, 186, 191
Hundert, A. J., 532
Hunt, D. E., 86, 88, 253
Hunt, J. G., 648, 649
Hunt, J. McV., 157, 502, 623, 624
Hunt, M., 185, 196, 198
Hunter, R., 97

Hurley, J., 325
Husa, F. T., 325
Husband, R. W., 560
Huston, T. L., 301
Hutchinson, R. R., 220
Hutt, C., 544
Huxley, A., 441, 602
Hyman, H. H., 62, 64, 591
Hymovitch, B., 569

Ickes, W. J., 559
Ikemi, Y., 634
Ilg, F. M., 264
Ilgen, D. R., 469
Ingham, R., 518, 519
Ingram, A., 31
Inkster, J. A., 371
Insko, C. A., 318, 339, 346, 354, 355, 356, 358, 360, 361, 362, 365, 372, 393, 394
Irle, M., 372
Isaacs, S., 264
Isen, A. M., 296, 297
Israel, J., 31
Ittelson, W., 511, 512, 544
Iverson, M. A., 163
Ivey, M. E., 449
Izzett, R., 342, 589

Jaastad, K., 563
Jacklin, C. N., 448, 450, 458
Jackson, J., 328, 464
Jackson, D. N., 63, 103, 616, 627
Jackson, V. W., 339
Jackson-White, R., 461
Jacobs, R. C., 428
Jacobson, L., 69, 495
Jacoby, J., 594
Jaffe, D., 578
Jahoda, M., 587, 613, 614, 615
James, J. W., 518, 541
Jamieson, B. D., 631
Janis, I. L., 31, 354, 391, 458, 560, 561, 564
Jarmecky, L., 295
Jellison, J. M., 393, 461
Jenkins, J. J., 19
Jenkins, L., 280
Jenkins, M. D., 480
Jenness, A., 560
Jensen, A. R., 479, 485, 486, 487, 500, 501
Jensen, B. T., 399
Jensen, D. L., 134
Jensen, L. C., 274
Jerdee, T. H., 327, 469
Joesting, J., 327
Johnson, D. L., 563, 631
Johnson, H., 588
Johnson, R. C., 594
Johnson, R. F. Q., 634
Johnson, V. E., 193, 194, 195
Johnston, S., 100

Jones, E. E., 18, 22, 100, 101, 102, 103, 119, 120, 125, 130, 131, 132, 133, 628
Jones, J. M., 337
Jones, K., 520
Jones, R., 348
Jones, R. A., 6, 367
Jones, R. G., 132
Jordan-Edney, N. L., 526
Jorgensen, B. W., 162, 459, 564
Jorgensen, C., 183, 476, 477
Jourard, S. M., 138, 139
Jovanovic, U. J., 205
Julian, J. W., 654

Kaats, G. R., 88, 89, 177, 178, 192, 196, 199, 200, 201, 202, 203, 204, 207
Kafrissen, S. R., 420
Kahn, R. L., 35, 61, 64, 213, 661
Kaiman, I. P., 594
Kalven, H., Jr., 565
Kamin, L. J., 485, 487
Kamzan, L., 303
Kamzan, M., 304
Kanter, R. M., 574, 575, 578
Kaplan, A., 532
Kaplan, B. E., 390
Kaplan, J. A., 161, 310
Kaplan, K. J., 153, 619
Kaplan, M. F., 501
Karabenick, S. A., 304, 594
Kardiner, A., 495
Karlin, R. A., 541, 542, 545
Karlins, M., 331, 393, 394
Karnes, M. B., 503
Karoly, P., 164
Karon, B. P., 495
Katchadourian, H. A., 185, 189, 191, 207
Katcher, A., 222
Kateb, G., 601
Katz, D., 382, 383, 385, 661
Katz, I., 494, 495
Katz, J., 202
Katz, L. B., 85, 86
Kauffman, D. R., 130
Kaufmann, H., 6, 7, 20
Kavanagh, M. J., 653
Kawash, G. F., 206
Kaye, D., 391
Keasey, C. B., 273
Keen, S., 602
Keiffer, M. G., 327
Keller, K., 137
Kelley, H. H., 20, 21, 22, 24, 31, 102, 104, 167, 354, 569, 631
Kelly, G. A., 86, 87
Kelly, G. F., 191, 192
Kelly, M., 360
Kelman, H. C., 72, 342, 589, 610, 613
Kemeny, J. G., 36, 38
Kemp, C. G., 594
Keniston, K., 63, 261, 268, 435, 436, 437

Kenna, J. C., 182
Kenny, J. W., 527
Kepner, C. R., 230
Kerckhoff, A. C., 162, 169
Kerlinger, F. N., 592
Kerner, O., 235
Kerr, N. L., 565
Kerr, R., 496
Kerr, S., 645, 648
Key, W. H., 303
Kibler, B. K., 324
Kiesler, C. A., 342, 354, 358, 373, 379, 382, 383, 384, 385, 386, 518, 608, 610, 613, 617
Kiesler, S. B., 130, 465, 466, 608, 610, 613
Kilham, P., 477
Kilham, W., 600
Kimble, G. A., 19
Kimbrell, D. L., 272
Kimmel, E., 327
King, D., 535
King, D. C., 424
King, K., 202
King, M. G., 518, 541
Kinkade, K., 577
Kinkead, E., 611
Kinsey, A. C., 183, 184, 195, 196
Kipnis, D. M., 167
Kirmeyer, S., 546
Kirschner, P., 391
Kirscht, J. P., 587, 589
Kirtley, D., 594
Klaiber, E. L., 449
Klaus, R. A., 491, 492, 494, 500, 503
Kleck, R. E., 516
Kleeman, J. L., 91
Kleiber, D., 83
Kleinke, C. L., 380
Klevansky, S., 542
Klimoski, R. J., 341
Kline, N. S., 528
Kline, P., 254
Klineberg, O., 329, 480, 482, 491, 495
Klopfer, P. H., 477
Kluckhohn, C., 434
Knapp, M. L., 140
Knapper, C., 96
Knight, G. W., 118
Knight, H. C., 560
Knob, K. A., 205
Knobloch, H., 494, 501
Knowles, E. S., 523
Knox, R. E., 371
Knurek, D. A., 224
Kobayashi, Y., 449
Koenig, K., 589
Koffka, W., 21, 22
Kogan, N., 623, 629, 630, 631
Kohl, J., 309, 619
Kohlberg, L., 253, 254, 259, 260, 261, 263, 264, 267, 268, 269, 273, 274, 435

Köhler, W., 22
Kolstoe, R. H., 220
Komarovsky, M., 461
Komorita, S. S., 335, 403
Konečni, V. J., 298
Koning, H., 419
Korman, A. K., 644
Korn, R. R., 305
Korner, A. F., 502
Korte, C., 295, 301
Koulack, D., 362
Kovel, J., 345
Kramer, B. M., 335
Kramer, R., 268, 269
Krasner, L., 83
Krauss, R. M., 38
Kraut, R. E., 123
Krebs, D. L., 300, 306
Krebs, R., 265
Krech, D., 6, 317, 321, 322, 496, 610,
    617, 618
Kremer, M. W., 188
Kris, E., 216
Kronhausen, E., 206
Kronhausen, P., 206
Krug, R. E., 590
Krupat, E., 112, 545
Kruskal, W. H., 35
Ktsanes, T., 162
Ktsanes, V., 162
Kuhn, D., 459, 460
Kuhn, D. Z., 227
Kuhn, T. S., 31, 36, 40, 73, 641
Kurtines, W., 270
Kushner, H., 149
Kutchinsky, B., 51, 206, 207
Kutner, B., 319, 343

Lagarspertz, K., 218
Lake, R. A., 122
Lambert, W. E., 120
Lambert, W. W., 20
Lamberth, J., 515
Lamm, H., 563
Lana, R., 394
Landsberger, H. A., 655
Landsman, M. J., 139
Landy, D., 165
Landy, E., 653
Lang, G., 634
Lang, J., 511
Langer, J., 272
Langman, B., 111
Langmeyer, D., 463
Lanier, L. H., 482, 491
Lantz, H. R., 539
Lanzetta, J. T., 31
Lao, R. C., 83, 325, 495
LaPiere, R. T., 342
Larson, D. L., 659
Lasakow, P., 138, 139
Lasater, T. M., 392
Latané, B., 36, 38, 39, 42, 43, 44, 56, 57,

Latané, B. (continued)
    81, 150, 288, 289, 290, 293, 294,
    295, 300, 303, 306, 310
Laufer, R. S., 438
Laughlin, W. S., 476, 477
LaVoie, J. C., 69, 272
Lawler, E. E., 638, 659
Lawrence, J., 9, 25
Lawrence, L. H., 589
Lawson, E. D., 325
Lawton, S. F., 535
Lay, C. H., 103
Layton, B., 541
Layzer, D., 487
Lazarus, R. S., 537
Leach, C., 100
Leaman, R. L., 87
Lear, J., 71
Leavitt, E. A., 499
Leavitt, G. S., 63
Leavitt, H. J., 566
LeBon, G., 553
Lee, D., 594
Lee, E. S., 491
LeFan, J., 163, 165
Lefkowitz, M. M., 231
Legant, P., 100
Lehmann, S., 415, 416
Lehrer, L., 273
Leipold, W. D., 516
Lemert, E. M., 23
Lennox, V. L., 125
LePage, A., 224, 225
Lerner, E., 264
Lerner, M. J., 84, 85, 86, 298
Lerner, R. M., 304
Lesser, G. S., 480, 504, 505, 623
Lesser, I. M., 246, 254
Lett, E. E., 528
Levenson, H., 31
Lever, J., 453
Levin, F. M., 138
Levin, H., 228, 239, 254, 413, 452
Levin, P. F., 297
Levine, E. M., 453
Levine, F. J., 112
Levine, J. M., 617
Levine, S., 502
Levinger, G., 138, 139, 161, 162, 163
Levinson, D. J., 15, 319, 588
Levy, J., 616
Levy, L., 620
Levy, M., 135
Levy, S. G., 235
Lewin, A. Y., 469
Lewin, K., 25, 26, 27, 138, 416, 417, 420,
    511, 658
Lewis, E. C., 457
Lewis, L. D., 295
Lewis, O., 547
Lewis, R. A., 169
Lewis, S. A., 165
Lewis, S. K., 122

Leyens, J. P., 230, 233, 234
Leyhausen, P., 522, 528
Li, C. C., 478
Libman, E., 120
Lieberman, M. A., 571
Liebhart, E. H., 303
Lief, H. I., 194
Lien, D., 295
Lifton, R. J., 48
Lindgren, H. C., 589
Lindner, R., 97
Lindzey, G., 6, 7, 12, 13, 215, 237, 600
Lingle, J. H., 603
Linn, L. S., 343
Linton, P. H., 205
Lipetz, M. E., 172
Lipinski, C. E., 155
Lippitt, G. L., 418
Lippitt, R., 418, 569, 658
Liptzin, M. B., 205
Little, K. B., 516
Livesay, T. M., 496, 499
Llewellyn-Thomas, E., 231
Lobitz, W. C., 424
Loewenstein, R. M., 216
Loftus, E. F., 112
Logan, R. W., 475, 478
Loiselle, R. H., 205
Lombardo, J. P., 280, 291
London, P., 300, 305
London, R. S., 516
Lonetto, R., 638
Long, B. H., 594
Loo, C. M., 544
Lopes, L. L., 97
Lorenz, K., 213, 214, 216, 217, 229, 237,
    522
Lorge, I., 560
Lott, A. J., 569
Lott, B. E., 569
Lottier, S., 539
Louis-Guérin, C., 563
Lubell, S., 438
Lublin, S. C., 554
Lucas, O., 9
Luce, R. D., 284
Luchins, A. S., 98, 99
Luckey, E., 201
Luft, J., 516
Lund, F., 394
Lunde, D. T., 185, 189, 191, 207
Lussier, R. I., 83
Lyman, S. M., 523
Lynch, S., 435
Lynn, D. B., 182
Lyons, T. F., 653

Macaulay, J. R., 225, 292
Maccoby, E. E., 228, 239, 254, 448, 450,
    452, 458
MacCrimmon, K. R., 654
MacDonald, A. P., Jr., 155, 375, 377
MacDougald, D., Jr., 194

Machiavelli, N., 134
Mack, R., 434
Mackenzie, K. D., 629
MacKinney, A. C., 653
MacKinnon, C., 261, 268
MacNeil, M. K., 429
MacRae, D., 264
Madaras, G. R., 348, 632
Madsen, C. H., Jr., 227
Madsen, M. C., 287
Magruder, J. S., 124
Mahoney, E. R., 517
Maitland, K. A., 269
Majumder, R. K., 375, 377
Malamud, P., 231, 239
Maller, J. B., 252
Mallick, S. K., 220, 239
Mandell, W., 394
Mander, A., 221
Mann, F. C., 660
Mann, J., 205, 206
Mann, J. H., 321
Mann, L., 600
Mann, R. D., 563, 638
Maracek, J., 100
Marcia, J. E., 246, 254
Marcus, S., 204
Marcuse, H., 601, 602
Markle, A., 488
Markley, O. W., 360
Marks, E. S., 64
Marks, R. W., 601, 602
Marlatt, G. A., 390
Marlowe, D., 128, 392, 623
Marony, J. H., 188
Marquis, D. G., 631
Marriott, C., 5
Marrow, A. J., 657, 658
Marsden, H. M., 539
Marsella, A. J., 539
Marshall, J. E., 542
Marston, W. M., 560
Martella, J. A., 648
Martin, C. E., 183, 184
Martin, J., 342, 588
Martindale, D. A., 529
Marx, G. T., 235
Masangkay, Z. S., 264
Maslow, A. H., 534, 659
Massie, R. K., 8, 10, 14
Masters, R. E. L., 196
Masters, W. H., 193, 194, 195
Matas, C., 624
Mathewson, G. D., 169
Matlin, M. W., 168
Matthews, D., 84
Mattson, A., 9
Mausner, B., 659
May, M. A., 252
Maykovich, M. K., 325
Mayo, C. W., 87, 99
Mayo, E., 655
Mbiti, J. S., 495

McArthur, L. A., 100
McArthur, L. Z., 452
McBride, D., 568
McBride, G., 518, 541
McCain, G., 544
McCall, G. J., 169
McCandless, B. R., 220, 239, 588
McCarrey, M., 532
McCarthy, J., 594
McCarthy, P. J., 64
McCary, J. L., 179, 181, 191, 193, 194,
    195, 196, 199
McCauley, C. R., 633
McClay, D., 518
McClearn, G. E., 218
McClintock, C. G., 384, 385
McCluskey, K. A., 264
McConnell, H. K., 380
McCord, J., 228
McCord, W., 228, 235
McCorkle, L. W., 305
McCrimmon, J., 173
McDavid, J. W., 20, 325, 458
McDill, M., 329
McDonald, F. J., 272, 273, 274
McDonald, P. J., 461
McDougall, W., 244, 253
McDowell, K. V., 518
McGarry, J., 393
McGarvey, W., 365
McGee, R., 432
McGhee, P. E., 621
McGinnies, E., 356, 393, 394, 650
McGinniss, J., 142
McGrath, J. E., 552
McGregor, D., 655, 659
McGrew, P. L., 541
McGuire, W. J., 31, 73, 318, 351, 352,
    391, 392, 415, 623
McHugh, M. C., 467
McIntyre, C. W., 264, 273
McKay, H. D., 539
McKeachie, W. J., 285
McKinley, J. C., 62
McKinney, T. T., 478
McKusick, V. A., 15
McLaughlin, C., 545
McLuhan, M., 24
McMahon, I. D., 467
McManis, D. L., 245
McMillan, D., 572
McMillen, D. L., 298
McNamara, W. J., 646
McNeel, S. P., 378
McNemar, Q., 457, 498
McPartland, J., 491
McPherson, J. M., 539
Mead, G. H., 18, 19, 117, 250
Mead, M., 228, 436, 437
Meadow, A., 563
Meehl, P. E., 62
Meek, D., 565
Meeker, M., 504

Megargee, E. I., 229, 238
Meggyesy, D., 654
Mehrabian, A., 515, 516, 518, 533
Meier, G. W., 502
Meir, E. I., 659
Meisels, M., 516
Melville, K., 573, 574, 576, 577, 578
Menaker, S. L., 83
Menne, J. M. C., 531
Merbaum, A. D., 494
Mercer, J., 492
Meredith, H. W., 218
Merrens, M. R., 300
Merrill, M. A., 457
Merton, R. K., 27, 167
Messé, L. A., 301
Messick, D. M., 378
Messick, S., 63, 616, 627
Mesthene, E. G., 433
Meter, K., 301
Mettee, D. R., 164, 168
Meyberg, V., 205
Meyer, R. G., 423
Meyer, T. P., 224
Mezei, L., 340, 624
Michael, S. T., 586
Michelini, R. L., 301
Michelson, W., 511, 531, 540
Midlarsky, E., 293
Midlarsky, M., 236
Milavsky, B., 222
Miles, M. B., 571
Miley, C. H., 154
Milgram, S., 53, 71, 81, 82, 265, 310,
    431, 545, 559, 595, 596, 597, 598,
    599, 600
Miller, A. G., 287
Miller, G. A., 94, 411
Miller, H., 87, 394, 632
Miller, J. S., 186
Miller, K. S., 479
Miller, L. K., 286
Miller, N. E., 19, 218, 219, 220, 229, 342,
    354, 382, 383, 391, 630, 631
Miller, Norman, 153, 362
Miller, W. E., 64
Mills, C. W., 657
Mills, J., 169, 370, 379, 394
Milton, G. A., 127
Milton, O., 589
Mintz, N. L., 534, 535
Mischel, H., 465
Mischel, W., 231, 452, 456, 623
Mitchell, R. E., 238, 541
Mitnick, L., 356
Modigliani, A., 118
Moleski, W., 511
Mollenauer, S., 205
Monahan, L., 459, 460
Money, J., 181, 182, 183, 449
Monson, T. C., 142
Montagu, M. F. A., 218, 477
Montgomery, R. L., 429

Mood, A., 491
Moore, B. S., 297
Moore, W., 428
Moorehead, A., 18, 25
Morgan, L. B., 440
Moriarity, T., 295
Morin, S. F., 186, 187
Morris, D., 229
Morton, J. R. C., 502
Moscovici, S., 31, 563, 608, 617, 618, 632, 633
Mosher, D. L., 204, 205, 206
Moss, H. A., 454
Moss, M. K., 161, 291
Mosteller, F., 40, 64
Mostert, N., 433
Mouchanow, M., 14, 15, 16
Mouton, J. S., 532
Mowrer, O. H., 218
Moyer, K. E., 217
Mullens, S., 517
Mulvihill, D. J., 221
Munson, P. A., 373, 386
Munter, P. O., 159
Munz, D. C., 138
Murphy, C. J., 648
Murphy, R. J., 235
Murray, E. J., 341
Murstein, B. I., 166
Mussen, P., 395, 494, 588
Mutterer, M. L., 252
Myers, D. G., 563, 564, 632, 633

Nadler, A., 309
Naeye, R. L., 501
Nakagawa, S., 634
Nangle, J., 51
Nass, G. D., 201
Nataupsky, M., 370
Nathanson, M., 273
Neary, J., 489
Nebergall, R. E., 357
Neff, F. W., 423, 434
Neidermayer, H., 159
Neiman, L. J., 16
Nelson, C., 96, 136
Nelson E. A., 252
Nelson, P. A., 528
Nelson, S. D., 29
Nelson, Y., 515
Nemecek, J., 532
Nemeth, C., 285
Neufeld, E., 463
Neulinger, J., 328
Newbrough, J. R., 421, 428
Newcomb, T. M., 161, 317, 352, 378, 531, 553
Newman, O., 512, 530
Newton, P., 186
Newtson, D., 119
Nias, D. K. B., 591
Nicolay, R. C., 325

Noble, F. C., 90
Nobles, W. W., 495
Noel, B., 268
Noel, R., 56
Nord, W. R., 617
Nosow, S., 303
Novak, D., 84
Nutt, R. L., 199
Nuttin, J. M., Jr., 31

Oakes, W. F., 69, 415
Oberschall, A., 431
O'Connor, J., 243, 269, 284, 395
Oetting, E. R., 519
O'Hara, J., 518
O'Leary, V. E., 470
Oliver, L., 453
O'Neal, E. C., 220, 222, 223, 461, 536
Orlofsky, J. L., 246, 254
Orne, M. T., 67, 599, 634
Orpen, C., 590
Orris, J. B., 648
Orwell, G., 41, 441, 603
Osborn, A. F., 560, 564
Osgood, C. E., 365
Oskamp, S., 77, 105, 168
Osmond, H., 534
Osterhouse, R. A., 391
Ostrom, T. M., 565
Ovesey, L., 182, 495

Pack, S. J., 126
Packard, V., 201, 203
Page, B., 300
Page, E. B., 504
Page, M. M., 225, 356
Page, R. A., 291
Paige, J. M., 32, 235
Palmer, J. C., 112
Panos, R. J., 154
Parke, R. D., 156, 233, 239, 272
Parker, E. G., 51
Parker, H. B., 538
Parlee, M. B., 449, 450
Parnes, S. J., 563
Parry, H. J., 62
Parsons, H. M., 655
Pasamanick, B. A., 494
Paskal, V., 280
Patchen, M., 385
Patterson, A. H., 544
Patterson, M. C., 516, 517, 519
Paulus, P., 544
Payne, S. L., 64
Peabody, D., 593
Peck, R. F., 12, 252, 253
Pederson, D. M., 138
Pellegrini, R. J., 489
Penman, K. A., 590
Penner, L., 40
Pepitone, A., 369, 553
Percival, E., 220
Perin, C. T., 88

Perlman, D., 32, 168, 202, 203, 293
Person, E., 182
Peters, D. R., 644
Peterson, J., 491
Peterson, J. H., 334
Peterson, L., 532
Peterson, M., 423
Peterson, P. D., 362
Peterson, V. J., 482
Petronko, M. R., 88
Pettigrew, T. F., 329, 336, 479, 487, 491, 501
Pfeiffer, J. R., 516
Phares, E. J., 83, 393
Pheterson, G. I., 465
Phillips, D. P., 5
Piaget, J., 253, 255, 256, 257, 286
Piliavin, I. M., 57, 294, 295, 303, 304, 307, 309
Piliavin, J. I., 57, 151, 279, 294, 295, 303, 307
Pilkey, D. W., 206
Pinner, B., 238, 541
Pintner, R., 496
Pisano, R., 220
Pizer, S. A., 427
Pliner, P., 309, 619
Plog, S. C., 138
Polanyi, M., 40
Polefka, J., 104
Poley, W., 589
Pollock, H. M., 539
Pomazal, R. J., 303
Pomeroy, W. B., 183, 184
Poor, D., 589
Poppen, P. J., 266
Popper, K. R., 40
Porter, E., 516
Porter, J. A., 330
Poser, E. G., 120
Potter, D. A., 104
Potter, E. H., 453
Prentice, N. M., 273
Preston, M., 560
Price, C. R., 419
Price, G. H., 516
Price, J. L., 544
Price, K. O., 378
Primrose, C., 182
Prince, V., 182
Prociuk, T. J., 83
Proshansky, H., 186, 319, 511, 512, 544
Proster, J. J., 542
Prothro, E. T., 329
Pruesse, M., 206
Pruitt, D. G., 285, 306, 631, 632, 633
Pruyn, E. L., 573
Puthoff, C., 341

Rabbie, J. M., 31, 153, 285
Rada, J. B., 598, 600
Radloff, R., 150
Raiffa, H., 284

Rakosky, J. J., 223
Rall, M., 238, 541
Ralls, K., 217
Ramchandra, V., 367
Rance, D. E., 650
Rand, A., 281
Ransford, H. E., 238
Rapoport, A., 284
Raser, J., 602
Ratcliffe, J. M., 310
Rather, D., 566
Raven, B. H., 155, 285, 286, 569
Raven, J. C., 499
Rawlings, E. I., 297
Rawson, H. E., 270
Raymond, B. J., 624, 625
Rechy, J., 185
Redl, F., 28
Redlich, F. C., 539
Reed, T. E., 478
Reedy, G., 642
Rees, M. B., 591
Regan, D. T., 137
Reich, C. A., 437, 601, 602
Reichart, S., 438
Reifler, C. B., 205
Reis, E. E. S., 157
Reiss, I., 199
Renz, P., 495
Resko, B. G., 452
Resnick, S., 541, 543, 545
Rest, J. R., 268, 269
Restle, F., 560
Rettig, S., 270
Reuben, D., 180
Revelle, W., 319
Rhamey, R., 167
Rhead, C. C., 532
Rhine, R., 357
Richards, J. M., Jr., 110
Richardson, S. A., 63
Rider, R. V., 501
Riesman, D., 64, 253, 625, 626
Riess, M., 518
Rifkin, A. H., 188
Ring, K., 155, 412, 413
Ritchie, E., 393
Rittle, R., 559
Rivlin, L., 511, 512, 544
Roberts, P. F., 478
Roberts, R. E., 574, 576, 577, 578
Robinson, D., 64
Robinson, D. L., 395
Robinson, E., 393, 394
Robinson, J. E., 202, 339
Rodgers, H. L., Jr., 360
Rodin, J., 57, 159, 294, 295, 303, 449
Roethlisberger, F. J., 655
Rogers, C. R., 79, 658
Rogers, E. M., 165, 420
Rogers, R. W., 453, 598, 600
Rohde, S., 64
Rohe, W., 544

Rohrer, J. H., 495
Rokeach, M., 40, 85, 161, 316, 317, 338, 339, 340, 592, 593, 594, 624
Rollin, B., 180
Romano, J., 517
Roper, G., 633
Rorer, L. G., 63, 591
Rose, A. M., 334
Rosen, B., 327, 469
Rosen, B. C., 494
Rosen, E., 342, 588
Rosen, S., 370
Rosenbaum, R., 308
Rosenberg, L. A., 617
Rosenberg, M. J., 352, 372
Rosenberg, S., 96
Rosenblatt, P. C., 285, 528
Rosenfeld, H. M., 126, 515
Rosenhan, D. L., 297, 300, 504
Rosenkoetter, L. I., 273
Rosenkrantz, P. S., 99, 328, 463, 464
Rosenthal, A. M., 281
Rosenthal, R., 67, 68, 69, 495, 588
Rosner, S., 623
Rosnow, R. L., 67, 97, 393, 394, 415, 588
Rosow, I., 167
Ross, A. S., 295
Ross, C., 46, 453
Ross, D., 20, 226, 227, 231
Ross, H., 533
Ross, H. L., 50
Ross, L. D., 139, 159
Ross, M., 372, 380, 381, 541, 542
Ross, S., 20, 226, 227, 231
Rossi, P. H., 202, 496, 498
Rost-Schaude, E., 563
Roszak, T., 436, 573
Rothbart, M., 394
Rothbart, M. K., 154, 452
Rothman, G. R., 273
Rothschild, G. H., 566
Rotter, J. B., 81, 83, 251
Rottmann, L., 164
Rozelle, R. M., 392
Rubin, I., 195, 196
Rubin, Z., 170, 171, 172, 173
Rudé, G., 235
Rule, B. G., 220, 624
Rusk, H., 309
Russell, J. C., 153
Russo, N. F., 519
Rutter, D. R., 518
Ryan, W., 84
Rychlak, J. F., 26

Saari, D., 309, 619
Saegert, S., 168
Sagarin, E., 23
Sagatun, I., 118
Sahakian, W. S., 20
Sahlein, W. J., 309
St. Jean, R., 631, 632
Saks, M. J., 565

Sales, S. M., 168, 559, 603, 604
Salinger, J. D., 115
Salter, V., 516
Saltz, E., 300
Saltzstein, H. D., 254
Sampson, E. E., 154
Samuel, W., 624
Sandiford, P., 496
Sandilands, M. L., 624
Sanford, F. H., 219, 589, 654
Sanford, N., 15, 319, 416, 584
Sarbin, T. R., 18, 19, 624, 633
Sarkin, R., 201
Sarnoff, I. R., 153, 385
Sarup, G., 360
Satow, K. L., 301
Satterfield, C. H., 89
Saul, B. B. B., 128
Saxe, L., 100
Scarr, H. A., 553
Scarr-Salapatek, S., 486
Schachter, S., 147, 149, 150, 151, 154, 156, 157, 158, 159, 167, 531, 563, 568
Schaffner, P., 168
Schaller, G. B., 214
Schanie, C. F., 423
Schaps, E., 303
Scheidt, R., 225
Schein, E. H., 48, 611, 654, 655, 657, 659, 660
Schein, V. E., 469
Scheinfeld, A., 458
Schellenberg, J. A., 215, 230, 334
Scherer, S. E., 517
Scherwitz, L., 552
Schleifer, M., 273
Schlenker, B. R., 31, 32, 372
Schloss, G. A., 571
Schmideberg, M., 156
Schmidt, G., 205
Schmidt, L., 151
Schmitt, R. C., 539, 541
Schmuck, R., 586
Schneider, B., 659
Schneider, D. J., 96, 104, 126
Schneider, F. W., 290
Schoenfeld, W. N., 478, 480
Schofield, M., 203
Schoggen, P., 28, 48
Schönbach, P., 370
Schooler, C., 154
Schopler, J., 238, 318, 346, 541, 542, 546
Schreisheim, C., 645, 648
Schroder, H. M., 86, 88, 253
Schroeder, H. E., 632
Schuelke, N., 482
Schuman, H., 64, 320
Schur, E. M., 23
Schwartz, J., 487
Schwartz, M., 487
Schwartz, R. D., 63
Schwartz, S. H., 265, 294, 296, 301, 305,

Schwartz, S. H. (continued)
    306
Schwartz, T., 229, 232, 239
Schweitzer, D., 393
Scodel, A., 588
Scott, J. P., 218, 226
Scott, M. B., 523
Scott, W. A., 62, 321
Sears, D. O., 340, 370, 386
Sears, R., 218, 228, 239, 254, 452
Seashore, H., 499
Seaver, W. B., 69
Sebastian, R., 234
Sechrest, L. B., 63, 516
Secord, P. F., 31, 44, 165
Sedlacek, W. E., 199
Sedlacek, W. F., 205
Seeman, W., 463
Seidel, H. E., 503
Seiden, R., 199
Seidenberg, B., 63
Sekerak, G., 559
Selltiz, C. A., 44, 346
Senn, D. J., 138, 139, 162
Sensenig, J., 367
Severance, L., 357
Severy, L. J., 89, 279, 301
Seyfried, B. A., 162
Shafer, E., 537
Shaffer, D. R., 246, 380
Shantz, C. U., 255
Shapira, A., 287
Shapiro, S. P., 309
Sharp, G., 424
Shaver, K. G., 101, 102, 104
Shaver, P., 31, 207, 459, 460
Shaw, C., 539
Shaw, E. A., 469
Shaw, G., 654
Shaw, J. I., 369
Shaw, M. E., 16, 19, 552, 553, 559, 560,
    562, 566, 567, 568, 638, 651
Sheatsley, P. B., 591
Sheehan, P. W., 634
Sheldon, E. B., 429
Sherif, C. W., 239, 357, 359, 360
Sherif, M., 239, 240, 357, 359, 413, 431,
    432, 616
Sherman, J. A., 458
Sherman, M., 127
Sherman, S. J., 631
Sherrod, D. R., 310, 542
Sherwood, I. J., 424
Sherwood, J. J., 257, 366
Sheth, J. N., 318
Shields, S. A., 450
Shils, E., 592
Shima, H., 650
Shipman, V. C., 503
Shockley, V. L., 150
Shoffeitt, P. G., 254
Shotz, M., 264
Shuey, A. M., 479, 494

Shulman, R. F., 380, 381
Shure, G. H., 31
Sidman, J., 205, 206
Siegel, A. E., 231
Siegel, P. M., 496, 498
Siegelman, M., 188
Siegman, C., 591
Sigall, H., 165
Sigelman, C., 239, 277
Sigusch, V., 205
Siiter, R., 463
Sikes, J., 396
Silver, M. J., 69
Silverberg, G., 111
Silverman, I., 373, 374, 375, 377
Simmons, C. H., 84, 85, 86
Simon, J. G., 466
Simon, L. M., 499
Simon, S., 239
Simon, W., 177, 191
Simons, H. W., 588
Simons, L. S., 225, 538
Simpson, E., 270, 274
Sims-Knight, J., 264
Singer, D. G., 231
Singer, J. E., 136, 150, 157, 531, 536,
    542, 554
Singer, J. L., 231
Singer, R. D., 233, 335, 416
Sinnett, E. R., 531
Siroka, E. K., 571
Siroka, R. W., 571
Sistrunk, F., 458
Sizer, M. F., 244
Sizer, T. R., 244
Skinner, B. F., 20, 41, 79, 274, 441, 443
Skolnick, P., 369
Skrzypek, G. J., 652
Skubiski, S. L., 293
Sladen, B., 542
Slater, P. E., 436, 439, 564
Slavin, R. E., 396
Slomovitz, M., 111
Slosnerick, M., 544
Small, L., 269
Smigel, E. O., 199
Smith, C. R., 339
Smith, D. B., 205
Smith, E. E., 18
Smith, H., 342
Smith, H. L., 64
Smith, M. B., 31, 161, 265, 266, 338,
    382, 383, 435
Smith, P. W., 338, 385
Smith, R. E., 295
Smith, R. F., 538
Smith, R. G., 393
Smith, R. J., 611
Smith, S., 230, 496, 544
Smith, T. E., 542
Smythe, L., 295
Snapp, M., 396
Snow, R. E., 69

Snyder, M., 121, 122, 137, 142, 380, 381,
    394
Snyder, R., 56
Snyderman, B., 659
Sommer, R., 513, 516, 517, 519, 520,
    521, 522, 525, 526, 527, 532, 533
Songer, E., 365
Sorrentino, R. M., 84, 85, 138, 139
Southam, A. L., 449
Southwick, C. H., 538
Spanos, N. P., 634
Spence, J. T., 163, 460, 462
Spiller, G., 642
Spreitzer, E. A., 659
Stack, L. C., 81
Stang, D. J., 168, 617, 621, 639
Stanley, J. C., 52, 69
Stapp, J., 462
Starr, J. M., 439
Starr, S., 205, 206
Staub, E., 294, 300, 301
Stea, D., 511
Steele, L., 359
Stein, A. H., 234, 452, 459
Stein, D. D., 161, 338, 339, 341
Stein, R. T., 643
Steiner, I. D., 18, 130, 552, 564, 588
Steinzor, B., 520, 534
Stephan, C., 167, 396, 397
Stephenson, G. M., 518
Stern, S. E., 487
Stevenson, L. G., 528
Stewart, L. H., 496
Stewart, N., 499
Stikes, C. S., 341
Stinchcombe, A. L., 329
Stires, L. K., 130, 625
Stith, D., 503
Stodolsky, S. S., 505
Stogdill, R. M., 638, 643, 644, 645, 648
Stokes, J. P., 631
Stokols, D., 238, 537, 538, 541, 542, 543,
    545, 546
Stoller, R. J., 182
Stone, G. C., 63
Stone, W. F., 589
Stoner, J. A. F., 629, 632
Stonner, D., 224, 230
Storms, M. D., 160
Stotland, E., 163, 382, 385
Stratton, L., 516
Strauss, P. S., 593
Streufert, S., 370
Stricker, L. J., 616, 623, 627
Strickland, L. H., 653
Strodtbeck, F., 520
Stroebe, W., 357, 564
Stroop, J. R., 560
Stroud, J., 246
Stuckert, R. P., 478
Sue, D. W., 326
Sue, D. W., 326
Sue, S., 326

Suedfeld, P., 148, 149, 290, 624
Sullivan, H. S., 248
Sulzer, J. L., 220
Sunday, E., 545
Sundstrom, E., 511, 515, 520, 522, 528, 529, 537, 538, 541, 543, 545, 547
Swap, W., 168
Swingle, P., 284
Szabo, D., 625

Taback, M., 501
Taft, R., 109
Tagiuri, R., 96, 112
Tajfel, H., 31
Tannenbaum, A. S., 654
Tannenbaum, P. H., 352, 365
Tanner, K. L., 495
Tanser, H. A., 482
Tanter, R., 236
Tapp, J. L., 112
Taub, D., 359
Tavris, C., 207
Taylor, D. A., 138, 139, 528
Taylor, D. W., 560, 563
Taylor, F. W., 654
Taylor, J. B., 303
Taylor, M. G., 119
Taylor, S. E., 168
Taylor, S. P., 220
Taynor, J., 465
Teddlie, C., 543
Tedeschi, J. T., 372
Teevan, R. C., 621
Teger, A. I., 295, 305, 545, 631, 632
Teich, A. H., 432
Teichman, Y., 153
Telaak, K., 359, 362, 363
Temoshok, L., 450
Terborg, J. R., 469
Terebinski, S. J., 399
Terman, L. M., 457
Tesser, A., 306
Test, M. A., 292
Thayer, G., 225
Thayer, R. E., 424
Theman, V., 480
Thibaut, J. W., 20, 21, 31, 132, 167, 631
Thistlethwaite, D. L., 631
Thomas, E. J., 16
Thomas, L. E., 439, 440
Thomas, R., 287
Thomas, W. I., 22
Thompson, R. J., Jr., 220
Thorngate, W., 31, 32
Tilker, H., 295
Tilly, C., 234
Tinbergen, N., 216, 217, 522
Tipton, R. M., 280
Tittler, B. I., 360
Titus, H. E., 587, 589
Tocantino, L. M., 9
Toch, H., 431
Toder, N. L., 254

Toffler, A., 411, 431, 440, 441
Tognoli, J., 138
Tomkins, C., 603
Tomlinson, T. M., 235
Touhey, J. C., 378, 470, 471
Toynbee, A. J., 492
Travers, J. R., 427
Tresemer, D., 460
Triandis, H. C., 29, 31, 94, 337, 338, 340, 341, 343
Trimble, J. E., 325, 326
Triplett, N., 559
Tripodi, T., 87
Trommsdorff, G., 563
Truax, C. B., 138
Truman, D. B., 64
Trumbo, D., 51
Tucker, J., 544
Tulkin, S., 489
Tumin, M. M., 221
Turiel, E., 268, 273
Turner, C. W., 225
Turner, R. H., 317
Tyler, L. E., 458, 479, 484, 495, 498

Underwood, B., 297
Unger, R. K., 463, 624, 625
Urban, T. F., 594

Vacc, N. A., 87
Vacc, N. E., 87
Vacchiano, R. B., 593
Vachon, D., 511
Vaizey, M. J., 544
Valins, S., 159, 174, 544
Vance, F. L., 164
Van der Schyff, L., 590
Varela, J. A., 653
Vassiliou, V., 337
Vaughn, B. E., 264
Veach, T. L., 630
Veitch, R., 161, 535, 541
Veldman, D. J., 83
Vernadsky, G., 9, 11
Vidmar, N., 564, 631
Vidulich, R. N., 594
Vincent, J. E., 122, 298
Vivekananthan, P. S., 96
Vockell, E. L., 154
Vogel, S. R., 328, 463, 464
Vogel, W., 449
Vollmer, H. M., 419
Vonhoff, H., 300
VonKulmiz, P., 532
Vontress, C. E., 325
Vraa, C. W., 567
Vroom, V. H., 660
Vukcevic, D. P., 516

Wack, D., 559
Wainwright, L., 81
Walbek, N., 293
Walder, L. O., 231

Walder, P., 300
Walker, D., 329
Walker, E. L., 83
Walker, N., 221
Walkley, R., 396
Wall, P. M., 112
Wallace, B., 376
Wallace, D. L., 40
Wallace, W. P., 35
Wallach, M. A., 623, 629, 630, 631
Waller, W. W., 165
Wallston, B. S., 303, 304, 309
Walsh, J. J., 404
Walster, E., 151, 164, 169, 170, 172, 173, 279, 298, 299, 393
Walster, G. W., 151, 298, 299
Walters, C. E., 485
Walters G., 331
Walters, R. H., 20, 219, 227, 228, 231, 239, 245, 272
Walton, M., 542, 546
Wandersman, A., 168
Ward, C. D., 393
Ward, L., 173
Ware, E. E., 206
Ware, R., 88, 89
Warner, W. L., 504
Warr, P. B., 96
Warren, J. R., 154
Warren, N., 482, 484, 485, 489
Warriner, C. H., 553
Warwick, D. P., 72
Washburn, S. L., 477
Waters, H. F., 231, 239
Watson, G., 334, 395
Watson, G. B., 560
Watson, J., 418
Watson, J. B., 270
Watson, J. D., 40
Watson, J. M., 235
Watts, R. E., 539
Watts, W., 435
Webb, E. J., 63
Weber, M., 433
Weber, S. J., 67
Webster, S. W., 397
Wedge, B., 532
Wegner, M. A., 205
Weick, K. E., 65, 638
Weigel, R. H., 396, 397
Weil, R. J., 228
Weinberg, G., 186
Weinberg, M. S., 127
Weinfield, F., 491
Weinrub, A., 487
Weisberg, D. K., 578
Weiss, R. F., 280, 291
Weiss, W., 65, 393
Weissberg, N. C., 345
Weissenberg, P., 650
Weitz, S., 141, 344
Weitzman, L. J., 46, 453
Weizmann, F., 487

Welch, S., 539, 540, 541, 546, 547
Wells, H. G., 442
Wells, M. G., 415
Wells, W. D., 233
Werner, E. E., 327, 485
Wesman, A., 499
West, S. G., 101, 102, 103, 205, 263
Westhues, K., 572
Westie, F. R., 337, 342, 344, 404, 588
Westin, A. F., 603, 604
Westley, B., 418
Wheeler, D., 122
Wheeler, L., 159, 230, 528
Wheeler, L. R., 500
White, B. J., 239
White, C., 583
White, G. M., 292
White, L., 467
White, R. K., 658
White, R. W., 382, 383
Whiting, B., 448, 451, 452
Whitmyre, J. W., 563
Whittaker, D., 435
Whyte, W. H., Jr., 81, 167, 531, 625, 626
Wiback, K., 469
Wicker, A. W., 28, 112, 342, 343, 344,
    346, 347, 546
Wiesenthal, D. L., 618
Wilbur, C. B., 188
Wilder, D. A., 618
Wilder, J., 251
Wilkens, G., 285
Wilkins, C., 343
Wilkins, P. C., 164
Willems, E. P., 631, 632
Willerman, B., 163, 164
Willerman, L., 487
Williams, C. J., 127
Williams, D., 638
Williams, L., 339
Williams, R. M., Jr., 395
Willis, F. N., 515, 516
Willis, R. H., 339, 365, 613, 627, 628

Willitz, J. E., 304
Willows, D., 227
Wilner, D. M., 396
Wilson, E. O., 214
Wilson, G. D., 591
Wilson, J. P., 301
Wilson, W., 394, 594
Wilson, W. C., 204
Winch, R. F., 162
Winer, B. J., 644
Winkel, G., 511
Winsborough, H., 539
Winsome, R., 325
Winter, D. G., 35, 36, 45
Wiser, P. L., 396
Wishner, J., 96, 97
Wishnov, B., 118
Wispé, L. G., 277, 304
Witcover, J., 142
Witty, P. A., 480
Wnek, D., 290
Wodarski, J. S., 285
Wohlwill, J., 511, 513
Wolf, R. M., 506
Wolfe, B., 15
Wolfgang, M., 221
Wolins, L., 653
Wolkon, G. H., 591
Wolosin, M. A., 631
Wolosin, R. J., 631
Wong, T. J., 161, 341
Wood, D. A., 659
Wood, F. A., 641
Wood, R., 194, 196
Woodmansee, J., 318, 319
Woodyard, E. R., 501
Worchel, S., 230, 367, 543
Word, L. E., 295
Worthington, M., 516
Worthy, M., 488
Wrench, D. F., 495
Wright, B. A., 303
Wright, P. C., 264

Wright, P. H., 161
Wrightsman, L. S., 44, 49, 79, 81, 89, 90,
    92, 153, 154, 156, 219, 251, 284,
    321, 339, 406, 407, 504, 572, 586,
    588, 589
Wynne-Edwards, V., 522

Yakimovich, D., 300
Yalom, I. D., 571
Yancey, W. L., 513
Yankelovich, D., 47, 48, 439
Yarrow, P. R., 343
Yerkes, R. M., 480, 499
York, R., 491
Yoshioka, G. A., 167, 532
Young, C. E., 411
Young, J., 90
Youssoupoff (Yussoupov), F., 10
Yukl, G., 650

Zablocki, B., 574
Zacker, J., 588
Zagona, S. V., 594
Zajonc, R. B., 22, 168, 364, 365, 368,
    559, 631
Zander, A., 639, 646, 658
Zanna, M. P., 126
Zarrow, M. X., 502
Zavalloni, M., 563, 633
Zdep, S. M., 149
Zeisel, H., 565
Ziller, R. C., 594, 629
Zillman, D., 222, 230
Zimbardo, P. G., 54, 55, 153, 159, 352,
    380, 554, 555, 557, 559
Zimmerman, E., 449
Zlutnick, S., 537, 539, 540
Zucker, L. G., 616
Zuckerman, M., 179, 205
Zurcher, L. A., Jr., 284, 303, 594
Zusman, J., 420

Subject Index

Abstract conceptual system, 88–89
Acceptance, in attitude change, 354, 356–357
Achievement:
  and birth order, 154
  in peaceful societies, 228
  and personal motives, 35
  in postindustrialized society, 418
  sex differences, 457–458, 459–461
  sex-role socialization of, 450
  social-class differences, 499
Achievement motivation, 251
  as process variable in development of intelligence, 506
  sex differences, 459–461
Acquaintance potential, as factor in attitude change, 396, 400–401
Acquiescence, as response set, 63, 587, 591, 593
Acquisition, as an ingratiation motive, 130–131
Action research, 416 (see also Social action)
  and planned change, 416–418
Activism, 435–436
Adaptation:
  to noise, 536
  to overload, 545–546
Adaptation-level theory, and attitude change, 357
Additive model, in impression formation, 97–98
Adjustive function of attitudes, 382
Adolescence, 249, 250
Advocacy research, 412–413
Affective component of attitudes, 318–321
Affiliation, 147–175
  and anxiety, 150–156
  and birth order, 153–156
  and furniture arrangement, 532–534
  interpersonal attraction, 161–169
  love, 169–175
  need, 149
  need and conforming behavior, 621
  needs in women, 459
  neo-Freudian view, 13
Africans, Black:
  developmental rates, 482, 484–485
  discrimination against, 329–330

Aftereffects, of aversive conditions, 536
Age differences:
  interpersonal distance, 516
  in Machiavellianism, 135
  in philosophies of human nature, 91–92
  and social change, 435–439
Aggregates, 552
Aggression, 211–241 (see also Violence)
  and attitude change, 395
  control of, 236–239
  cross-cultural comparisons, 228–229
  ethological theory, 216–218, 237
  experimental control of, 239–240
  and frustration, 218–225, 238, 417
  hereditary determinants, 218
  high temperatures and, 535
  and inside density, 540–541, 542, 546
  instigators, 221–222, 422
  and level of moral maturity, 265
  mass media and, 230–234, 239, 416
  in psychoanalytic theory, 13, 212–213, 215–216, 237
  sex differences, 448–449, 450, 455–456
  social-learning theory, 226–228, 238–239
Aggressive cues, 222–225, 424
Agnew, Spiro, 375, 604
Alexandra, Tsarina, 7–11, 13–16, 18–19, 21, 25, 27
Alexis, Tsarevich, 7–11
Ali, Muhammad, 37, 163
Alienation:
  and helping behavior, 300
  and social class, 504
  of youth, 435–436, 438
Alinsky, Saul, 424, 425
Allport, Floyd H., 553, 559
Alternatives Foundation, 577
Altruism, 279–311 (see also Helping behavior)
  dimension of human nature, 81, 89–92, 93–94
  and impression management, 121–122, 123, 137–138
  and overload, 545
Ambiguity, intolerance for:
  and authoritarianism, 588
  and conforming behavior, 622

Ambisexuals, 186 (see also Homosexuality)
American Civil Liberties Union (ACLU), 604, 627
American Indians, see North American natives
Amish, 607–608
Anal stage, of psychological development, 12, 247, 249
Anchors, and attitude change, 358–364
Androgens, 448
Androgyny, 462–463
Anger arousal, 222
Angry aggression, 215
Anomie scale, 407–408
Anti-Black attitudes, see Racial attitudes; Racism
Anticonformity, 611, 612, 616, 627
Antidemocratic orientation, 335–336
Anti-intraception, as component of authoritarianism, 584, 585
Anti-Semitism, 583 (see also Discrimination; Prejudice)
Antisocial behavior, 279
Anxiety:
  and birth order, 153–156
  in conceptual systems theory, 88
  and isolation, 148, 150–154
  and personal distance, 516
  and racial attitude change, 407
  reaction to transgression, 271
Apathy, 81
Aphrodisiacs, 194
Applied research, versus pure science, 412–416
Approach-approach conflict, 27
Approach-avoidance conflict, 27
Approval-seeking behavior (see also Ingratiation):
  impression formation, 125–128
  and interpersonal distance, 515–516
Aptitude, sex differences in, 457–458
Arapesh society, 228
Architecture:
  barriers, partitions, and privacy, 532
  and crime, 530
  and density, 542
  functional distance, 531
  and interpersonal behavior, 512–513, 530–536

Architecture (continued)
  office landscaping, 532
  room arrangement and interaction,
    532–534
Archival research, 35, 45, 46–47
Area sampling, 60
Army Alpha Test of mental ability, 480,
  482, 491, 499
Artifacts, 107
  in person perception, 107–108
Asch, Solomon, 22, 458, 611–613,
  616–620, 627–628
Asch situation, 458, 611–614
Assassination, 84, 85, 90, 111, 300
A-S scale, 587
Assimilation-contrast theory:
  assumptions about human nature,
    360
  in attitude change, 358–364
Assumed similarity, 106, 108
Assumed Similarity of Opposites
  (ASO) scale, 648
Assumptions about human nature, 6,
  29, 30, 37, 70, 77–98, 327
  and aggression, 211–215
  and alienation, 435
  and attitude change, 353, 355, 360,
    405–408
  and authoritarianism, 588
  in communes, 575
  complex man, 654, 659–660
  consistency theories, 368–369
  empirical-rational, 418
  in experiments, 70
  functional theories, 384
  homeostatic principle, 513
  and impression formation, 77–86
  and impression management, 143
  and leadership, 654–660
  of men and women, 447–473
  normative-reeducative, 420
  and organizational effectiveness,
    654–660
  power-coercive, 422
  and prejudice, 327–332
  psychoanalytic theory, 11–13
  rational-economic man, 654–655
  reinforcement theory, 29, 30, 355
  role-construct theory, 86–88
  self-actualizing man, 654, 659
  self-perception theory, 380
  as sexual beings, 177–179
  social-judgment theory, 360
  social view, 654–659
  stimulus-response theory, 355
Atheoretical research, in social
  psychology, 32
Athletic coaches, and authoritarianism,
  590
Athletic performance, race differences
  in, 488
Athletic teams:
  authoritarianism of coaches, 590
  cohesiveness, 567–568
  performance at home versus away,
    529

Attention, in attitude change, 354,
  356–357, 391
Attitude(s), 315–322
  and behavior, 315–349
  components of, 319–321
  definitions, 316–318
  functions of, 382–383
  intensity of, and persuasibility, 395
  love as, 170–171
  measurement of, 316–317
  toward minority groups, 322–325 (see
    also Discrimination; Prejudice)
  and moral behavior, 264–269
  polarization in groups, 563–564
  as predictors of behavior, 342–348
  prejudice, 315–322
  sexual, 169–170, 177, 196–204
  and sexual behavior, 201
  similarity and attraction, 161–162,
    167
  simple versus complex, 321–322
  survey, 47–48
  about violence, 213
Attitude change, 32, 389–409
  attempts, 91, 397–405
  toward authority, 434–435
  causes, 389–392
  face-to-face contact and, 395–405
  intergroup-contact hypothesis,
    394–395
  and nonchange, 352–353
  parent-child, 436–439
  sexual, 198–204
  and social change, 432–435
  theories, 25, 31, 351–387
  toward work, 432–434
Attitude-change theories, 25, 31,
  351–387
  behaviorist, 379–382
  consistency, 364–379
  field, 357–379
  functional, 382–385
  Gestalt, 357–379
  interracial, 397–405
  reinforcement, 353–357
  self-perception 379–382
  social-judgment, 357–364
  stimulus-response, 353–357
Attitude-measurement methods,
  316–317, 319
Attitude measures:
  California F scale, 63, 342, 587–592,
    600, 603, 621
  E scale, 587, 591, 592, 593
  Gough Sanford Rigidity scale, 406
  "Kiddie Mach" scale, 135
  Machiavellianism scale, 134–135,
    407–408
  Marlowe-Crowne Social Desirability
    Scale, 128
  North-Hatt Occupational Prestige
    Scale, 496–498
  P-E-C scale, 587
  Philosophies of Human Nature
    (PHN) scale, 89–92, 407, 408
  Rehfisch Rigidity scale, 406

Attitude measures (continued)
  Rubin's love scale, 170–172
  School Segregation scale, 403–404
  Sentence-completion test, 404
  Social Desirability Scale, 128
  Welsh Figure Preference Test, 406
  Wesley Rigidity Scale, 406
Attraction, see Interpersonal attraction
Attractiveness (see also Physical
  attractiveness):
  and rate of being helped, 303
  of a victim, 84–86
Attribution theory, 22, 24, 25, 78–79,
  100–104
  attitude change, 372
  and internal states, 160–161
Audience:
  in attitude change, 354, 394
  response to censorship, 367
  effect on performance, 559
Authoritarian aggression, 584, 585
Authoritarianism, 581–605 (see also
  Authoritarian personality
  syndrome)
  and conforming behavior, 622
  in the future, 603–604
  in government, 582–583
  and obedience, 600
  within the person, 583–594
  societal, 600–602
Authoritarian personality syndrome,
  15–16
  and behavior, 342–343
  and helping behavior, 300
  and prejudice, 335–336
  and social change, 429
Authoritarian submission, 584, 585
Authority, changing attitudes toward,
  434–435
Authority figures:
  and dogmatism, 594
  and obedience, 594–600
Autokinetic effect, 428–429, 616–620
  sex differences, 458
Autonomous morality, 255
Autonomy:
  versus doubt, as stage of
    psychosocial development,
    249–251
  in moral development, 274
  neo-Freudian view, 13
Averaging model, in impression
  formation, 97–98
Aversive racism, 345
Avoidance-avoidance conflict, 27

Bacon, Francis, 442
Balance theory, 25
  attitude change, 364–365, 367–368
  and attraction, 165–167
Bantustans, 329–330
Barker, Roger, 417
Barriers, and privacy, 532
Base rate, 103
Basic research, versus applied research,
  412–416

Beauty, *see* Physical attractiveness
Behavioral-constraint model of crowding, 545, 546
Behavior = f(Person, Environment), 25, 343–346
Behaviorist theory, of attitude change, 379–382
Behavior settings, 18, 28, 49, 546 (*see also* Situational factors)
  cross-cultural differences, 93–94
  over- and underpopulation of, 546, 547
Behavior therapy, 79, 81, 342
Belief(s):
  and attraction, 161–162, 167
  and sexual behavior, 201, 203
  and social distance, 337–342
  survey, 47–48
  systems, 88–89
Belief prejudice, 340
Bellamy, Edward, 442
Bereiter-Engelmann intervention, 503
Berkeley Free Speech Movement sit-in, and level of moral maturity of participants, 266–267
Berrigan brothers, 424
Biased sampling, 59
Binet tests of intelligence, 479
Biofeedback, effects of false heart rate, 159–160
Biological aspects:
  sex differences, 448–450
  of transsexual persons, 181–183
Birth control, and intelligence of the human species, 500
Birth order, and affiliation and anxiety, 153–156
Bisexuality, 191–192
Blackfoot Indians, 325–326
Blacks, in the U.S., 37, 85, 169, 267–268
  definition of race, 476–479
  discrimination against, 331, 332–333, 343–345
  environmental deprivation, 489–495
  ghetto riots, 235, 238
  impression formation, 80
  intelligence, compared with Whites, 479–495
  personal space, 517
  prejudice against, 141–142, 318–321, 322–324, 327–329, 332–333, 362–364, 383–384, 588
  as recipients of help, 304, 346
  reducing prejudice toward, 394–408
  reverse discrimination, 122–125, 213
  social class and intelligence, 499, 504–506
  social distance from Whites, 337–342
  social movement, 431–432
  stereotypes, 331
Blaming the victim, 84–86, 298, 333
Blind scoring, 188
Blood types, and race, 476–477, 478
Body language, 141 (*see also* Nonverbal behavior)
Boredom, and isolation, 148

Brainstorming, 560–563
Brainwashing, 392
Breeding populations, 476, 489
Bucher, Lloyd, 392, 608
Busing, for desegregation, 418
Byrd, Admiral, 148
Bystander effect, 293–296

California F scale, 63, 342, 587–592, 600, 603
  and conforming behavior, 621
California Psychological Inventory (CPI), 62
Calley, Lieutenant, 589, 594
Canada, prejudice in, 330, 334
Capital punishment, 221
Carlyle, Thomas, 639
Carnegie, Dale, 82
Castration anxiety, 246–247
Causation:
  in correlational research, 44–45, 47, 48, 50
  in experiments, 51, 54, 67, 69–70, 73
  in science, 40–41
Cause, attribution of, 100–104
Ceiling effect, 617
Cell assemblies, 502
Censorship:
  public speaking on unpopular issues, 490
  reactance theory, 367
  in the Republic of South Africa, 330
Central Intelligence Agency, 582
Central traits, 96–97
Change agents, social psychologists as, 418–427
Character Education Inquiry, 252
Charisma, 639
Charity (*see also* Helping behavior):
  donating behavior, 291–293
  enlisting support for, 301, 302–303, 308–309
Chauvinism, male, 464
Chavez, Cesar, 418, 424, 425
Cheating behavior, 135, 252, 265, 273
Chichester, Sir Francis, 148
Child-rearing practices:
  and aggressive behavior, 228, 239
  and authoritarianism, 588
  and conformity, 622
  and developmental rates, 484–485
  and development of conscience, 254
  and homosexuality, 188–189
  and level of moral maturity, 266
  sex-role socialization, 452–453
Children:
  bystander effect, 294
  conforming behavior, 623
  response to crowding, 543–544
  frustration and aggression in, 220–221, 229
  helping behavior, 293, 305, 308
  imitation, of aggressive behavior, 226–227
  interpersonal distance, 516

Children (continued)
  intervention projects and IQ, 491–492, 501–504
  moral development, 247–269
  prejudice in, 335, 339
  race differences in IQ, 504–506
  regional differences in IQ, 491
  sex-role socialization, 450–453
  similar beliefs versus race, 339
  social-class differences in IQ, 498–506
  television influence on, 230–234
Children's books, and sex-role socialization, 453
Chinese Americans:
  intelligence, 495–496
  prejudice against, 342–343
Chitling Test, 493–494
Choice shift, 632–633
Christian beliefs, 244
Civil disobedience, and level of moral maturity, 267–268
Civil disorder, 421 (*see also* Revolution; Riots)
  Report of the National Advisory Commission, 420, 421
Classrooms, crowding in, 543–544
Client-centered therapy, 79
Clockwork Orange, A, 41, 239
Closed-ended questions, 61
Closet queens, 186, 187 (*see also* Homosexuality)
Closure, 25
Codification of rules stage, 255
Coding, 58, 66–67
Cofigurative culture, 437
Cognitions, 366 (*see also* Cognitive-dissonance theory)
Cognitive abilities, sex differences in, 449, 450, 457–458 (*see also* Intelligence)
Cognitive complexity, 87–89
Cognitive component of attitudes, 318–321
Cognitive consonance, in attitudes, 322
Cognitive-dissonance theory, 25, 27, 29
  attitude change, 366, 368, 370–379, 380, 381–382
  attitudes and behavior, 347–348
  of interpersonal attraction, 169
Cognitive stages of moral development, 255–259
Cognitive state, and emotion, 157–159
Cognitive theory:
  of moral behavior, 245, 254–270
  in social psychology, 21–25, 86–88
Cohesiveness, group, 285–286, 567–569
Coitus:
  men, 203–204
  women, 202–203
Coleman Report, 491, 498
Coleridge, Samuel Taylor, 130
Commission on the Year 2000, 441
Commitment mechanisms, in communes, 575–576

Common effects, in causal attribution, 103–104
Communal groups, 572–579
Communes, 441–442, 572–579
Communication:
    in groups, 566–567, 568
    persuasive, 354
Communication networks, 566–567
Communicator:
    credibility of, and attitude change, 360–361
    persuasive, 354
Communism, dogmatism in, 592–593
Community participation, and authoritarianism, 589
Compassion, 85–86
Competence:
    as an antecedent of attraction, 163–164, 167
    and conforming behavior, 621
    versus race in social distance, 341
    as a sex stereotype, 463–464
    and social influence, 618
Competition, 27, 278
    versus cooperation, 283–287
    and density, 542
    development of, 286–287
    in postindustrialized society, 418
Competitive motive, 284
    and productivity, 285
Competitive reward structure, 283, 286
    and attitude change, 396–397
Complementarity of need systems, and interpersonal attraction, 162–163, 167
Complexity, as dimension of human nature, 86, 87, 88–92
Complex worker theory, 654, 659–660
Compliance, 610–616, 627–628
    and impression management, 137–138
    process, in conformity, 613, 615
    reaction to forced, 370–373
Comprehension, in attitude change, 354, 356–357
Compulsive resistance, 615
Conative component of attitudes, 318–321
Conceptual systems theory, 88–89
Concomitant variation, 44–45
Concrete conceptual systems, 88–89
Confederates, in research, 72
Conflict:
    field of force analysis, 27
    in organizations, 54
    reduction, 239–240
    resolution in communes, 576
Conformity, 607–628
    Asch studies, 611–613
    in conceptual systems theory, 88
    in dress, 607, 609, 624–625
    as a dimension of human nature, 81–82, 89–92
    and identity status, 254
    as a tactic in ingratiation, 130, 132

Conformity (continued)
    needs and attitude change, 384–385
    as a cause of prejudice, 334
    process, 615
    sex differences, 458
    in society, 624–627
Congruity theory, and attitude change, 365–366, 368
Conscience, 254 (see also Moral behavior)
    psychoanalytic theory, 12, 246–247
    social-learning theory, 273
Consciousness I, II, III, 437, 602–603
Consent, informed, in research, 70–71
Consequences versus intentions, in determining morality, 256
Consideration, as dimension of leadership behavior, 644, 645–648
Consistency theories, 31
    assumptions about human nature, 368–369
    attitude change, 352, 364–379
    balance theory, 364–368
    cognitive-dissonance theory, 366
    congruity theory, 365–366
    application to desegregation, 378–379
    reactance theory, 366–367
Consonance, in attitudes, 321–322
Constructs, 6–7
    role-construct theory, 86–88
Contemporary causes, of interpersonal behavior, 29, 30
Content analysis, 46–47, 57–58
Contingency theory of leadership, 648–654
Contrast and assimilation in attitude change, 358–359
Control:
    in experimental research, 42–43, 45, 51, 56
    in quasi-experimental research, 52
    in research, 42–56
    as a goal in science, 41
Conventionalism, as component of authoritarianism, 584–585
Conventionality, 610
Conventional level of moral maturity, 259–260, 265, 266–269
Conventional prejudice, 340
Cooperation, 27, 278, 283–287 (see also Prosocial behavior)
    development of, 286–287
    mixed-motive games, 284–285
    teaching, to children, 308
Cooperative motive, 284
Cooperative reward structure, 283
    and attitude change, 396–397, 401
    and productivity, 285–286
Coping behaviors, and crowding, 538, 543–544
Correlational method, 40, 43–45, 46–50
    versus experimental method, 42–45
Cost-reward analysis, of helping, 306–308
Counterconformity, 611, 612

Counterculture, 436–437
Countermovements, 431, 432
Creativity, 89
    and conforming behavior, 622
Credibility, of the source of a communication, 360–361, 365–366, 390, 393–394
Crime:
    architecture and, 530
    and police training, 422–424
    and population density, 539, 540, 541, 546
    preventive treatment, 603, 604
    sex, 51, 206–207
    statistics, 236, 237–238
Cross-cultural comparisons:
    aggressive behavior, 228–229
    interpersonal distance, 513
    moral development, 264
    population density and social pathology, 541
    sex-role socialization, 450–452
Cross-sectional studies, in moral development, 268
Crowd behavior, effect on passersby, 53
Crowd consciousness, 553
Crowding, 536–548 (see also Overcrowding)
    models, 545–548
Cues, aggressive, 222–225, 422, 424
Cultural deprivation, see Environmental deprivation
Cultural disadvantagement, 506 (see also Environmental deprivation)
Cultural relativism, 492–493
Cultural value, risk as, 632
Culture:
    and intelligence, 492–493
    nature and functions of, 13
Culture-free tests, 480, 498
Culture shock, 440
Cumulative scaling, 317
Cybernetics, see Technology
Cynicism, as component of authoritarianism, 584, 585

Dale Carnegie human relations courses, 128–130, 136
Data banks, 603–604
Davis, Sammy, Jr., 169
Death:
    instinct, 237
    as a social behavior, 4–5
Deception:
    in impression management, 140–143
    in research, 71–72, 252
Decision verifiability, and leadership effectiveness, 651–653
Deduction, 38–39, 40
Deductive reasoning, 250
Defense mechanisms, 12
Defensible space, 529–530
Defensiveness, 62
Dehumanization, 436

Deindividuation, in groups, 553–559
Demand characteristics, 67, 281
Demonstrations, and social change, 424
Density, *see* Population density
Dependence, neo-Freudian view, 13
Dependency, as characteristic of
   recipients of help, 302–303
Dependent variable, 42, 54, 57, 73
Depersonalization, 334
Deprivation index, 506
Description, in science, 40
Desegregation:
   application of consistency theories to,
      378–379
   residential, 395
   school, 396–397, 418, 427
Designated leader, versus leadership,
   643–644
Despair, versus integrity, as stage of
   psychosocial development, 249,
   250
Destructive obedience, 594–600
Destructiveness, as component of
   authoritarianism, 584, 585
Determinism, 39, 83–84, 639–642
Devaluation, of a victim, 84–86
Developmental rates, race differences,
   482, 484
Deviance, 23
Dewey, Thomas E., 60, 64
Differential accuracy, as component of
   accuracy of person perception,
   107, 108, 110
Differential elevation, as component of
   accuracy of person perception, 108
Diffusion of responsibility, 39, 56, 57,
   294
Diffusion of responsibility hypothesis,
   in risky shift, 631
Discrimination, 315–349
   causes, 332–337
   costs of, 325–327
   earned-reputation theory, 337
   historical theory, 332–333
   phenomenological theory, 336–337
   versus prejudice, 322–325
   psychodynamic theory, 335–336
   reverse, 122–125
   sex, 447, 467–470
   situational factors, 334
   and social distance, 337–342
   sociocultural theory, 333–334
Disinhibitory processes, in aggression,
   227, 230
Dispositional attribution, 100–104
Dissonance, *see* Cognitive-dissonance
   theory
Distance zones, 514–515
Distraction, and persuasibility, 391
Distributive justice, levels in
   development of concept of, 258
Divorce, sexual activity after, 198
Dogmatism, 592–594
   and persuasibility, 393
Dogmatism scale, 406, 592

Dominance hierarchies, in confined
   groups, 527–528
"Door-in-the-face" effect, 122, 124
Dormitories, residents' response to
   density and arrangements, 544–545
Double-barreled questions, in surveys,
   61
Double standard, for sexual behavior,
   200–201, 203
Dove Counterbalance General
   Intelligence Test, 493–494
Draw-a-Horse test, 492–493
Dress, conformity pressures in, 607,
   609, 624–625
Driving behavior, drunk, 50–51, 51–52
Drugs, and sexual behavior, 207
Dying, *see* Death

Eagleton, Thomas, 375
Early childhood, and mental ability,
   501–504
Early Training Project, 491–492, 503
Earned-reputation theory, of prejudice,
   337
Eating, and persuasibility, 391
Ecological model of crowding, 545–546
Ecological psychology, 27, 28, 417,
   511–513
Economic-exploitation theory, of
   prejudice and discrimination,
   332–333
Economic factors:
   and authoritarianism, 603
   in discrimination, 331, 332–333
   and societal pressures to conform,
      627
Eddy, Mary Baker, 82
Education, race differences in U. S., 491
Ego, 12, 215–216, 245–246
   in authoritarianism, 584
   Erikson's conception of, 248, 254
Ego-defensive function of attitudes,
   382–383, 384
Ego ideal, 246
Ego involvement, and attitude change,
   359, 362, 363
Ego-strength scale, and conforming
   behavior, 621
Eichmann, Adolf, 594–595
Electra complex, 15
Elevation, component of accuracy of
   person perception, 108
Ellsberg, Daniel, 419
Emergency behavior:
   bystander effect, 293–296
   helping intervention, 288, 293–296
Emergent leadership, 643
Emerson, Ralph Waldo, 133
Emotional constructs, and moral
   behavior, 244
Emotional states:
   and aggression, 215
   determinants, 157–161
Empathy, 85–86, 250, 255, 274, 280

Empirical approach, 39
Empirical prediction, 41
Empirical-rational strategy for change,
   418–420, 421, 425–427
Employment, equality of sexes in,
   467–470
Encounter groups, 569–572
   in communes, 577
Environment, and interpersonal
   behavior, 511–549
Environmental cues:
   to aggression, 222–225, 229
   pornography, 204–207
Environmental deprivation, and
   differences in intelligence-test
   scores, 479–480, 489–492, 494, 495,
   500, 501–504
Environmental equivalence, in
   race-difference research, 483, 489
Environmental factors (*see also*
      Situational factors):
   heritability coefficient, 486
   influencing development of
      intelligence, 506–507
   and intelligence, 489–495
   and race differences, 476–477, 487
   social-class differences in
      intelligence, 500–504
Environmental intervention projects,
   491–492, 503–504
Environmental process variables, in
   development of intelligence,
   506–507
Environmental psychology, 511–549
Environment versus heredity:
   race differences in intelligence-test
      scores, 479–496
   sex differences, 448–457
Epigenesis, 251
Equality, 258–259
   between the sexes, 447–448, 467–471
Equal Rights Amendment, 447
Equity, 258–259
Equity theory, and helping, 298, 299
Erikson, Erik, 248–251, 259, 273–274
Erotic stimuli, 204–207
Esalen, 570
E scale, 587, 591, 592, 593
Estrogens, 448
Ethical-risk hypothesis, 270–271, 273
Ethical standards:
   Milgram's study of obedience,
      598–599
   of research, 70–72, 73–74, 282
Ethnic groups, 476 (*see also* Racism)
   attitudes toward, 318–349
   and helping behavior, 304
Ethnocentrism, 492, 583, 591, 592, 593
Ethological theory, 522
   aggression, 213–215, 216–218, 237
   assumptions about human nature,
      213–215
Evaluative apprehension, 371, 373
Evolutionary theory, of altruism, 280
Expedient resistance, 615

Experimental method, 36, 42–43
  versus correlational research, 42–45
  field experiment, 53–54
  laboratory experiment, 56–57
  natural experiment, 50–51
  quasi-experimental research, 51–53
  simulation research, 54–56
Experimental realism, 72
Experimenter effects, 68–69
Experimenter-expectancy effect, 68
Experiments, 415
  ethical issues, 70–73
  problems, 67–73
  social aspects of, 6
  social relevance, 73–74
Expiatory punishment, 256–258
Expressiveness, as a sex stereotype,
    463–464
Externalization process, in prejudice,
    335–336
Externalizing function of attitudes,
    382–383
External locus of control, as a
    dimension of human nature, 82–83
External validity, 69–70
Extramarital sexual activity, 196, 197,
    198
  bisexuality, 191–192
  trade homosexuals, 186, 187, 191
Eye color, self-pacing versus reactivity
    and, 488
Eye contact:
  and ingratiation, 133, 137
  and interpersonal distance, 518–519
  and self-disclosure, 139–140
Eyewitnesses, accuracy of, 111–112

Face-saving behavior, 117–118
Face-to-face contact, and prejudiced
    attitude change, 395–405
Factor analysis, 406
Factorial design, 43
Facts, in social psychology, 31–32, 37
Failure:
  and approval-seeking behavior, 126
  and helping behavior, 296, 298
  sex differences, 459–461
Faking bad, 62
Familiarization hypothesis, and
    risky-shift phenomenon, 631
Family, in psychoanalytic theory, 13
Family ideology, and authoritarianism,
    588
Fantasy, and sexual arousal, 205–206
Farm, The, 574, 576, 578
Fear:
  and anxiety, 150–151, 271
  and sexual attraction, 173–174
Fear of success, 459–461
Federal Commission on Obscenity and
    Pornography, report, 420
Federalist Papers, The, 40
Feedback, effects of false heart-rate,
    159–160
Femininity, 461–463

Femininity (continued)
  sexual aspects, 192
Fiedler, Fred E., 648–654
Field experiment, 45, 53–54, 73, 282
Field study, 45, 48–50, 73
Field theory, 25–27, 28, 29, 30, 33,
    416–418
  attitude change, 357–379
  sex differences, 457
FIGHT (Freedom, Integration, God,
    Honor, Today), 425
"Filtering factors" of mate selection,
    162–163
First impressions, 98–100
Fixation, 247
  in stages of moral development, 261
Fixed-action patterns, 216–217
Flattery, as an ingratiation tactic, 130,
    132
Followership, 654
"Foot-in-the-door" effect, 121–122, 123,
    309, 618–619
Forced-choice technique, 62
Forced compliance, and attitude
    change, 370–373, 379, 380
Freedom:
  and attitude change, 378–379
  versus determinism, 83–84
  and reactance theory, 366–367
  restriction under high-density
    conditions, 546
  and society, 600–602
Freud, Sigmund, 11–13, 29, 79, 189,
    212–213, 214, 215–216, 237,
    244–254, 255, 258, 259, 273–274,
    600–602
Friends:
  and helping behavior, 294, 295, 296
  and interpersonal distance, 515–516
  as recipients of help, 303
Friendship, residential proximity and,
    531–532 (see also Friends)
Frustration, 219
  and aggression, 216, 218–225, 417,
    546
  as a cause of prejudice, 335
Frustration-aggression hypothesis,
    218–221, 229, 238 (see also
    Aggression; Frustration)
  Berkowitz's revision, 222–225, 229,
    238
Frustration-induced behavior, 219
Frustration tolerance:
  and noise, 531
  and spatial density, 542
F scale, see California F scale
F-syndrome, 584 (see also
    Authoritarianism; California F
    scale)
Functional distance, 531
Functional proximity, 531
Functional theory:
  assumptions about human nature,
    384
  attitude change, 382–385

Functional theory (continued)
  applications to attitude change,
    383–384
Funnel sequence, of questions in
    surveys, 61
Furniture arrangement, and interaction,
    532–534
"Future shock," 439–443
Fuzz, 231

Games, sex differences in preference,
    467
Gamesmanship, 117
Ganda children, developmental rates,
    482, 484–485
Gandhi, Mahatma, 300
Gaskin, Stephen, 576, 577, 578
Gay persons, 186 (see also
    Homosexuality)
Gender identity:
  bisexual, 191–192
  versus choice of sexual partner, 181
  homosexual, 183–191
  transsexual, 181–183
Generation gap, 436–439
  in interviewing, 64
Generative mechanism, 44
Generativity versus self-absorption, as
    stage of psychosocial development,
    249, 250–251
Genetic factors, in intelligence,
    476–477, 485–489
Genetic transmission:
  of altruism, 280
  race, 476–477
  sickle-cell anemia, 476
  Tay-Sachs disease, 476
Genital stage, of psychological
    development, 12, 247, 249
Genotypes, 476
Genovese, Kitty, 35–36, 38–39, 81, 281,
    282, 291, 294–295, 296
Gesell Developmental Schedules, race
    differences in, 484, 485
Gestalt theory, 21–25, 29, 30, 33, 96–97
  assumptions about human nature, 29,
    30
  attitude change, 352, 357–379
  of interpersonal attraction, 169
  sex differences, 457
Ghetto, riots in, 235
Gift giving:
  and control of others, 305
  as an ingratiation tactic, 130, 137–138
Goal clarity, and leadership
    effectiveness, 650–653
Goldwater, Barry, 589
Good-boy/nice-girl orientation, stage
    of moral maturity, 260
Goodenough Draw-a-Man Test, 493
"Good Samaritan" laws, 310
Gough Sanford Rigidity scale, 406
Gravel, Mike, 419
"Great man" theory of leadership,
    639–643

Great Whale River Eskimo society, 228
Group(s), 551–553
    cohesiveness, 567–569
    communication networks, 566–567,
        568
    problem solving, 559–563
    size, 564–566
    size and conformity, 617
Group behavior, 551–559
    polarizing effects, 563–564
    problem solving, 559–563
    risk taking, 628–633
    and size, 564–566
Group cohesiveness, 285–286, 567–569
Group dynamics, 27, 416, 418, 552
Group functioning, and leadership,
    642–648 (see also Organizational
    effectiveness)
Group-induced shift, 632–633
Group marriage, 198, 573
Group polarization, 632–633
Group psychology, and psychoanalytic
    theory, 12–13
Group space, 523–524
Groupthink, 560, 561, 564, 568
Guilt:
    and helping behavior, 297–298
    versus initiative, as stage of
        psychosocial development, 249,
        250–251
    reaction to transgression, 271
Guru, stage of moral maturity, 261

Habits, 30
Hallucinations, and isolation, 149
Halo effect, 22, 64
Handicapped, stigmatized role of,
    127–128
Haphazard sampling, 59
Happiness, and helping behavior, 297,
    298
Harmful behavior, and helping
    behavior, 297–300
Harmful consequences, in research, 71
Harrad West, 573
Harris, Louis, 624
Harvard Program on Technology and
    Society, 441
Hawthorne effect, 655
Hawthorne Works studies, 655–659
Head Start Program, 69, 503
Heart-rate feedback, effects of false,
    159–160, 174
Heat, and interpersonal behavior, 535
Hedonic relevance, in causal
    attribution, 103, 104
Hedonistic orientation, stage of moral
    maturity, 259
Heider, Fritz, 100, 165–167, 364–365
Helpers:
    background and personality, 300–302
    and recipients of help, 302–304
Helping behavior, 35–36, 42–43, 44, 57,
    81, 278, 287–308
    altruism, 279

Helping behavior (continued)
    in conceptual systems theory, 88
    costs and rewards, 306–308
    cross-cultural differences, 93–94
    learning, 286–287
    psychological states and, 296–300
    recipients of, 302–304
    social influence, 291–296
Helping professions, 309–310 (see also
    Helpers; Helping behavior)
Heredity:
    and aggression, 218
    race differences in intelligence,
        481–489
    social-class differences in
        intelligence, 499–500
Heredity versus environment:
    intelligence-test scores, 479–496
    sex differences, 448–457
    social-class differences in
        intelligence, 499–504
Heritability:
    coefficient, 486
    of IQ, 486–487
Hermaphrodites, 181–182
Heteronomous stage of moral
    development, 255
Heterosexual behavior, 196–204 (see also
    Sexual behavior)
Historical causes:
    of interpersonal behavior, 29, 30
    of prejudice and discrimination,
        332–333
Hitchcock, Alfred, 230
Hitchhiking, 137, 303–304
Hitler, Adolf, 639
Homeostatic principle, 513
    and crowding, 537–538, 545, 546
    in personal space, 518–519
    in privacy, 524–525
Homicide, 221, 225, 547 (see also
    Genovese, Kitty)
Homosexuality, 23, 182, 183–191
    female, 191
    incidence rates, 183–186
    personality, in males, 187–191
    self-identification of male
        homosexuality, 186–187
    stigmatized role, 127–128
Hoover, J. Edgar, 225
Hormones, sex differences, 448–450
Hostility (see also Aggression):
    neo-Freudian view, 13
    and racial attitude change, 407
House Committee on Un-American
    Activities, 607
Humanism, beliefs about human
    nature, 94
Human products, analyzing, 57–58
Hunt, E. Howard, 263
Hunter College Aptitude Scales for
    Gifted Children, 504
Hutterite society, 228, 229
Huxley, Aldous, 442
Hypnosis, 633–634

Hypocrisy, 293
Hypotheses, 7, 38, 49, 54, 56

Id, 12, 215–216, 245
    in authoritarianism, 584
Identification:
    and helping behavior, 300
    process, in conformity, 613–614
    in psychoanalytic theory, 246–247
Identity:
    development, 149, 250, 254
    versus identity diffusion, stage of
        psychosocial development, 249,
        250
    sexual, 181–192
Ideological gap, between parents and
    children, 438–439
Idiosyncracy-credit model of
    conformity, 628
Image, see Impression management
Imitation, 19–20 (see also Modeling)
    of aggressive behavior, 226–228
    and prejudice, 334
    sex-role behaviors, 456
Immanent justice, 258
Implicit personality theories, 95–96, 108
Impression formation, 22, 77–113
    accuracy of judgments of others,
        104–112
    adding versus averaging, 97–98
    and attitude change, 372
    attribution of cause, 100–104
    central traits, 96–97
    conceptual systems theory, 88–89
    first impressions, 98–100
    future trends in study of, 112
    group stereotypes, 95
    implicit personality theories, 95–96
    philosophies of human nature, 79–86,
        89–94
    role-construct theory, 86–88
Impression management, 115–145
    detection of, 140–143
    and human nature, 143
    ingratiation, 128–134
    nature of, 116–118
    consistent public image, 121–125
    self-disclosure, 138–140
    self-presentation, 118–121
    quest for social approval, 125–128
    and social influence, 134–138
Incentive, see Reward
Incipient cooperation, 255
Income, race differences in, 483
Independence:
    and conformity, 610–611, 616, 622,
        627
    as a dimension of human nature,
        81–82, 89–92
Independent consent, 615
Independent dissent, 614
Independent variable, 42, 52, 54, 57, 73
Index of Status Characteristics, 504
Indians, see North American natives

Individual characteristics, and attitude
    change, 397, 401
Individual conscience orientation,
    period of moral maturity, 261
Individual differences (see also Overlap):
    beliefs about, 85–86
    interpersonal distance, 516–517
Individualistic motive, 284
Individualistic orientation versus group
    orientation, 552–553
Individualistic reward structure,
    283–284
Individual level of analysis, of causes of
    prejudice, 334
Individuation, 436
Induction, 38–39, 40
Industrial society versus
    postindustrialized society, 418 (see
    also Technology)
Industry versus inferiority, stage of
    psychosocial development, 249,
    250
Infancy:
    developmental rates, 482, 484
    mental ability, 501–504
Inferiority versus industry, stage of
    psychosocial development, 249,
    250–251
Influence, see Social influence
Informational appeal, 384–385
Informed consent, in research, 70–71
Ingratiation, 119, 128–134
    conformity as, 628
Inhibition, of aggressive behavior,
    226–228
Initiating structure, dimension of
    leadership behavior, 644–648
Initiation rites, and attraction to the
    group, 168–169, 370
Initiative versus guilt, stage of
    psychosocial development, 249,
    250–251
Inner-directedness, 626
Innocent victim, 84–86, 298
Inside density:
    and aggression, 541
    dormitories, 544
    and social pathology, 539–541
Insomnia, and sleeping pills, 160
Instincts, 211
    death, 237
    territoriality, 217–218
Instinctual behavior, 229
    aggression, 215–218, 219–220, 226,
    229
    in psychoanalytic theory, 13
Institute for Social Research, 418, 583
Institute for the Future, 441
Instructor evaluation, 91–92
Instrumental aggression, 220
Instrumental function of attitudes, 382
Instrumental-relativist orientation, stage
    of moral maturity, 259

Integrity versus despair, stage of
    psychosocial development, 249,
    250–251
Intelligence:
    as an antecedent of attraction,
    163–164
    as a culturally defined concept,
    492–493
    and environmental deprivation,
    489–492
    heritability of, 486–487
    versus intelligence-test scores, 481
    and leadership, 638
    Level II, 500–501
    occupation and, 499
    race differences in test scores,
    479–496, 504–506
    sex differences, 457–458
    social-class factors, 496–506
    characteristics of the testing situation,
    494–495
Intentions versus consequences, in
    determining morality, 256, 264
Interaction, in experimental research, 43
    (see also Interpersonal behavior;
    Social interaction)
Interaction context, and impression
    management, 119–120 (see also
    Situational attribution; Situational
    factors)
Interaction territory, 523
Interconnectedness, in attitudes, 322
Intergroup contact hypothesis, 395
    factors facilitating attitude change,
    395–397
    test of validity of, 397–405
Internal-External (I-E) scale, 83
Internal factors, in interpersonal
    behavior, 29, 30
Internalization, 258
    process, in conformity, 613–614
Internal validity, 69–70
International Association for the
    Advancement of Ethnology and
    Eugenics, 479
Inter-Nation Simulation, 56
Interpersonal accommodation, 112
Interpersonal attraction, 147, 161–169,
    365
    antecedents, 161–167
    love, 169–175
    mate selection, 162–163, 166
    theories, 167–169
Interpersonal behavior, 3–6
    affiliation, 147–161
    aggression, 211–241
    attitude change, 351–409
    attitudes and, 315–349
    attraction, 161–169
    conformity, 607–635
    in groups, 551–579
    impression formation, 72–113
    impression management, 115–145
    leadership, 637–654

Interpersonal behavior (continued)
    love, 169–175
    obedience, 594–600
    and the physical environment,
    511–549
    prosocial, 277–312
    sex roles, 447–473
    sexual, 177–208
    society and institutions, 411–444
    theoretical differences, 27–29
Interpersonal concordance, stage of
    moral maturity, 260
Interpersonal distance, 513–521
Interpersonal perception, see Social
    perception
Interpersonal relationships, and
    leadership effectiveness, 644–654
    (see also Interpersonal behavior)
Interpersonal trust, 81, 251
Interpretational appeal, 384–385
Interracial contact:
    and reduction of prejudice, 394–405
    residential, 395
    in South Africa, 329–330
Intervention, educational, 491–492,
    503–504
Interviewer effects, 63–64
Interviews, 35, 45, 48, 49, 58–65
Intimacy (see also Love):
    and interpersonal distance, 513–514,
    516
    versus isolation, stage of psychosocial
    development, 249, 250–251
    race versus similarity of values as
    determinant of, 340
    and self-disclosure, 138–140
Intimate zone, 514
Intrapersonal factors, see Personality
    factors
Introversion, and personal space, 516
Intrusion, into personal space, 517–518
    compensation, 518–519
Invasion of privacy, 603–604
    protestations of, 604
    in research, 70, 73
Invention, rates, 431
Involvement, and attitude change, 359,
    362, 363
Irrationality, as a dimension of human
    nature, 82–83, 89–92
Isolation:
    versus intimacy, stage of
    psychosocial development, 249,
    250
    neo-Freudian view, 13
    and physical surroundings, 512–513
    reactions to, 147–149

James, William, 639
Japanese Americans:
    discrimination against, 330–331
    intelligence, 495–496
Jefferson, Thomas, 24, 424

Jensen, Arthur, 479, 485–489, 490
Jesus people, 573
Johnson, Lyndon B., 71, 420, 421, 589
Jorgenson, Christine (George), 183
Judgments, groups versus individuals, 559–560
Juries, 565–566
Justice (*see also* Just-world hypothesis):
  children's conception, 256–259
  distributive, 258–259
  immanent, 258
Just-world hypothesis, 84–86, 224, 298

Kennedy, Edward, 336, 369, 373–375, 378
Kennedy, John F., 51, 60, 62, 90, 163, 561, 642
Kennedy, Robert F., 111, 326
Kernel of truth hypothesis, 337
  sex differences, 463
Kerner Commission, 235
"Kiddie Mach" scale, 135
King, Martin Luther, 85, 267–268, 418, 420, 431–432, 642
Knowledge explosion, 431
Knowledge function of attitudes, 383
Kob, territoriality in, 217
Kohlberg, Lawrence, 244, 254, 258, 259–270, 273–274
Koinonia, 573
Kpelle, and cultural definitions of intelligence, 493
Krogh, Egil, 263
Kuhlmann-Anderson test, 483
!Kung people, 451, 537

Laboratory experiment, 45, 56–57 (*see also* Experimental method; Experiments)
LaGuardia, Fiorello, 142
Laine, Steven, 82
Landon, Alfred, 59
Language development, as process variable, in development of intelligence, 506
Latency period, 247, 248, 249
Latitudes of acceptance, and attitude change, 359, 360–364
Latitudes of rejection, 359, 360–364
Laughter, and room size, 543
Law, scientific, 38
Law-and-order orientation, stage of moral maturity, 260
Leader Behavior Description Questionnaire (LBDQ), 645, 646
Leadership, 12–13, 637–662
  authoritarian, 658–659
  behavior, 643–646
  in communes, 576
  and communication networks, 566
  and conformity, 628
  democratic, 658
  "great man" theory, 639–643

Leadership (continued)
  laissez-faire, 658
  and organizational effectiveness, 654–660
  and risky shift, 631–632
  and seating arrangements, 520
Leadership style, 648, 658–659
Learning, *see* Social-learning theory
Learning ability (*see also* Cognitive abilities; Intelligence):
  and dogmatism, 594
  Level I, 500–501
Learning provision, as process variable, in the development of intelligence, 506
Least-preferred coworker (LPC) measure, 648–654
Legalistic orientation, stage of moral maturity, 261
Legal reform, 50–51, 425 (*see also* Legislation)
Legislation (*see also* Legal reform):
  and discrimination, 331–332
  and prosocial behavior, 310–311
  and social change, 420, 425, 427
Leisure, 434
Lepcha society, 229
Lesbianism, 191 (*see also* Homosexuality)
Level I and II abilities, 500
Lewin, Kurt, 25–27, 415, 416–418, 569–570, 657–659
Libido, 12, 13, 247
Liddy, G. Gordon, 124
Lie detector, in research, 122, 125
Life space, 26, 27, 30
Likert method of summated ratings, 317
Likert-type scale, 62–63, 317
  PHN, 89–92
Liking:
  balance theory, 364–365
  and interpersonal distance, 515–516
  and self-disclosure, 138–139
Linnaeus, Carolus, 476
Literary Digest poll, 59
Locus of control, 82–83
  and persuasibility, 393
  race differences, 491
  and reaction to high density, 542
Locus of reinforcement, *see* Locus of control
Longitudinal studies, of moral development, 268, 269
Love, 147, 169–175
  adolescent, 250
  measurement, 170–172
  and sexual behavior, 199–204
  stimulants, 171–172
Love scale, 170–171, 172
LPC, *see* Least-preferred coworker measure
Luck, as an explanation of performance, 466, 467
Lynching, 335

MacArthur, Douglas, 589
Machiavelli, Niccolò, 134
Machiavellianism, 134–136
  and competitive behavior, 347
  and helping behavior, 300
Machiavellianism scale, 134–135, 407, 408
Magruder, Jeb, 595
Maladjustment, 23 (*see also* Psychopathology; Social pathology)
Male hustlers, 186, 187, 189–190 (*see also* Homosexuality)
Managerial strategy, 654–661
Manipulativeness, and social influence, 134–138 (*see also* Machiavellianism)
Mao Tse-tung, 424
Marcuse, Herbert, 600–602
Marijuana, and sexual behavior, 207
Markers, as space reservers, 526–527
Marlowe-Crowne Social Desirability Scale, 128
Marriage:
  complementarity in mate selection, 162
  and self-disclosure, 138, 139
Marx, Karl, 418
Masculinity, 461–463 (*see also* Sex roles)
Maslow, Abraham, 175
Mass media:
  prejudice and, 330–331
  and repressive society, 604
  sex-role socialization, 452–453
  violence and, 230–234, 239, 416
Masturbation, 194–195
Mate selection, 162–163, 166
Mate swapping, 198
Mattachine Society, 186
McCarthy, Eugene, 333
McCord, James, 595
Memory:
  errors in interviews, 61
  groups versus individuals, 559–560
Mennonite society, 228, 229
Menstrual cycle, performance and mood, 449
Mental illness, and population density, 539
Mental patients, stigmatized role of, 127–128
Mental set, by subjects in experiments, 57, 89 (*see also* Response set)
"Mere exposure" hypothesis, 168
Methods, in social psychology, 35–74
  archival research, 46–47
  field experiment, 53–54
  field study, 48–50
  future, 73–74
  laboratory experiment, 56–57
  major, 45–57
  natural experiment, 50–51
  problems, 57–73
  quasi-experimental research, 51–53
  simulation research, 54–56

Methods, in social psychology
(continued)
survey, 47–48
Milgram, Stanley, 81–82, 265, 269, 414,
581, 595–600
Milwaukee Project, 503–504
Minnesota Multiphasic Personality
Inventory (MMPI), 62, 63
Minority groups (see also Ethnic groups):
attitudes toward, 322–325, 327, 329
and conformity, 618
earned-reputation theory, 337
Mitchell, John, 263
Mixed-motive games, 284–285
Mobs, 553
Modeling:
aggressive behavior, 227–228,
229–230, 535
helping behavior, 291–293
and resistance to temptation, 272–273
sex-role socialization, 452, 456
Modesty, in self-presentation, 118–119,
120, 125, 130, 132
Monday night class, 577
Moods:
and helping behavior, 297
menstrual cycle and, 449
Moral behavior, 243–275
cognitive theory, 244, 254–270,
273–275
integrative approach, 274
psychoanalytic theory, 244, 245–254,
273–275
social-learning theory, 245, 270–275
in Western culture, 244–245
Moral development:
cognitive theories, 254–270
Erikson's psychosocial stages,
248–251
Kohlberg's stages, 259–270
Piaget's cognitive stages, 255–259, 264
psychoanalytic theory, 12, 244–254,
273–275
social-learning theory, 270–273
Wilder's interpretation of superego
as values, 251
Moral independence stage, 255, 256,
258, 434–435
Morality (see also Moral behavior):
changes in, 434–435
development in Western culture,
244–245
social-learning theory, 270–273
Moral judgments, 243–275
and moral behavior, 264–269, 273
stories to measure, 259, 260, 262–263,
264, 265
Moral knowledge, 274
Moral realism stage, 255, 256
More, Thomas, 442
Morningstar Ranch, 577–578
Morris, James (Jan), 183, 184
Mother-child interaction, 154, 454 (see
also Child-rearing practices;
Parent-child interaction)

Mother-child interaction (continued)
and developmental rates, 484–485
and mental development, 503
Motivational base, 432
Motivational factors, in the testing
situation, 489, 494–495, 504
Motives:
affiliative, 149
and moral behavior, 244
and persuasibility, 393
Movies, see Mass media
Moynihan, Daniel P., 337
Moynihan Report, 479
Multiplex attitudes, 321–322
Mundugumur society, 228–229
Murder, see Homicide
Music:
and persuasibility, 391
and sexual activity, 207
Mutual commitment, 117
My Lai massacre, 589

Nader, Ralph, 418, 425
Names, stereotypes of, 324–325
National Commission on the Causes
and Prevention of Violence, 231,
232, 233, 234, 236, 238
National Institute of Mental Health, 420
National Training Laboratory in Group
Development, 418, 570
Natural experiment, 45, 50–51, 416, 417
(see also Experimental method;
Experiments)
Naturalistic observation, 65
Naturalistic research, 415, 417
Nay-saying, 63
Nazi Germany, 582, 583
Need systems, complementarity and
attraction, 162–163
Negative aftereffects, of noise, 536
Neo-Freudianism, 13, 246, 248
and aggression, 216, 237
Neutral thwarting, and crowding, 547
New Communities Project, 577
New Year's resolutions, 389–390
Nicholas, Tsar, 7–11, 14–15
Nixon, Richard M., 60, 101, 169,
375–378, 420, 566, 595, 627
Noise:
and frustration tolerance, 531
and interpersonal behavior, 535–536
Nonaggressive societies, 228–229
Noncommon effects, in causal
attribution, 104
Nonmanipulative method, 43–45
Nonreactive methods, 47
Nonverbal behavior:
and detection of prejudice, 141–142
in ingratiation, 133
and personal space, 517–519
and self-disclosure, 139–140
self-presentation, 126, 140–142
Nonviolent strategies for change,
420–425, 431–432

Normative-reeducative strategy for
change, 420
police training, 422–427
Norms, 16 (see also Sex roles)
and activism, 435–436
and alienation, 435–436
and attitude change, 396, 401
autokinetic effect, 428–429
and change, 420, 428
and helping behavior, 304–306
moral, 244
personal distance, 513–521
sexual, 177–178
and social-desirability bias, 61–62
North American natives, 248
cooperative and competitive
behaviors, 287
cultural determinants of change, 420
cultural relativism of intelligence,
492–493, 495
equity theory and, 299
prejudice against, effects of, 325–326
Northern Ireland, prejudice in, 329
North-Hatt Occupational Prestige Scale,
496, 497–498
NTL Center for Applied Behavioral
Science, 418
Nuclear conflicts, in personality
development, 248–251
Nurturance, sex-role socialization of,
450
Nutrition, and mental development of
the fetus, 501

Obedience, 81–82, 594–595
and authoritarianism, 600
destructive, 594–600
and level of moral maturity, 265, 269
orientation stage of moral maturity,
259
sex-role socialization of, 451
Object appraisal function of attitudes,
383
Objectivity:
in question wording, 61
in science, 39–40
Obscenity, 204
Observation:
in experimental research, 42
groups versus individuals, 559–560
naturalistic, 65
in social learning, 20
in social psychology, 32, 49
Observational method, 35, 45
research problems in, 65–67
Occupation:
as index of social class, 496–498
and IQ, 499, 507
and Machiavellianism, 135
and philosophy of human nature, 91,
92
sex differences, 469–470
Occupational status, 497–498
sex differences, 469–470, 471
Oedipus conflict, 246–247, 456

Office landscaping, 532, 533
Oglala Sioux, 248
One-upsmanship, 117
Open-ended questions, 61
Operational definitions, 39
Opinion molecules, 360
Opinion polls, 32
Opposition, response set, 63
Oral anxiety, and affiliation, 153
Oral stage, of psychological
    development, 12, 247, 249
Organizational effectiveness, 642–643,
    654–660
Organizational philosophies, industrial
    versus postindustrialized society,
    419
Organizational practices, industrial
    versus postindustrialized society,
    419
Orgasm, 180, 195, 198
Oriental Americans:
    discrimination against, 330–331
    intelligence, 495–496
    prejudice against, 342–343
Orwell, George, 442
Other-directedness, 626
Other-enhancement, see Flattery
Outside density, 539–541
    in dormitories, 544
Overcategorization, 324
Overcrowding, 214, 237–238
Overdifferentiation, in person
    perception, 109
Overlap:
    racial similarities, 455
    social-class similarities, 507
Overload model of crowding, 545–546,
    547
Overload theory, in city life, 310
Overpopulation, 214, 237–238

Panel of Privacy and Behavioral
    Research, 71
Paradigm, in social psychology, 31
Parametric study, 53
Parent-child interaction (see also
    Child-rearing practices):
    and gender identity, 182, 188–189,
        190
    generation gap, 436–439
    and helping behavior, 300
    sex-role socialization, 452
Participant-observation method, 49, 51
Partitions, and privacy, 532
Passionate love, 172–174
Paul, St., 82
Peaceful societies, 228–229
Peale, Norman Vincent, 82
P-E-C scale, 587
Penis envy, 15, 247, 456
Penis size, 194
Perceptual development, 501–504
Performance, of tasks:
    presence of others, 559–563
    and spatial density, 542–543

Perinatal environment, and mental
    ability, 501
Peron, Isabel, 11
Personal constructs, 86–88
Personal-distance zone, 514–515
Personalism, in causal attribution, 103,
    104
Personality characteristics (see also
    Personality factors):
    of Blacks, 495
    and cooperative behavior, 285
    and level of moral maturity, 265–267
    of male homosexuals, 187–191
    and personal space, 516–517, 542
    sex differences, 457–463
    social-class differences, 499, 504
Personality defects, and prejudice,
    335–336
Personality development:
    Erikson's psychosocial stages,
        248–251
    psychoanalytic theory, 13, 247–248
Personality disorder, and personal
    space, 516
Personality factors (see also Personality
    characteristics):
    and affiliation, 153
    in attitude change, 389–390,
        391–392, 457–463
    and conformity, 620–624
    and helping behavior, 300–302
    and interpersonal attraction, 161–162,
        167
    and leadership, 637–643
Personality integration, in conceptual
    systems theory, 88–89
Personality measures:
    California F scale, 63, 342, 587–592,
        600, 603, 621
    California Psychological Inventory
        (CPI), 62
    Internal-external (I-E) scale, 83
    Minnesota Multiphasic Personality
        Inventory (MMPI), 62
    Role Construct Repertory Test, 87
    Self-Monitoring Scale, 142–143
    Thematic Apperception Test (TAT),
        173–174, 233
Personality style, and leadership,
    639–643
Personality-test scores, and helping
    behavior, 300–302
Personality theories:
    implicit, 95–96
    psychoanalytic, 12
    and social psychology, 25–26, 30
Personality traits, 96–100
    versus situational factors in behavior,
        623–624
Personality-trait words, likableness of,
    98
Personal responsibility:
    and attitude change, 373
    bystander effect, 293–296
    in emergencies, 289, 295

Personal space, 513–521
    invasion, 517–519, 520, 547
Personal thwarting, and crowding, 547
Personnel Research Board of Ohio State
    University, 643–648
Person perception, accuracy of, 104–112
    (see also Impression formation;
    Social perception)
Persuasibility, 31 (see also Attitude
    change)
    sex differences, 458
Persuasion, see Attitude change
Persuasion hypothesis, in risky shifts,
    631–632
Persuasive communications, 354,
    384–385, 389–409
Petting behavior, 201–202, 204
Phallic stage, of psychological
    development, 12, 247, 249
Phase sequences, 502
Phenomenological approach, 22, 30, 33,
    86–88 (see also Functional theory)
    attitude change, 382–385
    to prejudice, 336–337
Phenotypes, 476
Philosophies of human nature, 79–98
    (see also Assumptions about
    human nature)
Philosophies of Human Nature (PHN)
    scale, 89–92, 407, 408
Physical attractiveness:
    as an antecedent of attraction,
        164–166
    and credibility, 394
Physical environment, and
    interpersonal behavior, 511–549
Physiological arousal:
    and emotional state, 157–159
    and pornography, 205
Physiology:
    orgasm in women, 195
    sex differences, 448–450
    of sexual behavior, 197
    of transsexual persons, 181–183
Piaget, Jean, 245, 254–259, 264, 269–270,
    272, 273–274
Placebo, 157–159
Plato, 442
Pleasant behavior, as an antecedent for
    attraction, 165, 167
Plessy v. Ferguson, 478
Polarization, of responses in groups,
    563–564
Polarization hypothesis, of group shift,
    632–633
Police training, 422–424, 604
Political views:
    and attitudes, 318
    and authoritarianism, 589, 592–593,
        600–602
    and level of conceptual system, 89
    and level of moral maturity, 265–268
    and racism, 346
    social-psychological research,
        412–416

Polls, 32, 48, 58–65, 624
Population:
    explosion, 214, 237–238
    genetic, 476–477
    racial percentage and prejudice, 327,
        329–330
    research, 48
    effects of zero population growth,
        500
Population density, 537–541
    personality and reactions to, 542
    sex differences in reaction to,
        541–542
    and social pathology, 538–541
    task performance and, 542
Pornography, 51, 204–207
    Federal Commission on Obscenity
        and Pornography, 420
    reactance theory, 367
Porter, Bart, 263
Position power, and leadership
    effectiveness, 650, 651
Postconventional level, of moral
    maturity, 260–261, 266–269
Postdecision dissonance, 370, 371
Postfigurative culture, 437
Postindustrialized society, 418, 419,
    441–442
Postnatal environment, early, and
    mental ability, 501–504
"Postulate of Commensurate
    Complexity," 31
Potter, Stephen, 117
Power:
    and leadership effectiveness, 650
    and prejudice, 329
Power and toughness, as component of
    authoritarianism, 584, 585
Power-coercive strategy for change,
    420–425, 427
Power orientation, 35, 36, 89
Power themes, and presidential
    achievement, 35, 36
Preconventional level, of moral
    maturity, 259, 266–269
Prediction, in science, 41
Prefigurative culture, 437–439
Prejudice, 315–349
    and the authoritarian personality,
        583, 588
    causes, 332–337
    costs, 325–327
    versus discrimination, 322–325
    earned-reputation theory, 337
    extent of, 327–332
    factors, 340–341
    historical theory, 332–333
    effects of interracial contact on,
        394–405
    phenomenological theory, 336–337
    psychodynamic theory, 335–336
    racial, 35, 89, 315–349
    reducing, 394–395
    situational factors, 334

Prejudice (continued)
    and social distance, 337–342
    sociocultural theory, 333-334
    universality, 327–332
Premarital sexual behavior, 196, 197,
    198, 199–204
Prenatal environment, and mental
    ability, 501
Preschool books, 46
Primacy effect:
    in attitude change, 394
    in impression formation, 98–100
Primary environments, crowding in,
    546–548
Primary territories, 523, 525
    territoriality in, 528–530
Principled level, of moral maturity,
    260–261, 266–267, 434–435
Principles, acquisition of universal, 244
Prison, isolation in, 149
Prisoner's Dilemma, 284–285
Prison study, 54–55
Privacy:
    barriers and partitions, 532
    in communes, 578
    crowding, 537
    invasion of, in research, 70, 73
    in public, 520
    in public territory, 525–527
    territoriality, 524–525
Private acceptance, 610–611, 612, 616
Private attitude versus public behavior,
    in attitude change, 372, 379–380
Probability sampling, 59–60
Problem solving:
    and group size, 564–566
    groups versus individuals, 559–563
Productivity (see also Organizational
    effectiveness; Performance;
    Problem solving):
    and cohesiveness, 567–569
    and communication networks, 566,
        568
    and group cohesiveness, 285–286
    and leadership, 642–643, 654–660
Projection, 15, 106
Projectivity, component of
    authoritarianism, 584, 585
Propinquity, as an antecedent of
    attraction, 167
Prosocial behavior, 277–311 (see also
    Cooperation; Helping behavior)
    fostering, 308–311
    importance of, 279–283
Prostitutes, 197
    male hustlers, 186, 187, 189–190
    use of by males, 196, 198, 203
Protection, as an ingratiation motive,
    131
Protestant Ethic, 433–434
Proxemics, 511
Proximity, residential and friendship,
    531–532
Proxmire, William, 322

Pruitt-Igoe housing project, 512–513
Psychoanalytic theory, 11–16, 26, 29,
    30, 33, 79, 83
    aggression, 215–216, 237
    assumptions about human nature, 29,
        30, 212–213, 215–216
    attitude change, 382–385
    authoritarianism, 584, 587
    bisexuality, 191–192
    female homosexuality, 191
    moral behavior, 245–254, 273–275
    of prejudice, 335–336
    prosocial behavior, 279
    research in, 251–254
    sex-role development, 456
    stages of psychological development,
        247–248, 249
Psychodynamic theory, of prejudice,
    335–336
Psychological development,
    psychoanalytic stages, 12, 247–249
Psychological reactance (see also
    Reactance theory):
    and helping behavior, 305–306
    in high-density conditions, 546
Psychological states, and helping
    behavior, 296–300
Psychopathology (see also Social
    pathology):
    and authoritarianism, 586
    and population density, 539–541
    reaction to transgression, 271
Psychophysics principles, in
    social-judgment theory of attitude
    change, 357–359
Psychosexual stages of development,
    247–248, 456
Psychosocial stages of development,
    248–251
Psychotherapy:
    and assumptions about human
        nature, 79, 81
    and homosexual persons, 186
    sexism in, 328
    and transsexual persons, 183
Public behavior versus private attitudes,
    372, 379–380
Public-distance zone, 514–515
Public image, see Impression formation;
    Impression management
Public-opinion polls, 32, 58–65, 624
Public territories, 523, 525
    defense of, 525–527
Punishment:
    and attitude change, 373
    expiatory, 256–258
    and imitation of aggressive behavior,
        227–228, 239
    orientation stage, of moral maturity,
        259
    reaction to transgression, 271
    reciprocal, 256, 258
    and resistance to temptation, 272
    seeking, 271

Quality of life, and assumptions about human nature, 92–94
Quantification, in experimental research, 42–43
Quasi-experimental research, 45, 51–53, 73
Questionnaires, 32, 45, 48, 49, 58–65
Question wording, in surveys, 60–61
Quota sampling, 59

Race, 475–479
    of examiner, and test scores, 489, 494
    interviewer effects, 64
    popular definition, 477–478
    and social distance, 337–342
    technical definition, 476–477
Race differences:
    athletic performance, 488
    collective violence, 235
    developmental rates, 482, 484
    genetic, 476–477
    helping behavior, 304
    identification with television violence, 232
    income, 483
    intelligence-test scores, 479–496, 504–506
    philosophy of human nature, 92
    research problems, 478–479, 495
Racial attitudes, 32, 161, 315–349 (see also Discrimination; Prejudice)
    change, 378–379, 394–409
Racial prejudice, 35, 89, 122–125, 337–342 (see also Discrimination; Prejudice; Racial attitudes; Racism)
    effects of interracial contact on, 394–405
    nonverbal cues to, 141–142
Racism, 322–349
    attitude change, 352–387
    attitudes and behavior, 342–348
    aversive, 345
    costs, 325–327
    history, in the U.S., 332
    and social distance, 337–342
    stereotypes, 331
Radical social psychology, 413
Railroad Game, 399–402
Randomization, in experimental research, 42
Random sampling, 60
Rapport:
    in interviewing, 61
    and test results, 495
Rasputin, and influence over the Tsarina of Russia, 7–11
    field-theory view, 27
    Gestalt view, 25
    psychoanalytic view, 13–16
    role-theorist view, 18–19
    social-learning view, 21
    stimulus-response view, 21
"Rasputin phenomenon," 11
Rational approach, 39

Rational-economic theory of man, 654–655
Rationality, as dimension of human nature, 82–83, 89–92
Rational prediction, 41
Reactance theory:
    and attitude change, 366–367
    and romantic love, 172
Reactive methods, 47
Real similarity, 106, 108
Rebellious orientation, 24
    and attitude change, 395
    in conceptual systems theory, 88
Recency effect:
    in attitude change, 394
    in impression formation, 87–88, 98–100
Recipients of help, characteristics of, 302–304
Reciprocal punishment, 256, 258
Reciprocity:
    and attraction, 165–167
    norm of, and helping behavior, 305–306
    and self-disclosure, 138
Reference scales, 358
Regional differences, in intelligence-test scores, 480, 491
Rehfisch Rigidity scale, 406
Reinforcement theory, 19, 30 (see also Stimulus-response theory)
    affiliation, 149–150
    assumptions about human nature, 29, 30, 94, 355
    attitude change, 352, 353–357
    and control of violence, 239
    and helping behavior, 291
    interpersonal attraction, 167–169
    and passionate love, 172–173
    verbal, 355–357
    vicarious, 20
Relationships, in science, 40
Relative deprivation:
    as a characteristic of social movements, 432
    as a trigger for collective violence, 236
Relatives, as recipients of help, 303
Releasers, 217, 222
Reliability:
    in experimental research, 43, 58
    in observational research, 67
Religious views:
    and attitudes toward sex, 197–198, 199
    changes in, 434–435
    and commitment to a communal group, 578
    and self-presentation behavior, 119–120
Replication, of experiments, 69–70
Report of the National Advisory Commission on Civil Disorders, 420, 421

Representative sampling, 59
Repression, societal, 600–604, 625–627
"Rep Test," see Role Construct Repertory Test
Republic of South Africa, prejudice in, 329–330
Reputational method, of defining social class, 496
Research Center for Group Dynamics, 27, 418
Research methods, in social psychology, 35–74
    experimental versus correlational, 42–45
    future, 73–74
    major, 45–57
    problems, 57–73
    scientific method, 36–41
Research problems:
    analyzing human products, 57–58
    asking questions, 58–65
    experiments, 67–73
    observation, 65–67
    in studying prosocial behavior, 281–283
    in studying sexual behavior, 179–181
Residential desegregation, 395
Residential environments, inside and outside density in, 539–541, 544–545
Residential proximity, and friendship, 531–532
Response, 19
Response set, 62–63
    acquiescent, 63, 587, 591
    in social perception, 107, 110
Reverse discrimination, 122–125, 213
Revolution, 235–236, 422, 424
    and technological society, 601–602
Reward:
    and altruistic behavior, 280, 289, 291, 306–308
    attitude change, 354–357
    and imitation of aggressive behavior, 227–228
Reward structures, 283
    and attitude change, 396–397
Rigidity:
    neo-Freudian view, 13
    and racial attitude change, 407
Ring, Kenneth, 412–416
Riots, 235, 423
    and social change, 424
    and temperature, 535
Risk-taking behavior, 628–633
Risky shift, see Risk-taking behavior
Robber's Cave experiment, 239–240
Role, 3, 16–19, 26, 30, 33, 87–88, 118
    confusion versus identity, stage of psychosocial development, 249, 250
    sex as, 456–457
    stigmatized, 127–128
Role conflict, 16–17, 33

Role Construct Repertory Test, 87
Role-construct theory, 86–88
Role expectations, 16, 18, 33 (see also
    Sex roles)
    of the stigmatized, 127–128
Role obligations, 18, 33, 127–128
Role-oriented behavior, and attitude
    change, 396
Role theory, in social psychology,
    16–19, 29, 30, 33
    assumptions about human nature, 29,
    30
    sex-role development, 456–457
Romantic attraction, see Love
Romeo-and-Juliet effect, 171–172
Roosevelt, Franklin D., 59
Rules:
    and cognitive stages, 255–256
    and commune success, 576–577
    and moral behavior, 244
Russell, Bertrand, 173

Salience, of initial attitudes, 380–382
Sampling, 47, 48, 49, 57–58
    in a survey, 59–60
Sampling error, 48
Scapegoating, 335, 395
Schachter, Stanley, 147–148, 150–161,
    173
Schlesinger, Arthur, 561
School desegregation, 396–397, 427
School Segregation scale, 403–404
Schweitzer, Albert, 300
Science, pure versus applied, 412–416
Scientific method, 36–41
    characteristics of, 39–40
    goals of, 40–41
Scoring, 58
Seating arrangements:
    effect on behavior, 519–521
    and interpersonal distance, 516
Secondary environments, crowding in,
    546–548
Secondary territories, 523, 525
Selective breeding, for aggressive
    behavior, 218
Selective exposure, 370
Selective migration, 496
Self (see also Impression management;
    Self-concept):
    goals and motives, 119–120
    presentation of, 117–121, 130
    and society in youth, 436
Self-absorption versus generativity,
    stage of psychosocial development,
    249, 250
Self-actualization:
    as goal in postindustrialized society,
    418
    and homosexuality, 186
    and self-disclosure, 138
Self-actualizing theory, of the working
    man, 654, 659
Self-concept, 18, 104

Self-concept (continued)
    in adolescence, 250
    and attitude change, 405–408
    Black, 495
    in conceptual systems theory, 88
    and homosexuality, 185, 186, 188
    and interpersonal attraction, 169
    and level of moral maturity, 265–267
    and self-presentation, 120–121
Self-concern, and helping behavior,
    296–297, 298
Self-confidence, and persuasibility,
    391–392
Self-disclosure:
    and impression management,
    138–140
    and mate selection, 162–163
Self-discrimination, 470
Self-enhancement, as an ingratiation
    tactic, 130
Self-esteem, 32
    and conforming behavior, 621, 622
    intelligence and attraction, 163–165
    and persuasibility, 391–392
    and sex-typing, 462
Self-evaluation:
    sex differences, 466–467
    through social comparison, 150, 155
Self-fulfilling prophecies, 69, 441
    of prejudice, 325–327
    sex-role stereotypes, 464
    test scores, 495
Self-identity, see Identity;
    Self-concept
Selfishness, as dimension of human
    nature, 81, 89–92
Self-monitoring individuals, 142–143
Self-Monitoring Scale, 142–143
Self-perception, 104
Self-perception theory:
    assumptions about human nature,
    380
    attitude change, 379–382
    attitudes and behavior, 347–348
    and internal states, 160–161
Self-presentation, 115–145
    as an ingratiation tactic, 130, 132
Self-revelation, see Self-disclosure
Semantic differential, 317
Sensitivity training, 569–572
    effects on philosophy of human
    nature, 90–91
    and sexual arousal, 174
Sensory stimulation in early childhood,
    and mental ability, 501–504
Sentence-completion test (Getzels and
    Walsh), 404
Sequence of variables, 44, 45
Sesame Street, 331, 452
Sex (see also Sexual behavior):
    attitudes toward, 169–170, 177
    and love, 170, 172–174
Sex appeal, and playing "hard to get,"
    151

Sex crimes, 51
    and pornography, 206–207
Sex differences, 447–473
    achievement, 457, 459–461
    aggressiveness, 448–449
    aptitudes, 457–458
    in attitudes toward sexual behavior,
    199–204
    biological, 448–450
    conformity, 458
    employment practices, 468–470
    evaluation of performance, 465–466
    eye contact, in self-disclosure,
    139–140
    game preference, 467
    helping behavior, 296–297, 300, 302
    heterosexual behavior, 196–204
    hitchhiking success, 137, 303–304
    homosexuality rates, 183–186
    intellectual abilities, 127
    intelligence, 457–458
    interpersonal distance, 515, 516,
    517–518
    level of moral maturity, 266, 268
    liking and self-disclosure, 139
    Machiavellianism, 135
    masculinity-femininity, 461–463
    nonverbal self-presentation, 126
    occupational status, 469–470
    perceptions of, 463–467
    persuasibility, 31–32
    philosophy of human nature, 92
    reactions to high density, 541–542
    self-evaluation, 466–467
Sexism, 327 (see also Sex roles)
    economic, 333
    in psychotherapy, 328
Sex roles, 447–473
    in the future, 470–471
    image, 126–127
    socialization of, 450–453
    stereotypes, 46, 127, 139–140, 171,
    328, 450–453, 463–464
    stereotypes, in peaceful societies,
    228–229
    theories, 456–457
Sexual arousal, see Sexual response
Sexual attraction, 172–175
    and fear, 173–174
Sexual behavior, 23, 26, 32, 177–208
    assaultive, 178, 185
    bisexuality, 191–192
    development, 181–192
    environmental effects, 207
    heterosexual, 196–204
    homosexual, 183–191
    identity, 181–192
    mistaken beliefs, 192–196
    pornography and, 206
    premarital, 196, 197, 198, 199
    problems, in studying, 179–181
    social influences, 204–207
Sexual development, 181–192
Sexual identity, 181–192

Sexual identity (continued)
  bisexuality, 191–192
  gender, 181
  homosexuality, 183–191
  in peaceful societies, 229
  transsexualism, 181–183
Sexual intercourse, see Coitus
Sexual needs, 178–179
Sexual physiology:
  mistaken beliefs, 192–196
  transsexual persons, 181–183
Sexual response (see also Sexual behavior):
  mistaken beliefs, 192–196
  and pornography, 204–207
Shame, reaction to transgression, 271
Shockley, William, 490
Sickle-cell anemia, 476
Significance level, in experimental research, 43
Signification, as an ingratiation motive, 131–132
Similarity:
  as an antecedent of attraction, 161–162, 167
  and attitude change, 397
  as a dimension of human nature, 85–86
  and friendship, 531–532
  of helper and recipient, 304
  and interpersonal distance, 515, 518
  and successful communes, 576–577
Simplicity, as dimension of human nature, 86, 87
Sims Score Card, 483
Simulation research, 45, 54–56, 416
Sirhan, Sirhan, 111
Situated identity, 118
Situational attribution, 100–104
Situational factors:
  in attitude change, 390–391
  in conformity, 611–613, 616–620
  in impression formation, 77
  in interpersonal behavior, 29, 30, 511–549
  in leadership effectiveness, 650–654
  versus personality traits in behavior, 623–624, 639
  in prejudice and discrimination, 335
  in race differences, 489–495, 496–507
Skinner, B. F., 442
Skin pigmentation, and intelligence-test scores, 482, 483–484
Social acceptance, similarity of beliefs versus race as determinant, 337–342 (see also Social distance)
Social action:
  by social psychologists, 411–444
  strategies, 418–427
Social approval (see also Social-approval need):
  and affiliation, 153
  quest for, 125–128
  and self-disclosure, 139

Social-approval need, 125–128, 149 (see also Social approval)
  as a cause of prejudice, 334
  and helping behavior, 300
  and persuasibility, 391–392
Social behavior, 3–6 (see also Interpersonal behavior)
  and psychoanalytic theory, 11–16
  and unplanned social change, 427–432
Social change, 411–444
  definition, 427–428
  and ethics of research, 72
  measurement of, 428–431
  strategies, 418–427
  unplanned, 427–432
  utopias, 439–443
  youth and, 435–439
Social class, 496–497 (see also Socioeconomic status)
  and helping behavior, 300
  and heritability coefficients, 486–487
  and intelligence, 498–506
  motivation and personality factors, in tested performance, 504
  and personal space, 517
  and race differences in IQ, 489
  sex-role stereotypes, 454
  similarities and differences, 496–504
Social-comparison theory:
  anxiety and affiliation, 153
  intelligence and attraction, 163
  self-evaluation through, 150, 155
Social contract, 13
  and productivity, 655–659
Social-contract stage, of moral maturity, 261
Social control, processes in communes, 575–576
Social density, 541 (see also Crowding)
Social desirability:
  bias, 61–62
  as a determinant of causal attribution, 103
  needs of survey respondents, 61–62
Social Desirability Scale, 128
Social determinism, 639–642
Social distance, 119, 337–342
  Summated Difference scale, 404
Social-distance zone, 514–515
Social engineers, 441
Social ethic, 625–626
Social-exchange theory, 19, 20
  affiliation, 149
  ingratiation, 128–134
  interpersonal attraction, 167–169
Social facilitation, 559
  and office landscaping, 532
Social indicators, 73, 429
Social influence, 607–635
  and causal attribution theory, 104
  group risk taking, 628–633
  in helping behavior, 291–296
  hypnosis, 633–634

Social influence (continued)
  and impression management, 134–138
  and leadership, 643–648
  Machiavellianism, 134–136
  in society, 624–627
Social interaction:
  impression formation, 77–113
  impression management, 115–145
  and productivity, 655–659
Social interference, as an antecedent of crowding, 537, 543, 547
Social issues, and justice, 258–259 (see also Social movements; Social problems; Social reform)
Socialization, of the individual:
  moral behavior, 243–275
  psychoanalytic theory, 12
  sex roles, 450–453
  sexual, 181–192
Social-judgment theory:
  assumptions about human nature, 360
  attitude change, 352, 357–364
Social-learning theory, in social psychology, 19–21
  aggression, 215, 219–220, 226–229, 238–239
  assumptions about human nature, 215
  moral behavior, 270–275
  sex-role development, 456
  utopia, 441, 442
Social movements, as predictors of social change, 431–432
Social norms, see Norms
Social pathology, and population density, 538–541
Social-penetration theory, and self-disclosure, 138
Social perception, 77–113
  accuracy, 104–112
  and authoritarianism, 588
  future trends in research, 112
  impression formation, 77–113
  and impression management, 118
  processes of, 79–104
Social problems:
  applicability of research to, 72–74, 411–444
  future shock, 439–443
Social psychology:
  definition, 3–6
  methods, 35–74
  and social change, 411–444
  theories, 6–33
Social reform, experimental approach to, 430 (see also Social change)
Social relevance, of research, 73–74
Social responsibility, norm of and helping behavior, 300, 304–306
Social service, and law-enforcement agents, 423–424
Social structures, 428

Social view of human nature, 654, 655–659
Society:
  authoritarianism in, 600–604
  changing, 411–444
  conformity in, 624–627
  nature and functions, 13
  origins, 13
  and youth, 435–436
Sociocultural causes, of prejudice and discrimination, 333–334
Socioeconomic status:
  and attitudes toward sex, 197
  and collective violence, 235–236
  and cooperative versus competitive behavior, 287
  and counterculture, 437
  and identification with television violence, 232
  and moral development, 270
  and prejudice, 333–334
Socioemotional orientation, function of leadership, 645
Sociofugal spaces, 534
Sociopetal spaces, 534
Solution specificity, and leadership effectiveness, 651–653
Source, of a communication (see also Communicator):
  credibility, 360–361, 365–366, 390, 393–394
  race, 394
South Africa, segregation of races in, 329–330
Spatial behavior, 511–549
Spatial density, 541
Specimen record, 66
S-R theory, see Stimulus-response theory
Standard deviation, 404
Stanford-Binet Tests of Intelligence, 457, 494–495, 498–499
Statisticized group technique, 560
Statistics, in experimental research, 43
Status (see also Socioeconomic status):
  and attitude change, 396, 401
  and conformity, 628
  and experimenter effects, 68
  and ingratiation tactics, 132–133
  of occupations, 469–471, 497–498
  orientation, 89
  and physical attractiveness, 165
  and self-presentation, 126
  social class, 496–506
  and social influence, 618
Stereotype accuracy, 107, 108, 110
Stereotypes, 319, 324–325, 331
  changes over time, 334
  and fear of success, 459–461
  and impression formation, 78, 95
  of names, 324–325
  as self-fulfilling prophecies, 325
  sex differences, 463–464

Stereotypes (continued)
  sex-role, 450–453
Stereotypy, component of authoritarianism, 584, 585
Stigmatization, roles, 127–128
Stimulation, effects in early childhood, 501–504
Stimulus, 19
Stimulus generalization, 21
  in attitude change, 357
Stimulus overload, 310
Stimulus-response theory, in social psychology, 19–21, 21–22, 26, 29, 30, 33, 97 (see also Social-learning theory)
  assumptions about human nature, 355
  attitude change, 352, 353–357, 372
  prosocial behavior, 279–280
  sex-role development, 456
Stimulus-value-role theory of marital choice, 166
Strategic aggression, 215
Stratified random sampling, 60
Strength of will, as dimension of human nature, 82–83, 89–92
Stress, and crowding, 537–543
Subjective method, of defining social class, 496
Subjects, research:
  ethical issues, 70–72, 73–74
  volunteer, 67, 415–416, 588–589
Success:
  and approval-seeking behavior, 126
  fear of, 459–461
  and helping behavior, 296, 298
  sex differences in evaluation of performance, 465–466
Suggestibility, 31
  and hypnosis, 633–634
Suicide, 212, 214
Summated Difference scale, 404
Summated rating method, 317
Superego, 12, 237, 246–247, 254
  in authoritarianism, 584
  as values, 251
Superordinate goal, 240
Superpatriots, 586
Superstition, as component of authoritarianism, 584, 585
Supervisor, successful, 661 (see also Leadership; Organizational effectiveness)
Surveillance, in our society, 603 (see also Central Intelligence Agency)
Survey method, 45, 47–48, 58–65
Survival, and altruistic behavior, 280–281
Symbolic interaction theory, 18, 117
  of interpersonal attraction, 169
Symonds, Martin, 84
Sympathy, and helping behavior, 297–298

Systematically biased sampling, 59
Systematic sampling, 60
Systems approach, to human problems, 73

Taft, William Howard, 475
Task orientation, function of leadership, 645
Task performance:
  groups versus individuals, 559–563
  and spatial density, 542
Task structure, and leadership effectiveness, 650–653
Tay-Sachs disease, 476
Tchambuli society, 228
Teacher's expectancy effects, 69
Technocracy, 436
Technology:
  advance and cost, 432–433
  and attitudes toward work, 432–434
  and dehumanization, 436
  and repression in society, 601–602
  and utopias, 441
Television (see also Mass media):
  sex-role socialization, 452–453
  and violence, 230–234, 239
Temperature, and interpersonal behavior, 535, 545
Temptation, resistance to, 245, 270–271
  effects of punishment on, 272
  modeling and, 272–273
Tension system, 26, 27
  balance theory, 364–365, 367–368
Territorial behavior, 521–530
Territoriality, 513, 522–523
  and aggression, 217–218, 226, 237–238, 522
  in confined groups, 527–528
  functions of, 524–525
  in nonhumans, 217–218, 226, 522–523
  in primary territories, 528–530
Testing-situation characteristics, and test scores, 494–495
T-groups, 27, 569–572
Thematic Apperception Test, 173–174, 233
Theories, in social psychology, 2–33, 37–38
  cognitive, 21–25, 86–88
  comparison of, 27–29
  field, 25–27, 28–30, 33, 416–418
  future of, 29–32
  Gestalt, 21–25, 29, 30, 33, 96–97
  need to build, 415, 416
  psychoanalytic, 11–16, 26, 29, 30, 33, 79, 83
  role, 16–19, 29, 30, 33, 415
  social-learning, 19–21
  stimulus-response, 19–22, 26, 29, 30, 33, 97
Theory X, 655
Therapy, see Psychotherapy
Threshold analysis, 343

one scale, 316–317
amples, 65
ism, 122–125
homosexuals, 186, 187, 191 (see
so Homosexuality)

ral, 96–97
bleness of trait words, 98
gression, reaction to, 245, 271
sexualism, 23, 181–183
vestites, 182
ls, in social psychology, 73–74
eau, Pierre, 330
e believers," 13
an, Harry S, 60, 64
:
rsus mistrust as stage of
psychosocial development,
248–249
d self-disclosure, 138
tworthiness:
dimension of human nature,
79–81, 89–92, 93, 251
d helping behavior, 300
n Oaks, 441, 573, 577, 578
n studies, of intelligence, 485–487
-factor theory:
emotion, 156–161
expression of aggression, 216–217
assionate love, 173

conscious, in psychoanalytic theory,
245, 335
dermined independence, 614
iformity, 610
its of analysis, 29, 30, 58
iversal ethical principles orientation
stage, of moral maturity, 261
obtrusive measures, 47, 49, 63, 73
ntrustworthiness, as dimension of
human nature, 79–81, 89–92, 93
pward mobility, and prejudice,
333–334
rban dwellers, and helping behavior,
300, 310–311
rbanization:
and discrimination, 333–334

Urbanization (continued)
rate, 431
USSR, education for cooperation in,
308
Utilitarian function of attitudes, 382
Utopias, 441–443

Validity:
in experiments, 69–70
of a survey, 58–65
Value-expression function of attitudes,
383
Values:
and activism, 435–436
and alienation, 435–436
and attraction, 161–162, 167
change, and social change, 432–435
changing work ethic, 432–434
industrial versus postindustrialized
society, 419
parent-child, 436–439
and research on sexual behavior,
179–180
and sexual behavior, 201, 203
similarity versus race, 337–342
and social class, 504
survey, 47–48
unplanned social change, 427–432
Value stretch, 504
Variability, as dimension of human
nature, 85–86, 89–92
Verbal ability, and birth order, 154
Verbal reinforcement, of attitudes,
355–357, 365
Verification, 38–39, 40
Victim, blaming the, 84–86
Vietnam War, attitudes toward:
authoritarian, 589
and dogmatism, 594
and social influence, 119
Violence, 211–241, 281
attitudes toward, 35, 40–41
collective, 234–239
and the mass media, 230–234
and social change, 422–425
Vocabulary, of questions in surveys, 61
Volunteer subjects, 67
and authoritarianism, 588–589

Voting behavior, 89 (see also Political
views)

Wagler, Evelyn, 231
Wallace, George, 369
War, 234–239 (see also Vietnam War)
in psychoanalytic theory, 13
and social change, 422, 424
Warmth, and experimenter effects, 68
as a sex stereotype, 463–464
"Watered down" theory, of attitudes
and behavior, 345–347
Watergate break-in, 101–103, 115, 122,
124
attitude change toward, 375–378
moral maturity of participants, 263
"Weapons effect," on aggressive
behavior, 224–225
Wechsler Intelligence Scale for
Children, 499
Welsh Figure Preference Test, 406
Wesley Rigidity scale, 406
Wilson, Harold, 58
Wilson, Woodrow, 83
Withdrawal, under conditions of high
density, 544, 545, 546
Women's Movement, 448, 467–471
Wording, of questions in surveys,
60–61
Work, attitudes toward, as an example
of social change, 432–434
World Future Society, 441

Xenophobia, as measure of prejudice,
588

Yale University Communication
Research Program, 354, 355
Yea-saying, 63
Yellow Kid Weil, 134
Youth, 435–436
and social change, 435–439
Yussoupov, Prince, 10–11

Zeitgeist theory of history, 639–642
Zero population growth, effects on
intelligence, 500